LOOKING FORWARD through the LIFESPAN

To the memory of my father, Arthur Clifford,
this book is affectionately dedicated

LOOKING FORWARD
through the LIFESPAN

4 *edition*

DEVELOPMENTAL PSYCHOLOGY

Candida Peterson

Copyright © Pearson Education Australia (a division of Pearson Australia Group Pty Ltd) 2004

Pearson Education Australia
Unit 4, Level 2
14 Aquatic Drive
Frenchs Forest NSW 2086

www.pearsoned.com.au

Senior Acquisitions Editor: Nicole Meehan
Senior Project Editor: Carolyn Robson
Senior Editorial Coordinator: Jill Gillies
Copy Editor and Indexer: Jo Rudd
Proofreader: Felicity Shea
Cover and internal design by designBITE
Cover image supplied by Illustration Works
Typeset by Midland Typesetters, Maryborough, Vic.

Printed in China

1 2 3 4 5 08 07 06 05 04

National Library of Australia
Cataloguing-in-Publication Data

Peterson, Candida.
Looking forward through the lifespan.

    4th ed.
    Bibliography.
    Includes index.
    ISBN 1 74103 150 8.

    1. Developmental psychology. I. Title.

155

An imprint of Pearson Education Australia (a division of Pearson Australia Group Pty Ltd)

BRIEF CONTENTS

DETAILED CONTENTS

Part 3 The Preschool Period: From Age Two to Age Six

Part 5   The Adolescent Phase

PREFACE

A book, like a person, begins life as an idea, uniquely conceived, struggling into the world, and then shaped throughout its developing lifespan by the unique environment that nurtures its growth. This book owes a special debt of gratitude to its roots in Australasia and to my students and professional colleagues who taught me to appreciate the relevance of local conditions, and of uniquely Australian, New Zealand, European and Asian research, as lenses through which the broad outlines of human lifespan development can more clearly be perceived. While selecting the best contemporary research from developmental psychologists' laboratories around the world, this text is enriched with uniquely Australian, New Zealand and Asian examples.

I believe that the basic facts of growth are both universal and timeless. Yet intriguing differences exist between, say, teenagers on the beach at Bondi versus Malibu, or between infants growing up in Aboriginal- versus Anglo-Australian families, or between Maori and Pakeha New Zealand preschoolers, or among elderly nursing home residents of Brisbane, Boston, Bristol and Beijing. Cross-cultural variations like these are explored in depth in this book.

A rich array of real-life examples is included in boxed features and in the main text to highlight developmental differences that are linked to gender, ethnic background, historical era and socioeconomic conditions. Through all of these contrasts, we see the uniqueness of each human lifespan and enjoy the personal idiosyncrasies that make the study of lives in progress such a fascinating enterprise. The book's chronological organisation connects these threads and simplifies the story of psychological change from conception through extreme old age by revealing the unity of each human life course around a small and coherent set of developmental themes. (These are outlined in Chapter 1.)

My writing has also been guided, through this and the three previous editions, by a strong commitment to a lifespan approach. I believe human psychological growth and functioning can best be understood by beginning at the beginning of prenatal life and following the developing person through each step along our shared developmental journey. Unlike many other textbooks, I have therefore devoted an evenly balanced coverage to each of the major phases in the lifespan, highlighting the important discoveries of researchers and theorists who specialise in infancy or in gerontology, as well as in all the key phases in between.

The older I have grown, the more fascinated I have become with the connections that exist between the simple psychological changes that take place at each successive life stage. The story is rarely a simple one, and it has taken many decades of systematic

Oodgeroo Noonuccal (Kath Walker) was born in Queensland in 1920 and is jointly recognised as Australia's foremost Indigenous poet and a leading civil rights campaigner. She left school at age 13 to enter domestic service, then volunteered for the Army in 1939. She married during World War II and had two sons. Awakened from her conventional life as a 1950s housewife by an article in a Communist newspaper, Walker gradually became politically active. Her leadership of the campaign for Aboriginal civil liberties grew over the decade and she achieved national prominence in 1961 at the age of 41 through her election as Queensland State Secretary of the Council for the Advancement of Aborigines and Torres Strait Islanders. For the next seven years, Walker travelled throughout Australia, often giving as many as ten speeches per day advocating Aboriginal equality, citizenship and the right to vote. As the major force behind the national referendum of 1967 she was eventually successful and

longitudinal research to unravel the predictability in some seemingly disjointed lifespan trajectories (I have included some vivid examples in the section on 'life-cycle surprises' in Chapter 1). But after many decades of concerted research endeavour, the lifespan approach has clearly come into its own. It is evident from the current body of empirical evidence that development and change are inescapable facets of the human condition.

For this reason, psychological processes (cognition, personality, social relationships, and so on) can best be understood by following them through their full course over time. The lifespan approach that guides this book offers new insight into human nature in all its complexity. Practical solutions to life's problems, and fresh ideas about how a person's present and future selves reflect earlier antecedents also emerge when psychological processes are examined developmentally.

As the title of this book suggests, I am confidently optimistic about the possibility of development through all stages of the lifespan. Based on my reading of the current research evidence, I believe that every person, however old, or however young, is capable of genuinely incremental psychological growth. Of course, setbacks, losses and blockages of development are also possible at any age. However, the last decade has seen significant scientific breakthroughs that strengthen grounds for optimism. It is an exciting time to be writing about human development. As this book goes to press, in the wake of the mapping of the human genome and the discoveries that have arisen out of new, non-invasive techniques for examining the functioning of the human brain, it is clearer than ever before that genuine psychological growth continues long after a person's physical growth in size and stature has ceased. The recent genetic and neurocognitive findings that are highlighted throughout this edition reinforce behavioural evidence of human capacity for lifelong psychological growth. The plasticity of psychological functions is no longer a matter for mere speculation and, contrary to earlier ideas, the human brain has the optimising potential to recover from loss or injury well into old age.

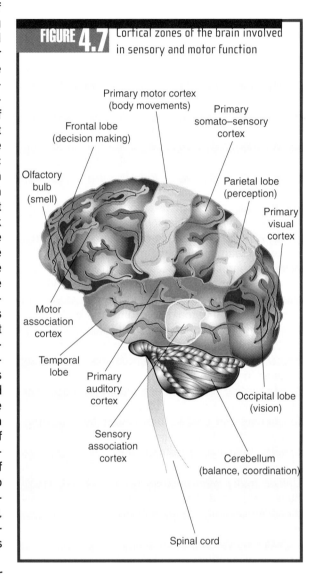

FIGURE 4.7 Cortical zones of the brain involved in sensory and motor function

Primary motor cortex (body movements)

Primary somato–sensory cortex

Frontal lobe (decision making)

Olfactory bulb (smell)

Parietal lobe (perception)

Primary visual cortex

Motor association cortex

Temporal lobe

Primary auditory cortex

Occipital lobe (vision)

Sensory association cortex

Cerebellum (balance, coordination)

Spinal cord

The world grows even smaller in this information age, and exciting new anthropological and sociological discoveries have also been incorporated into this edition of the book. Much of the social evidence reinforces neurobiological findings of developmental plasticity throughout life by highlighting the benefits of relational and cultural supports for overcoming losses of capacity that used to be seen as inevitable markers of ageing. With the wealth of new evidence that has emerged in the last five years, the revision of my text has been timely, and this edition includes hundreds of new studies published since the 21st century began. I believe we can all look forward to future phases in our own lifespans even more optimistically now than was conceivable when I chose the title for the first edition of this book almost a quarter of a century ago. Nevertheless, the scientific enterprise still continues. Consequently, rather than simply listing the facts of development as we know them now, I have incorporated information on new methodologies into the present edition, so that readers will be able to intelligently and critically keep abreast of the research developments that are bound to arise in the years ahead.

The book's organisation is chronological, but within each age period a carefully structured topical treatment serves to pinpoint the areas of most rapid and significant developmental change. In my own teaching, I have used the book with both chronologically and topically organised course curricula.

Instructors who favour a topical approach will note that the new, topically labelled chapter titles and contents show how the core psychological domains are examined in recurring sequence throughout each of life's major phases. This makes it easy to link reading assignments with topics like neurobiology, cognition, personality and so on. Other pedagogical features new to this edition are 'milestone' summary tables that condense the key developments of each era in the lifespan (infancy, early childhood, etc.) for each separate developmental domain (cognition, emotion, etc.).

	Domain of development		
	Sensation and perception	Emotion	Cognition
	Senses of hearing, smell, taste and touch are well developed at birth.	Soon after birth, infants show alertness, distress and general upset.	Even before birth, infants have a capacity for memory and simple learning.	At en we dis to wi fo
kill ny o	Neonates can distinguish among the sounds, smells and tastes of the world outside the womb with fine acuity.	By two months they display social smiling. At three to four months they laugh in response to predictable and mildly surprising social and physical stimuli over which they can	Discriminative learning is possible at birth and by two months infants can learn complex contingencies.	
om	Vision develops rapidly over first four mo which baby	trol.	Attention develops over the early m and is trigger by	By at ca

Instructors with a topical curriculum can reference these by column as topic summaries, while those opting for a chronological approach may prefer to use the rows to help students appreciate how all the component psychological capacities of a 'whole' human being connect together at a given phase in life. As part of the chronological organisation of Chapters 4 through 17, my focus is as much upon pointing out the connections between earlier and later developments as upon outlining the unique features of each successive age period. To encourage revisions and topical clarity of developments that span more than one age period, I frequently refer the reader back to earlier chapters with page references while the new milestone summaries can also be used as advance organisers for readers wanting to glimpse what future age periods will hold in store.

BOX 11.5 Expressing individuality
Gender differences in the logic of morality

To illustrate gender differences discussed in the text, consider the answers Gilligan (1982, pp. 19–20) received when she asked one 25-year-old man and one 25-year-old woman what it meant to be ethical.

Interviewer: What does the word 'morality' mean to you?
Young man: I think it is recognising the right of the individual, the right of other individuals and not interfering with those rights. Act as fairly as you would have them treat you.

Interviewer: Are there really right and wrong answers to moral problems, or is everybody's opinion equally correct?
Young woman: We need to depend on each other, and hopefully it is not only a physical need but a need of fulfilment in ourselves, that a person's life is enriched by cooperating with other people and striving to live in harmony with everybody else, and to that end there are right and wrong; there are things which promote that end, and things that move away from it.

BOX 10.10 A case in point
A babe in the woods

When Louise was 15, she went out alone with a boy for the first time. She had met him only the day before in a northern New Zealand campground. Her father described the event and his ensuing conversation with his daughter as follows.

14 December 1964. *When the park manager's son Bryan offered to go walking with Louise and, to our surprise, picked her up in a car, it turned out in effect to be her first date. The young fellow, who is 18, good-looking, and evidently sure of himself, assumed either he had a babe in the woods in Louise or else, being American, she was ready for anything. He didn't go farther than putting an arm about her but he made a longer date for tonight and Louise seemed convinced he meant to go farther. Though what this might involve she hadn't the foggiest notion.*

I had half suspected she was uninformed though I recall Peg talking to her about sex some years ago, too long ago, as it happened, for her to remember. I thought perhaps her girl friends may have shared their knowledge, as children do; but they too apparently know very little. Still I didn't want to bring the subject up out of the blue.

evening it ... *aturally o* ... *ed at leng*

Sprinkled throughout each chapter are boxes containing anecdotes, diary excerpts and vignettes from everyday life which bring important concepts to life through personal examples. Some of the boxes are one-offs while others recur in most chapters so they become familiar pedagogical features with distinctive icons to identify them. As well as making key concepts familiar, the boxes are useful to students as content organisers and study tools.

Each box is closely linked conceptually to the main text, and their varied content includes case histories that track 'whole' people across major portions of their growing up, novel cross-cultural examples, historical glimpses, practical activity suggestions that enable readers to try out simple research techniques, and prediction exercises that test the reader's theoretical ingenuity and point out the unexpected in contemporary research.

My writing style is clear and engaging and I have aimed for a book that is as intellectually stimulating as it is enjoyable to read and easy to understand. Knowing how they grate upon the thoughtful student, I have avoided oversimplifications and bland prescriptiveness. Instead, I try to encourage readers to think freely and critically about the core concepts, theoretical clashes and methodological approaches that define the essence of the discipline of lifespan development. By supplying glimpses of the scientific procedures that underpin the research findings that I describe, I have tried to give students the flavour of the lively debate that makes the scientific study of human development come alive. In this I have been aided by my experience as a researcher and by my genuine love for my subject matter, as well as by my enthusiasm for teaching that has not worn thin after more than 30 years of lecturing, each semester, to theatres of over 100 and discussion groups as small as 15.

More ambitious projects and Internet links are suggested at the end of each chapter, along with a selection of web-based and multimedia resources for those wishing to study particular topics in greater depth.

For further interest

Looking forward on the Internet

For ideas about the development of the human brain, both prenatally and postnatally, go to: **http://faculty.washington.edu/chudler/dev.html**. For more information on pregnancy and birth planning, try: **http://www.pregnancy.org**.

For resources, ideas, activities and other items of interest in conjunction with this chapter, visit the Companion Website for this textbook at:

http://wps.pearsoned.com.au/peterson

Activity suggestion

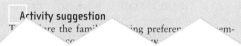

personal acquaintances. Ask them (a) how many children they hope to have, (b) what sex they prefer their eldest and youngest to be, and (c) what they would choose if they could opt either for twins or for more widely spaced offspring. If possible seek informants from a variety of cultural backgrounds, and compare your findings with those of your classmates.

Multimedia

For a provocative glimpse of prenatal development and the adverse effects of alcohol on the growing fetus, view the video: *Alcohol and Pregnancy* (Penn State, PCR Video in the Behavioural Sciences 5:

As an experienced teacher, I am well aware of the power of a textbook to influence students' learning and the pleasure and lasting insights they gain from a course. I have therefore grounded this book in a careful selection of classic and contemporary research and theory that, in my opinion, defines the essence of lifespan developmental psychology.

Piaget's theory

Jean Piaget (1970) put forward a theory of development spanning four major stages, each characterised by a qualitatively different mode of thought. The mechanism of transition between stages is a dialectical conflict between the processes of *assimilation* and *accommodation* that he had derived from biology. Assimilation in biology describes the incorporation from the environment into an organism,

In prelingual infants and toddlers, gesture has an important role to play, in line with Piaget's observations of the cognitive role of motor symbols in assisting thinking, memory and problem-solving. As Susan Goldin-Meadow (2000) explains:

> Gesture thus allows speakers to convey thoughts that may not easily fit into the categorical system that their conventional language offers ... Gesture reflects a global-synthetic image. It is not constructed out of segmented movements

I have taken care to avoid reiteration of long lists of facts or concepts which conduce towards mindless memorisation, and have relied, instead, on clear definitions of essential ideas in the chapter context where they first occur, supplemented by a full glossary of technical and key concepts at the end of the book that will prove

articulation of rules An index of *conscience* in which the individual explains why something is right or wrong.
artificialism The child's belief that natural phenomena are fabricated by people.
asceticism Anna Freud's term for the adolescent's extreme rejection of all pleasurable experiences and impulses.
ASL (American Sign Language) The sign language used by deaf people in the USA.
assimilation Piaget's term for the incorporation of new information into an existing mental category or *schema*.
asynchrony Discrepancies in growth rates either among various parts of the same person (*intra-in*

useful to readers who may not have studied psychology or human development before.

My aim has been to encourage the reader to share in the fun and suspense of scientific discovery and also to think critically about the ideas presented in these pages. My own view is that no one theory or experiment will ever supply a final answer to any of the mysteries of the lifespan. Furthermore, while all research should aim for eventual applicability to improving practice, the facts presented here are not prescriptive recipes that will give simple formulae for how to work with and care sensitively for, growing, changing human beings. Instead, the understanding of human development develops in all of us over time, both with the accumulation of new knowledge and with the testing of accepted wisdom through critical study and analysis. The discipline of developmental psychology is itself a lively and ever-changing enterprise, growing with each fresh scientific discovery as well as with the sudden new insights emerging when a thoughtful person has the audacity to challenge an established truth. Therefore, my prime goal has been to supply readers with the basic understanding, the critical thinking skills and the sense of curiosity that are all

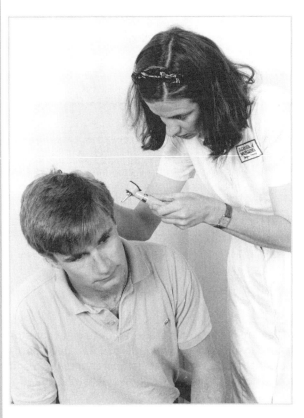

needed in order to make the study of human psychological growth an exciting, lifelong enterprise.

This book is meant for everyone with an interest in human behaviour and its exciting developments over the lifespan. This includes professionals who are working, or will work, with people of different ages. My own students typically span a broad range of career interests, often including present and future clinical psychologists, teachers, therapists, career counsellors and personnel managers, social workers, child care staff, nurses, doctors, lawyers, elder carers and members of the clergy. The study of human development over the complete lifespan offers important benefits for each of these professional groups.

By coming to understand the connections that exist between earlier and later developmental outcomes across the full lifespan, adults who work with the young can plan their teaching or therapeutic interventions with a view to long-term benefits, while helpers of the elderly can assist their clients to make the most of psychological strengths acquired earlier. Those whose careers bring them into contact with people who are much younger or much older than themselves likewise have much to learn from the contemporary research findings that are described in this book. As they read, they may at times be surprised to discover how much capacity for psychological growth exists at each life stage, and at other times be struck by how hard it sometimes is to bring developmental potential to fruition. Correspondingly, a lifespan approach to psychology challenges the insightful researcher to discover meaningful patterns of change within the complexity of a lifetime's experience and to develop new ways of using that knowledge in practical application.

A genuine interest in human development over the lifespan can be a hobby, as well as a profession. Even if they have no interest in raising children or pursuing a person-centred career, students are likely to gain personally from reading about human psychology in the balanced lifespan framework that characterises this book. As each of us progresses along a unique developmental trajectory, we face many of the same issues that lifespan researchers have investigated scientifically. While needing to find our own personal solutions to life's myriad problems and possibilities, the research findings described in this book can serve as a useful backdrop. As we all mingle with other people of varied ages – parents, grandparents, friends, children, intimate partners and work colleagues – we come likewise face-to-face with development in action. It is my hope that by assisting readers to look forward through the lifespan, armed with knowledge and data-grounded optimism, this book may help to sustain and nurture their enthusiasm for participating in the challenging life-long adventure of psychological growth.

Many people deserve special thanks for their contributions to this book. First and foremost, my husband Jim, and my children Megan and Kim, who have all developed through significant stages of their own lives in very close company with this book's development through its four editions. Their patience, good humour, practical help, useful ideas, critical feedback and constant emotional support have sustained me throughout many long hours of research and writing. Work on this edition was enriched by two important new developments in my family life: I thank my son-in-law, Marcus, and my grandson, Rafael, for their treasured contributions. Too numerous to list by name, yet a crucial part of all the thinking behind this book, are my academic colleagues and the many students over the years who have shared their ideas about development with me inside and outside of class, and have given me feedback about the textbook in person, by letter and by email. It is very gratifying to make contact with former students again after many years, when new developments in their own lifespans draw their thoughts back to these pages – like Karl who recently emailed me: 'I still have your old *Through the Lifespan* book – one of the few I retained from all those years ago. And as I write this my sister-in-law is having a baby – my brother's first child … the lifespan begins!'

I am particularly grateful for the input from instructors who have used earlier editions of this text and helped to shape the present edition through thoughtful responses to survey questions, by commenting on outlines, by providing reviews and critiques of manuscript drafts and generally by sharing with me their enthusiasm for the unique features of my book and their ideas for further improvement. Your resonance with my pedagogical approach is genuinely appreciated, as are the many constructive suggestions you have given me. These have helped to shape the many new and improved features of this edition and my thanks go to all of you. The editorial board for the fourth edition consisted of a large number of anonymous participants, and the following academics:

Dr Shirley R. Wyver, Institute of Early Childhood, Macquarie University
Dr Nerina Caltabiano, School of Psychology, James Cook University
Dr Pia Broderick, School of Psychology, Murdoch University
Dr Verity Bottroff, School of Medicine, Flinders University
Dr Dawn Butterworth, School of Education, Edith Cowan University
Ms Jeni Grubb, School of Nursing, Monash University

Last, but in no way least, I wish to express my gratitude and appreciation for the two superb editors at Pearson Education Australia, Nicole Meehan and Carolyn Robson, who have raised the format, design and overall quality of this edition to new heights of excellence. Nicole's energy, enthusiasm and keen sense of the academic environment were fundamental strengths as this radical revision of the third edition was conceptualised, planned and implemented. Throughout all stages of the manuscript's editing and the book's production, Carolyn's wise good sense, cheerful efficiency, diplomatic problem-solving and keen attention to detail made a huge difference in achieving an overall quality and finish that I could barely imagine when the project began. My heartfelt thanks go to both of you, as well as to the many other behind-the-scenes members of the editorial, sales and production teams at Pearson Education Australia for excellent contributions.

Candida Peterson
September 2003

STUDYING HUMAN DEVELOPMENT OVER THE LIFESPAN

PART 1

Contents

Overview

The study of how people grow and change psychologically over the complete span of human life from conception to death in old age is an ambitious, multifaceted undertaking. This is *lifespan developmental psychology*.

The period of time encompassed by the discipline is impressive in itself. For example, a typical infant born in Australia or New Zealand today can count on living for more than three-quarters of a century (78 years if Australian, 76 if a New Zealander: Valkonen, 2001); your own statistical odds may be even better, given that you have survived infant and child mortality to reach an age where you can read this book. However, it is not simply the breadth of the stretch of time encompassed that lends fascination to the lifespan approach.

From a personal perspective it can be exciting, but also a little daunting, to think about what the future is likely to hold for ourselves and those we care about as we progress through adulthood in the 21st century. Think of all the important social and technological changes that have happened during your own and your parents' lifetimes – perhaps spanning the advent of television through to the internet.

From a scientific perspective, too, a study of development over the lifespan is essential in order to gain a full understanding of human psychology. Studying the processes of change that hold a person's life together from its beginning moment at conception right to its end in extreme old age reveals the coherence of human psychology amid all its complexity. Thus the story of human development, tracking patterns of psychological growth over the whole of life, can be compared to reading a mystery story from start to finish.

In a crime story, plots thicken, suspects emerge and new evidence arises to discount initial suspicions. Were you to stop reading after only a few chapters, you would probably end up with a hazy or completely distorted impression of the crime and its perpetrators. But by the time you reach the final page of the thriller, the whole story has come together. A human life is just the same. By examining continuities and changes in people's psychological functioning as they pass through all life's exciting milestones, pitfalls and opportunities, we come to understand human behaviour as an integrated story with a clear pattern and consistent plot amid all the intriguing suspense and individual variation. This is the story we follow chronologically through this book.

A study of psychological development also provides useful insight into the discipline of psychology. The complete lives studied in this book weave their complex patterns by drawing together threads from theoretical orientations as diverse as humanistic psychology, cognitive psychology, behaviour genetics, psychoanalysis, social psychology, cognitive science and

neuropsychology. The kinds of research strategies that are needed to track development through the complete life course likewise encompass all psychology's varied methodologies. These include naturalistic observation of people in their ongoing life settings, consultation of historical and autobiographical records, administration of tests and interviews, questionnaires and other self-report measures, media analyses and clinical interviews, as well as controlled experimentation. With its integrating theme being the understanding of behaviour over the whole of life, the discipline of lifespan human development is also enriched by contributions from all psychology's separate subdisciplines and from related fields ranging from neuroscience and biochemistry to sociology and cultural anthropology.

The first three chapters trace the broad outlines of this overall pattern. Chapter 1 supplies an overview of the discipline. We examine the kinds of insights about human nature that we gain through knowing a person's chronological age, and the benefits of studying these age-related regularities in behaviour objectively, through the lenses of science. Chapter 1 also tracks the history of people's fascination with childhood as the source of adult uniqueness, and the new insights we gain through the lifespan approach by following the human life story to its conclusion in old age. Core concepts needed for following the process of psychological development over the whole of life are defined and explained.

Chapter 2 introduces the building blocks of lifespan psychology. We learn about the basic research techniques that enable us to study changes in psychological functioning over the years and decades of a person's life, together with the seminal theories that inform our chronological journey through the life course in the rest of this book. Chapter 3, the final chapter in Part 1, is devoted to the study of the earliest beginnings of life in a new human being. First, we trace those beginnings back to a time even before conception has taken place by analysing how the biological processes of genetic inheritance convey information that reaches back through myriad generations of human ancestry. Then we explore the new baby's fascinating, though largely invisible, developmental journey from conception through the first nine months of life inside the womb.

LIFESPAN DEVELOPMENTAL CHAPTER PSYCHOLOGY

1

Nothing is permanent except change.

Heraclitus, 513 BC

Contents

This chapter begins by examining the lifespan developmental researcher's most important, yet most enigmatic, clue to human psychology: chronological age. We know that human behaviour changes in predictable ways as a person gets older. This predictability gives age its importance as a basis for psychological understanding. But we also know that age alone does not *cause* developmental change. Think about people who spend years in a coma. Even though they get older, they do not pass through normal developmental milestones during this time. This absence of a straightforward causal link is what makes the age clue enigmatic.

In this chapter we analyse what age means to each of us, now and as we reflect on our past and future lives. We also explore some of the varied ways in which chronological age has shaped the fabric of human life in general – across cultures, through history and in our contemporary technological society. Then we return to the lifespan researcher's quest for a scientifically responsible account of human psychology, overviewing what researchers and theorists have discovered about age as a signpost to change over the whole of life, and noting some caveats of using age on its own as a scientific clue.

A contemporary model of how human psychological functioning develops over the whole of life is presented, and we glimpse a few of the fresh insights and 'lifecycle surprises' that arise out of this lifespan model of development as a continuing process. The chapter concludes with a foretaste of some of the practical applications of developmental science that emerge in the rest of this book. We see how professionals from varied disciplines and walks of life can use lifespan psychology to optimise their own developmental journeys, and those of Australians and New Zealanders of any age.

Adults can grow psychologically through the whole of life

People stop growing taller at the end of adolescence. Some decades ago it was thought that the same might be true of psychological growth. For example, in 1890 the pioneering experimental psychologist, William James, proposed that: 'In most of us, by the age of 30, the character has set like plaster and will never soften again' (Rubin, 1981, p. 18). But, owing to recent lifespan developmental research, we now know that this view is wrong. Unlike physical growth, psychological development can continue in a genuinely progressive sense throughout the whole lifespan. Some examples of adults becoming more complex, flexible, creative, effective and far-sighted throughout old age are included in Box 1.1.

BOX 1.1 Four luminary lifespans

George Bernard Shaw, born in 1856, dropped out of high school prematurely at age 15 after very mediocre academic careers in four different schools where he continually failed many subjects. He spent his pocket money on books and theatre tickets and, to earn more, briefly took up a clerical job in real estate. Bored with this, he elected to become unemployed and to depend financially on his mother in order to teach himself creative writing, in line with his early passion for plays and literature. He first tried novels but had trouble getting them published, and so became a drama critic. Then, contrary to his own oft-quoted line 'Every man over 40 is a scoundrel', Shaw finally discovered his true calling at the age of 36 with the completion of his first play. He continued as a prolific and accomplished playwright throughout the remainder of his long life, rapidly achieving international acclaim. Shaw was honoured with the Nobel Prize for literature at the age of 68, wrote his last play during his late 80s and died at the age of 94.

Bertrand Russell, born into the English aristocracy in 1872, achieved world acclaim as a philosopher and mathematician for the books on mathematical theory that he published in his early 30s. In 1950, at the age of 78, he was awarded the Nobel Prize for literature in recognition of his philosophical writing. However, despite his exceptional literary, theoretical, philosophical and scientific achievements, Russell could never be described as an 'ivory tower' academic. Developing a strong social conscience during his early 20s, he was imprisoned during World War I for his pacifist activities and lost his lectureship at Cambridge University as a consequence. Undaunted, he continued throughout his long life to vigorously and courageously oppose war, gender inequality, political exploitation and social injustice. Over time, his fame as an academic was eclipsed by the international recognition he earned through his political activism. As one of the most outspoken critics of the nuclear bombing of Hiroshima and Nagasaki by the United States during World War II, he was again imprisoned at the age of 89 for taking part in an anti-nuclear demonstration. At the age of 94, Russell achieved 'the climax of his anti-war campaigning' (Morris, 1983, p. 94) when he founded the International War Crimes Tribunal in Stockholm and gathered leading intellectuals from around the world to hold a trial protesting against war crimes by the United States in Vietnam.

In blatant instances of ageist bigotry (see page 19 of this chapter for a discussion of this concept) Russell, from age 80 on, was frequently attacked by journalists and politicians who claimed the only explanation for his protest activities was that he had become 'senile'. With wry humour he parried these accusations, commenting in his autobiography: 'I daresay it is about their only retort. In any case, if the charge is true, I fail to see why anyone troubles to remark on my babblings' (Russell, 1975, p. 661). Russell died in 1970 at the age of 97, commenting on his deathbed that, for all its woes and political upheavals: 'I do so hate to leave this world' (Morris, 1983, p. 97).

Oodgeroo Noonuccal (Kath Walker) was born in Queensland in 1920 and is jointly recognised as Australia's foremost Indigenous poet and a leading civil rights campaigner. She left school at age 13 to enter domestic service, then volunteered for the Army in 1939. She married during World War II and had two sons. Awakened from her conventional life as a 1950s housewife by an article in a Communist newspaper, Walker gradually became politically active. Her leadership of the campaign for Aboriginal civil liberties grew over the decade and she achieved national prominence in 1961 at the age of 41 through her election as Queensland State Secretary of the Council for the Advancement of Aborigines and Torres Strait Islanders. For the next seven years, Walker travelled throughout Australia, often giving as many as ten speeches per day advocating Aboriginal equality, citizenship and the right to vote. As the major force behind the national referendum of 1967 she was eventually successful, and Indigenous Australians were at last allowed to cast their vote and were counted in the Census for the very first time.

Throughout this time Walker was also writing poetry. Her first book, *We Are Going*, published in 1964 when she was 44, was a signpost for Aboriginal rights that swiftly won national and international acclaim. The first print run of the book sold out in just three days, breaking the Australian record for poetry sales previously set by C.J. Dennis in 1916. She was awarded the MBE (Member of the Order of the British Empire) by the Queen in recognition of her outstanding literary achievements. However, in 1988 at the age of 68, Walker sent this award back as a gesture of protest against the injustices Aboriginal people still continued to suffer two decades after winning their right to vote.

At this point, she entered a new phase in her life. A return to her ancestral land on North Stradbroke Island enabled her to forge a new identity (see Chapter 11) that melded together her triad of lifelong interests in children, Aboriginal culture and race relations. She invited children, both black and white, to come and share her life in her educational camp on Stradbroke Island. There, she taught them to appreciate nature, conservation of the land and Aboriginal culture. Over 30 000 children had visited Moongalba (this poetic name, translated, is 'resting place') by the time Oodgeroo died there peacefully in 1993.

Emily Kame Kngwarreye was born about 1919 (her exact birth date was never recorded) at the Alkahere Soakage on

Children learned to appreciate nature at Walker's camp at Moongalba.

the edge of the Utopia cattle station in Central Australia, some 250 kilometres northeast of Alice Springs. She received a strictly traditional Aboriginal upbringing as a member of the Anmatyerre language group, and was well into adolescence before she saw a white person. This first glimpse was disturbing: she was gathering wild yams in a thicket with a friend when, on the horizon, a pair of Anglo-Australian policemen appeared on horseback with an Aboriginal prisoner in chains.

Before taking up a paintbrush for the first time in 1988, when in her mid-70s, Emily Kame Kngwarreye had risen to the rank of tribal elder, a respected leader of her people who held important responsibilities for her land and her kin, and as a keeper and teacher of sacred culture and religious knowledge.

In the eight short years from the time of her introduction to oil painting until her death on 2 September 1996, Emily Kngwarreye created a legacy of remarkable paintings that established her position as foremost among Australia's contemporary artists. Her abstract depictions of desert landscapes, harvest scenes, and the roots, vines, fruits and flowers of the yam plants for which she bore ceremonial responsibility, play on light and colour in a manner reminiscent of Monet's impressionism. Many of these large canvasses now grace the permanent collections of leading public and private art galleries throughout the world. Their size alone bears amazing tribute to the tireless dedication of the elderly artist who created them, in the open air, often racked with arthritis. Kngwarreye was spurred on as she painted, not only by her artistic inspiration, but also by a strong sense of personal responsibility for her cultural heritage and for the many members of her extended family who depended on her art sales for their financial support.

Thus, until the moment of her death and afterwards, Kngwarreye continued to earn the respect of younger members of her community. She was a senior elder with vast traditional wisdom and experience of Aboriginal culture. She was a great artist, and she was a powerful community leader and economic provider. Her inner strength, coupled with faith in herself, in her people and in her position within the larger spiritual scheme, enabled her to paint with inspiration until the moment of her death, while also equipping her to negotiate, with enviable dexterity, humour and generosity, 'the pressures that worldly success brings to individuals living in communal bush societies' (A.M. Brody, 1998, p. 19).

Hallmarks of the lifespan approach to psychological understanding

The four lifespan vignettes in Box 1.1, while describing adults whose political and creative achievements were undeniably of higher quality, broader scope and greater impact on society than most of us are ever likely to achieve, illustrate the typical patterns of ordinary men's and women's lives in most other ways. When we begin to chart development chronologically in later chapters of this book, we shall see that formative childhood experiences, such as Shaw's difficulties at school or Kngwarreye's first glimpse of white policemen, can continue to shape adults' thoughts, reminiscences and life plans many decades later. Similarly, core elements of a person's early identity, such as Russell's passion for social justice or Walker's love of poetry, can lie dormant for many years and then surface in undertakings for the first time during mature adulthood or old age.

Lifelong development
The perspective that guides this book – lifespan psychology – brings core elements like these, which all human lives share, into sharp relief. Guided by the scientific research evidence that we examine as we follow chronological psychological development through this book, we shall see that there is no stage in life when a person has become 'too old' to develop new plans and ideas, cultivate and express long-standing talents or contribute productively to the welfare of younger friends, family and future generations. Each of the four life stories in Box 1.1 gained productive new dimensions in maturity and old age.

Continuity and change
Another core theme of lifespan development, the notion of a delicate interplay between the constancy of certain core processes in the context of inevitable, unstoppable change, was first articulated by the Greek philosopher Heraclitus during the 6th century BC: 'Nothing is permanent except change' (van Doren, 1941, p. 559). The life stories in Box 1.1 reveal many instances of continuities over time of core elements of each personality; this continuity is also seen in life

goals that played themselves out in changing ways at both earlier and later stages in the four adults' lifelong patterns of development. For example, the youthful idealism that led Walker to join the Army during World War II, and Russell to go to prison for anti-imperialist protests during World War I, took a more mature form in the political activism that both individuals engaged in after the age of 40.

Similarly, there was continuity over many decades of changing life circumstances in the personal strength of character and the creative inspiration that fuelled the artistic genius of both Shaw and Kngwarreye. These creative individuals continued to produce great works to the end of their lives, in spite of physical frailty and social opposition. We return to this core theme later in this chapter, after exploring some of the other essential features that enrich the lifespan perspective on the scientific study of human psychological development from conception through old age.

Biology and culture
Another key feature of the lifespan approach to human psychological development is the recognition of how each person's lifelong pattern of psychological growth is shaped in predictable and idiosyncratic ways by an interplay between biobehavioural and sociocultural forces. For example, consider the life stories in Box 1.1. In her later years Kngwarreye suffered from the normal, age-related decreases in visual acuity (see Chapter 16) that made large canvases and wide brushstrokes a more effective painting style for her than finely detailed miniatures or delicate line drawing. Her Aboriginal cultural heritage similarly influenced her painting. The themes she chose to depict were bound up with her ceremonial responsibilities as an elder. She preferred to paint in the open air, surrounded by friends and kin, rather than isolated in an indoor studio where protection from the physical forces of wind, dust, rain and searing summer temperatures might have made the task of mixing and applying paint to canvas much easier.

In every human lifespan, from conception to old age, the complete pattern of developing psychological functioning, across the domains of cognition, emotion, personality and social relationships, is continually subject to changes that have biological underpinnings and take place in a sociocultural context. In other words, human psychological development occurs in a physical body that is situated socially within a cultural context. Lifelong growth is nurtured by others in changing ways over time, and historical and cultural forces also regulate development. Cultural diversity adds new elements to the plot of our developmental story and, in periods of rapid social change such as the present, the contrasting experiences of each new generation also contribute to the development of diversity among members of different age groups.

We look more closely in Chapter 2 at how the science of lifespan psychology accommodates these complexities, and keep an eye on the joint influences of biology and culture on psychological growth throughout the remainder of this book.

Normative transition events

Some of the developmental changes that punctuate any person's life story are idiosyncratic and unpredictable; many others are as regular as the hourly chiming of a town hall clock and can be forecast with reasonable certainty long before they occur, simply because they happen to almost everyone who reaches a particular age. These predictable developments, often known as 'milestone events' or 'turning points', occur throughout the lifespan. Some, like an infant's first social smile, a toddler's first meaningful word, a child's first friendship, an adolescent's departure from the parental home and an adult's transitions to work, marriage, parenthood, grandparenthood and widowhood, are universal across most cultures and most eras of human history. Others, like learning to read, attending school or university, conscription into military service, running for political office, pursuit of a demanding career or retirement from employment into a leisured way of life, are of a more restricted scope across the human population and yet are predictable in particular cultures at particular historical times.

Lifespan developmental psychology makes use of the inherent predictability conferred by the normative nature of many of the most important transitions and challenges that shape our lives to assist in the task of scientifically understanding how people change as

they grow up and grow older. Development carries the individual forward through each milestone transition and, at each of these important junctures from infancy through adulthood, new opportunities for psychological growth present themselves. At the same time, the range of available life choices may narrow, the loss of developed capacities may arise and problems and disappointments will almost certainly occur. In responding to these opportunities and adversities, the individual's life course takes shape from conception through to death. Many changes can be foretold with reasonable accuracy simply by knowing how old someone is, as we see in the next sections of this chapter.

Why is age so important to psychologists?

Psychology distinguishes itself from other disciplines that focus on human lives (like history or literary biography) by being concerned to achieve a reliably objective, scientific understanding (Bond & McConkey, 2001). Within this disciplinary framework, developmental psychology uses chronological age as an important guide to the science of development (Peterson, 2001).

Let us take a closer look at why age can provide useful insights to scientists and lay people alike. What can we learn about a person's overall patterns of psychological functioning simply from knowing how old they are? Why do we so often focus, when observing strangers, on clues like skin texture, body shape, hair colour and hairline which can suggest how old they are? What does it matter how old you and your closest friends are? Answers to these questions highlight how significant age can be, as does Box 1.2. In fact, the overall influence of age on human psychological functioning is, as noted above, partly a biological matter of inhabiting a body that has been around in the world and actively used for a certain number of years. As we see in later chapters, many biobehavioural processes take time to mature and wear-and-tear can eventually undermine bodily functioning in the same way that it may have affected your old car or vintage computer.

Age group membership also exerts important sociological and cultural influences on human psychological functioning. Although what it means specifically to be aged 15, 35 or 50 will vary considerably from culture to culture and, within a culture, across successive generations in that culture's history, the fact that age group membership has a meaning is constant through them all (Baltes, Staudinger & Lindenberger, 1999). To gain a sense of how age as a psychological variable can assist in the explanation and prediction of human behaviour and its development through time, let us examine some of these personal, cultural and sociohistorical correlates of the chronological age construct.

Normative life events, such as retirement from work or a grandchild's school entry, are markers which shape the life cycle for many adults in our culture.

The personal meaning of age

If someone asked you how old you will be at your next birthday, would you be eager to give a truthful answer? Are you impatient for that birthday, so that you can be one year older than you are at present? Do you feel flattered when someone thinks you are older than you really are? Do you believe you feel, look and act exactly your age?

If you said 'yes' to most of these questions, there is a strong chance that you have not yet reached the age of 25 years (Hori, 1994; Peterson, 2003). If you hesitated or said 'no' to most or all of these questions, you could be any age from 30 to 90.

In fact, according to the results of a recent survey of a group of 103 Queenslanders aged 20 to 89 years (Peterson, 2003), most Australians over 30 would prefer to be younger. Specifically, as shown in Figure 1.1, whereas average Australians aged 20 to 29 perceived no gap between their real age and the ideal age in life, this gap had appeared by age 30 and grew wider up to the age of 89. Thus, Australians who were actually in their 50s felt as if they were in their 40s and wanted, like Jack Benny, to be 39. Those who were aged 75 and over felt like 61-year-olds and thought the ideal age in life was 45. Studies of mature adults in Finland (Uotinen, 1998), in Japan (Hori, 1994) and in the United States (Barak et al., 1988; Montepare & Lachman, 1989) have revealed similar patterns of difference across successive age groups within the same culture. But, as shown in Figure 1.2, there also appear to be important cross-cultural variations in the absolute age considered to be ideal. North Americans seem to be the ones most likely to

Reactions to growing older are shaped by personal experience.

express the wish to be forever in their 20s; Australians favour the 40s; and Finnish adults are more inclined to favour older ages than both of these groups (see Figure 1.2).

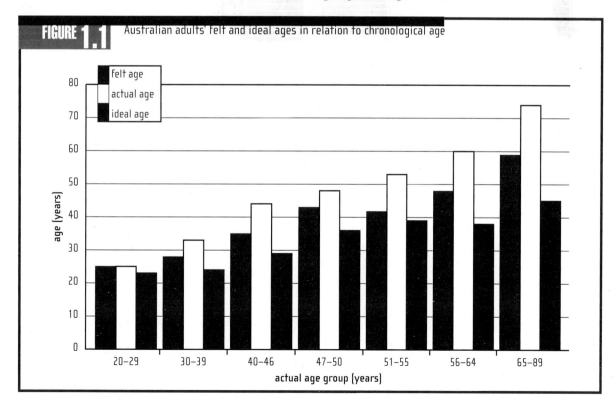

FIGURE 1.1 Australian adults' felt and ideal ages in relation to chronological age

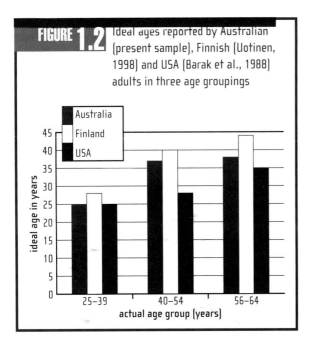

BOX 1.2 Taking things personally: How old are you?

If you would like to get a sense of what age means to you and a taste of how lifespan researchers go about studying this question, try completing this quiz.

1. How old are you now? _____ (years)
2. How old do you feel? _____ (years)
3. What is the best thing about being the age you are right now?_____
4. What is the worst thing? _____
5. What is the ideal age in life to be? _____
6. What is the worst stage in life? _____
7. Name one change for the better _____ and one change for the worse _____ that have happened to you over the last 10 years.
8. What change(s) do you look forward to most over the next 10 years? _____

Answers: For comparisons with the viewpoints of other people in your age group, see Figures 1.1 and 1.2 and the accompanying text.

Your answers to questions like those in Box 1.2 may help you to appreciate some of the dimensions of personal age consciousness that could help to shape your plans, goals and thinking about the future right now, along with your level of sensitivity to age as a criterion for personal reflection and social categorisation. It could be interesting to see whether your viewpoint on your age changes after you read about the recent studies of adult development included in Chapters 13 to 17.

Like it or not, however, age is a fact of life for all of us. No matter how hard we try to disguise its symptoms with the aid of hair colouring, anti-wrinkle creams, wigs, facelifts or cosmetics, or how steadfastly we refuse to disclose our age on documents or avoid celebrating birthdays, it is hard to keep chronological age completely private. Think back to the last time you had to produce your birth certificate or give your birth date. Chances are, it was not that long ago. Age is relevant to applications for jobs, courses of study, foreign travel, medical treatment and borrowing money from the bank. Legal age limits govern our eligibility to leave school, drive a car, get a tattoo, vote, drink alcohol and remain in full-time employment in many occupations (Peterson & Siegal, 1998).

Informally, each age group in a society is segregated to some extent from their juniors and seniors, either in schools or inner-city neighbourhoods, or through their various clubs and friendship networks. At each phase in life people are subjected to cultural attitudes that may range from adulation to bigotry. The sense of being a particular age also shapes our thoughts and feelings about ourselves, as well as many aspects of our outward behaviour. However, by no means are all these thoughts negative, whatever age you are. Group surveys suggest that most adults aged 30 to 60 years old are reasonably content to be whatever age they currently are, and only a few would prefer to be in their 20s again, as shown in Figure 1.1. Culture is a major shaper of favourable versus antagonistic feelings towards old age, as we see later in this chapter.

BOX 1.3 Expressing individuality
What it means to be 50

Despite the significance of normative trends, it is important to note the individual differences among the members of any age group in the personal meanings they attach to their age. Consider the contrasting autobiographical accounts by two distinguished French women, the philosopher Simone de Beauvoir and the actress Simone Signoret, of what it felt like to turn 50.

de Beauvoir wrote:
Perhaps the people I pass in the street see merely a woman in her fifties who simply looks her age, no more, no less. But when I look, I see my face as it was, attacked by the pox of time for which there is no cure. My heart, too, has been infected by it ... My powers of revolt are dimmed now by the imminence of my end and the fatality of the deteriorations that troop before it; but my joys have paled as well ... Yes, the moment has come to say: Never again! It is not I who am saying goodbye to all those things I once enjoyed, it is they who are leaving me; the mountain paths disdain my feet. Never again shall I collapse, drunk with fatigue, into the

smell of hay. Never again shall I slide down through the solitary morning snows. Never again a man. (1968, p. 673)

While this image of the 50s is predominantly negative, de Beauvoir's compatriot, Simone Signoret, agreed with many contemporary women in Australia, New Zealand and the United States (see Figure 1.2 and Chapter 15) that age 50 was 'the best that life can be'. As an actress, the lines of age freed Signoret from the confines of acting shallow roles reserved for nubile young stars. Signoret wrote:

It's miraculous when life brings you parts that seem to grow better each year; stronger, laden with the memories and personal experiences that have put those lines on your face. They are the scars of the laughter, the tears, the questions, the astonishments and the certainties that are also those of your contemporaries ... Does one act better after one has aged? Well, one doesn't act better, one doesn't act anymore. One is. The compliments you get from people who speak about 'the courage to show oneself in an unflattering aspect' are just pious remarks. It isn't courage: it's a form of pride, possibly vanity, to show yourself as you really are in order to better serve the character that has been offered you as a gift. (1978, pp. 358–60)

In her interviews with a group of nine contemporary Australian women who had recently turned 50, Jan Bowen (1995) discovered other positive personal experiences of this and future decades in life. Sara Henderson won the Australian Businesswoman of the Year Award in 1991 for almost singlehandedly pulling her remote cattle station back into financial solvency after being widowed the year she turned 50. She said:

> I think you look back and analyse your life as you get older. I look back over my life and the older you get, you philosophise a lot more. I think strength builds as you go, I really believe that. A lot of people aren't tested so they never find their inner strength, but if you are tested a lot, you keep finding more and more and it develops and grows ... My challenges started at the age of fifty ... I think it took fifty years of experience to have been able to deal with what I have had to handle. I don't think I would have been capable at thirty; maybe at forty I might have been halfway capable. (pp. 15–16)

Ambivalence about growing older tends to be particularly poignant during adolescence when change occurs so rapidly that the body, personality and intellect seem to be transforming themselves almost overnight. Sixteen-year-old Tina de Varon gave the following account of how a sense of her age first took on meaning for her:

> When I was thirteen or fourteen, I felt bereft of the time of my childhood. I knew that this time could never come back, that I would only get far-

ther and farther away from it. I wanted to be little all over again. But at the same time I couldn't wait to be grown up; I was buying bras and eye makeup, and holding hands with boys. I can remember saying to myself 'You are stupid to want to be big and little at the same time'. Somehow I knew that by wanting to be more grown-up, I was making my precious childhood go away too fast. This mixture of feelings used to frighten me and make me sad. (Kagan & Coles, 1972, p. 346)

For this teenager, personal consciousness of having crossed the threshold of her teens aroused a mixture of conflicting thoughts and emotions. She looked forward eagerly to the independence and privileges of adulthood, but at the same time she felt such a poignant nostalgia for her childhood that she was filled with sadness and anxiety.

To a younger child, age may mean little more than the criterion for membership in a peer group or a source of smug pride after a birthday. But parents are likely to be even more keenly aware of their children's ages than their own, for the child's passage through successive milestones on the road to maturity clocks the speed of the parents' ageing process (see Chapters 14 and 15).

Personal plans for lifespan development

Personal impressions like these about our present age and about future age periods can have important consequences for mental health, emotional well-being and psychological development, indicating that we need psychological research evidence in order to make sure that such personal beliefs about age are objectively accurate. Indeed, as adults engage in life planning (Lawrence & Valsiner, 1993), their implicit beliefs about future age periods, and their anticipations of the problems and possibilities of later stages in the lifespan can prove crucial for enabling them to make realistic choices that will foster lifelong psychological growth.

Fortunately, even without the benefit of formal study in the discipline of lifespan psychology, many mature men and women hold surprisingly positive and optimistic views about what later stages of the adult lifespan may have to offer. When Carol Ryff and Susan Heincke (1983) interviewed a group of 308 North American women ranging in age from 19 to 73, they discovered positive images of future age periods even among the oldest group. As illustrated in Table 1.1, when asked how facets of their personalities would change over the next 10 to 15 years, even women over 70 generally had things to look forward to. At least a third of them foresaw positive gains in one or more areas of life functioning.

Furthermore, when Ryff and Heincke looked at the factors that predicted the strongest sense of confidence in possibilities for future personality growth among their sample of elderly women, a combination

Respondent age group	Young adults (19 years) (n = 123)		Middle-aged adults (46 years) (n = 95)		Elderly adults (73 years) (n = 90)	
TABLE 1.1 Women's anticipations of developmental gains in adulthood in the next 10 years						
Anticipated direction of change	Positive gain (%)	Loss or no change (%)	Positive gain (%)	Loss or no change (%)	Positive gain (%)	Loss or no change (%)
Sense of purpose	89	11	62	38	31	69
Close relationships	89	11	67	33	35	65
Autonomy and self-sufficiency	92	8	67	33	44	56
Personal control	92	8	58	42	29	71
Personal growth	71	29	48	52	25	75
Self-acceptance	94	6	73	27	42	58

Source: Based on data in Ryff & Heincke (1983).

of higher education (especially at university), employment history and current involvement in learning and/or creative pursuits emerged as the best predictors. The authors concluded that:

> [Findings] illuminate age differences by showing that, among prior life experiences, it is the realm of work and education that is most strongly implicated in the sense of purpose and continued growth. As such, the effects underscore the observation that current institutions may lag behind the added years of life the elderly now experience. (Ryff & Heincke, 1983, p. 204)

Recent dramatic improvements in population health care and longevity have led demographers to suggest that most adults alive today can count on considerably more years of life than their parents or grandparents experienced, or even imagined possible (see Chaper 18 for detailed longevity projections). Yet most of us have only a sketchy idea of what those extra years will bring us, and of what our lives will be like 10, 20 or 50 years from now. Take a moment to examine your own views. Do you look forward to middle or old age with as much optimism as the North American women interviewed by Ryff and Heincke (1983)? Or does the thought of becoming a decade older, or even passing the threshold to your next birthday, inspire feelings of dread and denial? To help think about the lifespan as a conceptual entity, you may wish to complete the exercise in Box 1.4.

Social changes in personal age consciousness

By the time most children enter primary school, they generally have some idea about growing up, as well as a set of impressions, however sketchily defined, about their own future life course. By early adolescence, a firm set of anticipations about the major turning points in life is likely to be in place, together with views about whether or not to marry, have

children, take time out of a career for childrearing and so on (see sections on adolescent identity development in Chapter 11).

Even so, in youth, as in maturity, there is plenty of room for individuality and surprise, and it is hard to get a firm fix on subjective beliefs about the lifespan, owing to the rapid pace of social change. As a result of contemporary changes in the average length of formal education and of the nature of career options and the labour market, adults' plans for the future now require more compromise and tolerance for change than was true in the past (Pryor & Taylor, 1986). The wider range of options available today for age at entering or leaving a career, university or marriage means that our implicit models of the life course need to remain more open and flexible. According to Bernice Neugarten (1987), 'We are less sure today where to place the punctuation marks in the life line and just what those punctuation marks should be' (p. 30). But Neugarten went on to explain:

> Whether or not historical change is occurring, it is fair to say that one's own age remains crucial to every individual, all the way from early childhood to advanced old age. A person uses age as a guide in accommodating to others, in giving meaning to the life course, and in contemplating the time that is past and the time that remains. (p. 30)

BOX 1.4 Activity suggestion
Life-line drawing

This life-line drawing measure (Ruoppila & Takkinen, 2001) provides a window on your personal anticipations of future phases in the lifespan, as well as a graphic portrayal of how you now view your life as a complete whole.

Instructions: Draw the stages of your life as you conceive of them from birth to death. Don't worry about your ability as an artist. Relax and sketch in whatever way you like. Then draw lines to mark *periods* in your life. You may define as many or as few as you think appropriate. Finally, assign a name to each period in the drawing. (An example of a 16-year-old Australian girl's response to this question is shown below.)

When this measure was administered to a large group of Japanese adults (Kojima & Aoi, 1987) it was found that they viewed middle age as the least differentiated phase in their life course, and elderly Japanese people generally divided their lives into more phases than young adults. One group of 19- to 50-year-old Australian students used between three and 15 periods to describe their lives, with a mean of nine.

Try giving this exercise to groups of people of mixed age. Count the number of phases used by each person and graph this against their age in years. Also analyse the frequencies of positive terms ('happy', 'relaxation', 'exciting', etc.) and negative labels ('loss', 'lonely', 'sick' etc.) used for each major life phase. Are certain age periods consistently

viewed with greater optimism than others? Is the general shape of the life-line flat, upward-sloping, steadily downward or U-shaped? What could this mean?

Interpretation: As noted in the main text, adults of all ages are apt to think both optimistically and pessimistically about previous stages in the life cycle and what the future may hold in store. This exercise enables a pictorial exploration of your feelings about the shape of your past, present and future life cycle. If you gave the same task to friends younger and older than you, compare their pictures with yours. If your classmates also complete this exercise, you could check, using group averages, which age groups have the most positively sloped lines or the highest number of differentiated stages. According to Sanna Takkinen and Isto Ruoppila (2001), life lines with a genuinely upward trend (after averaging out the dips and peaks over short spans within the overall picture) are associated with sense of purpose, life satisfaction and socioeconomic well-being in mature adults.

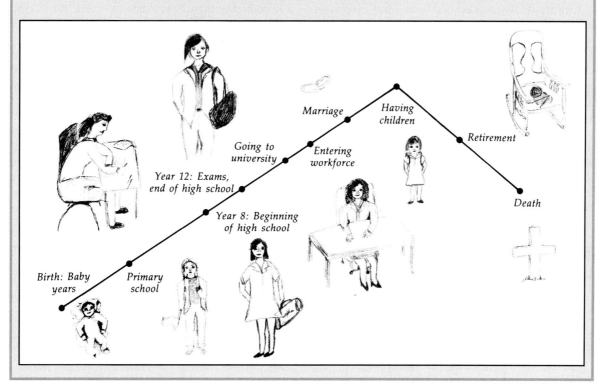

Culture, age and lifespan development

Personal feelings about the pros and cons of being 6, 16, 50 or 80 clearly vary among members of the same age group and culture, as illustrated in the preceding examples (see especially Box 1.3). However, age variations are much more pronounced when we compare across cultures (see Figure 1.2). This is not surprising, since the age-related practices and values of different cultures vary markedly from one another, while also

changing within each culture with the progression of historical time. Consequently, as Jacqueline Goodnow and W. Andrew Collins (1990) explained, it is impossible to understand fully the development of any individual in isolation from their cultural milieu. To understand age-related changes in a person's psychological make-up, we must take account of their culture's shared beliefs about age-appropriate behaviour and development, together with the culturally significant network of social roles and relationships in which each individual lifespan is embedded. Developmental patterns and plans are shaped by attitudinal factors within the culture, and by cultural institutions like schooling which may be restricted to specific age groups (like primary school for children aged 5 to 13) or broadly accessible to many age groups (like university with mature-age entry options and the University of the Third Age). Cultures also hold their own specific sets of beliefs about how development does, and should, happen. According to Goodnow and Collins, these beliefs, of which we may be only dimly conscious, actively guide progression through the life cycle of all members of a given culture, inspiring the decisions we make as we lead our lives, and the ways we influence the developmental journeys of our offspring, parents, partners and work colleagues.

It is useful to examine the models and beliefs about the life course that different cultural groups adhere to in their everyday thinking about their own and others' lives. Mark Byrd and Trudy Breuss (1992) explored the beliefs of New Zealand men and women about how to subdivide the adult life cycle into chronological age periods. As shown in Table 1.2, their results revealed highly uniform agreement among New Zealanders of both sexes and all ages with regard to the chronological boundaries of youth and old age. But New Zealanders' beliefs about middle age were much more variable. In line with findings reported earlier in this chapter about personal age ideals (see Figure 1.2), the point at which middle age was seen to begin for New Zealand adults in general seemed to depend a lot on the respondent's own age. Young adults tended to locate middle age at the middle of average life expectancy (which, in New Zealand at the time of the survey, was 76 years), whereas those aged 30 believed people did not become 'middle-aged' until their 50s. According to

Byrd and Breuss: 'Middle age is a particularly ill-defined phase of life and subject to much individual interpretation as to what personal characteristics one should use to define middle-age'. (p. 145)

Filial piety and attitudes to age

Many cultures in Asia share norms of filial piety, collectivism, and respect for Buddhist teachings and Confucian philosophy (Takahashi, 2000). Consequently, culturally shared attitudes and practices with regard to middle and old age may be more positive in Asian cultures than those prevailing among contemporary adults in New Zealand, Australia and other industrialised societies with an Anglo-European tradition. To investigate such a possibility, Shigeo Hori (1994) tested a sample of approximately 800 Japanese adults aged 19 to over 60 years on an attitude measure similar to that employed by Byrd and Breuss (1992) in New Zealand. The results are shown in Table 1.2, together with those for the New Zealand group. Although Japanese adults tended to set the chronological boundaries of youth and old age a little higher than New Zealanders did, the overall similarities between these two cultures were more marked than any contrasts between cultures.

Similarly, when Matthew and Jana Sharps and John Hanson (1998) compared young adults' attitudes to the elderly in Thailand and the United States using an anonymous survey, they found no support for the hypothesis that Thailand's traditions of filial piety would produce positive attitudes. Indeed, the anonymous Thai students used more negative terms than Americans did to describe old people. However, when interviewed face to face, the Thai students were 'uniformly enthusiastic and positive' (p. 658) in their responses to the question 'How do you feel about

TABLE 1.2 The age boundaries of adult life according to contemporary adults in New Zealand and Japan (mean ages in years)												
	Participants who responded to the questionnaire											
	Men						Women					
	Young (18–29 years)		Middle-aged (30–59 years)		Old (60 plus years)		Young (18–29 years)		Middle-aged (30–59 years)		Old (60 plus years)	
	NZ	Japan	NZ	Japan	NZ	Japan	NZ	Japan	NZ	Japan	NZ	Japan
End of youth	20	28	20	29	20	30	18	27	19	28	19	29
Beginning of middle age	38	39	45	44	56	49	39	38	50	43	58	47
Beginning of old age	66	65	67	69	68	72	63	64	61	69	61	71

Source: Based on data in Byrd & Breuss (1992) and Hori (1994).
Note: Japanese respondents were asked when 'youth ends'; New Zealanders were asked the 'age of youth'.

older people in general?' This may have been due to politeness norms that required concealment of their true feelings. The authors concluded that 'Even strong traditions of filial piety may not shield elders from negative attitudes to the degree that might be desired' (p. 659). Clearly the question of how cultural norms intersect with beliefs about the lifespan warrants study.

Age-grading: The ascent to elder status

In non-Western cultures with longstanding oral traditions and time-honoured cultural practices that tend to be carried over with little change from one generation to the next, there is good reason to value the knowledge and skill of an older person who has had many more years than a young adult to acquire the culture's lore and wisdom. Thus the social position accorded to an elder may be superior in such a culture to that of the older adult in a modern industrialised society where urbanisation and the rapid pace of technological change have severed links with younger generations, while making the old person's skills and knowledge seem irrelevant and obsolete (Cowgill & Holmes, 1972; see Chapter 16).

Anthropological evidence provides some support for these suggestions. For example, the remote-dwelling Lepcha people of the upper Himalayas looked forward to old age so much that they would manipulate their clothing, hairstyle and appearance, not in order to seem young, as a Westerner might, but rather to fool people into believing them older than they really were. In Lepcha culture it is a special mark of respect when a younger sibling calls an older sister 'mother'. Fathers and fathers-in-law are equally flattered when their children are thoughtful enough to address them as 'grandfather', or to tell them that they are looking ancient (de Beauvoir, 1977, p. 83).

The traditional Maori people who lived in New Zealand before the arrival of the Pakeha (Anglo) settlers also had strong cultural norms of respect for age, along with a clear set of social mechanisms for recognising the gains in wisdom and social prestige that ageing could bring. Although social advancement was not an automatic consequence of growing older, positive achievements in adult roles led to personal pride and public tribute. One way in which traditional Maori culture accorded social recognition to adult achievers was the process of ceremonial tattooing, or *moko*. Reminiscent of contemporary Anzac Day parades where war veterans display their medals and ribbons, the traditional Maori warrior who achieved distinction on the battlefield aspired to the reward of a facial tattoo authorised by the King. The *moko* was tattooed on the face by a special artisan during a public ceremony. The tattooing process was painful, but the occasion was one of rejoicing for the warrior who would carry this public record of achievement on his face for all to see for the rest of his life. *Moko* decorations were also granted for adults' intellectual and creative achievements. For

women, exceptional ability as a dancer or musician or in the domestic arts might earn the award of a facial tattoo. But a mature outlook on life and sense of social responsibility were additional implicit criteria. As Michael King (1972) explained, women's *moko* was 'the mark of adulthood and an indication that women were able to bear pain and ready to take on responsibilities, domestic and public' (p. 88).

The practice of formally according increasing social status to people as they grow older is called *age-grading*. Among the tribal Masai of East Africa, another tradition-oriented culture, there are seven age grades for males: uninitiated youth, apprentice warrior, senior warrior, junior elder, senior elder, retired elder and ancient elder. Each grade has its own code of dress and diet and its own residential, social and occupational characteristics. For example, apprentice warriors run messages and build fences and are not allowed to marry or eat meat (Cain, 1964).

There was an especially strong culture of respect for the elderly among the indigenous Australian Aboriginal people before they came into contact with Europeans and, as seen in Box 1.1, much of this veneration of the wisdom born of age and experience remains intact among Aboriginal Australians today. Recall the position that the painter Emily Kngwarreye held when over the age of 80, not only as a respected artist but also as an elder with economic, political and religious authority (Brody, 1998). In Aboriginal culture, however, respect for the elderly was, and is, earned on merit, rather than simply being an automatic right once a person reached a particular age in years. According to anthropologists Ronald and Catherine Berndt (1964):

> Wisdom is not assumed to come automatically with increasing age. Personal factors are involved, too. A man, or woman, who by middle life has achieved a reputation for incompetence or foolishness is not *normally* expected to improve as he grows older. On the whole, however, there is an emphasis on age, especially when it comes to providing a final decision on some debatable point – in much the same way that in our own society precedents are cited as a basis for legal judgments. Other adults do have an informal say, but they are considered to be less familiar with all the issues which may be involved. And because in the great religious sequences men take a more active role than women, some men come to have increased authority as ritual headmen. This lends weight to their opinions. Knowledge of sacred matters is a pre-eminent criterion, and people who qualify on this score are regarded as final authorities, or as human spokesmen for those authorities. (pp. 338–9, courtesy Estate of R.M. & C.H. Berndt)

The practice of age-grading was formalised in many traditional Aboriginal communities, such that a series of ceremonial initiations was required in order

In traditional Aboriginal culture, the older men and women occupy a special place in religious, political and educational life.

enforcement and the transfer of knowledge and spiritual matters. New privileges accompanied these added responsibilities. Yet, at each step, the individual had to prove himself worthy in the eyes of others before this higher social recognition could be accorded.

Traditional Aboriginal women in many communities also underwent initiations into elder status through their adult lives, though details are less fully documented than in the case of the male life cycle of ceremonial initiation (White, 1985). Thanks, however, to the painstaking record-keeping of amateur anthropologist Daisy Bates, a teacher and journalist who migrated to Australia from Ireland in her late teens and spent the last half of her life, until her death at age 91, living in traditional Aboriginal communities in Southern and Western Australia, the following account has survived. It tells how the elder status of *yogga biderr* (meaning 'great, strong woman' or 'vein of strength') was accorded to an older woman who had borne many children, had gained and displayed specialised secular and traditional knowledge and had become influential in her community:

> The ceremony was usually at some big gathering … The privileges conferred upon the woman were a continuous and plentiful supply of food, clothing, shelter and fire by the younger members amongst her relatives, and immunity from capture by raiders. She was also henceforth sacred from revenge in a tribal fight, but she was powerful in stirring her people up to fight against offending outside tribes and she was equally privileged to allay family feuds within the tribe, and other quarrels. If family feuds arose and a fight was anticipated, the *yogga biderr* could go into the midst of the combatants and disarm them of their spears and other fighting weapons, and her harangues, either directed towards war or peace, were always listened to with respect. As she was generally supposed to possess [wisdom] she was some-

to ascend to higher levels of seniority and elder status. These traditions were based on the community's recognition that the junior member was worthy of such a promotion, based on past achievements and leadership potential. The Berndts (1964) described how these successive initiation ceremonies punctuated the life cycle for indigenous Western Australian Aboriginal men, as illustrated in Figure 1.3.

This traditional Aboriginal conceptualisation of the life cycle implicitly depicts adulthood as a ladder or staircase ascending towards ever higher levels of power, social service and spiritual purity for adults of both sexes. For example, from the time of the first initiation at puberty through the successive ceremonies that segmented the mature lifespan, a man was seen to gain wisdom and respect progressively with his years (Maddock, 1974). As he progressed through the initiation sequence, a man was also accorded increasing social responsibility for law-making, law

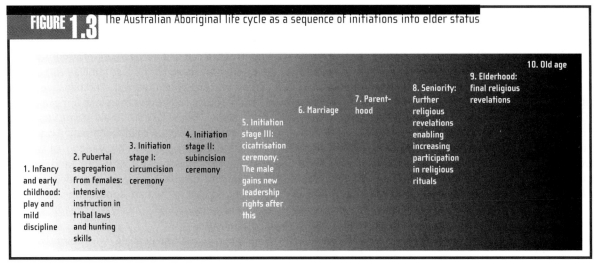

FIGURE 1.3 The Australian Aboriginal life cycle as a sequence of initiations into elder status

									10. Old age
								9. Elderhood: final religious revelations	
							8. Seniority: further religious revelations enabling increasing participation in religious rituals		
						7. Parenthood			
					6. Marriage				
				5. Initiation stage III: cicatrisation ceremony. The male gains new leadership rights after this					
			4. Initiation stage II: subincision ceremony						
		3. Initiation stage I: circumcision ceremony							
	2. Pubertal segregation from females: intensive instruction in tribal laws and hunting skills								
1. Infancy and early childhood: play and mild discipline									

Source: Based on data in Berndt & Berndt (1964), p. 183, courtesy Estate of R. M. & C. H. Berndt.

times consulted as to the favourableness or otherwise of a hunting expedition and was also frequently requested to smoke the magic out of a dog or spear after an unsuccessful day's hunt. (White, 1985, pp. 145–6)

Development in historical perspective

As illustrated in Box 1.4, it seems quite natural today to subdivide the lifespan into separate phases and we tend to view each phase in life, from infancy through old age, as unique in certain ways. Adolescents have fewer obligations and social privileges than middle-aged adults, for example, but more flexibility and tolerance for error. However, when we look back through history, we see that segmentation of the lifespan is a recent development for Western technological societies. In medieval Europe there were only three phases in life: infancy, maturity and (occasionally) senility (Aries, 1962). From the time that children could walk and speak, they were integrated into the mainstream of adult life. They were not excused from manual labour, and they worked alongside adults on the same jobs and for equally long hours (de Mause, 1976). On the other hand, neither were they denied access, as modern children are, to bawdy or boozy adult entertainment. Breughel's paintings provide a graphic record of the mixed-age drinking and lewd amusements that occurred in Dutch villages during the early 16th century. All ages, similarly, mingled together to play games like knucklebones or hide-and-seek and to listen to nursery rhymes – activities that we might now consider suitable only for preschoolers.

The history of childhood

The medieval psychology of childhood reflected society's refusal to attend to any differences other than size between the very young and their elders (Aries, 1962). Such a view of childhood is illustrated visually in the frescoes of pre-Renaissance artists like Giotto and Fra Angelico. These painters depicted the infant Jesus as a tiny man with mature facial and bodily proportions. The dwarf-like statues of family members that decorated the tombs of Elizabethan England supply another permanent record of the use of miniature adults to represent infants and children (Plumb, 1971). The clothing styles of 13th-century Europe also reflected the belief that children were merely 'adults-in-miniature' – people of all ages dressed in identical long gowns (Aries, 1962). No words existed in medieval European languages to describe young people specifically. Terms like 'boy' and 'girl' could refer to elderly peasants and servants as well as children, while the word 'child' described kinship without reference to age. The distinction of being physically small was not seen as important enough to warrant a separate word to describe it. The few

Children in past centuries were dressed, and treated, as little adults.

attributes of children that were recognised, such as economic dependency and generational lineage, were in no way unique to childhood.

Court physician Jean Herouard, who kept a diary on Prince Louis of France from his birth in 1601 until 1628, gives detailed accounts of the young monarch's participation in mixed-age recreation which included betting, gambling, listening to obscene jokes and attending plays where nudity and explicit sexuality were featured. One of the two 'toys' he owned was a small-scale sword with a real tip which frequently drew real blood from his playmates. No one seemed to believe that five-year-olds needed special protection, nor that their skills or wisdom differed markedly from those of a mature person.

According to Lloyd de Mause, who described the history of childhood as 'a nightmare from which we have only recently begun to awaken' (1976, p. 1), this ignorance of children's special disabilities and vulnerabilities led to harsh, inhumane forms of discipline. Children of the past were sent to the gallows for minor crimes, just like adults. Even in the home, punishments for behaviours that we now consider characteristic of children, such as showing fear, interrupting or failing to answer an adult's question or wetting the bed, ranged from burnings and beatings to incisions with a knife, icy baths, sexual abuse and being forced to swallow their own urine. De Mause accounted for this callous treatment by citing an old proverb: 'A man should not trust on a broken sword, nor on a fool, nor on a child, nor on a wraith, nor on a drunkard' (p. 229). In other words, because there was no separate 'psychology' of childhood, children's behaviour was judged by adult standards and deviations dealt with accordingly.

Until recently artists depicted children as miniature adults, as in this 18th-century spelling book. The head is too small and the trunk too long to look like a real toddler.

Historians link the emergence of adolescence with an increased emphasis on schooling in the 19th and 20th centuries.

The history of adolescence

Adolescence, as a separate phase in life spanning the teens (see Chapter 10), has an even shorter history. Indeed, according to Gillis (2001), 'It was not until the twentieth century that everyone was seen as being entitled to both a childhood and an adolescence' (p. 8814). Before that, teenagers worked, married (witness Romeo and Juliet) and had children while mingling with older men and women on a largely equal footing. The historical shift that contributed most to setting adolescents apart from other age groups was the advent of compulsory schooling, though where this first arose is the subject of some controversy. In England, Frank Musgrove (1964) argued that the discovery of 'a specific group of "young persons", neither children nor adults' (p. 33), had occurred with the advent of the public school, pinpointing its origin more narrowly to the publication of the book *Tom Brown's School Days* in 1850. John and Virginia Demos (1972) agreed that 'The concept of adolescence, as generally understood and applied, did not exist before the last two decades of the nineteenth century', but they suggested that 'adolescence was on the whole an American discovery' (p. 632).

As well as being fed by the prolongation of formal schooling (Musgrove, 1964), by the delaying of young people's entry into full-fledged adult occupations (Aries, 1962) and by advertisers' appeals to a separate 'youth market' (Demos & Demos, 1972), popular consciousness of the unique needs and behaviour of adolescents grew with the separation of youthful from adult offenders within the penal system and the consequent concept of the 'juvenile delinquent' (Bakan, 1974). This aspect of the invention of adolescence is one that Australia can claim credit for. According to John Collins (1975):

> Australia has a special place in the history of the study of adolescent delinquency. In South Australia in 1889 the first ever special children's court was set up to deal with juvenile offenders. Its aim was to achieve a blend between legal and welfare considerations, to take into consideration the welfare of the child, his previous conduct and the nature and seriousness of the offence. (p. 150)

The history of adulthood, old age and the lifespan

The modern adult's preoccupation with chronological age (see Figure 1.2) had no equivalent in the past (Gillis, 2001). Indeed, in Europe three to five centuries ago, there were no birth registries or birth certificates and most adults lacked the necessary literacy and numeracy skills to compute their own ages exactly. Even the word 'adulthood' was unknown in the English language until 1870 (Jordan, 1978). The only exception was 'old age' which has always held a special place in popular consciousness, perhaps because of its obvious signs of grey hair, wrinkles and muscular weakness.

One of the earliest surviving documents commenting on old age was composed by the Egyptian philosopher Ptah-hotep, in 2500 BC:

> How hard and painful are the last days of an aged man! He grows weaker every day; his eyes become dim, his ears deaf; his strength fades; his heart knows peace no longer; his mouth falls silent and he speaks no word. The power of his mind lessens and today he cannot remember what yesterday was like. All his bones hurt. Those things which not long ago were done with pleasure are painful now; and taste vanishes. Old age is the worst of misfortunes that can afflict a man. His nose is blocked, and he can smell nothing any more. (de Beauvoir, 1977, p. 104)

In ancient Greek and Roman times, old age had an earlier onset than today. Cicero claimed that old age began at the age of 46, while in the fourth century BC the Greek philosopher Hippocrates placed the beginning of old age at 55 years for men and 50 for women (Covey, 1992). However, a perceived early onset of ageing did not imply that the Greeks and Romans shared Ptah-hotep's belief that old age consisted of unmitigated gloom or unbroken decline. Hippocrates divided old age (which he saw as lasting over four decades) into five substages:

1. *Age 50 to 65*. The 'springtime' of old age: a person is gaining wisdom and maturity, yet also has reasonably good health and physical power.
2. *Age 65 to 75*. The phase of 'green' old age: a person is beginning to show signs of physical decline but, ideally, can maintain activity while enjoying a certain social respect accorded to venerability.
3. *Age 75 to 80*. 'Real' old age: a person is definitely becoming physically frail and should begin to withdraw gracefully from social life.
4. *Age 80 to 90*. The 'ultimate' stage of old age: though physically frail, the old person is capable of reaching a peak of wisdom and spiritual insight through solitary contemplation.
5. *Age 90 onwards*. The stage of 'caducity': this is inevitably a period of senility and painful infirmity from which death provides a welcome relief.

This mixed model of old age was carried forward with slight modification into ancient Roman custom. The social position of the elderly family patriarch was enviable. He (patriarchs were always male) had the power of life and death over his children and his slaves. Politically, the votes of elderly men counted for more than those of young adults, so that an affluent man might look forward to growing old despite physical aches and pains or disabilities. According to Plato: 'As age blunts one's enjoyment of physical pleasures, one's desire for the things of the intelligence and one's delight in them increase accordingly' (de Beauvoir, 1977, p. 123).

However, the notion of ageing as the 'worst of misfortunes' was prevalent during eras in European history when the physical attributes of beauty, strength and endurance were highly prized. In medieval Europe, for example, where military and courtly exploits served to brighten an otherwise harsh and physically stressful style of existence, old age was scorned. On the other hand, in China from as early as 600 BC, wisdom and continuity with tradition were valued more highly than physical strength or athletic prowess, so that the same distinctive physical characteristics of old age that were despised in the West were viewed in a favourable light (Takahashi, 2000). Confucius wrote:

When I was 15 years old, I set my heart upon the study of wisdom.
At thirty, I planted my feet on firm ground and grew stronger in it.
At forty, I no longer had doubts.
At fifty, I understood Heaven's bidding.
At sixty, there was nothing on earth that could shake me.
At seventy, I could follow the dictates of my own heart without overstepping the boundaries of what was right.

Confucius, *Analects II*, 4

Indeed, throughout his own lifetime, circa 551–479 BC, Confucius himself exemplified these principles. Married at 19, he entered a teaching career in his mid-20s. Deploring the poverty and social unrest of the feudalistic society around him, he read and lectured on the ancient Chinese classics and preached the values of virtue, moderation and respect for tradition both within and beyond the family. In mid-life, Confucius attained a political career as magistrate or minister of crime in his local province. Retiring prematurely at 55 because of political sabotage, he travelled for a short period and then settled in retirement to a life of scholarship, teaching and contemplation until the time of his death (Takahashi, 2000). As noted earlier, the values he cherished continue to be reflected today in the importance placed on scholarship and in the respect accorded to the elderly in many contemporary Asian cultures with a Confucian or Buddhist tradition.

Though evident in Confucius's writing, the lifespan as a framework for viewing the connections between different age periods, and the idiosyncrasies within them, was not fully incorporated into popular consciousness until the 1990s, according to historian J. R. Gillis (2001). Gillis suggested that, as a consequence of this lifespan perspective, a new era in the social history of adult life is just beginning to unfold. He wrote:

Today age is seen as more subjective, more contingent [than during the twentieth century] ... We are told that how we age is up to us, dependent on how we eat, exercise and medicate ourselves ... Ageing has ceased to be seen as some invariable law of nature, to be discovered and obeyed. It is no longer a problem to be formulaically solved, but a challenge that confronts every generation and to which there is no one answer, only an ongoing dialogue with ourselves and others about the meaning of age. (p. 8816)

Older men and women today no longer feel constrained by the images of old age that pertained in previous centuries.

In other words, the account that the historians of the future may write of ages and stages in the lifespan as we know them today is likely to be multifaceted. With no single clear recipe or prescribed pattern for how to conduct our lives through adulthood and old age, the opportunities for continued psychological development are likely to be wider than ever before, and the possibilities for new styles of ageing that may remould history are exciting to contemplate. All the more reason why the scientific study of lifespan development is imperative in order to redefine the boundaries of psychological developments that have already stepped outside many of the rigid frameworks of the past.

Age and society

In addition to its key place in personal plans, cultural practices and popular consciousness across eras in history, chronological age plays a role in society through formal laws regarding the legal age to marry, drink alcohol, drive a car, vote, run for political office or have a cosmetic procedure like a tattoo or body piercing (Peterson & Siegal, 1998) and also informally through society's reactions to people of different age groups who either conform to, or deviate from, social stereotypes about how people of different ages should conduct themselves. You need only pick up a newspaper to see this for yourself, as illustrated in Box 1.5.

The normative social clock

Pressure to conform to age-appropriate standards of behaviour is applied to people of all ages. The command 'Act your age!' means something different to a toddler than to a 12-year-old, and something different again to an adult of 50. However, at each of these ages the precise meaning of this phrase is usually perfectly clear. Preschoolers are chided for crying or kicking rather than using language to persuade (see Chapter 6) and for generally behaving like babies. Teenagers should not be childish, but nor should they grow up too quickly. Adults in their early 20s are expected to prefer techno, dance and rock music to orchestral classics or opera, and older men and women are expected to have reversed these preferences.

When people step out of line by behaving in a way deemed more appropriate for a person who is much younger or older than themselves, they may incur social disapproval. In 1965 Bernice Neugarten (1968) asked a group of middle-aged American adults to name the upper and lower age limits for behaviours like wearing a two-piece bathing suit, getting married, starting a career, having one's last child or moving across the country to be near married children. In each case, the socially approved age range was quite narrow. Neugarten (1979) found that adults tended to describe their own timing of important life events in terms of a normative social clock.

BOX 1.5 Age makes the news

Have you noticed how often simply being unusually young or unusually old makes an otherwise commonplace achievement newsworthy? To prove this to yourself, search your local newspaper for items in which people's ages are mentioned.

The Australian, Monday, 8 April 2002: Italian physician Severino Antinori reports that his 62-year-old patient, Rosanna Della Corte, has given birth to a healthy baby boy, Ricardo, following an artificial insemination operation. Della Corte is the oldest woman on record to give birth to a live infant.

Time, Monday, 1 April 2002: Maude Farris-Luse dies at the age of 115 years in Coldwater, Michigan. Luse credited a diet of boiled dandelion greens and fried fish as the reason for her long life.

The Australian, Saturday, 11 May 2002: Chinese chef Li Tao, age 24, sets a world record by hand making 2,097,152 individual noodles out of 1 kg of dough. Each was so thin that 18 could pass simultaneously through the eye of a needle.

Time, Monday, 27 January 2003: Within hours of each other Linda Braidwood, age 93, and Robert Braidwood, age 95, died of pneumonia in Chicago. The Braidwoods were married for 66 years and worked collaboratively as archaeologists throughout that time, discovering Turkey's earliest building in 1964.

Time, May 2001: Adam Ezra Cohen, age 17, wins the Westinghouse Science Talent Search for his 153rd patented invention: an electrochemical paintbrush.

London Times, Friday: Thompson Horan, age 89, is furious that officials have stopped him from enjoying hang-gliding. They think that Mr Horan, though sprightly, may be a little long in the tooth for such an adventurous sport, despite having made a dozen successful flights. He will be 90 next week.

The West Australian, Monday, 10 January 1983: Mrs Madeline Landers of Narrandera, NSW, age 65, jumped from 800 metres in a parachute jump and landed only 20 metres outside the ground target at Corowa airport on the NSW–Victorian border. Of the jump, Mrs Landers said: 'I felt completely at ease once I got out of the plane.'

For instance, they were able to tell her that they had married 'early' or started their careers 'late', and went on to justify their deviation as having been due to some special circumstance such as the Great Depression. She concluded that adults' behaviour is guided by what she called a 'normative social clock'. By this term, she meant our implicit beliefs about cultural expectations for age-appropriate behaviour – both the content of what adults of a particular age should and should not do, and our own plans and intentions either to adhere to or violate these norms.

The social clock, according to Neugarten's research during the second half of last century, exerted a tightly constraining influence on most men's and women's behaviour. But it may be loosening its hold today. It would seem that the rules embodied in the social clock are far fewer than in the past, and that the expectation of adherence to whatever rules remain may be less rigid today than for previous generations.

To the extent that contemporary adults abide by a social clock at all, they are apt to interpret the meaning of being 'on-time' much more generously than their parents or grandparents did. For example, Figure 1.4 illustrates the beliefs of a group of contemporary Australian students about the social clock for marriage. They were asked to name the 'best' ages for a man and a woman to marry, and at what age a person of each sex would be 'too old' or 'too young' to marry for the first time. As Figure 1.4 shows, most students believed adults were not too old to marry until their mid-60s. Nor was any age after 18 years too young. This offers a range of more than 40 years in which to go through this developmental transition without the social stigma of being 'off-time'. The ranges of acceptable age limits for parenthood, grandparenthood and entering university were found to be similarly broad, each lasting a minimum of two decades (Peterson, 1996).

Thus the issue of being 'on-time' or 'off-time' is an excellent illustration of the impact of recent socio-historical change on lifespan development. It would seem that the specific issue of whether or not deviation from the social clock hampers psychological development must be considered in the context of the particular era in a culture's history in which the adult happens to be enmeshed.

The problem of ageism

The fact that society enforces rules about the penalties and privileges of membership in particular age groups by punishing deviants from these age norms with ostracism and ridicule, if not outright legal penalties, has led to allegations of age prejudice. In 1969 the gerontologist Robert Butler coined a new word, 'ageism', to describe a form of bigotry. Like racism and sexism, ageism unfairly limits people's access to certain valued opportunities and prerogatives on the basis of an irrelevant criterion – in this case, how old they happen to be. Not everyone is vulnerable to sexism or racial prejudice, but ageism is a wider problem. In most societies, bigotry on the basis of age is something that everyone must face eventually. Provided people live through a complete life cycle, the existence of ageism implies that they will be treated unfairly some of the time.

Butler was especially attentive to situations that gave the elderly an unfair disadvantage, since adults over the age of 65 are particularly vulnerable to ageist discrimination. Many subtle and not so subtle social messages portray old people as rigid, ailing, incompetent and obsolete. Older workers who re-enter the job market are told they are inflexible, unfit, overqualified or less in need of a job than younger workers, irrespective of their level of health or expertise (Perlmutter & Hall, 1992; for a fuller discussion

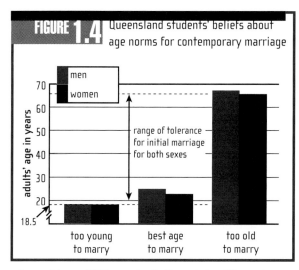

FIGURE 1.4 Queensland students' beliefs about age norms for contemporary marriage

Source: Peterson (1996), reproduced with permission of Baywood Publishing Company, Incorporated.

Adults who escaped the problems of discrimination and bigotry earlier in life may encounter prejudice in old age, and become politicised by it.

of ageism and employment see Chapters 15 and 16).

Other instances of prejudicial treatment of the elderly include residential segregation, the economic inadequacy of the age pension in an inflationary economy, discriminatory portrayals of elderly citizens in the media and a special vocabulary of insulting terms like 'old fogey', 'crock', 'crone', 'old bat', 'old bag' or 'dirty old man' that are applied specifically to the aged. But the disability of age prejudice is not confined to people over 65. According to Edgar Friedenberg (1969), adolescence is another frequently stigmatised age period. He argued that:

> A juvenile may not legally withdraw from school even if he can establish that it is substandard or that he is being ill-treated there. If he does, as many do, for just these reasons, he becomes prima facie an offender; for, in cold fact, the compulsory attendance law guarantees him nothing, not even the services of qualified teachers. It merely defines, in terms of age alone, a particular group as subject to legal restrictions not applicable to other persons. (p. 67)

Although children might appear to be exempt from ageism to an adult's eyes, it is often apparent through their own. The following interview extract reveals the ageist practice of unfair disadvantage through a neglect of children's rights and competencies, as perceived by an Australian seven-year-old:

Adult: 'Do you know what it means to be discriminated against?'

Child: 'It means when you're not allowed to do something.'

Adult: 'Are you ever discriminated against because you're a child?'

Child: 'Yes, when they won't let you into something, like the movies or a restaurant ... When they won't give you your own menu ... When Dad won't let me do something like steer the tractor ... When the shop lady won't serve you even though you were there first.'

Box 1.6 illustrates some further stereotypes about age groups that may make them the butt of ageist humour.

The science of lifespan human development

The accusation that society is ageist highlights the need for clear, detailed and accurate knowledge of what the genuine developmental and age-related changes in psychological functioning over life actually are. We need scientifically valid and reliable descriptive evidence about age groups and age differences. Further, to enable well-informed social planning and lifespan decision making, and to bring ageist discrimination to light, information is needed about the limits of individual variability. Many stereotypes are not complete fabrications. Instead,

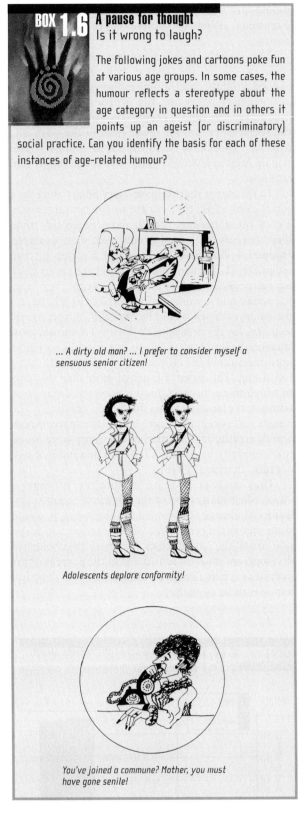

BOX 1.6 **A pause for thought**
Is it wrong to laugh?

The following jokes and cartoons poke fun at various age groups. In some cases, the humour reflects a stereotype about the age category in question and in others it points up an ageist (or discriminatory) social practice. Can you identify the basis for each of these instances of age-related humour?

... A dirty old man? ... I prefer to consider myself a sensuous senior citizen!

Adolescents deplore conformity!

You've joined a commune? Mother, you must have gone senile!

they reflect inappropriate generalisations from the problems of a few to an image of the majority.

In addition to combating unfair attitudes and unrealistic institutional discrimination, factual information about each phase in the lifespan can be put to a wide variety of positive uses. Like the people quoted at the beginning of the chapter, we all have impressions about what it means to be a particular age and what our futures are likely to hold in store as we grow older. But are our ideas accurate? Or do they reflect unquestioning adherence to time-worn clichés and 'old wives' tales'? We need objective information to be sure. Also, just as we think back to our childhood experiences to try to explain some puzzling aspect of ourselves as we grow older and continue to change, how well we know ourselves at any age will depend partly on our understanding of our continuing patterns of lifelong development.

Sensitive social planning for special age groups also demands detailed knowledge about them. Daycare centres, recreational and educational facilities, dwelling units and hospitals are some of the many institutions where successful planning depends on accurate understanding of the needs, interests and capabilities of people of various ages.

Finally, and most importantly, we need systematic scientific study of age–behaviour relationships over the lifespan for the simple reason that behaviour does change regularly and reliably as a function of age (Baltes, 2001). It is therefore not possible to fully understand trends that emerge later unless their beginnings are known. These beginnings themselves cannot be fairly evaluated except in relation to their final outcomes. Thus, psychology, the discipline which attempts to describe and explain all human behaviour, must necessarily include the study of behaviour changes over chronological age from conception through to senescence.

Studying change

Psychology is not alone in its search to understand the process of change. As Larry Goulet and Paul Baltes (1970) pointed out, almost every discipline on a university campus includes a branch or subdiscipline devoted to the measurement of alterations in phenomena with the passing of time. Microbiologists note how cell structures vary over periods of hours or days, historians and anthropologists examine changes in social structures or cultural customs over decades or centuries, and geologists measure variations in the earth's crust across millions of years.

Within psychology itself, the lifespan developmental approach focuses on longer-term changes than most other branches of the discipline. Learning theorists might measure changes in a learner's performance over minutes or hours, health psychologists might chart diet and exercise over days or weeks, and a clinical therapist might keep track of a client's progress over months or years, but the ultimate aim of lifespan developmental psychology is to account for the entire range of behaviour from conception through to extreme old age.

A definition of lifespan developmental psychology

Lifespan developmental psychology is the scientific study of the links that exist between chronological

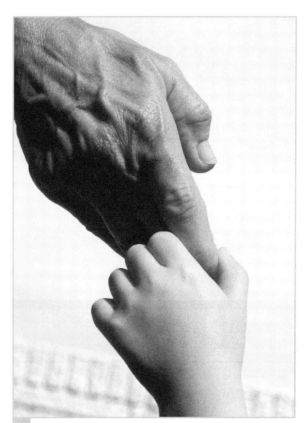

Like the predictable biological changes transforming a young hand into an old one, equally predictable psychological changes are the focus of the science of lifespan development.

age and human behaviour, together with the patterns of change in psychological functioning that arise in predictable ways as human beings grow up and grow older. Consequently, lifespan developmental psychologists strive to understand the continuities and changes that punctuate an individual's lifelong developmental course from conception to old age (Baltes, 2001). Lifespan developmental researchers are interested in all facets of human behaviour, including biobehavioural and cognitive processes, emotion, personality, social relationships and mental health.

By comparing adjacent age groups, developmentalists examine the changes in psychological functioning that reliably take place as people grow up and grow older. At the same time, developmental researchers are interested in those aspects of the person that do not change with time – for example, in the periods of stable functioning that often arise before and after a developmental transition (Levinson, 1986) and the continuities over time that enable recognition of the infant's budding temperament in her adolescent, adult and old-age personality.

These continuities and changes can take different forms over the lifespan. According to Paul Baltes and his colleagues (Baltes, 2001; Baltes, Staudinger & Lindenberger, 1999), three distinct sets of developmental variables are of special interest:

1. **Inter-individual regularities in development.** These are the age-related patterns of constancy or change

in psychological functioning that apply to most people as they grow up and get older. Two examples are the toddler's acquisition of language and the mellowing of personality in late middle age.

2. **Inter-individual differences in development.** These are contrasts in the developmental patterns of groups of people growing up and growing old in different geographical, historical, cultural or socioeconomic environments, who may also differ on variables like gender, health, temperament or socioeconomic background.

3. **Intra-individual plasticity in development.** This is the extent to which patterns of stability or change over the lifespan are flexibly modifiable in positive ways. Plasticity in development contributes to positive developmental gains in psychological capability and affords resilience in offsetting, correcting or minimising loss or damage arising with age.

Core assumptions of the lifespan approach

Researchers who study human development from a lifespan perspective employ a unique set of research methodologies (examined in Chapter 2) and generally agree on a number of basic assumptions about how development over the whole of life unfolds (Baltes, 2001). Some of these core postulates are outlined in Table 1.3. These concepts are examined further when we look at theories of development in Chapter 2, and then throughout the rest of the book in the context of studying specific developmental changes obeying these properties.

TABLE 1.3 Core assumptions of lifespan developmental psychology

Assumptions about human psychological development	Theoretical proposition
Development is a lifelong process, with no age period reigning supreme.	Psychological development can, and does, occur at all ages throughout life. No age period holds supremacy in its influence over the life course, and later developments can be as important as early ones in shaping the directions and nature of psychological growth. No age period in life is either too early or too late to permit some developmental change.
Development involves both qualitative (discontinuous) and quantitative (continuous) changes.	At all stages in life, some developments build on one another gradually in a cumulative way (quantitative change) while others create innovative patterns totally distinct from what went before (qualitative change).
Development is multidirectional.	There is pluralism in both the nature and direction of developmental change. During the same developmental periods, some systems and domains of behaviour and psychological capacity show increases in levels of functioning, some stay steady and others decrease.
Development involves a changing dynamic of biology against culture over the lifespan.	There is a growing gap between biological and physical growth after adolescence, and culture becomes increasingly important as a regulator of psychological growth in adult life.
Development involves a balance of gains and losses.	The process of development is not always a linear movement towards greater effectiveness and competency. Instead, throughout life, development always involves the joint occurrence of gain (growth) and loss (decline) in psychological capacity.
Development is plastic, flexible and modifiable over time.	It is almost never too late to grow in genuinely productive new psychological directions or to overcome developmental blockages and adversities. There is flexibility in human developmental directions which remain largely modifiable across the life course. Recovery from insult or injury, like development in general, reflects the constant interplay of biological and environmental precursors with current life conditions, and will vary according to individual initiative, resilience and degree of nurturant support surrounding the individual.
Development is embedded in multiple contexts.	The developmental course that each person charts through life is uniquely their own. When considered collectively across groups of people, lifelong developmental patterns are infinitely diverse and are shaped by normative (culturally general) and non-normative (idiosyncratic) life events. These combine in an interactive (dialectical) fashion to shape patterns of change in psychological functioning over time.

Developmental psychology as a discipline draws upon multidisciplinary contributions.	Psychological development needs to be understood in relation to processes that are: • biological (e.g. genetic, physiological and neurocognitive), • cultural/anthropological, and • sociohistorical (e.g. demographic, economic, sociological and historical).
Development is more than the linear sum of separate influences.	Interactions among biological and sociocultural influences shape behavioural development from conception to death.

Source: Adapted from Baltes (1987); Baltes & Staudinger (1996); and Baltes, Staudinger & Lindenberger (1998), p. 1043.

The concept of development

While the field of lifespan human development is concerned with *all* changes in behavioural, psychological and social functioning that obey a predictable relationship to chronological age, there is a special interest in those changes that are genuinely *developmental*. As James and Betty Birren (1990) explained:

> *Development*, as scientists have defined it, implies changes in the organization of behavior from simple to complex forms, from small to large repertoires of behaviors, from fixed ways of responding to demands and needs to large repertoires of behaviors that can be strategically chosen. This suggests that development ends at no specific time and that the organism may continue to differentiate behaviors long after physical maturity, and move toward increasing complexity. (p. 9)

Generally speaking, truly developmental changes correspond to the word's etymological derivation from the notion of 'unwrapping'. In each case some relatively small, indistinct, simple or powerless potentiality is transformed over time into a clearer, stronger, more complex or unique actuality. As Robert Kastenbaum (1993) explained:

> Development proceeds as form moves from its potentiality to its actuality. An acorn and an oak are obviously very different from each other, yet also obviously intimately interconnected … The oak is the actuality of the acorn and the acorn is the potentiality of the oak. (p. 113)

More specifically, changes that qualify as genuine psychological developments usually possess four additional properties:

1. *permanent*, as opposed to merely cyclic or continually reversible;
2. *qualitative*, in addition to mere quantitative increments in an already extant capacity;
3. *generalisable* across many different generational cohorts within a culture, as opposed to being either idiosyncratic to a particular individual's life history or unique to only one cohort in a particular culture or population; and
4. *progressively enhancing* of the individual's capacity to function psychologically, as opposed to regressive or degenerative changes.

Let us examine what these criteria tell us about changes that are true developments in human psychological capacity, together with some specific examples.

Permanent change

The notion of development as a relatively permanent change is in contrast to brief changes in human psychological functioning that fluctuate regularly or reverse themselves – such as the alterations in mood that may accompany a woman's monthly menstrual cycle, or the changes in attentiveness, creative capacity and irascibility that parallel daily sleep/wakefulness and hunger rhythms (Luce & Segal, 1966), or the waxing and waning of sexual powers and urges — despite the fact that these may occupy major portions of the life cycle (Kohlberg & Kramer, 1964). In general, developmental changes are relatively permanent and irreversible except in the context of atypical events such as brain injury or physical or mental illness.

Qualitative and quantitative change

The notion that lifespan development involves qualitative as well as quantitative change means that lifespan growth is not simply a matter of gradual changes along a given dimension of psychological functioning. Surprising transformations can also take place, as in biological growth when an earthbound caterpillar develops qualitatively into a soaring butterfly. As the humanistic psychologist Abraham Maslow said of human development:

> Change becomes much less the acquisition of habits or associations one by one, and much more a total change of the total person, i.e. a new person rather than the same person with some habits added like new external possessions. (1968, p. 39)

The infant's transition from creeping to walking upright is one example of a qualitative developmental change. Once up on two legs, the baby's patterns of posture, muscle use and balance all differ dramatically from the 'four-legged' mode of locomotion that most infants perfect before reaching the age of one (see Chapter 4). Further along in the lifespan, the teenager's transition from a companionable friendship with a same-sex chum to an intimate late-adolescent heterosexual dating relationship is another example of a qualitative developmental change (see Chapter 12). New issues of commitment and intimate sexuality are apt to transform the entire nature of the close relationship (Noller, Feeney & Peterson, 2001). A visual example of qualitative developmental change in children's pictorial representation (see Chapters 6 and 7) appears in Box 1.7.

Qualitative development (as from a mini into a Rolls) is possible for humans but not cars.

Generalisable change

In Chapter 2 we examine some of the research methods that developmentalists use to tease apart general developments from those that are somewhat idiosyncratic. Ideally, the science of human development strives to explain general developmental changes that apply to most people most of the time, rather than changes that are confined to particular cohorts of people or to particular eras in a culture's history.

Progressive change:
The actualising of hidden potential

To be described as 'development', a change should improve the individual's ability to cope independently with a wide range of varied situations. That is, development entails 'an increased capacity for self-regulation, a larger measure of relative independence from environmental fluctuations' (Nagel, 1957, p. 16). For example, during toddlerhood, the child's acquisition of meaningful speech opens new vistas of communication and the acquisition of information

---

BOX 1.7

Activity suggestion
Development through art

Instructions: Scan horizontally across the rows. You will notice changes in style which are so marked that it may be difficult to believe that each picture is the work of the same artist. These are *qualitative* changes which have developed over several years. Now scan down the columns. Each picture was sketched at about the same time as its partner(s). Only quantitative differences are evident. Yet the artist is a different person in each case, though of a similar age to the others in the same column.

For further interest: Visit a day-care centre or primary school and ask several children of various ages to draw a picture of a person. Look through the drawings and list all the qualitative changes you can discover between younger and older artists' work (e.g. inclusion of a torso, differentiation of fingers and toes, realism of bodily proportions, etc.).

Reference: For general reading about the fascinating topic of children's artistic development, consult Goodnow (1977).

Qualitative developmental change

Style 1   Style 2   Style 3   Style 4   Style 5   Style 6   Style 7   Style 8

through what others say, as opposed to merely through direct experience. Similarly, during old age some (though not all) healthy adults acquire 'wisdom' (see Chapter 16). This new cognitive attribute qualitatively enhances their abilities to plan, reason and give sensible advice (Baltes, 1993). The life stories in Box 1.1 illustrate this. For example, the concern for the future of the human race that Bertrand Russell expressed through his anti-nuclear activism, and the abiding concern for Aboriginal Australians that Kath Walker expressed through her political activism, her poetry and her educational innovations were qualitative advances in personal self-expression that had cognitive attributes similar to Baltes' (1993) definition of wisdom. The increases in optimism and life satisfaction that were observed in a recent Australian comparison between adults in their 20s and in their 70s (see Figure 1.5) is another vivid example. Significant gains on both dimensions arose in Australians who were over the age of 70 (Maher & Cummins, 2001).

Life-cycle surprises

As the lifespan approach studies genuinely developmental changes of these kinds, it provides an integrating perspective that can help to clarify the long-term consequences of early developmental trends. Sometimes, the outcomes of this longer view are surprising; as it seeks continuities and discontinuities in behaviour patterns from one age to another, the lifespan outlook frequently reveals unexpected links that clarify the meaning of particular behaviours at a particular age. For example, motorically active infant girls are found to be exceptionally extraverted and aggressive when they reach adolescence (Bayley, 1965), suggesting that mature personality may be an offshoot of a congenital energy surplus. On the other hand, anticipated lifespan links sometimes do not emerge, and this too is informative. For instance, the infant boy's level of activity predicts

later task persistence, but not extraversion (Bayley, 1965), indicating that sex-typed socialisation experience plays an important role in the way an early disposition will emerge in later behaviour. When she charted personality development through the first half of the lifespan, Jean Walker MacFarlane (1975) noted that an individual's position in relation to the group may change, with some precocious children becoming ordinary adults and vice versa. She wrote:

> We had not appreciated the maturing utility of many painful, strain-producing, and confusing experiences which in time, if lived through, brought sharpened awareness, more complex integrations, better skills in problem solving, clarified goals, and increasing stability. Nor had we been aware that early success might delay or possibly forestall continuing growth, richness, and competence. (p. 221)

MacFarlane gave two examples of optimistic lifecycle 'surprises' from among the group of 10 per cent of men and women who turned out far better in adulthood than their troubled early development had led the researchers to expect. One was a girl who, as a teenager, had seemed to spend all her time and energy defying regulations. She had an extremely poor relationship with her parents, had been expelled from school at 15, and had appeared in juvenile court numerous times. But by her mid-thirties she had settled down. MacFarlane described her as a wise,

BOX 1.8 How can you explain it?
Cheerfulness and longevity

Imagine you are a member of a research team that has just embarked on a comprehensive study of the lifespan development of a large group of healthy 11-year-olds. The sample has been carefully selected to ensure good physical and mental health, and all the boys and girls included in it are above average intelligence. Your task is to track the personality dimension of cheerfulness over time. Using a standard, well-refined cheerfulness measure, you discover a subgroup of children (let's call them Sunny, Joy, Mike and Bobby) with unusually positive dispositions. These children earn higher cheerfulness scores than the other children in the sample. Another subgroup (let's call them Dolores, Cassandra, Richard and Brian) have the lowest scores. You now have to wait 60 to 70 years to observe your outcome measure – longevity – but you manage to keep careful track of all the children in your sample as they develop through adolescence and adulthood. If your findings match those of a similar longitudinal study (Freidman et al., 1994) that was begun in the United States in 1921, you will observe a survival difference as a function of cheerfulness.

Who will live longest – Sunny, Joy, Mike and Bobby or Dolores, Cassandra, Richard and Brian? (*For an answer see the text.*)

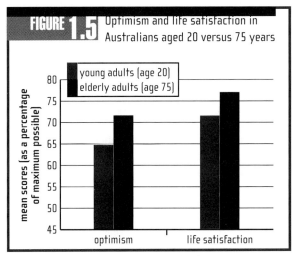

FIGURE 1.5 Optimism and life satisfaction in Australians aged 20 versus 75 years

Source: Based on data in Maher & Cummins (2001).

steady and understanding parent whose exceptionally close and sensitive style of relating to her offspring was characterised by a captivating blend of humour and compassion.

Another of MacFarlane's life-cycle surprises was a man who described himself as 'a listless oddball' when in high school, an opinion confirmed by the independent team of clinical psychologists who had entertained grave doubts about his mental health and intellectual capacity when they assessed him as an adolescent. The surprise arose when the research team assessed him again after he had turned 30. He had emerged from the gloom of his troubled adolescence to blossom as a talented architect with a happy marriage, a rich home life and an active interest in community affairs.

In 1921 Louis Terman began a longitudinal study (see Chapter 2 for a description of the longitudinal methodology) of a group of intellectually gifted 11-year-olds. Seven decades later, researchers were able to track the length of life of these healthy and highly intelligent children, now that the survivors were all in their 80s (Freidman, et al., 1994). Their results produced an intriguing life-cycle surprise: personality was a statistically significant predictor of longevity. If you attempted the exercise in Box 1.8, you will know which dimension of personality unexpectedly came to the surface as linked with a long life – cheerfulness. You may be surprised by the strength of the association. It was equal to that of such well-known and powerful physiological predictors as serum cholesterol and blood pressure. What was even more surprising, however, was the direction of the association. The happiest, most cheerful children in Terman's sample had significantly shorter lives than children who had been low in cheerfulness at age 11 and were most likely to be survivors at the age of 80.

What could account for this unexpected link? A number of possibilities suggested themselves to the research team and we examine several of these when we look at health and longevity in old age in Chapters 16 and 18. Meanwhile, it is important to remember that this important information would never have come to the surface if Terman and his team had not had the foresight to (a) measure personality in the first place and (b) follow the participants through seven decades of life to the point where the differences became clear.

As well as integrating psychological concepts between one life phase and another, the lifespan approach also enables a clearer understanding of individual people, since a person's behaviour at any given age includes some characteristics which are elaborations of past developments and some which have newly emerged, and which may themselves later be elaborated, reorganised or even contradicted. As Paul Baltes put it: 'As development unfolds it becomes more and more apparent that individuals act on the environment and produce novel behaviour outcomes, thereby making the active and selective

nature of human beings of paramount importance' (1979, p. 2).

George Vaillant (1990) also conducted a longitudinal study in the United States, beginning with a sample of 94 men in their second year at university and continuing as the men grew through adulthood into their 50s. Based on family home visits, psychiatric examinations and in-depth psychological assessments, he assessed one subgroup of undergraduates as having poor coping skills, poorer academic aims and social achievements than the rest of the group and a generally poor prognosis for future development in adult life. While some of these men's later life histories were in line with these gloomy predictions, a subgroup of them confounded the original forecasts and became 'lifecycle surprises'. In fact, these men emerged in their 40s and 50s with significantly better developmental outcomes (such as a creatively productive career, a happy marriage and warm, loving involvement with offspring) than the subgroup that had seemed to have the greatest psychological potential and developmental promise at the initial undergraduate assessment.

The examples in Box 1.1 likewise illustrate the benefits of a lifespan perspective for discovering developmental potential that can sometimes remain concealed until adult life. Both George Bernard Shaw and Kath Walker were ordinary students in school who showed no signs of the creative literary genius that was to emerge during mature adulthood. Both these exceptionally talented adults fit the criteria of life-cycle surprises. As early 'drop-outs' from high school, it is unlikely that anyone assessing their developmental potential during their teens or early 20s would have been able to predict the qualitative and genuinely developmental changes that were to arise in their lives after the age of 40.

Nurturing development through the lifespan

As we have seen, opportunities for genuinely developmental gains in psychological capacity continue throughout life and this fact is likely to have special meaning for people who are involved with the lives of others in a nurturant capacity – including parents of the young, spouses and adult caregivers of the elderly and professionals from many different walks of life, from teachers to gym instructors, retirement planners and personnel managers, as well as therapists, doctors, nurses, counsellors and members of allied health fields.

Given that psychological development is a valued, but not inevitable, aspect of an individual's nature, the nurturant other, whether an intimate family member or a professional caregiver, can play a special role in assisting it to happen. At every stage in life, the actualisation of a person's development potential requires a supportive, nurturant environment, social as well as physical. Just as an acorn may fall on bitumen and fail to sprout, or a mature oak tree may be stunted by drought or broken by storm, so also can unfavourable personal circumstances conspire against human development at any age and block psychological growth. Conversely, just as a plant's exceptionally rapid growth or abundant foliage and fruit can be enhanced by nurturant care, so too can the growth of human beings rise to peak levels when the environment is optimal. As we see in later chapters, psychological development through all stages in the lifespan is shaped in important ways by the people we share our lives with. Nurturant and capable parents, teachers, health professionals, counsellors, friends, lovers, children and colleagues can all foster individual growth, even under otherwise unpropitious circumstances. This important fact may help to explain some of the life-cycle surprises described in the previous section. For example, according to Paul Baltes and Ursula Staudinger (1996): 'Spouses, professional colleagues and members of older generations most likely represent the primary social forces in the acquisition and refinement of generativity' (p. 23).

On the other hand, the unfavourable attitudes or practices of a person's advisers, helpers and social supports can conspire to block development, even for an individual who possesses all the inner requisites for growth. This unfortunate possibility demonstrates how important it is to know as much as we can about the developmental potential of all age groups, so that such anti-developmental outcomes

can be avoided. In addition to generative concern, patience and respect for individuality, practitioners who work with developing human beings of all ages require a sound understanding of the overarching principles and solid empirical facts of lifespan developmental psychology. The descriptions, explanations and research discoveries about development that make up the rest of this book are designed to pave the way towards this kind of understanding among those who spend their lives with others, as offspring, parents, friends or helping professionals. Table 1.4 outlines some of the fundamentals of the optimisation approach.

Developmental optimisation

Optimisation can be defined as any applied intervention that is designed to maximise individuals' opportunities to develop their potential to the full. The broad goals of developmental optimisation (Baltes, 2001) are shown in Table 1.4 and can begin even before a baby is born. Expectant parents, for example, can optimise their child's chances of a healthy and normal birth by refraining from smoking cigarettes during pregnancy (see Chapter 3). Health educators might similarly optimise physical growth and psychological adjustment during adolescence by providing accurate information on diet, body shape, exercise and practices to ensure safe sexual intercourse (see Chapter 10).

After a brief overview of how the principles in Table 1.4 are put into practice by parents, teachers and other professionals working with people, we explore in Chapter 2 how optimisation is put into practice as one of lifespan developmental psychology's basic scientific goals. But before we consider what is entailed in the process of facilitating psychological development, we briefly consider some of the special concerns and requirements of the people whose role it is to provide care, support and psychological guidance to human beings ranging in age from unborn infants to senior citizens.

Parents and developmental optimisation

A lifespan perspective on parenting suggests that the parents' role in nurturing their offspring's development need not come to an abrupt end with the termination of physical growth during adolescence, or even after the grown child leaves home. Instead, the fact that psychological growth is possible throughout life implies that concerned parents will still have opportunities to nurture their sons and daughters as adult equals. At the same time, the concept of life-long development suggests that interaction with children and the tasks entailed in parenthood may themselves stimulate parents' own progress towards higher levels of maturity, with offspring nurturing the parents' cognitive, social and broad psychological development.

By nurturing the growth of those younger than themselves, mature adults develop generativity.

TABLE 1.4	Strategic directions for lifespan optimisation research	
Optimisation goal	**Developmental process**	**Example**
Developmental enrichment	Psychological growth	• Lifelong educational opportunities (e.g. University of the Third Age). • Second-language learning in retirement in preparation for travel or reading of a new world of literature.
Maintenance of functioning	Prevention of age-related decline or loss	• Environmental design to facilitate mobility and prevent falls in community dwellings. • Sports programs to help older men and women find new recreational interests (e.g. golf, bowls) when age precludes youthful sports like football or weightlifting.
Regulation or alleviation of age-related loss	Compensation for age-related declines and losses	• Teaching deliberate memorisation strategies and list-making to compensate elderly people who have memory problems. • Teaching sign language to elderly people who have become profoundly deaf so they can communicate in this modality and, perhaps, volunteer to help signed deaf children in school.

Source: Adapted from Baltes (1989).

Optimisation through education

Teachers who have a sound knowledge of lifespan development, and hence an astute awareness of the developmental opportunities and pitfalls affecting different age groups, can play a crucial role in helping to optimise development at all ages through the lifespan. This role may be particularly critical at important educational transitions and turning points in the life cycle. This includes preschool and kindy teachers, who can smooth the preschooler's initial route into formal education (see Chapter 7), as well as the gifted teachers we all remember who inspired and sustained our learning and social development in primary school (see Chapter 9), or contributed importantly to our academic or vocational interests and future life planning as adolescents in high school (see Chapter 11). But it is also crucial to make available educational opportunities later in life to cultivate and enhance the cognitive potential of mature and elderly men and women who may continue to exercise their minds and develop new cognitive strengths throughout extreme old age (Baltes, 1993; see Chapter 16).

In fact, teachers of mature adults encounter some of the same problems faced by teachers of children and adolescents. These include questions of how to motivate learners to do their best, how to help them organise their learning and how to assess their progress. But there are also special challenges and rewards in the teaching of mature students. An important prerequisite for optimising both teaching and learning is an accurate knowledge of the unique psychological characteristics, strengths and problems of adulthood and old age. A positive attitude towards the learning potential of older men and women, grounded in the research evidence that is discussed in Chapters 15 and 16, will help teachers to bring out the best in their mature students. We now know that the learning process as a psychological attribute has no age boundaries.

According to G. Fischer (2001), a lifespan approach to education is even more critical for the 21st century than adequate early schooling. This century is accelerating the already fast pace of technological change in conjunction with job redesign, occupational obsolescence and rapid individual job change and career restructuring (see Chapters 14 and 15). According to Fischer, this means that fewer adults in future decades will still be pursuing the same careers at 40 that they were educated for at high school or university. He explains:

> Most people see schooling as a period of time in their lives that prepares them for work in a profession or for a change of career. This view has not enabled people to cope well with the new realities of our world that: (a) most people change careers several times in their lives even though what they learned in school was designed to prepare them for their first career, and (b) that the pace of change is so fast that technologies and skills to use them become obsolete within 5 to 10 years. (p. 8837)

The optimising roles of health and helping professionals

As a consequence of their varied crisis interventions and their many opportunities to provide nurturant care for people of all ages, most nurses, doctors, therapists, social workers and other professional caregivers are closely attuned to the unique physical characteristics of each age period in the lifespan, and exceptionally aware of the striking bodily changes that emerge as people grow up and grow older. The risk is that an understanding of the normal processes of healthy biobehavioural and psychological development may become undermined when contacts are limited to sufferers of atypical illnesses and injuries encountered in the atypical environment of a hospital or doctor's surgery. To counteract false preconceptions, a sound understanding of research evidence on normal patterns of healthy growth through the lifespan is needed.

Some studies of attitudes towards old age suggest that members of the health professions are more vulnerable to myths and ageist (see page 19) prejudices and stereotypes about old age than members of the general public (Gatz & Pearson, 1988; Peterson, 1993a; Pruchno & Smyer, 1983). According to Gene Bocknek (1976), the view held by many counsellors that adulthood at best permits stability in psychological functioning and more often is characterised by unmitigated loss and decline of functioning has led to the mistaken belief that 'counselling is of dubious value with people of middle age and older' (p. 38) and to intervention strategies limited to medication or resignation. These views, as shown in later chapters, are no longer tenable in the face of recent lifespan research.

Looking forward

Thus a lifespan outlook offers to supply developing adults, as well as parents, carers and the members of many person-oriented professions, with a more accurate understanding of the promising developmental opportunities arising throughout life, and with useful feedback about the lifelong antecedents and consequences of their immediate plans, projects and intervention efforts. As a result of this integrating continuity within the discipline itself, certain core ideas and key issues arise again and again as we explore human development chronologically in this book. These guiding themes offer an integrating perspective that provides a sense of continuity through the book and across the human lifespan.

Chapter summary

Healthy human beings can continue to grow and develop psychologically throughout the lifespan, long after biological growth in stature has ceased. A lifespan perspective seeks to understand this developmental potential by watching how humans grow and change psychologically over the whole of life, from conception to extreme old age.

The lifespan approach to developmental psychology reveals that both biology and sociocultural experience influence how people progess through life's stages. This progression reflects the continuity and discontinuity of developments. The lifespan is punctuated by normative transition events (e.g. career entry, marriage), which happen to most people at roughly the same point in life. These predictable upheavals are important triggers of developmental change.

Chronological age, or the duration of a person's life, is usually measured in months and years since birth. A person's age has enormous significance for understanding their overall patterns of psychological functioning.

Age has huge personal meaning for most of us. Personal age consciousness shapes how we behave, feel and think about ourselves and our future. Many adults over 50, in many cultures, feel younger than their true age. People's ideal age increases as they get older; even after the age of 70, many adults foresee positive personality growth in future years.

There are cultural differences in models of life stages and in the pattern of the human life course. Traditions of filial piety and reverence for elders as repositories of culturally significant knowledge afford the elderly a higher social status in some societies. The practice of age-grading unifies a culture's attitudes towards different age groups through the ceremonial honouring of achievements of successive milestones along the route to maturity.

Over time, popular attitudes and the treatment of different age groups have undergone great change. In Europe during the Middle Ages, there was no clear awareness of childhood as a distinctive life stage and children worked and played alongside adults without provision for their special needs. Adolescence did not emerge as a clearly distinct age grouping until the mid-1800s, and only much more recently have the fine segmentations of adulthood been recognised (e.g. '30-something'). Old age, on the other hand, has always had a special place in popular consciousness.

Today we mark age in many public ways through laws that accord privileges (e.g. driving a car) and responsibilities (e.g. serving on a jury) in terms of chronological age.

The normative social clock consists of a set of socially shared beliefs about the appropriate timing of transition events. 'On-time' adults who adhere to the dictates of this imaginary clock may enjoy a smoother passage through the lifespan than those who are 'off-time' in either a premature or delayed direction. Modern societies are more flexible in their clocking of life's journey and fewer negative sanctions now apply to adults who, for example, delay first marriage and parenthood until their 40s.

Yet society continues to practise ageism, a form of bigotry that unfairly limits people's access to valued opportunities and prerogatives on the irrelevant basis of age.

Lifespan developmental psychology is the scientific study of the links that exist between chronological age and human behaviour, together with the patterns of change in psychological functioning that arise in predictable ways as human beings grow older.

Recent lifespan research identifies several core principles that govern changes in psychological functioning over age: (a) lifelong developmental potential and plasticity, (b) a combination of qualitative and quantitative change, (c) multidirectionality, (d) non-linear interactions between biological and socio-cultural forces with increasing emphasis on culture in adult life, (e) a progessive striving to maintain a positive balance of gains against losses, and (f) multi-contextual and multidisciplinary embeddedness.

Genuine psychological development is defined as changes in the organisation of behaviour from simple to complex, from small to large repertoires and from rigidity to increasing flexibility, so that the individual's capacity to cope with life's challenges is increased. These changes are mostly permanent, qualitative, broadly generalisable and progressive.

Life-cycle surprises are outcomes in later life that could not have been predicted on the basis of short-term developmental trends. Examples show the importance of lifespan research.

Developmental optimisation can be defined as applied research or intervention designed to maximise an individual's genuinely progessive psychological growth and a positive psychological balance of gains against losses over the lifespan.

For further interest

Looking forward on the Internet

Use the Internet to visit the following websites. Examine them for further information and varied perspectives on issues raised in this chapter. Also search for other relevant websites for yourself, using keywords like 'ageism', 'old age', 'lifespan', 'life cycle', 'childhood', 'adulthood', 'age stereotypes', 'longevity' and 'adult development' in your search engine.

In particular, for further ideas on issues of age stereotypes, age discrimination and images of age groups in society, visit:

http://www.aarp.org/bulletin
http://www.aoa.gov

For resources, ideas, activities and other items of interest in conjunction with this chapter, visit the Companion Website for this textbook at:

http://wps.pearsoned.com.au/peterson

Activity suggestion

As a practical activity in conjunction with themes in this chapter, try examining images of age groups in the media. When visiting the different websites above, you might like to think about how different age groups in society are portrayed. In addition, using examples like those in Box 1.5 on page 18 and Box 1.6 on page 20, search for images of different age groups in magazines, on television, in greeting cards and other popular media. Group the images by age (approximately). Then, with a friend, rate each image in terms of whether it portrays the person (or age group) in (a) a positive light, (b) neutrally, or (c) in a negative light. Compare frequencies of favourable and unfavourable images across age groups. Are older men and women viewed negatively?

Multimedia

For a fascinating glimpse of the history of childhood in Australia, schedule a viewing of the following film in class, or borrow it as a video: *Australian Childhood: Changes over 200 Years* (Equality Videos, Sydney, 1994: 24 minutes). To learn more about Oodgeroo Noonuccal (Kath Walker) whose lifespan development as a poet and activist featured in Box 1.1, take a look at the video: *Kath Walker: Poet and Activist* (Equality Videos, Sydney, 1995: 16 minutes).

THE SCIENCE OF LIFESPAN DEVELOPMENT: Goals, theories and methodology

CHAPTER 2

*What is now proved
was once only imagined.*

William Blake, 1757–1827

Contents

The fascinating process of lifespan human development has both personal and practical relevance. As we come to understand the regular patterns of psychological change that occur as people grow up and grow older, we gain a sharper understanding of our own past and future lives, and a more accurate set of guideposts by which to chart plans for our own lifelong psychological development. One thing that all human beings have in common is a finite lifespan. As we see in later chapters, some of the changes that arise between the moment of birth and the instant of death are identical for everyone, while others are unique to individual, historical and sociocultural circumstances.

For those who spend their adult lives working with other people, the study of lifespan developmental psychology has additional practical significance. It may be hard to remember exactly what we ourselves were like at the age of 8 or 18, and equally difficult to imagine what it would be like to be 48, 68 or 80. Studying developmental researchers' discoveries makes this task easier. As we progress through our study of the lifespan, age by age, it will become increasingly clear that lifespan development is punctuated by predictable regularities as well as the occasional exciting life-cycle surprise (see Chapter 1). Thus knowledge of the complete process of human psychological development provides a useful reference point for work with individuals who are much older or younger than ourselves.

Chapter 2 supplies the tools needed to make sense of recent research discoveries and their theoretical interpretations. It begins with an overview of research methodology. We see *why* developmentalists strive to observe human behaviour through the lens of science, and *how* research is conducted so as to study the processes of change over the complete lifespan. Many research techniques and strategies are available to the developmental scientist, each with unique strengths as well as inevitable limitations. By thinking critically about the methods and measurement strategies underlying a piece of psychological research, you will become skilled in drawing your own conclusions from research you read about and in weighing up scientific evidence realistically. In this way, you can continue to inform yourself of research breakthroughs that occur in the future.

The remainder of Chapter 2 is an exploration of the seminal theories that had begun to guide the understanding of human development even before there was a separate scientific discipline of lifespan developmental psychology. We approach these theories from four broad perspectives: (a) the psychoanalytic approach of Sigmund Freud and Erik Erikson, (b) learning theories, (c) the cognitive-developmental approaches of Jean Piaget and Lev Vygotsky, and (d) adult developmental stage theories. After examining the strengths and weaknesses of each approach, we see how all the theories can be drawn together around some of the core concepts of development that were introduced in Table 1.3.

The scientific goals of lifespan research

When first embarking on the study of lifespan human development, it is worth pausing for a moment to reflect on what kinds of new knowledge are likely to be gained, over and above the insights about people of different ages that we already carry around in our heads, after years of living and interacting with people. I often ask my students this during our first lecture together. Some of their answers are shown in Box 2.1. You might like to complete the exercise in this box to clarify your own expectations of what development research may be able to contribute.

The goals of the developmental scientist align themselves nicely with those of many students who are just embarking on the study of human development (see Box 2.1). In both cases, there is interest in simple questions of fact – 'How do humans [will I] live?' 'Do people [will I] lose memory capacity when they [I] get to be aged 60?' and so on. There is also interest in causal questions and explanations – 'What causes [will help me achieve] increased life satisfaction during retirement?' 'How do children [can I help my child] learn to read?' – and in questions of

BOX 2.1 **A pause for thought**
What can research tell us that we don't already know?

Activity suggestion: Add to the list in the cartoon by examining your own goals and asking friends of various ages to play '5-Questions': *What are the five most important things to be learned from studying human development through the eyes of the research scientist?* Make your own list and ask friends who are older or younger than you to suggest additional questions about how people develop over the lifespan to which they would like to know the answer. Add these to your list.

With your composite list in front of you, consider doing a preliminary assessment of how much you already know about human development, based on your lifetime of practical experience with people and your own common sense. Next to each question on your list, write a number to reflect your present degree of certainty regarding its answer, using the following scale:

1 = Totally uncertain: I have no knowledge at all about this.

2 = Mostly uncertain: I have a few ideas, none of which I'm
   sure of.

3 = Partly sure: I have some ideas, but could definitely use
   some more information.

4 = Quite sure: I know a lot, and am mostly confident about
   the truth of what I know.

5 = Totally certain: I know the answer and am completely
   sure about it.

Put this list aside now and return to it when you have read
to the end of this book. At that point, it will be interesting to
see whether any of your unanswered questions have been
resolved or whether any of your ideas about development
have changed. In this context, consider the ideas of New
Zealand adult attachment researcher Garth Fletcher (1984)
about the pros and cons of scientific knowledge versus
common sense:

*Common sense may fruitfully be conceptualized as a form
of psychological theory. At the fundamental, bedrock level
of that theory, I have argued, it is impossible to do without some of our commonsense beliefs or concepts. At a
less fundamental level, I have argued, it is both desirable
and possible to treat common sense as a valuable resource
that can be utilized in various ways by psychologists.
What makes common sense, viewed as a way of thinking,
such a difficult and dangerous resource for psychologists
is its propensity to operate silently in the unconscious
infrastructure of the mind. Accordingly, it tends to be
recalcitrant to analysis while at the same time exerting a
powerful hidden influence over psychologists' thinking
that is often both unanalyzed and unevaluated. [p. 212]*

Note: For more on Fletcher's own research into the development of close emotional attachments in adulthood, see
Chapter 13.

practical significance for everyday life – 'What qualities in a parent, infant nurse or primary school
teacher contribute best to the healthy psychological
development of the children in their charge?'.

At a more general level, these three types of question reflect the three main scientific goals of research
in lifespan developmental psychology. When they
conduct research studies, or develop and interpret
theories, developmental scientists seek to (a) *describe*,
(b) *explain*, and (c) *optimise* human psychological
development over the lifespan. These three research
goals are listed in Table 2.1 with examples of
research designs that serve each goal.

Descriptive research: Picturing psychological development age by age

The descriptive goal of developmental psychology is
to gather facts and figures about age groups and age-
related changes. For example, a descriptive develop-

mental researcher with an interest in mental ability
might administer a standardised test of intelligence
(an IQ test) to groups of adults of three different
ages: (a) 25 to 30 years, (b) 45 to 50, and (c) 65 to
70. The results of one such study (Kaufman, 1990),
in which mean (average) IQ scores were plotted by
age group supply a simple descriptive picture of
how adult intelligence relates to chronological age
(Figure 2.1).

Descriptive developmental research has many
uses. One important use is to catalogue the progress
of development for a particular psychological
attribute. When the developmental characteristics of
large and sufficiently representative samples of people
at different ages are collected to provide *generalisable*
descriptions (see pages 37 and 44 for discussions of
generalisability), they can be grouped together to
produce averages at each age level. Known as *age
norms*, these averages suggest the qualities or behav-

TABLE 2.1 Three scientific goals of research in developmental psychology		
1. Description of psychological development	2. Explanations for developmental phenomena	3. Applied optimisation
• Cataloguing of age-related changes in behaviour to produce age norms and other summary information • Developing psychological profiles of age groups • Comparisons between age groups to discover age-related differences between them • Delineation of average rates of change in behaviours over time, along with the periods of stability that punctuate the changes • Descriptions of individual differences in developmental patterns and their links with variables such as culture, ethnicity or historical era.	• Searching for systems of causality behind the descriptive patterns identified through the descriptive aim • Using theories and models to organise information about development • Generating and testing predictions from contrasting theories and models in order to select the best explanation for a particular developmental phenomenon • Devising parsimonious and encompassing explanatory systems to link developmental phenomena across age groups and behaviour domains.	• Using research findings generated through descriptive and explanatory studies to improve people's developmental outcomes • Testing ideas about development through practical field work. When an intervention that is designed to enhance development is carefully monitored and evaluated, insights about the causes for change can be inferred through success or failure • Applying descriptive knowledge about normal development to diagnose individuals' developmental difficulties or delays • Microdevelopmental studies in which an intensive intervention (e.g. teaching memorisation strategies to elderly adults) is designed to stimulate normal developmental processes.

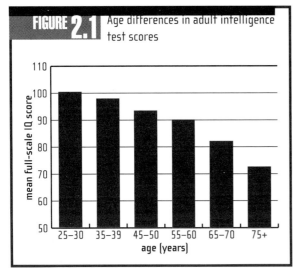

FIGURE 2.1 Age differences in adult intelligence test scores

Source: Based on data in Kaufman (1990).

Age norms and other descriptive developmental information can be used to assist in the design of playground equipment.

iours that can be expected from members of different age groups, or a picture of what is typical. Figures 2.2 and 2.3 depict age norms for Australian children's growth and development. Figure 2.2 shows the average rates of growth in height and weight for Australian boys and girls who are typical members of their age and gender group (50th percentile), together with the norms for children who are among the slowest of healthy children to gain height and weight (25th or 10th percentile). Figure 2.3 shows the norms for the infant's biobehavioural development of

FIGURE 2.2 Age norms for Australian children's physical growth

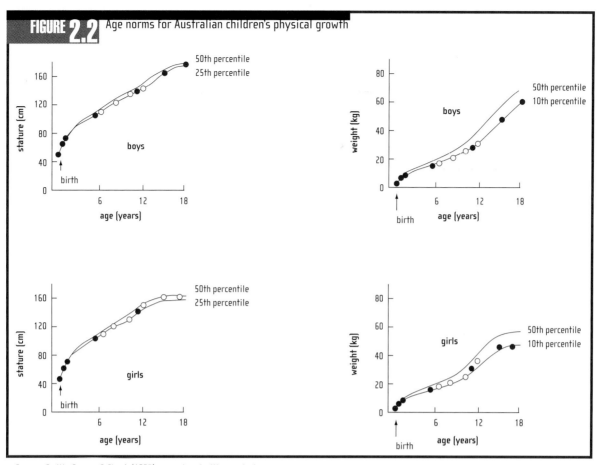

Source: Smith, Spargo & Cheek (1982), reproduced with permission.
Norms for Aboriginal children in Western Australia are shown in open circles, Aboriginal children in South Australia in shaded circles.

locomotor skill, a topic examined in more depth in Chapter 4.

In addition to providing the database upon which developmental theories are constructed, age norms can be practically useful to parents, teachers and health professionals who want to judge whether a child in their care is developing at a typical, average rate. Parents might use height and weight norms like those in Figure 2.2 to check whether their children are relatively fat, thin or average for their age, and consider adjusting their diet or exercise regimes accordingly. Child-care staff could make use of Figure 2.3 norms as a rough guide to when to introduce highchairs, playpens and climbing toys to infants in their care. Norms also facilitate social planning and environmental design for particular age groups. Height and weight (in Figure 2.2) can be used to guide construction of school desks and neighbourhood playground equipment. Simple descriptions enable a comparison between one person and other members of the same age group, thereby pinpointing the need for special intervention in cases where the individual's development appears to be blocked, delayed or exceptionally accelerated, suggesting ideas for remedial or giftedness education.

Limitations of the descriptive approach

Important cautions and limitations apply both to age norms specifically and to the fruits of the descriptive developmental research goal more generally. Although age norms can suggest general trends, it is essential to consider the range of variability among healthy individuals of a particular age group, not only the group average. Few children's development exactly matches the average normative timetable in every way. Consequently, although age norms are very useful when treated cautiously, they are frequently misinterpreted. It is easy to forget, when looking at averages, that the norm is in fact based on a wide range of individual scores. Thus, while the age norm for sitting alone in a highchair was six months, according to researcher Mary Shirley (1933), she arrived at this figure by averaging the separate scores of the 25 normal children in her sample, some of whom achieved this milestone as early as four months and others not until they were nearly eight months old. So it would be unwise for parents to conclude that their children are either delayed or advanced for sitting alone on the basis of a deviation from the norm of a month or so. Variations like these are perfectly normal. A chart in the format of Figure 2.2 is preferable, since it displays the range

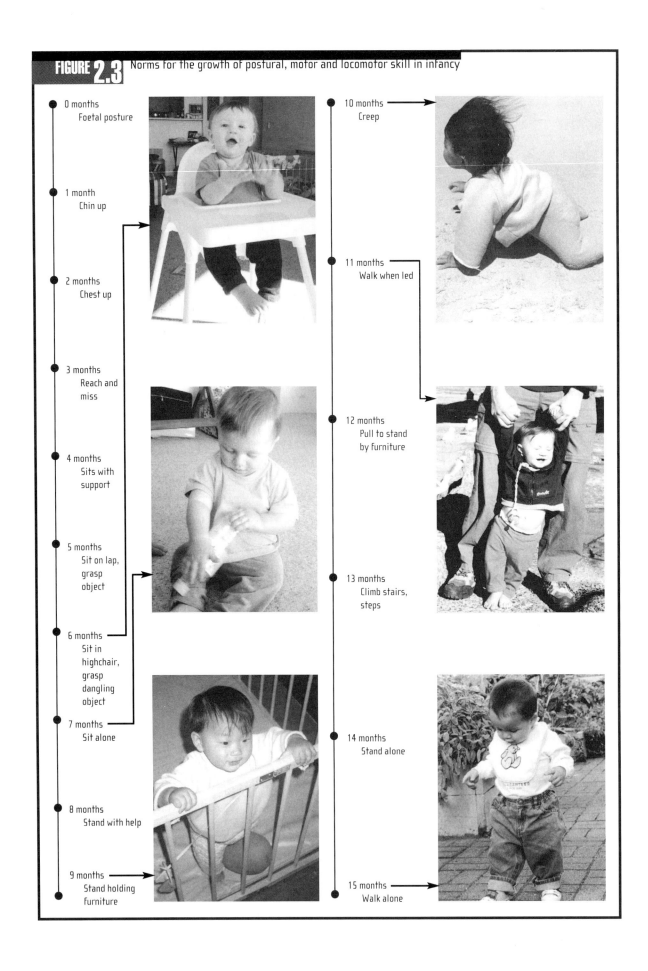

0 months
Foetal posture

1 month
Chin up

2 months
Chest up

3 months
Reach and miss

4 months
Sits with support

5 months
Sit on lap, grasp object

6 months
Sit in highchair, grasp dangling object

7 months
Sit alone

8 months
Stand with help

9 months
Stand holding furniture

10 months
Creep

11 months
Walk when led

12 months
Pull to stand by furniture

13 months
Climb stairs, steps

14 months
Stand alone

15 months
Walk alone

Age norms are group averages. A height norm for 18-month-olds is computed by measuring a group of toddlers of this age and computing their mean height.

of variation among normal, healthy children of the same age, as well as the average.

Age norms are also liable to differ as a function of the child's ethnic background. While the North American data collected by Mary Shirley in 1933 placed the average age for sitting with support at the four-month norm shown in Figure 2.3, in Australia Annette Hamilton (1981) discovered an age norm of two months two weeks for the same skill when she studied Aboriginal children who were being reared in a traditional indigenous environment in a remote community in Arnhem Land. Norms for growth in height and weight also differ for Aboriginal versus Anglo-Australian children, as Figure 2.2 illustrates. Discrepancies like these indicate the risks involved in applying descriptive data generated in one cultural setting to diagnostic or intervention work with a different population. Even seemingly similar cultures can yield contrasting norms. One large-scale study of the first independent steps taken by more than 1000 children in Brussels, London, Paris, Stockholm and Zurich yielded two different walking norms: 13.2 months for Parisian, Swiss and English children, compared with 12.2 months in Brussels and Stockholm (Hindley et al., 1966). Possible explanations for these differences are considered in Chapter 4. But such variations among subgroups within an age category indicate how misleading it can be to regard normative trends as fixed, absolute and inevitable.

This is particularly true of norms that strive to subsume the psychological functioning across long spans of adult life, as in Figure 2.1.

One solution is to compute separate norms for different cultural, gender and socioeconomic groups within a population. In addition, whether the norm is designed to be specific to subgroups or broadly generalisable, its validity as a scientific tool depends heavily on the principle of *representative sampling*. This means that the people chosen to represent a particular cohort or age group in a normative study should be typical of other members of that cohort who did not happen to be chosen. Thus it is misleading to choose only university students when hoping to generalise the norm to all 18-year-old Australians,

and even more misleading to sample nursing-home elderly as representative of everyone over the age of 65.

Adults gain such widely different experiences over the course of a lifetime and are affected so much by their present circumstances, with all that this implies in terms of physical health, income, gender, level of education and cultural background, that the descriptive search for normative averages may seem like 'combining chalk with cheese'. As John Flavell (1970) explained: 'Experience is a far more promising source of interesting adult cognitive changes than are biological events' (p. 250). Thus, when creating normative descriptions of adult development, it is often necessary to come up with separate norms for adults with different backgrounds and varying kinds of lifestyles and life experiences.

Perhaps the most important limitation of descriptive developmental information is its failure to explain *why*. This includes answering questions about why particular age groups differ from one another, and why a particular pattern of behaviour happens to be the norm for people of a given age. To demonstrate this to yourself, try completing the exercise in Box 2.2.

Explanatory research: Creating theories and testing predictions

In the words of Cicero (106–43 BC): 'The causes of events are more interesting than the events themselves'. A causal explanation for developmental change adds interest and clarity to 'facts' or 'events' by helping to resolve the paradoxes that may arise when purely descriptive information is examined on its own. Explaining development involves finding a reason *why* a particular behaviour or psychological attribute (like an IQ score) shows its descriptively observed relationship with chronological age. At a broader level, explanatory research seeks causal connections between antecedent conditions and developmental outcomes, as a basis for theoretical integration and future prediction of facts uncovered through descriptive research. For example, the descriptive data in Figure 2.1 might be explained by a learning theory (see page 60 for a fuller discussion of this theoretical approach) that focuses on the quality of education as a major factor in the growth of the kinds of cognitive skills that enhance performance on IQ tests. In fact, systematic comparisons of schooled and unschooled children and adolescents in rural and urban Mexico prompted the conclusion that:

> Schooling helps children develop specialized strategies for remembering and so enhances their ability to commit arbitrary material to memory for purposes of later testing. (Cole & Cole, 2001, p. 524)

So perhaps the longer years of generally better schooling that the 25-year-olds in Figure 2.1 enjoyed explains the finding that they outperformed the 70-year-old 'children of the Great Depression' in

BOX 2.2

How can you explain it?
Age differences in IQ

The dilemma: Descriptions of age groups and age differences tell us what *does* happen as people grow up and grow older. However, as we note in Chapter 1 (see pages 23–25), chronological age on its own does not cause developmental change. Consequently, there is often more than one plausible explanation for any given piece of descriptive information about an age group. Consider Figure 2.1 again. One explanation for the normative difference in IQ scores between younger and older adults could be that intelligence declines with age. But that is not the only plausible explanation. Can you think of an alternative reason why the North American adults aged 65 to 70 in Figure 2.1 earned a lower mean score for intelligence than the group aged 25 to 30 who were tested in the same year (Kaufman, 1990) on the same standardised IQ test?

Possible solutions: There are at least two possible alternative explanations for the results in Figure 2.1, other than the (depressing!) possibility that our minds grow duller with every passing year after we reach age 30. These include:

(a) *The ageist nature of IQ tests.* K. Warner Schaie (1983) points out that the format and content of many standard IQ tests are biased in favour of young adults who have only recently completed formal education, and against the cognitive styles more typical of older men and women. Not only is an extremely rapid response to most items called for, but vocabulary and knowledge measures often selectively favour words and concepts that have entered the lexicon in recent years (e.g. 'cyberspace', 'download'). Furthermore, as Schaie pointed out, some standard test items build on an 'unnecessarily ageist stereotype' (p. 179) such as the following example which he chose from a published cognitive test:

Fill in the blank:
Youth Beauty Life; Age _____ *Death* (p. 179)

(b) *Cohort obsolescence.* When we compare cross-sectional with longitudinal research designs later in this chapter, we see that a cross-sectional study of the kind that produced the Figure 2.1 data involves comparing age groups of people who have had different life experiences, many of which may have been relevant to their cognitive development. For example, the 70-year-olds in Kaufman's (1990) study would have been born around 1920, as compared with 1960 for the 30-year-olds. The former group would have lived through two world wars and the Great Depression, with many consequent disruptions to their education that the younger generation would have been spared. Consequently, the higher IQ scores of the younger group in Figure 2.1 could simply be a product of better education, or of some other difference between the cohorts.

In other words, being older may have nothing directly to do with the lower mean IQ score of the 65- to 70-year-olds in Figure 2.1 – they would have registered the same score if they had been tested at the age of 25 to 30 years.

Kaufman's (1990) study of adult intelligence (Box 2.2). Of course, developmental descriptions supply the data from which the explanation is generated, so the descriptive and explanatory goals of development often go hand in hand.

The task of coming up with plausible and experimentally testable explanations for psychological development has been compared to the exercise of discovering 'who-dunnit' in a mystery story. In each case, the first step is to get a clear picture of the facts (descriptive data). Next, a *hypothesis* (or possible explanation) is formulated. Finally, further information is sought that will either confirm or refute the hypothesis, using one of the research designs that we consider later in this chapter. To try this out for yourself, complete the hypothesis-generating exercise in Box 2.3.

Hypotheses are testable predictions that suggest ideas requiring scientific data collection for their answers. In addition to deriving these kinds of predictions from a descriptive data-gathering exercise, as in the examples above, it is also possible to work in the other direction. Theories, like empirical data, can be the inspiration for a testable hypothesis. For example, consider the age norms for Australian children's growth in height and weight shown in Figure 2.2. The biobehavioural theory that rapid healthy physical growth reflects a combination of optimal nutrition, exercise and freedom from childhood disease (see Chapters 4 and 9) leads to the prediction that the Figure 2.2 norms for indigenous Australian children, suggesting a slower growth rate than for Anglo-Australian children in the mainstream majority, could be tested through further descriptive data-gathering research. Information on frequency of illnesses and hospitalisation, dietary intake and

Schooled children develop different cognitive strategies from their peers who do not attend school.

BOX 2.3

Activity suggestion
Test your sleuthing skill

Figure 2.4 shows some descriptive evidence about the relationship between age and hearing loss for men in the United States. By looking at the graph we can see that the young men in this study (all in their early 20s at the time of taking part) had suffered no discernible hearing losses at any sound frequency. But older men (aged 60 and above) showed moderate losses of hearing acuity at intermediate frequencies and serious loss for high-frequency sounds.

This is descriptive evidence. But description begs an explanation. Can you think of a reason why older men differ from younger men in their capacity to hear high-pitched sounds? What aspects of ageing could have caused the difference?

Try to devise two distinct explanations (hypotheses) that explain the age-related hearing losses shown in Figure 2.4. See if you can frame your explanations in terms of distinctly different principles of sensory ageing.

There are many ways of testing developmental explanations. For a solution to the mystery of aged hearing loss, turn to Box 2.4.

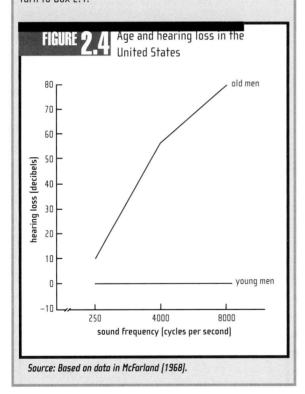

FIGURE 2.4 Age and hearing loss in the United States

Source: Based on data in McFarland (1968).

observational studies of daily exercise and health habits could be gathered from children like those included in the Figure 2.2 samples, together with normative data on height and weight for indigenous and non-indigenous children of various ages. If the patterns of association suggested by the theory were borne out, this would lend it stronger support.

Explanations for individual age-related phenomena, such as changes in stature, handedness, IQ scores and modes of locomotion, are sometimes called 'mini-theories'. They are theoretical because they demand assumptions and deductions that go beyond the tangible level of directly measuring, observing or graphing the behaviour of various age groups. But they are miniature because their scope is limited to making a few specific age contrasts within a relatively narrow area of psychological functioning. Major theories and explanatory systems, on the other hand, are designed to encompass and interconnect large fields of behavioural development. They incorporate a great many specific deductions which are themselves derived from a large number of basic assumptions, or axioms (Reese & Overton, 1970). Later in this chapter, we examine several of the major theories that have guided contemporary thinking about developmental psychology.

Pre-theoretical models

As Hayne Reese and Willis Overton (1970) pointed out, the important theories in developmental psychology that we examine later in this chapter are grounded in an implicit model or analogy. This hidden but crucial component of every major theory is not a formal part of the theory, although it flavours, guides and constrains the way explanations are formulated. According to Reese and Overton, most relatively new areas of inquiry borrow simple and well-explained phenomena from other fields to serve as models for theory-building. The model acts like a lens that lends shape and colour to complex and disorganised patterns until they come to look familiar and manageable. Three different kinds of pre-theoretical models are prevalent in lifespan developmental psychology – the environmental-mechanistic model, the organic-maturational model and the dialectical model.

THE ENVIRONMENTAL-MECHANISTIC MODEL

Theories built on this model emphasise the role of the external environment in guiding and building developmental change. Think about assembling a computer from its component parts. The basic chips, circuit boards and other components resemble the biological and physical factors that provide the foundation for human development. But psychological functioning, in all its complexity, is built up over time through experiences like social interaction, informal learning, parenting, schooling and so on. In the same way that computer circuits or car engines do not assemble themselves without help, active intervention from a developmentally nurturant environment (see Chapter 1) is essential for psychological growth to take place, according to learning theories and other theories that adopt the mechanistic analogy. Consequently, this model leads to theories that concentrate on dissecting complex, mature behaviour into its simpler primitive precursors.

An example of a mechanistic theory of sensory functioning in adulthood appears in Box 2.4, together with a solution to the deductive exercise presented in Box 2.3.

BOX 2.4 Using science: From description to explanation via the mechanistic model

As noted in Box 2.3, the mystery of why old men's hearing is less acute than younger men's has a number of plausible explanations. Perhaps the ears decline in acuity with the changes in their physiological structure and operation that inevitably arise during old age (see Chapter 16). Compared with a young person's body, the body of an older adult has several distinctive characteristics, including slower nerve conduction speeds and a decreased diameter, number and reactivity of muscle fibres. Do these changes explain the reduction in acuity of aged ears?

An alternative explanation is that the ageing of the ears reflects the amount and ways they have been used over the lifespan, in much the same way that a car's decline in function can often be expressed more accurately by the number of kilometres driven than by years since it was built. According to this theoretical explanation (sometimes called 'wear-and-tear', see Chapter 16), the losses of auditory acuity shown in Figure 2.4 are the result of decades of listening to loud noise.

To test alternative developmental explanations like these, a curious researcher might be tempted to design an experiment. But it would clearly be unethical to expose subjects in an experimental group to loud noise for many years in order to test the prediction from wear-and-tear theory that their rate of auditory ageing would be faster than that of a matched control group exposed only to normal levels of noise over the same time period.

Fortunately for science, nature often performs experiments like these without a researcher's deliberate intervention. Consider the patterns of hearing loss shown in Figure 2.5.

These curves collectively show that losses in hearing acuity experienced by older men in the United States (see Figure 2.4) are not unique to ageing. Young pilots (aged 20 to 29 years at the time of being tested) show patterns of hearing loss at higher sound frequencies that resemble those of older men, even though they have not yet lived long enough to have experienced the physiological changes to their muscles and nerve fibres that are described in more detail in Chapter 16. It seems that the noise of plane engines is to be blamed for their premature loss of sensitivity to high-frequency sounds.

On the other hand, ageing itself does not produce identical hearing losses, according to the descriptive evidence in Figure 2.5. This figure shows that older women in the United

States show less loss at higher frequencies than American men of the same age. But the most dramatic evidence against an 'age-only' explanation for auditory decline emerges in the curve for elderly Africans that is included in Figure 2.5. These old men were tested for hearing sensitivity while in their 60s, after spending their entire lives in the African bush (McFarland, 1968), away from the drone of city traffic or the noise of farm machinery. The fact that aged Africans' hearing acuity at all sound frequencies was nearly as perfect as that of a young American who had escaped noise pollution on an airfield suggests that age alone does not diminish auditory sensitivity.

The five curves shown in Figure 2.5 also illustrate the symbiotic relationship that exists between most descriptions and explanations of development. Although each curve by itself does nothing but describe, all five curves taken together suggest a reason behind the evident decline in hearing efficiency during old age. Since urban Americans are exposed to more loud noise than African bush dwellers, since American working men typically encounter more noise on the job than their wives do at home, and since young pilots in the 1940s and 1950s experienced especially severe exposure to loud noise, it would seem that the wear-and-tear to the hearing system that builds up over a lifetime in a noisy environment accounts for the observed declines in auditory acuity.

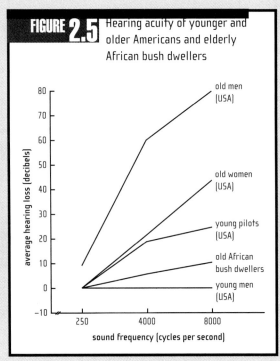

FIGURE 2.5 Hearing acuity of younger and older Americans and elderly African bush dwellers

Source: Based on data in McFarland (1953, 1968).

THE ORGANIC-MATURATIONAL MODEL

Theories built on this pre-theoretical model emphasise biological factors such as the human genetic blueprint (see Chapter 3) and maturational processes within the brain and body that are seen to unfold developmentally into ever more complex psychological capacities with minimal intervention from the environment (apart from the basic nutrients and protection from harm that are needed to sustain life and basic health). As the name implies, the organic model compares human psychological development to a plant's growth cycle. First a seed is planted, then (given adequate soil, water and sunlight) it grows, sprouts up out of the ground, increases in size, flowers, fruits and, eventually, even under ideal conditions, withers and dies at the end of the biologically ordained timetable for the life cycle of that kind of plant.

Theories built on the organic model often draw on the similarities between the increasing complexity of children's psychological make-up and the transformation of an apple blossom into a ripe fruit. Thus the growth of intelligence through childhood and adolescence might be seen in terms of the maturation of modular neurobiological processes within the brain, as opposed to the active intervention of teachers as in the mechanistic analogy. Similarly, organic theories often presume that fixed sequences of qualitative (see page 23) transformations govern human psychologi-

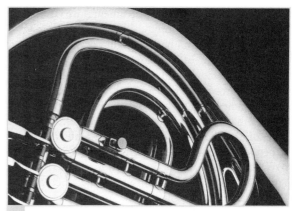
Dialectical models compare human development to the development of a musical theme.

cal development, similar to the natural, organic growth sequence that transforms a caterpillar into a butterfly. Thus a parallel might be noted between the stages that toddlers go through to master independent locomotion (see Figure 2.3) and the butterfly's emergence from the chrysalis. According to this view, babies will crawl before they walk, despite any efforts on the part of parents or other environmental engineers (such as the designers of wheeled walkers, see Chapter 4) to distort this natural sequence. Organic theories do not necessarily expect earlier psychological attributes to be discernible in, or even functionally related to, those that emerge later.

THE DIALECTICAL MODEL

Dialectical models present human psychological development in terms of the progressive resolution of essential contradictions and challenges to reach ever higher and more effective levels of complexity, integration and organisation. The name, originating in the Greek philosopher Plato's analysis of the teaching style of his mentor, Socrates, helps to explain the core elements of the dialectical position. One of Socrates' pupils might make an assertion which Socrates, the teacher, would then challenge by astute questioning that drew out the inherent contradictions in the student's original position. These opposing viewpoints could then gradually be resolved through open discussion until a higher-order synthesis was eventually achieved.

Applied to human development, the dialectical analogy suggests that psychological growth is set in motion by contradictions, or opposing forces, that lend meaning to one another, struggle for ascendency, and eventually yield a genuinely developmental change that incorporates the best features of the polar opposites by drawing them together into a higher-order synthesis (Riegel, 1975). Dialectical development can therefore be compared to an orchestral symphony. As a symphony develops, the musical counterpoints, or seemingly discordant elements, are resolved as the melody builds a more complex and integrated texture. Likewise, in modern jazz, discordant notes and disharmonious elements are synthe-

The organic model compares human growth to the sprouting, blossoming and fruiting of a tree.

sised through rhythm and instrumental variation into a more complex harmony.

Nancy Datan and her colleagues (1987) described the development of the parent–child relationship in dialectical terms. Initially, the infant's helpless dependency creates a conflict with the parent's formerly independent lifestyle, which is thrown into chaos by the new baby's arrival (see Chapters 3, 5 and 13). The pole of the dialectic involving the infant's extreme dependency and demandingness could completely overwhelm the parent's own need for self-expression and continuing development unless the inherent contradiction is openly confronted. Similarly, the infant's development needs could be ignored if the caregiver's pole rises to overwhelming ascendency. Neither of these outcomes is as growth-promoting for either generation, according to Datan, as the development of a higher-order synthesis in which both elements of the initial contradiction are clearly represented. This might initially take the form of a balanced parental nurturance in the context of independent interests that align themselves with childrearing. However, even this higher-order synthesis itself is merely a temporary harmony, according to the dialectical model's view of life as a never-ending process of change through contradiction. Thus the growing child's demand for independence will eventually clash with the parent's need to nurture and protect. As time passes, the child progressively grows more self-reliant and the parent cedes control (or is forcibly 'dethroned') until, as two grown adults, parent and child achieve a new kind of partnership which eliminates the imbalance of nurturance versus dependency.

The dialectical model, inspired as it is by Karl Marx's theory of economics and history, also lays special stress on the interdependence between an individual's development and the current historical and cultural context (Baltes, 1979, 1987).

The ancient Greek philosopher Heraclitus was one of the first Western thinkers to apply the dialectical model to human life and relationships. He argued that both harmony and conflict were so essential to human functioning and social organisation that growth and change were inevitable. 'There is nothing permanent except change,' concluded Heraclitus (Evans, 1978, p. 95). Dialectical approaches to development were also an important component of ancient Oriental philosophies. Traditional Chinese philosophers identified a polarity between the *yin* forces of weakness, softness and passivity and the *yang* forces of power, heat and activity that matches the modern masculinity/ femininity dialectic. A dialectical model also stresses the unity of opposites:

> Dialectic polarities not only exhibit opposition, thereby partially excluding one another, but they also complement and provide a definitional base for each other. For example, the idea of interpersonal harmony implies and helps define interpersonal conflict, and vice versa … The yin–yang

concept of Chinese philosophy assumes that some amount of either pole of an opposition is always present, no matter how powerful the other. If one pole completely dominated the other then the larger system of which they were parts and to whose coherence they contributed would not exist. (Altman, Vinsel & Brown, 1981, p. 121)

In contemporary developmental psychology the dialectical model has broad appeal because, possibly, it solves the vexing puzzle of why behaviour continually develops and changes as individuals grow older, even well into adult life. Instead of viewing stability as normal and change as unusual, the dialectical model argues that growth-driving forces are inevitable and periods of apparent stability (or stagnation) are the deviant phenomena that a developmental theory must explain.

Another strength of the dialectical position is its role in inspiring key elements of many of the major theoretical positions that guide contemporary psychology, including the theories of Erikson, Piaget and Vygotsky that we examine more closely later in this chapter.

Optimisation: Goal of applied research

As noted in Chapter 1, the lifespan approach to human development has a very optimistic 'bottom line': genuine growth and gains in psychological capacity are possible throughout the whole of life. But this fact places a burden of responsibility on people whose lives, careers and leisure pursuits are intertwined with the lives of other human beings of any age. How can we foster optimal psychological development in ourselves and those we care for throughout the whole lifespan? Applied, optimisational researchers strive to answer these questions, while contributing to the progress of scientific understanding at the same time. By testing intervention strategies in the laboratory of real life, optimisational research can supply useful new insights to guide the construction and evaluation of developmental explanations and theories. In fact, when striving to weigh theories about development against one another (see Box 2.7), two very important considerations are (a) whether or not a theory can suggest useful applications to nurturing development, and (b) whether or not those interventions actually work.

Thus, optimisational research stretches one step beyond explanation. With its roots in well-tested description and theory, applied optimisational research seeks 'to modify and optimize individual development in a more robust, long-tested manner by programmatic individual and ecological intervention' (Baltes, Reese & Nesselroade 1977, p. 88).

Applied interventions to boost development, or remove obstacles in its path, can supply ways of testing models, explanations and theories of human development. If a prediction from a theory can be made to 'work', in the sense of boosting an individual's developmental progress, this provides verification of its underlying ideas about the causes of development. But not all optimisation strategies derive directly from theory. Some of the most promising have grown out of the recognition of the special problems that certain children, adolescents or adults were facing, or as a result of an articulated community need. For example, the 'Head Start' educational program for disadvantaged preschoolers originated in the discovery (based on descriptive data-gathering) of serious lags in the cognitive development of poverty-stricken children as compared with their middle-class peers. Descriptive accounts of the extent of television's daily broadcasting of scenes of violent death and destruction have likewise driven applied researchers in Australia, New Zealand and overseas to examine the effects of viewing aggressive television on children's and adolescents' development (Sheehan, 1983). Many other instances of problem-centred approaches to understanding and improving people's developmental opportunities are considered in more detail in later chapters of this book.

In designing and evaluating interventions to optimise development, it is especially important to maintain a lifespan perspective. As we saw in Chapter 1 when we examined Jean Walker MacFarlane's 'life-cycle surprises' (see pages 25–26), unexpected events sometimes arise when we examine development over long spans of time. This highlights the need to evaluate optimising interventions over the whole of life. Short-term gains may not be maintained in the long run. Conversely, development that appears problematic at one stage in life does not necessarily breed problems at later stages. Nor does exceptional developmental progress early in life guarantee exceptional progress or the absence of problems later on. Thus the task of the researcher adopting the optimising goal is highly complex.

Consider an example. When Lorelle Futterweit and Holly Ruff (1993) analysed the long-term results of an early-intervention program at Yale University which had provided emotional support, dietary supplements and day-care assistance to low-income families up to the time the infants were 30 months old, they made a surprising discovery. Some 9 to 10 years after the termination of the intervention, these children scored no higher than children from the non-intervention control group on tests of intelligence and academic achievement that had been the main focus of the researchers' optimising efforts. Taken on its own, this result would suggest that there had been no optimising benefits from the applied intervention. But when other aspects of the children's functioning during middle childhood were examined, clear developmental gains did emerge with striking force. The children from the intervention group had better school attendance records in primary school and high school, and they were also significantly less likely than children in the control group to require special services from remedial teachers, guidance officers, disciplinarians, clinicians or therapists. Their mothers' developmental prospects also seemed to

have been improved. Although matched for education levels at the beginning of the study, mothers of children in the intervention group were found to have completed more years of schooling than the control group mothers by the final assessment point 10 years after the educational intervention program for the children had been completed and the environment had returned to normal. In other words, it seemed that the provision of early assistance had benefited the children both directly and indirectly, over the longer term. In a direct way, the children were less likely to need the kinds of special services that are indicative of deep-seated learning deficits, behaviour problems or psychopathology. Indirectly, since maternal education is a correlate of positive developmental outcomes in offspring (White & Watts, 1973), the children in the intervention group were more likely to benefit, throughout childhood and adolescence, from having mothers who had improved on the education levels they had achieved prior to their child's birth. Furthermore, by boosting mothers' educational achievements and opportunities for further adult development, as well as their self-esteem and self-efficacy, the well-being of the entire family was undoubtedly improved as a result of this optimising intervention.

Futterweit and Ruff concluded that:

Frequent, ongoing long-term evaluation processes need to be built into studies to capture periods of stability and change in individual children. In this manner, we learn more about the processes underlying change than by studying limited outcomes less frequently. Interventionists, therefore, can monitor how well the intervention is working, what processes are being affected, and when states of transition are occurring. Individual differences in the timing of developmental changes provide a basis for modifying interventions accordingly. (pp. 167–8)

As well as highlighting the need for long-term evaluation studies of applied interventions that are designed to nurture and enhance psychological development, this example teaches another important lesson about optimisational research. As Paul Baltes (2001) explained:

Lifespan psychology does not prescribe the goals of development. Rather, it has taken on the mission to accumulate and disseminate knowledge about which processes and characteristics contribute under which circumstances to the optimization of development. Eventually, it will be this kind of knowledge that every individual may use to compose his or her life in a fulfilling manner (p. 8848).

The methods of developmental psychology

In pursuit of these broad scientific goals, developmental researchers use a variety of techniques to gather descriptive information about development and to test theories and optimising interventions. These techniques can be grouped into four main categories:

1. case studies;
2. naturalistic observation of spontaneous behaviour in real-life settings;
3. interviews, questionnaires, tests and other self-report techniques;
4. experimental research conducted in laboratories or other settings where extraneous variables can be controlled.

Let us briefly examine the main characteristics of each approach, including their strengths and weaknesses.

Case studies

The case study method involves an in-depth focus on one person – a child, an adolescent or an adult – in order to compile a detailed portrait of that person's overall patterns of development in each of the major psychological domains (cognition, personality and so on). Clinicians compiling a case study often consult indirect sources such as hospital records (birth complications and admissions for illness or injury) and school records (standardised test scores, academic achievement results, behaviour problems, diagnostic referrals). They may interview all the key players in a person's life (e.g. a child's parents, teachers and peers or an adult's spouse, offspring and work colleagues) while at the same time assessing the subject on a broad range of measures, including perhaps interviews, tests and behavioural observations. The goal is to compile as complete a picture as possible of all the interconnected facets of that individual's overall psychological functioning. The portrait that emerges, while idiosyncratic, can serve not only to inform the diagnosis and treatment of the individual's clinical problems, but can also suggest hypotheses about development that can be followed up using broader sampling techniques. Neuropsychological case histories of adults who have suffered head injuries or strokes are one example; Sigmund Freud's psychoanalytic insights based on patients' retrospective memories and clinical case notes are another (see pages 54–5).

Case studies of typically developing children without clinical problems have also been compiled by developmental psychologists (including Jean Piaget, see Box 2.10) and interested, well-educated parents (including the naturalist Charles Darwin, who kept a diary on his son Doddy's early development, and Bronson Alcott, father of the author of *Little Women*). Often the primary purpose was personal reminiscence or for family records, much as parents today might compile a photo album or videotape. Although the developmental patterns discerned in a case study of a healthy, normally developing person may lack generalisability, even to other children or

adolescents of the same age, gender and background, a carefully recorded case study can provide a vivid glimpse of a real, whole person that can serve as a useful adjunct and reality check when we dissect development into separate cognitive, personality or social dimensions using other styles of research. An example appears in Box 2.5.

The validity of a case study depends largely on how accurately and objectively it depicts the chosen target person. No claim is made that a case study like the one in Box 2.5 would fit any other child of the same age, or even that it will accurately depict Louise herself when she is a few months older. Like a photographic snapshot, it permanently records just one point in one person's lifespan. Thus idiographic descriptions tend to raise further questions, the answers to which require other descriptive techniques. For example, we might wonder after reading the description in Box 2.5:

1. Is Louise precocious, average or delayed in her development of motor skills like climbing and running?
2. Are most 16-month-olds able to climb, open and close boxes and speak in single words?
3. Is Louise's way of responding to the frustration of losing her toy a feature of her being the age she is (e.g. at the threshold of the 'Terrible Twos', see Chapter 6)? Or is it more likely to reflect the specific character of Louise's own personality (e.g. one of the core temperament patterns in infancy that we study in Chapter 5)? Will Louise herself develop different ways of reacting to frustration as she grows older?
4. Is Louise 'spoilt', perhaps through being an only child? If she is, what could her parents do to rectify the problem?

Answers to questions like these would require systematic studies of larger groups of children, using one of the developmental research strategies that we examine next.

Naturalistic observation

One way to think about developmental research methods is in terms of how intrusive they are, or how much they disrupt the ongoing activities of the people being studied. At the least intrusive extreme, together with some case studies, is the technique of naturalistic observation. As noted above, observational procedures

BOX 2.5 A child called Louise

This example of the case study approach comes from the diary of an advertising executive named Arthur Clifford, who kept a record of the development of his daughter, Louise, from her birth until her eighteenth birthday.

19 July 1949. *Today our daughter is 16 months old. She is 31 inches tall and weighs over 24 pounds—above average I believe. She is very much a real person. She talks, in single words, she runs, climbs, gets down by herself, enjoys pictures, likes to close and open boxes and understands a surprisingly large amount of what we say. She is almost always amiable, is cross only when hungry or tired, or when barred from some place she wants to go. When she is cross, she hollers, but even her hollering is largely a matter of form: if it works, all right; if not, too bad. Except last Friday when she came out of the doctor's office crying as though her heart was broken. It was over a blue plastic duck she had specially selected among the toys made available in the waiting room for children to play with. She kept it all during her examination and bitterly resented having to give it up when she left. For a half hour in the car she cried for her lost 'ducko'. We got her something else and that made a little difference. Still from time to time she would say 'ducko' and sob.*

© Peterson, 1974, pp. 60–1, reproduced with permission.

Note: We meet up with Louise again in later chapters. Her father's diary is used to show some of the links between the science of development and a child growing up in real life. Sometimes, points that her father noted or wondered about have been investigated by psychologists in the laboratory or in natural settings. Sometimes they have been incorporated into the major theoretical explanations of psychological growth, examined later in this chapter. Most often they are merely incidental details which, though unimportant in themselves, motivate the search for more accurate and general facts about development by showing how fascinating the study of a growing child can be.

Louise at 16 months.

involve watching people of different ages in their normal habitats while taking precautions to ensure the objectivity of conclusions drawn. For example, a researcher who was interested in children's temper tantrums might sit quietly in the kitchen of a child's home, or on a bench in a preschool playground, waiting for an anger outburst to occur. Alternatively, the observer might borrow a shopping trolley and track children through supermarkets as their parents shopped, waiting for confrontations over purchases of toys, sweets or a cool drink. Each time a child spontaneously displayed anger in one of these settings, the researcher would record the details. The use of two independent observers is one way of checking accuracy and objectivity. When observers do their recording of the same behaviours without conferring, a high level of agreement with one another indicates both that the behaviours being observed arose as indicated and that their definitions are clear.

One major advantage of the naturalistic style of data-gathering is real-life validity. Since the behaviours being observed arise in their natural context, a researcher can feel quite confident that they are genuine. But there are also problems involved in using this method. In the first place, it is only useful for gathering data on events that occur reasonably often and are overtly visible or audible. Thus a child's understanding of death and dying (see Chapter 18) is normally not accessible to direct observation. To get at the child's underlying ideas about death, questions would need to be asked, since children rarely discuss this 'taboo' topic spontaneously. It would likewise be extremely impractical for observers to strive to be present to watch how children behaved when their pets or relatives died, given the (fortunately) quite infrequent occurrence of these traumatic events.

Other possible problems with naturalistic observation involve the risk of subjectivity in interpreting behaviour, and the danger that individuals may behave unnaturally when they realise they are being watched. One solution to subjectivity bias is to have several independent observers watch the same events. Some assurance of objectivity is given if all the separate observations agree closely. The problem of 'acting for an audience' or 'hamming it up' can often be overcome by using video cameras, one-way glass observation rooms or other ways of shielding participants from contact with the observers. Another approach is to train, as observers, individuals who (like mothers or teachers) are a normal part of the developing person's natural environment.

It is nevertheless often difficult, given the many factors that influence everyday behaviour in a natural setting, to decide on causal chains to explain patterns of behaviour observed. For example, a child might throw a tantrum in a supermarket because temper tantrums are part of the normal 2-year-old's repertoire. Equally, something temporarily unique to the child (such as fatigue or boredom) or specific to the supermarket setting (such as noise, being restrained in a trolley, boredom or the overwhelming availability of forbidden treats like lollies) might trigger such behaviour in children who rarely or never throw tantrums at other times or in other places. Thus multiple observations in several different natural settings may be needed to establish generalisability and possible causal links.

Experimental studies

In an experimental study the researcher is able to test causal hypotheses. By controlling some variables, and systematically manipulating one or more other variables, specific conclusions can be drawn about the influences of changes in the manipulated variable (known as an IV, for *independent variable*) on some measurable outcome (known as DV, for *dependent variable*). Often there is a control group, matched to the experimental group in variables likely to influence the DV, who do not receive the IV manipulation. This helps to pinpoint the IV as the factor influencing any changes that are unique to participants in the experimental group. In addition, by conducting the experiment in a controlled laboratory setting, other causal influences apart from the IV can also be excluded. Consequently, in contrast to the naturalistic observational method, the behaviours being observed are protected from the intrusion of distracting aspects of the natural, social and physical environment.

We look at many specific examples of developmental experiments in later chapters. For instance, in Chapter 4 a study of infant learning is described. To test whether newborn babies can deduce causal connections between their own bodily movements and outside events, Hanus Papousek (1974) brought infants into a carefully engineered laboratory setting from which all extraneous sights, smells and sounds were excluded to control for these distractions. After eliminating these possible reasons for a baby wanting to turn its head, Papousek was able to show, in infants who were only 4 months old, reliable increases (his chosen DV) in head-turning as a function of the independent variable (which consisted of signals from an electric light). To create the chance to learn about a causal connection in the physical world, Papousek placed the infants in a headrest where a motion-sensitive switch turned on the light bulb so that it flashed in front of the baby's eyes. The babies' awareness of causality was demonstrated when they not only reliably increased their head-turning to make the light go on, but were also able to master complicated sequences (such as first turning left then right) to bring the interesting stimulus of the light flash under their own control.

Laboratory experiments like these have definite advantages. Indeed, this is the method of choice for testing specific explanatory predictions in a controlled manner. But there are limitations to laboratory experiments when it comes to generalising their findings outside the laboratory into everyday life. For

Direct testing and questioning of children yields much useful information about development.

example, a baby at home would rarely encounter contingencies as pure and simple as the connections to be learned in Papousek's laboratory where all potentially confusing visual, auditory and tactile stimuli were eliminated. Mastery of real-life causal chains would conceivably take longer for infants to acquire than under Papousek's perfectly controlled conditions.

Self-report techniques

Many researchers who study the development of preschoolers, older children, adolescents or adults employ self-report methodologies. These include interviews, questionnaires and standardised tests in which the participant answers a select set of questions, or performs selected tasks, in response to verbal instructions. To probe inner feelings, thoughts and plans, as well as to examine overt behaviour that might not occur frequently enough to be readily accessible to direct observation, the self-report approach is the method of choice. For example, a child psychologist with an interest in young children's concepts of death (see Chapters 7 and 18) might use an interview methodology to probe the child's understanding of (a) how to distinguish living and non-living things (e.g. plants versus bicycles), (b) causes of the deaths of humans or pets, and (c) awareness of death's finality.

When studying the development of adolescents and adults, a written questionnaire is often used in preference to a face-to-face interview. Not only is this more economical in permitting groups of people to be tested all at once, it also enables ethical precautions to ensure the privacy, anonymity and confidentiality of the information the participant is asked to supply. This is particularly important when the topic under investigation is personally sensitive (e.g. sexual experience, contraceptive use or attitudes to controversial topics) or when the information disclosed in the study could harm the participant or someone else were it made public.

In this context, a telephone interview is another useful alternative, as in a study by Reed Larson (1995, 1997) of teenagers' changing moods. Recognising that adolescents crave privacy, both in their everyday lives and when it comes to revealing aspects of their inner selves to psychological researchers, Larson devised an innovative new twist on the interview methodology. Each of the teenage boys and girls who participated in his study was fitted with a pager that 'bleeped' at randomly selected intervals throughout the day. When contacted in this way, participants simply had to report where they were, what they were doing and how they were feeling. Larson found that the desire to spend periods alone in the bedroom increased significantly from childhood into the teens, peaking around the ages of 13 and 15. Furthermore, periods of solitude had a beneficial influence on psychological development. As compared with classmates who spent large amounts of time in interaction with friends, those who regularly spent between one-third and one-half of their time alone scored lower on measures of depression and higher on teacher-rated scales of adjustment and popularity. It seemed that spending periods alone assisted adolescents with the tasks of self-development and the consolidation of social experience, especially when listening to music.

The type of music also made a difference. When listening to soft rock music, most adolescents preferred to be with friends, as opposed to alone, possibly because the romantic themes of longing, disappointed love and sadness evoked a craving for companionship. But when listening to hard rock and heavy metal music, as well as popular songs in the Top 40 and rap music, positive moods were most common when the adolescents listened alone in their bedrooms. Conversely, when they listened to heavy metal music with family members, adolescents typically experienced very negative moods and emotions, possibly owing to dissonance between the themes portrayed in these styles of music and the family environment. Larson (1995) consequently concluded: 'Media experiences provide adolescents with an important context for dealing with stress and negative emotion. Popular music listening allows adolescents to internalize strong emotional images around which a temporary sense of self can cohere' (p. 535).

Other related questioning techniques include standardised tests (like the IQ tests considered in Figure 2.1 and Box 2.2) and non-verbal procedures in which a participant points at an object, chooses or creates a drawing or engages in some other informative action in response to the tester's instructions.

Numerous examples of these approaches are discussed in later chapters of this book. Collectively, self-report methods have the advantages of easy administration and capacity to delve into aspects of behaviour that are not readily observable. But there are some corresponding disadvantages. These include the self-report study's possible vulnerability to such problems as:

- Reporting bias or concealment (as when participants paint untruthful pictures of themselves to impress the researcher) or leave questions blank out of fear of embarrassment.
- Communication problems (as when young children, who are not yet familiar with the sophisticated styles of language a tester might use, or with the experimenter's purpose in asking questions to which he or she must already know the answer, respond in ways that mask their true understanding (Siegal, 1991, see Chapter 7).
- Genuine forgetfulness on the part of adults who are asked to recall events in their lives that arose briefly, possibly several decades ago (see Chapters 14 and 16).

Developmental research designs: Tracking psychological functioning over time

As well as having to make decisions about what method to use to gather data, and how much control to exert over subjects' spontaneous behaviour, developmental researchers need to make hard choices about how best to include the age variable in their research design. For researchers who hope to incorporate the entire lifespan into a single study, this design issue can be especially vexing. Should development be allowed to follow its natural course, with the researcher waiting for each participant to grow up and grow older, while measuring their behaviour at regular intervals? (As explained below, this is an example of the longitudinal design.) Or should they adopt the more immediate solution of testing people whose ages span the entire life cycle, and then comparing the responses of older and younger groups? (As explained below, this is a cross-sectional design.) Each approach has its strengths and weaknesses, and other more complicated choices are also available, as we see later in this section.

The cross-sectional design

How well a developmental explanation accounts for what actually happens to people as they grow older depends in part on the design used to map behaviour onto age. In a cross-sectional study, members of different age groups, chosen to be similar to one another on other dimensions besides age, are compared at a single point in time and the inference is drawn that differences between them reflect developmental change.

Figure 2.1 shows an example. This plot of intelligence against chronological age was obtained cross-sectionally by testing groups of young, middle-aged and elderly adults in the same year (Kaufman, 1990). As noted in Box 2.2, one possible explanation for the pattern of results obtained is developmental: IQ may decline as adults grow older from age 30 to age 70. But, given that the adults of different ages in this study were born in different years (in other words, belonged to different *cohorts*), differences between them could conceivably be a product of cohort-specific experiences rather than being in any way linked to age. The possibility of cohort differences in educational opportunities and attainments is canvassed in Box 2.2.

The rapid progress of social change, particularly in areas of health care, education, technology and attitudes to women's employment, has meant that different generations of Australians and New Zealanders, as in other modern industrialised nations throughout the world, have had quite different experiences over their lifespans. For example, between 1844 and 1867 in New South Wales and Victoria, less than half the colonies' children attended any kind of formal schooling (Burns & Goodnow, 1985). A child who grew up in this generation would differ throughout the remainder of the lifespan from an individual born in a later cohort after compulsory schooling was introduced. In fact, since the age groups included in a cross-sectional study are invariably born in different years, almost all the contrasts revealed in any cross-sectional study's results could conceivably have been caused by experiences that differ between cohorts that are not specifically a product of age (from having to curtail education to fight in World War II or seek employment in the Great Depression, to having had the chance to watch *Sesame Street* as a preschooler or to learn to browse the Internet before ever entering a library).

Box 2.6 shows another example of results from a cross-sectional study.

One of the biggest assets of the cross-sectional design is its ability to collapse a whole lifetime of development into one single episode of testing. (No individual researcher could count on living long enough to use a longitudinal design to follow participants from their 8th to their 100th birthday, which was the time span encompassed by the handedness study illustrated in Box 2.6.) The drawback is the possibility of mistaking cohort variations for true developmental change. In fact, cross-sectional studies have the disadvantage, as noted earlier, of vulnerability to cohort differences that have nothing to do with age. In the case of the handedness study in Box 2.6, for example, one non-developmental explanation relates to cohort differences in educational experiences. There were marked changes in educational

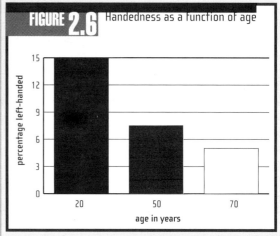

FIGURE 2.6 Handedness as a function of age

Source: Porac, Coren & Duncan (1980), figure 1. Copyright © The Gerontological Society of America.

For answers see the text.

policy during the 20th century with regard to pupils' handedness. Adults from cohorts born before 1950 (i.e. the two oldest groups in Box 2.6) would have gone to school in an era when left-handedness was strenuously discouraged. In fact, in the United States and Canada, as in Australia and New Zealand at that time, primary school teachers were under strict

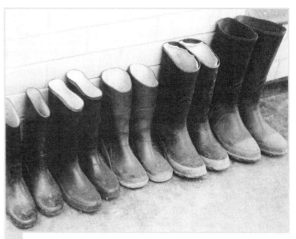

The cross-sectional method measures people at different ages at the same point in time.

instructions to make sure all children wrote with their right hand, sometimes resorting to strategies like immobilising the child's left hand in an effort to force this to happen. But by the 1950s this policy had changed. Few of the younger participants in this study who entered school with a left-hand preference would have been compelled to switch to right-handedness.

Even more dramatic than this change in educational philosophy are the social changes that have taken place over the past 150 years in the roles, positions and opportunities for women in modern society. Figure 2.7 lists some of these in a historical time line depicting salient events in women's situations in Australia, New Zealand and other Western nations. The cohort contrasts that are likely to be bound up with lifespan research into gender roles and women's attitudes and life plans are obvious from these events.

The longitudinal design

In a longitudinal study the same group of participants is followed through time, being tested at regular intervals as they grow up and grow older. This is clearly a more time-consuming way of assessing development than a cross-sectional study. There are compensating advantages, however. Individual patterns of change can be tracked over time, linking each

In a longitudinal design, an adult might take an IQ test every 10 years from age 20 to age 70.

person's earlier behaviour patterns with their developmental outcomes later in life. This allows for the discovery of *life-cycle surprises* (see Chapter 1), as well as for a fine-grained analysis of which qualities within people or within their environment best

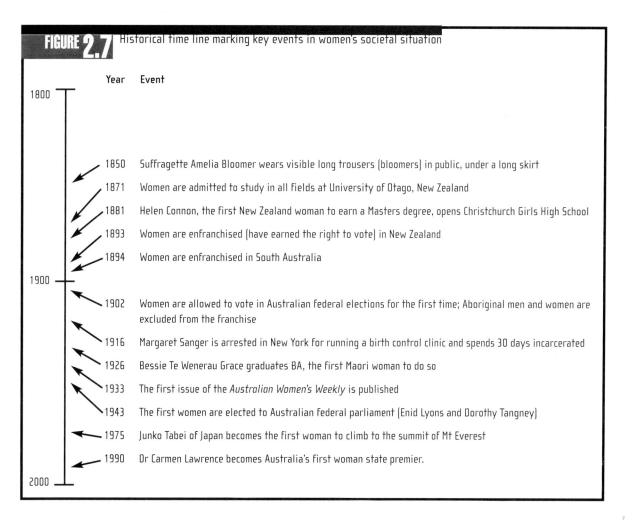

FIGURE 2.7 Historical time line marking key events in women's societal situation

Year	Event
1850	Suffragette Amelia Bloomer wears visible long trousers (bloomers) in public, under a long skirt
1871	Women are admitted to study in all fields at University of Otago, New Zealand
1881	Helen Connon, the first New Zealand woman to earn a Masters degree, opens Christchurch Girls High School
1893	Women are enfranchised (have earned the right to vote) in New Zealand
1894	Women are enfranchised in South Australia
1902	Women are allowed to vote in Australian federal elections for the first time; Aboriginal men and women are excluded from the franchise
1916	Margaret Sanger is arrested in New York for running a birth control clinic and spends 30 days incarcerated
1926	Bessie Te Wenerau Grace graduates BA, the first Maori woman to do so
1933	The first issue of the *Australian Women's Weekly* is published
1943	The first women are elected to Australian federal parliament (Enid Lyons and Dorothy Tangney)
1975	Junko Tabei of Japan becomes the first woman to climb to the summit of Mt Everest
1990	Dr Carmen Lawrence becomes Australia's first woman state premier.

(time line axis marked: 1800, 1900, 2000)

predict positive long-term outcomes and optimal growth gains throughout life.

Figure 2.8 illustrates how the patterns of development discerned through longitudinal research can contradict the results of cross-sectional studies of identical developmental phenomena. This figure duplicates the cross-sectional results on IQ and age that were described in Figure 2.1, while superimposing on them the results of K. Warner Schaie's (1983) longitudinal studies of adult intelligence. The same standardised IQ tests were used in both studies. But in Schaie's longitudinal studies, the same groups of participants took the test initially when they were in their 20s and were then invited to return for testing at decade intervals through to their 70s.

The results from the longitudinal design certainly paint a more optimistic picture of lifespan changes in intelligence (at least for adults over 30!) than the cross-sectional results. Does this mean we should believe them? Unfortunately, before deciding to do so, two problems plaguing the longitudinal approach to developmental data-gathering must be taken into account.

The first of these is a problem known as *selective attrition*. Inevitably, people drop out of longitudinal studies for many reasons: they may move and fail to leave a forwarding address, they may become bored or frustrated with the prospect of taking the tests repeatedly, they may fall ill or even die. If the dropping out were purely random, no real harm would be done to the research design (other than possible concerns over generalisability if the research sample grew too small). But often dropping out (i.e. attrition) is selective. In other words, as time goes by, the people who are lost from a longitudinal sample are apt to differ in highly relevant ways from those who remain in the study. For example, a disproportionate number of the subjects who were less intelligent at the beginning of a longitudinal study might die from causes that a person of higher intelligence would manage to avoid, such as drink-driving or unprotected sex with an AIDS-infected partner. This could spuriously inflate intelligence test scores obtained at later stages since the survivors would have been more intelligent throughout all stages in life. The suggestion in Figure 2.8 of a rise in IQ score from age 30 to age 50 would then be spurious, reflecting changes in the sample over time rather than any gains in intelligence for the individuals who chose to continue being tested.

The need for repeated testing is another major liability of longitudinal methodologies. Schaie's (1983, 2000) participants would increasingly have known what to expect when tested at older ages, not to mention the possibility of memory for, and reflection upon, specific test items, so the higher IQ scores registered by the older groups could merely reflect the fact that they had become 'test-wise', or had had so much practice in taking the tests that their scores rose as a result of learning rather than any age-related tendency that could be generalised to other adults in the population.

The problem of selective attrition can also distort attempts to discover whether, in developmental studies of handedness, preferences change systematically with age. Even if the researchers who studied handedness cross-sectionally in the study shown in Box 2.6 had opted, instead, for the longitudinal approach, their results would not necessarily have produced a pure picture of development because of the likelihood of selective attrition. The possibility that left-handed individuals have shorter average life expectancy than the right-handed majority is not as outlandish as it might seem. Left-handed adults frequently complain that the physical environment is designed for the right-handed majority. Thus, risks of accidental injury may be greater for people who have to cope with such potentially lethal devices as motor vehicles, industrial machinery or firearms by using the 'wrong' hand. In fact, from a survey of 1896 right- and left-handed Canadians, Stan Coren (1989) found that left-handers were 89 per cent more likely than right-handers to suffer an accident requiring medical intervention during the two years surveyed. He argued that accidental death may be correspondingly more probable as a result of the environment's bias against safety for left-handers and, with Diane Halpern (Halpern & Coren, 1993), found that in one sample left-handers were indeed five times more likely than right-handers to die of injuries incurred in accidents. Furthermore, according to Halpern and Coren (1993), left-handedness is associated with depression, attempted suicide, early onset of breast cancer and elevated use of tobacco. As all these are risk factors for reduced longevity, Halpern and Coren concluded that the apparent increase in right-handedness with age (see Box 2.6) is not really a developmental change (see Chapter 1), but instead

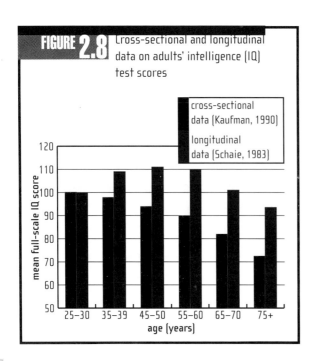

FIGURE 2.8 Cross-sectional and longitudinal data on adults' intelligence (IQ) test scores

cross-sectional data (Kaufman, 1990)

longitudinal data (Schaie, 1983)

b. 1879 Aged 25   b. 1911 Aged 25   b. 1944 Aged 25   b. 1974 Aged 25

A time-lag design studies individuals of the same age from different cohorts at different points in historical time

reflects the shorter average life expectancy of left-handed members of the population.

Time-lag and sequential designs

Given that cross-sectional and longitudinal designs are both potentially vulnerable to bias, K. Warner Schaie (2000) has recommended that cross-sectional and longitudinal investigations be supplemented by a third kind of research design, known as the time-lag method. This entails assessing the same age group at two or more points in time. For example, over a period of ten years, each incoming class of first-graders at a particular school might be given the same test of intelligence. A comparison of the average scores earned by successive classes could conceivably reveal a difference over time. Time-lag data like these tell us nothing directly about development, since all the groups in a time-lag study are the same age. But the method does give an indication of whether the climate of the times and/or membership in a particular cohort influences the phenomenon in question. If either of these factors is operative, differences will emerge between the various groups in the study.

A less biased picture of development can therefore be drawn when all three measurements – cross-sectional, longitudinal and time lag – are taken on the same group of people. Then the pure effects of age (obtained from cross-sectional and longitudinal data) can be distinguished from cohort influences (obtained from cross-sectional and time-lag data) and from distortions due to time of testing (obtained from longitudinal and time-lag data). Short-cut techniques that accomplish the same objectives are also afforded by the sequential methodology developed by K. Warner Schaie (1965, 2000) and Paul Baltes (2001); one of their designs is illustrated in Figure 2.9.

In this case, different groups of people (Cohorts A, B and C) are studied on four different testing occasions (1957, 1967, 1977, 1987). A comparison of each cohort's later results with their own earlier scores supplies independent longitudinal estimates of age-related change. For example, in 1987 a longitudinal study over the age period from 10 to 40 years could have been performed by comparing members of Cohort C at age 10 in 1957 with their later scores at 20, 30 and 40 in 1967, 1977 and 1987. Contrasts between the scores of the three separate cohorts in 1957 and again in 1967, 1977 and 1987 provide comparable cross-sectional age difference measures in each of these years. Time-lag data on 40-year-olds can likewise be obtained by comparing Cohort A's score in 1967 with Cohort B's in 1977, Cohort C's in 1987 and Cohort D's in 1997. In addition, sequential designs make use of combinations of longitudinal and cross-sectional tests. For example, a cohort-sequential (or longitudinal-sequential) design could compare Cohort C and Cohort D over the longitudinal age span from 10 to 40 years from 1957 to 1997, as shown in Figure 2.9. Alternatively, a cross-sequential study could compare Cohorts B, C and D at multiple testing points, as also shown in the figure. Mathematical formulae enable the compilation of these three separate sources of information into a global estimate of how much of the evident variation in scores is due to age, due to cohort and due to the time when the tests were given (Schaie, 1965).

Since sequential and combined designs like this one are quite expensive, both financially and in terms of the time and effort invested by the researchers and their subjects, they have yet to see very wide application to the investigation of psychological functioning over the lifespan. Instead, most of the up-to-date research studies examined in the following chapters of this book continue to rely on the economical cross-sectional method, with supplementation from longitudinal research. The sequential design alternative has, nevertheless, served the very useful purpose of drawing attention to the possibility of multiple causes for observed age differences.

The likelihood of generational and era contrasts

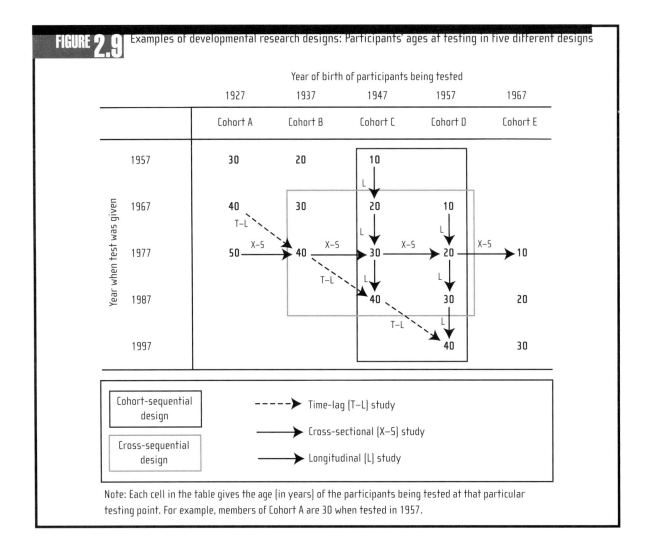

FIGURE 2.9 Examples of developmental research designs: Participants' ages at testing in five different designs

Year of birth of participants being tested

	1927	1937	1947	1957	1967
	Cohort A	Cohort B	Cohort C	Cohort D	Cohort E
1957	30	20	10		
1967	40	30	20	10	
1977	50	40	30	20	10
1987			40	30	20
1997				40	30

Year when test was given

- Cohort-sequential design
- Cross-sequential design
- - - - → Time-lag (T–L) study
- ⟶ Cross-sectional (X–S) study
- ⟶ Longitudinal (L) study

Note: Each cell in the table gives the age (in years) of the participants being tested at that particular testing point. For example, members of Cohort A are 30 when tested in 1957.

does need to be continually borne in mind when interpreting cross-sectional or longitudinal data. On the other hand, there is no justification for discarding the baby with the bath water. According to researcher Norval Glenn:

> All too often students of aging now fail to recognize that cross-sectional data properly analyzed and supplemented with information from other sources can often provide more nearly conclusive evidence about the effects of aging than can any other kind of data. (1981, p. 362)

Theories of lifespan development

'A favourite theory is a possession for life' wrote William Hazlitt (1779–1830) and, in fact, theoretical developments have played a major role in the emergence of lifespan developmental psychology as a scientific discipline.

An encompassing theory of development collects facts about psychological growth together and organises them systematically. This inspires further research and assists in the interpretation of data generated by the various research methods and designs examined earlier in this chapter. Theories themselves

are dynamic, evolving in response to the new empirical evidence that their initial postulates inspired. Theories are also highly practical. By explaining why development occurs, they can suggest intervention strategies to foster and optimise lifelong patterns of genuinely developmental change.

Some theories are designed quite specifically to explain particular developmental changes within just one life stage and/or one domain of psychological functioning – for example, children's sex-role development, adolescents' moral reasoning, adults' career development and theories of successful social ageing. We examine these theories in later chapters, in the context of the chronological age period to which most of their explanations and predictions are confined.

Other theories are far-reaching ones that strive to account for developmental change across many core domains (cognition, personality, social relationships) and across either the whole of life or a substantial portion of it. In this chapter we examine the guiding premises of these 'grand' theories that have exerted a seminal influence in inspiring, guiding and interpreting contemporary research in lifespan developmental psychology. They are (a) psychoanalytic theories,

(b) learning theories, (c) cognitive-developmental theories, and (d) stage theories of adult development.

Before looking at each of these approaches in turn, you may wish to evaluate your personal orientation to the key theoretical issues in lifespan psychology by completing the exercise in Box 2.7.

BOX 2.7 A question of taste: Examining your own theoretical orientation

Theories occupy different positions along a number of core dimensions of beliefs and viewpoints about human development. This exercise will help you understand the theories presented in this chapter, while also bringing your own assumptions and preconceptions about development into conscious awareness. You could also try it again after you have read about the theories to see if your viewpoint has changed.

Instructions: Mark one of the boxes to indicate your standpoint on each issue.

Nature/Biological	□ □ □ □ □ *versus*	**Nurture/Sociocultural**
Psychological development is the unfolding of genetically ordained, maturational changes in line with neurobiological structures and programs that are minimally influenced by experience.	1 2 3 4 5	Psychological development is the product of experience. Children are shaped by their social interactions and the surrounding sociocultural context. In general, learning takes precedence over simple maturation.
Continuity	□ □ □ □ □ *versus*	**Discontinuity**
Change consists merely of gradual quantitative additions or subtractions to a set of ageless psychological characteristics.	1 2 3 4 5	Change includes dramatic transformations which cannot be boiled down simply to having more or less of some earlier psychological characteristic.
Activity	□ □ □ □ □ *versus*	**Passivity**
Development is self-initiated. The individual actively seeks growth and change.	1 2 3 4 5	Human development is shaped by powerful forces which are beyond individual control.
Lifespan stability	□ □ □ □ □ *versus*	**Lifespan plasticity and change**
Most psychological development takes place early in life (infancy and childhood); continuity and stability prevail from then on as already developed capacities are exercised; once a developed capacity is lost it will not be regained.	1 2 3 4 5	Change is normal throughout the whole of life; each new development sows the seeds for future developments and changes; plasticity is the rule so that many lost capacities can eventually be recovered.
Macroscopic	□ □ □ □ □ *versus*	**Microscopic**
By standing back from minute-to-minute details, we see the essence of development – its broad, lifelong trends.	1 2 3 4 5	If the fine-grained, short-term detail of developmental change can be grasped, the broad trends will fall into place by themselves.
General	□ □ □ □ □ *versus*	**Differential**
People are all essentially similar, despite surface differences. We must search for general principles that apply to everyone.	1 2 3 4 5	Only after understanding the range of differences that make each human being unique will general trends become apparent.

The psychoanalytic approach: Freud and Erikson

Freud's theory

Sigmund Freud conceptualised development as a series of age-related conflicts between the child's primitive, hedonistic desires and the limitations imposed on them by society for the sake of cooperative living. Three separate personality structures are assumed to take part in this conflict: the id, the ego and the superego. The id is an unconscious reservoir of selfish instincts. The ego, also operating at a purely unconscious level, represents reality and serves to guide the id to gratification through realistic, appropriate and punishment-free channels. The third structure, the superego, represents 'the ethical standards of mankind' and limits both ego-based and id-based gratification of desires that conflict with the well-being of society as a whole.

There are five stages of development in Freud's theory. Each is defined partly in terms of unconscious conflict, partly in terms of a balance of id, ego and superego, and partly by which area of the body serves as the main focus of pleasure or gratification during that stage. In order of development, they are as follows.

THE ORAL STAGE

(First year of life). Pleasure is centred around the mouth. The id is the dominant personality structure at the beginning of the oral stage, and the child is unable to make a distinction between itself and the outside world. But since no baby's needs are always satisfied fully and instantaneously, an ego begins to develop. It first manifests itself as tolerance for short delays and is elaborated during weaning, which Freud saw as the first major conflict between the infant and the surrounding social world. He argued that this conflict was inevitable, but that parents could intensify it either by undue frustration (e.g. harsh and abrupt weaning) or by undue gratification (e.g. overfeeding or prolongation of breast or bottle feeding to a late age). He proposed that babies whose oral conflict was intensified in these ways often failed to grow out of the oral stage completely, and that such 'fixation' led to an 'oral character' and an excessive preoccupation with the mouth (characterised by such habits as eating disorders (see Chapter 10), chain smoking or excessive drinking).

THE ANAL STAGE

(One to three years). Freud postulated a shift in the focus of pleasure to the anal region during the second year of life. Conflict in the anal stage is between the requirement of hygiene imposed by the parents through toilet training and the toddler's narcissistic wish to void on impulse. Again, Freud felt that either overfrustration or overgratification during toilet training would intensify the conflict and potentially lead to an anal fixation and thence to traits such as messiness, stubbornness and greed.

THE PHALLIC STAGE

(Four to six years). The genital region becomes the pleasure centre near the age of four. During the next

During Freud's oral stage, pleasures centre around the mouth.

Freud's life

Sigmund Freud (1856–1939) was born in Freiburg, Moravia, and died in London. Trained as a medical doctor and researcher, he initially took up private psychiatric practice for purely economic reasons. (He had six children and the prospects for advancement as a Jewish university lecturer in Vienna were bleak.) However, it turned out that the direct contact with neurotic patients which his practice provided inspired some of his most important theoretical ideas.

Most of Freud's patients were adults. Surprisingly, though, as he analysed their innermost thoughts and feelings, Freud found a far heavier preoccupation with the events of infancy and childhood than with contemporary adult experience. A major component of his theory is therefore a developmental one: the notion that 'the child is father to the man' or that salient early experiences play a major role in shaping adult personality.

Another important concept which Freud introduced was that of infantile sexuality. During an era of rigid Victorian sexual morality, the idea that an infant's feeding experiences were conceptually analogous to adult orgasm seemed even more revolutionary and distasteful than it does today. As Freud himself observed:

Sigmund Freud traced personality development during the phallic stage to special conflicts between parents and their children of like and opposite sex.

Freud was a very courageous man. He was subjected to harsh personal and theoretical criticism for most of his working life. This was augmented, during his later years, by Nazi oppression and severe physical pain. He suffered from cancer and had surgery for it in 1923, the same year that his classic text, *The Ego and the Id* was published. Undaunted by either pain or politics, he continued writing, teaching, seeing patients and developing his theory up to the eve of his death at age 83.

year or two the child is in the phallic stage, and the major development-inducing conflict is an unconscious drama of lust and love for the parent of the opposite sex, coupled with antagonism and jealousy towards the same-sex parent. This conflict, named after the Greek tragedy as the Oedipal conflict for boys and the Electra conflict for girls, creates intense unconscious anxiety over incest taboos and fear of reprisal from the same-sex parent. Resolution is achieved when the child *identifies* psychologically with this parent, striving to become a carbon-copy of him or her in every way. Conscience and sex roles are acquired via identification; children emulate these qualities by studiously copying the parent who was formerly their unconscious rival.

THE GENITAL STAGE

(Puberty onwards). Biological reproductive maturity ushers in the final conflict in Freud's theory, since the coping mechanisms that were developed during the oral, anal and phallic stages are normally insufficient to deal with the full force of mature sexual desire. If the conflict during the genital stage is resolved successfully, adolescents gain the capacity for productive creativity, and for genuine and mature sexual styles of love.

Erikson's theory

Another psychoanalytic developmental theorist, Erik Erikson, was a pupil of both Sigmund Freud and Freud's daughter, Anna (see Chapter 12). But in his later theorising, Erikson departed from Freud's classic psychoanalytic position by downplaying Freud's notion of unconscious sexuality. Erikson accorded much greater importance than Freud to the influences of the sociocultural environment. He also viewed qualitative stage transitions as a feature of adult development as well as childhood and adolescence. In defining the essence of his unique approach, Erikson wrote:

> I shall present human growth from the point of view of the conflicts, inner and outer, which the vital personality weathers, re-emerging from each crisis with an increased sense of inner unity, with an increase of good judgment, and an increase in the capacity 'to do well' according to his own standards and to the standards of those who are significant to him. (1968a, pp. 91–2)

Thus, like Freud before him, Erikson saw dialectical conflict as the basic mechanism of development and defined cumulative stages of personality growth in terms of the unique forms of that conflict. However, whereas Freud used the concept of sex energy (libido) as a basic unifying theme, Erikson coined the term 'epigenesis' to describe what he saw as common to all the conflicts and developmental changes arising at different stages in life. Epigenesis states that 'anything that grows has a ground plan and that out of this ground plan the parts have arisen to form a functioning whole' (1968a, p. 92). In human psychological growth, this epigenetic 'ground plan' sets up a series of eight potential conflicts, each with two contradictory facets. The resolution of each conflict entails unification of these contradictions to create a newly emergent 'part' of the total personality. Each of the eight conflicts constitutes a stage in Erikson's system.

BASIC TRUST VERSUS MISTRUST

(Birth to one year). The quality of the parental care that infants receive during this stage largely determines the balance of trust with mistrust in their budding psyches. Resolution of unconscious conflict entails finding a realistic compromise between blind faith in the primary caregiver, as the source of total pleasure, and an acceptance of the unavoidable pain of delay and frustration. The outcome of a satisfactory resolution brings babies their first 'psychosocial strength', which Erikson described as *hope*, and which will form a cornerstone for all manifestations of faith later in life.

AUTONOMY VERSUS SHAME AND DOUBT

(One to three years). In this stage children acquire a sense of autonomy, or independence, as they explore their environments and interact with others. A sense of shame and doubt also emerges through the caregivers' inevitable curtailment or disapproval of some of the child's early social and exploratory activities. A satisfactory resolution of the conflict between shame and self-assertion transcends them both, and entails a mature feeling of free choice bounded by the societal limitations of law and custom. Too much autonomy, relative to shame, produces a child who is uncontrolled and defiant. Too much shame results in an overly inhibited child who is a compulsively zealous conformist.

INITIATIVE VERSUS GUILT

(Four to five years). Children in this stage know the limits of ordinary social behaviour and have largely mastered their body and their language, so that they are capable of functioning adequately without a lot of parental assistance. Parents are still very important in this stage, however. They encourage the child to initiate play and constructive activities, and they curb the child's unrestrained initiative to inculcate feelings of personal responsibility and guilt. As in the earlier stages, a balance between spontaneous, free-flowing initiative and its conscientious limitation through guilt is required for a satisfactory resolution of the unconscious conflict that is unique to this stage. The resulting healthy sense of purpose consists, according to Erikson, of 'the courage to envisage and pursue valued and tangible goals, guided by conscience but not paralyzed by guilt and by the fear of punishment' (1968a, p. 289).

INDUSTRY VERSUS INFERIORITY

(Six to 11 years). When children enter school, their lives become geared to working hard (industry) in the school-room. The school's evaluation of each child's achievements compared with those of other children fosters a sense of superiority or inferiority. In Western society, school's demands for hard work and accomplishment also extend into out-of-school activities, so that play takes new forms such as competitive sport, the building of forts and tree houses, and publicly evaluated art, drama or music. The conflict in this stage is between the joy of work, with the feelings of unlimited power it engenders, and the limiting sense of incompetence and inferiority which may result from an unfavourable comparison of the child's prod-

ucts with those of other children. A satisfactory resolution requires the development of cooperation with other people, so that children can freely and successfully exercise their own unique competencies in contribution to a larger productive effort.

IDENTITY VERSUS ROLE CONFUSION

(12 to 18 years). Perhaps the best known concept from Erikson's theory to emerge into popular consciousness is that of the *identity crisis*, which is the pivotal focus of this fifth stage in development. Both his own protracted adolescence (devoted to dabbling in a range of vocations) and the ideological searching and personal confusion that he observed among European and North American youth, immigrants and minority groups contributed to Erikson's formulation of this stage and to the major emphasis he accorded it in his own writing and theorising. The adolescent's central task, in Erikson's view, is to define a comprehensive sense of self, or identity, which incorporates the relics of past identifications and aligns the adolescent's own unique attributes with the opportunities society offers. The problem is enhanced in contemporary society by the wide range of alternative roles available and by their inconsistency with one another and with the traditions of the past. A satisfactory resolution of the identity conflict entails the development of a coherent sense of self that integrates all the essential features of the individual's past and sets the direction for further personal growth and a productive contribution to society.

INTIMACY VERSUS ISOLATION

(Early adulthood). Once young people attain a workable identity, they are ready to commit the new-found self to a close relationship with another person. The outcome of this integration can be a new kind of identity as a couple, which includes, but transcends, the particular identities of each partner. There are two risks:

1. The refusal to commit oneself to another completely, leading to psychological isolation;
2. One's own identity being overwhelmed by the partner's, leading to a loss of sense of self.

Ideal love, or intimacy, according to Erikson, is 'a mutuality of devotion greater than the antagonisms inherent in divided function' (1968a, p. 139).

GENERATIVITY VERSUS SELF-ABSORPTION

(Middle adulthood). The crisis of the middle years, according to Erikson, relates to socially significant accomplishment. In mid-life people need to produce things (generativity) which carry beyond the finite limits of their own lives to influence future generations. Possible solutions include the raising of healthy and happy children or a creative, political or constructive vocation that helps to better the world. The crisis comes about through doubt about the magni-

BOX 2.9 Erikson's life

Erik Homberger Erikson (1902–94) was born in Frankfurt, Germany, to Danish parents and died in California, USA, at the age of 92. During his late adolescence he had a series of important personal experiences which were later incorporated into his theoretical work. After graduating from high school he set out alone through Europe as 'a young man with some talent and nowhere to go'. Eventually, he returned to Germany and enrolled in art school. He crystallised his joint interests in art and childhood, first by painting children's portraits and later as a Montessori teacher. In Vienna he met Anna Freud, the daughter and colleague of Sigmund Freud. She encouraged him to train as a psychoanalyst.

With the threat of war erupting in Europe, Erikson migrated to the United States in 1933, obtaining a position at the Harvard Medical School in Boston. He spent the remainder of his life in America, acquiring a joint identity as a displaced person, an American intellectual and a European by tradition. Erikson's varied career included teaching university students, treating child and adolescent patients, studying normal children from a range of cultures and class backgrounds (including Sioux and Yurok Indians) and, most importantly, drawing all these diverse facets of his life and experience together into a theory of lifespan psychological development.

Erikson's theory grew out of Freud's. But the contrasting cultures to which Erikson's studies, travels and migration exposed him, in combination with his consciousness of the dramatic significance of recent historical events, led him to place a far greater emphasis than Freud on interactions between the individual and the current historical and cultural climate. Also, Erikson carried the psychoanalytic theory of human psychological development well beyond adolescence, where Freud had left it, to postulate that a series of predictable crises and conflicts continues to spark development during early and middle adulthood and into old age. These two unique emphases in Erikson's theory have captivated the imagination of a great many contemporary developmental psychologists (Havighurst, 1973).

Erikson was constantly concerned with the rapid pace of social change in contemporary life and was a strong critic of exploitation, social injustice and militarism. During much of his adult life, in line with his own theory of *generativity*, he taught and spoke publicly on behalf of young people and the future of a just society. His later writings included works on the generation gap, racial tensions, changing sex roles and the dangers of nuclear war.

destroyed, superseded or put to bad use, are faced with a helpless sense of waste and frustration which may lead to bitter and stagnating self-preoccupation. To achieve a satisfactory resolution to the conflict, people must recognise the finite limits of their own endeavours and yet must persist in striving to assist future generations.

INTEGRITY VERSUS DESPAIR

(Old age). This is a stage for looking back over one's life, for reminiscing, tying up loose ends and integrating one's whole life into a coherent picture. Erikson called it 'a new edition of an identity crisis' (1968a, p. 141) because it is also a time for thinking about life as a whole and for locating one's complete life cycle into the larger scheme of things. The conflict often begins when the recognition of the imminence of death upsets complacent satisfaction with life as it has been, and brings poignant regret for the unrealised possibilities that might have been. A satisfactory resolution enables a transcendence of the conflict, as the ageing person undertakes to 'transfer his strength to the upcoming generation' (Clayton, 1975, p. 121) and achieves a belief in some higher unity of human life which is free of temporal relativity. An adult who attains mature integrity thus comes to know

> that an individual life is the accidental coincidence of but one life cycle with but one segment of history, and that for him all human integrity stands and falls with the one style of integrity of which he partakes. (Erikson, 1968a, p. 140)

The cognitive-developmental approach: Piaget and Vygotsky

Piaget's theory

Jean Piaget (1970) put forward a theory of development spanning four major stages, each characterised by a qualitatively different mode of thought. The mechanism of transition between stages is a dialectical conflict between the processes of *assimilation* and *accommodation* that he had derived from biology. Assimilation in biology describes the incorporation of elements from the environment into the organism, as when a plant assimilates carbon dioxide or when an animal eats food, digests it and converts its nutrients into bodily tissue. Accommodation arises when organic structures are modified to suit the constraints of the external environment, as when animals grow thick fur to combat the cold of winter and shed their coats in the heat of summer.

In Piaget's theory, assimilation and accommodation interact with one another through a process of adaptation so as to rise dialectically (see page 42) to a higher order of equilibrium. By analogy with biology, assimilation in cognitive development arises for Piaget when some new item (which could be tangible like food, or intangible like a new idea) is incorporated into

tude or worth of one's contribution or through failure to make a contribution at all. Parents who feel alienated from their children, or workers who see the things to which they have devoted their lives being

an existing cognitive structure which he called a *schema*. For example, during Piaget's first stage of sensorimotor development, schemas consist of action patterns, and the process of assimilation might be seen when an infant who started off with a largely reflex schema for sucking on the human breast (see Chapter 4) is able to assimilate new items like rubber teats, pacifiers or her own thumb into the sucking schema, making it more versatile, or better 'adapted'. The schema is the psychological counterpart for Piaget of an organ of the body and consists of an integrated pattern of behaviour elements. Just as a structure in biology can be as simple as a toe or as complex as a digestive system, Piaget's mental schemas range from the newborn's simple sucking reflex to the *schema of intuitive qualitative correspondence* (a method used by school-age children for deciding the numerical equality of groups of numbers).

The process of accommodation is triggered, according to Piaget, when assimilation fails: for example, when a breast-fed baby has trouble assimilating the inanimate nipple of a bottle into his sucking schema. Accommodation consists of altering the schema to enable it to assimilate the new item. This interplay between assimilation and accommodation leads to ever more sophisticated conceptual structures and modes of cognitive functioning. But development, for Piaget, is more like the ascent of a staircase than a steady climb up a hill. Because of the joint contribution of biological maturation of the brain and the varied experiences the child encounters while growing older, qualitative changes (stages) occur at specific points in development. Each stage gives rise to a new kind of thought. The stages are described below.

SENSORIMOTOR STAGE

(Up to age two). The sensorimotor stage is a period during which the infant learns to deal effectively with the physical and social world at the level of overt behaviour. It ends with the beginnings of symbolic thought.

PREOPERATIONAL STAGE

(Two to seven years). The preoperational stage is a period during which the ability to think about objects, words and other symbols, and to manipulate them mentally, evolves and spreads into the areas of play, moral awareness and social functioning. Thinking in this stage is 'prelogical', according to Piaget. The preschooler is intrigued by many natural and social phenomena and their causal origins, as seen in the average three-year-old's perpetual question 'Why?'

Preschoolers are also quite adept at devising their own intriguing explanations for puzzling dilemmas like what makes the sun come up and go down, or how dreaming occurs. But their line of reasoning is more likely to be *transductive* (linking one idiosyncratic particular to another, see Chapter 7) than

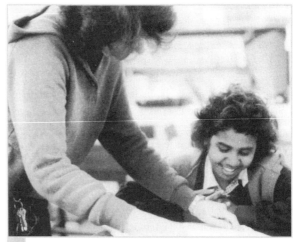

Piaget's theory explores children's and adolescents' ideas about scientific phenomena.

inductive or *deductive*. Hence it is likely to seem illogical to an adult. This illogicality is drawn out into the open when children argue with one another or with a parent, motivating cognitive development through an overt dialectical clash between opposing points of view in which more advanced logic eventually triumphs over prelogicality to progress development to the next stage. Indeed, for Piaget, arguments make a major contribution to qualitative developmental progress towards higher stages, a belief reinforced by more recent research findings of contemporary Swiss developmental psychologists including Anne-Nellie Perret-Clermont (1980), examined in more detail in Chapter 7.

CONCRETE-OPERATIONAL STAGE

(Seven to 11 years). During the concrete-operational stage, the child's thoughts become organised into an integrated system of logical operations called groupings. As a result, the child acquires a rational and

BOX 2.10 Piaget's life

Jean Piaget (1896–1980) was born in Neuchâtel, Switzerland, and died in Geneva, Switzerland, at the age of 84. His father was a professor of medieval literature at the University of Neuchâtel and Piaget himself taught there briefly, from 1925 to 1929, before moving to the University of Geneva where he spent most of the remainder of his academic life.

Piaget is often deemed to be the greatest developmental psychologist of the 20th century, and his remarkable discoveries of children's unique ways of thinking about the world have earned him the nickname 'Giant in the Nursery' (Elkind, 1978). However, as Piaget himself (1976a) explained, he was drawn to the study of child psychology almost by accident. His scientific career began precociously with the publication of an article on the albino sparrow in a biology journal at the age of 11. He continued publishing at a rapid rate until one of the journal editors (who would nowadays be dubbed 'ageist') learned how young he was and refused further publication on the grounds of age alone.

At about the same time, Piaget was whiling away boring intervals in his high school classes by drafting a theory of philosophy, which he 'imprudently' published as a novel at age 21. His dissatisfaction with this high-flying venture eventually brought home to him the need for an empirical basis around which to organise the analysis of consciousness; some years later, after completing a doctorate in biology, he discovered this basis in psychology.

In 1923 he married Valentine Châtenay, a fellow scientist. During the early years of his marriage he tested children in Paris to standardise the IQ test that Theodore Simon and Alfred Binet had recently developed. The children's wrong answers piqued Piaget's curiosity, and he gradually evolved his own style of interviewing, the *clinical method*, which enabled him to probe beneath the surface of children's replies by posing challenges and investigating their underlying reasoning.

For the next 50 years Piaget continued to interview children, using games, scientific dilemmas and verbal challenges that still have their place in the contemporary developmental psychologist's repertoire of investigative techniques.

Piaget's unique approach to child psychology is best captured in an incident he recorded in his autobiography (Flavell, 1963). He tells of being commissioned by Albert Einstein to discover whether Newtonian mechanics or the relativity theory had primacy in the developing mind. The crucial test was whether children first understood the concept of time and derived velocity from it (which is the position taken by classical mechanics), or whether they began with velocity as a first given and constructed time in relation to it (the approach taken by relativity theory). Piaget eagerly set about testing these two views, using some of the tasks described in Chapter 7. Disappointingly, though, while he found some support for relativity's priority, the notions of velocity that young children began with were themselves derivative of even more basic spatial relationships. In other words, he found that the children's first implicit 'theory' of physics was different from both Newton's and Einstein's.

This experiment illustrates, on a small scale, what Piaget's basic approach to cognitive development entailed. He endeavoured to understand the organisation of the human mind by witnessing the first glimmerings of thought in early infancy and tracing them through their ever-increasing shades of complexity as the mind developed. By this means he enhanced not only the understanding of children and how they think, but also supplemented the philosophy of knowledge. Until Piaget, philosophers had focused primarily on adult cognition, thus missing out on the rich store of insights to be derived from observing the growth of thought in the mind of a child.

consistent understanding of tangible objects and events. Thinking is still limited, however, when it comes to higher-order abstractions and intangibles.

FORMAL-OPERATIONAL STAGE

(After age 11). For Piaget, the formal-operational stage is the pinnacle of logical thought. When fully mastered, formal operations enable the adolescent to think rationally, hypothetico-deductively and thoroughly about even such remote abstractions as friction and momentum, the mechanisms of human thought or the possible future of the world. Genuinely qualitative cognitive development ceases, according to Piaget, with the attainment of formal operations. But the quantitative assimilation of further information and its integration into existing formal thought structures can continue through the remainder of the lifespan.

Vygotsky's theory

Lev S. Vygotsky developed a sociocultural theory of cognitive development that, like Piaget's, emphasises the role of social interaction, including logical disagreements, as a motive force behind cognitive gains. According to Vygotsky, the cultural tools that a child receives from the social environment, through interactions with parents, peers and teachers, are essential in enabling the human mind to grow. There are three ways that these tools can be acquired. One is through imitative learning where the child watches and copies the actions of an interaction partner. The second is through internalisation of lessons that are socially conveyed through play, teaching, coaching or other kinds of explicit instructional communication. Gradually, ideas that first entered the child's mind via the speech of others become internalised as implicit, covert speech. 'Thus, with the help of speech, children ... acquire the capacity to be both subjects and objects of their own behaviour' (Vygotsky, 1978, p. 26). The third route for the acquisition of cultural tools is via collaborative learning with peers. Using a dialectical model Vygotsky proposed that, by mutual striving to understand and convince one another,

According to Vygotsky's theory, children can perform tasks with help from others that they cannot yet perform on their own.

BOX 2.11 Vygotsky's life

Lev Semyonovich Vygotsky (1896–1934) was born in Beloruss, Russia. He studied law at the University of Moscow during the heady days preceding and following the October Revolution of 1917 from which Russian socialism was born. His experiences as a student activist and moral thinker (see Chapter 11) inspired him to contribute to children's development through education. He also developed a sensitive appreciation of the importance of cooperation with other people and the support of human society for both individual and political development.

After graduation, Vygotsky worked as a teacher. He published his first theoretical volume, *The Psychology of Art*, in 1925 before joining forces in psychological research with Alexander Luria and Alexei Leontiev, working on his theory of cognitive development. In spite of its premature curtailment by Vygotsky's untimely death from tuberculosis at the age of 38, his seminal sociocultural theory remains alive and well today, having exerted major influences upon the disciplines of both developmental and educational psychology.

children working collectively can eventually surpass their earlier levels of private understanding.

While resembling Piaget's theory in many respects, Vygotsky's is more explicitly social, and more attentive to the unique features of the child's own sociocultural environment that can drive cognitive development in a different direction from that seen among children of the same age in a very different social milieu. According to Vygotsky:

> From the very first days of a child's development his activities acquire a meaning of their own in a system of social behaviour and, being directed towards a definite purpose, are refracted through the prism of the child's environment. The path from object to child and from child to object passes through another person. (1978, p. 30)

Another important theoretical construct introduced by Vygotsky was his notion of a zone of proximal development (ZPD). The zone is a range of capacity stretching from sole performance to assisted capability. What this implies, in line with Vygotsky's discoveries about the benefits of collaborative social learning, is that children who work on a cognitive problem with a skilled partner are able to accomplish tasks that they could not solve alone. The ZPD is the gap between the child's private problem-solving capacity and the level of potential development that can be achieved by working under adult guidance, or in cooperation with a cognitively advanced peer. Eventually, after mastering cognitive concepts through this kind of collaborative social interaction, the new knowledge is internally assimilated and the ZPD extends to a more developmentally advanced style of

problem-solving. Here again, the sophistication of the child's cultural environment is the major determiner of the extent of development that can be achieved.

Learning theories: Classical theories and the social-learning approach

At its broadest level, the learning perspective views human development primarily as the product of experience, postulating that the basic principles governing the acquisition of new knowledge and skills by organisms ranging from a rat in a Skinner box to a university student taking a course in microbiology also contribute importantly to developmental change over the lifespan. A number of these core learning concepts are listed and explained in Box 2.12.

Classical learning theories

In 1928 John B. Watson, the father of behavioural learning theory, wrote:

> Give me a dozen healthy infants, well-formed, and my own specified world to bring them up in and I'll guarantee to take any one at random and train him to become any type of specialist I might select – doctor, lawyer, artist, merchant-chief, and, yes, even beggar-man and thief, regardless of his talents, penchants, tendencies, abilities, vocations, and race of his ancestors. (1928, p. 104)

According to Watson, a person's developmental future rests in the hands of parents, teachers, peers and others who engineer that individual's overall learning environment. Disputing the relevance of hereditary, physiological and neurobiological predispositions, Watson argued that it was possible to shape human development in all its complexity using nothing but the simple teaching devices of classical and operant conditioning (see Box 2.12 for definitions).

Another classic behavioural learning theorist, B. F. Skinner (1953), proposed that learning principles of reward, extinction and punishment are responsible for much of the behaviour and psychological functioning that human beings develop, including language. Wise and consistent parenting is critical, according to this view, to ensure that children acquire the right habits and avoid learning the wrong ones.

Developmental learning theories not only use learning principles to explain how children develop new capacities, but they also strive to explain how the process of learning itself changes as the learner gets older. While they vary in detail, several theories (e.g. Pavlov, 1927; Luria, 1961; Kendler & Kendler, 1972) agree that there are two separate stages in children's learning. During the first, learning is viewed as the gradual building of relatively simple and direct sensorimotor associations. In the second stage, more advanced and abstract cognitive strategies and func-

BOX 2.12 A glossary of learning terminology

Classical conditioning: The classical conditioning procedure involves the repeated pairing of a neutral stimulus with a stimulus that instinctively or 'unconditionally' evokes a response. Eventually the neutral stimulus comes to evoke the same response. (*Example*: Pavlov's dog was conditioned to salivate to a bell after repeated pairings of the bell with the taste of food.)

Operant conditioning: Operant conditioning alters the frequency of designated behaviours by delivering reward or punishment whenever they occur. (*Example*: a hungry rat gropes randomly around its cage until it chances to press a lever. Food reinforces the lever-pressing – the rat learns to press reliably.)

Reinforcement: A reinforcement is anything that changes the probability of a response with which it is associated. (*Example*: earning pocket money reinforces a teenager's tidying of his room.)

Punishment: An aftermath that decreases the frequency of the behaviour with which it has come to be associated. (*Example*: rats learn to avoid a bar producing an electric shock.)

Mediation: Mediation is the learning of an abstract concept linking a stimulus to a learned response. (*Example*: after learning to select a small red diamond and a small red heart, a child learns to select all *small* or *red* objects.)

Vicarious reinforcement: Observing positive consequences for others of a particular behaviour pattern increases the likelihood that the observer will copy it.

Generalisation: Generalisation is the spontaneous transfer of learned responses to similar situations. (*Example*: the dog salivates to the sound of a buzzer.)

Extinction: Extinction reduces the strength of a conditioned response. In classical conditioning this occurs by repeated exposure to the conditioned stimulus without the unconditioned stimulus. (*Example*: the bell is rung without food being given. Eventually the dog no longer salivates when hearing it.) In operant conditioning this occurs by repeated failure to gain reinforcement after the response. (*Example*: food is withheld when the lever is pressed. Eventually the rat ceases lever-pressing.)

Behaviour modification/cognitive behaviour therapy: The principles of classical conditioning, operant conditioning and instructional learning can be applied in a practical way to the treatment of behaviour problems, the central assumptions being:

- a person's behaviour is his problem (as opposed to the view that the behaviour is a symptom of some underlying conflict); and
- the problem is due to learning – for example, the child has either learned to do the wrong things or has not learned to do the right things. If she has learned to do the wrong things, extinction is called for. If she has not learned to do the right things, conditioning is called for.

Modelling: Modelling is learning to do something by observing someone else (the model) do it. (*Example*: a child copies an adult's patting of a dog.)

---

tions come to control the learning process. This implies both (a) that theories of learning need to include age in their explanatory frameworks, and (b) that developmental theories postulating learning to account for changes in behaviour must incorporate different learning models for individuals of different ages.

Also, although developmental learning theories have so far dealt systematically with only the first half of the lifespan, recent research suggests that qualitative changes in the learning process may occur during the latter half of life, not all of which can be equated with weakening or loss of capacities developed earlier (Baltes, 1989). Thus, additional theoretical stages for learning may need to be formulated in the future.

Social learning and Bandura's social-cognitive learning theory

A different learning approach, known as *social learning theory*, initially proposed in 1941 by Neal Miller and John Dollard, was elaborated and applied to children, first by Robert Sears (Sears, Maccoby & Levin, 1957) and then by Albert Bandura (1969).

Children learn to do new things by observing others.

Bandura (1989, 1997) has continued to refine the theory to include a new role for cognition (Bandura, 1989), renaming it 'social-cognitive theory' to reflect this added emphasis.

Social learning theory, in both its original and its social-cognitive incarnations, strongly emphasises observational learning. Through processes of imitation, modelling and vicarious reinforcement (see Box 2.12), children may acquire complex social behaviours ranging from aggression to altruism. They can also acquire sex roles and standards of conscience in this way, supplemented by classic learning principles of reward, extinction and punishment. Throughout their growing up children have ample opportunity to watch others, copy their behaviour and learn from others' observed successes as well as their mistakes. For example, a toddler might observe an older sibling pumping a swing or building a sandcastle at the beach, and try to copy these behaviours via modelling. If the model (the older sibling) earns a reward for expressing the behaviour (e.g. a peer admires the sandcastle) the learner's chances of copying it are likely to increase still more, through the principle of vicarious reinforcement (see Box 2.12).

In some of his early research, Albert Bandura (1969) showed that aggression can also be acquired through observational learning and modelling. Children who watched a video tape of adults beating up a rubber clown were more likely than children who had not watched the film to behave aggressively towards the clown doll when they were put in a room alone with it. Bandura showed that people effectively learn to do things they have never done before by observing a model do them, and that observational learning occurs even when no reward accrues to either the model or the observer. Even new behaviours that are not directly observed can be acquired through imitation. For example, when children watch violent fights on television, they are found not only to copy the aggressive actions they saw the televised model perform (Bandura, 1973) but even to do totally different hurtful things—such as choosing to press a button that will burn the fingers of another child in preference to one that will help the other child win a game (Liebert & Baron, 1972). In other words, social learning through modelling can be abstract as well as specific.

Also, observation can sometimes diminish the tendency to copy—as when a child who sees another fall off a playground slide becomes wary of going on it—and its effects can show up months (and possibly years) after a single observational opportunity (e.g. Hicks, 1965).

Bandura's social-cognitive theory also includes a stronger emphasis on self-regulatory motivational mechanisms than classic learning theories. He proposed that the core observational learning process, modelling, has cognitive elements. Modelling, for Bandura (1989), is a four-step process:

1. *Attention*. The learner must notice the model and keep attention focused on the behaviour to be modelled.
2. *Retention*. Using memory processes, which may include imagery and language, people can store behaviours they have observed so as to reproduce them days, or weeks, later.
3. *Reproduction*. When learning complex behaviours through observation, mental organisation of the behaviour pattern is called for rather than simple repetition or echoing. This improves with age and practice.
4. *Motivation*. In order to want to copy a behaviour, the person needs an incentive, sometimes an anticipated or vicarious reinforcement.

Two other important features of Bandura's social-cognitive learning theory are his notions of self-regulation and self-efficacy. *Self-regulation* involves (a) becoming aware of one's own behaviour, (b) assessing it against internalised standards, and (c) a self-response of reward or punishment. Thus, a 7-year-old girl might help a younger child tie his shoelaces, reflect on her helpful act, judge it positively and then self-reward with feelings of gratification at her adherence to the moral standard to be helpful.

Self-efficacy is the collection of beliefs people have about their own abilities and areas of incompetence. These influence the decision to imitate others. Thus, a

Feelings of self-efficacy develop out of successful learning experiences and reflection on one's own achievements, such as growing an attractive garden.

boy who believes himself incompetent at sewing will be unlikely to model his sister's mending of her school blazer, despite the vicarious reward of watching the praise she earns for her successful sewing efforts.

Stage theories of adult development

Buhler's theory

Charlotte Buhler (see Box 2.13) was an influential lifespan theorist both in her own right and through the influences she had on the stage-linked and humanistic approaches to adult development of theorists such as Robert Havighurst (1973), Daniel Levinson (1986), Abraham Maslow (1968), Donald Super (1990) and George Vaillant (Vaillant & Vaillant, 1990). She presented adult development in terms of intentionality, goal-setting and actualisation. Through her observational research and her clinical case histories of adult patients in therapy, she discovered a lifelong pattern that she labelled *intentionality*. Evident in all but the most forlorn of lives, intentionality is a developmental process of (a) choosing life goals, (b) working towards them, (c) evaluating goal achievement, and (d) selecting new goals, revisiting neglected ones and revising life plans in order to fulfil one's full human potential for self-actualisation and self-determination.

According to Buhler, most of us are not consciously aware of these core life goals, which can often only be discerned through deep psychotherapy, or by piecing together a person's complete life story after they have died. Nevertheless, a basic assumption of Buhler's theory is that each human life is coherently organised from birth to death around a goal activity. These goals manifest themselves in all the various spheres of the person's life endeavour (from vocational activities to intimate relationships and private thoughts). Goals also change in predictable ways over life as they are worked towards, achieved or amended, and reformulated or abandoned.

Buhler divided intentionality into five major goal tendencies (Havighurst, 1973):

1. need satisfaction (creature comforts, love, trust, etc.)
2. adjustment (self-limitation in accordance with social standards)
3. creative expansion
4. inner harmony
5. self-fulfilment.

Buhler suggested that changes over the lifespan in the way that goal tendencies are expressed can be understood partly in terms of the biological life curve (which she saw as ascending to a zenith of vigour and skill in early adulthood and then declining to its lowest ebb in very old age) and partly in terms of social roles (such as employment, friendship, childrearing and retirement), which also set up various possibilities and limitations for people of

different ages. Her resulting adult stage theory is shown in Figure 2.10 on page 64.

Wise choices and considerable effort are needed in order to develop successfully through all these adult stages. Many lives fail to attain fulfilment, according to Buhler (1968), and she offered these examples.

- Myron, at 34, had still not completed the second phase, tentative self-determination. He had not yet married and had no career. Buhler attributed his non-committal uncertainty to his extreme dependence on a domineering mother.
- Georgia, age 35, faltered in the third phase because she had undertaken two irreconcilable goals. She was trying to care for her demanding mother and make a success of a demanding marriage, and she found that the conflict engendered by these two aims led to frustration in both of them.
- Gary, age 58, failed to master the fourth phase of assessing his life pattern realistically. He had had three marriages, and each one failed because he took up extramarital affairs. He loved his third wife deeply and was hurt when he lost her, but he refused to hold himself to account and could not see the repetitious pattern in his life.

In other words, for Buhler, a successful course through life entails:

1. The realistic selection of a range of goals that are consistent with the individual's creative potential, personal values and possibilities;
2. An honest and hard-working endeavour to meet

FIGURE **2.10** Buhler's stage theory

Post self-determination stage (age 65 to death)

A period of reminiscence and self-acknowledgment of the degree to which goals were fulfilled; followed by repose, aimless activity, devotion to others or to charity or, in rare cases, a continuation of expansive pursuits.

Assessment stage (50 to 65 years)

A period of critical evaluation of the extent to which life goals have been met. Biological and/or social losses may trigger this process. A sense of failure can lead to a hurried attempt to remedy the loss (by taking on a new job, remarriage, etc.). A successful resolution of the phase entails a revised orientation to the future in view of the limited time still available, and an emphasis on self-definition of goals rather than the acceptance of conformist societal evaluations.

Definitive self-determination stage (25 to 50 years)

A period of accomplishment of consolidated goals in a career, in marriage, in childrearing and in relation to the self. Life contains the greatest quantity and variety of purposeful activities during this phase.

Tentative self-determination stage (15 to 25 years)

A period of making initial life plans and preliminary commitments to a job, to other people and to a sense of self. The person may adopt a career but be prepared to change it, and become committed to another person but also on a tentative basis. Basic personal values have become clearer by the end of this phase.

Pre self-determination stage (birth to 15 years)

As biological growth combines with the family and school environment to foster skills and interests, children and adolescents gain the necessary preparation for goal-setting by becoming increasingly aware of their own talents and limitations.

these goals; and

3. The monitoring and modification of goal direction to suit the current life phase and its biological and social circumstances.

Levinson's theory

Daniel Levinson collected longitudinal data on the overall patterns of adult men's (Levinson, 1978) and women's (Levinson, 1986) lives and devised a theory of adult development as 'the evolution of the life structure' (1986, p. 3). His model of adult development from age 17 to age 65 is shown in Table 2.2.

Levinson (1986) reports being surprised, when he examined his longitudinal data, to discover an orderly pattern of qualitative (stage-wise) changes in all the adult lives he analysed. Furthermore, the stages themselves were very similar for everyone. As shown in Table 14.7 on page 500, Levinson's model of the lifespan consists of a regular alternation between stable periods of life functioning (the 'life structures') and periods of developmental upheaval (the 'transitions') during which life goals and life activities are evaluated in a manner somewhat similar to that proposed by Buhler, and new developments take place at a rapid rate. As Levinson explained:

A *transitional* period terminates the existing life structure and creates the possibility for a new one. The primary tasks of every transitional period are to reappraise the existing structure, to explore possibilities for change in the self and the world, and to move toward commitment to the crucial life choices that form the basis for a new life structure in the ensuing period. Transitional periods ordinarily last about five years. Almost half our adult lives is spent in developmental transitions. No life structure is permanent – periodic change is given in the nature of our existence. As a transition comes to an end, one starts making crucial choices, giving them meaning and commitment, and building a life structure around them. The choices are, in a sense, the major product of the transition. When all the efforts of the transition are done – the struggles to improve work or marriage, to explore alternative possibilities of living, to come more to terms with the self – choices must be made and bets must be placed. One must decide: 'This I will settle for', and start creating a life structure that will serve as a vehicle for the next step in the journey. (p. 7, © American Psychological Association, reprinted with permission)

TABLE 2.2 Levinson's stage theory of adulthood

Developmental era	Developmental stage	Age in years	Developmental task
Era of Pre-adulthood (Age 0–23)	1. Early adult transition	17–23	Moving out of parents' home Finding employment Shopping around for appropriate vocation
Era of Early Adulthood (Age 24–45)	2. Entry life structure for early adulthood	23–28	Settling on an appropriate career Creating a stable life structure with options open
	3. Age 30 transition	28–33	Reappraising and modifying the initial structure
	4. Culminating life structure for early adulthood	33–40	Establishing a niche through ambitious goal achievement
	5. Mid-life transition	40–45	Reappraisal and reformulation of goals to allow neglected parts of the personality to express themselves
Era of Middle Adulthood (Age 45–65)	6. Entry life structure for middle adulthood	45–50	Creating a productive self-expressive life structure
	7. Age 50 transition	50–55	Assessing, modifying and improving the middle adulthood structure
	8. Culminating life structure for middle adulthood	55–60	Achieving the goals formulated during the fifties transition
Era of Late Adulthood (Age 65 ++)	9. Late adult transition	60–65	Preparing for retirement
	10. Entry life structure for late adulthood	65++	Pursue retired life

Chapter summary

This chapter sets the stage for the study of human development through the rest of this book by examining the guiding assumptions, interdisciplinary perspectives, research methods and theoretical insights of a lifespan approach to developmental psychology. In studying changes in human psychological functioning through the whole of life, researchers seek to understand the individual, cultural and historical diversity that makes each human life story unique. At the same time they seek general patterns across all human lives in their pursuit of goals to describe, explain and optimise lifelong psychological growth.

The study of human development over the lifespan is integrated by a set of premises (see Tables 1.3 and 2.1) describing researchers' shared interests and mutually agreed assumptions. These include an empirical orientation prescribing the gathering of objective data to test ideas about development, the view that patterns of growth in physical, cognitive, personality, emotional and social domains unfold coherently and

predictably with increasing age and the notion that all human beings have the potential to grow psychologically from conception through extreme old age in directions that positively balance gains against losses.

Methods for gathering developmental data are richly diverse. They include case histories, naturalistic observations of people's spontaneous ongoing behaviour, self-report interviews and questionnaires, standardised psychometric tests, and tightly controlled experiments conducted in laboratory or field settings. The developmental researcher must also decide whether to use a cross-sectional, longitudinal, time-lag or sequential design to carve out a portion of the lifespan and infer how psychological functioning changes over time.

The theoretical approaches that have guided the field of lifespan developmental psychology are also very diverse. Because of their overarching importance for understanding behaviour and change throughout life, we examine four major theoretical approaches in this chapter: (1) the psychoanalytic theories of Freud and Erikson, (2) the cognitive-developmental approaches of Piaget and Vygotsky, (3) learning theories, both classical and social-cognitive, and (4) adult stage theories including the work of Buhler and Levinson. As well as offering plausible accounts for a variety of developmental findings, each of these broad theoretical approaches has implications for the optimisation of human development by assisting people of all ages to grow to their full potential.

For further interest

Looking forward on the Internet

Use the Internet to visit the following websites. Examine them for further information and varied perspectives on issues raised in this chapter. Also search for other relevant websites for yourself, using keywords like 'research methodology', 'cross-sectional', 'longitudinal', 'Erikson', 'Piaget', 'Freud', 'Bandura' and 'life cycle' in your search engine.

In particular, for further ideas on some seminal theories that continue to guide thinking and research on lifespan developmental psychology, visit:

http://www.piaget.org (This site includes a short biography of Piaget.)

http://www.marxists.org/archive/vygotsky (This site includes a short biography of Vygotsky.)

For resources, ideas, activities and other items of interest in conjunction with this chapter, visit the Companion Website for this textbook at:

http://wps.pearsoned.com.au/peterson

Activity suggestion

As a practical activity in conjunction with themes in this chapter, and as a way to consider likely cohort contrasts in recent generations in your own community that could have an impact upon the study of lifespan psychological development using cross-sectional or longitudinal methodologies, try completing the following exercise. **Step 1:** Visit local libraries and newspaper offices to obtain access to news articles from last century (1930 to 1990). **Step 2:** Choose a topic and an age group (e.g. sporting achievements by children, marriage ages of bride and groom, news items about elderly citizens). **Step 3:** Find examples of news items fitting your topic from at least three different decades. **Step 4:** Locate similar items in a contemporary newspaper. **Step 5:** Scan the examples you have collected and try to come up with ideas about general patterns of historical continuity and change in your chosen area. Further activities are given on the Companion Website for the book (see above).

Multimedia

1. For a vivid account of the theories of Bandura, Erikson and Piaget, schedule viewings of the following films (or borrow them on video via the web address: **http://www.davidsonfilms.com**):
   - *Bandura's Social Cognitive Theory: An Introduction* (Davidson Films, San Luis Obispo, CA, 2001: 30 minutes)
   - *Erik H. Erikson: A Life's Work* (Davidson Films, San Luis Obispo, CA, 1989: 38 minutes)
   - *Piaget's Developmental Theory: An Overview* (Davidson Films, San Luis Obispo, CA: 25 minutes)
2. For an activity involving theoretical orientations to the lifespan, try the CD-ROM activity 'Understanding Human Development' (Lawrence and Dodds) published by Pearson Education.

IN THE BEGINNING:
CHAPTER 3
Heredity, prenatal development and birth

The nine months preceding birth [are] far more interesting and contain events of greater moment than the three-score and ten years that follow it.

Samuel Taylor Coleridge (1772–1834)

Contents

CHAPTER OVERVIEW

In this chapter we begin the study of development at its earliest beginning. We go even further back than the moment during intercourse when a new life is conceived to examine the genetic blueprint that carries the lessons of evolutionary ancestry forward to shape the new human being.

Behaviour genetics is the science devoted to the study of the roles of genes and heredity in human psychological development. Recent dramatic breakthroughs have been made in this field with the mapping of the human genome at the dawn of the 21st century and researchers now have a clearer idea than ever before of how the biological information contained in the genetic blueprint joins with life experience to shape human psychological development. At the instant of conception, when the genes carried in the father's sperm unite with those in the mother's ovum (egg cell), a course is set, within broad parameters, that will carry development forward through the lifespan. Equally decisive, from that moment onward, are the environmental forces, first within the mother's body and then, from birth, in the wider physical and social world, that combine with genetic information to define development in its many and varied aspects.

We first examine the unfolding of the genetic blueprint and the exciting new developments in bioscience that, with the mapping of the human genome (Jasny & Kennedy, 2001), have 'unlock[ed] the secrets of our genetic heritage' (p. 1153). We also explore the methodologies that behaviour geneticists use, including their intriguing comparisons of the developmental patterns of identical and fraternal twins, and the new light that these discoveries cast on an age-old question of concern to all of us: the balance of nature versus nurture in the growth of human individuality. In other words, how much is our human uniqueness the product of the genes we inherit from our biological ancestors and how much is it due to the nurturant experiences we have while growing up and growing older?

We examine what we now know about the joint roles of heredity and environmental experiences in shaping human nature, not only early in life but also through the lifespan. Genes continue their varied and intricate interactions with experience to instigate developmental change not just in early life but throughout adulthood and old age: witness the important role family history plays in longevity (see Chapter 18) and in vulnerability to diseases that have psychological overtones, like schizophrenia or Alzheimer's disease (see Chapters 3 and 16).

The second half of Chapter 3 is devoted to prenatal development. In line with the descriptive goal of developmental psychology (see Chapter 2), we begin by tracking the amazing transformations over the first nine months of life inside the mother's womb that gradually turn the single-celled zygote into a fully equipped human being. We also examine closely the development of brain and behaviour, step by step, through (a) conception, (b) the period of the zygote, (c) the period of the embryo and (d) the fetal period, since the physical growth and differentiation of the brain has crucial relevance for cognition, behaviour and all the new human being's other psychological characteristics.

From an optimising perspective, after considering healthy development, we look at risk factors in the prenatal environment, such as drugs ingested by the pregnant mother which, when they strike at a critical period of prenatal life, may threaten or disrupt this normal process, especially in fetuses with a genetic predisposition to vulnerability. Knowledge of these risk factors enables intervention to overcome them. This area of research has also seen recent important breakthroughs, so that well-informed parents in Australia and New Zealand today who are eager to optimise their new child's developmental journey through the lifespan have many more practical strategies available to them than even their own parents had.

The gradual awakening of psychological functioning, first in simple reflex movements and sensory reactions and later in more complex behavioural patterns, raises important questions (e.g. When does the mind, as opposed to the brain, emerge? Can fetuses think and learn? If yes, at how young an age?). New arenas for optimisation are opened up by exciting new findings, explored in this chapter, about the fetus's prenatal psychological capacities.

We look at the birth process and choices and decisions about it that are available to expectant parents in Australia and New Zealand today, and at some of the variations that can be played on the childbirth theme by culture and ethnicity.

The chapter concludes with a portrait of the neonate. Freshly arrived in the world, what psychological capacities does a newborn possess? How will any such capacities guide, stimulate and direct future developments during the chronological journey to infancy, childhood and beyond?

Heredity's blueprint

At a fateful moment soon after intercourse, when one of the father's ejaculated sperm cells finds its way to one of the mother's ripe ovum (egg) cells, conception occurs. This is the merging of sperm and ovum, triggering the biochemical reaction that will gradually create a fully formed human being. The sperm and ovum cells each contain 23 chromosomes. Chromosomes are carriers of genetic material. At conception, as the sperm penetrates the ovum, the 23 individual chromosomes in the nucleus of the sperm join together in matching pairs with the 23 individual chromosomes from the nucleus of the ovum, producing a single-celled *zygote*, with a full complement of 46 chromosomes (see Figure 3.1). Thus genetic

Heredity is responsible for many physical resemblances between relatives.

material is passed on in equal proportions from the maternal and paternal hereditary lines, linking the new human being with all the parents' genetic ancestors in their family trees.

Genes and chromosomes

As shown in Figure 3.1, chromosomes are tiny threadlike bodies with distinctive shapes. As noted later in this chapter, chromosomes can influence development directly through disorders that can arise when their numbers or structures are abnormal. But, in normal development, their primary function is to carry the basic units of heredity, the genes.

The genes are located in specified segments along each chromosome. They code for biochemical compounds, each supplying a specific set of instructions for development. The complete set of genes contained on the 46 chromosomes of the newly conceived zygote is known as that new human being's *genotype*. The genotype, in conjunction with environmental influences, produces a *phenotype*, or the observable expressions of hereditable characteristics in that person, including physical and psychological characteristics.

The recent breakthroughs in genetic and biochemical research that resulted in the mapping of the generic human genotype (or *genome*) (Paabo, 2001) have been spectacular. We now know quite a lot about individual genes and how they govern the development of certain physical traits that are *species-general*, applying to all humans (like the distinctive shape of the human skull, as compared with a chimpanzee's), and others that are individually distinctive and vary from person to person within the human race (like eye colour).

It is now believed that the human genome contains between 26 000 and 50 000 genes. For comparison, it is interesting to note that the fruit fly genome contains 136 000 genes, whereas the chimpanzee genome has about the same number of genes as the human – and, moreover, 'The overall DNA sequence similarity between the human and the chimpanzee is about 99%' (Paabo, 2001, p. 1219).

Genes synthesise the enzymes and proteins that build and regulate the physical body. They provide the instructions that, according to a precise developmental timetable, lead certain embryonic cells to become brain cells, others to become bone or muscle cells and still others to become specialised organs like the lens of the eye. They have a long-term influence, through on–off switching mechanisms, on the timing of events like puberty (see Chapter 10), menopause (see Chapter 15) and longevity (see Chapter 18). Within the brain, genes direct the maturational processes of various neural pathways and brain structures at specified points throughout childhood and early adolescence, as we note later when we examine the processes of neurobiological and neurocognitive change (Plomin et al., 1997).

Genes and individual differences

So far, the genetic influences we have mentioned have been species-general. But, given the obvious fact that human beings are genetically different from chimpanzees or fruit flies, what about the differences among members of the human species, or even among members of the same family? How do genes influence the fact that you are taller or shorter than your brother? How is it possible for a blue-eyed child to be born from parents who are both brown-eyed?

The answer to questions like these relates back to the formation of *gametes* (sperm or egg cells), a process known as *meiosis*. Each gamete has only 23 chromosomes, in contrast to the 46 in the rest of the parent's body cells (see Figure 3.1). Furthermore, the selection of chromosomes to go into a particular gamete's cell nucleus is a purely random process, like drawing a number in Lotto or out of a hat. Consequently, given the vast number of different chromosomal combinations that are possible within one individual parent's full complement of gametes (mathematically 2^{23} or about 8 million) it is safe to say that no two sperm or ovum cells will be identical, even when they come from the same parent. Given the different chromosomes, the genes carried on them will also, of course, be different. Thus the differences

---

FIGURE 3.1 Human chromosomes come in distinctive shapes

This drawing shows a normal body cell's complement of 46 chromosomes, including the XX pair at the bottom right, which denotes a female.

that exist among genotypes of siblings in the same biological family are in part a reflection of the 'lottery' of chromosomal assortment during gamete production; the set of genes that any one child receives from its parents at conception will be different from those of all other siblings, apart from the special case of identical twins (see page 74). No two siblings, apart from some twins, have exactly the same genotype, nor is any child's genotype a 'clone', or carbon copy, of either biological parent's genotype.

Nevertheless, the fact that biological siblings draw their sets of genes from the same finite pool ensures that brothers' and sisters' genotypes will be more similar to each other's than to the genotype of an unrelated person. As a rough estimate, we can say that non-twin siblings in the same biological family are likely to share approximately 50 per cent of their genes with one another, a fact that will be important when we examine the polygenic inheritance of behavioural characteristics later (see page 72). From the perspective of family planning, this fact is also very important in helping parents estimate the risks to future offspring when they have already borne one child with a genetic disorder such as haemophilia (see Table 3.1). In the next section we examine how genetic counsellors calculate these risks in order to give advice on the optimisation of developmental outcomes.

Mendelian inheritance: Pairs of genes

In the simplest instance of hereditary influence, the trait in question is determined by just one pair of genes. As might be expected, to the extent that they are influenced by genes at all, none of the most interesting psychological attributes (like intelligence, cheerfulness or schizophrenia) is simple enough to be inherited in this way. But a number of physical traits (such as eye colour, hair curl, blood group) are influenced by just one gene from each parent, as are some of the hereditary diseases that have important consequences for psychological as well as physical development. So it is important to understand the role of heredity at its simplest level, before going on to consider the more complex techniques required for behaviour-genetic analysis of polygenetic traits like intelligence.

Dominance–recessivity

In the 1860s an Austrian monk, Gregor Mendel (1822–84) carried out some innovative breeding studies of pea plants that led to the discovery of an important genetic principle known as *dominance–recessivity*. As the name implies, this principle is applicable to single-gene-pair traits in which one gene in the pairing completely dominates the other, so that the phenotype reflects only the dominant gene's trait. An example is eye colour. Since the gene for brown eyes is *dominant*, and the gene for blue eyes is *recessive* (see Figure 3.2), any genotype that includes a dominant brown-eyed gene will produce a brown-eyed phenotype (a baby with brown eyes), and a blue-eyed phenotype can only result from a genotype with a matching pair of blue-eyed genes.

When an individual has two identical genes in a particular pairing, that individual is *homozygous* for the trait in question. An example is the blue-eyed mother in Figure 3.2 whose genotype is homozygous with a matching pair of recessive, blue-eyed genes. *Heterozygosity* arises when the two genes in a pair are different. An example is the brown-eyed father in Figure 3.2 whose genotype is heterozygous for eye colour. He received a blue-eyed gene from one parent and a brown-eyed gene from the other, but his own eyes are brown, owing to the dominance of this gene over its blue-eyed partner. Because of the random assortment of chromosomes during meiosis that we examined earlier, it is impossible to foretell exactly which of the father's eye-colour genes will find its way into the particular sperm cell that will end up successfully penetrating the ovum when these parents conceive a new baby. If conception selects a sperm with the recessive gene, the new baby will end up with a homozygous genotype and a pair of blue eyes just like its mother. But if a sperm with the dominant gene reaches the ovum first, the baby will inherit a heterozygous genotype like the father, together with his brown-eyed phenotype.

On average, therefore, if the couple were to have a large number of children, roughly 50 per cent of them would have a homozygous genotype and a blue-eyed phenotype, while the other half would have brown eyes and a heterozygous genotype for eye colour. Figure 3.2 illustrates these possibilities.

Co-dominance and additive gene effects

Not all single-gene-pair traits obey the principle of dominance–recessivity. Sometimes each member of a gene pair is equivalently dominant, a situation known as *co-dominance*. If the individual's genotype is heterozygous with respect to this gene, a compromise, or combined outcome, will emerge in the phenotype. An example is the AB blood group. A child who inherits an A gene from the father and a B gene from the mother ends up with the blood group AB, with equal proportions of A-antigens and B-antigens in their bloodstream. *Incomplete dominance* arises when people with heterozygous genotypes express a recessive trait less strongly in their phenotypes than individuals who, with homozygous recessive genotypes, have the recessive gene's phenotype in fully developed form.

Although more complicated in the case of polygenically determined traits than for single-gene-pair combinations, the effects of co-dominance and incomplete dominance are essentially similar. Thus, multiple pairs of co-dominant and incompletely dominant genes tend to produce phenotypes that

FIGURE **3.2** The inheritance of eye colour

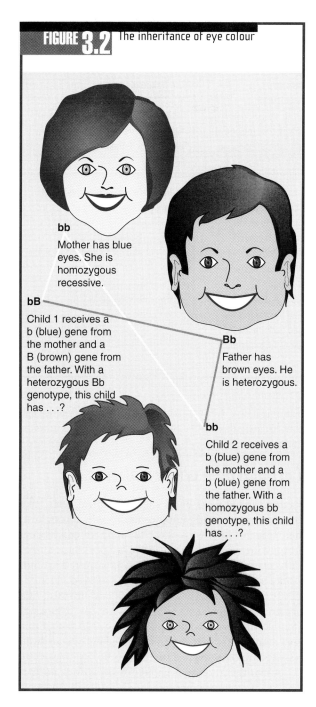

bb
Mother has blue eyes. She is homozygous recessive.

bB
Child 1 receives a b (blue) gene from the mother and a B (brown) gene from the father. With a heterozygous Bb genotype, this child has . . .?

Bb
Father has brown eyes. He is heterozygous.

bb
Child 2 receives a b (blue) gene from the mother and a b (blue) gene from the father. With a homozygous bb genotype, this child has . . .?

During pregnancy, the question of which parent's eye and hair colour the new baby will inherit remains a topic for suspense and speculation.

reflect an average between the phenotypes of pure-bred strains. An example is a child's height. Since height is determined by multiple pairs of genes (as well as environmental factors like nutrition and exposure to disease), a child whose mother is unusually short but whose father is exceptionally tall may end up somewhere between these two parents' heights once physical growth in stature is complete at the end of adolescence.

Sex-linked traits

Some of the genes involved in Mendelian inheritance are located on the X or Y chromosome rather than on one of the other 22 chromosomes. In this case, inher-

itance patterns will differ depending on the baby's gender. Girls receive an X chromosome from each of their parents. But since boy babies have the mismatched XY chromosome set (see Figure 3.1) they receive only one copy of the X chromosome and it always comes from the mother. Furthermore, they alone have a Y chromosome, contributed by the father. Consequently, any genes located exclusively on the Y chromosome reflect the paternal genetic history only. Given that the Y chromosome is smaller than the X, however, this is less common than the expression of recessive X-linked traits in the sons, but not the daughters, of mothers who are heterozygous for the traits in question. Several genetic disorders are inherited in this way (see Table 3.1).

Genetic counselling

Using genetic family trees like the one shown in Figure 3.2, ideally carried back for several generations, a trained counsellor who gathers a detailed family case history of the presence of traits and diseases that are known to be transmitted in a Mendelian manner can offer invaluable information to couples whose ancestral lines show evidence of these diseases or disabilities. Some of the most common of the conditions that are known to be passed on through a single dominant or recessive gene are listed in Table 3.1.

Dominant gene diseases cannot skip generations in a family. A parent must have the disorder in order to pass it along to a child. Unfortunately, however, some dominant disorders (e.g. Huntington's chorea)

	Dominant single-gene-pair disorders	**Recessive single-gene-pair disorders**	**Sex-linked disorders**

	Dominant single-gene-pair disorders	**Recessive single-gene-pair disorders**	**Sex-linked disorders**
Who is affected?	All offspring (homozygous and heterozygous) whose genotype includes the defective gene	Only the offspring with a homozygous recessive genotype that includes the defective gene	For X-linked recessive disorders: all males and homozygous recessive females; for Y-linked disorders: males only
Examples	• Huntington's chorea (a degenerative disease) • Extra digits (more than the normal five fingers per hand) • Early-onset (familial) Alzheimer's disease	• Tay-Sachs disease (a degenerative disease of the nervous system, culminating in early death) • PKU (a metabolic disorder) • Thalassaemia (abnormal blood cells; becomes progressively crippling with age) • Cystic fibrosis (a disease characterised by respiratory problems and early death) • Gaucher's disease (a metabolic disorder)	• Duchenne's muscular dystrophy (progressive wasting of muscles) • Haemophilia (a disease of impaired blood coagulation • Spinal ataxia (degeneration of the spinal cord) • Colour blindness • Optic nerve degeneration

do not show their symptoms until the sufferer has reached middle age, by which time child-bearing has usually already taken place. This makes genetic counselling more complicated. Recessive disorders do not manifest themselves in the heterozygous parent's phenotype, allowing generations to be skipped. Thus detailed multigenerational family histories of the diseases listed in the second two columns of Table 3.1 are desirable, in order to discover blood relatives, even in the distant past, who may have suffered from the disease. If they are located on both sides of the family, the increased possibility of a homozygous recessive offspring makes it advisable to conduct further tests, which may include molecular genetic assays such as genotyping and DNA analysis (Plomin & Rutter, 1998).

When the chance of a couple's transmitting one of the genetic diseases listed in Table 3.1 is high, they may decide not to risk parenthood, or opt for an alternative such as adoption or AID (artificial insemination by donor) to short-circuit their biological danger zone. In a few cases, knowledge of the faulty gene's influence enables a cure. For example, the recessive disorder known as PKU (phenylketonuria) leads to mental retardation if it is left untreated. This is because the faulty gene limits the body's ability to metabolise a chemical called phenylalanine, which occurs naturally in many foods. But when a physician knows that an infant has inherited PKU, a cure is possible. Normal intellectual development can be guaranteed, provided the infant is placed on a strict diet to prevent contact with phenylalanine as soon as it is born, and the diet continues throughout childhood. In this case, the disordered genotype need exert no adverse effect at all on the brain's development.

Thus nurture outwits nature and a faulty genotype has no negative consequences for the child's phenotype.

Chromosome abnormalities

Genetic counsellors may suggest clinical tests, like blood analysis and amniocentesis, which can also help parents to assess the risk of their child being born with a *chromosome abnormality*. Such disorders are not strictly genetic, since an entire chromosome, rather than a specific gene located on it, is faulty. Sometimes, when gametes are formed, the sperm or ovum can emerge with an abnormal number of chromosomes, possibly one too few or one too many. This is more frequent when one or both parents are over the age of 35 to 40.

When the abnormal gamete fuses with a normal one from the other parent, the zygote will not have the normal total of 46 chromosomes, resulting in a number of chromosomal disorders (or *syndromes*), including those listed in Table 3.2.

Polygenic inheritance

Although an understanding of the Mendelian inheritance of traits via pairs of dominant and recessive genes, of single-gene-pair genetic disorders and chromosome abnormalities, can be of untold value to genetic counsellors and would-be parents with family histories of genetic disorders, this form of inheritance is of far less significance to the developmental psychologist than another pattern of hereditary contribution: *polygenic inheritance*. This refers to traits that are influenced by many different gene pairs,

TABLE 3.2	Developmental difficulties resulting from abnormal numbers of chromosomes	
Syndrome	**Chromosome problem**	**Symptoms**
Down syndrome	An extra copy of chromosome 21	Mental retardation, thick tongue, distinctive facial appearance
Fragile X syndrome	Part of the X chromosome is shrunken and damaged	Mental retardation is highly probable, though not inevitable; delay in sociocognitive skills is also likely
Klinefelter syndrome	An XXY or XXXY sex chromosome complement	Phenotypically male appearance, often accompanied by learning difficulties; reading problems or mild intelligence deficits; at puberty, penis growth is delayed and testes are underdeveloped; sterility is common
Turner syndrome	An XO chromosome complement	Phenotypically female with stubby fingers, short stature and small breasts; infertility; verbal intelligence is often normal but there are frequently problems with spatial reasoning
Supermale syndrome	XYY	Phenotypically male; unusually tall; generally of normal or near-normal intelligence

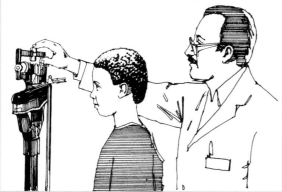

During infancy, childhood, and through the remainder of life, individual differences in stature reflect polygenic inheritance along with environmental variations like nutrition and health.

often located on several different chromosomes. To the extent that they are inherited at all, important psychological attributes like intelligence, creativity, conscientiousness, cheerfulness and sociability are polygenic, rather than Mendelian, in their complex patterns of heritability. As Peter McGuffin, Brien Riley and Robert Plomin (2001) explain:

> Single genes do not determine most human behaviors. Only certain rare disorders such as Huntington's disease have a simple mode of transmission in which a specific mutation confers the certainty of developing the disorder. Most types of behavior have no such clear-cut pattern and depend on interplay between environmental factors and multiple genes. (p. 1232)

In order to study the contribution of polygenic inheritance, in interaction with the environment, to the development of psychological characteristics, behaviour geneticists cannot rely on techniques like the gene mapping, genetic assays, DNA analysis, chromosome inspection and family histories that are such useful tools in the study of Mendelian traits. Instead, multivariate quantitative methods are normally required, and the outcome is more often a probabilistic estimate of the extent to which variations among people in the same psychosocial environment can be attributed to nature or nurture than any exact diagnosis or prediction about a particular child. Among the quantitative methodological techniques that are commonly used to investigate polygenic inheritance are (a) the method of twin comparison, (b) family resemblance studies, and (c) the adoption design.

Behaviour genetics

Using quantitative techniques, the behaviour geneticist compares the psychological attributes of people with a genetic relationship to one another (such as twins) and those being reared together (such as adoptive siblings). The aim is to identify the contributions of nature (genetics) and nurture (environment and experience) to the attribute in question. The basic assumption made by the behaviour genetic approach is that nature and nurture together determine the development of psychological characteristics, either in a simple linear manner (as via additive influences) or in complex, interactive combinations. Whereas the focus on genetics might seem to imply little interest in the role of experience, behaviour geneticists in fact consider the relevance of nature and nurture together. As Alison Pike and Robert Plomin (1997) explained:

> A common pitfall is the belief that the goal of genetic research is to demonstrate that everything is genetic. This is not the case. Behavioural genetic research merely takes the first step toward understanding the aetiology of individual differences by asking whether genetic differences are important. If genetic differences are found to be important, the next steps include … exploring the developmental interplay between nature and nurture. Genetic designs are equally important for understanding the role of the environment because they take genetic factors into account [and] provide the best available evidence for the importance of nongenetic influences (p. 649).

Let us now examine genetic designs involving comparisons (a) between pairs of twins, and (b) among adopted and biological offspring in a family.

Twin studies: A window on nature versus nurture

While most of us have our mother's womb to ourselves during our first nine months of life, some babies share a womb and are born in pairs (Figure 3.3). Twinning is an intriguing 'experiment in nature' which has been of enormous assistance to

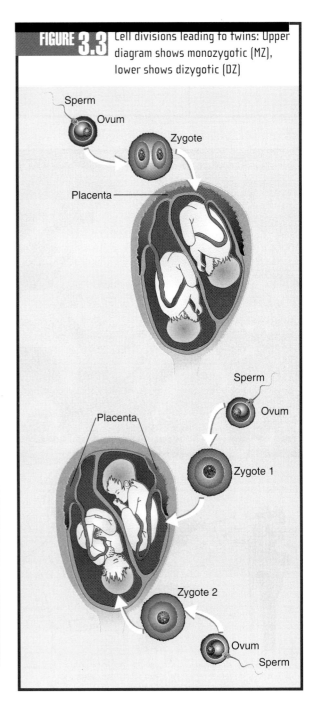

FIGURE 3.3 Cell divisions leading to twins: Upper diagram shows monozygotic (MZ), lower shows dizygotic (DZ)

Sperm
Ovum
Zygote
Placenta

Placenta
Sperm
Ovum
Zygote 1
Zygote 2
Ovum
Sperm

For a mother pregnant with twins, the question of zygosity may be almost as intriguing as it is to a developmental psychologist.

behaviour geneticists in their exploration of the processes of polygenetic inheritance. There are two different types of twins, each with a different life history from the moment of conception. Approximately once in every 250 pregnancies (Plomin, 1990) twins are born *monozygotic* (or identical). These twins are the product of a single zygote (fertilised ovum) which splits in two shortly after fertilisation. The result is two separate babies with identical genotypes – in other words, individuals who are completely identical genetically. *Dizygotic* (or fraternal) twins, on the other hand, occur once in about 70 normal pregnancies (more frequently if the couple is using fertility drugs). Each twin develops from separate sperm and egg cells. Since they are no more genetically alike than ordinary brothers and sisters, any differences that develop between them later in life could be caused either by heredity or by the environment, or by both these factors in combination.

If monozygotic twins are found to differ consistently and dramatically from their co-twin in some particular attribute (e.g. intelligence, personality, sociability), the only plausible explanation is nurture. Since their hereditary 'nature' (i.e. the genotype) is identical, it is difficult to account for differences between members of a monozygotic twin pair on the basis of genetics.

On the other hand, if members of monozygotic twin pairs are consistently found to resemble their co-twin more closely than pairs of same-sex dizygotic twins on a particular trait, the role of heredity is implicated in that trait's development. Dizygotic twins can differ by reason of both nature and nurture, since their genotypes differ (see page 74). Furthermore, it makes sense to assume that their environments (parenting, family experiences, schooling and so on) differ from twin to twin about as much as do those of monozygotic twins. To the extent that this is the case, the environmental source of variation (i.e. nurture) is held constant when differences in developmental outcomes between pairs of monozygotic and dizygotic twins are compared.

Like non-twin siblings, fraternal twins develop from two separate sperm and two separate ova. On average, only about half of their genes are the same.

The results of twin comparisons: Intelligence and personality

A large body of research over several decades has employed the twin comparison methodology to examine sources of individual variation in cognition and personality. In a typical study, behaviour geneticists administer standard tests of cognitive ability (such as an IQ test) and/or personality – for example, a standardised inventory measuring extraversion (outgoingness) versus introversion (shyness) – to pairs of monozygotic and dizygotic twins. By comparing each twin's score with that of the co-twin, an estimate of the within-pair difference is obtained. To examine similarities across groups of twins who are monozygotic or dizygotic, a *correlation coefficient* is often used. When repeated over a large number of twin pairs, correlation coefficients (denoted r) will range between $r = +1$ (for a perfect positive association), through $r = 0$ (for no reliable links) to $r = -1$ (for a perfect negative relationship, such that the higher the score of one twin, the lower the score of the co-twin).

Table 3.3 shows the combined correlation coefficients from several independent studies (Loehlin, 1985; Scarr, 1992) of identical and fraternal twins' IQ and personality test scores.

As the Table 3.3 results indicate, the average pairwise resemblance between monozygotic twins is greater than for dizygotic twins, both in intelligence and in personality. This suggests a role for heredity in the development of each of these traits. To obtain a more precise estimate, behaviour geneticists sometimes obtain a *heritability coefficient* (H) using the formula: $H = r$ (MZ pairs) $- r$ (DZ pairs) $\times 2$.

This coefficient can range from 0 (= no effect of genes on the trait) to 1.00 (= the trait is totally heritable). Using this formula on the data in Table 3.3, we can see that, for IQ scores, H = 0.62, suggesting that heredity plays a moderately important role in shaping intelligence for the particular population from which these twins were drawn. For the Table 3.3 personality scores, a somewhat lower heritability coefficient emerges (H = 0.40), suggesting that, while heredity does play a part, the environment is also a crucial contributor to variability among people's overall personality patterns.

Thinking critically about twin studies

The twin design provides a rich natural resource for evaluating heredity's contribution to development. However, being naturalistic (see Chapter 2), the method of twin comparisons is not amenable to the same strict experimental controls that might be employed in a laboratory breeding study using rats, mice or fruit flies as subjects.

For example, in the interests of scientific rigour, it would be desirable to be able to vary systematically the environments in which twins grow up, to be sure of accurately representing all the rearing situations

TABLE 3.3	Average resemblance (correlation coefficients) between pairs of MZ and DZ twins		
Kinship relationship	Genotypic similarity within pairs	Correlation coefficient
Monozygotic (MZ = identical) twins reared together	100%	IQ: $r = 0.86$ Personality: $r = 0.50$
Dizygotic (DZ = fraternal) twins reared together	Approximately 50%	IQ: $r = 0.55$ Personality: $r = 0.30$

Source: Based on data in Loehlin (1985) and Scarr (1992).

that shape human development. But for obvious ethical and practical reasons, it is not feasible for a scientist to consider separating large numbers of identical twins at birth and placing them in homes spanning the gamut of a population's socioeconomic levels, or matching them with parents selected to epitomise particular personalities or rearing methods. Instead, the validity of the twin comparison method rests on two basic assumptions.

The first is that the various environmental influences acting on twins are just as diversifying as those that apply to the entire non-twin population. The best way of confidently meeting this assumption is with a large sample size. Fortunately, the continued popularity of the twin comparison procedure, ever since Francis Galton pioneered it in 1875, has meant that there are sufficient collective data on widely tested characteristics like intelligence to afford such confidence (Plomin, DeFries, McClearn & Rutter, 1997).

The second basic assumption of the twin comparison procedure is that the diversifying influences of the environment are no greater for fraternal twins than for identical twin pairs. This is the assumption that researchers most often challenge.

Identical twins: Identical treatment?

It is obvious that dizygotic twins of opposite sex (brother and sister) are not treated identically by parents, peers or teachers. Since pairs of monozygotic twins are inevitably of the same gender, they are not exposed to this diversifying influence. (See Chapter 8 for discussion of some of these gender-related differences in childrearing.) Thus direct pairwise comparisons between monozygotic and dizygotic twins can really only make use of brother–brother and sister–sister fraternal dyads. Even so, researchers have argued that the fact that monozygotic twins bear a closer physical resemblance to one another, on average, than dizygotic pairs could produce more similar environments for the monozygotics. Parents' expectations of similar personalities and behaviour in monozygotic twins, whom they know to be genetically identical, could also motivate greater similarities in the way the twins are treated at home and at school. But if the rearing environment is more similar for identical than fraternal twin pairs, the environ-

ment's role in promoting differences between individuals will be underestimated by the twin comparison method.

To evaluate this possibility, Robert Plomin, John DeFries and Gerald McClearn (1980) examined how 354 pairs of identical twins and 496 pairs of same-sex fraternal twins were actually treated at home on a number of significant dimensions of parenting. Some of their findings are illustrated in Figure 3.4.

These results suggest that monozygotic twins are treated more similarly than dizygotic twins when growing up together in the same household. But what about monozygotic twins who are separated at birth and reared in different families, totally out of contact with the co-twin? Surely these pairs of twins, despite being monozygotic, would be treated differently by the environment than pairs of twins being reared together by the same parents, with the same siblings, under the same roof?

To test this hypothesis, Thomas Bouchard and his colleagues (1990) undertook the task of tracking down pairs of monozygotic twins from around the

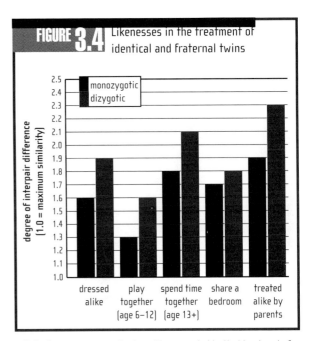

FIGURE 3.4 Likenesses in the treatment of identical and fraternal twins

Note: Scores are on a scale where '1' represents identical treatment of both members of any given pair of twins.
Source: Based on data in Plomin, DeFries & McClearn (1980).

world who had been separated from their co-twin in infancy and reared in very different family environments. When they were reunited and tested on standard intelligence and personality scales in Bouchard's laboratory, most of the previously separated monozygotic twins showed at least some similarities to one another, and the resemblances in personal idiosyncrasies in some of the pairs was almost uncanny – for example, choosing the same occupation, having identical preferences for unusual foods and beverages or adopting the habit of flushing the toilet before and after use. In addition to noting these anecdotal likenesses, Bouchard compared the correlations on standard IQ tests between these separated monozygotic twins. For comparison, recall the correlations for monozygotic and fraternal twins being reared together (see Table 3.3). The correlation for the sample of 137 separated monozygotic twins was $r = 0.76$. Although this is somewhat lower than the correlation for monozygotics who shared the same family environment ($r = 0.86$), it is nevertheless greater than that observed among dizygotic twins reared together ($r = 0.55$). Thus it would seem that the factor of more similar treatment for monozygotic than dizygotic twins, while playing a part in their IQ similarities, will not completely explain away the evidence from all the twin comparison studies, taken collectively, that heredity makes a moderately strong contribution to individual differences in IQ scores.

Studying twins in Australia, David Hay (1985) argued that a valuable lesson could be learned from cases where parents were misinformed about the twins' zygosity at birth. In some cases, dyads that were actually monozygotic were thought to be fraternal because there were two placentas. In other cases, fraternals were thought to be monozygotic because they looked so much alike at birth. DNA testing eventually gave the true answer. When parental treatment of these twins later in childhood was compared, the genuinely monozygotic pairs were found to be treated significantly more similarly by parents than those whom the parents had believed were identical, but who were actually no more genetically similar than non-twin siblings. Thus genetic similarity does seem to provoke environmental similarity via parental childrearing strategies.

In collaboration with his colleague Pauline O'Brien (Hay & O'Brien, 1983), Hay studied a large sample (N = 1356) of twins at La Trobe University in Melbourne, Australia. They concluded that the following additional features of growing up as a twin in a family environment that includes at least one twin pair could seriously limit the validity of generalising heritability estimates derived from twins to the non-twin population:

1. *Stress*. Multiple-birth households encounter more stresses than families where all the siblings are of different ages. These stresses include financial problems, more physical illnesses for all members of the family, and marital and legal problems for the parents. The developmental consequences of the family's strategies for coping with problems like these may limit the validity of generalisations to non-twin households where, on average, fewer stresses operate.

2. *Lags in mental growth of twins*. Both dizygotic and monozygotic twins are found to suffer delays in cognitive and language development compared with non-twin children. Whether these are due to the often more complicated deliveries arising for twins, the effects of sharing a womb prenatally, or to some other feature of the postnatal twin situation is not known for certain. There is evidence that twins may catch up on some of their deficits after about four years of age. But, until they do, comparisons of intellectual growth may be problematic.

3. *Sibling rivalry*. There is an especially acute problem of competition between same-sex dizygotic twins in some households. This boosts the observed differences in behaviour between competitive fraternal twin pairs who strive to carve out different terrains for themselves, compared with non-twin siblings of different ages whose rivalry is less intense. It also artificially boosts any estimates of heritability derived from contrasting fraternal twin pairs with identical twins.

4. *Paradoxes in twins' performance of specific tasks*. A puzzling finding emerged in the La Trobe twin data. Identical twins scored well below the averages earned by fraternal twins, cousins and non-twin siblings when asked to recite strings of numbers forwards. However, when the same numbers were repeated backwards, no differences among the sets of relatives emerged. Paradoxes like these suggest that 'something unusual is going on in the twin situation' (Hay & O'Brien, 1983, p. 324), making it risky to form general conclusions about heredity's contribution to the development of ordinary children based exclusively on the study of twins.

Shared and non-shared environment

Even when growing up in the same household with an identical twin, children do encounter experiences that are uniquely their own. The term *non-shared environment* refers to the distinctive situations and experiences a child has that are not replicated for any other member of the family, even the co-twin. These could include being treated more affectionately or more strictly by a parent than the sibling (Noller et al., 1995), being in a different class in primary school with a different teacher and peer group from the sibling or the child's deliberate cultivation of a special talent or interest – such as art, sport, a musical instrument or a particular haircut and clothing style.

Monozygotic twins may be even more strongly motivated than dizygotic twins or non-twins to identify, nurture and emphasise any minor differences in

These twins are monozygotic; their facial features and overall physical appearance are highly similar.

themselves or their environments that might set them apart from their siblings. Thus their exposure to non-shared environment could be heightened. This deliberate cultivation of differences is an effective way of carving out an identity that is uniquely their own. It has been labelled the *sibling contrast effect* (Farber, 1981).

Susan Farber (1981) drew on the sibling contrast effect to explain her otherwise perplexing discovery that some pairs of identical twins who had spent little or no time together at any stage during their growing up resembled one another more closely than identical twin pairs who had lived throughout childhood in the same household. In fact, her data showed that the longer twins had been apart, the greater the behavioural similarities between them! It seemed that minor differences between twins in the same household had been overemphasised by the family, due to the sibling contrast effect. Identical twins who live together may also resent being mistaken for each other, and so may consciously cultivate their own marks of distinction. Among separated twins, neither of these tendencies would operate, allowing any genetically based resemblances to emerge to the full extent. However, the fact that the contrast effect is more likely to operate in families rearing identical twins than in those with fraternal twins also creates problems for the twin comparison method, at least when it comes to generalising heritability estimates derived from twins to members of the non-twin population.

Eventually, a lifespan approach to data collection may open up new avenues for twin research (Plomin, Loehlin & DeFries, 1985). When twins grow up, marry and have offspring of their own, an intriguing phenomenon emerges: parents from pairs of identical twins are as closely related genetically to the children born to their co-twin (their nephews and nieces) as to their own sons and daughters. Thus comparisons among cousins and siblings, and across generations, in the families of identical-twin and fraternal-twin parents should shed new light on the contribution of parental treatment and genetic similarity to psychological development.

Studying polygenic inheritance with the adoption design

Owing to the concerns with twin comparisons (see above), some behaviour geneticists favour a different method for teasing apart the respective contributions of nature and nurture to the development of polygenic traits. The *adoption design* resembles the method of twin comparisons in its reliance on naturally occurring variations in family environments. But adoption is the deliberate decision by parents to rear children who, while not their biological progeny, are in all other respects their planned, chosen and parentally nurtured sons and daughters. As a behaviour genetic technique, the adoption design relies on the fact that adopted siblings are nurtured by parents who are not genetically related to them, often in the company of siblings to whom they also have no particular genotypic similarity. In addition to childless couples who adopt children to whom neither parent has a biological kinship tie, adoption arises frequently in a 'blended family' situation involving step-parenting (Phillips, Nicholson, Peterson & Battistutta, 2002). For example, a divorced father might remarry and be rearing one or more children from his previous marriage together with step-children who are the biological offspring of his new wife. Or remarried fathers and mothers may have children together, as well as having some from previous marriages, so that some siblings in the family will be related biologically to only one of their rearing parents, while others will have genes in common with both parents and possibly some siblings.

The results of adoption studies: Intelligence and personality

Comparisons between adopted and biological siblings in blended households offer new windows into the respective roles played by heredity and shared environmental experiences in the development of psychological attributes like intelligence and personality. In this approach, the genotypic similarity of biological relatives is pitted against the adoptive relatives' sharing of a common living environment. If an adopted child is found to be more similar to the biological than the adoptive parents, genetics are clearly implicated. In fact, assuming that their environments and lifestyles are no more similar than would be the case among any randomly chosen members of the population, the only possible basis for a behavioural (or phenotypic, see page 69) similarity between biological parents and offspring they had borne, but not reared, is the partial overlap of their genotypes. (Recall that biological siblings share only about 50 per cent of their genes in common with one another and the same is true of the probable genotypic overlap between parents and their biological children.)

However, the absence of any distinctive psychological resemblance between biological parents and their children who were separated from them at birth to be raised in adoptive homes does not necessarily prove that genes have no influence over the particular psychological characteristic in question. An alternative possibility is that a different pattern of heredity influences that trait during childhood compared with adulthood. By the same token, the discovery of a strong resemblance between adopted-away children and their biological parents demonstrates not only that the behaviour being evaluated is heritable, but also that it is influenced by some of the same genes in childhood as in adulthood. In other words, such a resemblance demonstrates the genetic continuity of the behaviour being evaluated.

Motivated by these theoretical advantages of the adoption design, John DeFries, Robert Plomin and Michelle LaBuda (1987) set an ambitious longitudinal adoption study in motion in Colorado in 1975. The aim was to assess the heritability and genetic stability of intelligence and personality. The sample included 196 adoptive families who were followed from the child's placement in an adopting home in early infancy. There was also a matched control group consisting of 161 families from the same communities, whose children were the natural, biological offspring of both parents. In addition to complete intelligence testing of all members of these families, the adopted children's biological parents were contacted and given regular IQ tests.

When the data accumulated over many years were grouped together, results were interpreted as showing that adult intelligence is shaped to an important degree by heredity. Comparisons between adopted and biological siblings suggested that the environment plays a larger role in the development of intelligence in childhood than in adulthood, though there was a decrease in its effect from birth through to age four. The researchers concluded that:

> Although genetic variation accounts for a smaller proportion of the observed variation in cognitive ability in infancy and early childhood than in adulthood, the effects of many of the same genes may be manifested increasingly as development proceeds. (DeFries et al., 1987, p. 11)

They also noted that childhood intelligence predicted adult intelligence moderately well. 'These data point to both genetic change and genetic continuity during cognitive development,' they argued. 'A little bit of genetic change might go a long way toward altering the course of development. For this reason, developmental behavioral genetics must continue to focus on genetic change as well as genetic continuity' (1987, p. 12). This finding brings out the important possibility of different roles played by heredity at different stages in life, and highlights the need to continue studies of genetic influences on behaviour through the lifespan.

Richard Weinberg and Sandra Scarr (1987) also used an adoption design to explore how heredity influenced the growth of intelligence. The children in their study included 130 African-American children who had been adopted by Anglo-American parents. Over the period from age four to age 12, these children earned IQ scores that were above the average scores earned by their Anglo classmates in primary school. Their academic achievement was also above that of their biological parents at the same age, and even higher than the average for the entire population growing up in the same region of the United States at that time. However, the biological offspring of the families who had adopted an African-American child did even better academically than their adopted siblings. During adolescence, there was a larger drop in IQ for the African-American adoptees than for the other children in the same family, possibly resulting in part from the teenager's growing sensitivity to racial discrimination. Weinberg and Scarr (1987) also suggested that adolescents were probably less influenced by the intellectual climate of the family than younger children, because of a need to break away and 'seek their own niches'. We return to some of these issues in Chapters 11 and 12.

Heredity's influence on personality has also been explored using the adoption method. Shyness is argued to be one of the most heritable of all the dimensions of human personality (Plomin, 1986). As part of the Colorado Adoption Project, Denise Daniels and Robert Plomin (1985) tested the sociability versus shyness of biological and adoptive mothers, and measured adopted infants' shyness at the ages of 12 and 24 months. A genetic basis for shyness was shown by the fact that extreme shyness on the part of the biological mother predicted that her biological children would be unusually shy at age two, even though there had been no contact between mother and child since birth. On the other hand, the family atmosphere also contributed significantly to the development of shyness. Toddlers whose adoptive mothers were unusually shy likewise scored above average in shyness, indicating that nurture is important.

Table 3.4 summarises the results of a large number of adoption and family resemblance studies of IQ scores.

Thinking critically about adoption designs

Only in a science-fiction universe would children be matched with adoptive parents in a scientifically controlled manner to meet the rigours of experimental design. But the fact that adoption research relies on pre-existing social practices does pose scientific limitations when using this information to examine the influences of nature and nurture on psychological development. Systematic bias is, for example, introduced when adoption agencies place children with adoptive parents who resemble their biological parents in intelligence, education, social factors and personality. This complicates the logic of the

TABLE 3.4 Correlation coefficients among family members' IQ scores as a function of adoption versus biological kinship		
Kinship relationship	Estimated genotypic similarity	Mean IQ correlation
Between adopted (biologically unrelated) siblings being reared together	0	+0.34
Between adoptive parents and their adopted offspring	0	+0.19
Between biological half-siblings being reared together	0.25	+0.31
Between biological parents and their reared biological offspring	0.50	+0.42
Between biological siblings being reared together	0.50	+0.47

Source: Based on data in Bouchard & McGue (1981) and Scarr (1992).

adoption design which relies on there being no greater genetic similarity between biological and adoptive parents than between any randomly selected members of the adult population (Hay, 1985). To the extent that adoptive children are selectively placed in families with whom they may share genetic similarity, the presumed contribution of the environment to development may be overestimated.

A child's knowledge that she is adopted may also limit the relevance of data drawn from adoption studies to children growing up with biological parents. Like identical twins who, via the sibling contrast effect (see page 78), deliberately emphasise their minor differences so as to carve out distinctive personalities of their own (Farber, 1981), adopted children may consciously cultivate any unique personal traits that are noticed. Thus a casual comment that the adopted child seems artistic, musical or even exceptionally shy may lead to a special focus on this quality, because the child believes it to be a special legacy of her distinctive line of heredity. The contrast effect observed in the parenting of identical twins may likewise help to diminish family resemblances in adoptive households. The parents' knowledge of the mechanisms of heredity may sensitise them to the possibility of intellectual or temperamental differences in adopted offspring, and cause them to attribute to genetic causes any behavioural differences they happen to notice. In this way, parents too may enhance and cultivate adopted children's unique talents or traits, rather than expecting them to grow up to become carbon copies of their adoptive relatives.

Effects of adoption on psychological development

Contrary to popular myth, an adopted or blended family situation is not, in itself, a developmental risk factor, nor do adopted children automatically feel rejected or unwanted by their adopted families. Indeed, quite the opposite – adopted children and adolescents on average are found to enjoy somewhat closer relationships with their adoptive parents, and to experience them as more loving and helpful, than

A child's tendency to be shy or outgoing reflects both nature and nurture.

average biological offspring feel in relation to their natural parents (Marquis & Detweiler, 1985; Weinberg & Scarr, 1987).

When Kathlyn Marquis and Richard Detweiler (1985) matched a group of 46 adopted adolescents and young adults in the United States with a group of individuals of the same age, sex and cultural/economic background who had not experienced adoption, they found that the adoptees felt significantly more self-confident, competent and generally positive about themselves. They also held more positive views about other people, including their parents, and were more open, self-assured and trusting in their interactions with people in general. Marquis and Detweiler suggested that these differences could be due partly to the more frequent use of optimal child-rearing strategies in adoptive families. Perhaps the fact that the adopted children were, by definition, 'wanted' offspring explained why their parents were more likely than the average American parent to rear their children in nurturant, protective, comforting and reliably predictable ways. But Marquis and Detweiler further suggested that knowing that their adoptive parents had chosen to adopt them might boost adopted children's self-confidence, while also reinforcing their belief in their parents' good qualities. Thus, offsprings' subjective reports of their adoptive parents' favourable childrearing practices may have been distorted by 'rose-coloured glasses'.

On the other hand, using a naturalistic observational design, in which mothers and their adopted or biological offspring were videotaped while playing together at home, Robert Plomin and his colleagues found that adoptive mothers were more attentive and responsive to their adopted children than biological mothers were to their offspring (Rende, Slomkowski, Stocker, Fulker & Plomin, 1992). Thus subjective biases do not entirely explain the more positive interactions reported in adoptive families.

Nature and nurture together: The interaction between heredity and environment

In addition to the specific insights they supply about how resemblances among family members in polygenic traits like IQ or personality may develop, the results of twin comparisons and adoption studies are also important at a broader level. Collectively, the findings we have just examined point out the mutual roles of heredity and environment in the development of polygenic psychological attributes. In fact, polygenic inheritance is clearly not the 'either–or' dichotomy that the phrase 'nature *versus* nurture' might seem to imply. Instead, it should now be evident that *both* heredity *and* environment jointly contribute to psychological development and that their respective influences are interconnected and inseparable from one another.

The study of how nature and nurture jointly contribute to the growth of a trait like intelligence is complicated still further by the fact that heredity and environment do not always combine in a simple, additive way. Instead, there are many instances where genotypes reverse their standing relative to one another when the environment is changed. Gardening provides many convenient examples: a genetic stock of seeds that has been selectively cultured to grow well in dry sandy soil will not do as well in moist clay as seeds cultured specifically for humid growing conditions, and vice versa. In this case, neither type of seed can be said to be intrinsically genetically superior or inferior to the other. Instead, before selecting a particular hereditary strain of seed to plant, something must be known of the garden where it will grow. No valid prediction about whether, or how well, the plant will grow can be made without specific knowledge of both heredity

The growth of a plant reflects the interactive contributions of nature and nurture.

(the seeds) and environment (the quality of the soil, exposure to sun and rain, cultivation).

The term *interaction* describes this kind of situation. When an interaction is operating, the developmental outcome cannot be attributed to either heredity or environment alone, but to the joint effects of the two of them acting together. Furthermore, in behaviour genetics, heredity and environment may combine in non-linear ways (Plomin, DeFries & McClearn, 1980). The concept of interaction, and some of its implications for the study of heredity and development, were brought out with exceptional clarity in an experiment by Daniel Freedman (1958) on the emotional development of puppies.

As subjects for his investigation, Freedman chose puppies of four different breeds: fox terriers, beagles, Shetlands and basenjis. He used pedigree dogs because the controlled mating of pure-bred parents had ensured that puppies of one breed were genetically like one another and genetically distinct from pups of other breeds. Then Freedman created two different canine-rearing environments.

Half the puppies of each breed grew up in a warm, indulgent atmosphere. The trainers played with the pups, engaged in mock fights with them and encouraged them to be curious and vigorously active. The other half were subjected to a harsh upbringing. Their trainers used strict discipline and painful smacking to teach these puppies to sit, obey, shake hands and come to the trainer on command. There was little cuddling or free play.

To evaluate the influences of heredity and environment on emotionality, Freedman then set up the following test situation: each dog was deprived of food and ushered into a room containing a bowl of fresh meat. If the dog attempted to eat, it was spanked and shouted at by its trainer. Then the trainer left, and Freedman measured how long each dog waited before approaching the meat. He found that all the basenjis ate immediately, whereas none of the Shetlands ever approached the food – their genes and not their training evidently accounted for the difference. But the indulged terriers and beagles were significantly more reluctant to approach the food than their severely handled litter-mates. So for these breeds the environment had played the crucial role.

In other words, Freedman's experiment showed that 'emotionality' in dogs reflects the genes that all members of a breed share and also the type of handling that each puppy grows up under. Heredity obviously makes a contribution to the dog's emotional development, but the role of heredity cannot be understood in isolation from the environment.

Whether dogs of a genetic breed like fox terriers will grow up to be 'conscientious' or 'undisciplined' cannot be predicted without knowing something of what their home environment is like. On the other hand, knowledge of whether the rearing climate has been harsh or lenient is of little use unless the breed of dog is also specified. This mutual dependency of nature upon nurture, and vice versa, shows an interaction between the hereditary and the environmental determinants of the puppies' emotional behaviour. When interactions like these occur, global generalisations about the proportional contributions to development of heredity and environment will mask essential differences between various gene–environment combinations, and will therefore be misleading. The same is true of human development.

Consequently, to understand the lifespan development of polygenic psychological capacities, we need to consider the whole person in the context of their genotype and the environment, noting that the interconnected relationship between these two forces will propel development in changing ways throughout life. No two developmental courses are ever identical. The same genotype will respond differently to varying environmental circumstances, and the same outward environment will influence different genotypes quite differently.

The possibility of non-linear interactions in development, while complicating the study of the roles of nature and nurture, raises interesting questions that our new genetic knowledge may help us to answer. These include practical questions about how to optimise individual development in the context of a

person's genotype, the environmental situation and the interaction between the two. Theoretical questions are also raised about the limits of developmental optimisation, and about the balance and interplay of environmental and genetic factors in normal development and psychopathology. Genetic information alone will not solve these problems, nor environmental engineering on its own. Instead, a new way of thinking about both nature and nurture is required. As Peter McGuffin, Brien Riley and Robert Plomin (2001) explain:

> Although in many ways behavior presents geneticists with the same challenges as other complex physiological and medical traits, behavior is unique in that it is the product of our most complicated organ, the brain. Most valuable for behavioral genetics will be the sequencing of multiple human genomes and identification of the several million DNA base pairs that differ among us . . . However, there are two built-in limitations to this DNA revolution. The first is that all behavior involves gene–environment interplay. The second is the unsolved question of the distribution of effect sizes of [some genes which] may involve effects so small or so complicated that they will never be detected. (pp. 1248–9)

To see how a consideration of the whole person in change developmental situations can raise questions about nature, nurture and their interplay, consider the snapshot in Box 3.1 of a moment in one 6-year-old's unique developmental journey.

This example of personality and cognitive functioning at age 6, though unique to one particular child, raises broader questions that may help to illustrate the way a consideration of nature and nurture as interacting developmental forces can assist our understanding of human development generally. Louise's father discerned an individual difference variable in his daughter's personality, pronouncing her 'shyer than most children'. In fact, shyness is a trait of temperament that does have an important hereditary component (Plomin et al., 1997; see page 79). However, it is also clearly a product of environmental experiences (e.g. in the case of Louise, it is possible that being an only child may have contributed, while her access to peer contact in the neighbourhood may have mitigated to some extent the effect of not having siblings).

Louise's father also raised practical questions of a kind likely to trouble many parents at some point during their child's development: were Louise's parents responsible for her shy nature? Should they have spent more time inviting other children over and sending her out to play with friends, rather than allowing her to engage in favourite solitary pursuits like playing with cuddly toys, drawing or reading? The question of how to optimise his daughter's adjustment to the impending environmental disruption of a move interstate was also a source of concern to Louise's father, as to many other parents who plan

All human behaviour involves an interplay between genes and the rearing environment. Family resemblances reflect these dual influences.

Expressing individuality
A 'whole' child of six

When Louise (see Box 2.5) was six years old, the family moved to a new residential environment in southern California. Just before they left Michigan, her father contemplated the move and how Louise would adjust to it. He made the following entry in his diary:

Louise at age 6 with her new friend Jill.

1 June 1954. *Louise's sixth birthday has come and gone and I have been so distracted with leaving Michigan after a lifetime of residence that I failed to record even her birthday party. Our house is up for sale. As soon as it is sold, we'll be off for California. A couple of times it looked as though buyers would take the house immediately and both times I found myself resisting it, reluctant to leave old friends and associations. Louise, with friends of far shorter acquaintance, does not disguise her reluctance. She'd like nothing better than to hear we've decided to stay.*

I feel sure she'll make new friends, although she is anything but a glad-hander. She is shyer than most children, lacks their self-assertiveness when away from home. Her dolls and playthings form a large part of her life, especially when she rediscovers one.

Not long ago the rediscovery was an air-filled plastic bunny, and this absorbed her. She had to have it with her every minute. Then it was a hand-puppet she had bought in St Louis last fall. When the puppet's monkey head broke I substituted the head of a plastic rabbit, and this became her inseparable companion. Now it is a rubber cow named Bessie that she has owned since infancy. It languished in the attic a year or so until she discovered it again and brought it down. She holds it almost constantly, sleeps with it under her pillow, dresses it with fancy clothes, and sucks its nose when she feels hungry or forlorn.

Next to playing with her cuddly toys, she likes best to draw and make things – cards, stamp albums, books of various kinds. She likes to write her name, address, and such other words as she may know or can have spelled for her. She likes to add and subtract, using her fingers as a calculator. She likes television and she especially likes being read to. She also likes to cut out and paste up pictures from magazines.

© Peterson, 1974, pp. 215–16, reproduced with permission

the future not only in terms of its impact on themselves but also, perhaps more pressingly, in relation to its likely impact on their children's opportunities for optimal psychological growth.

Questions like these are bound up with the possibilities and challenges that a consideration of heredity and environment as interactive, rather than either/or influences can open up. How to optimise the social development of a shy child about to be uprooted from a familiar and stable circle of friends is an apt illustration of the possibilities for non-linear interactions in development. It is impossible to answer Louise's father's queries without considering the potential interactions between her genetic disposition towards shyness and the unique environmental circumstance of an interstate move. For a child with a more extroverted genetic predisposition, the move would almost certainly have different consequences than for a shy child like Louise.

Let us examine what recent research can tell us about how to make sense of non-linear relationships between nature and nurture. We also look at how this knowledge of complex interactive relationships between heredity and environment can be used to optimise children's healthy psychological development.

Niche-picking: Children as active environmental engineers

Children are not simple passive recipients of environmental input (Scarr, 1992). Instead, they actively seek out the particular environmental situations that best suit their genetic predispositions (Scarr & McCartney, 1983). Box 3.1 illustrates this: Louise, being shy, had evidently selected favourite toys and leisure pursuits (like drawing, reading and making things) that could be pursued in a solitary situation. A more extroverted 6-year-old might have picked different leisure niches – perhaps team sports or dramatic play (see Chapter 1) that would demand high levels of social interaction with peers.

As Sandra Scarr and Kathleen McCartney (1983) noted, active niche-picking by a child with a particular genetic disposition creates non-linear inter-actions between heredity and environment. From the moment of birth, children actively select certain aspects of the environment to attend to and others to ignore. Thus, even when they are very young, infants are capable of shaping and modifying their social and physical environments through personal initiative. (Several instances of the infant's exercise of personal control are presented in Chapter 4.) Genetic disposi-tion can help to guide this active selection process. When a child whose genetic endowment disposes her towards shyness is placed in a day-care environment with rich potential for social companionship, the option of electing how much or how little social interaction to take part in is still available. The cumu-lative effect of day-care might be to raise the child's sociability above the level likely if she had remained alone with a shy mother throughout the preschool years. But relative to other day-care children, such a child might still seem quite shy. In this case, a genetic predisposition towards shyness actively directs and shapes the social environment to make it different from the social worlds of other children in the same family, school or day-care centre.

Thus, while it might be tempting to assume that all children in the same day-care class share the same environment, or that all the brothers and sisters in a particular family are treated in the same way by their parents, these assumptions are probably not accurate. The non-shared aspects of the environment that chil-dren experience or engineer for themselves are much harder to study scientifically than shared environ-mental features. But the former are apt to exert a stronger environmental influence on development than the latter.

The range-of-reaction principle
A person's genetic disposition can also set upper and lower limits on the environment's possible range of influence (Gottesman, 1963). For example, when Sandra Scarr (1992) looked at the IQ scores of ado-lescents who had grown up in adopted families, she found that their absolute scores were higher than those of their biological parents. But there was also a linear relationship to the biological parents' level of intelligence. When the biological parents' IQ scores were above average, their adopted-out children were found to profit to the full extent from the intellectu-ally enriched environment provided by the adoptive family. Thus, they earned higher IQ scores than chil-dren adopted into the same families whose biological parents had been of only average intelligence. Conversely, below-average intelligence in the biologi-cal parents appeared to create an intellectual ceiling for the adopted child. An adoptive family environ-ment that was rich in intellectual stimulation pro-vided some benefit, boosting the child's IQ above the biological parents' own scores. But relative to the adoptees with a more favourable heredity, the gains were smaller.

If children with a genetic disposition towards high intelligence are given the opportunity to engineer their own intellectual environment via niche-picking, the chances are that cognitively stimulating pursuits will be chosen and further intellectual growth will occur. But a sibling in the same family who lacks this genetic giftedness disposition might select an envi-ronment with minimal cognitive challenge, thus narrowing the range for environmental boosting of cognitive potential.

In the case of a genetic personality disposition towards shyness (see Box 3.1) the range-of-reaction concept suggests that, irrespective of environment, a child like Louise would probably never become as phenotypically extroverted as a child with a genetic disposition towards sociability, even in the kind of environment best able to stimulate and promote the growth of extraversion. The results of a cross-cultural study of men's career development, a later stage in the lifespan (see Chapter 15), in Sweden and the United States supply a practical illustration (Kerr et al., 1996). American men who were painfully shy had delayed career advancement compared with average men and extroverts. But in Sweden shyness was unconnected with men's rate of career progress. The working environments in these two cultures moderated the influence of the genetic disposition.

Evolutionary preselection and specialisation
Behaviour patterns that confer a survival or breeding advantage on organisms in a particular environment may become preprogrammed in the human nervous system, according to the theory of evolution by nat-ural selection propounded by Charles Darwin (1802–92). This may help to explain some rather paradoxical relationships between heredity and envi-ronment in human psychological development. For example, when Paul Rozin (1991) studied the food preferences of parents and their adolescent offspring, he came up with one such puzzle. Rozin began with the assumption that human taste preferences have adaptive survival value and may therefore be grounded in genetic predispositions that were selected via evolution. In fact, strong aversions to plentiful, nutritious foods can have adverse conse-quences for health and social behaviour. A child who refuses to eat green vegetables may be at risk of a vitamin deficiency, while an adult with an aversion to onions, mushrooms or cheese may find it awkward to eat out with others who relish these foods. Yet we probably all have one or more intense taste aversions with no clear rational or biochemical basis (in other words, pure preferences that have nothing to do with food allergies or genetic intolerance to certain foods). Where do these 'psychological' tastes and distastes come from?

As food dislikes are evident in young children and are often quite durable throughout life, Rozin rea-soned that food aversions probably either have a genetic basis or are acquired through early childrearing experiences with food in the home. To test these possibilities, he examined the food preferences of 118 late-adolescent university students and both their biological parents. To ensure that the offspring had had continual exposure to parental 'nurture' when it came to food, Rozin selected only intact families in which both parents had lived continuously with the teenager and shared meals on a daily basis, at least until the adolescent entered university. To simplify things still further, he concentrated on those food preferences over which the parental generation displayed a consistent position, with mother and father being in complete agreement that they both either loved or hated a particular food. When he looked at the offspring's preferences for these same foods, he found surprisingly little similarity.

For example, in households where both parents adored lima beans, their adolescent sons and daughters were just as liable to dislike these nutritious vegetables as in a home where the parents themselves modelled an aversion to them. Similarly, an adolescent's liking for cheddar cheese, chicken livers, broccoli or wholemeal bread could not be predicted to any significant degree by knowing that the parents had a consistent preference or aversion for these foods. In fact, on his long list of popular and unpopular foods, Rozin discovered only two clear links between offspring preferences and the agreed parental position: chilli and red meat. If both mother and father either loved or hated hot pepper sauce or medium-rare steak, their sons and daughters were also likely to display the same preferences at a level greater than chance. Since no adopted children or stepchildren were included in the design, such family resemblances could have had either a genetic or an environmental basis.

But the puzzle was why so few of the other food tastes displayed any clear inheritance or nurturance patterns. If a teenager's love for broccoli is not the result of a genetic predisposition nor of his experiences with this vegetable at home while growing up, where does such a taste disposition come from? Similarly, how could this boy's sister have developed an aversion to mashed potatoes that no one else in the family shares?

One possibility is that food preferences, being related to survival, do have a covert basis in our species' genes but require an environmental triggering to emerge into the phenotype. Thus a child who comes down with a bout of stomach flu immediately after her first exposure to mashed potatoes may acquire a distaste for this food after a single occurrence, in the same way that child cancer patients undergoing chemotherapy are found to develop learned aversions to distinctive tastes that they connect with the experience of nausea (Peterson, Beck & Rowell, 1992).

An experimental demonstration of the joint requirement for a hereditary disposition and a unique environmental trigger was reported by Robert Hinde

Children's food preferences may reflect influences of nature and nurture.

(1992). The behaviour he looked at was fear of snakes in rhesus monkeys. In the wild, all normal monkeys acquire this fear at an early age without needing to be bitten or even confronted by a snake. Either nature or nurture could conceivably account for this fact. An in-built, hereditary snake phobia would have species-survival value. But infant monkeys might also learn to be afraid by observing the reactions of older monkeys to snakes encountered by the troop in the wild. Hinde reported that monkeys reared exclusively in the laboratory showed no fear when snakes were first presented to them, discounting a simple genetic explanation. Yet the results of an intriguing experiment suggest that heredity does play a role.

A group of laboratory monkeys with no prior exposure to snakes (and hence no fear) was shown a videotape of a feral monkey grimacing at a snake in utter terror. The laboratory monkeys acquired a snake phobia from this single, indirect exposure. Yet when they were shown a 'doctored' videotape in which the wild monkey appeared to be terrified of an unfamiliar flower, they showed no fear at all of the flower when it was subsequently placed in their cage. Hinde therefore concluded that rhesus monkeys inherit a disposition to fear snakes, but not flowers, as part of the genetic blueprint for their species. When the social stimulus of a monkey clearly dreading a snake is experienced, this hereditary predisposition is drawn into the behavioural phenotype. Perhaps a similar interaction between hereditary disposition and environmental experience is bound up with humans' reactions to foods.

Resolving the paradox of nature versus nurture

It is clear that there is no simple solution to the nature–nurture debate. At one level of the interactive relationship between these two variables, heredity seems all-important. As Sandra Scarr (1992) explained:

> Feeding a well-nourished but short child more and more will not give him the stature of a basketball player. Feeding a below-average intellect more and more information will not make her brilliant. (p. 16)

Here, genetic dispositions directly predict developmental outcomes, regardless of enrichment of the environment. At another level, however, even a child with the genetic disposition to become a genius will not develop normal intellect in an impossibly cruel, utterly unstimulating or completely cold and impersonal institutional environment. At this level of the interaction, the environment completely predicts development with no contribution from heredity. At other levels, both factors play a part.

From a parent's point of view, these findings are reassuring. The interaction between heredity and environment that has been observed in recent research relieves parents of the heavy burden of responsibility they would bear if heredity were irrelevant and the environment made all the difference to a child's cognitive or personality development. Scarr argued that 'good enough, ordinary parents' probably have the same overall effect on their children as 'super-parents' who create the ideal rearing environment for their offspring. As she explained:

> Children's outcomes do not depend on whether parents take children to the ball game or to a museum so much as they depend on genetic transmission, on plentiful opportunities, and on having a good enough environment that supports children's development to become themselves. (p. 15)

Heredity's lifespan influence

The passage of time also shapes variations in the ways in which heredity and environment contribute to behavioural development. This is because:

- Many aspects of the genetic blueprint that are set out in the genotype at conception do not show their effects on the phenotype until years (or decades) later.
- The genes themselves are subject to change with time.
- The environment and the individual's relationship with it change over the lifespan.

In other words, heredity is itself a developmental process. Its influence changes with the passage of time, and patterns of interaction between nature and nurture vary with the age of the developing person.

Heredity continues to exert an influence on psychological functioning at all stages in the lifespan. This grandmother's resemblance to her grandchild, like each of their respective traits, reflects the interactive inputs of nature and nurture.

The process of mutation

One way that genes change is through the process of *mutation*. Mutations are spontaneous changes in a gene's structure. Cells that descend directly from the mutated gene carry the new genotype. Thus, a succession of mutations over a long span of time could conceivably be responsible for evolutionary changes to a whole species. If a new, mutated gene produces a physical or behavioural characteristic that enhances survival capacity, offspring carrying the gene will have improved odds for reproducing. Thus the new genetic strain is retained and bred into each successive generation. But to the extent that mutations are random, there is no guarantee that they will produce behavioural or structural improvements. Many mutations yield unfortunate results and many others produce inconsequential changes.

Mutations can occur either in bodily cells or in the sperm and egg cells. If a mutation occurs in a body cell, it dies out when the person dies. If it occurs in a sex cell (or gamete), it can be passed on to the next generation. The rate at which mutation occurs spontaneously is unknown. Estimates range from once in two thousand cell divisions to once in several million divisions (Burnet, 1973). Mutation rates increase with exposure to X-irradiation and ultraviolet light, as Sir MacFarlane Burnet (1973) discovered when he examined albino children and adults in the Trobriand Islands. Albinism, a defect in pigmentation, is inherited via a single recessive gene. Burnet observed that Trobriand babies who inherited this condition were born with completely 'clean', or unpigmented, skin. But adult albinos had patches of skin pigmentation due to mutations in the skin cells themselves, apparently brought about by exposure to intense sunlight. This observation is of special significance for the study of genetic contributions to ageing – as people grow older, opportunities for mutations in their cells increase, particularly if they have been X-rayed a lot, or have lived in sunny climates (see Chapter 16). Because of their location, gametes are probably less prone to genetic mutation than exposed cells in the skin, but the increased likelihood of genetic defects among children of older parents does seem partly due to gamete mutation. Fathers over the age of 40, in particular, run an increased risk of having children with genetic defects.

A further intricacy in this already complex pattern is the finding that mutations can have different effects as a result of certain experiences arriving at critical times in development. For example, there is a mutation that causes mice to throw epileptic fits when exposed to loud noises (Burnet, 1973). But mutant mice become seizure-prone only if they are exposed to noise during the 18th or 19th day after birth. When insulated from noise during this critical period, their mutant genetic inheritance exerts no noticeable effect on their subsequent behaviour. Time-linked processes like these are undoubtedly also involved in human heredity, though ethical and practical obstacles to precise control over human breeding and early experience make their discovery far more difficult.

Delayed gene action

The passage of time is also significant to the study of genetic effects because some normal, unmutated genes exert their influence at different times during the lifespan. One example is a disease known as Huntington's chorea. Its degenerative effect on the nervous system does not begin until adulthood. The time of a girl's first menstrual period is also partly influenced by heredity, but does not show itself until adolescence. Even the timing of 'natural' death is seen to have a hereditary component (Kallman, 1953). The fact that genes can have delayed effects like these, which extend beyond the normal 'growing period', is a further reason why the study of psychological development must include age periods beyond childhood and adolescence (see Chapter 1). It also complicates the problem of explaining how genes influence development, since their timing as well as their immediate function must be accounted for.

In order to explain latent gene effects, Gerald McClearn (1970) postulated that there are two different types of genes: structural genes, which determine the emergence of physiological structures or behaviour traits, and regulator genes, which determine when a particular structural gene will show its effect. If this theory is correct, it suggests that both hereditary characteristics themselves and the timing of their effects can vary from person to person as a result of individual differences in genotype.

Gene–environment interactions in adult development

A lifespan focus on the entire process of psychological development from conception through to old age (see Chapter 1) also sheds new light on contemporary behaviour genetics. When the balance of inputs from heredity and environment is examined in the context of mature adults' personality growth, the picture that emerges is not always the same as in childhood (Bergemen-Klackenberg, Plomin, McClearn, Pederson & Friberg, 1988). As Robert Hinde (1992) has explained: 'To understand the bases of adult personality we must come to terms with [a] dialectic between individual characteristics and relationships which starts at birth and continues throughout life' (p. 607).

Nevertheless, a number of exciting new insights are emerging in recent research. When the growth of adult personality is studied, it is tempting to turn to twins as a source of information. Indeed, some of the problems that were seen to plague the use of twin comparisons as a source of insight into the intellectual and personality development of singletons are spontaneously overcome during adulthood (Hay & O'Brien, 1983). Once they become adults, twins typically do not share the same household, regardless of their zygosity. Thus the variations between monozygotic and dizygotic twin children in the same family that are explored earlier in this chapter (such as sibling rivalry, differential parental treatment and the deliberate accentuation of differences to establish personal identity) no longer interfere with comparisons between the two types of adult twins. On the other hand, the accumulation of many decades of life experience adds to the complexity of the environmental component in studies of adult personality.

Irving Gottesman (1963) conceived of the possibility that the timing of genetic influences on personality might vary over the lifespan. In other words, a trait that had low heritability in childhood might jump to showing high heritability in old age, or vice versa. He used a longitudinal twin study method to test this theory.

When he gave a series of psychometric tests to 178 pairs of teenage twins, Gottesman observed greater similarity between identical than fraternal pairs in the areas of intelligence, psychopathology and achievement. He concluded that heredity had a strong influence on the way these three traits had developed from birth to adolescence. Paradoxically, in a follow-up study 12 years later, Gottesman found that identical twin pairs were no more alike than fraternal twins in IQ, psychopathology or achievement once they reached adulthood. In other words, hereditary similarity had been a more important basis for resemblances between the twins during adolescence than in adulthood. On the other hand, Gottesman found that three other traits on which fraternal and monozygotic twin pairs had been about equally varied when tested in their teens showed stronger within-pair similarities among adult monozygotics than fraternals. These traits, which Gottesman concluded were more heavily influenced by heredity later in life than during childhood or adolescence, were self-confidence, insightfulness and emotional stability.

He concluded that:

> It is no longer possible to assume that studies of the heritability of personality traits in one age group yield valid information with regard to other age groups, and it is no longer meaningful to review twin studies of personality without taking into account the ages of the different samples studied. (p. 27)

Researchers in Sweden have made a particularly important contribution to the study of hereditary and environmental influences on adult personality. The Swedish Twin Registry contains information on both members of nearly 25,000 pairs of same-sex monozygotic and dizygotic twins who were born between 1886 and 1958.

One study assessed a subsample of Swedish twins on the personality dimension of 'sensation-seeking'. At one extreme, high sensation-seekers continually thirst for excitement, take risks, seem to thrive on variety and new experiences, and despise monotony. At the other extreme are 'boredom-tolerant' individuals who gravitate to humdrum routines, fear change, avoid risks and rarely become impatient with repetitive stimulation. Data from the Swedish twins suggested that heredity and environment interact in a non-linear manner in shaping this particular aspect of personality. As adults, twins who were strongly disposed by their genes to seek sensation, but grew up in highly controlling home environments, were much more tolerant of monotony than other adult twins with an equally strong hereditary disposition to crave novelty whose homes as children had been highly permissive. But the adult twins who had no genetic history of sensation-seeking were relatively unaffected by the degree of control their parents had imposed on them as children and adolescents. Thus, becoming a risk-taker required a unique, interactive combination of heredity and early experience. The same may be true of many other dimensions of adult personality.

Also, as we note in later chapters, adults are active shapers of their own development, no less so than infants or children. By selecting the lifestyles, interests and people they relate to, adults may act either to augment or overcome the cognitive and personality dispositions instilled in them in childhood by the forces of nature and nurture.

Prenatal development: *From zygote to fetus*

According to the English Romantic poet Samuel Taylor Coleridge (1772–1834), the story of a person's life during the nine months before birth is 'far more interesting and contains events of greater moment than all the threescore and ten years that follow it'. Having examined the genetic beginnings realised at the moment of conception, let us now look at the next instalments in this fascinating story of development before birth.

The newly conceived human being begins life as a single fertilised egg cell and continues to develop, only partially visible, for the 40 weeks that lead up to birth. Much has been learned in recent years about this fascinating process of prenatal development, despite the difficulties of observing the fetus inside its protective cocoon deep within the mother's body.

The zygote's growth from a single cell of pinhead size into a fully formed newborn baby normally takes about nine months. Because of the three dramatic changes that take place in fetal development over this nine-month period, the prenatal phase is typically subdivided into three separate episodes – zygote, embryo and fetus.

The period of the zygote

The first short phase of a normal pregnancy occupies about three weeks. During this time, the baby-to-be travels down the mother's fallopian tube to find a resting place in the wall of her uterus. The single-celled new baby, known at the start of this stage as a *zygote*, divides rapidly during the first few hours after fertilisation, turning into a multi-celled, hollow sphere called a *blastula* during the time it takes to migrate down the fallopian tube. Once the wall of the uterus is reached and the blastula embeds itself, the second phase of prenatal development begins (see Figure 3.5).

The period of the embryo

The period of the embryo, spanning the time from three weeks after conception to the start of the third month of prenatal life, is in many ways the most dramatic developmental period in the entire lifespan. This is the time when all the major organs and physiological systems in the body take shape. Consequently, when it leaves this phase, the embryo, though tiny, is recognisably human. First, the part of the blastula nearest the uterine wall differentiates into the *placenta*, or the new baby's prenatal life-support system. The placenta's blood vessels are connected to the mother's bloodstream, enabling the placenta to 'breathe' and excrete waste for the baby. It continues to grow with the fetus. When it emerges into the world as the afterbirth, it can be the size of a dinner plate and weigh up to one kilogram.

The outer edge of the blastula becomes the *amniotic sac*. This membrane encases the baby in a protective liquid, called *amniotic fluid*, which absorbs shocks and helps to maintain a constant temperature. At three weeks, the newly differentiated embryo appears little more than a small grey lump of flesh, but during the period immediately after implantation it separates into three distinct layers.

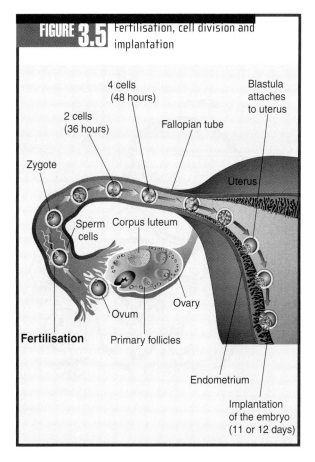

FIGURE 3.5 Fertilisation, cell division and implantation

4 cells (48 hours)

Blastula attaches to uterus

2 cells (36 hours)

Fallopian tube

Zygote

Uterus

Sperm cells

Corpus luteum

Ovum

Ovary

Fertilisation

Primary follicles

Endometrium

Implantation of the embryo (11 or 12 days)

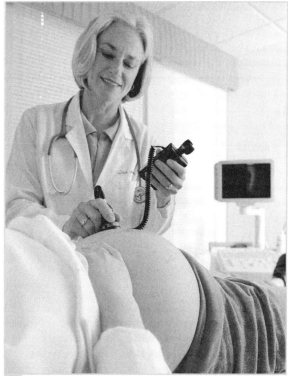

In contrast to later pregnancy, the fertilised ovum does not have contact with the mother's bloodstream until after implantation in the uterine wall.

The outside layer, known as the *ectoderm*, folds around the mid-line to make a tube. A smaller tube folds in along the length of one of the larger tube's outside edges, and this eventually becomes the spinal column and the nervous system. Most of the rest of the ectoderm becomes the skin. The *mesoderm*, which is the middle layer inside the tube, will later become muscle and bone, and the innermost layer, the *endoderm*, differentiates to form the internal organs. In sum, at three weeks

> a human is really no more than a complicated worm with an outer skin, with a gut running through the middle, and with various extras like muscles and bone and blood vessels in between. (Smith, 1970, p. 151)

During the fourth and fifth weeks after conception, the embryo grows to a length of 1.25 centimetres. Part of the heart forms and begins to beat, and the limbs, hands and even the fingers become apparent. The sixth and seventh weeks are busy ones for the growth and functioning of physiological systems. Organs such as the lungs, stomach, brain and kidneys develop rapidly and the first real signs of physiological activity begin to appear. The stomach produces digestive juices, the liver produces blood cells, circulation begins and the kidneys excrete wastes. Simple reflex movements can be produced by direct stimulation of a muscle.

By the end of the ninth week, sex differentiation of the gonads has occurred. Minute testes and ovaries are visible, and tiny amounts of male and female hormones are produced. Thus a different developmental course for the two sexes is possible from about this time. Spontaneous movement (as distinct from reflex responding) also emerges at about nine weeks.

The period of the fetus

The final period in prenatal development begins when the first bone cells emerge, about 12 weeks after conception. Most of the baby's organ systems are fully differentiated by now and the fetal period is one of rapid growth. Behaviour also develops dramatically during this phase and, by the 14th week after conception, the fetus's repertoire of activities is already rather impressive. Milestones of biological and behavioural growth during the fetal period are highlighted in Table 3.5 and Figure 3.8.

Growth during the fetal period is spectacular. By the time the full-term infant is born at 40 weeks after conception, the weight of the original fertilised cell has increased about 5000 million times, compared with an increase of only 20 to 30 times over the remainder of the lifespan. Proportions also change, so that by 16 weeks the head is only one-quarter of the total body size, compared with almost one-half at 3 weeks (see the diagram in Table 3.5). The various organs and physiological functions that will enable independent survival, including breathing, heartbeat and temperature regulation, are also perfected towards the end of the fetal period. Meanwhile, many new behavioural developments are occurring

TABLE 3.5	Milestones of fetal development
Age post-conception	**New developments**
3 months	Blood forms in the bone marrow; muscles spurt in growth; head is about half the total size of the fetus.
4 months	Hair appears; bones and joints are distinguishable; ear is fully formed; the brain is separated into two hemispheres; rapid bone growth.
5 months	Neurons in the brain begin to acquire a substance called *myelin* which facilitates rapid neural transmission; hair growth begins.
6 months	Eyes are completely formed, as are fingernails and sweat glands; lungs begin to produce *surfactin*, a chemical that will assist survival if the baby is born prematurely; fat has formed.
7 months	The nervous system is functioning well enough to support life outside the womb; lungs are able to extract oxygen from the air; eyes become responsive to light; electrical activity of the brain suggests periods of sleep and wakefulness.
9 months	Interconnections among neurons develop rapidly; weight doubles in one month; reflexes are now highly responsive.

simultaneously. The baby acquires hearing between the 13th and 29th weeks – it now kicks vigorously when loud noises are made outside the womb. Taste also develops at about this time, together with neurological reactions to stress hormones. Thus, pregnant women who experience extreme emotional upsets often report that their five- to seven-month fetus reacts with vigorous kicking to its mother's feelings of distress (Sontag, 1966).

Fetal brain development

The growth of the human brain is spectacular but its most dramatic phase, without doubt, takes place prenatally. At the peak rate of brain growth during prenatal life, as many as 250 000 new neurons (nerve cells) are added every minute. Figure 3.6 shows how the brain evolves from the 16th day after conception to the time of birth. It starts off as a neural plate differentiating out of the embryo's ectoderm. The plate folds over into a groove and then, by the seventh to eighth week of development, a discernible brain has formed out of this tubelike structure.

Figure 3.7 shows an even more intriguing aspect of prenatal brain development. Contrary to the belief that the death of cells in the central nervous system (including the brain and the spinal cord) does not begin until old age, when it is accompanied by cognitive deficits (see Chapters 1 and 16), brain cells actu-

ally begin to die (a process known as *apoptosis*) prenatally. Figure 3.7 shows the total count of motor neurons (nerve cells) in the fetal spine at 10 weeks and 30 weeks after conception. As the graph shows, the complement of neural cells declines markedly from its peak at about two months after conception. Rather than being a symptom of mental deterioration, it seems that the death of cells is a normal part of development right from the start. By pruning itself developmentally, the brain can specialise in the structures and functions that are required for human neurobiological and cognitive operations.

The emergence of behaviour

Prenatal development is not simply a physiological process of organ differentiation, development and growth. Physiological functioning also sources its origins prenatally. By the early age of 14 weeks, the tiny embryo is already capable of rudimentary forms of behaviour. It can swallow and digest amniotic fluid, urinate and move its fingers. It has developed a variety of reflexes, such as frowning and thrusting its limbs in response to a touch on the skin.

Brain impulses coordinate these reflex reactions as well as highly competent physiological functions that include the production of digestive juices in the stomach, the removal of uric acid from the blood by the kidneys, the heartbeat and hormone production.

FIGURE 3.6 The development of the human brain during prenatal life

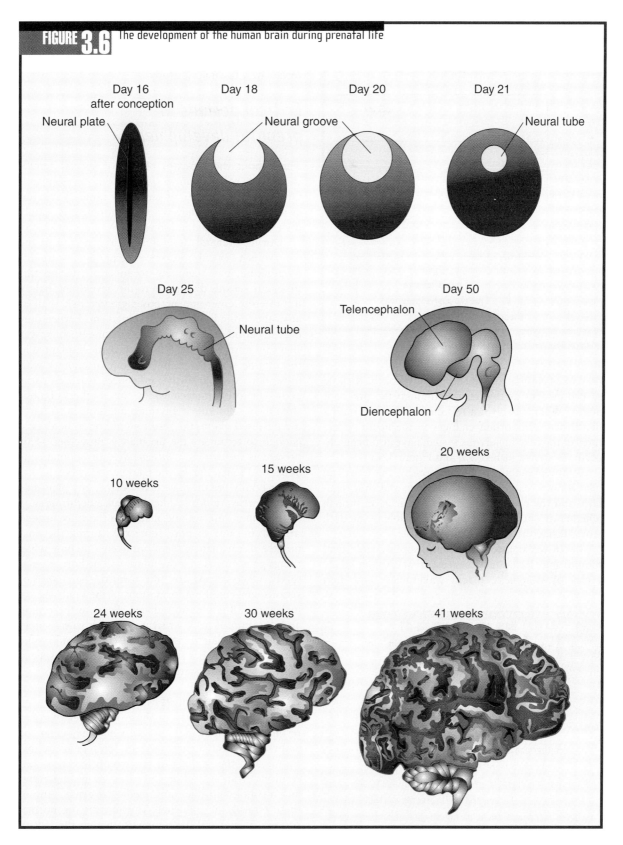

By the end of the third month after conception, the fetus is capable of more sophisticated forms of behaviour, including specialised responding by individual parts of the body (such as the eyelids, legs or arms) to external stimulation. Thus, if the eyelid is stroked, the fetus will squint; if the palm of the hand is touched, it will clench its fist; if the lips are touched, it begins to suck. These reflexes persist during the first months of postnatal life, as we see in Chapter 4.

Thumb-sucking, a behaviour that might seem a little sophisticated even for a newborn, is actually

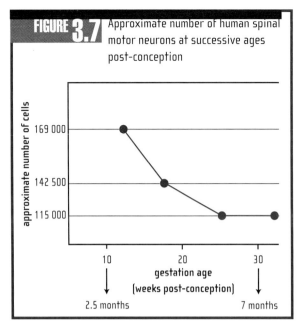

FIGURE 3.7 Approximate number of human spinal motor neurons at successive ages post-conception

Source: Based on data in Forger & Breedlove (1987).

present as early as the third prenatal month. Kicking is also evident at this stage, although the pregnant mother will probably not feel the baby's kicks until a month later. Important changes in the neural structures of the central nervous system have also begun to occur, as shown in Box 3.2 and Figure 3.6.

By the prenatal age of six months, the fetus can hear sounds readily. The eyelids open and shut regularly and the eyes appear to shift their gaze, though whether or not anything would be visible in the dark world inside the womb is questionable.

By 28 weeks after conception, sophisticated fetal monitoring techniques suggest that regular daily cycles of sleepiness, placid wakefulness and alert

BOX 3.2 How can you explain it? Does the nervous system 'age' before birth?

We are all familiar with the warning that we may kill neurons in our brains by drinking alcohol. But the notion that neural death begins prenatally in normal fetuses whose mothers have never had an alcoholic drink while pregnant is somewhat more surprising. Figure 3.7 shows evidence that this does happen, however. The results are from a study by N. G. Forger and S. M. Breedlove (1987) which involved mapping a count of the number of motorneurons present in the spines of human fetuses against prenatal age.

Can you think of an explanation for the steady death of neurons as the fetus progresses from 2.5 months to 7.5 months post-conception? (For an answer, see the section on infant neuropsychological development in Chapter 4, page 116.)

activity have become established. Further important changes in sensory, motor and cognitive development have emerged by seven months (see page 96 for the results of a fascinating study).

Critical periods in prenatal development

Throughout the lifespan, phases of special significance are called *critical periods* in development. Often, these are times of especially rapid change or, as in prenatal life, times when development is readily disrupted by damaging forces.

During prenatal development, the period of the embryo is a critical one. Since organ systems are differentiating and beginning to function during this time, any serious disruption to the developing baby's intrauterine environment poses greater risk than at any other point in prenatal development. Earlier, during the period of the zygote, the risk of deformity was slight because, until the blastula became implanted in the uterine wall, the baby was out of contact with most potentially intrusive influences (such as virus germs or drug molecules) in the mother's bloodstream. In addition, if anything did happen to harm the fertilised ovum, the result would often be drastic enough to terminate the pregnancy altogether. (This process is known as a *miscarriage*, or spontaneous abortion.) Later, during the fetal period, when all the major bodily organs have taken shape, any problems that do arise are not so likely to cause deformities.

Although injuries and insults to the fully formed organs continue to pose some risk during the final months of pregnancy, the more likely outcome when things go wrong is that the infant will be born prematurely. Once organs are fully formed, the chance of serious congenital malformations of the kinds shown in Figure 3.8 is greatly reduced. Because the timing and duration of peak structural growth varies somewhat from organ to organ, the critical embryonic period can be further subdivided into times of special risks to particular parts of the body.

Teratogenic influences

Teratology is the study of those influences that can result in developmental damage when they enter the embryo's protected environment. Teratogens are disruptions to the ecology of the womb (see Box 3.3) resulting from such things as virus germs, cigarettes and alcohol, and illicit and medicinal drugs. Any of these teratogenic influences can disrupt the normal process of prenatal development, though the risk of this occurring is undoubtedly much lower than many parents fear. In fact, approximately 95 per cent of newborns are born perfectly healthy, with no congenital birth defects of any kind (Gosden, Nicolaides & Whitting, 1994).

In line with the critical period concept, the timing of a teratogenic influence is generally more important than the specific teratogenic agent encountered, since the outcome will depend on the particular organ or physiological system that is developing most rapidly when the harmful influence intrudes.

Figure 3.8 shows the critical periods of maximum risk to the brain, the sense organs and other bodily parts in relation to the stage in embryonic or fetal development when the harm occurs. Of course, the risk does not reduce to absolute zero at any prenatal stage, especially for pervasive problem conditions such as severe maternal malnutrition or drug dependency (including alcohol and cigarettes) which can undermine the growth and functioning of the brain and other fetal systems through the pregnancy.

The nature of the congenital defect can also be influenced by timing. A cleft palate arises at the stage in embryonic development when the two sides of the roof of the mouth are in the process of joining together. If fusion is incomplete, cleft palate develops. Other critically timed birth defects include club foot (bones in the foot and ankle are twisted), spina bifida

Diet and exercise can optimise pregnancy for both mother and baby.

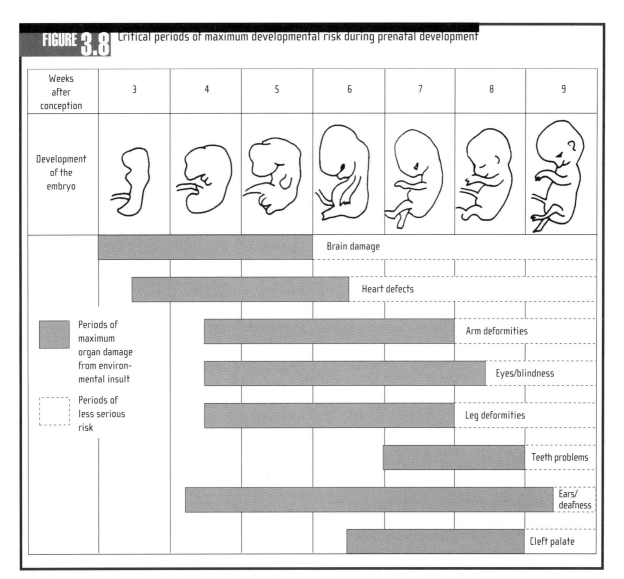

FIGURE 3.8 Critical periods of maximum developmental risk during prenatal development

Source: Moore (1993), Fig. 9-12 © Elsevier Inc., reprinted with permission from Elsevier.

(the neural tube that forms the spinal column fails to close, resulting in paralysis) and anencephaly (part of the brain and skull is missing). In each case, the flaw is due to the organ having formed itself wrongly during its critical process of differentiation from the embryo's other bodily structures. Figure 3.8 illustrates the most common forms of abnormality arising week by week during pregnancy.

Optimising prenatal development

From an optimising standpoint, a sound knowledge of patterns of normal prenatal development and of the potentially teratogenic influences or growth-retarding fetal environmental influences that are shown in Box 3.3 can be an invaluable asset for expectant parents who are motivated to optimise their baby's

BOX 3.3

Optimising development: The ecology of the womb

Though rather bland by adult standards, the normal, natural uterine environment is an exceptionally safe and comfortable one for the growing fetus. The amniotic fluid, the placenta and the mother's body all combine to provide nutrition, waste removal, a constant temperature and protection against disruptive outside forces. But, just as in any other environment, upsets to the ecological balance can occur, sometimes with disastrous results. Listed here are several 'ecological' precautions for pregnant women, with reasons why they are advisable and references for further study.

Precaution: Eat an adequate and balanced diet. (This applies before as well as during pregnancy.)
Reason: The fetus's nutritional needs and the mother's own health both depend on a sound diet. Serious malnutrition can interfere with normal prenatal growth and may limit the baby's intelligence (Goldenberg, 1995).

Precaution: Avoid excessive alcohol consumption.
Reason: Although studies of chronically alcoholic mothers are complicated by additional related factors such as poor health, poor diet and inadequate medical attention, it is a fact that alcohol crosses the placenta to the fetus. This, in concert with the findings of poor developmental progress and reduced intelligence among the children of alcoholics, indicates that large amounts of alcohol should certainly be avoided. *Fetal alcohol syndrome* (FAS), a congenital defect associated with alcohol abuse by the pregnant mother, results in a characteristic set of facial deformities together with a repressed IQ and irritability (Abel, 1998). Even moderate social drinking (1 to 3 drinks per day) can produce milder forms of the same problems, known as *fetal alcohol effects* (FAE) (Abel, 1998).

Precaution: Avoid any medicinal drugs not prescribed by a doctor who knows of the pregnancy.
Reason: The well-known thalidomide tragedy of the early 1960s alerted the public to the possible dangers of drugs taken during the first three months of pregnancy (Lenz, 1966). There is some evidence that certain barbiturates, antibiotics and even asprin in large doses can be harmful (Barr, Stressguth, Darby & Sampson, 1990).

Precaution: Avoid illicit drugs such as cocaine, heroin, methadone and amphetamines.
Reason: Growth retardation and prematurity are clearly implicated. There is also some evidence of long-term irritability and learning problems (Chavkin, 1995).

Precaution: Take a folic acid supplement or eat foods rich in this B vitamin throughout the early months of pregnancy.
Reason: Spina bifida and other neural tube defects are more common in mothers who were low in folic acid during pregnancy.

Precaution: Avoid exposure to virus diseases.
Reason: Rubella (or German measles) may produce malformations if contracted by the mother during the embryonic period (Hardy, 1973). Immunisation against this disease (by injection or exposure well before planning a pregnancy) is therefore advisable. No other virus disease has been linked as clearly and consistently to prenatal difficulties. But since a virus can traverse the placenta, avoiding unnecessary exposure to viruses against which the mother has no immunity is a sensible ecological precaution.

Precaution: Avoid cigarette smoking.
Reason: The infants of mothers who smoke while pregnant more often have medical complications during labour and delivery. They are more likely to be underweight, to develop slowly and to suffer from viral and respiratory infections such as bronchitis and pneumonia through the first year of life. There is also evidence of increased learning difficulties, reading problems and vulnerability to respiratory infections in the offspring of mothers who smoked while pregnant (Chavkin, 1995).

Precaution: Avoid radiation.
Reason: X-rays can cause harm to the developing fetus. Fortunately, the modern technique of ultrasound enables doctors to photograph the fetus inside the womb without the risk of exposing it to radiation.

Precaution: Avoid extreme emotional stress.
Reason: Stress hormones also cross the placenta from the mother to the baby. Babies born to highly stressed mothers are often very restless at birth and may have unusual difficulty adjusting to changes in routine and establishing normal feeding, sleep and bowel habits (Lobel, 1994).

developmental opportunities. By following the precautions listed in Box 3.3, expectant parents can maximise their baby's chances for optimal brain development and physical health, while also reducing the risk of prematurity and infant adjustment difficulties.

But it is important to keep things in proportion. In the first place, the risk of an infant being born in Australia or New Zealand today with a congenital birth defect is quite small. Furthermore, vulnerability to teratogens is thought to reflect an interactive relationship between heredity and environment. Thus, even if a teratogenic agent is encountered at a critical point in prenatal development, the babies most likely to be affected are those who have a genetically determined vulnerability in addition to the prenatal environmental disruption. In other words, the odds are strongly on the side of normal developmental progress through the dramatic first 9-month stage of the new human being's developmental journey through the lifespan.

Prenatal cognitive development

The sensory capacities of a fetus (such as hearing and taste) develop long before birth, together with the capacity for voluntary movement like kicking. Does this mean that a baby might use its senses to notice things, and begin to learn about these things while still in the womb? If so, this could open up exciting possibilities for optimising interventions to smooth the baby's transition into life outside the mother's body during birth and the neonatal adjustment period. New avenues for optimising the infant's readiness for postnatal learning might also appear.

The human mind before birth

But are fetuses actually able to cognitively process the sensory information that finds its way into the protected environment of the womb? Can they learn about the internal or external environment? Will they remember these things after they are born? Can they grow bored?

In an imaginative study designed to answer these questions, Barbara Kisilevsky and Darwin Muir (1991) studied fetuses' heart rate and movement responses by placing recording devices on the mother's abdomen. Then a simple experiment was conducted. While the fetus was still in the womb, one of its ears was located using ultrasound. Choosing the spot on the mother's belly that was nearest to the fetal ear, the researchers repeatedly played two different types of sound at low volume. One sound was a steadily vibrating noise. The other was a pure tone. To rule out the possibility that the mother herself might react to the sounds, she was fitted with headphones broadcasting loud rock or classical music. Thus, in the mother's ears, music completely drowned out the noises being presented to her unborn baby. The fetus's heart rate and rhythms of kicking during and immediately after the sounds

were played gave an indication of its responsiveness to each type of auditory stimulation.

The results suggested that, even before birth, the fetus is cognitively sophisticated enough to become bored when exposed to monotonous sound patterns. The researchers used an *habituation procedure* to demonstrate this fact. The habituation task, developed in order to study sensation and perception in young infants (see Chapter 4), involves presenting the same stimulus repeatedly and evaluating any changes in responsiveness over successive presentations. In their study of fetal hearing, Kisilevsky and Muir discovered that fetuses were capable of becoming habituated. In a manner similar to infants and older individuals, they reacted by kicking vigorously the first few times that either type of sound (vibration or tone) was presented. But as the same sound was repeated again and again, their responsive kicking activity gradually waned. Eventually, after up to eight repeats, most fetuses quit responding altogether. Had they simply become too exhausted to kick any longer?

To test this possibility, Kisilevsky and Muir presented a new type of sound on the ninth trial. The changes in the fetuses' response patterns were dramatic. Those that had been exposed to the pure tone so often that they had ceased reacting to it roused themselves and began to kick forcefully as soon as the vibrating noise was presented. The same pattern of recovery emerged when the pure tone replaced the vibrating noise. So, the gradual cessation of kicking and cardiac responsiveness over repeated trials appeared to reflect the fetus's cognitive awareness of monotony rather than simple physical exhaustion. Heart rate slowed down selectively, also, to the familiar but not the novel sound.

What effect would this prenatal learning about sounds have on the infants after they were born? As newborns, would they still remember the sounds they had heard as fetuses and respond differentially to them? Kisilevsky and Muir explored this possibility by paying a hospital visit to all the newborn babies who had taken part in their prenatal study, within a week of their birth. When they played the vibrating noises and pure tones again to the newborns, Kisilevsky and Muir could not be sure of any differential response to either of the sounds. However, before dismissing altogether the possibility of postnatal memory for prenatal stimulation, the researchers highlighted the need for further research using a broader range of stimuli and response measures and more extensive periods of prenatal exposure.

Evidence that newborn infants can remember things they experienced during prenatal life did emerge in another intriguing longitudinal study spanning the last six weeks of the fetal period (DeCasper & Spence, 1986). Two groups of fetuses were studied. One group experienced specific auditory stimulation prenatally. Every day during the last six weeks of pregnancy, their mothers read aloud the same passage from a chosen children's book (e.g. *The Cat in the Hat* by Dr Seuss). The other group experienced no such repeated stimulation. A few hours after the babies were born, their preferences for novel and familiar story passages (as read either by their mother or a female stranger) were measured. The researchers rewarded sucking responses by presenting a particular passage. When the familiar passage produced more reliable sucking than the novel one, this testified to a preference based on prenatal exposure. As predicted, the babies who had had stories read to them prenatally displayed a consistent and statistically significant preference for familiar passages after they were born. The results are illustrated in Figure 3.9. No consistent preference among the passages emerged for the group that heard them for the first time after birth in the hospital nursery. It therefore seemed that sounds heard consistently during pregnancy were remembered by the fetuses, explaining their consistent preferences when they heard these same sounds again as newborn infants. Of course, there was no implication that the infants understood the content of what had been read!

In another experiment using the sucking response, it was found that newborn babies sucked longer while listening to a tape that played their parents' native language than to a tape of the same material spoken in a different language (Moon, Cooper & Fifer, 1993). Since this ability was already present at birth, the researchers suggested that the necessary learning had taken place prenatally as the fetus in the womb listened to its parents speaking.

Naturalistic observation of newborns' attention and soothing patterns (see Chapter 4) support the results of these imaginative experimental studies. For example, it has been noted that neonates relax more to the sound of their mother's voice than to the voice of another woman, and that the smell of amniotic fluid is more soothing to neonates than any other type of odour, including no smell at all (Porter et al., 1992). Presumably, these differential reactions reflect

memories for the auditory and olfactory experiences of prenatal life, together with a preference for familiar, rather than novel, types of sensory stimulation.

The expectant parents during pregnancy

During the nine or so months that they will have to wait from the time of discovering the pregnancy to the point of being able to welcome their newborn infant into the world, the lives of the expectant parents are likely to undergo predictable changes. These are undeniably less dramatic than the changes the developing fetus is undergoing, but they are nevertheless important for facilitating the parents' own patterns of psychological growth and adjustment to their new life roles, and for creating the family environment into which the new baby will be welcomed.

Regardless of whether this baby is a first or subsequent offspring, major adjustments to the mother's and father's lifestyles are normally required. This is a time for the expectant parents to come to grips with the reality of having this particular child, and for putting plans for the baby's arrival into action. In the case of a first baby, a major reorganisation of the couple's lifestyle may be attempted, including at least some of the following changes: moving into more spacious quarters; curtailing a career; changing, or curtailing, leisure plans and activities; making both immediate and long-term child-care and babysitting arrangements; working out a new style of couplehood that will accommodate parental responsibilities and a third member of the household; evolving a new relationship with the expectant grandparents; worrying over present or future economic strains; enjoying 'last flings' (travel, theatre, etc.); making medical preparations (from childbirth classes to charting the shortest route to the hospital); and obtaining the items of clothing and furniture that the baby will need. When the expected child is a second or later birth, preparations may also include briefing older

FIGURE **3.9** Newborn infants' preferences for rhymes read to them in the womb

prefer novel passage

prefer familiar passage

Source: Based on data in DeCasper & Spence (1986).

The nine months of pregnancy allow new parents time to prepare for this major transition in their lives.

children about what to expect, and arrangements for post-hospital care of the baby.

While all these practical preparations are going on, first-time expectant parents are liable to go through a phase of self-examination in which they consider what their new roles will be like and how they will change as people with the transition into parenthood. Anxiety over whether they lack some of the requisite skills or emotional qualities necessary for successful childrearing is apt to surface as the birth draws near, even among couples who satisfied themselves on this score before venturing to become pregnant. Worries about the child being born with a congenital defect or whether the mother will suffer injury to her own health during the birth process are also extremely common.

If a couple has taken the sort of precautions discussed in Box 3.3, fears like these are usually quite unrealistic. Still, the need to wait so many months to be sure can itself be a source of stress. One way of minimising these psychological discomforts during the anticipation period is active preparation. Expectant parents who read books about pregnancy, birth and child development, or attend lectures on these subjects and take part in childbirth preparation classes are found to have an easier time of it, not only during pregnancy but also after their child is born (Wente & Crockenberg, 1976). It is most important, too, for the expectant husband and wife to be able to discuss their concerns and plans for the future together. As well as providing assurance, discussions may help new parents to guard against the misunderstandings that so often arise when they try on their new parental roles.

Expecting a boy or a girl

During the nine months of pregnancy, waiting for the baby to arrive, parents develop expectations about whether their new child will be a boy or a girl. Sometimes, the suspense of waiting nine months to find out is too great and the expectant parents undertake some form of fetal screening (e.g. ultrasound or amniocentesis) for the express purpose of learning the fetus's gender. But other parents are glad to wait, and may elect not to be told the baby's sex even if a diagnostic procedure like amniocentesis has revealed it to their doctor.

For some parents, the preference for one sex or the other becomes very strong, as illustrated in Box 3.6 on page 102. What happens if a parent's prenatal gender preference is frustrated? Are infants of the wanted sex treated differently from those who disappoint their parents in this one respect during the crucial initial moments of making each other's acquaintance postnatally?

To answer these questions, Hakan Stattin and Ingrid Klackenberg-Larsson (1991) conducted an ambitious longitudinal study of 212 Swedish families. During pregnancy, the expectant mothers and fathers were independently interviewed to discover which sex they hoped the new baby would be. Only families in which the mother and father shared the same sex preference were followed further. After the baby was born, the researchers visited the babies at home and observed each parent's patterns of interaction with the infant. Interviews were also conducted with the mother and father separately to assess stress, adjustment and satisfaction with the parental role. Follow-up visits were made at regular intervals until the babies reached the age of 25 years. As adults, they themselves were also interviewed to obtain a retrospective picture of their experiences of family life while growing up.

The results showed that a parent's prenatal gender preference exerted a powerful influence on a child's development. Even after 25 years of exposure to a wide range of other diversifying experiences, consistent differences emerged between the men and women whose expectant parents had hoped that they would be the sex they actually turned out to be and those whose gender at birth had frustrated both parents' hopes. The objective observations conducted in the home revealed that sons and daughters who had been of the wanted sex enjoyed more attention from their parents during infancy, were happier and closer to both parents during childhood, and showed better conflict-resolution skills and fewer maladaptive acting-out behaviours during adolescence than those whose sex had initially been 'wrong'. Despite the fact that many parents in the latter group later claimed to have forgotten which sex they had actually preferred during the pregnancy, or even claimed to have wanted a child of the sex they eventually ended up with, their patterns of childrearing from infancy onward were less favourable than in families where reality matched prenatal preference. Parents spent less time playing with children of the 'wrong' sex and reported having more problems with these children during childhood and adolescence. The adverse impact on father–child relationships was greater than on mother–child relationships, especially if a son had been wanted and a daughter was born instead. Retrospective reports by the offspring themselves at age 25 confirmed that family relationships had been less positive throughout for children whose sex had been a disappointment to their parents than for those of the gender both expectant parents had hoped for.

Thus, these data indicate that the period of pregnancy can begin indirectly to affect the baby's future social development by establishing parental expectations and attitudes. At least over an issue as basic as gender, prenatal preferences would appear to exert a major impact on the parents' behaviour, even after the fetus emerges as a responsive, interactive human being.

The baby's birth

Birth is an important transition for the infant as well as for the parents. From the baby's point of view,

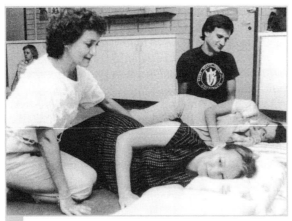
Many women today elect to prepare for childbirth by attending classes.

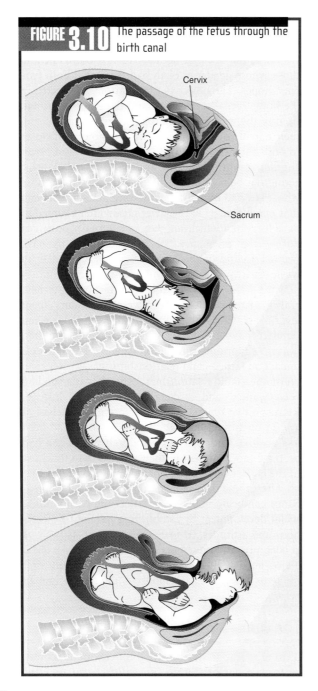
FIGURE **3.10** The passage of the fetus through the birth canal

Cervix

Sacrum

birth ends one important phase in life and begins another. Now that the period of largely invisible, but all-important, prenatal physical and psychological development has reached its end, the baby's transition out of the uterus and into the world is the beginning of its developmental journey through the lifespan as an independent human being.

Birth is a psychological as well as a biological process. Though it may be difficult to appreciate the complete gamut of the newborn infant's psychological reactions to the sudden jolt out of the quiet, protective womb into the 'blooming, buzzing confusion' (James, 1890) of the world outside, what we now know of the sophisticated sensory and cognitive capacities of fetuses even before birth (see pages 95–6) tells us that the event will be experienced by the baby, who is an active participant in the entire process.

The birth process itself typically begins 266 days after conception with irregular contractions of the mother's uterus that are felt as labour pains. The process occupies three stages.

Stages of labour

The *first stage* in the birth process typically lasts for between 8 and 20 hours in women who are giving birth for the first time, and usually a shorter period for experienced mothers. Before this stage begins, the fetus takes up a position in the womb that is most often head down (cephalic presentation) but may occasionally present buttocks (breech presentation) or shoulders (transverse presentation) first. Stage 1 begins when the mother feels the first contraction and ends when the cervix (the opening of the uterus) is fully dilated to a width of about 10 centimetres. Contractions begin mildly and irregularly but grow in strength and frequency. At the end of the first stage, known as the *period of transition*, contractions become intensely painful and last for between 45 and 90 seconds. During periods between contractions, a mother in the transition stage may employ psychological strategies such as relaxation exercises or mental preparation to get ready for the next contraction.

The *second stage* of birth begins when the cervix

BOX 3.4 Lessons from culture: Birth in a traditional Aboriginal community

Daisy Bates (1861–1951) studied and wrote about the traditional Aboriginal people of the western deserts of Australia. Bates came to Australia from Ireland as a journalist and lived for a while on a cattle station. Early in the 20th century she moved into a small tent in the outback and lived until the eve of her death at age 90 in remote Aboriginal communities, learning 188 indigenous languages and becoming a full participant in the lives of the people she studied. In this way she gained insight into traditional Aboriginal childbirth practices, which she described as follows:

Birth had no pangs for the young mother. She knelt down, rested her buttocks on her heels, pressed her breath, and the baby was born, so easily, so free from pain or obstruction, that there was rarely a cry. The operation performed on young girls and their initiation to womanhood at an early age tends to this painless birth. The baby is left on the ground, a mother or elder sister will snip the umbilical cord with her strong and long nails, leaving two or three inches on the navel. This is tied in a loose knot and flattened down, and later, when it dries and falls off, hair is netted about it in a little ring, to be hung round the baby's neck and left there for weeks and months. It is supposed to contain part of the child's spirit existence, and when it withers off the baby has absorbed the spirit. The baby is massaged tenderly with soft ashes and charcoal. (Bates, 1966, p. 235)

Unique in Australia, I believe, and perhaps unique in the world, is the legend of the dream-child, ngargalulla, as told me by the Broome tribes ... They believed that below the surface of the ground, and at the bottom of the sea, was a country called Jimbin, home of the spirit babies of the unborn, and the young of all the totems. In Jimbin there was never a shadow of trouble or strife or toil, or death, only the happy laughter of the little people at play ... The ngargalulla is still a spirit in the first months of its existence, but when it begins to laugh and cry, to touch and talk, and to manifest its personality as a little human being, its link with the dream world is gone, and it becomes cabajerra—in other words, a normal baby. Thenceforward, through its whole life, the fathers who have dreamed its existence are the controllers of its destinies, within the relentless circle of tribal law. (Bates, pp. 26–8)

is fully dilated and ends when the baby is born. The baby's head moves into the birth canal and intense contractions, lasting 45 to 60 seconds, propel the baby into the outside world. A few minutes later the placenta is expelled, completing the *third stage* of the birth process.

The uncomplicated delivery

Most babies in Australia and New Zealand today are born in hospital, and this is certainly a sensible optimising strategy to ensure that mother and baby have access to appropriate medical or surgical attention, should the delivery become complicated. In contrast to common practices up to the middle of last century, however, when the hospitalised mother was placed under general anaesthesia and the father and other relatives were kept strictly away, modern childbirth hospital procedures are far less strange, drug-dependent or intrusive. With her partner and/or other familiar and socially supportive friends and relatives surrounding her, the mother in labour is able to make many of her own choices about the type and amount of pain relief she requires at each stage of the delivery, while remaining fully conscious. Most first-time mothers today use some medication to reduce the pain of delivery, even when they have attended 'natural' childbirth classes and have hoped for a totally unmedicated delivery (Hetherington, 1990). However, attending birth preparation classes is still helpful, both for alerting women to what they can expect in the delivery room, and also for teaching them relaxation strategies to assist their pain management. While still reporting pain and still generally needing some pain-relief medication, most mothers who have attended childbirth preparation classes use less medication and tend to delay its use until more advanced stages in the delivery (when the risk of uptake into the baby's bloodstream is less) than do unprepared mothers (Bennett, Hewson, Booker & Holliday, 1985; Hetherington, 1990). Still, contrary to the saying 'The pains of childbirth are quickly forgotten', pain is not only felt but remembered by first-time mothers, despite childbirth preparation classes and irrespective of choices made regarding natural or medicated births. The results of one study in which 398 Sydney women were interviewed three weeks after they had given birth for the first time showed that the average new mother expressed mild agreement with the statement 'Labour was so bad, I'd *hate* to have the experience again' and mild disagreement with the opposite view ('Labour was so good, I'd like to have the experience again') (Bennett et al.,

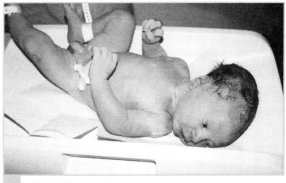

A healthy, full-term newborn.

1985). Still, the thrill at the moment of delivery, when a healthy newborn emerges into the world, is apparently more than adequate compensation, since a majority of women do go on to repeat the experience at least once (Australian Bureau of Statistics, 2001).

How is the health and normality of a newborn to be judged? Table 3.6 shows the standard instrument. Known as the Apgar scale (after Virginia Apgar [1953] who devised it), the measure assesses the newborn's functioning on five dimensions: (a) heart rate, (b) breathing, (c) muscle tone, (d) colour, and (e) reflex responsiveness, all rated on a scale from 0 to 2. Infants who earn a total score of 7 or more are in good health, while those who score 4 or less are in need of further medical attention.

Childbirth complications: Prematurity and low birth weight

More than 90 per cent of infants are born *on time*. In other words, birth begins within a healthy range of variation of roughly two weeks either side of the exact due date of 266 days post-conception. And the vast majority of babies in Australia and New Zealand today are of adequate size when they are born (over 2500 grams). But in a minority of cases, when the baby is born either too early or too small, psychological as well as medical optimisation efforts may be needed to make sure that the child's long-term developmental future is not adversely affected by this initial setback.

Prematurity refers to a birth occurring more than three weeks before the due date, resulting in an infant weighing less than 2500 grams and showing other signs of immaturity, such as difficulty with sucking and breathing. The small-for-dates newborn, on the other hand, arrives on schedule but weighs less than the acceptable figure of 2500 grams. Even when born into well-equipped hospitals, premature and small-for-dates infants require more medical intervention in the aftermath of the birth than the average newborn. However, their odds of survival have improved dramatically in recent years (Chomitz, Cheung &

Lieberman, 2000). In fact, one study in the United States showed a 33 per cent survival rate among very tiny infants who weighed only 500 to 749 grams at birth (Lin, Verp & Sabbagha, 1993). For those with a birth weight of 1250 to 1499 grams, the survival rate was 91 per cent, which compares favourably with the 98 per cent survival rate for full-term newborns of normal weight.

However, even after they have managed, in hospital, to recover their health and the gains in weight and mature capacities that normal full-term infants achieve during their last few weeks in the womb, the small-for-dates or premature infant may impose extra burdens of psychological adjustment and developmental challenge on the parents (Silcock, 1984). This is especially so when parents blame themselves for the stresses and complications their small and/or premature infant has been experiencing (Silcock, 1984).

Long-term developmental consequences of birth complications

Fortunately, longitudinal studies have been conducted to test whether any long-term setbacks to healthy psychological growth emerge reliably in children as a function of their exposure to birth complications, prematurity and low birth weight. One of the most impressive of these is a study by Emmy Werner and Ruth Smith (1992) who followed a sample of 670 Hawaiian babies longitudinally from birth to late adolescence.

Werner and Smith's results were reassuring in relation to risk factors from delivery complications. Their findings also serve as an excellent illustration of the interactive relationship that exists between biological and social influences on lifespan development (see Table 1.3). Of their sample of 670 infants, a total of 107 (16 per cent) had experienced severe complications of delivery owing to extreme prematurity, extremely low birth weight or other severe stressors (e.g. a dangerously low Apgar score, see Table 3.6). A further 208 had mild birth complications and 53 per cent had been born full-term, of adequate weight and without delivery complications of any kind.

TABLE 3.6 The Apgar scale of neonatal well-being			
Physiological function	Score		
	0	1	2
Respiration	Absent	Slow and irregular	Good; baby cries
Heart rate	Absent	Slow/less than 100 beats per minute	Over 100 beats per minute
Muscle tone	Limp	Some weak flexing	Strong, active motion
Colour	Blue or pale	Body is pink; extremities are blue	Pink
Reflex responses	None	Grimace only	Coughing, sneezing, crying

Source: Apgar (1953).

BOX 3.5 Optimising development: Helping parents cope with prematurity

Anne Silcock (1984) studied a group of 24 Brisbane mothers and fathers of premature and low-birth-weight infants longitudinally over several months following the birth with the object of gaining a better understanding of their adjustment process. She concluded that this process progressed through four stages, each with its own specific coping task.

TASK 1 COPING WITH GRIEF

The relatively high mortality risk for babies born more than 10 weeks premature, with weights under 1500 grams, meant that all the parents in Silcock's sample had grounds for believing that their newborn might not survive. In addition, many of them experienced reactive grief for the 'normal' full-term newborn they had been expecting throughout the pregnancy. Their anticipatory or reactive grieving took a variety of forms. Anxiety was paramount for some parents. Several mothers reported agonising next to the telephone, afraid to call the hospital lest they be told their baby had died, yet driven to do so for reassurance. Silcock argued that another important component of the grief reaction involved surrendering the fantasy of a 'perfect' baby and accepting the preterm infant as theirs. Several mothers who proved unable to do this continued to disparage their formerly preterm offspring when, by age two, their development had objectively returned to normal.

TASK 2 DEALING WITH A SENSE OF FAILURE

Mothers and, to a lesser extent, fathers are apt to feel they have failed in the task of child-bearing when they produce a premature baby. The resulting losses in trust, self-confidence and self-esteem can be minimised or exacerbated, depending on how the spouse, friends and extended family members react to the situation. Silcock found that those mothers whose husbands and extended families reacted with fear and unhappiness, and refused to visit the infant during its time in the Special Care Nursery, were most vulnerable to feelings of personal failure and inadequacy. In two cases of second marriage, the problem was further intensified by the husbands' invidious comparison with their former wives who had delivered only healthy full-term births. On the other hand, little or no loss of self-esteem was reported by the nine mothers in Silcock's sample who

had histories of previous miscarriages, stillbirths or preterm infants, or were carrying twins. In their case, the birth of a live, though premature, infant was viewed as a success relative to other possible outcomes.

TASK 3 RESUMPTION OF NORMAL PARENTING

Depending on the duration and extent of the intensive care needed to sustain the premature baby's life initially, the parents must readjust, once the baby's health improves, to a normal mode of parenting. Before conducting her study, Silcock had anticipated that successful accomplishment of Tasks 1 and 2 would greatly assist this process. But her results revealed that another factor was even more important. Her data showed that the frequency of the mother's visits to the baby during the hospital stay was the best predictor of a satisfactory mother–infant relationship once the infant went home. Tasks 1 and 2 were bound up with this factor for those mothers who chose not to visit the hospital, out of dread that the baby would die, or denial of the abnormal birth, or the father's unsupportive attitude. For these mothers, as predicted, adjustment to mothering was poor even after the baby regained its health and returned home. But even when the reasons precluding hospital visits were such impersonal causes as living a long distance from Brisbane or the lack of transport or babysitters for older children, the mother's later adoption of a normal style of parenting was somewhat hampered. Silcock therefore concluded that practical factors as well as the emotional crises she had identified could interfere with the effective parenting of prematures, and that 'the best predictor of the quality of future maternal–infant relationship is the mother's frequency of visiting during the infant's stay at hospital' (p. 267).

TASK 4 UNDERSTANDING THE NEEDS OF PRETERM BABIES

Despite the educational efforts of hospital staff and a lengthy adjustment period during the baby's month or more in hospital, 10 of the mothers in Silcock's group proved either unable or unwilling to recognise that their premature babies were unusual and would require a special style of care when they returned home. Five of these mothers were teenagers and two were migrants who were not fluent in English. Since Silcock was able to follow these mothers for only two months after the baby's discharge, she could not determine whether this group's initial problems became permanent or were merely temporary.

When they compared the three groups at age 2, Werner and Smith found that those who had had severe birth complications were outperformed by the healthy, full-term group on standard tests of language and intellectual and social development. But by the age of 10, after the children had been exposed to several years of schooling and to a decade of influential developmental stimulation within the family environ-

ment, birth complications were no longer a significant predictor of intellectual performance. Instead, IQ scores were linked with the quality of the children's home environments. Children whose parents were aloof and unresponsive, and whose homes were relatively impoverished in sources of social and academic stimulation earned significantly lower IQ scores than those from warm families rich in social stimulation and intellectual challenge. However, for the former group, birth complications created a situation of 'double jeopardy'. The lowest IQ scores of all were earned by the survivors of prematurity and other severe birth complications whose parents were cold and aloof and whose home environments were unstimulating. The same general pattern was seen to persist through adolescence.

In other words, as in the case of the gene–environment interactions considered earlier in this chapter, the effects of the biobehavioural setbacks of birth complications, like those of an adverse genotype, cannot be understood in isolation. Their meaning in terms of lifespan development depends on the quality of the rearing environment.

The transition to parenthood

The transition to parenthood is a developmental milestone for first-time parents, just as it is for their newborn sons and daughters. How they adjust can be an important predictor of their ability to provide a family environment that is warm and stimulating enough to foster optimal cognitive, social and emotional development for their infants (see above) and for one another. An illustration of one father's reaction to his child's birth and early development appears in Box 3.6.

Ross Parke (1977) compared fathers' and mothers' involvement with their newborn babies in a series of studies all conducted within three days of delivery. In the first study he observed both parents together in the baby's company. The fathers in this study were rather special. They were all middle class, and had mostly attended Lamaze classes and assisted at the birth. Parke found that both fathers and mothers looked at, spoke to, smiled at and kissed the babies equally often. But fathers held them and rocked them more than mothers did. In subsequent studies of lower-class parents, of fathers who were uninvolved in the birth and of parents alone with the infant, similar results were obtained. In short, Parke found that, regardless of background or prior experience, fathers tended to involve themselves at least as fully as the mothers in all forms of care for their newborns, with the possible exception of feeding. Also, the average father was as competent as the average mother at reading the baby's signals and adjusting his style of care to suit the needs of the baby. It would seem that both parents can, with motivation and deliberate and well-informed preparation, learn how to make the transition into parenthood an optimal one, especially when they have supported each other through the momentous events of their infant's prenatal development and delivery.

We examine the parenthood transition from the standpoint of adult development in Chapter 13.

BOX 3.6 A father's reaction to childbirth

When his infant daughter was 10 months old, Louise's father recorded the following description of her birth in his private diary:

29 January 1949. *Louise at ten months and ten days. Some day I'll try to remember what she was like at this time. Even now, I've half forgotten her earlier personality.*

The morning when she was born, when I dozed in a chair in Peggy's hospital room: how my teeth chattered after the nurse told me to come up to the delivery room. The message was so non-committal; it could mean anything. Partly from lack of sleep and partly from until then well guarded fear for Peggy, I felt a momentary panic that was only relieved when I met young Dr Roberts (for the first time). 'You have a baby girl.' 'A girl? Dr Flaherty said it would be a girl.' I had of course predicted a boy, just as I often predict against my wishes, so that the consolation of being right may partly balance disappointment.

'Would you like to see her?' 'Yes.'

There they were out in the hall, Peggy and Louise. Peggy was sleeping heavily, her face very red (from the scopolomine as I learned later). Louise was in a canvas basket. Her skin was very tight over the bones of her face and forehead. Her eyes were closed and she lay very still, but neither the doctor nor the nurses seemed to consider this extraordinary, so I guessed it was all right too.

© Peterson, 1974, p. 15, reproduced with permission

Later, Louise's father went on to describe the emotional meaning his daughter's birth and first 18 months of life had had for him.

7 November 1949. … *Yes, I'm perfectly satisfied that nothing that's ever happened or ever could happen to me comes within miles of meaning as much as Louise. I would like to write a great book, good poetry, a novel, a play; but when I feel discouraged because I haven't, I think of her and I'm quite happy. I would like a second child but I know for certain that the second child would also have to take second place in my affections.*

© Peterson, 1974, pp. 15–16, reproduced with permission

Chapter summary

Psychological development over the lifespan is shaped by the genes that the new person draws together from the paternal and maternal sides of the biological family tree. The new baby's genotype is established by the union of 23 chromosomes from each parent at conception. From this moment to the end of life, the new individual's unique genotype interacts in complex ways with their distinctive experiences and life circumstances to determine the course of development through life.

Polygenic inheritance, involving multiple gene combinations, is responsible for many of the most interesting psychological developments in cognition, personality, sociability and adjustment. Developmentalists and behaviour geneticists rely on methods such as twin comparisons and adoption designs in their efforts to unravel the distinctive contributions of heredity and environment to human psychological growth. But genetic influences may change at different points in the life cycle because (a) there are varied, non-linear interactions between heredity and environment, and (b) the individual may play an active role in selecting directions for psychological growth. Thus, there can be no simple apportionment of development to either nature or nurture alone.

Recent evidence from twin-comparison and adoption studies shows that complex interactions between heredity and environment may allow for greater flexibility in parenting than was previously supposed, without the risk of thwarting the optimal development of the child's genetic potential.

Prenatal development can be divided into three phases. The period of the zygote covers roughly the two-week interval from conception until implantation in the mother's uterus, culminating in the differentiation of the future baby from its surrounding life-support systems. The period of the embryo, continuing until bone cells appear about three months after conception, is a critical phase when disturbances to the ecology of the womb may cause congenital malformations. The brain and bodily organs undergo rapid differentiation and formation during this phase. The period of the fetus, from three to nine months after conception, is a time of rapid behavioural and physiological growth that will fit the baby for independent life. Genuine psychological functioning emerges in this phase, including some remarkably sophisticated sensory, motor and cognitive accomplishments.

The birth process is a major developmental milestone for mother and child. A healthy birth, arising for the vast majority, gets the baby's life outside the womb off to a good start with good muscle tone, neurological function, reflex responsivity and strong functioning of the heart, circulation, lungs and other bodily organs. Birth complications, such as prematurity, difficult labour, oxygen deprivation or low birth weight, may have an impact on later development. Psychological interventions can help parents and infants to cope with early setbacks like these.

Giving birth is a significant and memorable event in the mother's own life cycle and fathers are increasingly coming to share this perspective. Fathers today tend to become 'engrossed' in their newborn child and involve themselves fully in caring for the neonate at home. The lifespan psychological development of both generations is fostered by this early mutual involvement with one another's lives.

For further interest

Looking forward on the Internet

For ideas about the development of the human brain, both prenatally and postnatally, go to: **http://faculty.washington.edu/chudler/dev.html**. For more information on pregnancy and birth planning, try: **http://www.pregnancy.org**.

For resources, ideas, activities and other items of interest in conjunction with this chapter, visit the Companion Website for this textbook at:

> **http://wps.pearsoned.com.au/peterson**

Activity suggestion

To explore the family-planning preferences of members of your community, interview as many recently married adults as you can locate among your personal acquaintances. Ask them (a) how many children they hope to have, (b) what sex they prefer their eldest and youngest to be, and (c) what they would choose if they could opt either for twins or for more widely spaced offspring. If possible seek informants from a variety of cultural backgrounds, and compare your findings with those of your classmates.

Multimedia

For a provocative glimpse of prenatal development and the adverse effects of alcohol on the growing fetus, view the video: *Alcohol and Pregnancy* (Penn State, PCR Films & Video in the Behavioural Sciences, 1985: 17 minutes). For a video of childbirth, watch: *Birth at Home* (Australian Film & TV, 1977: 14 minutes).

INFANCY — FROM BIRTH TO AGE TWO

PART 2

Contents

Overview

When parents of grown children look back over their entire experience of parenting, the phase of infancy, or the period from birth until about age two, is likely to stand out as the time when both the pleasures and the pains of parenthood were the sharpest. The first moments, days and weeks of life with a new baby, while dimmed for many new parents by lack of sleep and the stresses and anxieties connected with early infant care, are nonetheless momentously moving, ever fascinating and exciting. The pleasures of early parenthood increase still more at around two months when infants confer their first social smiles upon their charmed caregivers and their sensory and motor capacities have matured to the point where they can take a more active role in their own development within the family.

The most nostalgic moments of all are likely to be at points when the key developmental milestones of infancy are reached. The baby sits alone for the first time, rolls over, tastes the first spoonful of solid food, walks a few steps without holding on, speaks a meaningful word, buries her face in her mother's skirt while chortling her joy in reunion after a separation.

In the next two chapters we examine these exciting psychological developments of the infancy phase.

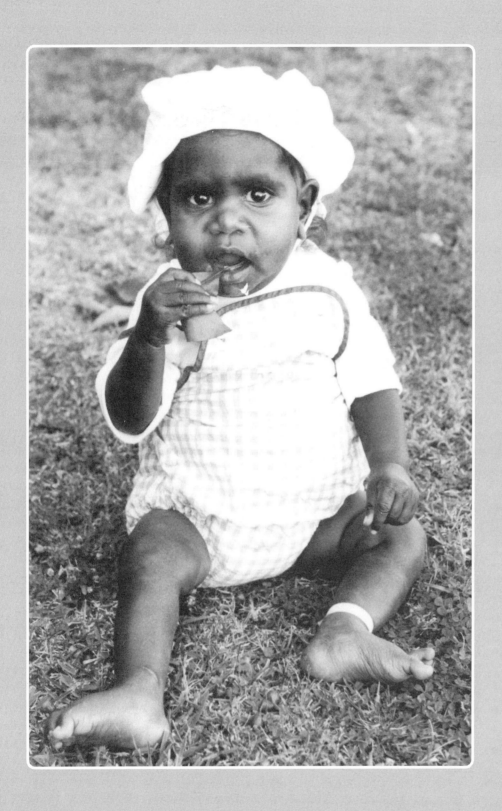

INFANCY: Physical, neurobiological, sensorimotor and cognitive development

CHAPTER 4

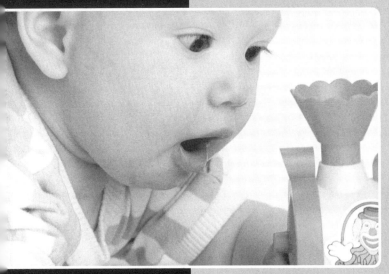

Where did you come from, baby dear?

Out of the everywhere into here.

Where did you get your eyes so blue?

Out of the sky as I came through.

George MacDonald (1824–1905)

Contents

The phase in the lifespan known as *infancy* begins at birth and ends around the second birthday when the baby begins to use language in a meaningful way. Despite its brief duration of only two years, this portion of the lifespan is filled with an impressive number of significant developmental accomplishments. At the start of infancy, the new-born child, while a far more competent thinker, perceiver and active agent than researchers could have imagined just 20 years ago, still has a long way to go before being able to get around in the world independently. But by infancy's end, most babies have quadrupled in size. They have a sophisticated brain which, combined with the maturation of neonatal sensory capacities, equips them to perceive their world more or less as adults do. They are now generally sleeping mostly at night, walking upright and using their hands with skill and dexterity to manipulate objects as fine as a pencil or as intricate as a bottle cap or door latch. Thanks to these motor skills, they have become adept at controlling and exploring the physical and social stimuli in their immediate environment, and know quite a lot about how the world is organised. This knowledge combines with irrepressible curiosity to prompt the rapid cognitive development that characterises the infancy phase. They have completed the sensorimotor stage of cognitive growth (Piaget, 1970, see Chapter 2) and are communicating and socialising effectively, even if in primarily non-verbal ways.

In this chapter, we discuss each of the important developmental changes that conspire to create this dramatic transformation. First, we examine the nature of the psychological being that the new parents take home from the maternity hospital or birthing room, looking at the patterns of sleeping, crying and reflex responding that define the neonate's behavioural repertoire and at how these change over the first six months of postnatal life. Then we examine the major developmental accomplishments across the whole of infancy in terms of (a) physical growth and health, (b) neurocognitive development, (c) motor development, (d) the growth of sensory and perceptual skills, (e) the development of learning, (f) cognition, information processing and problem-solving, and (g) the development of motivation for cognition and self-efficacy.

Chapter 5 then completes our portrait of the competent infant by examining social, emotional and personality growth over the first two years of life.

The first three months: Crying, sleeping and reflex responding

Despite being tiny (about the size of a tall man's foot) and far less ready than a newly hatched chick or a newborn horse or puppy to manage the world without parental help, the full-term neonate is nonetheless already a remarkably competent human being. The baby is equipped with a set of automatic reflex behaviours (like sneezing, coughing, blinking and sucking) that assist survival during the first few months of life as the cortex of the brain develops the readiness to take over voluntary control of behaviour. Rhythms dictating the right time for sleeping, feeding and elimination are also present.

However, from the new parents' standpoint, the first few months of learning to adjust to life with a new baby can be fraught with difficulty, even for well-informed and well-adjusted men and women who welcome their new parental roles wholeheartedly (see Chapter 13). Three of the biggest problem areas involve the baby's basic survival activities: sleeping, crying and feeding. Ignorance is one cause of stress, with few first-time parents possessing an accurate knowledge of the typical newborn's habits or needs in any of these domains. But difficulty also stems from the fact that these three aspects of the infant's life are apt to demand at least as much change to the parents' habits as to those of the infant. In modifying their routines to suit life with a new baby, parents too may suffer 'growing pains'.

An accurate understanding of the baby's bodily functions and early behaviours can prove indispensable for a relatively smooth adjustment to the new parenting role. Having a parent who understands the nature of an infant's first behaviour patterns and capabilities is very important, both for optimising the infant's own development and ensuring a smooth uptake of the parenting role.

This section of the chapter therefore focuses on three important areas of the infant's behaviour in the first three months of life: reflex behaviours, crying and sleeping.

Reflex behaviours

Reflexes consist of largely automatic behaviour patterns that are controlled by subcortical neural mechanisms. Infants at birth have a wide repertoire of reflexes, some of which are shown in Table 4.1. Some of these (like coughing, sneezing and blinking) have essential survival value and are retained, largely unchanged, throughout the lifespan. Others have specific functions that are important only in early infancy (such as rooting, sucking and swallowing, which assist in the establishment of nursing), while still others have no obvious benefits either during infancy or later on (such as the Babinski reflex, which curls the toes in response to stimulation on the sole of the foot). These last two groups of reflexes disappear after a few months (see Table 4.1) in line with the processes of cortical brain development that we examine in more detail later in this chapter.

TABLE 4.1	Some reflex responses of very young infants		
Reflex	Description	Function	Developmental course
Moro	In response to either (a) a loud noise or (b) a sudden jolt of the head backwards, the infant stretches its arms to the side, and hugs them back to the chest, clenching fists.	Today, it assists diagnosis of a normal nervous system (its absence signals possible brain defects in the infant). During evolution, it might have assisted tree-dwelling ancestors to cling to the mother, or to break a fall by grabbing a branch.	Disappears by about six months of age while infant is awake and alert; may reappear briefly while falling asleep.
Sucking	When the lips or tongue are touched, the infant begins to suck.	Assists the establishment of feeding.	Uncontrollable reflex disappears by about six months of age; voluntary sucking ability remains lifelong.
Rooting	In response to a stroke of the cheek or corner of the mouth, the infant turns its head and tongue in that direction.	Assists in locating the nipple.	Uncontrollable reflex disappears by five or six months of age; voluntary head-turning remains lifelong.
Grasping	Curling of fingers around an object pressed on the palm of the hand.	Today, it assists in diagnosis of a normal nervous system. During evolution, it may have assisted in clinging to the mother.	Disappears by three months; voluntary grasping appears by six months.
Babinski	Toes fan, then curl, when the sole of the foot is stroked.	Today, it assists in diagnosis of a normal nervous system. During evolution, it may have assisted in clinging to the mother.	Disappears by one year of age.
Pupillary	Pupils of the eye grow smaller in bright light, larger in dim light.	Protects the eyes against bright light; assists vision in dim light.	Lifelong.
Eyeblink	Blinking the eyes.	Protects the eyes from foreign objects and bright light.	As a reflex, it remains lifelong; voluntary blinking is gradually mastered in conjunction with the primitive reflex response.

In addition to their specific functions for physiological maintenance and survival, reflex behaviours pave the way for the development of voluntary behaviours and serve as their initial building blocks, according to Jean Piaget's (1970) theory (see Chapter 2). They also have value for the diagnosis of abnormalities of brain development. If reflexes are consistently absent, or unusually weak, during the early weeks of life, this can indicate brain impairment, as can the unexpected persistence of those non-survival reflexes that normally disappear by the age of six months (see Table 4.1).

Crying

Like the survival reflexes, an infant's crying may also assist well-being by drawing attention to the infant in distress. Peter Wolff (1969) recorded the cries of 18 newborns when they were still in the hospital. He found he could distinguish three different patterns of crying sound. He called the most common pattern the 'rhythmic' cry because it consisted of a steadily pulsating sequence of gasps and hollers. It was made before meals, but also in many other situations when the baby seemed uncomfortable or unhappy. Wolff labelled the second pattern the 'mad' cry because it was made when he frustrated the babies by repeatedly pulling a nipple out of their mouths. It sounded more shrill and turbulent and less regular than the rhythmic cry, to which it often reverted after some minutes. The third pattern, the 'pain' cry, was most specific of all, since in most babies' hospital experience it occurred only once – when their toes were pricked to draw a blood sample. This cry consisted of one long scream followed first by total silence and then by a gasping intake of breath.

Wolff followed his babies home from the hospital to see if mothers actually treated these different cries differently. He found that they did. The rhythmic cry

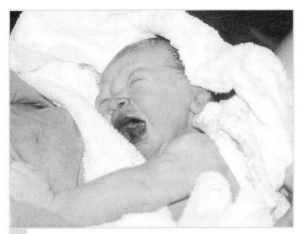
At birth, infants produce three distinctly different cries.

was allowed to go on for longer than the mad cry, whereas a mother's typical response to the pain cry was to drop everything and rush to the baby, looking anxious. (Needless to say, relief was mingled with annoyance when they discovered it was only a tape recording of the blood-sample cry which Wolff had played to test them.) This suggests that crying communicates more than just simple distress and, consequently, is an important early vehicle for the establishment of child–parent communication and the sensitive parental responsiveness to infants' needs that will facilitate the development of a bond of attachment between parent and child (see Chapter 5).

Common sense suggests that the crying reflex has evolutionary survival value as a call for help. But there is a problem with this theory. Most adults find the loud cries made by distressed babies aversive. Our instincts may therefore tend to avoidance rather than approach or soothing. In fact, Ann Murray (1979) found that parental reactions to crying include both an 'egotistical' and an 'altruistic' component, with

the former causing escape from the vicinity of the crying infant (or closing the door or plugging the ears), and only the altruistic component leading to concerned attention and efforts to comfort the baby. She argued that socialisation into parenting roles during childhood (e.g. through babysitting) and contact with easy-to-soothe infants as an adult could intensify the altruistic mode of response, whereas exposure to a disconsolate baby who refused to be comforted might foster egotism.

In support of this hypothesis, Ann Frodi and Michael Lamb (1980) found that mothers who had committed child abuse react differently from non-abusive mothers to videotapes of a crying five-month-old. The abusive women felt more annoyance (egotistical response) and less sympathy (altruistic response) than their non-abusive counterparts (Figure 4.1). They also showed more intense physiological changes in blood pressure and heartbeat than the non-abusers and, unlike these latter women, reacted with physiological upset even to a smiling baby. Frodi and Lamb suggested that the abusive women's egotistical response pattern was learned 'through transactions with children who, because of their temperament or their parents' incompetence, are difficult to care for' (p. 241).

Adult judges who were unacquainted with the infant to whose cries they were asked to listen were also found to react with more physiological stress and more self-reported aversion to the cries of infants who had been born prematurely or small-for-dates (see Chapter 3) than to the cries of full-term infants (Frodi & Lamb, 1978). This may help to explain why premature babies incur a higher risk of child abuse.

There are also important cross-cultural differences in caregivers' responsiveness to infant crying. Murray (1979) noted that parents in African hunter–gatherer cultures were more responsive to infants' cries than parents in developed Western countries. In fact, she reported that the average interval between the onset of crying and the caregiver's reaction was

In infancy, as in childhood, crying may evoke either sympathy or annoyance from a caregiver.

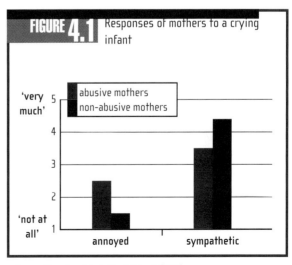

FIGURE 4.1 Responses of mothers to a crying infant

- abusive mothers
- non-abusive mothers

Source: Based on data in Frodi & Lamb (1980).

6 seconds among hunter–gatherers compared with an average of 3.83 minutes among middle-class mothers in Boston. She concluded that, for the infant in Western culture, 'an important lesson is how little effect his crying has on his caretakers' (p. 200).

Crying also follows a developmental timetable. By about two months of age, the infant's crying repertoire has broadened to include cries of annoyance (as when a toy the infant is playing with is snatched away); by eight months of age, babies display their awareness of the communicative function of crying by pausing during the crying cycle to check whether the caregiver is attending (Bruner, 1983b).

Soothing the crying infant

Cultures differ not only in the speed with which they respond to fretful infants but also in the methods they use to comfort them and encourage them to sleep. In Australia, Aboriginal mothers rocked their babies in hand cradles and sang them lullabies (Berndt & Berndt, 1964). Another technique used widely in tribal and pre-industrial cultures is swaddling. This entails wrapping the infant tightly in bands of cloth which stimulate the skin while restricting movement of the arms and legs. Lullabies and rocking are almost universal practices, even though the cradle may be anything from a bundle of sticks to a moving car.

A novel method of soothing babies was discovered by Lee Salk (1973). He played a tape of an adult's heartbeat loudly throughout the day and night in one newborn nursery ward and found that the babies in this ward cried less and gained more weight

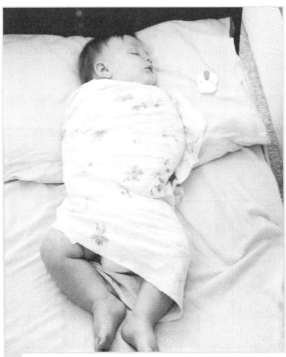

Traditional and modern methods of soothing each have their place. This infant has been swaddled, but also has a modern 'soother' (the dummy or pacifier) standing by.

over a four-day period than their counterparts in a quiet hospital nursery. Salk interpreted this result in terms of prenatal experience. He suggested that fetuses grow so accustomed to the continual pounding of their mother's heart while in the womb that they pine for the sound after birth. Thus he believed that he had diminished the fretfulness of his 'heartbeat' group simply by sparing them this particular source of postnatal anguish. Appealing as this explanation is, it does not account for why swaddling or lullabies are soothing, and it must be stretched even to explain the quieting influence of rocking since, while the heartbeat sound is continuous, the fetus is only rocked when the mother is moving about.

Yvonne Brackbill (1979) noticed that all methods of soothing, from swaddling bands to cradles and heartbeats, shared one common feature. They all involve intense steady stimulation to one of the baby's sense organs, such as the skin, the ears or the vestibular balance receptors. Perhaps the soothing comes about through the stimulating properties of the soothing practice, rather than as a result of any of its specific characteristics. To test this idea, Brackbill exposed infants aged three to four weeks to each of the following types of stimulation:

1. a steady 85-decibel noise
2. a 400-watt light
3. being swaddled
4. a 31°C temperature stimulus.

She found that all four of these intense forms of sensory input led to a decrease in the babies' crying, while increasing quiet sleep, as compared with an unstimulating 'control' condition. Also, even though no one stimulus was more soothing than any of the others, several stimuli together were more effective than any one alone. Sweetened pacifiers, gentle rocking and foot baths have also been shown to be more comforting to babies than the absence of stimulation (Birns, Blank & Bridger, 1966). In other words, unlike adults, who are kept awake by hot rooms, tight clothing, continual noise or bright lights, very young infants seem to be soothed into quiescence by all steady forms of stimulation.

In addition to being rocked and sung to more frequently than their Anglo-Australian counterparts, Aboriginal babies growing up in traditional bush communities also have more access to the soothing tactile sensations of close physical contact with the human body. Instead of being left alone on a blanket or in a cot, the Aboriginal infant under the age of six months is usually in contact with the warmth of human skin, even when asleep. Annette Hamilton (1981) conducted naturalistic observations (see Chapter 2) of wakeful and sleeping infants aged zero to six months at the Maningrida Aboriginal community in Arnhem Land and found that Aboriginal infants cried very little and were in tactile contact with a caregiver almost all the time (see Figure 4.2). Thus the stimulation of the mother's heartbeat,

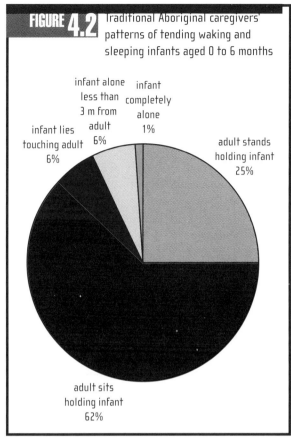

FIGURE 4.2 Traditional Aboriginal caregivers' patterns of tending waking and sleeping infants aged 0 to 6 months

infant alone less than 3 m from adult 6%

infant completely alone 1%

infant lies touching adult 6%

adult stands holding infant 25%

adult sits holding infant 62%

Source: Based on data in Hamilton (1981).

walking rhythms and body heat may have facilitated soothing.

The continuity of such traditional soothing techniques as rocking and cradling, lullabies or swaddling from generation to generation within the same culture suggests that parents learn some of their caregiving strategies by imitation or coaching from their elders. But when tradition fails, or when the new family is geographically out of touch with experienced older kinfolk, innovative parents may develop their own effective soothing strategies, such as a ride in a car or a tape of dance music, by a process of trial and error. The rewards of a calm baby and a quiet household are powerful incentives to parents to learn any methods that seem to work. This is likely to be beneficial for infant learning, too. Distressed babies in an uncomfortable physiological state are likely to have little spare energy to devote to the mastery of the complex challenges of motor coordination, perception, learning and thinking that set the stage for physical, intellectual and social growth through the rest of the lifespan. Thus, parents' skills in comforting and soothing are crucial for the baby's optimal psychological development, especially during the initial months of postnatal life.

Sleeping

For the first few months of life, a challenge that may occupy even more of the parents' thoughts and energy than dealing with crying is the task of trying to coax infants to sleep for longer stretches of time. In fact, although very young infants sleep for a longer total number of hours (about 16) per day than older infants, children or adults (see Figure 4.3), they tend to take their sleep in short naps of no more than two or three hours, rather than in larger chunks of time, even during the night. Some wakeful intervals between naps are punctuated with periods of quiet alertness, while others progress into excited crying. Nor are these sequences usually consistent, either from baby to baby or for the same baby from one day to the next. An example of one two-month-old infant's 24-hour sleeping, waking and crying cycle is shown in Figure 4.4.

Consequently, both because of the disruption to the household created by the infant's irregularity, and because of the need to attend to wakeful infants at repeated intervals when older family members would normally be asleep, one of the first lessons in manners which most parents attempt to instil when their babies come home from the hospital is the custom of sleeping steadily through a sizeable portion of the night. The elongation and stabilisation of the typical baby's feeding cycle after about six weeks may aid this process, but the socialisation of sleep is rarely accomplished with complete success during infancy. Sleep disturbances are some of the most common behaviour problems of childhood for which parents seek professional help (Roffwarg, Muzio & Dement, 1966). In addition, most parents are familiar with the minor stresses of bedtime: 'Why do I need a nap?' the toddler asks. 'Why do I have to go to bed so early?' asks the older child. 'You need your sleep,' the child's mother probably answers. But how much sleep is really needed? And what is it needed for?

Figure 4.3 shows the average total amount of sleep taken by normal individuals of various ages. As people grow older, the amount of sleep they need each night gradually declines. But among people of the same age there are also wide individual variations in the duration of nightly sleep without an alarm clock. Adult men seem to need slightly more sleep than women. Feeble-minded adults also sleep longer than normal adults. But perhaps the most striking evidence of individual variability came from a study of 783 Minnesota 2-year-olds, some of whom slept on average only 8 hours out of 24 (or no more than a typical adult) while others slept as many as 17 in every 24 hours (Smith, A., 1970).

Box 4.1 illustrates another common characteristic of certain phases in the sleep cycle of young infants – an active phase of moving around vigorously, breathing fast and making noise, while still deeply asleep. Louise's father suspected that his daughter was dreaming during this phase, and such a conjecture is consistent with research which shows that, when adults are awakened from a stage known as REM (for 'rapid-eye-movement') sleep (Luce & Segal, 1966), they report dreaming more often than when

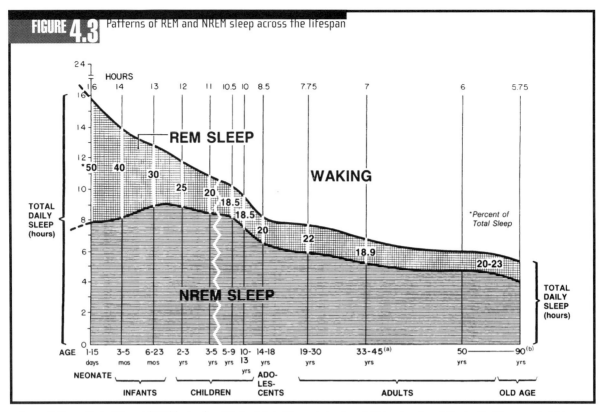

FIGURE 4.3 Patterns of REM and NREM sleep across the lifespan

Source: Roffwarg, Muzio & Dement (1966) (revised), p. 608. Reprinted with permission. Copyright American Association for the Advancement of Science.

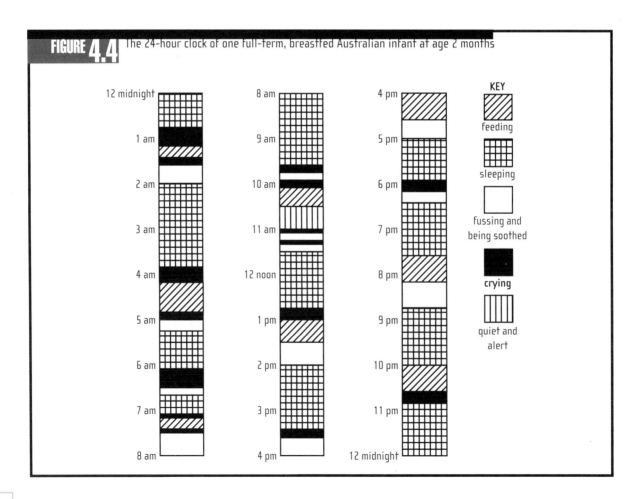

FIGURE 4.4 The 24-hour clock of one full-term, breastfed Australian infant at age 2 months

KEY

- feeding
- sleeping
- fussing and being soothed
- crying
- quiet and alert

A case in point
Pleasures and dreams at 10 months of age

Louise's father made the following entry in his diary as he reflected back over his only daughter's first 10 months of life. His observations illustrate several characteristically infantile behaviours – feeding, sleeping, making playful faces and making noise. In addition, this extract clearly illustrates the power of the infant's restricted repertoire of behaviours to command parental attention and affectionate responsiveness.

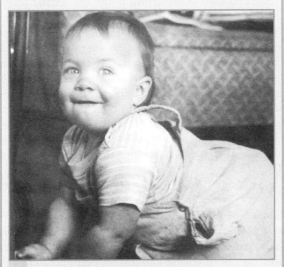

She hums when the vacuum cleaner hums.

29 January 1949. *Is Louise happy now? I don't know. She is not unhappy. She laughs a great deal – more, I believe, than most babies. She takes delight in any new article she gets hold of, and says, 'Hiss-s-s, hiss-s-s' over it. She enjoys imitating and being imitated. She hums when the vacuum cleaner hums, barks softly when Blackie barks, and she and I have a game we both get a big bang out of: a grimace that she invented, drawing back her lips with her mouth open as if she were ready to scream but is holding it back. I copied it and she recognised it on me. Now she does it expecting me to imitate her, and when I do it she imitates me. In moments like those I presume she's happy. But what of most of the time, when she's eating, standing up and sitting down in her play-pen as she does most of her waking time, going out in her buggy, bathing, sleeping? At night – right now for instance – she tosses a good deal, kicks the rails of her crib, and whimpers. I presume she's dreaming. Is she after something? Is she already dissatisfied with things as they are and looking forward to something better? She gets along very well with people: she likes them and smiles at them—unless she's either hungry or sleepy.*

© Peterson, 1974, p. 16, reproduced with permission

roused from the other type of sleep, NREM ('non-rapid-eye-movement') (Roffwarg, Muzio & Dement, 1966). Figure 4.3 shows the changes that occur over the life cycle in the balance of REM to NREM sleep. NREM sleep epitomises what most people expect sleep to be: a period of quiet rest and relaxation during which breathing slows down, the muscles of the body relax, the body's temperature cools and the electrical activity of the brain falls into a slow, synchronised pattern. By contrast, during REM sleep, not only do the eyelids flutter but the heart rate may speed up, bodily movements often occur and the brain's electrical activity resembles wakefulness, even though the sleeper is as difficult to arouse as during NREM sleep.

Lifespan changes in dreaming

Howard Roffwarg, Joseph Muzio and William Dement (1966) made the rather puzzling discovery, as shown in Figure 4.3, that young infants spend at least half their total sleep allotment in the REM state. For adults, the proportion is less than one-quarter. The difference seems paradoxical. If the REM electrophysiological state corresponds to dreaming, surely adults would have more use for it than newborns. Why should very young infants dream more than adults when they have had so much less wakeful life experience to dream about? According to Roffwarg and his colleagues, this paradox can be explained by the *autostimulation theory* of REM sleep. This theory holds that REM sleep serves the important developmental function of providing young infants with challenging mental stimulation. Just as spontaneous kicking by the fetus (see Chapter 3) is thought to pave the way for later locomotor control, it may be that REM sleep activates the nerve pathways and brain centres that will be used at later ages to process input from the outside world. This would explain why the ratio of REM to NREM sleep declines as babies mature. As they grow older, infants and children are able to gain mental stimulation from the outside world during their waking life activity.

In support of this theory, the results of studies in which very young infants were deprived of REM sleep (e.g. by being deliberately awakened every time they began to move into the REM stage; or naturalistic observations of infants who were kept awake by illness or the pain of circumcision) have shown a decreased proportion of REM sleep relative to NREM when the babies returned to their normal sleep cycles (Emde & Metcalf, 1970). By contrast, if adults are selectively deprived of REM sleep, it is REM sleep that subsequently increases, relative to NREM sleep, in compensation (Emde & Metcalf, 1970). If the function of REM sleep in the very young infant, unlike the adult, is mental stimulation, it makes sense that stressful experiences of enforced wakefulness would reduce the infant's need for REM sleep by providing a compensatory source of cognitive stimulation. Premature infants are found to spend a larger proportion of their total sleep in the REM stage than full-term infants do; this is also consistent with the autostimulation theory since the premature baby's less mature brain development at birth would make the mental stimulation to be achieved during REM sleep even more essential than for the full-term neonate (Halpern, Maclean & Baumeister, 1995).

Culture and infant sleep patterns

Given that the important physiological functions served by REM and NREM sleep are universal, it is no surprise that infants the world over spend roughly the same amount of time asleep during the period from birth to three months. Nor is it very surprising that there is strong cross-cultural uniformity in the proclivities of very young infants to take their sleep in bursts of two to three hours, rather than sleeping steadily through the night.

However, by the time babies reach the age of four to five months, parents are often able to encourage them to sleep for longer periods at a stretch, and to increase their proportion of nightly sleep, relative to sleep taken during the day. At this point, the influences of cultural beliefs (Goodnow, 2001) become more apparent. In many Western cultures, parents who are affluent enough to be able to afford separate sleeping quarters for each family member move their infant's cot out of the parental bedroom into a private room at this stage (Morelli, Rogoff, Oppenheim & Goldsmith, 1992). By contrast, Mayan mothers in rural Guatemala elect to keep their infants in the parental bed until the birth of their next baby. Even then, the move is generally to sharing a bed with a sibling on the grounds that close relationships among family members are fostered by sharing a bed (Morelli et al., 1992).

There are also important cross-cultural variations in the amount of effort parents elect to invest in the struggle to shift their baby's sleep cycle towards one long burst of nightly sleep (Super & Harkness, 1997). Research indicates that Anglo-Australian parents, like their counterparts in New Zealand and North America, tend to place a high premium on nightly sleep from as early an age as possible. They therefore tend to make strenuous efforts to coax their infants to remain awake for much of the day (apart from scheduled naps at prescribed times) and expect them, as a consequence, to remain asleep for up to eight hours at night with brief, semi-somnolent interruptions for feeding only. But in many countries in Western Europe, parents are less concerned about infants who have irregular sleep cycles, equal balances of daily and nightly sleep and no interval of sleep lasting more than four hours. These European parents report the anticipation that a shift to predominantly nightly sleep will occur naturally around the age of two years, without the need for parental intervention.

Studying Australian infants in Melbourne, Margot Prior and her colleagues (Prior, Garina, Sanson & Oberklaid, 1987) also discovered important ethnic differences in parental reports about their baby's sleep. Her sample of families included a rich melting pot of diverse cultural backgrounds. Though all the infants had been born in Melbourne, their parents came from all around the world (see Figure 4.5).

As the transition to longer periods of nightly sleep progresses, short daytime naps remain important.

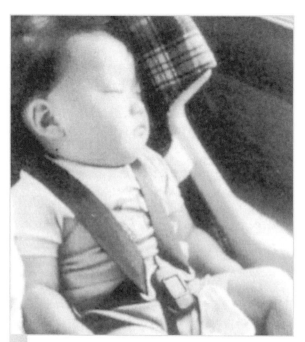

Parents use many methods to soothe fretful infants, but feelings of tenderness and relief when the baby falls quietly to sleep are universal.

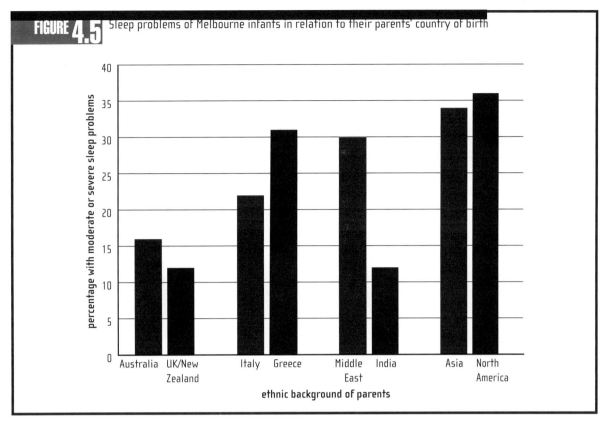

FIGURE 4.5 Sleep problems of Melbourne infants in relation to their parents' country of birth

Source: Based on data in Prior et al. (1987).

When she queried the parents about their infants' patterns of nightly sleep, and about the presence or absence of sleep disturbances, Prior found that parental nationality was a significant predictor of the pattern of responses she received. As shown in Figure 4.5, parents from Asia, North America, Greece and the Middle East were more likely to report that their infants had sleep problems than those from Australia, New Zealand, the UK and India.

Neurobiological and neurocognitive development in infancy

Growth of the brain

At birth the human brain is only about 25 per cent of its adult weight; by the end of infancy (for convenience, this can be marked by the second birthday) the brain will have increased to 80 per cent of the weight it will sustain throughout most of the rest of the lifespan. This rapid neurocognitive growth spurt during infancy is differentially distributed across different areas, structures and functioning of the brain (see Figure 4.6). At birth, subcortical structures are the most mature, whereas the cerebral cortex (the outer layers of brain tissue) has the most growing to do. Within the cortex itself, the frontal areas (see Figure 4.7) are less mature at birth than areas further back, explaining why mechanisms of voluntary self-control and deliberate self-regulation of reflex

BOX 4.2 How can you explain it?
Cot death: the mystery killer

Babies today have a much brighter developmental future than their counterparts just one century ago when infant mortality was substantially higher throughout the world than it is now. Yet even now, infant death has not been completely eradicated, even in affluent societies. Approximately one in every hundred neonates born today dies during infancy (Australian Bureau of Statistics, 2002). The leading killer of infants between the ages of 1 and 12 months is a mystery condition known as *sudden infant death syndrome* (SIDS), or 'cot death', which strikes apparently healthy infants without warning while they are asleep. SIDS is especially prevalent in Australia and New Zealand, relative to other Western nations with a similar standard of living (Hassall, 1987). In Australia at present, one in every 500 babies born will die of cot death before celebrating their first birthday. Despite extensive research, the cause of cot death is not yet fully understood. Each new wave of research into this perplexing condition seems to create more mysteries than it solves. Some of the most baffling results are identified in the following exercise.

Test your ingenuity: Can you think of an explanation that covers *all* (or even *some*) of these mysterious facts about cot death?

1. Aboriginal babies are three times more likely than Anglo-Australian infants to die of cot death.
2. Maori infants are twice as likely to die from cot death as Pakeha (Anglo) New Zealand infants.
3. The most common age for SIDS to occur is between 2 and 4 months after birth.
4. In surprising contrast to Maori infants, babies born to recent Polynesian immigrants to New Zealand incur a significantly lower risk of cot death than Pakehas. Despite their shared genetic ancestry, five times as many indigenous Maori infants as migrant Polynesian infants succumb to cot death.
5. SIDS is most frequent in boys, later-borns, low-birth-weight infants and the offspring of smokers or less educated mothers. But infants who fit into none of these categories are also vulnerable to cot death.
6. Cot death usually occurs when the baby is peacefully asleep and, in sharp contrast to death by suffocation at older ages, there are usually no signs that the victim struggled to regain breathing.
7. Cot death is more common in babies living at higher altitudes than at sea level.
8. Although about half the victims of cot death have mild colds at the time of their death, very few show symptoms of more serious illness.
9. The rate of cot death for the younger siblings of a baby who died from SIDS is no higher than among infants from similar families where no cot death has ever occurred.
10. Babies who sleep on their stomachs (prone) are more likely to suffer SIDS than babies who sleep on their backs (supine).
11. SIDS is more common in the winter months, and frequently, though not universally, parents report that the victim had heavy bedding, including lamb's wool rugs.
12. Parents who smoke even moderately (say 9 to 12 cigarettes a day) treble the risk that their infant will get SIDS.

Can you think of a theory of SIDS that fits these facts?

A possible explanation. While no theory of SIDS is yet definitive, one hypothesis links SIDS with infant brain development and the transfer of subcortical reflex response patterns to cortical control at 2 to 4 months of age, as noted earlier in this chapter. Possibly, if the brain's cerebral cortex is not mature enough to assume control of breathing during sleep, the normal mechanisms for sensing inadequate oxygen and triggering awakening, crying and changes in heart rate fail to click in, especially in an infant who is suffering respiratory distress due to illness or cigarette smoke. In addition, abnormalities in the arcuate nucleus of the brain may be involved, at least in a proportion of SIDS victims (Kinney, Filiano, Sleeper, Mandell, Valdes-Dapena & White, 1995).

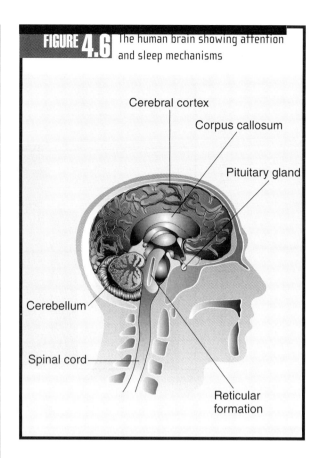

FIGURE 4.6 The human brain showing attention and sleep mechanisms

Cerebral cortex

Corpus callosum

Pituitary gland

Cerebellum

Spinal cord

Reticular formation

responses are not fully functional in infants under about four months of age.

Brain cells are of two basic types – neurons and glial cells. Both types are present at birth in almost their full complement and, within each neuron, the basic structures like axon, dendrites and cell nucleus (see Figure 4.8) are also mostly present in the brain at birth. The rapid prenatal spurt in neuron development described in Chapter 3 (see pages 92–3) is responsible for these developmental achievements. However, at birth the infant's neurocognitive systems do not yet function like an older child's. Over the first four months of life outside the womb, rapid growth in the dendrites and synaptic connections among brain cells combines with cortical maturation to enable the important changes in behaviour that occur at about four months. These include the capacity to control the neck muscles to support the head, enabling the infant to sit unsupported, to ride upright in strollers and car seats, to use a highchair and make other important strides in socialisation. The cortex also takes over voluntary control from lower brain centres and assists with the changes in reflexes, attention and sleep patterns that we examined earlier.

After the neonatal period, the dramatic gains in brain weight that occur throughout the rest of infancy are due primarily to (a) the growth in size of the already present neurons, (b) the addition of dendrites and axon terminals to form interconnections with one another, (c) the pruning of unwanted synapses to simplify the brain's 'wiring', and (d) the

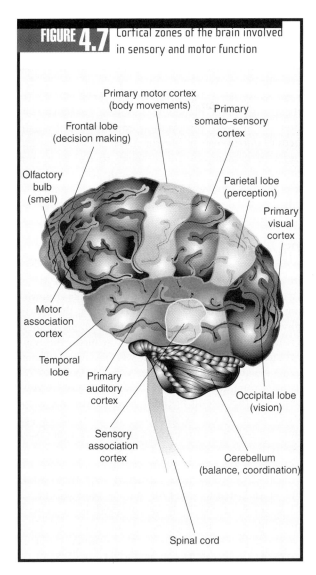

- Primary motor cortex (body movements)
- Frontal lobe (decision making)
- Primary somato–sensory cortex
- Olfactory bulb (smell)
- Parietal lobe (perception)
- Primary visual cortex
- Motor association cortex
- Temporal lobe
- Primary auditory cortex
- Occipital lobe (vision)
- Sensory association cortex
- Cerebellum (balance, coordination)
- Spinal cord

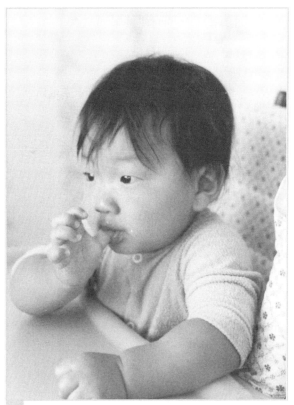

The motor skill of bringing the thumb up to the mouth to suck it involves coordinated activity in many areas of the brain.

myelinisation of neuron channels, pathways and modular interconnections.

Connecting neurons into networks

A basic brain cell, the *neuron*, consists of a cell body with a single cable (the axon) extending from the cell body in one or both directions, and a root-like web of transmitter connections at each end of the axon, known as dendrites, and terminal fibres (see Figure 4.8).

The axon terminals and dendrites develop and expand rapidly during infancy to create *synapses*, or connections between nerve cells, that enable messages to travel from one neuron to another. This dendritic growth and interconnecting of neurons with one another in dendritic arbours via the synapses contributes to the brain's weight gain. It also allows the brain to organise itself in response to stimulation received from the outside world.

Initially, as dendrites begin to form, they proliferate in a dramatic burst of growth known as *transient exuberance* (Nowakowski, 1987). To get an idea of the scale of this phenomenon, it has been estimated that an individual neuron might develop as many as 15 000 interconnections with other neurons (Thompson, 2000). The proliferation of neural connections allows the brain to construct pathways of information on the basis of all the stimulation and experience that infants gain in encounters with their physical and social worlds during the early months of life. Once the major pathways are laid out, transient exuberance is replaced by a phenomenon known as *synaptic pruning*. Unnecessary connections among the brain's neurons are discarded. In other words, the brain selectively prunes itself of unused neural pathways and connections, which simply shrink away and disappear. Consequently, by the age of three years, there are far fewer connections among neural networks in the brain than at the peak of transient exuberance around the second birthday. This is another instance where a process (loss of neural connections) that might initially appear to be a degenerative change (i.e. 'ageing', see Chapter 1) actually turns out to be a progressive developmental change.

It seems that a major purpose of the early neural proliferation of transient exuberance is to make the brain physically ready to receive the stimulating input of experience. Once the neural pathways that are necessary to transmit the kinds of information the infant encounters through experience have been mapped out, synaptic pruning is useful in order to streamline the brain's activities with maximum efficiency. For example, before the age of 12 months each skeletal muscle appears to have multiple synaptic connections

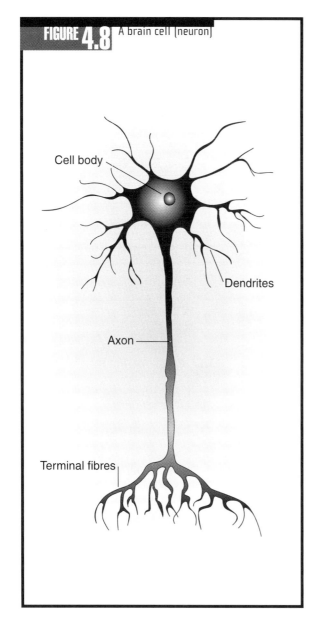

FIGURE 4.8 — A brain cell (neuron)

Cell body

Dendrites

Axon

Terminal fibres

Myelinisation

Another developmental process that contributes to efficient neural transmission is myelinisation, or the coating of the axon with an outer sheath made of a fatty substance called *myelin*. This substance speeds the transmission of neural impulses, enabling children to process information rapidly and to gain better control over motor functions. There is a rapid burst of myelinisation from birth to age four, and then a steady but slower increase up to adolescence. The process of myelinisation is governed by glial cells which, unlike neurons, continue to form throughout life (Tanner, 1990).

Physical growth during infancy

In addition to the important growth changes in the structure and functioning of the neural cells comprising the brain and central nervous system, the child's physical body also grows rapidly throughout infancy. From weighing about 3 kilograms at birth, the typical infant doubles in weight by four months and then gains weight at a gradual rate, as bones and muscles grow throughout the body, to weigh about 13 kilograms at the second birthday. Length also increases steadily, with babies gaining 2.5 centimetres per month on average for each of the first 12 months of postnatal life, reaching an average height of 85 centimetres by age two. In other words, by infancy's end, typical 2-year-olds have achieved half their adult height and roughly one-fifth of their adult weight.

Growth of the body is governed by a genetic timetable which unfolds itself in interaction with the environment's capacity to provide optimally nurturant conditions for growth, including adequate nutrition and freedom from disease. The directions of physical growth are *cephalocaudal* (head-to-feet) and *proximodistal* (from the centre outwards). The trunk grows more rapidly than the head. In fact, from birth to adulthood the head merely doubles in size whereas the trunk triples, the arms quadruple and the legs and

with different motor neurons in the spinal cord, but after synaptic pruning has occurred each muscle cell has only a single neural connection (Thompson, 2000). Neurons that are stimulated by input from the baby's motor activity establish new synapses and flourish. Those that are rarely or never stimulated die off. The same is true for neurons in other areas of the brain and nervous system that respond to perceptual, cognitive, emotional and social experiences.

An intriguing aspect of this process from a lifespan point of view is that the 12-month-old's brain is actually denser, with a richer set of synaptic interconnections, than the brain of an adolescent or a young adult. Yet the young adult is clearly superior in cognitive competence. This illustrates the fallacy of drawing any simple analogies between brain size and cognitive development or competency – a theme we return to in Chapters 14 and 16 when we examine decreases in adult brain mass in late adulthood and speculate on their possible cognitive correlates.

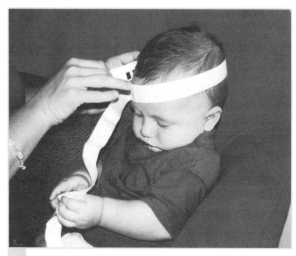

The child's brain and body both grow rapidly during infancy.

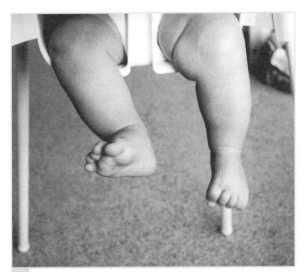

Voluntary motor control over the movement of the toes is a late acquisition.

When they studied the physical growth patterns of a group of Aboriginal Australian infants and young children who were growing up in a remote desert community in Western Australia, M. Gracey, H. Sullivan, V. Burke and D. Gracey found that the family's ownership of a television was a predictor of how fast their infants were gaining height and weight. As television sets are expensive, especially in a remote region where appliance transport costs alone are substantial, it seemed logical that affluent families who could afford a TV would also be able to provide their children with better nutrition through being able to afford to buy more food, including more varied and expensive grocery items. So the logic seemed to be that Aboriginal infants and children in television-owning families would display the best health and most rapid rates of physical growth.

However, the results showed just the opposite: Aboriginal families in the Kimberly region who owned a television had offspring with the most serious growth delays.

Activity suggestion. Before reading on in the text, try to think of two possible explanations for this unexpected finding. Write them down. Then, using the ideas about research strategy that were raised in Chapter 2, try to design a study that would allow you to gather data to test one of the explanations you came up with.

feet expand to five times their newborn dimensions. Motor skills also move down from the head to the feet and out from the centre to the periphery. Thus, babies acquire control over their neck muscles before the muscles of their chests, backs and shoulders. Control over movement of toes and fingers is gained last of all. (The growth of motor skills is examined in more detail later in this chapter.)

Cultural influences on physical growth: Aboriginal children

Within the parameters set down by these universal growth patterns, there is considerable room for individuality. As noted earlier, differences in the rate of growth among young infants have some genetic basis but also reflect the health, diet and quality of life to which the baby is exposed. In one study of Aboriginal children growing up in remote communities in the Kimberley region of Western Australia, poor rates of growth were a cause for serious concern (Gracey, Sullivan, Burke & Gracey, 1989). Aboriginal girls were found to weigh 1.1 kilograms less and to be 3.6 centimetres shorter than urban Anglo-Australian girls by the age of two, while Aboriginal boys weighed 1.5 kilograms less and were 4.5 centimetres shorter than their Anglo counterparts (see Figure 2.2).

Psychological factors may be as important to optimal infant growth as the family's physical health and economic well-being. In the Kimberley study, the family's balance of contact with Anglo-Australian society compared with traditional Aboriginal culture emerged as an important predictor of individual differences in Aboriginal infants' growth rates. The direction of the association between individual Aboriginal families' economic circumstances and the offsprings' degree of growth retardation was an intriguing and unexpected one, as noted in Box 4.3.

As described in Box 4.3, the results of the Kimberly growth study revealed poor rates of growth

in height and weight among Aboriginal children whose parents owned a television set, while babies who were being reared in Aboriginal households without a television set generally displayed near normal growth patterns. What is more, even though a healthy balanced diet and good food hygiene were positively associated with growth in these Aboriginal communities, the results of this study paradoxically showed that the family's ownership of a refrigerator was linked with infants' growth delay and frequent ill health. It seemed that the fridge was less a means of ensuring healthy nutrition in these desert Aboriginal homes than a symbol of cultural values.

Those families with stronger subjective ties to non-indigenous, mainstream Anglo-Australian culture may have expressed this both through refrigerator and television ownership and in their childrearing patterns. Conversely, families with a more strongly Aboriginal sense of cultural identification may have been helped by traditional knowledge of diet and nutrition, and/or by social support and advice from experienced members of their local Aboriginal community, to optimise their offspring's health and physical growth.

Along similar lines, it has been found that infants

being reared by impoverished mothers in Bangladesh and Brazil who had elected to reject traditional breastfeeding practices in favour of bottle-feeding had greater growth delays and poorer health than other infants from the same economically deprived circumstances whose mothers had chosen to adhere to their culture's tradition of breastfeeding (Cunningham, Jelliffe & Jelliffe, 1991).

The growth of beauty

Although a newborn may appear beautiful to doting parents and grandparents who rejoice in the child's birth, from a strictly objective standpoint most newborns are rather ugly. The head has often been twisted out of shape by passage through the birth canal and may be bald, bruised or unevenly matted with lanugo hair. With puffy eyes, receding chin, red skin, scrawny limbs and a pot belly, the newborn is likely to be described as beautiful only by parents blinded by love. However, the progress of normal growth after the neonatal period leads to radical changes in the baby's overall shape and facial appearance which promote a more conventionally attractive appearance. Again, individual variation is marked and striking differences between babies in degrees of 'cuteness' or physical beauty are evident throughout infancy. Cookie Stephan and Judith Langlois (1984) designed an experiment to test whether adults were prejudiced in favour of beautiful babies. They first collected a set of 193 photographs of Afro-American, Hispanic and Anglo-American babies. Infants posed for the photographs on three separate occasions – at birth, three months and nine months of age. Paid adult judges then rated each photograph on a series of physical and behavioural qualities that included their impressions of the baby's health, responsiveness, intelligence, affection for its mother, cheerfulness and so on.

The results showed that, even as newborns, some babies of each race were consistently perceived as more beautiful than others from the same racial background. But, in line with the changes outlined above in the proportions of facial features, infants in general were found to become cuter between birth and three months. After three months, as voluntary facial expressions like smiling came in, the judges became even better at making fine discriminations between beautiful, average and ugly babies. The 'beautiful is good' stereotype which characterises children's and adults' impressions of their peers (see Chapter 9) was also found to apply even to very young infants. The adult judges believed the babies from each racial group and age category whom they saw as most beautiful to also be the most intelligent, cheerful, socially responsive and physically healthy. These were the babies the judges thought their parents would love most, and the ones least likely to cause problems for their parents when they grew older. Average-looking babies earned intermediate scores on these behavioural dimensions, and unat-

tractive infants were viewed as dull, difficult trouble-makers. Figure 4.9 illustrates some of these relationships.

It would seem from these results that an infant who enters the world with the blend of features our culture perceives as attractive (many of which are shaped by heredity) has a distinct early advantage when it comes to both physical and social development. On the other hand, a genetic disposition towards unattractive physical features is likely to evoke its own, distinctively less favourable, rearing environment. This is yet another example of the interactive relationship between nature and nurture that we explored in detail in Chapter 3.

In a more recent study, Langlois, Roggman and Rieser-Danner (1990) found that babies are also responsive to physical attractiveness in adults. They used an experimental procedure in which the facial attractiveness of an adult experimenter was manipulated by having the adult put on either an attractive or an unattractive mask. One-year-old infants were given the opportunity to interact with the adult under both conditions. The results showed that the infants approached the attractively masked person more, played with that person for longer periods and expressed more positive vocalisations while doing so. The same preference for physical attractiveness also emerged when the infants were given a choice between two dolls to play with: one that had a classically pretty face and another that looked quite ugly. Infants more often chose the first doll, and played with it longer when the choice was made for them. While beauty may be 'only skin deep', it would seem that a bias in its favour emerges very early in the life-span.

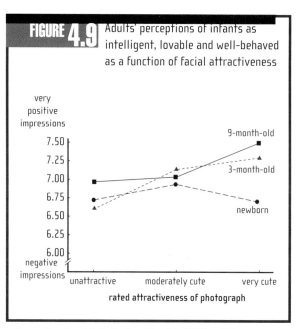

FIGURE 4.9 Adults' perceptions of infants as intelligent, lovable and well-behaved as a function of facial attractiveness

Source: Based on data in Stephan & Langlois (1984), p. 580.

The development of motor skills

Motor skills are the muscular and coordination abilities that enable children to move around, pick up things and generally control the positions and movements of their bodies. Several sophisticated motor skills are described in Box 4.4.

BOX 4.4 | A case in point
The motor skills of a one-year-old

According to her father's diary, at 13 months Louise was capable of a wide range of motorically skilled actions. He wrote:

28 April 1949. At 13 months Louise walks well, without holding on. She can't run or anything like that, but she can turn around in the middle of the room, stoop over and pick something off the floor, and only when she has to get somewhere in a very great hurry does she now drop to her hands and knees. She is into everything, knows how to open cupboard doors, even if they don't have handles—and most of ours don't. She enjoys pulling books off their shelves, pulling or tearing off the dust jackets, and throwing the books on the floor. In fact, she likes to throw practically anything she sees on the floor: her toys if they are not already there, my ties, my brush and comb, Peggy's combs, papers of all kinds (though in recent times she has been letting magazines alone; they were her major interest for a while). On the other hand, she likes to pick things off the floor as long as there is someone to hand them to. She enjoys going after her ball and she carefully carries it all the way back to be rolled or bounced away again. Somehow she just can't see the idea of rolling or bouncing it herself; it must be carried.

© Peterson, 1974, pp. 24–5, reproduced with permission

In this example, Louise at age one demonstrated motor skills that are quite typical of infants her age. She was walking independently (see Figure 2.3), though not yet able to run, and could bend over from a standing posture to retrieve an object. In addition, she had enough hand–eye coordination and fine motor skill to pick up objects, open cupboard doors, pull books out of bookshelves and retrieve a ball. The normative ages of development (see Chapter 2) for these and several other motor skills are shown in Table 4.2.

Nature versus nurture in motor skill development

Motor skills are also studied cross-culturally to compare the developmental progress of babies growing up in widely different environmental circumstances. These studies reveal important differences in the rate of motor skill mastery from one culture to another. For example, tribal babies in Uganda are found to take their first unaided steps at the precocious age of nine months (Geber & Dean, 1964) compared with an average of about 12 months for middle-class infants in London, Stockholm and Sydney (Hindley, Filliozat, Klackenberg, Nicolet-Meister & Sand, 1966; Jones, Hemphill & Meyers, 1973). Tribal Ugandan babies are similarly advanced in many other motor skills from an even earlier age. In fact, as newborns they resemble four- to six-week-old Western infants in their remarkable control of their heads and trunks, and in the relative absence of subcortical distress reflexes like the Moro reflex (see page 108).

Two different hypotheses have been put forward to account for cross-cultural differences like these. The first, known as the *maturation* theory, postulates a biologically ordained timetable of growth which unfolds without the need for specific intervention from the environment. According to this view,

At 13 months, Louise was into everything.

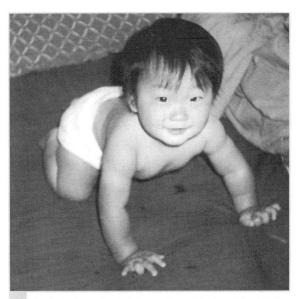

By developing locomotor skills for crawling and, later, walking, infants develop cognitively through exploration of hitherto inaccessible parts of their world.

TABLE 4.2 The sequence of motor skill development during infancy		
Motor skill	Average infant develops skill at	90% of healthy infants develop skill by
Lifts head to face forward when lying on stomach	3 months	4 months
Sits with support	4 months	5 months
Rolls over from stomach to back	4 months	6 months
Sits without support	6 months	7.8 months
Walks holding on	9 months	13 months
Walks alone well	12.5 months	14.3 months
Walks backwards	18 months	21.5 months
Kicks ball	20 months	24 months

Source: Bayley (1993); Frankenberg & Dodds (1967); Shirley (1933).

Ugandan babies walk early because they are genetically programmed to do so. The second hypothesis argues that *experience* regulates the speed with which babies master motor skills. Thus, Ugandan babies may learn to walk at a younger age than those in London or Sydney because they are carried around outdoors on their mother's back all day instead of being left lying in cots or pushed around in prams. Perhaps the former style of childminding enables Ugandan babies to practise holding themselves erect and making the leg movements prerequisite to walking. Or perhaps the stimulation of viewing the changing landscape while being carried, or the example of

While the experience of being upright may be beneficial, there is no evidence that coaching or training assists infants' learning to walk.

the slightly older tribal children who walk unaided, motivates them to strive for independent mobility.

Controlled experiments testing the heredity-driven maturation theory against the theory that experience (or practice) governs the development of motor skills have yielded contradictory and inconclusive results. Arnold Gesell (1940) studied a pair of twin girls. One was given specific instruction on how to position her body for stair-climbing, plus plenty of opportunities to try getting up and down stairs. But she developed the skill at exactly the same age as her sister who had been denied all access to staircases until the time of the crucial test. Gesell concluded that maturation alone was the operative factor. On the other hand, when Myrtle McGraw (1939) studied a different pair of twins from a similar middle-class background in the United States, she found that skills like swimming and roller-skating did not develop in the untutored control twin until the specific training that led to early emergence of these skills in the other twin were eventually given.

Marcella Ridenour (1982) also used a twin comparison method to contrast maturation with a newer kind of experience: the wheeled infant 'walker', which supports a baby in an upright position with feet on the floor while a table with casters provides balance and mobility. Many Australian and New Zealand parents put their infants into walkers like these from as early as four months of age, in the belief that the walker encourages the child to learn to walk early. But without a control group it is never possible to know whether walking skill would have matured in the baby at the same age, without the walker.

To test the theory that these mechanical walkers 'teach' babies to walk, Ridenour randomly assigned one member of each of 15 sets of twins to the use of a walker. This twin was required to spend at least one hour per day in the walker, beginning at the age of four months. The co-twin was not allowed to use the walker at all. When she compared the twin siblings with one another, Ridenour found no significant difference in age of first independent walking between the one who had used the walker and the one who had not. Across the group as a whole, these twins mastered walking at around the normative age of 12 months, suggesting no particular acceleration or delay as a result of being in the experiment. Maturation therefore seemed a better explanation than learning in this instance. However, the fact that only one very specific type of learning was assessed in this study does not rule out the possible contribution of other kinds of practice or motor learning to the growth of walking skill.

The combined research suggests, therefore, that to try to prove that motor development is due only to maturation or only to practice is as fruitless as trying to find behaviours that develop independently of heredity, or without influence from the environment (see Chapter 3). Instead, it now seems that both maturation and practice interact in the growth of almost all motor skills. Thus, even genetically ordained changes in the way nerve cells mature and interconnect can be influenced by specific experience: kittens reared in completely dark environments are found to develop fewer nerve connections in the visual part of the brain than their normal litter mates from light environments. Those kept in 'planetariums' (where the only visual stimulation consists of small bright spots in the ceiling) develop normal brain cells for registering points of light, but fail to acquire the cells that react specifically to lines or movement (Rose, 1973).

Culture and skill: Aboriginal infants' motor development

The image of an infant careering in a wheeled walker across the linoleum of a contemporary Australian or New Zealand suburban kitchen presents a sharp contrast to the experience of learning to walk in traditional Aboriginal culture. Like many other non-Western societies, Aboriginal infants in traditional communities in the remote regions of Australia are carried around for most of the day on someone's hip or back, for much of the time in a woven cradle or *buratya* (Hamilton, 1981). Does this lead to a faster rate of mastery of motor skills like walking than the urban Australian child's typically somewhat passive existence in a cot or pram? In fact, as we saw, one theory to explain Ugandan babies' mastery of walking some three months ahead of their counterparts in urban London, Sydney or Stockholm is the fact that Ugandan babies have a similar experience of being carried everywhere on their mother's back.

To test the possibility that being carried upright on a caregiver's body accelerates the acquisition of motor skills by Aboriginal infants, Annette Hamilton (1981) conducted a study among the tribal Anbarra Aborigines living at Maningrida in Arnhem Land.

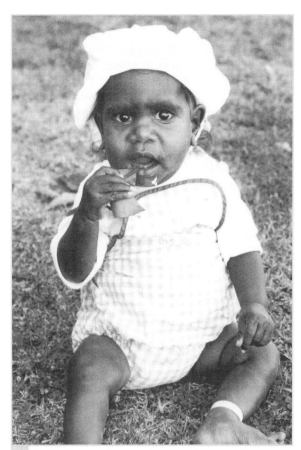

Aboriginal children learn to sit without support at an earlier age than their Anglo peers.

The average ages of acquisition of selected motor skills by the small group of Aboriginal babies that she followed longitudinally over their first year of life are shown in Figure 4.10. Hamilton's norms for Anglo-Australian infants are included for comparison. It would appear that Aboriginal babies in traditional communities resemble Ugandan infants in being motorically precocious relative to Anglo-Europeans. According to Hamilton, the traditional Aboriginal family's distinctive childrearing practices undoubtedly contributed to this effect. She noted that Aboriginal mothers and substitute caregivers actively encouraged the early development of motor skills. Given the outdoor lifestyle and cooperative group work, certain skills were of particular value in a traditional Aboriginal way of life. Independent walking was one such skill, since a mother burdened with an infant was less mobile on long journeys into the bush to gather food. So was the skill of remaining seated near the mother while she cooked. Hamilton noted that the Anbarra infants were propped into a sitting position on the lap from an early age, freeing the adult for working:

> While the European mother considers it obvious that a child with no spinal control should not be propped upright for long periods, the Anbarra mothers constantly pulled their 8-week-old babies into a sitting position, leaning the baby's back

against their crossed legs or nestling them into their laps. Frequently a mother would prop her baby in the sitting position, its trunk curled forward, and leave it momentarily unsupported until it was about to fall over. (p. 136)

Judith Kearins (1986) also studied traditional Aboriginal families, this time in remote Western Australian communities. She found that Aboriginal mothers typically carried their very young infants without offering head and neck support. Anglo-Australian mothers usually provide such support at least until the baby reaches 20 weeks of age. This difference in early experience is undoubtedly related to another aspect of the Aboriginal infant's precocity observed by Hamilton (1981) who noted that, from as early as six months of age, Aboriginal infants in Arnhem Land were capable of sitting unsupported on their mother's shoulders, clutching the mother's hair, throughout a 5-kilometre walk. Few Anglo-European infants would be capable of this degree of postural control before 12 months of age. The link with the mother's carrying practices suggests the relevance of nurture or practice, rather than simple maturation, to the growth of head and neck control.

Kearins also noted several additional differences between Aboriginal and Anglo mothers' infant care practices that could conceivably enhance Aboriginal infants' mastery of the cognitive and problem-solving skills discussed later in this chapter and again in Chapter 7. As Kearins explained:

Informal observations reveal other differences between the groups in ways which may be important to the development of cognitive habits. Many Aboriginal children of both traditional and non-traditional families, for instance, appear to enjoy greater permissiveness, become more socially skilled, more independent, better and earlier judges of their own physical capacities, and learn more to ignore the commands of another than White Australian children. They also seem to be treated as autonomous and competent decision-makers from infancy. These attributes of child-rearing mean that Aboriginal children have more freedom to learn for themselves than White Australian children (reared generally for greater dependence, compliance and obedience) and it is probable that such freedom leads to greater use of a visual learning strategy. (p. 211)

The development of sensation and perception

The five senses at birth

Through the five senses infants take in and process information about the outside world. As we saw in Chapter 3, sensory development begins even before birth. Consequently, the neonate has functional use of all five senses, as detailed in Table 4.3.

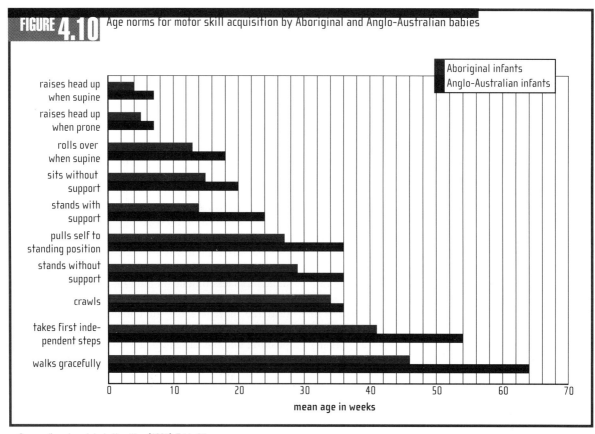

FIGURE 4.10 Age norms for motor skill acquisition by Aboriginal and Anglo-Australian babies

Aboriginal infants
Anglo-Australian infants

raises head up when supine
raises head up when prone
rolls over when supine
sits without support
stands with support
pulls self to standing position
stands without support
crawls
takes first independent steps
walks gracefully

mean age in weeks

Source: Based on data in Hamilton (1981), Table 21.

TABLE **4.3** The newborn's sensory capacities

Sensory system	Developmental status	Description/Evidence
Touch	Developed	Beginning during the embryonic period of prenatal development (see Chapter 3), reflex movement is evoked by touching the baby's skin. Thus it is no surprise that newborns respond sensitively to touch and pain.
Smell	Developed	Newborns have a highly acute sense of smell – by just 6 days old they can distinguish the smell of their own mother's milk from the smell of milk from a different nursing mother (MacFarlane, 1975).
Taste	Developed	Fetuses have a keen sense of taste, shown by their preference for swallowing amniotic fluid that is sweetened rather than plain. Taste is equally acute at birth, and preference for sweet flavours remains.
Hearing	Developed	Fetuses have acute hearing (see Chapter 3). Immediately after birth, auditory acuity often declines temporarily owing to fluid that enters the inner ear during the birth process. But at three days most infants are displaying acute hearing again, and by one month they display the capacity to distinguish fine sound contrasts such as *ba* versus *pa* (Eimas et al., 1971).
Vision	Developing	The newborn's retina and optic nerve have not yet fully developed, and the ability to turn their eyes and focus them has yet to mature. Thus vision is quite limited at birth and acuity does not reach the 20/20 level of a mature human until six months of age.

Development of vision and hearing during infancy

VISION

The ability to use the sense of sight to direct walking or crawling across a room, to retrieve small objects on the floor or to explore a magazine (see Box 4.4) represents the culmination of many months of development. At birth the baby's vision is seriously limited. The muscles that control eye movement are not yet under complete voluntary control, so the baby has trouble tracking moving objects or even keeping the two eyes oriented in the same direction. The ability to focus the lens is absent, causing anything at a distance of more than about 20 centimetres to appear blurry. In combination with a total lack of experience in looking at objects, these limitations imply that, though newborns are by no means blind, they see the environment in a different and much more limited way than older human beings.

The development of visual expertise is very rapid, however. Figure 4.11 shows the sequence of changes over the first six months in how infants come to view one of the sights they are most interested in: the human face.

Four-month-old infants can respond to configurations of relationships between the separate elements of a complex visual pattern (Bower, 1966). They have adult-like colour vision (Bornstein, 1976), move their eyes across patterns to scan their edges and middles (Cohen, DeLoache & Strauss, 1979) and look longer at complex shapes than at simple ones (Fantz & Fagan, 1975). By six months, size constancy enables the infant to give the correct interpretation to the apparent changes in the size of objects that occur when they are moved closer to, or further from, the eye (McKenzie, Tootell & Day, 1980). Depth perception likewise enables the eight-month-old baby to recognise a sheer drop before crawling over it (Gibson & Walk, 1961). Thus, by the first birthday, vision has become for practical purposes fully functional.

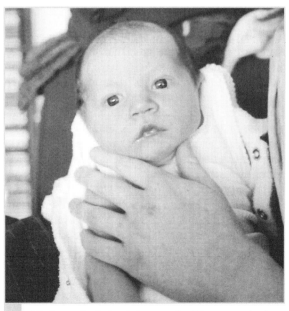

At birth, the muscles that control movements of the eye are not yet under voluntary control.

FIGURE 4.11 Developmental changes in face perception

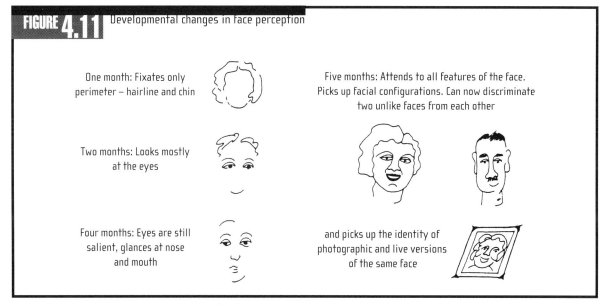

One month: Fixates only perimeter – hairline and chin

Two months: Looks mostly at the eyes

Four months: Eyes are still salient, glances at nose and mouth

Five months: Attends to all features of the face. Picks up facial configurations. Can now discriminate two unlike faces from each other

and picks up the identity of photographic and live versions of the same face

Source: Based on data in Cohen, DeLoache & Strauss (1979).

Charles Nelson and Kim Dolgin (1985) also studied infants' perceptions of faces. Using a paired-comparison procedure, they demonstrated that seven-month-olds could discriminate happy from fearful expressions on the faces of male and female models, provided that the infants were always allowed to become familiar with the happy face before the fearful expression was presented. Fearful faces, when shown separately, elicited longer looking times than happy ones. These differences suggest that babies' lesser familiarity in real life with faces contorted through fear may make it harder for them to recognise this emotion in photographs.

HEARING

Newborns can distinguish the human voice from other kinds of sound, but they are not good at making fine discriminations within a particular sound category. By six months, babies have mastered a range of sounds in the spectrum of a high-pitched human voice, but continue to have difficulty distinguishing among low-pitched sounds, including deep voices.

Because of infants' special interest in the sounds of the human voice, the baby's impressive early development of hearing emerges most clearly when a habituation task is used to test it. With this procedure, the baby is allowed to grow accustomed to a particular vocal sound pattern. Then a new sound is presented. If the baby reacts, his or her capacity to distinguish the old from the new is demonstrated. Habituation tasks for language perception often make use of phonemes, or the units of sound that convey meaning in language (such as syllables 'ta' and 'tee'). The results of habituation research clearly demonstrate acute perceptual ability. Even when only one month old, babies are capable of distinguishing between sounds as similar as /bah/, /pah/ and /dah/,

when spoken by the same high-pitched human voice. Because these auditory skills are closely bound up with the mastery of spoken language, we analyse this aspect of sensory development in more detail in Chapter 6.

Perceptual development

The word 'perception' describes the brain's organisation and interpretation of the vast quantity of information conveyed to it by the sense organs. *Perception* builds upon sensation but also entails coordination among sensory modalities to mentally interpret sensory experience. Eleanor Gibson (1989) argued that perception can best be understood within a framework 'in which the traditionally separated senses are considered to form part of a single "perceptual system" acting to extract the invariant, intermodal information that defines the physical world' (Crassini & Broerse, 1980, p. 145).

At what age does the baby begin to perceive the world in an integrated, coordinated way? Finding an answer to this question is made more difficult by the baby's limited repertoire of motor skills. However, researchers have come up with a number of innovative ways for overcoming these limitations and getting a glimpse of what the world looks and sounds like to a newborn baby. For example, Boris Crassini and Jack Broerse (1980) capitalised on the fact that even though motor coordination of the large muscle groups is underdeveloped in infants at birth, neonates are capable of turning their eyes in the direction of sounds they hear. This enables researchers to study perceptual coordination between the senses of vision and hearing by examining eye movements.

The sample of babies studied by Crassini and Broerse consisted of 32 healthy, full-term newborns in Brisbane. They ranged in age from 2 to 11 days at the time of taking part. The study began when they were lying on their backs in a testing chamber in a relaxed, alert state. The mother assisted the experimenter by steadying the infant's head at midline while a sound was played either to the baby's right ear or to the left. Video recordings of the infants' eye movements showed that the most frequent response to a sound was not to move the eyes at all. (This occurred on 61 per cent of the test trials.) But when the neonates did turn their eyes, they looked in the direction that the sound was coming from significantly more often than to the other side (25 per cent compared with 14 per cent). A signal detection analysis confirmed this evidence of perceptual coordination between the senses of vision and hearing as early as the first week of life.

In another research project, Jack Broerse, Carol Peltola and Boris Crassini (1983) studied coordination between auditory and visual channels of perception at a more advanced stage in infancy. They tested a sample of Queensland babies who were within six weeks of their first birthday. The infants were studied under three conditions:

1. *Auditory–visual coordination condition.* In this condition the infant was seated in a car seat inside a tiny room that looked something like a space capsule. There was a window at the front, and the mother looked through it and conversed with the infant through a microphone.
2. *Visual channel alone.* The microphone was turned off in this condition so that the infant inside the capsule could see the mother's face and lip movements, but could not hear her voice.
3. *Auditory channel alone.* In this condition, the microphone was on but the window was closed. Thus, the baby could hear the mother, but not see her.

The key assumption the researchers made was that the infants in all three conditions would attempt to relate these experiences in the laboratory to the knowledge of the world they had built up through perceptual learning at home over the first year of life. Thus, the babies' levels of emotional distress were compared across the three conditions on the grounds that an unfamiliar perceptual situation would prove more distressing than a familiar one. Broerse, Peltola and Crassini argued that, for an infant who is aware of the interdependency between visual and auditory information coming from the same source, conditions 2 and 3 present a paradox. In condition 2, a familiar face can be seen visually to be talking. Knowledge of the link between the visual and vocal channels of speech alerts the infant to the fact that the visible face should be making a sound. But no sound reaches the ears, presenting a dilemma for the baby. In condition 3, an infant with auditory–visual coordination would realise that conversation should similarly have a visibly moving face to go with auditory signals that indicate the person is talking.

The results of this study indicated that an awareness of perceptual interdependency is clearly present by the end of the first year of life. Significantly higher levels of distress were manifested by these Australian babies in the paradoxical situations of conditions 2 and 3 than during the predictable perceptual experiences of condition 1. And the paradox of a faceless voice (condition 3) distressed the babies more than the paradox of a voiceless face (condition 2). Possibly, at home, babies learn that mothers can contort their faces in mobile but soundless ways during games like 'Peek-a-boo', whereas a loudly audible voice generally implies the visible presence of a human speaker to go with it.

Coordinating perceptual and motor skills

Perception is an active process, one that both fosters and profits from the baby's own increasingly skilled motor activities (see pages 121–4). Infants need to use perception to negotiate locomotion and to pick things up. At the same time, by looking and feeling as they crawl or walk across a room, they gain perceptual input that would not be as readily accessible if they were being passively carried. Gradually, infants develop skills that enable them to coordinate sensory and perceptual domains cognitively; one-year-old Louise was clearly able to do so in several of her skilled actions, as described in Box 4.4.

When Jeff Field (1982) compared New Zealand adults with six-month-olds in a task that required turning the head to locate the source of a brief burst of sound, he found that the infants were quicker than the adults and equally accurate. Even more impressively, competent sensory coordination was demonstrated by a group of American five-month-olds who were shown two films of moving cars. When the sound track accompanying the films was the noise of an engine growing louder, the babies looked consistently at the approaching car. But when the noise of the engine on the sound track grew softer, they shifted their focus to the vehicle that was driving away. These selective patterns of looking showed not only that the babies could accurately perceive and comprehend visual and auditory distance and motion cues, but also that they knew how to match cues from the two modalities together in the appropriate way (Walker-Andrews & Lennon, 1985).

In Australia, Beryl McKenzie, Ross Day and E. Ihsen (1984) studied the ability of a group of 60 Melbourne infants to locate events in space. The infants were between the ages of six and eight months when they took part in the study. Using a laboratory-experimental procedure (see Chapter 2) in the setting shown in Figure 4.12, the researchers trained the infants to anticipate an interesting event (e.g. the experimenter popping up like a jack-in-the-box, smiling and waving an attractive toy). On different trials of the procedure, the baby was turned around so as to encounter the event from several different positions. Accuracy in localising the event was measured.

The results were impressive. They showed that

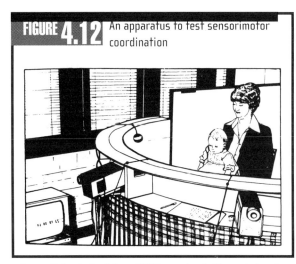

FIGURE 4.12 An apparatus to test sensorimotor coordination

Source: McKenzie, Day & Ihsen (1984), reproduced with permission of authors and the British Psychological Society.

most eight-month-old babies were able to pinpoint the interesting event with ease and precision, regardless of which way they were moved around. They seemed to have a mental map of the world outside their own body on which sights and sounds were consistently positioned, irrespective of their own location. Furthermore, even the six-month-olds were not as egocentric as Piaget's theory might have predicted. According to Piaget's theory of egocentrism (see Chapters 2 and 7), perceivers who are egocentric will imagine that sensory events can take only one form: the one they see, feel or hear. Thus, they cannot conceive of alternative perspectives from other vantage points. If the infants in the apparatus shown in Figure 4.12 were egocentric, they should have continued to look to their left to locate an object they had previously seen on the left, even after their own position had been rotated through 90°. But the six-month-old Australians were more sophisticated than this. They searched for the interesting display in the direction where it was really located, rather than in the orientation to their own eyes and ears that strict egocentrism would predict.

As babies grow older, they come to explore the world actively by crawling and, later, walking around it. Joan McComas and Jeff Field (1984) wondered whether infants' exposure to fixed landmarks while crawling independently facilitated their mastery of sensorimotor coordination between locomotion and vision or hearing. To test this possibility, they compared two groups of middle-class infants aged 9 to 10 months in Auckland, New Zealand. One group had been crawling independently for only two weeks at the time of being tested. The other group, while similar in age to the first, had learned to crawl much earlier and had at least eight weeks of independent crawling experience when they entered the study.

Infants were initially trained to expect an interesting event (a popping jack-in-the-box) at one of two windows. Landmark information was provided at the correct window. Then the babies were moved to the other end of the testing room where their view of the landmarks was at a 180° angle from the original. The test was whether the infants could now locate the event correctly. If crawling experience made a difference, the veteran eight-week crawlers should have succeeded more often than the novices who had been crawling for only two weeks. But no such difference emerged. The same number in each group (about half) located the event accurately on the first trial from the new vantage point. The researchers concluded that the ability to localise events in space in a non-egocentric manner develops relatively independently of the experience of being able to crawl.

Cognition and learning during infancy

'Infants are far more cunning than grown-up people are apt to suppose,' remarked Bertrand Russell in 1924. Recent research has repeatedly proved the truth of this assertion across a wide range of cognitive activities, including the learning of complex contingencies, the deliberate deployment of attention, reasoning about causality and other manifestations of *sensorimotor intelligence* (Piaget, 1970).

Learning complex contingencies

Human beings have a rudimentary ability to learn even before they are born, as was demonstrated in the studies of fetuses' reactions to familiar auditory stimuli that we examined in Chapter 3. At birth, even more sophisticated learning feats are possible, as was shown in a study of learned contingencies by E. Butterfield and G. Siperstein (1972). Studying very young infants, they used the sucking reflex in a contingent discrimination task. In this task, the baby was taught that sucking on a nipple brought a reward in the form of the chance to listen to a piece of soft music. Infants who were only two days old learned to suck reliably when their sucking turned the pleasant music on. When the contingency was reversed so that a suck instantly switched the music off, the babies learned to inhibit sucking, despite the reflex tendency to suck when an object is placed in the mouth (see page 108).

Hanus Papousek (1967, 1974) also developed a set of complex contingency learning problems which drew out several intriguing facets of the very young baby's sophisticated cognitive capacity. The first task taught infants to turn their heads for the reward of a taste of milk. Papousek found that two-month-old infants easily learned a rather complex discrimination. They had to turn in one direction when a bell rang and in the other direction to the sound of a buzzer. A subsequent complication challenged them still further. They now had to turn their head in the opposite direction from the one already mastered to receive the reward. Surprised at first, the infants responded with a burst of intense activity and soon learned to bring the milk reward under their own head-turning control once again.

A further variation in the procedure entailed the substitution of an array of flashing lights for the milk. Papousek (1974) found that four-month-old babies not only learned to turn their head left or right in order to turn on the lights, but they could even learn complicated sequences where a left turn had to be followed by a right turn to elicit the reward, or where only every second left or right turn was rewarded.

The fact that young infants could solve complex problems like these, remarkable in itself, was not the only thing that interested Papousek. He watched the babies after they had made an incorrect response. They became more alert, looked around, frowned, moved their limbs and sometimes fussed or cried. On the other hand, finding the correct solution was accompanied by signs of pleasure and relaxation. Papousek speculated: 'Sometimes we even had the impression that successful solving of the problem elicited more pleasure in the subject than did the reward' (1974, p. 576).

In other words, there was evidence that the babies' learning was motivated as much by curiosity (or a desire to discover reliable relationships between their own behaviour and outside happenings) as by a desire for the appetitive reward of a taste of milk or for the sensory pleasure of brightly flashing lights. In fact, Papousek found that the lights tended to lose their appeal after the baby had learned to make them come on at will. But if the problem contingency was changed once the babies showed signs of boredom, their interest was apt to perk up again. This desire to learn new things, first evident in early infancy, will prove an asset to cognitive development through the lifespan, provided appropriate learning experiences continue to be provided (see sections on 'learned helplessness' later in this chapter).

Curiosity and attention

The infants tested in the complex contingency experiments were curious. Why else would they have worked so hard to obtain tiny tastes of milk, to hear a melody or turn on a pattern of lights? They also seemed prone to boredom, since they stopped working once the solution to a problem had become obvious. In life outside the laboratory, the same delicate interplay between boredom and curiosity governs what infants pay attention to and, hence, what they learn about and what further mental abilities they develop. The diary entry in Box 4.5 shows one instance of this interplay when Louise was 16 months old.

BOX 4.5 The world of a 16-month-old

When she was sixteen months old, Louise's father wrote:

29 July 1949. *I find it hard to imagine what Louise's world must be like. Simple, surely. When Peggy carried her into the house this evening, still sleeping, I slammed the car door and she woke enough to say 'Dot'. To her I and an automobile exist together; when she sees a picture of a car or hears a horn blow she associates it with me. Her world has a small radius. Things far away are uninteresting to her, yet the tiniest picture close at hand of a dog, a 'pony', or something else she recognizes will at once claim her attention. She delights in the familiar, perhaps because it is relaxing in a world so full of the unfamiliar. She enjoys doing or saying the same things over and over, though when it comes to toys, nothing pleases her more than a new one. What's more, she will know immediately at the first brief glimpse that it is new, that she has not had it before*

© Peterson, 1974, p. 61, reproduced with permission

Infants are curious about the interesting sights and sounds around them. The desire to explore and understand motivates learning and thinking.

At the age of 16 months, Louise delighted in doing and saying the same things over and over.

Each age has its attention-getting stimuli. Louise's father was surprised by Louise's lack of attention to things far away, and by her interest in familiar pictures and oft-repeated sayings which most adults would find rather boring. On the other hand, the attention of Papousek's four-month-olds was captivated by simple blinking lights, which 16-month-olds like Louise would undoubtedly find rather dull. The typical six-month-old is eager to attend to a lively conversation or a smiling face. A mechanical rabbit can hold the attention of a toddler, as can a comic strip that of a school-aged child. In short, attention preferences change with age. Even during adulthood the changes in attention preferences continue. Thus in one study young adults showed a greater proclivity to attend to fantasy dramas on television than did older men and women. The latter group paid correspondingly more attention to science shows and current affairs broadcasts (Riley & Foner, 1968). In other words, as attention patterns change, so does the focus of cognitive activity, through the lifespan.

Jerome Kagan (1976) has suggested that one factor underlying developmental changes in attention preferences is 'optimal schema discrepancy'. By attending to something repeatedly, the individual develops a mental image or 'schema' of it. Once the schema has been built up, attention to the object is no longer necessary and boredom sets in. But if some minor change in the object then arises, curiosity is piqued again and attention is mobilised until these new features become incorporated into the old schema. Major changes sometimes capture attention too, but if they are too drastic they may be ignored, either because fear is evoked instead (e.g. by the distorted faces in monster movies) or for lack of a schema to relate them to (e.g. when a book filled with mathematical formulas fails to interest a person who has never studied higher mathematics). The activity in Box 4.6 illustrates this.

Kagan (1970) tested this theory of schema discrepancy by asking a group of mothers to show a simple mobile to their infants every day for three weeks. Then, in the laboratory, the babies were shown a mobile that was either identical to, similar to, or very different from, the mobile they had seen at home. Kagan measured the amount of time each baby spent attending to the laboratory mobile. He found that the mobile that was somewhat like the one at home (rather than being either identical to it or very different from it) was the one that received the longest attention. He concluded that the infants had formed a schema of their home mobile and that the laboratory mobiles proved most captivating when they were similar enough to be related to this earlier schema but different enough to demand slight cognitive modification.

Piaget's Sensorimotor Stage

Jean Piaget identified the infancy period as the stage of sensorimotor development, the first step in his

BOX 4.6 **Activity suggestion**
Grabbing attention over the lifespan

At which of the pictures in each pair did you look longest when you first turned to this page?

Estimate the time you spent on each picture and record it in the space provided. Then, if you have children in your range of personal acquaintances who would enjoy doing the task, repeat the procedure, estimating their looking times by monitoring their eye movements with a stopwatch.

Interpretation: Drawings (a) and (c) are apt to be only slightly attention-getting to most adults because they depict familiar objects for which schemas are well established. Drawings (b) and (d) should hold the attention longer because they involve novel distortions of familiar objects, thereby provoking schema discrepancy. For young children, the differences may be less marked, owing to less familiarity with the standard items.

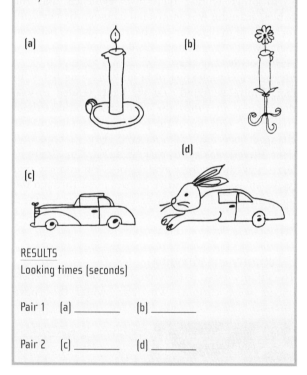

RESULTS
Looking times (seconds)

Pair 1   (a) _____   (b) _____

Pair 2   (c) _____   (d) _____

four-stage theory of cognitive development (see Chapters 2 and 7). Piaget (1970) conceptualised infant mental development as a process of building up mental schemata through *assimilation*, or altering existing ideas to make them consistent with new information through *accommodation*. During the sensorimotor stage, this cognitive growth takes place exclusively on the plane of motor action and direct perception but, at this level, becomes quite sophisticated by infancy's end. Piaget proposed six discrete steps, or substages, in the growth of sensorimotor intelligence, as shown in Table 4.4.

TABLE 4.4	Six substages in the growth of sensorimotor intelligence	
Substage	Age	Description
1	Birth to 1 month	**Reflex reactions**
2	1 to 4 months	**Primary circular reactions:** Infants adapt reflex schemas to new situations (e.g. by sucking a toy differently from the mother's breast).
3	4 to 8 months	**Secondary circular reactions:** Repeating and extending actions that produce interesting changes in the perceptible world.
4	8 to 12 months	**Coordinating secondary circular reactions:** Combining schemas purposefully.
5	12 to 18 months	**Tertiary circular reactions:** Active means–ends experimentation and cause–effect concepts.
6	18 to 24 months	**Beginnings of symbolic representation:** Using a symbol to stand for, or represent, something else (e.g. opening the mouth to represent the opening of a matchbox).

The concept of object permanence

Piaget (1970) suggested that one conceptual change, occupying the whole of the sensorimotor period, was so important as to bring about a 'veritable Copernican revolution' (p. 705) in the baby's mind. This is the concept of *object permanence*. Before this revolutionary discovery infants are, according to Piaget, complete adherents to the adage that 'out of sight is out of mind'. Once they lose sensory contact with an object very young infants behave as though the object has ceased to exist. Piaget described one such instance involving his eight-month-old daughter Jacqueline: as she was about to reach for a toy duck, Piaget threw a sheet over it. She immediately withdrew her hand. Even when Piaget took hold of her hand and made her feel the duck through the sheet, she made no attempt to reach for it, though she could easily have done so.

Piaget first observed the next stage in the development of the object concept when his 13-month-old nephew, Gerard, paid him a visit and began rolling a

Infants of 12 months have a peculiar way of searching for hidden objects; they seem to believe a missing item will be found in a previous hiding place, even when this does not happen to be the spot where the object was seen to disappear.

ball. It went under an armchair and Gerard immediately dropped to his hands and knees and, with some difficulty, retrieved it. Later, the ball rolled under a sofa, too low to crawl under. After watching this disappearance, Gerard returned to the armchair and carefully explored the place where the ball had been found before. Consistently, infants of approximately 12 to 18 months will search for hidden objects in this peculiar way. They act as if hidden objects do still exist but can only be located in places where they were found before, rather than where they were seen to disappear. Piaget's explanation was that children at this stage could not fully separate objects from actions and locations. Thus, for Gerard, the ball that could be retrieved was conceived as the 'ball-under-the-armchair', which was not quite the same as the 'difficult-to-retrieve-ball' resting under the sofa.

In the next stage, beginning at around 18 months, searching is still limited. Having overcome the tendency to hunt in formerly fruitful hiding places, the child will now only explore the place where the object vanished, seeming unable to conceive that objects may shift location while out of sight. Children at this stage are perfect dupes for the simple trick of hiding a coin in one hand and then switching it to the other behind one's back. The child will persistently search in the hand in which the coin was first hidden, unable to imagine its being anywhere else. Eventually, the child learns that invisible objects not only continue to exist but may also be moved while out of sight. Having attained this level of development, Jacqueline Piaget, perhaps in reaction to her father's persistent experiments, contemptuously refused to search in 'obvious' hiding places like a closed fist, and could cope with any number of invisible displacements.

Investigations of larger samples of babies from a wider range of backgrounds than Piaget's own family, using standardised testing procedures, have provided impressive support for his delineation of the sequence of steps in the growth of object permanence (Escalona & Corman, 1967; Gratch & Landers,

1971). Table 4.5 illustrates this sequence. A similar sequence also characterises the development of infants' understanding of the permanence and uniqueness of their mothers, though babies with secure attachments to the mother (see Chapter 5) develop this concept of human constancy (called *person permanence*) slightly before object permanence (Bell, 1970; Bower, 1974).

The concept of causality

Piaget also followed infants' development of a practical understanding of causality through the six substages of sensorimotor development (see Table 4.4). In substage 1, before the age of three months, infants' thoughts about cause and effect are governed by a kind of 'causal anarchy' in which no recognition of any cause–effect relationship is apparent. But, between three and four months of age, Piaget noticed that each of his babies in turn began to use a very simple causal rule which he called the *secondary circular reaction*. The infants continually repeated actions which had produced interesting outcomes in the past, suggesting that they saw a predictable connection between what they did and what subsequently happened. Thus three-month-old Laurent, who had a chain of rattles hanging over his crib, would glance up at the rattles before pulling the chain. He seemed to anticipate the sound they were about to make and to connect it with his own action of pulling. Papousek's experiments (see pages 128–9) likewise indicated a basic grasp of the causal connection between head-turning (cause) and the lights flashing (effect).

Causality at the stage of the secondary circular

reaction is nonetheless limited. Unaware of the need for a physical or spatial connection between a cause and its consequences, infants will kick to move the moon as readily as to shake a blanket or a string of beads on their pram. They also seem relatively insensitive to causes located outside their own bodies. As Piaget put it:

> ... the child's whole behaviour seems to indicate that at the time the interesting sight is interrupted he has recourse to a single causal agent only – his own activity. (1952b, p. 247)

This special sensitivity to the potential causal significance of our own actions is not unique to babies. Even adults may resort to belief in superstitious contingencies when the emotional stakes are high. For example, a person might carry an umbrella to attempt to cause clear weather, or avoid the number 13 for fear of bad luck. There is, however, a difference from the infant's secondary circular reaction: adults who cross their fingers over a bet at the races know that they are being 'irrational', whereas the infant does not yet understand the rudiments of physical causality.

By about age one, all three of Piaget's children had acquired a rather mature practical understanding of physical causality. They were aware of causes that originated outside their own body, and they limited the search for potential causes only to those events that were closely associated in both space and time. Through repeated practice, they had learned that sticks had to touch objects in order to move them, that a string had to be attached to a toy before it was worthwhile trying to tug on it, and that an empty cup was not as much fun to tip over as a full one. They had also learned to infer a cause after viewing only its effect, and to anticipate effects when only the causes had been seen. Thus, when his son was 13 months old, Piaget recorded the following observation:

> Laurent is seated in his carriage and I am on a chair beside him. While reading and without seeming to pay any attention to him, I put my foot under the carriage and moved it slowly. Without hesitation Laurent leans over the edge and looks for the cause in the direction of the wheels. As soon as he perceives the position of my foot he is satisfied and smiles. (1952b, p. 296)

It is important to note that this seemingly sophisticated grasp of causality at an intuitive level, while representing an important advance over the secondary circular reaction, still entails one very important limitation: babies cannot discuss or cognitively reflect on the causal rules that appear to govern their practical activities. In fact, according to Piaget, the acquisition at a conscious verbal level of the same sophisticated understanding of causality that is mastered in practical terms during infancy will occupy the remainder of childhood (see Chapter 7) and may not be completed by adolescence (see Chapter 11) or even adulthood (see Chapters 11 and 16).

TABLE 4.5 Steps in the growth of the concept of object permanence	
Infant's age	Search behaviour
Less than 6 months	'Out of sight' is 'out of mind': no search for a covered object once it has been hidden.
8 to 13 months	'A-but-not-B' searching: the infant will search for a hidden object in a place where it was previously found, rather than at the spot where it was seen to disappear.
13 to 18 months	No concept of invisible displacement, but effective searching strategies at the locus of disappearance.
18 to 24 months	Fully-fledged object permanence: invisible displacements can be tracked in the imagination, enabling effective retrieval.

Personality, emotion and cognition

The many examples of skilled cognitive performance described in earlier sections of this chapter testify eloquently to the versatility of the human mind as early as the first year of life. However, while infants are remarkably skilled thinkers in many ways, their competence is also quite fragile. Skills displayed in one situation may fail to generalise to other seemingly equivalent tasks. Skilled action is also liable to deteriorate seriously when feedback about the influence of one's own actions upon the outside environment is withheld. Thus, the motivation for learning is another crucial factor in the rapid developmental gains in learning, cognition and problem-solving that we have just examined. Four factors are especially important for fostering the motivation to explore and make sense of the physical and social world. These are:

1. A sense of basic trust
2. The development of a sense of personal control over events in the environment
3. Escaping the problem of learned helplessness
4. Developing a sense of self-efficacy.

Gaining trust

In Erik Erikson's theory of personality (see Chapter 2), the most important developmental achievement of infancy is the acquisition of a realistic sense of trust. Erikson defined the mature hope or trust that grows out of a dialectical contradiction between blind infantile gullibility and instinctive mistrust as follows:

> A basic sense of trust means both that the child has learned to rely on his (or her) caregivers to be there when they are needed, and to consider himself trustworthy … Out of the conflict between trust and mistrust the infant develops hope, which is the earliest form of what gradually becomes faith in adults. (1983, p. 27)

Thus a realistic sense of trust represents a balance between irrational optimism and utterly unshakable pessimism. A blindly trusting infant who indiscriminately has confidence in everything and everybody is clearly ill-equipped for dealing with a world fraught with the physical hazards of roads, cliffs and poisons, not to mention the possibility of human hostility and aggression. On the other hand, an infant who grows up totally devoid of faith in anything has no basis for believing in the future or for valuing human relationships, or even life itself. Basic trust, as an intermediate, dialectical resolution of these two extremes (see Chapter 2), consists of the enduring belief that the social world is benign and reliable enough that our basic wishes and needs will ultimately prove to be attainable, despite setbacks and disappointments, and some untrustworthy elements.

According to Erikson, clear contingencies in the physical environment and, especially, in the baby's social relationship with the mother or primary caregiver serve as joint cornerstones for the development of basic trust. By learning to anticipate the consequences of their own acts on objects, babies begin to acquire trust in the outside world. The social contingencies of parental care are likewise capable of teaching the baby to have faith in the reliability and goodwill of people in general. As Erikson explained:

> The newborn infant's more or less coordinated readiness to incorporate by mouth and through the senses meets the mother's and the society's more or less coordinated readiness to feed him and to stimulate his awareness. The mother must represent to the child an almost somatic conviction that she (his first 'world') is trustworthy enough to satisfy and to regulate his needs. But the infant's demeanor also inspires hope in adults and makes them wish to give hope; it awakens in them a strength which they, in turn, are ready and needful to have confirmed in the experience of care. This is the ontogenetic basis of hope, that first and basic strength which gives man a semblance of instinctive certainty in his social ecology. (1968a, pp. 287–8)

Developing a sense of personal control

L. Alan Sroufe (1983) described the positive emotions that arise when an infant gains cognitive control over the environment. One five-month-old he was studying was inclined to burst into exuberant laughter whenever the caregiver made loud clucking sounds while face to face with the baby. But when the identical sounds were made from behind, the baby grew distressed. Evidently, in the face-to-face condition, the adult's expression taught the infant to anticipate the sound. Another infant showed signs of fear the first time his mother wore a mask. But as she continued to put the mask on and take it off, the changes to her face became predictable and the baby's fear turned into delight. Sroufe explained these findings as indicating the strength of the infant's emotional investment in being able to trust and predict events. When an occurrence matches the infant's mental anticipation of it, delight arises. But a sense of not

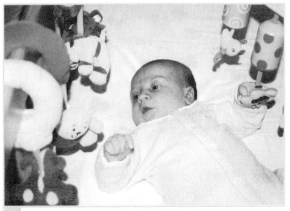

By learning the contingency between striking a mobile and its movement and sound, infants begin to gain a sense of personal control over their environment.

being able to control, or even anticipate, what will happen next produces distress. As Sroufe explained:

> The tendency to impose order on experience is ever present. When order can be attained from novelty, incongruity, or uncertainty, or through mastery or repetition, there is positive affect. When the orderly flow of cognition or behavior is inalterably interrupted, there is negative affect. (p. 467)

Learned helplessness

A richly stimulating home environment stocked with toys and other objects providing learnable contingencies, coupled with a trust-engendering social environment in which the infant's signals evoke parental responses, jointly form the basis for the rapid advances in learning which make the period from birth to age two such an exciting and crucial one. As noted earlier, babies are curious about the world. They seek causal connections between their own actions and important outside events. Once they discover that such connections do exist, they experience the double pleasures of new knowledge plus a stronger sense of their own personal efficacy. Armed with the concepts and schemas which successful learning provides, they are set to tackle more advanced and difficult problems. At the same time, the emotional stability provided by basic trust in their caregivers combines with infants' curiosity and growing confidence in themselves as successful learners to make the seeking of solutions to problems enjoyable in itself. Thus each new cognitive and emotional achievement motivates striving for further mastery.

What would happen to a baby whose world was

Learning to manipulate and control a toy rabbit may confer feelings of self-efficacy and personal control.

not built around the kind of causal connections that infants so readily attend to and are eager to learn about? What if the child's actions had no influence at all on interesting people or enjoyable events in the environment? Under circumstances where the possibility of exerting control over fate is totally lacking, would babies instead learn how not to learn?

Undoubtedly they would, according to the results of a study that exposed very young babies to one of three different kinds of toy (Watson, 1971). The infants in the first group had a responsive mobile hung over their cots. They could make this object move in a variety of interesting ways by turning their heads. The second group had a stationary display which was like the first group's mobile except that it never moved. The third group was the crucial one. Their mobile moved, but on a purely random basis – no action by the baby in the cot bore any consistent relationship to any aspect of the toy's motion.

After enough time to become familiar with their respective playthings at home, the babies were brought into the laboratory for a learning trial. They were placed in a cot with a different mobile which (like the first group's home one) could be controlled by the infant's own movements. The measure was how quickly the babies mastered the task of bringing the motion of the laboratory mobile under their own voluntary control. Infants in the first two groups learned to do so with ease. Furthermore, although the second group had had no prior experience of successfully solving a similar problem at home, their rate of learning was not noticeably inferior to the first group's.

The babies from the third group were the ones who seemed handicapped. They proved unable to master this relatively simple learning problem. Even some six weeks later, a learning deficit continued to impair the progress of babies who had been exposed initially to the uncontrollable mobile. It seemed that the frustration of their early efforts to find a way of manipulating this perverse toy had led to a generalised state of helplessness, at least as far as mobiles were concerned. What they seemed to have learned was that this category of problem was totally 'unlearnable', or else not worth the effort of trying. This produced a sense of *learned helplessness*. Fortunately, in this case, the problem was limited to a very specific kind of toy. But, if infants develop a pervasive sense that *all* contingencies in their environments are beyond their personal power to control, active interventions to develop feelings of self-efficacy may be needed, as explained below.

Developing self-efficacy

Albert Bandura (1989, see Chapter 2) coined the term *self-efficacy* to describe an individual's expectation of competency in any given situation. As he explained, the motivation to learn is enhanced when a person anticipates being capable. The same is true of young babies. But experiences early in life can teach an opposite lesson – that one's own efforts to learn are unavailing. When this happens, motivation for learning in general may be undermined. A bleak stimulus-free cot or room is another obvious example of such an unfortunate situation. But even a play-room stocked with toys could conceivably engender helplessness if all the objects happened to be too intricate to manipulate, too heavy to move or too random and unpredictable in their actions for an infant to be able to gain control over them.

Conversely, the provision of controllable toys is likely to be an enjoyable way to exercise the baby's mind and foster feelings of self-efficacy. Indeed, toys (like rattles) that afford the pleasure of sensory stimulation in direct response to the baby's actions are universal favourites. Furthermore, such toys may assist the development of emotional well-being as well as cognitive growth. Megan Gunnar-Vongnechten (1978) found that 12- to 13-month-old boys, who were initially frightened by a mechanical rabbit, changed to playing with it happily when she taught them how to operate the switch controlling the toy's movements. According to Bandura's theory, their motivation to learn about other toys and mechanical objects should similarly have increased as a result of gains in feelings of self-efficacy arising from learning to control the switch.

Throughout the remainder of the lifespan similar strategies are effective for boosting efficacy and the desire to learn. A sense of self-efficacy in getting the world to respond to our efforts to influence or control it is a powerful weapon against learned helplessness at all ages. In Chapter 9 we explore self-efficacy in the primary school classroom, and in Chapter 17 we see how the ability to exert control shapes not only the health but the sheer survival of elderly nursing home residents.

Chapter summary

This chapter examines the developing sensory, motor, perceptual, emotional, social, neurobiological and cognitive capacities of infants over the first 18 months of life.

From the moment of birth, infants are remarkably competent human beings. With a repertoire of inborn reflex behaviours that equip them to survive independently in the world outside the womb, newborn infants can breathe, suck, cry, shiver, cough, sneeze and hiccup, just like older children and adults.

They also have a uniquely neonatal set of reflexes like the Moro (startling grabbing in response to a sudden noise or fall) and the Babinski (toe curling) that will disappear around three months of age when the brain's cortex takes over control from lower brain centres. These reflexes assist survival by preventing suffocation and enabling the infant to feed; they also help in the early acquisition of more complex patterns of behaviour (or schemas) – for example, the reflex of sucking the breast is modified to accommodate a pacifying plastic soother, a bottle's teat or the infant's own thumb.

The gradual expansion, modification and adaptation of reflexes arises together with three other important behaviour patterns – sleeping, crying and the dawning of social awareness. Changes occur in infants' rhythms of sleep, wakefulness and dreaming, and motor skills like neck muscle control and reaching develop during the first few months of life.

Sensation and perception also develop in important ways over this time. The sense organs are all functional from birth, and newborns are acutely sensitive to smells, sounds, tastes and touch. The acuity of vision is limited at birth, and objects more than a few centimetres from the eye appear blurred. The range of clear vision and the ability to focus the eyes and to scan, by moving the eyes systematically across an object, picture or scene, all improve substantially during the first six months of postnatal life.

From age 6 to 18 months, equally rapid progress is made in the mastery of more advanced motor skills for sitting, rolling over, reaching, grasping, crawling, walking and coordinating the movements of the body in a skilled and efficient way. There are marked variations in rates of motor skill development from baby to baby and from one cultural group to another.

Babies are capable of simple learning and memory even before birth. They enter the world with an eager curiosity and attentional focus that further facilitates the learning process. By attending to the consequences of their own deliberate actions (like batting or kicking a mobile toy), infants acquire the cognitive skills to solve increasingly complex problems of contingency between causes and effects. In this way, they come to gain a sense of personal control over responsive features of their environments.

According to Piaget, infants spend the first 18 months of life in the Sensorimotor Stage of cognition, developing mastery over notions of object permanence, causality, and the nature of the physical world.

Before age two, they typically progress through the 'Copernican revolution' embodied in the concept of object permanence. This enables them to search for hidden objects in increasingly sophisticated ways. At the same time a practical understanding of causality as a contingent relationship between a prior adjacent cause and a subsequent effect emerges, even though the infant cannot yet put a theory of cause and effect into words.

Young infants' learning and cognitive growth may

be thwarted if no contingencies or opportunities for mastery exist in the environment they inhabit, a state known as learned helplessness. The inability to control important events can produce acute distress at any age. Conversely, throughout the lifespan, opportunities to master learnable contingencies are rewarding and are a source of motivation to tackle ever more complex challenges.

Infants are made happy when shown how to control hitherto uncontrollable phenomena, such as toy rattles, mobiles or mechanical rabbits.

Parents' morale improves as infants acquire sensory, motoric, cognitive and emotional competence, become socialised into sleeping and eating more like their older family members, and become active social partners in their delighted discoveries of all the interesting things the world outside the womb has to offer to their eager young minds.

For further interest

Looking forward on the Internet

Use the Internet to visit the following website. Examine it for further information and varied perspectives on issues raised in this chapter. Also search for other relevant websites for yourself, using keywords like: 'infants', 'toys', 'learning', 'walking', 'play' and 'early development' in your search engine. Visit **http://www.verybestbaby.com**.

In particular, for further ideas on crying, soothing and sleeping visit: **http://www.colic-baby.com** and to extend your understanding of neurobiological development, including a quiz exercise, visit: **http://zerotothree.org/brainwonders**.

For resources, ideas, activities and other items of interest in conjunction with this chapter, visit the Companion Website for this textbook at:

http://wps.pearsoned.com.au/peterson

Activity suggestion

As a practical activity in conjunction with themes in this chapter, visit your local toy shop or department store and examine the toys designed for infants aged 0 to 2 years (the age the toy is intended for often appears on the box). For each toy you select, make a note of the skills and capacities required in order to enjoy the toy, the kinds of abilities playing with it would be likely to develop, and any hazards or safety issues that may be relevant.

Multimedia

For an instructive account of neonatal behavioural capacities, view the film/video: *The Amazing Newborn* (Case Western Reserve University, 1978: 33 minutes). For a vivid picture of early brain development, view the video: *Love's Labours* (DLGHS [USA], 1992: 60 minutes).

INFANCY: Social, emotional and personality development

'Begin at the beginning,' the King said gravely, 'and go on till you come to the end: then stop.'

Lewis Carroll (1832–98)

Contents

CHAPTER OVERVIEW

Think for a moment about what makes you unique – for each one of us, including twins, is refreshingly different from every other human being – and try to explain the reasons why. Can you account for how you came to possess the quirks of temperament, the distinctive habits and mannerisms and the outlook on life that helps to define your individuality? Were you born that way? Or is your character as it expresses itself today a product of the distinctively formative experiences you had while growing up?

This chapter begins with an exploration of the distinctive personality qualities, or patterns of temperament, that each infant is born with. We examine the contrasts, keenly noted by new parents, between babies who cry loudly and fret much of the time and those who are almost always either cheerful or asleep. We also look at recent research into the causes and consequences for individual variations in infant temperament patterns that make some infants easier, and others more difficult, for parents to bring up. The long-term developmental outcomes of these early patterns of infant personality will be tracked, and we will see how temperament, in interaction with individual differences in parenting styles, can guide development along predictable channels that will further ensure that, while every person differs from every other person in the world, adult outcomes can at least partly be foretold through an astute understanding of emotional, social and personality growth during infancy.

The nature and quality of the intimate social relationship that evolves between the infant and a caregiver is also partly shaped by infant personality, as well as by the caregiver's astuteness and skill in understanding that baby's unique disposition, in order to provide the responsive, sensitively modulated style of care that will evoke a bond of trust and love between them. This process of forging an emotional bond of loving mutual attachment may begin for the parent at the infant's birth. But babies themselves take several months to acquire the sensory, cognitive, motor and emotional maturity to be able to recognise their caregivers as distinctive, familiar people and then only gradually become specifically attached to them.

This chapter takes a close look at stages in the attachment process and at the crucial psychological developments that come together when an infant becomes so firmly bonded to a parent that contact with him or her is intensely pleasurable and a source of relief from emotional distress, whereas separations from that parent are, correspondingly, uniquely painful. The infant's personality and early experiences contribute in interaction with parental personalities and cultural background to the formation of a secure attachment. We examine variations in the ways babies form these bonds of love to their caregivers and at factors that predict whether the bond will be secure or insecure and tinged with anxiety or ambivalence.

As we will see, although this developmental milestone or early attachment formation is typically reached between 7 and 12 months of age, the consequences of variations in the attachment process and of individual differences in the bonds of affection, and the internal working models of people and relationships that result from it, will persist to shape development throughout the lifespan. In later chapters of this book we examine how adolescent and adult developmental changes in personality, cognition, social behaviour and emotional balance can be linked directly with the ways attachments were formed during early infancy. For these reasons, and also because of the significant roles that bonds of love, trust and close friendship play in all of our lives, the attachment process that we examine in this chapter is deemed by many to be one of the most significant developments in the entire lifespan.

The roots of personality: Infant temperament

BOX 5.1 Expressing individuality
Two different babies

Consider the following description of two Australian neonates when they were one week old:

Baby A was born in a Darwin hospital to a healthy mother who experienced no complications during pregnancy or delivery. He was full-term at birth, weighing 3 kilograms. When observed by hospital staff during the first three days of his life, he was rated as extremely alert for a baby his age; but now, despite his wide-eyed appearance, he fails to track moving objects with his eyes, and does not often turn his head in response to loud sounds. His mood seems generally placid and happy. He cries rarely, and is easily consoled when in distress. He also

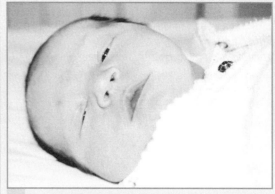

Even as neonates, all babies are different.

calms himself if left alone. The ongoing noises of the nursery do not seem to irritate or excite him. He supports the weight of his body when held upright.

Baby C is also a full-term male, born in the same hospital after a similarly uncomplicated pregnancy and delivery, weighing 3.5 kilograms. The observers rate him high in activity and irritability. He moves continuously even while asleep and shows vigorous startle reactions to mild sounds. His mood is turbulent. He cries loudly for long periods and is difficult to soothe. He resists being held or cuddled but cannot easily soothe himself when left. His legs crumple when he is supported in an upright position.

Infant personality is by no means as complex or multifaceted as adult personality, yet the basic elements of individuality emerge very early. Several key dimensions of temperamental difference among babies are evident almost from birth. Developmental researchers study the precursors to mature personality in infant temperament for many reasons. For one thing, temperament is likely to influence all the aspects of the baby's development that we examined in Chapter 4. The ease with which motor skills are mastered, for example, may reflect the baby's activity level and interest in getting up and about and exploring. Attention to sensory and perceptual stimuli will be shaped by temperament. A cheerful, complacent or rebellious mood may also contribute to the infant's early cognitive development via attentiveness and exploratory efforts. Furthermore, as they develop social skills and person recognition, infants' attachments to caregivers (see page 151) are likely to be shaped in important ways by their own and the caregiver's personality. Another reason for scientific interest in infant temperament is practical. Researchers who wish to optimise parents' adjustment to parenting and their adoption of effective strategies for soothing, stimulating and caring for their babies can tailor their advice to best effect by knowing something about the infant's temperamental dispositions.

Thus the caregiving strategies that would work best with Baby C in Box 5.1 would probably be very different from the ones most suited to meeting the needs of Baby A.

All babies are different

In George Bernard Shaw's play *Back to Methuselah* (1920) Eve exclaims to Cain:

Oh I have heard it all a thousand times. They tell me too of their last-born: the clever thing the darling child said yesterday, and how much more wonderful or witty or quaint it is than any child that ever was born before. And I have to pretend to be surprised, delighted, interested; though the last child is like the first, and has said and done nothing that did not delight Adam and me when you and Abel said it. (p. 34)

This is a dramatic statement because, outside the fantasy world of the theatre, no experienced mother is likely to express the view that all babies are exactly alike. In a large family each sibling, from birth, may have a distinctive way of behaving that is as unique as their physical appearance. During subsequent pregnancies, expectant mothers may even notice differences in temperament between fetuses long before birth. 'This one is not going to be anything like little Mary,' said one pregnant mother. 'She hardly kicked at all. This one is kicking all the time' (Sontag, 1966, p. 783).

If you have not had children of your own but have had the opportunity to visit a hospital's neonatal nursery or crèche for very young infants, you will undoubtedly be aware of some of the dimensions of temperament that distinguish infants from one another, almost from the moment of birth.

Some newborns in a nursery will be active and vigorous. Some will seem cheerful and alert. Some may be so sluggish and passive as to appear drugged, even though they have not been exposed to obstetric medication during childbirth (see Chapter 3). Still others appear angry and discontented through much of their wakeful time. These and other dimensions of difference have been observed reliably in babies within hours of their birth and 'temperamental individuality is well-established by the time the infant is two to three months old' (Thomas & Chess, 1977, p. 153).

The two newborns described in Box 5.1 differed along many of the dimensions of temperament commonly measured by researchers. Thus one baby was very active and vigorous while the other was placid and quiescent. One reacted irritably to the slightest touch, sight or sound, whereas the other ignored weak stimulation, responding only to intense sensory input, and even then in a mild manner. One was alert and attentive for long periods and was easy to soothe when distressed. The other was just the opposite. Finally, the mood tone of one was positive and cheerful while the other's was rather negative and angry. These dimensions of infant character are described and defined more systematically in Table 5.1.

A pioneering longitudinal study in New York by Alexander Thomas, Stella Chess and Herbert Birch (1963) highlighted several of the personality traits that can be reliably discerned in babies at birth. More recently, Ann Sanson, Margot Prior and Frank Oberklaid (1985) conducted a large-scale study of 2443 representative Australian families in Melbourne with infants aged between four and eight months. These researchers confirmed that distinctive dimensions of personality are evident in infants from a very early age. Also, Australian parents appear to be as capable as the middle-class North American mothers and fathers interviewed by Thomas and his associates of rating these temperament qualities reliably and

TABLE 5.1	Dimensions of temperament in Australian infants		
Label	Description	Low score	High score
Activity level	The level and extent of motor activity	Not active	Very active
Irregularity (versus rhythmicity)	The regularity with which behaviours such as sleeping and feeding occur	Rhythmic, regular	Arhythmic, irregular
Approach–withdrawal	The nature of the response to a new person or stimulus	First response is approach	First response is withdrawal
Adaptability	The ease with which a child adapts to changes in the environment	Very adaptable	Not adaptable
Intensity	The energy level of a response or reaction	Not intense	Very intense
Threshold of responsiveness	The strength of stimulation necessary to evoke a discernible response	High threshold	Low threshold
Mood	The amount of friendly, happy behaviour as contrasted with unfriendly, unhappy behaviour	Positive, happy	Negative, unhappy
Distractability	The degree to which extraneous stimuli alter ongoing behaviour such as crying	Distractable, soothable	Not distractable or soothable
Persistence or attention span	The amount of time devoted to an activity, and the effect of distraction on the activity	Persistent, long attention span	Not persistent, short attention span

Source: Sanson, Prior & Oberklaid (1985), p. 186, reproduced with permission of the authors and by courtesy of the Australian Psychological Society.

accurately. The dimensions of temperament discovered by Sanson and her colleagues are shown in Table 5.1.

Patterns of temperament

When they compared Australian infants' temperament patterns with those of North American infants of the same age, Sanson and her colleagues discovered some interesting variations. On average, Australian babies were rated as less active than their counterparts in the United States. They slept longer and more peacefully, and moved less frequently and strenuously when awake. While greater placidity could make caring for an Australian infant easier, two other differences from the American norms are likely to make the Australian parent's task more difficult – compared with American babies, Australian

infants were found to be less regular in their daily rhythms of feeding, sleeping and eliminating, and also less adaptable when confronted with new situations.

In fact, the ease or difficulty of caring for a young infant is determined to a large extent by temperament. Some combinations of traits, such as cheerfulness, placidity and regularity of rhythms, make the baby a delight to look after, but other combinations can make the caregiver's task considerably more difficult. The parents of an infant who is easily irritated but hard to soothe (like Baby C in Box 5.1) are bound to experience more frustration in their caregiving and comforting efforts than those whose offspring combine these two personality traits in the opposite manner (like Baby A). In fact, infants can be grouped into three basic types on the basis of their

 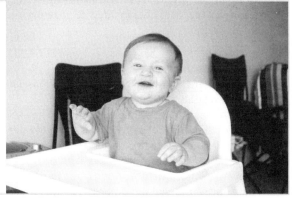

A positive reaction to a new experience, like the taste of a new food, is a component of an easy temperament pattern.

combined dispositional qualities, as shown in Table 5.2 (Thomas, Chess & Birch, 1970).

The 'easy' row of the table describes the type of child that the average parent is delighted to care for. Easy children are not overly active nor too lethargic, and they show a favourable balance of cheerful, happy behaviour over negative moods. They follow a regular schedule of sleeping, waking, hunger and elimination, so that their parents can quickly learn to predict their needs. It is also much easier for the rest of the household to fit in with the baby's routine if that routine follows a constant schedule from day to day, rather than being erratic and unpredictable. Finally, the baby's speed of adapting to new situations or routines will shape the parents' lifestyle in important ways. A baby who adapts readily and quickly can be fed a varied diet easily, and can be left in the care of relatives or taken along with the parents on outings, visits and holidays. The baby who is slow to adjust, however, may tax the parents' patience to the point where they feel compelled to curtail their own activities; they may also give up trying to introduce the baby to potentially pleasant or stimulating new tastes, people or things to do.

The chances of an Australian baby being born with the entire gamut of traits defining a difficult or slow-to-warm-up nature are fortunately not high (Sanson, Prior & Oberklaid, 1985). Figure 5.1 shows the distribution of the infants from the Melbourne temperament study in each of the three temperament patterns outlined above, plus a fourth, 'average', pattern subsuming babies who were rated in the middle of most of the dimensions that distinguish an easy personality from a difficult one. The vast majority of Australian babies appear to be 'easy' or 'average', with slightly fewer 'slow-to-warm-up' and 'difficult' infants than the corresponding New York percentages of 10 and 15 respectively (Thomas, Chess & Birch, 1970).

The 'slow-to-warm-up' temperament classifica-

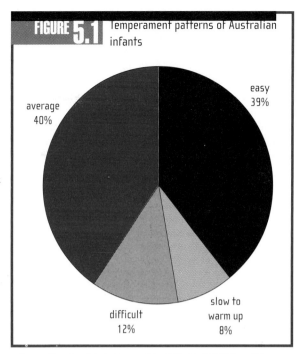

Source: Based on data in Sanson, Prior & Oberklaid (1985), p. 189.

tion describes infants who are apt to pose a challenge to many eager parents. Such babies have a low level of spontaneous activity, which may result in their being left alone too often, without the interesting sights and sounds needed to rouse their curiosity (see Chapter 4). Their variable schedules of hunger and sleep make it hard for their caregivers to predict their needs and, since their first reaction to a new experience is usually to withdraw from it, they are usually slow to adjust to even minor changes of routine. Parents consequently have trouble helping them to fit in with home life. The parents of such infants will not gain as much reward as the parents of the baby with an 'easy' temperament, who will enjoy the child's positive responses and general ebullience of mood.

TABLE 5.2 Infant temperament type

Temperament type	Dimension of behaviour								
	Activity level	Rhythmicity	Distract-ability	Approach/ withdrawal	Adaptability	Attention span and persistence	Intensity	Threshold of responsive-ness	Quality of mood
EASY	Varies	Very regular	Varies	Approach	Very adaptable	High	Low or mild	High or low	Positive
SLOW TO WARM UP	Low to moderate	Varies	Varies	Withdrawal	Slowly adaptable	High or low	Mild	High or low	Slightly negative
DIFFICULT	Varies	Irregular	Low	Withdrawal	Slowly adaptable	High or low	Intense	High or low	Negative

Source: Thomas, Chess & Birch (1970), Table 1.2, reproduced with permission.

The hardest child of all to cope with is probably the one with the 'difficult' temperament, as outlined in the last row of Table 5.2. Such infants resemble their slow-to-warm-up counterparts in being irregular in their habits, and resistant to novel experiences and to parental efforts to modify their routines. They show more intense reactions than the slow-to-warm-up children, however, and have a greater predominance of unhappy, unpleasant moods over neutral or happy states. Thus much of their time is likely to be spent in vigorous protest and unsoothable crying, raising parenting problems.

The simple knowledge that some babies are liable to enter life with difficult or slow-to-warm-up temperamental patterns can be of enormous assistance to concerned caregivers. They can then tailor their childrearing strategies to suit the infant's needs. Since both types of babies seem to have special problems in coping with novelty and change, they are likely to do best when new experiences, like solid foods and toilet training, are introduced gradually with plenty of time for the babies to make up their own minds about them.

The influence of heredity and environment

Two questions that are central for many parents of temperamentally difficult children are:

1. What causes a difficult temperament in the first place?
2. Can it be changed?

These questions have obvious links with issues explored in Chapter 3, including the biological contribution of the genetic blueprint to development and the influences of early experiences, including those arising during prenatal life.

Although the discovery that the basic dimensions of temperament are evident in babies from the moment of birth might appear to favour the genotype as the source of all temperament variation, we must not forget that the human being's formative experiences begin well before birth, and so does susceptibility to adverse environmental influences such as teratogens (see Chapter 3). In addition to potential harm from nicotine or virus diseases, the fetus is affected by the hormones that circulate in the mother's bloodstream. These hormones are reactive to the mother's own activity level as well as to exposure to stimulation, like loud noise. And, as we saw in Chapter 3, the fetus itself can perceive and react to sounds outside the womb, at least from six or seven months after conception. Thus auditory and vestibular stimulation (e.g. when the pregnant mother listens to loud music or walks home from work) could conceivably begin to influence the growth of the new baby's temperament many months before he or she is actually born.

On the other hand, studies comparing monozygotic and dizygotic twins (Braungart, Plomin, DeFries & Fulker, 1992; Emde et al., 1992) have shown a closer resemblance between monozygotic twin pairs than dizygotic same-sex twins (see Figure 5.2), indicating an important role for heredity in shaping variability in temperament within the population (see Chapter 3).

The fact that the heritability of temperament is not complete means that the environment and the experiences that a baby has after the genotype has been determined also play a role in deciding whether the infant will be difficult, easy or slow to warm up. One plausible common-sense view is that the birth process (including birth complications and exposure to obstetric medication) might play a role. However, systematic experimental investigation has failed to support this hypothesis. For example, using their Melbourne sample, Ann Sanson, Margot Prior and Frank Oberklaid (1985) compared Australian infants who had an uncomplicated delivery with those who had suffered the following obstetric complications: (a) prematurity, (b) low birth weight, (c) complications of delivery, and (d) perinatal stress. No differences in frequencies of easy, difficult or slow-to-warm-up patterns emerged between the groups. A study conducted in Canada also examined temperament in relation to (a) the mother's use of pain-relieving medication versus a

The balance of happiness to sadness and moodiness is one of the most important dimensions of infant temperament through the lifespan.

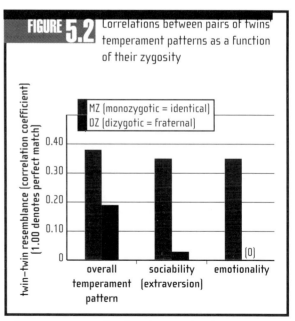

FIGURE 5.2 Correlations between pairs of twins' temperament patterns as a function of their zygosity

Source: Braungart et al. (1992) and Emde et al. (1992).

'natural' (unmedicated) delivery and (b) the use of Leboyer procedures and other 'gentle' birth techniques as compared with standard birth practices (Maziade, Boudreault, Cote & Thivierge, 1986). No important differences were found at any point from birth to age one between those infants who had been born gently and their counterparts who had had a standard, medicated hospital birth.

Some parents subscribe to the view that eldest children are more apt to be temperamentally difficult than the second or third babies in a family. However, when they tested the effect of birth order, Sanson and her colleagues (1985) disconfirmed this common-sense theory. Firstborns showed no consistent differences in temperament from later-borns, nor did rural children differ in any systematic way from urban infants. Similarly, contrary to the popular stereotypes that portray boy babies as active, vigorous and persistent and girls as cheerful, quiet and cuddly, no significant sex differences were observed among these Australian infants on any of the individual dimensions of temperament listed in Table 5.1. Nor did the infants' sex predict whether their overall temperament classification would be difficult, easy or slow to warm up.

However, the notion of a partly physiological basis for temperament was suggested by a significant association between colic, sleep disturbances and temperament classification. Only 20 per cent of the Australian infants with easy temperaments had suffered from moderate to severe colic, compared with more than 50 per cent of those with difficult personalities. Nurses likewise reported more serious sleep disturbances and crying problems in the difficult babies compared with the easy babies.

These monozygotic twins have a similar temperament. Their identical genotypes and shared rearing experiences are both responsible.

Cultural variations in temperament

Parents' cultural backgrounds are likely to shape their ideas about which patterns of infant temperament are desirable and which undesirable qualities parents should (and could) modify. So variations across cultures in parental belief systems (Goodnow, 1996) could conceivably influence infant temperament, as could cross-cultural variations in disciplinary, socialisation and childrearing practices (such as the differences in sleeping arrangements that were examined in Chapter 4).

The ethnically diverse community of a cosmopolitan city such as Melbourne provides opportunities for testing the influence of cultural beliefs and childrearing strategies on the development of personality. Michael Kyrios, Margot Prior, Frank Oberklaid and Andreas Demetriou (1989) compared the temperament patterns of infants who came from either an Anglo-Australian or a Greek-Australian family. Their results showed that the parents' cultural background exerted a significant influence on infant temperament. Despite the fact that all the babies were born and reared in similar households in Melbourne, and the researchers had carefully matched them in terms of antenatal history and family income, education, health and other environmental variables, the findings showed that Greek-Australian infants were more likely than their Anglo-Australian peers to display the various qualities of difficult temperament that are identified in Table 5.2. Even after the effects of parental education and income were statistically controlled, the Australian babies whose parents had been born in Greece were found to have more negative moods on average, and also to be less adaptable, less easily distracted and less positive in mood and approach than Anglo-Australian infants of the same age and sex.

Aboriginal Australian infants

Other studies confirm the idea that there is a link between culture and temperament (De Vries, 2001; Freedman, 1974). One that gives a particularly intriguing illustration of the possible influences that cultural variations can exert on early and later personality was conducted in Darwin and supplied the examples used in Box 5.1.

Although the two babies described in Box 5.1 were both Australian, they differed in ethnicity. Baby A was a full-blooded Aboriginal infant whose parents lived on a mission station near Darwin, whereas Baby C was a Caucasian infant from urban Darwin whose parents were Anglo-Australians of British descent. The contrast between these two cultural backgrounds does have a bearing on such personality differences as those listed in Box 5.1 and Table 5.1. When Daniel Freedman (1974) compared a larger group of Aboriginal and Anglo-Australian newborns in Darwin, he found striking differences between the two groups on five dimensions of temperament: (a) alertness, (b) reflex reactions, (c) threshold of responsiveness, (d) mood quality, and (e) muscle tone and activity, as explained below:

- *Alertness.* Aboriginal newborns were more quietly alert than Anglo-Australian newborns. From their earliest days of postnatal life, Aboriginal infants spent considerable periods of time wide awake with their eyes open, while the Anglo-Australian neonates had their eyes closed for much of this time and appeared sleepy and lethargic.
- *Reflex reactivity.* Another index of developmental status is provided by the reflex behaviours that were described in detail in Chapter 4. Freedman found that efforts to elicit the Moro reflex were less successful among Aboriginal than Anglo-Australian babies. Since this reflex is more pronounced among premature than full-term infants, and dwindles among the latter over time, such a difference may testify to greater neurological maturity among Aboriginal babies at birth. In addition, the visual tracking reflex was harder to elicit in Aboriginal than Anglo-Australian newborns, possibly for similar reasons.
- *Threshold of responsiveness.* Aboriginal babies seemed to be much less tense and irritable than Anglo-Australian infants. They were less prone to cry or to become over-excited and less often disturbed by stray sounds or such discomforts as a wet nappie.
- *Mood quality.* Aboriginal infants displayed a more positive balance of happy, cheerful moods over unpleasant distress than Caucasian newborns. They were also more responsive to cuddling and other soothing stimulation (see Chapter 4) and more adept at comforting themselves after bouts of crying.
- *Muscle tone and activity.* The average weight of an Aboriginal child at birth is slightly less than that of the average Anglo-Australian infant, in line with the differences in neonatal and infant physical growth that were charted in Chapter 2 and described in more detail in Chapter 4. (In fact, Freedman recorded an average of 3016 grams for the Aboriginal infants in his sample group and 3516 grams for those of Anglo background.) Yet, despite their slightly smaller body mass, the Aboriginal newborns were found to have better muscular control over their necks, backs and legs than the Anglo babies. They were also more likely to extend their legs reflexively when supported in an upright posture. This led to a more controlled pattern of activity in Aboriginal newborns.

Nature and nurture in cross-cultural differences in temperament

The contrasts described in Boxes 5.1 and 5.2 between Aboriginal and Anglo-Australian infants admit of several possible explanations. Perhaps heredity endows infants with different dispositional proclivi-

BOX 5.2 How can you explain it?
Cultural paradoxes in early temperament

Paradox 1. The differences between Anglo and Aboriginal infant temperaments that were illustrated in Box 5.1 and described in more detail in the section above were present at birth, before parental childrearing strategies could have exerted an influence. Can you think of a reason why the typical Aboriginal Australian newborn would already display a different pattern of temperament from an Anglo newborn? Try to suggest two different possible explanations.

Paradox 2. Marten De Vries (2001) conducted a longitudinal study of temperament in Masai infants who lived in a drought-stricken region of East Africa. He measured temperament in a group of 13 impoverished Masai infants at the age of four months and returned to study them several months later. Distressingly, he found that six of the infants had already died. Intriguingly, however, the infants' personality traits of easy versus difficult temperament as 4-month-olds were significant predictors of their survival. Can you guess which group survived the best?

Answers can be found in the next sections of the text.

ties, some of which may be based in faster or slower rates of maturation of the brain and body. Given their different ancestry, survival pressures operating in their ancient environments may have contributed to the genetic selection of different temperament qualities for the indigenous inhabitants of Australia and their European counterparts (see Box 5.1).

Alternatively, the cultural contrasts in temperament that have been observed between Aboriginal and Anglo-Australian babies as newborns could reflect nurture. Cultural differences in patterns of pregnancy and childbirth for Baby A (see Box 5.1) in a remote bush settlement versus Baby C in urban Darwin could conceivably explain the temperament patterns. Baby A may well have had less (or no) obstetric medication and this environmental influence during the birth process could account for his greater alertness and more relaxed mood. In addition, the known effects of maternal mood and behaviour on fetal development (see Chapter 3) could be implicated in cultural differences (see Chapter 4).

In fact, each of these possibilities is consistent with the findings of other cross-cultural comparisons of infant temperament. In one study (Freedman, 1974), newborn infants of Chinese descent were found to resemble Aboriginal babies in their more positive mood quality, lower levels of irritability and readier soothability than Caucasians, while infants of African descent displayed consistently higher gross motor ability, in line with their advanced development of motor skills (see Chapter 4).

To probe possible explanations for these observed cultural contrasts in infant temperament more deeply, Margot Prior and her colleagues in Melbourne undertook an intriguing extension of their Melbourne study (Kyrios et al., 1989). In addition to their sample of Australian-born infants of migrant Greek parents, they included a sample of Greek babies who still lived in Greece with their Greek parents. If being a migrant in an unfamiliar culture led the Greek-Australian parents to behave in ways that enhanced their offspring's chances of acquiring a difficult temperament, these non-migrant Greek babies should resemble Anglo-Australians. On the other hand, if the basis for the difference is hereditary, the Greek infants in Greece should most closely resemble Greek-Australians.

A total of 36 Greek infants from the city of Thessalonike and the isle of Chios were tested. The results ruled out the possibility that the parents' stress over being migrants explained the Greek-Australian infants having more difficult temperaments than Anglo-Australians. Greek infants in Greece were also found to be more irritable, less readily soothable, more negative in mood, less adaptable and generally more difficult than Anglo-Australian babies. The researchers suggested that cultural differences in the family atmosphere and philosophies of childrearing might help to explain these differences:

> Within the context of an immediate need gratification approach, Greek infants may learn from the earliest stages that even the most subtle expression of hunger or fussiness will result in their needs being met. Hence, in contrast to Anglo-Australian infants, Greek infants may not learn to adapt as well to demands outside of the self and, as a result, may become less easily distracted from their attempts at self-gratification. With regard to discipline, Greek mothers are reported to be punitive, inconsistent and, as a result of social pressures such as those related to migration, may be less tolerant of problem behaviours. Hence, it was not surprising to find cross-cultural differences in the quality of mood, with Greek infants consistently rated as more negative in mood. (pp. 599–600)

In other words, the results of this study suggest that early experiences, in the form of the childrearing strategies parents use to soothe, feed and train their young infants, may help to shape the growth of personality.

The study by De Vries (2001) of temperament in Masai infants, described in Box 5.2, may also help to shed light on the influences of nature and nurture in personality development. De Vries found, as shown in Figure 5.3, that a distressingly high 71 per cent of Masai infants with easy temperaments at four months died before their first birthday. Yet in the same harsh, drought-stricken circumstances, only 17 per cent of infants with difficult temperaments died by the same age. Parental childrearing patterns may have been influential, supporting the nurture hypothesis. If the difficult infants cried more persistently and demanded to be fed more often, they may have received more nourishment from starving parents than an infant with a more placid, 'easy' mood. At the same time, it is possible to account for the results shown in Figure 5.3 from a nature perspective. Maybe a genetic disposition towards easy-going yielding to fate (like the 'easy' infant) versus resisting and fighting against adversity (like the 'difficult' baby) may have been transmitted from parents to children, with the more 'difficult', resistant parents being more able to eke out an existence in conditions of severe drought than the parents and infants whose biological temperaments disposed them to be easy-going (see Box 5.2).

Does early temperament predict later personality?

Several studies have explored the persistence of temperament patterns from the newborn period through the remainder of infancy. In a classic longitudinal study, Betty Jo McGrade (1968) measured 24 babies at birth on many of the dimensions of temperament described in Table 5.1. When she returned eight months later, she found that the only newborn measure which related significantly to an individual difference at eight months was how the babies had reacted to having a nipple pulled rudely out of their mouth just as they began to suck. Babies who had shown little or no reaction to this frustration as newborns were rated happier, more active and less tense than other babies at eight months. In other words, a happy mood in infancy may have its origins in tolerance to stress as early as the third day of life.

Another longitudinal study of 80 infants in New York also demonstrated a high degree of consistency of mood tone throughout the first two years of life

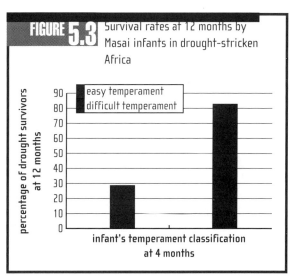

FIGURE 5.3 Survival rates at 12 months by Masai infants in drought-stricken Africa

Source: Based on data in De Vries (2001).

(Thomas, Chess & Birch, 1970). Some 92 per cent of these babies were given identical mood ratings by their mothers throughout infancy, making this the most consistent of all the temperamental characteristics shown in Table 5.1.

Michael Lewis (1993) followed a group of infants longitudinally from early infancy to the start of formal academic instruction in preschool at age four. He found that the temperament dimension of negative mood tone (frequent expression of intense negative emotions like anger and distress), measured at three months of age, predicted poor cognitive performance at four years of age, even after the influence of other variables, including the mother's sensitivity and responsiveness, had been statistically controlled.

A longitudinal study of over 800 New Zealand boys and girls from birth to age 18 revealed remarkable continuity in temperament over this major segment of the lifespan (Caspi & Silva, 1995). In line with the infant temperament styles of (a) responsiveness, (b) activity and (c) distractability (see Table 5.1), Avshalom Caspi and Phil Silva discovered a temperament pattern in 3-year-old Otago children that they labelled 'lack of control'. Toddlers who exhibited this pattern were rated by observers as rough and aggressive in play, distractable and hard to keep still and prone to dramatic mood swings. When these same children described their own personality patterns at age 18, similar characteristics were clearly evident. Teenagers who had shown lack of control at three years of age were inclined to be risk-takers or sensation-seekers with a preference for thrills and danger and relatively low regard for rules and

authority. Following on from the anger and aggression they had displayed as toddlers, these 18-year-olds 'were prone to respond with strong negative emotions to everyday events, they described themselves as mistreated and victimized, and they reported they were enmeshed in adversarial relationships' (p. 495).

Caspi and Silva considered a number of possible explanations for these clear longitudinal continuities in temperament over time. In line with the notion discussed in Chapter 3 that babies from birth select their own environments to match hereditary dispositions (Scarr & McCartney, 1983), these New Zealand data were consistent with a lifespan process of environmental engineering. As Caspi and Silva explained:

Early individual differences may be elaborated over the life course because the person's pattern of interacting with others tends to recreate the same conditions over and over again. (p. 496)

For example, a shy toddler in a milieu such as the United States, which favours extroversion (Chen, Rubin & Li, 1995), persistently withdraws from social situations. Consequently, he or she is less likely to participate in the social learning experiences that peer interaction provides (see Chapter 8) and thus may carry forward a non-assertive, meek and solitary nature into adolescence or adulthood. But in an environment such as China, where shyness is deemed a desirable quality by adults and peers alike, shy children are found to enjoy greater peer popularity than active, outgoing children (Chen et al., 1995) and so may gain opportunities that foster appropriate social entry and cooperation skills, thus developing increasing social outgoingness throughout childhood.

The goodness-of-fit hypothesis

In other words, while it is frequently the case that infants will retain the temperament patterns they are born with throughout their lives, this is not inevitable. According to Thomas and Chess (1977), the chance that an infant personality disposition, such as a high activity level, will persist through childhood depends very largely on how tolerant the parents are of active, rambunctious offspring. They coined the phrase *goodness-of-fit* to describe the degree of overlap between the particular style of temperament an infant starts out with and his or her parents' image of an ideal child. When the fit is close, temperament will show strong continuity. But if the match is poor, parental socialisation efforts are usually capable of considerably modifying the infant's initial tendencies. To the extent that they are successful, this will result in a discontinuity of temperament between infancy and later childhood.

Research evidence suggests that individuals are active shapers of their own environments and highly responsive to the contingencies that these environments supply (Scarr, 1992; see Chapter 3). Thus a temperament pattern that brings the social rewards of affection and enjoyable social contact with inti-

The tendency of temperament to persist over time suggests that this one-year-old's cheerfulness would have been discernible shortly after birth as tolerance to frustration.

mate others is likely to persist unchanged over time. In contrast, traits that earn disapproval from important members of the chosen social environment are likely to decline or vanish as time passes. During childhood and adolescence, this goodness-of-fit hypothesis (Thomas & Chess, 1977) explains how family influences contribute to the selective retention of valued personality patterns, along with the loss or modification of negatively valued qualities. According to this model, a cultural or parental image of the ideal child will influence treatment of offspring with particular temperament qualities. Over time, this may lead to change in devalued traits of temperament but maintenance of valued ones, so that the question of whether personality is stable or changeable with development becomes a relative one.

The goodness-of-fit hypothesis suggests a reason for the common observations of dramatic discontinuities of temperament over time for some children, along with remarkable persistence and continuity in other children. When newborn infants' idiosyncratic dispositional tendencies match up neatly with their caregivers' temperaments, habits and expectations, there is little incentive on either side to alter this congenial state of affairs. But when the match is poor, parents will undoubtedly strive to change their infants' personalities in more congenial directions. If their socialisation strategies are effective, as when the parents of a difficult infant display patience, warmth and consistency while introducing new routines gradually and remaining sensitive to the infant's special needs and wants (Thomas, Chess & Birch, 1970), a change over time is highly probable. On the other hand, a poor fit between infant temperament and parental ideals will not provoke a change if the parents use ineffective childrearing strategies like anger and unjustified physical punishment (see Chapters 9 and 12 for a further discussion of effective versus ineffective parental styles of childrearing).

Parent–infant reciprocity in personality expression

The degree of overlap between infant temperament and parental ideals also influences the extent to which the mother's and father's own adult personalities will alter with the transition into parenthood. Eleanor Maccoby, Margaret Snow and Carol Jacklin (1984) measured mothers' and sons' temperaments, together with the intensity of the mother's efforts to modify the boy's behaviour. At 12 months, mothers of boys with difficult temperaments exerted more strenuous teaching efforts than mothers whose sons were temperamentally easy. A longitudinal follow-up at 18 months showed that the sons of the mothers who had made the most intensive teaching efforts at 12 months had indeed become significantly less temperamentally difficult during the subsequent six months. However, the difficult boys had also managed to modify their mothers to some extent. When their sons were 18 months old, mothers of difficult

boys were making less effort to change their sons' personalities than they had done when the boys were only 12 months old. Perhaps the effort of coping with a temperamental personality had facilitated the mother's development of a more relaxed and flexible attitude, and greater tolerance, through her own personality change.

A parent who is exhausted from lack of sleep may find it harder to be patient with a sleepless and difficult infant than the parent of one who, while equally difficult temperamentally, manages to sleep soundly throughout the night. In line with our earlier discussion in Chapter 4 of individual differences in infants' durations of nightly sleep (see page 111), Joy Osofsky and Karen Connors (1979) tried to discover why some babies sleep steadily through the night from as early as four months of age, while other equally healthy babies wake several times each night throughout their first year of life. These investigators ruled out obvious differences like breast versus bottle feeding, scheduled versus demand feeding, the baby's weight and the frequency of minor illnesses, since none of these bore any clear relationship to the age at which infants were able to sleep steadily through the night. But parents' personalities did make a difference. Mothers who had displayed anxious dispositions at the beginning of the study, and parents of both sexes who showed either unusually high levels of anger or unusual levels of concern over sleep and insomnia generally, were the ones most likely to end up with infants who continued to wake regularly during the early morning hours. By contrast, the offspring of parents who were neither unusually anxious nor angry tended to settle in to steady sleeping throughout the night by the age of about four months.

Since the parents' personalities predated the babies' sleeping habits, it seems most probable that both parental and infantile temperaments contribute to complex relationships like these, and that all the time anxious parents are communicating their tension to their infants, they themselves are being made more or less anxious by the baby's own particular style of mood and degree of adaptability.

Marged Goode, Loris Alexander and Gillian Arthur (1982) studied parental reactions to the nightly crying of 25 Melbourne infants. The father's and mother's personality both exerted an influence on how the baby behaved at night. Fathers who earned high scores on a standardised measure of anxiety were more likely than non-anxious fathers to spend time trying to settle their infants for sleep. Depressed fathers did so the least. Anxious fathers also got up more at night and spent more time soothing their crying infants than other fathers, especially if the mother's personality included a mixed (or 'androgynous': see Chapters 8 and 13) blend of masculine and feminine traits. Mothers who scored high in depression had infants who cried more than average and had more difficulty in establishing regular patterns of

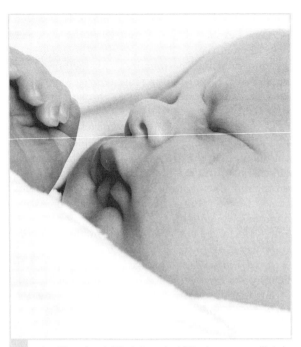

Parents with a relaxed attitude towards nightly sleep are more likely to have infants who sleep through the night from an early age.

daily and nightly sleep. Again, the possible causal explanations for these relationships are multiple. Mothers could well become depressed, and fathers anxious, as a result of exposure to a temperamental baby who refuses to sleep through the night. However, links noted between infant behaviour at six months and such enduring parental qualities as masculinity and femininity suggested that the parents' personalities also shaped that of the baby. As the researchers explained:

> The findings suggest that if labile emotions accompany pregnancy and childbirth, it is extremely difficult to establish whether the emotions of one influence the behaviour of another or vice versa or both. However, where relatively stable personality traits are concerned, the suggestion of the personality of one affecting the behaviour of another rather than vice versa seems sound. While some interaction between personality and emotional state is to be expected, the separate effects of each variable may be a function of time. The relationships surrounding the emotional responses appeared to be strongest at one and three months, while the effects of personality were greater at six months than they had been earlier. (p. 186)

The fact that parents' temperaments and patterns of behaviour, like those of their infants, are apt to change with the passage of time raises the question of who shapes whom the most. Though such a comparison is hard to make in view of the great diversity of an adult's range of habits, styles and mannerisms as contrasted with the infant's rather limited behavioural repertoire, there is nevertheless ample evidence to show that adults are modified in sometimes quite

striking ways by their infants and by their experiences as parents, not only during infancy but up to and even after the grown children leave home.

On the basis of his own comparisons of the attitudinal and behavioural matches and mismatches between a group of older children and their parents in Queensland, Michael Siegal (1985) was led to the conclusion that:

> Parent–child relations can be viewed in a context of reciprocal determinism. Neither the behaviour of children nor the socialization behaviours of mothers can be regarded as dependent variables but as interlocking determinants of each other. Mothers' childrearing practices alter children's behaviour, and children's behaviour alters mothers' childrearing practices. (p. 70)

Richard Bell (1971) similarly summed up the combined evidence from lifespan reciprocity research when he noted that:

> If we can come out of the shadows of old ideological conflicts, the child can be recognized as a very lively educator himself … The value of marriage is not that adults produce children but that children produce adults. (p. 71)

Emotional development in infancy

We have seen how infants' expression of emotions like anger or cheerful pleasure may vary as a function of temperament. However, alongside these individual differences, there are overall developmental changes in emotional expression that are true of most children as they develop.

Newborn infants have a far more restricted range of emotions in their repertoires than do older children and adults, but versatility in emotional expressiveness develops rapidly over the first year of life, as shown in Table 5.3.

In order to study the development of the infant's emotional repertoire, Carroll Izard and his colleagues (Izard et al., 1995) took videotapes of infants, ranging in age from two and a half to nine months, as they were being exposed (off camera) to positive or negative emotion-provoking situations such as being reunited with their mother after a separation, watching a toy jack-in-the-box pop out unexpectedly or having a toy rudely snatched away. Izard observed clear differences in the types of faces babies made to these different affective stimuli, along with consistency from baby to baby in the expressions that arose on their faces in response to a given triggering event (like the toy grab). Furthermore, there was consistency between the youngest and oldest infants in the sample, suggesting that different emotions were being evoked reliably by the various types of affectively charged events.

To establish how closely the infants' facial expressions matched conventionally recognisable emotional states, Izard asked adult judges (who did not know the babies concerned) to view the videos of the

TABLE 5.3	Developmental changes in emotional expressiveness over the first year of life
Birth	Reflexively distinctive-sounding 'anger' and 'pain' cries (Wolff, 1969)
1 month	Displays irritability through the 'fussy' cry (see page 108)
2 months	Smiles socially
3 months	Displays a consistent preference to look at a photo of a smiling, rather than an emotionally neutral, stranger
4 months	Laughs in response to familiar sounds, simple social games, and other stimuli over which the infant can exert control (see Chapter 4)
6 to 12 months	Displays fear (e.g. stranger fear, see page 151). Other primary emotions (anger, sadness) also become clearly recognisable in the infant's facial and vocal expressions

BOX 5.3 A case in point
Pacifying temper with a thumb

When his daughter was 14 months old, Louise's father made an entry in his diary which illustrates how she employed emotional self-regulation by sucking on her thumb to ease herself out of a temper tantrum.

2 June 1949. Louise has been ill with tonsillitis, a fever, and a rash. Not too seriously, not seriously enough to stay in bed or even indoors. But it has made her cross and given her temper tantrums. Even so, she seems philosophical about them, half ready to call one off if it doesn't seem to be working.

Tonight, for instance, she was put to bed and got impatient for her bottle. By the time Peggy had bathed her, put her shirt on, and laid her on her back in her crib, Louise was fuming. She cried and kicked and flailed in all directions, and banged her head. When I offered her the bottle she called for her mother to pick her up. Realising that this would have settled nothing, we decided to wait her out. She slowed down kicking, put her thumb in her mouth and then accepted the bottle. But from Mom not from me.

infants' faces without being given any information about the triggering events that were provoking their changes in expression. When asked to name the emotion the grimacing infant was experiencing, adult judges consistently identified the feelings of anger, disgust, interest, joy, surprise and sadness in the faces of babies only two months old, and by seven months they could consistently identify fear. These 'basic' emotions are evoked directly by stimuli and events in the outside world. But more complex emotions, like shame and embarrassment, include a cognitive component of self-awareness and so do not enter the infant's repertoire until the second year of life (Lewis, Sullivan, Stanger & Weiss, 1989).

Emotional self-regulation

As they develop, infants not only gain greater versatility of emotional experience, but they also learn to regulate and control their own emotions. By six months of age, some capacity to limit the upset ensuing from negative emotion is evident in many infants, who consistently turn their faces away from upsetting stimuli or suck vigorously on objects as a calming strategy (Mangelsdorf, Shapiro & Marzoff, 1995). Box 5.3 illustrates a more complex instance of emotional self-regulation in a child aged 14 months.

Attachment: The first relationship

Possibly the most important development of the first year of life, and one of the most significant develop-

ments of all during the lifespan, is the infant's formation of a bond of loving attachment binding him or her to a cherished caregiver. The foundation that is laid by this growth of feelings of mutual love and closeness to a caregiver will exert an important lifespan influence, shaping the formation of close relationships to other people, not only during the infancy period but throughout all successive stages in life via friends, romantic love, parenthood, and so on. As we see in later chapters, those individuals lucky enough to have forged secure attachments to their caregivers in infancy enjoy many cognitive, social and emotional advantages over their peers who, through an accident of personality incompatibility, or some basic deficiency in themselves, their caregivers or their environments, fail to become securely attached.

We therefore look closely now at how attachment develops. We begin with an outline of what leads up to attachment, and then look at what the process of attachment consists of from the infant's point of view.

Before attachment: General sociability

Newborn infants are sociable. As noted in Chapter 4, if given a choice among different sounds to listen to that seem equally pleasant to the adult ear (such as a woman's voice reading poetry, a piece of soft orchestral music, a flute song or a melodious bird's warbling), neonates display a consistent preference for the human voice (Brazelton, 1984). The sound of a human voice likewise calms the newborn – soothing heart rate, relaxing tense muscles and diminishing crying – more effectively than most other kinds of sound (Brazelton, 1984).

However, there is an important difference between feeling sociable towards people in general and having specific feelings for one individual caregiver whose absence is felt even when other friendly and affectionate substitute caregivers are present. As the first close relationship (Noller, Feeney & Peterson, 2001), the baby's initial attachment to a caregiver possesses many of the same properties as the other close emotional relationships that will emerge later in life. H. R. Schaffer (1996) described these as follows:

> A relationship has characteristics of its own, such as faithfulness, involvement or devotion, none of which can be applied to any one specific instance of interaction … [Interactions] are a here-and-now phenomenon, [relationships] imply continuity over time and are more than the sum of a series of interactions. (p. 99)

Because infants are sociable from the moment of birth, preferring human companionship to contact with inanimate objects, it may seem as though they have this special devotion or 'love' for their parents instantly. However, until they reach three to five months of age, babies' sociability and attraction to people is largely indiscriminate. Very young infants will happily accept comfort from almost anyone who holds, feeds or soothes them. In fact, an experienced grandmother, babysitter or health professional who has become adept at these infant care skills through experience with many babies may sometimes be preferred by an infant in the general sociability stage to a novice mother lacking in such expertise.

When they begin to smile socially (approximately 6 to 8 weeks), babies display this same generalised sociability in smiling. Grins are bestowed freely upon grandparents, neighbours, casual acquaintances and even total strangers in supermarkets.

However, by about four months of age, things are beginning to change. The first indications of *differential sociability*, or special friendliness towards one or two chosen people in the baby's life space, begin to appear. Infants now smile more at familiar faces than strange ones and engage in routines like peek-a-boo more enthusiastically with familiar partners. But there is little protest when the parent leaves, provided another competent, even though unfamiliar, caregiver is present to supply comfort and attention.

The development of attachment between six and eight months of age heralds a dramatic departure from this earlier pattern of friendly sociability to all and sundry. In sharp contrast to 2-month-olds, infants aged six to eight months are liable to cry and cling when their parents leave, and react with fear or aversion to the smiling face of a stranger. The need to cling to someone and be soothed is no longer appeased by just anyone who has the skills to rock or stroke a baby (see Chapter 4). Particularly when the baby is tired, sick or frightened, distress abates only when the familiar attachment target comes to the baby's aid. Table 5.4 illustrates the transition from generalised sociability to a genuine and specific attachment to a chosen caregiver, as defined by the pioneering attachment researcher, John Bowlby.

Prerequisites for attachment

Part of the reason that an infant's attachment takes time to develop is the need for a number of perceptual, cognitive, motoric and emotional building blocks for a specific, discriminating preference for a particular caregiver to develop first. One of these is the ability to recognise and distinguish people by sight. The important changes in visual acuity over the initial months of life (described in Chapter 4) are central to this skill. Also in Chapter 4, we noted how infants cognitively develop a concept of object permanence. Applied to people, the corresponding understanding of basic person permanence equips the infant to realise that his or her mother is a distinct and 'permanent' individual who continues to exist even when she is out of sight.

Stranger fear, or the infant's special wariness towards people outside the immediate family circle, develops at about the same time as the first clear-cut attachment and may be a related phenomenon.

		Phases in the growth of an attachment relationship during infancy
TABLE 5.4		
Infant's age	Phase	Description
0 to 2 months	Pre-attachment	Generalised sociability; indiscriminate social responsiveness
3 to 7 months	Attachment in the making	Maturation of readiness for attachment through visual face recognition, person permanence, stranger wariness, etc.
8 to 24 months	Clear-cut attachment	Differential proximity seeking, separation protest, clinging to attachment target(s) more than to other people
2 years onwards	Goal-directed partnership	Relationships are mutual: child is sensitive to parent's needs

Source: Adapted from Bowlby (1973); Noller, Feeney & Peterson (2001).

Infants who are in the grip of stranger fear often display their most intense negative reactions to an approach from an unfamiliar adult who resembles the target of their first attachment. For example, if the baby's initial attachment is to the mother, the mother's biological sister (who hasn't seen her infant niece for a few weeks) could provoke an intense fear reaction, especially if she approaches the baby too closely and smiles or tries to hold her. The little brow may pucker and, if auntie persists, crying will no doubt ensue. It seems that a cognitive appraisal process enables the infant to compare the facial features of the stranger to her familiar cognitive schema representing the mother's face. A mismatch signals threat and evokes the emotion of fear (see page 149).

Figure 5.4 illustrates the developmental correspondence between the onset of stranger fear and the infant's first attachment.

First signs of true love

While newborn babies are sociable, they cannot be said to 'love' their parents in the same way that parents might almost instantly 'fall in love' with a newborn baby (see Chapter 3). When we speak of true love, we generally mean that the lover feels a special affection for the loved one, preferring him or her to people in general. The first signs of this in infants often appear between the ages of five and seven months when babies single out a caregiver for special treatment. By carefully and systematically observing the infant's behaviour when with caregivers, with other family members and with strangers, and by comparing the baby's patterns of social responsiveness to various figures in the social environment, it is often possible to glimpse an attachment being formed. Telltale signs include, in general terms:

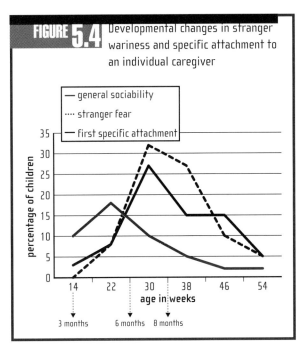

FIGURE 5.4 Developmental changes in stranger wariness and specific attachment to an individual caregiver

Source: Based on data in Schaffer & Emerson (1964a).

1. The expression of special positive emotional attraction for the target of the attachment
2. Evidence that the attraction is specific to this one person, or felt more strongly for him or her than for people in general

While parents may fall in love with their infants at birth, the baby takes several months to develop a bond of attachment.

3. Reluctance to be separated from the attachment target
4. Evidence that this reluctance is greater for the target than for people in general
5. Delight in reunion with the target after a separation.

Thus, newborn infants who display a preference for being held in human arms rather than laid on a mattress cannot be said to be attached to a caregiver in the full sense of the term. Although fond of humans in general, they do not yet seem to distinguish one set of arms from another. But an older infant who clings to the mother but resists being held by a stranger can be said to have an attachment, according to the specificity (or differential sociability) criterion.

At a more fine-grained level of analysis, Mary D. S. Ainsworth (1973) catalogued the following list of specific behaviours as evidence of a baby's attachment:

1. Crying to attract the caregiver's attention
2. Smiling more at the caregiver than at other people
3. Vocalising more in the caregiver's presence than when alone or with strangers
4. Crying when the caregiver leaves or puts the baby down, even if another person is present
5. Following the caregiver with eyes or on foot
6. Looking selectively at the caregiver or in the direction of the caregiver's voice when he or she is out of sight
7. Greeting the caregiver by grinning, crowing and general excitement after a separation
8. Lifting arms to be held by the caregiver
9. Clapping hands with or scrambling over the caregiver
10. Burying the face in the caregiver's lap
11. Embracing, hugging, kissing the caregiver
12. Exploring the environment with a caregiver's presence as a secure 'home' base; reduced exploration in the caregiver's absence

Exploration of the environment with the caregiver as a secure base is a sign of specific attachment.

13. Flight to the caregiver when in danger
14. Clinging physically either to the caregiver or to one of the caregiver's familiar possessions (such as a handbag).

Some of these signs of attachment occur more frequently than others. A few cannot occur at all until the prerequisite motor skills have developed (e.g. locomotion is necessary to follow the caregiver out of the room). Furthermore, any one indicator of differential responding to the caregiver, when taken in isolation, does not unequivocally show that a baby has a secure, personalised attachment (Gewirtz & Boyd, 1976). Each behaviour on the list could be evoked by a variety of causes. For example, as L. Alan Sroufe and Everett Waters (1977) pointed out, babies may sometimes smile as a gesture of affiliation towards the caregivers to whom they are attached, but smiling can also be evoked by successful problem-solving, by the reduction in tension that accompanies a non-threatening interaction with a stranger or as part of an exploratory visual inspection. Nevertheless, in combination with one another, the behaviours on this list help to provide a concrete picture of attachment, or that insubstantial 'psychological tether which binds infant and caregiver together' (Sroufe & Waters 1977, p. 1186).

The Strange Situation

To provide a more precise measure of the quality of an infant's attachment to the primary caregiver than that obtained through naturalistic observation, Mary D. S. Ainsworth created a laboratory testing procedure known as the 'Strange Situation'. Figure 5.5 illustrates the layout of the laboratory in which the test for attachment takes place. The sequence of events in the Strange Situation during which the infant's reactions are observed and recorded is shown in Table 5.5. Throughout each of the sequential episodes, the observer measures the infant's patterns of (a) contact-seeking, (b) exploratory play behaviour and (c) crying. The quality of the infant's play when the mother is present is compared with play during her absence.

The Strange Situation permits comparisons between the infant's social interaction with the mother versus with a female stranger. In addition, the infant's emotional reactions to separations from, and reunions with, the mother are carefully noted, together with the feelings and non-verbal emotions the baby expresses when entering the room, during play, and when left completely alone. The time it takes infants to regain their composure during any periods of upset, together with their mother's skill in comforting them when this happens, is another important element in the structured observation. When all this information is put together, a clear picture emerges of each infant's attachment behaviour. After testing many infants in the procedure, Ainsworth discovered that infants' attachment patterns generally fell into one of three broad categories. Labelled Type A, Type B and Type C, these distinct styles of attachment are described below.

- *Type A: Insecure avoidant attachment.* Babies with this attachment classification show relatively little upset when the stranger enters or the mother leaves and are reluctant to cling to the mother at any stage. Relative to infants in other classifications, they display indifference to the mother throughout the experimental procedures, generally showing no particular attention to her or delight in reunion with her after the separation.
- *Type B: Securely attached.* These babies display their secure bonds of affection and attachment for the mother by protesting vigorously when she departs, actively searching for her during her absence and displaying intense delight in reunion with her on her return to the room.
- *Type C: Anxious-ambivalent insecure (or insecure-resistant).* These babies often cling to or hover near their mothers and show distress when the mother leaves. Yet, they are likely to give little corresponding evidence of joy upon reunion with her and may continue crying during Episodes 5 and 8. Throughout the task, the emotional reactions of Type C infants generally appear disorganised, anxiety-ridden and negative.

Ainsworth discovered that Type B was the most common classification for infants in the United States, with roughly 65 per cent of babies falling into this category. Type A was the next most common with 20 to 25 per cent of babies, followed by Type C

Episode	Participants	Duration	Procedure
			TABLE 5.5 Steps in the Strange Situation test
1	Mother, baby and researcher	30 seconds	Tester guides mother and baby to the experimental room, then leaves. (The room contains appealing toys.)
2	Mother and baby	3 minutes	Mother sits quietly while baby explores; if necessary, play is stimulated after 2 minutes.
3	Stranger, mother and baby	3 minutes	Female research assistant (Stranger) enters. First minute: Stranger is silent. Second minute: Stranger converses with mother. Third minute: Stranger approaches baby. After 3 minutes, mother leaves unobtrusively.
4	Stranger and baby	3 minutes or less	*First separation episode*. Stranger remains in the room and responds to the baby's initiatives.
5	Mother and baby	3 minutes or more	*First reunion episode*. Mother returns and greets and/or comforts baby, then tries to settle the baby again into play.
6	Baby alone	3 minutes or less	*Second separation episode*. Mother leaves, saying 'bye-bye'; the baby remains alone in the room until a reaction is noted; then the Stranger arrives.
7	Stranger and baby	3 minutes or less	Continuation of second maternal separation. Stranger gears her behaviour to that of the baby.
8	Mother and baby	3 minutes	*Second reunion episode*. Mother enters, greets the baby, then picks the baby up. Meanwhile, the Stranger leaves unobtrusively.

FIGURE 5.5 The Strange Situation laboratory, used to test quality of attachment

one-way observer mirror

stranger's chair

mother's chair

attractive toys

A B

with about 10 per cent. (A very small proportion of infants cannot be reliably classified using the Strange Situation procedure.)

Cultural variation in attachment classifications

The Strange Situation has shown itself to be a reliable index of the quality of babies' attachments to their caregivers in societies such as the United States, Australia, New Zealand and Canada, where most infants are familiar with similar real-life situations. For example, when parents go out, these children are often left in the care of a babysitter. On a visit to a doctor's surgery, the infant might encounter strangers. While playing on the loungeroom floor while the mother chats with a neighbour, the infant would have an opportunity to explore. If mother leaves the room briefly to answer the phone while the neighbour watches the baby, an experience similar to Episode 4 is encountered.

When the Strange Situation test was used with infants in Japan, however, percentages in the various classifications were found to differ from those observed in the United States (Miyake, Chen & Campos, 1985). As shown in Figure 5.6, an unexpectedly high percentage of Japanese babies were classified as Type C. While displaying separation protest when their mothers went away, they displayed

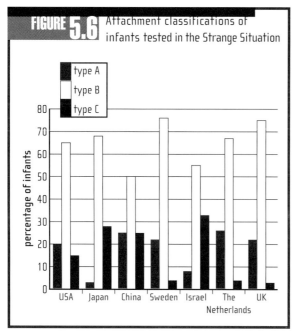

FIGURE 5.6 Attachment classifications of infants tested in the Strange Situation

- type A
- type B
- type C

(bar chart: percentage of infants on y-axis, 0 to 80; categories on x-axis: USA, Japan, China, Sweden, Israel, The Netherlands, UK)

Source: Based on data in Miyake et al. (1985) and Schaffer (1996).

As compared with his own father or grandfather, the contemporary Australian father seems much more eager to spend time holding the baby.

little or no abatement of their distress when she returned, refusing to accept her soothing and continuing to cry vigorously. Other cultural variations in frequencies of the attachment classifications have also been observed. Some if these are shown in Figure 5.6.

It is not known whether cross-cultural variations like these reflect actual differences in attachment security, resulting perhaps from cultural variations in childrearing patterns, or are some artifact of the Strange Situation testing procedure. Possibly the procedure is so unlike anything a Japanese infant would encounter in everyday life that even securely attached babies become upset, not by caregiver separation but rather by the total artificiality of this particular laboratory simulation (Miyake, Chen & Campos, 1985).

Optimising development: Causes and consequences of secure/insecure attachment

The developmental advantages of acquiring a secure attachment during infancy are likely to persist throughout the lifespan and may include self-confidence, emotional well-being, a happy marriage or a warm relationship with one's own offspring. Consequently, for the sake of optimising lifespan psychological growth, as well as infant adjustment, it is important to understand what causes infants to become securely attached.

Caregiver sensitivity

A father, as well as a mother, can become the target of the infant's first secure and specific attachment, indicating that neither (a) female gender, (b) the biological prenatal or birth relationship between mother and child, nor (c) the bond arising during breastfeeding are necessary ingredients for a secure attachment's development (Schaffer & Emerson, 1964a). In fact, even when the mother is the primary caregiver who remains at home with the baby full-time and engages in most of the routine comfort-giving activities of feeding, changing, soothing and bathing, some infants perversely attach themselves to their working father first, only gradually broadening the circle of love to include the mother. Other infants forge their first secure attachment with a live-in grandparent or a sibling (Schaffer & Emerson, 1964a). Clearly quality, not quantity, of care is what makes the difference.

But what specific qualities in caregivers are likely to inspire an infant to become securely attached to them? The factor that seemed to trigger attachment in the pioneering study in Scotland that gave rise to these intriguing results (Schaffer & Emerson, 1964a) has been highlighted again and again in more recent research using the Strange Situation. This is the *sensitivity* of the caregiver. Table 5.6 lists some of the specific components of parenting that make it 'sensitive'. In general, parents who recognise and respond cheerfully and appropriately to their infants' moods, social signals and needs when in distress are the ones most likely to inspire an early attachment. Some caregivers – fathers, grandparents and siblings, as well as mothers – seem to possess a special knack for knowing what the baby wants, together with the skill and willingness to fulfil that need. They come quickly when the baby cries and can usually pinpoint the source of the infant's discomfort while expertly supplying a remedy.

Another important aspect of sensitivity is *synchrony*, or the caregiver's awareness of the level of stimulation the baby can comfortably tolerate. Thus, the sensitive parent gears up the tone of interaction at

TABLE 5.6 Characteristics of sensitive parenting	
Situation	Parenting behaviour
Caregiving interaction	• Parent accurately distinguishes distress from non-distress. • Parent identifies cause for distress and responds appropriately.
Social interaction	• Parent displays *synchrony* (approaching when infant wants to socialise; withdrawing when infant wants solitude). • Parent displays interest and engagement towards infant (not aloof or detached). • Parent plays with infant with enjoyment. • Parent stimulates child's cognitive development.
Emotional tone	• Parent is not hostile. • Parent displays positive emotional regard for the child. • Parent displays responsive affect.

Source: Based on data in National Institute of Child Health and Development (1997).

times when the baby wants fun and excitement, and tones it down when the infant seems too stressed, tired or overstimulated to want to be played with or cuddled.

Since the baby's tendency to seek attachments is increased by distressing states such as anxiety, stress, fear, fatigue and ill health, a caregiver's sensitive responsiveness to a baby who is suffering from any of these forms of discomfort is apt to prove especially potent in the formation of a specific attachment. So, even when not enjoying 24-hour-a-day access to the infant, a parent can become an attachment target by displaying sensitivity. Insensitive, emotionally aloof parenting may interfere with the attachment process even, or perhaps especially, if the caregiver and child are constantly and exclusively in each other's company. As Mary D. S. Ainsworth (1979) explained:

> Within the limits represented by our sample, however, we found that it was how the mother holds her baby rather than how much she holds him or her that affects the way in which attachment develops. (1979, p. 934)

The caregiver's attachment history

Inge Bretherton and Everett Waters (1985) studied the parents of a group of 160 infants whose attachment classifications had been rated Type A, Type B or Type C in the Strange Situation test. These caregivers were given in-depth interviews exploring their early recollections of childrearing experiences and the emotional tone and quality of their parents' treatment of them when they were young. The results produced clear evidence of generational continuities

in insensitive parenting. For example, one father of a Type A baby reported that he had been so terrified of his mother that he had avoided telling her when he broke his hand. Many other parents of insecurely attached infants recalled similarly extreme instances of parental insensitivity, together with other unusually stressful experiences such as the traumatic loss of an early attachment figure or severe parental hostility and rejection.

It was the parent's interpretation of these experiences rather than the experiences themselves that seemed to prove the decisive factor in the subsequent quality of their parenting. Some parents of Type B babies had also suffered traumatic early experiences in relation to attachment but, unlike the insensitive parents, they placed the blame for the experience elsewhere rather than on their own 'inadequate' personalities. Thus one Type B mother, who had told the interviewer she would need hours to catalogue all the faults in her own mother's early treatment of her, went on to explain: 'Okay, well to start with my mother was not cheerful, and I can tell you right now, the reason was that she was overworked' (p. 96). Bretherton and Waters felt that this woman's ability to account for her early rejection on grounds other than some defect in her own character as a baby had enabled her to exhibit sensitivity and affection when mothering her own child. Conversely, as they explained, 'a child whose parents are consistently lacking in responsiveness, who threaten abandonment or who actually abandon the child will tend to build a representational model of self as unworthy and unlovable' (p. 212).

On these grounds, Bretherton and Waters came up with a theory to explain why some well-informed and well-motivated parents, who hope to interact effectively with their infants, end up proving incapable of the sensitive responsiveness that forms the foundation for a secure attachment. They wrote:

> Parental 'insensitivity' to infant signals, then, may originate in the parent's need to preserve a particular organization of information or state of mind. Attachment-relevant signals originating externally from the infant and internally from memory may be similar in the 'rules' they evoke for parents who are insecure in terms of their own internal working models of attachment. The need to restrict or reorganize attachment-relevant information, whether it originates internally or externally, may result in an inability to perceive and interpret the attachment signals of the infant accurately and, in some cases, in an active need either to alter infant signals or to inhibit them. To summarize, where the parent's own experiences and feelings are not integrated, restrictions of varying types are placed on attention and the flow of information with respect to attachment. These restrictions appear in speech in the form of incoherencies and in behavior as insensitivities. (p. 100, reproduced with the permission of the Society for Research in Child Development)

Infant temperament and attachment

Although a parent's sensitivity is a critical factor in the infant's optimal development of a secure attachment, attachment as a social relationship is a mutual process. In fact, the patterns of temperament discussed earlier in this chapter have a lot to do both with attachment and with its precursor, parental sensitivity. It is obviously much more difficult for any parent to decipher the wishes of an infant whose schedules of hunger, wakefulness and elimination are completely irregular than to minister sensitively to the needs of a child who eats, sleeps and wets in a predictable pattern 'by the clock'. Nor is it as easy to express affection to a bad-tempered infant who resists change and expresses predominantly negative moods as to one who almost invariably reacts cheerfully and adaptively to parental overtures.

In fact, over and above the observed differences in attachment due to the mother's sensitivity, the results of Ainsworth's longitudinal study also showed an influence due to the baby's disposition. She found the 'difficult temperament' pattern (see page 142) to be disproportionately represented among the babies who ended up in Type C with an anxious, insecure attachment. The tendency of babies in this group to reject their mothers and express negative emotions during reunions in the Strange Situation could be viewed as just one manifestation of the 'difficult' baby's vigorous and angry rejection of most new or mildly stressful experiences.

Byron Egeland and Ellen Farber (1984) also found that babies who had been rated by their paediatric nurses in hospital as having difficult temperaments when they were between one and two days old were more likely to have become insecurely attached to their mothers by the time they reached the age of 12 months. The infant's inherent character appears to be a better predictor than parenting style of the adverse outcome in this case, since the difficult-temperament tendency was evident to objective observers in the hospital, even before the mother's sensitivity had had a chance to impinge on the baby.

Inge Bretherton and Everett Waters (1985) suggested that the infant's and parent's personalities interacted continually from the moment of their first meeting so as to shape either a secure or an insecure attachment by the age of 12 months. When they looked at the newborn temperaments and mothering patterns of the 16 children in their sample who had received a Type B (securely attached) classification in the Strange Situation as one-year-olds, they found that having had *either* a favourable temperament classification *or* a sensitive mother predicted a baby's ending up as securely attached nearly as well as both qualities together did. Thus, 44 per cent of the group who had been either above the median on temperament but below the median for maternal sensitivity, or vice versa, had ended up with a secure attachment, as compared with 50 per cent of those who had

scored above average both for newborn temperament and for sensitive mothering.

Beginning life with a favourable temperament pattern undoubtedly boosts the baby's chances of achieving a secure attachment, because easy, alert infants are cheerful and willing to interact. By rewarding the mother's initial caregiving efforts with smiles and mutuality, temperamentally easy babies can effectively teach their novice mothers what their needs are and how to satisfy them. On the other hand, an easy temperament could also foster a secure attachment without any modification of the insensitive parent's attempts to parent, simply because highly flexible and adaptable infants who are generally alert, cheerful and responsive have the disposition that most effectively promotes their parent's gradual development towards a more sensitive parenting style.

Day-care and attachment

BOX 5.4 A case in point
Day-care – a brave new world

When infants and toddlers attend day-care, they have opportunities to become attached to substitute caregivers, while also experiencing routine separation and reunion episodes when their primary caregivers drop them off at child care and collect them later. Louise's father described his daughter's adjustment to entering a half-day infant nursery when she was two years old.

5 October 1950. *Louise has the same attitude toward nursery school as toward a new food. She'll take a bite, taste it thoughtfully, swallow it, and say, 'It's good'. That's the faint praise that damns. She'll have no more of it. In the planning stage of nursery school, she looked forward to it eagerly, and she went off bravely and expectantly with her mother the first morning. But the teacher would not allow her mother to stay and Louise, never having played with children on her own before, cried when she saw her go. When her mother returned for her at noon, she learned Louise had made a couple of tentative tries for some of the toys, only to have them snatched away by some of the other children. This was enough to discourage her and she spent the rest of the morning standing in silence.*

A weekend intervened ... The next morning at breakfast, I mentioned nursery school and her face fell. No, she stated flatly, she didn't want to go. 'All right,' I said, as before. 'You don't have to go if you don't want to.' That was fine with Louise. 'How would you like just to go, say hello to the teacher and come right home?' I thought if she went thus for a few mornings, she'd get over the strangeness and could be left for

The case history in Box 5.4 illustrates one child's gradual adjustment to the prospect of separation from her primary caregiver in order to attend child care. Though Louise entered the nursery at age two, after the stage when her initial attachment would have developed, other infants begin day-care before, or during, the formative period for attachment development during the first year of life (see Table 5.4). What effects will early day-care have on the ease with which infants develop the first attachment to a parent, and on the security of that attachment bond?

Beginning with John Bowlby (1982), a scientific debate has raged for decades in developmental psychology over the likely effects of regular separations between infants and their primary caregivers to attend day-care, while both parents pursue employment outside the home. Concerned parents are often preoccupied by the same question. Does day-care attendance invariably weaken the bond of attachment that the infant is struggling to forge with the primary caregiver? If so, do hours of attendance or age of entry matter? What is the mechanism responsible? Could it be the stress of continual separation or is it a question of the total amount of time that infants and their parents spend together? Until recently, attempts to answer these questions were based on small-scale studies which often produced contradictory results.

However, persuaded of the importance of a conclusive answer to the vexing question of whether child care is a risk factor for insecure attachment, with all its potentially damaging consequences through the lifespan (see pages 158–9), the National Institute of Child Health and Development (NICHD) in the United States invested in a comprehensive large-scale study (NICHD, 1997). Its aim was to provide a definitive test of the hypothesis, based in Bowlby, that infants who attend child care outside their homes on a regular basis have a higher risk of developing insecure (Type A or Type C) attachments than infants, matched on other variables, who are reared exclusively at home by one or both parents.

The sample chosen for this study consisted of 1153 infants and their mothers who were recruited to represent the full range of demographic diversity (economic status, ethnicity and parental education) of the US population. Fifty-three per cent of the children were in full-time child care, 23 per cent attended child care on a regular part-time basis and the remaining 24 per cent were exclusively home-reared. The infants' attachment styles were assessed in the Strange Situation at age 15 months, and their patterns of interaction with their mother and (where relevant) their day-care providers were assessed using naturalistic observation (see Chapter 2) at regular intervals. The quality of the infants' child-care environments was also examined and found to range from poor to excellent.

The results of this comprehensive investigation are likely to be greeted with optimism and relief by employed parents throughout the world: out-of-home child care had no effect per se on the probability of an infant developing either a secure or an insecure attachment. This lack of any significant influence of non-parental care applied to infants in institutional or family-run day-care, and the infant's age at entry and hours of weekly attendance likewise made no difference. The researchers concluded:

There were no main effects of child-care experience (quality, amount, age of entry, stability, or type of care) on attachment security or avoidance ... The results of this study clearly indicate that child care by itself constitutes neither a risk nor a benefit for the development of the infant–mother attachment relationship as measured in the Strange Situation. (p. 877)

One of the advantages of day-care from the child's point of view is the opportunity for regular contact with playmates of one's own age and a wide variety of toys.

In other words, when tested systematically, the hypothesis that day-care is harmful received no scientific support. This result is in keeping with the observation noted earlier in this chapter that the quality of a caregiver's sensitivity, rather than the sheer quantity of time infant and caregiver spend together, is what influences attachment security.

Attachment through the lifespan

Though attachments first develop in infancy, their effects are felt throughout the rest of the lifespan. To explore the link between infant and childhood attachment processes, Inge Bretherton and Everett Waters (1985) reassessed a group of 40 six-year-olds whose attachments to their mothers and fathers had first been measured in the Strange Situation (see Figure 5.5) at 12 months of age. Data from home visits, interviews and a two-hour session in a laboratory playroom were combined to provide a picture of the children's functioning at the age of six. The laboratory measures included a series of spontaneous separation and reunion episodes as the father and mother were called out of the room by the experimenter, and then allowed to return. The children were also shown a short film about a 2-year-old child of their own sex who underwent a 10-day separation from their parents in foster care. They were asked to explain what the child in the story would do, as a way of evaluating their own attitudes towards issues of parenting and separation.

Some of the replies Bretherton and Waters obtained are shown in Box 5.5. Before reading on, you may wish to consider how infants with Type A, B or C attachments would be likely to respond to a projective story-telling task like this by completing the exercise in Box 5.5.

An attachment to a blanket can serve the useful function of consoling infants and older children during necessary separations from their human caregivers.

BOX 5.5 A pause for thought
Can you typecast these 6-year-old story-tellers?

Instructions: Listed below are three children's responses to the question of how a 2-year-old would cope with a two-week separation from parents. During infancy, one of the respondents had been classified as Type A, one as Type B and one as Type C in Ainsworth's Strange Situation. Can you guess which was which and why?

Interviewer	What will he do?
Daniel	Chase them.
Interviewer	Chase who?
Daniel	His dad and mom in his new toy car ... And then he's gonna ... toss a bow and arrow and shoot them.
Interviewer	Shoot his mom and dad?
Daniel	Yeah, if he wants to.
Interviewer	What will she do?
Lisa	She's gonna stay up until she gets tired ... And she's gonna cry ... And she's gonna get a flu ... And she's gonna get dressed in the morning with that dress [a present from the mother] all the time.
Interviewer	What will she do?
Mary	Run away.
Interviewer	Where's she going to run to?

Source: Bretherton & Waters (1985), pp. 103–4.

For answers see the section below.

Consequences of infant attachment in childhood

The effects of having a secure or insecure attachment as an infant may persist later in life. Inge Bretherton and Everett Waters (see Box 5.5) found that children who had been securely attached (Type B) as infants displayed a very different pattern of response to these measures from the children who had been anxiously or avoidantly insecure in their attachments during infancy.

Throughout the various parental separations and reunions in Bretherton and Waters' playroom, the secure children appeared relaxed, open and outgoing. During the parent's absence, they engaged in pleasant chitchat with the unfamiliar experimenters. When the parent returned, they showed pleasure in welcoming them back and confidently sought proximity while resuming the fluent, free-ranging dialogue that had been interrupted by the separation.

The children who had had insecure Type A and C attachments, on the other hand, seemed tense and tongue-tied both with the parent and with a stranger in the playroom. Those who had had an insecure-avoidant attachment to the mother (Type A) in infancy continued to avoid both verbal and physical contact with her in the playroom at the age of six. Though responding politely when addressed, they preferred to attend to toys and activities rather than to either parent during reunion episodes, and sometimes tried to move subtly away from the parent to a different part of the room.

By contrast, those children who had been anxiously ambivalent in their infant attachments (Type C) were more overtly hostile to the parent in the playroom than either of the former Type A or Type B children. They also seemed tense and uncomfortable when conversing with the experimenters during the parent's absence. When the parent returned, they were overtly rejecting. Sometimes they even reversed roles and punitively lectured the parent on the naughtiness of having gone away. When shown a photo that had been taken of the whole family when they entered the laboratory, the Type C children, unlike children in the other groups, showed signs of depression and disorganisation.

The film about the child in foster care elicited equally distinctive reactions from the three attachment groups. Box 5.5 includes some of the comments three of the 6-year-olds in Bretherton and Waters' sample made after viewing the film. Have you guessed the attachment classifications of Daniel, Lisa and Mary when they were babies?

When the combined responses of each of the three attachment groups to the interview about separation were analysed, Bretherton and Waters concluded that:

> The secure six-year-olds seemed to have free ranging access to affect, memory, and plans, whether in forming speech in conversation with the parent or in discussing imagined situations relevant to attachment ... These children seemed at ease in exploring feelings during the separation interview and had ideas (interestingly unique to each child) regarding constructive interactions that a child might take in response to a projected two-week separation from the parents. (p. 95, reproduced with the permission of the Society for Research in Child Development)

On the other hand, the children who had been insecurely attached in an anxious and resistant manner as infants lacked a stable image of the parent as accessible. They therefore became 'distressed, silent, irrational, or occasionally self-destructive' (p. 96) in response to questions about separation. Yet another style of responding was shown by children who had been avoidantly attached. This group seemed highly conflicted and resisted allowing themselves even to think about an event as traumatic as a 10-day separation. Thus their story endings were vague and ill-thought-out and they gave mostly 'don't know' responses to the interviewer. (In line with these general conclusions, Lisa in Box 5.5 had been classified Type B as a baby, Daniel was Type C and Mary was Type A.)

Attachment in maturity

Adolescent and adult developmental patterns also bear witness to the pervasive long-term influence of secure versus insecure attachments during infancy. As we see in Chapters 9, 12, 13 and 14, securely attached infants, who grow up to become securely attached children, adolescents and adults, are likely to enjoy different experiences with peers, romantic partners, spouses and colleagues at work than those whose attachment styles remain insecure. Indeed, according to Cindy Hazan and Phillip Shaver (1987), romantic love is itself an attachment process that mirrors infant–parent attachment. Thus, adults who were securely attached to their mother or father during infancy stand a better than average chance of developing a secure, trusting, intimate relationship when they fall in love. But an adult who was an anxiously attached infant carries the risk of being unable to feel secure with a romantic partner in later life.

In support of their theory, Hazan and Shaver found that adults' descriptions of their styles of love were closely analogous to Mary D. S. Ainsworth's Type A, B and C attachment patterns of infancy, with the Type B secure love style being characterised in adulthood by trust, intimate self-disclosure and comfort in being emotionally close. By contrast, Type C anxious-ambivalent adult love style was identified by an overwhelming preoccupation with love, coupled with self-doubt and a jealous fear of being rejected or abandoned. This style parallels the Type C anxious-ambivalent attachment pattern of infancy. Similarly, in line with infants with a Type A avoidant infant attachment, a group of avoidant adults described their romantic relationships as cold, aloof and superficial and their beliefs about love in terms of discomfort with closeness, disappointment and reluctance to make a long-term commitment to a relationship.

Research also shows that, during childhood and adolescence, securely attached infants generally score higher than their insecurely attached counterparts on measures of (a) self-esteem, (b) popularity with peers, (c) skills for coping with difficult cognitive problems or social situations, (d) skills for coping with failure, (e) enthusiasm and persistence in learning, (f) curiosity, (g) mature independence from parents, and (h) freedom from problem behaviours such as aggression, hyperactivity or anxiety (Sroufe, 1985). These are ideal qualities with which to embark not only on future social relationships but upon a life of learning, creative expression and self-discovery (see Chapters 9, 12, 13 and 14).

Fathering

Infants become attached to their father as well as their mother. As noted earlier, some infants forge their first attachment to their father and only later generalise it to their mother and other close family members. But for most infants who form their first attachment to their primary-caregiver mother, the father nonetheless soon becomes a highly valued attachment target whose relationship to the infant can be equally secure and significant for immediate and long-term well-being. Infants who are securely attached to their father are especially likely to turn to him for companionship and stimulation through play, games, story-telling and other cognitive challenges (Lamb, 1997).

When two parents are present in the household, the mother and father can play complementary roles. An example is seen in Box 5.3 where infant Louise, angered by illness and the frustration of bumping her head, alternated between her parents in her attempts to obtain soothing and the comfort of her feeding bottle.

In the long run, an intact family with both father and mother present is beneficial because it gives the baby with an insecure attachment to one of the parents the chance to form a secure (Type B) attachment to the other parent. Figure 5.7 shows the results of a study of 950 infants using the Strange Situation (van Ijzendoorn & De Wolff, 1997). As shown, only 17 per cent of these babies had insecure (Type A or Type C) attachments to both their mother and their father. In most cases, even when the attachment to one parent was insecure, a compensatory secure attachment had formed with the other parent.

Despite their potential to exert beneficial direct and compensatory influences on their children's psychological development, however, not all fathers become as actively involved in parenting as mothers do, especially while their children are young infants. The playwright Oscar Wilde once remarked: 'Fathers should neither be seen nor heard. That is the only proper basis for family life.' Over the past quarter of a century, a number of empirical studies have shown that many contemporary fathers continue to live by this precept (Edgar & Glezer, 1992; Parke & Stearns, 1993).

In one of the classic studies on this topic, Freda Rebelsky and Carolyn Hanks (1971) measured the contact between American fathers and infants on a 24-hour-a-day basis by the use of a microphone pinned to the baby's T-shirt. They found the typical father spent only 38 seconds a day talking to his baby during the first quarter of the infant's first year of life. Even the most devoted father in this study favoured his baby with just over 10 minutes of daily conversation. Though this dearth of contact may possibly have been due to the infants being so young, there was no suggestion of an increase over the three months that the study continued. In fact, 70 per cent of the fathers spent progressively *less* time with their baby as the infant grew older.

In an effort to determine the causes of such a reluctant uptake of fatherhood and also to verify the extent to which this applied in Australia, Graeme Russell (1978) recruited 43 two-parent families with a preschool child by approaching people in Sydney's suburban shopping centres and on the streets of two small country towns in New South Wales. All the fathers worked full-time, their occupations covering a wide cross-section that was typical of the population as a whole. Approximately half the mothers were full-time housewives, and half were employed outside the home on a full-time or part-time basis. The hours per week that these fathers spent in activities with their children are shown in Table 5.7.

These results indicate that, like their American peers, Australian fathers were relatively uninvolved in day-to-day care for their children. The total of some 12 hours a week that the average father devotes to parenting is less than many Australian men spend in leisure pursuits like watching television, playing sport or drinking at the pub. The average Australian father was less involved than his wife in every child-related activity Russell looked at, including playing with the child. However, play was the one role in which the father invested the bulk of his parenting time. A decade later, using data from a new sample of Sydney families as well as from similar studies in the United States, Graeme and Alan Russell (1987) concluded that the situation had changed very little, with fathers in the United States and Australia continuing to spend far less time on child-care tasks than their wives, as well as less time in face-to-face interaction with their infants and preschool children.

Other cross-cultural contrasts have shown New Zealand fathers to be similarly uninvolved in parenting compared with mothers (Ritchie & Ritchie, 1978) and the same is true in Canada (Lytton, 1980). Fathers in contemporary China appear to take a more active role than their American, Australian or

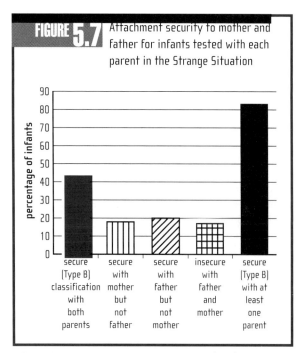

FIGURE 5.7 Attachment security to mother and father for infants tested with each parent in the Strange Situation

Source: Based on data in van Ijzendoorn & De Wolff (1997).

TABLE 5.7	Mean hours per week of parent–child interaction for Australian fathers and mothers								
	Feed	Dress	Change napkins	Bath	Attend at night	Read stories	Help at school	Play	Total
Fathers	1¾	½	⅓	½	¹/₁₀	½	¹/₁₀	9	12
Mothers	10½	3½	1½	1½	⅓	1½	⅓	14	33

Source: Russell (1978), p. 1177. Reproduced with the permission of the Society for Research in Child Development.

When both parents are available, many infants and toddlers prefer to play with their fathers.

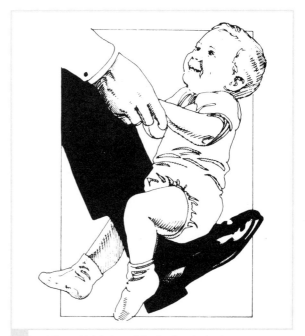

When fathers pick infants up, it is often in order to play.

New Zealand counterparts in caring for their single child (Su, 1982). But in other less affluent nations, such as Guatemala and Uganda, even lower levels of father participation are found than in the West (Parke, 1979). While expressed attitudes about fathers' participation in child care have become very positive in industrialised nations like Australia, New Zealand and the United States in recent years, there is little evidence of these attitudes carrying over into practice. Harry McGurk (1995) found that fathers in the mid-1990s remained less involved than mothers in the many tasks associated with caring for children, even when both parents were employed full-time outside the home.

Michael Lamb (1975, 1997) observed fathers and mothers of 8-month-olds in interaction with their infants. He noted that parents of each sex were inclined to provide qualitatively distinct kinds of input when they picked up the baby from its cot. Mothers typically gathered up the baby in order to perform one of the physical caretaking routines of feeding, changing, bathing, dressing or soothing the child. When a father picked up the infant, it was almost always in order to play. As a result, the infants

responded more positively to physical contact with their father than with their mother. Even when both parents were willing to play, the babies preferred to go to their father, presumably because the kind of play the father initiated was more interesting. Lamb observed that fathers tended to play more physical games like tossing the baby in the air, and also devised more idiosyncratic, made-up games than mothers did; mothers tended to confine themselves to standard routines like peek-a-boo or counting toes.

Graeme Russell (1982) made a detailed analysis of an atypical Australian lifestyle: families with the father as the primary caregiver and the mother in a secondary caregiving role. Though such households were uncommon in the early 1980s and remain so today, Russell managed to recruit 50 of them in the Sydney area. The random sampling in shopping centres, which had yielded his estimates of the typical caregiving patterns of Australian families, netted a group of 10 families. Their circle of friends and acquaintances yielded a further 10, and the rest responded to advertisements. Approximately one-third of the fathers in this group were unemployed. The remainder worked part-time or irregular hours.

The average mother in the group spent 40 hours a week at work, and the average father 28. However, in contrast to the traditional Australian family, where a full-time working mother usually means the sharing of child care between the mother and an outside helper, the primary-caregiver fathers in Russell's non-traditional sample had sole responsibility for their children for an average of 26 hours each week. (The corresponding figure for their wives was 15 hours, and for the average Australian father with a full-time working wife, two hours).

Russell was intrigued by what had led these families to adopt such an atypical pattern of childrearing. The most common motivation was financial. Thirty-eight per cent of these families explained that their combined income was greater with the non-traditional pattern than it would have been with the wife as the children's primary caregiver. But a further 26 per cent had elected to share parenting out of an ideological commitment to the need for both parents to be equally involved in their children's upbringing. They felt strongly that the children's gains from having extensive periods of regular one-to-one contact with the father as well as the mother outweighed any other disadvantages of this atypical parenting pattern. Once they had embarked on it, other parents also perceived clear benefits to their children from the new way of life. Seventy-four per cent of the fathers felt they had grown closer to their children after becoming primary caregivers, and 28 per cent also said they had gained a better understanding of their children's personalities and day-to-day needs. Some additional costs and benefits of the lifestyle, as reported by these Sydney fathers and mothers, included stronger family ties on the positive side of the equation, and the father being teased by male friends on the negative side.

Graeme and Alan Russell (1987) recorded patterns of interaction among family members in a set of 57 Sydney households with two or more children, the eldest of whom was six years old. They also interviewed the father and mother separately about the extent of their own, and their spouse's, involvement with the offspring. One important question was whether the above-noted findings of far less involvement by fathers than mothers in parental duties might have been a function of researchers mainly asking parents what they did, rather than observing them directly. The researchers reasoned that fathers might be unwilling to admit to engaging in behaviours like feeding or nappy changing which violated their sex-role stereotypes about masculinity (see Chapters 8 and 13). This possibility highlights one of the advantages of the naturalistic observational method outlined in Chapter 2.

But when they analysed the results of their observational study, Russell and Russell concluded that the data generally failed to support their hypothesis. Instead, the observational findings reinforced the data obtained in interviews, by showing that Australian mothers interacted more frequently with their children than did Australian fathers. The mothers were also more directive and more involved in caring for the child's needs (e.g. telling the child to put toys away, to eat dinner using a knife and fork, to clean their plate, take a bath, or that it was time for bed). In line with the data on infants cited earlier, however, fathers were found to spend more time than mothers in outdoor play, and children were found to initiate playful pursuits with their father more often than with their mother. On the other hand, contrary to a popular stereotype, fathers were no more competitive in play, and no more encouraging of competition between siblings, than mothers were.

Overall, their observations of these Sydney families led Russell and Russell to conclude that:

Although there are major mother/father differences, it is obvious that most fathers were actively involved and that they did have strong relationships with their children – confirming the attachment studies in infancy. The present results suggest that fathers make a significant contribution to their child's socialization, although they did not appear to take major responsibility for their day-to-day care or needs. Given the affective quality of their relationships with their children, however, they are obviously in a position to exert considerable influence, especially as their children become older and caregiving becomes less important. (p. 1583)

These researchers also found that Australian fathers showed more negative reactions to dependency bids on the part of sons than daughters, and were also more negative than mothers in reacting to their son's dependency. Similarly, fathers reacted more negatively to their son's misbehaviour than to similar misdeeds by their daughter. These contrasts in parental reactions to misdeeds and dependency are shown in Figure 5.8.

Fathers also gain developmental benefits (as do mothers) from intimate involvement with their

Fathers make a significant contribution to their children's development of social, cognitive and sporting skills.

infants and children while growing up. We examine how adult development is shaped by the experience of parenting in Chapters 13 and 14.

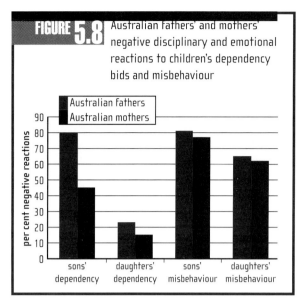

FIGURE 5.8 Australian fathers' and mothers' negative disciplinary and emotional reactions to children's dependency bids and misbehaviour

Source: Based on data in Russell & Russell (1987).

Chapter summary

Infants come into the world with their own idiosyncratic patterns of temperament. Reflecting the joint contributions of genetics and prenatal experience, these variations in temperament may express themselves through irritability, high or low activity, the duration and intensity of the infant's crying, how easy the infant is to soothe, or how cheerful, fretful, cuddly or adaptable. The diurnal rhythms of the infant's digestive and sleeping schedules also reflect the vagaries of temperament. As well as varying from baby to baby, personality patterns also vary systematically with cultural backgrounds. Aboriginal infants are apt to be more alert and soothable than Anglo-Australian infants. Infants from European immigrant backgrounds also show distinctive temperament styles.

We can classify infants' temperaments as 'difficult' or 'easy' in terms of their readiness to adapt to the parenting strategies that prevail in Western culture. Yet, as research among the Masai people shows dramatically, such classifications are specific to a particular culture. Qualities like angry irritability which may seem 'difficult' in one environment can be highly adaptive in harsh surroundings such as drought-stricken Africa.

Parents' own personalities and childrearing strategies may help to shape infant temperament. At the same time they are subject to modification as they learn to interact with, and accept, the personality that their baby brings into the world.

Over the first year of life, a development that remains of crucial significance throughout the lifespan begins to emerge. This is the infant's first close relationship: a bond of attachment to a caregiver. A secure, personalised attachment is demonstrated by a converging set of behaviours first displayed by the baby at about six months of age. These include delight in the caregiver's company, special attentiveness to the caregiver, following and cuddling with the caregiver especially closely even when other affectionate people are available, and protesting vigorously when the caregiver goes away.

Attachment is fostered by sensitive caregiving and, on present indications, seems to develop equally readily among babies who spend time in day-care as among those who are exclusively home-reared.

Secure attachments are important throughout the lifespan. As well as supplying the emotional support, self-confidence and comfort we all gain from being in love and knowing that love is reciprocated, a secure attachment during infancy and childhood encourages cognitive exploration, the acquisition of social skills and language development, as we see in the next few chapters.

For further interest

Looking forward on the Internet

Use the Internet to visit the following websites. Examine them for further information and varied perspectives on issues raised in this chapter. Also search for other relevant websites for yourself, using keywords like 'attachment', 'personality', 'parenting', 'family', 'mother love' and 'fathers' in your search engine.

In particular, for further ideas on infant temperament, go to **http://www.zerotothree.org/tips/temperam.htm**; for details of the Australian temperament project described in this chapter, go to: **http://www.aifs.org.au/atp/pubs.html** and for information on toys and play in infancy and childhood go to: **http://www.cfw.tufts.edu**.

For resources, ideas, activities and other items of interest in conjunction with this chapter, visit the Companion Website for this textbook at:

http://wps.pearsoned.com.au/peterson

Activity suggestion

As a practical activity in conjunction with the themes raised in this chapter, you may wish to examine contemporary attitudes to fathers being the primary caregivers for their young infants. Try collecting glossy magazine advertisements, television commercials, and pictures from children's story books that display an infant under age 2 with a caregiver. Count up the number of times that caregiver appears to be (a) the father, (b) the mother, or (c) some third party (e.g. grandparent). Do mothers continue to outnumber fathers in these situations? Does the source of the image (e.g. magazine versus picture book) make a difference?

Multimedia

For a provocative discussion of fathers' roles in early infant development that is still timely today, view the video *Fathers* (Film Australia, 1980: 16 minutes, colour).

Milestones of development in infancy

	Domain of development			
Physical and motor skill	Sensation and perception	Emotion	Cognition	Social relationships	Personality
By six weeks of age babies begin to master the skill of supporting their heads in a steady, erect posture. This skill is generally fully developed by four months when infants also lift their heads from a prone position and can sit with support. Five months brings rolling from stomach to side or back. By eight months the typical infant can pull up to a standing posture and sit with support. The average infant walks alone for short distances at 12 months. Fine motor skills for reaching and grasping develop by three months. By nine months the infant can pick up small objects with thumb and first finger like a pincer.	Senses of hearing, smell, taste and touch are well developed at birth. Neonates can distinguish among the sounds, smells and tastes of the world outside the womb with fine acuity. Vision develops rapidly over the first four months, by which time a baby can perceive colour like an adult, track moving objects visually, and systematically move the eyes to scan complex contours and designs. By five months infants can accurately discriminate between faces of similar-looking people in live and photo portrayals and can recognise facial expressions of emotion. Visual acuity improves to adult (20:20) levels between six and eight months, as do depth perception and size constancy.	Soon after birth, infants show alertness, distress and general upset. By two months they display social smiling. At three to four months they laugh in response to predictable and mildly surprising social and physical stimuli over which they can exert control. Between six and twelve months fear is clearly expressed. This includes the fear of strangers with a resemblance to a familiar caregiver (stranger fear) which plays a role in the formation of a social attachment (see social relationships). Anger, surprise and shyness emerge by six months. Pride and embarrassment do not emerge until age two.	Even before birth, infants have a capacity for memory and simple learning. Discriminative learning is possible at birth and by two months infants can learn complex contingencies. Attention develops over the early months and is triggered by optimal discrepancy from a familiar pattern. During the first four months after birth, while in Piaget's stage of Primary Circular Reactions, infants adapt inborn reflexes to suit new situations. From four to eight months, they begin to develop personal control over objects and events they can move, manipulate and explore. Before six months, they have no concept of the existence of hidden objects, but from eight to 12 months they will search for hidden things where they have previously been found. By 18 months they can search maturely. By age two they can imagine invisible displacement.	At two months the social smile emerges. By four months it is well established and infants display general sociability towards friendly people without singling out caregivers for special attention. By six months signs of specific attachment to a familiar caregiver emerge. Between seven and 12 months the typical infant forges a bond of emotional attachment to a caregiver. This bond may be secure (Type B), avoidant (Type A) or anxious–ambivalent (Type C).	Infants are born with distinctive temperament patterns involving variations in levels of alertness, mood activity and irritability. Babies with an easy temperament adjust more readily to novel situations than those whose personalties at birth are either difficult or slow to warm up. Over the first year of life, according to Erikson's theory, infants forge a sense of basic trust that grows into a secure attachment and fosters hope later in life.

THE PRESCHOOL PERIOD – FROM AGE TWO TO AGE SIX

PART 3

Contents

Overview

The years from the time when toddlers learn to speak to the start of primary school are magical ones in both the child's and the parents' lives. As children begin to explore the world independently, their curiosity sharpens, their mental ingenuity seeks explanations for the paradoxes they encounter, and budding language skills equip them with the capacity to offer captivating spoken commentaries about all these things. Parents who listen closely to toddlers' early words, phrases and questions gain fascinating glimpses into the workings of a growing mind.

As the 17th-century French writer La Bruyere (1645–96) noted, 'Children have neither past nor future; they enjoy the present which very few of us do'. Adults who have time to share the preschooler's playful day-to-day present are treated to a rich world of the child's imagination, as well as, in many families, fluent verbal negotiations over rules and routines of meals, play, bedtime, toys and sharing as 2-year-olds express their self-confidence and a growing urge for independence. As parents engage in these everyday routines with their incessantly active, walking and talking toddlers and preschoolers, they are likely to be kept so busy they may almost lack the time to notice the delightful developmental changes in the child's maturity that take place almost daily as new vistas open up and familiar challenges are mastered. Suddenly, and all too soon, the child is no longer a speechless infant, a lisping toddler or a playfully mischievous preschooler but a confident, social and knowing 6-year-old, ready to venture forth into the outside world of peers and formal education in primary school.

In Chapters 6 and 7 we examine the dramatic developmental changes that punctuate the preschool years.

TODDLERS: Cognitive, social and personality development in the context of language acquisition

CHAPTER 6

*He gave man speech, and speech created thought,
Which is the measure of the universe.*
Percy Bysshe Shelley (1792–1822),
Prometheus Unbound

Contents

CHAPTER OVERVIEW

Toddlerhood, the period from age one to three, stands out in the lifespan for one remarkable developmental achievement: the acquisition of language. This momentous development transforms the entire fabric of the child's psychological nature and mode of existence. New powers of thought are gained with the capacity to represent concepts in words. Communication with others opens new vistas of mental life while also advancing social and emotional development to a higher plane. Toddlers who converse with parents and peers gain sophisticated new social skills for questioning, persuading, negotiating, teasing, sharing in the imaginary worlds of stories and make-believe places, and giving and receiving emotional solace when distressed by pain, anxiety or frustration.

New social opportunities open up with the growth of language. Children can talk with a wide variety of older, younger and same-aged conversational partners and use language to meet new playmates, sustain group play and join in complex styles of fantasy play, reminiscence and negotiation that require insight into what is going on in the conversational partner's mind.

In this chapter we explore these developments from a primarily chronological perspective. We link to the previous two chapters by looking at the cognitive representational thought processes that precede language. We examine prelanguage skills like hearing sounds, making speech-like noises and engaging with caregivers in 'pseudo-conversations' that are real apart from being devoid of meaningful words.

We explore the infant's discovery of word meaning, a developmental change that many would argue is the most significant of all the psychological developments in human evolution, and in a child's lifespan. Vocabulary grows rapidly once this initial discovery has been made. We look first at individual differences in this process, and then at the transition from using single words as names for things to holophrastic grammar, or the child's rules for constructing sentences that are only one word long.

Next we explore steps in syntactic development from two-word sentences and telegraphic speech to the mastery of rules for changing simple assertive sentences into questions and negative forms.

Syntactic development takes place so rapidly that some have argued it must be largely inherited. Nativist approaches postulate a pre-wired innate device in the brain that governs language growth. This theory is compared with learning approaches and with an interactive model that emphasises the social interaction, conversation and parental language input. This is done in the context of a human brain that is ready to receive language and of a social world that nurtures and challenges the child's communicative potential.

We then focus on social development, first examining how language influences children's play. Then we explore the new styles of persuasion, negotiation and conflict resolution that become available to the child once language is acquired. These skills contribute to further cognitive and social growth as children begin to learn how to comprehend other people's emotional states and take them into account in their efforts to persuade and reason.

Toddlerhood is sometimes known in popular speech as the 'terrible twos'. This undoubtedly reflects the conjunction, at this age, of the developmental trajectories for language, social development and personality growth. As the child's personality unfolds over the first two years of life, self-awareness becomes increasingly evident. New linguistic and social skills enable the toddler to translate this awareness into the extreme self-assertion that may sometimes seem 'terrible' to a parent. By saying 'No!', throwing temper tantrums and rejecting parental efforts at persuasion or placation, 2-year-olds display their self-hood through extreme and frequently explosive independence. Eventually, as better language skills emerge and effective parenting strategies encourage compliance without jeopardising the important personality strengths that a mature style of autonomy confers, children outgrow the 'terrible twos'.

Getting ready to speak:
The cognitive, social and vocal prerequisites for language

Human beings stand out from other species for their eloquent use of symbols, including that most complex symbol system of all – language. As adults we employ symbols with such versatility and dexterity that virtually every aspect of our daily lives is coloured by symbolism of some kind. For the infant it is different. *Symbolic representation*, or the capacity to use mental categories as substitutes for physical objects and events, does not develop until early in the second year of life. Until then, the baby's thinking is very different from the cognitive activities of

an older child or an adult who has the benefit of language.

Symbolic representation
Like a drawing or a doll's house, a symbol substitutes for, or represents, some other thing. Language is perhaps the most sophisticated of all human symbol systems. But adults use many other representational devices to supplement the linguistic symbols conveyed through spoken, signed or written words. These devices include graphic symbols (when we sketch a picture or an invisible outline with a finger, or write music or read maps), motoric symbols (when we recall how to tie a knot, or play an imaginary piano tune on the table), gestural symbols (when we illustrate the length of something as a space between

thumb and forefinger, or insult a careless driver using a manual expletive) and sensory or 'iconic' symbols (when memory floods the mind with pictures, sounds or smells of past experiences).

Symbols are implicit in most thought processes, from the murky obscurity of dreams to the sophisticated complexity of calculus. The physical environment, like most social situations, is also replete with symbolic meaning. Thus, the clothes we wear convey messages (such as black or white for mourning), the movements of our bodies and faces betray our thoughts and feelings without our knowing it (a grimace may indicate fear) and objects from clocks to traffic lights speak a socially defined language.

As noted in Chapter 2, the Russian psychologist Lev S. Vygotsky (1962) and the Swiss psychologist Jean Piaget (1970) both made major contributions to the understanding of how children develop cognitive skills, including language. They both searched for the roots of symbolic thinking in late infancy, months before the toddler discovers meaningful speech. Vygotsky (1962), in fact, believed that the development of symbolic representation began quite independently of the development of speech. Thus, the first symbols that children use are not early cries, gurgling or babbled syllables, which may sound like speech but have no meaning for the baby. Instead, most babies show their first signs of being able to represent ideas symbolically by developing gestures, or *motor symbols*, to which they assign a private meaning.

Piaget observed his own children carefully during their development through infancy and toddlerhood, keeping diary records (see Box 2.10) to remind himself of their significant developmental achievements. He (1962) witnessed the following instance of the use of a motor symbol by his second daughter, Lucienne, on her first birthday:

> She was sitting in her cot when she unintentionally fell backwards. Then seeing a pillow, she got into the position for sleeping on her side, seizing the pillow with one hand and pressing it against her face ... But instead of miming the action half seriously, she smiled broadly (she did not know she was being watched) ... She remained in this position for a moment, then sat up delightedly. During the day she went through the process again a number of times, although she was no longer in her cot; first she smiled (this indication of the representational symbol is to be noted), then threw herself back, turned on her side, put her hands over her face as if she held a pillow (though there wasn't one) and remained motionless, with her eyes open, smiling quietly. The symbol was therefore established. (pp. 96–7, reproduced with the permission of Thomson Publishing Services)

In other words, Lucienne used the motor symbol of stretching out on an imaginary bed and placing her hands around an invisible pillow to playfully repre-

The gesture of clapping can symbolise approval, while the action of 'riding' a rake is a symbol for galloping on a horse.

sent the act of falling asleep. A few weeks later, Piaget observed her pretending to eat a napkin ring and then demonstrating her awareness that it was sheer pretence by laughing and shaking 'no' with her head. At the age of one year and seven months, she pretended to drink from a box and then offered the 'cup' to the lips of all the adults present.

These motor symbols are clearly representational. Lucienne was well aware (as indicated by smiling, laughing and shaking her head) of the difference between the serious acts of sleeping, eating and drinking and the symbolic copies of these actions that she produced while pretending. In line with the role of representational thought in complex problem-solving, Lucienne was able to use motor symbols to mentally represent problem solutions, and thus clarify in her mind the steps she needed to take to achieve a solution. As Piaget (1962) explained:

> At one year and four months, Lucienne tried to get a watch chain out of a matchbox when the box was no more than an eighth of an inch open. She gazed at the box with great attention, then opened and closed her mouth several times in succession, at first only slightly and then wider and wider. It was clear that the child, in her effort to picture to herself the means of enlarging the opening, was using as 'signifier' her own mouth, with the movements of which she was familiar tactually and kinesthetically, as well as by analogy with the visual image of the mouths of others. (p. 65, reproduced with the permission of Thomson Publishing Services)

In other words, Lucienne's opening and shutting her mouth was her idiosyncratic way of symbolising the box as a cavity whose 'mouth' needed to be wider.

Gestural symbols also serve a representational purpose (e.g. sketching the outline of the Australian coastline with a finger) and frequently also a communicative function. Between the ages of 8 and 10 months, most infants begin to use gestures for genuinely communicative reasons (Acredolo & Goodwyn, 1990a). Among the first gestures that emerge early are conventional signals like waving the hand to indicate 'good-bye', shaking the head to say 'no' and pointing with the index finger to draw another person's attention to an object, person or action that the infant is aware of (see Box 4.1).

Gestural communication is especially important for severely and profoundly deaf children whose auditory disabilities limit their access to the sounds of speech (Marschark, 1993). But hearing children gesture too, and even totally blind children who have never visually witnessed a gesture use hand motions in systematic ways when explaining ideas to blind listeners (Goldin-Meadow, 2000).

In prelingual infants and toddlers, gesture has an important role to play, in line with Piaget's observations of the cognitive role of motor symbols in assisting thinking, memory and problem-solving. As Susan Goldin-Meadow (2000) explains:

> Gesture thus allows speakers to convey thoughts that may not easily fit into the categorical system that their conventional language offers … Gesture reflects a global-synthetic image. It is idiosyncratic and constructed at the moment of speaking – it does not belong to a conventional code. In contrast, speech reflects a linear-segmented, hierarchical linguistic structure, utilising a grammatical pattern that embodies the language's standards of form and drawing on an agreed-upon lexicon of words. Taken together, gesture and speech offer the possibility of constructing multiple representations of a single task. These multiple perspectives may prove useful, particularly in domains that lend themselves to visual thinking. (p. 237)

Sign language and spoken words

Deaf babies whose parents are also deaf are in a unique position to acquire not simply these idiosyncratic symbolic gestures but rather a complex language that expresses itself through hand signs coupled with bodily movements and facial expressions. Conventional sign languages such as ASL (American Sign Language), Auslan (Australian Sign Language) and BSL (British Sign Language) have similar syntactic structures and equal complexity to spoken languages like English, French or Chinese. But since the code these languages use is visual, they

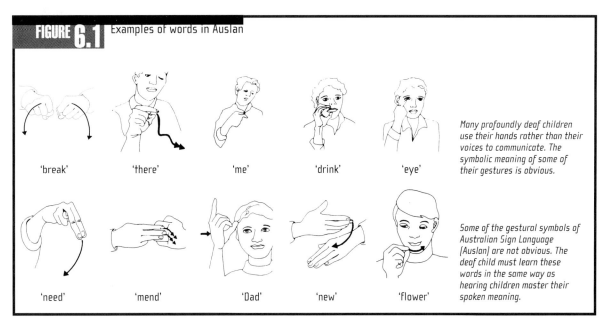

FIGURE 6.1 Examples of words in Auslan

'break' 'there' 'me' 'drink' 'eye'

'need' 'mend' 'Dad' 'new' 'flower'

Many profoundly deaf children use their hands rather than their voices to communicate. The symbolic meaning of some of their gestures is obvious.

Some of the gestural symbols of Australian Sign Language (Auslan) are not obvious. The deaf child must learn these words in the same way as hearing children master their spoken meaning.

are accessible to individuals whose severe hearing impairments preclude access to the sounds produced by vibrations of the vocal cords.

When deaf infants and toddlers do learn sign language from their signing deaf parents, language acquisition is unusually rapid. Raymond Folvern and John Bonvillian (1991) were intrigued by the suggestion that the symbols used in sign language may develop ahead of spoken words because of their independence of the articulatory vocal apparatus of the human body and their direct link with the motor symbols that all infants produce spontaneously. To test this possibility, Folvern and Bonvillian followed a group of nine infants of deaf parents who used Ameslan or ASL (American Sign Language) as their native language. Sure enough, these children developed their first signed words much earlier than the age norm of 12 to 13 months, when most hearing children acquire symbolic representation in the form of spoken words. In fact, on average, the signing infants produced their first clearly recognisable symbolic signs at the precocious age of eight months. By the age of 13 months they had a vocabulary of at least 10 signed words, and they had begun to combine signs into sentences at the age of 16 months. This contrasts with the average hearing infant's failure to produce any spoken sentences until after the second birthday. Folvern and Bonvillian concluded that:

> According to the perspective of a gestural advantage, early sign language acquisition is synchronized more closely with cognitive underpinnings, and the delay in the manifestation of milestones of speech is attributable to motoric rather than cognitive factors. This study's results showed that there is a temporal advantage for the production of early non-referential language in sign ... Our results also suggest that the gestural advantage may reappear at the time of the onset of two-sign combinations. Taken together, these findings highlight important similarities and marked differences in signed and spoken language acquisition. (p. 815)

Representing by pretending

When children engage in pretence, like imagining that a doll is a baby or that a fork is a doll, they make vivid use of symbolic representation. The older child's elaborate fantasies and dramatic games are full of even more complex and abstract symbolism. Like adult actors, they use language, gestures, mannerisms, costume, visual imagery and symbolic objects to create vivid play scenes. At the same time, a child who engages in pretence is clearly aware of the difference between representations and their real counterparts. The objects, persons and events being symbolised are public in a way that pretend images are not. Thus, a real balloon can be seen, touched or blown up by anyone, while an image of a balloon is both private and

fleeting. Similarly, if a person pretends that a banana is a telephone, the toddler is aware that a real call cannot be taken on it, and that it really can be eaten (Wellman, 1993). Box 6.1 includes an exercise to demonstrate these contrasts.

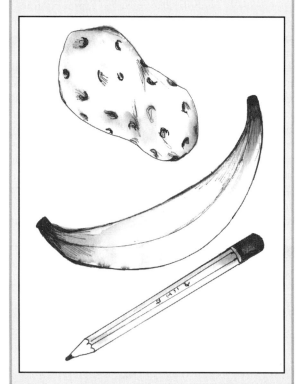

BOX 6.1 | **Activity suggestion**
Let's pretend

The task of pretending is a simple one. Try these activities yourself.

1. Take a potato and pretend it is a bar of soap. How would you wash your hands with it?_____

2. Take a banana and pretend it is a mobile phone. How would you answer a call?_____

3. Take a pencil and pretend it is a spoon. How would you stir up cake batter with it?_____

Now try the same activities with young children from your range of personal acquaintances. What is the youngest age at which children can reliably display pretending?

Speech sounds before meaning

Lev Vygotsky (1962) agreed with the German psychologist William Stern (1905) that the child's discovery that 'each thing has its name' is the 'greatest discovery of his life' (p. 108). However, he noted that, for many months before words begin to be used in a meaningful way to symbolise ideas, children produce vocal noises to which they themselves attach no meaning or representational properties. In fact, as we saw in Chapter 4, neonates use their voice to make noise while still in the stage of reflex behaviour, long before self-consciousness, awareness or any understanding of speech as a form of symbolic representation.

Some parents jump the gun and imagine that the first time an infant says 'da' or 'ma' this sound pattern is deliberately intended to symbolise Daddy or Mummy. But sounds that resemble speech are actually produced with consummate fluency and versatility long before the infant discovers how to use the voice symbolically to convey meaning. Up to that point, the 'speech' a baby hears and utters is more appropriately described as noise than as language. Despite their representational potential, spoken sounds at this stage have no conceptual significance to the baby. However, the fact that an infant's mastery of prelanguage skills plays an important role in shaping later progress with meaningful speech makes these skills worthy of attention.

Three important prelanguage skills are (a) *production*, or the use of vocal organs to generate speech-like 'noise', (b) *reception*, or the infant's physiological and behavioural reactions to the speech of others, and (c) *pseudo-conversation*.

Producing noises

During the first year of life, while the rudiments of motor or visual symbolism are developing, the speech apparatus is also becoming prepared for meaningful language. Cries are the first vocal sounds a baby makes. Within a few weeks, new gutteral sounds known as 'coos', 'goos' or 'grunts' also enter the repertoire. While making these sounds, the baby exercises and masters some degree of control over areas of the brain and vocal apparatus to be used

later for spoken language. By four months of age, when a more sophisticated form of vocal exercise known as 'babbling' begins, practice with speech-like noise-making gains momentum. A baby's first babbled sounds are strings of vowels and consonants which resemble such 'words' or syllables as babba, abba, maymaymay or gugugu. An adult listener may attempt to superimpose meaning onto these strings of sound but to the baby they have no meaning.

Babbling typically continues for six to eight months and then declines when meaningful speech begins. The speech-like quality of babbling gave rise to the belief, once widely held, that infants began to babble as an attempt to imitate their parents' speech. However, this theory was discounted when systematic observations of deaf babies revealed that infants who had never had language models to imitate because they were born deaf babbled as much as normal babies in their early months. Nonetheless, as babbling continued, hearing infants began to outstrip their deaf counterparts, both in the frequency and the variety of the sounds they produced. So it seems that being able to hear the babbled sounds themselves is essential for maintaining interest in babbling.

An additional proof that babbling does not develop as a copy of adult speech came from the discovery that the repertoire of sounds made by hearing babies towards the end of the babbling period includes virtually all the sounds of all human languages (Bower, 1977). Babies who have never heard anything but English can babble Chinese tones, German gutterals, Russian consonant clusters and numerous other tongue-twisters with an ease to be envied by older foreign-language learners.

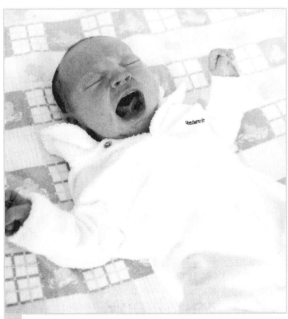

When infants cry, they communicate their distress to their concerned caregivers.

While babbling, infants produce speech-like sound patterns that have no meaning.

During later stages of babbling, children are also able to produce the intonation patterns used by mature speakers to express questions, exclamations, wheedling pleas and so on. They can also mimic non-human sounds. But these sound effects are not yet used symbolically, any more than the babbled 'words' themselves are.

Listening to others' speech

All the time this cacophony of vocal exercise is going on, the baby is also busy listening to adults' spoken language. As noted in Chapter 4, even newborn babies show special interest in the range of sound frequencies characterising human vocalisation (Aslin, Pisoni & Jusczyk, 1983). By the age of two weeks, they can discriminate human speech from other similar sounds like rattles, bells or the stereo. Soon after, by the age of one month, babies are capable of perceiving very minute differences among speech sounds. In the usual sound discrimination test, the experimenter initially presents one particular sound whenever the baby sucks on a pacifier. For a while, sucking increases. Then, as the same sound is presented over and over, the baby grows bored and sucking declines. At this point a new sound is introduced. If the baby fails to discriminate the new sound from the old one, sucking will remain at its same low level. A reliable increase in sucking, on the other hand, indicates that the baby has noticed the difference. Using this procedure, 1-month-olds have been shown to distinguish 'bah' from 'gah', 'pah' from 'pee' and 'tah' from 'tee'. They even notice the slight difference between 'bah?' spoken with a rising intonation and the same sound 'bah!' said with a falling voice (Eimas, Siqueland, Jusczyk & Vigorito, 1971; Trehub & Rabinovitch, 1972).

William Condon and Louis Sandor (1974) found that even very young infants could distinguish the end of one word in a flow of human dialogue from

By the age of one month, infants can distinguish between speech sounds that are as similar to one another as 'bah' and 'pah'.

the beginning of the next word. After filming movements made by newborn and 2-week-old babies while adults spoke to them, Condon and Sandor observed an impressively close match between the infants' body movements and the beginnings and endings of words in the continuous flow of adult speech. For example, one baby began twisting his shoulders as the adult voice articulated the word 'come'. Exactly at the point when this word ended and the adult began to say 'over', the infant's form of shoulder movement also changed. This changing of movements at word boundaries went on in precise synchrony across the full 89 words in the adult's utterance. The same patterning occurred when tape-recorded Chinese speech was played to these English-speaking infants, but they did not synchronise their bodies to the tapping of a pencil or a meaningless string of vowel sounds. In other words, their sensitivity to segmentation seemed to apply specifically to natural language.

This sensitivity is obviously important for language acquisition. Without clear boundaries between words, speech would be as hard to decode as the following written 'nonsense': LI FEEX PECTA TI ONH ASINC REA SEDIN RE CENTDEC ADES. (Can you decode this message? If not, check the answer at the end of this chapter.)

The infant's ability to notice fine differences between speech sounds is not entirely dependent on exposure to these sounds while listening to the parent's speech. Instead, infants whose parents speak only English are capable of discriminating sound contrasts in foreign languages that do not arise in English and which adult English-speakers are often unable to hear (Aslin et al., 1983). Thus, in one experiment, babies aged from one to four months who had never heard the Czech language were exposed to a contrast in this language between two 'z' sounds that can be symbolised phonetically as /řa/ versus /za/. The babies picked up the difference easily, while a comparison group of English-speaking adults had great difficulty in doing so (Trehub, 1976). According to Aslin et al. (1983), the results of studies like these combine to demonstrate the following important facts about infants' speech perception:

1. Infants from birth are capable of perceiving a wide range of subtle contrasts between speech sounds ('phonemes').
2. Infants are more sensitive to some sound contrasts than adults are, suggesting that the adult's ability to distinguish among meaningless variations in sound declines through disuse.
3. Infants from diverse language environments show similarly adept speech-perception abilities, suggesting that: 'the most important factor controlling the young infant's responsiveness to speech appears to be a basic set of innate perceptual mechanisms rather than exposure to specific types of early linguistic experience' (p. 642).

During the babbling stage, infants develop a rudimentary understanding of conversational turn-taking.

Pseudo-conversations

Infants six months old and younger might seem to be unpardonably rude: they frequently continue to babble all the time a parent is trying to speak to them. But by about seven months of age, most infants have a rudimentary understanding of vocal turn-taking. They generally pause to listen to a speaker, and only begin to babble again when the other speaker has stopped. This simple conversational rule of turn-taking is an instance of the *pragmatics* of language: practical rules that govern the appropriate uses of language to communicate in social contexts. Children acquire it early, before they are able to use sounds to convey meaning.

When parent and infant imitate one another in sequence, this may contribute to the child's mastery of pragmatic skills like turn-taking. The babbling infant's matching of his or her speech sounds to noises in the environment likewise reflects a planful element in early presymbolic speech that may later facilitate the pragmatic engagement in conversation when word meaning has been acquired. Two such instances in the pseudo-conversation of a 10-month-old infant were included in Box 4.1. Louise's father wrote:

> She hums when the vacuum cleaner hums, barks softly when Blackie barks, and she and I have a game we both get a big bang out of: a grimace she invented, drawing back her lips with her mouth open as if she were ready to scream but is holding it back. I copied it and she recognized it on me. Now she does it expecting me to imitate her, and when I do it she imitates me.

Three months later, Louise had made the transition into meaningful speech, as shown in Box 6.2.

The greatest discovery in life: Word meaning

As noted earlier, Lev Vygotsky (1962) deemed the child's discovery that speech sounds can be used

BOX 6.2 **A case in point**
'Ba' means 'ball'

One month after her first birthday, Louise's father made the following entry in his diary.

'Ball' or 'ba' is one of the words she knows and speaks.

28 April 1949. *She will hunt for her ball if you ask her where it is; and ball or 'ba' is one of the words she knows and speaks. Others are 'bottle' (very distinctly), 'bok' for box, 'puk' for paper, 'book', 'nut', 'ti' for tongue, 'tik' for stick or toothpick, 'bah' or 'bop' (with great emphasis on the final p) for Blackie, and 'da', 'dot', or 'dottle' for daddy. Some words stand for several things. 'Bottle' means first of all her nursing bottle, then any bottle or container that looks like a bottle. 'Bottle' also means 'give me', probably because she wants every bottle she sees. Hence, by transference, 'bottle' is the name she gives to any new thing that does not fall into one of her other categories of names.*

'Dot' means 'take me' or 'pick me up' or 'yes, I wanted you to pick me up'. This might be because, about the time that she began to take an active interest rather than mere passive acquiescence, in being picked up, I used to ask her, 'Want to come to Daddy?' Her answer was to raise her arms and say 'da'. Peggy gave her a pebble today and she immediately called it a 'nut', probably because it was about the size and shape of a walnut. For a while she was saying 'bikie' for Blackie but has since relapsed to the simpler 'bop'. And after being once told worriedly, 'Be careful of Daddy's glasses', she combined the two words 'daddy's' and 'glasses' into a single 'doggle'. This word, too, has now dropped out of her vocabulary. Another thing she lost for a time, and that I missed, was her special grimace. But now and then – as a favour to me, I suspect – she does it again fleetingly. She likes to make a door swing and says 'doe!'

© Peterson, 1974, pp. 24–5, reproduced with permission

representationally to be the 'greatest discovery' in a lifetime of cognitive and social development. His colleague, the Russian psychologist A. R. Luria (1981), explained why:

> In the absence of words, humans would have to deal only with those things which they could perceive and manipulate directly. With the help of language, they can deal with things which they have not perceived even indirectly and with things which were part of the experience of earlier generations. Thus, the word adds another dimension to the world of humans … Animals have only one world, the world of objects and situations which can be perceived by the senses. Humans have a double world. (p. 35)

For most children, the awareness that speech sounds, like gestures, body movements and acts of pretence, can be used to represent concepts symbolically dawns gradually, beginning in the second year of life. There is often a 'grey' area between vocal noise-making and genuinely meaningful speech when children can sometimes be seen to comprehend speech sounds, provided they are tested under ideal conditions. In one such test, Sharon Oviatt (1980) assessed comprehension of the words 'rabbit' and 'press it' by infants who ranged in age from 9 to 17 months.

She found some evidence of meaningful understanding even in these very young infants. Both sets of words were unknown to the children before the experiment began. During the study, 'rabbit' and 'press it' were repeated over and over in very attention-getting ways. For example, when the adult said 'rabbit', a live rabbit might be shown. Or the child might be asked to turn on a battery-operated Pluto dog whenever 'press it' was spoken. After training, comprehension of the word 'rabbit' was tested by asking 'Where's the rabbit?' A look in the right direction was scored as correct. Nonsense questions ('Where's the kawlow?') and questions with other meanings ('Where's the book?') were included to control for spontaneous head-turning or guessing. Comprehension of the phrase 'press it' was scored correct if the child responded by activating the mechanical dog when asked to do so. Although these measures showed some comprehension even by 9-month-olds, Oviatt concluded that:

> By 12–14 months of age, a major shift was observed in the quality of language comprehension such that infants appeared more flexible and categorical in their use of words. (p. 105)

The child's awareness of an association between a few distinct sound patterns and a matching set of objects or actions does not necessarily prove that he or she has made Stern and Vygotsky's 'greatest discovery', however. According to Eric Lenneberg (1969), even 'Aunt Pauline's favorite lap dog' can respond distinctively to a few words like 'ball' or 'sit', and we do not conclude that the dog has a mastery of language as a symbolic representational system.

Lenneberg suggested that genuine comprehension of word meaning requires:

1. Consistent recognition and use of the word in the same context
2. The ability to conduct a phonetic analysis which dissects complete words into the component phenomes (or sounds) they are made up of
3. A semantic ability which enables children to recognise that anything can potentially have a name, even if they have never heard its name before
4. The ability to analyse sentences or phrases to extract words.

Box 6.2 illustrates the representational awareness of word meaning. When the word 'ball' was spoken, Louise displayed her understanding of its role as a symbol for a real object by searching for the ball. The fact that she knew the word when someone else said it combined with the appropriateness of the context to indicate that when she produced her own 'ba' sound she meant it to refer to the ball.

Similarly, her deliberate distinction between use of 'ti' for 'tongue' and 'tik' for 'stick' betrayed her phonetic awareness of the difference between the sounds of these words in adult speech, along with conceptual knowledge revealed by her consistency in matching the sounds to corresponding real-world objects.

Between the ages of 18 and 24 months, it is common for toddlers to go through a 'naming explosion' (Reznick & Goldfield, 1992) when new words are added to the vocabulary at a very fast rate, sometimes up to 20 words per week. At this point, it is clear that they meet Lenneberg's semantic knowledge criterion of realising that anything can have a name.

Vygotsky saw the discovery of word meaning as so significant, not only because of the new possibilities for communication arising with spoken language, but also because the child's thought processes are revolutionised as a result of this discovery. As he explained: 'Speech begins to serve the intellect and thoughts begin to be spoken' (1962, p. 43). And: 'The child begins to perceive the world not only through his eyes but through his speech. As a result, the immediacy of "natural" perception is supplanted by a complex mediated process, [and] as such, speech becomes an essential part of the child's cognitive development' (1978, p. 32).

The development of a vocabulary

Owing in part to developmental limitations on the delicately coordinated motor skills needed in order to twist the tongue around such tricky speech sounds as 'ndm', 'th', 'dz', 'ing' and 'gri', a child of 18 months who has begun the 'naming explosion' may want to name many more things than those whose names can comfortably be echoed from adult speech. Thus children may develop names with a distinctively childlike pronunciation ('mama' for 'mother', 'gaga' for 'grandma') or may create their own names which they apply consistently to selected objects (like Louise's creation, as noted in Box 6.2, of the name 'Bop' for the dog, Blackie – a pseudonym that the whole family eventually chose to adopt).

This creation of names to match word meanings often entails the processes of *overextension* and *underextension*, which reveals that the child's semantic production is an active, constructive process rather than a mere passive attempt to echo adult usage. It takes some time before the 'dictionary' in the child's head comes to match that of an adult speaker.

Overextension

Overextension describes the child's tendency to have a broader range of referents for a word than the conventional meaning of that word in the adult's vocabulary.

Boxes 6.2 and 6.3 illustrate the process of overex-

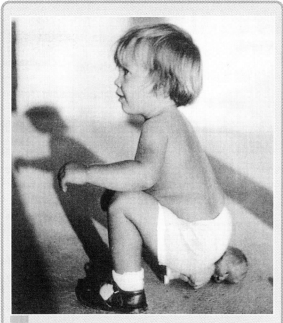

'Doll', correctly pronounced, was one of the first words Louise could speak.

BOX 6.3 The range of things a word can mean

Once Louise began to use words meaningfully, her vocabulary grew rapidly. When she was 14 months old, her father wrote:

24 May 1949. *Generally speaking, Louise divides her physical world into three large categories: 'bottles', 'bocks', and 'oddles'. 'Bottles' are containers of almost any description, but especially of glass, and articles that have a distinct hole or cavity in them, like bottle caps and toothpaste tubes. (I imagine she senses the cavity because they give so easily when bitten.) 'Bock', derived from box and block, is anything resembling those things, anything squarish or cubical, and sometimes, by inference, just anything. 'Bock' also means 'give it back'. An 'oddle' – her way of saying handle – is anything long and anything easy to grasp and put in the mouth.*

Those are the three largest categories, but there are several others, smaller and more precisely identified. 'Ball', for example, means just that: a ball. A 'nut' is a kind of small ball of irregular shape. A 'piece' is something very small, like a crumb or a hair, something that has to be picked up with the fingernails. And quickly got rid of, I might add, because when Louise goes to the trouble of picking such a thing up she strongly insists that you take it from her.

Most of the things she identifies are firm, solid things. Among them are her 'doll', correctly pronounced, and 'ti' for stick, 'dah' for jar, and a special word for the garden tractor which Peggy understands but that I have as yet not heard too clearly. For the genera of limp things, she has no term, but she particularizes 'tie', 'puh' for paper, and 'tok' for sock. 'Boy' is any kid heard yelling or the sound of a bicycle. 'Dirl' is a girl, i.e. Louise herself.

© Peterson, 1974, reproduced with permission

tension of word meaning. Louise had initially learned 'bottle' as a symbol for her nursing bottle. Later, she used it for other containers. Next, it was generalised further to convey the meaning 'give me'. Likewise, when she saw a pebble for the first time, she gave it the name 'nut' which she had acquired in her previous encounters with walnuts. Some additional examples of children's early generalisations of a few words to symbolise a wide range of referents are shown in Table 6.1.

These examples all illustrate the child's overextension of word meanings beyond their normal adult range of reference. The same phenomenon was also observed by Allen and Beatrice Gardner (1969) when they taught a chimpanzee named Washoe to name things with her fingers using ASL (American Sign Language). One instance of Washoe's overextension occurred just after they taught her the sign 'listen' for a timer on the stove. Washoe herself extended the meaning of this sign to include a clock, a wrist watch, a bell with a clapper and a shiny, flickering flashlight. Though no fluent speaker of sign language would use the 'listen' sign for all these items, the underlying consistency in Washoe's usage is apparent. Washoe also used the sign for 'dog' (which she first learned as a symbol for a picture of a dog in a book) to describe the sound of a dog barking. Another chimpanzee, Lucy, ingeniously created a name for her first taste of a radish by rapidly combining the signed gestures for 'cry-hot-food' (Linden, 1977).

Why do beginning language learners generalise word meanings in this way? Wouldn't it be just as easy to learn a new name to symbolise each of the new objects in the third column of Table 6.1?

According to Eve Clark (1983), children sometimes

TABLE 6.1	Early word meanings: Making a few words go a long way		
Toddler's word	First used to symbolise	Generalised to	Source
'Dog'	Blackie, the family dog	other dogs, cows, horses, ponies	Peterson, 1974
'Bow-wow'	the landlord's dog	a pattern on the rug resembling a line drawing of a dog, a horse (viewed from the child's balcony), a baby in a pram (also seen from the balcony), some hens, horses, prams, cyclists, the landlord himself	Piaget, 1962
'Bow-wow'	a porcelain figurine	a dog barking in the yard, a fur stole, feline and canine animals at the zoo, a toy dog, a clock, a squeaking rubber doll, pearl buttons, a bath thermometer	Vygotsky, 1962
'Moon'	the real moon	grapefruit halves, flat shiny leaves, lemon slices, mounted steer horns	Nelson et al., 1978
'Ball'	a toy ball	whole beets, chopped beets, grapefruit skins (but not the juice)	Peterson, 1974
'Ticktock'	the child's father's wrist watch and his parents' buzzing alarm clock	a picture of a wooden cuckoo clock, watches, buzzing radios and telephones, a chevron-shaped medallion on the dishwasher	Nelson et al., 1978
'(T)atta'	departures or 'all gone'	opening and closing doors, raising a box lid, any disappearance of an object	Clark, 1983

overextend words because their conceptual definitions of the word are broader than an adult speaker's. In other words, the child's own mental image of 'dog' in fact amounts to something like the adult category of 'furry animal'. But, in other cases, children use overextension because they want to talk about things whose names they have not yet learned or have temporarily forgotten. They know the overextended word is not quite appropriate, but are forced to rely on it as a convenient approximation. In support of this latter possibility, Clark cited the case of a little girl who overextended the word 'bird' in her own speech to represent any moving animal. But when someone else said 'bird' she would look around until she saw something flying and was not satisfied if the only visible animal was a cat.

Longitudinal data support the view that toddlers do recognise that many of their overextensions are inadequate. But they use overextension as a convenient temporary measure while the vocabulary is small. As a child's command of language increases, the proportion of words whose meaning is overextended correspondingly declines. Figure 6.2 illustrates this process. The subjects in this study were six toddlers who had total vocabularies of 25 words or less initially. At this point, between one-third and one-half of the children's words were extended beyond their normal meaning in the adult vocabulary. But at each subsequent longitudinal follow-up,

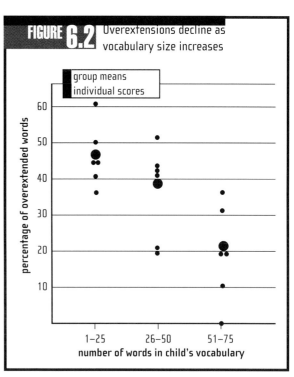

FIGURE 6.2 Overextensions decline as vocabulary size increases

Source: Based on data in Clark (1983), p. 804.

the percentage of overextended words was noticeably less. By the time their vocabularies had stretched to 50 words or more, one child had abandoned overextension altogether and the others used it much less often than formerly (Clark, 1983).

The meanings conveyed by children's early overextended words are strikingly similar across languages, regardless of the diversity of adult vocabulary in Russian, German, French, Chinese or English. This also suggests that children's early vocabulary development entails more than simple copying of adult meaning by successive approximations. Instead, children seem to begin the language acquisition exercise with their own ideas about the kinds of things they wish to talk about.

Underextension

Not all the new words in a toddler's vocabulary are extended beyond their conventional adult usage. Sometimes the range of referents for one of the child's early words is much narrower than it would be for an adult. This is the phenomenon of *underextension*. An example, given in Box 6.3, is the use of the word 'dirl' (= girl) by 14-month-old Louise. It had only one reference: Louise herself. Any other child encountered or heard yelling or playing was classed as a boy, irrespective of the child's gender.

In one systematic study of the underextension phenomenon, Katherine Nelson and her colleagues (Nelson, Rescorla, Gruendel & Benedict, 1978) tested four toddlers individually. All the children had the word 'car' in their early vocabulary, using it spontaneously to refer to the family vehicle. To see if the children would apply the word, as an adult would, to photographs of cars and/or to toy car replicas, several examples of each of these kinds of stimuli were arranged in plain sight of the child. The tester then said, 'Where's the car?' Each child systematically and deliberately walked past the toys and photos, ignoring them, in order to point out the window at their only acceptable target for the label: the family car. In other words, the word 'car' was underextended to have just one referent.

How children learn word meaning

The phenomena of overextension and underextension fit in well with Roger Brown's (1965) pioneering observation that children's early development of word meaning proceeds in two directions simultaneously. Some meanings progress towards greater abstraction (overextension), others move away from adult usage towards ever greater narrowness and concreteness (underextension). Still other words, like Louise's 'tie', 'put' (= paper) and 'tok' (= sock), retain approximately their adult meaning.

According to Brown, children come to the task of language learning with their own preconceived ideas about many of the concepts they want to learn how to label. Take the example of 'dog' or 'bow-wow' (see Table 6.1). This word may be less useful to a toddler than a more general word like 'animal' which could include other equally familiar household pets like cats, hamsters or rabbits, as well as the many other intriguing four-legged creatures that children encounter in picture books, on television or on visits to zoos and wildlife parks. But adults rarely use the word 'animal' when talking to children. So children accommodate by fitting the concept they want a label for ('animal' or 'mammal') into the name their adult conversational partners have chosen to supply. On the other hand, when it comes to flowers, fruits and plants, parents often teach a general word (e.g. 'flower') before introducing a more specific label like 'rose' or 'daffodil'. If the child wants to talk about roses only, the word 'flower' might be used but in an underextended manner.

In other words, Brown argued, children's early development of word meaning proceeds in both directions – towards concreteness and towards abstraction – from a middle level which is partly determined by adults' standard ways of labelling things for children. There is, however, another advantage of the middle-level names that parents most often initially supply. These can often be represented as conveniently by a gesture as by a spoken word. For example, actions of pretending to pat a dog or sniff a flower transmit the concepts of 'dog' and 'flower' nearly as effectively as their respective names, while the more specific 'bop' and the more general 'animal' defy such non-verbal characterisation.

Katherine Nelson (1979) tested the development of vocabulary experimentally by showing a group of 24 toddlers a set of novel objects whose nonsense names were repeated equally often in a series of laboratory sessions. The items and their names follow. Can you guess which name a child would learn first?

- *weedle*: a metal kitchen whisk
- *nutty*: a plastic screw-driven nutcracker
- *bickers*: a set of five small plastic boxes
- *linky*: a commercial toy consisting of a long, flexible metal spring (marketed as 'Slinky')
- *mobol*: a wooden triangular toy with a central open space and wheels at each point.

Nelson (1979) found that the names for these objects were acquired in a predictable order. 'Linky' and 'bickers' were the easiest words of all. This was indicated both by the fact that they were learned first by those children who mastered the entire list, and by their being the only names that some of the children ever managed to acquire. Next came 'nutty', followed by the two hardest items, 'mobol' and 'weedle'.

Nelson proposed that this fixed order of vocabulary development was due to a tendency for function to take precedence over other factors, such as the shape or colour of the object or the pronunciation of its name, as a basis for bringing new words into the vocabulary. Thus the toddlers in her experiment could find many interesting and varied practical uses for the Slinky spring and the plastic boxes. The nutcracker's potential was more limited, but it did lend itself to twisting, banging and being put into the mouth. On the other hand, there were almost no interesting uses for the wheeled toy, 'mobol'. Therefore, despite the fact that it was more distinctive than all the other objects – in shape, colour and the sound of its name – it was the slowest to enter the vocabulary.

This finding suggests that the development of names for objects is not a purely imitative process. Instead, words evolve to reflect the child's own ideas about concepts that are meaningful and worth talking about. An observational study of Australian mothers (Wales, Colman & Pattison, 1983) lent further support to this conjecture.

The 40 mothers in this study were asked to name a variety of objects for their 2-year-olds and to predict how the children themselves would name the same objects. The items belonged to groupings such as vehicles, fruit or furniture which could be described in three ways – specifically ('double-decker bus'; 'Granny Smith'), at a basic level ('bus'; 'apple') or using an abstract categorical label ('vehicle'; 'fruit'). The results showed that the mothers greatly overestimated the frequencies of both specific names and abstract categorical words in their children's vocabularies. The toddlers never used abstract names and only rarely gave the highly specific labels. Of greatest interest, in light of the theory that children learn names for their own concepts rather than borrowing labels and ideas from adults, was the discovery that, while only 49 per cent of the names given by mothers were at the basic (intermediate) level of abstraction, some 99 per cent of the names given by

A ball is an interesting toy, and the word 'ball' is often one of the first to enter a child's vocabulary.

their children to the same objects belonged at this level (e.g. apple).

Katherine Nelson (1973) also conducted a naturalistic study in 1-year-olds' homes. She recorded the first words spoken by each toddler, and then noted how the mother reacted to her child's first efforts to speak meaningfully. Since all the children had acquired concepts before they learned any names, they first tried to construct a match between the words they had heard adults using and their own prelanguage meanings. Sometimes they were successful, either because their own concepts happened to coincide closely with adult usage, or because their mothers were very tolerant of discrepancies. In such cases, vocabulary growth proceeded rapidly. After the children had learned between 10 and 100 words as names for their own concepts, they typically reversed the process and began to discover the meanings behind their mother's most common words.

In confirmation of Brown's hypothesis, Nelson discovered that the children's acquisition of meaning at this stage proceeded both up and down the breadth hierarchy. Sometimes children gradually curtailed their usage of words with initially broad meanings so as to conform eventually to the narrower adult range of reference (e.g. one girl first used 'Daddy' for her father, donkeys and her toy duck, and then later narrowed it to mean only the father). But they also occasionally broadened their own initially overly specific meanings (e.g. one boy had used 'Mommy' at the outset only in reference to his mother but later applied it to all adult women). This suggests that vocabulary development is not altogether one-sided. Although the child may choose which names to learn first, the ability to use them socially for purposes of communication also depends on the interests and decoding ability of the adult listener.

The growth of grammar also interconnects with vocabulary development. In one study, Elizabeth Bates (1999) discovered a positive correlation between the number of words a child knew the meaning of and that child's capacity to produce grammatically complex sentences. As shown in Figure 6.3, children with vocabularies of 500 words or more were particularly skilled in producing grammatical sentences.

Using a laboratory training procedure, Nameera Akhtar, Malinda Carpenter and Michael Tomasello (1996) examined the role of the social and conversational context in teaching children new vocabulary items. In the first phase of their procedure, three objects that the 2-year-olds in their sample had never encountered before were introduced by two adult research assistants. Depending on the child's experience, the objects might have comprised a liquid timer, a beanbag Frisbee and a novelty yo-yo. The adults encouraged each child to play with these novelty toys, demonstrating their functions to the child, and simultaneously labelling each one with a nonsense word (e.g. 'modi'). Then one of the adults left the room and a fourth novel object was introduced into

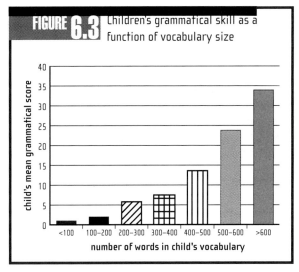

FIGURE 6.3 Children's grammatical skill as a function of vocabulary size

Source: Based on data in Bates (1999).

the set. Later, the adult who had been away returned and said 'Look, I see a gazzer, a *gazzer*!' without pointing or looking at any of the toys. There was also a control group of children who were tested without being exposed to the mention of the gazzer.

The test phase involved asking the child to select a 'gazzer' and bring it over to the experimenter. The results suggested social learning. Even though the name could conceivably have referred to any of the four novel items, a large percentage of the children in the experimental group selected the item that had been introduced into the set during the adult's absence. They seemed to have taken account of her conversational strategy of using a new word to describe a new, rather than a familiar, item, and were also able to put themselves in her shoes by realising that she would not have seen the 'gazzer' at the point when they did, but only upon return to the room when her exclamation was uttered. The researchers concluded that:

> Twenty-four-month-old children demonstrated an ability to use a broad range of pragmatic cues in determining adults' referential intentions in a wide variety of discourse situations. The ability indicates a deep and flexible understanding of the behavior of other persons and their referential intentions. In our view, it is this understanding that forms the foundation of the process of language acquisition. (pp. 643–4)

Setbacks in vocabulary development

A developmental danger zone for language learning was also discovered by Katherine Nelson (1973). She found that some mothers in her longitudinal study consistently rejected their child's early efforts to acquire verbal labels for prelanguage concepts. One case was a child called Robert. When he first began talking at 12 months, Robert was exceptionally intrigued by movable objects, along with their actions and spatial positions. Thus, his first words

described movements and physical relationships instead of being names for people, pictures or social situations. His mother, on the other hand, persisted in offering him words that she used as names for the people and things she pointed out in his picture books. She seemed unable to understand or accept his motion-oriented meanings. Consequently, Robert's language development slowed down drastically. Throughout the study, he remained the most delayed language learner of any child in the sample. He also showed frequent temper tantrums, which Nelson attributed to the frustration engendered by 'his world being distinctly at odds with his mother's expectations and her reward systems' (p. 113).

A case like Robert's demonstrates the importance of parental sensitivity to a child's communicative intent. When children develop word meanings that are totally at odds with their parents' definitions of the same words, no communication is possible. At this point, a child may discard his working vocabulary and come up with a new set of hypotheses about his native language. But this is not easy. Furthermore, if the new hypotheses happen still to be mismatched, a child may eventually give up trying to learn to speak. To avoid creating a situation of 'learned helplessness' about word meaning (see Chapter 4), it is crucial that at least one of the child's conversational partners should comprehend at least some of the child's early symbolic efforts. This may be one of the reasons why infants raised in poorly staffed institutions are slow to acquire language. It is also an area of concern to paediatric nurses and other health professionals who may be charged with the care of infants or toddlers during their parents' absence.

The example of Robert also illustrates the importance of the baby's own unique contribution to the parent–child relationship. The discussion of infant temperament in Chapter 5 shows how much easier it is for most parents to behave sensitively to infants whose signals are both regular and similar to those made by most other babies. For the same reason, a child like Robert, who begins the task of learning to communicate with an eccentric set of ideas about what words should mean, poses a much greater challenge to his parents and caregivers than a child whose hypotheses about word meanings happen to coincide closely with adult usage.

Box 6.4 is an activity that provides practice in coming to terms with some imaginative toddlers' more idiosyncratic hypotheses about language.

Syntactic development: The rules of language

Once children have developed a modest vocabulary of meaningful words, they are ready to go beyond naming to put language to more sophisticated uses. This entails the development of syntax or grammar.

Descriptive grammar (or *syntax*) is defined as the

BOX 6.4 A pause for thought
Can you decode the toddler's lexicon?

Instructions: Mismatches between the notions of toddlers and their caregivers about what words should mean can delay language acquisition. So, if you plan to take up communication with a toddler, either as a caregiver, teacher or medical helper, it is crucial to bring as much skilled knowledge to the task as possible. This 'sleuthing' exercise involves guessing what each child intended the 'words' in the first column to mean, using the limited clues available. Answers are at the bottom.

What does 'doggie' mean?

Word	Usage pattern – objects or situations to which the child consistently applies the name	What word or phrase would you use if writing a 'dictionary entry' for the child's meaning?
1. 'Car'	Car, motorcycle, bicycle, propeller aeroplane, helicopter, steering wheel	
2. 'Hi!'	Hands under blankets, hands in mittens, shirt falling over foot, finger puppets wiggling on fingers	
3. 'Cotty-bars'	Abacus, toast rack, photo of Greek temple	
4. 'Kutija'	Matchbox, cardboard box, bedside table, chest of drawers	
5. 'Kuck'	Cat, self-kicking, fluttering moth, turtle on TV, throwing a ball	

Answers: 1. Something with a moving wheel, 2. Something that conceals a hand or foot, like a finger puppet. 3. Something with stripes or bars on it, like a cot. 4. A container that opens and shuts. 5. Moving legs, arms or wings. (Clark, 1983)

complete set of rules needed to construct all the sentences a native speaker might use in a lifetime. It is quite distinct from the traditional *prescriptive grammar* of the schoolroom, which offers rules like 'Don't say ain't'. This more familiar form of grammar strives to alter language usage in prescribed ways. Descriptive grammars, by contrast, are actually miniature theories about language. For example, a descriptive grammar of the English language would include rules for producing grammatically correct sentences of the form 'The sun is shining' without ever producing such an ungrammatical sentence as 'Shine sun the is'. As children acquire language, they approach these encompassing rules of syntax by gradual approximations. Thus in the early stages of sentence construction, the descriptive grammar of the child's language is very different from the rules used by a mature speaker. Some of the rules governing the child's first sentence constructions are described in the next three sections of this chapter.

The holophrastic stage

After an initial period in which words function only as names for things, children enter a phase when they use single words to convey meanings complex enough to require full sentences in adult language. This phase is known as the stage of the one-word sentence, or *holophrastic speech*. The basic rule of descriptive grammar during this stage is 'word + context'. The child supplements the word's naming function by means of non-verbal contextual cues. The transition from simple naming becomes apparent when listeners find themselves unable to translate a child's utterance into a name. For example, if a child says 'Daddy!' while pointing to her father, the naming interpretation seems valid. But if she says 'Daddy?' inquiringly, while pointing at a car, the meaning 'Is it Daddy?' would seem a likelier translation, as would the possessive 'Daddy's' if she uttered the word affirmatively while pointing at his briefcase. Box 6.5 includes some examples.

The social skills developed by toddlers during the holophrastic stage allow them to orchestrate sophisticated dialogues, provided their conversational partners are cooperative. Eve Clark (1983) found that some children, whose own sentences were limited to one word, seemed to plan conversations which enabled their partner to articulate the longer sentences they were not yet capable of uttering by themselves. One example was the following exchange between a mother and her daughter aged 15 months (p. 318):

Child [looks at electric fan]: Fan.
Mother: Hmmm?
Child: Fan.
Mother: Bathroom?
Child: Fan.
Mother: Fan! Yeah!
Child: Cool!
Mother: Cool, yeah. Fan makes you cool.

The examples of a 15-month-old's speech in Box 6.5 include a number of holophrastic sentences. Louise used the single word 'door' to mean things like 'Close the door' and 'Open the door'. Then she created more ingenious holophrases which coupled a word with the negating gesture of a headshake. The context in which these sentences were spoken helped to reveal their meaning. The sound of the horn of a car not belonging to her father elicited the headshake with the word 'Dot' (meaning 'That's not Daddy'), while a strange dog barking led to the headshake plus 'Blackie' (meaning 'That's not Blackie barking').

There is evidence to show that holophrastic grammar is genuinely productive (Ingram, 1971). Children in the one-word stage spontaneously create a variety of novel holophrases. They have their own set of rules for combining words with gestures and intonations to convey specific meanings. Paula Menyuk and Nancy Bernholtz (1969) discovered that at least part of the meaning conveyed by a holophrase is accessible to a listener who knows neither the child nor the non-verbal context in which the utterance was spoken. These researchers played recordings of holophrases to a group of adult judges who were able to classify them as exclamations, questions or declarations. No clues were given other than the child's tone of voice.

The young child's skill in creating meaningful pantomimed gestures (such as Louise's enactive symbolising of mosquito bites in Box 6.5) makes the gesture-plus-word style of holophrase similarly effective. As shown in this box, 15-month-old Louise also understood simple adult sentences even when they were not accompanied by gestures or pointing. However, being at the holophrastic stage herself, she probably comprehended only the main words (such as 'tractor') and filled in the rest of the sense by inference. In fact, one experiment showed that holophras-

What can a single word mean?

When Louise was 15 months old, her father made the following entries in his diary:

13 June 1949. *This record seems to be mainly on the subject of vocabulary. I suppose it interests me because it is the most concrete, or at any rate the most direct, evidence of Louise's thinking ... If you say 'mosquito' or 'bites', she will slap at her hand ... Today she was saying 'Dot' and shaking her head. What could it mean? Peggy figured it out. Whenever Louise hears an auto horn she says 'Dot', meaning either that it must be I or, more probably, somebody doing what I do when I come home. When it isn't I, Peggy says, 'No, that isn't Dot'. So now Louise says 'Dot' and shakes her head, her way of saying, 'No, that isn't Dot', but he's doing what Dot does.*

Until recently her vocabulary consisted entirely of nouns or of nouns made to do the work of verbs. 'Door', for instance, also means 'close the door' or 'open the door'. Curiously enough, her first word that is not a noun is 'Why'. She loves the word without yet having a clear idea what it means, possibly because it evokes such a satisfactory response from her parents. Hence she says it often and sometimes most appropriately.

At 15 months, Louise was producing holophrastic sentences.

9 July. *Today she put a gasoline spout back with the tractor when I asked her to. No gestures or pointing; I just said, 'Put it back with the tractor.' She also handed me the saw which we had carelessly left out.*

© Peterson, 1974, reproduced with permission

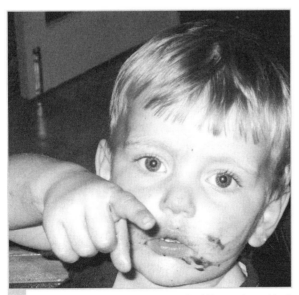

During the holophrastic stage, the gesture of pointing may be combined with a single word to produce a sentence.

tic toddlers were even more accurate in responding to holophrastic commands like 'Ball!' than to complete sentences like 'Throw the ball to me!' (Shipley, Smith & Gleitman, 1969). It would seem that comprehension of the subtleties of meaning conveyed by the way words are combined in sentences awaits the next step in speech development, when children use syntax to begin to produce word combinations.

Two-word sentences

Several different theories (or grammars) have been advanced to account for the kinds of sentences that children create when they first begin putting words together. Initially, three independent research teams (Brown, 1973) came up with a system most often referred to as 'pivot' grammar. In this grammar, all words fall into one of two classes: 'pivot' or 'open'. There are relatively few words in the former category and all are in heavy use, because the rule for *pivot grammar* is that each sentence consists of a 'pivot' word plus an 'open' word. Some examples from three of Martin Braine's (1963) child subjects are shown in Table 6.2.

Children with pivot grammar can be both ingenious and prolific in their creation of sentences. Gregory's 'more taxi', for example, was his unique and highly effective way of requesting that driving around in the taxi be continued. Braine reported an increase for one child from 14 to over 2500 distinct pivot sentences over a mere six months.

However, some dissatisfaction with the pivot theory of two-word speech has been expressed. It appears that, while the grammar gives an excellent account of the early two-word sentences of some children, it is not universal. There are children who learn to speak without ever using the pivot rule (Bowerman, 1973). Also, the theory focuses almost exclusively on the structure rather than the meaning of early sentences.

An alternative view of two-word speech that overcomes these problems was put forward by Braine in 1976. He analysed the first-word combinations of 11 children whose native languages included English, Samoan, Finnish, Hebrew and Swedish. In spite of the many differences among the adult grammars of these languages, Braine found that all the children he studied used the same basic grammatical system to create

their first two-word combinations. This included a set of positional rules which mapped words into specified places in sentences and special sets of meanings defined by each type of sentence. Each child had a small number of these rules and, because each rule was acquired independently, no two children possessed exactly the same set at a given time. Also, before the positional rules were mastered, many of the children showed a 'groping pattern' in which they put words together in a disorganised way. They seemed to want to express a given meaning before they had learned the correct positional rules by which it was conveyed. Here are some of the early meanings these children expressed, and examples of the positional formulas by which they expressed them:

1. *Identification*: 'See car', 'Here pink', 'That lady' and 'Kurt boy' ('Kurt is a boy').
2. *Description*: 'Big balloon', 'Shirt wet', 'Hot fire' and 'Old cookie'.
3. *Possession*: 'Mommy mouth', 'Daddy coffee', 'Kendall turn' and 'This Nina' ('This belongs to Nina').
4. *Plurality*: 'Two fly' and 'Two bread'.
5. *Recurrence*: More plane', 'More raisins' and 'Other ball' ('The ball again').
6. *Disappearance*: 'All gone sticky' and 'All gone blow' ('The matchbox is empty – no matches to blow out').
7. *Negation*: 'No bed', 'No mama' ('I don't want to go to mama'), 'Not eat' and 'No want it'.
8. *Actor–action relations*: 'Mother build', 'Daddy work', 'Stone daddy' ('Daddy threw a stone') and 'Kendall turn page'.
9. *Location*: 'Sand eye', 'In Daddy' (as she shuts her father in a room), 'Bill here' and 'Lotion tummy'.
10. *Requests*: 'Want more', 'Gimme ball' and 'Want pocket' ('Give me whatever is in the pocket').

Telegraphic grammar and overregularisation

Once the two-word limit is overcome, children construct multiword sentences that are often clearly understandable, even without assistance from the surrounding non-verbal context. But these sentences have a distinctive flavour, somewhat similar to a newspaper headline or a telegram. When words cost money, adults commonly omit articles ('the', 'a') as well as many grammatical 'extras' that improve the grammatical polish of speech without radically adding to the meaning (prepositions, conjunctions and some adjectives, adverbs and auxiliary verbs). Thus, the sentences are very short and contain only the main content words that convey maximum meaning. A child's telegraphic speech is similar, as illustrated in Table 6.3. The more sophisticated inflected grammar of a slightly older child is also shown in Table 6.3.

In the early telegraphic stages, all grammatical inflections ('-ing', '-ed', etc.) tend to be left out. But

TABLE 6.2	Some sample sentences with 'more' as the pivot word	
Child	Sentence	Meaning
Gregory	'more taxi' 'more melon'	'Let's ride in the taxi some more.' 'Give me more melon.'
Andrew	'more car' 'more sing'	'There's another car.' 'Sing another song.'
Steven	'more ball' 'more book'	'Throw the ball again.' 'Read some more.'

Source: Based on data in Braine (1963).

Age 22–23 months: Telegraphic speech	Age 32 months: Inflected speech
TABLE 6.3 Examples of telegraphic and inflected speech in the language of one girl	
'Mom helping you'	'Dot, are you expecting me to have these?'
'Mom help you?'	'Do you mind if Mom puts the toothpaste away?'
'Poor head'	'I tore the picture by accident'
'Louise see it'	'Mom, why are your eyes like fish and mine are like fish and Bop's are round?'
'Dot found it'	'Pogue's my friend, so I let her eat my peanut'
'The chairs were nice'

'The little bed were nice' | 'When I get to be a big girl, can I color my fingers red?' |

Source: Peterson (1974), reproduced with permission.

since these are relevant to meaning, they are added progressively as telegraphic speech develops, as seen in simple sentences like 'Louise see it' and 'Mom helping you' (see Table 6.3), which convey information not only about the actors and their actions but also, via the inflections, about when the event occurred. In fact, the present progressive verb ending ('-ing') is generally one of the first inflections to be incorporated into telegraphic speech, followed closely by the plural (add 's') and simple prepositions ('in' versus 'on') (Clark & Clark, 1977). Eventually,

telegraphic grammar is outgrown as speech becomes fully inflected. Table 6.3 shows some examples from Louise's speech over the period from 22 to 32 months.

As children gradually add inflections to telegraphic speech, they often go through an apparent regression, known as *overregularisation*. Susan Ervin (1964) observed this phenomenon as she watched how children began to add past tense inflections to previously uninflected verbs and to put plural markers onto nouns. At first it seemed as though some children were regressing. Having used correct past tense forms such as 'Dot found it' or 'Louise saw it', or plurals like 'Mommy feet', for some time, they suddenly began saying things like 'Dot finded it' or 'Louise seed it' or 'Baby footses all wet'. But in these 'mistakes' Ervin saw sure signs of progress, not regression. This was because, as soon as they began producing the incorrect past tense and plural forms of 'irregular' verbs and nouns, the children Ervin studied also began uttering their first correct inflections of regular verbs (like 'Mommy walked', where the simple rule to add 'ed' applied) and regular nouns (like 'two cats', where the simple rule is add 's' to the singular). These regular verbs and nouns had previously been uninflected in the children's speech. Ervin concluded that the first correct irregulars like 'came' and 'feet' had been learned by rote. But once the children discovered that rules existed for converting singular to plural and present to past tense, rote memory gave way. Thus they made the mistake of applying the new rules even to irregular exceptions.

When children create their own overly regular plurals and verb endings, this shows clearly that language acquisition is a process of mastering rules, not simple parroting. At first, the rules a child comes up with are too simple and too widely generalised to duplicate adult usage. But this very lack of conformity to adult grammar shows that the child's concept

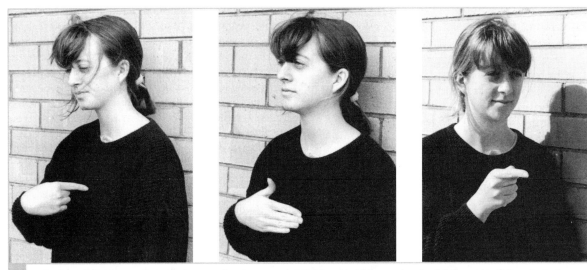

One rule of descriptive grammar that many languages have in common is S-V-O (i.e. object follows verb and verb follows subject). Thus, the Auslan (Australian Sign Language) sentence above keeps the same word order when translated into English as 'I like you'.

of language includes far more than rote memory for set phrases and expressions. Instead, children often apply their 'linguistic genius' to the task of devising rules that transcend all the specific phrases they have ever heard. These rules allow them to produce totally original utterances that have a consistent, rule-governed structure (e.g. the rule that all past tenses are created by adding 'ed' to the present tense form of the verb), even though the rules are not the same as in the mature grammar of their language. This phenomenon reveals compellingly that language acquisition is a sophisticated cognitive accomplishment that cannot be reduced simply to rote learning or memorisation.

Transformational grammar: Questions, negatives and complex sentences

Transformational grammar (Chomsky, 1967) describes the rules that allow simple declarative statements (like 'Mom helps Louise') to be modified to convey a range of more complex meanings, including (a) questions ('Is Mom helping Louise? Why is Mom helping her?'), (b) negations ('Mom is not helping Louise'), (c) passives ('Louise is being helped by Mom'), (d) conjunctive assertions ('Mom is helping Louise and Dot is watching her') and (e) embedded sentences ('Louise said that Mom was helping her'). These constructions emerge in children's speech over the period from age two to age four. Questions and negatives are usually acquired first (see Box 6.5 and Box 6.6 for examples) and develop by a series of gradual approximations towards the mature transformational rule, as explained below.

NEGATION

From the time they first begin to speak, children often want to say things that contradict rather than affirm the ongoing verbal or non-verbal state of affairs. Lois Bloom (1970) noted that children use negative words to express at least three different kinds of negative meanings. In her longitudinal study, she found that the first of these to develop was the notion of non-existence (as in Box 6.5 when Louise said 'Dot' and shook her head to indicate that her father was not home yet). Next came rejection, in which a negative term was used to indicate a desire to be rid of something or to prevent an undesirable occurrence (as in Box 6.6 when Louise said 'No Dot doing that!'). Finally, Bloom's subjects began using negative sentences like 'That not lollypop' and 'It's not cold out' to convey denial or to assert that an implied or previously spoken statement was not true. (One of Louise's negatives of denial was reported in her father's 24 May 1950 diary entry as follows: 'Mom went up to the attic to rummage around for some things. She didn't take Louise with her. Louise hollered up: "Mom, you don't like to see a lot of junk but I do!"')

Two other developmental studies of negation have analysed sequential changes in the structural rules which enable children to create negative sentences like these. Henning Wode (1977) found that after first using 'no' exclusively as a single-word utterance, his daughter Inga developed a structure he called anaphoric negation, in which a negative word or gesture was joined with another word to create simple negative sentences like 'No want' (meaning 'I don't want it') or '[headshake] Boppie' (meaning 'That's not Boppie'). As sentences grew in length, the negative word remained for a time in front of the affirmative word, but negative and affirmative meanings were clearly integrated with one another. Louise's 'No Dot doing that' at 22 months was typical of this rule.

Edward Klima and Ursula Bellugi (1966) suggested that the child's first grammatical rule for forming negative sentences was to preface an otherwise affirmative statement by the word 'no' or 'not', and that children who were at this stage probably could not even understand embedded negative contractions (such as 'That isn't Dot').

The next stage occurs when the child begins to embed negative words inside the sentence to produce utterances like 'This no candy', 'Kathryn not

BOX 6.6 A case in point
The magic of a child's early sentence constructions

When Louise was 22 months old, her father made an entry in his diary that illustrates the rich versatility of a child's early efforts to convey complex meanings using telegraphic grammar. He wrote:

27 January 1950. *This is the time more than any other in my life that I shall look back on with nostalgia. Merely anticipating it, I can feel it as keenly as though the experiences I am living through now were already in the dim and distant past. When I'm playing with Louise and she laughs and gasps out, 'No Dot doing that!', I feel a pang as though it were something long ago that I shall never know again. So it is when she pleads, 'Mom help you?', or on the other hand, says with so much satisfaction in her throaty voice, 'Mom helping you'. So it is in a hundred other things she says and does: her languid way of waving goodbye or goodnight; her play at table, holding her spoon in her teeth or sticking her finger in her mouth to pretend she doesn't want to eat; her 'no, no' when I ask her something and her repeating 'no, no' until I agree that she doesn't have to do it or have it, whatever it is; her banging her doll's head against her own and then saying 'Poor head', so that Peggy or I will caress it (her head, not her doll's); her pushing her face into mine and crying, 'Do-at!' or 'Dot-tee!'*

© Peterson 1974, reproduced with permission

quite through' and 'I can't do it' (Bloom, 1970). The words 'can't' and 'don't' were at first used only in the negative as interchangeable variants of the earlier negative words 'no' and 'not'. Children at this stage showed no awareness of the relationship between 'not' and the auxiliary verbs 'can' and 'do'. It was only at the third stage that children's use of 'do' and 'can' in affirmative sentences showed that they understood the derivation of the negative contractions. At this final stage, the ability to negate other auxiliaries, like 'is' and 'will', gives them the same versatility as adults and they create fully negative sentences like: 'Louise will do it, Dot won't', 'I'm not finished yet' or 'Mom, you don't like to see a lot of junk, but I do' (Peterson, 1974, p. 114).

QUESTIONS

The rules needed to convert an affirmative sentence into a question are likewise acquired sequentially. At first, in the holophrastic stage, the child may use tone of voice to distinguish questions from affirmatives (e.g 'Car?' said in a rising tone implies uncertainty compared with the same word spoken in a descending voice, implying certainty). During the stages of two-word and telegraphic speech, the same intonation strategy is employed, producing sentences like 'Mom help you?' in Box 6.6. Next, question words like 'who', 'where', 'when' and 'why' are appended in front of declarative sentences to produce questions like 'What me think?' or 'Why you smiling?' Then, corresponding to the third stage in the development of negation, the child masters auxiliary verbs and includes them in questions like 'Where the other Joe will drive?' or 'Why the kitty can't stand up?'

Finally, the rule for inverting the subject and the auxiliary verb is brought in, and the child begins to ask questions like 'What can dinosaurs eat?' This stage in the development of questions is illustrated in questions like 'Mom, why are your eyes like fish and mine are like fish but Bop's are round?' (see Table 6.3).

COMPLEX SENTENCES

Two-year-old Louise's sentence 'Do you mind if Mom puts the toothpaste away?' joins together two separate ideas – Mom's actions with regard to the toothpaste and Dot's mental attitude towards those actions. This kind of complex sentence construction begins to emerge at around age three, but is still developing in most children up to the age of five (de Villiers & de Villiers, 1999). In Chapter 7 we examine some of the cognitive and social implications of the acquisition of syntax that is sophisticated enough to enable children to talk about cognitive states ('We pretended we were horses', 'He thought he saw a ghost', 'She said her glass was empty') for the development of children's awareness of their own and other people's minds (de Villiers & de Villiers, 1999).

Theories of language acquisition

There are three main theoretical approaches to language acquisition. The first assumes that language development is innate and unfolds through a process of genetically ordained maturation. The second explains language development as a learning process in which children store the language they hear others speaking in memory and modify their own speech based on these memories, in response to positive or negative reinforcement. A third approach explains the acquisition of language in terms of social input as an interaction between the genetic program for language in the human brain and environmental stimulation arising out of social interaction. The kinds of social experiences that foster language, according to this account, include the child's important social role as a conversational partner in family dialogue, disputes, play and commentary. The next sections explore these three contrasting theoretical approaches.

The nativist approach

The rapid progress in sentence construction that is illustrated in Table 6.3 is quite typical of toddlers the world over. Yet the system of grammatical rules necessary to produce sentences like Louise's at 32 months is highly complex. Consider Louise's sentence, 'Dot, are you expecting me to have these?' It involves sophisticated vocabulary ('expecting') and sophisticated grammatical rules such as (a) inversion of the auxiliary verb with the subject to denote a question, (b) use of the progressive inflection '-ing' to denote ongoing activity, and (c) embedding of the

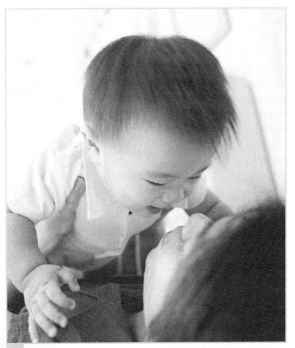

The nativist approach ascribes language development to neurocognitive maturation, while learning theories highlight the importance of parent–child conversation.

inverted, future, possessive phrase ('me to have' ['I will have']).

Do children actually learn all these complex linguistic constructions after only a few years' experience with speaking and being spoken to? Or are babies endowed at birth with a brain that is organised in such a way that language development follows its own course with only a marginal contribution from experience? Noam Chomsky (1967) espoused the latter view when he inaugurated the nativist approach to language acquisition. Chomsky proposed that the human brain comes equipped with an 'innate concept' of the grammar of human languages, encoded in a Language Acquisition Device, or LAD.

It is obvious that even a nativist theory cannot dispense with experience entirely. The grammars of all humanity's varied languages differ from one another in certain important respects. For example, the Russian and French languages employ more inflections than English, as shown in Table 6.4. By contrast, Chinese verb forms occur mainly in a single tense, requiring fewer inflections than English. But the phonology of Chinese is extremely complicated, employing intonation to distinguish meaning in a manner very different from that of European languages. Table 6.4 illustrates some of these syntactic variations.

Since babies the world over acquire their native language with approximately equal ease, only those universal aspects of grammar that are shared by all languages (such as the rule that a sentence consists of a subject plus a predicate) could be completely innate. But the acquisition of rules that are specific to a given language would also be relatively easy if, as the nativists suggest, the LAD includes both the universal rules of grammar and a template for cross-linguistic syntactic variations. In fact, the LAD is thought to contain hypotheses about all the rules that could conceivably apply to any human signed or spoken language. In addition, it is thought to have 'operating procedures', which enable it to test whether one of these rules happens to be included in the grammar of the particular language spoken by a particular infant's parents (McNeill, 1970).

Thus, according to nativist theory, language acquisition is biologically programmed, and all the child is required to do is to compare innately specified rules against the speech of his or her community. Obviously, such a process is far less tedious than the cognitive discovery of grammar and the creation of new rules 'from scratch'. Unfortunately for the proof or refutation of Chomsky's theory, no one has yet managed to pinpoint the relevant brain structures that the LAD is believed to reside in, nor mustered conclusive empirical evidence that they exist. So the nativist view remains an unproven, though logically plausible and widely favoured, hypothesis.

Learning theories

The notion that language is acquired through learning has a long history but, as in the case of the

TABLE 6.4 Some differences in grammatical rules among languages

English (no inflection)	Russian (adjectives and possessive pronouns are inflected according to the gender of the noun)
My red book	МОЯ КРАСНАЯ КНИГА (MOYA KRASNAYA KNEEGA)
My red pen	МОЙ КРАСНОЙ ПЕРО (MOI KRASNOI PERO)
English (no inflection)	French (verbs are inflected to match the pronoun)
I eat	Je mange
You eat	Vous mangez

Chinese (tonal variations give different meanings to the same sound patterns)	
Low-pitched tone	Falling (high to low tone)
ma — mother	mà — to swear
shi — lion	shì — business
fan — sail	fàn — meal
yao — to invite	yào — to shine
High-low-high tone	Rising (low to high tone)
mǎ — horse	má — linen
shi — arrow	shí — ten
fǎn — return	fán — to be vexed
yǎo — to bite	yáo — to shake

nativist approach, some controversy and uncertainty still exist over which specific learning mechanisms are primarily involved. One view is that simple reinforcement plays a major role (Staats, 1970). This assumes that children acquire grammar by being rewarded for speaking correctly formed sentences and being either ignored or punished when they speak ungrammatically. But Roger Brown's (1973) tape-recordings in children's homes told a different story.

Throughout the massive number of conversations he recorded between toddlers and their mothers, he found only scattered instances of a parent attempting to provide positive or negative feedback about the grammar the child was using. Instead, mothers give the 'yes' and 'no' answers that Staats equated with reward and punishment primarily in terms of the meaning of whatever the child was trying to say. Thus, when one child expressed the grammatically flawed sentence 'Mommy not boy he girl', the mother responded affirmatively, but when another said 'Walt Disney comes on on Tuesday' (a sentence that is grammatically perfect) the mother said 'No', because the child had the day wrong.

Even in those rare instances when mothers did attempt to instruct their offspring on correct grammatical usage, the children appeared to resist their teaching efforts. For example, a child who began by saying 'Nobody don't like me' and was told to repeat 'Nobody likes me' eight times over, without effect, was eventually persuaded to amend the original sentence; but the new version was even less grammatically regular than the first. The child garbled his own rule together with the adult's to produce 'Nobody don't likes me' (McNeill, 1966, p. 69).

However, although the simple notion that children acquire grammar by being rewarded for correctly formed sentences and punished when they speak ungrammatical ones appears incorrect, it is nevertheless possible that reinforcement of another kind does have an important role to play in language mastery. This is the satisfaction of being understood by a listener, and the corresponding punishment of not being able to communicate. Katherine Nelson's (1973) account of the frustration experienced by Robert (see p. 181) when his mother persisted in misunderstanding his movement-based word meanings gives one instance of the unpleasant feelings that communication failures are likely to produce. Conversely, the joy in being understood by a conversational partner is rewarding in itself.

IMITATION

As an adjunct to simple reward and punishment, learning theorists have argued that modelling, observation or copying may assist language acquisition (Ervin, 1964). The notion that children acquire grammar by storing memories of sentences they have heard from other people and later imitating these models is one of the oldest of all language-learning theories.

In fact, all normal children do imitate a portion of what is said to them, but they do not repeat everything they hear, nor is everything they say an immediate or even a delayed repetition of something someone else has said. One child used the sentence 'More book' (see Table 6.2) to request that reading be continued and 'All gone sticky' to describe washed hands. Clearly, no adult had ever spoken such phrases in his hearing (Braine, 1963). Even when children are obviously echoing adult speech, there are several important variations in their manner of imitation. Sometimes they repeat exactly what they hear (Adult: 'That's not a screw'; Child: 'Dat not a screw'). Sometimes they seem to understand what they repeat (Adult: 'Are they all there?'; Child: 'All dere?'). But at other times no comprehension is evident (Adult: 'But he was much bigger than Perro'; Child: 'Big a Perro'). (All these examples are from Brown, reported in McNeill, 1970, p. 1103.)

In view of this diversity, no learning theorist is prepared to assert categorically that the child's language is an exact copy, or replica, of adult speech (Bloom, Hood & Lightbown, 1974). Instead, the basis for the theory that children acquire language through imitation is that the act of copying an adult speech model in some way enhances the child's own understanding of the rules of grammar. But does it?

In one of the first attempts to provide an empirical answer to this question, Susan Ervin (1964) made detailed recordings of the sentences produced by a group of five children who were just beginning to put

*While some toddlers do imitate a portion of what they hear, **all** children produce novel sentences that they cannot possibly have copied.*

words together. She divided their utterances into two categories: (a) imitations and (b) spontaneous speech. The former were phrases copied from an immediately preceding utterance by an adult, while the latter included everything else the child said. Ervin then wrote a grammar to describe all the spontaneous sentences produced by each child. By seeing whether the sentences they had copied from adults were consistent with these rules or more advanced, she was able to test whether the process of imitating had demonstrably aided the growth of grammar. In all cases but one, the imitated sentences matched the rules for spontaneous sentences perfectly. But if imitation had been a means of acquiring new grammatical rules, Ervin reasoned, grammatical progress should have shown up first in the imitated utterances. Therefore, copied sentences should have reflected more complex rules than spontaneous speech. Ervin concluded that 'We cannot look to overt imitation as a source of the rapid progress children make in grammatical skill in these early years' (p. 172).

One problem with Ervin's study was that she looked only at rules of word order. Such rules were possibly too general to reveal subtle lexical and grammatical benefits accruing from imitation. Also, Ervin's sample was small and the children were all at a similar stage in language development. So Lois Bloom, Lois Hood and Patsy Lightbown (1974) designed a subsequent study that analysed the spontaneous and imitated words and sentences of six children as they developed from single-word utterances through telegraphic speech. First, and somewhat disturbingly, these researchers found huge differences in the frequency of imitation, even among as few as six children. One boy copied one out of every three of the utterances he spoke, while another child created 15 spontaneous sentences for every one that was imitated.

Variations like these suggest that any conclusion about whether imitation facilitates language acquisition will depend on the child, since frequent imitation would be bound to have a greater impact than the rare exercising of the prerogative to copy. This, in fact, was the conclusion reached by Bloom, Hood and Lightbown when they examined the children's speech. The process of imitation had clearly assisted the linguistic development of those children who imitated frequently. Several new words and new grammatical relationships had first entered these children's repertoires as imitations and had only later emerged in their spontaneous speech, but the children who imitated infrequently seemed to derive no benefit from the rare instances when they did imitate. As in the case of the children in Ervin's sample, their imitations were no different, either lexically or grammatically, from their spontaneous utterances. Nor was their progress in language acquisition apparently inferior to that of the prolific imitators who were picking up new words and grammatical rules by copying.

Thus, while the act of imitating can apparently help some children to learn language, it is not an essential means of language acquisition for all children. Perhaps, as Bloom, Hood and Lightbown suggest, whether particular children will use imitation effectively depends on their intelligence, their personality and their parents' style of interacting with them. Furthermore, imitation is selective. Even those children in the study who imitated a lot did not repeat everything that was said to them. They tended to copy only those utterances incorporating particular grammatical rules or vocabulary items that were just beyond the reach of their own spontaneous speech. Some children copied new words only, while others concentrated exclusively on new grammatical expressions. Therefore, it would seem that imitation, when effective, is selectively chosen. In other words, it is an active language-learning strategy that cannot be equated with 'parroting' or the simple passive encoding of external models.

Henrietta Lempert (1984) used a training procedure to test whether being forced to imitate can effectively teach children to use new grammatical rules. The participants in her study were 60 three- and four-year-olds who did not yet use the passive voice in their spontaneous speech. Before beginning the experiment, Lempert tested their comprehension of passive sentences using a set of plastic toys. She asked each child to use the toys to act out such sentences as 'The horse is pushed by the cow' or 'The truck is being pulled by the car'. Children who did not yet understand passives usually made the horse and the truck perform the action. Children who made these mistakes were subsequently exposed to a training program requiring them to imitate correct passive sentences while looking at pictures where the actor and acted-upon were clearly differentiated. One picture, for example, showed a girl running with a boy

behind her. The passive sentence was 'The girl is being chased by the boy'.

Lempert found that her imitation training procedure was very effective in teaching children a new grammatical construction. As a result of their practice in imitating as few as 20 passive sentences, children learned both to comprehend and to produce phrases relying on the passive rule. Since they had had no previous understanding of the rule, this was clear evidence of grammatical growth. Furthermore, the benefits from training generalised. After their practice with imitation, the children were able to create new passive sentences that they had never heard before. Thus when Lempert showed them a novel set of pictures and asked them to describe the actions portrayed 'in the new way', the children gave replies such as 'The monkey is chased by the tiger' or 'The horse is being washed by the lion'. This versatility suggests that children are capable of achieving full mastery of a new grammatical structure simply by being made to imitate it sensibly.

However, it should be noted that Lempert took great care to avoid a situation of blind imitation, where children simply repeat nonsensical sound patterns 'parrot-fashion'. In her study, participants had to see and comprehend the pictured action before being asked to imitate a sentence describing it.

Lempert's discovery that a child's imitation of advanced grammatical rules in adult speech can promote grammatical development suggests the usefulness of incorporating systematic imitation training into the optimisational repertoire of speech therapists working with language-delayed children. It also has broad implications for how research studies of grammatical development should be conducted. According to Lempert:

> Current beliefs about how children learn language are mostly derived from samples of utterances children have produced spontaneously under uncontrolled or unspecified conditions. Consequently, models of language acquisition are largely descriptions of what children choose to say rather than models that generate testable predictions. Although the study of children's naturally occurring speech has an essential role in understanding language acquisition ... the current studies demonstrate that the acquisition of syntax can be subjected to controlled study. (p. 59)

A conversational approach

We noted earlier that infants begin to play the role of conversational partners by engaging in meaningless pseudo-conversations even before their discovery of the representational significance of word meaning. From then on, language continues to develop in a social way, as children make efforts to understand the speech of people around them and to express meanings that others understand correctly.

Consequently, over and above any contributions

to language made by reward or punishment, children are helped to acquire language by the experience of speaking and being spoken to. Becoming the conversational partner of another human being who treats the infant as someone to talk and listen to, and someone whose non-verbal expressions and spoken noises make sense, is a crucial factor in language acquisition, according to the conversational approach. Box 6.7 includes a thought problem incorporating these ideas.

Conversations and motherese

Children encounter the social patterns of conversation long before they begin to speak meaningfully. Catherine Snow (1977) analysed everything that one pair of mothers said to their babies from the time the children were three months old until they reached the age of 18 months. Even at three months, these mothers treated their infants as though they were partners in a dialogue. Whenever the baby burped, yawned, sneezed, coughed, gurgled, smiled or laughed, the mother replied with simple expressions like 'Pardon you', 'That's better' or 'What's so funny?' As the children progressed into naming and holophrastic grammar, these questions and rejoinders became more varied, as shown in Table 6.5. Snow felt that these maternal conversational techniques gave infants optimal opportunities to join in a conversation once they were ready. As noted earlier, skills like taking turns and making eye contact with a speaker apply as much to pseudo-conversation as to real dialogue. Thus, these responses may give the baby a head start. Once meaningful language begins to be acquired, they can use it socially.

The style of speech mothers address to 2-year-olds, as compared with 10-year-olds, has also been analysed. Speech to younger children, called *motherese*, is briefer and grammatically simpler than that addressed to older children. It also contains fewer verbs and third-person pronouns, but more partial and complete repetitions (Snow, 1972). Juliet Phillips (1973) found that the vocabulary mothers used when addressing toddlers was simpler and less varied than that used with adults. In other words, adults seem instinctively to tailor their language to suit toddlers' modest comprehension and production skills. Even 4-year-olds tend to use simpler speech when speaking to younger children than they would use with peers (Shatz & Gelman, 1973).

Toni Cross (1978, 1981) tested whether the use of motherese actually does encourage language acquisition. Her subjects were well-educated middle-class Australian mothers of toddlers. Interestingly, Cross found that all the mothers in her sample used motherese to some extent. Furthermore, when she compared the toddler's rate of language development to the extent of the mother's use of motherese, a positive relationship emerged. In other words, simplifying

Adults typically simplify their speech when addressing children who are just beginning to acquire language.

speech was clearly beneficial. Cross found that mothers who made the most radical and frequent simplifications had offspring with the best language skills by the age of 36 months.

Studies of second-language acquisition by young children also highlight the usefulness of motherese, or simplified speech. Catherine Snow and Marian Hoefnagel-Hohle (1978) conducted a longitudinal study of preschoolers from English-speaking families who were given the opportunity to acquire Dutch as a second language during their parents' temporary residence in the Netherlands. They found that children who were exposed only to complex adult-oriented speech made little or no progress. Thus one group of three- to five-year-olds who heard an average of 700 complex Dutch utterances a day during their five months' attendance at a Dutch-language kindergarten showed little or no evidence of speaking or understanding Dutch by the end of the trial period. By contrast, another group exposed to a smaller amount of Dutch in the form of motherese, which was simplified, spoken directly to them and relevant to things they were doing, did learn elements of the Dutch language. It was found that Dutch children who regularly watched large amounts of German language television did not learn any German at all (see Box 6.7). Clearly, face-to-face conversation in general, and motherese in particular, are crucial to the language mastery.

Some of the specific conversational strategies that these mothers used to especially good effect in facilitating their toddlers' early language mastery are shown in Table 6.5.

Conversational expansion

As Table 6.5 shows, one of the effective strategies of motherese is *expansion*, in which the parent adds a grammatical improvement to a child's conversational opener. This may be an especially effective teaching device, because expansions supply the child with especially relevant information, including the following:

1. By expanding, the parent is letting the child know that what he or she has just said is inadequate or confusing.
2. Expansions link in with the immediate non-verbal context.
3. Expansions provide examples of how to construct more grammatically advanced utterances around the concepts the child is eager to talk about.

Roger Brown and Ursula Bellugi (1964) felt that it was virtually impossible for a parent to avoid using expansion when conversing with toddlers. As they explained: 'A reduced or incomplete English sentence seems to constrain the English-speaking adult to expand it into the nearest properly formed complete sentence' (p. 138). On the basis of their tape-recordings of conversations between parents and toddlers they estimated that the mother of a tele-

TABLE 6.5	Some features of motherese
Feature of motherese	**Example**
Short sentences	*Mother*: 'She's funny.' 'See Daddy.'
Expansions	*Child*: 'Broke.' *Mother*: 'It broke.'
Simple recasts	*Child*: 'Built it.' *Mother*: 'She built the house.'
Continuations	*Child*: 'Swim him ocean?' *Mother*: 'Yes, he does.'
Exaggerated intonations	*Mother*: 'Now *that's* my *sweetie*, isn't he?'

Note: For further information on the effectiveness of these features, see Cross (1978) and Nelson, Denninger, Bonvillian, Kaplan and Baker (1984).

graphic speaker typically expands about one in every three utterances her child addresses to her.

Courtney Cazden (1965) performed an intervention study to test whether expansion really does assist the child's development of grammatical competence. Her subjects were preschoolers. She divided them into three groups. The experimental (expansion) group had a conversation hour every day during which an adult expanded everything the children said. There were also two control groups, one that met with the adult to play silently and another where the adult conversed, without expanding, by making

Adults use the nonverbal context (like pointing) and linguistic strategies like expansion and topic extension to assist in communicating with young children.

new comments on what the child had just said. After three months Cazden tested the grammatical progress of the children. She found that the expansion group had improved a little more than the no-conversation control group, but the simple conversation control group progressed as well, if not better, than those exposed to expansion.

The results of a later study by Sharon Penner (1987) demonstrated that the expansion process can boost the growth of grammar when used judiciously by a parent who is closely in tune with the child's current level of language development. Her subjects were 20 toddlers aged 21 to 40 months and their primary-caregiver parents (18 mothers and two fathers). Penner recorded parent–child dialogues on tape and later counted the frequencies of expansions and expatiations (or topic extensions) in the parent's speech. As shown in Figure 6.4, she discovered that parents used these two forms of conversational follow-on differentially, depending on whether the child's previous utterance had been grammatically correct or incorrect.

Penner concluded that this selective use of expansion should aid grammatical development by showing children exactly how to produce a grammatical advance on their own ambiguous or incorrect utterances. For example, if a child said 'Ball fall' and the parent replied 'Yes, the ball fell', the child was in an ideal position to realise that the verb had to be changed to indicate past tense. Furthermore, parents' tendency to expand selectively in this way suggests that parents indirectly supply feedback about grammaticality. Children's recognition of the similarity between their own ungrammatical statements and the parent's expanded ones may diplomatically imply to them that their own utterances are not quite adequate, as well as supplying an accurate model of how to correct the grammatical mistake. As Penner explained:

When parents extend the topic of an utterance, the child receives indirect information that the utterance was understood. Perhaps the more frequent use of topic extensions after grammatical utterances provides a kind of selective pressure favouring children's use of more mature grammatical forms. (p. 382)

Culture and motherese

Some parents have difficulty adjusting their speech to suit the needs of an immature listener. Others disapprove in principle of exposing children to the incorrect grammar and patronising intonations of 'baby talk'. For example, among the Kaluli of Papua New Guinea, parents and grandparents who simplify their speech when addressing children are considered to be poor teachers of language who will delay their children's language acquisition by setting a bad example. Thus Kaluli mothers compensate by requiring toddlers to repeat any complex adult sentences they seem to have difficulty understanding (Nelson et al., 1984). Interestingly, language development appears to keep the same timetable in New Guinea as in middle-class urban Australia or New Zealand.

On the other hand, the effective use of motherese is a well-developed parenting skill in traditional Australian Aboriginal communities (Walsh & Yallop, 1993). In order to cope with the complexity of adult Aboriginal languages with their sophisticated vocabularies for describing kinship relations, food groups and other important categories of information, children are introduced to language gradually with the aid of a type of motherese that the whole community endorses and is fluent in. For example, the Walpiri language, spoken in the Yuendumu, Willowra and Lajamanu Aboriginal communities near Alice Springs, includes a special form of baby-talk or motherese that offers toddlers substitutes for tongue-twisting adult words like 'ngati' (mother), 'ngawurri' (younger sister) and 'kapirdi' (elder sister). The Anglicised 'mamiyi' is Walpiri baby-talk for mother, while the phonetic and conceptual complexity of adult words for older and younger sister is overcome in baby-talk by calling both of them 'yayi'. The word 'jiji' (taken from the Australian colloquial 'gee-gee' for a horse) is also a common substitute for the adult 'nantuwu' (horse). When Walpiri adults address infants and toddlers they are likely to use 'jiji', though they would never use this baby-talk word when speaking to one another.

As a result of these well-understood speech modifications, Aboriginal infants are encouraged to participate in conversations with mature speakers from an early age. As their speech skills develop, children are expected to graduate naturally into adult language. When they fail to do so, parents and older siblings may tease them by mimicking their childish speech or by pretending not to understand a familiar baby-talk word (see the section on 'Raising the ante' later in this chapter).

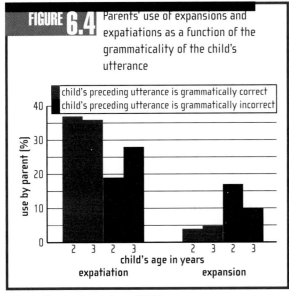

FIGURE 6.4 Parents' use of expansions and expatiations as a function of the grammaticality of the child's utterance

child's preceding utterance is grammatically correct
child's preceding utterance is grammatically incorrect

use by parent (%)

child's age in years

expatiation   expansion

Source: Based on data in Penner (1987).

This systematic use of baby-talk is highly effective when measured in terms of the Aboriginal child's rapid rate of language learning. As Edith Bavin (1993) explained:

> By the age of two, Walpiri children produce connected utterances that contain recognizable forms ... The adult shows pride in the knowledge gained by the child, and teases the child, repeating words as they are pronounced. (p. 92)

In a Japanese study of profoundly deaf mothers who used sign language as their medium of communication (Masataka, 1996) it was found that motherese transcends the medium of speech. These Japanese deaf mothers, whose 6-month-old infants were also profoundly deaf, modified their signed communications when addressing the baby compared with their signed communication to their adult deaf friends. The specific modifications of conversational style that were made for the babies were in line with the features of motherese listed in Table 6.5. Compared with their signing to friends, the mothers' signing to their infants was slower, contained more repetitions and had more exaggerated movements and facial expressions. Furthermore, deaf babies found motherese appealing. When videotapes of the deaf mothers signing to their own infants were replayed to a different group of deaf Japanese babies of the same age, they showed greater interest in, and responsiveness to, the motherese than the adult signing.

Conversational supports and challenges: Raising the ante and listening sympathetically

Adults can also facilitate toddlers' language acquisition by strategic use of either comprehension or deliberate misunderstanding.

RAISING THE ANTE

Jerome Bruner (1983) discovered that pretending not to grasp a lazy or badly constructed utterance is another effective device that parents can use to assist their toddlers' mastery of language. Bruner called this strategy 'raising-the-ante', by analogy with a poker game. On the basis of extensive longitudinal video recordings of mothers' dialogues with their toddlers, Bruner discovered a regular pattern of changes over time. In the first place, before the child had begun to babble, mothers engaged in pseudo-conversations similar to those noted by Snow (1977). But as soon as their infants began to show that they could use their voices for more than mere involuntary cries, belches and grunts, Bruner's mothers refrained from reacting to these inadvertent non-linguistic noises and confined their dialogue to times when the child appeared to be making sounds deliberately.

Later, the entrance of symbolically meaningful words into the child's repertoire caused the mother to raise the stakes still further. Now, she ignored babbling and insisted that the child utter a real word in order to get her attention. Finally, during the stages of two-word sentences and telegraphic speech, some of the mothers in Bruner's sample adopted the technique of deliberately misunderstanding 'lazy' utterances which they knew to be beneath the child's operating level of competence. For example, if a child who had once been heard to say 'Want jam' later used pointing, grunting or a holophrase like 'gimme', the mother might pretend not to know what he meant. Perhaps she might offer him the wrong thing or simply ignore him until he spoke a complete sentence.

Some examples of a mother's synchronising her dialogue to match the language level of her child are illustrated in Table 6.6.

BEING A SYMPATHETIC LISTENER

In addition to the conversational benefits of motherese, expansion, the simplifying of speech and upping the conversational ante, a parent's sheer presence as an interested human companion offers a powerful motive for language acquisition which no radio or television set can ever hope to equal. Babies enjoy communicating and being understood even before they master language as a means for doing so. The fact that each new aspect of children's language mastery extends the range of what they can talk about and the ease with which they can understand and be understood must in itself constitute a powerful incentive for language learning. Furthermore, the emotional bond that develops between parent and child before language learning effectively begins (see Chapter 5) gives parental approval of toddlers' linguistic offerings special value.

Conversely, each new linguistic advance lessens the baby's immature dependency on others and widens social, cognitive and exploratory horizons. Some of the most important social consequences of language learning are explored later in this chapter.

Personality development in the context of language growth

The acquisition of language provides the child with new cognitive skills for self-reflection and representational thinking and opens new avenues of social experience with important implications for the child's personality development through (a) self-awareness and (b) a mature sense of autonomy (Erikson, 1968a).

Self-awareness

At what age do children become aware of themselves as permanent and distinctively recognisable human beings? Michael Lewis and Jeanne Brooks-Gunn (1979) developed an ingenious methodology to answer this question. In their procedure, known as the *rouge test*, mothers are instructed to surreptitiously apply a dot of rouge or lipstick to the infant's nose during routine caregiving. The infant is later

TABLE 6.6	Example of a mother 'raising the ante' for conversation	
Age	Child's highest language level	Sample dialogue
4 months	Meaningless babbling	*Child:* 'An-bah-bah-bah-ah-bah-boo.' *Mother:* 'Ah baby! Hi baby! That's right!'
15 months	Meaningful names	*Child:* (pointing to the refrigerator): 'Uh-uh-uh?' *Mother:* 'Do you want something?' *Child:* 'Uh-hu-hu!' *Mother:* 'Come on, tell me what you want. You can tell me.' *Child:* 'Muk.' *Mother:* 'Milk? That's good! Here it is.'
2 years	Two-word grammar	*Child:* 'Door.' *Mother:* 'Yes, that's a door.' *Child:* 'Door!' *Mother:* 'I see the door, what about it?' *Child:* 'Door open.' *Mother:* 'Okay, here, I'll open it for you.'

shown a mirror. If the face in the mirror is recognised as being an image of self, babies should touch their own nose in order to locate, examine or remove the unusual mark which they correctly locate on their own anatomy. But if the baby ignores the mark or attempts to touch only the mirror image of it, it makes sense to assume that the face seen in the mirror is not connected with self.

When they tested a group of infants aged 9 to 24 months, Lewis and Brooks-Gunn found that almost no infants under 15 months passed the rouge test. Between 15 and 17 months, a small minority did so, whereas between 18 and 24 months the vast

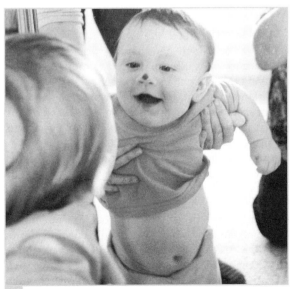

An infant of 9 months being exposed to the rouge test.

majority were able to pass the test by touching their own nose as soon as they noticed the red spot in the mirror. At the same age, infants are often able to label a photograph of themselves with their own name, suggesting that the advent of language may assist in the construction of a stable sense of self.

Social experiences are likely to contribute, together with cognitive development and language, to the growth of self-awareness during toddlerhood. When Gordon Gallup (1979) gave the rouge test to groups of captive adolescent chimpanzees, he found that those who had been reared with other chimps routinely passed the test. However, chimpanzees who were social isolates because they had been raised alone by humans in a laboratory were unable to pass the rouge test during adolescence and early adulthood. Perhaps children, as well as chimpanzees, learn to understand self through interacting socially with other children and adults, learning the boundaries between self and others through face-to-face social contact.

Autonomy versus shame and doubt

According to Erik Erikson (1968a, see Chapter 2), the central personality crisis of the toddlerhood period is a conflict over feelings of independence and autonomy versus feelings of shame and self-doubt. As Erikson explained: 'This stage ... becomes decisive for the ratio between loving goodwill and hateful self-insistence, between co-operation and willfulness, and between self-expression and compulsive self-restraint or meek compliance' (p. 109). To resolve the crisis successfully, the infant needs to learn about self. The self-confidence and sense of personal agency that the infant develops by learning how to predict and control important contingencies in the physical and social world (see Chapter 4) contribute to a successful resolution of the crisis, as does firm but warmly affectionate parenting. As Erikson explained:

> As he gets ready to stand on his own feet more firmly, the infant learns to delineate his world as 'I' and 'you', and as 'me' and 'mine' … But his environment must also back him up in his wish to stand on his own feet, while also protecting him against the now newly emerging pair of estrangements, namely the sense of having exposed himself prematurely and foolishly, which we call shame … and that 'double take' which we call doubt – doubt in himself and doubt in the firmness and perspicacity of his caregivers. (pp. 108–10)

In other words, according to Erikson, the emergence of a clearly delineated sense of self during toddlerhood combines with the greater independence that skilled language and skilled upright locomotion both confer to cause the toddler to want to become a fully autonomous individual, free of parental restriction and control. At the same time, the infant's realistic recognition of the need for parental restraint, coupled with firm but nurturant parenting, helps to rein in this autonomy within manageable bounds. Consequently, when an effective foundation of trust has been laid via secure attachment in infancy, the toddler is able to resolve the crisis by developing a maturely realistic sense of personal agency. This is a lifespan asset. According to Erikson, the child's sense of self acquires a new dimension with successful resolution of the autonomy crisis, producing a belief that 'I am what I can will freely' (1968a, p. 114).

Toddlerhood negativism: Nexus of social, personality and language development

The personality developments of self-awareness and autonomy, the distinctive social behaviours of toddlers, who are prone to throw tantrums, defy parental commands and refuse reasonable offers of assistance, and the new syntactic skills developing with the transformational grammar of negation all come together during toddlerhood in a unique phenomenon known as *negativism*. The phenomenon is so striking that the 24 months spanning the second and third years have acquired a special name in popular speech: the terrible twos.

Negativistic self-assertion

From a naturalistic observational study (see Chapter 2), Louise Bates Ames (1974) produced the following descriptive account of one child's negativistic non-compliance:

> 'Come here, dear,' calls Mother to 18-month-old Tommy. Tommy gives her a look and then runs the other way. Mother catches up with him and commands her son to 'Give me that piece of candy. You know I've told you not to take candy'. Tommy clutches his candy even harder and yells a rebellious 'No!' 'Come into the house this minute, Tommy. I won't have you behaving so badly.' Tommy stands his ground and refuses to budge. (p. 118)

This behaviour pattern clearly reflects language skill (saying 'No!'), interpersonal awareness (e.g. checking the mother's facial expression before defiantly disobeying) and a sense of personal autonomy as an agent with a will independent of his parent's. From the point of view of a parent like Tommy's, in the throes of grappling with a toddler's supermarket temper tantrum, the most striking developmental achievement may be the social power to bring proceedings to a standstill through obstinate refusal to get ready for an outing. But this episode also testifies to the growth of language skills for negotiation and for saying 'No!'. Indeed, the social skills for sizing up opposition and the consequences of refusal, along with the social and linguistic capabilities for negotiating, are striking testimony to psychological development during this formative period.

Thus, negation can be seen to epitomise toddlerhood in terms of social and emotional growth as well as in a linguistic sense (negation being one of the important markers of transformational grammar) (see page 186). As Charles Wenar (1982) explained:

> 'No' [represents] the first conquest of an abstraction. It contrasts with the concrete global words of the period between the 15th and 18th months of life by conveying the specific concept 'I do not want this'. The process underlying this abstraction consists of distinguishing essential elements from unessential ones; specifically, the toddler abstracts the common element of prohibition from the many situations in which the caretaker says 'No'. The shift from situational, physical resistance of infancy to the 'No' of the toddler is a shift from action to symbolic representation of action. Thus freed, the symbol can be employed at will and with considerably less expenditure. Because of its availability, 'No' is more conscious and volitional than the reactive resistance of infancy … the toddler now has entry to the arena of semantic communication. Discussion and negotiation – those uniquely human achievements – become possible. (pp. 19–20)

The toddler's skill in using the word 'no' as an answer to parental suggestions or commands is only one aspect of the broader development of a social behaviour pattern known as negativism. *Negativism* is defined operationally as 'the toddler's intentional noncompliance to adult requests, directives, and prohibitions' (Wenar, 1982, p. 5). Observational studies of parent–child interaction at home have shown that negativism increases abruptly in most children between the ages of 18 and 24 months. In other

Being non-compliant is often a sign of maturity in 2-year-olds.

BOX 6.8

A case in point
The terrible twos

Two instances of Louise's non-compliance were recorded in her father's diary in the months following her second birthday.

6 April 1950. *Sometimes, for other reasons than hunger or weariness, Louise loses her temper. Then the slightest opposition, especially having to do with something over which she has had a previous battle, is apt to set it off. One of these sensitive issues is the game of Alley Oop that she has long enjoyed playing with. It consists of an assortment of thin round wooden sticks with little wooden bulbs attached to one end. She once had her Alley Oop taken away from her because she was chewing on the sticks and bulbs. Since then, whenever she plays with it, she seeks to learn how far she can go in the direction of chewing before she is told not to. Being told not to, when one of these sensitive issues is involved, provokes the explosions.*

This happened the other morning. She flew into a rage and began issuing her commands in a loud voice. Her mother tried reasoning with her, but Louise only shouted more. Her mother took the toy away and told her she could have it when she stopped hollering. There was no immediate effect. Louise still hollered. Little by little she quieted down as her interest was taken by other things and it seemed she had forgotten all about the disputed toy. Then, with tears still in her voice, she asked: 'Have I stopped hollering?'

2 July 1950. *She likes to dawdle, which is normal for children of her age. Even when she is hungry, she will stall around rather than get ready to eat. She is reluctant also to get into her bath and equally slow about getting out. We resort to various stratagems, and one of the best is to offer her a choice. 'Which would you rather do, wash your hands at the basin or with a washrag at your table?' 'With a washrag at my table,' she says, climbing promptly in. Last evening she was sitting at her table while her mother dawdled at getting the washrag ready. 'Mom,' Louise ordered impatiently, 'wash L-O-U-I-S-E'.*

© Peterson, 1974, reproduced with permission

words, however compliant or non-compliant a toddler may have been before the age of 18 months, a sudden upsurge in defiance to parents can be anticipated after that age. Studies also show a marked drop in the average child's negativism at around age three, followed by a more gradual decline over the next two years (Wenar, 1982), though many children are actually almost four by the time their relationships with parents become fully harmonious again. Some typical examples of early childhood defiance appear in Box 6.8.

Day-care and negativism

Toddlers who attend day-care centres on a weekly basis tend to be more negativistic than their counterparts who spend all day at home, at least when it comes to obeying a command from a parent (Rubenstein, Howes & Boyle, 1981; Siegal & Storey, 1985). According to Michael Siegal's (1985) observations of teacher–child interactions in child-care centres in Brisbane, Australia, this is probably partly due to a tendency for day-care staff to adopt a more lenient approach than parents to rule enforcement. He noted that day-care teachers were apt to ignore children's minor misdemeanours. They also spent less time reprimanding toddlers than mothers did. Thus the day-care veteran may acquire a looser or less consistent standard about which adult directives must imperatively be obeyed. They may also gain the confidence to defy at home any particular parental rules which don't happen to apply or be enforced at the day-care centre.

But Siegal's observations suggested that, in addition, peers exerted perhaps an even stronger influence

Like many other children her age, Louise at two was reluctant to get into her bath and equally reluctant to get out again.

than teachers on the social skills of his Queensland day-care veterans. He found that these children had a more sophisticated grasp of social norms and rules of social interaction than stay-at-home toddlers. He attributed this largely to the day-care child's intensive daily contact with peers at the centre. As Siegal explained:

> Rule-guided behaviour may be practised in the peer group where it undergoes modifications leading to a consciousness of cognitions – in this case, relations between rules and behaviours in their social contexts. Children can come to reflect on the applicability of rules to themselves and others through the social knowledge gained in peer-group interaction. They come to internalize rules for behaviour and follow these even when external surveillance is withdrawn. (p. 81)

Gaining social skills: Language, negativism and negotiation

Progress through the successive milestones of language development outlined in earlier sections of this chapter may also contribute to the toddler's eventual outgrowing of the negativism characterising 'the terrible twos'.

Barbara Lawrence (1984) discovered this when she brought a group of 60 North American toddlers and their parents into her research laboratory, which was outfitted to resemble a normal home. She made extensive video recordings of the children's speech during a series of prearranged tasks where parents had to try to involve the toddler in helping them perform simple household chores such as dusting, sweeping and picking up litter. The maturity of a child's language growth was a better predictor of compliance with parental directives than either sex or chronological age. Lawrence found that those toddlers in her sample who had reached the stage of telegraphic speech (see page 184), and were speaking in simple sentences averaging three or more words long, were significantly less overtly defiant and also less passively negativistic than their peers with less mature speech. She found that the typical response by children at the one-word and two-word sentence stages of grammatical development, when asked by parents to help with household chores, was either to defy or ignore the parental request, whereas the telegraphic speakers responded favourably to such requests and compliantly assisted their parents with jobs like making beds, cleaning and tidying up.

Better language skills may have promoted compliance in the telegraphic speakers by enabling them to understand more fully the vocabulary and syntax of verbal requests for help from parents. Lawrence found greater compliance by all children to requests that were phrased simply and concretely ('Pick up those red books and put them on the table') than to grammatically complex and abstract expressions

('Would you mind helping me clean up?'). But another important feature of parents' interaction with offspring who had advanced language skills was more extensive use of mutual discussion and verbal negotiation. Lawrence noted that, before agreeing to comply with their parents' requests for help, telegraphic speakers typically engaged in intensive 'rapid-fire' dialogues. The aim was not only to elicit a valid reason from parents for why they should assist with the chores, but also to work out a 'contract' composed of strings of explicitly agreed conditions and verbal guarantees acceptable to both parties. Some of the language-advanced toddlers paused after each successive parental request to renegotiate terms. Others were willing to comply consistently and enthusiastically to each subsequent parental plea on the basis of the verbal agreement reached during the initial dialogue.

While the toddlers with delayed language development were generally more negativistic, their parents did sometimes manage to gain their compliance. The strategy of simply asking and repeating requests or demands for help was not a very effective way of doing this. In fact, one father who directly asked his son for help on 25 occasions was overwhelmingly unsuccessful. The boy ignored or flatly refused the vast majority of these requests, so that the father ended up doing three out of every four of the assigned household chores entirely by himself.

On the other hand, some parents of toddlers with relatively immature language did manage to overcome their child's negativistic tendency to defy by a method somewhat resembling the 'expansion' features of motherese (see page 192). Parents employing this technique preface their requests for help with some comment on whatever activity the child is engaged in (e.g. 'That's a very nice tower of blocks you've made. Now would you like to help me pick up these bits of paper and put them in the rubbish bin?'). Lawrence suggested that this diplomatic strategy may have been effective in overcoming the toddler's reluctance to comply because parents who acknowledged the importance of the child's ongoing activity before suggesting something new were placing the child on a more equal footing and reinforcing the child's claim to take independent initiative, while at the same time suggesting the positive social benefits of cooperative compliance.

Such diplomacy was not only unnecessary but possibly a hindrance in families with toddlers whose language was advanced. The most effective parental strategy for this group appeared to be a rather noisy verbal harangue. The statistical method known as *multiple regression* enables an evaluation of independent contributions of separate variables to a complex causal process. Using this technique to see which of the above factors separately predicted parental success in gaining compliance from telegraphic speakers, Lawrence discovered the following rather surprising facts:

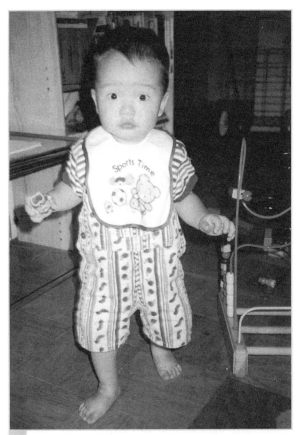
A toddler who hears and comprehends a parental command does not always elect to comply with it.

1. The more loudly and vociferously the parents expressed their commands, the greater the child's compliance.
2. Forceful, unequivocal orders produced more compliance than polite, indirect requests prefaced by 'please'.
3. Parents who conversed about topics their child was interested in were less effective in maintaining compliance than those who confined their conversation exclusively to the chore at hand.
4. Seeking help using a questioning tone of voice ('Would you like to help?') was less effective than a straight command ('Make that bed').

Parents who believe in the value of modelling politeness and consideration when interacting with offspring might find these conclusions disconcerting. But Lawrence was quick to point out that the apparent link between parents' rudeness and toddlers' compliance might actually have been an indirect consequence of longer dialogues in families where parents ended up by issuing loud, imperative orders. When she analysed her videotapes sequentially, she discovered that almost all parents in both groups had first attempted to cajole their child into helping by means of politely phrased queries and pleas. Only when these efforts failed did the more persistent parents resort to loud, forceful orders.

Lawrence was not able to decide conclusively from her data what actually causes the clear link she observed between advanced language development and diminishing negativism. Her finding of lengthier and more sophisticated dialogues between the more compliant toddlers and their parents suggests that the acquisition of sophisticated verbal negotiating skills might reduce the toddler's felt need to resort to blanket, unflinching defiance. Conversely, the more compliant children's better language skills may have resulted from a long-term parental preference for mutual dialogue and simplified speech, dating back well before their offspring had reached the stage of toddlerhood negativism. The obvious linguistic similarities between the most effective parental commands in Lawrence's study and the beneficial characteristics of motherese (see page 191) lend support to this second possibility.

In Australia, Rosemary Leonard (1993) studied how politely children aged two and a half to five years replied to adults' requests and refusals. Politeness was defined as a combination of the use of (a) indirectness ('Could it be your turn to do it?' in place of 'You do it') and (b) softeners (words like 'please'). Children who made use of these linguistic forms in preference to plain statements or threats or insults were rated as polite. To examine this important dimension of linguistic and social behaviour in a systematic way, Leonard encouraged the sample of children in her study to make a series of attempts at resolving conflicts among puppets. The results showed that both the type of situation and the adult's manner of asking influenced the child's level of politeness. But even children as young as three were capable of using diplomatic negotiation rather than defiance or passive non-compliance to achieve their goals.

Request situations were more likely to evoke polite language and skilled negotiation than refusal situations. An adult who asked nicely was less prone to evoke negativism. In addition, the adult's use of a reason was beneficial on two counts. Children who encountered a reason used more polite forms of refusal than those who encountered a simple command. Also, if an adult gave a reason, the child typically replied with a more sophisticated negotiation strategy (e.g. compromise, appeals to logic) than when the adult simply stated a rule or denied a request by the child.

These findings support Lawrence's suggestion that even toddlers are likely to respond initially with negotiation rather than blind defiance to conflicts that encourage verbal discussion and polite argument. However, when frustrated, negotiation may be abandoned in favour of aggression or passivity. These methods of responding to frustration are less mature but may endure throughout the lifespan if negotiation skills fail to develop, even though later aggression will be expressed in more subtle and sophisticated ways than as a toddler's temper tantrum.

Cultural differences in parenting for self-assertion

Children gradually gain skill as verbal negotiators in step with their development of linguistic competence and social sensitivity. But their culture's attitude to verbal assertiveness, as transmitted to them by their parents and older siblings, also influences their modes of negotiation and the balance of politeness to bland directness in their verbal behaviour. In cultures where children are expected to be passively acquiescent, and where it is deemed impolite for a child to express a point of view that contradicts the opinion of an adult, the skills for sophisticated debate and effective negotiation that are considered to be hallmarks of linguistic and cognitive maturity by Anglo-Australians and Anglo-New Zealanders may be slow to develop.

Jacqueline Goodnow and her colleagues (Goodnow, Cashmore, Cotton & Knight, 1984) explored beliefs about children's verbal assertiveness in a sample of migrant and mainstream parents in Sydney. The Anglo-Australian and Lebanese-Australian mothers and fathers in this study were asked:

1. How old should children be before asserting their own point of view in disputes with peers and adults?
2. At what age do you expect verbal negotiation skills – such as being able to reason and justify their own point of view – to develop?
3. Who is responsible for training the child as a negotiator – the family, or teachers and peers in school?

The results revealed a number of similarities between Anglo-Australian and Lebanon-born parents.

Both groups, for example, believed that children should preface their requests to an adult with 'please' by the age of four at the latest. Parents in both cultural groups likewise felt that they themselves were responsible for teaching such polite forms to their toddlers and preschoolers. Interestingly, this was in contrast to a report by Goodnow and her colleagues of an earlier finding that most Japanese parents did not expect their children to use the Japanese equivalent of 'please' until close to the child's sixth birthday. However, it is difficult to equate parental attitudes across languages where the grammatical demands of polite forms of address may be very different.

There were also several important differences between the Anglo-Australian and Lebanese-Australian parents' expectations about their children's verbal assertiveness. Three of these contrasts are illustrated in Figure 6.5. In every case, the Lebanon-born parents expected skilled negotiation and self-confident assertiveness to develop at a later age than the Anglo-Australian parents. Cultural differences like these in adults' expectations about children's development of appropriate forms of spoken self-assertion in their social dealings with others also extend forward through the lifespan to shape teachers' reactions to their pupils' behaviour in primary school and high school. In Chapter 9 we examine contrasting expectations among Aboriginal, Maori and Anglo pupils and their Anglo teachers about what level of independent self-assertion is most appropriate in mixed-ethnic Australian and New Zealand classrooms today.

Aboriginal-Australian parents typically adopt a more egalitarian approach to childrearing than Anglo-Australian parents, tempered by strong nurtu-

---

BOX 6.9

Activity suggestion
Developing assertiveness

Instructions. The items below, taken from Goodnow et al. (1984), describe self-assertion skills that are often observed in young children. From your range of personal acquaintance, locate experienced parents who would be willing to indicate the age at which

they believe (a) a typical boy and (b) a typical girl develops these skills in your community today. Are differences in ages reported as a function of the sex of the child? If you can contact parents from different ethnic backgrounds, compare their responses and see how well their responses match cultural differences reported in this section of the text.

Response options:

	A. By age 3 years or younger	B. Between age 4 and 5 years	C. At age 6 or older	D. Never

1. Shares toys with other children
2. Resolves disagreements without fighting
3. Gets own way by persuading friends

4. Can explain why he/she thinks something is true
5. Asks for an explanation when in doubt
6. Disagrees without biting, hitting or throwing
7. Resolves quarrels without adult help

8. Stands up for own opinions and rights with peers
9. Stands up for own opinions and rights with adults
10. Modifies own viewpoint when presented with conflicting evidence

---

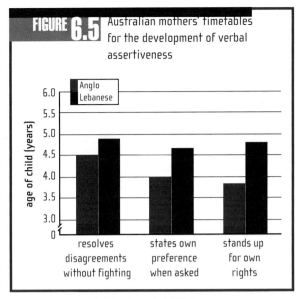

FIGURE 6.5 Australian mothers' timetables for the development of verbal assertiveness

Source: Based on data in Goodnow et al. (1984).

rance and affiliation (Malin, 1990). From the results of a participant-observer study involving the vidoetaping of urban Aboriginal and Anglo-Australian parent–child interactions at home, Merridy Malin concluded that middle-class Anglo parents used more reprimanding, directive ordering, punishment and verbal censure of their children's behaviour than Aboriginal parents. Anglo parents tended to view their children's non-compliance as a threat to their own parental authority. But Aboriginal parents, taking a more egalitarian approach, did not necessarily expect compliance from their children any more than they would from another adult. As one Aboriginal mother told Malin:

> Kids are kids … if a kid don't want to listen to you, they won't … You know kids, they playing, they don't know anything else but their little mates. Same as adults, when they sitting down having a drink, the wife won't hear the husband or the husband won't hear the wife. They don't take notice to the kids. So they don't expect their kids to hear them straightaway. (p. 315)

The situation is similar for Aboriginal infants and toddlers in Walpiri language communities near Alice Springs, according to Edith Bavin (1993). She noted that the Aboriginal parents in these communities involved young children in the activities of older members of the group from an early age. Thus independence was granted early and new rights and responsibilities were introduced as soon as the child seemed ready to assume them. As Bavin explained:

> Children are encouraged to be independent and are not protected from potential danger in the way that many white middle-class children are. Walpiri adults will protect children from serious dangers, such as snakes, but they do not normally stop children from playing with a knife or a piece of broken glass. When a baby cries the mother provides milk but when infants cry or scream for attention they are likely to be left alone and not fussed over, unless a real reason for the crying is determined. (p. 87)

As a method of encouraging autonomy, self-confidence and appropriate levels of self-assertion at home, the style of childrearing adopted by these Aboriginal parents has the advantage of encouraging cooperative and nurturant interactions among siblings. But Aboriginal pupils in primary school may be at a disadvantage when teachers interpret their off-hand, though friendly, social overtures as negativistic and disrespectful. In fact, Malin found that Aboriginal pupils were reprimanded more often for misbehaviour than their Anglo-Australian classmates and praised less often for their prosocial and academic achievements. This highlights the importance of cultural sensitivity in the early years of school, a topic that is examined in more detail in Chapter 9.

Chapter summary

Even before they begin to speak meaningfully, toddlers develop cognitive capacities for symbolic representation. Representational thinking will eventually form the basis for language and social understanding. Early symbols can be expressed as actions, gestures or in make-believe play. At the same time, infants and toddlers make vocal noises and engage in pseudo-conversations that have the form of speech but are devoid of meaning. Between 12 and 18 months, the child typically makes what Vygotsky dubbed 'the great discovery in life' – the power of language to express representational meaning.

With the awareness of word meaning, new vistas for cognitive, personality and social development open before the child. Language growth and social interaction skills escalate rapidly. Vocabulary blossoms as the child masters names for people, actions and things.

Setbacks in vocabulary development may occur if adults persistently misconstrue the toddler's idiosyncratic use of single words to symbolise whole concepts. But most children move rapidly through the stage of using a word simply as a name for something into a holophrastic style of grammar, where single words are made to do the work of entire sentences. By the age of two, most toddlers can combine two words into a sentence. With the onset of telegraphic speech, the child gains further grammatical versatility, is able to ask questions, express negative feelings, and put nouns into the plural and verbs into the past tense.

Theories of syntactic development include the nativist approach, learning theories and a conversational view that emphasises the benefits for language development of exchanging discourse with a range of conversational partners. Parents assist language learning when they accommmodate their language input to the level of the young speaker. They use techniques like motherese, expansion, sympathetic listening, and the deliberate misunderstanding of toddlers' immature or lazy utterances in order to motivate acquisition of more fully grammatical forms.

Toddlerhood is also a phase of rapid development in personality and social interaction. Self-awareness develops as children converse with others and learn about the distinction between their own and others' perspectives. Opposition to the will of others emerges with the 'terrible twos'. Blind negativism is gradually overcome as the toddler learns to discuss, persuade and negotiate.

In their dealings with adults and their play with peers, young children use language to converse, to initiate activities and assert themselves, and to resolve disputes by means of negotiation. As a result of social interaction and conversation, they acquire social skills that will help them later in the serious business of living.

Culture exerts an important influence on parental expectations regarding negotiation, politeness and self-assertion. Cultural variations in childrearing strategies set the timetable for children learning to assert themselves. Culturally shaped expectations and parenting strategies can also have far-reaching influences later in life on children's early peer relations and behaviour in school.

For further interest

Looking forward on the Internet
Use the Internet to visit the following websites. Examine them for further information and varied perspectives on issues raised in this chapter. Also search for other relevant websites for yourself, using keywords like 'language development', 'early childhood' and 'parenting' in your search engine.

In particular, for a useful description and evaluation of a range of web materials on early language development, go to: **http://www.cfw.tufts.edu**.

For resources, ideas, activities and other items of interest in conjunction with this chapter, visit the Companion Website for this textbook at:
http://wps.pearsoned.com.au/peterson

Activity suggestion
As a practical activity in conjunction with themes of toddlerhood negativism and negotiation in this chapter, visit a toy store or supermarket and take note of children shopping with their parents. Record all the requests parent and child make to one another, as well as the partner's verbal and nonverbal responses. Does any evidence of negativism emerge? Is it more frequent in certain areas of the store (e.g. trolleys, sweets aisle, checkout)?

Multimedia
For interviews with Chomsky and Bruner along with a step-by-step journey through children's acquisition of language, schedule a viewing of this film: *Baby Talk* (Insight Media, 1985: 60 minutes).

Answer to 'nonsense' message on page 174: 'Life expectation has increased in recent decades.'

PRESCHOOLERS: Physical, neurocognitive, emotional, intellectual and social development

CHAPTER 7

I am not young enough to know everything.

J. M. Barrie (1860–1937)

Contents

CHAPTER OVERVIEW

In an angry letter to his teenage daughter, who had just been threatened with dismissal from boarding school, the novelist F. Scott Fitzgerald (1896–1940) wrote with exasperation:

> You have reached the age when one is of interest to an adult only insofar as one seems to have a future. The mind of a child is fascinating, for it looks on old things with new eyes – but at about age twelve this changes. The adolescent offers nothing, can do nothing, say nothing that the adult cannot do better. (1963, p. 33)

While some might disagree with Fitzgerald's disparaging attitude towards adolescent intellect, the utter fascination of the young child's outlook for thoughtful adults is undeniable.

In this chapter, after a brief look at the physical growth and motor skills of children aged from two to six years, we examine the neurocognitive basis for some of the exciting cognitive changes that make the preschooler's mind so fascinating. Then we chart these cognitive developments in more detail, exploring how preschoolers think about their physical and social worlds and their surprisingly creative, if somewhat illogical, explanations for dilemmas drawn all the way from human psychology and the wonders of nature to the mathematics of quantitative measurement.

Piaget's and Vygotsky's theories of early childhood cognition (see Chapter 2) are examined, and we briefly consider information-processing models and contemporary sociocognitive explanations for the dramatic cognitive developments that follow close on the heels of language development (see Chapter 6) and continue to the point where most children become immersed in formal classroom instruction at around age six.

In conjunction with language and social experiences, the influence of these cognitive changes on children's emotional life and understanding is explored, together with other important changes in social cognition and behaviour that arise during the preschool years as children become full participants in play and conversation with family members and peers.

Culture exerts an important influence on the cognitive development of preschoolers. We make a special study of recent research into Australian Aboriginal and Maori children's cognitive, emotional and social development, exploring how cultural variations in childrearing patterns and parental values and beliefs can shape children's memory, problem-solving, empathy, social cooperation and capacity to learn from peers in group settings.

The chapter concludes with a close look at one of the special provinces of preschoolers' psychological development: the wonderful world of make-believe that they enter through pretend play. We examine how this mode of play unfolds and its likely influences on psychological functioning during the preschool years and throughout the remainder of the lifespan.

Physical growth and motor skills during early childhood

Physical growth

At the end of infancy, the average 2-year-old is approximately half the height that he or she will eventually reach as a mature adult. While growth is now somewhat slower than it was during infancy, it nevertheless remains impressive throughout the preschool period. On average, the healthy child in Australia and New Zealand today gains 6 to 8 centimetres in height each year between the second and the sixth birthdays (see Figure 2.2) and gains about 3 kilograms in weight each year over the same period. The average rate of growth in height for girls and boys relative to earlier and later stages in development is shown in Figure 7.1.

Motor skills

At infancy's end (see Chapter 4) major qualitative gains in motor skills culminate in toddlers who, at age two, walk upright without assistance and display the hand dexterity and other fine motor movements that enable skills like those catalogued in Table 4.2 and Box 4.4. Yet gains continue to be made throughout the preschool period in strength, coordination and refinement of all the major motor skills. Some of these developments are listed in Table 7.1.

Gross motor and coordination skills enable children to take part in many different kinds of sport and recreational activities, alone and in the company of

At infancy's end, the average child has achieved roughly half of his or her adult stature.

Children become skilled at climbing, hopping, skipping and throwing during the preschool years.

peers. Participation in sports and games can teach valuable social lessons (turn-taking, cooperation, graceful acceptance of victory or defeat) as well as supplying healthy exercise and the practice that is needed to refine and perfect motor skills still further.

Safety is an important priority for preschoolers' motor activity and athletic exercise because their motor skills remain far from fully developed, and their cognitive capacities for planning and judging physical ventures are also underdeveloped. Careful monitoring and appropriate adult supervision is necessary to guard against accidental injury. While infrequent in absolute terms, deaths by accidental injury are the leading threat to longevity for contemporary Australian and New Zealand children during the preschool years.

The risk of accidental death and disability among children of preschool age highlights the need for parents, teachers and health professionals to take an active role in anticipating the danger zones in children's physical play. Several preventive health strategies may prove useful in reducing accidents. Optimisers of children's safe play need to have an accurate awareness of the major milestones of motor development over the period from three to six years of age. The dramatic gains in physical skill, strength and coordination that normally arise during this phase of bodily development open up new areas of risk, both inside and outside the home. One example is the typical preschooler's dexterity at shifting furniture and climbing up on it to reach previously inaccessible parts of the house. This new physical skill:

virtually ensures exposure to numerous home health hazards such as sharp instruments and toxins found in kitchen and bathroom cabinets and to outdoor hazards such as motor vehicles, broken glass and unfriendly animals. As the child advances in size, strength, and coordination, he or she begins to engage in increasingly more complex and hazardous recreational activities including the use of bicycles and skate-boards and participation in team sports that involve potentially deadly projectiles and potentially crippling bodily contact. (Maddux, Roberts, Sledden & Wright, 1986, p. 27)

Fine motor skills enable children to participate in many artistic, constructive and creative pursuits that can be undertaken alone or in company with peers. By perfecting fine motor skills for tying shoelaces, combing hair and doing up zips and buttons, children become increasingly independent of parental assistance for self-help and personal hygiene. Many families encourage preschoolers' participation in simple

New motor skills bring new risks of accidental injury during the preschool period.

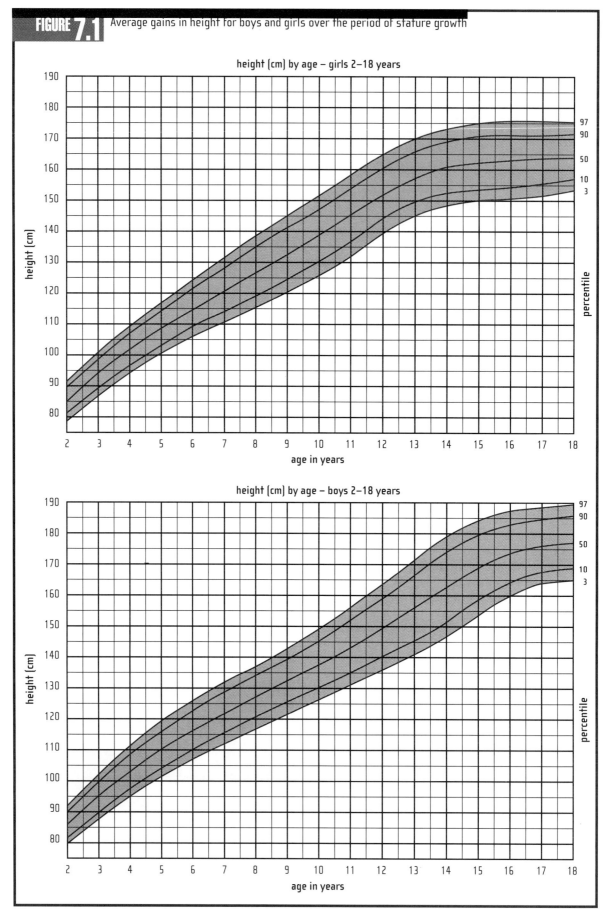

Source: Based on data in Tanner (1970).

TABLE 7.1	Summary of motor skill development from age three to age six		
Age	Gross motor and locomotor skills	Motor coordination skills	Fine motor and manual dexterity skills
3 years	• Runs easily but cannot stop or turn quickly • Climbs on furniture and playground equipment without help	• Kicks a ball forward • Pushes large toys around • Can jump a distance of just over 30 centimetres	• Can stack blocks, turn pages, pick up small objects
4 years	• Can stop, start and turn while running • Can hop on one foot for up to six steps	• Pedals and steers a bicycle • Can jump about 60 centimetres	• Can hold a pencil and draw with it • Cuts paper with scissors, though not always on the line
5 years	• Can descend a staircase without help, alternating feet • Can hop for 5 metres on one foot • Walks on tiptoe	• Can catch a ball • Swings on a playground swing without help	• Can copy a square or triangle with a pencil • Threads beads on a string, threads a needle

household chores, like setting the table or putting groceries away, as a way of exercising motor skills and coordination and also of teaching the child the value of cooperative participation in jobs that the whole family benefits from (Goodnow & Bowes, 1994).

Neurocognitive development during the preschool period

The patterns of brain growth, synapse formation and myelinisation that we examined during infancy (see Chapter 4) continue through early childhood. In addition, a process of lateralisation, in which areas on the left and right cerebral cortex of the brain acquire distinctive functions, becomes more pronounced in the preschool years, with implications for language development and handedness.

These general directions of early childhood neurocognitive growth are outlined in the biogenetic map of the human brain, but life experience also plays a critical role in the way the brain develops over the preschool years, just as it did in the prenatal period (see Chapter 3) and during infancy (see Chapter 4). Perhaps the most striking lesson of recent developmental neurocognitive research has been to point out the extent of the brain's *plasticity*, the ability to grow in new directions in response to individuating experiences during early childhood, as well as throughout life. Mark Rosenzweig, Marc Breedlove and Arnold Leiman (2002) explain:

> During the past few decades, however, psychologists and other neuroscientists have produced many concrete demonstrations that changes in behavior are due to brain changes. Indeed, it is now clear that constant change is one of the brain's defining features. Just as important is the now abundant evidence that the relationship between changes in the brain and changes in behavior is bi-directional: experience also can alter neural structure. (p. 643)

In this section of the chapter, we examine brain plasticity during early childhood, together with the important changes in myelinisation and lateralisation that make a contribution to the distinctively developing linguistic, cognitive, physical and socioemotional capacities of children aged two to six years.

Myelinisation

Myelinisation is, as noted in Chapter 4, the developmental process in which selected neurons become coated with a fatty insulating substance (*myelin*) that improves the conductive speed of nerve impulses. The brain's myelinisation follows a definite sequence. At birth, the sensory pathways responsible for vision, hearing, touch and smell are mostly fully myelinised. But other brain centres take longer. For example, the myelinisation of the *reticular formation* (or the region in the brainstem that governs alertness and arousal: see Figure 4.6) and of the frontal cortex (see Figure 7.2), while beginning to be evident in the preschool period, are not fully completed until after puberty (Tanner, 1990; see also Chapters 9 and 10). This may help to explain why preschoolers have only a limited attention span relative to older adolescents and adults. During the preschool period, as the reticular formation and associated regions of the frontal cortex of the brain become partially myelinised, alertness and conscious control of attention increase, relative to younger infants and toddlers (Case, 1992).

Neurons in the inner *hippocampus* region of the brain also gain myelin during the years from age three to age six, possibly helping to explain some of the improvements in deliberate memorisation ability that arise late in the preschool period (see later in this chapter).

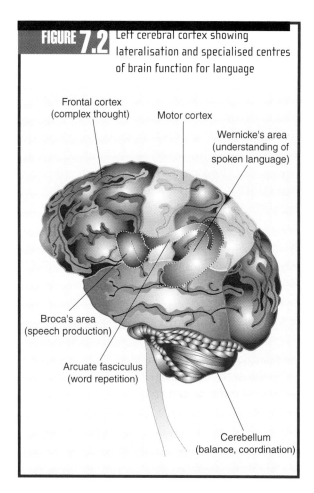

Frontal cortex
(complex thought)

Motor cortex

Wernicke's area
(understanding of
spoken language)

Broca's area
(speech production)

Arcuate fasciculus
(word repetition)

Cerebellum
(balance, coordination)

Lateralisation

The cerebral cortex, or the outer surface layer of the cerebral hemispheres of the brain (see Figure 7.2), gradually becomes specialised for certain cognitive functions, beginning in infancy. Clearly differentiated specialisation for handedness and language is generally evident by the preschool period, although the process continues into adolescence (Coren, Porac & Duncan, 1981). In other words, the specialised emphasis acquired with lateralisation means that some cognitive abilities (such as speech or music perception) are connected to one side of the brain rather than the other. Connecting the two hemispheres of the brain is a structure called the *corpus callosum*. This band of axons enables the two hemispheres of the cortex to communicate with one another.

Cortical dominance is connected with the phenomenon of handedness that we examined in Chapter 2. As noted there, most adult humans (over 80 per cent) display a preference for using their right hand for skilled tasks like writing, drawing or gesturing (Coren, Porac & Duncan, 1981). Although education may play a minor role in establishing hand preferences for writing, studies of early humans, chimpanzees and even toads have revealed the lateral dominance of limbs (Rosenzweig, Breedlove & Leiman, 2002), indicating that the tendency for right-hand dominance is probably built into the human genotype.

Lateralisation of the brain is involved in language and hand preference for motor skills.

Some of the cognitive functions that are presumed to be emphasised by either the left hemisphere or the right hemisphere are listed in Table 7.2. Between the ages of two and six years, the lateralisation of language processing and production becomes more

TABLE 7.2	Some of the cognitive functions believed to be lateralised in each hemisphere

Left hemisphere	Right hemisphere
Speech production	Music perception
Comprehension of speech	Artistic and musical production
Logical problem-solving	Form/shape perception
Analytic thinking	Synthetic thinking
Language	Spatial cognition
Processing of embedded and logically connected propositions	Intuitive thought

pronounced in the average child (Spreen, Risser & Edgell, 1995), which may have implications both for language acquisition (see Chapter 6) and for older preschoolers' increasing success on the many cognitive tasks that rely on language, as we see later in this chapter.

Recent studies of deaf children (see Chapter 6) suggest that experience interacts with the genotype in establishing lateralisation. For example, congenitally deaf children with limited exposure to language (owing to lack of access to sign language coupled with a severe auditory impairment that curtails their access to speech) are found, in adulthood, to display patterns of language-related brain activation that are importantly different from those of both hearing adults and natively signing deaf adults who acquired sign language in childhood (Neville et al., 1997).

On the other hand, deaf native signers (who acquired sign language at roughly the same age as hearing/speaking children acquire speech) show similar patterns of left-hemisphere dominance to those observed in spoken-language users – namely, pronounced left-hemisphere dominance of activation and heightened activity in the specific areas of the left hemisphere that are known to be involved in the comprehension and production of speech (Neville et al., 1997). In addition to activating these language centres in the left hemisphere, signing also activates areas in the right hemisphere that appear to have a role in the special spatial and/or motoric components of communication via hand, body and facial movement (Neville et al., 1998).

In one behavioural study of the development of lateralisation, preschoolers and adolescents were asked to perform four tasks: (1) kicking a ball, (2), picking up a crayon, (3) looking through a small hole, and (4) lifting a box to their ear to hear a sound. Only one-third of preschoolers, compared with a majority of adolescents, displayed lateralisation by consistently using the same side of their body for all

four tasks (Coren et al., 1981). Thus lateralisation continues to develop during middle childhood.

Plasticity

Throughout the lifespan the human brain retains a high degree of *plasticity* – the flexible ability to change in response to experience and to recover function after injury or cell loss. However, brain plasticity is especially apparent during infancy and early childhood. Infants and toddlers learn language very rapidly (see Chapter 6) and, if a brain injury occurs during infancy, recovery is generally faster and more complete than for the same injury in adult life (Rosenzweig et al., 2002). Once an initial language has been acquired, a second language can be learned at any age. However, in line with the *critical period* hypothesis (see Chapter 3) it is believed that, in order to acquire pronunciation and other subtle features of the new language with the same degree of fluency as a native speaker, the learning of the second language should begin during the preschool years, or by age seven at the latest (Rosenzweig et al., 2002). Interestingly, while the left hemisphere localises the language functions for the second (or third or later) language that a person acquires, the areas most heavily implicated are close to, but not the same as, the areas of the brain that are involved in processing the native language (Kim, Relkin, Lee & Hirsch, 1997).

Cognitive development: Preoperational thinking

As children become fluent in language, windows into their thought processes open up as they ask questions, discuss concepts and solve dilemmas put before them by developmental psychologists. One of the first people to exploit the rich possibilities for learning what children think by giving them open-ended probe questions in a 'clinical-style' interview format was the Swiss psychologist Piaget whose theory of cognitive development is outlined in Chapter 2.

Preoperational concepts of biology and physics

During the late 1920s, Piaget (1929/1973) recorded numerous instances of preschoolers' unique ideas about people, nature and the universe. Here is an example:

Adult: If you pricked this stone, would it feel it?
Child: No.
Adult: Why not?
Child: Because it is hard.
Adult: If you put it in the fire, would it feel it?
Child: Yes.
Adult: Why?
Child: Because it would get burnt.
Adult: Can it feel the cold or not?
Child: Yes.

'Can a boat feel it is in the water?'

BOX 7.1 | **A case in point**
Animistic thinking

Animism: Animistic thinking is illustrated in the following extract from Louise's father's diary, recorded when she had just turned seven.

14 April 1955. *More than any other child I know, Louise puts life into her dolls. To other children here and in Livonia dolls are simply toys. Often they have given their dolls no names before meeting Louise. They apparently get the idea from her. Louise's dolls are almost real people. She talks to them and tells of what they say and do, greets them in the morning, neglects them when they fall out of favor, and restores them to her good graces. Shortly before Christmas she took up with Sleepy again and had to have new clothes for her. Then a new doll that she named Mary claimed nearly all of her love and has held it since. Day before yesterday she was playing with Melissa and came home crying her heart out. Melissa had torn off Mary's arm. It wasn't 'my doll's arm'. Louise rarely breaks her own toys, yet she sheds no tears when other children break them as they frequently do. But Mary was a person and needed that arm. Peggy went back to Melissa's house with her, and Melissa's mother, by some magic I was unable to conjure when Sleepy lost her arm, got Mary's arm back on. Because Louise gives so much personality to her dolls, they have also come to have a personality to her mother and me. I felt almost as bad as she did when Mary lost her arm and I made no attempt to convince her that Mary was only a doll. I knew better.*

© Peterson. 1974, p. 235, reproduced with permission

Adult: Can a boat feel it is in the water?
Child: Yes.
Adult: Does the grass feel it when you pick it?
Child: Yes, because you pull it.

The preschooler that Piaget interviewed in this example was attributing human feelings to plants and inanimate objects. This common characteristic of children's thinking, known as *animism* (see Box 7.1), helps to illustrate how wide the gap is between preschoolers' and adults' understanding of the world. Even though both child and adult appear to speak the same language, the concepts to which their words refer are radically different. This can create frustration for both generations. But a discrepancy in viewpoint does not always indicate that the child is wrong.

Margaret Donaldson (1978) cited the case of a child whose first day at school was spoiled by disappointment. He had entered school eagerly and was even more excited when, some time during his first morning class, his teacher asked him to remain seated at his desk 'for the present'. On the basis of his experience with the language used by his family at home, this boy got his hopes up. He anticipated a gift. When none was forthcoming, he felt cheated by the teacher. But the teacher herself was sublimely unaware of her young pupil's disappointment. She had used the idiomatic expression 'for the present' to denote a span of time, without awareness of any other possible meaning. According to Donaldson, 'She failed to decentre and consider what her words would be likely to mean to a small child' (p. 18).

Communication gaps like these between children and adults involve more than just language. It is true that a child of three does not yet have the adult's breadth of vocabulary or a mature command of complex syntactic structures (see Chapter 6). However, according to Piaget (1970), misunderstandings like those in the above examples, between preschoolers and older people, are as much conceptual as they are linguistic. The diversity of outlook separating the child's world from that of the adult is consequently a central theme in Piaget's theory.

On the basis of interviews like the one above, he discovered three defining characteristics of children's beliefs about biological and physical concepts: animism, realism and artificialism (see Table 7.3). Box 7.2 illustrates Piaget's concept of realism.

Artificialism, the belief that nature is a product of human engineering, is illustrated in the following extract from one of Piaget's naturalistic observations in a primary school:

Renee, age seven, had a new baby sister. She looked up from the modelling clay she was playing with to ask the teacher: 'Mademoiselle, what part of my little sister did they make first? The head?'

'Did your Mummy tell you how babies were made?' the teacher cautiously inquired.

The child's understanding of physical and biological phenomena differs from the adult's.

Piaget's realism

Piaget (1973, p. 135) recorded drawings and an interview with an 8-year-old named Fav. They vividly portray the *realism* in preoperational children's thinking about dreaming.

While Fav slept, he believed he was in bed and running around at the same time.

Interviewer:	While you are dreaming, where is the dream?
Fav:	In front of your eyes.
Interviewer:	Where, quite near?
Fav:	No, in the room ...
Interviewer:	Were you really there?
Fav:	When I was in bed I was really there, and when I was in my dream I was with the devil, and I was really there as well.

TABLE **7.3**	Three core concepts of preoperational thought

Concept	Definition
Realism	Attributing tangible substance to intangibles
Animism	Attributing animal or human characteristics to objects
Artificialism	Viewing natural things as humanly engineered

'No, but I know,' replied Renee. 'Mummy still had some flesh left over from when I was born. To make my little sister, she modelled it with her fingers and kept it hidden for a long while.' (Piaget, 1973, p. 408)

In addition to using concepts of animism, realism and artificialism to explain nature, preschoolers' methods of arriving at explanations and logical deductions are importantly different from the reasoning methods of older thinkers. Adults generally reason either inductively or deductively. *Induction* occurs when a series of specific instances is seen to imply a general rule – 'All the people born more than 200 years ago have died; therefore, human beings cannot live for as long as 200 years'. *Deduction* is

when a specific proposition is inferred from a general fact or principle – 'Human beings are all mortal; therefore, Mr Smith will die eventually'.

Preoperational thinkers, by contrast, are inclined to reason transductively. *Transductive reasoning* is also seen in the child's explanations of natural phenomena – for example, a log floats because it is big, whereas a leaf floats because it is small, or because it is green. Here, the search for an explanation is limited to pinpointing some salient detail in the situation, rather than attempting to find a more encompassing rule that cannot easily be contradicted. Being bereft of the organising framework of concrete operations, the young child is likewise less sensitive to contradictions than the older thinker. Thus there is no inherent contradiction between both large and small size causing buoyancy in the transductive thinker's mind.

William Tunmer, Andrew Nesdale and Chris Pratt (1983) tested the reasoning skills of 96 Western Australian children, aged five to seven years, by reading them stories like the following:

Does this make sense? When bikes have broken wheels, you can't ride them. One morning a car ran over Johnny's bike and broke the wheel. Johnny then picked up his bike and rode it to a friend's house. (p. 101)

A preoperational thinker may believe that ice cream is alive because it crawls over your fingers.

To a child whose reasoning is transductive, a stick floats because it is little, whereas a log floats because it is big.

By age seven, most children were adept at detecting the logical inconsistencies in such stories. Their deductive style of reasoning led them through a series of inescapable logical steps which, when put together, made the final clause of the story impossible. Their train of thought went as follows: 'Whenever P is true,

Q is true. P is true. Therefore, Q must be true.' (The bike is broken and therefore could not be ridden.) This is the way an adult would approach the same problem. But the 5-year-olds, whose reasoning was transductive, did not do at all well on the task. They tended either to accept the stories in full as perfectly clear and sensible or to query the empirical truth of one individual sentence. The latter strategy gave rise to such comments as 'I rode my bike when the wheels were broken' or 'Cars don't break wheels when they run over bikes'. Neither memory failure nor inexperience with items like a bicycle could explain the 5-year-old's poor performance. Instead, it seemed that their transductive reasoning style had obviated the discomfort with the violation of deductive logic that so disturbed the older group.

The problem of conservation

One of the hallmarks of preoperational thinking in Piaget's theory (1970; see also Chapter 2) is the failure to understand *quantity conservation*, or the notion that amount remains constant over a number of perceptual transformations of physical appearance. For example, a 5-year-old girl is shown two buttons positioned at opposite ends of a table. After placing a cardboard barrier between the buttons, her teacher asks: 'Are the buttons as near one another now as they were?' 'They're nearer,' the girl replies. The adult cuts a small hole in the cardboard and asks the same question again. 'They're further now,' says the child. Then the teacher replaces the cardboard with a thick book. Now the child replies, 'They're much nearer!' 'Why?' 'Because it's thicker'.

Conservation of distance

The child in the above example is a preoperational thinker. She has not yet grasped the concept described as the conservation of distance. In other words, she does not realise that the distance between the two objects is a function only of the location of the objects themselves. To her, the distance between the two buttons is reduced when something comes between them, and the amount of reduction depends on the size of the intervening object. To an adult, the buttons themselves would have to be moved before the distance separating them would increase or decrease. In Piaget's terms, the adult conserves distance while the 5-year-old does not (Piaget, Inhelder & Szeminska, 1960).

Conservation of number

'Want to earn some money?' says a father to his son. 'Here are six 50-cent coins. Can you count them?' The boy counts and agrees there are six. 'Now,' says the father, 'here are some more coins.' The boy counts the second bunch and states there are six again. Then the father spreads the first group of coins out into a long row and leaves the second set clumped together (see Figure 7.3). 'Take your pick,'

FIGURE **7.3** Conservation tests developed by Piaget

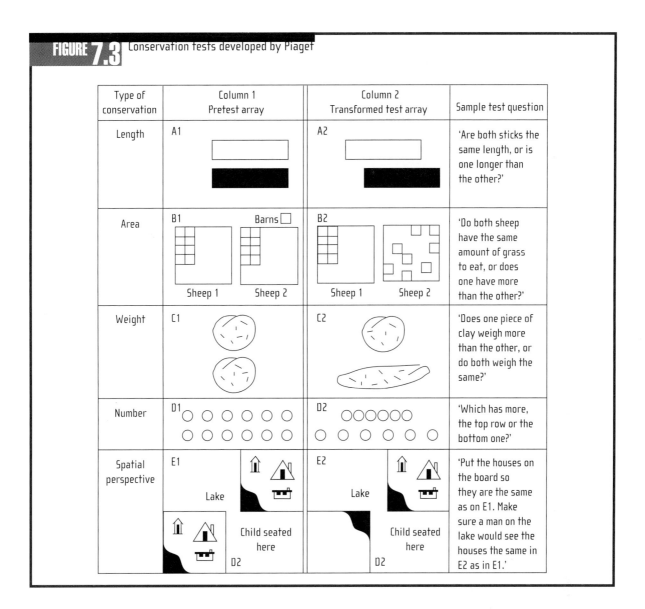

Type of conservation	Column 1 Pretest array	Column 2 Transformed test array	Sample test question
Length	A1	A2	'Are both sticks the same length, or is one longer than the other?'
Area	B1 Barns □ Sheep 1 Sheep 2	B2 Sheep 1 Sheep 2	'Do both sheep have the same amount of grass to eat, or does one have more than the other?'
Weight	C1	C2	'Does one piece of clay weigh more than the other, or do both weigh the same?'
Number	D1	D2	'Which has more, the top row or the bottom one?'
Spatial perspective	E1 Lake Child seated here D2	E2 Lake Child seated here D2	'Put the houses on the board so they are the same as on E1. Make sure a man on the lake would see the houses the same in E2 as in E1.'

he says. 'You can have these or these.' The boy reaches eagerly for the long row. 'Just a minute,' interrupts his father. 'Why did you choose those?' 'Because there are more dollars here.' 'More here than here? Why don't you count them to be sure?' The boy counts each group again and comes up with a total of six again in each collection. 'So there are six here and six here?' questions the father. 'I'd still rather have these,' says the boy, and pockets the long row of six, convinced he has worked a bargain. To this boy, who lacks conservation of number, a widely spread array clearly contains more coins than an array in which the coins are bunched together, even though their number was initially the same, and even though no coins were added or subtracted while the money was being moved around.

Conservation of substance

When the tokens used in a number conservation experiment happen to be coins, or pieces of fruit or chocolate, a child's decisions about quantity are likely to take on more than sheer academic interest. In fact,

a dinner table stocked with a child's favourite foods can provide a rich testing ground for quantity conservation. Thus, in a test for conservation of substance, a little boy might be shown two chocolate cupcakes, both exactly the same size. An adult says, 'This is mine, that's yours – do we both have the same amount to eat, or does one of us have more cake than the other?' 'We have the same,' the boy says. Then the adult slices the cake nearest him into six pieces and repeats his question. 'I have more now,' the boy answers. 'Why?' 'Because mine's round and yours is all cut up.' Again, this child's understanding differs from an adult's. To the adult, a cake may be less attractive when it is cut into small pieces but cannot be said to contain any less food. The only way to alter its quantity is to eat or drop some of it, or add another piece. Piaget found that young children thought quantity could fluctuate along with simple changes in shape or appearance. If a ball of clay or pie dough was flattened into a pancake, a preschooler might believe that the amount of substance in it had substantially increased.

INSTRUCTIONS

1. Tell these jokes to children of your acquaintance aged four, five, six and seven years. Note their reactions and comments (McGhee, 1979).

   Mr Larsen went into a restaurant and ordered a whole pizza for dinner. When the waiter asked him if he wanted it cut into four or eight pieces, he said: 'Oh, you'd better make it four! I'm hungry enough for four, but I'd get too full if I tried to eat eight pieces!'

   One day George and Betty found an old raft. They decided to take their picnic lunch and eat it on the raft. When they got to the middle of the lake, George took out his flask of lemonade and drank it all at once. The raft started to sink. 'That'll teach me,' said George. 'Drinking all that lemonade made me too heavy for the raft!'

2. Try giving one or more of the conservation-of-quantity tests shown in Figure 7.3 to children aged five, six or seven. Then tell them the 'pizza joke'. Is their laugh at the joke predictable because they passed the test(s) of conservation? According to Piaget, it should be. For further insight into the links between humour and cognition in childhood, consult McGhee (1979).

The conservation of quantity in situations like these accounts for the typical 7-year-old's disproportionate enjoyment of jokes like those in Box 7.3 (McGhee, 1979). Preschool children do not find them very funny because, as non-conservers, they believe that quantity actually does change when a whole item is cut up into pieces. Adults, on the other hand, are apt to be so well aware of conservation that the joke seems merely absurd or simple-minded. But to a child who has only recently acquired conservation, the humour is irresistible.

Conservation of fluid

Similarly to conservation of substance, tests for conservation of liquid amounts tap children's notions about liquid quantity before and after a transformation. To conduct such a test at the dinner table, pour the child's favourite soft drink into two identical glasses. Make sure it reaches the same height in both glasses, seeking the child's assistance if necessary. After the child has agreed that both glasses contain the same amount, pour the contents of one glass into a taller but narrower vessel. Most preschoolers watching this demonstration will reach eagerly for the taller glass, believing that it now contains substantially more drink than the shorter glass. A few may opt for the short, squat container if they happen to focus on width. But a lack of conservation is evidenced by the belief that quantity has changed even though no liquid was added or taken away. Figure 7.3 illustrates some of Piaget's conservation tests. (In each case, the correct answer is that the transformation has not affected quantity or, in the case of conservation

This child is being tested for conservation. To the non-conserver, quantity may change with any alteration of the superficial appearance of the array, such as pouring it into a taller container.

of spatial position, the relative placement of the houses in relation to one another and the lake.)

When Piaget analysed the growth of quantitative thinking with age, he discovered that some types of conservation (like length and number) seemed easier, and were mastered earlier, than other types (like weight or spatial relations). For each type of conservation, he noted a series of three stages – an initial period where conservation was completely absent and quantity was judged simply by appearances; a stage of on-and-off conservation in which children seemed to waver between perception and conservation (e.g. they might conserve number when the objects in one row were flowers and in the other, vases; but not conserve it when both rows contained identical items like buttons or coins); and a final stage of complete conservation in which children expressed a belief in conservation and backed up their judgments with appropriate explanations such as 'You didn't add any so they must be the same' or 'You can tell they are the same if you pour back the lemonade' (or '... press the row of buttons together' or '... roll the clay back into a ball'). During this last stage, children were frequently surprised, or even scornful, that the examiner could think quantity could vary or ask such 'obvious' questions.

Piaget proposed that conservation develops with the child's transition out of the preoperational stage into the next stage in his system, that of *concrete operational thinking* (see Chapter 2). Preoperational children judge things according to how they look. Quantity is estimated from appearances, like the shape of a container or spatial position, even after the skills of measuring and counting have been mastered. Children with concrete operations, on the other hand, rely on their logical understanding of how things must be. The preoperational child cannot conceptually transform a situation or mentally

The sharing of tasty foods at a birthday party may tax preschoolers' understanding of quantity conservation.

reverse it in the way a concrete thinker can. Preschoolers do not come up with the idea of moving the row of coins back into a cluster. Nor can they mentally equate the height of the tall, thin container of juice with the greater width of the short, squat container. In short, preoperational children have not yet managed to organise their thoughts about objects into the logical systems that Piaget dubbed *concrete operations* (see Table 7.4).

Numerical and mathematical concepts

Though conservation is undoubtedly the most thoroughly studied of all the unique attributes of

TABLE 7.4	The concrete operations	
Operation	**Definition**	**Example**
Closure	Logical and mathematical operations are mentally grouped according to the principle that any two operations can be combined to produce a third operation that will also be part of the logical group.	Selecting all the *boys* then selecting all the *girls* is equivalent to selecting all the *children*.
Associativity	The order in which operations are combined does not affect the outcome.	'All the girls and boys' is the same as 'All the boys and girls'.
Reversibility	Any operation in the system has a corresponding, opposing operation that cancels or undoes its influence.	Pouring the same amount of liquid from a tall, thin glass back into the short, squat one it started out in cancels the transformation that led to the apparent increase in amount.
Identity	In any grouping of operations, there is a null operation that changes nothing.	$2 + 0 = 2$; or, selecting the boys plus no one else is the same as just selecting the boys.

preschoolers' thinking pinpointed by Piaget, several of his other discoveries are also likely to have practical interest to parents, educators and health professionals who work with this age group. As a basis for mathematical learning in school, concepts of *classification* and *seriation* develop together with number conservation during the period from age four to age seven. These concepts, together with the development of *numeracy*, are examined next.

Classification

The acquisition of concrete operations provides the basis for an understanding of logic and mathematics, according to Piaget (1970). *Classification* refers to the ability to group sets of discrete items into a logical category. Hierarchical classifications could, for example, teach a child that her pet dog Blue belongs to the broader class of dogs, and dogs are a subclass of animals.

The broader hierarchy, heading or principle gives organisational structure to the discrete items falling within it. Most preschoolers can classify successfully when all the items are similar and when the organising rule is concrete and unidimensional. Thus they know that parents, children and grandparents can be grouped together as members of the 'family' and that dogs, horses and kangaroos all belong to the category of 'animals'. But a preschooler who has not yet developed the concrete operation known as *class inclusion* cannot deal with more than one level of hierarchical classification at the same time. Thus, when asked whether a bouquet containing twelve roses and six daisies has more roses or more flowers, the preoperational thinker typically falls into the trap of replying 'more roses', even though the child is prepared to assert that roses and daisies are both a type of flower when asked about them separately. Without the benefit of operations integrating thoughts about roses and daisies as components of the hierarchical 'flower' class, the young child cannot keep both the inclusive class and its separate components in mind at the same time.

Similarly, when asked 'Are there more people in Perth, or more people in Western Australia?', preoperational children may argue that Perth has more. Without the concrete operation of closure (see Table 7.4) they cannot conceive of all the people in the state as the sum of those in the capital city plus all those in rural areas.

A study by Ellen Markman and J. Siebert (1979) suggested that the preoperational thinker's confusion over class inclusion might stem from familiarity with subtle stylistic patterns of adult language use. They noted that adult speakers tend to use words like 'flowers', 'trees' and 'musicians' when all the items in a class are either identical or very similar to all the other items. Conversely, a collection made up of horn, string and percussion players is more likely to be labelled 'a band' than simply 'musicians'. The stand of trees shown in Table 7.5 is more likely to be described as 'a forest' than as 'trees'.

To test whether the type of noun used to refer to the collection could influence children's class inclusion performance, Markman and Siebert presented 6- and 7-year-olds with a series of modified class inclusion questions in which the collection was always labelled with a noun connoting diversity of membership within the class. (Some examples are shown in Table 7.5.) The resulting improvement in children's class inclusion scores was dramatic. Compared with a success rate of only 40 per cent using the standard questions, 70 per cent of their subjects succeeded when asked the modified questions shown in Table 7.5.

Robert Grieve and Alison Garton (1981) also challenged Piaget's interpretation of class inclusion on the grounds that the way he worded his questions is apt to mislead even those children with an adequate understanding of the logical operations involved. They found that 4-year-olds did well on symmetrical questions where the contrasting classes were evenly balanced, as in sentences like: 'Are there more horses or more cows?' or 'Are there more white horses or more black horses?' But their performance

TABLE 7.5		Preschoolers' typical responses to standard and modified class inclusion questions			
Standard question	Typical reply	Stimulus picture		Modified question	Typical reply
'Are there more pines or more trees?'	'More pines.'			'Who would have more trees, someone who owned the pines or someone who owned the forest?'	'The forest.'
'Are there more dogs or more baby dogs?'	'More baby dogs.'			'Who would have more pets, someone who owned the baby dogs or someone who owned the family?'	'The family.'

on asymmetrical questions where items came from different positions in a class hierarchy (e.g. 'Are there more boys or more children?') was uniformly poor. Thus Australian preschoolers did equally badly on questions of the form: 'Are there more horses or more black cows?' as on standard Piagetian questions of the type: 'Are there more horses or more black horses?'

Since questions of the former variety can be answered correctly without any knowledge of the rules of class inclusion, Grieve and Garton challenged Piaget's explanation and proposed instead that simple confusion about language provides a more concise explanation for his findings than preoperational thought. However, this theory was challenged, in its turn, by Graeme Halford (1985) whose sample of Brisbane preschoolers had difficulty even with class inclusion questions phrased in a familiar symmetrical format. As we discovered when analysing conservation research, it seems that awkward testing procedures can add further dimensions of difficulty to Piagetian tasks. However, some prerequisite level of logical development is also evidently necessary for children's success even when questioning formats are simplified.

Seriation

When preschoolers are asked to order objects like sticks, dolls or jam-jar lids from smallest to largest, they often have trouble. In fact, Piaget found that most 4-year-olds were unable to construct an evenly graduated, ordered series. They could not even insert a single missing item (e.g. a 7-centimetre stick) into a series that had already been constructed (between the 6-centimetre and the 8-centimetre sticks in an ordered row). Piaget decided that this was because they could not simultaneously compare one particular stick with the shorter and longer sticks in the series. To do so would require the recognition that stick 'n' is longer than stick 'n – 1' while shorter than stick 'n + 1'. The preoperational child seems unable to view a stick as both long and short, depending on which of the other sticks it is being compared with (Piaget, 1952a).

Once acquired, the logic of seriation enables the concrete-operational thinker to deal with the mathematical concepts of measurement and numerical relationships that are essential for comprehending addition and subtraction. *Seriation*, or the capacity to order quantifiable objects and events on a continuum, also enables the child to arrange remembered experiences according to their position in time, and to solve the problem of transitive inference. This entails deducing from such information as 'A is taller than B' and 'B is taller than C' that C must be shorter than A. Thus the child with concrete operations uses transitive inference to deduce relationships among quantifiable items without needing to measure or directly compare them.

Transitive inference

According to Graeme Halford (1993), cognitive development consists of both qualitative and quantitative increases in the mind's capacity to process information. This theory predicts that a particular type of concept cannot be acquired until the requisite level of mental and relational complexity has been reached. According to Halford, children at Level 0 have no symbolic representations. Cognition consists purely of the facets of Piagetian sensorimotor intelligence that were examined in Chapter 4. But at Level 1 the child gains the capacity to represent binary relations symbolically. Thus the child knows that the harder you push an object, the faster it will move. The concept of one object being larger than another is understood. But, because there is a strict limit on the amount of information the child can integrate into a single decision or representation, differences in size among a series of items of varying length cannot be processed all at once. Consequently, the child at Level 1 cannot cope with the task of arranging three or more objects in order from shortest to longest. Thus Level 1 children fail Piaget's test of seriation requiring the arrangement of sets of objects by quantity.

Such failures are predicted by Halford's (1993) model of Level 1 processing. But at Level 2, Halford argues, the child masters the notion of compositions of binary relations. Thus 'Doll A is taller than Doll B' can be combined with 'Doll B is taller than Doll C' to yield an accurate ordering of all three dolls by relative height. Solutions to transitive inference problems therefore become possible at this stage. Finally, at Level 3, compositions of binary operations can be represented symbolically. We return to this notion when we examine Piaget's theory of formal operations in Chapter 11.

Numeracy

Piaget suggested that a mature understanding of number depends on concrete operations for classification (e.g. recognition that three chairs, three books and three shoes all belong to the class of 'threes'), for seriation ('two' is more than 'one' but less than 'three') and also for number conservation ('two' shoes cannot become 'three' through mere displacement).

Although these achievements do not normally occur until after school entry, many children learn to count before they go to school, particularly today with exposure to programs like *Sesame Street* on television. Rochel Gelman (1979) found that even some children as young as two and a half understand the following basic principles of counting:

1. There must be one-to-one correspondence between the number names and the things being counted (i.e. each thing must be tagged with only one distinctive label).

Children learn the importance of counting, measuring and the arithmetic of money outside of school, as well as in the classroom.

2. Number names must be listed in a stable order.
3. The list of numbers must always be run through in the same order.
4. Any set of items may be collected together for a count.
5. The last label used designates the number of items in the collection.
6. The order in which objects are tagged does not matter, provided the other principles are adhered to.

The following example of a 5-year-old's use of the 'finger-abacus' illustrates how knowledge of the names and sequencing of numbers up to ten was coupled with one-to-one correspondence to assist in developing the concept of simple addition.

> In the car this morning, Louise counted on her fingers up to ten, then announced, 'Five and five are ten'. She had figured it out for herself. She followed with, 'One and one are two, two and two are four'. 'How much is three and three?' I asked. 'Just a minute and I'll tell.' She counted on her fingers. 'Six!' (Peterson, 1974, p. 189)

Piaget's theory: Mechanisms of developmental change

Piaget proposed that preoperational thought eventually gives way, as children develop, to a new stage of concrete-operational thought. The developmental mechanism in his theory (see Chapter 2) is an internal cognitive process that he termed *equilibration*. Equilibration draws upon the tools of *assimilation* and *accommodation*, which were considered in Chapter 4 in the context of the infant's development of sensorimotor intelligence.

Equilibration

The process of equilibration, for Piaget, consists of a dialectical struggle between the mechanisms of assimilation and accommodation. By assimilating new information, the child takes in ideas uncritically from the outside world. Accommodation involves modifying existing conceptual schemes to suit the new information. Through equilibration, the two processes are brought together into a higher-order, balancing structure. For example, in a standard conservation test, the preoperational thinker is quite content to 'assimilate' the apparent results of a conservation transformation (see Figure 7.3) into a rigid preoperational concept of quantity. For instance, a sausage of clay and a tall glass of juice are assimilated into the notion that longer means bigger. The cut-up cake, the spread-out row of coins and the barns scattered throughout the paddock are likewise assimilated into the simple notion that 'the more separate pieces there are, the greater the amount'.

The factor needed to trigger accommodation and, consequently, equilibration, is the child's own inescapable recognition that this oversimplified assimilation strategy is illogical or inconsistent with reality. When children are allowed to play freely with the materials (clay, coloured water, coins and so on) used in conservation experiments, this sometimes happens spontaneously. For example, after rolling clay sausages into balls and back into sausages many times, a child might suddenly notice 'reversibility'. Rural Mexican potters' children, who have ample opportunities to play with clay in these ways, acquire the conservation of substance earlier than other children in the same community who have no access to clay (Price-Williams, Gordon & Ramirez, 1969). Presumably their play provides experiences like reversing balls of clay into sausages and vice versa that challenge their preoperational beliefs.

Cognitive conflict

In addition, Piaget proposed that children's thought processes can be thrown into disequilibrium by having arguments with peers. Once the brain has matured to the point where transition to a higher level of thinking is in order, the experience of engaging in a debate with a slightly older, or more cognitively advanced peer can challenge preoperational beliefs. The cognitive activity that this then stimulates can provoke genuinely progressive developmental change through a dialectical process (see Chapter 2). By assimilating and accommodating cognitively the peer's more advanced arguments (e.g. when the peer appeals to reversibility when discussing a conservation problem), the less mature

By discussing or disputing with an older child, the preoperational thinker is forced to accommodate his thinking to the mature reasoning offered.

child can be helped to achieve a higher level of understanding. As Piaget explained:

> It may well be through quarrelling that children first come to feel the need for making themselves understood. (1955, p. 83)

Responding to Piaget:
Contemporary extensions and alternatives

Piaget's conservation tasks and other cognitive problems have generated a wealth of research in Australia (Halford, 1982; Keats, Keats & Liu, 1982; Seagrim & Lendon, 1980) and in New Zealand (Mackie, 1980), as well as in the UK (Donaldson, 1978) and in Piaget's native Switzerland (Perret-Clermont, 1980). In general, the results of these studies have provided impressive confirmation of Piaget's initial discovery that conservation is non-existent among toddlers, rare among preschoolers, but almost universal in children over the age of six or seven. The root cause for the preoperational child's eventual decision to abandon one seemingly adequate mode of logic in favour of another is still not completely understood, but the results of several recent research studies have made important contributions to narrowing the gap in our understanding. Some of these newer ideas are outlined below.

Social influences on cognitive development: Peer discussion and conflict

As noted above, Piaget (1970) proposed that debates with other thinkers could disrupt the cognitive equilibrium of preoperational thought and stimulate cognitive progress. When children are forced to defend their beliefs during a conversation with someone else who sees things differently, flaws in their logic may become self-evident, provoking further thought to resolve the contradiction.

Although he made one early study (Piaget, 1955) of children's spontaneous quarrels with their siblings and peers, Piaget himself did not directly test the possibility of cognitive gains arising via such arguments. But, in 1975, Gilbert Botvin and Frank Murray conducted a pioneering study in which the effects of peer disagreement on non-conserving children's subsequent conservation performance were systematically investigated. Botvin and Murray brought children into the lab and organised them in groups of five, asking them to agree on solutions to conservation problems. The composition of each group was pre-arranged to include two non-conservers and three conservers who had consistently given conserving judgments and concrete-operational reasons during a series of individual pretests. After listening to their conserving peers' arguments during the discussion sessions, a substantial number of initially non-conserving children became conservers. That this was more than simple mimicking or 'parroting' of the conservers' views was shown when the discussion participants generalised to new problems and gave reasons which, while valid, were different from any used by the conservers during the argument sessions.

The value of peer debate as a stimulus to the growth of conservation was demonstrated even more forcefully by Anne Nellie Perret-Clermont (1980) when she put two non-conserving children together to discuss conservation problems to which neither child knew the correct answer. Figure 7.4 illustrates

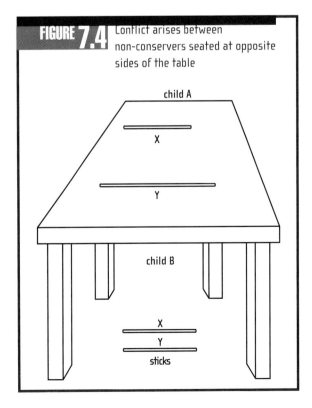

FIGURE **7.4** Conflict arises between non-conservers seated at opposite sides of the table

Throughout infancy and childhood, peer interaction and observation of peers are important instructional experiences.

one of the situations she used. In this arrangement, both non-conservers are likely to agree that the stick extending further to the right is longer than the other one. (Actually, they are identical in length.) But when seated face-to-face, child A thinks X is longer while child B thinks that Y is. Perret-Clermont (1980) found that experiences like these led to subsequent gains in conservation when the children were tested individually. Presumably the experience of being contradicted by a peer generated doubts, or 'cognitive conflicts', in each child's mind. Resolution of these contradictions through a covert dialectical synthesis of assimilation with accommodation could then account for the sudden emergence of concrete-operational reasoning skills in non-conservers who had never been exposed to a conserver's correct viewpoint.

Culture, peer debate and cognitive development

The child's ability to profit from social experiences of this kind may be influenced by the attitudes prevailing in the child's home and in the wider cultural environment. Parents, grandparents and the wider society all have beliefs about how good or bad it is for a child to disagree openly with a peer or an adult. They also hold views about whether it is better to settle a dispute with a peer by discussion or fighting, and whether the best solution to a conflict with a parent or teacher is egalitarian negotiation or deferential conformity to the views of the authority figure. Research supports this diversity of parental outlooks.

To take one example, Jacqueline Goodnow and her colleagues (Goodnow, Cashmore, Cotton & Knight, 1984) discovered that Japanese mothers were much less tolerant of debates and disagreements among playmates than mothers from similar socio-

economic backgrounds in the United States. Whereas most American mothers expected that from an early age their child would be able to (a) 'state his/her own preferences or opinions when asked', (b) 'stand up for his/her own rights with others' and (c) 'get his/her own way by persuading friends', the Japanese mothers accorded these same qualities a very low priority and hoped that they would develop either late in childhood or not at all.

A comparison between groups of Australian mothers who were born in Sydney or in Lebanon reflected similar cross-cultural variations in attitudes towards children's assertiveness (Goodnow et al., 1984). As noted in Chapter 6, Anglo-Australian women resembled mothers in the United States when it came to setting an early timetable for the child's development of the verbal skills needed to persuade and negotiate with others. But the Lebanese-Australian mothers were like the Japanese in favouring unquestioning obedience in their children and discouraging open disagreements with peers.

In New Zealand, Diane Mackie (1980) designed an intervention study with the aim of boosting the attainment of conservation by Maori children. Her results also supported the view that cultural attitudes play an important part in shaping children's willingness to recognise the inherent contradictions in their preoperational views of the world. Mackie's subjects were 18 non-conserving children from Pakeha (Anglo) families plus a corresponding group of 18 non-conserving Maori children. The task was the spatial conservation problem illustrated at the bottom of Figure 7.3. Two different kinds of interventions were attempted with both groups. The first involved intra-individual conflict. Here the child's board was made of clear plastic so that when he or she had finished placing the houses on it, the whole tray was turned around and superimposed over the experimenter's model, making explicit the inadequacies of a non-conserver's placements. The other intervention involved a peer debate procedure (see page 219). Here, conflict was created between two children's viewpoints by making them sit on opposite sides of the table. A child who adopted an egocentric approach could not agree in this situation with another egocentric thinker who viewed the board from a different perspective. Their task was to discuss the problem together and find a mutually acceptable solution. Mackie's results are illustrated in Figure 7.5.

Whereas gains were made by the Pakeha group in response to both types of intervention, the Maori children profited from the peer debate procedure but showed no clear gains after the individual demonstration with the plastic tray. Mackie concluded that the peer-oriented structure of Polynesian society, with its emphasis on negotiating satisfactory solutions to community problems through cooperative discussion, could plausibly explain the differential effectiveness of peer debate as a boost to conservation in Maori children.

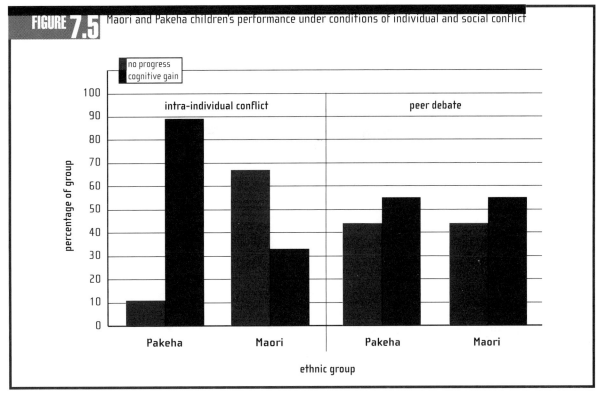

no progress
cognitive gain

intra-individual conflict | peer debate

percentage of group

ethnic group

Pakeha   Maori   Pakeha   Maori

Source: Based on data in Mackie (1980).

She argued that if teachers in New Zealand wished to capitalise on these findings, they might boost the cognitive attainments of Maori pupils by using peer teaching, team debates or other classroom techniques that required children to interact with each other while solving cognitive problems. Similar methods might also prove effective for teaching academic and social skills in Australian classrooms where children from many different cultural backgrounds come together to learn. Adrian Ashman and John Elkins (1990) argue that peer collaboration can be especially beneficial to children with physical or intellectual handicaps, who may find it easier to comprehend the perspective of a peer than to deal with the conceptual gap between child and adult understanding.

Peer collaboration is an effective stimulus to cognitive development.

Learning to interpret conserving transformations

Graeme Halford (1982) argued that the development of conservation results from children's mastery of a system of rules allowing them to categorise transformations as either relevant or irrelevant to quantity. To become a genuine conserver, a child must be secure in the knowledge that, short of accidental spillage, there is no *possible* way of ever changing the quantity of a liquid simply by pouring it into any of the conglomeration of containers found on supermarket shelves. This is a broader rule than Piaget's 'reversibility', as exemplified by a child being able to imagine pouring the doubtful amount back into a comparison container. According to Halford, true conservers define all the transformations – pouring, shaping or spatial rearrangement – that are used to test conservation as 'quantity-irrelevant' procedures. Even though each of these manipulations can have a drastic effect on the appearance of the items in the array, the child who knows this rule is aware that no transformation, apart from addition or subtraction, can possibly alter quantity in the slightest. Halford proposed that the acquisition of a system of rules like these is the primary factor responsible for the child's eventual development of a full-blown unshakeable understanding of conservation. As he explained:

> Interpretation of conserving transformations reflects an important new acquisition, the ability to interpret an ambiguous stimulus in a way that is consistent with an overall system ... a conserving

transformation is ambiguous because there are no cues in the immediate situation indicating that quantity has remained the same. Those cues that do exist are usually misleading. We still conserve, however, because we know that to regard quantity as changing when it is simply poured or re-arranged is inconsistent with our conception of quantity; that is, we adults conserve because to do otherwise would run counter to a whole network or system of beliefs that such a conception of quantity must exist before conservation can occur. Thus, precisely because the conservation situation is ambiguous, the participant is thrown back on interpreting the transformation, and this can only be done correctly by referring it to the systematic concept of quantity of which it is a part. (Halford & Boyle, 1985, pp. 174–5)

To test this explanation for conservation's development, Graeme Halford and Frances Boyle (1985) presented a group of 138 Brisbane preschoolers and primary school children with arrays of counters similar to those illustrated in Figure 7.6. Rows of 20 counters like these clearly exceed the counting capacity of most 4-year-olds as well as many 7-year-olds. But it was Halford and Boyle's deliberate aim to prevent the child from counting the items after the transformation. Instead they wanted to know whether children would think the original number of items had changed or remained the same after the simple move to new positions. So, after showing children the first two rows of Figure 7.6 and asking them to point to 'the row with more beads', they changed the array into the patterns shown in rows 3 and 4 of Figure 7.6 and repeated the question. Conservation was indicated not by the child's initial choice of row, but rather by the decision to point to the *same* row after the move. Such perseverance testified to the child's underlying knowledge that rearrangement does not alter quantity, so that the row that first had the most continued to have the most after the beads were moved around. Children who changed their minds were seen to lack a firm grasp of this basic rule.

Using this procedure, Halford and Boyle concluded that few Australian 3- and 4-year-olds understood the transformational basis of conservation. However, by age six most Queensland children firmly resisted the suggestion that number could be changed by simply moving beads to new positions. Halford and Boyle felt that their results provided 'some vindication of Piaget's viewpoint, because they indicate some kind of conceptual shift in quantitative understanding' (p. 174) at around age six.

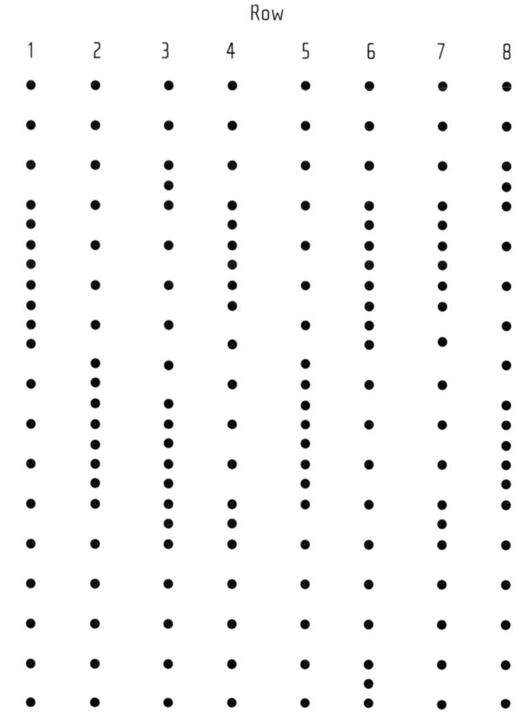

Lessons from bilingual children

Research studies of bilingual children growing up in Australia and Asia have also helped to shed light on how children make the transition from preoperational to concrete-operational thought. One study involved a group of primary school children who had

FIGURE 7.6 Uncountable arrays testing number conservation: Can you tell which array has more without counting?

Row

1 2 3 4 5 6 7 8

been born in Greece, lived there until the age of four or five and then migrated to Sydney where they had been living for at least two years at the time of the testing. After establishing that the children understood the words 'more', 'longer', 'same amount' and 'same length' in both Greek and English, standard tests for conservation of length and substance were carried out in both languages. These bilingual children were found to reason at a significantly more advanced level when tested in Greek, their native language, than when the identical conservation questions were posed in English, the language of their schooling. In fact, 35 per cent of the children who scored as non-conservers in English were able to conserve consistently when the same interviewer questioned them in Greek. Of these, 29 per cent reverted from conservation to non-conservation when the questions were asked again in English (Keats & Keats, 1978).

Daphne and John Keats conducted several studies in which non-conserving bilingual Australian and Asian children were given extensive training in only one of their two languages or dialects (Keats & Keats, 1978; Keats, Keats & Liu, 1982). In addition to providing practical insights to aid the teaching of bilingual pupils in primary schools, another purpose of these studies was to test Piaget's theory that concrete-operational thought processes are independent of language. If this is so, bilingual children who learn to conserve in one language should immediately become conservers in their other language. On the other hand, if conservation skills are language-specific, training given in one language (say English) should have no impact at all on the children's thinking in their native dialect (Chinese, Polish, German or Malay).

The results of the Keats' lengthy program of research were generally consistent with Piaget's theory. It was found that, when Polish, German and Malay children who had initially scored as non-conservers when tested both in English and in their native language were successfully taught to conserve weight by means of an exclusively English-language training procedure, they immediately achieved conservation in Polish, German or Malay as well. However, the results for the 5- and 6-year-olds who were bilingual in Chinese and English showed that the language used to teach conservation did make a difference. These children displayed greater gains in conservation skill in both languages after being trained in Chinese than when they had been exposed to an identical training program using English, their less fluent language.

A further study was then conducted in the People's Republic of China to test whether this effect would generalise to other Chinese-language bilinguals (Keats, Keats & Liu, 1982). Two groups of bilingual Chinese 5- and 6-year-olds were tested and trained for weight conservation in their native dialect and also in Mandarin Chinese, the official language of their schooling. The results for Shanghai children who spoke the Shanghai dialect at home and Mandarin at school were the same as for the Chinese–English bilinguals. Training in their native Shanghai dialect produced higher conservation scores on subsequent tests in both dialects than did training in the children's less fluent second language, Mandarin Chinese. But the differences, though significant, were not large. The authors therefore concluded that:

When adults talk to young children, they sometimes fail to take account of what their words mean to an inexperienced conversationalist.

Although examples of possible interaction between language and thinking were observed, they were few in number, of very minor significance and of brief duration. It is concluded that language and thinking are essentially independent in children of five to six years of age. (p. 134)

On the other hand, the combined results of all the Keats' conservation training studies did reveal an interesting and important relation between cognitive development and bilingual preschoolers' progress in learning their second language. For all the Australian migrant groups, except Germans, the breadth of a child's vocabulary in the new language, English, was a better predictor of concrete-operational thinking than breadth of vocabulary in the native language.

This suggests that the learning of English may enhance cognitive development in bilingual children. In the case of German immigrant children, however, delays in beginning to learn English predicted high scores on conservation tests given in both English and German. There is a plausible explanation for this seemingly contradictory result. German-Australian parents are found to favour early and exclusive exposure to English more strongly than other migrant groups (Taft, 1985). Thus there may be an optimum age for learning a second language. When English is introduced too early in a bilingual household, parent–child communication may be impaired, with consequent delays in children's acquisition of concrete-operational reasoning.

Finally, the Keats' studies showed that, out of 21 bilingual groups, all but one earned higher mean conservation scores when given delayed post-tests in their native language than when the same tests were administered in their newly acquired 'school' language (English or Mandarin). There are implications of these findings for education. Teachers in bilingual classrooms must be careful not to underestimate the cognitive capacities of children whose skills with the English language may not have reached the same standard as their underlying cognitive capabilities.

Conversational biases in experimental testing

Based on his extensive investigations of the cognitive development of preschool children in Brisbane, Australia, Michael Siegal (1997) came to the conclusion that conversational factors in the standard Piaget testing situations, like the conservation experiment, may limit young children's capacity to express their genuine understanding of abstract concepts. He says:

Children are both sophisticated and limited users of the rules of conversation that promote effective communication: sophisticated when it comes to the use of conversational rules in everyday, natural talk; limited in specialised settings that require knowledge of the purpose intended by speakers who have set aside the rules that characterise the conventional use of language. Such situations may often involve children in experiments where they inadvertently perceive adults' well-meaning questions as redundant, insincere, irrelevant, uninformative or ambiguous. (pp. 1–2)

In other words, according to Siegal, Piagetian measures like conservation or classification may pose incongruous or unfamiliar dilemmas to children, using unwieldy language and a style of experimental conversation they have never previously encountered. Thus, young children may be biased against revealing their genuine levels of cognitive understanding by any, or all, of the problems listed below (Siegal, 1991).

1. *Vacillation.* Children who are not absolutely certain of their initial answers may change their minds if subtle conversational cues suggest that is what they are supposed to do. The experimenter's repetition of the same question supplies such a cue. Thus, in a standard conservation test (see Figure 7.3), a child may misinterpret the experimenter's repetition of the query: 'Are they the same length/size/amount?' after the transformation as a subtle hint that the child's initial answer was wrong and should be changed.
2. *Insincerity.* Children may be quite certain of the correct answer but may give a different answer if they suspect the experimenter wants to hear it. Their motives for this can be various, ranging from misplaced cooperativeness to mischievous noncompliance or a desire to terminate the testing session as quickly as possible. Thus one girl might pretend to agree with an experimenter's suggestion that a transgressor could catch a cold from being naughty because she mistrusts the researcher's motives for asking about misbehaviour. A boy might find it so distressing to think about illness and accidents that he would prefer to escape back to the classroom. So he likewise claims to agree with a suggestion he privately considers preposterous.
3. *Trust in the experimenter.* Young children are inclined to trust adults and want to please them. A preschooler might claim she would be willing to drink from a glass of milk that had previously contained a cockroach, not from any real misunderstanding of the origins of contamination but simply out of a misplaced desire to be polite. Her blind faith in adults might lead her to believe that an experimenter would never ask her to drink something unsafe.
4. *Fascination with the task.* If an experimental task is unduly attractive to children, they may say or do whatever seems necessary in order to prolong it. They may vacillate in their conservation judgments, not because they are genuinely uncertain whether two quantities are the same or not, but rather because they are enjoying pouring out the liquid or squeezing the plasticine so much that they do not want to be forced to abandon those activities and go on to something that might be boring.
5. *Being 'cute'.* Children might judge some of the questions experimenters ask them when measuring preoperational thought to be naive, preposterous or silly. But, instead of saying so forthrightly, they may give the response they believe an adult would expect from a child. The goal may be simple politeness or they may wish to convey an impression of being cute, desirably innocent or childlike. Thus children with no real concept that objects are animate might claim that a stone would feel a pinprick because, like expressing a belief in Santa Claus or the tooth fairy, they imagine that is what an adult would expect a child to say.
7. *Confusion over language.* If adult experimenters use words that children are unsure of, or apt to define in a slightly different way (see the discussion of the meaning of telling lies in Chapter 8), or if the experimenter's questions are unduly wordy, intricately detailed or long-winded, the child may become confused. But, as noted in Chapter 6, a young child's response to a breakdown in conversational meaning may not be to challenge the speaker. Instead of asking for clarification, the child may simply respond at random or echo the final words in the adult's incomprehensible question.

Vygotsky's sociocultural approach

Lev S. Vygotsky's theory of cognitive development (see Chapter 2) resembles Piaget's in its emphasis on the child as an active learner and on the preschool period as a crucial stage in development. This is a time when social forces combine with the neuro-cognitive developments examined earlier in this

Through guided participation with an older skilled performer, children learn to do things with help that they will eventually do independently.

chapter to make the child especially receptive to developmental opportunities. However, Vygotsky's sociocultural theory places heavier emphasis than Piaget's on variations in cognitive skills in different cultural environments, the value of social interaction for promoting cognitive growth and cross-cultural variation in developmental patterns. These themes are echoed in many of the recent extensions and alternatives to Piaget's stage of preoperational thought that we have just been considering.

According to Vygotsky (1978), children learn by participating socially in cooperative activities and conversations, especially with peers and adults who are more expert than they are. He proposed a *zone of proximal development (ZPD)* in which the child can perform cognitive tasks through guided participation with a skilled collaborator that they are incapable of performing on their own. Cognitive development, for Vygotsky, can be compared to an 'apprenticeship in thinking' (Rogoff, 1990) in which the culture's intellectual traditions are passed on to the preschool apprentice by guided instruction and involvement in activities that the socially supportive teacher deems important and worthwhile. Eventually, the child apprentice is able to internalise the lessons learned through social cooperation and becomes capable of independent problem-solving.

Memory development

One afternoon in Neuchatel, Switzerland, a nanny was pushing a baby in a carriage through the park. The baby was wide awake and looked around brightly at the trees, buildings and the signpost on the edge of the park that marked the tram stop. Suddenly a big, ill-shaven character charged up to the carriage, forced the nurse aside and made as if to abduct the baby. The nurse fought the vagrant off bravely and, in the process, received two long scratches across her cheeks from his unkempt fingernails. Just then a policeman in a short cape hurried over and chased the intending kidnapper away.

The baby in the pram was Jean Piaget, and for many years Piaget believed this incident to be one of his earliest memories of a true event. Even though the adults around him had often talked about the attempted kidnapping in his hearing when he was older, he remembered details of the visual scene that only he and the nurse could have known – what the man looked like, for instance, and the position of the carriage in relation to the tram sign. Such details could not have been conveyed to him by the nanny, for she had left the Piaget household shortly after the scene in the park.

Imagine Piaget's disillusionment, then, when his parents received a letter from his former nurse confessing that there had been no kidnapping, no kidnapper and no policeman. She had concocted the whole story herself and had scratched her own face to lend authenticity. Now, as a convert to the Salvation Army, she wanted to confess her misdeed and return the gold watch that she had been awarded for her bravery.

This incident gives grounds for some scepticism concerning the factual validity of anyone's very early memories. How can we be sure that the mental image we are left with is really a picture of the events as they happened, and not a reconstruction which the mind has unconsciously fabricated around some later verbal rendition of it? This question is of special relevance today in light of the many legal cases that have come to court in recent years involving adults' memories of abusive experiences and other traumatic events from early childhood. Kevin McConkey's (1995a) thoughtful discussion of how Australian forensic and clinical psychologists might approach these issues is summarised in Box 7.4.

BOX 7.4 Applying psychology: Memories in court

In recent years, the question of how accurately people can remember traumatic events from their childhood, such as sexual, emotional, physical or verbal abuse, has come to prominence in the media (McConkey, 1995a). A number of high-profile legal cases have drawn public attention to the possibility that an adult, with or without a therapist's help, might be able to recall incidents of abuse that occurred during infancy or early childhood. For example, in the United States, a woman won over $1 million in a lawsuit against the primary school she had attended. She claimed to have uncovered a memory that had lain repressed in her mind for more than two decades – one of her teachers had repeatedly raped her.

Questions about the psychology of childhood memories are brought into practical focus by cases like this. Is it possible for a memory that has been repressed for decades to surface either spontaneously or with the aid of therapy or

As with Piaget's imaginary kidnapping, a child's memory for events in the distant past may be shaped by more recent experiences such as an adult's recounting of a shared event.

hypnosis? How accurate are such distant, repressed memories likely to be? Is it possible to distinguish genuine memories of real events from inadvertent, unconscious fabrications like Jean Piaget's 'memory' of his near escape from kidnapping?

At present, research evidence is not strong enough to provide an unequivocal basis for either accepting or dismissing legal allegations of abuse that are supported primarily by adults' recall of repressed childhood memories. Kevin McConkey urges that further research into memory processes be conducted in the hope of providing conclusive answers. At present, he says, we know more about what we do not yet know than might be hoped for by the media, the legal profession, or clients and family members who are involved in allegations of early abuse. According to McConkey:

> 'Memories' that are reported either spontaneously or following the use of special procedures in therapy may be accurate, inaccurate, fabricated, or a mixture of these. The presence or absence of detail in a memory report does not necessarily mean that it is accurate or inaccurate. The level of belief in memory or the emotion associated with the memory does not necessarily relate directly to the accuracy of the memory. The available scientific and clinical evidence does not allow accurate, inaccurate, and fabricated memories to be distinguished in the absence of independent corroboration. (1995a, p. 20)

Nevertheless, psychologists are frequently called on to offer opinions about cases involving an apparently repressed childhood memory. Recognising this, McConkey made a number of suggestions for how to deal with these issues in a clinically, ethically and legally responsible manner:

1. In dealing with a client who reports recovering a memory of abuse, the therapist should take pains to explain the current state of knowledge in childhood memory research and explore with the client the possibility that the memory 'may be an accurate memory of an actual event, may be an altered or distorted memory of an actual event, or may be a false memory of an event that did not happen' (1995a, p. 21).

2. Given that 'memories' of traumatic events may be stressful and damaging to mental health, irrespective of their truth or falsity, therapists should treat their clients with empathy and understanding, recognising that the needs and well-being of the client should be the primary focus of therapeutic intervention.

3. Given that the accuracy of repressed childhood memories cannot be established without corroboration, psychologists should proceed cautiously when questions of litigation arise and should explore with the client the possibility of objectively testing the accuracy of the memory (McConkey, 1995a).

On the other hand, Piaget's story also helps to explain how a child's memory operates. It would seem that remembering the events of the distant past involves the active reconstruction of a total situation from a few isolated fragments or traces, so that memory itself is dynamic, creative and constantly changing. Piaget confirmed this suggestion experimentally when he and Barbel Inhelder (1968) gave memory tasks to a large group of schoolchildren. In one task, 6- and 7-year-olds were shown a partially full bottle of wine held at an angle over a table top as shown in Figure 7.7. The children were asked to draw what they saw, while the tilted bottle was still in full view. They correctly traced the level of the wine parallel with the table surface. One hour later, with no bottle to refer to, they were still able to draw what they had seen correctly. But when tested again about one week later, many children made the error of drawing the level of the wine parallel to the base of the bottle. Their originally accurate memory image had become distorted over time to correspond with what they believed happened to liquid when a bottle was tilted.

This result is perhaps not too startling. It is well known, after all, that memory deteriorates over time, though the deterioration is typically conceptualised as a fading away rather than a gross distortion. But there was a more surprising result from another memory task in the same series. This time, Piaget and Inhelder gave children a seriation test (see page 217), showing them a graduated series of sticks, each slightly taller than the stick on its left. Here, recall was not as accurate after one week as it was six months later, even though the sticks had not been presented during the interim; memory of this array had actually *improved* over a long period of time. Presumably, many of the children who had been preoperational when the display was first shown had come to understand the concept of seriation during the intervening six months, and had used this new knowledge to correct their previously disordered memories of the set of sticks.

Because the suggestion that a memory could actually become more accurate over time seems implausible, Piaget and Inhelder's procedure has been repeated many times by independent investigators. These researchers have consistently agreed that

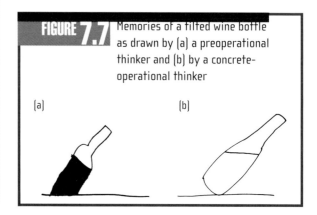

FIGURE 7.7 Memories of a tilted wine bottle as drawn by (a) a preoperational thinker and (b) by a concrete-operational thinker

(a)   (b)

improvements do occur when the memories of children who initially lack a concrete-operational understanding of seriated sticks or tilted liquids are reassessed later on, once concrete operations have developed (Furth, Ross & Youniss, 1974). It seems that the transition from preoperational to concrete-operational reasoning promotes the logical reorganisation of memory traces that were initially set down without the benefit of concrete operations. On the other hand, preschoolers sometimes astound adults with the vivid detail of their visual or auditory memories, whereas the recollections of older children or adults who use abstract logic or broad conceptual categories to organise memory may lack sensory detail. Some of these unique characteristics of early childhood memory are illustrated in Box 7.5.

Strategic memorisation by preschoolers

Cognitive growth contributes to memory by enabling children to master and utilise deliberate memorisation strategies. Four special strategies are particularly useful when it comes to memorising lists of difficult or meaningless material (e.g. telephone numbers or words for a spelling test):

1. *Organisation*, or mentally rearranging listed items into sensible clusters like 'fruit', 'furniture' or 'multiples-of-seven'.
2. *Labelling*, or giving names to non-verbal items like locations or pictures (e.g. 'the tall one', 'the mountain with the cross').
3. *Rehearsal*, or repeating the material to be recalled during the interval preceding the test.
4. *Elaboration*, or constructing mental pictures, rhymes or other easily remembered slogans to serve as mnemonic aids (e.g. the jingle 'Thirty days hath September', or the 'memory walk' whereby each item in a list is visualised in successive key locations along a familiar walk, such as from home to the office).

The fact that young children do not spontaneously employ strategies like these to assist their remember-

---

BOX 7.5 A case in point
Effortless memory at 20 months and at age four

Two instances of his daughter's seemingly effortless incidental memory for detail that greatly impressed Louise's father were recorded in his diary. The first took place when Louise was 20 months old.

9 January 1950. *Christmas was indeed a special occasion, taking me all the way back to the days when I was young – though not quite as young as she – and Christmas was the one big day of the year. Louise enjoyed opening her presents and playing with her new toys, especially a doll that she readily agreed to call Peggy. She got two bears from outside the family and these were also named with our help, one Frank, the other Bruno. But to a little dog pull-toy she herself gave the name of Dasher and she also by herself named a reindeer: Cranberry. A hammer and peg toy claimed her attention for a minute or so; unfortunately it was badly put together, so Peggy packed it away, meaning to exchange it. Louise raised no objection, for there were many other things to distract her. Peggy forgot to exchange the toy, forgot indeed the toy itself until suddenly, several days later, Louise began crying for her hammer. What hammer? Nobody dreamed it could be the toy she had played with so briefly. She was shown a couple of other hammers that she used to play with, but Louise stoutly insisted on having a special one. Then a couple of days after that, while Louise was outdoors, I remembered the forgotten and still unexchanged toy and managed to repair it. Louise came in. Nothing was said by any of us. She played with it a while, then spoke up: 'Dot found it.' (pp. 85–86)*

Christmas is a memorable part of childhood.

Two and a half years later, her father was still impressed with Louise's memory.

20 September 1952. *She has returned to nursery school; goes mornings Wednesday and Thursday. One of the rooms has a piano and some other furniture in it. The children were asked, after their summer's absence, if they noticed anything different about it. Only Louise did: the wallpaper. I have often observed this talent for observation she has: how she will describe down to the last detail the appearance and apparel of some person at the time of her last encounter. But it, like others, has gone unrecorded.*

© Peterson, 1974, p. 172, reproduced with permission

---

ing helps to explain their poor performance on strategic memory tasks. But why do they not use them? Is it because they are unfamiliar with the techniques, or because the effort of using them seems too great, or because they do not see the need for strategies in the first place?

All these factors are probably relevant. Until the child enters school, there is little need to memorise information deliberately and the child is probably not taught how to use mnemonic devices. However, knowing a strategy does not guarantee its use, as John Hagen (1971) discovered when he trained a group of retarded children aged eight to 12 to rehearse. Their memories improved almost to the level of an adult's when they practised rehearsal. But once the experiment was finished they abandoned the technique. Perhaps they were not motivated enough. According to John Flavell (1971): 'When you deliberately memorize, you are intentionally doing something now that will only pay off later, at recall time. Memorizing is like storing nuts for the winter: it has a planful quality about it that ordinary perceiving and remembering do not have' (p. 272).

Deliberate, voluntary memory

Even at recall time, the child's payoff in school may not be great enough to seem to justify the effort of rehearsal. In fact, Soviet researchers have distinguished between memory as a goal in itself and memory as part of a motivated, meaningful activity (Zaporozhets & Elkonin, 1971). In their experiment, children were subjected to identical memory demands in three different situations:

1. in the laboratory (the child was simply instructed to remember, no reason being given)
2. in a game with peers (memory was required for the child to be successful in a playful activity such as a treasure hunt)
3. in a practical task on behalf of an adult (memory was necessary for the child to fulfil an important assignment given to him by the teacher, such as delivering a message to the principal).

Children performed better in the play task than in the laboratory, but their memories showed up best of all in the practical activity. It appeared that the added motivation of being trusted by an adult to do something useful accounted for the gain.

Graeme Halford, Murray Maybery and Dianne Bennet (1985) developed a task that allowed for the separate assessment of (a) developmental gains in memory resulting from use of strategies, and (b) gains resulting from the growth of the span of memory itself. Their 38 Brisbane subjects ranged from six to 13 years of age. Over this age period, considerable gains in overall memorisation ability were noted, consistent with earlier findings. Some theorists had previously attributed these gains purely to the implementation of strategies. But when Halford, Maybery and Bennet teased span and strategies apart, their findings indicated that a simple extension of memory span with age also contributes importantly to improvements in memorisation ability during the primary school years.

On the other hand, while less efficient than older children when it comes to deliberate memorisation using strategies, preschoolers often display quite remarkable memory for incidental detail, as Box 7.5 illustrates. The difference seems to be one of control. The adult who has the option of using memorisation strategies can also decide when not to use them. To the young child, on the other hand, memory is more of a spontaneous, effortless occurrence. So the preschooler who makes no particular effort to remember anything sometimes ends up remembering more than an older child, despite the latter's more adept command of specialised techniques for registering and retaining difficult-to-remember items in memory. (See Chapters 9 and 16 for further discussions of memory in older individuals.)

Metamemory

Another reason why young children do not always spontaneously employ mnemonic strategies is that they are blissfully naive concerning the limitations of their own memory and the process of memory itself. An accurate understanding of memory and its limitations is known as *metamemory*. When asked: 'If you wanted to phone your friend and someone told you the phone number, would it make any difference if you called right away after you heard the number or if you got a drink of water first?', approximately half of one group of 5-year-olds thought it would be quite all right to have a drink first (Kreutzer, Leonard & Flavell, 1975). The overwhelming majority of older children in grades one to five were sufficiently aware of memory's fallibility to know that if they wanted to succeed they should phone immediately. Another question was the following:

One day two friends went to a birthday party and they met eight children that they didn't know before. I'll tell you the names of the children they met: Bill, Fred, Jane, Sally, Anthony, Jim, Lois, and Cindy. After the party one friend went home and the other went to practise a play that he was going to be in. At the play practice he met seven other children he didn't know before, and their names were Sally, Anita, David, Maria, Jim, Dan, and Fred. At dinner that night both children's parents asked them the names of the children they met at the birthday party that day. Which friend do you think remembered the most, the one who went home after the party, or the one who went to practise the play where he met some more children? Why? (p. 40)

By age nine, many children seemed implicitly to be aware of the phenomenon called *retroactive interference*. This occurs when newly memorised material limits recall of items mastered previously. In the above example, the child who went to the play would be more confused about the names from the party. Kindergarten children did not seem to appreciate this. Furthermore, these young children were the only ones who asserted categorically that they never forgot anything. Nonetheless, the metamemory of this youngest group was better than might have been expected. The researchers found that, like the older children, 5-year-olds were aware that it was easier to learn items they had once known but forgotten than totally new information, and that a lot of items are harder to remember than a few. Henry Wellman (1977) added to this list of preschoolers' metamemorial competencies by finding that most 5-year-olds understood that noise distracts memory, that adults remember better than babies, that prompting by someone else can assist recall and that a longer time to study the items is also an aid to memory.

Emotional development during early childhood

Over the period from age three to age six children acquire increasing control over their feelings, with associated gains in the ability to self-regulate negative emotions like fear and sadness (see Chapter 4) and in the capacity to curb impatience, in order to wait quietly while paying attention (Eisenberg et al., 2000). These emotional regulation skills are important assets to the young child in preschool and primary school who needs to inhibit outbursts of tears or angry tantrums, while being able to sit patiently and attend in class.

Emotional understanding develops along with emotional control during the preschool period. Children learn to identify emotions from facial expressions, to identify likely causes for emotional reactions and to show empathy by comforting playmates who display signs of distress. The neurocognitive developments discussed earlier in this chapter may play a role in these new developments of the preschool period, and it is clear that language acquisition makes a major contribution, together with social interaction. When family members converse about feelings, children gain insight into their own emotions and those of others. Judith Dunn (1996)

BOX 7.6 Culture and cognitive performance: The amazing memory skills of Aboriginal children

L. S. Vygotsky's (1978) sociocognitive theory (see page 224 and Chapter 2) suggests that those cognitive skills that adults in a culture value highly will be transmitted to children during collaborative activity as the adult instructs and 'scaffolds' the child's mental activity and challenges them within the ZPD (see page 225). In tradi-

tional desert life, memory was a crucial safety skill for Aboriginal Australian children who might wander away from the family camp to play, hunt and explore. Thus, spatial memory skills might be expected to develop especially swiftly in traditionally reared Aboriginal children, according to Vygotsky's theory.

In an experimental test of this possibility, Judith Kearins (1981) examined the memorisation capacities of Aboriginal children who still lived in traditional communities in the remote desert regions of Western Australia. In one of her experiments, children were shown a box with 20 compartments with a different manufactured object in each (button, thimble, compass and so on). In another task, the 20 items in the box were natural (twig, leaf, seashell and so on). The children had 30 seconds to view the full array of 20 items. Then the box was upturned, the items were shuffled, and it was the children's task to replace each one in the position it had initially occupied. The results are shown in the graph.

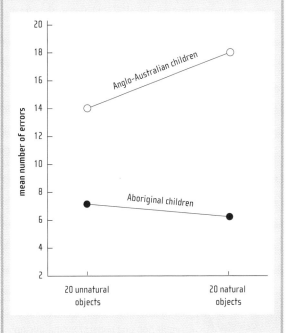

Aboriginal children made significantly fewer memory errors than a control group of urban Anglo-Australian children of the same age with both the natural and the manufactured arrays.

Kearins suggested that the Aboriginal children's superior performance might be due in part to their strategy of sitting very still and concentrating on the array while it was in position. The white children's moving lips gave evidence of their efforts to employ a verbal labelling strategy which was clearly less effective for this type of task. It is likely that the Aboriginal child's expert attention strategy develops as part of the traditional desert child's socialisation practices, since Betty Drinkwater (1976) found that Aboriginal children growing up in urban and suburban communities in Queensland displayed no special expertise for spatial memory.

While sharing snacks with one another preschoolers learn about other people's idiosyncratic likes and dislikes.

found that 3-year-olds who came from families where feelings and their causes were freely and frequently discussed displayed a better understanding of their friends' emotional states three years later when they were starting primary school. They were also better at resolving disputes with peers because of a more astute awareness of the causes and consequences of positive and negative emotions. Table 7.6 shows a summary of some of the milestones of emotional development during early childhood.

Understanding emotion and desire

Preschoolers develop an awareness of the links between emotion and desire from as early as age three (Wellman, 1993), enabling them to predict that a person whose desires are gratified will feel positive feelings, whereas if desires are frustrated they will feel negative emotions like anger, sadness or disappointment. Figure 7.8 shows some of the stimuli and experimental situations that have been used to assess this understanding (Peterson & Slaughter, in press). For example, a protagonist in a cartoon story might

TABLE 7.6	Developments in emotional self-regulation and understanding during the preschool period
Age	**New developments**
2 to 3 years	Sympathy is displayed towards others in distress; discussions of emotions and their causes become more frequent; emotions based on evaluations of own behaviour (shame, guilt, pride) appear.
3 to 6 years	Child understands the likely causes and consequences of many basic emotions; child can self-regulate emotions reasonably well and is aware of some basic emotional display rules, leading to the masking of inappropriate emotions in social situations.

be pictured reaching for a glass of juice, imagining it (see Figure 7.8) or looking at it with an expression of eagerness. Children as young as three can generally state that the character wants the juice under these conditions. In a more challenging task, as shown in Figure 7.8, a boy who wanted juice is pictured drinking milk. When asked how this boy feels, many 3-year-olds and most older preschoolers say he is unhappy because his initial desire was frustrated. Similarly, they are able to ascribe negative emotions to characters who are given disliked foods or who accidentally fall in the water. Even though the preschoolers taking these tests might have different desires themselves (liking bananas, for example, or enjoying going swimming), they are generally able to accurately predict that the characters in the cartoons will experience negative emotions when their (admittedly idiosyncratic) desires are frustrated in these ways (Peterson & Slaughter, under review).

Self-esteem

Another important development of the preschool period is in the domain of *self-esteem*, or the evaluative component of a child's concept of himself or herself. Building on the *self-awareness* that was cultivated towards the end of infancy (see Chapter 6), most preschoolers have a notion of themselves which they can describe in words. For example, by age three most preschoolers know their own names, can recognise themselves in photographs and mirrors and can accurately answer the basic gender identity question (see Chapter 8) 'Are you a boy or a girl?' (Slaby & Frey, 1975). However, when asked to describe themselves, preschoolers typically focus on superficial, outward features such as their physical appearance, their first name or some of their prize material possessions. This is in contrast to the more meaningfully idiosyncratic, psychological or personality qualities like shyness, tomboyishness or laziness mentioned by school-age children in response to the same question (Harter, 1980). The following self-portrait by a 50-month-old boy is typical of the preschool age group:

I have a bike.
I go to kindy.
I'm four years old.
My name is Charles.
My hair is black.
I like to suck my thumb when I watch television.

In order to examine the evaluative component of the self-concept, Susan Harter and Robin Pike (1984) developed a pictorial self-esteem test using dimensions of self-worth that were framed in terms of contrasts like those shown in Table 7.7. They tested a group of 90 four-year-olds in the United States on this measure by showing the children pictures of children who were high and low in the specified trait (e.g. 'good at doing puzzles') and asking them to rate their own competence by choosing one of four alter-

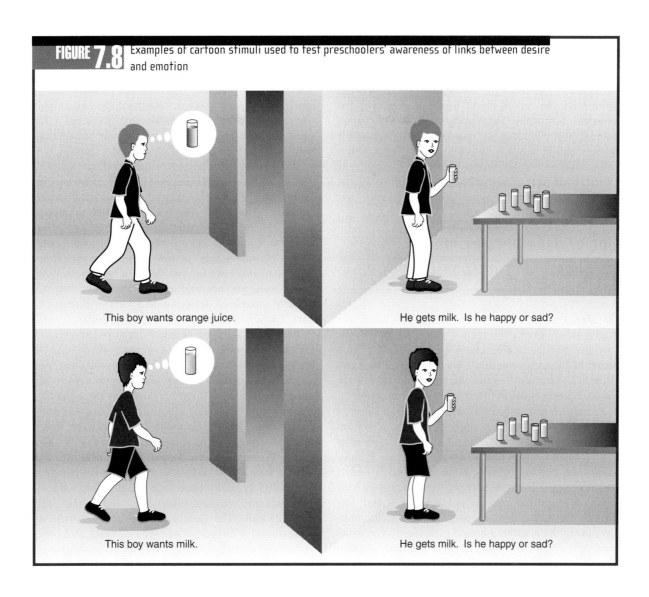

FIGURE 7.8 Examples of cartoon stimuli used to test preschoolers' awareness of links between desire and emotion

This boy wants orange juice.

He gets milk. Is he happy or sad?

This boy wants milk.

He gets milk. Is he happy or sad?

Physical skills play an important part in boosting the self-esteem of preschoolers.

TABLE 7.7 Dimensions of self-esteem in preschoolers

| | Area of competence | |
	Cognition	Physical and motor skill
High self-esteem	Is good at doing puzzles Knows colour names Knows the alphabet Is good at counting	Is good at climbing Can tie shoelaces Runs fast Is good at swinging on the swing set
Low self-esteem	Not good at doing puzzles Doesn't know names of colours Doesn't know the alphabet Can't count	Not good at climbing Can't tie own shoelaces Can't run very fast Is not good at swinging

Chapter 7 Preschoolers: Physical, neurocognitive, emotional, intellectual and social development 231

natives: 'not very true of me', 'only sort of true of me', 'pretty true of me', 'really true of me'. The children's preschool teachers then rated each pupil on the same scales. When pupils' and teachers' ratings were compared, the match in the areas of cognitive and physical competence was almost perfect. In other words, even children as young as four accurately understood how adept they were at the various academic and motor skills appropriate for their age. In other words, accurate evaluative dimensions of the cognitive and physical self-concept seemed to have developed by the age of four.

Social development in early childhood: Social cognition and social play

As cognition develops during early childhood, the topics of children's thoughts are not limited to the notions about nature, quantity and number that many of Piaget's seminal studies examined (see pages 209–17). Instead, for the young child, as for the adult, a lively topic of interest is human psychology. Children observe other people, try to make sense of their behaviour and plan and predict others' actions and emotions based on their own implicit ideas of how human beings operate. This is the field of *social cognition*, defined broadly as an individual's understanding of human behaviour, human psychology and all the other human elements of social life. Within this broad domain, one topic of special interest during the preschool period is children's construction of a *theory of mind*, or their understanding of people's mental states and the influences of them on their behaviour.

Theory of mind

The *theory of mind* is the concept of human thought that children over the age of five infer mental states like intentions, memories and true or false beliefs, and to use these for understanding and predicting the behaviour of self and others. Such a theory of human psychology is, according to Simon Baron-Cohen (1995), 'one of the quintessential abilities that makes us human' (p. 3). Theory of mind is often assessed using false belief tasks that require children to infer what protagonists will do, say or think in situations designed to create beliefs that are discrepant from reality (Wellman, Cross & Watson, 2001). As adults, we are aware that a person who has not witnessed (or been told about) an event will not know the event has happened. Thus, if you parked your car in the driveway and did not see your spouse come home and borrow it to go to the shops, you would be quite surprised to find it was not there when you opened the door. Children without a theory of mind cannot predict these feelings of surprise. If they themselves know that the car is truly parked at the shops, they

think everyone else also knows this. Thus they would expect you to just go to the shops to get your car, even though you actually never saw it being moved. Without an awareness that your search behaviour is mediated by your mind, or that your mind is capable of retaining beliefs that events have rendered false, these children have no way of accurately anticipating your actions, thoughts and emotional responses.

Because of this, children without a theory of mind are apt to be at a serious disadvantage in social situations that call for empathy or psychological understanding. They have no real awareness of mental states like intention, belief and memory. Thus they are often confused when other people act upon irrational intentions, false beliefs or mistaken memories. They may also have limited skills for communicating, empathising and negotiating with others and may not be fully capable of detecting deception or humour or participating in fantasy play (see page 236).

However, a theory of mind develops rapidly during the preschool period, equipping most children to engage effectively in the full range of social situations requiring an astute grasp of mental states before they are ready to enter primary school. On the basis of a meta-analytic review of 178 separate theory-of-mind studies that were conducted in several different countries including Australia, Japan, Canada and the UK, Henry Wellman, David Cross and Julianne Watson (2001) found that older preschoolers (4.5-year-olds and older) typically pass false belief tasks, while 3-year-olds and children under four and a half years typically fail. The developmental change arose so consistently, irrespective of types of tasks and other variations among the studies, that the authors concluded: 'Understanding of belief and, relatedly, understanding of mind exhibit genuine conceptual change in the preschool years' (p. 655).

Thus, most 3-year-olds have trouble making sense of other people's behaviour in many everyday situations. For example, they generally cannot predict the search patterns of someone who entertains a false belief about the location of a hidden object; or they may imagine that other people will omnisciently see through their trick of replacing the lollies in a Smarties box with buttons. They say that a newcomer who does not know about the substitution will nonetheless reply 'buttons' when asked what is in the box. In other words, they seem to assume that human thoughts are like mirrors, microscopes or X-ray machines in always reflecting the true state of the real world, rather than being subject to distortion by ignorance, forgetfulness or misinformation. By age five or six, on the other hand, most children succeed readily on false belief tasks like the Sally-Ann problem (Baron-Cohen, Leslie & Frith, 1985) that is illustrated in Figure 7.9.

In contrast to children with typical patterns of development, failure on false belief tasks persists to more advanced stages in children with certain sensory and developmental disabilities.

FIGURE 7.9 A false belief test for theory of mind

Part 1 The girl hides her marble in the basket and leaves.

Part 2 The boy moves the marble to the (covered) box.

Test phase The girl comes back: *'Where will she look for her marble?'*

Autism and theory of mind

Autism is a developmental disorder characterised by a triad of severe impairments in (a) language and communication, (b) social relationships, and (c) imagination (Frith, 1989). Autism is generally diagnosed during infancy or early childhood and arises more frequently in boys than girls. Although 75 per cent of people with autism also have mental retardation, intellectual impairment is not a characteristic of autism itself. Furthermore, even when their intelligence is normal most children and adolescents with autism continue to have problems with a theory of mind. Many studies conducted in Australia, Europe and North America over several decades have shown that many autistic people never develop a fully functional theory of mind even when intelligence is normal (see Happé, 1995, for a review). Throughout their adolescence and adulthood, autistic people tend to have difficulty imagining other people's thoughts or conceptualising the consequences of believing something that is not realistic or factually true.

Francesca Happé (1995) reviewed 28 separate studies of the development of a total of more than 300 individuals with autism (all with mean verbal mental ages of five and over). The results of these studies consistently revealed higher failure rates on false belief tests of theory of mind than were seen in normal developers of similar verbal and non-verbal mental ages. For example, pass rates for autistic subjects in 14 studies conducted from 1985 to 1993 with samples predominantly in their teens ranged from only 15 to 60 per cent, with a mean of just 33 per cent passing.

Blind and deaf children

Failure on false belief tests is also found to persist into the upper primary school years in many children with blindness (McAlpine & Moore, 1995; Peterson, Peterson & Webb, 2000) and in many profoundly deaf children who grow up in hearing families where no one apart from the deaf child uses sign language (see Chapter 6) as fluently as a native speaker (Peterson & Siegal, 2000). Yet natively signing deaf children, who acquire sign language in infancy and have other signing family members as conversational partners show no delays in developing a theory of mind (Peterson & Siegal, 1999a). It seems that the problem for deaf children in hearing families is the absence of any one with whom to share conversations about false beliefs, desires, emotions, mistaken memories and other invisible mental states until they enter a sign-language community in primary school (Power & Carty, 1990).

Siblings and theory of mind

For normally developing preschoolers too, the presence of a diverse range of conversational partners in the family and the neighbourhood is a predictor of early theory-of-mind development. Children who have siblings are found to develop concepts of false belief ahead of only children, even after the effects of language ability are statistically controlled (Jenkins & Astington, 1996; Peterson, 2000).

The opportunity to play and converse with a sibling at home even before entering preschool, kindergarten, child care or a playgroup may help to explain the sibling advantage in theory-of-mind development, since children learn important social lessons through playing with peers that would be much more difficult for a parent to teach. Box 7.7 illustrates one such instance. Some of the positive social lessons in generosity that 4-year-old Louise was beginning to learn through playing with her 4-year-old neighbour, Merry, nearly backfired into deception when her father intruded his views about Merry's theory of Louise's mind.

Social play

Through social play, children gain rich opportunities for varied conversational exchanges with peers over topics of mutual interest and involvement. In addition, their social horizons are likely to extend to include ever wider networks of playmates and other congenial social partners.

Developmental changes in social play

Social play can be defined as voluntary, pleasurable interaction that places children into direct physical or communicative contact with one another. Its roots stretch back to infancy. When placed on the floor together, babies as young as 10 months are capable of poking or touching each other or engaging in a tug-of-war for a toy. By 18 months, children who have been in contact with peers regularly begin to show signs of rudimentary cooperation (Garvey, 1977). For example, one may take the lead while the other follows, or they may take turns modelling and copying each other's activities. But this is only a beginning. After observing the spontaneous social activity of many infant and toddler pairs, Catherine Garvey wrote:

> We can conclude that the two-year-old still has a great deal to learn about how to play with others. His social expertise rests on his experience with cooperative adults and he must now learn how to sustain a mutually enjoyable encounter with a volatile and equally inept playmate. Human infants and infant primates (who unlike puppies and kittens are not normally reared in litters) do

BOX 7.7 Social lessons – giving gifts and gaining insight into donors' and recipients' minds

When Louise was four, she grappled with several of the social and cognitive dilemmas bound up with the giving of gifts, as the following extract from her father's diary indicates.

Louise with her friend Merry. Between visits, Louise devoted much time to deciding what to give Merry the next time they met.

9 December 1952: *Lately her great enthusiasm has been giving things, especially to her friend Merry. 'Wasn't I generous?' she asks, and I don't know whether the pleasure comes from giving or the praise she expects for it. Anyhow, she devotes much time and thought trying to decide what to give Merry next time they meet. The other day she told me she had given Merry her best teddy bear, Frank, given to her one Christmas by Frank Bayer. The same Christmas, she received another and much cheaper bear, Bruno, but it, perversely, has always been her favourite. So I could appreciate why she gave Frank away.*

Still, I didn't think it was the right thing to do and tried to explain why. The bear, I told her, was a present and she should keep it because the person who gave it wanted her to have it. It didn't sound too convincing even to me so we ended up with a little game of going through her things, deciding what she could and what she ought not give away. It turned out that most of the things it was proper to give she could not, either (1) because she wanted it herself, (2) because Merry already had one like it, or (3) because Merry had given it to her.

A few weeks ago she was busy deciding to give something to Merry. I've forgotten what it was but after she had said for the umpteenth time (saying a thing once or twice is never enough), 'I'm going to give this to Merry because I don't want it any more', I protested mildly. 'Well, don't tell her you don't want it or Merry won't want it either.' 'Oh no, I won't,' she enthusiastically agreed. 'I'll tell her I want it. I'll tell her I want it, Dot. I'll tell her I want it.' How easily the diplomatic lie is cultivated! I suggested she not say anything at all, because if she told Merry she wanted it, that would not be true.

not appear to be able to interact with their peers before they are weaned, mobile and able to use the communication systems unique to their species. (p. 39)

When play with peers first begins, children may spend considerable time alone, engaging in simple repetitive exercises – such as pulling wheeled toys around, digging in the sandpit or rolling a ball. Much of their time may be spent inactively on the sidelines of peers' play, simply watching. But as age increases and peer experience grows, more varied and sophisticated forms of play are likely to emerge, together with genuinely social interaction. Language assists in these developments and, conversely, gains momentum from active participation in social play. When Anthony Pellegrini (1984) conducted a naturalistic observational study (see Chapter 2) of preschoolers' play in a nursery school setting that had separate areas allocated to play with blocks, sand, water, art materials and housekeeping toys, he found that play in the housekeeping corner was a particularly strong predictor of 3- and 4-year-olds' aptitude for imaginative, symbolic language. Somewhat unexpectedly, Pellegrini also found that the boys in his sample used imaginative language more often and more competently than their female classmates. However, he also noted that the boys he was studying spent more time in the housekeeping corner than the girls. Pellegrini explained his observation of male superiority with representational language on the basis of this difference in play patterns, noting that:

> More 3-year-old boys than girls tended to play in the housekeeping center. Presence in this center, in turn, was a good predictor of imaginative language. Thus, boys' propensity to play in the housekeeping center may have been responsible for the gender difference for imaginative language ... [because] this type of activity center elicited language that defined players' roles and transformed props. Players must interact socially and verbally define the transformation of their roles if other players are to understand their transformations. For example, by stating 'I'll be the daddy' a child is using an explicit verbal definition to convey to other players the role transformation from child to daddy. (p. 138)

Another unexpected finding was Pellegrini's discovery of a statistically significant negative relationship between an adult's presence in the play environment and the quality of functional language play. In other words, while the child's generating of imaginative language while playing alone or purely with peers seemed to boost language competence, the presence of an adult detracted from it. Part of the reason might have been intimidation by the adult. Many of the 4-year-olds were too shy to continue playful monologues or to speak directly to one another when an adult appeared to be listening. They also refrained from correcting each other or giving each other orders when the teacher was with them. Pellegrini

found that, when left alone by an adult, 4-year-olds took the initiative more than children of two or three in generating ideas for play. They typically came up with games and sequences of fantasy play spontaneously when left alone, but were inclined to hold back and wait for adult direction if the teacher was present.

However, there are other times when a teacher's intervention is clearly beneficial. A New Zealand study conducted by Jan Halliday, Stuart McNaughton and Ted Glynn (1985) in a mixed-race kindergarten in Auckland illustrates such a situation. The children attending this kindergarten ranged in age from two and a half to four years and, unlike those in Pellegrini's US sample, were displaying highly sex-stereotyped play before the experiment began. Boys, in particular, were reluctant even to enter the housekeeping corner, let alone play there. Thus they were missing out on the language benefits of sharing in fantasy play, while the New Zealand girls' development of motor and constructive skills was being curtailed by their exclusion from play with blocks and outdoor toys. An intervention study was therefore designed (Halliday, McNaughton & Glynn, 1985) to correct these imbalances. Teachers were instructed to participate with the children in block-building and housekeeping. Under these conditions, role stereotyping relaxed somewhat so that children of both sexes gained opportunities to take part in each type of play.

Malcolm Watson and Kurt Fischer (1980) also studied the growth of social play from age 18 months to seven years. They identified toddlerhood as the period when children gained sufficient understanding of social roles to allow them to act out such simple imaginary sequences as pretending to drink from an empty cup, 'walking' a wooden block as though it were a person, or making a doll take a nap. But the toddler's knowledge of the requirements of familiar adult roles such as mother, father, doctor or nurse was still extremely limited. In Watson and Fischer's middle-class American sample, the ability to accurately mimic a doctor's behaviour began to develop after age three. By age six, most children could coordinate and switch their make-believe roles with great versatility. For example, one 6-year-old boy simultaneously enacted the overlapping roles of doctor, husband and father with an ease that many role-conflicted real-life fathers (see Chapter 4) might be disposed to envy. Thus he switched appropriately from examining a sick patient to chatting with his wife and then disciplining his 'daughter' doll over and over again during a single play sequence.

Differences in social play are seen not only between age groups but also across cultures (Garvey, 1977). Play patterns vary within the same society as a function of such factors as presence of siblings at home, length of acquaintance among peers and the child's attendance at day-care (Howes, 1985). Some of these differences may persist past toddlerhood into

Pretend play with toy animals and constructive play with blocks, or sand, are common activities during early childhood.

Ken Rubin and his colleagues (Rubin, Maioni & Hornung, 1976) studied the play of a group of Canadian preschoolers from middle- and working-class families. Play was subdivided into three broad categories:

1. **Functional play**
   Definition: Simple repetitive exercising of muscles or routine actions
   Example: Digging in a sandpit or tossing and catching a ball
2. **Creative, constructive play**
   Definition: Use of tools or objects to make or create something
   Example: Building a tower of blocks, making a sandcastle, finger painting
3. **Pretend play**
   Definition: Use of symbols, or toys in representational substitution of the symbol, for something real
   Example: washing a doll's hair or feeding a doll with air from an empty bottle substituting for shampoo or milk; acting out imaginary dramatic sequences, such as crouching and pretending to steer an invisible car's wheel, making car-like noises: 'Vroom! Vroom!'

The most frequent type of play was constructive, (see Figure 7.10). But with development from age four to age five, pretend play became more frequent, a phenomenon that is likely to have implications for developmental advances in theory of mind and in social skills and social cognition more generally, as we see in the next sections of this chapter.

Pretend play as a boost to development

Jerome Singer (1973) gave an apt illustration of the fascinating complexity of the typical preschooler's pretend play when he wrote:

> We observe these little creatures talking to thin air, treating a bit of blanket fluff or a stick like a baby that needs cuddling, having a teddy bear talk on a toy telephone in phrases suspiciously like mother's. Sometimes we see a quiet little boy carrying on bloody and bitter battles punctuated by imitative cannon noises, diving airplanes, with only the help of some props of wooden blocks …
> A 5-year-old boy has a toy giraffe of felt and plastic which he declares is a visitor from outer space, a Martian who has a long neck because that's what all the people look like up there. (p. 1)

While all forms of play can assist children's psychological development, pretend play is likely to prove especially beneficial during the preschool period. As we have already seen, this mode of social play is a particularly rich source of language stimulation (Pellegrini, 1984). In addition, playing fantasy and make-believe games can assist children's mastery

later phases of the lifespan. When Russell and Mollie Smart (1980) contrasted the complexity of social play in American and New Zealand primary schools, they found a higher rate of sophisticated social play in New Zealand. There were no differences between boys and girls, but Maori children played more complex social games than Pakeha New Zealanders. The Smarts suggested that a lower rate of solitary television viewing might be one of the factors responsible for New Zealand children's superiority over Americans. The Maori children's advantage could also reflect low television viewing, coupled with cultural norms favouring collective cooperation and mutual group activity (see page 220).

Functional play provides opportunities for the exercise of motor skills.

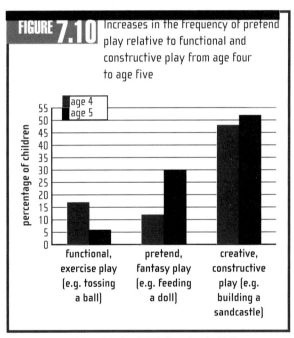

FIGURE 7.10 Increases in the frequency of pretend play relative to functional and constructive play from age four to age five

Source: Rubin, Watson & Jambar (1978). Reproduced with the permission of the Society for Research in Child Development.
Note: Percentages do not total 100 because other infrequent styles of play were not coded.

of the cognitive skills that are needed to achieve Piaget's transition from preoperational thinking, while at the same time boosting children's creativity, emotional understanding, theory-of-mind development and skills in negotiating with parents and peers. Some of the special developmental benefits deriving from playing games of pretend are outlined below.

Cognition, conservation and pretend play

Success in the Piagetian quantity conservation tasks described earlier in this chapter (see Figure 7.3) requires children to simultaneously consider the test array (e.g. balls of clay) both before and after a critical transformation (rolling one ball into a sausage). Maybe children can be helped to visualise these two situations together in their 'mind's eye' by playing pretend games in which an object is simultaneously itself and some pretended alternative (e.g. a real clothes peg can also be an imaginary person). To test this possibility, Claire Golomb and Cheryl Cornelius (1977) pretested a group of children for conservation of substance. Those who failed were then given six different experiences of engaging with an adult in pretend play. The pretences they enacted together included:

1. pretending to eat 'food' made of plasticine
2. pretending a chair was a car
3. a more elaborate dramatic scenario involving puppets and stuffed toys.

At the end of each game, an adult either challenged the pretence or carried it beyond reasonable bounds (e.g. by arguing that a chair could not be a car because it had no wheels or by actually beginning to chew on the plasticine). These actions were designed to force the children to argue with the adult, and to come to grips with the *reversibility* of pretending (see page 215). In other words, children were forced by the adult's intervention to notice that the toy or symbol could alternate between being its real self (say, a chair) and being whatever the pretence required it to symbolise (a car), and could then return to its ordinary nature again.

This play experience dramatically enhanced preschoolers' conservation concepts. The group of children who were exposed to the make-believe play experiences showed a statistically significant improvement on their own previous performance on a set of quantity conservation problems. Their mastery of conservation skills after playing these pretend games was also nearly six times greater than that of a control group who had spent the same amount of time engaged in a construction task with the experimenter – results that were especially notable, since no direct experience with the conservation materials, as such, had been given.

Creativity and cognitive flexibility

Jerome Singer (1973) divided a group of children aged six to nine years into high-fantasy and low-fantasy groups on the basis of their frequency of playing pretend games as contrasted with other kinds of play (see Figure 7.10) and their replies to these questions:

1. Do you ever have pictures in your head? Do you ever see make-believe things in your mind or think about them? What sorts of things? Do you have a make-believe friend?

2. Do you have an animal or toy or make-believe person you talk to or take along with you? Did you ever have one, even though you don't any more?

('Yes' to both questions denotes high fantasy.)

Although both groups were equivalent in general intelligence, as measured by their IQ scores, Singer found that the high-fantasy children stood out from those with low fantasy in the following ways:

- more creative
- more verbally fluent
- more ingenious, flexible and skilful when asked to make up a story
- more patient when required to sit quietly for 15 minutes.

Although it is difficult to infer causality from correlations like these, Singer theorised that extensive experiences with make-believe play during early childhood among high-fantasy children might have fostered the development of inner language, creativity and vivid mental imagery. These assets would then have provided enough resources for mental stimulation to stave off boredom and frustration during the patience test. Also, since linguistic and creative abilities are valued in school (see Chapter 9), imagination is likely to boost subsequent academic learning and performance. However, the fact that highly imaginative Australian children are found to watch less television than their peers (Peterson, Peterson & Carroll, 1983) also raises the possibility of basic personality differences which may dispose for and against fantasy play, or of adverse influences on the less imaginative by the activities they happen to opt for in place of make-believe.

The frequency and variety of children's dramatic make-believe during their free-play time at preschool has been found to predict children's skill in understanding others' emotions and taking account of their feelings empathetically (Fein, 1986). With differences due to age, sex and intelligence partialled out, those children who sustained the longest episodes of fantasy play and incorporated the widest variety of social roles into their dramas were found to score higher than their classmates on tests of affective role-taking (see Figure 7.8). They were also singled out by their preschool teachers as being exceptionally competent at social role-taking during spontaneous interactions with their peers at school.

Adolescents who remember having imaginary companions during early childhood are found to score significantly higher than their peers on measures of creative achievement in scholastic, artistic and literary fields (Singer, 1973). L. S. Vygotsky (1962) likewise concluded that children learn about real life through imaginary play. He noted that the reproduction of real meanings and rules in the context of make-believe helps them to understand these rules and consequently apply them appropriately to serious situations.

Piaget's (1962) observations of his own three children's play suggested that fantasy assisted their solution of real-life problems, thereby encouraging the development of logical thought. He often noticed his children dramatically re-enacting puzzling everyday situations and coming up with solutions that could be applied outside the context of play. His son Laurent even taught himself geography in order to draw accurate maps of an imaginary kingdom he called Siwimbal.

Pretend play and theory of mind

Marjorie Taylor and Stephanie Carlson (1997) tested a group of 3- and 4-year-old children who resembled Singer's high-fantasy older children in having an imaginary companion and using animals and toys as impersonated characters and found that they scored higher on standard false belief tests than children of the same chronological age who rarely engaged in fantasy play. The children with rich imaginary lives displayed a more astute grasp of human psychology in theory-of-mind measures even after the effects of verbal ability had been statistically controlled. Taylor and Carlson concluded:

We suspect that engaging in pretend play develops children's understanding that mental representations may not constitute an accurate reflection of the external world. This insight might be more obvious in the domain of fantasy than in the domain of belief. Whereas beliefs are representations of the external world, fantasy often has no counterpart in real life. (p. 452)

Playing make-believe games with dolls or toy animals is linked with advanced language and creativity development.

Pretend play, emotional self-regulation and emotional understanding

Judith Dunn (1983) recorded episodes of make-believe play in families containing an infant and a preschool-age sibling. She found, surprisingly, that in fantasy games with the mother the firstborn child frequently took on the role of pretending to be a baby. This seemed odd, as children in other contexts typically elect to mimic higher-prestige, adult roles. Dunn suggested that one of the benefits for the older child of adopting the role of the infant brother or sister in play was the opportunity to overcome feelings of jealousy, anger and aggressiveness towards the infant sister or brother. Since negative emotions like these are socially unacceptable, the motivation to self-regulate and diminish these feelings (see page 149) is strong and fantasy may supply a useful outlet. In fact, during play, the 'pretend baby' (that is, the older sibling) can claim the same favours and attention from the mother that are a source of jealousy when bestowed on the real baby in everyday life.

In addition, Dunn noted a continual alternation between self and sibling during these episodes of make-believe play. She argued that these playful exchanges helped the preschooler to master a personal sense of identity. Consequently, the older siblings in her study displayed an exceptionally confident grasp of the differences between male and female, good and naughty, and younger and older. Unlike children of the same age without siblings, they were aware, for example, that babies need protection in circumstances an older child can negotiate independently. They also recognised that the baby's likes and dislikes were different from their own, and that rules that applied to the baby were different from those applying to older members of the household. It seemed that:

> The enthusiasm and adroitness with which the children played with the categorization of their own identity leaves little room for doubt about the confidence and certainty with which they understood the dimensions of age and gender as applied to themselves and to their parents. (Dunn & Kendrick, 1982, p. 112)

Emotional understanding can also be enhanced through pretend play. During her naturalistic obser-

Emotional understanding can be enhanced through pretend play.

vations, Dunn was struck by the sophistication of the older siblings' emotional understanding and social cognitive skills, not only while they played make-believe games but also afterwards in serious conversation with their mother about the behaviour of their baby sibling. Dunn found that many siblings as young as three displayed a clear understanding of the contrast between the feelings, intentions and thoughts of the baby sibling and their own. Thus one 3-year-old named Bruce commented, while watching his baby brother play with a balloon: 'He's going to pop it in a minute. And he'll be frightened … I like the pop' (p. 106).

Pretend play and negotiation skills

Yet another function of make-believe for the children in Dunn's study was as a strategy for negotiating with their mothers. She noted that the theme of pretending to be a baby was used frequently by older children when they wanted an excuse to do something parents would disapprove of in someone their age. Thus, having outgrown the bold negativism of the 2-year-old (see Chapter 6), many of the 3- and 4-year-olds in Dunn's sample appeared to use make-believe as a more diplomatic means of refusing to comply with their mother's requests.

The following conversation arose when a 3-year-old boy named Harvey pretended to be his infant brother, Ronnie. The mother asked Harvey to help her and he refused, explaining that he couldn't because he was the baby:

Harvey: 'No, I'm Ronnie.'
Mother: 'Well, pretend you're Harvey for a little while.'
Harvey: 'Pretend I'm Harvey baby.'
Mother: 'Harvey baby?'
Harvey: 'Mammammamma gagaga gagaga. Bababa.'
Mother: 'You'd better not leave that plasticine on the floor. You know what Ronnie'll do with it.'
Harvey: 'I'm a little baby boy.'
Mother: 'I don't care what you are.'
Harvey: 'I'm a little boy.' (Dunn & Kendrick, 1982, p. 112)

By this more diplomatic means, Harvey was able to resist his mother's request to clean up the plasticine, while at the same time gaining an opportunity to gauge how strong her reaction to this refusal would be in a playful context. If the mother's opposition was strong enough, Harvey could always revert to his serious self and demonstrate helpfulness.

How do children acquire a preference for pretending?

These important developmental benefits of fantasy play reveal its value. How can children be helped to enjoy both the pleasures of experiencing games of pretending and the benefits to psychological functioning and development that can derive from engaging in fantasy play? Not surprisingly, given the early age at which pretence develops, the family is an important consideration.

Greta Fein (1981) discovered that fathers, who have an important role as playmates during early infancy before the baby begins to engage in make-believe (see Chapter 5), are critically important in developing their children's enjoyment of pretence. Fathers of preschoolers who are high in imagination and intellectual ability and who spend longer than other children in pretend play at preschool (see Figure 7.10) are found to spend more time with their sons and daughters than other fathers. Though such a relationship could be due to fathers' delight in the company of offspring who stand out for their dramatic skills, an observed link between children's imagination and parenting during infancy suggests an alternative direction of causality. Greta Fein (1981) noted that the security of an infant's attachment to the mother and/or father at the age of 18 months (see Chapter 5) predicted the imaginative quality and variety of the child's make-believe play as a two-year-old. Also, preschoolers in crowded households with many closely spaced siblings, or in homes suffering from marital discord, are found to play less imaginatively than other children. Finally, parents who make frequent use of physical punishment tend to have offspring who earn low scores on measures of fantasy and imagination (Singer & Singer, 1981).

Taken together, these results suggest that parents can optimise the cognitive and social advantages to be gained by their children from make-believe play by creating a safe, warm and relaxed home atmosphere where fantasy can be given free rein.

Chapter summary

The preschool phase, from age two to age six, is a 'magical' era in development. Preschoolers make important strides in physical growth and in motoric and neurobiological development, while also gaining socially and emotionally from their increasing exposure to the social world outside the family, including opportunities to play with peers in informal and organised settings.

From a cognitive perspective, preschool children are impressively astute in their capacity to devise ingenious miniature theories for physical, biological and psychological phenomena (Wellman & Inagaki, 1997). In their play and conversation, they spontaneously put their minds to work to account for the aspects of their physical and social worlds that they find humorous, puzzling or disturbing.

Despite thinking along different lines from older children or adults, and using sequences of 'preoperational' (Piaget, 1970) inference that defy the rules of formal logic, preschoolers' thought processes are coherent and predictable with a structure all their own.

We examined preschoolers' animistic, realistic and artificialistic concepts of causality, their transductive inferences and their understanding of number, seriation, classification and the physics of quantitative transformation. Piaget's pioneering discoveries about young children's understanding of quantity conservation give us insight into an aspect of preschool cognition that continues to excite psychological researchers and theorists today. According to Piaget, the acquisition of a concrete-operational system of logic eventually enables the school-aged child to overcome the limitations of preoperational thought by understanding that quantity is conserved under logically reversible transformations.

With the transition from preoperational to concrete-operational thinking, children acquire more sophisticated theories of emotions and social relations, along with sophisticated new skills for adopting other people's roles and perspectives. The acquisition of a 'theory of mind' at age four or five enables preschoolers to go a long way towards appreciating the feelings and mental perspectives of others, especially when they have rich access to play and conversation with siblings and peers.

Memory also develops in notable ways during the preschool period. Involuntary memory may become less efficient as children gain experience with strategies like labelling, rehearsal and elaboration which aid deliberate memorisation. Lacking a sophisticated metamemory, 5-year-olds often have difficulty reflecting on the limits of their own memory. This can inhibit deliberate memorisation and may lead to unrealistic beliefs about the circumstances under which memory breaks down.

While fostering cognitive and social cognitive growth, play also makes other important contributions to the preschool child's psychological development. Social play, rule games, physical sports and creative pursuits all confer distinctive benefits, but perhaps the most far-reaching developmental advantages derive from make-believe and fantasy play. Pretend play boosts growth of psychological understanding (including theory of mind), social skills and emotional well-being in the family and on the playground.

For further interest

Looking Forward on the Internet

Use the Internet to visit the following websites. Examine them for further information and varied perspectives on issues raised in this chapter. Also search for other relevant websites for yourself, using keywords like 'children', 'memory', 'early childhood' and 'children's growth' in your search engine. General sites include: **http://www.srcd.org**.

In particular, for further ideas on children's play and development visit: **http://www.ncb.org.uk/cpc** and **http://www.culture.gov.uk/education_and_ social_policy/children's_play.html** and **http://www. zerotothree.org/magic**.

For resources, ideas, activities and other items of interest in conjunction with this chapter, visit the Companion Website for this textbook at:

http://wps.pearsoned.com.au/peterson

Activity suggestion

As a practical activity in conjunction with themes in this chapter, try exploring children's safety. Collect posters, pamphlets and labels on medicine bottles and household products that convey health messages, or warnings, to children. Also visit: **http://www. kidshealth.org/kid/ill_injure** and check out information available for kids on the Internet. Consider the cognitive demands this information places on a child (or parent) and discuss how age-appropriate various items are.

Multimedia

For a vivid account of Piaget's methods of testing children's thinking, view *Piaget's Development Theory: 'Conservation' and 'Classification'* (Davidson Films, 1972: 29 + 16 minutes, colour).

Milestones of development from age two to age six

Domain of development

Physical and motor skill	Emotion	Cognition	Language	Social relationships	Personality
By 18–24 months, toddlers run, walk well both forwards and backwards, climb stairs with both feet on each step and jump in place. By three to four years, they are able to walk up stairs with one foot per step, walk on tiptoe and skip rope. A 2-year-old has the manual dexterity needed to turn the pages of a book one by one, stack four or five blocks and throw a ball. By age five, skills like catching a ball, threading beads on a string, kicking a ball and striking a ball with a cricket bat have usually developed. The typical 3-year-old has cultural exposure to the relevant tools, can ride a tricycle, draw with a pencil and paint with a brush.	By 18–24 months, many toddlers display the emotions of shame, pride and embarrassment which require a sense of self and a consciousness of personal autonomy. The child's vocabulary for labelling feelings develops rapidly from age three to age five, along with the ability to recognise the emotions of others and predict how people will feel in certain emotionally charged situations (e.g. after receiving a gift or getting lost in the supermarket). Empathy also becomes more common during the preschool period and children acquire simple strategies for comforting others in distress.	The development of a capacity for mental representation at around 18 months enables the child to imagine invisible displacements of objects, manipulate symbols and play simple games of pretend. According to Piaget, the period from age two to age seven is the preoperational stage of cognitive development during which children use language and other mental representational systems to manipulate ideas in their minds. They store memories, engage in fantasy and pretence and develop 'prelogical' theories about the physical and social world. During the preoperational stage, children have difficulty with concepts of quantity conservation, seriation and logical classification. They may explain physical phenomena animistically and biological phenomena artificialistically. Between age three and age five children typically acquire a theory of mind that enables them to predict and understand their own and other people's behaviour on the basis of mental states like true and false beliefs.	By the age of two months, most infants make cooing and gooing sounds that have no communication meaning. From four to nine months, babbling of speech sounds becomes more versatile, and sequences of vowels and consonants are produced. By 12 months, many infants can produce simple meaningful gestures (e.g. nodding the head, 'yes', or waving 'bye-bye'). Some have begun to use a single word as a meaningful name (e.g. 'Mama', 'bow-wow'). Between 16 and 24 months vocabulary expands rapidly. Holophrastic sentences (consisting of a word plus context to convey a subject–predicate clause) generally emerge, soon to be followed by two-word sentences. By age three, children typically produce sentences of three or more words that include grammatical markers. Between age three and age six, there is continuing improvement in children's comprehension and production of grammatical rules for plurals, negation, past tense and so on.	In addition to the close relationships with parents, forged during infancy through the process of attachment formation, preschoolers enjoy increasingly important relationships with siblings and peers outside the family as they grow from age two to age six. Those who attend preschool, day-care or playgroup learn social skills through peer interaction. They become increasingly capable of communicating, asserting their opinions and rights, and resolving conflicts amicably rather than through aggression and physical force. A concept of gender identity, enabling the child to correctly label himself or herself as boy or girl, emerges between age two and age three, as do increasing capacities for self-control and self-regulation (see Chapter 8).	Toddlers typically assert their independence and self-awareness at age two with bouts of non-compliance. In Erikson's theory, the period from age one to age three is a time when the sense of shame emerges; also a sense of autonomy arises out of a clash between the child's will and the constraints imposed by reality and the needs of caregivers, peers and society as a whole. From age three to age five, children encounter a stage of conflict within the personality between personal initiative and guilt. Parents assist the successful resolution of this stage conflict, according to Erikson, when they foster moral values and conscience while allowing the child to take the initiative and assume responsibility within reasonable limits.

MIDDLE CHILDHOOD:
PART AGE 6 TO AGE 12

4

Contents

Overview

Most children enter primary school eagerly, proud of having moved through one of the major gateways along the road to maturity, and keen to face the new challenges that schooling and entry into a classroom of peers provide. For the lucky majority, such optimism is fully justified. Middle childhood tends to be an exceptionally calm and happy phase in the lifespan, when health is sound and the cognitive, social and physical skills acquired during early childhood are consolidated and put to varied use. Psychological development progresses steadily as children exercise their imaginative, linguistic, motoric and social skills in the playground and refine their cognitive aptitudes for attending, learning, remembering and solving problems in the class-room. With mastery of new academic skills like reading, writing and computation, whole new vistas of knowledge are opened up to the child in school. At the same time, growing contact with the world of peers during middle childhood teaches children the rules of friendship, morality and gender roles.

Chapters 8 and 9 chart these important psychological developments together with the equally important biological changes of physical and neurocognitive growth with which they are intimately interconnected.

MIDDLE CHILDHOOD:
Social, personality and sex-role development

CHAPTER

8

Children have never been very good at listening to their elders, but they have never failed to imitate them.

James Baldwin (1924–1987)

Contents

CHAPTER OVERVIEW

During middle childhood, as the child journeys from the start to the end of primary school, important social and personality changes occur as peer relationships form, moral reasoning crystalises and the self-concept and a gender role develop. Parents and siblings play a central role in this process. Schooling, peer groups and other contacts outside the family also help to shape children's psychological growth around the core values of their society, culture and ethnic group, as we see in the cross-cultural examples in this chapter.

In school and on the playground, children learn skills for making friends and influencing people, establishing a social position in their classroom and forging links with out-of-school peer groups. We examine research into the factors that promote these key social developments, which may lead to peer popularity or rejection and to stable mutual friendships or loneliness during middle childhood. The influence of siblings on the child's development is analysed and we also study the links between peer status, moral development and social cognitive understanding, while considering how to optimise the social development of children who have difficulty making friends. Links with the lifespan are explored, since the social strategies that children forge in middle childhood and their social status as popular, controversial, rejected or neglected members of the peer group can exert lifelong influences on social relationships and personality growth.

As we all know from our own interactions with different families, there are important differences among households in ways of disciplining and teaching children, in childrearing philosophies and in the overall climate of the home. In this chapter we examine the consequences for children's psychological growth and well-being of different approaches to parenting, and of different constellations of siblings.

One important sphere of parental influence is children's moral development. We take a cognitive focus on the growth of moral understanding, but also explore behaviourally how children learn to obey their parents, resist the temptation to do wrong, display conscience and show empathy and other prosocial behaviours like generosity, helpfulness, compassion and the striving for justice.

Similarly, this chapter explores sex-role, or gender-role, development from both a cognitive and a behavioural perspective. We see how children learn to recognise and understand the social and biological attributes of masculinity and femininity and look at their gradual acquisition of a socially defined gender role. The socialising influences of parents, siblings, peers, schooling and the overall culture on gender-role development is noted, and we critically evaluate four different theories to explain this process: psychoanalytic, social-learning, cognitive developmental and gender-schema. Individual differences in these developments are marked, and we look at some of the reasons why.

Together with moral standards and resistance to the temptation to do wrong, children's socialisation during middle childhood includes important lessons in prosocial behaviour, helpfulness and altruism, in the social conventions of politeness, in the fairness of a just distribution of assets and in the dynamics of political influence. These important social developments make up the final sections of this chapter.

Parental influences on social and personality development

School separates children from their parents for many hours each day and gradually dilutes the parents' exclusive influence over their child's development by introducing the sometimes competing socialising forces embodied in the peer group, children's friendships, teachers' influences and the values inherent in the culture of schooling. Despite this, most parents are eager for their children to attend school and have high expectations of formal schooling as a source of important social, as well as academic, benefits for their offspring. When Peggy Fairburn-Dunlop (1986), for example, asked a group of parents of preschoolers who had recently emigrated to New Zealand from Samoa what they hoped for their children as a result of formal schooling, social gains were almost as salient in these parents' minds as the 'three Rs' (reading, writing and arithmetic). Even though many did not speak English to their children at home, they mentioned the school's

Parents' disciplining and teaching styles influence their children's development.

role in teaching English much less often than its role in teaching social skills. The Samoan parents all had high hopes for their children's acquisition of poise, peer acceptance, self-confidence and social adjustment as a result of school. Among the specific benefits of schooling mentioned by the Samoan parents were 'mixing with other children' and 'overcoming shyness'. These social gains were named only slightly less often than the mastery of literacy and numeracy (see Chapter 9).

Parents' childrearing styles and philosophies

The dilemma that 6-year-old Louise's father faced when he made his September diary entry (see Box 8.1) is one shared by many parents: how can a mother or father assist the child to make a smooth transition into the social and academic constraints imposed by formal schooling? More specifically, is there anything parents can do to overcome problems like painful shyness, low self-esteem or crippling anxiety? Is parenting effective in developing the kinds of social and academic skills that children need to make a satisfactory adjustment to school?

Answers to questions like these are bound up with parents' broad philosophies of childrearing. To study these, Diana Baumrind (1971, 1991) undertook a pioneering longitudinal study in the United States during the 1960s that yielded results which continue to shape contemporary understanding of parenting styles in Australia (Phillips, Nicholson, Peterson & Battistutta, 2002) as well as New Zealand, Europe, the United States and many other parts of the world (Baumrind, 1991).

When she interviewed parents and observed their childrearing practices naturalistically at home, Baumrind discovered that two dimensions of parenting style, *warmth* (or affectionate, supportive responsiveness to the child) and limit-setting, or *control*, varied across the households she observed. She discovered that a four-way typology of parenting captured the overall childrearing philosophies and strategies of most of the families in her longitudinal sample. Table 8.1 displays this scheme.

In order to examine the influences of these broad approaches to childrearing on children's social and emotional development, Baumrind assessed the young children in her sample on a number of dimensions of social adjustment and personality development, including moodiness, self-reliance, self-esteem (see page 256), social outgoingness, peer acceptance, emotional maturity and self-control. When the longitudinal sample reached middle childhood, participants were reassessed between their eighth and ninth birthdays on similar dimensions of social and emotional adjustment. Baumrind discovered that parents' childrearing styles were strongly correlated with their offsprings' developmental outcomes. Children whose parents used the *authoritative* parenting style were developing especially well. Baumrind (1991) defined optimal social competence during middle childhood

BOX 8.1 | A case in point
One 6-year-old adjusts to the novelty of school

When Louise was six, her parents moved interstate and she entered a new primary school soon after her arrival in a suburban Californian community. Her father made the following three entries in his diary, recording the progress of his daughter's adjustment to school from her first day to her changed attitudes several months later.

7 September 1954. *Louise went to school this morning, entering the first grade. She seemed a trifle unhappy with all the strangeness around her, but bravely fighting back the tears. Her teacher is Miss Solari. Her mother went with her to register and left as the school bell rang. Louise has been looking forward eagerly to school again, especially to the romance and prestige of being in the first grade. No longer is she a 'kindergarten baby', but a real first grader.*

4 December 1954. *Yesterday Miss Solari told Peggy she might like to borrow books from the library for Louise to read ... Peggy told Miss Solari about Louise's shyness and how she wanted to ask questions but was afraid. So to break down her reserve, Miss Solari called Louise up to her desk the following day and Louise came, her mouth quivering and two big tears about to fall. Miss Solari said, 'Why don't you smile like your mother does?' and Louise essayed a weak smile, forcing her mouth up at the corners. When I think of something like that, I feel like crying myself, wanting so much to help her overcome her fears.*

4 March 1955. *She loves school, and the worst thing that can happen to her is to have to stay home on account of illness. We've planned to go down to Los Angeles the later part of this month. But because that will take her out of school for a few days, Louise vigorously opposes the trip. She has I think definitely made the break from Livonia to Carpinteria, and now even Merry who for so long she described as her 'best friend' has become little more than a nostalgic symbol. She still misses Merry as she misses snow but she is quite able to get along without them.*

© Peterson, 1974, reproduced with permission

as a positive blend of strong prosocial assertiveness skills and strong social responsibility and moral values. Her rationale for this two-dimensional model of social adjustment was as follows: Children who lack assertiveness are not deemed to be optimally adjusted socially because they are likely to miss out on positive peer experiences and instructive social interactions with adults (see Box 8.1) that contribute to self-esteem and useful learning of social skills.

TABLE 8.1 Baumrind's typology of parenting		
	Warmth/Responsiveness	
Control	*High*	*Low*
High	AUTHORITATIVE Parents set reasonable rules which are introduced firmly but with sensitivity to the child's needs and developmental changes, monitored through open communication.	AUTHORITARIAN Parents set many rules and make many demands which are enforced firmly and sometimes punitively, with little attention to the child's perspective and little opportunity for discussion.
Low	PERMISSIVE/INDULGENT Few rules are set and enforcement of them is lax and inconsistent; parents are warm and loving but unwilling to restrict their children's freedom.	INDIFFERENT/UNINVOLVED Few rules are set and enforcement of them is lax and inconsistent; parents are distanced from childrearing and low in awareness, monitoring and sensitivity to their children's needs.

High levels of social responsibility are equally important for optimal adjustment since irresponsible children, whether antisocial in orientation or simply immature and overly dependent, will miss out on important social opportunities; they will also fail to express the qualities that contribute to self-esteem and satisfactory social relationships with peers and others outside the family.

Baumrind discovered that many of the offspring of parents who had an authoritative style stood out as high in both assertiveness and social responsibility (see Figure 8.1). They tended to be outgoing, altruistic and strongly concerned to do the right thing; generally, perhaps for these reasons, they had high self-esteem. A few of the 9-year-olds whose parents had an authoritarian philosophy also displayed these qualities of high social competence (see Figure 8.1). But more often, these children were only moderately competent socially, often scoring low in self-esteem and assertiveness and having only weakly internalised moral standards (see page 277).

Children whose parents were permissive/indulgent did still worse and those whose parents were indifferent/uninvolved fared worst of all. In the offspring of both these categories of lax, permissive parenting, immature dependency was common and the children frequently displayed low levels of both assertion and responsibility, with low self-esteem, antisocial behaviour and unsatisfactory relationships with peers.

Reasoning or punishment? Parents' disciplinary tactics

In addition to adhering to one of the broad stylistic philosophies of parenting that Baumrind identified, parents are also called upon to make many small, day-to-day decisions about how to deal with specific instances of misbehaviour in their children. Traditionally, the accepted approach was clear: 'Spare the rod and you'll spoil the child', parents were told.

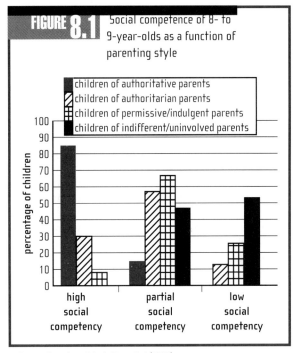

FIGURE 8.1 Social competence of 8- to 9-year-olds as a function of parenting style

- children of authoritative parents
- children of authoritarian parents
- children of permissive/indulgent parents
- children of indifferent/uninvolved parents

Source: Based on data in Baumrind (1991).

Thus, if a child threw a tantrum in a supermarket or snatched a toy from a younger sibling, a parent might administer a swift smack. Serious disciplinary breaches were often curbed with a scheduled spanking conducted some time after the disobedient event.

While some parents continue to use this physically punitive disciplinary approach today, recent psychological research from the perspective of social learning theory (Bandura, 1989; see also Chapter 2) has called it into question. For one thing, use of physical violence by the parent sets a bad example for the child. As noted in Chapter 2, children learn by *modelling* or (copying) their parents' behaviour. Parental hitting or smacking can breed corresponding aggression in the young child.

Indeed, the results of one large-scale study of spanking (Larzelere, 1986) revealed just that. Children aged three to 17 years whose parents frequently employed spanking as a disciplinary tactic were found to be more aggressive in their behaviour towards their peers and siblings than the offspring of parents who avoided spanking and used non-violent forms of discipline.

Another problem with parental use of physical punishment is that even when it is effective it is apt to teach fear rather than social understanding. Kenneth Dodge (1994) studied the parents of a group of 584 five-year-olds in the United States, interviewing them about their use of a range of physical disciplinary tactics, including spanking, slapping, hitting or kicking the child and beating with a rod or strap. Later, the children's social cognition skills (see Chapter 7) were tested using a specially prepared videotape that displayed child actors engaging in unintended negative acts (e.g. spilling paint on another child's drawing or knocking over a tower of blocks in a fall). Compared with the offspring of parents who never or rarely used physical punishment, children who were frequently spanked and beaten made many errors in judging the motivations and intentions of the video-taped actors. They tended to perceive violence and hostility everywhere, misjudging accidental mishaps as intentional, premeditated acts of deliberate aggression and harm.

If physical punishment has these many, potentially negative, repercussions, what are parents to do when their children misbehave? An alternative to punishment, for many contemporary parents, is the use of *reasoning* (see also the discussion of parental negotiation strategies in Chapter 6). When parents explain things and reason with their children, they often supply them with rational justifications for the desired behaviour that can go beyond fear of punishment or the desire to win parental affection. Similarly, when children accept parental reasons, they gain a cognitive understanding of why the disciplined behaviour is wrong.

As a disciplinary strategy, a parent's use of reason-ing either on its own or in conjunction with other tactics is *induction*. For example, a mother who uses inductive discipline might tell her child not to pick the neighbour's flowers 'because Mr Jones has spent lots of time planting and watering them and wants the flowers to stay there to make his garden pretty'. It has been common for parenting researchers to compare induction with other parental disciplinary tactics. Among the repertoire of punitive behaviours that some contemporary parents use are *power assertion* (forceful control, such as slapping the child's hand, which includes the physical forms of punishment described above as well as other forceful tactics such as dragging the child bodily out of the garden as she reaches for a flower) and *love withdrawal* (registering emotional displeasure over the child's transgression, but without a clear explanation of *why* the mother feels angry or unhappy).

Research evidence over many years (Hoffman 1970, 1993) has indicated that induction is more effective than other approaches. *Other-oriented induction* is especially valuable. In this variation of the inductive technique, parents point out the negative effects of the child's misbehaviour on other people. Studies show that other-oriented induction is more likely to result in future resistance to the temptation to transgress than either power assertion or love withdrawal. But there are exceptions to this rule. If the child ignores the parents' reasons, induction on its own offers no emotional motivation for compliance. Also, if children misunderstand the parents' inductive messages, they may backfire in ways the parent could not have foreseen.

One example was pointed out by Leon Kuczynski (1983). He suggested that self-oriented parental rationales may imply to children that their parents want them to operate according to self-interest rather than morality. For example, if a parent says 'Stop kicking your sister's toy or you'll hurt your foot', the implication is that the transgressor's own comfort is the main issue at stake. By contrast, the use of other-oriented induction (e.g. 'Jane will be very unhappy if her toy is broken') highlights the parents' expectation that their children will think about other people's welfare in addition to their own.

The child's chronological age or level of cognitive maturity may also influence the effectiveness of other-oriented induction. A child of three or four is likely to have difficulty conceptualising other people's minds, intentions and emotional perspectives (see Chapter 7). Thus a parent's attempt to use other-oriented induction with a 4-year-old could fall on deaf ears, whereas the same kind of inductive appeal could promote socially responsible behaviour very effectively in a child of seven or eight.

Optimally effective parenting

In a thoughtful and comprehensive analysis of the effectiveness of parents' use of such disciplinary techniques as induction, love withdrawal and power

When parents use reasons ('you might fall off if you don't wear a belt') they are often more effective in motivating children's compliance.

assertion, Joan Grusec and Jacqueline Goodnow (1994) drew attention to the child's active role as a processor of disciplinary information. Children think about the lessons their parents offer through the medium of disciplinary intervention. But they do not automatically accept and internalise the message, no matter which strategy the parent happens to use. Instead, even when the lesson is fully comprehended (which doesn't always happen), the child has a choice of either accepting or rejecting it. Only the former decision leads to internalisation.

In addition to the child's own active role in the process, a number of other factors influence the effectiveness of parental discipline, according to Grusec and Goodnow. These include the quality of the emotional bond between parent and child and the communicative effectiveness of the disciplinary message. When a child is securely attached to a parent (see Chapter 5), the threat of parental disapproval may carry more meaning than when the emotional relationship between parent and child is aloof and distant, or when the attachment between them is insecure. Similarly, in order for a disciplinary message to be taken on board by the child, he or she must notice it, understand it and feel motivated to comply with it. The interconnections among these factors, according to Grusec and Goodnow's (1994) model, are shown in Figure 8.2.

In other words, as Figure 8.2 shows, a disciplinary message must be clear, meaningful and suited to the child's present level of cognitive maturity in order to be influential. But this by itself is not enough. The child must also want to comply. The motivation to do so can be boosted by the child's believing that the message is logical, important and in the child's best interests. Desire to please the parent, fear of punishment or parental displeasure, and recognition of how much the issue means to the parent can also boost the child's motivation to behave in accordance with the parental directive.

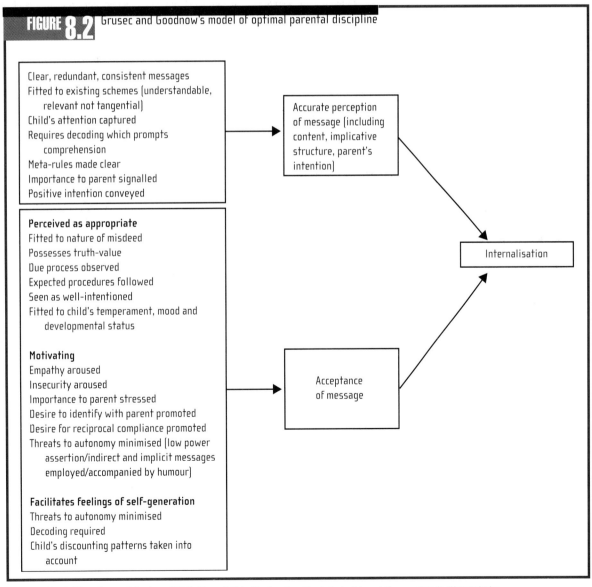

FIGURE 8.2 Grusec and Goodnow's model of optimal parental discipline

Clear, redundant, consistent messages
Fitted to existing schemes (understandable, relevant not tangential)
Child's attention captured
Requires decoding which prompts comprehension
Meta-rules made clear
Importance to parent signalled
Positive intention conveyed

Perceived as appropriate
Fitted to nature of misdeed
Possesses truth-value
Due process observed
Expected procedures followed
Seen as well-intentioned
Fitted to child's temperament, mood and developmental status

Motivating
Empathy aroused
Insecurity aroused
Importance to parent stressed
Desire to identify with parent promoted
Desire for reciprocal compliance promoted
Threats to autonomy minimised (low power assertion/indirect and implicit messages employed/accompanied by humour)

Facilitates feelings of self-generation
Threats to autonomy minimised
Decoding required
Child's discounting patterns taken into account

Accurate perception of message (including content, implicative structure, parent's intention)

Acceptance of message

Internalisation

Source: Adapted from Grusec & Goodnow (1994), Figure 1, © by the American Psychological Association, reprinted with permission.

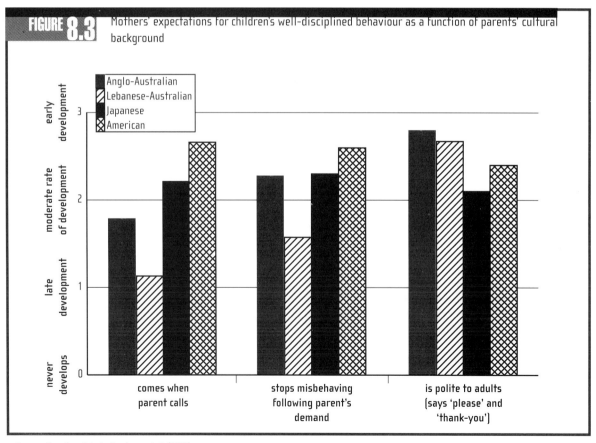

The quality of the emotional bond between parent and child can influence the effectiveness of the parent's disciplining and teaching efforts.

Cultural variations in parenting

Parents from different cultural backgrounds may hold distinctive ideas about the ideal outcomes for their children's development and about the ages at which important developmental milestones are likely to be achieved. In Chapter 6 we looked at cultural differences in parents' developmental timetables for verbal assertiveness and in Chapter 12 we examine variations in high school students' levels of academic achievement as a function of culture and parental preferences for one of Baumrind's four childrearing styles.

In addition, comparative research conducted in Australia, Japan and the United States by Jacqueline Goodnow and her colleagues (Goodnow et al., 1984) has revealed that parents' expectations about the ages at which resistance to disciplinary transgressions like impolite speech, disobedience and misbehaviour can be anticipated also varies with the parents' cultural background. These researchers studied Australian mothers who came from mainstream Anglo-Australian backgrounds together with a group of Lebanese-Australian mothers who had migrated to Sydney before their children were born. Japanese mothers in Japan and Anglo-American mothers in the United States were also included for comparison. The mothers were asked at what age they anticipated that their child would obey them and display polite speech to the mother and other adults. Results are shown in Figure 8.3.

FIGURE 8.3 Mothers' expectations for children's well-disciplined behaviour as a function of parents' cultural background

Source: Based on data in Goodnow et al. (1984).

Interestingly, the Lebanese-Australian mothers expected obedience and curtailment of misbehaviour at considerably later ages than mothers in all the other groups. This lenient attitude towards disobedience is likely to have implications for the mothers' use of the disciplinary practices examined above, and for the Lebanese-Australian children's adjustment to the early grades of primary school where teachers' norms are apt to align themselves with those of the Anglo-Australian mothers.

Earl Schaefer and Marianna Edgerton (1985) found that American parents who belonged to ethnic minority groups valued obedience and conformity in their children more than parents from the Anglo-American mainstream. Highly educated, middle-class members of most ethnic groups were also found to tolerate independence in children more, and to value a child's blind obedience correspondingly less, than working-class parents from the same ethnic background. The results of one study by Ailsa Burns, Ross Homel and Jacqueline Goodnow (1984) of 305 representative Sydney households containing at least one 9- to 11-year-old child likewise showed that family income, immigrant status and the overall qualities of the neighbourhood the family lived in and the schools the children went to were all predictors of the stress parents placed on obedience rather than self-assertion (see Chapter 6) in their offspring. In low-income families headed by a welfare recipient, lone mother or underemployed father, the values of inner direction and self-control were de-emphasised, perhaps because the family situation 'militate[d] against these virtues being greatly rewarded' (p. 234). Immigrant parents likewise placed less emphasis than mainstream Anglo-Australian parents on the 'good sense and sound judgment' seen to go along with an internalised conscience, while valuing conventional conformity, politeness, cleanliness and 'good manners' extremely highly.

Siblings and psychological development

In addition to these direct efforts, parents influence their children's development indirectly through their family planning decisions. Often, the strategy to become pregnant for the second time is guided by a goal of providing a companion and playmate for the first child. Even when subsequent offspring arrive unplanned, or via plans other than the hoped-for impact of a sibling upon the eldest child, the overall family constellation (consisting of a given number of brothers and sisters separated from one another by specified age groups) is likely to exert an important influence on each child's unique direction of psychological development (Parke & Kellum, 1994). Siblings can supply one another with comfort, companionship and valuable play and learning opportunities (e.g. see Chapter 7 for a discussion of the developmental benefits of engaging with a sibling in

When there are several children in the family, parents do not always treat each of them the same.

fantasy play). At the same time, the presence of a sibling can be a source of friction, conflict and jealousy. Parents may contribute to feelings of resentment between siblings when they practise favouritism, or *differential treatment*. This occurs when parents display different degrees of affection and disciplinary control towards the children in the family. For example, the eldest child might be punished more harshly than the youngest, or a mother might shower her only daughter with love and affection she fails to lavish on her sons. This can be painful, especially for the child who is slighted. Yet there are both social and cognitive advantages to learning how to settle disagreements with siblings when it comes to children's development of the levels of social understanding they will need in order to function effectively in peer groups and friendship networks in school, and siblings can provide moral support when confronting the outside world. Let us examine some of these sibling social influences in more detail.

Sibling rivalry and differential parenting

When a new baby arrives on the scene within a year or two of the elder brother or sister's birth, the older child's relationship with his or her parents is likely be disrupted, at least temporarily (Dunn, 1994). Mothers typically devote less time and attention to the older child, who may react with hostility to the new arrival. Based on a naturalistic observational study of preschoolers and their infant siblings, Judith Dunn (1994) reported that angry clashes between siblings reached frequencies as high as 56 outbursts per hour.

With time, however, these rivalrous exchanges are inclined to abate as the older child develops emotional self-regulation (see Chapter 7) and the young sibling becomes an active participant in play and everyday activity under the older child's direction (Dunn & Kendrick, 1982).

Deborah Vandell, Ann Minnett and John Santrock (1987) studied a group of 73 closely spaced sibling pairs between the ages of four and 11 years. As the pairs grew older, the young sibling was seen to gain steadily in power and status relative to the older brother or sister. Thus, by the end of middle childhood, being the eldest was no longer very distinctive from being the youngest. Instructions, teaching and direct help of the younger by the older brother or sister all declined over time, but pleasurable companionship and the positive emotional tone of siblings' involvement together increased with age. The researchers suggested that the new companion role developed during middle childhood could remain an important bond throughout the remainder of the lifespan.

Studies of siblings' interactions in adult life do reveal patterns of continued contact and emotional support, but also lifelong hostility and antagonism in some dyads. The latter outcome is especially probable among same-sexed sibling pairs who live in close geographical proximity. On the basis of a study of 65 North American siblings aged 25 to 93 years, John Santrock (1997) concluded: 'Sibling relationships in adulthood may be extremely close, apathetic or highly rivalrous' (p. 500).

Nicole Doherty and Judith Feeney (2003) studied attachment patterns in Australian adults' sibling relationships. In line with studies of lifelong continuity in attachment patterns, considered in Chapter 5, they found that sibling relationships have the potential to fulfil attachment functions in adult life, especially for females and adults who were not currently in a romantic relationship. Approximately half of the sister–sister dyads in their sample aged 16 to 90 years were genuinely attached to one another, as compared with one-third of the brother–brother dyads and one-quarter of the adult sibling dyads of mixed sex.

Parents who display comparable levels of affectionate responsiveness and disciplinary control towards all their children are more likely to have offspring that get along well with one another during middle childhood than parents who practise favouritism, or *differential parenting*, in which one sibling is given greater parental affection than another and allowed greater leeway in relation to disciplinary control.

As Patricia Noller, Judith Feeney and Candida Peterson (2001) explained:

> Siblings who perceive a brother or sister as gaining more favoured treatment than themselves may take this as a sign of parental hostility, or else as evidence of their own unworthiness for love … This process can be especially damaging to children who suffered insecure patterns of attachment to their parents during infancy. Furthermore, the fact that there is often a link between problems in the parents' marriage and parents' tendency to treat siblings differentially … suggests that adverse consequences of differential affection and control for children's development may be compounded by the direct effects of family discord. On the other hand, differential treatment by parents can also have positive effects on

children and on their relationships with siblings when this treatment reflects parental sensitivity to children's individuality and special needs. (p. 36)

The frequency and intensity of siblings' angry, hostile and argumentative interactions with one another is found to mirror the extent to which parents favour one sibling while displaying coolness and strictness towards another (Stocker, 1995). It seems that even the child who is favoured by parents has guilt, anger and resentment towards the less favoured sibling or siblings, erupting in rivalry from time to time. But the disfavoured sibling who receives disproportionately more disciplinary control and punitive sanctions from parents is, in addition, likely to express worry, anxiety and behaviour problems at school (Stocker, 1995).

Siblings as tutors

Children who have siblings have opportunities to learn from one another as well as from parents. Older siblings also have opportunities to take on the role of teacher while instructing their younger brothers and sisters in topics ranging from social relations, movies, music and television to academic skills.

The *sibling tutoring effect* (Zajonc & Hall, 1986) refers to the cognitive gains made by older brothers and sisters as a result of being allowed to teach new skills to younger siblings. Large-scale comparisons between the IQ scores of children from families of two or three reveal that first-born children with siblings score consistently higher than only children from similarly intellectually stimulating home backgrounds. Youngest children also lag behind the middle or oldest children in a family. The explanation seems to be that: 'Acting as a teacher helps a child's intellectual growth, but the only child never gets that opportunity' (Zajonc & Hall, 1986, p. 49).

Siblings and social cognition

Older siblings learn nurturance and empathy by being allowed to care for their infant brothers and sisters (Dunn, 1983). One observational study of tribal African children's caregiving strategies during their frequent periods of being in sole charge of their infant siblings revealed an even wider range of nurturant and teaching behaviours by these children than by their parents or extended adult kin in the same families (Whiting & Whiting, 1975). Parents' and older siblings' rates of scolding, helping and giving food and attention to the babies were quite similar. But brothers and sisters played with and teased the infants more, and were also more punitive than aunts, uncles, parents or grandparents.

In Western cultures, children's rapid development of social cognitive skill is partly a product of their opportunities to play and converse with younger and older siblings. Recall the discussion in Chapter 7 of children's acquisition of a *theory of mind*, enabling them to understand other people's mental states and use them to predict behaviour even when the person's

The development of social understanding and theory of mind may proceed more quickly for children like these with a sibling than for the only child.

increased in proportion to the variety of ages and conversational perspectives provided by the sibling constellation, with the presence of older brothers and sisters at home proving especially beneficial (Ruffman, Perner, Naito, Parkin & Clements, 1998). A close mutual understanding is likely to grow up among siblings in a family, and this is likely to motivate their interest in, and awareness of, the contents of one another's minds. Perhaps this shared awareness, fostered through play, conflict and conversation with siblings, explains the rapid development of concepts of false belief, as confirmed in five studies with varied populations of children from varied cultures, educational and family backgrounds. Sibling children may develop a theory of mind more quickly than only children because they have richer and more varied social experiences at home, especially in fantasy play. Sibling rivalry and conflict may also be beneficial, in line with Jean Piaget's (1970) suggestion that children's arguments teach them to appreciate the cognitive perspectives of others, and to effectively articulate their own (see Chapter 7).

However, if the sibling is too young to play or too old to be likely to interact in a distinctively different manner from a parent, no benefit is likely to arise for social cognition. This prediction was supported by the results of a recent study of Australian 3- to 5-year-olds who displayed advanced theory-of-mind development and had at least one sibling aged over 12 months and under 13 years. As shown in Figure 8.4, those whose nearest siblings were infants under one year old, or adolescents and young adults,

beliefs are out of line with reality. This important social-cognitive skill develops more quickly in children who have siblings than in only children who have no one apart from their parents to play and interact with at home (Perner, Ruffman & Leekam, 1994). Furthermore, even after differences in language ability are statistically controlled, children who have at least one younger or older sibling are found to develop a theory of mind at a significantly earlier age than only children (Jenkins & Astington, 1996).

The results of four separate studies of false belief involving a total of 265 normally developing children aged three to five years in Japan and the UK showed that children's rates of mastering theory of mind

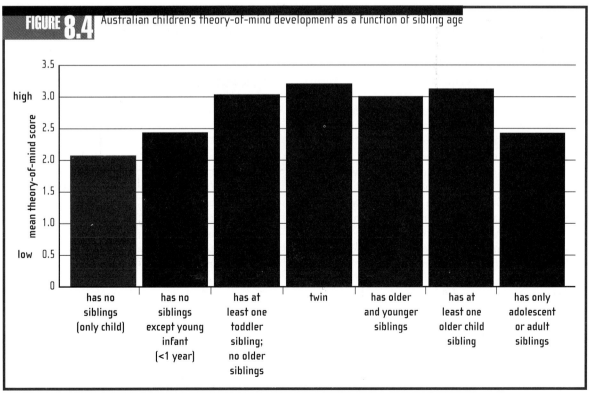

FIGURE 8.4 Australian children's theory-of-mind development as a function of sibling age

Source: Based on data in Peterson (2000).

performed no differently from only children (Peterson, 2000).

The only child

Despite not gaining the social understanding that can derive from play and conversation with siblings quite as rapidly, only children do eventually master a theory of mind during the preschool or early primary school period, and their overall rates of cognitive development are not markedly different from those of children from similar backgrounds who have siblings. Nor are any lasting social, emotional or personality deficits found to result from growing up without any brothers or sisters.

One ambitious longitudinal study followed some 3000 American children from high school into mature adulthood (Pines, 1981). The results showed that those adults who had grown up as only children continued to do better across a range of indicators of social and mental health than those adults who had siblings, even after moving out of the family environment. Adult only children earned higher than average scores in IQ tests, just as they had in childhood. They also had more distinguished academic achievements to their credit by the age of 29, and were rated as more mature, more socially sensitive and more cultivated artistically and intellectually than adults who had been reared with siblings.

Perhaps only children gain intellectual advantages from the extra stimulation and attention their parents are free to expend on them. But do they end up becoming 'spoiled', selfish or undisciplined as a result? To answer this question, Paul Amato (1987) compared socialisation patterns and adolescent developmental outcomes in two selected groups of Melbourne families. The first group had had only one child in the household throughout childhood and adolescence. The second group consisted of a matched set of two-child families of similar economic backgrounds. Amato compared the older offspring in the two-child homes with the only children, in order to control as far as possible for the advantages due to extra parental time, attention and financial resources available in one-child families. Across a large number of statistical comparisons, very few differences emerged between the Australian only child and the corresponding older child in a family of two. In fact, the two groups appeared identical when it came to parental punishment patterns, children's level of independent initiative or self-reliance and the number of household chores and duties the offspring performed. The only clear difference was a tendency by mothers (but not fathers) to exert less control over only children. Amato concluded that the notion of the only child as spoiled, selfish, temperamental or maladjusted was a myth, and that for the average only child growing up in an Australian family today the odds of encountering problems were no greater than for any other children of similar social backgrounds and family circumstances who have siblings in their lives.

In China, the one-child policy to curb the population explosion has resulted in concerns over only children growing up spoiled or selfish, similar to the unfounded myths about only children prevailing in the West. But in China, likewise, the results of systematic research comparisons have shown that only children have personality characteristics that are completely on a par with Chinese children who have siblings. Furthermore, Chinese only children tend to weigh more and be more advanced in verbal abilities than second and third borns with an older sibling (Falbo & Poston, 1993). Possibly better health care and more intensive parental language input may help to explain these effects.

Personality and the self-concept

In Chapter 7 we examined the growth of self-esteem in preschoolers. During middle childhood there is further development in the child's awareness of self as a psychological entity. William Damon and Daniel Hart (1988) explored age differences in the self-concept by asking children aged from four to 15 years to describe themselves in a few words. They discovered a developmental progression, as shown in Table 8.2, from simple, superficial and categorical descriptions through comparative judgments to a highly differentiated self-concept that took note of the implications of personal characteristics for social relationships and friendship.

Industry versus inferiority

Self-concept development is also bound up with the core personality conflict that propels psychological development through the period of middle childhood, according to Erik Erikson's theory (1968a; see also Chapter 2). Over the period from age six to

TABLE 8.2	Developmental changes in children's self-concept	
Age	Type of self-concept	Example
4 to 7 years	Concrete, physical or categorical description	I have blue eyes. I play football.
8 to 11 years	Comparative social assessment	I'm taller than most others in my class. I am good at reading but useless at maths.
12 to 15 years	Nuanced interpersonal implications	I understand people, so friends come to me with their problems. I'm very shy so I have trouble making friends.

age 11, children in primary school gain many opportunities to work hard to achieve academic, social, creative and athletic goals. Within the unconscious personality, this promotes a feeling of *industry*, or a work ethic, according to Erikson's theory. At the same time, children in school are continually in a position of being forced to compare their achievements and levels of industrious application to scholastic and extracurricular activities with those of classmates of their own age. Depending on the outcomes of these evaluations, feelings of relative superiority or inferiority to peers may emerge, with implications for the self-concept and, according to Erikson, for a realistic appraisal of the limits on what can be achieved through individual, competitive work, relative to the greater goals to be achieved through cooperative achievement with peers. As Erikson (1968a) explained:

> Since industry involves doing things beside and with others, a first sense of division of labor and of differential opportunity … develops at this time. Therefore, the configurations of culture and the manipulations basic to the *prevailing technology* must reach meaningfully into school life, supporting in every child a feeling of competence – that is, the free exercise of dexterity and intelligence in the completion of tasks unimpaired by an infantile sense of inferiority. This is the lasting basis for cooperative participation in productive adult life. (p. 126)

Peers as developmental influences

The peer group offers children the opportunity to achieve recognition and respect among a group of equals. Within the family, the child's status is always at least partly subordinate to that of the parents. Sibling status is likewise influenced as much by age as by the individual's own temperament and behaviour. Nor do children choose their parents or their siblings, even though some occasionally claim to wish they had such a choice. But in the peer group of children of roughly the same age who are not bound together by kinship ties, it is largely the child's own behaviour which determines liking and social approval or disapproval and dislike. Among peers, the child's status as a leader or follower, as popular or an isolated or rejected child, depends primarily on his or her social skills and on social behaviour. Being an 'enemy' or a 'friend' is a powerful punishment or reward. Thus, social behaviour that wins peer approval is maintained by reinforcement (see Chapter 2). The pain of being rejected by peers is illustrated in Box 8.2.

Measuring a child's status in the peer group: The sociometric technique

Research into a child's status in a group of peers has typically employed a technique known as *sociometric measurement*. Using this procedure, children who belong to an established group of peers (e.g. a class-

BOX 8.2 A case in point
The pain of social exclusion

When Louise was eight years old, her contact with two peers in the neighbourhood gave her a lesson in social relations. Her father recorded the incident in his diary.

> **1 January 1957.** *Melissa doesn't like sharing her friends with others and often when she and Louise are playing together the two of them will make it plain to another child that he or she is not wanted. I have tried, by reminding Louise how she feels when this is done to her, to get her to welcome the newcomer but she fears that, if she does, she will be the one left out in the cold. This happened to her twice yesterday. The first time she had the good sense to go off and read and in a short time the others were beside her eager to share in what she was doing. The second time she wouldn't try doing something on her own and came home in tears instead.*

© Peterson, 1974, reproduced with permission

In this extract, the pain of peer rejection is vividly depicted. Indeed, its sting was so sharp that it apparently superseded a lesson Louise's father had tried to teach her. She rejected his suggestion that she welcome another child into the group on the grounds that it would meet with Melissa's disapproval. Thus, the fear of peer rejection can serve as a powerful motive force in social development.

room at school, or a scout troop) are interviewed individually to determine who they do and don't like. Sometimes these questions are asked directly: ('Name someone you really like to play with.' 'Who do you like best?' 'Now tell me the name of someone in your class that you really do not like at all.'). In other versions of the task, specific behavioural indicators of liking and dislike may be elicited instead: ('Who would you like to invite to your next birthday party?' 'Who do you usually sit beside at lunchtime?'). A child's discomfort at being asked to articulate dislike for a peer can be minimised by using the 'class-play' variant of the sociometric procedure. Here, pupils suggest members of their class to occupy various type-cast roles such as 'someone who is very bossy', 'someone who can't get along with others' or 'the loner'. Similarly, with very young groups of children (such as preschoolers), the problem of not knowing everyone's name can be overcome by using a photograph of the class and having children point to the face.

Positive sociometric nominations are the votes a child gets when peers are asked who they like and want to play with. Negative nominations are choices of an individual in response to questions about disliked or antisocial behaviour ('Who is always hitting others and spoiling their games?'). After all members of the peer group have been interviewed and have given three nominations each in response to 'likes best' and 'likes least' questions, the total number of nominations of each type for each child in the group is derived. Based on these totals, children can be assigned to one of four distinct sociometric classifications: popular, neglected, controversial or rejected, as explained in Table 8.3.

As Table 8.3 indicates, being unpopular is not simply the opposite of being *popular* or having lots of 'likes best' nominations. There are *rejected* children who are unpopular in terms of active dislike by members of their peer group, but there are also *neglected* children who are unpopular in the sense of having very few positive sociometric nominations although they are not actively disliked. Never being chosen either as a desired or an undesirable companion, they are merely isolated or ignored. Perhaps an even more intriguing social situation is that of the *controversial* child who earns an exceptionally large number of both 'like' and 'dislike' votes from peers. While some playmates actively seek out this child as a companion, others are equally adamant in their desire to avoid the child's company.

Are sociometric classifications reliable?

A considerable body of research evidence has accumulated over many decades of measuring children's peer popularity using the sociometric technique. Taken collectively, the results of many studies have shown that a child's status as a popular, controversial, neglected or rejected member of the peer group is likely to remain stable over time (Dodge, 1983; Hartup, 1987; Rubin et al., 1998), stability is greatest in well-established peer groups, and older children tend to give more consistent responses to repeated sociometric testing than preschoolers. Classroom groups with a stable school setting yield more consistent sociometric results from longitudinal measurement than such *ad hoc* groups as day-camps, sporting associations or other groups of relatively recent acquaintance or infrequent contact with one another.

In addition, stability is greatest at the extremes of the popularity to rejection continuum than in the middle of the sociometric hierarchy. Thus, a child disliked by everyone is unlikely to emerge as popular at a later date, while a child who has once been highly popular will probably never become isolated or rejected. All in all, these results indicate that children recognise friendship hierarchies in their peer groups, and that sociometric measures of these hierarchies are reliable.

A more interesting question, especially in light of the powerful influences that group acceptance or rejection can exert on the individual child's development, is what qualities conspire to make a child popular with peers.

The correlates of peer acceptance and rejection

Some of the correlates of children's social acceptance, social rejection, controversial status and social isolation that have been discovered using sociometric techniques may seem unfortunate, unfair and largely irrational. It has been found, for example, that a child with an unusual first name (e.g. Norman, Archibald or Beryl) is less likely to be sociometrically popular than a peer whose first name (e.g. Mark, Steven or Allison) is common within their social cohort (Perry & Bussey, 1984). Similarly, a child with a trim, muscular body build is more likely to score high in sociometric acceptance then one who is obese or abnormally thin, and an attractive facial appearance is another observed correlate of popularity over which children themselves have little control (Langlois & Downs, 1979). Unpopular children (whether neglected or actively rejected) also display poorer academic performance and lower marks in school than their popular peers (Van Lieschout & Van Aken, 1987).

On the other hand, many of the attributes that show the strongest and most consistent correlations with peer popularity make intuitive good sense. Children who have outgoing, friendly temperaments and a good command of social skills are popular because they are skilled at participating in, and facilitating, harmonious social relationships within the peer group (Putallaz, 1983). When tested in novel social situations, children who are highly popular within their own familiar group of peers are apt to display advanced skills for establishing contact with unfamiliar playmates. Having broken the ice, children who are popular are also exceptionally adept at maintaining friendly interaction in novel groups through the use of social skills such as cooperative turn-taking, volunteering appropriate information ('My favourite sport is football') and expressing a friendly interest in others (Putallaz, 1983).

Some additional correlates of popularity and unpopularity in children's peer groups during early and middle childhood are shown in Table 8.4. Many of these characteristics are true of popular and unpopular children from early childhood through adolescence, though there is some developmental change. In a study of Sydney school children aged five

TABLE 8.3	The child's sociometric status in four categories		
		Positive (likes) nominations	
		Many	Few or none
Negative (dislikes) nominations	Many	Controversial	Rejected
	Few or none	Popular	Neglected (or 'socially isolated')

Popular	Neglected
Outgoing, sociable, friendly	Shy
High levels of cooperative play	Prefers adult to peer companionship
Frequently expresses affection and approval towards peers	Frequently plays alone
Is an effective group leader	Not aggressive
Has good social understanding	Withdraws in the face of others' aggression
Has advanced theory-of-mind development	Lacks skills for initiating or maintaining social interaction
Willing to share	
Not aggressive	
Controversial	**Rejected**
Displays high levels of attention-seeking	High in antisocial aggression
High activity level	High activity level
Exhibits high rates of both prosocial and antisocial aggression	High in disruptive behaviour
Frequently initiates helpful and friendly overtures towards selected peers	Slow development of theory of mind
Displays sound sociocognitive understanding (though possibly Machiavellian at times)	Is talkative but inclined towards egocentric or argumentative speech
	Lacks social understanding

to 11 years Ailsa Burns and Jacqueline Goodnow (1985) found that (a) a caring attitude, (b) avoiding aggression, (c) availability, and (d) common interests were equally important as features of friendship throughout middle childhood. But changes arose in other criteria for defining a person as a friend.

Australian children aged five to nine years saw having fun together as one of the most important criteria for becoming a person's friend. But with increasing cognitive (see Chapter 9) and social maturity, the superficial sharing of good times diminished in importance relative to intellectual and personality qualities as criteria for selecting friends and sustaining friendship. Mutual understanding was insignificant at age five, but equal in importance to the sharing of activities by the age of 11.

Loneliness versus unpopularity

Being alone and being lonely can be two quite different things, in childhood as well as adulthood. Nor is loneliness in any way synonymous with social rejection. Children who are actively disliked or rejected by their peers very often possess exactly the opposite traits from children who score high in peer popularity. Rejected children are likely to use aggressive or hostile methods to try to gain entry into new peer groups, and to show levels of social skill, empathy and interpersonal understanding that are all well

below the average for their age group (Dodge, 1983). But neglected or socially isolated children who spend much of their time alone without close peer companionship are not necessarily deviant in any of these ways.

Instead, the neglected child may simply be too shy, quiet and unassuming to attract either favourable or unfavourable notice (Asher & Hymel, 1981). But isolation can be as painful to a child as active rejection by others. In fact, when Steven Asher, Peter Renshaw and Shelley Hymel (1982) asked a group of 522 mid-western American children aged eight to 12 years how often they felt lonely, they discovered that approximately 10 per cent of each age group felt so lonely and isolated from their peers as to be extremely unhappy. Furthermore, not all the children who suffered severe loneliness would be picked out by a teacher using an objective sociometric measure to identify children with special social needs. In fact, some sociometrically popular children in this study reported (a) feeling alone, (b) believing others disliked them, and (c) feeling rejected or 'left out of things'.

Conversely, some children rated as socially neglected and socially rejected according to the sociometric procedure were highly satisfied with their social position in the peer group and not at all lonely. Asher and his colleagues suggested that 'some

Not all children who play alone feel lonely. Some may prefer solitary pursuits over group activities.

unpopular children simply may be unaware of their poor acceptance by peers' (p. 1463). Others may be well aware of their status but feel quite content to be left alone.

A longitudinal study of Western Australian schoolgirls by Marjorie Tidman and Peter Renshaw (1987) highlighted some of the factors associated with these variations in attitude. One girl, who had consistently been the most withdrawn and socially isolated member of her peer group from grade one to grade six of primary school, was seen to experience 'a crisis period of isolation and anxiety during her middle primary school years' (p. 197). However, by the age of ten she had emerged from this period of unhappiness as an extremely well-adjusted and independent child whose decision not to pursue the goals of peer group acceptance seemed to be self-chosen. The researchers described her at this age as:

> A quiet, yet strong-minded individual, actively making sense of her world and pursuing her own well-defined friendship goals. She has quite consciously rejected the goal of seeking wide group acceptance and sought instead to develop a single intensive friendship. Unless she manifests a desire to be a more active member of the peer group, direct intervention may disrupt the equilibrium she has deliberately sought to maintain. (p. 1975)

Peter Renshaw and Peter Brown (1993) studied loneliness longitudinally in a group of 128 children in Perth, Western Australia, over a one-year period. The results supported an additive model of loneliness. Children who lost friends over the year of the study were more likely to report feeling lonely at its end than those who either gained friends or maintained the same number of friendships throughout the year.

Similarly, children who began the study with relatively low levels of sociometric peer group popularity, and those whose popularity declined as the study progressed, reported more loneliness than other children, even when they had managed to retain one or more close friends.

But intimate friendship with one close 'chum' also counteracted loneliness throughout the study somewhat independently of group popularity. In other words, even a single friend could offset loneliness if the friendship was both intimate and mutual, whereas children with no close friends were apt to report loneliness even when they scored high in general popularity within the peer group. On the other hand, popular children with no close, mutual friends were somewhat less lonely than equally friendless children who were of low sociometric status. Renshaw and Brown reached the following conclusion on the basis of the overall pattern of results from this longitudinal study:

> Taken together, the findings suggest that loneliness in middle childhood is a stable phenomenon located in a complex web of interrelated aspects of social functioning. (p. 1282)

Compensating for peer group rejection: Mixed-age peer groups and mutual friendships

Children who are unpopular with their classroom peers in school can sometimes achieve a more positive peer experience when playing with mixed-age peer groups in the neighbourhood, or when they have a mutual friendship with one other child.

When children are allowed to mix with much older and much younger peers, there is often more nurturance, sharing and cooperation and less aggressive hostility than in same-age groups. David Perry and Kay Bussey (1984) described how play with much younger peers could assist in overcoming the tendency to avoid social contact by children with few friends of their own age. In this study, a group of children who had been picked out as isolates on a sociometric test were given a total of three to four hours' exposure to younger playmates. After this experience, the former social isolates were found to play much more effectively with classmates of their own age. Thus their social encounters with the younger child had proved therapeutic. Their subsequent rates of praising, greeting, cooperating, laughing and nurturing their same-age peers all increased to a greater extent than among isolates who had been given similar play therapy with playmates of their own age.

Perry and Bussey put forward two contrasting explanations for the exceptional gains arising from contact with younger children:

> Possibly interaction with a younger peer constitutes a gentle introduction into social intercourse, allowing withdrawn and frightened children to build up self-confidence as they establish patterns of nonthreatening, mutually reinforcing interaction. Or maybe therapy with a younger peer

Even children as young as 4 or 5 can sustain mutual friendships that remain stable over time.

Playing ball games can be fun for both sexes but traditional sex-role stereotypes prescribe them for boys rather than girls.

works because the withdrawn child can assume some degree of leadership ... can behave directively and assertively and can see these efforts reinforced in the form of compliance from the younger peer. (p. 327)

A mutual friendship arises when one child (e.g. Billy) nominates as a 'best friend' another child (e.g. Alex) who also nominates Billy among his top three friendship choices. When these mutual friendships remain stable over time, as even the friendships of well-acquainted preschoolers are likely to do (Peterson & Siegal, 2002), they may provide children who are neglected or rejected by the peer group at large with compensatory opportunities to acquire useful social skills. In forging and maintaining a friendship, children are required to display at least a basic level of social understanding and enough skill in resolving conflict and sustaining a pleasant interaction to make the friendship worth supporting by both parties. In fact, research evidence shows that children who are rejected by the peer group as a whole, yet have one stable mutual friendship, score significantly higher on measures of social cognition, theory-of-mind development (see Chapter 7) and moral understanding (see page 276) than rejected children without any mutual friends (Peterson & Siegal, 2002).

The development of sex roles

Socially defined sex roles (also known as 'gender roles') describe the stereotypic patterns of attitudes, personality and behaviour that distinguish males from females as social entities at certain ages within a particular culture during a particular phase in that culture's history. These roles vary from one age group to the next (so that wearing a necktie or lipstick is appropriate for adult males and females, respectively, but not for boys and girls) and are highly culturally specific.

Owing to their social roots, most social sex roles have no necessary biological preconditions. For example, wearing a skirt, lacquering the fingernails, comforting a doll or kicking a football are all behaviours that both boys and girls can effectively perform without prejudice or advantage from the presence of an XY or XX chromosome complement (see Chapter 3). Yet deeply ingrained cultural traditions prescribe that many behaviours like these are unacceptable for one sex but highly desirable for the other. Cultural variations in gender roles indicate how arbitrary these social codes can be. For example, in traditional Aboriginal culture last century, swearing was considered acceptable among adult women but was a breach of etiquette for children and adult males (Bates, 1966).

The term *gender identity*, which is quite distinct from the socially defined gender role, describes a person's sense of themselves as a biological male or female person, quite separate from the individual's allegiance to, or repudiation of, any particular features of the socially defined sex role (Bem, 1987). The distinction between these two aspects of the self-concept can be seen in cases of adult men and women who feel so confident of their basic biologically ordained masculinity or femininity (gender identity) that they can comfortably adopt such non-traditional social sex roles as househusband or corporate businesswoman (Hall, Lamb & Perlmutter, 1982).

Sex roles as broad social constructs can also be distinguished from sex-role myths and stereotypes which consist of simplified generalisations or global expectations about male and female behaviour ('women love to cook'; 'boys are adventurous') which are too general to be fully accurate. As with stereotypes based on age or race, these distort or oversimplify reality. While some sex-role stereotypes may be relatively innocuous, the term is often used in a negative sense to denote harmful myths or sexist beliefs which degrade one sex or the other, or serve as rationales for unfair treatment. For example, as Patricia Edgar and H. McPhee (1974) noted of some of the sex-role stereotypes they saw on Australian commercial television:

> TV commercials are an affront to men, women and children. Grown-up men buy powerful cars, drink lots of beer, kiss girls who are pretty enough, thin enough or fragrant enough to warrant it … grown-up women diet for love and approval, serve tough meat and have their husbands rush out the door despite the pathetic plea 'it's your favourite pudding'. (p. 42)

The socialisation of children into gender roles

As children grow up, increasingly boys and girls are treated differently in ways that are likely to dispose them to adopt traditional masculine or feminine gender roles. For example, at birth a child is apt to be called by a gender-specific first name and may be clothed in pink or blue so that relatives and strangers will instantly recognise the clothed infant as belonging to one gender and not the other. Parents' perceptions of their newborn infants also reflect gender-linked expectations, with baby girls seen as 'tiny', 'pretty' or 'cute', while boys of the same objective weight and length are seen as 'big', 'coarse-featured' and 'strong' (Rubin, Provenzano & Luria, 1974). Unfamiliar adults also spend more time cuddling, talking with, singing to and giving toys to babies they believe are female than when the same infant is introduced to them as a boy (Blakemore, 1981).

During middle childhood, differential treatment of the sexes continues and intensifies. Boys in primary school, for example, are given more freedom than girls to roam the neighbourhood across a wider terrain and without an adult chaperone (Sidorowicz & Lunney, 1980; Cunningham, 1987), as shown in Figure 8.5.

At school, differential social treatment of the sexes is also the norm, even today, in most Australian and New Zealand classrooms as well as in North America and Europe (Liben & Signorella, 1993). The same is true in many families, especially when there are siblings of both sexes to compare and contrast. Even the seemingly private and personal environment of a bedroom may reflect the cultural differentiation of the sexes, as the activity in Box 8.3 illustrates.

Using a group of 96 North American preschoolers as subjects, Harriet Rheingold and Kay Cook (1975) found that the furnishings, décor and toys in boys' and girls' rooms were strongly stereotyped by sex. Compared with girls, boys possessed more toy machines, vehicles and military equipment, more educational toys and art materials, more live and toy animals and plants, more sports equipment and more scientific toys designed to enhance reasoning about space and time (clocks, magnets, telescopes, chemistry sets, outer space models and so on). With fewer toys overall, the girls' rooms outstripped boys' only in the number of dolls and toy domestic appliances. Rheingold and Cook suggested several possible ways that these differences in the home environment might contribute to children's sex-role development:

> The rooms of children constitute a not inconsiderable part of their environment. Here they go to bed and wake up; here they spend some part of every day. Their rooms determine the things they

Traditional sex-role stereotypes depict little boys as more adventurous than little girls.

By performing chores around the house, children acquire sex-role socialisation.

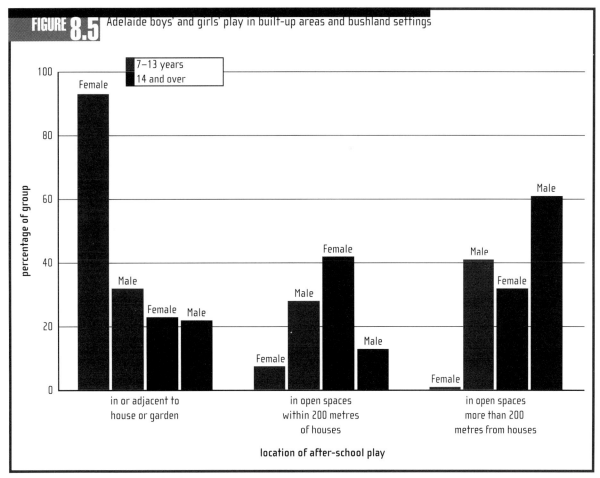

FIGURE 8.5 Adelaide boys' and girls' play in built-up areas and bushland settings

Source: Based on data in Cunningham (1987).

see and find for amusement and instruction. That their rooms have an effect on their present and subsequent behaviour can be assumed; a standard is set that may in part account for some differences in the behaviour of girls and boys. Clear in the findings of this study was the extent to which the boys were provided objects that encouraged activities directed away from the home – toward sports, cars, animals and the military – and the girls, objects that encouraged activities directed toward the home – keeping house and caring for children. (p. 463)

Domestic chores are also a route through which older children and adolescents are socialised into gender roles. Many household jobs are gender stereotyped. For example, it is less common for mothers than fathers to perform car repairs, plumbing maintenance or minor carpentry around the home, while wives more often than husbands do the cooking and cleaning, and are much more likely than other family members to be the ones who get up at night to sick children, and to wash the bathroom, including the toilet (Goodnow & Bowes, 1994; see Chapter 14). Consequently, children are apt to acquire sex roles by being asked to do jobs around the house. When Jacqueline Goodnow and Pamela Warton (1991) quizzed a group of Sydney young people about what

household chores they did, traditional sex stereotyping was clearly evident, as shown in Figure 8.6.

Television and sex-typing

Most Australian children spend many hours each week watching television, and this can be an important source of input contributing to their development of sex-typed attitudes and behaviours. With a

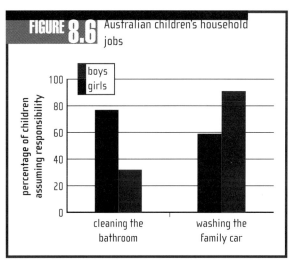

FIGURE 8.6 Australian children's household jobs

Source: Based on data in Goodnow & Warton (1991).

BOX 8.3 Activity suggestion
Conducting an inventory of a child's bedroom

Aim. The aim of this exercise is to provide a taste of the style of research pioneered by Rheingold & Cook (1975). For this activity you will need access to two children's bedrooms. Be sure to obtain parental consent to visit the rooms as well as the occupants' permission if they are old enough to understand.

Subjects. Select one boy and one girl of the same birth order (only child, older of two, etc.) and roughly similar ages (both must be over two and under eight years old) and comparable family economic background. To be eligible, each child should have his or her own room, not shared with a sibling.

Procedure. After obtaining parental permission, visit each child's bedroom without the child being present. Record the presence or absence and number of each of the items on the inventory checklist below. For items in quantities of ten or more, you may estimate in multiples of ten.

Inventory checklist

___ Male ___ Female Child ___ years old Birth order ___

Furnishings	Present	Quantity
Animal or fantasy (e.g. outer space) furnishings		
Ruffled, lacy furnishings		
Dressing table, mirror, accessories		
Brightly coloured furnishings		
Pastel-coloured furnishings		
Large movable furnishings (e.g. cubby house, rocking horse)		
Paintings, posters or wall charts		
Desk or work table		

Large toys	Present	Estimated quantity
Musical instruments		
Television set		
Computer		
Radio/record player		
Bicycle/pedal car/etc.		
Large domestic toys (e.g. toy stove, fridge, washer, etc.)		
Doll's house		
Doll's equipment (e.g. pram, stroller, change table, etc.)		
Garden sets, wheelbarrow, etc.		
Train set		
Motor depots (e.g. toy garage, rocket launching pad, car track, etc.)		

Books	Present	Estimated quantity
Picture reading books		
Text-only reading books		
Colouring books		
Cut-out books		
School books		
Comic books		

Military toys	Present	Estimated quantity
Guns, rifles, water pistols		
Swords, knives		
Police gear (handcuffs, helmets, shields, etc.)		

Others (specify)

Dolls/animals/robots	Present	Estimated quantity
Baby dolls		
Child dolls		
Dolls' clothes		
Teen/adult dolls		
Stuffed cloth animals		
Plastic/metal animals		
Space/transformer/robots		
Soldiers/fantasy figures		

Others (specify)

Sports or games equipment	Present	Estimated quantity
Balls		
Computer games		
Swimming gear		
Roller skates, skateboard		
Darts, ring toss		
Board games (chess, etc.)		

Others (specify)

Art equipment	Present	Estimated quantity
Painting sets (complete sets of 5++ colours)		
Texta/crayon sets (number of complete sets of 10++ colours)		
Clay		
Weaving loom, textile sets, knitting wool sets, etc.		

Others (specify)

Construction toys	Present	Estimated quantity
Block sets (20++ pieces)		
Lego sets (20++ pieces)		
Meccano/metal construction sets		
Carpentry tools		

Others (specify)

Toy vehicles	Present	Estimated quantity
Large cars, trucks (over 8 cm high)		
Small cars, trucks		
Aeroplanes, rockets, spaceships		

Others (specify)

few exceptions, the sex roles typically portrayed on television tend to be highly traditional and stereotyped. For example, Kevin Durkin and his colleagues (Mazzella, Durkin, Cerini and Buralli, 1992) examined sex-role stereotyping in contemporary Australian television commercials, analysing 281 commercials broadcast on prime-time evening television. The results indicated that men and women were portrayed in accordance with a narrow range of highly traditional sex-role stereotypes.

In the first place, men were overrepresented in Australian television advertisements and were depicted as mature, unemotional and career-oriented. They played roles in advertisements as expert authority figures wearing the trappings of success who provided objective, logical reasons for their purchases of consumer products. Women, on the other hand, were presented as young, flighty, domestic creatures who purchased inexpensive products for no particularly logical reason. The researchers concluded that Australian television advertising is no different in terms of sex roles from that broadcast in the northern hemisphere. Sadly, despite vigorous public debate, there appears to be no evidence of a decline in sex-role stereotyping on commercial television at the present time. According to Durkin and his colleagues (1992):

> The present analysis indicates that Australian television commercials conform to widely criticized patterns within Western television, and present a highly stereotyped picture of males and females. (p. 258)

Partly, perhaps, because they watch less television, Aboriginal children growing up in rural Australia have been found to be less rigidly con-strained by traditional sex-role stereotypes than their Anglo counterparts (Barry, 1978), as shown in Figure 8.7. However, the beliefs, toy preferences and play patterns of Aboriginal children become more restrictive and sex-stereotyped with increasing age, matching a similar trend for urban Anglo-Australian children.

The cognitive development of gender understanding

Children's development of a social sex role also has a cognitive component. If they are deliberately to adopt the mannerisms, attitudes and practices of a traditionally masculine or feminine role, children must be able to identify themselves and other people as male or female. The implications of adopting masculine or feminine roles will be different for children who believe gender is as temporary as being a 6-year-old or a Grade 1 pupil from those who are aware that biological gender is a permanent personal characteristic. These cognitive aspects of gender develop in a predictable sequence, beginning at the end of toddlerhood. Collectively, a cognitive awareness of gender as a permanent personal characteristic is known as *gender constancy*.

Gender constancy, the realisation that one's biological gender as male or female is unchangeable, short of something as drastic as a sex-change operation, develops through three stages:

1. Gender identity
2. Gender stability
3. Gender consistency.

Vigorous physical activity, such as surfing, is more consistent with the masculine than the feminine sex-role stereotype.

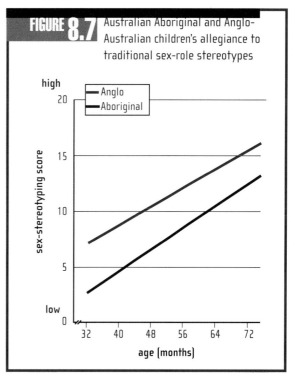

FIGURE 8.7 Australian Aboriginal and Anglo-Australian children's allegiance to traditional sex-role stereotypes

Source: Barry (1978), reproduced with permission.

Words like 'boy', 'girl', 'man' or 'lady' do not usually enter a child's vocabulary until age two or later. Even then, these words may be used without a clear awareness of their relevance to biological masculinity or femininity. In one pioneering study, Spencer Thompson (1975) found that, until the age of 30 months, less than half of a group of normally developing toddlers could correctly label themselves 'boy' or 'girl', a finding that was subsequently replicated in several studies by Beverley Fagot (1985).

Between the ages of 27 and 36 months, most children learn to give the correct answer to the central question of gender identity: 'Are you a boy or a girl?' (Bem, 1989). When this happens, other obvious social consequences of superficial masculinity and femininity may also be clearly understood. Most 3-year-olds know, for example, that 'John' is a boy's name and that a male isn't called 'Alice'. They believe that girls talk a lot, cry, and help their mothers to clean the house, whereas boys are loud, mow the grass, hit people and can grow up to be a doctor, a senator or a 'boss'. They also recognise certain toys and other objects as appropriate only for females (dolls, dolls' furniture, skirts, cosmetics) and others as being mainly for boys (trucks, trains, weapons).

Despite being able to apply the word 'girl' accurately to those who are fully clothed in sex-appropriate ways, many preschoolers aged three to five years have surprising difficulty in doing the same for a naked infant or child. In fact, when Ronald and Juliet Goldman (1982) asked a sample of 5-year-olds in Australia, Sweden, the UK and the US 'How can anyone know whether a newborn baby is a boy or a girl?', the replies given by many children in all four countries betrayed considerable confusion. For example, one 5-year-old said: 'The doctor tells you. He looks through a magnifying glass at their eyes and he can tell by the eyebrows' (p. 282).

Replies like this betray the absence of another concept that is critical to a fully mature understanding of sex roles, namely the concept of gender constancy.

GENDER STABILITY

Most adults realise that, short of major surgery, a person's biological sex, evident at birth, is theirs for life. This notion of the stability of biological gender over time is not obvious to young children. Perhaps this is not so surprising. Children are surrounded by other human characteristics, like height, hair colour and the ability to grow a beard, which can and do change with age. They know of many other changes which, though not inevitable, are readily possible. They are told that they will probably marry eventually and have children, that their parents will become grandparents. Many toddlers have already had the opportunity to witness the transformation of the family kitten or puppy into a mature cat or dog. In addition, they are allowed to choose whether to become teachers or lawyers or firefighters or airline pilots when they grow up. So why should gender alone remain invulnerable to change?

Lawrence Kohlberg (1966, p. 95) was struck by the young child's failure to view gender as a fixed and unchangeable human attribute when he overheard the following conversation between two 4-year-olds.

Johnny: 'I'm going to be a pilot when I grow up.'
Jimmy: 'When I grow up, I'll be a Mommy.'
Johnny: 'No, you can't – you have to be a Daddy.'
Jimmy: 'No, I'm going to be a Mommy.'
Johnny: 'You're not a girl so you can't be a Mommy.'
Jimmy: 'Yes, I can.'

In other words, 4-year-old Jimmy did not have a concept known as *gender stability*. He did not realise that his gender could not be changed. He probably knew that he would eventually be transformed from a boy into a man, so why not from a male into a female? In fact, Kohlberg found that many young children believed that boys could grow up to become women, wives and mothers and that girls could later become men. These beliefs seem odd to most adults. Yet for children without a clear awareness of the biological basis for masculinity or femininity, there is no unequivocal reason to expect continuity in biological gender over the lifespan.

GENDER CONSISTENCY

The final step in a full mastery of a cognitive awareness of gender, or gender constancy, is the understanding of the biological basis of gender and its independence from such superficial qualities as dress or hairstyle. This is the concept of *gender consistency*. Sandra Bem (1989) illustrated its absence in a typical preschool classroom. Her son Jeremy went to preschool on a particular day, wearing a pair of his sister's hair slides (barrettes). His classmates called him a girl, noting that 'only girls wear barrettes'. Four-year-old Jeremy already understood gender consistency and pulled down his pants to demonstrate unequivocally that he was a boy and not a girl. But his peers without gender consistency remained unconvinced. 'Everybody has a penis', one classmate commented, 'but only girls wear barrettes' (Bem, 1989, p. 662).

Ages and stages of gender constancy understanding

Robin Slaby and Karin Frey (1975) found that a cognitive awareness of gender constancy developed in three steps from age three to age seven. First, gender identity was acquired, and then gender stability gradually emerged over the period from age four to age six. Most of the 4-year-olds in their sample were able to tell accurately the sexes of a range of male and female dolls, photographs and people. But nearly a quarter of them still had Jimmy's problem of not

Children who lack gender consistency do not yet realise that dressing up in girls' clothes or playing with dolls is not what makes this girl female.

knowing whether they themselves had always been, and would always be, the gender they were at the moment. By age six, most were aware they could not grow up to be opposite-sex adults. Yet many six-year-olds and almost half of the 4-year-old group still confused gender with its outward trappings, believing that if a girl wished to become a boy it would suffice for her to put on male clothes, cut her hair and engage in boys' activities. It was not until age six or seven that most children displayed a complete appreciation of gender constancy through the recognition that superficial clothing or behaviour do not alter the biological gender a person is born with.

Rheta De Vries (1969) found that this lack of complete gender constancy was part of a larger problem with generic invariance which plagues children under the age of five or six. In her study, a group of American children aged three to six years were allowed to pat a cat named Maynard. After the preschoolers had become well acquainted with him, Maynard, somewhat reluctantly, permitted the experimenter to fit him out in a series of life-like masks. These presented him in quite authentic-looking disguises, first as a rabbit and than as a small schipperke dog.

De Vries found that 3- and 4-year-olds perceived no problem at all with the species transformations. They appeared to believe that animals could belong to several distinct species at once, or could change from one species to another in a matter of minutes. But for older children Maynard's crossing of the borders between species created a cognitive dilemma. Most 6-year-olds realised that he was a cat, and a cat only. They viewed species membership as a basic invariant attribute that no amount of masks or other

magic tricks could alter. Thus they were quite disturbed when Maynard, who had been a cat, reappeared as a dog or rabbit.

Valerie Jordan (1978) similarly found that 5-year-olds had difficulty with conservation of kinship concepts. They were unsure whether they would still be their parents' sons and daughters when they grew into adulthood. Nor were they convinced that brothers could be librarians, or daughters could be pilots. As in the case of conservation of animal species, a consistent understanding of these concepts developed gradually around age six or seven.

Maureen McConaghy (1979) studied gender constancy in Swedish children. She reasoned that the cues a child uses to decide a person's gender could be critical to whether gender is viewed as a permanent or a changeable attribute. Using a 'gender jigsaw' made up of dolls with male and female genitals that could be overlaid with transparent boys' and girls' clothes and hairstyles, she discovered three distinct stages in the development of gender understanding. In the first, children understood neither gender constancy nor that the genitalia determined a person's sex. In the second stage, some awareness of gender's fixedness was displayed but without clear knowledge of the relevance of the genitalia to biological masculinity and femininity. Finally, children came to understand that a person's gender can only be unequivocally determined by viewing the genital organs, and that it cannot be changed except by sex-change surgery. Box 8.4 illustrates the growth of one child's understanding of the anatomical basis for gender.

Ronald and Juliet Goldman (1982) testing Australian children studied the development of *gender consistency* or the awareness that the genitalia provide a better guide to biological gender than such mutable surface features of appearance as haircut or clothing. Accuracy increased gradually with age. However, progress was slower than expected. Even by age nine, some 40 per cent of the Australian participants in the Goldmans' sample did not yet have an accurate concept of the crucial differences between the naked male and female anatomies.

Sandra Bem (1989) found that approximately 53 per cent of preschoolers aged three to five years could distinguish between male and female toddlers when shown nude photographs like that in Figure 8.8. Furthermore, the children who could distinguish had a better understanding of gender stability than their classmates of the same age who could not. In fact, 74 per cent of the children who could accurately distinguish between male and female toddlers in nude photographs recognised the same toddlers when they appeared in other photos wearing cross-sexed clothing (see Figure 8.8).

Box 8.4 illustrates the development of one child's expression of her budding awareness of gender identity and gender consistency in spontaneous conversation.

FIGURE **8.8** Examples of photographs used in Bem's experiments

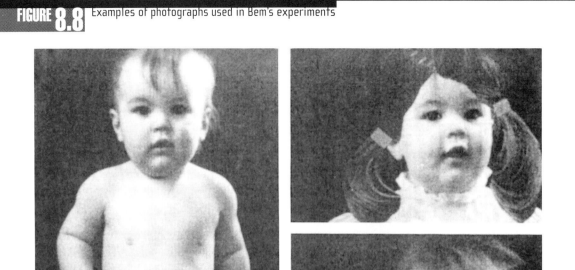

Source: Bem (1989). Reproduced with the permission of the Society for Research in Child Development.

The development of androgyny

From the 1950s to the early 1970s, many developmental psychologists shared with parents and teachers the belief that weak adherence to sex-role stereotypes was symptomatic of abnormality and the need for therapy in children of primary-school age (Sears, Maccoby & Levin, 1957). This view was based on an oversimplified model of masculinity and femininity as opposite ends of a single continuum. Children could not be both masculine and feminine, it was thought, so it was healthiest for girls to gravitate to the feminine extreme and boys to the masculine one. Boys who were identified as 'sissies' were deemed to require psychological intervention and counselling to promote their adoption of a more masculine pattern of social behaviour, and girls who behaved like tomboys were also thought to be maladjusted.

However, in 1975, Sandra Bem revolutionised these views, together with the psychological understanding of gender roles as an aspect of personality development, when she proposed the concept of androgyny. As Bem defined it, androgyny consists of a flexible blend of socially desirable masculine and feminine sex-role attributes. Research by Bem (1975) and others has shown that androgyny is associated with optimally effective psychological functioning in adult men and women. Table 8.5 shows how androgyny emerges when masculine and feminine personality traits are measured.

Some parents view androgyny as a desirable outcome for their young children. To encourage it, they may urge their children to cultivate playmates of both sexes, they may provide androgynous toys (like art materials and tennis gear) or cross-sex toys (dolls for boys and trucks or tools for girls) at birthdays and Christmas, and may suggest non-traditional careers when older children start to think about their future. Figure 8.9 shows the opinions of a group of 120 contemporary Australian men and women about whether parents should encourage their children to take part in activities that have traditionally been stereotyped for members of the opposite sex (Peterson, 1995).

BOX 8.4 Why can't a woman be just like a man?

At the age of two, Louise's attention was drawn to the outward attributes of hair and clothing which distinguished masculinity from femininity. Her father wrote:

> **24 December 1949.** *There are some round butter cookies that she especially likes and she calls them 'cakes'. This is partly because they resemble the cake pictured in her pat-a-cake story. We haven't had any in the house for the past few weeks, but when we last did, she was given the empty box with the Baker Maid trademark on it. I called her attention to the baker man (as in the pat-a-cake rhyme), then corrected myself and said 'Baker Girl'. Peggy bought a new package yesterday, evidently under Louise's eyes. This noon she asked for 'Cookies; no, cakes, Baker man – baker GIRL'.*
>
> © Peterson, 1974, reproduced with permission

Louise was already aware of the facial features that distinguish the sexes, and remarked that her father had a moustache ('tash') which her mother did not.

By the time she was eight years old, Louise revealed her explicit awareness that possession of a penis constituted the one unequivocal anatomical basis for sex differentiation. Her father wrote:

> **5 July 1956.** *Here at the Bedloes' in Western Michigan on our way home to California there's one little anecdote I want to record. I was waiting in the car with Louise, Merry, and Merry's older sister Kim while Peg and Sara were shopping. Kim said something about what if she and Merry were boys. 'Why,' I said, teasing them, 'I thought you were boys.' Louise speaks up: 'Merry isn't anyhow. I've seen her undressed and she doesn't have one of those little things boys have.' Kim (11) giggled. Merry (8) joined in but just to keep her company. Louise saw nothing to laugh at.*
>
> © Peterson, 1974, reproduced with permission

Thus, by the age of eight, Louise was using anatomy to define the basic differences between the sexes. With this criterion as a guide, she presumably also understood that gender was not readily alterable.

The results of one study (Boldizar, 1991) that classified children aged eight to 13 years into one of the four categories shown in Table 8.5 concluded that 25 to 30 per cent of children in this age range are androgynous.

Studying a sample of more than 400 children and their parents in the United States, Phyllis Katz and

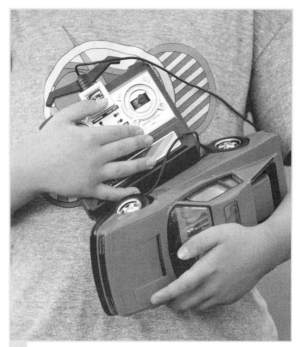

Some parents view androgyny as a desirable outcome, encouraging their sons to enjoy dolls and their daughters, toy cars.

TABLE 8.5 Androgyny as a product of masculine and feminine personality traits

		Masculine personality traits (leadership, logically minded, makes decisions easily, etc.)	
		Many	Few
Feminine personality traits (nurturance, expresses feelings, intuitive, etc.)	Many	Androgynous	Feminine
	Few	Masculine	Undifferentiated

Keith Ksansnak (1994) found that when parents made efforts to encourage androgynous behaviour in their offspring they were often reasonably successful. The subgroup of parents in their study who encouraged their children to think about non-traditional vocations (e.g. nursing for boys, engineering for girls), who gave their children cross-sex chores to do around the house (e.g. boys making beds while girls mowed the lawn) and who actively cultivated their children's interest in cross-sex films, television and literature tended to have sons and daughters who were less rigid in conformity to traditional gender roles than the offspring of the parents in the sample who disapproved of cross-sex options for their children and actively encouraged them along traditional masculine or feminine paths.

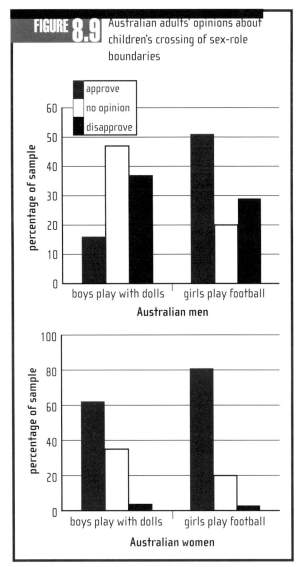

FIGURE 8.9 Australian adults' opinions about children's crossing of sex-role boundaries

Source: Based on data in Peterson (1995).

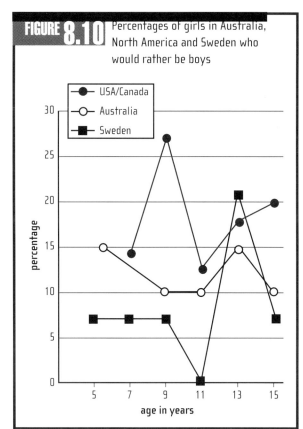

FIGURE 8.10 Percentages of girls in Australia, North America and Sweden who would rather be boys

Source: Based on data in Goldman & Goldman (1982), p. 171.

In a cross-cultural interview study, Ronald and Juliet Goldman (1982) asked groups of girls and boys in Australia, Sweden and the United States whether they ever wished they were a person of the opposite sex. Few boys expressed preferences to be girls. But, possibly because the feminine role allows less room to exercise adventurous, athletic and cognitive problem-solving skills, a substantial minority of girls did claim to want to be boys, as shown in Figure 8.10. On the basis of a study of 64 children growing up in a small town in northern New South Wales, John Shea (1983) concluded that:

> Working class girls who start with a fairly narrow range of sex-typed behaviours may become even more rigidly sex-typed in adolescence, while middle class girls may undergo a profound transformation in the range of sex-typed behaviour [preferences] as they move from middle childhood into adolescence. (p. 249)

On the other hand, Australian boys of all social classes are found to favour things masculine from as

early as age three (Bussey, 1983; Shea, 1983). Kay Bussey (1983) also found active rejection of female models and companions and feminine stereotyped activities by Sydney boys as young as five. Australian 7-year-old boys were not even able to describe the rules of familiar girls' games like knuckle-bones or netball, while 7-year-old girls displayed full awareness of the rules of all the games being played by their male peers (Rickwood & Bussey, 1984). Bussey suggested that Australian boys were taught to devalue and ignore feminine activities as a mandatory part of the preference for male ones. Girls, on the other hand, appeared to acquire whatever allegiance they eventually came to feel for the female gender and the feminine sex role without ever experiencing such a strong need to repudiate or denigrate masculinity.

In the United States, Phyllis Katz and Keith Ksansnak (1994) similarly found that girls expressed a stronger inclination towards androgyny and traditional masculinity than boys did towards either femininity or androgyny. However, they also noted a developmental trend towards increasing sex-role flexibility as children progressed from middle childhood through adolescence. At age nine, most children were unwilling to deviate very far from traditional sex-role stereotypes in their own behaviour and were generally disapproving of other people who did so. They believed, for example, that it would be wrong for a wife to accept a job where she would earn more than her husband or for a man to remain at home to care

From an early age, boys are taught to value adventure and risk-taking and to devalue feminine or sedentary pursuits.

for offspring while his wife worked. By age 15, these attitudes about sex-role conformity in others were less rigid, and teenagers themselves reported engaging in many more cross-sex recreations, chores and career plans than their peers at the age of nine.

As Katz and Ksansnak explained:

> Between preschool and late childhood, a curvilinear relationship between gender-schema flexibility and age has been obtained … Very young preschool children express more flexibility prior to stereotype acquisition, which decreases as stereotype information is learned and increases again in middle grade school. The question raised in the present investigation, however, was what happens from middle childhood through adolescence. Our findings suggest a continued increase in flexibility on most measures. (p. 281)

Some researchers have noted a brief resurgence of sex-role rigidity at the time of puberty (see Chapter 10), a phenomenon known as *gender-role intensification*, followed by a swift return to role flexibility in late adolescence (see Chapter 12).

Theories of gender-role development

Middle childhood sees dramatic gains in children's understanding of gender as an invariant human attribute, together with important changes in children's gender-role behaviour. But why do these developments take place? And why do some children adhere to traditional roles so much more firmly than others? Four major theoretical approaches have offered explanations for these developments.

Freud's psychoanalytic theory

The first formal theory of sex-role development was put forward by Sigmund Freud (1957), who proposed that children's sex roles developed, along with a sense of morality and conscience, out of the resolution of the *Oedipal conflict* (for boys) or the *Electra conflict* (for girls) at around the age of five (see Chapter 2).

With the Oedipal conflict, a process called *defensive identification* emerges. According to Freud, the nature of the boy's love for his mother, which in infancy grew out of his dependence on her care, changes during the phallic stage. In place of pure dependency, a new kind of love emerges accompanied by vague sexual feelings. (The boy himself is not aware of these erotic feelings or of the conflicts they engender, because they are buried deep in the unconscious part of the mind, according to Freud's theory.) The result is an unconscious desire for sexual intimacy with the mother. Thus, during the phallic stage, the boy comes to perceive his father as his rival. Because of the father's strength, control and power, however, the boy fears a direct confrontation, particularly one in which his own sexuality will be vanquished. (This was called *castration fear* by Freud.) Rather than provoke a direct challenge, the little boy therefore resolves the conflict by unconsciously striving to make himself into an exact replica of his father. By identifying with his father completely, he is motivated to adopt *all* his father's traits, including a masculine sex role and a mature set of moral values. The fruits of this identification process are great. As the boy comes to recognise how closely he now resembles his father, he has the added pleasure of enjoying his father's triumphs vicariously as though they were his own. Consequently, jealousy and fear of castration gradually diminish and the latency stage of personality development begins (see Chapter 2).

For a girl, the Electra conflict involves a similarly unconscious struggle. According to Freud, girls initially desire their father sexually and perceive their mother as a rival. Freud believed that, during the phallic stage, the girl discovered her 'anatomical inferiority' to boys (in other words, her lack of a penis), blamed her mother for it and then shifted her affection to her father, so that the mother became both the rival and the model to be emulated, through the same defensive identification that emerged when boys resolved the Oedipal conflict.

Freud's concept of identification has some appeal, because the child's overruling desire to become identical to the same-sex parent accounts for the fact that the child copies very complex and quite subtle patterns of behaviour. Parent–child resemblances

According to Freud, children acquire sex-roles through a process of emotional identification with the same-sex parent.

pervade virtually every aspect of overt and covert behaviour. The similarities between father and son or mother and daughter in middle childhood may range from unmistakable quirks, such as a particular way of laughing or of holding one's shoulders, to such deeply rooted and relatively unobservable qualities as a strict moral sense or firm self-control.

There are also reasons for feeling dissatisfied with Freud's Oedipal account of the process of identification. His prediction that boys who have cold, domineering (and therefore fear-inspiring) fathers will identify more strongly with parental models than boys whose fathers are warm and lenient does not tally with observational evidence. If anything, the opposite appears to happen (Sears, Maccoby & Levin, 1957).

Furthermore, Freud's theory is not really amenable to empirical test or validation, based as it is on clinical judgment and the psychoanalytic case histories of adult psychiatric patients (see Chapter 2). Nevertheless, Freud's notion of identification has played a major role historically as the inspiration for one of the three major contemporary theories of gender-role development (see Table 8.6): social learning theory.

Social learning theory

Social learning theorists like Robert Sears (Sears, Maccoby & Levin, 1957) and Albert Bandura (1986) have drawn on Freud's notion of identification with the same-sex parent as a stimulus to both gender-role and moral development. However, social learning theorists give parental identification a different causal explanation from Freud's postulate of unconscious sexual personality conflicts.

According to the social learning explanation for gender-role development, the identification process results from principles of learning rather than from the psychosexual dynamics of rivalry and unconscious sexual desire. Social learning theorists argue that children are motivated to copy sex-role attributes partly because they perceive themselves as more similar to the same-sex parent than to the cross-sex parent. Also, the parent role is one of the most nurturant, meaningful and powerful in the young child's life. In laboratory experiments, similarity and power have been shown to enhance the learner's wish to emulate a model. Selective imitation of the same-sex parent also brings reward when it strengthens the parent's feelings of gratification and affiliation with the child. Thus children learn to copy their same-sex parent through reinforcement (see Chapter 2), while parents' own perceptions of similarity bind them in a very special way to the child of their own gender. As Eleanor Maccoby and Carol Jacklin (1974) explained:

> Each parent expects and wants to be a model for the same-sex child. He will be especially interested in teaching that child the 'lore' that goes along with being a person of their shared sex. (p. 306)

In addition to explaining why children imitate their same-sex parent, social learning theory also draws together several other factors which are seen to facilitate the child's learning about gender roles. Reward and punishment both contribute. Children typically win the approval of their peers, parents and teachers when they behave in accordance with their own culturally prescribed sex role.

In one recent Australian study, Kay Bussey and Albert Bandura (1992) showed a group of Sydney youngsters aged two to four years a series of video clips of older boys and girls in a toy store. These older children acted out a scene in which they selected an extremely cross-sex toy (e.g. a baby doll for boys or a dump truck for girls) from a set of other toys that would have been more in keeping with traditional sex-role stereotypes. The child actors then played with these cross-sex toys in stereotypic ways for two and a half minutes. When asked for their reactions to the boy they had seen on video changing the baby doll's nappy and to the girl who enacted removal scenes with the dump truck, the preschoolers were quite disapproving. Using a scale made of light switches, boys and girls at all ages from two to four years described the boy and girl actors' cross-sex behaviour as being on the 'awful' end of a scale ranging from 'real awful' to 'real great'.

Thus it would seem that peers from an early age do react negatively to children's deviations from traditional sex-role stereotypes. Such punishing reactions could discourage children who value their peers' opinions from deviating from traditional roles. Bussey and Bandura (1992) also asked the children themselves how they would feel if they played with a toy designed for the opposite sex. Boys and girls of

According to social learning theory, children acquire sex roles by copying their same-sex parents and learning to do all the things that parent does.

four claimed they would feel bad. This is also consistent with the cognitive postulate of social learning theory (see Chapter 2). Self-evaluative reactions come to replace the need for direct copying of observed models as children develop.

Using a modelling procedure, Bussey and Bandura (1984) tested another premise of social learning theory – that the power and influence wielded by parents over their offsprings' lives will enhance children's tendency to identify with and copy parents rather than casual strangers or men and women on television. The results were consistent with this prediction. Children selectively modelled the behaviours of actors of their own sex more than actors of the opposite sex. But boys also imitated female models who had power significantly more than powerless females, thus confirming 'modelling as a basic mechanism in the sex-typing process' (p. 1292).

Ann Sanson and C. DiMuccio (1993) also obtained evidence supporting a social learning account of sex-role development from a large-scale longitudinal study of a group of Melbourne infants. The babies were followed from shortly after birth until their eighth birthday. The 300 families who took part were selected to represent a group of over 2400 infants of varied ethnic background whose temperament patterns were measured when they were four to nine months old (see Chapter 5). By the time the children reached the age of eight, a total of seven yearly waves of data collection had been completed. At each assessment point, parents reported on their children's behaviour and development. The children also took a number of standardised tests of temperament, sex roles and aggression.

During infancy and toddlerhood, few gender differences were observed. However, as the children moved through preschool and primary school, the differences between boys and girls became more and more apparent. Boys displayed more physical aggression, more violent anger outbursts and more competitive behaviour in early and middle childhood than girls did. They were also less compliant with adult directives from toddlerhood onwards (see the discussion of toddlers' negativism in Chapter 6) and displayed more 'acting-out' behaviour problems than girls. Boys were more likely to score as hyperactive and temperamentally difficult. They were also slower in motor development and more prone to language delay.

The results were in line with social learning theory. The fact that differences in aggression between boys and girls emerged only after infancy, and increased dramatically with the child's entry into the wider social worlds of preschool and primary school, highlighted the influence of peers and schooling together with parents in rewarding, punishing and supplying models of sex-typed behaviour.

As Sanson and her colleagues explained:

At a global level it is almost inevitably males who make wars, not only in the fighting of them but in the creation of the precipitating conditions, the decision to go to war, and the massive development of weapons and technology which contribute to warlike states of mind. Whilst it would be simplistic to claim that there is a direct link between childhood aggression and the making of wars, it is important to consider the socialisation processes operating, particularly for males, which contribute to the conditions where conflict, violence, and war appear to be a 'normal' part of life. (p. 86)

Kohlberg's cognitive-developmental theory

Lawrence Kohlberg (1966) argued that, before they can reasonably adopt a coherently organised gender role, children must develop a cognitive understanding of gender as a permanent personal attribute. The cognitive developments of concepts of gender identity, gender stability and gender consistency are prerequisites for the child's deliberate cultivation of a socially prescribed masculine, feminine or androgynous gender role.

Kohlberg's idea of sex-role development as a form of cognitive rule learning fits in with Piaget's view of how children come to understand the world in general (see Chapter 7). If sex-role development is a form of cognitive rule learning, Kohlberg's model predicts that it should follow the same pattern as rule acquisition in other domains. In other words, a small set of relatively simple rules should be learned and observed rigidly at first, followed by:

1. the acquisition of additional, more sophisticated, rules

2. the modification and complication of existing rules to take account of new data and exception
3. a looser and more flexible attitude towards the rules once they have been completely mastered.

Young children very often do adhere rigidly to a restricted set of ideas about what males and females should do, while older children show greater flexibility and tolerance for exceptions (e.g. Garrett, Ein & Tremaine, 1977).

One telling instance of rigid sex-role stereotyping was reported by Eleanor Maccoby and Carol Jacklin (1974). They were acquainted with a 4-year-old girl whose mother was a medical doctor. Yet the little girl asserted categorically that girls could become nurses if they wished, but only boys could become doctors. It is hard for the notion of parental identification to explain this child's tenacious insistence on a rule that was violated by the (admittedly somewhat atypical) example of her own mother. But her behaviour is consistent with the process by which young children master other rules, like the syntactic rules of language (recall the discussion of overregularisation in Chapter 6).

Kohlberg proposed that, once children develop a cognitive understanding of gender constancy, they become motivated to align themselves with gender roles socially prescribed for individuals of their

Young children are likely to believe, rigidly, that only boys can play football and only girls can dance.

biological sex, while repudiating cross-sex role attributes. Since biological gender is theirs for life, it makes good psychological sense to accept the inevitable by striving to become traditionally sex-stereotyped.

Eventually, children may become more flexible again as the cognitive changes of adolescent formal operational thinking (see Chapters 2 and 11) permit them to conceptualise multiple possible futures and to think abstractly and creatively about rules and how they can be improved upon or transcended (see Chapters 11 and 12).

One longitudinal study of primary school pupils in Queensland by Michael Siegal (1984) provided some support for Kohlberg's cognitive-developmental model. The 67 participants were six years old at the start of the study. They were tested at yearly intervals through to age nine. Observations were conducted either during the normal nap time at school for the Grade 1 pupils, or during the silent reading period provided for pupils in Grades 2 and 3. Because these lessons imposed constraints on activity and social interaction they enabled a child's aggressiveness and conformity to rules to be measured in some detail. Masculine sex-typed behaviour was identified as such disruptive actions as poking or touching a classmate, or fidgeting, talking and generally flouting school rules. Measures of the children's level of emotional identification with their mother and father were also taken.

While the boys' 'masculine' disruptive behaviour in Grade 2 was unrelated to the strength of identification with the father in Grade 2, there was a significant positive association between masculine behaviour in Grade 2 and subsequent father identification by the time the boy reached Grade 3. The finding that overt sex-typing of behaviour preceded the child's identification with the same-sex parent by one year is consistent with Kohlberg's view that identification is a tool rather than a root cause of sex-role development.

Siegal's more complex pattern of findings for girls was also broadly in line with the cognitive-developmental position. Masculine behaviour by girls in Grade 2 was a negative correlate of degree of father identification in Grade 2, but a positive predictor of strong paternal identification by the time the girl reached Grade 3. Siegal interpreted these relationships to mean that: 'Girls who flout rules would appear to be inappropriately sex-typed and they may later opt to emulate the father' (p. 40).

In other words, gender-role preference (expressed in this case by absence of a clear favouring of the female sex role) again seemed to precede, rather than follow from, the decision to emulate a cross-sex parental model.

Gender schema theory

Also cognitive in its focus, Sandra Bem's (1983) gender schema theory explains the child's mastery of a sex role in terms of information processing. From an early age, according to Bem, children struggle to make sense of the social world. As an aid to memory and understanding, they develop *heuristics*, or simple rules that draw diverse experiences together and give them structure and meaning. In searching for the rules of human social behaviour, gender stands out as an obvious categorisation mechanism. Even before they learn to speak, children take note of sex differences in adults' appearances and behaviour.

The social world is in fact consistently subdivided into masculine and feminine sectors. From the way toys are arranged on supermarket shelves to the choice of a public toilet, children are taught to use gender as an organising principle. Imagine a world that was organised quite differently – for example, with separate restrooms for people of different ages, or for those with curly or straight hair. In such a social environment, gender might not intrude itself so forcefully into children's cognitive organisation. But in most human societies today, the male/female dichotomy is a more informative one than subdivision by almost any other physical or behavioural characteristic. Consequently, according to gender schema theorists, the child rapidly learns to use gender as a mechanism for introducing order into sometimes chaotic social experience and masters sex-role stereotypes initially as useful clues for remembering information and making predictions about people's behaviour.

Bem suggested that gender schemas begin to exert an impact on social development from about the time children learn to label people accurately as males or females, between ages two and three. Their cognitive importance increases with age. But, at any given age, gender schemas are also a source of individual difference. Children who are highly gender-schematic use the male/female dichotomy as a rule of cognitive organisation to a greater extent than their gender-aschematic age peers. For example, when asked to remember the activities of a group of actors displayed on television, gender-schematic children are likely to score higher than aschematic children if the behaviours they watched are all highly consistent with traditional sex-role stereotypes. But a gender-aschematic child might display a better memory for an actor's cross-sex behaviour (Bigler & Liben, 1990).

Table 8.6 summarises these three major contemporary theories of gender-role development and notes a representative research study supporting each of them. Since there is evidence in favour of each one, it would be premature to abandon any of these three persuasive theoretical explanations. But possibly we do not have to. Douglas Kendrick (1987) argued that cognition, social learning and biologically ordained gender attributes all go hand in hand in contributing to gender-stereotyped behaviours like aggression and nurturance. As he explained:

Although psychologists have tended to view sociobiological approaches as incompatible with emphases on learning and cognition, there is no inherent reason to see genetic influences as

TABLE 8.6 Summary of contemporary theories of gender-role development

Theory	Key propositions	Supportive research evidence
Social learning theory (Bussey & Bandura, 1992)	Children learn sex roles by imitating same-sex models, especially parents and peers. As learning progresses, children become aware that gender-role-appropriate behaviour brings reward and are motivated to self-regulate their own behaviour based on their internalised gender-role standards.	When given the chance to imitate actions they have witnessed a model displaying, children are more likely to imitate same-sex than opposite-sex models and to copy actions by the model that are sex-typical rather than sex-atypical (Perry & Bussey, 1984).
Cognitive-developmental theory (Kohlberg, 1966)	Over the years from birth to age 7, children develop a cognitive awareness of gender as a permanent biological trait (gender constancy). Once this cognitive understanding is in place, children are motivated to emulate same-sex roles and to avoid cross-sex behaviour.	Children's self-reported reactions to hypothetical stories about boys and girls who behave in cross-gender ways (e.g. a boy plays with dolls) are relatively neutral at age 4 to 5 years but become markedly more negative at age 8 to 10 years, after gender constancy is acquired.
Gender schema theory (Bem, 1983)	Children use the male–female distinction from an early age (*before* gender constancy) to organise information and learn about the social world. This leads them to remember and copy gender-role-consistent behaviour and to ignore role-atypical acts. There are also individual differences in children's preferences for use as gender schemas to think about the social world.	When 2-year-olds who had learned to identify their own gender early (highly gender-schematic) were compared with 2-year-olds who did not yet know their own gender (gender-aschematic), the former group displayed more sex-stereotyped play (Fagot & Leinbach, 1989).

incompatible with either learning or thinking …
For instance, whether an act of violent aggressiveness if performed by an individual could be seen to be a function of characteristics of the biological organism (aggression thresholds will differ as a function of sex-related characteristics such as testosterone levels and large muscle development); in interaction with the objective characteristics of the situation (there are contexts in which aggression is appropriate, as in some male-dominated sports); and the subject's interpretation of the situation (males would be more likely to have aggressive behaviours as part of their self-perceived script repertoire, and to have had more recent activation of dominance-threat schemata). (p. 33)

Moral development

Together with the development of gender roles during early and middle childhood, children are also developing concepts of right and wrong, and the motivation towards ethical behaviour (conscience) that is increasingly governed by this moral sense of right and wrong. According to Martin Hoffman (1970), moral maturity requires that children behave in accordance with ethical principles even when they are not ordered to do so by authority figures, and even when no one else will ever know whether they did the right thing or yielded to the temptation to lie, cheat, steal, do harm or behave selfishly. In other words, moral development requires that moral principles become *internalised* within the child to serve as an inner voice of conscience prompting ethical behaviour and confession of transgression even when there is no possibility of a parent or other authority ever learning about or punishing their transgressions.

Hoffman described four kinds of overt behaviour, each testifying to the presence of an internal conscience:

1. *Resistance to temptation.* A child with a conscience refrains from doing wrong even when alone or when external threats of detection and sanction are minimised.
2. *Guilt.* A child with an internalised conscience experiences feelings of guilt after a transgression. This distinguishes conscience from blind obedience, which induces not guilt but rather the fear of punishment.
3. *Articulation of rules.* A child with a conscience has reasons for behaving morally that go beyond the simple fear of punishment. Thus, explanations like 'It's not yours to touch' or 'That's unfair' testify to an internalised conscience.
4. *Confession.* When a child publicly confesses a transgression that would not have been discovered without the confession, there is strong evidence that conscience has become internalised, since if external sanctions were the main reason

for abstaining from transgression this behaviour would make no sense at all. For a child with a conscience, taking the blame and being punished can often be less painful than the sting of guilt.
5. *Reparation.* Restoring the previous situation by making amends or helping to clear the damage is similarly powerful evidence of conscience.

BOX 8.5 **A pause for thought**
Do the best minds produce the strongest consciences?

In their classic investigations, Hugh Hartshorne and Mark May (1928) discovered a statistically significant relationship between children's IQ scores and the strength of their resistance to the temptations to cheat, lie and steal. Can you predict the direction of the link? Would brighter or duller children display a stronger conscience?

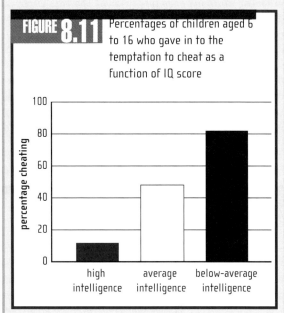

FIGURE 8.11 Percentages of children aged 6 to 16 who gave in to the temptation to cheat as a function of IQ score

Source: Based on data in Hartshorne & May (1928).

SOLUTION
The link between higher intelligence and strong resistance to temptation is shown in Figure 8.11. Children who were brighter were also more morally advanced. But was this because intelligence boosts the growth of conscience? Or that conscientious children work harder in school? Or might it be that advanced development in both the cognitive and moral domain is stimulated by some third factor, such as a nutritious diet or parental education?

But there is another less obvious explanation for the relationship shown graphically in Figure 8.11. Can you think what it might be? (Hint: According to this hypothesis, the strength of a person's conscience has nothing to do with mental ability.)

For the answer, see the next section of the text.

The development of moral behaviour

In a classic study using a range of observational and self-report methodologies, Hugh Hartshorne and Mark May (1928) set out to perform what they hoped would be the definitive study of the growth of moral behaviour. Their vast sample of over 11 000 New York children aged six to 16 years, from a broad range of economic, religious and ethnic backgrounds, was given a large number of 'honesty' tests at school, at church, at home and at parties.

For example, in one test of resistance of the temptation to cheat, children were asked not to look at the answer keys that were 'accidentally' left on the desk beside them while they took a test. They were allowed to correct their own papers and it seemed they could change their original answers without anyone ever knowing. In another test, involving the temptation to steal, children were told to deposit some money in an anonymous-looking box (which actually contained a live spy) in an empty room. As they were given the money as a loose collection of small-denomination coins, and as no one (so they thought) was in the room with them, it seemed plausible to many children that they could pocket a few of the coins without anyone knowing. When they analysed the children's patterns of responses across the different tests of conscience that each child had taken, the researchers came to a surprising and disturbing conclusion. There was no such thing as a moral child! Most children transgressed on some of the moral tests. There was a link between IQ scores and performance (see Box 8.5) but these links were relatively weak. More importantly, it was discovered that almost all the children were dishonest at least some of the time.

Hartshorne and May were led to question whether even the significant association between IQ and honesty shown in the tests was a genuine phenomenon. They suggested it might have been an artifact of the experimental procedures they used to assess conscience, with smarter children appearing to resist temptation not because they actually had stronger consciences but because they could 'smell a rat'. Why would a money box, supposedly designed to hold a few loose coins, be as big as a seated human being? Such a child might wonder. In the end, the researchers concluded that:

> These studies show that neither deceit nor its opposite 'honesty' are unified character traits, but rather specific functions of life situations. Most children will deceive in certain situations and not in others. Lying, cheating, and stealing as measured by the test situations used in these studies are only very loosely related. Even cheating in the classroom is rather highly specific, for a child may cheat on an arithmetic test and not on a spelling test. (pp. 411–12)

This conclusion frustrated the aims of the inquiry because it gave no clear guidance on how to optimise children's moral growth. Even the institution of Sunday School, which many parents subscribed to, partly as a source of moral socialisation, was of no direct benefit. Children who had been enrolled in Sunday School but had never attended resisted temptation just as well as those who had attended faithfully every Sunday.

Box 8.6 offers an instance of a different kind of social learning that proved to be an indirect result of Sunday School attendance for one individual 9-year-old.

BOX 8.6 A case in point
Louise and Taffy in awe of adults

When Louise was nine years old, her father ascribed her over-zealous compliance with her teachers' wishes to her fear of their disapproval, coupled with confusion about the rules behind their praise and reproof and the situations to which the rules applied. His thoughts are recorded in the following diary entry.

1 February 1957. She received a postcard from Sunday School to say that her meeting room has been changed. This worried her terribly since it would mean asking directions of someone in the office. I suggested she walk with Linda. 'Linda's father drives her. He won't let her walk.' 'Then walk to her place and ride with her.' The frown left her face; the problem was solved. Neither she nor Linda might be able to find the room but with a friend along she has no fear of speaking to grown-ups. She boasted to me once that when Linda is with her she, Louise, is the one who does all the talking to people. It doesn't work in school however. She is still afraid to ask her teacher the simplest and most necessary questions. Something about adults, especially those in authority, intimidates children. I remember the same feeling when I was a child.

Our neighbour's little dog Taffy obviously felt it when she came over to get meat from Boxy's abandoned plate yesterday. Three times she approached with trepidation, snatched a piece of meat, and slunk away casting a fearful eye at us inside the house. Does a dog respect the commandment against theft? Or is it that the world of mankind is so full of incomprehensible rules and taboos for dogs that any contact with humans carries the risk of breaking one of them? So I suspect it is with children in the almost equally incomprehensible world of adult rules and taboos. In this case, an extreme desire not to disobey authorities combined with uncertainty over what they defined as wrong to produce an overall inhibition of any social behaviour. It is true that Louise's fear of her teachers would undoubtedly have induced her to refrain from such morally innocuous actions as asking directions to her Sunday School classroom and asking necessary questions in school. Like the dog, Taffy, she was inclined to keep on the safe side of 'incomprehensible' adult rules and taboos.

© Peterson, 1974, reproduced with permission

The development of moral understanding during childhood

According to the cognitive-developmental theories of moral growth proposed by Jean Piaget (1932/1965) and Lawrence Kohlberg (1984), children require a cognitive understanding of *why* forbidden acts are wrong if their obedient behaviour is to be deemed truly moral or ethical. If a child avoids lying, cheating or stealing purely out of fear of adult reprisal, caution or prudence may be at stake, along with a hedonistic desire to escape pain, but not genuine morality. Box 8.6 illustrates an instance of how blind fear of adult authority may prompt inhibited behaviour.

In order to examine children's understanding of the logic behind the ethical rules to avoid transgressions like theft and deception, Piaget (1932/1965) posed dilemmas about issues like lying using the semi-structured clinical-interview methodology discussed in Chapter 2. Here is an example:

Piaget: (pointing to his student assistant) 'You see this gentleman?'
Child: 'Yes.'
Piaget: 'How old do you think he is?'
Child: '30.'
Piaget: 'I would say 28.' (to student) 'How old are you?'
Student: 'I am 36.'
Piaget: 'Have we both told a lie?'
Child: 'Yes, both lies.' (Piaget, 1965, p. 140)

In this instance, the child believed he had told a lie because he had made a statement that was factually untrue. The fact that he had not intended deceit, and could have no possible basis for knowing the research assistant's exact age, did not remove the overtones of moral condemnation bound up with his consciousness of having lied.

When Piaget quizzed a group of Swiss children aged six to 12 about what it meant to tell a lie, he discovered that many children under the age of nine expressed rather odd ideas. They seemed to equate lies with anything that was factually untrue, as well as anything a person could conceivably get into trouble for saying. Thus, when a 6-year-old named Lud was asked what a lie was, he said: 'It's when you say naughty words.' 'Such as?' Piaget prompted. Lud hesitated and blushed. 'Fire away!' said Piaget, and Lud came up with a juicy four-letter word. When Piaget probed, Lud insisted this expletive was a lie.

Most of the children who defined lies in this way considered untruths that escaped disapproval not to be lies. At the very least, lies that went unpunished were judged not to be very naughty. Thus, it was considered more acceptable to lie to a peer than to an adult, because peers were both more credulous than adults and less able to mete out punishment even if they knew they were being deceived. Lies told to adults were sometimes condoned, if the liar was clever enough not to be found out.

In this story, a little girl who was frightened by a chicken exclaimed that the chicken was 'as big as an elephant'. A majority of Australian children aged five to nine years described this exaggeration as a 'naughty' lie.

When Piaget asked the children to judge which of the two boys was naughtier – one who, after being frightened, romanced that he had seen a dog as big as a cow, or one who calmly told his mother he had received good marks in school when he hadn't – most children under the age of nine said that the first child was naughtier. His lie was 'bigger' (in the sense that it was unlikely for dogs to grow to the size of cows, but not impossible for a boy to get good marks, even though the speaker hadn't). Furthermore, the adult would know instantly that the first boy's statement was untrue, while she might be gullible enough to believe the second. According to these young children, a lie the listener believes is not a lie at all. Rather than judging lies by the motivations and intentions of the speaker to deceive a listener, lies were defined purely 'objectively' in terms of their discrepancy from objective fact and probability, a phenomenon Piaget dubbed *moral/lexical realism*.

A more recent study of young Western Australian children revealed similar tendencies to equate lying with any utterance that is factually untrue (Peterson, Peterson & Seeto, 1983). The 200 participants in this study were shown films of children who exaggerated when frightened, uttered a swear word, falsely claimed to like a friend's new hairstyle (white lie), told a self-serving lie (that the dog was guilty of spilling milk that the liar had actually spilled) and so on. The results appear in Table 8.7.

Piaget's theory

Piaget (1932/1965) proposed that moral reasoning develops through the two stages between early and late childhood, as shown in Table 8.8.

While some recent research supports Piaget's position, it seems that, as in the case of his tests of quantity conservation (see Chapter 7), the exact ages at which children make the transition from one stage to another may vary, both with the child's educational and social circumstances and with the procedures researchers use to assess children's moral understanding (Siegal, 1997; Siegal & Peterson, 1994). For example, in one study of Brisbane preschoolers, results revealed that many children as young as three years of age were able to distinguish between deliberate lies and accidentally untrue mistakes in a manner that would not have been predicted by Piaget's theory

TABLE 8.7 Percentage of people at five age levels who defined specified statements as 'lies'					
Age	5 years	8 years	9 years	11 years	Adult
Statement					
Exaggeration	60	85	88	95	50
Age guess	55	45	20	8	5
Directions guess	89	69	65	48	30
White lie	80	95	95	88	92
Practical joke	75	72	75	65	50
Altruistic lie	95	100	95	87.5	80
Swearing	38	12	8	15	2
Self-protective lie	100	100	100	100	9

Source: Peterson, Peterson & Seeto (1983). Reproduced with the permission of the Society for Research in Child Development.

TABLE 8.8 Piaget's cognitive-developmental stages of moral reasoning			
Stage	Age	Description	Example
Heteronomous morality	5 to 9 years	Authority figures determine what is right and wrong. Right is to obey the will of the adult, wrong is whatever authorities disapprove of: the motivational intentions of the transgressor are irrelevant to any judgment of morality.	It is morally worse to break a dozen eggs while helping a parent with the groceries than to break one egg by deliberately hurling it at the cat.
Autonomous morality	10 years and over	Morality is determined by the intentions of the actor (to help or do harm) and by the meaning of the action in the context of the greater good, irrespective of obedience pressures.	It is worse to lie deliberately to a young child who may believe you than to make a preposterous statement to an adult, who will know instantly it is untrue.

of heteronomous morality (Siegal & Peterson, 1996, 1998). In this study, the test of moral reasoning was presented in a manner designed to optimise children's understanding. Children were told puppet-play stories about two characters who both falsely told an unsuspecting friend that a mouldy sandwich was safe to eat. One protagonist did so deliberately, in full knowledge, after having seen the grey-green mould on the bread before it was concealed by a thick spread of Vegemite. The other character genuinely wanted to tell the truth, and genuinely did not know about the mould on the bread. He had simply made an unintentional mistake.

Figure 8.12 shows the percentages of Australian children at age three and age five who made correct moral judgments that the first character had lied and the second had made a mistake.

As shown in Figure 8.12, even 3-year-olds were accurate at a level that was significantly above what would be expected by chance when the task involved the domain of food safety, a situation where truthful communication is paramount and lying can cause serious harm. Five-year-olds were accurate in both food safety and food preference situations, realising that a protagonist who knew that the bread beneath a thick layer of Vegemite was brown would be telling a lie if they told a friend who did not like wholemeal bread that the bread was white. But a person who did not know what type of bread it was because they had not seen it would, contrary to Piaget's theory of lexical realism, only be making a mistake.

Social conventions versus moral rules

Judith Smetana (1981) found that even children as young as three are aware that moral transgressions that violate the rights and needs of others (such as lying, stealing, cheating, hitting and malicious breakage) are more serious than violations of politeness rules like forgetting to say 'please' or 'thank you', eating with fingers instead of a spoon or sucking one's thumb in public. Politeness rules belong to a broad category of social norms known as *social conventions*. These codes of social etiquette and conduct are determined by group consensus and may be specific to certain social situations. They prescribe the 'right' and 'wrong' way to behave without recourse to human rights and in a manner unique to a particular social situation (Turiel, 1983).

For example, the social conventions of a particular preschooler might prescribe (a) that each child should sit in a fixed place on the rug during story time, (b) that each child should speak briefly to the whole class and not whisper to friends during show-and-tell, (c) that teachers should not be addressed as 'Teacher' or by their first name, and (d) that a child should remain indoors when the others go out to the yard to play (Smetana, 1981). While useful for maintaining order and regularity in the school setting, these rules are as morally neutral as the sex-role conventions that most contemporary Australian and New Zealand children abide by, such as the rule that boys do not wear dresses to school or that it is wrong to name a girl 'Jack'.

Moral rules, on the other hand, define inalienable rights and wrongs of behaviour in an absolute manner, transcending the peculiarities of a given social situation. Basic ethical values apply to all age groups, cultures and historical eras. To the extent that they define the essential ingredients of social justice, rules against hurting other people, deceiving them or stealing or destroying their property are essential to social cooperation at all levels in all societies and social groups (Turiel & Wainryb, 2000).

Most children aged five and older realise that basic moral rules are universal (Turiel, 1977). They agree that stealing would be wrong even at a school that did not have a specific rule against it. They also realise that social conventions are subject to negotiation, and can be changed. Consequently, 5-year-olds in one study (Turiel, 1983) agreed that it would be all right to use a familiar form of address with a teacher who had explicitly said that this was okay. They also thought it was acceptable to drop litter or run in the corridors of a school that lacked rules prohibiting such conduct. Michael Siegal (1985) found a similar level of awareness among Australian children from as young as three years of age, particularly if they had had some experience with organised peer group activities such as day-care or kindergarten. The 3-year-old Brisbane day-care veterans in his sample realised it was worse to hit someone in the playground than to put a toy away on the wrong shelf, and that refusing to share a toy with a playmate was a more serious transgression than eating ice-cream with a fork. They also liked a teacher better when she disciplined children for moral violations, whereas her enforcement of social violations had little effect on their preferences.

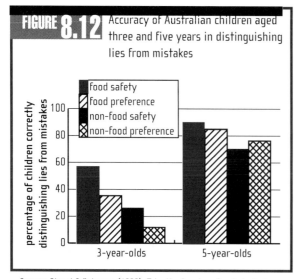

FIGURE 8.12 Accuracy of Australian children aged three and five years in distinguishing lies from mistakes

Source: Siegal & Peterson (1996). © by the American Psychological Association. Reprinted with permission.

The positive side of morality

While morality may sometimes be equated simply with resisting the temptation to do wrong, there is also a moral obligation to take positive steps to do things that benefit other people. In a child's life, two of the most important aspects of this *prosocial*, or positive, side of morality are helpfulness and fairness.

Helpfulness

When parents socialise their children into becoming ethically responsible adults, they usually want them to learn to try actively to do the right thing as well as to avoid doing wrong.

In other words, for a full understanding of moral growth we need to understand the development of *prosocial* behaviour as well as the factors that contribute to curbing *antisocial* misdeeds as children grow older. One highly important prosocial skill is *helpfulness*. Psychologists' concern over how to optimise this behaviour escalated in 1964, in the wake of newspaper accounts of the tragic murder in New York City of a young woman named Kitty Genovese, whose several dozen neighbours had watched her being stabbed for a full 35 minutes before one of them picked up the phone to call the police. Since that time, a growing body of research (e.g. Krebs, 1970) has shown that some situations seem almost invariably to induce this sort of passive non-intervention in the face of an emergency. Such passive failure to help has come to be known as *bystander apathy*. Most adults are apathetic bystanders in some cases. However, research has shown that adults are most and least likely to help in the following situations:

Least likely	Most likely
• When the nature of the emergency is ambiguous	• When the problem is obvious (e.g. a car crash)
• When there are many observers present	• When the bystander is alone
• When the required intervention demands special qualifications or is unusually difficult	• When no one else has the skills needed to help and the bystander does have them

Ervin Staub (1970) ingeniously created a child-sized version of the bystander dilemma to test this question. In his experiment, a subject child who had been left alone in a room to work (on the pretext that the adult experimenter had to fetch something) suddenly heard cries of distress which seemed to come from a child in an adjoining room. The measures of helpfulness included:

1. Spontaneously hurry to the rescue of the 'child' in distress (the noise actually came from a tape recorder);

Children learn prosocial moral acts by copying parental examples and helping parents with tasks like recycling on behalf of the environment.

2. Report the incident to the experimenter who came back into the room moments later.

When Staub tested a group of US children aged five to 13 in this paradigm, he paradoxically observed a decline in helpfulness from age seven to 12. Were children actually becoming more selfish with age? Or was the problem one of unreasoned obedience to an unwritten rule of adult authority (see Box 8.6).

Staub reasoned that the older children might have sensed that they were not supposed to leave the room when the experimenter was absent. To test this possibility, Staub told the children who took part in a subsequent study that they might find they needed more pencils to draw with. If so, they were allowed to fetch some from the next room. In other words, under this condition of the experiment, the children were made aware that they were under no obligation to remain in the room during the experimenter's absence, yet any implication that helpfulness might be called for was deliberately avoided. In this condition, nearly all the older children spontaneously went to the rescue of the needy child. One girl's approach dramatically illustrated the inner conflict between obedience and altruism. As soon as the child heard the victim's cries, she deliberately snapped the lead in one of her pencils and then marched purposefully into the adjoining room. In this way, she ensured that her helpfulness could not be misinterpreted as disobedience. Clearly, the motive to be helpful is present in many children throughout middle childhood.

Fairness and distributive justice

As they interact with groups of peers in school, children develop notions of justice and fairness, both in relation to the distribution of rewards and benefits (called *distributive justice*) and also at a broader level.

When it comes to distribution payments for work done and other desirable resources within a peer group, there are at least four different justice principles that may be seen as fair, depending on the ages and circumstances of the recipients and the type of resources being shared (Deutsch, 1975).

When they start to earn, and spend, pocket money, children begin to learn about fair wages for work done.

1. *The principle of need.* The rule 'to each according to his/her needs' allocates goods and services to compensate individuals who suffer hardships and deprivations. Adults are inclined to this principle when distributing rewards within the family, as when spending a disproportionate share of the family income on medical treatment for a sick child. Australian children also use the need rule more often when allocating to family members than to strangers (Peterson, 1975), and when they feel a strong sense of identification with their mother rather than their father (Siegal, 1985). However, children under the age of seven may have difficulty taking account of need in hypothetical situations (Damon & Hart, 1988).

2. *The equality rule.* The belief that 'everyone is equal' prescribes that each recipient's share of the collective reward should be exactly the same. This rule is favoured by adults for friendships, teams and other solidarity relationships (Deutsch, 1975). Young children and girls endorse strict egalitarianism across a wider range of task situations than older children and boys (Peterson, Peterson & McDonald, 1975). Australian children aged five to 11 years also opt overwhelmingly for equal distribution when no particular performance requirements of a task are specified.

3. *The equity rule.* The notion that resources should be given 'to each according to his/her contribution' is the rule of *equity*, or *proportionality*.

When this rule is used, the recipients' rewards are in direct correspondence to their input into the group effort. This rule is the predominant basis for adults' impersonal business dealings. William Damon (1988) found that the child's ability to consider the claims of equity increased with the transition from preoperational to concrete-operational reasoning. When he interviewed children about their hypothetical strategies for distributing payment among child workers, he found that the majority of children aged six to seven favoured the rule of equity. Michael Siegal (1985) found that a preference for equity as the basis for setting salaries at work increased in Australian children from age eight to age 18.

4. *Winner takes all.* This rule prescribes that one individual should gain exclusive possession of the entire reward. Such a rule applies to competitive achievement and underlies many school challenges and sporting competitions. Given all parties' prior acceptance of the principle and equal chances for anyone to be the winner, this rule is viewed as appropriate in specified circumstances.

Comparisons between the distributive justice reasoning of Australian and Japanese children and adolescents (Siegal, 1985; Mann, Radford & Kanagawa, 1985) have also yielded interesting cross-cultural contrasts. Michael Siegal (1985) noted that Japanese children made more use of the need principle than their Australian peers, particularly when distributing payments among highly productive workers. He attributed this difference in part to contrasting parental socialisation practices in the two countries, especially the Japanese mothers' more frequent tendency to use 'feeling-oriented' appeals against misbehaviour. But a 'trickling down' of adult occupational mores and economic realities into children's consciousness also appears to play a part in shaping the two cultures' very distinctive ideas about 'fair pay'. As Siegal explained:

Western children perceive the pursuit of individualism as a pathway to successful economic performance; often the world of the family is regarded as a separate issue. In Japan, company policies are geared to integrate the two worlds of work and family by providing for family needs. (p. 110)

Chapter summary

Parental influences, including parents' disciplinary strategies, teaching styles and explanations for family rules and regulations, can influence children's development in many areas – their mastery of social skills, the growth of self-esteem, their academic performance and their moral understanding and behaviour.

Siblings also influence a child's development.

Parents' differential treatment of siblings, the styles of sibling conflict management and play, rivalry and teaching each other all contribute to individual differences in patterns of psychological development during middle childhood.

Developments in personality take place in relation to the school child's resolution of the central personality conflict, in Erikson's theory, between feelings of industry versus inferiority, and through the processes of dialogue and peer cooperation and competition in school and in the playground.

Peer relationships evolve in important ways during middle childhood as children earn a position in their peer group as popular, neglected, controversial or rejected. Friendships develop, which are important in protecting children from feelings of loneliness, and in fostering the growth of moral understanding, conflict-resolution skills and social cognition.

Social influences, together with cognitive growth and cultural and biological factors, are instrumental in shaping the child's development of a gender role. From birth, males and females are treated differently in our culture. By about age three, most children are aware of their social categorisation as boys or girls and of our culture's fairly arbitrary stereotypes about which sex should play with dolls, cook meals, roam the neighbourhood, drive a truck, or aspire to be a doctor or airline pilot.

By age eight, an understanding of gender constancy and the biological determinants of gender generally emerges. Middle-class girls are slower to acquire a preference for their gender role than boys or working-class girls, and Aboriginal children are less rigidly sex-stereotyped than Anglo-Australian children of the same age.

Before the concept of gender constancy develops, children may believe that males can grow up to be females and vice versa. Kohlberg saw gender constancy as a prerequisite for developing a sex role, arguing that children are not fully motivated to acquire gender roles until they realise the immutability of biological gender.

Bem's gender schema theory also highlights cognitions about gender but considers that the process of schema acquisition begins in early childhood. Freud believed that the sex role develops with the child's resolution of phallic-stage conflicts as a result of identification with the same-sex parent. Social learning theorists account for a similar process of identification without recourse to infantile sexuality, viewing sex-role development as the outgrowth of observational learning.

Looking forward through the lifespan, we catch a glimpse of the changes in sex-role development that occur between middle childhood and adolescence, and at the possibility of transcending a sex role to become androgynous during late adolescence and early adulthood.

Many theorists link the development of a sex role to the growth of moral values and conscience. During middle childhood there is an important transition for most children from blind obedience to authority to an internalised 'conscience'. This guides the child's ethical behaviour without the need for policing, threats, rewards or punishments. Parental disciplinary practices are thought by some to be responsible for internalisation, but Piaget stressed the joint roles of cognitive maturation (enabling the child to understand the logic behind moral rules of conduct) and play with peers (motivating the child to behave in ways that earn social acceptance and approval).

Children show some understanding of the difference between morality and social conventions from as young as age three, especially when exposed to peers in day-care or kindergarten. Compared with children in other cultures, older Australian and New Zealand children have a growing awareness of social and political issues like justice and economics, and an accelerated understanding of social conventions about nudity.

Children are motivated to be helpful but may fail to express these tendencies when obedience pressures or bystander variables conflict with their prosocial inclinations. Cultural variations in childrearing practices may influence political and moral thinking and behaviour.

For further interest

Looking forward on the Internet
Use the Internet to visit the Companion Website for this textbook at **http://wps.pearsoned.com.au/peterson** and explore activities and projects related to material in this chapter. Also visit **http://www.aboutourkids.org/articles/friends.html** for more information on children's peer relationships and friendships, including intervention suggestions for parents who are concerned about their children's peer popularity. Also search for relevant websites for yourself by entering terms like 'friends', 'obedience', 'children's peer groups', 'sex roles' and 'gender roles' in your search engine.

MIDDLE CHILDHOOD: Physical, neurobiological, cognitive and emotional development in the context of schooling

CHAPTER 9

There is always a moment in childhood when the door opens and lets the future in.

Graham Greene (1904–1991)

Contents

CHAPTER OVERVIEW

The phase of middle childhood begins with the child's entry into primary school at around age five or six. It ends at the juncture of three important transition events: (a) the onset of biological puberty, (b) commencement of high school, and (c) the chronological passage to becoming a 'teenager' on the 13th birthday.

Middle childhood is a time of important neuropsychological, biological and physical growth, heralding changes in athletic, cognitive and emotional capacities, in line with the equally important social and personality changes examined in Chapter 8. The body and brain develop steadily, abilities consolidate and new aptitudes are discovered. As in earlier development, this process arises partly through neurobiological maturation and partly through the stimulating influences of experience, including formal schooling.

On primary school entry, children are faced with new opportunities for physical exercise, bringing chances to acquire and use motor and athletic skills and the fine dexterity needed to write, draw, sew or play a musical instrument. With participation in classroom instructional activities, organised games and sports and informal physical play with peers at recess and after school, children have a chance to compare their performance with that of peers. Primary school children acquire the motivation to achieve, a realistic awareness of their own potential relative to other children's and the social development derived from cooperation in groups and teams, ranging from maths and reading classes to choirs, bands, drama, football or even skipping rope.

In this chapter we examine all these important developmental changes as well as their consequences for the child's physical and emotional health. We look at the crucial health issues of diet, nutrition, exercise and resistance to infection, and also the child's development of the cognitive health understanding (Siegal & Peterson, 1998) that will help them to optimise well-being and cope with the emotional upsets and physical illnesses that they will inevitably encounter. Emotional development throughout the remainder of childhood is examined in this context.

Entry into primary school also stimulates cognitive development. During the early primary grades, children gain new skills for processing complex information and developing new solutions for challenging academic and real-life problems. We note the significant changes in attention span and focus, memory, reflection, executive control and decision-making that take place over the period from age six to age 12. Creative thinking helps children solve academic and everyday problems for which there may be no predetermined correct answer.

At the same time, cognitive development is boosted, as are the child's social and emotional horizons, by the growth of literacy. Learning to read is easier when children enter school with an awareness of books, speech sounds and rhyme. But schooling itself is also highly influential via teachers' attitudes and instructional strategies, peer support and the cultural significance of the printed word. We explore how children acquire literacy skills, and look at cultural variations in attitudes to literacy and the future consequences of reading for psychological development through the lifespan.

Academic achievement in school is more than simply the conjunction of cognitive aptitude with access to formal education. Children's motivation to learn and confidence in their abilities as learners, built up over many informal learning experiences in infancy, toddlerhood and preschool, combine with the social and cultural parameters of the school situation to set the pace for each child's academic development.

We look at children's attitudes to school, their patterns of ascribing causes for their scholastic successes and failures, and the culture of the classroom in Australia, New Zealand and other multicultural societies of the world today. The unspoken assumptions and preconceptions that pupils and their teachers bring with them to their encounters in schools can have both productive and counterproductive effects on the academic and psychosocial development of each child in school. In examining matches and mismatches between the cultures of home and school, we pay special attention to indigenous children, bilingual children and children from migrant and minority ethnic backgrounds.

Health and physical growth during middle childhood

The brain, body and physiological support systems develop steadily from age six to age 12, as evidenced by the rapid rate at which primary school children discard outgrown clothing and move up in hat and shoe size. Figure 9.1 displays some of these trends.

Illness is on the decline during middle childhood. Though all children suffer a few bouts of colds, flu and other minor infections every year, the period of primary school is a time of relative freedom from serious health problems for most children, particu-larly those who have been effectively immunised, and who have acquired sound hygiene habits and immunity to everyday illnesses in day-care or preschool.

With good teaching and plenty of chance for exercise at play and in school, children gain new physical skills, polish old ones, and increasingly come to display the delicate motor control and coordination that are necessary for the artistic, musical and athletic accomplishments that many children display towards the end of the primary school years.

Growth trends

Most girls and boys gain height and weight at a regular rate each year between the ages of six and

Growth in height and weight is steady for most children throughout middle childhood.

12 years (see Figure 9.1). On average, the yearly increase in height is about 6 centimetres and the yearly weight gain about 2.25 kilograms. Different parts of the body and internal organ systems grow at different rates, as illustrated in Figure 9.2. This graph shows the comparative rates of growth of bodily and physiological systems during childhood and adolescence (Tanner, 1970). As can be seen, the brain approaches its full adult size early in middle childhood, while other systems undergo dramatic growth spurts in early adolescence.

Growth problems: Obesity and malnutrition

The gains in physical growth shown in Figures 9.1 and 9.2 pertain to the average child. But not all children are lucky enough to be average, and some do encounter health and growth problems. These problems may limit their mastery of the motor skills typical of their age, restricting chances for social participation and causing difficulties with peer acceptance and additional psychological hardships. For these reasons, optimisation of the health and physical development of the child can have far-reaching consequences and benefits.

OBESITY

For the average child in Australia, New Zealand and other developed societies, two of the most common risks to optimal physical and motor development in middle childhood are nutritionally inadequate diets and obesity. For example, a recent Western Australian survey (Stanley, 2003) revealed that being overweight and underweight pose serious health risks

to contemporary Australian children, in line with findings in the United States that approximately 25 per cent of children are obese (US Department of Health, 1996). Defined medically as a body weight that is 20 per cent or more above the child's ideal weight, obesity is becoming more frequent in affluent nations throughout the world. The proportions of Australian boys and girls displaying obesity and other abnormal weight patterns are shown in Figure 9.3 (Caffin, Binns & Miller, 1981).

Another study in Western Australia pinpointed one source of this problem by finding that, between ages nine and 11 years, approximately one-third of the average child's total nutritional intake consisted of 'junk' foods deemed to be of poor nutritional value. Of the 'junk' consumed, 'fast foods' contributed 9 per cent, with the rest consisting of 'empty-calorie' snacks or foods high in sugar and fat (e.g. sweets, ice cream, potato crisps), which cause disproportionate weight gain without nutrients for optimal growth and health (Caffin, Binns & Miller, 1981).

A longitudinal survey following a group of 850 obese children in the United States into adulthood (Cowley, 2001) revealed that 50 per cent of the children who had been obese at age six remained so throughout the rest of childhood, adolescence and early adulthood. In other words, weight problems originating in middle childhood are likely to persist to pose difficulties later in life. During childhood, too, obesity is problematic for health and optimal psychological development. Children who are obese suffer more frequent illnesses than children of normal weight. They miss school more often and take less physical exercise, further limiting their opportunities for optimal health and social and cognitive growth. A boy or girl who is obese is also at a serious social disadvantage. Decades ago, Robert Staffieri (1967) discovered that children as young as six were prejudiced against fatness, and research over intervening decades has consistently confirmed that there is an association between popularity and a slim physique (Reaves & Roberts, 1983; Rees & Trahms, 1989; Gortmaker, Must, Perrin, Sobol & Dietz, 1993). In fact, even after getting to know their obese peers as people, primary school children are able to maintain a bias against fatness. Overweight children receive fewer invitations to visit peers after school and at weekends than their classmates of average build (Reaves & Roberts, 1983). They are also less popular in the classroom and less happy (see Chapter 8).

Thus, effective treatment for obesity may be necessary to optimise not only children's physical health but their social and emotional development as well. However, Leonard Epstein and Rena Wing (1987) suggested that a risk associated with dietary treatment of childhood obesity could be the development of anxiety over fatness. Later in life, a preoccupation with weight could lead to eating disorders. In adolescence, such serious eating problems as bulimia or

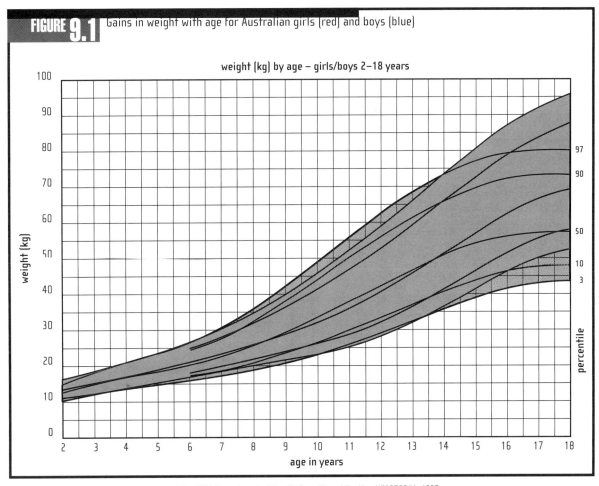

weight (kg) by age – girls/boys 2–18 years

Source: Reproduced with the permission of the NSW Department of Health from its publication HPA970044, 1997.

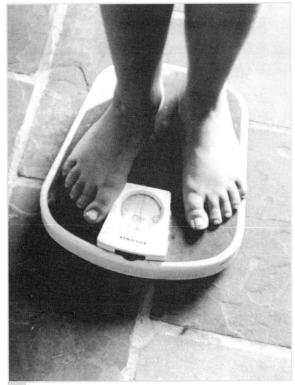

Weight increases steadily through middle childhood.

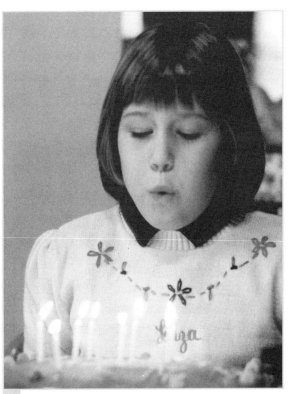

Children gain about 2 kg between one birthday and the next.

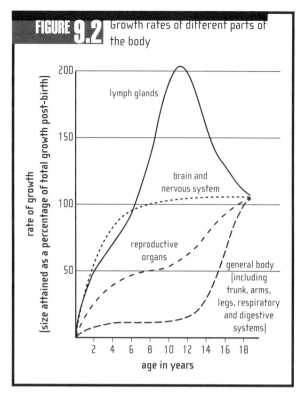

FIGURE 9.2 Growth rates of different parts of the body

Source: Tanner (1970), p. 85, reproduced with permission.

Children who are overweight tend to have more illnesses and fewer friends than their peers of average build.

anorexia nervosa might develop. We analyse these problems in more detail in Chapter 10.

Children who watch more TV than average also

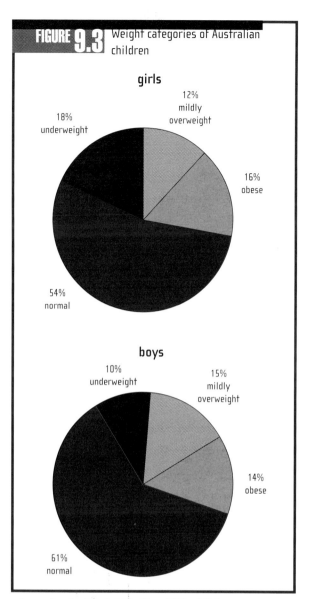

FIGURE 9.3 Weight categories of Australian children

Source: Based on data in Caffin, Binns & Miller (1981).

run an above-average risk of becoming obese. Television tempts children with advertisements for high-calorie, low-nutrition snacks and also limits the time available for the physical exercise and outdoor play that helps to burn off unwanted calories. In one US study, it was found that 10- to 14-year-olds who watched five or more hours of TV per day were eight times more likely to be obese than those whose daily TV consumption was only an hour or less (Gortmaker et al., 1993). A survey of commercial television broadcasts in South Australia showed that television advertising during children's prime viewing times placed the emphasis on vitamin-deficient over-processed foods and high-calorie junk foods rather than fresh, nutritious alternatives (Slee, 1993).

In a longitudinal study of a large group of North American children (Dietz & Gortmaker, 1985) it was found that heavy television viewing during middle childhood predicted obesity several years later, during adolescence. By spending more time in front

BOX 9.1 A case in point
Counting calories at age nine

When Louise was nearly 10, owing perhaps to the prepubertal 'fat spurt' (see Chapter 10), she gained weight and had to go onto a junk-food-free, reducing diet. Her father described the motivational difficulties this caused:

1 March 1958. The doctor found her 10 pounds overweight yesterday and put her on a strict reducing diet, 1000 calories a day. Louise suddenly felt the full force of it at dinner, when she was forbidden a second serve of grilled fish. She wept and stormed and said she wasn't going to eat anything. The more she looked at the diet, the worse it seemed. I conceived the idea of offering her a dollar for every pound she loses.
I disclosed the plan at breakfast and she accepted it but there was no doubt she'd rather earn her dollars an easier way.
'I'm going to save the money and spend all of it on food!' she exclaimed angrily.

© Peterson, 1974, reproduced with permission

Children who watch excessive amounts of television are more likely than their peers to favour sweet treats over nutritious fresh fruit and vegetables.

of a TV set, children have less chance to develop muscular fitness by exercising and, since there are few television advertisements promoting fresh fruit and vegetables, it can be very tempting to sit and consume fattening snacks while watching television. Like adults, children may not pay attention to how much they are eating when distracted by television programs, compared with dining at the table, and while children are sitting watching TV their metabolic rate decreases dramatically (Gortmaker et al., 1993). Thus most of the calories consumed are converted to body fat.

Obesity is not consistently disparaged by all cultural groups. In New Zealand, where obesity may be a hardship to Pakeha (or Anglo) children, the reverse may be true for Maoris and migrant New Zealanders from the Polynesian Islands. Box 9.2 describes the distress encountered by a Polynesian schoolgirl in the Cook Islands whose efforts to achieve an obese body shape were unavailing.

MALNUTRITION

For children in the developing world, dietary growth problems are very different from the obesity and empty-calorie junk-food consumption plaguing children in affluent countries. In much of Africa and

BOX 9.2 Lessons from culture
If only I was plump!

In an autobiographical essay, a Cook Island woman (Stewart, 1982, p. 128) gave the following account of her childhood unhappiness at being too thin.

Being plump is considered by my society as the ideal standard of beauty, the symbol of attractiveness and health. To be on the thin side is regarded as inappropriate, and not matching up to society's expectation. Thus, as a child and right through to the age of twenty-one, I regarded my thinness as a curse.

Moreover, the fact that I wasn't plump like the rest of the girls of my age was of great concern to my parents. Mum would cook all sorts of food just to make me eat, and on top of this I was given a tablespoon of cod liver oil with an iron tablet every morning. I loathed those doses after breakfast but more than often I was told: 'Be a good girl and swallow it, if you want to be fat and beautiful.' The desire to be beautiful, accepted, and loved by my parents forced me to go through that every morning.

Every day while dressing for school, I used to stand in front of the mirror to see if I had gained any weight. On the way, I'd stop at the nearest shop and weigh myself. But every time I was disappointed. At school I faced all sorts of names such as 'bony', 'stick', and 'skinny'. Therefore, to avoid being ridiculed, I buried myself in my work and kept away from the other children. Many times I desperately wanted to play basketball and tennis but the thought of being laughed at held me back. So I slowly became an isolate. (Reproduced with permission)

South America and many parts of Asia, children live in poverty and are malnourished. Severe malnutrition can delay physical growth. One study comparing affluent with poverty-stricken families in Nigeria revealed that sons in the poor families were an average of 4 inches shorter than sons in affluent households with more nutritious diets (Tanner, 1990). In the United States, vitamin, zinc and iron deficiencies are common in children from lower socioeconomic backgrounds and are associated with growth delays (Pollitt et al., 1996). It remains open to question whether lack of sufficient food or over-consumption of an empty-calorie and nutritionally inadequate diet is to blame. However, whatever the underlying cause, children with iron and zinc deficiencies run a higher risk of learning problems in school than well-nourished children.

Illness poses a greater threat when a child is malnourished, since malnutrition depresses the effectiveness of the body's immune system. It is estimated that seven million malnourished children in developing countries die every year from infectious diseases (World Health Organization, 2000).

Health, illness and health understanding

While obesity and malnutrition can interfere with children's optimally healthy physical growth, the risk of acute illnesses during middle childhood is somewhat lower than among preschoolers. During the primary school years, the average child will have roughly five brief illnesses per year, mainly colds and influenza. While these minor ills are unpleasant and will probably lead to missed days of school, they also exert developmental benefits when they help children to acquire a better understanding of health, illness and hygiene precautions to prevent the contraction and spread of disease. Over the period from early childhood to adolescence, children's understanding of health and illness becomes increasingly complex and biologically driven, though even young children have a sound basis for understanding simple health rules of sound diet, cleanliness and avoidance of contagion. Terry Au, Laura Romo and Jennifer DeWitt (1999) explain:

> Perhaps because illness and health figure so prominently in everyday life, children have relatively sophisticated and rich beliefs in this domain from quite early on. It makes sense to capitalize on such a rich store of knowledge in helping children reason about illness causation and prevention. (p. 231)

In fact, when they designed an HIV/AIDS education program for children aged eight to 14, they found that even the younger children (who, before being trained had many misconceptions about the risks of AIDS, modes of spread of the HIV virus and the likely prognosis for individuals infected with HIV) could learn effectively to reason biologically about this unfamiliar disease, with consequent benefit for their attitudes to AIDS patients and for their sensible health practices to guard against contracting the disease.

Some general developmental trends in the understanding of health and illness from the preschool period through middle childhood to adolescence are shown in Table 9.1.

Older children and adults are aware of regular sleep as a long-term health-promoting strategy as well as sharing younger children's awareness of the importance of sleep in recovery from disease.

TABLE 9.1	The development of children's understanding of health and illness
Age period	**New developments**
Age 3 to 5 years	Children are aware of invisible contamination of foods by disease germs and other noxious substances. They know, for example, that a glass of juice that had a cockroach dunked in it is not safe to drink, even after the cockroach has been removed and all traces of its presence have disappeared (Siegal, 1991).
Age 6 to 8 years	Children are aware of the biological processes of nutrition, blood flow, germs and contagion. However, in contrast to older children and adults, they favour *vitalistic* biological explanations over those based on physical and mechanistic causality. For example: a child of six says the blood's circulation through the body occurs 'because our heart works hard to send our life energy through the blood' (vitalistic) while adults say 'because the heart sends the blood by working as a pump' (mechanistic) (Inagaki & Hatano, 1999).
Age 12 and over (adolescence through adulthood)	Adolescents and adults are aware of an interdependence between mind and body in health and illness (e.g. psychological stress can increase illness susceptibility) and recognise the importance of health-promoting practices like exercise, sleep and a nutritious diet for enhancing the body's resistance to infectious disease (Inagaki & Hatano, 1999).

Neurocognitive development in middle childhood

Figure 9.2 (on page 288) charts the growth trajectory of the brain and central nervous system over infancy and childhood. After a rapid spurt of growth during infancy, continuing into early childhood, the brain's rate of growth begins to taper off. By about the age of seven, the brain's weight has increased to 90 per cent of its full adult size (Lecours, 1982; Tanner, 1990). This may account for the nearly universal tendency for cultural groups throughout the world to begin formal instruction of children in the knowledge and skills necessary for productive contributions to society (e.g. in our culture, the teaching of reading, writing and computational skills in primary school) at around age seven.

However, even though the brain's overall size changes relatively little throughout the rest of middle childhood, important developments continue into adolescence. Along similar lines to those charted in Chapters 4 and 7, there are developments in the brain's internal neurocognitive processes of myelinisation of nerve fibres, interconnections between synaptic pathways, hemispheric specialisation and changes in the brain's patterns of electrical activity.

Myelinisation

Myelinisation involves the building up of a fatty, insulating coating of myelin around the neuron's axon (see Chapter 4), increasing the transmission speed of neuronal messages. After a rapid spurt in early childhood, myelinisation of nerve fibres continues throughout middle childhood and adolescence in certain areas of the brain. The neurons in the frontal cortex of the brain continue to acquire myelin (Janowsky & Carper, 1996), as do certain parts of the reticular formation deep within the brain. Since these cortical areas are involved in the deployment of attention and concentrated cognitive activity, it is possible that increases in attention span over the early grades of primary school may have a partly neuro-maturational basis. It is also conceivable that school's demands for a child to sit still, pay attention and focus on discrete cognitive tasks for long stretches of time may help to trigger the myelinisation of these regions. Robbie Case (1992) suggested that the changes in the speed and efficiency of neuronal activity in the frontal cortex that arise with myelinisation are responsible for the increased attentiveness of older primary school children (witness the classroom behaviour of children in Grade 4 as compared with Grade 1). These changes may also be responsible for the frontal cortex's capacity to coordinate the cognitive activities involved in deliberation, planning and reflective thought, and the capacity to sustain a coherent line of thinking despite distractions or interruptions. In addition to becoming myelinised, nerve fibres increase in size and interconnections so that the brain continues to gain weight.

Neurocognitive activity

As noted in Chapter 4, the brain's patterns of electrical activity can be measured using a recording process known as an *electroencephalograph* (or EEG). When EEG recordings are made of children's brains during alert wakefulness, important changes are seen to arise during the period from age four to age ten. The EEG wave pattern known as *alpha*, which in adulthood is associated with alert activity, becomes more frequent over childhood. Furthermore, the balance of alpha waves to theta waves (which in adulthood are associated with sleep) shifts gradually over the same period (Thatcher, 1994). Up to the age of five, *theta* activity dominates over alpha activity even when the child is alert. Between age five and age seven, the balance of theta to alpha is roughly equal; in late middle childhood an adult pattern is established with alpha as the dominant EEG pattern during attentive cognitive activity.

Lateralisation

The cerebral cortex, or outside layer of the brain, has two distinct hemispheres, the left and the right. The left is more specialised for language and the right for wholistic, spatial and pictorial information. Inside the brain, a structure called the *corpus callosum* connects the two hemispheres. During middle childhood, the corpus callosum grows and continues to become myelinised, supporting sophisticated reasoning and problem-solving that requires transmission of information across the two hemispheres (Thompson, 2000).

The development of motor and athletic skills

Table 9.2 presents a summary of some of the important changes in motor skills and motor coordination that are achieved by the average child during middle childhood. By age 12, children can run faster, throw further, jump higher and react more rapidly than they could at the start of primary school. Relative to toddlers and preschoolers, the changes in motorically skilled action and sporting performance are even more dramatic. For example, the maximum height of a 12-year-old's jump is roughly five times that of a preschooler (Espenschade, 1960). There are few differences in motor skills between the two sexes during middle childhood. Girls, on average, have 5–10 per cent less muscular strength and aerobic capacity than boys, as displayed by their maximum force in gripping a lever or the amount of air exhaled with a deep breath (Sherman, 1973). But their sporting skills and athletic achievements in running, jumping, aiming and throwing are roughly on a par with those of boys, in contrast to the marked differences that will emerge after puberty (see Chapter 10).

Opportunities for physical exercise and the

TABLE 9.2 Development of motor and sporting skills during middle childhood	
Type of skill	**Skill development**
Throwing a ball	Throwing speed, distance and accuracy of arm all improve steadily from age 6 to age 12
Running speed	Running speed improves; children at 12 can, on average, run 1.3 to 1.5 times as fast as they could at age 6
Jumping ability	The distance children can jump, both vertically and horizontally, increases from age 6 to age 12
Kicking a ball	Speed and accuracy of kicking improve from age 6 to age 12, but are better at all ages in boys than in girls
Hopping	Skill in hopping directionally on one foot in small squares (as in the game of hopscotch) improves from age 6 to age 9 and then levels off
Eye–hand coordination	By age 9, children are proficient in the eye–hand coordination needed to play games like jacks and knuckle bones
Reaction speed	Reaction times diminish from age 6 to age 10, assisting in children's performance in speeded games, races, and so on

Cycling is a favourite activity of middle childhood.

cultivation of sporting skills are a normal feature of the primary school curriculum in Australia and New Zealand today. But many children also participate in sport and fitness exercises outside school hours. In fact, Russell and Mollie Smart's (1980) analysis of play patterns in New Zealand suggested that 75 per cent of school-age boys and girls took advantage of Auckland's well-equipped school playgrounds after school and at weekends. A similar number were regularly involved in sports clubs and sporting team

The exercise and cultivation of motor skills contributes to physical health and self-esteem during middle childhood.

fixtures. Australia's and New Zealand's temperate climates, as well as what Smart and Smart took to be 'the New Zealand ideology of vigorous outdoor play at all ages' (p. 90), could both help to explain this somewhat higher rate of athletic activity by children of primary school age in Australia and New Zealand than among a comparable group of preadolescents in the United States.

During early and middle childhood, motor skills and physical growth are important contributors to the child's self-esteem and self-image (Damon & Hart, 1982). Children value their overall gains in coordination and athletic competence as well as the specific skills they acquire by taking part in team sports like football, hockey, cricket and netball. Cycling and swimming are also favoured activities of middle childhood. These increase strength and fitness, as well as providing opportunities for enjoyable peer relationships. Susan Harter and Robin Pike (1984) studied self-perceptions of motor skills in a group of 255 children who were approximately evenly divided into preschool (ages four and five) and primary school (ages six to eight) age groups. The children were asked how good they were at a range of motor and athletic skills. Their physical self-concepts improved somewhat with age, but there was also more variability in self-perception of skills during middle childhood than at ages four and five, probably because school provides opportunities for putting motor skills to the test in peer competition or team sports. The results of a study of 1267 Australian children aged six to 13 (Ellerman, 1980) revealed similar increases between Grade 2 and Grade 4 in self-esteem related to athletic competence.

Emotional development

Sigmund Freud called the span of years from age six to age 12 the *latency* stage in personality development (see Chapter 2). For Freud, middle childhood was an unusually calm period of emotional stability and freedom from anxiety, compared with the emotionally fraught conflicts of infancy and early childhood (see Chapter 8) and the turbulence of adolescence (see Chapter 12). But recent research shows that the emotions do not lie dormant during middle childhood (Haviland & Walker-Andrews, 1992).

Instead, children become increasingly skilled at understanding their own and others' emotions, experiencing and expressing subtle and nuanced emotions, self-regulating inner feelings to maintain a balanced mood, and conforming to social pressures and expectations regarding emotional display rules (Harris, 1989). These trends continue patterns that began to develop during infancy (see Chapter 5) and early childhood (see Chapter 7). Some of the new developments of middle childhood are summarised in Table 9.3.

The development of emotional competence

Carolyn Saarni (1999) proposed that the development of an ability to experience, understand and express positive and negative emotions appropriately includes a set of eight component skills:

1. awareness of one's own emotional state
2. perception of the emotional states of others
3. acquisition of a vocabulary of emotion terms
4. the capacity for empathic involvement in emotional experiences
5. a capacity to self-regulate and cope with strong negative feelings
6. an awareness of the need for emotional display management, which may include control and concealment of emotions in certain social situations
7. awareness of the role played by positive and negative emotions in social relationships
8. emotional self-acceptance and self-efficacy.

To a younger child, birthdays are synonymous with happiness. Older children are aware that some people may feel sad or angry even if they're having a party.

As well as developmental changes in emotional life and emotion understanding, researchers have discerned changes in specific emotions during middle childhood. In terms of social interaction and emotional well-being, two of the most important of these are anger and fear.

Anger

Older children may not erupt into anger as often as toddlers and preschoolers, but the duration of their rarer bouts of sulking is seen to increase. Thus the total amount of time spent in an angry state remains about the same from age two to age 12 (Goodenough, 1931/1975). But the causes of anger change with age. School-age children's cognitive sophistication sensitises them to many subtle and indirect provocations which fail to make younger children angry because they lack perception. For example, a preschooler is aware of direct teasing and ridicule but is not as sensitive as an older child to a

TABLE 9.3	Emotional development during middle childhood
Age period	New developments in the emotion domain
6 to 8 years	• Children are aware that two opposite emotions can be felt at the same time (e.g. happiness at going to the zoo and sadness that their best friend cannot come along). • Children can integrate conflicting cues to understand others' emotions (mother's angry tone of voice indicates she is upset despite her smile and the statement that she is happy). • Children are aware that the same objective event can evoke different subjective emotions in different people. • Masking and feigning emotions in conformity with socially acceptable display rules improves.
9 to 13 years	• Children are aware of both deliberate and involuntary processes of emotional control and emotional fading; they realise that if you force yourself to think happy thoughts your mood can improve and that, over time, by not thinking about an emotion, the feeling fades. • Children have a full and explicit understanding of emotional display rules; they know how to decode the true feelings of a person who has masked or distorted their facially expressed emotion in accordance with social norms. • Children are aware of their emotional needs and are able to seek experiences that will favour them (e.g. retreating to their room and playing quiet music to calm down).

speaker's use of sarcasm and irony to endow a seemingly complimentary comment with a derogatory meaning (Winner, 1988). Thus an older child will take umbrage in conversational situations that are emotionally neutral to preschoolers with limited sophistication in discourse (Siegal, 1991). In addition, older children are capable of becoming angry about injustices inflicted on others besides themselves, and may even display generalised outrage at human cruelty, social inequality and environmental degradation. Culture and age intensify concerns over broad issues like these. For example, adolescents in Australia are more likely to express outrage at harm to the environment than their peers in Singapore (Poole, De Lacey & Randhawa, 1985).

Ken Rotenberg (1985) studied anger in children aged six to 12 years by asking them to give a detailed description of their most recent loss of temper. He found that most of the school-age child's anger was reactive rather than proactive. Almost all the outbursts reported were in response either to someone else's hostility or to a frustration with the physical environment. The three most frequent triggers were (a) physical attack, (b) verbal insult, and (c) blocking of the child's achievement of an important goal. No significant age differences were found during middle childhood in the duration or intensity of anger outbursts. However, in line with Piaget's theory (see Chapters 2 and 7), children over the age of eight were found to discriminate more clearly between accidental and intentional causes of harm than very young school children. Five- to seven-year-olds in fact responded just as angrily to unintended frustrations as to deliberate provocations. But older children showed greater outrage than preschoolers at breaches of promise and violations of interpersonal trust, possibly due to their more accurate awareness of the element of deliberate intentionality that goes into making promises and keeping them (Rotenberg, 1985).

The factors triggering the anger outbursts during middle childhood may also differ between the sexes. In her in-depth interviews with girls at a North American boarding school, Carol Gilligan (1982) found that many girls equated injustice with not being listened to. They cited numerous instances when other people had unfairly dominated conversations on topics they cared about, or ignored what they said after allowing them a chance to speak. Gilligan suggested that this distinctively feminine source of anger may ultimately become translated into a set of moral values based on care for others and mutual respect. (We talk more about this when examining adolescent moral reasoning in Chapter 11.)

Fear

Fears also develop and change as children mature. Some fears decline. The infant's fear of loud noises or the toddler's fear of the dark are no longer as intense in middle childhood, possibly because the older child

While frightening to a younger child, a ride in an amusement park can bring pleasure to an older one.

has mastered strategies for dealing with them, such as turning on a light. On the other hand, fears that depend on a cognitive capacity for imagination and fantasy (ghosts, monsters) or on the building up of experiences with disasters actually befalling self or others (death of a loved one, snakes, car accident) grow more common in middle childhood. Some fears depend on the cognitive capacity to consider hypothetical possibilities (e.g. nuclear war) and this may not develop until adolescence or later (see Chapters 11 and 14).

As children become more competent and gain the capacity for self-control and emotional self-regulation (see Chapters 4 and 8), many of the things that formerly terrified them no longer seem as frightening. Changes in targets of fear from childhood to adolescence are shown in Figure 9.4, based on a survey of 3118 Australian pupils aged eight to 16 (King et al., 1989). Eight-year-olds reported an average of 17 different things that frightened them 'a lot'. By age 16, only 12 things fell into this highest fear category. Across all age groups combined, 72 per cent of children were intensely afraid of nuclear war, making this a more widespread fear than any of the other 79 frightening things. Also high on the list of frequent and intense fears for Australian children were:

- not being able to breathe (63 per cent)
- being hit by a car or truck (62 per cent)
- earthquakes (59 per cent)
- a burglar in the house (48 per cent)
- snakes (41 per cent)

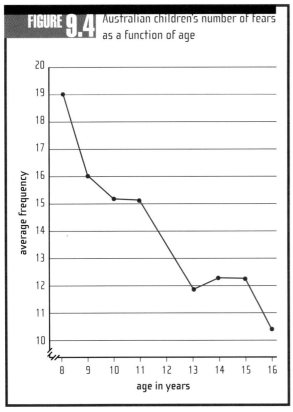

FIGURE 9.4 Australian children's number of fears as a function of age

average frequency (y-axis, 10 to 20)
age in years (x-axis, 8 to 16)

Source: King et al. (1989), © 1989 Elsevier Science Ltd, reprinted with kind permission.

• death or dead people (39 per cent). (The fear of death in childhood is examined in depth in Chapter 18.)

Children who lived in Melbourne reported more fears than children living in rural areas of Victoria.

Some of these fears reflect genuine risks in children's lives (e.g. the fear of a road accident or of suffocation by being smothered, drowned or in a fire). But the fact that the Australian girls in this study tended to report more intense fears of these realistic risks, and to be frightened of a greater range of things than boys, goes against reality. Boys are significantly more likely than girls to suffer accidental death or injury through risks like these during middle childhood.

The finding that fears decline with age during middle childhood was confirmed in another study of Australian children using a longitudinal methodology (Spence & McCathie, 1993). Like their peers in Melbourne (King et al., 1989), the fears of these urban Sydney children at the start of the study tended to cluster around genuine dangers (traffic, fire, death) and physical injury. Boys reported fewer fears than girls and described the fears they did suffer as less intense than their female peers'. The same children were followed across a two-year period. There was a significant decline in the overall range and level of fear that the children were reporting by the time they were two years older. The fears that displayed the largest decrease over time were darkness, getting sick,

punishment by parents and parental criticism. Boys also feared strangers and physical injury less by the end of the study than they had at the beginning, but neither of these fears changed for girls. On the other hand, boys became significantly more frightened of having to speak in front of an audience as time went on, while girls did not.

Though fear declined for the group as a whole as they grew older, individual differences in fearfulness remained constant over the two years. The boys and girls who had reported the most fears at the start of the study were still more fearful than the rest of their peers two years later. The results of this longitudinal study are important, as they suggest that the decline in Australian children's fears that is shown in Figure 9.4 is a genuine change with age, rather than a tendency for later cohorts to report more fears than children born a few years earlier into an Australian climate that was conceivably a little less frightening and dangerous. Box 9.3 illustrates how one girl's fears changed from toddlerhood to adolescence.

One of the most striking results of the cross-sectional study conducted in Melbourne and rural Victoria (King et al., 1989) was the discovery of how frightened Australian children are about cataclysmic disasters, including nuclear war, holocaust, annihilation from chemical or biological weapons and pollution from nuclear reactors or atomic tests. Similarly, the results of one New Zealand survey showed that the fear of being harmed by a nuclear disaster was one

BOX 9.3 Do fears grow as the child does?

The following excerpts from Louise's father's diary show some of the consistencies and differences in one child's most pressing fears and worries, as she grew up from age two to age 16. The first incident arose when Louise began attending nursery school just before her third birthday.

18 January 1950. *She continues to find things to worry about. Now it is her next visit to the doctor, scheduled for March. Every so often out of the blue she'll say, 'I don't want to go to the doctor in March!' At nursery school she alone of all the kids won't go outdoors to play. She would like to because she sees how much fun the others are having. Why not go out then? 'I was afraid Mrs Hulett would close the door tight and I couldn't get back in.' Now she has agreed to ask Mrs Hulett not to close the door tight. It remains to be seen whether she does or prefers to hang on to her worry. And who am I to point the finger? I also worry over trivialities that could be taken care of by relatively slight action on my part, fearful to take that action because of the new worries that might rise in the old one's place.*

At the age of ten, the prospect of a separation from her parents evoked a range of specific fears.

> *22 June 1958. Day after tomorrow our ten-year-old girl will begin her first long stay away from home. She will spend two weeks at Girl Scout camp in the mountains of Ventura County. She is looking forward to it with mixed pleasure and worry: fear that something will happen to her mother and me while she is gone. But, as she says, she worries only at night; by day she looks forward to the vacation with enthusiasm.*

Similarly, when she was 16 and living in South Australia, Louise feared separation from her parents, not only for its own sake but also for other specific threats the separation might hold in store.

> *17 July 1964. As Peggy and I prepare to leave on a cruise to Northern Queensland Louise is worried over our being separated. At first she feared for our safety at sea. Lately her worries have pinpointed on the behaviour of Gillian, with whom she will be staying and who talks of having a boy friend over one night – thus involving Louise in the deception of her parents. This is two weeks off and she fears she'll be haunted by worry over it the whole two weeks. At bottom, though, her concern is over our separation, even as she realizes this is something she must become accustomed to when she goes off to college.*
>
> © Peterson, 1974, reproduced with permission

Interpretation. Although there are many differences between these three examples of fear, common factors run through all of them. In each case, the fear was over an unlikely but possible eventuality, and in each case a major advance in independence and a change in her routine lifestyle coincided with the expression of her fear (entry into nursery school in the first case, and several weeks' separation from her parents in the other two). Though fear remained a problem for Louise from age two to age 16, her coping skills for dealing with anxieties clearly developed to a more sophisticated level from childhood to adolescence, as did her awareness of the link between her fear and the attractions of undertaking new challenges.

of the most widespread and serious of all the fears expressed by school-age children and adolescents (Barnhart-Thomson & Stacey, 1987). In the New Zealand study, more than 500 students from urban and rural high schools in the South Island were questioned. Results revealed that a majority (76 per cent) would not want to survive a nuclear war or global nuclear accident, though nearly half (47 per cent) felt that there was likely to be one during their lifetime. One in four New Zealand teenagers claimed to have frightening dreams or nightmares about nuclear war,

and 35 per cent said that the prospect of a nuclear holocaust had affected their plans for having children. There was no suggestion of outgrowing the fear with age – 18-year-olds worried more than 13-year-olds and females were more anxious than males.

Cognitive development in the context of schooling

With entry into primary school, the child's cognitive growth is stimulated by the academic challenges that formal education provides. In addition to mastering the content of their lessons in literacy, number, science, life skills and so on, children need to learn the rules of classroom etiquette and behaviour (Goodnow, 1996). These include the need to sit quietly at one's desk while attending to the teacher, making a deliberate effort to remember material from one lesson to the next, reliably completing assigned homework or independent classroom tasks, answering politely when called upon by the teacher, and not speaking to the teacher or to classmates at other times.

There is of course wide variation in the specific rules and ways of teaching and learning that are used in earlier versus later grades of primary school, among different schools in the same community, and even between any two teachers instructing the same grade level in the same school. But in Australia and New Zealand today, certain distinctive cognitive and social experiences of schooling are shared by almost every child. In school, children are expected to pay attention. Their academic performance is publicly evaluated in relation to that of their peers. In place of freely exercising their powers of thought in play, primary school children are introduced to new academic skills like reading, writing, spelling and mathematics as structured lessons that everyone in the class is expected to follow at the same pace. They are also exposed to a new way of life in the classroom that may demand the inhibition of exploratory curiosity, creative insight, humour and peer-oriented sociability. Rapid and accurate response to oral questions is encouraged, but with a new set of rules for how to

From their first days in a formal classroom setting, children begin to learn the etiquette of how to behave in school.

take part in teacher–pupil dialogue. Not all lessons are interesting, but memorisation of dull material may be mandatory, and disciplinary sanctions can often be used in place of intrinsic interest to motivate learning. The social structure of the classroom sets up new possibilities for competition or cooperation with peers, as well as providing feedback on the pupil's own progress.

In the next sections of the chapter, we examine how these facets of classroom life are apt to combine with the progress of cognitive growth and brain maturation to influence children's cognitive performance in the domains of planning, attention, memory, problem-solving, reflection and creativity.

Cognitive planning

In the course of instructing them in specific skills, following a chosen curriculum and enforcing a fixed set of rules for classroom behaviour, teachers gradually modify the child's overall way of thinking.

In contrast to the preschooler, whose processing of information often appears to arise spontaneously as an unconscious by-product of play, socialisation and exploration of the world, the development of cognitive skills turns into a serious business during middle childhood. School teaches children to plan their approaches to problems before embarking on the search for a solution. This strategic approach to the processing of information is eventually likely to generalise from academic problems into the challenging dilemmas of everyday life. Consequently, most adults take a systematic, planned approach to solving everyday problems. They may plan ahead when purchasing a house or car, on deciding when and where to retire, and in making all the other small and large decisions that daily life presents (Chalmers & Lawrence, 1993).

For a preschooler, or a child in the early grades of primary school, the process of thinking a problem through to a solution is likely to be quite different. Young children may focus on some irrelevant feature of the situation and miss the real problem altogether. They may become distracted part of the way through solving a problem, and never go back to it. Or they may come up with a solution, seemingly at random, and express it at once without considering whether other solutions might be more accurate or elegant than the first one. In short, as a result of schooling, thinking and problem-solving become planful activities. For young children who are not yet fully acclimatised to the cognitive strategies of formal schooling, separate cognitive operations are largely disjointed and uncoordinated and attention to the task may be too fragmented to enable an effective solution (Lachman & Burack, 1993).

BOX 9.4 Activity suggestion
Brain teasers

Instruction. As you try to figure out the answers to the following problems, keep track of your thought processes, step by step, by thinking out loud. If you have a tape recorder, dictate your thoughts as they come into your head and transcribe them later. If not, perhaps a friend would help you by writing down your ideas as you speak them.

Problem 1
At West Lake in China, a botanist has developed a new variety of fast-growing lotus which doubles its size every 48 hours. One seedling started in the centre of the lake will fill the lake completely in 40 days. On what day after planting will it fill exactly half the lake?

Problem 2
Dave felt hungry after seeing a film. He bought popcorn at the theatre and then crossed the road to buy cashews. Next he went down the street for a cheeseburger and finally crossed the road again for a milkshake before returning to the theatre to pick up his school bag. Using the measurements in the diagram, calculate how far Dave travelled while consuming his snacks.

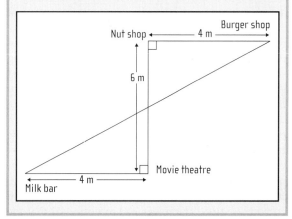

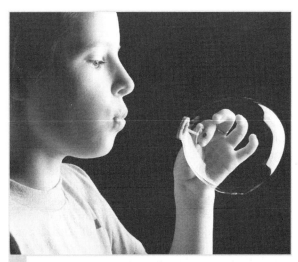

With school entry, children's approaches to thinking about puzzling aspects of the physical world become more systematic.

Developmental changes in attention during middle childhood

Children learn to think and solve problems in school, developing their capacities to:

1. focus on the relevant features of a problem (e.g. in Problem 2 in Box 9.4, focusing on the route Dave took rather than on the specific types of snacks he consumed)
2. attend to a cognitive task or problem for a sustained period of time rather than simply glancing at it and then turning to think about, or do, something else.

Developing a capacity for selective and sustained attention is crucial to a child's likelihood of success in school.

In the classroom, children need to concentrate at length on the teacher or on an academic task without becoming distracted. Their sustained attention must be deployed planfully and selectively. By deciding in advance what features of the situation are irrelevant and turning these out, the learner has more cognitive resources to bring to bear on the real challenges of the situation. Recall your own process of finding solutions to the problems in Box 9.4. One of the first steps towards solving each of these problems is to notice the relevant information while neglecting details that are distracting and irrelevant. For example, when confronted with the puzzle about the boy in the lift, you may have wondered initially whether the problem was one of human development, architecture, biophysics or human motivation. In fact, attention to three variables was needed for a correct solution. The solver had to notice (a) that the

actor in the problem was short in stature, (b) that operating a lift depends on access to the buttons, and (c) that buttons in a lift are normally arranged vertically in correspondence with the floors of the building.

When a teacher hands out an exercise sheet, writes a test item on the blackboard or asks a question out loud, it is unusual to be so inattentive as not to realise that there exists some information to be processed. But in everyday life, young children's cognitive effectiveness is often handicapped by the simple failure to notice that a problem exists. Thus attention is critical for everyday as well as academic problem-solving.

Selective attention

Over the period from age five to age eight, children gain skills in deploying their attention selectively to focus on the relevant features of a problem. At a noisy cocktail party, owing to problems with selective attention, newly arriving guests may at first notice only a chaotic cacophony of sound patterns. But as they join a group the amorphous mixture of noises resolves itself and only one conversation is heard clearly. This change reflects the cognitive process of attending selectively. Between early and middle childhood, selective attention in situations like this becomes more efficient. Thus primary school children are better able to tune out distracting sights and sounds while attending to their lessons, and can sustain attention to one of several competing stimuli for a longer period of time.

Another developmental change in selective hearing involves preferences for the potentially attention-getting features of a visual array. Sheldon White (1965) discovered a transition at about age six from colour to form dominance. When shown patterns of abstract, brightly coloured shapes, preschoolers are apt to focus on colour and neglect the form, while older children tend to prefer form but can also take note of colour when asked to do so. The young child's preference for attending selectively to colour could explain the following experience in an Australian Grade 1 classroom which puzzled a university student who was visiting the class on teaching practice:

Teacher: 'Johnny, how much is three plus three?'
Johnny: 'Brown.'

Johnny was using Cuisenaire rods (shown in Figure 9.5) to learn addition. His 'mistake' was evidently an inadvertent by-product of the same sort of error that adults often make in neglecting children's assumptions about conversation when asking them questions (Siegal, 1991). In an effort to be helpful, the makers of Cuisenaire rods used distinctive colours to draw attention to the differences in length that make the rods useful for teaching arithmetic. But a child like Johnny who attends to colour

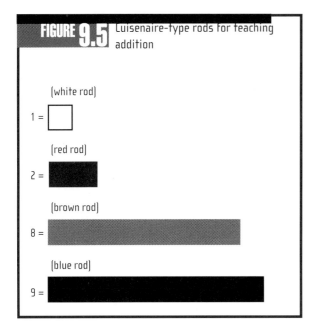

FIGURE **9.5** Cuisenaire-type rods for teaching addition

(white rod)

1 =

(red rod)

2 =

(brown rod)

8 =

(blue rod)

9 =

The use of instructional aids like computers, video, and other electronic technology requires pupils to deploy attention swiftly and flexibly.

rather than length will find this irrelevant dimension a source of misunderstanding.

Planful deployment of attention

Peter Coles, Marian Sigman and Karen Chessel (1977) recorded the eye movements of 3- and 6-year-old children as they looked at visual patterns like the one in Figure 9.6. These young children looked at the pattern longer than a comparison group of adults did, but their eyes moved across it in a rather chaotic way. Some looked only at the edges of the figure, others only at the middle, and many returned again and again to one small part of the drawing without ever viewing the whole thing. Thus, even the simple task of recognising what the drawing represented was hampered by not attending systematically and selectively to the distinctive features inside the windows that would enable the patterns to be distinguished from one another.

Older children and adults can scan systematically, and can plan to deploy attention efficiently to gather relevant information.

Attending to parts and wholes

A different kind of attentional problem was studied in Australia by Alan Watson (1983). He asked a group of 136 Sydney children, aged between three and 11 years, to say what the four drawings in Figure 9.7 looked like. He found that 3- and 4-year-olds experienced a lot of difficulty with the task. Many were not capable of giving even a single interpretation for any drawing. However, by the age of five years, most children could perceive the one most salient feature in each pattern – (a) tools, (b) face in profile, (c) scattered foods, and (d) an apple core. But perceptual processing was still limited at this age. Despite being prompted by the question 'Do you see anything else?', very few 5-year-olds were able to perceive the drawings' alternative possibilities –

(a) a man, (b) a front-on face (c) a pram, and (d) birds' profiles. There was a gradual increase in perceptual sensitivity from age five to age seven with a more abrupt gain between the ages of eight and nine. This suggested 'a genuine developmental surge in perceptual exploration during childhood' (p. 78), followed by stabilisation as the child moved into the upper grades of primary school.

According to John Flavell (1985), this ability to deploy attention flexibly enough to notice the subtle features of a visual array is a key element in mature information processing:

> My own mental image of a cognitively mature information processor is that of a conductor who directs his ensemble of musicians (attentional processes and resources) … now calling forth one instrument, now another, now a blended combination of several, all depending upon the effect desired. I think we do not so much 'pay attention' as 'play our attentional system'. That is, we intentionally exploit and deploy it in a flexible, situation-contingent, adaptive fashion. (p. 200)

Metacognition: Children's knowledge about attention

John Flavell, Frances Green and Eleanor Flavell (1995) told 4-year-olds a story about a woman who was trying to choose from a set of decorative brooches the best one to give as a gift. Unaware of selective attention, these preschoolers did not yet realise that the woman would be attending only to the brooches and so would not be able to notice other things or have other thoughts in her mind. Yet a study of children aged five to ten years revealed that those aged seven and older realised that, in order to remember detailed information, a person would need

FIGURE **9.6** Do these two houses have the same things inside?

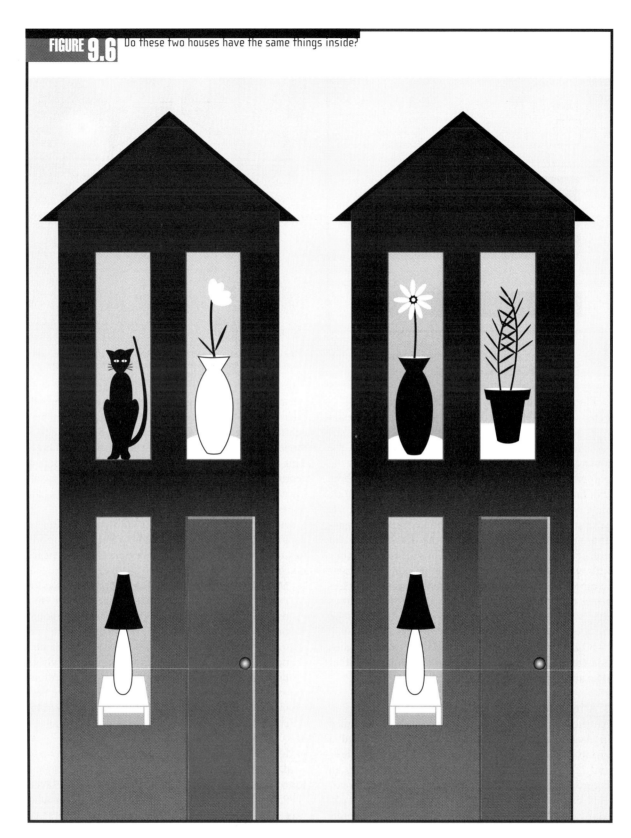

to focus selectively on the details to be remembered rather than globally on irrelevant features of the situation (Miller & Weiss, 1982).

This evidence indicates that a cognitive awareness of selective attention, like selective attention itself, shows a marked developmental improvement during middle childhood.

Memory and problem-solving

Developmental changes in cognitive problem-solving, including Piagetian operational thinking, memory storage and information retrieval, are considered in Chapter 7. But further changes occur during middle childhood and preadolescence in the ways children

FIGURE 9.7 Items from a perception test for Australian children

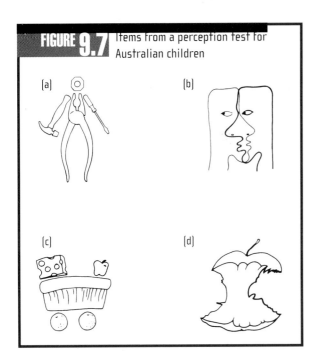

(a) (b) (c) (d)

Source: Watson (1983), p. 79, reproduced with permission.

Micheline Chi compared the memory skills of 10-year-old chess masters with those of adults who were mediocre at chess.

reason and remember, partly as a result of formal schooling. In Australia, Graeme Halford (1993) studied children's memory by drawing on a distinction made by psychologist William James (1890) more than a century ago between two types of memory. The first consists of *primary memory*, or a store containing all the information still present in consciousness at a particular point of time. This is different from *secondary memory*, which contains information that is stored somewhere in the recesses of the mind, but about which the person is not currently thinking. In other words, primary memory is an active, temporary process, while secondary memory is more passive and much longer lasting. Secondary memory stores can retain information for anything from a few seconds to a lifetime. However, this memory process does not actively evaluate, organise or manipulate the information to the same extent as a primary memory.

According to Halford, the capacity of primary memory doubles between the ages of eight and 18 years. In the experimental comparisons of Australian 8- to 9-year-olds and university students which he conducted with Murray Maybery and John Bain (Halford, Maybery & Bain, 1986), Halford discovered that the children performed on a par with adults when the number of items they were required to retain in memory and mentally manipulate was small (e.g. two or three items). But once this size limit was exceeded, children's performance fell apart. Adults, on the other hand, could recall larger amounts of information, partly because they were able to make effective use of the mnemonic strategy of *organisation* (see Chapter 7) to group discrete items to be remembered (e.g. banana, apple, pear) into larger clusters known as *chunks* (e.g. fruit).

In one intriguing study of 10-year-olds, Micheline Chi (1978) compared the cognitive processes of 10-year-old chess masters with those of university students who knew the rules of chess but rarely played the game. One unexpected difference emerged. When given a memory test that consisted of having to reproduce the arrangement of chess pieces on the board, Chi found that the child chess champions did significantly better than the adult novices. But when memory for random digits was tested, a more familiar developmental pattern emerged, with the adults doing much better than the child chess masters. Thus, expertise in the game of chess rather than overall differences in memory or intelligence appeared to explain the superior memory and processing of information about chess games by the child chess masters.

Presumably, their familiarity with the game also enabled them to chunk information in memory into large units like openings, or end-games, rather than as discrete series of individual moves. These skills are acquired with practice. Consequently, gains in memory and information-processing capacity arising during childhood can be as much a consequence of specific educational experiences and classroom practice as of universal developmental changes due to getting older. In fact, Michael Cole and his colleagues (Cole, Gay, Glick & Sharp, 1971) found that rural children in Liberia, aged nine to ten years, who lived in remote villages where they had no opportunity to go to school, displayed poorer memorisation skills than urban Liberian children of the same age who had the benefit of formal schooling. Furthermore, the schooled children rapidly learned with practice to improve their capacity for remembering the same sets of items used in the initial test. Even after extensive practice the unschooled group displayed little or no improvement. Without the years of learning at school how to deliberately commit items to memory, organise material and chunk, practice on the specific memory task itself was to little avail.

But even adult memory has its limits. In another study, Halford (1993) asked experienced researchers in the fields of psychology, education and architecture to interpret complex, multivariate interaction effects in the solutions of statistical computations. The content was familiar but the task was made more difficult than usual by the fact that the researchers had to give their interpretations directly, without making notes. In general, they performed well with two-way and three-way interactions, but their success declined dramatically when the task involved mentally considering four or more dimensions simultaneously. Halford argued that the cognitive load imposed by this task exceeded even the skilled adult's maximum processing capacity.

With exposure to complex problems at work or at school, adults and older children learn to combine discrete pieces of information into larger units, or chunks. This process of *chunking* assists memory and reduces the cognitive processing load. Instead of separate items to remember, recall of the chunk reduces the burden on memory to a single unit. By processing several chunks of information simultaneously, tasks can be maintained within whatever dimensional limit on cognitive load applies to the age group in question. The ability to organise information into discrete meaningful chunks is assisted by schooling and practice in solving memory and information-processing problems. Consequently, as they progress through middle childhood, children gradually become more expert at memory tasks as a result of the practice they receive inside and outside the classroom. As Halford explained:

> Expertise is not just a collection of strategies and skills, analogous to the software of a computer installation. Expertise entails the ability to develop new strategies and to adapt old strategies to changed circumstances. It is more dynamic than is often suggested. (p. 260)

Executive functioning and cognitive flexibility

The ability to shift attentional focus flexibly from absorbed attention to a particular detail (e.g. one person's conversation in a crowded room) back to the overall pattern or background makes an important contribution to cognition and problem-solving. As children grow older, their capacity to shift attention flexibly in these ways improves markedly, as does planning problem solutions ahead of time so that attention, memory and reasoning can be deployed efficiently and effectively. These developments, taken collectively, testify to an improvement with age in children's *executive functioning ability*. According to Claire Hughes (1998), 'The term *executive function* is used to encompass the processes (e.g. planning, inhibitory control, attentional flexibility, working memory) that underlie the flexible goal-directed behaviour' (p. 233).

An example of an everyday executive functioning task appears in Box 9.5. In this task, attentional focus is demanded by the need to ignore a card's

BOX 9.5 **Activity suggestion**
Sorting cards

Materials. For this task you will need a stopwatch and two standard decks of playing cards. (Choose decks with different patterns on the back.) Remove all the face cards and jokers from both decks. (If you are going to test young children, you should also remove all the number cards above 6 from the decks. Or you could use a special deck of children's picture cards.) *Remember, you will need the same set of cards for all your subjects if you intend to compare performance for different age groups.*

Instructions. In order to compare the executive functioning skills of children and adults of different ages, locate friends, relatives and neighbours who would be willing to try a simple card-sorting game. (If you include young children, make sure that their parents are happy for them to play, after you have briefly explained what the task involves.) Explain that the task is to sort the cards into separate piles, following a rule that you will give. As a practice run, turn the cards upside down and have the person sort them into two separate piles based on the patterns on the back of the two decks you used.

Next, tell them that the rule is to sort the cards into 10 piles (or 6 for young children) by number, with separate piles for aces, deuces, threes and so on. Start the stopwatch as the person begins to sort and ask them to work quickly. After three runs through, timing each run separately, announce: 'Now sort into four piles only, based on the suits of the cards – hearts here, diamonds here, clubs here and spades here.' Time this run and note any errors made.

Age comparisons. Compare the following measures across age groups in accuracy and mean time per sort: (1) difference in time between the last number sort and the first suit sort, (2) total number of errors made, and (3) difference in errors on the first suit sort compared with the last number sort.

Interpretation. Do scores on any of these measures appear to differ systematically by age? How well do any differences you observe fit with the hypothesis that there are improvements in executive functioning ability from early childhood to adulthood?

suit while sorting by number, or to ignore number when suit is the relevant dimension. Attentional flexibility is demonstrated by the ease of shifting from one sorting criterion to another, and inhibitory control by the capacity to ignore an obsolete though highly practical sorting criterion (e.g. number) when the sorting rule shifts to a new dimension (e.g. suit).

Creativity

Flexible thinking can be seen not only in attentional flexibility but also in children's original, creative and innovative solutions to cognitive problems. Children who can see beyond the obvious and come up with solutions that no one else has thought of may not always earn top marks on tests in school. However, creativity has its own rewards. A creative child's flexibility of thought can pay dividends when it comes to artistic, dramatic and creative endeavours, such as story writing. Jacob Getzels and Phillip Jackson (1962) gave a picture-based story-writing test to a group of children aged six to 12 in Chicago. Here are two examples of stories produced by two different children in response to a picture of a man gazing out the window of a plane. One child wrote:

> Mr Smith is on his way home from a successful business trip. He is very happy and he is thinking about his wonderful family and how glad he will be to see them again. He can picture it, about an hour from now, his plane landing at the airport and Mrs Smith and their three children all there welcoming him home again. (p. 39)

Another child wrote:

> This man is flying back from Reno where he has just won a divorce from his wife. He couldn't stand to live with her anymore, he told the judge, because she wore so much cold cream on her face at night that her head would skid across the pillow and hit him in the head. He is now contemplating a new skid-proof face cream. (p. 39)

It is clear that both children have a good command of language and are capable of writing coherent narratives. But the second story is more unusual and imaginative than the first.

The parents of children who wrote original, humorously creative stories like the one in the second example above differed from parents of equally intelligent children who were not creative. The former group had emphasised the importance of play, surprise and openness to experience in their approaches to childrearing, whereas the parents of other children, equally high in academic ability, whose stories were relatively pedestrian and stereotypic, had emphasised order, studiousness and obedience to a greater extent.

Fathers can play an important role in the child's development of creativity and cognitive flexibility. In line with early emphases on play rather than routine care in father–infant interaction (see Chapters 3 and 5), fathers who actively involve themselves in their primary school sons' and daughters' academic development can make a substantial difference. One comparison of girls in the United States who were growing up in either a father-present or a father-absent home (Fry & Grover, 1982) revealed significant advantages of daily interaction with the father when it came to rich ideas, cognitive flexibility, attentional selectivity, task persistence and achievement of elegant problem solutions (see Figure 9.8).

Evaluative thinking: Reflection versus impulsivity

Reflection versus impulsivity is another cognitive dimension related to executive control and cognitive flexibility. Reflective children are slow to offer solutions to cognitive problems but often earn high scores for accuracy and ingenuity. They seem to spend their lengthy problem-solving time considering alternative solutions and choosing the best one. Indeed, when struggling to solve a cognitive problem, a person's

Fathers who share activities with their children can boost their sons' and daughters' creativity.

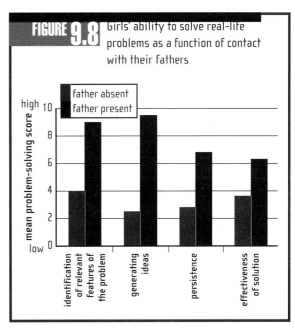

FIGURE 9.8 Girls' ability to solve real-life problems as a function of contact with their fathers

Source: Based on data in Fry & Grover (1982), p. 111.

In any classroom, some children's hands will go up faster than others when the teacher asks a question.

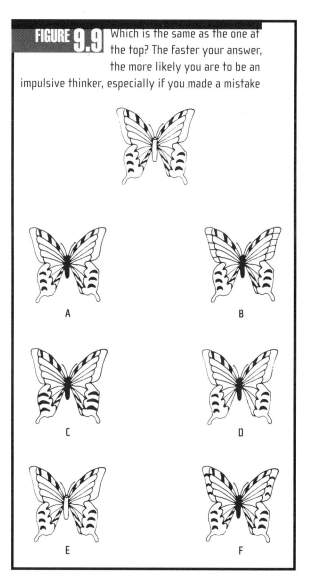

first attempt at an answer is not always their best one. (For example, you may have come up with a few false starts before hitting on the correct answer to the problems in Box 9.4.) Consequently, the process of problem-solving does not always come to an abrupt end when the first idea pops into mind. Instead, the capable, reflective thinker generally considers multiple options and strives for an elegant solution, discarding those that seem too simple-minded or cumbersome.

An impulsive problem-solver, on the other hand, solves problems quickly but makes many errors. These children appear to offer the first idea that pops into their head without considering alternatives. An inability to inhibit overly facile or incorrect solutions testifies to the lack of inhibitory control that is gradually overcome with the growth of executive functioning.

In the classroom, the cognitive style dimension of reflection–impulsivity is seen in the contrast between pupils who think long and hard about a problem, trying out many ideas in their minds before venturing a solution, and those who have their hands up instantly to offer the first solution that comes into their heads. Reflective pupils take longer to solve problems than impulsive thinkers, but also make fewer errors. Figure 9.9 shows an example of a problem used to measure reflection–impulsivity.

Developing literacy

The cognitive and neurobiological advances of middle childhood considered earlier in this chapter are important both in their own right and as a basis for the child's mastery of one of the most important skills that school has to teach – literacy, or learning to read and write. The developmental milestone of becoming literate is almost as significant in our culture as the acquisition of language (see Chapter 6). Reading is 'a prerequisite skill for nearly every form of employment and the primary key to lifelong learning' (Tunmer & Bowey, 1984, p. 144). Thus, in many countries in the world today, where formal education is still not a fact of life for every child, adults will put up with great hardships to enable themselves and their children to gain literacy. They recognise that, in addition to being a lifespan vocational and educational prerequisite, the skills of reading and writing open up a wide range of social possibilities, economic returns and intangible cultural advantages to the lucky few managing to acquire them.

This is in sharp contrast to contemporary Australian and New Zealand society where compulsory schooling and the ability to read and write are taken for granted. But, even in our culture, the process of gaining literacy is not as universal or effortless as it might at first seem. Unlike language acquisition, learning to read generally requires the intervention of formal schooling. Even with the aid of school, the task is likely to prove difficult for many children. In fact, on the basis of observations of monolingual English-speaking pupils in Australian schools, William Tunmer and Judy Bowey (1984) concluded that:

Somewhere between 10 and 15 per cent of school children having no apparent visual, hearing or mental deficits encounter unusual difficulty of one kind or another in learning to read … A significant number of children never learn to read efficiently or effectively. For those of us who can read, it is hard to understand why anyone should have trouble acquiring the skill, since once acquired reading seems to be easy and natural. But even the average child does not learn to read easily. (p. 144)

Developing reading readiness: Awareness of books and phonology

The task of holding a book in the correct position, perceiving lines of print and scanning the eyes across them is a complicated information-processing exercise, as the activity in Box 9.6 illustrates. To facilitate the smooth acquisition of the skill of literacy, young children need quite a bit of background knowledge about books, print and the general visual and auditory structure of words and sentences. To gain an appreciation of some of these 'prereading' assumptions, test yourself on the quiz in Box 9.6. Experiences at home as a preschooler can facilitate children's awareness of books, and longitudinal research evidence indicates that the number of books, newspapers and magazines in a preschooler's home predicts later success as a reader in school (Harris & Hatano, 1999).

Another important prereading skill that may also be acquired at home before school entry is *phonological awareness*, or the 'awareness of and access to the sound structure of a language' (McBride-Chang &

Experiences at home long before school entry can facilitate children's learning to read.

BOX 9.6 Activity suggestion
How do you hold a book?

Instructions. Among the prerequisites for learning to read are being able to distinguish the front cover of the book from the back, to distinguish the print from the illustrations, and knowing where to move the eyes and which way to turn the pages. Skilled adult readers of English are apt to take these items of insight for granted until exposed to a reading system, such as Chinese, which operates by different conventions. This illustration is modelled on a page from a beginning primary school reader used in China. Look at it and then work through the quiz.

Quiz
1. Point to the first word, or the place where you would start reading.
2. Now move your finger through the text to show the direction your eyes would move when reading from the start to the end of the page.
3. Point to the first word you would pause at if reading aloud.
4. Count how many sentences there are altogether.
5. Say what you think the text is about. (What clues did you use to decide this?)

Scoring: The answers are upside down at the bottom of this box. Give yourself one point for each correct answer.

Answers: 1. 同 2. Begin at the top right-hand corner and move down the column towards the bottom of the page, then up to the top of the second column from the right, and so on. 3. 跑 4. One. 5. Classmates playing in the playground.

Kail, 2002). William Tunmer and Andrew Nesdale (1985) measured phonological awareness in a group of 6-year-olds in Western Australia by asking them to tap with a pencil on a desk. For each separate sound they heard when a word was spoken, the children were to give a single tap. Thus the word 'cat' required three taps for its three separate sounds /k/, /a/ and /t/, while 'pea' required two (for /p/ and /ee/). They discovered that a child's accuracy in breaking down words into their component sounds was a strong predictor of subsequent skill in learning to read.

Sensitivity to rhyme is also a component of phonological awareness that can be demonstrated either productively (e.g. the child replies 'cat' when asked for a word to rhyme with 'pat') or receptively (e.g. the child agrees that 'toy' and 'boy' rhyme, whereas 'shop' and 'ship' do not). Alliteration, another component, refers to words that share the same initial sound pattern (e.g. 'street', 'strike' and 'straw').

Usha Goswami and Peter Bryant (1990) tested a large group of 4-, 5- and 6-year-olds in Britain and found that phonological awareness of rhyme and alliteration were remarkably good predictors of the children's rate of acquisition of literacy in primary school. It appeared that knowledge of rhyme was an essential prerequisite for reading, and not merely an accidental correlate or facilitator of the process. In the case of an affluent child, whose early experiences at home and in preschool include extensive exposure to nursery rhymes, musical lyrics and other forms of poetry, these three possibilities are hard to tease apart.

Longitudinal investigations and training studies provide an ideal means of sorting out causal relationships. In research of this kind with socially disadvantaged English children, evidence emerged to show that experience with rhyme is crucial to the child's success in learning to read, not simply a by-product. The results of one of these training studies (Bradley & Bryant, 1983) are illustrated in Figure 9.10. As the figure shows, children exposed to lessons in rhyme scored substantially higher than a control group on

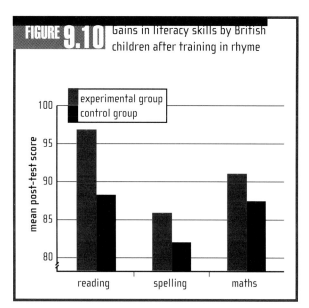

FIGURE 9.10 Gains in literacy skills by British children after training in rhyme

Source: Based on data in Bradley & Bryant (1983), p. 421.

reading and spelling tests but were no better on tests of maths. In other words, explicit training in phonological awareness was seen to boost the development of literacy, possibly by teaching children how to segment and analyse words phonologically by matching sounds to printed letters.

Research over recent decades has strongly confirmed that phonological awareness is 'one of the strongest predictors of learning to read in English' (McBride-Chang & Kail, 2002, p. 1393). It even predicts how readily Chinese children in Hong Kong learn to read Chinese characters, despite the lack of a direct correspondence between the way the character looks and the way it is pronounced (McBride-Chang & Kail, 2002).

Reading for meaning

Skilled reading involves not only decoding, or sounding out printed words phonologically, but also the ability to comprehend written material. In an irregularly spelled language like English, this entails a number of component cognitive operations, including the following (Bowey, 1994; Harris & Hatano, 1999):

1. Learn to distinguish visually among the shapes of printed letters (e.g. 'b' versus 'p' versus 'd').
2. Learn the rules for regular and irregular conversion of visual letters into sounds (e.g. 'b' always sounds like /b/, while 'c' sounds like /k/ in 'cat' and like /s/ in 'city').
3. Learn to discriminate whole words visually ('cap' versus 'cup').
4. Learn the correct pronunciation of visual word patterns, including irregulars (e.g. 'cough' versus 'though').
5. Learn to sound out sentences comprised of individual words.
6. Learn to match the sound patterns with their

Parents who read nursery rhymes to their children may boost later reading success.

meanings while reading rapidly with expression, or silently.

Judy Bowey (1994) studied 5-year-old Australian children who had not yet been exposed to formal reading instruction at school. She subdivided the group into two categories: novice readers and non-readers. Even though they had not yet been taught to read in school, the novice readers were able to read simple words accurately. The non-readers could not read any words as yet. Bowey compared the novice readers with the non-readers in terms of their levels of phonological skill, or the ability to dissect words into their component sounds. The novice readers scored significantly higher than the non-readers on several measures of understanding phonetic units and being sensitive to phonological cues. Furthermore, even after controlling statistically for spoken language ability and knowledge of the names of the letters of the alphabet, Bowey discovered robust differences between the non-readers and the readers in phonological sensitivity. Possibly, as suggested in Box 9.7, an awareness of the correspondence between phonetic sound patterns and written words had assisted the novice readers to master some of the elements of the decoding of print even before they had been exposed to formal reading instruction in school.

Even after decoding is fully mastered, however, there is often a gap between the ability to decode well enough to pronounce written material accurately and the ability to make accurate sense of what the phonologically decoded passages actually mean. The phrase 'barking at print' is sometimes used by teachers for children who can accurately pronounce a written passage that they don't understand.

To study the link between general cognitive development and reading comprehension, Alan Watson

In learning to read, children must discover how to sound out sentences comprising printed letters and words.

BOX 9.7 A case in point
Learning the logic of words

The following entries in her father's diary illustrate how 7-year-old Louise practised and perfected her reading skills.

4 March 1955. *Nearing her seventh birthday, she is learning to read very rapidly, and largely on her own. Road signs, advertising circulars, comics are all grist to her mill. She sets to work at figuring them out no matter how difficult they may appear. Usually she does figure them out herself, words like 'Ambassador', 'Bermuda', and such that often mean nothing to her as useful words but that reveal themselves phonetically. Sometimes she asks, 'What word is this?' but if I tell her to guess she will usually guess right. Occasionally I help her with the phonetics by breaking a word apart and having her sound each syllable; on other occasions I show her the similarity between the word in question and one she already knows. But this is becoming less and less necessary as she does it on her own initiative.*

20 August 1955. *Thus after a long vacation from reading she discovered a Tom Sawyer reading club at the Santa Barbara Library with the chance to whitewash a fence picket after reading four books and to win a certificate after reading ten. So Louise, whose other vacation interests had taken the place of reading, set to work on the ten books and earned her certificate. She reads conscientiously, perhaps too much so, skipping the little words to tackle the big ones and so sometimes losing the meaning. When this happens, she complains, 'This doesn't make sense', and wants to throw the book up in disgust. But I see she brought four more books home yesterday although the certificate was already hers.*

27 October 1955. *Louise has returned to books again after having been off them along with schoolwork in general. She borrows books from school and reads for an hour after supper as she is doing now. She reads for entertainment rather than instruction and usually brings home a thick rather than thin book because the thick books have more interesting stories. She brought one of the easy ones home on another child's recommendation and it bored her to actual tears. She was almost too angry to finish it and did so only because she had to in order to get credit for it.*

© Peterson, 1974, reproduced with permission

(1983) conducted a longitudinal study of Sydney children aged five to nine years, beginning when the children were in kindergarten and continuing as they moved through the first four grades of primary school. To assess possible cognitive contributions to the development of reading, Watson tested his subjects' thinking about several Piagetian operational problems like those described in Chapter 7, as well as performance on multiple classification matrices of the kind shown in Figure 9.11. To score correctly on this latter type of problem a child must simultaneously imagine the objects along two progressive dimensions (number of sides and light, dark or cross-hatched in Figure 9.11).

Watson found that the development of concrete-operational seriation and classification skills strongly predicted reading comprehension scores. Furthermore, scores on the operational thinking tests given when the children were still in kindergarten predicted reading comprehension during Grades 2, 3 and 4 even better than the same tests given in primary school. Vocabulary and oral language skills also made a significant, but statistically independent, contribution to comprehension ability. Watson concluded that Piagetian logical thinking skills may help children learn the logical rules of reading, and that children who are delayed in cognitive development may need to master the logical skills of classification and seriation (see Chapter 7) before formal reading will prove to be of optimum benefit. As Watson explained:

Teachers need to be made aware of the possibility of developmental delay and helped to diagnose its presence and to devise suitable teaching. The seriation and perceptual regulation tasks used in this project could usefully be extended for developmental diagnosis of those not learning as well as their peers, to provide an index of general cognitive and perceptual lag. They may also suggest cognitive and perceptual activities that teachers can use to stimulate the development of process abilities important for the mastering of the basic skills. (1983, p. 285)

The development of reading in Aboriginal children

For Australian children leading traditional lifestyles in remote communities where an Aboriginal language is spoken, the skill of reading English-language text may be mastered in a vacuum, without a clear awareness of the value of reading outside school. Michael Christie (1983) interviewed a group of 14 Aboriginal boys who lived in a remote community at Milingimbi in Arnhem Land. All the boys had been educated in schools that followed the mainstream Anglo-Australian curriculum, and all were competent readers. When questioned, each boy reported enthusiastic enjoyment of reading lessons at school. But none could see any place for reading in his life outside the classroom. Hence the boys failed to use reading recreationally or for the purpose of acquiring new knowledge. In school, they also minimised their chances to practise and perfect reading skills by electing to read the same unchallenging books over and over again. According to Christie, these Aboriginal pupils considered reading an arbitrary, meaningless ritual or ceremony, confined to precise 'reading-lesson' times inside the classroom. As he explained:

To them it is completely meaningful as a part of the school process; it doesn't need meaning in the outside world. To them, reading or doing maths outside of school would be akin to playing the didgeridoo when there is no ceremony. It's okay to do it if you really want to, but that is not its real function. (p. 68)

This tendency to consider reading a magical school ritual rather than a purposeful technique for seeking information or enjoyment also explains the Aboriginal child's preference for repetitious and unchallenging reading matter, as Christie noted:

They don't read at home and in the classroom will spend much time looking at picture books without reading a word. They love reading to the teacher and especially love reading easy stories, in groups, very loudly in strident, sing-song voices … To them, reading is like singing; it's something you do out loud in a group with your friends in a special context – not because it's meaningful but because it's enjoyable. To the ritual reader, one of the special charms of reading, like singing, is that you don't need to be concerned about what it means. (p. 69)

FIGURE 9.11 Which object belongs in the bottom right-hand corner of the board?

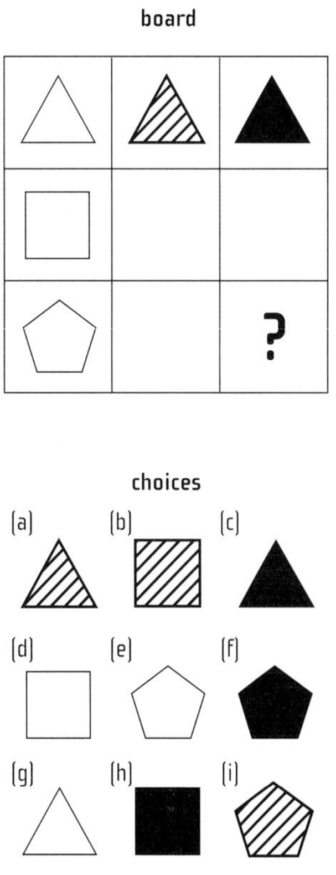

board

choices

(a) (b) (c)
(d) (e) (f)
(g) (h) (i)

Answer is (f).

The relevance of reading to life outside the classroom will vary in different cultural environments.

As a result of these observations, Christie came up with a school program designed to make the process of reading more meaningful and useful to Aboriginal children in everyday life. His argument was that any change in understanding the purpose of reading would also indirectly boost technical reading competence as a result of motivation. Eager readers would, in essence, teach themselves to read better. Christie's teaching suggestions included the following:

1. *Introduce newspapers into the classroom.* News stories, advertisements and announcements relating to the local community all help to demonstrate the relevance of reading to life outside school. Newspapers are also an ideal medium for motivating the effort of reading. Their topical relevance piques curiosity, while 'they have a few interesting pictures but not so many that reading is not necessary' (p. 71).

2. *Develop class activities and outside visits.* Practical opportunities to use reading in action also highlight the value of the skill in real life. For example, pupils could write away for, read and report on pamphlets before planning school excursions. They could also prepare written programs and make signs to advertise sports meetings and other school events. More reading should be introduced into science, art and other curriculum areas, since 'the more reading which is done outside the *reading lesson* the better' (p. 70).

3. *Allow children to choose their own reading matter.* Books, magazines or comics that are entertaining, informative and of personal interest are the best evidence of the fact that reading can be a pleasant form of recreation. Conversely, an Aboriginal child's impression that reading is a meaningless ritual is reinforced when lessons are confined to books with little intrinsic appeal. Christie also suggested that teachers in remote country regions might have to write their own story books or weekly 'newspaper serials', since books imported from cities may seem alien or irrelevant to the local populace.

Judith Kearins (1981) likewise suggested that instruction about 'reasons for reading' could prove useful to Aboriginal children in remote communities, as well as to other groups of children whose families emphasise talents other than literacy in their child-rearing approaches before their children enter school.

A similar analysis of the reading patterns of a group of 30 Aboriginal children in Grade 1 classrooms in Brisbane (Jones, 1979) yielded conclusions broadly consistent with the suggestions made by Christie and Kearins. The measure of reading achievement in this study was comprehension of the meaning of a list of written words. Each child's word comprehension score was evaluated in relation to the balance of teachers' approval and disapproval that prevailed in the class during reading lessons. Teachers who offered high rates of praise for correct answers, but rarely disapproved of incorrect answers, were not as effective with Aboriginal pupils as those whose rates of approval of accuracy and also disapproval of error were above average. Furthermore, Aboriginal children who had been exposed to teachers who praised freely but withheld rejection resembled the 'ritual' readers observed by Christie in older grades. As the researcher, D. Jones, explained:

> Whilst achieving relatively low reading scores at the time of testing, [Aboriginal children] gave every indication of being comfortable in the classroom situation and appeared to derive pleasure from reading and listening to stories being read to them. (p. 56)

On the other hand, teachers who rejected incorrect answers freely, but balanced this with equally high levels of approval for correct replies produced Aboriginal pupils whose reading comprehension was not only significantly better than that of their Aboriginal peers in other classrooms, but was also clearly up to standard for their age. Most had mastered reading effectively by the end of just one year of instruction in school. Jones saw the results as:

> suggesting that at least a moderate level of criticism and disapproval is a desirable feature for the Aboriginal child learning to read ... [There may be] a need for an intermediate level of stress for optimal growth in reading. It is possible therefore that excessive praise without criticism induces too little stress, and that a high degree of criticism without balancing levels of approval induces too much stress for the development of reading abilities. (p. 53)

Perhaps 'criticism' had combined with praise to enhance the children's motivation for reading to an optimal level (Christie, 1983; Kearins, 1981). But it is also possible that the content of the criticism (particularly any which may have related to poor comprehension) could have had the direct effect of boosting children's metacognitive understanding of the goals and process of reading (Paris, 1986).

The motivation to succeed academically

It takes motivation to learn to read, even under ideal teaching conditions. But a child's academic motivation accounts for more than just the acquisition of literacy. In fact, virtually everything that happens to a child in school from the start of Grade 1 to the end of Grade 12 is affected by *motivation*. Some children enter school eagerly and gain greater and greater motivation for schooling year by year. Often, these same children will aspire to higher education as a result of their love for school. Then, as adolescents and young adults, motivation for study may continue to grow stronger through the optional years they elect to spend in higher education. But other children do not have the good fortune to delight in going to school. When a pupil's poor academic performance can be attributed to indifference or failure to try, rather than lack of ability, the problem is one of motivation. Such children are often described as 'underachievers' on the grounds that their actual mastery of lessons in school is below what would be expected on the basis of their intelligence and learning ability.

Motivational problems may include poor academic self-concept, low morale, school phobia, academic underachievement and opting out of school at the earliest opportunity. The causes of problems like these are complex and not yet fully understood. But educational and developmental researchers have begun to gain some valuable insights into the dynamics of academic motivation.

In one pioneering study, Carol Dweck (1978) discovered that, from the earliest grades of primary school, there were important differences in the ways children processed the feedback their teachers gave them about their academic performance.

She compared children of identical ability who were exposed to identical kinds of positive and negative feedback from teachers and adult experimenters, and discovered a distinctive personality dimension which took the form of two contrasting ways of interpreting input about academic performance. One group displayed pessimism about their academic ability. The other group took in the feedback constructively while displaying a strong sense of their own ability to succeed.

Mastery orientation versus learned helplessness

Dweck described one group of children as *mastery-oriented*. These children stood out from their peers for their ability to maintain a self-confident, productive outlook even in the face of failure.

> Mastery-oriented children confront obstacles, they tend not to contemplate the causes for their difficulties nor, for that matter, to dwell at all on the fact that they are experiencing difficulty. Instead, they are likely to focus their attention on

strategies for solving the problem. (Licht & Dweck, 1984, p. 629)

The other group of children studied by Dweck were pupils who scored exceptionally low in mastery orientation, so much so that their reaction to academic tasks and feedback could be described as a learned helplessness (see Chapter 4). 'Helpless' pupils took a passive, self-defeating attitude to most of the tasks they were given in school. Unlike their mastery-oriented peers, they typically opted out of any task that seemed at all challenging academically. Even on routine tasks, they were likely to give up too quickly. Rather than boredom, the reason seemed to be an irrational fear of failure. Dweck also observed a number of other self-defeating features of the helpless child's processing of feedback about school work, including:

1. misunderstanding feedback about success
2. self-defeating views of causality
3. premature opting out of academic situations.

These problems, arising from a lack of mastery orientation, can be explained as follows:

1. *Mistaking feedback.* Unlike their mastery-oriented or average peers, Dweck found that helpless pupils were inclined to misjudge the 'raw data' of their own academic performance. These children adopted an unrealistically pessimistic perspective on their own ability and success in school. For example, if a maths teacher gave a test and then asked pupils to guess how many problems they had solved correctly before handing in their papers, helpless pupils would radically underestimate their own accuracy. Even when they were specifically told they had done well, pupils who displayed learned helplessness and were low in mastery orientation often imagined that the test was too easy or that most of their classmates had done even better than they had.
2. *Self-defeating causality.* Exceptional achievement in school is undeniable, objectively. Yet helpless children will still find ways to deny their achievements. For example, a child low in mastery orien-

Mastery-oriented children enjoy new puzzles and cognitive challenges.

tation might be told that she has just earned the top score for the entire class in a maths test. Or she might win a prize in an inter-school competition, or spell every word in a spelling test correctly. But, rather than accept at face value the tangible evidence of her ability, the helpless child is apt to explain the fact away in a defeatist manner by saying it was 'a fluke' or 'pure luck', or the rest of the class must have been deliberately trying to do badly. Conversely, when helpless children experience failure, they tend to perceive only one possible cause – their own irremediable lack of ability. Mastery-oriented children are the opposite. They typically explain failure as due either to bad luck or to not having tried hard enough, and consider success to be undeniable testimony to their own intrinsic aptitude.

3. *Premature opting out.* Perhaps as a result of these irrationally pessimistic impressions of their chances of success, Dweck noted that pupils with learned helplessness were also less persistent than other children when offered challenging tasks. Furthermore, if a free choice of problems to work on was allowed, pupils who were very low in mastery orientation were inclined to select boring or repetitive tasks that were far too easy to suit their level of ability and knowledge.

When Millicent Poole and B. C. Low (1982) compared the academic attitudes and motivation of a group of Australian pupils who had elected to drop out of school at the minimum leaving age with boys and girls at the same schools who had chosen to stay on for further studies, they found that unrealistically 'helpless' attitudes about their own scholastic abilities predominated among female premature school-leavers. Despite having achieved high grades in school so far, these girls had low achievement motivation and rated their chance of failure as extremely high if they had continued with further schooling.

Parents, children and academic achievement

Parents are likely to have beliefs about the causes of academic success, and about their offspring's probabilities of succeeding in school; these may begin to shape their children's feelings about academic success, their motivation to do well and their beliefs about the value of effort and their own talents for school, long before school entry.

To uncover links and gaps between parents' and children's ideas about academic success, Judith Cashmore (1982) interviewed a group of Sydney families from mainstream Anglo-Australian families and Italian-Australian backgrounds. The parents in the latter group had migrated from Italy to Australia before their children entered school, so that classroom experiences of both groups were similar. The child's, the mother's and the father's explanations for the child's achieving well in a range of school subjects, including mathematics, creative writing, art and music, were explored by asking respondents to indicate which of four possible causes best explained the child's academic successes and failures. The four factors were (a) luck (e.g. 'She passed the test because she guessed right'), (b) pupil effort ('He studied hard'), (c) pupil ability ('She is good at maths'), and (d) teacher's skill ('The lessons were clear').

Since few choices of teacher's skill or luck were given, Cashmore contrasted explanations based on pupil ability versus pupil effort. In both cultural groups, parents chose the former more often, while offspring favoured the latter. Since effort is more readily modifiable than skill, the children's explanations were more constructive.

Despite the lack of any cross-cultural differences among parents, there were differences for the pupils themselves as a function of both gender and ethnicity. As shown in Table 9.4, Anglo-Australian girls and Italian-Australian boys had the healthiest attitudes towards academic achievement.

Developmental changes in causal attributions for success or failure

Andrew Nesdale and Sherryl Pope (1982) similarly studied the perceived causes for academic success and failure in a group of 160 Western Australian pupils aged four to seven years who were given puzzles to solve that ranged from far too easy to practically impossible. An interesting age difference emerged in these Australian children's reactions to failure. The 7-year-olds were more resistant than the 4- and 5-year-olds to making any adverse inferences at all about their own effort or talent, even after consistently failing to solve any of the puzzles. They claimed either that the puzzles were too hard or that they had had bad luck. But the younger group more often blamed their own lack of skill or effort. This self-protective reaction to failure seen among 7-year-olds can be highly adaptive. Children who think they were just unlucky will be motivated in future to try again, while those who believe they lack ability for puzzles may not do so.

Culture and schooling

While competitive classroom tasks may provide a yardstick against which pupils can measure their

TABLE 9.4	Most frequent attributions of academic success and failure by Sydney pupils	
Respondents' gender	Ethnicity	
	Anglo-Australian	*Italian-Australian*
Daughters	Effort	Ability
Sons	Ability	Effort

ability relative to that of their peers, not all children achieve their best when made to compete against others. Cultural variations in beliefs about the value of competition as opposed to cooperation are particularly sharp in Australia and New Zealand today. Both Maori and Aboriginal cultures place greater emphasis on the value of cooperation and peer support than does the Anglo mainstream majority in each country. Thus Maori and Aboriginal children may be strongly motivated to downplay their own achievement in competitive classroom environments where the only way to succeed appears to be at the cost of classmates' failure.

Mismatches between the cultures of home and school

In one classic study of Aboriginal children's responses to cooperative and competitive classroom environments, Elizabeth Sommerland and W. P. Bellingham (1972) studied 64 Aboriginal students and 32 Anglo-Australian students attending a residential school in Darwin. Before coming to this school, most of the Aboriginal students had been exposed to a traditional, tribal upbringing:

> The majority have been socialised in terms of traditional Aboriginal goals and values, while kinship remains a dominant organizational aspect of their lives. Every student has a 'skin' name which defines his relationship to others in his life space, and even in the school situation avoidance taboos and reciprocal obligations are observed. The students have had very little contact with Europeans, and for most of them it is the first time they have had any meaningful personal contact with Aborigines from totally unfamiliar tribes. (pp. 150–1)

The children were assigned to groups of four to play cooperative and competitive games. The results indicated that Aboriginal children were significantly more cooperative than the Anglo-Australian students. Furthermore, even when they competed, the Aboriginal pupils did so in a mutually supportive manner – for example, by beginning with the player who had received the least reward on the previous trial so that he or she would have a better chance of winning. Unlike their Anglo peers, the Aboriginal children verbally reprimanded other players for being too competitive, with comments like: 'Don't worry about the money – you're just greedy for the money.'

However, there were differences within the Aboriginal group as a function of levels of aspiration for further schooling. Aboriginal students in a stream aiming for secondary education showed significantly more competitive behaviour than those who aspired only to training in domestic science or manual arts on completion of primary school. The emphasis placed by teachers on competitive academic achievement in the groups preparing for high school appeared to be one factor responsible for this difference.

Motivation might also have played a part. James

Chapman (1984) explored Maori children's perceptions of their chances of achieving success in school. He carefully matched a group of 13-year-old Maori students with Pakeha classmates who came from families of the same socioeconomic background and had similar levels of academic achievement. He found that, in comparison with their Pakeha peers, Maori students had lower expectations about their future chances of success in maths and science:

> Maori pupils tended to express lower expectations for future success in Maths and Science and to see the causes of successful event outcomes in school as being marginally less under their control than Pakeha pupils. The differences between groups were small, however. (p. 52)

Since the two groups had been matched for current ability and past performance in these disciplines, the Maori students' pessimism appeared to reflect an unrealistic or 'helpless' underestimation of their own mathematical or scientific potential. These data suggest that Maori children might benefit even more than their Pakeha peers from confidence-building efforts by their teachers and parents.

Teachers' expectations of diverse cultural groups

In addition to their possibly adverse reactions to the overemphasis on academic competition that is sometimes seen in Australian or New Zealand classrooms, these Aboriginal and Maori students' academic achievement might also have been undermined by their teachers' pessimistic misperceptions of their abilities and academic motivation.

Alison St George (1983) studied teachers' perceptions of 20 Maori and 67 Pakeha students in four urban primary schools in New Zealand. The children were all near the age of nine at the time of the study. She found that teachers rated the Maori children as significantly less successful academically than their Pakeha classmates. The teachers' unfavourable impressions of Maori students' academic skills stemmed in part from their perceptions of these children's home backgrounds. These New Zealand teachers viewed Maori parents as having more negative attitudes to schooling than Pakeha parents and as providing fewer books and less stimulation at home. Pakeha parents, on the other hand, were believed to provide optimal stimulation and to support their children's eagerness to learn consistently and enthusiastically. The group of students in whose academic ability the teachers believed most firmly was largely Pakeha (87 per cent), whereas the group seen to have the most doubtful ability was more than half Maori.

Teachers' classroom interactions reflected their expectations. Maori pupils received more public criticism of both their academic work and their classroom behaviour than their Pakeha classmates. By contrast, the Anglo pupils in the high-expectation group were asked more complex questions by their teachers than any other students in class, and lengthy explanations by these children were actively encouraged. Teachers meted out significantly less criticism to these students, while at the same time according them the public recognition of choosing them to answer questions when their hands were raised.

On the basis of previous research indicating comparable ranges of ability for Pakeha and Maori students in New Zealand schools, St George concluded that teachers' tendencies to expect less of Polynesian than Anglo children could play a causal role in underachievement by Polynesians as a group. Even though her study provided no evidence that overt discrimination was operating in New Zealand schools, she argued that education was needed for primary school teachers to alert them to the positive aspects of cultural diversity in the classroom:

> There will always be individual differences in pupil abilities and interests as well as a variety of group differences based on ethnic or cultural group. Hopefully, teachers will be encouraged to draw upon and react to positive aspects of such differences in ways which will result in greater similarity in levels of interests, efforts and positive self-regard in all children. In this way the cycle of maintaining the status quo of low minority achievement may begin to be broken. (p. 58)

At a more subtle level, the ethnic values and customs which children from other language communities have learned to take for granted at home may clash with the school's dominant Anglo style. For example, when Jan Harris (1980) interviewed a group of Australian primary school teachers about their experiences with 'multicultural' education, the problems that were mentioned extended well beyond difficulties with language. One teacher stated frankly that 'she had to struggle to guard against a tendency to dislike a child for something she's been taught at home which isn't acceptable here at school' (p. 34). Harris lamented the teachers' apparent disinclination to adapt their behaviour to the cultural differences and expectations of their students, and concluded that 'The child was expected to adjust to the school, rather than the school adjusting to the child' (p. 34).

Valerie Podmore and Ross St George (1986) found that differences between the tactics used by New Zealand Maori and Pakeha mothers to teach their children to solve puzzles and other problems were bound up with the mother's own level of educational attainment:

> Maternal education level was associated with notable differences on an extensive range of verbal behaviors. The more frequent use of Questions, Attending, Teaching, and Rewards among mothers from the higher education group could be related to their greater verbal facility, their tendency to model teaching behaviors used in classrooms or to different perceptions of the child-rearing role. Possibly, more mothers from the higher education group perceived their role as teaching their children, whereas more mothers from the lower education group focused on controlling their children's behavior. Further research concerned with parents' perceptions of child-rearing and their motivations could extend these findings and also explain some marked within-group differences in behavior. (p. 381)

The language of schooling

The languages of school and home are not always compatible. For example, when Australian children grow up speaking an Aboriginal language, or the non-English language of their migrant parents' country of birth, or when they come from a deaf family fluent in Auslan (see Chapter 6), their teachers may have no knowledge at all of the language the child is accustomed to using at home. The transition into school life is clearly made much more difficult under these circumstances. But for the bilingual teacher a different dilemma is apt to arise. To what extent should the teacher who is fluent in both languages maintain linguistic continuity with the home? Conversely, how soon should the child be encouraged to adapt to the dominant culture's requirement of speaking English? Nowadays, some schools in Australia and New Zealand allow a gradual transition, beginning bilingual language teaching as early as age two. But in other societies there is a total discontinuity between the language of the home and the language of the school. Box 9.8 describes the stresses and conflicts that can arise out of a clash between the languages of home and school.

Stephen Krashen (1988) argues that a large body of research on bilingual education programs indicates that they are most effective when teachers take careful account of the child's cultural circumstances at home, including the language spoken by the family, but also the parents' values, parenting practices and the full gamut of social experiences that children encounter at home. In addition, the following features of bilingual teaching programs in primary school are associated with greater success, according to Krashen's review of the published research literature:

1. high-quality teaching of English, using conversation and other techniques associated with rapid second-language learning
2. teachers who are fluent in the child's native language and can teach in it when appropriate
3. encouragement of children to continue developing skills in their native language along with encouragement of English-language mastery
4. peers in the classroom who share the same native language.

These factors apply not only to bilingual education in spoken languages but also to the effective education of children who are profoundly deaf and learn a sign language or Signed English in school. Until children are able to share a fluent language with teachers and classmates, the rest of the school curriculum is likely to have very little meaning for them.

Politeness, obedience and the culture of schooling

From extensive work with children from a range of cultural backgrounds in Australia, North America and Hong Kong, Jacqueline Goodnow (1996) concluded that beliefs about the rules of polite behaviour and pupils' expectancies for social approval constitute additional important dimensions of cultural difference which have clear relevance for academic performance in the classroom. She suggested that:

We might be able to pin down differences in 'motivation' by asking about the tasks regarded as calling for effort, the people whose requests are ignorable … and the techniques that are allowed in order to evade a task without a direct confrontation (e.g. work-to-rule, token efforts, talk without action, accepting the task but doing it

badly, doing something similar, failing to understand, etc.). (p. 21)

In particular, Australian Aboriginal children who are reared in a traditional manner in their home communities are often socialised to pay heed to commands from older children as well as from adults, and to show respect for seniority by not addressing an adult directly. These expectations tend to clash with the independence pressures of an Anglo-Australian upbringing, as Goodnow discovered in her comparison studies of Anglo-Australian, Lebanese-Australian and Japanese families (see Chapters 6 and 8), and have implications for pupil–teacher relations in school. In addition, the notion that to ask a teacher or a classmate for the answers to test questions is taboo may clash with children's experiences outside school of seeking help from older or more experienced members of the family or community who are eager to help whenever necessary.

For example, the implicit assumptions made by many mainstream Anglo-Australian teachers are (a) that rapid responding to tests and oral questioning is desirable, and (b) that original and creative problem solutions are more 'elegant' and appropriate than sheer repetition of something a teacher has just said, but these assumptions are not culturally universal. Many New Guinean and Ugandan adults consider fast answers to be a mark of disrespect for the questioner and condemn hasty responses as impolite. In China, originality may be perceived as disrespectful of tradition.

Children from different cultures and ethnic groups are liable to import their own expectations about how to behave in school without being aware of the clash with subtle conventions of the mainstream classroom. Nor are they always conscious of the criteria that define an 'elegant' solution to a classroom problem in the teacher's eyes. For example, Daphne Keats (1982) discovered that the Chinese model of an intelligent person was someone who was alert and attentive, used logic correctly, respected tradition and showed social responsibility and productive use of mental abilities to benefit other people. The contrasting Anglo-Australian model stressed individual academic attainment, creativity and powers of abstract, critical thinking.

Jacqueline Goodnow (1985) also noted that even something as seemingly objective as a score on a standardised IQ test can be shaped by cultural variations in concepts about intelligence and problem solving etiquette. One child, for example, may view working from analogies, using scratch paper or tracing the solution of a problem back from its answer as legitimate and sophisticated. To another, the same strategies may be construed as cheating.

Culture likewise influences children's ideas about the relative importance of striving for scholastic success and trying to win the teacher's approval by being 'law-abiding' and conforming to various classroom and school-based rules that have nothing directly to do with academic performance. In fact, one of the aims of school – in addition to the teaching of reading and problem-solving skills – is to train students to respect authority and conform to the laws and rules of the institution. Many of the rules initially encountered at school are in sharp contrast to home rules, even for children from a mainstream cultural background. For example, students are taught to sit perfectly still for long periods, to attend steadily to the teacher and to do whatever the teacher asks as swiftly and accurately as they can. At the same time, they are prohibited from making loud noises, daydreaming, chatting with classmates, looking at each other's test papers or leaving their desks without permission.

Most of these rules do have a logical rationale. The size of the class and the need to sustain the attention of the whole group on a single task for an extended time mean that regulations and prohibitions are essential for promoting efficiency. But, to the average student, who has never stood in the teacher's shoes, rules like these are apt to seem purely arbitrary. They resemble the social conventions discussed in Chapter 8. Conformity to stereotypically masculine or feminine sex roles, toy preferences, dress codes and sporting interests often increases as children join sex-segregated peer groups in school. Rules of etiquette or politeness, such as standing when a teacher enters the room or using 'Mr/Mrs' and 'Please' are also likely to matter more at school than at home and to be enforced more strictly by teachers than by parents.

For all these reasons, the transition to school is punctuated for most children by a sudden increase in rule consciousness. This was aptly illustrated in Michael Christie's (1983) interviews with a group of tribal Aboriginal girls in the Northern Territory. The girls themselves had up to ten years of formal schooling behind them, but Christie asked them to imagine that they had a younger brother or sister who would be attending school for the first time that day. Their task was to record on tape (in the Aboriginal language) whatever they felt the child would need to know in order to cope with school successfully. Christie summarised their advice as follows:

> The role is passive. Most girls emphasised sitting down and all stressed quietness. Listening was considered important, but no mention was made of trying, working, talking, thinking, or other active learning behaviours. The only active behaviours mentioned – fighting, yelling, following other children, and running away – were all condemnable. The children were exhorted to avoid all other children, and to concentrate upon sitting down and keeping quiet. (p. 66)

The contrast between Aboriginal and Anglo-Australian perceptions of appropriate behaviour was also illustrated by Bikkar Randhawa, Phillip de Lacey and Donald Saklofske (1986). Their sample consisted

Aboriginal pupils may perceive the rules of school differently from their Anglo classmates.

of 155 Australian children aged 11 to 14, of whom 49 were Aboriginal. Their Anglo-Australian teachers were asked to compare the levels of classroom responsiveness and involvement that they observed in their students on a normal day in school with the following seven behaviours, which collectively represent an Anglo-Australian ideal of a 'model' pupil's optimally responsive behaviour:

1. speaks up for own ideas
2. volunteers to speak in front of the class
3. raises hand and offers to answer questions
4. asks meaningful questions in class
5. looks people in the eye when answering
6. talks to others about school work at appropriate times
7. joins in the school's activities.

The results revealed significant differences in students' closeness of match to this ideal, due to ethnic group and gender. Aboriginal students were judged to be less responsive overall than their Anglo peers, and to engage in the seven desirable classroom behaviours less often. Girls from both ethnic groups were also deemed more desirably responsive than boys. These results are shown in Figure 9.12.

The findings confirmed what Randhawa et al. (1986, p. 401) described as 'the cautious, rather subjective and hitherto controversial suggestion' that Aboriginal students tend to display an overly reserved manner in mixed-ethnic classrooms. Instead of thrusting themselves forward to answer questions and give other public displays of their knowledge in a manner actively encouraged by their Anglo teachers, Aboriginal students seemed to be guided by a different set of norms about polite behaviour. As in several of the studies cited in this chapter, their model of polite behaviour in class appeared to be less assertive and less competitive and individualistic than the Anglo-Australian ideal. But by adhering to their own cultural norms, these Aboriginal students risked

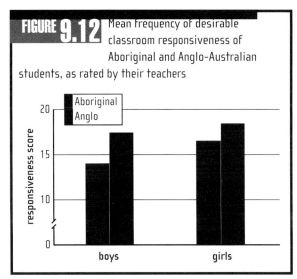

FIGURE 9.12 Mean frequency of desirable classroom responsiveness of Aboriginal and Anglo-Australian students, as rated by their teachers

Source: Based on data in Randhawa et al. (1986).

being misunderstood and having their academic abilities and motivation underestimated by their Anglo-Australian teachers and classmates.

Chapter summary

Middle childhood is a time of steady physical and psychological growth and consolidation of developmental gains. Children gain height and weight. The brain matures to nearly its adult weight through a series of important changes, including myelinisation of nerve fibres and the corpus callosum, alteration of EEG rhythms and lateralisation of the cerebral hemispheres, bringing gains in cognitive capacity.

Health is exceptionally sound during this age period, enabling children aged six to 12 to gain the polished motor skills, delicate control and coordination needed to achieve the notable athletic accomplishments that are observed in formal team sports and in informal exercise on the playground during the primary school years.

But the growth process can bring physical, social and psychological problems to children who are either obese or malnourished. These dietary problems are not exclusively a consequence of poverty, and may arise in affluent Australian and New Zealand children whose nutritional intake is dominated by empty-calorie junk foods, or whose recreational activities are dominated by television.

Emotional development in middle childhood continues the processes begun in infancy, toddlerhood and the preschool years. Children are likely to become somewhat less fearful as they grow older, at least up to adolescence. But fears of nuclear catastrophe loom large in the minds of many Australian and New Zealand children today.

Children's repertoires for experiencing joy, humour and anger also develop during middle childhood. Anger outbursts become less frequent but more prolonged. The positive emotions of happiness and humour become more versatile as the child develops linguistic skill and empathy. Sources of happiness gradually grow from personal pleasures to benefits accruing to other individuals or to humanity in general.

Entry into primary school stimulates cognitive development. During the early primary grades, children gain new skills for processing complex information. Advances in such cognitive processes as attention, memory and creative problem-solving are especially salient between the ages of six and nine years. These new skills enable adept solutions to the challenges children face during academic lessons and everyday life.

The acquisition of literacy is another important cognitive consequence of formal schooling. Learning to read is easier when children enter school with an awareness of books, phonemes and rhyme. But schooling itself is also highly influential, with teaching strategies, peer support and the cultural significance of the printed word all combining to shape how difficult it will be to master the skills of reading and writing.

Culture influences children's orientation towards academic achievement, their motivation, how well they can estimate their academic abilities relative to those of their peers, and their aspirations and attainments in school. Teachers' perceptions, the cooperative or competitive climate of the classroom, and parents' beliefs about the causes of academic success and failure likewise shape the process of cognitive development in distinctive ways for Aboriginal, Maori, migrant and mainstream pupils in Australian and New Zealand primary schools today.

For further interest

Looking forward on the Internet

Use the Internet to visit the following websites. Examine them for further information and varied perspectives on issues raised in this chapter. Also search for other relevant websites for yourself, entering keywords like 'schooling', 'cognitive development', 'reading' and 'emotional development' in your search engine.

In particular, for further ideas on fears, anger and emotional development, visit: **http://www.aacap.org** and for information on reading and the development of literacy visit: **http://www.brainconnection.com** and select the button entitled 'The Reading Brain'. For information on cognitive development and mental health, visit: **http://www.cfw.tufts.edu**.

For resources, ideas, activities and other items of interest in conjunction with this chapter, visit the Companion Website for this textbook at:

http://wps.pearsoned.com.au/peterson

Activity suggestion

As a practical activity in conjunction with themes in this chapter, try exploring children's fears by asking acquaintances aged 5 to 18 years to name three things that frighten them. Group responses by age and compare them with the research evidence described in this chapter.

Multimedia

For interest consider viewing the video *And Spare the Child* (Film Australia, 1981: 11 minutes, colour) which asks provocative questions about discipline strategies. Also of interest is *The Elementary Mind* (Insight Media, 1992: 30 minutes, colour) which presents seminal research findings on cognitive development.

Answers to Box 9.4
Brain teasers

Problem 1:
On the 38th day after planting.

Problem 2:
In addition to the 14 metres shown in the diagram, Dave travelled 10 metres diagonally, making a total of 24 metres in all. The diagonal distance is calculated using the formula: The hypotenuse squared equals the sum of the squared lengths of the other two sides of the triangle.

Problem 3:
He is too short to reach the eleventh-floor button.

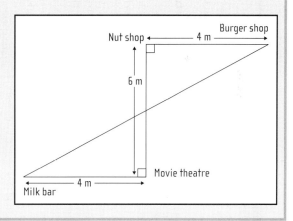

Milestones of development from age 6 to age 12

Domain of development

Physical	Emotional	Cognitive	Social	Personality
The brain reaches an almost mature overall size at the start of middle childhood but continues to grow neurologically through the processes of myelinisation, lateralisation and internal maturation.	Children's emotional expressiveness changes as they gain cognitive skills for comprehending multiple or conflicting emotions and for concealing their feelings from others.	The period of middle childhood coincides with Piaget's stage of concrete-operational thinking, during which logical reasoning is mastered for tangible, concrete concepts that can be seen, measured and manipulated.	Children acquire gender roles that organise their social behaviour in relation to cultural beliefs about toys, games, clothing and other features of the world that have gendered overtones.	The self-concept develops and children acquire beliefs about their own capacity to master challenges and gain self-esteem in academic, physical and social domains.
Physical growth of the body is slow but steady during this period and children refine motor skills in sport and athletic pursuits and vigorous social play.	The cause of basic emotions like happiness, fear and anger also changes with age.	At the same time, children who attend school gain literacy and numeracy skills and increase their cognitive capacities for attention, deliberate strategic memory, problem-solving, creativity, evaluative thinking and executive functioning.	They also develop an internalised set of moral beliefs, or a conscience, which helps them to do right and avoid wrong even when no parent is present to monitor them or mete out discipline.	According to Freud, middle childhood is a dormant latency phase in personality growth.
Diet and health understanding play increasingly important roles in optimising children's health status and rates of growth.	Children report more fears at the start of this period (age 6) than by its end (age 12) but the fears of the older child may be more difficult for an adult to dispel, involving pervasive threats and future possibilities.		In interaction with peers, children have opportunities to forge mutual friendships and to acquire a social status in the peer group as either popular, neglected, controversial or rejected.	But for Erikson, the school-age period is marked by a conflict between the sense of industriousness and a sense of inferiority as children engage in productive pursuits at school and compare their own achievements with those of their peers.

THE ADOLESCENT PHASE

PART 5

Contents

Overview

The teenage years define a phase of unusually rapid and significant psychological growth.
Puberty's impact on the body coincides with a series of new cognitive acquisitions and social
demands, making this one of the most exciting and dramatically changing phases in the lifespan. When adolescent development is successfully completed, the young person has gained
all the necessary requisites for full adult membership in society – including a mature physique,
reproductive sexuality, sophisticated logical thinking skills, a secure sense of identity, an
encompassing ethical code, self-sufficiency, good health and a balanced approach to the health
risks associated with cigarettes, alcohol, drugs and unprotected sexual intercourse. Last but
not least, the young adult has broken free of immature ties of dependency on parents to achieve
the capacity for intimate commitment to others. None of these prizes is won without effort, and
tragic setbacks must occasionally occur.

The next three chapters chart some of the landmarks, danger zones and optimising
guideposts that mark the developing person's journey through the adolescent years to adult
maturity.

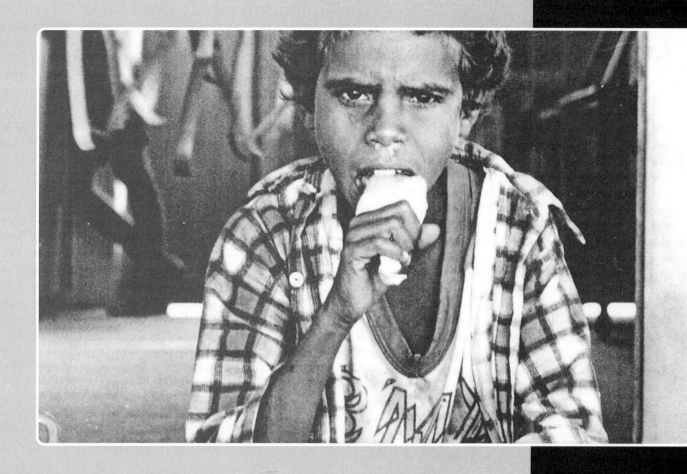

ADOLESCENCE: Physical, emotional and sexual development in the context of biological puberty

CHAPTER 10

That age is best which is the first, when youth and blood are warmer.

Robert Herrick (1591–1674)

Contents

CHAPTER OVERVIEW

Adolescence, the phase from age 12 to age 18, or from completion of primary school to graduation from high school, is a period of dramatic physical growth in stature, strength, neurobiology, physiology and reproductive maturity. At the same time, important changes arise in the adolescent's cognitive and social skills and in personality and emotional maturity.

In this chapter we chart the physical and biological changes of pubertal growth that culminate in a mature adult physique and reproductive capacity. At a broad level, these growth events are universal and timeless: all normal adolescents, irrespective of cultural background and historical era, achieve an adult physiology eventually. Yet their timing is largely idiosyncratic, with some children becoming fully reproductively mature even before reaching their teens and others continuing to grow physically well into their twenties. We study variations in the timing of each of the major steps in the pubertal growth process both between and within individuals. We also look at how variations in pubertal growth timing affect different individuals, depending on their gender, level of cognitive maturity, family and peer group circumstances; and at the social interpretations that the adolescent's culture and historical era assign to the hallmarks of physical beauty and to biological puberty as a transition event.

We analyse the psychological consequences for boys and girls who reach biological puberty either much earlier or much later than most of their peers. Interestingly, not only are there dramatic emotional and social impacts of variations in timing while pubertal growth is happening, but also many long-term psychological consequences that may endure for the remainder of the lifespan. Unexpected 'life cycle surprises' (see Chapter 1) are included among these.

We explore cultural variations in the ways adolescent pubertal growth can be experienced, including a close examination of the tribal initiation ceremony. This ritualised, culturally shared and sanctioned approach to the induction of physically mature teenagers into fully fledged adult roles contrasts sharply with the contradictions and uncertainties that surround the decade from age 13 to age 23 for many young people in contemporary, industrialised urban societies where the physical onset of manhood or womanhood is no guarantee of an immediate place in the adult world of employment, marriage, parenthood and mature responsibility. The psychological stresses that can often accompany adolescent uncertainties over jobs, higher education, intimate relationships and philosophies of life are also examined in this and the next two chapters.

BOX 10.1 A case in point
Puberty blues

When Louise reached her teens and began her pubertal spurt in physical growth, her father made the following two entries in his diary. As well as illustrating the dramatic changes in physical growth and maturity that occur with adolescence, they aptly illustrate the theme of generativity in middle adult personality development that we noted in the context of Erikson's theory in Chapter 2 and explore in more detail in Chapter 15.

2 August 1961. I have let a whole spring and nearly a whole summer go by without comment on Louise's progress. She celebrated her 13th birthday by going to dinner with Christine and to a Marx brothers movie afterwards. She finished the seventh grade with satisfactory marks though not, I am afraid, much else to show for her year of heavy homework. She has developed physically and is now taller than her mother. She studied typing in summer school, helped with the building of our back fence and the landscaping and weeding, played with Linda for the most part, welcomed Melissa back from Tucson, read a great deal. Now she is in her second week of Girl Scout camp with Linda, the only other girl from her troop who came to camp this year.

15 September 1961. When I looked at Louise standing up at the counter doing her algebra this evening I was again aglow with this sense of wonder that I sometimes experience that this is actually a daughter of mine. She is tall and thin, her hair today was wispy and light, having been washed last evening; she was wearing the blue corduroy skirt – now many sizes too small – that made me realize as she entered the fifth grade that she was on her way to womanhood. There is consolation in growing old, seeing her growing up and consolation in death knowing that she will live and continue to grow. I feel her inescapably a part of me and yet miraculously different.

Adolescence as a transition event

Though it has only recently come into its own, the 13th birthday is now one of the most momentous anniversaries in a modern person's life. It marks the transformation of a child into a teenager. With this passage from childhood into adolescence comes a new set of privileges and demands which combine to define a semi-adult social status. In Australia and New Zealand today, age 13 coincides for many children with entry into high school. As illustrated in Box 10.1, gains in height and the progression towards full reproductive maturity also make the

In late adolescence, opposite-sex friendships emerge, along with friendships between members of the same sex.

teens psychologically significant, while granting young people the adult physical appearance that will trigger different expectations from those around them.

Before attaining the legal age of majority at 18, the typical teenager will have learned to drive a car, completed high school and probably fallen in love at least once. The body will have grown almost beyond recognition, and new psychological capacities will have developed, ranging from emotional independence from parents to complex problem-solving. A mature ethical and political ideology will have emerged, along with a clear sense of one's future in the world of work and in intimate relationships.

Most of these changes are desirable ones. Yet the period of adolescence is rarely free of pain, stress and turmoil and the emotional reaction to turning 13 (like turning 30 or 50 later on) is apt to be one of ambivalence. Despite their eagerness to savour the delights and opportunities of this exciting period of rapid growth, many preadolescents are troubled by anxieties and doubts over whether they will be popular with peers, whether their mature bodies will be physically attractive, whether they will make wrong decisions, or whether they will be able to cope with the stresses of higher education, dancing, dating, driving a car and earning a living. The following extracts from an interview with one Australian girl before and after she became a teenager illustrate this ambivalence.

Wendy: Age 9

Q: 'You're nine now. In three or four years you'll be a teenager. Is that something to look forward to?'

A: 'Well, no, not really.'

Q: 'Why not?'

A: 'I'm embarrassed about how I'll look. I might have pimples all over my face. Also I'm scared to be in high school because I might not pass the exams and tests.'

Q: 'Do you think there's anything good about it?'

A: 'Well, yes, because you can wear nice clothes, shoes and makeup and stay up late and go dancing.'

Wendy: Age 14

Q: 'What's the best thing about being 14?'

A: 'Looking forward to things – like driving a car, going to uni, going out with boys.'

Q: 'Those things are in the future, aren't they? What about now compared to when you were younger?'

A: 'I suppose having intelligent friends with whom you can have intelligent conversations. Studying more interesting things in school.'

Q: 'What's the worst thing about being 14?'

A: 'The emotional turbulence.'

BOX 10.2 Activity suggestion
What is the worst age in life to be?

What is the worst age in life to be? Can you answer this question? What age, or age period, would you pick? Try putting these questions to your friends and acquaintances of different ages. You may also wish to ask them why they feel a particular stage in life is a disagreeable one. While old age is frequently mentioned by adults of all ages when research into concepts of different age periods in life is conducted systematically (Byrd & Breuss, 1992; Peterson, 2003), the teens are the next most popular choice. Adults who view ages 13 to 15 as 'the worst stage in life' typically mention 'confusion', 'self-doubt', 'awkwardness' and 'self-consciousness', traits that may reflect the speed of developmental change during that era being too rapid for optimally contented coping.

While adolescence has its pleasures and privileges compared with childhood, these are often mingled with negative feelings like self-consciousness and confusion.

Historical views of the adolescent transition

Adults are apt to have ambivalent feelings about teenagers, and one component of the transition is frequently the distancing of the child from adults in general, and parents in particular, a phenomenon known as the *generation gap*. Many centuries ago, the Greek philosophers Aristotle and Socrates described adolescents in terms many contemporary adults would find applicable to the teenagers in their home or neighbourhood. Aristotle said:

> Adolescents are in character prone to desire and ready to carry out any desire they may have formed into action. Of bodily desires it is the sexual to which they are most disposed to give way, and in regard to sexual desire they exercise no self-restraint. They are changeful too, and fickle in their desires, which are as transitory as they are vehement; for their wishes are keen without being permanent, like a sick man's fits of hunger and thirst … They are passionate, irascible and apt to be carried away by their impulses … They regard themselves as omniscient and are positive in their assertions; this is, in fact, the reason of their carrying everything too far. (Kiell, 1967, pp. 18–19)

Socrates said:

> Our youth now love luxury. They show disrespect for their elders … they contradict their parents, chatter before company, gobble up dainties at the table and tyrannise their teachers.

In Renaissance England, William Shakespeare was even more blunt:

> I would that there were no age between three and three-and-twenty, or that youth would sleep out the rest; for there is nothing in the between but getting wenches with child, wronging the ancientry, stealing, fighting. (*The Winter's Tale*, III, iii)

The generation gap

The mistrust of youth by the parent generation has been given many interpretations. Some see the tendency to draw a biased and unappealing picture of all adolescents as a reflection of the adults' jealous envy of youth's zest, beauty and freedom from responsibility. Others ascribe the gap to an intergenerational power struggle for jobs, income, privileges and respect. Still others view a generation gap in attitudes, values and styles of conduct as the inevitable result of children's need to become independent of their parents. This is reinforced by the ceaseless, cyclic parade of fashion which guarantees that, regardless of what their preferences for clothing or music may be, the adult generation is bound to appear old-fashioned to its adolescent children, and trend-following young people are bound to shock or offend their parents' tastes.

Regardless of the underlying reasons for it, this bigotry against teenagers is a form of ageism (see Chapter 1). Joseph Adelson (1979) argued that, as

The cyclic parade of fashion guarantees that the adult generation's tastes will seem outmoded to trendy teenagers.

such, it posed a threat to society. By cutting off trust between generations, the risk is that the dialectical exchanges which can so effectively foster the lifespan development of all interconnected age groups may be curtailed. Fortunately, according to Adelson, the gap between generations is more mythical than real. He coined the phrase 'generalization gap' to describe the tendency to group all teenagers together into one unfavourable stereotype. Most adolescents do not really differ from older and younger people as much as the public imagines, according to Adelson.

Whether real or largely mythical, the storm, stress and turbulence of the generation gap does not appear to impact adversely on young people themselves. Nor do they appear to share the pessimistic picture that many adults have of the teenage era from a subjective standpoint (see Box 10.2). Instead, most Australian adolescents would rather be teenagers than anything else (Goldman & Goldman, 1982). Figure 10.1 shows the replies of a group of Melbourne 13-year-olds to the question 'What do you think is the *happiest* [best] time to be alive?' A majority of these young teens chose adolescence. Their reasons for being pleased to have outgrown childhood centred around the enhanced status and independence accorded to adolescents: 'If you want some money you can take a part-time job'; 'You're allowed to make some of your own decisions'; 'Teenagers are much more free' (p. 112). Perhaps because of the ageist prejudice against the elderly, discussed in Chapters 1 and 17 of

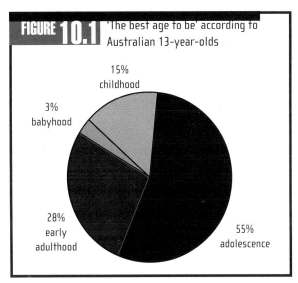

FIGURE **10.1** 'The best age to be' according to Australian 13-year-olds

- 15% childhood
- 3% babyhood
- 28% early adulthood
- 55% adolescence

Source: Based on data in Goldman & Goldman (1982), pp. 108–14.

In a traditional Aboriginal community the tasks and steps on the route to maturity are clear.

this text, no Melbourne teenager selected old age as 'the best time to be alive'. Early adulthood was ranked next in popularity after adolescence. But those who opted for the teens pointed out that adults were often more weighed down by worries, obligations and responsibilities than teenagers. As one teenage girl explained: 'If you are older, you are trapped in a family' (p. 112).

Cross-cultural views of the adolescent transition

Not all cultures view the transition from childhood to adulthood as a slow and complicated journey occupying all of the teen years. In many non-Western cultures today, as in Western society several centuries ago, the transformation of a child into an adult might require only a few days or could take place overnight. For example, in their traditional culture, the Australian Aborigines used a single brief ceremony to achieve essentially the same outcome as a five- to ten-year Western-style adolescence – namely, the marking of a clear boundary between childish freedom and indulgence and the power and responsibility of adult life. Similar ceremonial rites are practised in tribal Africa, in parts of South-East Asia and by indigenous groups in North and South America.

Initiation ceremonies

The ceremonial marking of the passage from childhood to fully fledged adult status is known as a pubertal initiation rite, a rite of passage or a pubertal initiation ceremony. The core practice is consistent across many cultures. The whole social group participates, either as actors or audience. There is a ritual to be performed which serves several different functions. The initiate is separated from the world he or she inhabited during childhood and is introduced to privileged skills and knowledge that the culture

reserves for its older members. Generational succession into a position of power is assured by the ceremony, and all members of the social group learn, by participating in the rite, not to treat the initiate as a child any longer. Once initiation is complete, the young person assumes a position alongside older men and women who now accord the initiate a higher level of social status.

The new status acquired through initiation is absolute. Once initiated, the fledgling adult can never go back to being a child, even momentarily. Some traditional ceremonies practised in Africa and Aboriginal Australia include the mock death of the child, followed by sudden rebirth as a totally different adult person with a new name. The pretence of slaughter may be carried out by throwing spears at young initiates as they are herded out of the camp before the ceremonial rite begins. Their wailing mothers and sisters pretend to believe that the young men have been killed, even though the elders' spears have been carefully aimed to miss their targets. When initiates come back after the ceremony as novice adults, everyone treats them with new respect. In one African village, a system of monetary fines is levied by the chief against anyone who forgetfully addresses the 'new' arrival by his childhood name. In such cultures, it seems that the gap between childhood and adulthood is too wide to be bridged by anything other than the dramatic, symbolic destruction of the childish personality and its immediate replacement by a mature character.

The initiation rites practised in tribal societies

throughout the world are also alike in other ways. Most include the following distinctive features:

1. They transform children into occupants of higher-status and more powerful social roles.
2. They force adoption of mature social and sexual traits.
3. They demand a complete cessation of the playful existence of childhood and a permanent separation of the initiate from the mother and/or younger siblings.
4. They dramatise the encounter between generations by allowing same-sex members of the older generation to inflict pain and physical mutilation on the young initiates while welcoming them into their own in-group.
5. They transmit cultural and religious knowledge, while at the same time testing the initiate's aptitude to receive it and hold it sacred.
6. They signal the adults' relaxation of legal jurisdiction and social control over the initiates.
7. They endow the novices with new authoritative roles of their own and guarantee them the respect of older and younger people.
8. They remove uncertainty about how to grow up and achieve independence, while at the same time offering the social support of mature members of the culture to ease the transition into adult roles.

Perhaps because of these important psychological and cultural benefits, some contemporary Aboriginal groups in remote communities continue to practise ceremonial pubertal initiation today. A ceremonial adolescence via initiation can certainly be seen to have advantages over the protracted Western-style adolescence, as Box 10.3 illustrates.

The physical changes of biological puberty

In spite of wide cultural variations in the social meaning of adolescence, the physical changes of puberty are basically the same for everyone. Physiologist J. M. Tanner highlighted the adolescent's psychological investment in physical growth when he wrote:

> For the majority of young persons, the years from twelve to sixteen are the most eventful ones of their lives so far as their growth and development are concerned. Admittedly during fetal life and the first year or two after birth developments occur still faster, and a sympathetic environment was probably even more crucial, but the subject himself was not the fascinated, charmed or horrified spectator that watches the developments, or lack of developments, of adolescence. (1972, p. 1)

The psychological impact of adolescent physical maturation is heightened by teenagers' awareness that the bodies they will inherit once pubertal growth has run its course will remain essentially the same

BOX 10.3 Lessons from culture
Pubertal initiation for Aboriginal Australian boys and girls

Anthropologist Robert Tonkinson (1978) gave the following description of a male initiation ceremony in Western Australia:

> Budjaga is about 14, tall for his age, with sandy-colored straight hair, a big smile, and several small cicatrices on his shoulders, put there by his ... friend Dabuni. His potbelly is gone, and he has the beginnings of a moustache. He is camped at Banngur rockhole ... with about 40 people, currently travelling in three bands. He and four or five boys are at the rockhole, killing finches with stones and eating them, so he has not noticed that a group of his relatives ... have just placed a quantity of vegetable food (fresh quandong fruits, bush tomatoes, and seedcakes) on the ground not far from his family's camp. With a highpitched, attention-getting cry followed by hand signs, the boys are called back to camp. Budjaga barely has a chance to notice the food before he is seized by two distantly related men ... The Mourners, who sit by the food, bow their heads and wail softly as Budjaga is brought over and surrounded by members of the Activist group. The younger children have stopped playing and are watching from what they judge to be a safe distance. Budjaga is held and comforted ... while one of the men pushes a sharpened spear point into his septum and another ... braces a *mulyayidi* (nose-bone) against the other side of his septum. The bone is from an eaglehawk's wing, chosen because Walawuru, the Eaglehawk-man, is the Dreamtime creator of this rite. Budjaga winces in obvious pain but makes no sound. (pp. 68–9, reprinted by permission of Holt, Rinehart & Winston, CBS College Publishing)

John Money, J. Cawte, G. Bianchi and B. Nurcombe (1970) also described a modern-day initiation ritual observed on a visit to the Yolngu Aborigines at Elcho Island in Arnhem Land. While involving a different operation, the ritual itself is very similar to the one observed by Tonkinson. Money wrote:

> ... the occasion is one of public rejoicing. The history of the people is celebrated in mimetic dance and chanting to the accompaniment of the rhythmic drone pipe, or didjeridoo, and clapsticks. The evening ceremony continues until the morning star rises. After daylight it continues until the climactic moment when the ceremonial initiates among the elders carry the boy off, safe from the view of girls and women, encircling him in close formation. One of them lies on his back on the ground, the boy lying face upward on him and pinioned in a locked embrace. Another man holds down the boy's legs. A third does the actual cutting. In ancient times a stone knife was used. Today the instrument is a razor blade. The cutting is more likely to be a series of dissection movements than swift incision. The boy may cry

out with the pain. Immediately the foreskin is removed, the men in charge carry the boy into the bush nearby where he is passed through the smoke of a fire for spiritual cleansing. The bleeding of his penis is stopped by cauterizing with a piece of hot charcoal and the application of hot, wet leaves. He returns to his home camp-fire and there rests and recuperates for about a week. (p. 384)

While by no means comparable in intensity or cultural significance to the circumcision ceremony for boys, the traditional Aborigines of former times did practise rituals in connection with a girl's first menstrual period. On the basis of interviews with Yolngu Aboriginal girls in Arnhem Land, physicians John Money, J. Cawte, G. Bianchi and B. Nurcombe (1970) gave the following description of the traditional ceremony, including elements surviving into the modern era: The unmarried adolescent girls who recorded interviews had been prepared for menstruation a year or two ahead of time by their mothers, and they also knew something from the talk of other girls. In an earlier era, the first menses would have been negotiated with ceremonial body-painting and chants which today have fallen by the wayside of cultural change. A girl is still expected, however, to pay lip-service at least to the ancient custom of menstrual isolation. Formerly she was isolated under a woven conical mat where she rested and slept. She conformed to dietary restrictions, notably the avoidance of fish and shellfish. Educated girls today, away in the city at school, still are likely to obey the dietary rule, so as to play safe and avoid the risk of falling sick. There is no further adherence, however, to the custom of concluding menstruation with a spiritual cleansing by being passed through the fumes of a smoky fire. (p. 407)

throughout the remainder of adult life, or at least until the process of physiological ageing sets in (see Chapters 15 and 16). Thus pubertal physical growth can affect psychological development not only during adolescence but also for decades after the body has stopped growing. This section of the chapter begins with a brief outline of the major aspects of the adolescent physical growth process, followed by a more detailed examination of how the adolescent's own construction of the meaning of bodily changes affects behaviour and adjustment during the teenage years and adulthood.

The milestones of pubertal growth

The word *pubescence* derives from a Latin word meaning 'to grow hairy'. But the darkening of body hair and the boy's need to shave newly emerging facial hair are usually not the first steps in the pubertal growth sequence. As Figure 10.2 shows, an abrupt increase in stature, known as the pubertal height spurt, generally heralds the onset of puberty in both sexes. Since girls begin pubertal growth an average of two years before boys, the average girl starts her

height spurt at around age ten with the peak normally occurring around her 12th birthday. The change is dramatic, with the average girl gaining 20 centimetres as a result of the spurt. Boys typically begin the spurt at 12 and are gaining height at their peak rate by age 15. As males grow more quickly and continue the spurt longer than females, the normal adult male/female height differential is established before the end of adolescence (Tanner, 1970). Interestingly, the size of the pubertal height spurt is largely independent of how tall the girl or boy was as a child. Therefore, to the dismay of would-be policemen and ballet dancers, a person's ultimate height cannot be foretold with certainty until late adolescence. Some adolescents who were taller than most of their classmates in primary school end up relatively short as adults, due to an unusually small pubertal growth spurt, and vice versa. Some 30 per cent of the variability in height among adults of the same sex is a function of the pubertal spurt (Tanner, 1962).

Hormonal changes arising soon after the onset of the height spurt stimulate the growth of the reproductive organs. Secondary sex characteristics like breasts, wide hips, a beard and a deeper voice emerge, to make the male and female appearance distinctively different. Figure 10.2 shows the timing of some these important pubertal events for an average boy and an average girl.

Hormonal balance also affects the adolescent's moods. Both the male hormone, testosterone, and the female hormone, estrogen, are linked with heightened emotional excitability. During phases of rapid pubertal growth, the hormones fluctuate irregularly, a possible explanation for negative feelings or moodiness. In one study, adolescents and adults carried electronic pagers everywhere they went for one week and, when beeped, answered questions about their moods. The adolescents reported more rapid and extreme mood swings than the adults, and more intense positive and negative moods (Buchanan, Eccles & Becker, 1992).

Growth asynchronies

Figure 10.2 illustrates the two-year gap between the sexes in the timing of the pubertal growth events, like the height spurt, that both sexes have in common.

In any classroom of young teens, pronounced differences in rates of physical growth are evident.

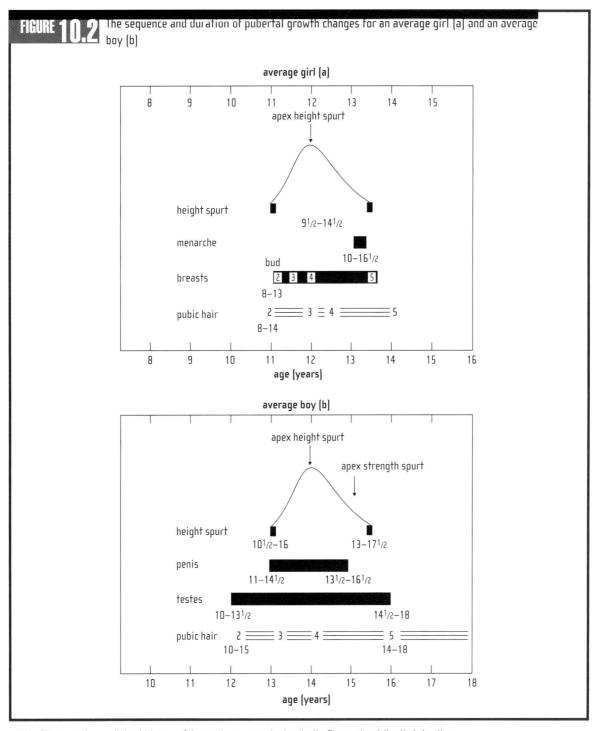

average girl (a)

apex height spurt

height spurt
9½–14½

menarche
10–16½

breasts
bud
2 3 4 5
8–13

pubic hair
2 3 4 5
8–14

age (years)

average boy (b)

apex height spurt

apex strength spurt

height spurt
10½–16
13–17½

penis
11–14½
13½–16½

testes
10–13½
14½–18

pubic hair
2 3 4 5
10–15
14–18

age (years)

Note: The range of ages within which some of the events may occur is given by the figures placed directly below them.
Source: Tanner (1970), reproduced with permission.

This mismatch, with girls averaging a two-year lead on boys, is an example of an inter-individual growth asynchrony. These asynchronies are the gaps that arise when one teenager's growth is compared with that of another teenager, and may also arise among members of the same sex. For example, Figure 10.3 illustrates inter-individual asynchronies in the timing of menarche (first menstruation) for average New Zealand girls as a function of race and year of birth.

To complicate things still further, individual differences in rates of growth are liable to be as dramatic as within-sex variations in the timing of puberty's onset. For example, some British girls in James Tanner's (1972) sample passed through the interval from the first sign of puberty to complete maturity in the record time of a year and a half. For others, the same growth changes took more than six years to complete. These differences in rate of maturation were found to bear no clear relationship to whether puberty began early or late. Some boys and

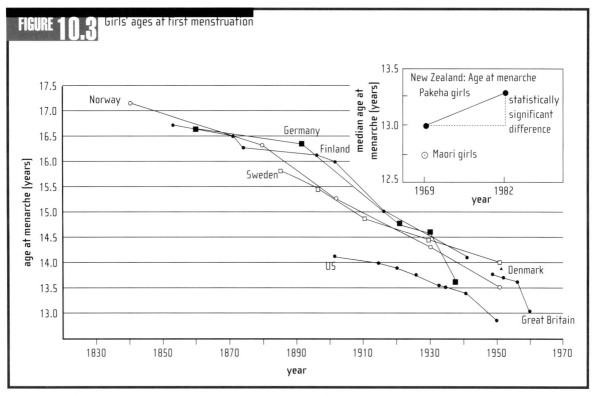

FIGURE 10.3 Girls' ages at first menstruation

Source: Tanner (1970), reproduced with permission; textual data from Coope et al. (1984).

girls who started the pubertal height spurt after the majority of their peers caught up quickly. Others began late and progressed at a slower rate than average. There are also intra-individual asynchronies in the timing of growth of different body parts. For example, adolescents' hands and feet typically grow faster than the trunk and limbs, contributing to a sense of clumsiness at the start of the 'awkward age'. Further embarrassment may arise from the following asynchronous aspects of pubertal growth:

1. The nose reaches its mature proportions faster than the rest of the face, producing a sense of looking like Pinnochio for a time.
2. When the sebaceous (oil-producing) glands of the skin are stimulated into activity by pubertal growth hormones, they develop more rapidly than their ducts. This can cause the blockages and infections known as acne.
3. The girl's shoulders typically grow at a different rate from the hips. When shoulder growth occurs first, a distressingly masculine shape may be the temporary outcome. When the hips grow first, the result is likely to be the embarrassment illustrated in Box 10.4.

A historical asynchrony: The secular trend

Between the 1830s and the 1960s, a historical phenomenon known as the secular trend was responsible for a steady decline in girls' ages at menarche, with each new generation of daughters reaching puberty about four months earlier than their mothers over

these 14 decades (see Figure 10.3). Now, the trend seems to have levelled out with, if anything, a new tendency for menarche to occur slightly later than in the 1960s and 1970s, according to a survey of some 900 boarders and day girls attending secondary schools in Christchurch, New Zealand (Coope et al., 1984). At 13 years 4 months, the median age of menarche was significantly higher in 1982 than in 1969 when a comparable group of Pakeha New Zealand girls was surveyed. The Maoris reached menarche ahead of Pakehas in 1969 at a median age of 12 years 8 months.

The results of another, recent New Zealand study in which a group of 500 Dunedin girls was followed longitudinally from age three to age 15 are shown in Figure 10.4. These girls' median age at menarche, which most of them had reached by the mid-1980s, was 13 years, 0 months. But some of the – mainly Pakeha girls (less than 2 per cent of the sample was Maori) – reached menarche as young as eight to nine years, and a number had still not reached it by the last testing session when they were 15. Thus the range among girls within the same culture and historical era is greater than the contrast in group averages reflected by the secular trend. In retrospect, it appears that the secular trend for menarche may have been a peculiarity of the late 19th and early 20th centuries. Historians have estimated that the average age for the first menstrual period in ancient Greece and Rome, and in medieval Europe, was close to the 13th birthday, or the present-day average (Amundsen & Diers, 1973). However, though the physiological

BOX 10.4 A case in point
A body out of control

Author Phyllis LaFarge described the asynchronous growth of curves during her adolescence in the 1940s and the embarrassment this caused her:

Along with the discontinuities specific to my circumstances came the discontinuities of puberty, the changes in my own body. The changes of adolescent bodies are subject matter for Goldoni or the Marx brothers, if only adolescents could feel that way. I had hips before I had breasts; it seemed cruel mismanagement. My mother, erect, and a puritan in her corseting as well as in the control of her emotions, bought me a girdle. I wore it with a Carter's knit undershirt, the kind with the little string tied about level with the breast bone. Cotton knit in contact with other fabrics is bound to roll itself into a little ridge. It is this ridge circumnavigating my hips which I remember above all else from the marriage ceremony of my uncle – this and the little string bow which kept popping out of the slit neck of my dress. It seemed impossible that the entire gathering, absorbed in a high nuptial mass, was not eyeing me. Self-consciousness about my body and appearance was overwhelming for several years. I did not put it into words, or even think it, but there was always the possibility that my body, like some not quite predictable tyrant . . . would betray me, that something else would bulge or sweat or all at once sprout hair and so depart from the firm, predictable body of childhood. (1972, p. 281, copyright by the American Academy of Arts and Sciences)

FIGURE 10.4 New Zealand girls' ages at menarche according to longitudinal evidence

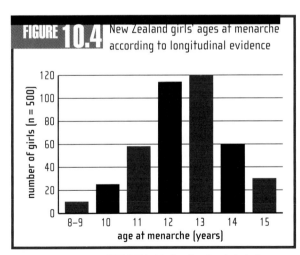

Source: Caspi & Moffitt (1991), © by the American Psychological Association. Reproduced with permission.

hastening of puberty may have ceased, the increase of psychological pressures for earlier and earlier social maturity appears to be a continuing trend in Western societies today.

One possible explanation for the apparent slowing of pubertal maturation today is the contemporary teenager's intense preoccupation with slimness and fitness. Underweight girls and athletes are found to have their first periods later than those who are stocky and non-athletic (Warren, 1983). Some additional correlates of age at menarche are explored in Box 10.5.

BOX 10.5 How can you explain it?
Early and late menarche

A number of perplexing correlates of the timing of menarche were uncovered when Michelle Warren (1983) tracked the onset of menstruation in North American girls from different cultural and socioeconomic backgrounds. Can you come up with a single coherent explanation to account for the asynchronies among the following groups of girls?

Menarche is significantly earlier than average in:

- blind girls
- girls living in large cities
- obese girls
- bedridden, retarded girls

Menarche is significantly later than average in:

- ballet dancers
- diabetic girls
- Olympic athletes
- long-distance runners
- girls with many brothers and sisters
- twins
- girls living at high altitudes

Answer: See the text, especially comments regarding the associations between body fat, exercise and pubertal timing.

Emotions, lifestyle and puberty

Michelle Warren's (1980) discovery that menarche occurred significantly later in girls who were training to be ballet dancers than in their sisters with a common genetic inheritance who shared the same household led to a search for other lifestyle correlates of delayed menarche. The combined results of this research (Warren, 1983) are shown in Box 10.5. Warren discovered that one prerequisite for the onset of puberty is an adequate level of body fat. This finding accounts not only for the slower attainment of puberty by ballet dancers, whose body weight averages 10 per cent less than the norm for their age, but also for the historical onset and termination of the secular trend, shown in Figure 10.3. Improvements between 1830 and 1970 in socioeconomic conditions led to better nutrition and protection from childhood disease, and hence to the earlier attainment of the critical proportion of fat needed to trigger menarche. But over recent decades no further nutritional improvements have been made in developed countries. A cultural preoccupation with dieting may retard growth and this possibly explains the reversal of the secular trend.

In addition to a psychological concern with slimness, puberty can also be delayed by emotional factors. Julia Graber, Jean Brooks-Gunn, R. Paikoff and Michelle Warren (1995) explored the effects of emotional well-being, family climate and stressful life events on the timing of menarche. The sample consisted of 75 affluent girls aged 10 to 14 years who were attending private schools in the north-eastern United States. Using a longitudinal design, the researchers assessed physical development, menarcheal age, stressful life events, depressive feelings and quality of family life on a yearly basis. The results revealed that psychological variables, including depressive moods, hostile relationships with parents, parental disapproval of the adolescent and family coldness were all significant predictors of a girl's age at menarche. Girls who matured early displayed more depression and experienced colder family relations and more hostile conflict than their peers who were later in reaching puberty. Furthermore, using multiple regression analyses, the researchers were able to demonstrate that family relations and depressive moods continued to predict pubertal maturation even after the influence of all biological variables, including heredity (mother's age at menarche), breast development, body fat, weight and height were statistically controlled. The authors concluded that:

> The results of this and related studies, in combination, suggest that multiple hormonal pathways may be influenced by internal and external environments. More definitively, this growing body of literature demonstrates the complexity of the associations among biological and psychological aspects of development and that the psychological system is responsive to a broader range of

influences ... The association of family affective environment with timing of maturation, along with the existing literature on maturational timing effects, on subsequent psychological development, is the beginning for demonstrating the interactive nature of early adolescent development. (p. 357)

In other words, emotional and attitudinal factors clearly influence pubertal physical growth. But the reverse is also true. The physical growth changes of puberty are found to shape psychological functioning and to determine personality differences, not only during the adolescent growth process itself, but possibly for the remainder of the lifespan. These influences are explored in the next sections of this chapter.

The psychological impact of puberty

In addition to its dramatic influence on the body, adolescent biological growth also shapes the self-concept and has a direct bearing on cognitive growth and performance in school (Simmons & Blyth, 1987; Petersen et al., 1993). The quality of intimate social relationships with parents, siblings, friends and dating partners changes with pubertal maturation and these influences can be quite long-lasting. Some of the longitudinal studies examined in this section have demonstrated that a biological event – like early or late passage through puberty – can continue to exert important psychological influences on men and women in their 30s and 40s, long after the physical effects of these growth changes have vanished and conscious memories of them all but disappeared. Research has likewise highlighted an important reciprocity between physical growth and adolescent social and emotional development (Buchanan, Eccles & Becker, 1992). The changing balance of hormones circulating through the bloodstream at puberty produces corresponding changes in adolescents' emotional adjustment and their relationships with parents and peers. At the same time, according to new longitudinal data (Graber, Brooks-Gunn & Warren, 1995; Steinberg, 1996), intense emotional intimacy between mothers and adolescent daughters may retard the biological passage through puberty, while a distant or conflict-ridden mother–daughter relationship may accelerate it. These complex interconnections between biology and psychology are examined in further detail after a brief look at the adolescent's subjective emotional reaction to the pubertal growth process.

Adolescent physical appearance and self-concept

One adolescent's self-concept fluctuations during the peak of pubertal growth are described in Box 10.4. Even though changes like these are normal and largely temporary, her reactions are quite typical. In fact, most adolescents experience acute distress at some time over such aspects of pubertal growth as facial acne, a large nose or an awkwardly shaped body. When newspaper advice columnist Abigail Van Buren analysed the estimated one million letters she had received from American teenagers over an eight-year period, she found that the following concerns arose most commonly:

'How can I be popular?'
'How can I get my parents to trust me?'
'Will a boy respect me if I give in?'
'I can't get along with my brothers and sisters.'
'I'm too fat.'
'I'm too thin.'
'I'm not stacked.'
'I've got pimples.'

In other words, four out of the eight most frequent problems of the teenagers who sought 'Dear Abby's' advice concerned some aspect of their physical development. An Australian survey asking adolescents whether there was any aspect of themselves they would like to change yielded similar findings (see Figure 10.5). Don Edgar (1974) questioned 661 boys and 555 girls from various high schools in the state of Victoria. Sixty-two per cent lived in urban Melbourne, while the remainder were from rural regions. Edgar found that the vast majority of these Australian teenagers were dissatisfied with one or more features of their physical appearance. When asked: 'What one thing about yourself would you most like to improve?' their replies were quite varied but almost no one said 'Nothing'. The list of desired changes included:

'My hair, it's dracky.'   'Not to be shy.'
'The pimples on my face.'   'My figure.'
'My sleeping habits.'   'My temper.'
'My looks.'   'My muscles.'
'I am too fat.'

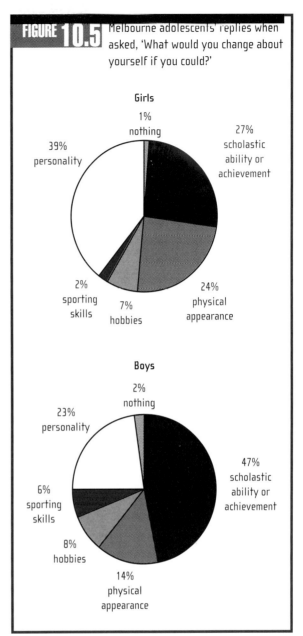

Source: Based on data in Edgar (1974), p. 40.

For an adolescent boy, the single most important prerequisite for feeling attractive seems to be the need to shave. Maryse Tobin-Richards, Andrew Boxer and Anne Petersen (1983) found that 'facial hair is the pubertal item which most influences positive perceptions of self, explaining twice the variance of other variables' (p. 144). They suggested that one reason for this might be the social significance of a beard as a sign of maturity:

Facial hair is a visually apparent change with powerful symbolic meaning for adult physical status. Thus the reactions from adults and peers to this physical change may stimulate a change in self-image. In order for this to happen, facial hair must be incorporated into a system of meaning regarding physical maturation. (p. 144)

The pubertal height spurt, in conjunction with the secular trend for increased height in younger cohorts, produces a large gap between teens and grandparents.

When they interviewed adolescent girls, Tobin-Richards and her colleagues (1983) found that the criteria for beauty were more complicated than for boys. Two factors were highly relevant: slimness and large breasts. But these interacted with pubertal timing. Large breasts, especially in early adolescence, are associated with chubbiness and early menstruation, as noted earlier. Consequently, because most girls wanted to be as slim as possible, early maturing girls, who were more advanced in pubertal growth, were generally less happy with their bodies than girls who had not yet begun to put on the weight associated with puberty. However, the counterbalancing factor that helped the heavier adolescent girl to feel satisfied with her physical body was breast development. Tobin-Richards et al. noted that:

> Interviews with adolescent girls reveal that all body parts, except breasts, are desired to be small and unobtrusive, and that big breasts are valued for their appeal to boys ... Thus while girls who perceive themselves as earlier maturers tend to hold a more negative set of self-perceptions, breast development is a positive marker for them. (p. 148)

In fact, for women of all ages, the relative value society places on a lithe, slim physique relative to well-rounded 'feminine' curves can be a crucial shaper of the self-concept. The influence of the media in prescribing these values is illustrated in Box 10.6.

In Australia, Sue Paxton and her colleagues (1991) interviewed a total of 562 adolescents in high school about their attitudes towards their height and weight. Disturbingly, she found that, even among girls who were not at all overweight and whose weight was normal for their height and build, 30 per cent described themselves as 'too fat' and wanted to be thinner. They believed a thinner build would not only make them more attractive to boys but would make them happier as well.

Figure 10.6 shows the responses of Melbourne girls and boys to a task requiring them to select a drawing of a human figure in silhouette as their ideal for their own body. A majority of boys chose a figure that equalled or exceeded their own current body shape in fatness, while 70 per cent of girls preferred a body that was more emaciated than their own.

Sexual maturation

Menarche, or the first menstrual period, generally arises midway through the pubertal growth sequence (see Figure 10.2) and may be associated with mildly unpleasant physical symptoms such as cramps, headaches and constipation, though many girls report none of these. While menstruation signals that ova are being released by the ovaries (see Chapter 3), the girl is generally infertile for about a year after the first period. Despite the inconveniences associated with it, menstruation is frequently a source of pride as the girl senses her transition into womanhood. It has a social meaning for most girls, who typically

BOX 10.6 Activity suggestion
Breasts versus legs

To assess what kinds of 'media pronouncements about what is feminine and beautiful' (Faust, 1983, p. 115) are being broadcast to the adolescent girls in your environment, you may wish to do a media 'spot check', using the following procedure.

MATERIALS
Assemble as many clippings as possible of full-length front-on photographs or sketches of women's fashion from recent issues of pattern books, women's magazines or the fashion pages of daily newspapers.

STEP A: LONG-LEGGEDNESS
Long legs relative to the torso distinguish late maturing from early maturing girls after puberty. To assess current fashion standards regarding this feature, first measure the total height of the model from top of the head to soles of the feet (excluding high-heeled shoes). Then measure the length from waist to soles. Compute a ratio of the latter to the former. Work out the mean across all the photographs you have collected.

STEP B: THE BUST
Breast size is a feature which remains more pronounced in early maturing than late maturing adolescent girls throughout the lifespan. To assess current standards, first measure the width of the chest at its widest point in one of your photographs. Then measure the waist width in the same photo, and compute a ratio of breast divided by waist size. Do the same for each photograph in your collection and compute a mean.

STEP C: INTERPRETATION
An American survey similar to this one was conducted in 1983 by Margaret Faust. She found that a leg/total height ratio of 0.70 was standard for high-fashion models. Are the ratios you obtained in Step A as high as this? If so, Faust suggests they should encourage feelings of attractiveness in late developers. Conversely, large breast dimensions in the media favour the self-image development of early maturing girls. Check the figures you obtained in Step B with those computed by fellow students. You could also test how consistently these cultural standards of beauty have been maintained over recent decades by doing the same computations on fashion plates from magazines going back to the 1940s.

communicate their changed status to their mother, sisters and girlfriends.

The comparable event for boys, spermarche, or the first ejaculation of semen containing sperm, is frequently a very private experience. When a group of American boys aged 13 to 16 was interviewed

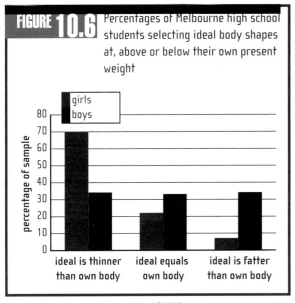

FIGURE 10.6 Percentages of Melbourne high school students selecting ideal body shapes at, above or below their own present weight

Source: Based on data in Maude et al. (1993).

(Gaddis & Brooks-Gunn, 1985), some 64 per cent reported that they had not mentioned their first ejaculation to anyone other than the interviewer. Even those who had told someone usually confined the news to one other person, typically their father. Nevertheless, despite the secrecy connected with it, most boys reported very positive reactions to this transition, as illustrated in Figure 10.7.

Adolescent physical appearance and self-esteem: A question of timing

Richard Lerner (1996) discovered that physical beauty is especially important to adolescents in the throes of making transitions to new peer groups, as when the family moves to a new neighbourhood or with entrance into high school. Longitudinal data indicated that, for 12-year-old primary school students in the United States who had been together with the same group of classmates for a number of

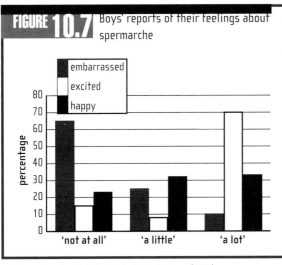

FIGURE 10.7 Boys' reports of their feelings about spermarche

Source: Based on data in Gaddis & Brooks-Gunn (1985).

years, physical attractiveness exerted very little influence over self-esteem. But a year later, these children entered junior high school. At this point, how attractive they had been as 12-year-olds became a significant predictor of self-esteem. Their self-rated popularity with peers and their athletic competence at age 13 was likewise a function of how superficially attractive they had been one year earlier. In addition, physical attractiveness predicted teachers' ratings of students' academic competence at the beginning of a new school year. But by the end of the year, when the teachers had gathered direct evidence of their students' work, there was no significant relationship between students' physical appearance and teachers' perceptions of their academic ability. In other words, like the physical features that determine a person's attractiveness in the first place, beauty's influence on psychological functioning is subject to change over time.

While it might seem that physical attractiveness is invariably advantageous, a study of 12-year-old girls from the midwestern United States suggested the opposite (Zakin, Blyth & Simmons, 1984). As a measure of beauty, school nurses classed the girls into one of three groups:

1. very good-looking
2. of average attractiveness
3. moderately unattractive.

Paradoxically, the unattractive girls were found to have much more positive feelings about themselves and their appearance, and to score significantly higher on objective tests of self-esteem, than their peers who were judged by adults to be extremely beautiful. The researchers concluded that: 'pubertal development ... meant a loss in self-esteem for attractive girls and a boost in self-esteem for average and unattractive girls' (p. 447).

This result is consistent with a *differential vulnerability* hypothesis. In other words, quite apart from how closely her features may match socially recognised standards of beauty, the adolescent girl's feelings about herself are shaped jointly by how much her appearance changes during the upheavals of puberty, and also by how much she valued her own beauty during childhood. According to the theory of differential vulnerability:

> The attractive girl is accustomed to receiving preferential treatment because of her looks. Presumably her self-esteem is more tied up with her physical appearance. Consequently, when the attractive girl begins to experience the pubertal transition the physical changes may be more traumatic and threatening for her because of the greater risk involved. The attractive girl's beautiful and highly valued features are now rapidly changing and she cannot know what the final outcome will be. During this time of physical metamorphosis the attractive child might thus be expected to be at a relative disadvantage. The

unattractive child, on the other hand, may welcome the onset of puberty. From her perspective there is nothing to be lost as her body changes; the final version can only be an improvement. The popular myth of the ugly duckling that grows into a beautiful swan may offer her hope that she will develop into an attractive adolescent. Thus, the unattractive girl may cope relatively better with the changes her body undergoes during puberty. (p. 448)

Another danger of extreme beauty in adolescence is that it may motivate its owner to think of nothing else. By being accepted too readily by peers on the grounds of appearance alone, stunningly beautiful girls, or tall muscular boys, may lack the incentive to acquire other desirable social and intellectual skills such as empathy, self-criticism or a mature sense of humour. On the other hand, an adolescent who is deprived by nature of this automatic ticket of entry into peer cliques may learn to cultivate these attractive personality attributes that have greater value later in the lifespan. The example in Box 10.7 illustrates this compensation process. Donald Horne, later to become a noted Australian humorist and critic, began to sharpen his wit in high school in reaction to a physique that equipped him to be neither a 'Sport' nor a 'Tough'.

Eating disorders and weight preoccupation

As noted above, another problematic aspect of adolescent growth, especially for girls, is an unrealistic fear of obesity (Warren, 1983). Taken to the extreme, such a fear can lead to the mental health problem known as *anorexia nervosa*. According to Michelle Warren (1983), anorexia, an extreme aversion to eating usually accompanied by symptoms similar to involuntary starvation, 'has fascinated physicians for centuries because of its bizarre manifestations, its seemingly self-imposed food restriction, and its distortion of the subject's mental image of the body' (p. 12). Though there may also be hidden biochemical abnormalities, a well-intentioned diet in an initially overweight individual frequently triggers the development of anorexia. When left untreated, the condition is found to prove fatal for 10 to 20 per cent of sufferers who literally starve themselves to death. The surviving remainder face serious physiological and psychological problems, including delays in pubertal growth, depression and impaired social adjustment, and an increased risk of serious mental illness, including obsessive-compulsive personality disorder, later in life (Nilsson, Gillberg, Gillberg & Rastam, 1999).

Medical aid, such as intravenous feeding, may be needed in serious cases of anorexia to prevent sudden death. But the most effective long-term treatments usually include psychological therapy aimed at altering the patient's deviant attitudes to food and body image, and improving relationships with friends and family. For example, after discovering that an exceptionally large proportion of anorexia sufferers came

BOX 10.7 A case in point
On not being a Sport

In the following excerpt from his autobiography, the Australian author and critic Donald Horne describes some of the social consequences at his new high school of not having an athletic physique.

At first there seemed to be an extraordinarily high number of Toughs at Canterbury. Since we were seniors there was no question of being hit, but some of the boys paraded their maleness with an indefatigable aggressiveness, using words and lurches of their bodies so effectively that a flick or two of their lowered eyelids might kill a conversation ... Then it became clear that there were very few bullies, that the more numerous kind of enemy was the Sport, the boy who, apart from masturbation, saw nothing in life except his own success in team games ... These boys were not necessarily bullies: it was simply beyond their comprehension that anyone should consider that the final reality did not lie in success in team games. Between them and someone who did not share their views there was no possibility of communication. I soon discovered, however, that I was not so surrounded by enemies as I thought: among those who appeared to be nothing but Toughs or Sports some were also Cynics, who liked talking so long as it was in the sardonic, chyacking style. I made my first friend among the Cynics. Then I discovered that a number of the boys were not Toughs or Sports at all, not even Cynics, more Humorists than anything else. With this discovery I took up the Humorists, with whom I found more possibilities for conversation than I had enjoyed at Parramatta. [1975, pp. 164–5]

The pleasures of belonging to a group of peers and the fear of being rejected are both acute throughout adolescence.

Preoccupations with food, dieting and slimness are common during adolescence.

from homes where interpersonal conflicts were routinely handled by avoidance and denial rather than through open communication and cooperative negotiation, Salvador Minuchin, Bernice Rosman and Lester Baker (1978) used family therapy (including the teaching of effective conflict-resolution skills to members of the victim's family) to successfully cure 86 per cent of their anorexic patients. (See Chapter 12 for a fuller discussion of patterns of resolving family conflicts during adolescence.)

Bulimia, or binge eating accompanied by vomiting or purging to rid the body of unwanted calories, is another eating disorder that often has its onset in adolescence (Maude, Wertheim, Paxton, Gibbons & Szmukler, 1993). Binge eating may or may not be accompanied by purging. Even when deliberate purging through laxatives or self-induced vomiting is employed, these disordered eating habits are not necessarily of the clinical proportions required to qualify as bulimia. The difference between bulimia (or bulimia nervosa) as a clinical condition and the more common binge–dieting cycles that large numbers of adolescents engage in, at least occasionally, is partly a matter of degree and partly one of attitude. Clinical victims of bulimia, like anorexics, often have very disordered images of their own bodies, believing themselves to be overweight when they are actually normal or unusually thin. Bulimia can pose severe health risks because of the damage done to the throat, stomach and colon by massive doses of laxatives or continual vomiting. The condition can also be life-threatening. The strain of sudden and extreme electrolyte imbalance resulting from a bulimic purge has been known to cause cardiac arrest (Hsu, 1990).

Australian estimates suggest that only 2 per cent of adolescent girls and 1 per cent of adolescent boys are clinically bulimic, and only one teenager in 1000 is anorexic (Maude et al., 1993). Similarly, in New Zealand, a recent survey showed that approximately 1 per cent of young women aged 18 to 24 currently had bulimia, with a lifetime prevalence of 2.6 per cent among contemporary New Zealand women (Bushnell, Wells, Hornblow & Oakley-Browne, 1990). This study also showed a strong cohort effect. Bulimia was more prevalent among recent generations of adolescents and young adults than among their mothers and grandmothers when they were in their teens and twenties.

While eating disorders that are serious enough to require clinical attention are still relatively infrequent, dissatisfaction with weight and occasional use of extreme weight-loss tactics are much more common, with more than one-quarter of one large sample of Melbourne schoolgirls reporting that they sometimes fasted and went on crash diets, and half reporting that they occasionally skipped meals in order to lose weight (Maude et al., 1993). Boys used these techniques less often than girls, possibly because their drive for thinness was weaker than that of their female classmates.

Depression and social anxiety are likely to result from learned helplessness about growth and weight, or the feeling that, despite one's best efforts to lose weight, gain muscle or alter one's appearance more generally, the process is totally outside one's power to control. In fact, an accurate sense of control over important developmental outcomes is crucial to psychological adaptation at all ages (Seligman, 1975). Given that the outcome of the growth process is very important to adolescents, a feeling of personal control over their weight, growth and attractiveness is crucial to emotional well-being.

Adolescents are not unique in this respect. Because the body's size and shape figure so largely in adults' impressions of themselves and others, the possibility of taking charge of this crucial aspect of the self is a key to emotional well-being throughout adulthood. When a change in weight (gain or loss) is needed or desired, personal control can determine the success of body building or dieting at any age. Australian research with overweight adults has conversely shown that a feeling of being helpless can undermine the success of even the most rigorous and conscientious of reducing diets. Even if the dieter does eventually lose weight, helplessness may lead to its being quickly put on again. A sense of personal control, on the other hand, fosters the maintenance of weight loss (McKenzie, 1985). If weight is a problem to you, or if you are simply curious about your feelings of control over gaining and losing it, you may wish to try the quiz exercise in Box 10.8.

However, for adolescents who are seriously overweight or underweight the solution may not be a simple one. It is clearly of little value to blame the victim – according to Jane Rees and Christine Trahms (1989, p. 205), 'Prominent myths pervade the work

BOX 10.8 Activity suggestion
Weight quiz

Instructions. To test your own views about weight control, indicate your opinion by marking each statement true (T) or false (F).

1. A person's weight is more a matter of genetics and physiology than of how hard he or she works at gaining or losing weight. T F
2. If they work at it, most overweight people can reduce to an ideal level. T F
3. Diet and exercise are more important than inherited factors in determining weight. T F
4. No matter how conscientiously they diet, people who were overweight as infants will be overweight as adults. T F
5. Almost all obesity could be prevented if people were willing to refrain from overeating. T F

Scoring. Give yourself one point each for choosing T answers to (2), (3) and (5) and one point for each F answer to (1) and (4). The higher your total, the more personal control you ascribe to weight control. Using a similar scale, Faye McKenzie (1985) found that overweight Australian women had lower control scores than their peers of normal weight. But the scores of one group of obese women rose significantly after they joined a weight-control program and succeeded in losing weight.

of professionals who may believe that obesity is curable or a temporary problem, that obesity is the person's own fault'. These myths are dangerous, say Rees and Trahms, because 'focussing on an unresolved weight problem promotes a sense of powerlessness that pervades development' (p. 206). Thus the adolescent's academic success, intellectual growth and social adjustment can suffer when dietary issues become an overwhelming preoccupation. At the same time, the cultivation of leisure interests involving physical activity or social interaction are undermined when learned helplessness about weight is allowed to get the upper hand. According to Rees and Trahms,

the most effective form of therapy for obese teenagers is eclectic, with an emphasis on gradual change:

> Strategies include an emphasis on support to keep the situation from further deterioration and to maximise the health of the obese teenager. Family interaction, or psychological problems that may have precipitated, or developed as a result of, the overfat condition need to be addressed ... The focus is on accomplishable actions that the patient can take to change attitudes and behaviour ... as well as the will to function productively regardless of body size. (p. 207)

The timing of puberty

The psychological consequences of puberty considered so far all apply to growth in general, irrespective of how old a child or adolescent happens to be when encountering a given set of pubertal growth events. But recent research shows that the factor of timing is at least as important as the nature of the change itself as a clue to understanding how puberty shapes the adolescent's feelings and behaviour. Thus, a girl who reaches menarche at the statistically average age of 13 is likely to differ in important ways from a peer who encounters the same change at a much older or younger age. The same applies to boys and the changes they experience. As mentioned earlier, the psychological consequences of variations in puberty's timing are capable of persisting throughout the adult lifespan. In the next sections of this chapter, we first examine the immediate impact of meeting pubertal growth changes either 'on time' or 'off schedule'. Then we analyse some puzzling lifespan data which illustrate how the short-term influences of puberty's developmental time clock may vary dramatically from the psychological effects emerging a decade or more later. Finally, we examine the delicate interplay that exists between pubertal timing and the social relationships that adolescents forge for themselves with their parents and other family members.

Early and late puberty in boys: Consequences during adolescence

A seminal longitudinal study begun in Berkeley, California, in the 1940s by Harold Ellis Jones, Mary Cover Jones and their colleagues explored the psychological impact of being off schedule in the timing of pubertal growth. Because of the males' two-year lag behind females (see Figure 10.2), the two sexes were studied separately. In the initial male sample, the 16 earliest maturing boys and the 16 latest maturing boys were selected from a sample of 90 healthy, well-nourished pupils in junior high school. The Joneses and their colleagues then studied these two groups intensively from age 14 until age 17. The criterion for physical maturity was fusion of the bones of the hand. But, not surprisingly, the early-maturing 14-year-olds were also heavier, taller by an average of 20 centimetres, more advanced in secondary sex characteristics like facial and bodily hair and further along in their progress towards reproductive sexual maturation than their late-maturing counterparts. What was surprising was that personality differences distinguished the two groups of boys as clearly and consistently as these physical traits.

During their teens, the early-maturing boys were more self-assured than the late maturers. They were also rated by clinical psychologists as more attractive and masculine in appearance, better dressed and groomed, more poised, relaxed and well-mannered, and possessing more self-assurance and a more out-going personality than either the late maturers or the average boys. Reports from classmates also showed early maturers to be more popular than late maturers with their male and female peers. Most of the elected class officers in school were picked from the ranks of the early maturers. These boys were also chosen by peers as team and group leaders in sport and other recreational pursuits, and by girls as dating partners. Neither late-maturing nor average boys earned these hallmarks of extreme peer popularity nearly as often.

Conversely, the late maturers stood out in the psychologists' ratings for symptoms of mild maladjustment. These included their display of nervous habits, like twitching or stuttering, immature dependency and their frequent misbehaviour in the classroom. Late maturers were also socially awkward with peers. Their adolescent classmates described them as bossy, physically unattractive nuisances, and rated them lower in popularity than either the average or the early-maturing boys. Late maturers' attitudes to girls and to adult authority figures were considered to be immature and irresponsible by the adult judges (Jones & Bayley, 1950).

Paul Mussen and Mary Cover Jones (1957) used a projective instrument called the TAT (Thematic Apperception Test) 'to investigate the relationship between maturational status and certain important, covert aspects of personality' (p. 244). Each boy was shown a set of 18 pictures of familiar life settings (e.g. a tea-table and two chairs, or a man and woman on a park bench). In response to each picture, the boy was asked to tell a story that described his feelings. The scoring procedure was based on the assumption that subjects had projected themselves into their stories. The hero's actions and feelings were therefore a guide to the boy's own hidden feelings. The strength of the technique was in allowing access to private needs and anxieties which most boys would have been loath to admit to themselves, let alone divulge in a public interview. Late maturers gave a far less attractive account of themselves on the TAT than early maturers. Derogations of competence (such as 'imbecile' or 'weakling') were particularly common in the former group. This result was consistent with the assumption that the late maturers' physical retardation, unfavourable reputation with male and female peers and competitive disadvantages at team sports had all combined to diminish feelings of self-worth.

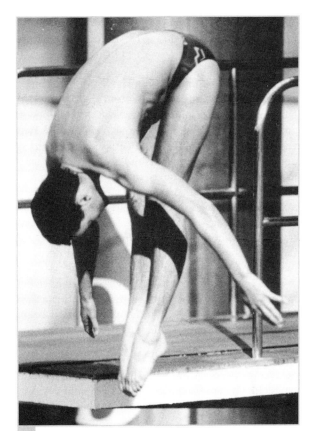

Early-maturing boys are chosen as leaders in sporting and social competitions.

Late maturers also expressed more delinquent themes in their stories, together with a strong need to defy parents, who were typically depicted as disliking or rejecting their late-maturing sons. A dependent theme likewise testified to the late maturer's reluctance to break free of parents and an immature reliance on parental advice, sympathy, help and encouragement.

According to Mussen and Jones, all these problems could be linked to the late maturer's physical underdevelopment. Because they still looked like 'little boys', their parents continued to treat them that way. The late-maturing boys' anger and frustration at being denied the independence accorded quite naturally by parents to sons who happened to look mature helped to explain the rebellion and hostility of the late developers.

It is perhaps not surprising that the late-maturing boys were at a disadvantage compared with early maturers in virtually all areas of behaviour and adjustment during adolescence. After all, the late maturers possessed the same physical traits of shortness, poor muscle tone and lack of facial hair that are found to cause most worry to boys in general. Socially, these same traits put the boys at a distinct disadvantage in competitive team sports, in situations requiring them to assert themselves with adults and in competition for girls' attention and admiration. The more interesting question from a lifespan standpoint is whether psychological after-effects remain from these upsetting adolescent experiences once late-maturing boys eventually grow to full stature. But before exploring this issue, let us consider the effect of pubertal timing on the adolescent girl.

Early and late puberty in girls: Consequences during adolescence

Due to the asynchronous growth of the two sexes, girls start the pubertal growth sequence some two years ahead of boys. Thus an early-maturing girl is apt to feel just as deviant and isolated as a late-maturing boy, since she is out of phase with the majority of her classmates and age peers of both sexes. The difference is that the girl's deviation is in a forward-looking direction. This leads to three contrasting predictions about the possible influence of the timing of puberty on the psychological development of adolescent girls. If being unusual is what matters most, the early maturing girl should have the most problems: her schedule differs from male and female classmates' alike. On the other hand, if being retarded in growth (and hence treated socially as a child) is the decisive factor, the late-developing girl should show poorer adjustment than her accelerated or average peers. A third possibility is that girls will be relatively unaffected by puberty's timing since, given the sex lag, even the very slowest girl is likely to complete puberty ahead of at least some of the same-age males in her class at school and so be able to consider herself within the range of average.

Early research evidence tended to favour the last of these hypotheses. For example, when Mary Cover Jones and Paul Mussen (1958) repeated their TAT study using adolescent girls as subjects, they found only two significant differences between early and late developers, compared with eight in their study of boys. Like the boys, late-maturing girls gave less favourable descriptions of themselves than early maturers, and expressed stronger needs for fame and social status. However, the most striking finding was how many fewer differences there were between girls than boys as a function of pubertal status. Similarly, when Juliet Harper and John Collins (1975) examined the popularity status of 631 Australian girls aged nine to 16 years, they found no relationship at all between a girl's social prestige and her recollection of how old she was when she reached menarche.

However, Roberta Simmons, Dale Blyth and Karen McKinney (1983) challenged the conclusion that the timing of puberty is irrelevant to girls' psychological adjustment. One problem with many of the earlier studies was reliance on the cross-sectional methodology. Cross-sectional comparisons not only fail to make allowances for differences that may have existed between early and late maturers' behaviour before the events of puberty, but are also apt to be biased by girls' notoriously faulty recall of the exact date of their first period. Simmons, Blyth and McKinney therefore employed a longitudinal design.

Beginning in 1968, they had collected enough data by 1983 to show quite convincingly that the timing of puberty was crucial to psychological adjustment in girls, just as it was for boys. Some of the differences that emerged from their first wave of data collection, when the girls were aged 11 to 13, are shown in Table 10.1. The two most striking differences involved independence from parents and academic performance. Late maturers did exceptionally well in school, while early maturers earned lower marks and had more disciplinary problems with parents and teachers than average or late developers.

TABLE 10.1 Some contrasts in girls' behaviour as a function of timing of puberty			
Age period	Menarche timing		
	Early	Average	Late
11 to 13 years	Poor marks on school work Low scores on maths and reading tests Does not plan to attend university Frequently misbehaves in school Allowed to babysit and travel on the bus alone	Average marks Average scores on maths and reading tests Does not plan to attend university Sometimes misbehaves in school Allowed to stay home alone when parents go out	Top marks on school work High scores on maths and reading tests Plans to attend university Behaves very well in school Not allowed to travel alone on bus, babysit or stay home alone
15 to 16 years	Very popular with boys Her parents like her close friends Allowed to go out without parental permission Her girlfriends expect her to date Dating boys	Not popular with boys Her parents dislike her close friends Not allowed to go out without parental permission Her girlfriends expect her to date Dating boys	Not popular with boys Her parents are neutral towards her close friends Not allowed to go out without parental permission Her girlfriends do not expect her to be interested in boys Not yet dating

Source: Based on data in Simmons, Blyth & McKinney (1983), pp. 243–57; Simmons & Blyth (1987).

But the early-maturing girls were allowed more leeway by parents than average or late developers, possibly as a result of the family conflicts over independence (see Chapter 12). By age 16, the most striking differences involved relationships with boys. Early-maturing girls began dating at a younger age than late maturers. They also considered themselves to be more popular with the opposite sex than the late or average developers did. But as Harper and Collins (1975) had found in Australia, there were no differences in same-sex popularity for these American girls as a function of maturity status.

Early menarche predicts an early onset of sexual experience and, in fact, is a stronger predictor than religious belief, ethnicity or coeducational schooling. A precocious interest in sex, boyfriends and dating may possibly distract early-maturing girls from their studies, causing the problems with academic achievement that were observed by Simmons and her colleagues (Table 10.1). Alternatively, the stress of being strikingly different from male and female peers, and the intense pressure she is under to reassure her parents that her precocious biological maturation will not lead to sexual immorality, unwanted pregnancy or sexually transmitted disease, can make early adolescent life very difficult for the female early maturer (Savin-Williams & Small, 1986).

Parents may also have different reactions to the timing of puberty in daughters than in sons. Ritch Savin-Williams and Stephen Small (1986) found that early-maturing daughters caused greater inner conflict, stress, doubts as to parenting ability and general anxiety to their parents than daughters who went through biological puberty at late or average ages. But early-maturing sons caused no such anxieties. Indeed, early-maturing sons, like late-maturing daughters were a source of the highest levels of parental pride and happiness.

Much of the research into the impact of pubertal timing has been conducted in the United States. Despite this, there are currently no grounds for supposing that the independent influences of timing on adolescent adjustment are the result of some peculiarity of North American culture. Instead, the existing cross-cultural data seem to indicate that teenagers in most contemporary Western societies are influenced in similar ways by the timing of their puberty in interaction with their gender. For example, a study by Hillevi Aro and Vappu Taipale (1987) in a small city in Finland made use of the longitudinal method to explore girls' stress reactions before and after the onset of menarche. The measure of stress was the frequency and intensity of the girls' self-reported suffering from such unpleasant psychosomatic symptoms as headache, insomnia, nausea, dizziness and excess perspiration. The investigators found that early maturers, who had reached menarche at the age of 12 or younger, were suffering from more of these bothersome symptoms by age 14 than either the average girls, who had reached menarche at 13, or the late

Girls who reach puberty late are more likely than other girls to do well in high school and to plan to attend university.

maturers who were just beginning to menstruate at the ages of 14 to 15 when the study began. Symptoms grew more troublesome for all the girls as they progressed through adolescence, but the early maturers continued to suffer most.

Aro and Taipale suggested that the increase in symptoms for all girls with age might 'reflect the general stressfulness of the female pubertal development process' (p. 266) relative to that of a male, who does not have to contend with menstruation and is less directly involved in contraception and the fear of pregnancy. In addition, the Finnish researchers noted that childhood is cut short for the female early maturer who has her first period at the age of nine or ten. Thus she may not have the same opportunity as other adolescents to complete the developmental tasks of middle childhood (see Chapters 8 and 9).

Hakan Stattin and David Magnusson (1990) likewise found that early-maturing Swedish girls completed fewer years of schooling and had their children earlier than women who, as adolescents, had reached menarche at an average or late age. These results parallel the North American findings of poor academic achievement and precocious sexual experience among female early maturers (see Table 10.1). But early-maturing Swedish girls were also shown to have more problems with the police, and to engage more often in shoplifting, truancy, use of illicit drugs and abuse of alcohol than other Swedish girls of the same chronological age, a finding that was not reported by researchers studying female pubertal timing in North America. Some of the variations in the timing of the social aspects of girls' dating and early couple relationships and their impact on a parent's thinking are illustrated in Box 10.9.

Lifespan consequences of puberty's timing

In line with the concept of *life-cycle surprises* discussed in Chapter 1, the data that emerged from the longitudinal follow-ups of the Jones's original Berkeley sample of early- and late-maturing males revealed that the psychological consequences of reaching puberty early or late remained with the men throughout their adult lives, long after any physical differences in height and build had all but disappeared. At age 30, the two groups of men were almost identical in physical appearance (Jones, 1965; Peskin, 1973). The late developers had emerged from their slow start a mere 2 centimetres shorter, on average, and 3 kilograms lighter than the men who had matured early. Nor were there any important differences between the two groups in fitness or muscularity.

Nevertheless, personality differences emerged almost as strikingly in adulthood as during adolescence. Mary Cover Jones (1965) rated the adult men who had matured early as more domineering, responsible and self-controlled, and as better able to make a good impression on other people than the men whose puberty had come late. On the other hand, the early maturers now had some negative qualities too. They were rated as more rigid and blindly conforming than late maturers, and as less capable of coping with stress. Late maturers, conversely, had a better sense of humour, clearer insight and a more sophisticated understanding of themselves and others. By age 38, the late maturers were likewise more perceptive, sensitive and egalitarian in their sex-role orientation than the early-maturing men (Livson & Peskin, 1980).

R. Ames (1957) also found that, although the early-maturing men continued to enjoy a more active outside social life in adulthood than males who matured late, the late maturers were the ones who seemed to enjoy the most satisfying intimate relationships with their wives and children. During youth and middle age, the early maturers continued, as in adolescence, to go out more socially and to be involved in more social activities related both to their work and to voluntary participation in clubs, lodges, sporting bodies and church affairs. They held more elected posts in volunteer organisations. Together with their wives, early maturers also entertained more in connection with the husband's job and had a wider circle of friends and social acquaintances. The early-maturing man's career typically demanded more leadership, supervision and management of others than the late maturers'. Over the same time in their job, they had advanced further up the organisational ladder, on average, than late maturers and, while still in their 30s, held more senior executive roles at work. On the other hand, Ames found that late maturers derived greater satisfaction from their marriages than the early maturers. They were also judged by their wives to be more understanding and considerate and were less likely to have considered or undertaken a marital separation or divorce.

Harvey Peskin (1973) hypothesised that the coping skills of late-developing males would be superior to those of the early developers, since the latter had had fewer opportunities as adolescents to cultivate strategies for coping with stress, owing to their relatively smooth passage through the pubertal growth process. He found, in fact, that in adulthood the late maturers scored higher on measures of creativity, openness, flexible thinking and intellectual curiosity. The early maturers were not only relatively rigid, conventional and closed-minded but also more psychologically vulnerable, due to an insatiable desire for prestige and an intense striving to be liked and approved of for their achievements and for 'doing the right thing'. Some of these characteristics match the symptoms of a problem known as *identity foreclosure* (considered in detail in Chapter 11). It would therefore seem that some positive qualities, such as leadership and social outgoingness, fostered in boys by early puberty, are maintained as psychological strengths throughout adulthood, but there are also some corresponding psychological costs for men of developing too early.

According to Michael Berzonsky (1983), the very experiences which combine to make adolescence pleasant for the early developing male – such as fitting in with prevailing social stereotypes and earning approval as 'good dates', 'good sports' and 'good-looking' – may be the factors which in the long run curtail their development of inner strengths. Thus, early-maturing boys 'are reinforced for becoming what others expect them to be; they foreclose on a ready-made identity and become (or continue to be) well socialized and outer-directed' (p. 217). On the other hand, the stresses that make adolescence such a traumatic period for the late-developing boy may force his acquisition of personal resources that will add greatly to his enjoyment of a productive adult life. Having learned to cope, however painfully, with the joint stresses of delayed physical growth and social ostracism, late-maturing boys seem to gain a deeper capacity for intimacy, greater strength for coping with stress and adversity, and a more tolerant and whimsical understanding of themselves and their attitude towards life.

Longitudinal follow-ups of the original female sample of early and late maturers at Berkeley yielded fewer differences in adulthood than were noted among men (Peskin, 1973). But where consistent differences did emerge, they tended to support the view that the compensation for growing through a stressful and troubled adolescence may be superior skills for coping with the stresses of adult life. In particular, Harvey Peskin (1973) found that, by the age of 30, women whose menarche had come early were more responsible, self-directed and objective in their thinking than their late-maturing peers. As adult women, the early maturers also appeared to be more poised in social situations, less rigid and less willing to withdraw or give up in the face of adversity. Like their late-maturing male counterparts, these women seemed to have gained skills and a clearer understanding of themselves as a result of going through puberty stressfully by being ahead of all their friends.

Therefore, whereas the specific consequences of being early or late are not identical for the two sexes, the underlying mechanism seems to be the same for both. Late-maturing males and early-maturing females, as a result of their deviant timing, encounter the most trauma and show the poorest adjustment during adolescence itself. But they are the ones who appear to enter mature adulthood with the strongest repertoire of psychological assets and coping strengths.

Social influences on the timing of biological puberty

Lawrence Steinberg (1988) conducted a series of longitudinal and cross-sectional investigations of the relationship between the hormonal changes that biological puberty sets in motion and the changing social dynamics of adolescent girls' and boys' relationships with their parents. Puberty was rated by independent medical assessments, not the adolescent's own self-report, while both generations supplied information on the quality of the parent–adolescent relationship.

The results revealed an intriguing interplay between biological growth events and changes in social relationships. On one hand, the combined cross-sectional and longitudinal analyses clearly showed that puberty produced changes in family relationships, irrespective of the adolescent's chronological age when the changes illustrated in Figure 10.2 began to occur. At the point when pubertal growth climaxed, there was an abrupt decrease in closeness between fathers and their offspring and an increase in conflict and angry arguments between adolescents and their mothers. These changes applied to both sexes. In addition, puberty led to more arguments and fewer calm discussions between daughters and their fathers, and to greater emotional distance between boys and their parents of both sexes. Such a direction of causality makes good intuitive sense. Puberty disrupts the adolescent's hormonal balance, heightening emotionality (Buchanan, Eccles & Becker, 1992). At the same time, the visible growth changes of puberty cause parents to view their offspring in a new light as young adults, with all that this implies about the likelihood of arguments between parents and offspring over household responsibilities (Goodnow & Warton, 1991), social and political issues (see Chapter 11) and adolescent risk-taking (see Chapter 12).

On the other hand, common sense would not have predicted the other causal chain that emerged equally persuasively from Steinberg's longitudinal analyses. This was the discovery that the timing of a girl's biological puberty was influenced by the quality of her social relationship with her mother during childhood. With other factors controlled, those girls who had an exceptionally close emotional relationship with their mothers were found to be delayed in reaching menarche, as compared with girls who were low in mother–daughter intimacy, according to the reports of both generations. Girls growing up in single-parent or step-parent families reached puberty earlier than girls in intact households, presumably owing to the greater emotional distance between parents and offspring in stepfamilies, according to Steinberg. Some of the results of this research are shown in Figures 10.8 and 10.9.

Can psychological intimacy between a mother and her daughter actually retard the girl's biological

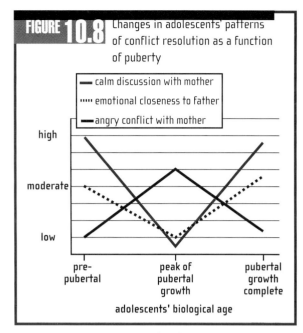

Source: Based on data in Steinberg (1989).

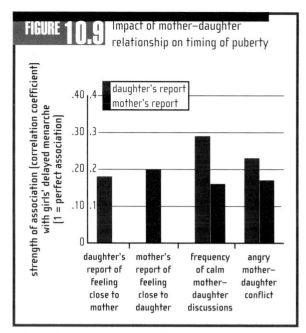

Source: Based on data in Steinberg (1988).

passage through puberty? Steinberg's data strongly suggest that it does and, furthermore, that this effect operated independently of pubertal maturation's tendency to increase the emotional distance between parent and child. But by what mechanism might parent–child social relationships exert their decisive effect on pubertal timing? One possibility involves *pheromones*. These chemical substances, secreted by one organism and picked up by other organisms through the sense of smell, are believed to be responsible for menstrual synchrony among women who live together in the same household (Kommenich, McSweeney, Noack & Elder, 1980). If pheromonal communication patterns were found to vary with the degree of emotional intimacy between a mother and her daughter, the observed relationship between pubertal timing and social distance might be explicable on this basis.

Steinberg argued that animal research supported the social triggering of biological menarche. Studies of species ranging from gorillas and monkeys to hamsters, wolves and dingoes have all shown that a daughter's fertility is suppressed until she moves out of the social group to which her mother belongs (Levin & Johnston, 1986, cited in Steinberg, 1989). Other research shows that ovulation is suppressed in pubertal female marmosets while they live near their mothers (Evans & Hodge, 1984, cited in Steinberg, 1989). If the same is true of humans, a close mother–daughter relationship could retard the girl's psychological development of independent self-reliance and emotional autonomy, consequently delaying biological puberty.

As an alternative to pheromones, Steinberg suggested that undue maternal closeness during adolescence might create emotional difficulties for girls. This theory is in line with the ideas of psychoanalysts

like Erik Erikson (1968b; see also Chapter 11) and Anna Freud (1958; see also Chapter 12), who felt that a trouble-free adolescence may be less healthy in the long run than a crisis-ridden period of storm and stress. As Steinberg explained:

> One hypothesis worthy of future investigation is … that a high level of maternal closeness at a time when the adolescent may be striving for autonomy is experienced by the adolescent as stressful, and that this stress in its turn inhibits certain endocrine activity related to pubertal development. (p. 89)

More recently, David Comings and his colleagues (2002) came up with an alternative explanation. Noting that girls exposed to extended periods of father absence during the first seven years of life reached menarche at an unusually early age, these authors proposed that an X-linked gene inherited by these daughters from their fathers (see Chapter 3) could dispose them towards precocious puberty. At the same time, the presence of this gene on the fathers' X chromosome could dispose these men towards behaviours that could lead to father absence. For example, the father might engage in extramarital sexual liaisons, predisposing him to divorce, or commit criminal acts, leading to prison sentences. High levels of sexual compulsivity and aggression are indeed linked with the genetic composition of the androgen receptor gene on the X chromosome, lending support to a genetic explanation for the observed link between early puberty and the social situation of prolonged father absence.

Adolescent sexuality

The fact that puberty equips the adolescent with mature biological capacities for reproduction and sexual enjoyment gives the psychological and social growth of sexuality special significance during this phase in life. One adolescent's first encounter with the new demands of a sexual role is described in Box 10.10.

BOX 10.10 A case in point
A babe in the woods

When Louise was 15, she went out alone with a boy for the first time. She had met him only the day before in a northern New Zealand campground. Her father described the event and his ensuing conversation with his daughter as follows.

14 December 1964. When the park manager's son Bryan offered to go walking with Louise and, to our surprise, picked her up in a car, it turned out in effect to be her first date. The young fellow, who is 18, good-looking, and evidently sure of himself, assumed either he had a babe in the woods in Louise or else, being American, she was ready for anything. He didn't go farther than putting an arm about her but he made a longer date for tonight and Louise seemed convinced he meant to go farther. Though what this might involve she hadn't the foggiest notion.

I had half suspected she was uninformed though I recall Peg talking to her about sex some years ago, too long ago, as it happened, for her to remember. I thought perhaps her girl friends may have shared their knowledge, as children do; but they too apparently know very little. Still I didn't want to bring the subject up out of the blue.

Last evening it came up naturally and we talked at length. Her chief fear is that she won't get dates if she refuses to allow a boy to take liberties. I told her she probably wouldn't have as many as the girl who was complaisant but she had a life to live beyond her dating age and it could be ruined by getting stuck with the wrong husband. I told her most young girls probably go no farther than petting but in some ways this is worse than going all the way because it arouses a desire now naturally dormant and then frustrates it. I told her specifically in a situation like last evening she should declare forthrightly that she didn't care for that sort of thing, that perhaps if she had a longer acquaintance and came to know a boy better she'd feel differently, and then he could put his arm around her and kiss her. I told her always to make clear that she had no personal aversion toward the boy himself, that she was sure he was a nice boy, but she'd have the same objection to anybody on such short acquaintance ... I must say I had no idea before they left that he was going to drive and that they were going so far away from everybody. Louise too thought he was inviting her for an afternoon walk. She'll have to obtain more definite details concerning future dates, and I on my part shouldn't have let her go off in the car. But one hates to be rude; and as it turned out it's best I wasn't because Louise would never have appreciated the danger without a glimpse of it herself.

© Peterson, 1974, reproduced with permission

It is not easy for adolescents who are just coming to terms with their own sexuality to form a satisfactory boy–girl relationship that takes account of both partners' sexual needs, knowledge, anxieties and capabilities. Several important areas are brought out in Box 10.10. These include an accurate understanding of the mechanics of reproduction and the dynamics of male and female sexual desire. The adolescent's desperate need for sex education and some of the difficulties in trying to obtain it from parents are also highlighted.

Sex education

The issue of whether, when and how to teach children about sexuality is a perplexing one. Though sexual attitudes have grown somewhat more liberal in recent decades (Moore & Rosenthal, 1993), even today the taboos attaching to frank discussions about sex may limit Australian and New Zealand adolescents' access to accurate information until many years after their physiological capacity for mature sexual performance is complete. When Ronald and Juliet Goldman (1982) examined the sexual knowledge of a group of Melbourne children and adolescents, they found widespread ignorance about many basic sexual concepts even among boys and girls as old as 15. As a basis for optimising the development of a mature understanding of sexuality, the Goldmans conducted a cross-cultural comparison of the relative effectiveness of the varied channels of communication through which young people learn about sex. In addition to a sample of 240 Melbourne boys and girls aged five to 15 years, the Goldmans and their associates interviewed a matched sample of 600 young people of similar ages and family backgrounds from large cities in England, North America and Sweden.

When primary sources of information were compared across nations, the most striking differences emerged between Sweden and the combined group of

For contemporary young people, a satisfactory level of health education should include sound knowledge of the risks associated with unsafe levels of sun exposure and with unsafe sexual practices.

English-speaking countries, including Australia. In Sweden, school was the predominant source of knowledge about sexuality. Compared with only 19 per cent of Australians, 32 per cent of Swedes claimed to have learned most of what they knew about sex from their teachers and school sex lessons. Conversely, fewer Swedish than Anglo-Australian teens cited their mothers or siblings as their best sources. The extent and quality of the sexual information available to adolescents in Sweden appeared superior to that available in English-speaking countries. In addition, the comments teenagers made to researchers in interviews highlighted a number of additional obstacles to effective sex education, especially in English-speaking countries. It seemed that lack of trust in their teachers' knowledge of sexuality had inhibited a number of British, Australian and American teenagers from approaching them for information. Others were put off by mistrust in their teachers' sympathy or discretion. For example, the Goldmans (1982, p. 308) collected the following spontaneous comments about teachers:

- *They might accidentally slip it out at staff meetings and it gets out to other kids* (Australian boy, 13 years).
- *I don't like teachers. I don't trust them, they tell other teachers* (English girl, 13 years).
- *Teachers can't handle it either, like parents. If you ask in class they call you an idiot and treat you as one* (Australian girl, 15 years).

According to Juliet Goldman (1990), the sexual awareness of Australian children and adolescents could be brought up to the level observed in Sweden by a number of simple educational strategies, such as agreement among primary school teachers on a consistent set of words to name the sexual organs and an honest, non-evasive approach to the presentation of simple facts about reproduction, menstruation and so on. She noted that the practical spin-offs of boosting children's sexual literacy might extend to more accurate reporting and courtroom testimony in cases of child sexual abuse (see Chapter 7). As Goldman explained:

It is now accepted that children should be both literate and numerate. Where language is concerned sexual literacy may be better described by the use of the word 'sexeracy'. Children have the right to be equipped with an adequate sexual vocabulary and to be sexerate, so that as they grow into adolescence and adulthood they do not develop into embarrassed tongue-tied individuals, exercising linguistically only a restricted code. This is surely what education is all about.

The inclusion of sex education as a mandatory component of the school curriculum has done little to remedy this situation for teenagers in English-speaking countries. The Goldmans conducted an extensive survey of the sex education programs available in high schools throughout Australia in 1992 and con-cluded that serious problems still existed, both in the content and delivery of the programs themselves, and in the preparation of the teachers who were called upon to conduct them. Susan Moore and Doreen Rosenthal (1993) similarly noted that Australian teenagers are not well educated about sex, and the sex education provided in Australian classrooms is far from adequate. They concluded that:

Many of the difficulties encountered in establishing effective programmes in schools arise from the controversial nature of the topic which gives rise to unique social, economic, political and legal problems. Teachers may well feel insecure in dealing with these complexities, especially if they have been poorly trained and have inadequate resources at their disposal. (pp. 141–2)

The timing of a teenager's access to sex education in school is also problematic, according to Moore and Rosenthal (1993, p. 142), who noted that:

Both in the United States and Australia, many schools introduce these programmes late in secondary school, at a time when a substantial number of adolescents have already left school and many are already sexually active.

In her own research with homeless young people in Melbourne, Doreen Rosenthal found little evidence that even the most basic classroom sex education messages, including those relating to AIDS, HIV infection and unwanted pregnancy, had been delivered or taken on board. Among the homeless 16-year-old boys in her survey, condom use was often either sporadic or non-existent. Yet these boys reported an average of 12 sexual partners in the preceding six months, with the maximum being 100 different partners. Homeless 16-year-old girls averaged seven, also with a maximum of 100 partners over six months.

Communicating with parents about sex

The inadequacy of sex education at school raises questions about where else Australian and New Zealand teenagers might go for accurate information. Figure 10.10 shows the most frequent sources accessed by the Goldmans' Melbourne sample.

Ashlea Troth and Candida Peterson (2000) questioned a sample of Australian teens aged 16 to 19 years in Brisbane about the frequency of their communication with their parents about such potentially difficult or embarrassing sexual topics as use of condoms, how to persuade a partner to have safer sex and the practicalities of contraception. Mothers were found to be more effective communicators than fathers, and daughters received more information than sons, as shown in Figure 10.11.

There were individual differences among these Brisbane adolescents in the quality of the sexual communication they enjoyed with their parents. Troth and Peterson found that mothers who communicated frequently about sexuality and safe sex across a broad range of topics had sons and daughters who

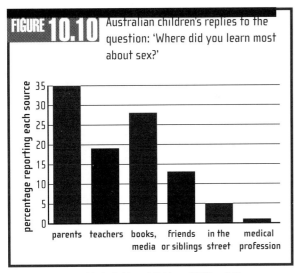

FIGURE 10.10 Australian children's replies to the question: 'Where did you learn most about sex?'

Source: Based on data in Goldman & Goldman (1982), p. 310.

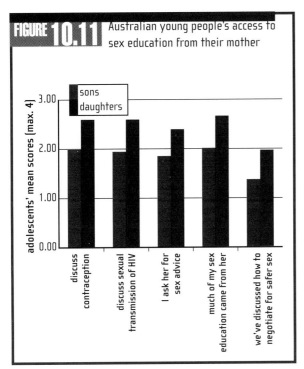

FIGURE 10.11 Australian young people's access to sex education from their mother

Source: Based on data in Troth & Peterson (2000).

Communicating with parents and partners about sex and sexual health is a challenging task for most adolescents.

felt more confident about negotiating with a partner for safer sex than those whose mothers were reticent. The former group was also more likely to use condoms in their actual sexual encounters, reducing their risks of encountering a sexually transmitted disease or an unwanted pregnancy.

Studying parents and teenagers in Melbourne, Kevin Collis (1991) discovered yet another reason for the inadequacy of the sex instruction parents offer their adolescent sons and daughters. The parents of 16-year-olds in this study were asked first to estimate the level of sexual activity among 16-year-old Australians as a group, and then about these teenagers' probable levels of knowledge about sexual matters, including the risks of HIV infection and unwanted pregnancy through unprotected intercourse. Their estimates were highly accurate. Yet when asked the same questions about their own teenage sons and daughters in particular, these same parents gave grossly unrealistic answers. Not only did they underestimate their teenage children's level of sexual activity and interest, but they frequently showed themselves ignorant of the basic fact of whether or not their son or daughter had ever experienced sexual intercourse. As well as radically overestimating virginity in their own households, these Melbourne parents displayed other overly optimistic beliefs about their children's rate of condom use, knowledge of sexual risks and willingness to approach the parent for sexual information. These misunderstandings were especially striking, given the parents' high level of accuracy in their beliefs about contemporary teenagers in general.

Sexually transmitted diseases

For adolescents in Australia and New Zealand today the risks of embarking on an active sex life in ignorance extend beyond unplanned pregnancy to the threat of serious venereal diseases, including infection by the potentially lethal HIV virus, the cause of acquired immune deficiency syndrome, or AIDS. This disease, which can be contracted through contaminated blood or the sharing of a drug needle, as well as sexually, has grown at an alarming rate in recent years. Teenagers are especially at risk owing to their tendency to experiment with multiple sexual partners without using a condom (Chapman & Hodgson, 1988). An increasing number of teenagers and young adults are being diagnosed as carrying the HIV virus (Moore & Rosenthal, 1993). In Australia at the end of 1993, two per cent of all new HIV infections were among teens aged 13 to 19 years, and 30 per cent were in young adults in their 20s, and in the United States it is estimated that one-quarter of all STD infections occur in the under-20s (Troth & Peterson, 2000). Yet teenagers in Australia, New Zealand and the United States continue to place themselves at risk of HIV infection by having sex with multiple partners in the absence of consistent condom use, AIDS testing or knowledge of the partner's sexual history.

Teenagers' sexual risk-taking may be enhanced by feelings of invulnerability. For example, the results of one study of unmarried Australians aged 17 to 25 years showed that 40 per cent of non-virgin males of Anglo-Australian ethnicity engaged in penetrative sex without a condom in casual relationships, while 69 per cent did so in relationships with a regular partner (Moore & Rosenthal, 1993).

Norman Barling and Susan Moore (1990) found that only 36 per cent of Australian male and female university students intended to use a condom in future sexual encounters. In the United States, a recent survey of tens of thousands of high school students aged 14 to 18 years similarly revealed that a majority of those who were sexually active had not used a condom during their most recent penetrative sex act (Ragon, Kittelson & St Pierre, 1995). Juliet Goldman (1990) found that only 40 per cent of Australian 15-year-olds knew the meaning of the words 'conception' and 'contraception', let alone details like how to purchase or use condoms. Box 10.11 includes an activity suggestion related to these findings.

Even when sexual knowledge is high and the risks of unprotected intercourse are perceived accurately, sensible attitudes and health-promoting behaviours do not necessarily follow. A disturbing 37 per cent of one sample of rural Australian teenagers viewed AIDS/HIV infection as a risk, yet agreed with the statement that 'If you don't take risks you don't have any fun'. (This peculiarly adolescent tendency to accept risk and/or to perceive oneself as uniquely immune from ordinary dangers is examined in more detail in Chapter 11.) So, in order to combat the spread of HIV/AIDS effectively, sex education for contemporary teenagers may need to incorporate the following components:

1. The promotion of more positive attitudes to condoms in adolescents of both sexes.
2. The eradication of mythical beliefs about causes of pregnancy or STDs.
3. Practical training in condom purchase and use.
4. Teaching communication skills so that adolescents become capable of discussing HIV risks with their partners and persuading them to use condoms or other safe-sex strategies where necessary.
5. Peer-group discussion and values clarification to promote the spread of positive attitudes, accurate knowledge, pro-condom beliefs and consistent safe-sex practices among teenagers.

Ethnic differences in STD and AIDS awareness

Knowledge about HIV/AIDS and attitudes to safe sex are partly a function of ethnic background, according to Doreen Rosenthal, Susan Moore and Irene Brumen (1990) who studied a group of 18-year-olds from Anglo-Australian, Chinese-Australian, Greek-Australian and Italian-Australian backgrounds. They found that migrant teenagers from non-English-

BOX 10.11 Activity suggestion
The sexual lexicon

PRELIMINARY CAUTION
Because the very mention of sexual topics can be controversial, do not attempt this activity unless (a) you know your child or adolescent subject well *and* (b) you have obtained his or her parent's or guardian's informed consent beforehand.

AIMS
The aims of this research exercise are twofold. First, it will give you an indication of whether the same levels of ignorance of sexual vocabulary that Juliette Goldman (1990) discovered in Melbourne apply to young people in your community today.

PROCEDURE
For each word in turn in the list below, ask your respondent (aged 9 to 19 years):
• 'Have you ever heard the word … ?'
• 'Can you tell me what it means?'
Words: abortion, AIDS, coitus, condom, conception, contraception, HIV, intercourse, menstruation, pregnancy, STD, uterus, virgin

SCORING
Score your subjects' answers by comparing them with the definitions in the Glossary at the back of this book.

DISCUSSION
By comparing results with your fellow students, see if there are apparent age differences in the distribution of accurate answers. Compare the percentages of accurate definitions for boys versus girls at each age.

One of the primary barriers against safe sex is the adolescent's fear, mingled with embarrassment, about discussing sexual topics.

speaking backgrounds knew less overall about AIDS than their Anglo-Australian peers. For example, only about half of the Greek-Australian teenagers, compared with a much larger proportion of Anglo-Australians, were aware that the HIV virus could be spread by semen and vaginal secretions, and 55 per cent of Italian-Australians believed that vaginal sex was safe without a condom, in contrast to a much smaller proportion of Anglo- and Chinese-Australians. Anglo-Australian boys and girls had equally high levels of knowledge about AIDS, whereas boys in each of the other cultures were better informed than their female peers.

Contrary to common sense, the accuracy of these adolescents' knowledge about HIV transmission did not predict their levels of risk-taking behaviour when they actually had sex. In fact, risky sexual practices were quite common among these Australian teenagers. Girls reported fewer sexual encounters with casual partners than boys but, in their relationships with 'regular' partners (which often meant a non-monogamous relationship with someone they had known for six months or less), a majority of all non-virgin females except the Greek-Australians had unprotected sexual intercourse at least some of the time. The researchers concluded that, although these teenagers were relatively well-informed about HIV and AIDS, they had not yet effectively made the transition from knowledge to behaviour. Thus, sex education may need to do a better job of shaping young people's attitudes and practical inhibitions about using condoms before it will manage to serve as a fully effective weapon against the spread of HIV.

Cultural variations in awareness of HIV and AIDS highlight the need for safe-sex education that is sensitive to cultural and ethnic differences. Peter Hill, Iris Smith and Colin Terare (1993) described one such program designed for use in the Aboriginal and Torres Strait Islander communities in North Queensland. Designated as education about 'caring' rather than 'safe sex', the program was built around three posters, each with an Aboriginal dot painting motif. The goals of the posters were to build self-esteem and reinforce pride in cultural identity as a prelude to direct confrontation of the risks of infection by HIV. As the researchers explained:

> By using the traditional symbols, we reinforce the value of our culture; but by using non-traditional colours, by changing the symbols, we show we are Aboriginal people living in a contemporary setting. We have choices, both good and bad – hopefully, through education we will make the right choices. (p. 42)

Coitarche

By analogy with the word 'menarche', *coitarche* refers to the first experience of complete sexual intercourse. This can sometimes be a source of ecstacy and rejoicing, but it can also bring feelings of disappoint-

ment, physical pain or guilt. Boys most often report enjoyment, though they may well be motivated by the masculine stereotype to conceal any ambivalence felt. The adolescent girl's reaction is more difficult to predict. One self-report study of Melbourne girls revealed that a majority had felt either distaste or indifference, with only 40 per cent being unequivocally satisfied (Kovacs, Dunn & Selwood, 1986). Figure 10.12 illustrates these Australian girls' reactions.

The timing of coitarche

The timing of coitarche is highly variable from one adolescent to the next. Most adolescents in Australia, New Zealand, Europe and North America today become sexually active while still in their teens (Bingham & Crockett, 1996; Noller, Feeney & Peterson, 2001) though a minority remain virgins until the age of 20, 25 or even later.

As in the case of early social dating, reaching coitarche ahead of most of one's peers can pose problems for long-term psychological well-being (Jessor, 1992). The results of one longitudinal study showed that early loss of virginity was a predictor of poor academic achievement among both boys and girls. Those teenagers who had reached coitarche ahead of their peers were also found to have poorer relationships with their parents, less interest in religion, greater tolerance for deviant or criminal activity and a high need for independence. Young people who had maintained their virginity later than most of their peers stood out from sexually experienced contemporaries for their highly conventional, perhaps old-fashioned, attitudes. They disapproved more of alcohol and marijuana, went to church frequently and hoped to marry a virgin. But, unlike the early sexual experimenters, they showed no signs of personal unhappiness or maladjustment. Instead, they

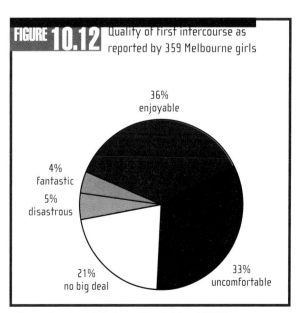

FIGURE 10.12 Quality of first intercourse as reported by 359 Melbourne girls

36% enjoyable

4% fantastic

5% disastrous

21% no big deal

33% uncomfortable

Source: Based on data in Kovacs, Dunn & Selwood (1986).

The timing of coitarche is subject to wide individual variability.

tended to be popular with peers and academically successful, and to enjoy good relationships with their parents. Thus, the decision to delay first intercourse had not seemed to hamper either their social lives or their emotional development.

On the other hand, when the timing is right, most Australian adolescents are found to value committed relationships and view sexuality as a normal and natural part of relationship development (Collins & Harper, 1985).

Cultural variations in sexual behaviour

Though the basic biological facts of puberty, intercourse and conception are essentially the same in human societies throughout the world, culture and social experience influence coitarche, both in its timing and in the psychological and social experiences surrounding it.

From a cross-cultural survey of 114 societies, it emerged that in 56 of these (49 per cent) it was the universal practice that all young people were initiated into penetrative sexual activity while still in their teens; in 23 societies (20 per cent) the notion of teenagers engaging in sex was unexpected and unusual (United Nations, 1991). Australia and other English-speaking countries fall somewhere in between these two extremes. Within Australia, there are also differences due to family cultural background and ethnicity. In one study of nearly 2000

unmarried tertiary students aged 17 to 20 in Melbourne and rural Victoria who came from four different cultural backgrounds, interesting ethnic differences emerged in patterns of sexual experience (Rosenthal, Moore & Brumen, 1990). The cultural groups sampled included Anglo-Australians, Chinese-Australians, Greek-Australians and Italian-Australians.

Results showed that significantly more Anglo-Australian females (68 per cent) were non-virgins, in contrast to the three other ethnic groups. In each of these, the vast majority of young women were still virgins in their late teens. There were some virgins in the sample of male Anglo-Australians (33 per cent), Greek-Australians (23 per cent) and Italian-Australians (39 per cent), but roughly two-thirds of the unmarried Chinese-Australian males were still virgins. This is in line with the attitudinal patterns reflecting disapproval of premarital sexual intercourse by Singaporean and Hong Kong students of Chinese descent. The double standard of premarital sexuality was reflected most clearly among Greek-Australian and Italian-Australian adolescents studied by Rosenthal and her colleagues in Victoria – some two-thirds of the males in each of these migrant groups were not virgins, while two-thirds of their female peers had retained their virginity. According to Rosenthal, Moore & Brumen (1990):

> The Greek- and Italian-Australian groups' behaviours seemed to reflect a traditionally male-oriented 'macho' culture, with young women in both groups being less active [sexually] but also less informed (p. 235)

Susan Moore and Doreen Rosenthal (1993) interviewed one Greek-Australian girl in Melbourne who explained her own impression of the double standard for premarital sexuality:

> [Virginity] is something you should take care of, something special. I think it symbolises that you are clean and that there is nothing dirty about you … You should keep it for your future husband even though he may have slept around. (pp. 14–15)

The double standard of premarital sexuality could not be articulated more clearly than this. However, to the extent that such beliefs contrast with normative beliefs in sexual liberality and equality between the sexes in the dominant Australian cultural mainstream, teenagers from migrant backgrounds may experience conflict and uncertainty. Indeed, conflicts over sexual and relationship issues are apt to persist through much of the remainder of the lifespan. As Moore and Rosenthal explained (1993):

> Today, young people in their twenties and even thirties may still have many sexual decisions to make before they choose a relatively stable path. Sexual conflicts are by no means over at the end of adolescence but, luckily, neither are sexual rewards. (p. 15)

Chapter summary

Human societies vary in their ways of marking off adolescence as a separate period in the lifespan. In some cultures, a protracted Western-style adolescence is replaced by a brief but dramatic pubertal initiation ceremony.

Historically, in Western society, adult observers from Socrates onwards have described adolescence as a time of personal stress, generational conflict and antisocial activity. Some of the 'storm-and-stress' may be rooted in the hormonal imbalances of adolescence. But teenagers in contemporary Australia and New Zealand also encounter stress in the form of uncertainties about their adult roles, society's changing sexual mores, changing patterns of family relationships and communication and the threat posed by the HIV virus to adolescents engaging in unprotected sexual experimentation.

Overriding cultural variations are the universal biological changes of puberty. A sudden spurt in height signals the onset of a striking sequence of growth changes, including the emergence of primary and secondary sexual characteristics. Menarche, or the first menstrual period, marks the biological transition to reproductive maturity for girls, as do the first shave or nocturnal emission, less dramatically, for boys.

To the distress of many adolescents, growth during puberty is apt to be asynchronous both within and between people. Body parts like the nose and feet grow at a faster rate than the face and legs, and no two adolescents can count on developing their secondary sex characteristics in exactly the same order or at exactly the same rate.

The timing of puberty exerts a major independent impact on psychological functioning, and the effects of early/late biological puberty appear to endure well into mature adult life. Late-maturing boys and early-maturing girls may feel severe disappointment over their physical appearance during puberty, and may acquire lasting feelings of helplessness or anxiety over beauty or weight as a result of misunderstanding the growth process.

Early pubertal maturation for boys and late menarche for girls can offer special psychological advantages during adolescence itself, ranging from exceptional social skills to outstanding academic achievement. But the results of longitudinal follow-ups of early and late maturers suggest that some of these advantages may reverse themselves by middle adulthood, where a stressful adolescence is seen to have promoted the acquisition of humour, sensitive understanding and productive coping skills that come into their own in adult life.

Ignorance and sexual problems accompany the attainment of puberty and coitarche for many contemporary Australian and New Zealand teenagers, in contrast to their peers in Sweden. Many Australian and New Zealand adolescents are disappointed with the quality of the sex education they receive, both informally from parents and peers, and in formal sex education classes in school.

Other sexual difficulties include the risks and anxieties associated with graduating into mature sexuality in a climate of threat from the HIV virus, the ambiguities and conflicts generated by double sexual standards, recent social changes and cultural variations in attitudes to premarital sexual intimacy. However, despite a few growing pains, coitarche is an important developmental milestone in the lives of most adolescents, and usually occurs during the late teens.

For further interest

Looking forward on the Internet
Use the Internet to visit the following websites. Examine them for further information and varied perspectives on issues raised in this chapter. Also search for other relevant websites for yourself, using keywords like 'adolescents', 'teens', 'health', 'menarche' and 'puberty' in your search engine.

In particular, for further ideas on teenage sexuality, pregnancy and contraception, visit: **http://www.childtrendsdatabank.org/socemo/childbearing/23SexuallyActiveTeens.htm** and for general information on child and adolescent health and health education visit: **http://www.kidshealth.org** and for specific information on diet and weight concerns visit: **http://www.aboutourkids.org/anorexia_nervosa.html**.

For resources, ideas, activities and other items of interest in conjunction with this chapter, visit the Companion Website for this textbook at: **http://wps.pearsoned.com.au/peterson**

Activity suggestion
As a practical activity in conjunction with themes in this chapter, scan advice columns in newspapers and glossy magazines for letters from teenagers. Code the problems mentioned into groupings such as: (1) physical appearance; (2) health; (3) pregnancy, sex and contraception; (4) weight; (5) relationships; (6) parents; and (7) school/career. In class, compare notes and compile a frequency hierarchy. Consider how many problems relate directly or indirectly to pubertal growth.

Multimedia
For insight into concerns of some Australian adolescent girls view the video '14's Good, 18's Better' (Australian Film Commission, 1980: 47 minutes, colour).

ADOLESCENCE: Cognitive, moral and personality development

*A boy's will is the wind's will,
And the thoughts of youth
are long, long thoughts.*

Henry Wadsworth Longfellow
(1807–82)

Contents

New cognitive abilities, new moral values and new personality strengths emerge during adolescence. These new capacities combine to transform the adolescent's mind in an even more dramatic way than pubertal growth transformed the body (see Chapter 10). Thus, when an adult renews acquaintance with a teenager last seen during middle childhood, the visible contrasts in body size and build may come to seem insignificant beside the enormous contrasts in thought processes, political and moral beliefs, sense of self and life interests.

In this chapter we begin our exploration of adolescent cognitive development with an examination of Jean Piaget's theory of the transition from the concrete-operational thinking of middle childhood into the highest cognitive stage of formal-operational thought. Recent research into Piaget's theory of formal operations is examined. We also consider the likely impact of these dramatic cognitive changes, bringing the adolescent's powers of logical reasoning into line with those of an adult, in terms of everyday social behaviours ranging from public speaking and philosophical debate to family disagreements over politics, politeness or household chores.

With the advent of formal operations, teenagers are apt to turn their minds to many of the same issues that preoccupy mature men and women. Instead of limiting their attention to toys, video games, fantasy play or classroom events, adolescents like to think and talk about such topics as politics, religion, fashion, health, the world, social justice, the future or the state of the environment – the same topics that interest and preoccupy many adults. These new interests combine with the adolescent's new capacity for logical thought and reasoned debate to create exciting new conversational opportunities at home and at school. At the same time, an awakening of interest in society and the future combines with more mature cognitive capabilities to raise the adolescent's moral consciousness. As they grapple with the personal need for a set of coherent values and ideals to believe in, and society's need for solutions to problems of exploitation, violence, injustice and global threats to humanity's survival, adolescents develop radically new moral outlooks. The more ambitious may apply their sophisticated cognitive skills to the task of a critical, imaginary overhauling of the entire moral, spiritual and political fabric of society.

Moral development is explored first from the perspective of Lawrence Kohlberg's influential stage theory, and then with a look at contemporary research that has validated, extended and suggested alternatives to Kohlberg's seminal theoretical position. Differences in patterns of moral reasoning due to gender and culture are examined, together with the question of how well adolescents' and adults' thoughts about moral problems predict their actual behaviour when faced with a situation of moral conflict.

The third major section of this chapter examines personality development during adolescence from the perspective of Erik Erikson's theory (see Chapter 2). According to Erikson, the central inner conflict that shapes the growth of personality during adolescence is a crisis over sense of self, or personal identity. Resolution of this crisis supplies the adolescent with a tentative answer to the core existential question: 'Who am I?' To resolve the crisis successfully, adolescents must explore their talents, needs and social roles along with their plans for the future in terms of relationships, a career and a philosophy of life. By bringing these disparate elements together into a coherently unified sense of self, a new dimension to the adolescent's personality emerges. This identity will guide psychological development through the remainder of life.

Not all adolescents manage to resolve the identity crisis satisfactorily during the teenage years. We examine variations on the identity theme that arise through problems of identity foreclosure, identity diffusion and identity moratorium, as well as the influences of gender, culture and socioeconomic background on this central personality development of the teenage years.

Cognitive development during adolescence: Piaget's theory

According to Jean Piaget (1970; see also Chapters 2 and 7), the final stage of cognitive maturity is reached by the end of adolescence. This is the stage Piaget labelled formal-operational thought. The adolescent who has mastered formal-operational thinking is able to reason logically and systematically about abstract problems and hypothetical possibilities, as is illustrated in the case history in Box 11.1.

The transition from concrete-operational to formal-operational thinking

In Chapter 7 we examined Piaget's stage of concrete-operational thought in which logical thought processes applied to concretely factual ideas and everyday experiences enable the child to solve problems like conservation, classification, seriation and deduction, which defied the younger, preoperational child. While sophisticated in many ways, concrete-operational thought does have its limitations. Being restricted to reasoning about the here-and-now, thinkers who are concrete-operational have no trouble classifying blocks by shape and size. They can place collections of sticks in regular order and have no difficulty discerning the effects on quantity of transformations of clay, coins or water which they can witness for themselves. But when problems extend beyond the realm of immediate, everyday experience, their logical reasoning is inclined to break down. Thus they fail tests of intangible concepts (like gravity or friction) as well as those involving

BOX 11.1 A case in point
Thinking concretely about a classic film

When she was 13, Louise's father described in his diary his surprise at the contrast between his teenage daughter's reaction to seeing a foreign film and his own. This aptly illustrates the distinction between Piaget's concrete-operational stage and the adult's formal-operational perspective.

21 February 1961. *Last evening we went to see* The Childhood of Maxim Gorki, *a Soviet film made in 1938. The decision to go was made on short notice when Louise came home from school with word that her class would be admitted free. The film is over 20 years old, had been shortened by cutting, but was still a moving experience. Louise and her Grade 6 classmates found it unusually sad. They identified themselves with young Gorki, his terrors, his unjust punishments, separation from his mother. They could not, like the average adult, relax in the reflection that after all, Gorki survived his trials and perhaps was made a better, more compassionate person because of them. They found it difficult or impossible to disassociate themselves from the events of the film or to view them as anything but potential experiences of their own. They might be sent down to a family of uncles squabbling over their father's property. They might suddenly be faced with the loss of their mother, left with a cruel grandmother in a community where their family was scorned and hated.*

This is the peculiar plight of childhood that all things are seen literally, with almost too much empathy. Hence, it is that the art of childhood – the drawing and painting done by children – thought superficially akin to adult abstract art, is at the opposite pole. Children's pictures are exact and concrete images of things and events in the child's own life.

So it is with Louise and such, I see, is the source of our misunderstandings. A passionate desire of hers all week has been to visit again a second-hand book sale that she saw for all too short a time. I told her to choose between the book sale and the movie and – after long thought – she finally chose the movie, but uncertainly. This shocked me. By all the rules of common sense the second-hand book sale should have been that and more; and anyhow our problem at home is too many books, not too few.

She was grumpy and listless and that also shocked me. We go to a movie once in a blue moon and have no TV. She should have been thrilled and gay.

What I failed to see was the spell this one short visit to the book sale had cast over her. Here was a world of its own: books of every conceivable description on every conceivable segment of life and sold for as little as 10 cents apiece!

© Peterson, 1974, reproduced with permission

A classic film about Maxim Gorki's childhood evoked concrete-operational thinking from a 13-year-old.

counterfactual or purely hypothetical propositions (such as an alien planet's world where ice is hot and fire is cold).

In his research with Barbel Inhelder, Piaget found that many 11-year-olds who could easily place concrete objects like pencils or sticks of varying lengths in serial order by size were unable to solve such seemingly comparable verbal problems as: 'Edith is lighter than Suzanne, and Edith is darker than Lily; who is the darkest of the three?' (Inhelder & Piaget, 1958). Similarly, preadolescents often cannot solve problems that require contrary-to-fact assumptions, such as:

The growth of thought during adolescence leads to concern over careers, politics, religion and the future of society.

'Imagine that the sun rose in the west and set in the east – where would it be at noon?' They also have trouble dealing with multiple attributes of a single concept, such as the disjunctive definition of a 'strike' in baseball as either hitting at the ball and missing, or failing to swing at a correctly pitched ball.

The inability to view present reality as a small piece in the puzzle connecting past experience with future expectation explains the problems associated with the concrete-operational perspectives on the Gorki film that were highlighted in Box 11.1. As Louise's father noted, a formal-operational adult can view the tribulations of a film character like Maxim Gorki as a fictionalised portrayal of someone both culturally and historically remote from their own lives. The future-oriented reasoning skills of formal operations likewise permit speculation about eventual gains (like compassion) emerging out of temporary setbacks (see the discussion of lifespan consequences of early and late pubertal maturation in Chapter 10). But concrete-operational thinkers are blinded to such possibilities by their cognitive fixation on the immediate present. With a focus on salient features of the immediate present, they are likewise less able than formal-operational adults to weigh up the pros and cons of a choice between a rare film screening and a readily available shop in a balanced, logical manner (see Box 11.1). Box 11.2 includes four additional tests of formal-operational thinking.

BOX 11.2 Activity suggestion
Testing for formal-operational thinking

Instructions. After practising these tests of formal thought on yourself, try giving them to willing friends of different ages. Compare age and gender groups in terms of proportions of optimally efficient, logical solutions.

Problem 1: The house with 4 windows
Instructions: Behind the shutters of the house, one of the four cards (A, B, C or D) is positioned so that the faces on it are at the windows. Any card could be there. What is the most efficient way (smallest number of moves) to open the window(s) in order to discover which card is there?

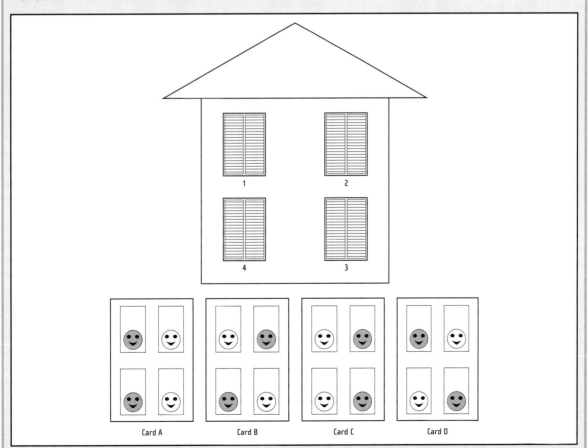

Card A   Card B   Card C   Card D

Answer: Two windows only need be opened. For example, open Window 1 first. If the face is red, open Window 4 (depending on whether the face in it is red or white, you will know if Card A or D is there). But if the face in Window 1 is white, open Window 3. You will know exactly which card is there in an identical two moves.

Problems 2 & 3: Are the conclusions logical?

Premise 1: All trains from Newcastle to Sydney Central stop at Hornsby.

Premise 2: The train on platform 2 stops at Hornsby.

Conclusion: The train on platform 2 goes to Sydney Central.

Premise 1: All trains from Newcastle to Sydney Central stop at Hornsby.

Premise 2: The train on platform 2 goes to Sydney Central.

Conclusion: The train on platform 2 stops at Hornsby.

Problem 4:

Question: In this imaginary world (see picture below) consisting of a total population of 12 people, what is the relationship between hair wave and eye colour? (Write your answer in the form of a rule. Be as exact as you can.)

Blue eyes

Brown eyes

Solutions: Concrete-operational thinkers are able to come up with answers that consider straightforward facts and univariate relationships, but they have trouble dealing with a range of hypothetical possibilities or with relational concepts such as probability. Thus, a typical concrete-operational solution to Problem 4 might be: 'Curly-haired people have brown eyes', ignoring the exception in the top row. A more exact solution is probabilistic. If her hair is curly, she has a 5:6 chance of having brown eyes.

The nature and measurement of formal-operational thought

Barbel Inhelder and Jean Piaget (1958) created a set of 15 tasks to measure contrasts between concrete-operational and formal-operational problem-solving. In describing and evaluating these, we can also glimpse the core defining features of formal-operational thought at its most general level.

The problem of the yellow liquid: All-combinations reasoning

In this task, children were given five bottles containing clear, odourless liquids. They were told that it was possible to produce a yellow colour by combining the contents of the bottles. Their task was to work out which combinations of bottles created the colour and which combinations remove it. In fact, each bottle contained a different chemical substance. Combining the first (acid), third (oxygen in water) and fifth (potassium iodide) made the colour appear, while the thiosulphate in the fourth bottle bleached it away.

Concrete-operational children typically approached this problem in a trial-and-error manner. After attempting a few haphazard combinations of the liquids, they sometimes succeeded in producing the yellow colour. But such success was short-lived. Their unsystematic approach gave no guidance about how to clear away the yellow stain or make it reappear. Quite often, concrete thinkers failed to produce the colour at all because they thought only of combining the bottles in pairs, or simply mixed all the jars together at once, without trying other combinations. Formal-operational thinkers, by contrast, tested every possible combination of the five jars in an orderly sequence. Being systematic, they also kept track of which combinations they had tried, and what each outcome was. Thus they were usually aware not only that combining the first, third and fifth bottles produced the colour, but also (a) that it could not be made in any other way (since they had tried all the other combinations), (b) that jar two had a neutral effect and (c) that jar four erased the colour.

In other words, formal-operational thinkers approached the problem as a scientist would. They spontaneously used the experimental design strategy (examined in Chapter 2) of holding other variables constant while manipulating a single variable and observing its effect (i.e. adding liquid from just one of the bottles in turn to a well-controlled, systematically tested, previously determined combination). They likewise approached the problem thoroughly, not stopping until all the combinations had been tried. By keeping trace of all possible combinations, they were able to test multiple hypotheses and to discover rules for how the colour could be both produced and eliminated.

As young people develop skill in all-combinations reasoning, they are able to combine variables mentally as well as through physical manipulation, and they gain an understanding of the large number of possible combinations when even three individual variables (say, A, B, and C) are combined in all possible ways (ABC, ACB, BAC, BCA, CAB, CBA). According to Piaget, this understanding of permutations and combinations develops spontaneously in adolescents who have reached the stage of formal-operational thought, even if they have never been exposed to lessons in formal logic or mathematics in school.

The pendulum problem: Hypotheses and possibilities

In a test of children's spontaneous understanding of physics, Inhelder and Piaget (1958) presented them with a set of pendulums consisting of different sized weights suspended by strings of different lengths. The researchers demonstrated how the pendulums could be dropped from positions of varying height or pushed with varying degrees of force. The children's problem was to predict the pendulum's rate of swing on the basis of one or more of these four factors. Concrete-operational thinkers typically approached the problem haphazardly, often manipulating several variables at the same time, and generally failing to solve the problem. They could not isolate the variables one by one. Instead, they either guessed at random or lengthened the string while also changing the size of the weight and pushing harder. Thus, even if the rate of oscillation did change, they could not determine which factor or factors were responsible. Formal-operational thinkers, on the other hand, seemed to possess an intuitive grasp of the scientific method; they successively held constant all variables but one. Thus they quickly discovered that only the length of the string made any difference.

Their approach to this problem showed that:

1. They were aware of all the variables (weight on the end, string length, height of drop, etc.) that might conceivably influence the swing of the pendulum; and
2. They could isolate and test the effect of each one individually while holding the others constant.

In other words, formal-operational thinking about the pendulum problem again displayed characteristics of the scientific method that were absent from the concrete-operational solutions to the same problem. Using formal-operational thought, the young person examined the situation systematically and formulated an exhaustive set of hypotheses about what might possibly contribute to the pendu-

In games like tug-of-war, children learn about the physical forces of pull, balance, gravity and inertia.

lum's rate of swing. Then, by systematically manipulating each variable in turn, while carefully holding all the other variables constant, they were able to exclude incorrect hypotheses and, hence, to arrive at the correct answer by a process of elimination. This is the essence of the scientific method, applicable in a wide range of domains, including psychology (see Chapter 2).

In formulating all possible hypotheses in this way, the formal-operational thinker makes use of the all-combinations mode of reasoning that we discussed in connection with the chemical combinations problem (see page 356). Another core feature of formal-operational thinking emerges in the scientific attitude towards the relationship between theory and empirical data. The theory expresses ideas that might possibly be true, and empirical evidence narrows down from this to a statement about ideas that happen to be true in the world as we know it (e.g. in a world where string length governs the movement of pendulums). The formal-operational thinker therefore treats possibility as the overarching condition, and observable reality as an item subsumed within the wider realm of possibility. Conversely, for the concrete-operational thinker, empirical reality as we know it is all that is possibly conceivable. The realms of reality and possibility overlap.

John Flavell and his colleagues (Flavell, Miller & Miller, 2002) offered the following fictitious example of a formal-operational thinker's verbal expression of this style of reasoning:

> Well, what I have just seen gives me the idea that W and only W might have the power to cause or produce Z, and that the presence of X might prevent W from causing Z, and that Y might prove to be wholly irrelevant to the occurrence of Z. Now if this idea is right, then Z should occur only when W is present and X is absent, whether or not Y is also present. Let's see if these are, in fact, the only conditions under which Z does occur … Oh no, that idea is shot down because I've just found that X also occurs sometimes when neither W or X is present. I wonder why. Hey, I have another idea … (p. 147)

The beam balance problem: Proportionality and reversibility

Beam balances like the one shown in Figure 11.1 were once familiar tools, not only in high school science labs but in post-offices, grocery stores and other everyday settings where they were used to weigh parcels, letters and other commodities. In these days of computerised computation, they might seem antiquated and irrelevant. But Inhelder and Piaget argued that no other physical tool or gadget is the equal of the beam balance when it comes to giving children concrete, hands-on experience with the mathematics of algebraic equations. In one of their typical tests for formal-operational reasoning, Inhelder and Piaget set up the beam balance as shown in Figure 11.1, gave the child a collection of standard weights and posed questions like the following: (a) How could you restore the beam to even balance (equilibrium)? (b) Is there any other way you could do that? (c) Why do these operations work? (d) Can you formulate a rule or proposition that explains in general terms what the conditions must be in order for the balance to achieve equilibrium?

When children and adolescents were given problems like these, concrete-operational and formal-operational thinkers approached them very differently. In a practical sense, provided they are given enough time to experiment, most concrete-operational thinkers manage eventually to restore the beam to equilibrium by trial and error. However, they are generally unable to give any coherent explanation for how they managed to get the sides to balance. Furthermore, their strategies for doing so are limited. Most concrete-operational thinkers are limited to solutions involving the addition or subtraction of weights of equal size. For example, at the very simplest level, the balance in Figure 11.1 can be brought level by taking the 2-gram weight off the white arm. In a slightly more sophisticated way, equilibrium can also be achieved by adding a 2-gram weight at a distance of three units down the black arm. According to Piaget, children at the concrete-operational stage are aware only of these kinds of

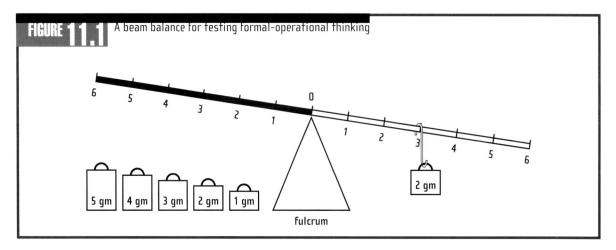

FIGURE 11.1 A beam balance for testing formal-operational thinking

fulcrum

reversibility by addition or subtraction. Consequently, it is inconceivable to them that the scale could be made to balance by using only the 1-gram weight. (Can you figure out how this could be done? You may wish to write down your answer before reading further.)

The formal-operational thinkers that Inhelder and Piaget tested were adept not only at the addition and subtraction of weights but also at restoring equilibrium by positioning the weights at different distances from the fulcrum. They even managed to formulate the rule that weights and distances along the arms have an inversely proportional relationship to each other: For example, if a new weight added to one side of the beam balance is twice as heavy as the one on the other side, it should be placed only half as far from the fulcrum to achieve balance, or, if three times as heavy, at one-third the distance.

Thus, in the problem in Figure 11.1, if the weight on the white arm (W) is 2 grams at length (L) of three units, then substituting a 1-gram weight for $\overline{W}$ (the weight on the black arm) produces the equation: $2/1 = \overline{L}/3$, so that $\overline{L}$ = six units. In other words, placement of the 1-gram weight at the very end of the black arm will restore the scale to equilibrium.

As well as testifying to the formal-operational thinker's capacity to create general rules, or propositions, to encompass and predict discretely observable phenomena, the beam balance demonstration shows that formal-operational thought includes:

- two kinds of reversibility, and
- the concept of proportionality.

When solving the balance problem, formal-operational thinkers were able to compensate mentally for an increase in weight on one of the arms either by the operation Piaget called 'negation' (e.g. taking away the weight that had been added, or adding weight to the other pan) or by using another form of reversibility that he called 'reciprocity' (e.g. moving the weight on the other arm). Concrete-operational children used negation in some situations (like pouring liquid out of a glass in a conservation test when too much had been poured in) and reciprocity in others (as when they realised that the longest stick in a series was short relative to an even longer stick), but they were unable to apply both operations at the same time in a coordinated manner. But formal-operational thinkers have an intuitive grasp of algebraic equations, even if they have not studied higher mathematics. Thus they can integrate the addition and subtraction of weights, and the multiplication and division of lengths along the arm into a coherent system of logical operations, with zero as the balancing point.

An adolescent needs to understand fractions and proportions in order to solve formal-operational problems. But probability and risk are also important in everyday life as adolescents think about health, danger and their future life roles. We examine these ideas in more detail in a later section of this chapter.

The horizontal plane: Higher-order abstract concepts and the logic of propositions

Inhelder and Piaget also asked children and adolescents to predict where wooden and metal balls of various sizes would stop when they were rolled along a horizontal plane. Concrete-operational children often made incorrect predictions. They seemed unable to imagine invisible forces like friction that would cause the balls to stop. But formal-operational thinkers accurately predicted the exact stopping point of each ball, explaining their predictions on the basis of the joint effects of friction and air resistance. This solution demonstrates an intuitive grasp of the concept of inertia.

Thus, another characteristic of formal-operational thought is the ability to think logically about hypothetical and intangible processes which can never be directly observed. These thinkers are also able to formulate logical propositions that have a truth value that is independent of concrete experience of real phenomena in the everyday world.

Table 11.1 summarises the characteristics of formal-operational reasoning.

TABLE 11.1 Summary of characteristics of formal-operational reasoning
• A scientific, hypothetico-deductive approach to problem-solving in which a range of possible solutions are formulated, followed by systematic empirical testing while controlling multiple variables.
• Awareness of reality as a specific case within an infinite range of possibilities.
• Systematic consideration of all possible combinations of variables, and all possible problem solutions, keeping track of all combinations.
• Awareness of reciprocity and negation as two kinds of reversibility, along with ability to coordinate negation and reciprocity with one another to restore equilibrium and solve problems formulated as equations.
• A clear understanding of ratios and proportionality, together with concepts of probability and partial association (correlation).
• A logical understanding of abstract, higher-order and intangible concepts like friction, gravity and air resistance.
• Understanding of formal properties of logical propositions like tautology and contradiction together with the ability to reason logically about scenarios that violate the factual conditions of everyday experience.

Formal-operational thinkers systematically consider all possible combinations of variables.

While formal operations begin to develop around age 11 and 12, most contemporary adolescents do not fully master this mature mode of thought until their late teens.

When do formal operations develop? Revisions of Piaget's theory

When he first formulated his four-stage theory (see Chapter 2), Piaget (1970) proposed that children begin to develop formal operations at the age of 11, and that most adolescents have fully mastered them by the age of 15. But more recent research evidence, including some of Piaget's own, while supporting the existence of formal operations as a distinctive mode of thinking, have challenged this proposed age of transition. For example, the results of one large-scale Australian investigation of several thousand adolescents and young adults aged 12 to 20, who were growing up in Sydney (Connell, Stroobant, Sinclair, Connell & Rogers, 1975) revealed that the vast majority were still reasoning at the concrete-operational level at the age of 15 (see Figure 11.2). In fact, though the percentages of Australian boys and girls who used formal-operational thinking grew gradually through the teens, the concrete-operational stage remained dominant throughout most of high school. Figure 11.2 displays the percentages of Australian adolescents of different ages who consistently solved Piagetian reasoning problems at either the concrete-operational or the formal-operational level.

In analysing their results, the Australian investigators concluded that even among that special group of teenagers who had elected to stay on at school past the minimum leaving age in order to prepare for university: 'It is not until 17–18 years of age that a majority of the subjects give evidence of the capacity for formal thought' (p. 127). Of the Sydney teenagers who had left school early to enter the workforce, only 8 per cent showed formal operational thinking at age 15, only 15 per cent at age 17 and still only 35 per cent by the advanced age of 20, after some five years

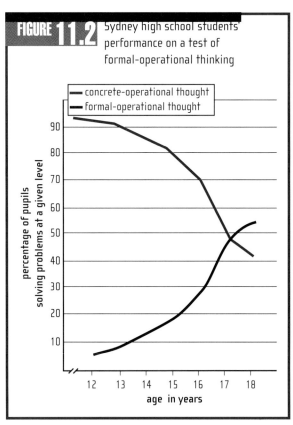

FIGURE 11.2 Sydney high school students' performance on a test of formal-operational thinking

Source: Connell et al. (1975), p. 126, by permission.

of on-the-job experience. These results indicate that the attainment of Piaget's highest stage of reasoning is not an automatic consequence of growing older.

Research conducted in the United States (Moshman, 1998; Neimark, 1975) and in Europe (Goossens, 1984; Piaget, 1972) has similarly challenged the notion that the formal operational stage is reached as early as age 15. It seems that few contemporary adolescents reason in a consistently formal-operational manner before the age of 17 or 18 and, even during adulthood, a substantial percentage of

According to the theory of cognitive specialisation, adolescents who think concrete-operationally about Piagetian problems like the beam balance may be capable of formal-operational thought in other domains such as football.

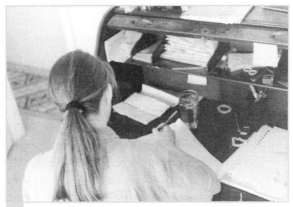

In cultures where adolescents attend school, academic lessons may stimulate early mastery of formal-operational thought.

the population continues to solve Piagetian problems by means of concrete operations (Neimark, 1975).

Late in his career, Piaget (1972) himself revised the ages for the stage transition that he had initially postulated. He also eventually concluded that formal-operational thought is probably not a universal stage in cognitive development. Piaget put forward three hypotheses to explain variations in the rate of mastery of formal thought. These are listed below and described in more detail in the following sections of the text.

- *Environmental causality.* Individual differences between cultures and between generational cohorts in the same culture, owing to different styles of education and other cognitively stimulating input.
- *Genetic causality.* Inter-individual developmental divergence in peak abilities and optimal developmental end-points, owing to inherited ability differences.
- *Nature–nurture interaction: Cognitive specialisation.* Each normally developing individual achieves formal operations only in his/her area of key interest, practice and cognitive specialisation.

Schooling and formal operations

In cultures where children do not go to school, even Piaget's stage of concrete-operational thinking is frequently slow to develop, particularly when children are tested on standard Piagetian problems. In a telling illustration of the difference the type of problem can make, Jean Retschitzki (1989) compared unschooled adults on the Ivory Coast on standard tasks and when playing 'the national game of Africa' which required a complex set of logical rules to balance defensive and offensive moves in capturing opponents' seeds. Formal operations were clearly evident among skilled players of the national seed game, yet they performed concrete-operationally on tasks like the beam balance.

The Sydney study described above likewise revealed individual differences linked with education (Connell et al., 1975). Those Sydney teenagers who had left school at the minimum age in order to enter trade apprenticeships or full-time employment were more likely to solve Piagetian problems at the concrete-operational level than their age peers who had elected to remain in school to complete matriculation classes in preparation for university entrance, and who more often solved the same cognitive problems using formal operations. Although the decision to leave school early may partly reflect differences in intelligence, it is likely that the added years of formal education to which the matriculation-bound students were exposed had played a role too. Lessons in physics, chemistry and higher mathematics in the upper grades of high school are likely to expose adolescents to the same kinds of challenging topics as were incorporated into Inhelder and Piaget's (1958) tests of formal-operational thinking.

However, the quality of the instruction children receive in school may be more important than mere exposure to additional years of high school. Piaget (1970) proposed that highly didactic instruction in which teachers state rules and require pupils to memorise them is far less effective than instructional situations that challenge pupils to think for themselves. He cautioned:

Remember also that each time one prematurely teaches a child something he could have discovered for himself, that child is kept from inventing it and consequently from understanding it completely. This obviously does not mean that the teacher should not devise experimental situations to facilitate the pupil's invention. (p. 715)

Not all high school classes achieve this ideal and hence may be of little benefit for fostering the transition from concrete- to formal-operational thinking. The case history in Box 11.3 gives an example of a high school lesson that was unlikely to prove optimally instructive in fostering pupils' higher-order thinking about physics, though it may have challenged their reasoning about gender-role stereotypes (see Chapter 8).

When Louise was 16 her parents moved to Elizabeth, South Australia, and she entered the Leaving (matriculation) class at the local high school, studying English, French, Latin, Mathematics and Physics. In his diary, her father recorded the following observation on one of her experiences in a science lesson.

24 April 1964. *Last week, in her Leaving Physics class, the teacher set the students experiments in electricity to work on in small groups. Louise's group was unable to make them confirm the theory and the teacher was scornful of them for flubbing such a simple experiment. He told the group, all girls, that it was just like cooking: all they needed to do was follow the recipe.*

'How's the cooking coming along?' he asked at last.

'I'm afraid it's burnt,' said Louise.

Pitching in to help, the teacher could arrive at no better results; and one after another he rejected resistances, declaring they were 'fried out' – an expression he seemed quite fond of. The girls picked it up, pretending innocently to believe that this was a correct technical expression. With serious faces they would say, 'I think this one's fried, sir.'

Hunting around for replacements among resistances used by students who had done the experiment successfully, one of the girls brought one back which was warm to the touch, handed it to the teacher and asked if he thought it might be 'fried'. Frustrated at his own lack of success in completing the experiment, the teacher finally lashed out at the class and vowed dire reprisals to any student he saw destroying school property.

His favourite recreation, Louise says, is tearing out pages of student notebooks.

© Peterson. 1974. reproduced with permission

As well as illustrating a teacher's efforts to link a stereotypically male domain, physics, with girls' presumed greater ability to understand cooking, this extract exemplifies some possible influences of teachers' and peers' attitudes on female academic achievement, a topic examined in more detail in Chapter 12.

Developmental divergence in peak abilities

Perhaps, even in the most optimally stimulating educational environment, not all adolescents will develop formal-operational thought. Piaget (1972) drew an analogy with outstanding achievements in art, music and gymnastics. While all children are capable, with proper training, of developing skills in each of these domains, only a few 'prodigies' or 'geniuses' develop artistic, musical or gymnastic talent to a peak level of giftedness, even with the best teaching and most extensive exposure to practice and expert coaching. If the same is true of mental development, an adolescent of only average intellectual potential might never attain formal-operational thinking, given that this represents the pinnacle of intellectual development, according to Piaget's (1970) theory. Of course, this would not preclude exceptional achievement in areas other than logico-mathematical problem-solving.

Cognitive specialisation

Piaget (1972) himself favoured his third, interactive hypothesis (see page 361). According to this view, each normally developing individual eventually becomes capable of formal-operational thought in certain narrowly specialised fields of thought. Formal operations are more likely to develop in these specialised areas of interest than when people think about problems in which they have no particular background knowledge or interest. Thus, the empirical question of when formal-operational thought develops is very much a question of which samples of adolescents and which tasks researchers select when assessing their cognitive capacities. If every adolescent of normal mental ability develops formal-operational capacity in at least some cognitive domain, and if that domain happens to be motor mechanics or rock music, Inhelder and Piaget's (1958) beam balance and chemical combination problems could never hope to assess their thinking adequately. The final proof of whether this hypothesis will explain the unexpected lag of contemporary Australian, New Zealand, United States and European teenagers behind Inhelder and Piaget's original norms awaits the creation of a new set of tasks that will test adolescents' ability to apply formal-operational skills to problems in areas like music, fashion, social relationships, history or even scientific psychology.

Supporting this hypothesis, one study of university students in the United States (De Lisi & Staudt, 1980) revealed that the student's field of academic specialisation predicted their use of formal operations or concrete operations to solve problems in that specialised domain. Students majoring in English literature en route to an Arts degree were scored as predominantly concrete-operational when tested on a Piagetian physics problem (the pendulum problem, see page 357) but were consistently able to produce sophisticated formal-operational solutions to comparably difficult tests of logical reasoning based on English literature. Conversely, science students majoring in physics scored as formal-operational on Inhelder and Piaget's (1958) pendulum test, but generally gave answers typical of the concrete-operational stage when tested on the English literature problems. This interactive association between problem type and students' fields of study is illustrated in Figure 11.3.

A student majoring in science is more likely than one who majors in English or fine arts to succeed on Piaget's pendulum problem.

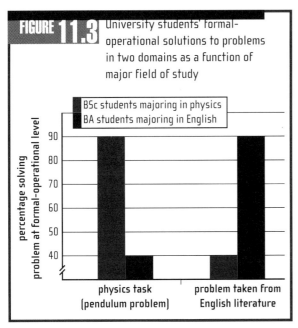

FIGURE 11.3 University students' formal-operational solutions to problems in two domains as a function of major field of study

■ BSc students majoring in physics
■ BA students majoring in English

Source: Based on data in Flavell et al. (2002).

Adolescent cognition in everyday life

The fact that many adolescents are capable of reasoning at Piaget's highest stage of cognitive maturity about topics in their own specialised field of academic study raises the question of how well they can reason logically about topics that are totally outside the formal academic curriculum of high school or university but of intense interest and preoccupation to many adolescents. Such topics may include recreational interests in sport, fashion, dating, popular music, dance, computer games, cars and broad social and political questions about the future of the global economy, the earth's environment or world peace. Adolescents may also give thought to their own future, planning their paths through developmental milestones like career entry, marriage or parenthood while also considering the philosophies, beliefs and ethical/moral values that they hope will guide their lives.

In later sections of this chapter, we examine the consequences of these cognitive changes for adolescent moral development and for personality growth through the core adolescent crisis over personal identity. But, first, let us look at some of the more immediate consequences of the adolescent's new cognitive capacities for thinking about real-life issues – health and illness, politics, and how to behave in social situations ranging from asking someone out on a date to having an argument with a parent over questions of social activism and hypocrisy.

Thinking logically about health and illness

Jean Natapoff (1982) linked children's thinking about health and health care to formal-operational reasoning. Her data showed that, unlike younger children, adolescents were aware that a person could be 'part healthy and part not, all at the same time'. Formal-operational thinkers were also conscious of the future, viewing health as a long-term issue in contrast to sickness, which was short-term. Adolescents also seriously considered the future health consequences of present behaviours such as diet, exercise and smoking. Finally, they related mental health to physical health and noted that changes in moods were symptomatic of disturbances in both.

Carol Nemeroff and Carolyn Cavanaugh (1999) studied concepts of fatness and thinness in children, adolescents and young adults as a means of gaining greater understanding of the health risks posed by eating disorders like bulimia and anorexia nervosa (see Chapter 10). They found that over 40 per cent of girls as young as age six consistently preferred body figures that were thinner than their own, while 80 per cent of preadolescent and young adolescent girls were either currently on a diet or had dieted in the past.

On the grounds that illogical reasoning about food and weight gain might help to explain the unhealthy eating habits of girls of normal weight who wanted to be thinner, Nemeroff presented university students with scenarios about an imaginary fellow student who was of average height and weight and enjoyed tennis and running. When she was depicted as liking to eat double-fudge ice cream, French-fried potatoes and steak, the protagonist was deemed to be more morally corrupt, untrustworthy, and 'bad' than when the same protagonist enjoyed a diet of fruit, chicken and homemade bread. The researchers concluded that even university students sustain irrational beliefs about food and eating, irrespective of their potential cognitive capacities for formal-operational thinking. As they explained: 'Not only are foods considered virtuous or evil depending on health value and caloric content ... but also immoral people are seen as polluting, and their residues and possessions avoided' (p. 192).

In other research with Paul Rozin, Carol Nemeroff likewise found that adolescents' and young adults' beliefs about sexually transmitted disease were often illogical, displaying the same tendency towards using magical reasoning in place of the logic of formal-operational reasoning as a source of causal explanations for infection and personal vulnerability (Rozin, Nemeroff & Markwith, 1993). They described adults' irrational beliefs about risk factors associated with HIV and AIDS as an instance of the

magical thinking that also explains adults' superstitious beliefs and use of rituals to bring luck in gambling or to ward off misadventure. They noted that even the most intelligent adults with fully developed capacities for formal-operational thought fall prey to superstition and magical thinking at times. However, when applied to the domain of HIV infection, magical thought can create exaggerated concern over possible contagion, leading to the stigmatisation of people with AIDS and other irrational discriminatory acts like refusing to donate blood, refusing to buy a home or car that a person with AIDS has used, or the refusal by United States postal workers to deliver mail addressed to an AIDS task force.

To explore the basis for irrational thinking about the causes of AIDS, Rozin and Nemeroff devised a questionnaire presenting hypothetical situations like those shown in Table 11.2.

Rozin and Nemeroff found that each of these rationally safe situations evoked fear and avoidance in a substantial proportion of university students. Such fear could only be explained by irrational beliefs in magical contagion, coupled with a lack of formal operational logic. The researchers concluded that:

> [irrational] attitudes or beliefs ... may be a major influence in responses of humans to infection, illness and interpersonal contact. The specific implication for understanding attitudes towards AIDS is that fear of AIDS cannot be dealt with only in terms of providing information that defines the risk and routes of infection. (1993, pp. 1090–91)

In other words, although formal-operational logic does boost the adequacy of adolescents' reasoning about disease, development is incomplete even in adulthood. A factually accurate and fully rational model of disease transmission does not appear to replace magical thought even among intelligent, well-educated teenagers and young adults. Consequently,

Even formal-operational university students may sometimes fall prey to irrational beliefs about food, nutrition and dietary health.

TABLE 11.2	Would you do it?	
Instructions. Rate your willingness to engage in each of these behaviours on a scale of 1 (Never), 2 (Maybe/Reluctantly) or 3 (Always/Gladly).		
• Food-related	Eating with a fork that a person with AIDS has used, after it has been through the dishwasher	Rating scale 1 2 3
• Clothing-related	Wearing a freshly washed jumper that had been worn by a person with AIDS	Rating scale 1 2 3
• General/futuristic	Staying the night in a luxurious hotel room that a person with AIDS is going to spend a night in next month	Rating scale 1 2 3

health reasoning represents another area of potential development through the adult portion of the life-span, and an area in urgent need of further exploration in order to overcome stigmatisation and prejudicial treatment of people living with HIV.

Thinking about politics and economics

Barry Stacey (1987) analysed New Zealand young people's understanding of politics, economics and social justice. He concluded that, although developmental patterns were partly a function of children's degree of exposure to buying, selling, banking and other realities of adult economic life, general trends were also apparent. With the transition from preschool to middle childhood, New Zealand children gradually overcame the simplistic beliefs that characterised preschoolers' thinking about politics and economics. Thus, the young child's notion that the physical size of a coin determines its monetary value was overcome. Nor did primary school children automatically believe that money is only safe in banks where staff wear uniforms. They had a better idea than younger children of the value of putting savings in a bank, and even a rudimentary understanding of what interest is and why banks pay it to their customers. For example, they understood, unlike preschoolers, that shopkeepers need to take commissions and make profits on their sales over and above the cost of the commodities they are selling. They also had some idea of what taxes were and how they helped to pay for the cost of government. Even quite sophisticated concepts, such as the vulnerability of businesses to market forces or fluctuations in

After important gains during middle childhood, children's concepts of money, banking, sales and finance continue to develop during adolescence.

currency exchange were understood by some of these New Zealand primary school students.

However, New Zealand children's concepts of finance, government and the economy continue to develop well into adolescence. Even in high school, the average teenager's understanding of many of these issues was incomplete. Stacey found that a majority of adolescents aged 13 to 16, for example, had only 'a rather low level of financial knowledge' (p. 13), especially if their parents were working class. After contrasting New Zealand children with their peers in Australia, Asia, Europe and the United States, Stacey concluded that a number of developmental trends were consistent across all these cultures. William Damon (1975) similarly studied the development of children's ideas about fair reward for work done and the just distribution of goods more generally. Some of the developmental trends observed in this research are summarised in Table 11.3.

Limitations of formal operational thought

According to Barbel Inhelder and Jean Piaget (1958), the adolescent's first taste of the logical power of formal-operational thought can be difficult to live with, both for teenagers themselves and for others around them. A temporary delusion of 'omnipotence' can produce a new kind of cognitive egocentrism (see Chapter 7). Adolescents become self-preoccupied and fail to perceive the limitations of pure logic. Nor are they yet socially experienced enough to temper formal logic with a sympathetic consideration of other people's points of view. In other words, the adolescent thinker may fall victim to problems known as the 'imaginary audience' and the 'personal fable'.

The imaginary audience syndrome

Everyday experience, as parents and high school teachers can amply testify, confirms Piaget's suggestion that adolescents' reactions to social situations frequently fluctuate between extremes of blatant exhibitionism and painful shyness. One day a teenager may colour her hair hot pink or have her nose pierced with a flamboyant earring, seemingly oblivious to being stared at by wearers of more conventional fashion. Yet the same girl might become tongue-tied when asked to make a phone call or greet a stranger, and refuse to go to a party in an old dress or stained jeans (Elkind & Bowen, 1979).

The term 'imaginary audience' reflects adolescents' mistaken belief that others are as single-mindedly preoccupied with the adolescent as an audience would be while watching Hamlet soliloquise on stage. In Australia, C. R. Lechner and Doreen Rosenthal (1984) developed a standardised measure of imaginary-audience thinking which supports the suggestion that it is heightened at the

TABLE 11.3	Developmental changes in the understanding of finance, economics and distributive justice		
Age period	Concepts of fairness	Concepts of money	Concepts of marketing, economics and finance
3 to 5 years	Simple concepts of sharing: It is good to give some of one's own treasures to others; no clear concept of merit or entitlement.	Money is nice to have but there is no clear awareness of where it comes from or how you spend it. Children believe money comes from shops, rich people, God or the Queen ... or that you just have it, as much as you want.	Children are fascinated by shopping and can enact rituals of buying and selling in their play, but they have no clear understanding of the economic interconnections of the marketplace and see shopkeepers as benefactors who give things away.
6 to 9 years	Rules of *equality* (everyone deserves exactly the same amount), *equity* (those who work more get more) and *need* (give to those who are disadvantaged and in need) emerge; no clear interconnections among these justice principles.	The numerical worth of different denominations of money becomes clearer; by age 7 to 9 years children understand you need a fixed amount of money to purchase items of specific worth or price.	Notions of employment as a source of money and economic position begin to emerge, along with a clear awareness of market transactions as exchange rather than gift-giving.
10 to 13 years	Fairness involves a coordination of justice norms so that hard work is rewarded, while everyone earns something and special consideration is given to those in need.	Concepts of the value of money are well developed and children can construct simple payment systems where work is done for a fair wage.	Children understand the basics of economic life, including relationships between primary producers, retailers and customers. They are also aware of theft, cheating and fraud and view money as a finite resource.

During early adolescence, teenagers sometimes imagine themselves parading before a nonexistent audience.

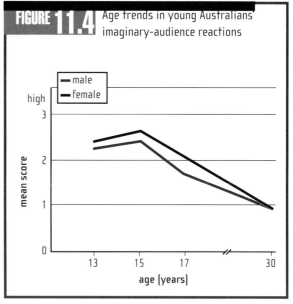

FIGURE 11.4 Age trends in young Australians' imaginary-audience reactions

Source: Based on data in Lechner & Rosenthal (1984).

age where young people would first be gaining capacities for formal-operational thought. Figure 11.4 shows the frequency of imaginary-audience cognitions in a sample of 180 Melbourne university students ranging in age from 13 to 30 years.

Health, dating and the imaginary audience
Adolescent cognitive egocentrism, as expressed in a belief in an imaginary audience, may relate as much to new social experiences in the early teens as to cognitive changes. Characteristically, adolescent self-consciousness and exhibitionism can both be enhanced by new social relationships with peers (see Chapter 12). Dating Australian boys have been found to display less imaginary-audience reaction than their peers who have not yet started going out with girls (Peterson, 1982a). Possibly this is because they are

Adolescent boys who go out on dates are less likely to believe in the imaginary audience than their peers who have not yet started dating.

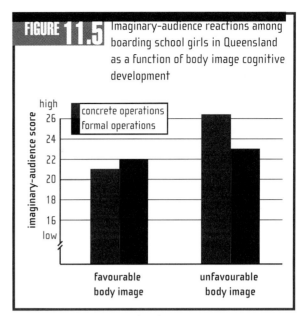

Source: Based on data in Allen (1992).

more confident about their attractiveness to members of the opposite sex. Similarly, in a study of boarding school girls in Queensland, Elizabeth Allen (1992) found that girls with favourable images of their own bodies showed only weak belief in the imaginary audience, regardless of their level of cognitive development. But concrete-operational girls who had developed negative feelings about their physical appearance as a result of pubertal growth changes (see Chapter 10) displayed a heightened imaginary-audience reaction. This reaction was absent among formal-operational thinkers who had equally unfavourable body images, possibly because formal-operational logic enabled them to consider the tribulations of pubertal growth from a balanced perspective (see Figure 11.5).

Formal operations and STDs

Adolescents represent a special risk group for the spread of HIV infection (see Chapter 10). Given that experimentation with multiple sexual partners and, possibly, injected drugs is typically more frequent during late adolescence than at other stages in the lifespan, educational intervention to promote safe sex and safe drug use in this age group is urgently needed. Formal-operational thinking skills enable adolescents to consider the future consequences of present risk-taking behaviour. But, according to Elkind (1967), the egocentrism of imaginary-audience and personal-fable cognitions can create a delusion of invulnerability. The sense of personal uniqueness that leads adolescents to construct narcissistic narratives and to feel themselves to be acting in front of an adoring audience can produce feelings of being immune from both present harm and untoward future consequences. Elkind noted that failure to take adequate contraceptive precautions could lead to unwanted pregnancy, attributable in part to belief in an imaginary audience. If a girl believes she is uniquely protected from risk, she may fail to use contraceptives despite awareness of how pregnancy is caused. The same is true of condom use and other precautions to prevent the spread of HIV. Educational interventions for adolescents may need to take the possibility of cognitive egocentrism into account. To be optimally effective, educational strategies for young people should target risky behaviour and the cognitions that go with it, in addition to presenting factual information about HIV and prevention strategies.

In their studies of Australian adolescents' beliefs about AIDS and HIV infection, Susan Moore and Doreen Rosenthal (1991a) discovered that an egocentric sense of personal invulnerability to the virus was common among adolescents of both sexes. Most believed that other teenagers were more vulnerable to contracting HIV than they themselves were, and females were particularly prone to underestimating their own risk of infection even after engaging in high-risk behaviours like unprotected intercourse with a promiscuous partner.

Moral development during adolescence

The onset of formal-operational thinking enables adolescents to speculate about broad philosophical, spiritual and social questions as well as to reflect on tactics of self-preservation in social situations. Recall (Chapter 2) that Jean Piaget himself whiled away

BOX 11.4   Strutting and fretting on an imaginary stage

In his autobiography, Australian author Donald Horne gives a vivid glimpse of the kinds of thought patterns typical of adolescents who are in the grip of the imaginary audience.

Just as my new body had grown up inside my old one, at first painfully and grotesquely, and then bursting out with such finality that I wanted to decorate it with floral ties and new suits and sun it in swimming trunks. I now had a sense of a new 'self' that was swelling and spreading, sometimes making me do things that startled me, at other times stopping me from doing anything at all ... I liked myself and I hated myself. Some of the things I most liked about myself could also make me prickle with shame. But even shame was an absorbing indulgence. I was both the movie and the audience. When I looked at the rushes of what I had done each day, I wanted to slap my own face or pat my own back. Usually I was pleased with what I thought I looked like,

although if I had a pimple on my face I might feel conscious of it all day. (1975, pp. 181–2)

many boring high school hours during his adolescence writing a novel with a moralistic, philosophical theme. He tells us that most of his classmates were occupied with similarly grandiose mental endeavours:

> One of them, who has since become a shopkeeper, astonished his friends with his literary doctrines and wrote a novel in secret. Another, who has since become the director of an insurance company, was interested among other things in the future of the theatre and showed some close friends the first scene of the first act of a tragedy – and got no further. A third, taken up with philosophy, dedicated himself to no less a task than the reconciliation of science and religion. (Inhelder & Piaget, 1958, p. 344)

The capacity to reason using formal operations also makes it possible for adolescents to think about ethical dilemmas and moral values, while questioning parental views and political, religious and legal codes that a concrete-operational thinker would simply take for granted. Some teenagers decide to become vegetarians at this time, others experiment with alternative lifestyles, philosophies and religions. But even those who maintain the status quo in their outward appearances of life are likely to think deeply about moral values and ethical uncertainties, giving rise to advances in their cognitive awareness of morality, building on the advances made during middle childhood (see Chapter 8).

Kohlberg's theory

Lawrence Kohlberg (1963) made a very important contribution to the understanding of how moral

reasoning and ideological commitment develop during adolescence. He began what was eventually to become a 20-year longitudinal investigation of moral thinking by presenting a group of 58 American boys aged 10, 13 or 16 with a set of dilemmas involving conflicts between legalistic rules and humanitarian needs. For example, one of the story-dilemmas Kohlberg used involved a man named Heinz whose wife was dying of cancer. Subjects were told there was a new drug that might save her, but the pharmacist who had developed this medication was charging $2000 for it (ten times what it cost him to make). Try as he might, the woman's husband could not raise that much money, nor would the pharmacist sell it more cheaply or let the man pay later. The dilemma was whether or not the man should steal the drug. As well as stating their opinion, the boys were asked to explain why or why not. Scoring depended less on whether they answered yes or no than on the rationale they used to support their judgment.

The scoring procedures and stage descriptions that Kohlberg developed in 1963 were used for almost two decades to assign subjects to six distinct developmental stages. But then, in 1983, shortly before his tragic death, Kohlberg and his colleagues (Colby, Kohlberg, Gibbs & Lieberman, 1983) made some radical changes to the stages and scoring system, which significantly altered the overall shape of Kohlberg's theory. The following discussion is based on Kohlberg's latest model of moral stages and the new scoring criteria, which have proved to be more reliable and objective than the earlier ones (Colby et al., 1983).

The older boys in Kohlberg's original longitudinal

sample used arguments that were qualitatively different from those used by younger boys to justify their decisions about theft of the drug. In addition, as the younger boys grew up, the longitudinal evidence showed that each boy's style of reasoning changed qualitatively. Eventually, these boys too offered the same argument that the older adolescents had expressed initially. In fact, after rescoring the interview transcripts from the adolescents, Kohlberg and his colleagues found that all of the young men progressed through a fixed series of qualitatively distinct styles of reasoning in a fixed order. The most basic level of argument had been used by most boys at age ten. Progress to a more advanced style of reasoning arose at different ages in different boys, but the kinds of arguments they would give once they made the change were highly predictable. No boy ever skipped a step and hardly anyone (less than 4 per cent of the group) reverted to lower-order thinking once the next level had been reached.

Kohlberg was thus able to identify five sequential stages which together formed an empirically verified developmental model of moral growth. When he examined the kinds of arguments used at each stage, Kohlberg discovered that the order of stages was also logically sound. Each earlier stage was a prerequisite for the next one, not only on the grounds of the longitudinal trends that emerged so consistently in the interviews, but also because each stage of reasoning was constructed from ideas that had been less fully or accurately developed at the previous stage. In other words, the moral views articulated at advanced stages in Kohlberg's system were philosophically, as well as empirically, more fully developed than ideas expressed earlier. Development can therefore be viewed as a dialectical synthesis or progression, where each argument builds on the arguments formulated at the previous stage and resolves earlier contradictions into a more persuasive and coherent totality. As Kohlberg himself explained:

> Moral development may be defined in terms of the qualitative reorganization of the individual's pattern of thought rather than the learning of new content. Each new reorganization integrates within a broader perspective the insights that were achieved at lower stages. (Colby et al., 1983, p. 1)

Kohlberg's overall model is illustrated in Table 11.4, together with examples of the kinds of arguments offered at each stage for what is right or wrong and to justify doing the right thing when faced with a moral challenge.

Kohlberg discovered that it was the type of moral justification an interviewee gave for a particular course of action, rather than the specific course of action recommended, that defined qualitatively distinct stages in moral reasoning. When faced with the dilemma about Heinz and the drug, for example, some respondents at each stage said 'Yes, he should steal it', while others at the same stage recommended

that he should not steal. But the arguments they used to justify their 'yes' and 'no' answers were distinctive at each stage level.

For example, an individual at Stage 1 might weigh the odds of punishment and decide that the husband should steal. Since the penalty for theft could be less than that for neglecting his wife, self-interest would be served in this manner. An individual from Stage 2, on the other hand, might justify the same decision to steal the drug on the grounds that the husband himself might fall ill and need his wife to do a similar favour for him, or that he would need to steal even more money if she died, because he would need to pay for her funeral. At Stage 3, a clear recognition of the claims of affiliation and duty enters moral reasoning for the first time, leading, for example, to the argument that the man should steal to save his wife because, if he is tried, the judge will like him better for being a worthy husband. By Stage 4, such considerations of personal liking and individual conscience are put aside in favour of an abstractly idealised respect for conformity to either the legal system (leading to a decision not to steal the drug) or religious law (leading, in many cases, to the decision to steal on the grounds that the pledge of marriage demands that the husband do everything in his power to protect his wife's life).

At Stage 5, young people are concerned with broad principles of justice, human rights and universal ethical values that transcend any unjust laws or

A moral dilemma such as whether to put back a fish that is smaller than the legal limit will evoke different levels of reasoning from younger and older adolescents.

TABLE 11.4 Kohlberg's theory of moral reasoning

Level and stage	Content of answers		
	What is right?	Why do right?	Basic philosophy
Level 1: Premoral Stage 1: **Heteronomous morality**	Avoid breaking laws or rules. Obey laws blindly because they are there. Avoid being punished.	Authorities will get even with those who break their rules even if they do so unknowingly or for humanitarian reasons.	No coherent moral theory; can't relate multiple viewpoints; can't separate abstract questions of right and wrong from concrete displays of power or punishment.
Level 1: Premoral Stage 2: **Instrumental hedonism**	Follow rules if you stand to gain by doing so. Allow and expect others to do the same. Keep bargains with others so they will keep theirs with you.	To serve your own interests best, you have to recognise systems which help everyone gain the most.	Right and wrong are relative to one's own immediate gain. No abstract moral values transcend 'enlightened' self-interest.
Level 2: Conventional Stage 3: **Conformity** (or 'good boy/good girl' focus)	'Being good' means having good motives and showing concern for others. Live up to other people's rules about how you should act, even if you don't gain materially by doing so.	The need to be liked and to be a good person in your own eyes means you have to behave according to everyone's stereotype of what 'goodness' consists of.	Can consider the Golden Rule ('Do unto others ...') at a concrete level. Is aware that feelings and expectations of others take primacy over self-interest, but has no ability to abstract beyond the values of other known people to consider an abstract or impersonal ethical code.
Level 2: Conventional Stage 4: **Law and order** (conformity to law or rule)	The most important guide to how to act is the legal rule book. If in conflict, abide by the rule rather than own or others' individual need.	To keep the 'system' (country, religion, etc.) going just as it is, you must obey all laws just as they are.	Is now able to distinguish the social system from individual personal relationships, but cannot go beyond existing sets of laws or rules to choose or formulate a more just and encompassing set of moral values.
Level 3: Principled Stage 5: **Principled morality**	Follow universal rules like 'life and liberty for all' regardless of majority opinion.	One's 'social contract' as a human being is to make and abide by rules which serve the welfare of all people, and promote the 'greatest good for the greatest number'.	Recognises conflicts between legal and humanistic or ethical viewpoints and strives to go beyond existing rules to integrate them. Will now view rule-abiding behaviour as immoral if it interferes with basic human needs.

Note: Kohlberg's (1969) original model also included a sixth stage of 'universal ethical principles'. This was dropped from the new theory 'because none of the interviews in the longitudinal sample seemed intuitively to be Stage 6' using the new scoring scheme (Colby et al., 1983, p. 5).
Source: Based on data in Colby et al. (1983), Table 1, pp. 3–4.

religious teachings that might conflict with them. Thus, an argument against theft might highlight the importance of considering the welfare of others in addition to Heinz's own wife, such as child cancer patients with better chances of survival than Heinz's wife, who might be deprived of access to the scarce drug if Heinz took matters into his own hands and acted unilaterally. But a different Stage 5 thinker might reason that the man should steal the drug. While acknowledging the pharmacist's right to have his property protected, the woman's right to life could be seen to have higher priority in any social contract that optimises the common good of humanity. This level of moral reasoning incorporates principles transcending all existing laws, religious doctrines or ethical codes in order to promote optimal concern for human welfare.

Kohlberg found that, whereas stages emerged in the same fixed order for all the members of his sample, the ages of transition varied. Roughly 80 per cent of the boys in his original sample reasoned purely at Stages 1 and 2 at the age of 10, whereas 57 per cent made some Stage 3 arguments by 13, and an impressive minority (19 per cent) had fully developed Stage 3 moral thinking by this age. Though some men did reach the higher stages of Kohlberg's scheme during their adult lives, he found that increasing chronological age did not itself guarantee progress, either during adolescence or later. By the age of 32, more than three-quarters of the original longitudinal sample of men were still using conventional moral arguments from Stage 4 or below. Using the 1983 scoring scheme, one of the most dramatic departures from Kohlberg's earlier theory was the failure of his latest analysis of the data to reveal any evidence at all of the development of principled moral thinking during adolescence. Once he had corrected the mistakes in his originally published analysis by rescoring all the interviews using the new Standard Issue Scoring scheme (Colby et al., 1983), Kohlberg found that not one of the 58 boys in his longitudinal study gave a single Stage 5 argument when tested at age 18 or younger.

Stage 5 reasoning had emerged in a small subgroup of men by age 24, according to the new scoring criteria. Figure 11.6 shows that, although the proportions of Stage 5 men increased from age 24 to age 32, the principled level of moral reasoning never managed to overtake conventional reasoning (Stages 3 and 4) as the predominant response pattern of adult men. Thus, throughout their lives, a majority of well-educated middle class men continued to reason at a less than fully mature level. This illustrates the need to track human development beyond adolescence.

The results of Kohlberg's latest data analysis present an interesting example of the value of studying psychological development as a lifespan process.

Adolescents and adults who reason according to Stage 4 in Kohlberg's theory often equate moral behaviour with obedience to the law.

Had Kohlberg stopped gathering data when his longitudinal subjects stopped growing physically at the end of their teens, convincing evidence of the growth of principled reasoning would never have emerged. Mature moral development is clearly an adult attribute – this qualitatively new level of reasoning cannot emerge until adulthood. Although most adolescents grapple intensively with moral problems, it seems that their solutions are limited to fixed rules and existing social, religious or legal conventions. More optimistically, the adult data show that at least some older men and women eventually manage to surmount familiar rules and doctrines, allowing them to develop a more encompassing set of moral principles. The emergence of Stage 5 reasoning after adolescence reinforces lifespan developmentalists' belief in the possibility of genuine psychological growth in the latter half of life, possibly because the experiences and responsibilities of adult life are a necessary ingredient for change.

A critique of Kohlberg's theory

Kohlberg's theory has had an enormous impact on the study of moral development. It has also stimulated research and theorising about the cognitive aspects of development, including the growth of faith and religious belief, which we examine in Chapter 15. At a broader level, Kohlberg's work has helped to bridge the gap between developmental psychology and the disciplines of philosophy (Boyd, 1986) and theology (Wilcox, 1986). But Kohlberg's theory has also provoked sharp controversy. Two major criticisms centre on (a) his use of male participants and male protagonists in the moral dilemmas, which meant that the effects of women's attitudes to moral issues could not be directly addressed, and (b) his

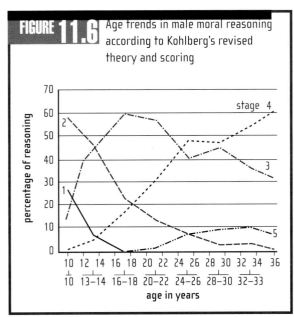

FIGURE 11.6 Age trends in male moral reasoning according to Kohlberg's revised theory and scoring

Source: Colby & Kohlberg (1987), Figure 3.1. Reproduced with the permission of Cambridge University Press.

changing of the descriptions and scoring criteria for the stages after the initial formulation of the theory had been published. Let us consider these arguments.

GENDER BIAS

Kohlberg's original longitudinal interviews included no female respondents and the chief protagonist in most of Kohlberg's dilemmas was male. According to Kay Bussey and Betty Maughan (1982), the simple fact of being asked to reason about the morally correct course of action to be followed by a man rather than a woman might elicit more sophisticated levels of reasoning from male than female subjects. To test this possibility, Bussey and Maughan administered Kohlbergian moral interviews to a group of 150 men and women in Queensland. Among the stimuli, they included a new 'female' version of the drug-stealing dilemma. The protagonist was a woman called Martha, while her husband was the cancer victim. The Australian men and women were asked whether Martha should steal the drug to save her husband's life. Interestingly, the vast majority of men as well as women scored at Stage 3 when presented with this dilemma. But a majority of the men scored at Stage 4 on the standard version of the cancer drug dilemma, just as Kohlberg's American men had done, whereas the Australian women gave predominantly Stage 3 responses to this masculine dilemma as well.

These results support the suggestion that Kohlberg's scheme may be intrinsically biased in a male direction. It would appear that traditional sex-role stereotypes depicting women as preoccupied with emotional feelings and intimate relationships had affected Australian men as well as women when they were asked to judge how a morally responsible wife should behave. But when challenged to justify the actions of a man, Australian men endorsed the stereotypically masculine focus on the legal obligations of marriage to a greater extent than women did, and consequently earned Stage 4 scores, in contrast to women's preponderant emphasis on the personalistic arguments for both male and female protagonists that placed them only at Stage 3 of Kohlberg's scheme.

THE IMPACT OF THE 1980s CHANGES

After a careful reanalysis of his interview transcripts some two decades after the initial publication of his theory, Kohlberg made a set of radical changes to the stage descriptions and the scoring criteria. Although he was able to rescore all his original longitudinal interviews using his improved stage definitions, other investigators who had published studies using the now outdated stage descriptions had no such opportunity, leaving their work somewhat in limbo.

Kohlberg (with Ann Colby and colleagues, 1983) argued that the changes were necessary for scientific reasons. The new Standard Issue Scoring technique is easier to use and has proved to be more objective and reliable than the old scheme. In fact, much of the criticism levelled against Kohlberg's original model related directly to the highly subjective nature of the scoring process, with attendant problems of rater bias and unreliability. The new system is clearly better. However, some confusion in the research literature has inevitably been created by secondary sources that have failed to keep abreast of the revised scheme, resulting in the ghost-like resurfacing of an outmoded 'Stage 6'. This stage was originally postulated by Kohlberg in 1963, but was later discovered not to exist as a discrete stage according to his fully updated and corrected scoring scheme (Colby & Kohlberg, 1987). Thus some criticism of Kohlberg may be unwarranted, generated by misunderstanding of the actual system of stages (see Table 11.4).

Actions speak louder than words: Moral reasoning and behaviour

The big question for theorists of moral development, however, is not just what causes sophisticated ethical thought, but whether advanced reasoning guarantees that a person will behave in an ethically responsible manner when faced with a moral conflict or temptation to do wrong. Do principled moral arguments from Kohlberg's higher stages lead to ethical action? Or are mature moral reasoning abilities largely irrelevant to everyday moral behaviour? We all know individuals who are capable of generating plausible after-the-fact justifications for their ethically questionable actions. Is this all that Kohlberg's developmental model really amounts to?

To test these possibilities, Kohlberg and his colleagues conducted a number of experimental tests and naturalistic observations. In one experimental study of university students, loosely modelled on the moral temptation tests devised by Hugh Hartshorne and Mark May (see Chapter 9), students were first given Kohlberg's moral reasoning interviews. Once their stage of moral-cognitive maturity had been identified, they sat a seemingly unrelated test, where it seemed that cheating was feasible without any risk of being detected (Colby & Kohlberg, 1987).

The results provided modest support for Kohlberg's postulate that moral reasoning predicts ethical action. Only 15 per cent of the university students who reasoned at Stage 5 in Kohlberg's scheme chose to cheat on the test, in comparison with 55 per cent of those whose reasoning was scored at the conventional level (Stages 3 and 4) and a full 70 per cent whose moral reasoning was at the preconventional level (Stages 1 and 2).

Student protests at the University of California against the Vietnam War provided Kohlberg and his colleagues with the opportunity to conduct a naturalistic-observational study of the relationship between moral thinking and real-life moral behaviour (Haan, Smith & Block, 1968). Undergraduate students completed Kohlberg's interviews and later had the opportunity to join an anti-war protest demonstration to express respect for peace and freedom of speech. Some students who reasoned at each of the stages sat in. However, support for Kohlberg's theory emerged in the finding that a higher proportion of students who reasoned at advanced levels chose to sit in than from lower levels. Stage 5 moral principles advocate self-sacrifice on behalf of non-violence, civil liberty and tolerance. A larger proportion of students at this level (73 per cent) than at any of the lower stages put their beliefs into action by protesting and allowing themselves to be arrested. Only 44 per cent of Stage 4s and 10 per cent of Stage 3s sat in, supporting a link between moral beliefs and behaviour. Their beliefs favoured simple obedience to the law and respect for university authorities, so relatively few took part in the demonstration.

A group of American soldiers who served in the Vietnam War were later brought to trial in the United States for military atrocities at My Lai and enabled another, more dramatic, test of Kohlberg's theory. In 1984 he had an opportunity to score the tape-recorded transcripts of war crimes trials in which the soldiers accused of murdering innocent civilians gave self-justifications for their actions. Kohlberg found that his moral stages predicted the actual wartime behaviour of each of these men in Vietnam. One soldier had steadfastly refused to obey orders to kill innocent people (Bernhart) and this man reasoned at Stage 4/5. Another (Meadow) had killed innocent women and children by his own hand, and reasoned purely at Stage 2. The officer who had given the order (Calley) reasoned at an intermediate (Stage 3) level. While, admittedly, based on a very small sample of people faced with a (fortunately) very unusual moral conflict, this analysis did support the direct derivation of ethical behaviour from the capacity to reason cogently about morality.

In other words, naturalistic observational studies, as well as experimentally controlled measures, provide some impressive support for Kohlberg's view that moral reasoning does directly and unequivocally predict moral action. When they were faced with moral challenges ranging all the way from the mildly reprehensible temptation to cheat on a test to the serving soldier's dilemma of whether or not to disobey a superior officer's order to commit a war crime, Kohlberg's interview-based assessment of young people's moral thinking was found to predict people's actual reactions when faced with crises of moral responsibility in their own lives.

Culture, collectivism and the morality of care

Kohlberg (1969) conducted a cross-cultural comparison of moral reasoning by interviewing middle-class boys aged 10, 13 and 16 years in Mexico, the United States, Turkey and Taiwan. Some were from urban centres and others lived in rural villages. The rate of progress through Kohlberg's stages was slower in villages than cities. Each of the cultures outside the United States likewise produced later ages of transition to successive stages than in Kohlberg's original North American sample. The sequence of stages was universal, however, supporting the cross-cultural validity of his theory. Critics have challenged the conclusion on two grounds.

First, they argue that moral concepts relating to theft and property that may be very salient to middle-class North Americans like those Kohlberg studied may have little relevance in other parts of the world. Second, Kohlberg's suggestion that people in non-Western cultures make slower progress through the stages may be the result of cultural biases in his methods of interviewing (Simpson, 1974). The relevance of the story about the cancer drug (see page 368) may escape many adults in subsistence cultures, as well as those in more advanced countries with economic and social structures that are radically different from those in the United States. For example, rural Taiwanese villagers are accustomed to buying all their goods from the local shopkeeper 'on credit'. They pay when they can, and are looked after by the store owner and the more affluent members of the community when they cannot (Dien, 1982). In such a society, the dilemma itself, and the behaviour of the pharmacist in particular, may seem too outlandish to warrant serious ethical deliberation.

Indeed, in Asian cultures with Buddhist and Confucian traditions (see Chapter 1) of filial piety, respect for elders and communally interdependent moral values (Bond, 1986), Kohlberg's dilemmas framed around individualistic moral choices and the competing claims of laws regarding property and respect for individual lives may not adequately sample the kinds of concerns that guide lifelong moral development.

A similar conclusion was reached by Anne Marie Tietjen (1986) when she investigated moral reasoning among children, adolescents and adult members of the Maisin tribe living in coastal villages in the Oro province of Papua New Guinea. A small tribe, the Maisin population numbered less than 1000 villagers at the time of the study. They eked out a meagre

In Asian cultures with a collectivist philosophy or Buddhist tradition, parents teach children to cooperate and care for others.

existence through subsistence gardening, gathering wild foods and fishing. Income was often supplemented by remittances from relatives working in the cities. Because the values of the Maisin are collectivist ones, cooperation and helpfulness figured strongly in the moral values children acquired before entering school. Traditional Maisin society is based on an ethic of egalitarianism, and 'placing oneself or one's needs above those of another or the community is regarded as antisocial and may be grounds for the use of Sorcery against a person who violates this norm' (p. 863).

Tietjen adapted Kohlberg's moral reasoning dilemmas to suit the local customs and familiar events in tribal life. The specific situations the Maisin were asked to think about included the following:

- Should villagers who have only enough food for their own needs donate some to people from another village whose gardens were destroyed by floods?
- Should a child miss a school picnic to get help for another child who has fallen and broken her leg?
- Should a child risk being hurt to protect another child who is being attacked by a bully?
- Should a medical student delay her studies and give up income in order to offer medical help to a village struck by a hurricane?

Tietjen used both cross-sectional and longitudinal methodologies to examine age-related changes in moral reasoning among the Maisin. Responses to each dilemma by children in each of Grades 1, 3 and 5 were gathered using a cross-sectional design and compared with the responses of groups of adolescents (aged 14 to 20) and adults (aged 24 to 60) to the same dilemmas. In addition, Tietjen used a longitudinal design to reassess the Grade 1 and Grade 3 children from the cross-sectional study one year after they took part in the initial assessments of moral reasoning, after they had entered Grade 2 or 4 respectively. The quality of respondents' moral thinking was scored on a continuum of moral maturity ranging from self-interested hedonism to internalised, self-sacrificing empathy. The results are shown in Figure 11.7.

Significant differences were found among age groups. In the cross-sectional study, the children in Grades 3 and 5 (aged 10 to 13), who were deeply immersed in Western-style schooling, scored significantly lower in moral reasoning than the adolescents and adults who had left school. More intriguingly, the Grade 1 children, who had only recently begun to be exposed to formal schooling, were also significantly more advanced in moral development than the children in Grades 3 and 5 who were older and had had time to become aware of the values of school (see Chapter 9). The explanation, that Western influences had undermined moral reasoning, was supported by the longitudinal responses of the Grade 1 children, who declined significantly in moral maturity on the second assessment. Although they were now a year older, the effects of age on moral growth appeared to

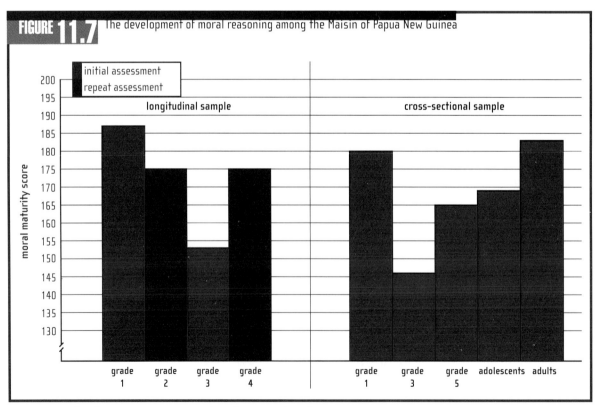

FIGURE 11.7 The development of moral reasoning among the Maisin of Papua New Guinea

Source: Tietjen (1986). Figure adapted from Table 1 (p. 864) and Table 2 (p. 865), from Developmental Psychology, 1986, 22, 861–868. Copyright © 1986 by the American Psychological Association. Adapted with permission.

have been outweighed by the clash of moral values between village tribal life and the world of school. However, these effects seemed temporary, as the children who were in Grade 3 at the first assessment gained moral maturity when they were longitudinally reassessed in Grade 4.

It seemed therefore that the initial result of exposure to Western moral values in school was a temporary increase in self-interested, competitive behaviour, with a corresponding loss of collectivist empathy and concern for the welfare of the community. But this trend reversed itself in adolescence with departure from school and return to the traditional Maisin community. As Tietjen explained:

> In more Westernized cultures, where the value of adopting a Western competitive orientation is evident, age and education could be expected to be related consistently to more competitive forms of reasoning and behavior. For the Maisin children, however, competition and individualism have no place in the adult society around them and they know that few of them will have the opportunity to leave their village to participate in Western culture. Thus, it would be maladaptive for Maisin children to become increasingly hedonistic in their reasoning. (p. 863)

Gender and moral reasoning

In other words, the moral reasoning of adolescents and adults in collectivist, socially oriented cultures may differ qualitatively from the individualistic judgments of competing justice claims that are implicit in Kohlberg's model of moral development derived from North Americans. For similar reasons, Carol Gilligan (1977) has argued that Kohlberg's theory and stage-scoring criteria may fail to adequately assess the growth of moral reasoning in women: 'The very traits that have traditionally defined the "goodness" of women, their care for and sensitivity to the needs of others, are those that mark them as deficient in moral development' (p. 484). Gilligan suggested that, when women face moral challenges, they reason about them in terms of the altruistic need to help others and to find ways of cooperating socially in an interdependent manner so as to draw the group together around the moral problem. Using data from qualitative interviews with adolescents and adults, she argued that the female moral orientation is built on the ethics of care, need and self-sacrifice. Women viewed moral dilemmas in an intimate social context and resolved them by appealing to principles of altruism, nurturance, attachment and sensitivity to others' concerns and needs. Some of these issues are illustrated in Box 11.5.

According to Constance Fischer (1992), the development of a distinctive female approach to moral reasoning has also been stimulated for affluent contemporary Australian, New Zealand, European and North American girls by the problem of how to come to terms with the rapid changes in social expectations about women's domestic, vocational and sexual roles

BOX 11.5 Expressing individuality
Gender differences in the logic of morality

To illustrate gender differences discussed in the text, consider the answers Gilligan (1982, pp. 19–20) received when she asked one 25-year-old man and one 25-year-old woman what it meant to be ethical.

Interviewer: What does the word 'morality' mean to you?
Young man: I think it is recognising the right of the individual, the right of other individuals and not interfering with those rights. Act as fairly as you would have them treat you.

Interviewer: Are there really right and wrong answers to moral problems, or is everybody's opinion equally correct?
Young woman: We need to depend on each other, and hopefully it is not only a physical need but a need of fulfilment in ourselves, that a person's life is enriched by cooperating with other people and striving to live in harmony with everybody else, and to that end there are right and wrong; there are things which promote that end, and things that move away from it.

The notion of individualistic competition and assertion of personal rights and claims may be more congenial to male than female ethical thinking, according to Gilligan.

that have arisen in their cultures in recent decades. Fischer argued that Matina Horner's (1972) classic studies of female university students' fear of success should be interpreted in these terms. Horner found that, despite their university education, more than 65 per cent of her sample of female undergraduates at a prestigious university in the United States responded to the sentence 'After her first term finals, Anne finds herself at the top of her medical school class...' by describing a host of negative outcomes for Anne, ranging from social rejection to psychotic breakdown. Such themes arose in less than 10 per cent of male undergraduates' corresponding essays about a student called John in the same situation. Fischer suggested that these data (which Horner had taken as evidence of a distinctly female drive to fail in mixed-sex competition) illustrate female moral reasoning. She argued that the women's negative images of achievement reflected their recognition of the moral conflicts that the self-interested pursuit of success can create. In these terms, Anne's dilemma is seen to pose the question of how to reconcile personal competitive striving with human interdependency and the obligation to consider others' needs and feelings. Fischer concluded that:

> In moral development ... new truth becomes apparent when male norms are set aside long enough to listen to female voices in their own right. (p. 120)

Men's and women's qualitatively distinct experiences during adult life (see Chapters 14 and 15) may likewise contribute to their moral development. To explore this possibility, Nancy Clopton and Gwendolyn Sorrell (1993) presented a set of moral dilemmas designed to elicit care-oriented reasoning to a sample of 40 US married couples, half of whom had a severely handicapped child. Dilemmas about parents of handicapped children were included in their tests, together with a standard Kohlbergian dilemma about the theft of a drug. The hypothesis that parents of handicapped children would have more advanced care-oriented reasoning than other parents was not supported. But the results were striking in another way, clearly showing that women and men used the same moral reasoning when faced with the same moral problems. In the light of Gilligan's theory, Clopton and Sorrell were surprised to observe that the fathers' responses to the parenting dilemmas 'were remarkable for their tenderness, concern and honesty' (1993, p. 99). The authors concluded that previous findings of sex differences in moral reasoning may reflect the different types of moral problems adults encounter and think about in their everyday lives.

Personality development: The identity crisis

According to Erikson's (1968a) theory (see Chapter 2), a sense of personal *identity* is the central psychosocial conflict in personality development during late adolescence and early adulthood. Teenagers think long and hard about future study, friends, social acceptance and plans for their lives. This is both understandable and necessary. Many of the decisions made during adolescence will have consequences that affect the rest of adult life.

As adolescents consider these issues, according to Erikson (1959, 1968a), an internal dialectical conflict or crisis over identity is triggered and this sets the chain of growth in motion. He wrote:

> Adolescence is not an affliction but a normative crisis, i.e. a normal phase of increased conflict characterized by a seeming fluctuation in ego strength and yet also by a high growth potential ... such developmental and normative crises differ from imposed, traumatic and neurotic crises in that the process of growth provides new energy as society offers new and specific opportunities. (1959, p. 116)

When adolescents resolve the crisis to develop the personality attribute of identity, they gain a coherent sense of self, not only for the present moment but in relation to their future life roles:

> Identity is a psychological process reflecting social processes ... it meets its crisis in adolescence, but has grown throughout childhood and continues to reemerge in the crises of later years. The overriding meaning of it all, then, is the creation of a sense of sameness, a unity of personality now felt by the individual and recognized by others as having a consistency in time. (p. 1968a, p. 13)

Thus Erikson viewed emotional upheavals as normal and a necessary part of adolescence (see Chapter 12). The identity crisis is a dialectical confrontation of opposites. The possibility of a higher-order developmental synthesis can arise only when the crisis is fully confronted and the ensuing conflicts satisfactorily dealt with. In other words, mature identity growth leads to a new, more complex and effective stage of personality organisation. As Erikson (1968a) noted:

> . . . it may be a good thing that the word 'crisis' no longer connotes impending catastrophe, which at one time seemed an obstacle to understanding the term. It is now being accepted as designating a necessary turning point, a crucial moment, when development must move one way or another, marshalling resources of growth, recovery and further differentiation. (p. 16)

One aspect of the identity decision is the choice of an occupation, since to adolescents a job means not so much a way of earning a living as 'something to be'. But a number of other choices are equally crucial, as Box 11.6 illustrates. In order to resolve the crisis and achieve a secure sense of identity, the adolescent must formulate:

1. a philosophy of life that includes moral values and an orientation to religion
2. a personality pattern that integrates enduring temperamental qualities (see Chapter 5) and basic dispositions into a comfortably fitting adult character
3. a decision about one's gender role
4. a sense of self as a sexual being (see Chapter 10)
5. a stance in relation to politics and social issues
6. a blueprint for future intimate relationships
7. a sense of self, including ethnic identity
8. an occupation or vocational identity.

The identity crisis is a necessary turning point when plans for the future are mapped out, however painfully.

The adolescent's resolution of the identity crisis organises and integrates all these separate elements of the personality into a coherent whole. The young person gains a sense of having a definite set of goals and sees a niche for their expression in the wider community. But this is not the end of personality growth. In fact, according to Jane Kroger (1989), identity development continues throughout the life-span. She studied a group of 100 middle-aged New Zealand adults and found that at least some of the identity issues listed above had continued to occupy most of these mature men and women for a major portion of adult life. But the identity decisions they had reached during adolescence provided the framework for a better understanding of their adult-development pathways. Thus Kroger's findings were consistent with Erikson's idea that:

> A sense of identity is never gained or maintained once and for all. Like a good conscience, it is consistently lost and regained, although more lasting and economical methods of maintenance and restoration are evolved and fortified in later adolescence. (Erikson, 1968a, p. 74)

Identity statuses

According to Erikson, adolescents must actively confront uncertainties and personality conflicts in order to achieve the dialectical synthesis of opposing elements in the self that will enable identity growth. This is because a secure sense of self must build upon genuinely essential personal characteristics. When adolescents opt out of the inner crisis through anxious avoidance, they outwardly display a super-

BOX 11.6 A pause for thought
How is identity development assessed?

In a study of a total of 622 Melbourne high school students, Doreen Rosenthal and her colleagues (Rosenthal, Gurney & Moore, 1981) posed the simple question 'Who am I?' and asked pupils to respond by listing answers to this question that reflected who they were, what they were really like and how they thought about themselves. The self-descriptions that respondents came up with were placed in one of two categories that can be described as follows:

- *Identity-resolved (I):* The person has a clear sense of identity
- *Identity-not-yet-developed (Not-I):* The person has no clear sense of self as yet.

Instructions. To assess your understanding of the identity construct, try grouping each of the following Melbourne students' responses as (I) or (Not-I) in terms of whether or not the response reflects a developed sense of identity. (Answers appear upside down at the bottom of the box.)

1. 'I've got it together.'
2. 'I feel mixed up.'
3. 'I like myself and I'm proud of what I stand for.'
4. 'I've got a clear idea of what I want to be.'
5. 'I can't decide what I want to do with my life.'
6. 'I change my opinion of myself a lot.'
7. 'I know what kind of person I am.'
8. 'I find I have to keep up a front and pretend I'm bigger and better than I really am.'
9. 'I don't know what I really feel about things.'
10. 'I'm up-front and I don't try to bluff my way through.'

Scoring: Give yourself one point for each answer you categorise correctly. Scores of 8 or more testify to a sound understanding of how thoughts about identity express themselves in teenagers' self-descriptions.

Answers

Category I: 1, 3, 4, 7 and 10
Category Not-I: 2, 5, 6, 8 and 9.

ficial appearance of having achieved a sense of identity, but it will be ill-fitting. This is to be expected of an identity that someone else has chosen for them rather than one of their own making. When this happens, the adolescent is said to be in a state of *identity foreclosure*. Individuals with foreclosed identities have an apparent commitment to identity choices that may have been made for them by parents (as when an eldest son is expected to follow in the father's footsteps in a family business) or by circumstances (as when special talent for a sport or music or ballet dancing leads to a decision from childhood to pursue this avenue of endeavour without exposure to alternative options).

Figure 11.8 shows how the identity foreclosure relates to the two intersecting developmental dimensions of (a) crisis confrontation and (b) a sense of certain commitment to an identity, together with the positions of three other identity statuses: identity achievement, identity moratorium and identity diffusion. Details of each of these statuses are outlined below.

IDENTITY ACHIEVEMENT

Identity achievers experience a period of crisis and turmoil, followed by active confrontation of the identity question, including exploration of a wide range of alternative identity options. An example of identity exploration in the context of dating appears in Box 11.7. Exploration and crisis confrontation are likely to become more urgent priorities as older adolescents are forced to make decisions about employment, higher education, relationships, sexuality and morality. After a period of crisis, doubt and extensive soul-searching and decision-making, adolescents in this status achieve a coherent sense of self that guides their philosophy of life and practical choices about a future lifestyle and life tasks to which they feel a sense of commitment.

IDENTITY MORATORIUM

Sometimes, identity achievement occurs smoothly after a relatively brief crisis and an efficient period of identity exploration. But, in other cases, identity development can be blocked – by the adolescent's own personality and/or by such life circumstances as poverty, educational deprivation, war or economic recession. In the face of such barriers, an identity moratorium may provide an effective long-term solution. The moratorium involves a protracted identity crisis, often entailing a painful period when all identity commitments are temporarily suspended and the individual feels lost and confused.

Erikson (1968a) illustrated the moratorium with

Graduation from university may force the identity moratorium to an abrupt conclusion.

the case of a family friend called Jill (not her real name). When Erikson first met her as a child, Jill seemed highly intelligent, but she was also obese, a tomboy and in bitter rivalry with her older brothers. After puberty, she 'straightened out and up', became popular and physically attractive, and earned good grades in high school. But then, part way through her university course, her moratorium began. She refused to return to university, deciding instead to remain on a ranch her parents had visited during the summer holidays. For a year she did no study and met few people her own age. She spent her time herding horses and cattle and bottle-nursing newborn animals by the campfire. After that, her moratorium over, she returned to university with a more complex identity. This new personality pattern incorporated the vivacious, bossy and masculine tendencies she had displayed as a child into a plan for 'nurturant activities' (perhaps veterinary studies?) which, according to Erikson, 'felt more like her', while at the same time being useful, worthwhile and practical.

When used in this way – as a breathing space prior to making irrevocable long-term commitments – the moratorium facilitates the effective resolution of difficult identity decisions. Thus the identities that eventually emerge in moratorium individuals are often exceptionally worthwhile, creative and self-expressive.

IDENTITY FORECLOSURE

When the adolescent assumes an identity without going through a crisis, the result is identity foreclosure. From the outside, a foreclosed identity may seem similar to an achieved identity. But it often lacks synthesis and fails to express the person's genuine interests and personality strengths, because it has been imposed by parents or other outside forces rather than deliberately chosen. Some adolescents opt out of the identity crisis by making a series of sudden and relatively irrevocable identity decisions, without ever seriously considering possible alternatives.

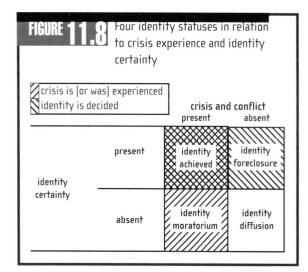

FIGURE 11.8	Four identity statuses in relation to crisis experience and identity certainty

crisis is (or was) experienced — identity is decided		crisis and conflict	
		present	absent
identity certainty	present	identity achieved	identity foreclosure
	absent	identity moratorium	identity diffusion

Exceptional early success in a demanding role such as ballet dancing or sport may contribute to identity foreclosure.

Intense pressure from parents is a common reason for identity foreclosure. Consider the affluent 16-year-old Australian who, when asked what job he hoped to get when he left school, replied with no trace of hesitation, 'I shall work at my father's factory, until he retires, then take it over' (Connell et al., 1975, p. 150). Foreclosure of vocational identity may arise as a result of strong parental influence.

From her interviews with New Zealand adults, Jane Kroger (1995) illustrated identity foreclosure with the case of a man, Frank, who had entered a celibate religious order in his teens in accord with his father's ambition for him and his own intention since childhood. According to Kroger, this early decision limited Frank's identity exploration as an adolescent and young adult by restricting his contact with people with whom he could form intimate relationships or identity alternatives.

IDENTITY DIFFUSION

Identity diffusion characterises those individuals who are unable to make even the simplest identity decision. Blocked in their development before beginning to grapple with the identity crisis, these young people lack both commitment and crisis confrontation. To a greater extent than any other identity status, identity-diffused adolescents are apathetic, profoundly confused, insecure and withdrawn. According to Erikson (1968a), the consequences of not facing the crisis – when coupled with the absence of any commitment

BOX 11.7 A case in point
Identity exploration through social comparison

During Louise's first term at the University of Adelaide, her parents spent six months travelling around New Zealand. She lived in a college near the campus and wrote to her parents regularly. Her father copied a passage from one of her letters into his diary. It illustrates how, as an identity-uncertain adolescent girl, she was somewhat overawed by the forceful identity a male acquaintance was already displaying as a first-year university student.

> **25 March 1965.** *We sent Louise a New Zealand greenstone pendant as a seventeenth birthday present. She had apparently not yet received it on the 20th when she wrote us: 'On Wednesday night ... all the freshers from the three boys' colleges in Adelaide were invited to St Martha's. It was smashing. I spent most of the evening with this type that is the sort you expect to find attending a university. He sort of brags but it isn't like bragging. He tells things he did as if it were the most ordinary thing in the world. For example, he told me about the time he and his friend pinched a fire hydrant and planted it in somebody's front yard and another time they pinched one of those red flags you find around construction work and painted a hammer and sickle on it and walked up and down the street with it. He was very amusing but he wanted me to go to some do at St Mark's (his college) Saturday (tonight) but I was already going to Diana's and besides I didn't really fancy that sort of thing on such short acquaintance.*

© Peterson, 1974, reproduced with permission

to an identity imposed from the outside – include a profound lack of interest in people, activities, values and even life itself, as well as self-doubt, anxiety, depression and procrastination. Even routine decisions like when to get up in the morning are fraught with stress.

Consequences of identity growth for personality and adjustment

As the central personality crisis during adolescence, development in the identity domain was postulated by Erikson to shape many other aspects of the growth of personality. Research findings have supported this prediction. Collectively, the empirical studies of correlates of the four identity statuses have included samples of young people in Australia (e.g. Moore & Rosenthal, 1993), New Zealand (e.g. Kroger & Haslett, 1991) and the United States (e.g. Grotevant & Cooper, 1985; Marcia, 1980). Collectively, the results of the research indicate that foreclosed adolescents tend to be conformist, stereotyped and conventional and to come from authoritarian families (see

Chapter 12). Identity-achieved and moratorium adolescents tend to be open-minded and androgynous (see Chapter 8) and to come from families emphasising individuality and connectedness (Grotevant & Cooper, 1985). Identity-diffused adolescents often report parental lack of interest or rejection and score lower than other groups on a variety of measures of personal adjustment. These contrasts are summarised in Table 11.6.

Cultural variations in personality and identity development

In multicultural societies like Australia and New Zealand, adolescents who have links with cultures and ethnicities other than the dominant Anglo-Australian or Anglo-New Zealand (Pakeha) majority may be forced to confront an additional dimension to the identity crisis – the question of ethnic identity (Phinney, 1996). In striving to reconcile their minority-group and majority-group identifications, these adolescents face additional challenges to their overall patterns of identity growth and personality development.

Developing an ethnic identity

On the basis of extensive interviews with African-American, Mexican-American and Asian-American teenagers, Jean Phinney and Linda Alipuria (1990) concluded that ethnic identity is a salient component of an overall resolution of the identity crisis for minority-group teenagers. The vast majority of them agreed that finding their own position on a contin-

uum ranging from total, undiluted allegiance to their minority ethnicity versus total repudiation of it in favour of unqualified identification with the Anglo-American mainstream was either 'important' or 'very important'. Furthermore, the researchers found that minority adolescents who did manage to incorporate elements of their Asian, African or Mexican roots into their identity choices displayed higher levels of self-esteem than those who identified exclusively with mainstream Anglo-American culture.

While there is added richness in a personality that contains multiple ethnic and cultural elements, resolving the identity crisis can be made more difficult by this additional burden of choice. Biased attitudes and discriminatory practices may also complicate the process of identity achievement for adolescents from minority-group ethnic backgrounds. On the basis of interviews conducted with adolescents in Melbourne, Jean Phinney and Doreen Rosenthal (1993) concluded:

> Minority adolescents may have to confront issues of prejudice and discrimination, structural barriers which limit their aspirations and hinder their achievements, and other features of the mainstream society that differentiate them from the majority. If minority youth are to construct a strong, positive and stable self-identity, then they must be able to incorporate into that sense of self a positively valued ethnic identity. (p. 145)

Phinney (1996) suggested that a secure sense of ethnic identity develops through three stages (see Table 11.7). These stages may or may not coincide with identity choices being made in other areas of the adolescent's life, such as careers, relationships or

	Identity status			
TABLE 11.6 Personality correlates of Marcia's four identity statuses				
Personality dimension	**Achievement**	**Moratorium**	**Foreclosure**	**Diffusion**
Sex-role orientation	Males masculine; females androgynous	Males feminine; females androgynous	Males masculine; females feminine	Undifferentiated sex roles
Authoritarian beliefs	Low	Low	High	Low
Prejudice	Low	Medium	High	Medium
Anxiety	Low	High	Low	High
Conformity to peer pressures	Low	Intermediate	Low	High
Dependency	Autonomous	Highly autonomous	Highly dependent	Dependent
Self-esteem	High	High	Low	Low
Ethnic identity	Strong	Medium	Strong	Weak

Source: Based on data in Berzonsky (1983); Bourne (1978); Grotevant & Cooper (1985); Marcia (1980); Waterman (1982).

TABLE 11.7	Stages of ethnic identity development	
Stage	**Definition**	**Description/Example**
Stage 1	Unexamined ethnic identity	Adheres without question to values of the mainstream culture with no consideration of other options
Stage 2	Ethnic identity search	Active exploration of own ethnic origins and options, sometimes accompanied by superficial adherence (e.g. dress) to markers of the alternative culture
Stage 3	Achieved ethnic identity	A personally congenial blend of qualities from mainstream and minority ethnicity, founded on rigorous examination of ethnic values and options

political beliefs. They define a developmental progression similar to Erikson's model of identity achievement, with Stage 1 reflecting foreclosure on the ethnic identity issue. However, despite the existence of stages, it is not necessary for individuals to progress developmentally through the complete sequence of ethnic identity stages in order to achieve psychological well-being.

According to Phinney, some individuals with multicultural roots spend their entire lives comfortably at Stage 1 of the ethnic identity continuum. Those who do progress further may, despite more advanced development, still experience psychological distress to the extent that social prejudice and economic disadvantage are inextricably bound up with the position in society of certain ethnic minority groups. As Michael Cole and Sheila Cole (2001) explain:

> The economic inequalities that go with some minority-group statuses make it very difficult to isolate minority-group membership as the crucial variable in the development of members' personal and social identities ... we cannot be certain why foreclosure occurs more frequently among minority-group adolescents or why some of them appear to identify less with their own ethnic or racial group than with the dominant group. (pp. 684–5)

Doreen Rosenthal and Shirley Feldman (1992) investigated the quality of the relationship between parents and 15- to 18-year-old Chinese-American and Chinese-Australian adolescents as a possible predictor of the adolescent's ease of developing a sense of ethnic identity. They found that whether the teenagers had grown up in the United States or in Australia made no difference. Nor did how closely the parents monitored their adolescents' activities. But other aspects of these migrant Chinese parents' behaviour did exert an important influence on their adolescents' identity development. In particular, a strongly positive identification with Chinese culture was observed among adolescents whose parents were warm, supportive and affectionate and who promoted the adolescent's autonomy by encouraging independent decision-making and open expression of dissenting points of view (see Chapter 12 for a discussion of parent–adolescent conflict). In other words, ethnic identification may have more to do with the quality of the emotional relationship between parent and child than with issues of ethnicity *per se*.

Ronald Taft (1985) studied the development of ethnic identity in a group of West Australian children and adolescents whose parents had migrated to Australia from Europe either before they were born or when they were young. He viewed ethnic identification as comprising six elements, as shown in Table 11.8.

To illustrate to yourself an example of the cultural competence dimension of Taft's model, you may wish to pause and take the quiz that appears in Box 11.8.

Taft (1985) studied the relationship between ethnic identification, as defined by elements in Table 11.8, and the psychological adjustment of Australian-born teens of British, Polish, Italian, Greek and German parents. He found that boys from each of these ethnic groups scored higher than girls on all the criteria for Anglo-Australian identification, possibly because European-Australian parents tend to keep their daughters closer to home than their sons.

On the whole, however, these adolescents appeared to be developing well and were remarkably free of negative symptoms such as identity diffusion and psychological maladjustment. In line with Phinney's model (see Table 11.7), many appeared to have reached Stage 3, in which they were able to select components of each ethnic identity that best suited their own personalities, and reported unusually high levels of satisfaction with their identity choices. In fact, one study comparing Greek-Australian teenagers with Greek adolescents in Greece showed that those in Australia 'were better adjusted in that they had higher self-esteem and fewer life problems' (Taft, 1985, p. 371). Taft suggested that a secure identification with one culture facilitated the achievement of satisfactory identification with the other. As in Phinney and Rosenthal's (1993) Melbourne study, the quality of the relationship between parent and child was a major predictor of the successful achievement of a secure sense of ethnic identity. According to Taft:

TABLE 11.8	Six elements of an Australian multicultural ethnic identity
Identity element	**Description**
Cultural competence	Knowledge of the key elements of mainstream and minority ethnic mores and practices.
Self-perceived identity balance	A person's composite response when asked (a) 'How Australian do you feel?' and (b) 'How Greek [parents' original nationality] do you feel?'
Feeling of belonging	The individual's self-reported attachment to, and involvement with, the mainstream Anglo-Australian community as contrasted with the tendency to be immersed in a segregated ethnic subcommunity, or in nostalgia for the former homeland.
Ethnic reference group	The cultural composition of the group whose opinions mean most to the person, and/or the group whose behaviour he or she emulates with greatest ease and consistency.
Citizenship	Immigrant residents in Australia may elect to take out Australian citizenship and/or retain the passport and prerogatives of their original nationality. As well as having various legal and social overtones, choice of citizenship may be viewed as an overt sign of a private sense of ethnic identification.
Social identity	This was measured by asking Australians who were unacquainted with the migrant subject to rate how 'foreign' or 'Australian' the person seemed to them to be on the basis of dress, spoken accent, style of bearing and so on.

BOX 11.8 Activity suggestion
Test your multicultural IQ

Instructions. The quiz below involves culturally specific knowledge similar to scales of *cultural competence* (Richardson, 1961; Taft, 1985) deemed to form a component of ethnic identity development by some theorists (see the text). Choose the one best answer for each item by marking choice (a), (b), (c) or (d).

1. **Skite** means (a) to brag (b) to skate on ice (c) to mine for gold (d) to hang-glide.
2. **To be crook** is (a) to break the law (b) to be a coward (c) to feel ill (d) to speak badly.
3. **Strides** are (a) fence posts (b) pig's trotters (c) gum boots (d) a pair of trousers.
4. **Dinkum** is (a) a starchy foodstuff extracted from the Australian native yam (b) a term of endearment for a baby (c) the genuine article (d) a musical instrument.
5. **To make a blue** means (a) to prepare a meal (b) to go sailing (c) to make a mistake (d) to give orders.
6. **Buckley's** is (a) a gold mine (b) a tall story (c) a type of kangaroo (d) no chance at all.

7. A **bowser** is (a) a morally conservative person (b) a petrol pump (c) a breed of dog (d) a kitchen utensil.
8. **Dill** describes (a) a small stream (b) a three-legged stool (c) a dunce (d) a native bird.
9. **To have a lurk** means (a) to come up with a tricky scheme (b) to take a rest (c) to conceal oneself (d) to consume a meal.
10. Which of the following differs from the other three? (a) puha (b) pipi (c) tuna (d) kina.
11. The opposite of an enemy is (a) manu (b) hoa (c) toru (d) marae.
12. A **koha** is (a) a fruit (b) a vegetable (c) a gift (d) a weapon.

Interpretation. Items (1) to (9) test knowledge of Australian slang and are based on Clifford (1968) and Richardson (1961). Items (10) to (12) test knowledge of New Zealand Maori culture and are taken from a 40-item quiz developed by Thomas (1988).

Answers. *The correct answers are : 1(a), 2(c), 3(d), 4(c), 5(c), 6(d), 7(b), 8(c), 9(a), 10(a), 11(b), and 12 (b). A score of 10 or better indicates excellent awareness of distinctively Australian and New Zealand cultural lore.*

Conflicts may, in certain groups, concern issues which are salient to particular cultures, such as restrictions on the social autonomy of Greek and Italian girls, but the evidence indicates that any such conflicts concern the parents' child-raising practices rather than differences in other values. (pp. 370–1).

Identity development in Aboriginal adolescents

Historically, in Australian Aboriginal culture the process of achieving a sense of personal identity was traditionally very different from the experiences of teenagers growing up in European societies. In place of the decade or more of indecision which a typical

European or Anglo-Australian adolescent now devotes to resolving the identity crisis, there was one brief event in traditional Aboriginal life: the pubertal initiation ceremony (see Chapter 10). Considered cross-culturally, the duration of an identity crisis provides no meaningful guide to the quality of the identity eventually achieved. In fact, Erik Erikson's own observations of the initiation rituals practised by North American Indians taught him to recognise 'the drama of puberty rites and the enormous existential experience a kid goes through'. He therefore concluded that, in a culture practising pubertal initiation, 'the transition may take a shorter time, but it may be terribly intense' (1983, p. 28).

However, for the contemporary indigenous Australian teenager, the identity question may no longer be as simple as it was before European influences entered Australia. According to Western Australian anthropologists Catherine and Ronald Berndt (1964):

> Children growing up in a traditional environment did not need to ask, 'Who am I? What am I here for? What is the meaning of life?' and so on. These questions were answered for them. Now the answers are less certain, even for children growing up on mission stations where indoctrination is most tenacious. As far as Aboriginal adults are concerned, the degree of control they can exercise over their children is diminishing rapidly. (p. 139)

John Money and his colleagues (Money, Cawte, Bianchi & Nurcombe, 1970) also noted problems in identity development among Aboriginal youth on Elcho Island in the Northern Territory of Australia. In 1970 this Aboriginal community continued to practise the traditional pubertal circumcision ceremony to initiate boys into tribal manhood. But Yolgnu adolescents were also exposed to mainstream Anglo-Australian influences at their high school in Darwin, as well as through contact with missionaries and occasional tourists visiting their local community. This intensified the identity dilemma. According to Money and his colleagues (1970), these Aboriginal adolescents were experiencing:

> acutely and at first hand the incompatibility of what their fathers and tribal elders stood for, versus what their school teachers and others of the mission staff stood for. The adults were unable to work out a compromise. Those youths who were unable to take sides, completely rejecting either the Aboriginal old guard or the mission new, had no model on whom to develop their teenaged sense of masculine identity. (p. 396)

Money's observations of profound uncertainty and occasional delinquent acts by these boys fit Erikson's (1968a) notion that risk of identity diffusion increases when a young person in a rapidly changing culture strives to integrate two essentially incompatible ('traditional' versus 'modern') sets of ideals. As Money went on to explain:

> The elders resisted modernization and the yielding up of their ancient traditions. In doing so they abdicated their responsibilities to their young people, who could not identify with the programme of traditional ways of behaving that the old men wished to perpetuate. Simultaneously, the young people, having no mandate from their elders, could not identify with the programme of modernization and Christianization as sponsored by the mission. Their solution was to escape their dilemma by putting together a programme of their own (p. 396).

Overall, however, Money found it remarkable that there were relatively few instances of delinquent or disorderly behaviour among these traditional Aboriginal adolescents. Their elders' tolerance of the teenagers' 'acting up' also augered well for the young men's chances of being able to progress beyond behavioural acting out, identity diffusion, identity moratorium (see Figure 11.8) and ethnic identity search (see Table 11.8) to achieve a secure sense of self-identity. In addition to supplying an optimistic model of the lifespan as a steady ascent towards wisdom and integrity (see Chapter 1), another advantage of traditional Aboriginal culture's model of a lifelong sequence of age-graded ceremonies and religious initiations may be the opportunity to gain a mature identity suddenly, once youthful 'wild oats' have been sown, in contrast to the protracted identity crises of adolescents growing up in mainstream Anglo-Australian culture.

For the Aboriginal adolescent, the identity crisis is further complicated by the need to integrate traditional and contemporary cultural patterns.

Identity development in New Zealand Maori adolescents

To examine Maori and Pakeha (Anglo) New Zealand adolescents' awareness of Maori culture, and to assess the extent of Maori teenagers' identification with it, David Thomas (1988) developed a test of Maori knowledge (see Box 11.8). When he administered the test to a group of New Zealand adolescents aged 11 to 16, Thomas found no difference between Maoris and Pakehas who lived in urban Hamilton – both groups did relatively badly, with an average of less than one in four items correct. But Maori teenagers from rural schools in small country towns possessing a Maori *pa* (settlement) did much better. Their average scores were more than double those of the urban Maoris. Thomas also found that the extent to which individual adolescents of Maori background identified with Maori culture and described themselves as 'all' or 'mostly' Maori, rather than Pakeha, positively predicted their scores in the quiz. Thus, cultural knowledge and ethnic identification appear to go hand in hand.

A comparison of statuses in resolving the identity crisis between Maori and Pakeha high school students in New Zealand was conducted by James Chapman and John Nicholls (1976). Their results appear in Figure 11.9. While still in high school, Maori teenagers were disproportionately more likely to experience identity diffusion than mainstream New Zealand teenagers.

It is possible that pride in Maori identification may have increased since 1976 when Chapman and Nicholls' pioneering study was conducted. Furthermore, heightened ethnic identification with Maori culture may be beneficial, according to Thomas (1988), since:

> Having some knowledge of Maori language and culture in the predominantly Pakeha (Anglo) New Zealand society means that such a child is, to some extent, bilingual and/or bicultural. Bilingual and bicultural children may be more likely to show competent behaviour, both in school settings and outside school, due to the greater social skills and more complex cognitive structures of bicultural individuals. (p. 387)

Some of the interpersonal benefits of a blending of the warmth and communal focus of a Polynesian or Maori social identity into the anxious reserve more typical of Anglo adolescents are illustrated in Box 11.9.

In addition to enhancing their self-esteem and pride in their Maori ethnicity, a strong ethnic identification with New Zealand culture may supply Maori adolescents with a rich social support network. According to Thomas (1988):

> For Maori people especially, participation in Maori cultural patterns may provide linkages to social support networks and social constraints which reduce the likelihood of criminal offences and other types of negatively sanctioned behaviour. These are issues which require further research. (p. 64)

BOX 11.9 A case in point
A charming age in Samoa

When Louise was 14, her parents migrated from California to New Zealand. En route to Auckland, their ship docked for a day in Samoa. Her father made the following entry in his diary:

22 June 1962. We arrived in Samoa, port of Pago Pago, last night. This morning we struggled down the ship's ladder, with too much assistance, and set out to the south along the edge of a long inlet from the wide harbour. We greeted and were greeted by men, women and children also walking, mostly toward the ship. We passed open-air markets and innumerable grocery and general merchandise stores, coconut palms, a banana tree laden with bananas, scores of different flowered trees and shrubs and houses built on piles with round thatched roofs. Louise wanted a souvenir so we stopped at a long thatch-roofed building lined with low tables displaying native crafts, mostly shell and seed jewellery. She was stand-offish at first, seeing no price tags and imagining the worst. But when we asked the price of a necklace and heard '50 cents' her fears were dispelled. Soon we were talking with a charming 13-year-old named Anne who was helping her mother at one of the tables. Louise bought a necklace from her mother. Our conversation continued and soon we were made a present of another necklace. Peg then bought one and before we left we were given another present. In the evening, after we had returned to the ship and were at sea again, Louise made some crayon sketches of her recollections. Her first thought was of the souvenir shop.

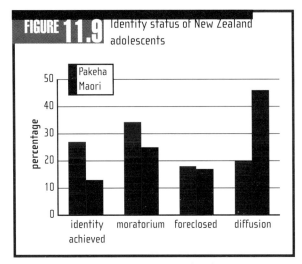

FIGURE 11.9 Identity status of New Zealand adolescents

Source: Based on data in Chapman & Nicholls (1976), p. 68.

Chapter summary

New cognitive skills emerge in adolescence. With the transition from the concrete-operational to the formal-operational stage in Piaget's scheme, new heights of logical reasoning are achieved. Teenagers can test abstract hypotheses scientifically and systematically by exploring all possible combinations of variables. They coordinate notions of probability, correlation and algebraic equivalence with ease. They can imagine unobservable and futuristic scenarios, and are aware that reality is only a small speck in the vast realm of possibility.

Thus, formal-operational thinkers can reason logically about personal and social problems, including health, ethics, relationships, politics and future plans. As a result, teenagers may become preoccupied with moral values and the search for a personal identity that integrates their present skills, ambitions and philosophy of life with future options across the looming span of adult life.

Contemporary adolescents typically do not fully master formal-operational thinking until the late teens or adulthood. Some never do. Though differences in ability and educational opportunity may account for some of these variations in rates of cognitive growth among contemporary young people, it seems that areas of interest are also relevant. Individuals are most likely to attain the formal-operational stage within their chosen area of cognitive specialisation.

While a powerful cognitive tool, formal thought is not without its limitations. An imaginary-audience reaction may produce an alternation between painful shyness and exhibitionism, while at the same time conferring a false sense of invulnerability to such risks as motor vehicle accidents, unplanned pregnancy and HIV infection. It is clearly relevant to adolescent health.

Moral reasoning also develops dramatically during adolescence and early adulthood, partly because of the teenager's improved cognitive abilities but also as a result of youthfully idealistic preoccupations with society, the environment and the future of the world.

Kohlberg outlined five stages of moral reasoning, grouped into premoral, conventional and principled levels. An individual's rate of progress through these stages may vary with gender and culture, but Kohlberg's latest analysis suggests that even the fastest developers do not complete the transition to the highest stage in his theory during their teenage years.

During adolescence, decisions about careers, relationships, moral values and a philosophy of life acquire new urgency as the teenager contemplates life as an independent young adult. The result, according to Erikson, is the identity crisis. This seminal period in lifespan personality development entails the search for a fully encompassing sense of self, along with goals and values to guide the rest of life.

Several outcomes to the identity crisis are possible. Foreclosure occurs when adolescents fail to explore alternatives, opting instead for an identity imposed on them from the outside. Identity achievement entails the gathering together of identity fragments from childhood and plans for the future, in the domains of career, religion, relationships and sexuality, to create an integrated sense of self leading to a satisfying role in society.

An identity moratorium arises when the identity crisis is unusually protracted, although this approach typically yields highly successful identity outcomes during adult life. Identity diffusion amounts to an opting out of the crisis, producing anxiety, low self-esteem and a desperate inability to decide on anything at all.

Cultural background exerts an important influence on these varied patterns of identity development. Migrant and minority adolescents are called upon to make ethnic identity choices in addition to their resolution of the universal themes of the identity crisis.

For further interest

Looking forward on the Internet

Use the Internet to visit the following websites: **http://www.piaget.org** and **http://www.eric.ed.gov** and select options relating to 'adolescent development', 'cognition' and 'formal operational thinking' to obtain more information about themes covered in this chapter. Also visit the Companion Website for this textbook at **http://wps.pearsoned.com.au/ peterson** for more ideas, resources and activities.

ADOLESCENCE: Social, personality and relationship development

When I was a boy of 14, my father was so ignorant I could hardly stand to have the man around. But when I got to be 21, I was astonished at how much he had learnt in 7 years.
Mark Twain (1835–1910)

Contents

CHAPTER OVERVIEW

When parents are asked to anticipate which period in their children's lives they think they will enjoy the most, and which one they believe they will find most stressful, it is something of a paradox that a majority of adults look forward eagerly to infancy and early childhood, while adolescence is dreaded. Despite the fact that adolescent offspring are independent enough not to need constant parental supervision or assistance in performing their daily routines and are mature enough to carry on intelligent conversations about sport, art, music, politics and social life, few parents look forward eagerly to this stage of parenting. Indeed, when Shelley Phillips (1982) questioned a group of 545 Sydney mothers and fathers about their parenting experiences, she found that those with young adolescents in the house were most likely to describe raising children as a 'nerve-wracking job'. They also found their children less cooperative than did parents of infants, preschoolers and primary schoolers, and were more concerned about the sacrifices entailed in parenting and their children's ingratitude for the sacrifices they made. These views are consistent with the attitudes of parents in other parts of the world, including the United States (Montemayor, 1983) and New Zealand (Smart & Smart, 1970).

Why is adolescence such a difficult phase in family life? Anna Freud, Sigmund Freud's daughter, thought there was one main reason:

> There are few situations in life which are more difficult to cope with than an adolescent son or daughter during the attempt to liberate themselves. (1958, p. 291)

This chapter begins with a look at the process of emancipation whereby teenagers become independent of parents. We examine the practical elements of the dialectic between freedom and responsibility, ranging from new expectations for participation in household work to being allowed to stay out late at night or, finally, move away from the family home to flat with friends or set up house with a romantic partner. Anna Freud's psychoanalytic theory of how adolescents become emotionally free of childhood attachments (see Chapter 5) is examined, together with alternative social-psychological explanations of the emotional 'emancipation' process.

We then look at parent–adolescent conflict, a process that presents a radical departure, both in frequency and strategies used, from the parent–child disputes of early and middle childhood. Continuities in parenting from childhood through adolescence are explored in the context of parental leadership and disciplining styles. These are seen to exert an important influence on adolescent behaviour, including such problem behaviours as delinquency, cigarette smoking, drinking and the abuse of hard drugs. Of all adolescent problem behaviours, none is as serious a subject for parents' or theorists' concern as suicide, especially in Australia where the rate of teenage suicide is one of the highest in the world.

After exploring the causes of adolescent suicide, including special aspects relating to Aboriginal Australian teenagers, we analyse a prime source of influence on adolescent social and emotional development – the peer group. Changing patterns of friendship with same-sex peers and the onset of dating relationships with friends of the opposite sex are explored in this context, and the chapter concludes with a look at gangs, cliques and the adolescent peer group as an organised, developing entity.

Becoming independent of parents

Adolescence can be a problematic time for both generations because of the difficult task that parents and teenagers must accomplish together during this turbulent phase in the family life cycle. The liberation (or 'emancipation' in the words of psychoanalytic theorists such as Anna Freud) of adolescents from the bonds of affection and dependency which have kept them close to their parents during their earlier growing up enables the establishment of mature intimacy as young adults (see Chapter 13). But how best to accomplish this developmental goal can be a source of doubt, friction and stress for both generations. Contemporary parents' anxieties over how to promote competence and mature self-reliance in their offspring are made worse by the lack of any firm cultural guidelines. Uniform religious and social beliefs (or initiation rites) create greater accord over these issues in other cultures (see Chapter 10). But in contemporary Western societies, it is largely up to the individual family to negotiate for itself what kind and

amount of independence is appropriate, and at what time.

Adolescents have a vested interest in drawing their parents' attention to extreme examples of 'liberated' behaviour within the peer group, such as the 11-year-old who is allowed to dispense with a babysitter when her parents go out at night, or the 13-year-old with a weekend curfew as late as 2 am. Most parents, on the other hand, are acutely aware of the dangers of premature independence for teenagers in Australia and New Zealand today, and it can be very hard for parents to push children out of the family nest into a world fraught with the risks and possible attractions of drugs, alcohol and fast cars, and the manifold effects of what many consider to be the breakdown of sexual restraint and moral values.

It can be equally hard for adolescents to accept gracefully the freedom their parents offer them without entering into it too fast and blaming parents for the consequent nicks and bruises, or holding back too long and suffering a sense of stagnation and failure. Many adolescents interpret parental involvement in the emancipation process as an act of unloving rejection, while parents who refuse to allow room to grow and free choice are seen as selfish and overprotective.

Evading the issue will not ease the situation either, according to Anna Freud. In fact, she saw parental failure to encourage the growth of independence as an even more serious risk than all the problems that can come about from the inappropriate pacing of independence. She noted that:

> We all know individual children who as late as the ages of fourteen, fifteen or sixteen show no such outer evidence of inner unrest. They remain, as they have been during the latency period, 'good' children, wrapped up in their family relationships, considerate sons of their mothers, submissive to their fathers, in accord with the atmosphere, ideas and ideals of their childhood background. (p. 282)

It was these children, Freud felt, who were perhaps in greatest danger of maladjustment during adolescence because, convenient though their compliance might seem, it signified the retardation or 'stunting' of a necessary part of normal pyschological growth, with the consequent risk of carrying an immature personality through the remainder of the lifespan.

Transitions in family life during adolescence

The ultimate goal of the emancipation process is a new, egalitarian style of relationship between parent and child that resembles close friendships among adults. But the route to such a relationship is never entirely smooth. In addition to the anxiety parents feel as they watch their children go forward freely into a world whose dangers they know only too well, they are also faced with the fact that they will never again be the sole objects of their offspring's unqualified devotion. And, though freedom may beckon irresistibly, the adolescent is also apt to feel poignant nostalgia for the security and parental support of the childhood years. Box 12.1 shows how some of these varied feelings were expressed in one father–daughter relationship.

The process of gaining and granting independence involves a delicate interplay between parents' and teenagers' values. When it comes to venturing into the outside world, the parent's role as guardian and

Growth towards independence

BOX 12.1

When Louise was 11, many of her classmates had already begun to boast that they were 'going steady'. Foreseeing that his own daughter would soon be doing likewise, Louise's father speculated in his diary on some of the implications of this new step towards fully fledged independence.

---

2 April 1959. I don't want Louise to fail to grow in independence but at the same time I don't want her to get hurt. Peggy sees the dilemma much less sharply than I do. She assumes, I feel, that independence and judgment will develop together. She wanted Louise to walk alone across the highway, for instance, at the age of 4 or 5; after all, other moppets were doing it. 'She'll have to learn some time.' To be sure. But the dangers involved in delay are as nothing compared to the risk of death by a speeding car. That however was a fairly easy problem to solve. Peggy took her to the road and watched while she crossed, saw whether she looked both ways, let her practise crossing. But how can a child be guided in sexual relationships? Or in drinking? Or even dating?

Louise herself had also become conscious of some of the penalties of growing up. First, she expressed this awareness rather lightheartedly. Her father wrote:

23 August 1959. Meanwhile this evening after going to bed she asked me: 'Why do I worry so much?' 'Well, what do you worry about?' 'Oh I worry about whether I'll enjoy my childhood.' 'Well, aren't you enjoying it?' 'Yes, except sometimes when I play with Linda.' 'But you have to have some bad times to appreciate the good ones.' Yes, that was so. It was all right then. What should she think about? How about Penrod? OK. She had just finished reading Penrod again. Tomorrow night it may be more difficult getting her to agree on what story to think about. It most often is.

Many years and many worries later, Louise had reconciled herself fairly well to the thought of an independent lifestyle. When she was 16, she moved into a residential college next to the University of Adelaide while her parents travelled through New Zealand and the eastern seaboard of Australia. Anticipating this change, her father made the following entry in his diary:

9 January 1965. Louise seems much less anxious about going it alone just a few weeks from now than I am on her behalf. I don't know how long her self-confidence will last but at the moment she couldn't be more serene. Partly this is the result of having been through a kind of dress rehearsal with Gillian's family and partly I suspect because she'll still be in Adelaide where she knows many people. Peggy and I are the ones who are venturing into strange places. Louise's heart is set on the university and St Martha's and she will face – at this distance anyhow – almost any trial or deprivation to obtain them. It will certainly be good for her: her first real taste of independence.

But her father, by now absolved of most of his anxiety over how to encourage his daughter's development of

protector favours caution and dependency, while the teenager's need to feel grown up or meet the standards set by peers leads to a desire for early autonomy. Thus, when asked at what age parents should relinquish control over their adolescents' day-to-day activities, Australian parents are found to set older limits than their teenage offspring (Farnill, 1987). The child's gender is also influential, with teenagers and parents both tending to agree that autonomy should be granted earlier to sons than to daughters. Figure 12.1 illustrates the opinions of a group of middle-class male and female Melbourne residents about the youngest acceptable ages for a variety of 'emancipated' behaviours for teenage boys and girls (Farnill, 1987).

On the other hand, in some areas of living, parents expect autonomy at younger ages than do adolescents themselves. This applies particularly to household duties and to helping parents with the care of the home, car, garden, pets or younger siblings. Jacqueline Goodnow and Pamela Warton (1991) interviewed a group of Sydney mothers and fathers who had at least one son or daughter aged eight to 14 living at home. Parents described the jobs their children did around the house and their methods of involving their children in household work. Children were also asked about their household responsibilities.

In line with the view that adolescence brings with it increasing responsibility for domestic contribution, these Sydney families reported more participation by 14-year-olds than by 8-year-olds in tasks involving care of communal household property (e.g. washing the car, weeding the garden, cleaning the bathroom). These jobs were also differentiated by gender. Thus, 77 per cent of 14-year-old Australian girls participated in cleaning the bathroom, compared with only 27 per cent of 8-year-old girls and 32 per cent of 14-year-old boys. Teenage boys compensated by being almost universally involved in car washing (91 per cent compared with only 59 per cent of 14-year-old girls and 67 per cent of 8-year-old boys). But some household responsibilities were undertaken as early as middle childhood. By age eight, 87 per cent of Australian boys and girls made their own bed and participated in setting the dining table, with no sex differences in these activities.

Thus the adolescent's transition into mature independence involves a two-way process of negotiating the balance between responsibility and freedom of choice. As they grow older, adolescents become less willing to accept parental advice about their recreational activities, clothes, hairstyle and selection of friends (Youniss & Smoller, 1985). But parental input into academic and career decisions continues to be tolerated. In Australia, adolescent girls are more

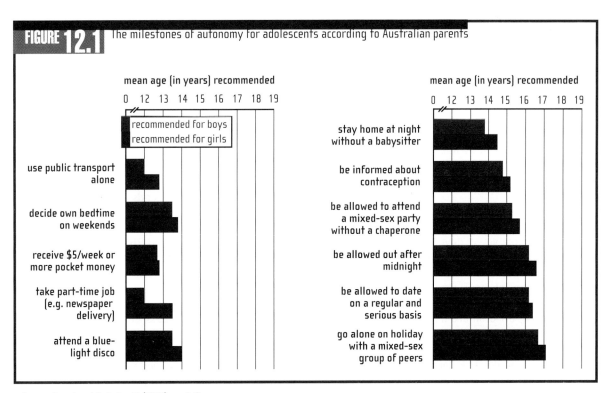

FIGURE 12.1 The milestones of autonomy for adolescents according to Australian parents

Source: Based on data in Farnill (1987), pp. 6–7.

Household roles for children and adolescents are frequently gender-segregated.

likely than boys to agree with their parents about values, the future and social issues like religion, politics or the environment, as well as about personal issues like drug use or sexuality (Feather, 1980). In part, this may reflect the Australian adolescent daughter's more frequent discussions of personal and social issues with her parents, as compared with an adolescent son (Noller & Bagi, 1985). Not only do daughters disclose more to their mothers about their friendships, sexual relationships and sexual problems, but they also talk with their fathers more often than Australian adolescent boys speak to either parent. Topics range over politics, society and the girl's general life problems and future plans.

So the emancipation process does not necessarily entail a total rejection of parental influence. But mundane issues of responsibility for housework and rights to self-determination in the domains of schoolwork, friendship and curfew are likely to be subjects of frequent discord and continual negotiation between adolescents and their parents. As each side makes a demand on the other, feedback is also sought to determine whether the anticipated level of autonomy is manageable and acceptable to both parties. With each concession granted, the terrain of the dispute is likely to shift, while the process of debating continues. Julius Roth (1971) offered the following description of this mutual and reciprocal decision-making process:

> Thus the parent attempts to some extent to impose upon his children his conception of the proper timetable of development, but he must make compromises in response to the spoken and unspoken pressures from his children and his anticipation of how they will feel about the demands that he will make upon them. At the same time, children are trying to do some things before they are expected or allowed to and are trying to avoid doing some other things at the time they should. The children too modify some of their behaviour and some of their pressures so as to avoid conflict with the parents. (p. 138)

The emancipation process

As an emotional process, the transition from childish dependency on parents to self-directed autonomy entails more than a simple rewriting of household rules. Nor is it even as straightforward as the negotiated transfer of responsibility for decision-making. Emotional bonds of intense love and attachment to parents must be broken, often painfully and traumatically. But, without this freedom, an eventual romantic relationship with an adult lover would be impossible. The adolescent who retains an intense attachment for a parent throughout the upheavals of pubertal physical growth and the social transition into adult life is in the most dangerous position of all, according to psychoanalytic theorists.

Anna Freud (1958) argued that emotional dependency on parents, though healthy during childhood, caused intense psychic conflict during adolescence. The only fully effective solution, according to her psychoanalytic theory, was a dramatic personality upheaval. Sigmund Freud, her father, viewed the pressing new sexual feelings and desires resulting from pubertal growth as an inevitable source of unconscious psychological conflict (see Chapter 2). Somehow, mature sexuality must be incorporated into the adolescent's personality. One alternative is to fit the new sexual feelings into existing personality structures and control them with primitive defence mechanisms like denial (pretending not to have sexual urges) and reaction formation (substituting for one's true wishes an aversion towards sexuality). But because the adolescent sex drive is so strong, this only works when the childish defences are implacably strong themselves. From a lifespan perspective, this is an ineffective solution, according to Anna Freud, because it implies a stunting of personality growth. The adolescent who fails to become emotionally free of attachment to parents, and controls sexual urges by means of childish defence mechanisms, is doomed to go through adult life equipped with the personality system of a child.

The other alternative implies a more turbulent adolescence. From a lifespan perspective, however, stress during the teens yields the potential for genuine personality development as an adult, according to psychoanalysts like the Freuds and Erik Erikson (see Chapter 11). In this approach, the adolescent must first unconsciously break free of childish attachments to parents so as to avoid the incest anxiety that would grow to impossible proportions after puberty. Once emotional independence is established, adolescents are free to fall in love with peers, who are legitimate targets for both emotional and sexual affection. But, in the process of breaking free, there is typically a number of personality struggles which are often so troubling that they would be readily interpreted as mental illness were they to occur at any other period in life. Anna Freud (1958), though, like Erikson, cautioned against viewing adolescent distur-

With the transition into adolescence, children begin to pull away from family pursuits they formerly enjoyed.

bances as pathological, since 'adolescence is by its nature an interruption of peaceful growth, and … the upholding of a steady equilibrium during the adolescent period is itself abnormal' (p. 270).

In her view, adolescents make use of a variety of unconscious processes to break the emotional tie that binds them to their parents. One tactic, known as *displacement*, severs the bond with a parent by means of a temporary emotional attachment to someone outside the family. The adolescent may literally leave home or may remain at home 'in the attitude of a boarder'. He or she no longer confides in the parents or seeks their reassurance. Sometimes the new attachment is to an adult, or a series of adults, usually possessing personality attributes exactly opposite to those of the parent to whom the teenager was formerly most closely attached. In other instances, adolescents become emotionally attached to leaders, 'demagogues' or 'heroes' who belong to a generation between their own and that of their parents and who typically command a youthful following as a result of the attitudes and beliefs they espouse. Yet another option is for the adolescent to forge a passionate new tie with someone their own age – possibly a single 'best friend' or 'chum' or perhaps with an entire 'gang'. The advantage of displacement as a vehicle for emancipation is that adolescent attachments to new figures are necessarily weaker than longstanding bonds with parents, if only because of their recency. Thus displaced attachments, being devoid of incestuous connotations, provide a temporary refuge before complete emotional autonomy is undertaken.

The main dangers of the process of displacement, according to Anna Freud, are either:

- that the break with parents might be too sudden; or
- that the new attachment might inspire the young person in antisocial directions.

A second unconscious process, known as *reversal of affect*, is 'less conspicuous outwardly' than displacement, but more 'ominous in nature inwardly'. Here, parental emotional ties are maintained but in such a way that adolescents' emotional feelings for their parents are turned into their opposites. Love becomes hate, admiration becomes contempt and dependence becomes rebellion. While, on the surface, adolescents may feel and seem emancipated, they are really no more independent than before, since compulsive opposition to the parents is just as constraining as compulsive obedience to them.

A third process involves a kind of *narcissism* in which the affection previously conferred on parents is turned inward, and adolescents literally fall in love with themselves. Usually, this happens only when the possibility of forming an attachment to someone else has been blocked in some way. Narcissism can be overcome if opportunities to love others outside the family present themselves. When left unchecked, however, the result may be 'delusions of grandeur' and other recognised symptoms of mental illness. If this happens, psychiatric treatment, according to Freud, is 'indicated as well as urgent'.

The same is true of two other adolescent pathologies identified by Anna Freud. In the first, known as *asceticism*, repressed sexual impulses produce such intense anxiety that all physical needs and desires are resisted, including the need for food, sleep and material comforts, leading to anorexia and depression. The second, known as *uncompromising adolescence*, is a state where even the elemental harmony necessary to coordinate life activities is considered unacceptable and therapeutic intervention is urgently required.

Emancipation through dialogue

James Youniss (1983) proposed a modification of this psychoanalytic model of emancipation. In place of the unconscious sexual drives viewed by psychoanalysts as the motivating force behind emancipation, Youniss viewed the development of emotional independence as triggered by a dialectical process of social construction. In this theory, the efforts of adolescents to persuade their parents to treat them as mature adults, and the parents' corresponding efforts to try to modify their impressions of, and rules for, their maturing offspring produce conflict that ultimately resolves itself into a higher-order synthesis. By *social construction*, Youniss meant the utilisation of cognitive and communication skills to boost the mutual understanding of interdependent people, such as parent and child. He outlined five elements of the social construction model:

1. Individuals continually construct and reconstruct their ideas of social reality through dialogue.
2. Discourse or argument reduces egocentrism by drawing attention to multiple conflicting views of social situations as well as providing a means for seeking the resolution of differences.
3. Skilled social construction depends on such communication skills as discussion, argument, debate, consultation, compromise and negotiation.

In becoming independent of their parents, adolescents seek social validation from their peers.

4. Individuals are motivated to seek social validation of their own views from others with whom their lives are entwined, and feel rewarded when their perspectives are validated and shared.

5. Individuals seek to maintain communication with others for emotional reasons and also as a guarantee against self-deception.

Given these postulates, Youniss concluded that the liberation process that is portrayed in psychoanalytic theories as the traumatic and complete severing of all attachments binding children to their parents might better be viewed as a last resort. While revolutionary emancipation of this kind is one possible outcome of the normal process of human development, it is by no means the only effective way of modifying the parent–child relationship to suit the demands of adulthood. In many healthy families, an adolescent's primary bond of attachment to parents is transformed, not eliminated, according to Youniss. Thus, provided family members have effective communication skills and sufficient motivation to carry through with the sometimes onerous process of social reconstruction, emancipation may take place through friendly dialogue rather than in pitched battle. Yet, in Youniss's view, the end result is the same. Parents and their offspring eventually gain a mutually respectful and emotionally satisfying style of friendship.

At the same time, the adolescent acquires enough emotional self-sufficiency to become attached to a romantic partner. In fact, Youniss argued, throughout the child's growing up most parents and children do strive to update their understanding of each other through communication. Thus 'the life world of mutual understanding is continually renewed' (1983, p. 107). He also suggested that relatively few adolescents are 'so trusting of their own rationality that they fail to seek validation of their ideas from their parents' (p. 93). So, provided the family is not hampered by hostility or impoverished communication skills, the development of emotional independence 'may consist not so much in breaking the bond as in transforming it and the persons within it' (p. 93).

Cultural variations in the process of becoming independent

The issues that trigger spoken or unspoken disagreements between adolescents and their parents during the push for independence are found to vary from one cultural group to another. In multicultural societies like Australia and New Zealand today, this means that whereas certain themes (like household work and staying out late at night) are common to most households with adolescents, other issues that greatly preoccupy the two generations in some homes are not even considered in others. According to studies of migrant and mainstream Canberra children aged 11 to 17 years by William Scott and his colleagues (Scott et al., 1991), academic achievement is much more of a preoccupation for some migrant teenagers and their parents than in most Anglo-

Australian adolescents from multilingual households experience multiple pressures in their search for independence.

Australian families. Possibly, in part, because of their strong drive to succeed in their new environment, parents who had recently come to Canberra (especially from countries where English was not the native language) put more emphasis on their children's success in school than mainstream Anglo-Australian parents. The migrant parents were also less satisfied than Anglo-Australians with their children's present performance in school, the amount of homework they did and their scholastic ambition, and this was true even of children who were performing above average. This might be expected to intensify parent–adolescent disagreement in migrant families. However, despite this, Scott found that migrant teenagers scored somewhat higher in emotional well-being than mainstream Anglo-Australian teenagers.

In an ambitious test of the effects of the migration experience itself on teenagers and their families, William and Ruth Scott and their colleagues (1991) measured teenagers' emotional balance, adjustment, self-esteem, friendships and dependency on their parents while they were still living in their home countries, before the move to Australia. They then followed these teenagers longitudinally through the process of migration and tested them again after they had been settled in Australia for three years.

The results of this study indicated that the adolescents' attitudes and level of emotional well-being before migrating combined with their position on the continuum between extreme emotional emancipation and extreme dependency on parents to predict their post-migration adjustment to Australian teenage life. Migrant adolescents who were rated as highly emotionally dependent on their parents before the move were rated as less stable and less emotionally well-adjusted by their new-found Australian friends some two years later. By contrast, migrant teens who had already made significant progress towards becoming emotionally emancipated from their parents before coming to Australia seemed to adjust to, and gain acceptance in, their new Australian peer group more quickly, possibly because they were not held back from making friends by immature parental dependency. The teenagers' original levels of self-esteem and optimism about the prospects for life in Australia likewise predicted better adjustment and satisfaction with friends after their arrival in Australia.

Doreen Rosenthal (1982) questioned a group of Melbourne 13- and 15-year-olds about the most common sources of friction in their dealings with their parents. The sample included migrant teenagers from Italy and Greece as well as mainstream Anglo-Australians. Disagreements between adolescents and their parents were rated on a 4-point scale, where a score of 1 represented little or no disagreement and 4 a very high amount. In the Anglo-Australian sample there were fewer reported areas of disagreement than between the Greek or Italian teenagers and their parents. In fact, the only issues that evoked even

a moderate amount of family disagreement (as indicated by an average score of 2 or higher) in mainstream adolescent households were the following:

- how often you go out with your friends and how late you stay out at night
- whether you are allowed to smoke cigarettes and/or drink alcohol
- your homework and study habits
- the jobs you do around the house.

In line with Jacqueline Goodnow's findings, reported earlier, the last of these issues of contention was bound up with Anglo-Australian parents' wish that their teenagers would take on more responsibility for household work than the teens themselves wished to shoulder. But in disagreements over the first of these issues, the tables were turned and children wanted more independence than their parents felt they were ready for. Either way, both topics are directly bound up with the family's need to emancipate and launch its teenage members into lifestyles that are independent of their parents.

Italian-Australian daughters recorded the highest level of family conflict of any subgroup in Rosenthal's sample, supporting the suggestion made in Chapter 11 that a clash between traditional Italian values and beliefs about women's roles and those of contemporary mainstream Australian society can complicate the emancipation process, along with identity development for Italian migrant girls. In addition to disagreeing with their parents at least moderately about the four contentious topics listed above, the Italian and Greek migrant youth also recorded higher than average disagreement scores in the following areas:

- your personal appearance (including length of hair and use of cosmetics)
- whether you are allowed out on a date with a member of the opposite sex
- your outlook on life
- how you spend your time away from home.

Rosenthal concluded:

In Anglo-Australian families, more individuality is tolerated, with greater stress on personal freedom. In Greek and Italian families, adolescents are subjected to more authoritarian, parent-centred control, with greater expectations that they will fit in or conform to family demands. For these adolescents, attempting to conform also to the attitudes and behaviours of their Anglo-Australian peers, disagreements with parents seem an inevitable price to pay. (p. 239)

Jane Kroger (1983) explored New Zealand teenagers' feelings about their families using a sentence-completion procedure. She also included a comparison with a group of North American adolescents whose feelings had been assessed by the same method. The emancipation process seemed to begin later in New Zealand than in the United States, especially for girls. Thus, at age 11 less than half as many

New Zealand daughters as girls in the United States, or boys in both countries, expressed negative feelings about their families (see Figure 12.2). But, with the transition to the teens, expressions of rebellion escalated dramatically in New Zealand. New Zealand sons at age 13 were critical of their parents more than twice as often as American boys at the same age, and the rate of negative comments by New Zealand daughters, trebled since age 11, was also higher than American girls'. Since a similar pattern of cross-cultural differences persisted through to age 15, the oldest age she tested, Kroger concluded that New Zealand parents may make the emancipation process more difficult for their adolescent offspring by setting stricter limits and retaining tighter control over their sons' and daughters' behaviour than their American counterparts.

Attachment to parents and peers

As teenagers become increasingly independent of their parents, they are inclined to turn to their peers for the kinds of comfort and emotional support that securely attached infants and young children gain from their parental caregivers (see Chapter 5). Table 12.1 shows how the attachment styles that infants forge with their caregivers in the first years of life relate to the dimensions of attachment that adolescents and young adults form with parents and romantic partners.

Figure 12.3 shows the developmental changes in secure-base attachment to parents versus friends that arose in one sample of North American adolescents over the age span from 12 to 17 years (Hazan & Zeifman, 1994).

As romantic partners enter the scene, they, too, are apt to become targets of attachment (see Table 12.2). This chart shows the relationship between adolescents' styles of attachment to parents, same-sex friends and opposite-sex romantic partners. As can be seen in this table, adolescents with a secure attachment to parents tend to replicate this healthy relationship style in their friendships and early romantic relationships.

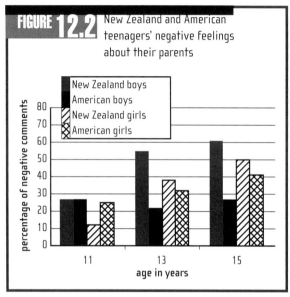

FIGURE 12.2 New Zealand and American teenagers' negative feelings about their parents

Source: Based on data in Kroger (1983).

		Attachment style	
Dimension of cognition	**Secure**	**Avoidant/Dismissing**	**Anxious-ambivalent/ Preoccupied**
Self-conceptions	• High self-esteem • Self-confident	• Moderate self-esteem • Lacking in confidence in others	• Low self-esteem • Low confidence in self and others
Memories of parents	• Parents warm and loving	• Mother aloof and rejecting • Parents lacking in honesty and integrity	• Father unfair and inconsistent
Beliefs about others	• Others are generally well intentioned and trustworthy	• Others are not trustworthy or dependable	• People have little control over their own lives
Attitudes about relationships and emotions	• Seek balance of closeness and autonomy in relationships • Express emotional distress constructively	• Need to maintain distance and independence from others • Suppress or deny negative emotions	• Desire extreme intimacy • Fear rejection • Deny own needs lest partner is rejecting

TABLE 12.1 Self-concepts, attitudes and beliefs in young adults with different attachment styles

Source: Based on data in Feeney & Noller (1996).

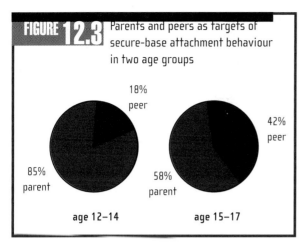

FIGURE 12.3 Parents and peers as targets of secure-base attachment behaviour in two age groups

18%
peer

42%
peer

85%
parent

58%
parent

age 12–14

age 15–17

Source: Based on data in Hazan & Zeifman (1994).

TABLE 12.2 Correlations between adolescents' attachment styles with their parents and their patterns of attachment with romantic partners and friends

Comparison	Attachment style		
	Secure	Preoccupied	Dismissing
Parent with friend	.41**	.61**	.47**
Parent with romantic partner	.24*	.45**	.17
Friend with romantic partner	.32*	.52**	.43**

*Note: * and ** denote statistically significant associations.*
Source: Furman (2002). Reproduced with the permission of the Society for Research in Child Development.

Parent–adolescent conflict and communication

The process of negotiating for emancipation could conceivably be conducted completely calmly and amicably, with no arousal of angry feelings on either side. But very often it is a source of further friction in an already conflict-ridden mode of interaction between parent and child. The observations by Socrates and Aristotle that teenagers in ancient Athens were irascible, regarded themselves as omniscient and took delight in contradicting their parents are equally valid today. After reviewing a number of observational studies of parent–child interaction in teenagers' households in the United States, Raymond Montemayor concluded:

> Taken together, the results obtained from studies of conflict with parents at the start, during, and after adolescence indicate that conflict and age are related in an inverted U-shaped function; con-

flict increases during early adolescence, is reasonably stable during middle adolescence, and declines when the adolescent moves away from home … In general, mothers indicate that parental satisfaction is higher with a preteenage child or an older child who has moved away from home than with a teenager … it appears that some worsening of the parent–child relationship occurs during early adolescence. This deterioration has two components, an increase in parent–adolescent conflict and mothers' loss of power and influence over their adolescents. (1983, p. 89)

Part of the impetus for intensified family disagreement may be the adolescent's acquisition of more sophisticated debating skills, resulting from the transition to formal-operational thought (see Chapter 11). If so, arguing with parents can serve beneficial ends. By enabling the exercise of logical thought and reasoned argument, the teenagers' cognitive and communicative skills are both extended. In fact, a positive association was found in one study (Peterson, Peterson & Skevington, 1986) between the emotional intensity of a group of Western Australian adolescents' habitual disagreements with their parents and the maturity of their reasoning, in relation to Piaget's theory of formal operations (see Chapter 11). Teenagers whose level of reasoning was still exclusively concrete-operational were inclined either to avoid disagreeing with their parents altogether, or else to drop contentious topics before the discussion grew too heated. Those with some formal reasoning skills, on the other hand, frequently reported engaging in heated, angry arguments with their parents.

One possible basis for this observed relationship could be that the adolescent's transition to the formal-operational level of reasoning increases the intensity of family disputes by equalising the debating skills of the two generations, and making disagreements seem more interesting and involving. However, it is also possible that heated conflict with parents triggers the mental disequilibrium that stimulates cognitive growth in adolescence.

Family negotiation strategies

Whether as a cause or a consequence of the acquisition of formal-operational thinking, the methods adolescents use to negotiate and resolve disputes with their parents are important determiners of the long-term effects of family arguments on adolescent development. In a study of 354 Australian adolescents from mainstream and migrant families, Peterson (1990) discovered the distribution of parent–adolescent conflict resolution styles illustrated in Figure 12.4. The styles of conflict resolution typically used in these Australian teenagers' debates with their parents can be viewed as being on a continuum of increasingly open dispute, ranging from anxious avoidance to violent fighting, as outlined in Table 12.3.

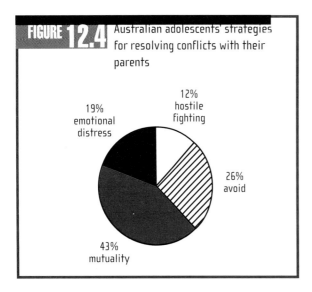

FIGURE 12.4 Australian adolescents' strategies for resolving conflicts with their parents

- 12% hostile fighting
- 19% emotional distress
- 26% avoid
- 43% mutuality

BOX 12.2 Conflict-resolution strategies used in familes with adolescents

Mutuality/open discussion. Parents and adolescents discuss and debate with one another in a full and open manner. Both parties to the conflict seek to understand the other person's position, while striving to express their own in a clear, full and rationally convincing manner. By paying attention to one another and keeping an open mind, it is often possible to achieve a mutually agreeable solution, as well as improved mutual understanding.

Conflict avoidance. When adolescents opt to avoid conflict, it is often because they fear that an overt confrontation, however mild, will cause friction and stress, or undermine the quality of the aversaries' social relationships. Families who use this strategy may feign agreement on issues where their opinions are actually divided. Family members may disguise their true feelings and pretend to agree in order to escape confrontation. Alternatively, the fact that the two parties hold different opinions may be admitted, followed by an immediate mutual decision not to say anything more about their disagreement. Either way, while minimising emotional upset and overt antagonism, this style of conflict management precludes the open exchange of views that is essential for full mutual understanding and so is apt to be less productive than some of the other tactics for resolving conflict.

Emotionality/post-conflict distress. Families who become emotionally energised during family disagreements but stop short of verbal or physical aggression may shout, scream or cry while arguing, and may feel upset at the end of a dispute, leaving in tears or giving one another the cold shoulder for a time.

Hostile fighting. In this approach to family conflict, disagreements between parents and adolescents, even about minor issues, are apt to trigger displays of verbal or physical violence from one or both generations. Tears, or rage, evoked initially by the subject matter of the disagreement typically escalate into emotional attacks of stronger magnitude on the other person as an individual. Conflict is managed through coercion rather than reason. Family members may hurl insults or profanities, or attempt to destroy each other's property. In extreme cases, they may even attempt to inflict injury on each other (see the section on family violence later in this chapter).

Learning to negotiate at home

Patricia Noller and her colleagues (Noller, Feeney, Peterson & Sheehan, 1995) explored the origins of adolescents' styles of conflict management by comparing the ways husbands and wives approached marital disputes with each parent's preferred strategy for negotiating with an adolescent son or daughter. The sample consisted of 164 Australian families with two or more offspring, at least one of whom was a teenager. Reports of conflict-resolution tactics were obtained from fathers, mothers and the adolescents. Results of this study are shown in Table 12.3.

As these findings show, the Australian adolescents who were studied by Noller and her colleagues tended to practise similar styles of resolving conflict with their parents to the styles employed by the parents themselves when they argued together as husband and wife. Consequently, spouses who practised mutual discussion with one another were developing adolescent offspring who used this approach when disagreeing with them. As other research has shown (Troth & Peterson, 2000), these adolescents are then likely to go on to have the skills to resolve conflict effectively through open discussion and mutual problem-solving when they form early couple relationships of dating and cohabitation. However, parents who practise less constructive conflict strategies in their couple disagreements, by nagging, getting angry, anxiously withdrawing from confrontation or attacking and hurting one another emotionally and/or physically, are likely to have adolescent offspring who use similarly maladaptive strategies in arguments with their parents. These teenagers will be less well equipped to communicate and resolve couple conflicts when they embark on early romantic relationships of their own (see Chapter 13).

When they looked at conflicts between adolescent siblings, Noller and her colleagues observed a similar pattern:

High levels of a particular style of conflict resolution in the parent–child relationship are mirrored by high levels of that same style of conflict resolution in the sibling relationship, possibly reflecting children's modelling of parental communication strategies in their interactions with one another. (p. 290)

In other words, these Australian data indicate that family conflict develops while children are growing up in either benign or vicious cycles. When the parents are skilled negotiators of marital disputes, who openly air their disagreements as a couple via mutuality (see Table 12.3) and hence achieve mutually acceptable solutions, there are benign carry-over effects in the

TABLE 12.3	Correlations between husband–wife and parent–child conflict-resolution styles		
	Conflict style		
Pairing	Mutual discussion	Coercive attack	Demand-withdrawal and avoidance
Mother–daughter	.48*	.34*	.47*
Mother–son	.24	.58*	.55*
Father–daughter	.55*	.34*	.41*
Father–son	.49*	.36*	.54*

Note: * Denotes statistically significant.

While physical fighting in sport has its place in adolescent life, the art of verbal debate and negotiation may be a more valuable asset in family life and close relationships.

form of exceptionally effective management of the conflicts arising between parents, offspring and siblings. On the other hand, when husbands and wives adopt hostile or coercive tactics such as threat, anger, insult and physical violence to deal with their conflicts with one another, a vicious cycle of escalating violence, distress or anxious conflict avoidance is likely to arise. Negative consequences of marital conflict may then spill over into parents' disagreements with their teenage offspring and into their children's own disputes with siblings and other family members.

Family conflict and adolescent self-esteem

The strategies families use to resolve their disagreements are found to have a bearing on adolescent self-esteem. Understandably, adolescents who find their parents receptive to their contrary opinions, and who report lively and extensive family discussions whenever opinions differ, are found to be more self-confident and relaxed than those for whom the expression of an opinion consistently leads to parental hostility, disparagement or anxious conflict avoidance. In one survey of a group of Melbourne primary and high school pupils, Paul Amato and Gaye Ochiltree (1986) linked self-esteem to patterns of communication in the family. The children and adolescents in this study were asked to answer 'Yes' or 'No' to:

1. Does your mother [father] talk to you much?
2. Members of my family yell and scream at one another.

The preadolescents who reported frequent discussions with their mothers had the highest self-esteem during primary school. But, among adolescents, frequency of talking to the mother bore no relationship to self-esteem. Instead, those who talked most often to their fathers had higher self-esteem than other boys and girls throughout high school, while frequent verbal violence at home was linked with self-disparagement. Similarly, when parent–adolescent communication consisted mainly of criticisms, adolescents were found to have low self-esteem (Patton & Noller, 1984). In a study of 313 young Australian teenagers and preadolescents, D. Andrew Ellerman (1993) found that mothers' support was a positive predictor of the offspring's overall self-esteem, and this relationship was particularly strong among girls.

In sum, the adolescent's self-concept appears to be linked more closely to the styles of negotiation families use in their efforts to resolve their disagreements than to the overall amount of conflict arising between parents and offspring. When conflicts are aired openly and debated vigorously, teenagers have a chance to refine their formal-operational reasoning skills by convincing their parents of the logicality of their points of view. At the same time, the open airing of differences promotes better mutual understanding in the family, whereas both hostile attack and the family's anxious avoidance of disagreement can lead to self-doubt and insecurity.

Family communication, conflict and identity exploration

According to Harold Grotevant and Catherine Cooper (1985), family communication to share ideas and resolve conflict provides adolescents with a medium through which identity issues can be explored and the identity crisis resolved (see Chapter 11). In their view, the optimal development of a sense of personal identity requires a psychological separation between teenagers and their parents. In order to consider personal choices and identity alternatives in sufficient depth to resolve the identity crisis, adolescents require the freedom to think and the courage to try out ideas and trust their own judgment, even when their views are at odds with those of their parents. At the same time, according to Grotevant and Cooper, a sense of connectedness within the family promotes identity exploration by continually demonstrating all family members' support, respect and sensitivity to other points of view.

To examine these issues in action, Grotevant and Cooper brought parents and adolescents together and taped their discussions of topics that were likely to evoke disagreement, such as where the family should go on their next holiday together, and what activities they should engage in while away.

The results supported their hypotheses. Daughters who were highly assertive in making suggestions to the rest of the family, and who readily disagreed with their parents' opinions, scored high in identity exploration, but girls who took a passive role in family discussion were less mature in their processes of identity development. Sons' advanced identity exploration was associated with their father's ability to compromise, tolerance for disagreement and willingness to modify his own position in light of the adolescent's persuasion.

These findings suggest that adolescents may learn to think deeply about identity issues as a result of arguing and debating openly with their parents. The parents' own style of resolving their conflicts as husband and wife may also provide a model of negotiation for their children to emulate (Noller et al., 1995). Grotevant and Cooper discovered that sons whose parents disagreed freely and vigorously as a couple scored higher in identity exploration than teenage boys in households where husbands and wives were overly conciliatory or conflict-avoidant.

Girls with mature identity development are often highly skilled in expressing their own opinions and asserting themselves with their parents.

Daughters who were advanced in identity exploration tended to have fathers who openly expressed individuality in disagreements with their wives, whereas, in a complementary pattern, the mothers of these girls frequently expressed mutuality with their husbands.

In other words, it appeared that, over and above their own direct learning of negotiating skills by arguing with parents and siblings, adolescents who observed models of open disagreement between their parents were encouraged to think independently about themselves and their future directions. At the other extreme, in households where the husband and wife typically avoided marital conflict, adolescent identity development was often delayed (Cooper & Grotevant, 1987). Janet, the eldest daughter in one such family, expressed a disagreement only once in the course of a 20-minute discussion about holiday plans that would affect her personally. Like her mother (who agreed with her husband 16 times more often than she disagreed), Janet seemed incapable of challenging, considering or modifying any of the opinions, suggestions or plans that her decisive father put forward. The result was an inhibition of Janet's ability to make decisions. Her identity development was therefore being foreclosed (see Chapter 11). As the researchers explained:

> Janet's low identity [score] may reflect a lack of exploration of issues outside the consensual family beliefs. In this family, in which signs of individuated spousal and parent–child relationships were less evident, the necessity for agreement and connectedness among family members and the family members' excessive involvement in each other's identity appeared to hinder the adolescent's development of individual ideas regarding career, dating and other issues. With regard to career choice, Janet commented, 'I'm having a hard time deciding what to do. It would be easier if they would tell me what to do, but of course I don't want that.' (p. 55)

Gender differences in adolescent family communication

In a later study using a similar method, Cooper and Grotevant (1987) similarly discovered that high levels of self-assertion and a focus on the differences between their own opinions and those of other family members during discussions were linked with adolescent girls' advanced development of a sense of personal identity vis-à-vis dating and intimate couple relationships. Girls who disagreed openly and frequently with their parents' stated views about a future family holiday (e.g. by saying 'I don't want to go on a train' or 'We don't have time to do all that') were found to have thought more deeply about dating than other girls and to have explored different modes and philosophies of couple relationships (e.g. by comparing cohabitation with marriage, or thinking relativistically about a variety of possible styles of couplehood, including platonic affairs and lesbianism).

Similarly, exploration of identity issues in the context of same-sex friendship was more advanced among girls whose parents disagreed openly but without force or animosity. As Cooper and Grotevant explained:

> The identity interviews suggested that females who were rated high in exploration on identity in the friendship domain had parents who stated their points of view but then let their daughters make their own decisions. Lower-exploring females had parents who showed little toleration of differences in terms of the types of friends who were acceptable for their daughters, little trust of their daughters' friends and greater intrusiveness in their daughters' peer world. In the domain of dating, higher-exploring females appeared more self-governing in terms of making decisions and had parents who respected their ideas and restrained their interference in their daughters' activities. Low-exploring females had little dating experience and had not considered their values about dating very extensively. (p. 288)

But sex differences again emerged. Boys who scored high in exploration of dating and friendship identity experienced more mutuality and connectedness in family discussions.

Gender is also an important influence on the way spontaneous conflicts are resolved in adolescents' families. Using the method of naturalistic observation (see Chapter 2), S. Vuchinich (1987) videotaped a group of 52 North American families with teenage offspring as they ate dinner together. He found that conflicts arose frequently in these dinner-time conversations and, when they did, were more likely to be confronted than avoided. In fact, argumentative responses were given to 64 per cent of the 'oppositional initiations' that arose at these dinners (as when family members challenged something another had said or shook their head, made a face, offered an insult, and so on). In most cases (61 per cent), the ensuing verbal conflicts were allowed to run their course without submission, retraction, compromise or withdrawal by either party.

But sex differences were observed in 'conflict-closing' and 'mediation' – the efforts made by family members to draw these conflicts to an amicable conclusion. Females of both generations made more efforts to mediate and terminate their own and other family members' disputes than did fathers or sons. In addition, mothers were found to initiate conflicts with their sons twice as often as with their daughters, whereas fathers disagreed with their daughters more than three times as often as with their sons.

No important differences between generations were observed in this study, with teenagers appearing no less willing than their parents to challenge a family member to a debate or to make efforts to bring conflicts to a close. But in an Australian study in which family interactions were similarly videotaped to examine family members' perceptions of their conflicting interactions, significant differences between teenage and parental generations did emerge (Noller & Callan, 1990). Australian teenagers viewed their family's communication patterns in a more negative light than their parents. When exposed to identical segments of their videotaped interactions and asked to rate each family member's behaviour, parents were inclined to perceive themselves, as well as their teenagers, as friendly, involved and cooperative. They rated their family's conflict-resolution style as more open and adaptable, and the family itself as more cohesive, than did the adolescents.

Parenting styles and discipline patterns in families with adolescents

Parents today employ a variety of different strategies in their efforts to socialise their children, teach them to obey family and societal rules, and prepare them for life as mature and responsible adults (see Chapter 8). Diana Baumrind (1991), the pioneering researcher who developed the typology of parenting in families with younger children shown in Table 8.1, modified her scheme slightly to encompass the variations she observed in families with adolescents in the United States. Table 12.4 shows the five distinct styles she observed, together with some of the consequences she noted for the behaviour and social competence of adolescent offspring.

Parenting styles and adolescent outcomes

After more than 15 years of exposure, varying approaches to parenting clearly have time to make their mark on adolescents' behaviour, and it does seem highly plausible that the differences in adolescent behaviour shown in Table 12.4 are the result of these variations in parenting style. However, there is an alternative possibility. Parenting styles could be a reaction to children's behaviour and parents gradually evolve their distinctive approaches to discipline over time, in response to the inherent personality characteristics of their offspring. Recall the variations in infant temperament that were outlined in Chapter 5. It is possible that a parent who attempts initially to use an indulgent or democratic style with a child who is high in activity level, low in self-regulation and temperamentally 'difficult' might eventually switch, in frustration, to a strictly autocratic style of control (Bell, 1968).

Regardless of the direction of causality, consistent differences are observed among adolescents growing up in households where these three different approaches to parental discipline are practised. In general, the offspring of authoritative-democratic parents appear to enjoy the smoothest passage through adolescence (Silverberg et al., 1992). They

TABLE 12.4 Baumrind's typology of the parenting of adolescents

Parenting style	Parenting behaviour	Adolescent outcomes
Authoritarian, directive parenting	Strict control and rule enforcement with minimal input from teens; high levels of monitoring and punitiveness for rule deviation; low expectations for autonomy	Sound academic achievement but low self-reliance and low to moderate self-esteem; low drug use
Authoritative parenting	Parent sets and enforces rules but allows input and negotiation to provide greater autonomy as teens seem ready to assume it responsibly; firm control and monitoring	Sound academic achievement; high social competence; high self-esteem; low drug use
Democratic parenting	Parents highly open to adolescent input with few demands and moderate to low levels of monitoring	Sound academic and social competence coupled with high drug use and other acting-out behaviour
Disengaged, non-directive parenting	Parents adopt a laissez-faire approach with little involvement in, or monitoring of, the adolescents' lives	High drug use; medium-to-low social and academic competence

generally score higher than other teenagers on self-report measures of (a) happiness, (b) self-esteem, (c) freedom from anxiety, (d) positive attitudes to parents, peers and schooling, and (e) mental health. Their performance in school also tends to be of a higher standard than that of adolescents exposed to laissez-faire parenting, and their risks of becoming involved in delinquent activities, truancy or alcohol and drug abuse are correspondingly lower.

The outcomes for adolescents exposed to authoritarian parenting tend to be more of a mixed bag. Risks of delinquency and substance abuse are typically low, but adverse outcomes like depression, poor self-concept and identity foreclosure (see Chapter 11) are somewhat higher than in authoritative households (Silverberg et al., 1992).

Single parents, step-parents and adolescent adjustment

Increasing numbers of people today are exposed to parental divorce or separation and it is becoming more common for teenagers to spend time in step-families, blended families or single-parent households. For example, as shown in Table 12.5 (Australian Bureau of Statistics, 2001), there was a roughly 2.5 per cent increase in single-parent families with dependent children aged 15 years or under in the Australian states between 1986 and 1996, with approximately 10 per cent of Australian families in 1996 being headed by a single parent.

Single parents typically display somewhat less monitoring and control of adolescents than in intact families (Amato, 1987). The risks of acting-out delinquency and other milder forms of misbehaviour can be expected to rise if increases in sole-parent households like those shown in Table 12.6 continue in future decades.

Another frequent outcome of parental divorce and remarriage is the stepfamily, in which adolescents live with one of their biological parents plus that parent's spouse or cohabiting partner. In some cases, the step-parent may also bring children from a previous relationship into the household, resulting in a blended family. In this case, the new parents may

TABLE 12.5 Single-parent families in Australia

	NSW	Vic	Qld	SA	WA	Tas	Total
1996							
Capital city	9.3%	9.1%	10.5%	10.4%	10.1%	12.1%	10.0%
Rest of state/territory	10.6%	9.5%	10.1%	8.4%	9.5%	9.6%	10.0%
Whole of state/territory	9.8%	9.2%	10.14%	9.9%	10.0%	10.6%	9.9%
1986							
Whole of state/territory	8.0%	6.7%	7.7%	6.5%	8.3%	7.6%	7.5%

decide to adopt similar childrearing strategies to one another or, alternatively, may carry forward the parenting styles they forged in their previous relationship into the step-parenting situation.

Jan Nicholson and her colleagues (Phillips, Nicholson, Peterson & Battistutta, 2002) studied a group of 136 Australian adolescents aged 17 to 21 years in stepfamilies. The majority lived with their biological mother and a stepfather (70 per cent) as opposed to a biological father and stepmother (30 per cent). Parenting styles of both the parent and the step-parent were examined separately, using Baumrind's typology. The adolescent's involvement in risk-taking and criminal behaviours was also explored. When both parents practised the same parenting style, consistent links were observed between parenting and risk-taking. Some of these relationships are shown in Table 12.6.

In general, as predicted by Baumrind, more problems emerged in adolescents who were exposed to a disengaged, laissez-faire style of parenting by both parents; these parents showed little control, interest or monitoring of their offspring's activities. (This style applied to roughly 1 in 5 of the study's participants.) Compared with Australian teenagers whose parent and step-parent were both authoritative in control, the children of disengaged parent dyads were four or five times more likely to report committing petty and violent crimes. They also displayed more negative mental health symptoms and engaged in more substance abuse.

Culture and parenting

More recent studies in Australia (Poole, Sundberg & Tyler, 1982; Rosenthal & Feldman, 1992) as well as overseas have confirmed these early indications of more positive outcomes for adolescents in democratic-authoritative than in authoritarian households. Adolescents from authoritarian homes tend to be conforming, dependent and submissive, while democratically reared teenagers are inclined to be independent, assertive and outgoing, as well as sometimes being rebellious, disobedient and disrespectful towards adult authorities. It would seem that authoritative or democratic rearing fosters independence by providing gradual, age-appropriate opportunities for independent behaviour. Authoritative parents accept and respect the child as an autonomous person.

The authoritarian parent, on the other hand, by making decisions without consultation, denies the child the chance to learn self-reliance. Although this might suggest that laissez-faire parents, who impose virtually no limits on their children's behaviour, would produce the most independent and self-reliant children of all, the research evidence does not support this conclusion. Presumably, authoritative democracy's gradual according of just as much freedom as the child can effectively cope with is necessary for the efficient teaching of independence skills. With laissez-faire parenting, independence is thrust on the child at possibly too early an age in doses that are probably too large to manage. In fact, recent studies of adolescents exposed to laissez-faire parenting have indicated a higher than normal risk of school misconduct (cheating, copying homework, truancy, lateness) and alcohol and drug use.

In a cross-cultural comparison of parenting styles and their effects on the rate at which adolescents gained independence from their parents, Millicent Poole, Norman Sundberg and Leona Tyler (1982) compared 462 boys and girls from rural towns in India, Australia and the United States, who were between the ages of 14 and 16 at the time of the study. In rural India, adolescents typically leave school at a younger age than in Australia or the United States. Thus, only 10 per cent of the Indian girls and 40 per cent of the Indian boys in the sample still attended school, compared with the vast majority of the Australian and North American teenagers. The measure of independence consisted of a checklist of items like 'Who decides the kinds of friends you should have?' (where an answer of 'myself' equals high autonomy) and 'I like to come and go as I wish' (where 'true' equals high autonomy). Parents' leadership styles were determined by the adolescents' self-reports.

The results showed that in India fathers exerted significantly more control over adolescent offspring than in either Australia or the United States. Australia came closest to a laissez-faire style of parenting, with Australian mothers exerting less control over their adolescent daughters than mothers in either India or the United States. The outcomes for adolescent autonomy are illustrated in Figure 12.5. As the graph shows, the American teenagers were

TABLE 12.6	Parenting style of parent and step-parent	
	Both disengaged	**Both authoritative**
Adolescent risk behaviours		
Depression	39%	18%
Anxiety	35%	14%
Stress	54%	27%
Criminal misdemeanour	58%	23%
Alcohol abuse	54%	32%
Cigarette smoking	46%	32%
Marijuana use	46%	32%
Use of heavy drugs	39%	4%
Unsafe sex	23%	0%

Source: Adapted from Phillips et al. (2002), Table 5.

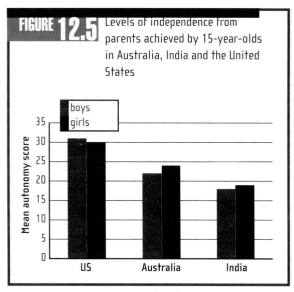

FIGURE 12.5 Levels of independence from parents achieved by 15-year-olds in Australia, India and the United States

Source: Based on data in Poole et al. (1982).

significantly more independent of their parents than Australian teenagers, who, in turn, were more independent than the adolescents in India. There were no significant differences between boys and girls in any of the three cultures.

William and Ruth Scott and their colleagues (1991) compared the effects of parenting styles on adjustment in over 2000 families drawn from Australia, Canada, Hong Kong, Japan, Taiwan and the United States. Parental affection and nurturance were related to adolescent self-esteem and all cultures. Interestingly, the direction of the relationship depended on who described it. For the teenagers themselves, high self-esteem was positively associated with high levels of perceived parental nurturance. But when parents described their own nurturance, the less of it they reported, the higher the adolescents' self-esteem. The Scotts and their colleagues concluded that when parents talked about their own

Australian mothers were found to exert less control over their adolescent sons and daughters than mothers in the United States and India.

nurturance, what they meant was probably closer to laissez-faire discipline than to how fond or affectionate they were. But adolescents seemed to take the latter interpretation in their descriptions of parents. Thus, the parental finding supports previous results of negative adolescent outcomes from laissez-faire parenting.

Another unexpected finding was that parental punitiveness was negatively related to adolescent adjustment within any given culture, yet the relationship between these two variables was positive when cross-cultural comparisons were made. In other words, the cultures that were highest in endorsement of strictly punitive parenting styles tended to produce better-adjusted adolescents. But when individual families from the same cultural group were compared, those who were especially high in punitiveness relative to other parents in that culture were relatively low in adolescent well-being. It would seem that parents who deviate from their own culture's accepted parenting norms in an unusually punitive direction have problems, but when the culture itself endorses a stricter stand than other cultures, no ill effects arise. It may be concluded that it is not possible to understand fully the process of human development in isolation from its cultural context.

Juvenile delinquency

By far the worst outcomes for adolescents are associated with the cold, aloof style of laissez-faire parenting known as the *indifferent-uninvolved approach*. Like the offspring of indulgent laissez-faire parents, teenagers subjected to this approach get into more trouble at school for truancy and misbehaviour, display less academic achievement, and use drugs and alcohol more extensively than adolescents from authoritative or authoritarian families. But, unlike indulgent parents, those adopting the indifferent-uninvolved style tend to produce offspring who are also at serious risk of major psychological problems. While indulgently reared teens tend to score high on measures of emotional adjustment, self-esteem and popularity with peers, those exposed to the indifferent laissez-faire style are more often depressed, anxious, rejected or neglected by peers (see Chapter 9) and lacking in social skills. Furthermore, recent research evidence consistently shows that indifferent-uninvolved parenting is associated with an unusually high risk of such serious forms of delinquency as theft, arson, carrying a weapon and being in trouble with the police (Silverberg et al., 1992).

Two hypotheses have been put forward to explain these unfortunate developmental outcomes from indifferent parenting. One is the *monitoring theory* (Patterson & Stouthamer-Loeber, 1984). According to this view, children and adolescents develop problem behaviours when their parents expose them to too much independence before they have the cognitive and social maturity to handle it, and cycles of antisocial or delinquent acts become self-perpetuating when parents fail to monitor, or react to, their children's misbehaviour. The other theory, by contrast, attributes the observed link between adolescent maladjustment and uninvolved-indifferent parenting to the lack of an intimate, affectionate, emotional relationship between parent and child.

According to this view, parental emotional rejection of the child breeds emotional difficulties in early childhood by disrupting the formation of a secure attachment (see Chapter 5). During adolescence, teenagers who continue to feel unloved and ignored by their parents may react by internalising the rejection and becoming depressed and low in self-esteem. On the other hand, if they externalise their emotional problems, the result may be aggressive criminal behaviour. Again, cycles may become self-perpetuating in the context of low parental monitoring or failure to intervene effectively when their children's problems are drawn to their attention by authorities outside the family.

In support of the monitoring hypothesis, Albert Bandura (1989) suggested that teenage boys' aggressive delinquency could result from their parents' disengaged or laissez-faire disciplinary methods. Delinquent sons frequently have mothers who assumed 'an attitude of passive intolerance' when directly confronted with evidence of misbehaviour. On the other hand, Diana Baumrind (1978) argued in favour of the warmth theory when she suggested that children who experience emotional neglect come to regard their parents as untrustworthy and pawns of the social order – a situation that undermines children's motivation to conform to their parents' or society's rules.

On the basis of studies of delinquent and non-delinquent boys in Queensland, Michael Siegal (1985) concluded that delinquents may actually prefer authoritarian parental discipline, not only to laissez-faire methods but even to democratic-authoritative childrearing. His subjects included twenty 14-year-old offenders who had been apprehended by the police, tried and incarcerated in a government correction facility for minors. A control group of twenty Brisbane boys chosen to match the offenders in age, IQ and family economic circumstances was also interviewed.

Siegal asked the two groups of boys to consider a set of hypothetical crimes. Some of the crimes were depicted cold-bloodedly, others included mitigating circumstances of various kinds. As compared with the non-delinquents, the offending boys made no allowances for economic hardship or emotional stress in their judgment of the criminals or in their recommendations for sentencing or punishment. They advocated equally harsh sentences for acts of theft, assault and arson committed by poverty-stricken or recently bereaved perpetrators as when no such mitigating circumstances were mentioned. Their explanations and recommendations regarding a

brain-damaged perpetrator were likewise more punitive than the non-delinquent group's. Delinquents spoke of 'putting the offender away' or keeping him locked up, whereas the non-delinquents mentioned hospitalisation and therapy.

Siegal concluded that:

> … behaviourally disordered youth are less likely to discriminate among degrees of responsibility underlying violations of the law … [Thus] delinquents may not view those who transgress as deserving of more autonomy but as requiring what is perceived to be authoritative, firm control and intervention … The issue for offenders may not be whether a law-breaker's actions are controllable but rather that he should have been stopped in the first place. (p. 91)

Siegal considered the possibility that these delinquents' preferences for forceful, autocratic parental control as a curb against misbehaviour might represent a 'post-hoc rationalization', or an attempt to blame their parents for their own delinquent behaviour, when this had not been the real cause. However, after surveying a range of British and North American studies of male delinquents, he concluded that parenting is genuinely implicated as a cause of delinquency. According to his reading of this evidence:

> … unclear rules, a lack of differentiation among situations and the absence of a noncritical parental interest are factors which contribute to children's problem behaviour … composite measures of family management techniques tend to be the most predictive of male delinquency. Altogether, the evidence suggests that a perceived lack of control underlying parents' childrearing techniques plays a considerable role. (p. 93)

Siegal also concluded, from another study of non-delinquents in Brisbane, that Australian teenagers in general take a relatively benign view of autocratic parental discipline. When asked to evaluate the discipline tactics used by a group of hypothetical fathers, these Queensland pupils rated physical punishment more favourably than permissive discipline or non-violent, love-oriented disapproval. Even inductive reasoning, the technique favoured by most parents and psychologists, was not seen by Australian 13- to 18-year-olds as any more effective or desirable than autocratically punitive slapping or smacking.

Family violence

Fortunately, in Australia, even verbal hostility appears to be used much less often than avoidance, discussion or argument to resolve adolescents' disagreements with their parents, and physical violence is infrequent in normal Australian and New Zealand families (Mathias, 1992). Nevertheless, when family violence does arise in adolescence, it can have serious repercussions throughout the remainder of the lifespan. A study of cycles of violence in New Zealand families found that mothers who were abused by their husbands tended to use similar forms of violence against their offspring. Thus New Zealand adolescents and younger children in families where husbands physically abused their wives were doubly at risk of physical attack – from their abusive fathers and from their abused mothers. Similarly, in New Zealand homes where husbands verbally abused their wives, mothers directed similar verbal abuse against their children. Violence triggered in one segment of the family unit was inclined to spread throughout the family and to beget further violence (Caspi, Lynam, Moffitt & Silva, 1993).

When asked about their own parents' behaviour at home when they were children, these abusive New Zealand mothers recalled frequent episodes in which they had been subjected to violence during childhood and adolescence. These results doubly confirmed the intergenerational transmission of family violence – violence in the couple relationship leads to violent treatment of offspring which, in turn, is likely to lead to further violence when the abused children have offspring of their own. However, it is important to point out that such family continuities in violent behaviour are not universal or inevitable. In one Sydney study, only 37 per cent of abusive mothers and 17 per cent of abusive fathers reported that they had, themselves, been abused while growing up (Mathias, 1992).

Another, more optimistic, finding of Caspi et al.'s New Zealand study was that, even in troubled families, physical violence and sexual abuse were far less common than purely verbal forms of abuse such as threats, insults, mockery and swearing. In the United States, the results of recent large-scale surveys similarly suggest that verbal violence (such as insults, nagging or swearing) and minor acts of aggression against property (such as throwing things or slamming doors) may occur as often as once a month in some 25 per cent of normal families with no history of criminal or psychiatric problems, while minor physical aggression (pushing, slapping, hitting) is reported as arising approximately once a year in these same families (Straus & Sweet, 1991).

In Australia, homeless youth frequently reported having left home owing to family violence (Pears & Noller, 1995). In one Queensland sample, 73 per cent of homeless young people had encountered abuse while still at home, ranging from hitting and slapping to broken noses, broken arms, burns, having one's head split open and violent rape (Pears & Noller, 1995). Almost half of these adolescents and young adults (48 per cent) reported that violence in their homes had occurred on a daily basis. Perhaps not surprisingly, even after they left their violent families these youth frequently engaged in self-destructive behaviours such as drug abuse.

Nonetheless, despite frequent media coverage of violent family homicide, extreme forms of violence entailing serious physical injury remain relatively rare occurrences in the United States population as a whole, as is the case in Australia, New Zealand and Britain.

Adolescents and substance abuse

Though abuse of alcohol and drugs is a correlate of indifferent parenting, most teenagers do some experimenting with alcohol and cigarettes, regardless of their parents' methods of discipline. Indeed, being allowed to smoke cigarettes or drink alcohol at home is viewed as one of the hallmarks of maturity by many teenagers in Australia (Farnill, 1987), New Zealand (Beaglehole, Eyles & Harding, 1978) and the United States (Urberg & Robbins, 1981). Freedom to indulge in these 'vices' testifies to their emancipation and maturity as fully fledged equals of their parents.

These habits are also sources of intense intergenerational controversy during early and middle adolescence. Most teenagers hope for greater autonomy to decide whether to drink or smoke than their parents are willing to accord them (Rosenthal, 1982). The fact that adults make use of a wide range of legal and illegal drugs for relaxation and recreation helps to explain the attractiveness of these substances to the contemporary teenager. But it is also true that simply being seen to hold a cigarette or a can of beer

Being seen with a cigarette can be valued by some adolescents as public proof of maturity status.

is valued by some adolescents as public proof of being grown up, sophisticated or 'cool'.

While these attractions are somewhat independent of the substance used, the various drugs commonly taken by teenagers differ in their effects on behaviour and development. Frequency of use and extent of physiological and psychological dependency on any given drug are likewise differentiating factors. The two drugs abused most commonly by adolescents are tobacco and alcohol.

Cigarette smoking

Accurate awareness of the health risks posed by tobacco has caused a decline in cigarette use by adults in Australia and New Zealand in recent years. But a great many teenagers continue to take up the habit. One large-scale survey (Holman et al., 1986) of Western Australian high school students revealed that more than 25 per cent of 15-year-olds smoked, and about one in five 13- and 14-year-olds. Throughout this age range, cigarette smoking was found to be more common among girls than boys and among country more than urban residents. Regular surveys conducted over recent decades suggest that cigarette use by Australian teenagers has declined in the wake of the anti-smoking campaigns initiated in the early 1980s, from a peak at age 15 of 40 per cent in 1977 to 35 per cent in 1983 and 28 per cent in 1993 (Australian Bureau of Statistics, 1993).

But after conducting a later study of the smoking habits of a group of over 6000 Canberra adolescents aged 13 to 17 years, D. G. Byrne, A. E. Byrne and M. I. Reinhart (1993) concluded that cigarette smoking is not a declining problem, at least among adolescents. Despite widespread awareness of the serious health risks posed by tobacco, their results indicated that young Australian adolescents are still taking up the smoking habit in large numbers. Indeed, the investigators described the rate of cigarette uptake by adolescent girls as 'particularly alarming' (p. 91) and concluded that tobacco-related health problems will pose a serious threat to older Australian women in future years.

Family and peer group influences both contribute to the uptake of smoking. In fact, out of 23 studies exploring the relationship between cigarette use by parents and offspring, a positive link was found in 19 of them, or 83 per cent of the research (Peterson & Peterson, 1986). In general, children take up smoking earlier and more heavily if both their parents smoke than if only one parent smokes. Older siblings' smoking is also found to increase the chances of a younger brother or sister taking up the habit in the United States (Brunswick & Messeri, 1984), in Australia (Peterson & Peterson, 1986) and among Pakeha children in New Zealand (Beaglehole, Eyles & Harding, 1978). But for some unexplained reason the use of cigarettes by Maori adolescents aged 13 to 17 bears no important relationship to whether or not their older brothers or sisters happen to be smokers

(Stanhope & Prior, 1975). Maori teenagers smoke more than Pakehas of the same age and sex, and more Maori girls than Maori boys are regular smokers.

The fact that the use of cigarettes by older family members in most cultures so strongly predicts the teenager's attraction to the habit has motivated some parents to quit smoking, not so much out of consideration for their own health as from a desire to avoid seriously handicapping the fitness and longevity of their children. In fact, when parents do quit smoking, for whatever reason, they substantially reduce their children's attraction to the habit.

One study of 344 Western Australian children between the ages of 10 and 14 showed that those children who had formerly been exposed to models of smoking in the family, but who presently lived in a household containing only ex-smokers, were almost indistinguishable from their classmates who had never been exposed to the use of cigarettes in their own homes (Peterson & Peterson, 1986). They had little intention of becoming smokers themselves in the future, and had fewer friends who smoked. They believed that cigarettes had more personal and social disadvantages of the types listed in Table 12.7 than their classmates who shared a household with an active smoker.

In fact, children in ex-smoking and non-smoking households agreed with less than one-third of the possible benefits of smoking listed in Table 12.7 (these were gleaned from the opinions of Australian smokers as well as from research studies and cigarette commercials). But when it came to the costs and disadvantages of smoking, the average Western Australian child from a family without active smokers endorsed about 80 per cent of the specific problems listed in the second column of Table 12.7.

Peers may also pressure each other to experiment with cigarettes. As noted in Table 12.7, another reason for taking up smoking can be the teenager's wish to gain acceptance into a peer group of smokers, or to impress members of the opposite sex with one's 'bravado' or 'maturity' as a user of cigarettes. But attitudes about smoking in society at large have undergone radical changes in Australia and New Zealand in recent years and so the adolescent's motivation to smoke is becoming two-edged. Contemporary teenagers are increasingly made to face the fact that, although some members of the peer group to which they aspire may be attracted by smoking, others will be repelled by it. Thus peer conformity may cultivate anti-smoking feelings in some teenagers just as it fosters the uptake of cigarette smoking in others.

Box 12.3 contains an exercise to help you judge what meaning smoking has for the adolescents in your own social circle.

When male and female smokers and non-smokers are compared, a different set of factors predicts cigarette uptake by girls as contrasted with boys (Byrne,

TABLE 12.7 Benefits and costs of smoking according to Australian teenagers

TABLE 12.7 Benefits and costs of smoking according to Australian teenagers

Reason	Benefits of smoking	Costs of smoking	Reason	Benefits of smoking	Costs of smoking
Social focus	Gain friends Dating partner smokes Be like an admired adult Increase enjoyment of parties	Parents disapprove Friends disapprove Dating partner disapproves Bad breath	Self-determination	Be stylish Assert own rights Proves you're not weak	Causes trouble with authorities Irresponsible towards non-smokers, and the community
Health focus	Feel good, relaxed Control weight, drinking Overcome stress, anxiety	Causes cancer More colds, flu Causes jittery nerves Less fit for sports Premature ageing Saps energy Makes you feel sick Can kill Causes heart disease	Pleasure, hedonism	Tastes good Combats boredom Gives you a lift	Dulls taste buds Bad odour in hair and clothes Expensive
			Achievement focus	Dulls intellect	Interferes with school work
Independence	Prove one's independence	Addictive, can't quit			

Source: Peterson & Peterson (1986), reproduced with permission.

BOX 12.3 **Activity suggestion**
Is smoking shocking?

On a tour of the Hebrides in 1773, Samuel Johnson was so distressed by cigarette smoking that he exclaimed: 'Smoking is a shocking thing – blowing smoke out of our mouths into other people's mouths, eyes and noses, and having the same thing done to us' (Evans, 1978, p. 640).

Many adults today have similar feelings about smokers. But what do contemporary teenagers think? To get some idea, ask as many adolescents as you can to complete the accompanying checklist (anonymously).

Imaginary situations. For each situation in the list, imagine that you have a choice of two companions who are identical in every way except that one smokes cigarettes and the other does not. Pick the companion you would prefer by ticking the appropriate column.

Scoring. To gauge the extent to which smoking is perceived as a social handicap, count up the number of times each subject explicitly selected the non-smoking friend. Totals ranging from 5 to 10 were average for Western Australian 13- and 14-year-olds in 1985 (Peterson & Peterson, 1986).

Situations	The friend who smokes	The non-smoking friend	It doesn't matter
1. Going in a car to a drive-in movie with:	☐	☐	☐
2. Sitting next to on a plane or bus trip:	☐	☐	☐
3. Bringing to dinner at my home:	☐	☐	☐
4. Going to dinner at a restaurant with:	☐	☐	☐
5. Going to a party with:	☐	☐	☐
6. Spending an evening at the home of:	☐	☐	☐
7. Playing sport with:	☐	☐	☐
8. Going on a double date with:	☐	☐	☐
9. Sitting next to in class:	☐	☐	☐
10. Going camping with:	☐	☐	☐
11. Borrowing clothes from to wear to a party:	☐	☐	☐
12. Studying for exams with:	☐	☐	☐

Attitudes to cigarette smoking vary with culture, historical era, family background and individual factors.

Byrne & Reinhart, 1993). Male Australian adolescents are found to be more concerned than their female peers with the adverse effects of cigarette smoking on sports performance. Girls express only slight concern over becoming less successful when playing sport if they smoke and, unlike boys, see no adverse effects of tobacco on physical fitness. Poor self-esteem was linked with smoking in both sexes, but again its degree of importance differed between the sexes – girls who took up smoking were less likely than boys to be drawn exclusively from the ranks of students with poor self-concepts.

The factors that best predicted cigarette uptake by girls were themselves a source of concern. It seems that many Australian girls still believe that a girl with a cigarette between her fingers is more attractive to boys, and likely to be more popular with her female peers, than a girl who refuses to smoke. Girls also believed that smoking was an effective means of achieving and maintaining an attractively slim physique (see Chapter 10). Thus female Australian teenagers who smoked viewed cigarettes as more of an advantage for peer popularity than did non-smokers, while those who did not smoke but intended to in the future more often believed themselves to be unattractively overweight.

These results have obvious implications for health education aimed at the prevention of tobacco-related illnesses in men and women. According to Byrne, Byrne and Reinhart (1993, p. 94):

> In terms of smoking prevention programs, the present results indicate that broad emphasis also needs to be given to the perceived linkages between smoking, health and fitness, and the notion that smoking endows social popularity. For boys, the evidence suggests that special attention should be given to developing strategies to overcome peer pressure to smoke, to developing adequate self-esteem as a nonsmoker, and to emphasise the fitness benefits of smoking abstinence. For girls, there would seem to be a need to focus on the importance of mothers' smoking habits, to emphasise the links between non-

smoking and favourable body image, and to encourage resistance to pressure from exemplar individuals and groups.

Drinking alcohol

Adolescents' drinking habits are also directly related to their parents' use of, and attitudes towards, alcohol. Many contemporary Australian and New Zealand parents view moderate social drinking as acceptable, or even as a desirable social skill, once the child reaches the legal minimum drinking age of 18 years. In fact, studies show that a majority of adolescents throughout the world take their first drink in their parents' company and with their parents' blessing (Jessor & Jessor, 1980).

Parents' own drinking habits predict drinking behaviour and drinking problems in their offspring. Adolescents who become heavy drinkers or alcoholics very often have one or more parents with the same problem. A genetic disposition towards alcohol abuse is suggested by the finding that biological offspring of alcoholics who grow up in non-drinking adoptive homes run a heightened risk of becoming alcoholics themselves in adolescence or early adulthood (Holden, 1985).

Over and above the salient influence of parents, however, the peer group, the community's laws about drinking, routes of access to alcohol and the adolescent's individual temperament can all contribute in important ways to the uptake of drinking. A study of New York adolescents aged 15 to 18 years showed, in fact, that peers, parents and personality all made separate and statistically independent contributions to alcohol use (Brook, Whiteman, Gordon, Nomura & Brook, 1986). Adolescents whose parents drank were more likely to have taken up drinking by age 17 or 18 than those whose parents were non-drinkers. But when parents' influence was statistically controlled, peers were also found to make a separate and substantial contribution to adolescent drinking. Thus even an adolescent with non-drinking parents was liable to become a drinker if he or she belonged to a peer group that approved of alcohol and made it freely available at parties or other social events. Finally, independently of these influences, teenagers whose temperaments were impulsive, energetic and outgoing and who placed a high premium on their independence were also more likely to be drinkers than placid, dependent introverts.

Other longitudinal studies of adolescents who drink heavily suggest that an opposite direction of developmental influence also operates, reinforcing the importance of studying development as a lifespan process. These studies show that teenage drinking problems may have consequences for the development of personality during mature adulthood. When the subjects reached university, students who had taken up heavy drinking as adolescents were more exuberant and sociable than their colleagues, but also suffered more from boredom, loneliness, unhappiness

Parental influences on adolescents' preferences to drink, or not drink, alcohol are more salient in Australia than in Norway or the United States.

and restless discontent. Due perhaps to anxiety about their drinking problem, they were less likely to continue to participate in research on alcohol use. But those who did remain with the studies as adults reported strained or distant relationships with their parents, many of whom were also problem drinkers (Conger & Petersen, 1984).

Interviews with 149 Australian adolescents, plus corresponding samples of approximately 100 teenagers from France, Norway and the United States, were used by Barbara Bank and her associates to test several contrasting theories of parents' and peers' contributions to the initiation of a drinking habit (Bank et al., 1985). One theory relates to the process of *internalisation* described in Chapter 8. Bank and her colleagues argued that teenagers may decide to drink in emulation of the behaviour of their parents or peers with whom they feel special bonds of unity or identification. Support for this theory was found in all four countries. The theory of internalisation did a better job than the second theory, known as *instrumentality*, of predicting teenage drinking patterns in all four nations. The instrumentality theory, which gained little support overall in the data, predicted that adolescents would either drink or refuse to drink for instrumental, or pragmatic, purposes. Thus one might accept a drink in order to win favour with the social companion offering drinks

around, while another might abstain to please a parent who disapproved of the use of alcohol.

Interesting contrasts in patterns of parental and peer influence were noted across the four cultures. In Australia and France, but not in Norway or the United States, parents were seen to be the major instigators of the adolescent's internalised drinking or non-drinking preferences. These results supported the researchers' initial prediction that: 'Adolescents are more likely to share drinking (or nondrinking) opportunities with their parents in Australia and France than in Norway or the USA' (p. 173).

In the United States and Norway, peer behaviours were more internalised and consequently exerted a stronger effect on adolescent drinking than in France or Australia. The researchers concluded that variations across cultures in family climate and parental discipline styles, and the tendency for adults to take a moralistic stance on alcohol, could all help to account for these important national differences in the balance of influence by parents as compared with peers on adolescent drinking.

Other drugs

In proportion to the number of teenagers who drink alcohol and smoke cigarettes, relatively few Australian and New Zealand adolescents make use of other legal or illegal chemical stimulants, hallucinogens or tranquillisers. Nevertheless, the small numbers of teenagers who do 'sniff' petrol, 'snort' cocaine, 'pop' pep pills, 'drop' acid (LSD) or 'shoot' heroin are the focus of serious concern, not only for their parents but also for teachers, members of the legal and medical professions and the community at large. The fact that most of the drugs abused by teenagers are not only illegal, but also highly expensive and addictive, links their use to other crimes such as theft, prostitution and drug-pushing. Without enough income to support a drug habit, the adolescent drug-user is apt to resort to these criminal pursuits as a way of finding money. The risk of spreading HIV by sharing infected needles is yet another reason for serious community concern.

Worried parents may find comfort in two important facts about adolescent drug abuse. In the first place, the high profile of the teenage drug addict displayed in the media is unwarranted and potentially misleading, in view of the relatively small number of adolescent users of hard drugs in Australia and New Zealand today. In fact, even at older ages, illicit drug use is described as 'a relatively minor problem' when compared with abuse of tobacco and alcohol (Holman et al., 1986, p. 62). For example, in Western Australia, crimes relating to alcohol are found to outnumber those relating to illegal drugs by a factor of more than ten to one.

In the second place, parents' own efforts do make a big difference in protecting their offspring from the risks of drug abuse. Recent research shows that young people who report close, warm relationships with their parents rarely engage in illicit drug use, even in the face of strong peer pressure to experiment (Glynn, 1981; Dobkin, Tremblay, Masse & Vitaro, 1995). In a longitudinal study of 139 San Francisco adolescents and their parents, Diana Baumrind (1991) discovered that an authoritative parenting style (see page 400) was a particularly strong predictor of the teenager's capacity to resist the temptation to experiment with illicit drugs, even in an environment like the San Francisco Bay area, where adolescent drug use is widespread. Baumrind obtained her first measures of parenting style when the children were four years old. She followed up the families in middle childhood and when the offspring were aged 15. Impressively, she found that parents who had consistently over the decade used an authoritative childrearing style, which combined high levels of warmth and affection with high demands and a clear set of rules, were universally successful in avoiding the problem of drug abuse when their children encountered the temptation to experiment with drugs in early adolescence. She concluded that authoritative parenting, though not a necessary condition to prevent adolescent drug abuse, was a sufficient one. In other words, parents who worry about adolescent substance abuse may have a solution at hand in the form of consistent, responsible, yet affectionate parenting.

Even during adulthood, abuse of hard drugs is a less frequent problem than the high media profile of drug addiction might suggest. Alcohol and tobacco pose far more real and serious risks, as Figure 12.6 indicates. Within a single year in Australia (1984) many more people died from the effects of cigarettes and alcohol than from all other drugs combined, including sleeping tablets (Australian Bureau of Statistics, 1993).

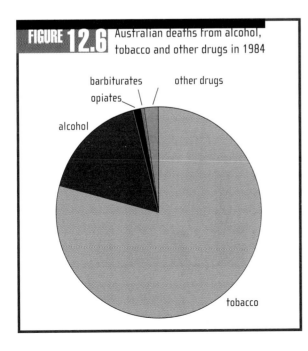

FIGURE 12.6 Australian deaths from alcohol, tobacco and other drugs in 1984

Adolescent suicide

The dramatic increase in adolescent suicide in recent years is a source of great concern to parents and professionals alike. In Australia, there was a doubling of the rate of suicide by boys aged 15 to 19 years between 1965 and 1985 (Kosky, 1987), with a further increase from 1985 to 1988 (Davis, 1992). At present, the suicide rates for adolescents and for the adult population appear to be levelling off, but the incidence of teenage suicide remains a serious problem. In New Zealand, there was a 53 per cent increase overall in male suicide from 1973 to 1988, and a more dramatic increase of 127 per cent by young males aged 15 to 24 years (Pritchard, 1992). Female suicide statistics in Australia and New Zealand over the same period were more varied but, generally, significantly fewer girls than boys killed themselves. However, in both countries, adolescent female suicide increased compared with that by older members of the female population.

After comparing teenage suicide patterns in Australia and New Zealand with contemporary statistics for 19 other nations, including Finland, France, Greece, Ireland, Japan and the United States, Colin Pritchard (1992) reached a disturbing conclusion. Australia and New Zealand together stood out from every other country in the survey for their disproportionately high rates of teenage suicide. In fact, Pritchard found that 'Australia and New Zealand were the only countries in the West whose male and female youth suicide levels exceeded the general rates [of suicide in the population]' (p. 616).

Why are Australian and New Zealand teenagers more prone than their counterparts in other modern, industrialised societies to kill themselves? What could make teenagers in these countries more eager to take their own lives than older members of the population? These findings are disheartening, as is the picture presented by Pritchard's multinational analysis of the absolute levels of teenage suicide in contemporary Australia and New Zealand. The frequency of youthful male suicides in Australia in 1987 was greater than in all but three other nations (Finland, Switzerland and Canada) and New Zealand's was the sixth highest. Relative to the population, more teenage girls killed themselves in New Zealand than in all but three other countries (Austria, Denmark and Switzerland).

Three other disturbing features of youthful suicide patterns in Australia and New Zealand have been noted (McIntosh, 1989):

1. Teenagers have made increasing use of firearms to commit suicide in recent years.
2. Rural teenagers are more likely than urban teenagers to commit suicide, especially in Australia. For example, a 1992 New South Wales survey revealed a five-fold increase in male teenage suicide in remote districts between 1964 and 1988.

3. Teenagers from the indigenous minority group (Aborigines in Australia and Maoris in New Zealand) are overrepresented among suicide victims.

The increasing use of guns is a source of concern, since teenagers who shoot themselves are unlikely to fail in the attempt at suicide and are more likely to take innocent victims with them than those who use techniques such as drowning or taking sleeping pills. Thus the chances of successful psychological intervention in response to a teenager's desperate plea for help are consequently minimised.

The high rate of suicide by Maori and Aboriginal teenagers is particularly disturbing. This finding parallels a similar pattern observed in other countries. For example, in the United States, native American Indians kill themselves more often than Anglo-Americans. But black and Hispanic teenagers in the United States are not overrepresented among suicide victims, so the problem appears to run deeper than simply being confined to ethnic minority groups or those suffering socioeconomic disadvantage. (The special problem of Aboriginal male suicide is examined in greater depth in the next section of this chapter.)

Official suicide statistics undoubtedly underestimate the actual rate of suicide, especially among teenagers (Davis, 1992). Supposedly accidental deaths from poisoning, drowning and motor vehicles are sometimes veiled suicides. Suicidal despair is more frequent than actual suicidal death, as reflected in estimates of attempted suicide by teenagers. A study in Perth showed that for every 'successful' suicide by a male aged 15 to 19, there were 14 additional 'unsuccessful' attempted suicides. Among Western Australian girls, there were 117 suicide attempts for every official recorded death by suicide (Avery & Winokur, 1978). About 40 per cent of Australian young people who end up as suicide victims have a history of one or more earlier attempts (Davis, 1992).

Hospital admissions for attempted suicides by Australian boys and girls doubled from the early 1980s to the early 1990s (Pritchard, 1992). In 1987, one in every seven deaths of Australian teenage boys was deemed to be suicide (Kosky, 1987). Across the age period from 15 to 24, suicide was likewise ranked as the second highest killer of males and the third most common cause of death among females. Many explanations have been given for the despair that drives teenagers to try to kill themselves. Family problems, including communication with the father (Cantor, 1977) and the feeling of being unwanted by one or both parents (Rosenkrantz, 1978), have been linked with adolescent suicide in some studies, and interventions to improve family communication have proven beneficial for some teenage suicide attempters. Nevertheless, the overall reason for so many adolescents deliberately seeking death during one of the most promising and exciting phases in life remains as mysterious as these deaths are traumatic for bereaved friends and family members.

Aboriginal suicide

Suicide by Aboriginal teenagers and young adults has also increased substantially in recent years from previously very low levels (Hunter, 1991). In the Kimberley Region of Western Australia, an area nearly twice the size of the state of Victoria with a population of approximately 14 000 Aborigines and a similar number of non-Aboriginal Australians, there were 25 Aboriginal suicides between 1957 and 1990. Of these a total of eight (32 per cent) took place during a single year, between late 1988 and late 1989. Alarmed by this indication of a sudden increase in despair among the rural Aboriginal community, Ernest Hunter (1991) made a detailed post-mortem examination of the life circumstances, personality patterns and family histories of the eight Aboriginal males who killed themselves in the Kimberleys in 1988–89. Seventy-five per cent of these Aboriginal suicide victims were under the age of 21 at the time of death. All died violent deaths: five by hanging, and one each by shooting, self-immolation and a leap from a moving vehicle. When compared with a matched group of Aboriginal teenage boys with no history of severe depression or suicidal behaviour, a number of distinctive characteristics of the eight adolescent suicide victims emerged, as illustrated in Figure 12.7.

Though both groups of Aboriginal boys had a history of heavy drinking, those who had subsequently committed suicide had been inclined to get more completely drunk more often than the boys in the comparison group. The suicide victims were more likely to have lived in town than in segregated

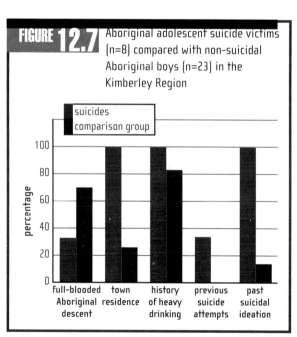

Source: Hunter (1991), Table 2, reproduced with permission.

Aboriginal communities where ancestral traditions are more closely adhered to, and were less likely to be of fully Aboriginal descent. Unsuccessful suicide attempts and suicidal intention had also been significantly more common among the boys who eventually killed themselves, reinforcing the previous suggestion that 'failed' suicide bids by teenagers are a warning sign and should lead to immediate and intensive therapeutic intervention.

According to Hunter, one reason for the drastic increase in youthful suicide in the Kimberleys may be the cumulative effects on Aboriginal adolescents of changing patterns of family life. As Fay Gale (1978) noted, the loss of employment on outback stations, the erosion of cultural and religious traditions and the advent of alcohol has drastically altered the life circumstances of many Aboriginal men in the generation containing the fathers of these teenage suicide victims. She observed that 'the path now followed by so many of the men, from hotel to gaol, is but an inevitable consequence of their loss of status and purpose in society' (p. 2). The consequent loss of successful adult male role models may well have undermined the suicide victims' will to live. As Hunter (1991) explained:

> Children in the 1970s were consequently increasingly confronted by a parental generation in which women 'appeared' economically privileged (in the unrelenting lifescape of poverty a little is a lot, such 'privilege' thus contributing to the vulnerability of Aboriginal women). Particularly in town settings, the conflicts arose around the scarce resources, often over the diversion of sustenance income to alcohol. Male role models were further compromised by absences (incarceration, illness and premature mortality) and the functional unavailability of intoxication and alcoholism. In many settings with heavy drinking the entire community is drawn into a weekly or fortnightly cycle of deprivation and 'abundance'. (p. 206)

The influences of family and friends

As we have seen, when deciding whether to experiment with cigarettes, alcohol or drugs, adolescents are often torn between their parents' disapproval of these activities and their peers' approval of them. Although friends may sometimes assist in the process of becoming emotionally independent of parents, it is also true that peers can hinder the individual adolescent's attainment of mature self-sufficiency. Genuine autonomy is curtailed when adolescents do things they don't really want to do (such as taking a drink or smoking a joint of marijuana) for the sake of gaining the approval of the peer group. Pressures on teenagers to behave according to the peer group's unspoken rules can be extremely intense, especially during mid-adolescence.

Conformity to peer pressures is shaped by culture as well as by age.

Peer pressures are exceptionally hard to resist if the teenager is shy, has recently entered a new social environment with the family's geographical move or entry into high school, or is ambitious enough to aspire to join a peer group of higher status than the immediate circle of friends. In the face of such parent–peer counter-pressures, the adolescent's chosen stance may be less a pull for independence than a yielding to whichever dependency ties are stronger, or more endangered, in a given situation.

Parent–peer cross-pressures

Clay Brittain (1963) questioned the stereotype that depicts adolescents as mindless conformists who blindly yield to peer pressures at every opportunity. He developed a set of stories, each structured around the indecision of an adolescent girl who had to choose between two alternatives, one favoured by her parents and one by her friends. For example, in one story the heroine's friends argue that she should not 'tell on' a culprit for fear of jeopardising peer group solidarity, whereas her parents thought it was unjust for the group as a whole to be punished for one individual's misdeeds.

The subjects who responded to Brittain's dilemmas were 338 girls from rural and urban high schools in Alabama and Georgia. To test these girls' conformity to the stated opinion of their parents versus their peers, independently of any preference for specific answers to the dilemmas, Brittain retested the students one or two weeks later using the same stories, but reversing the alternatives supposedly endorsed by parents and friends. When a girl chose either the parental or peer alternative on both occasions, she was clearly reflecting one or other group's pressure rather than her own personal decision as to which was the better course of action.

As he had anticipated, Brittain found that the area of behaviour largely determined which of the two cross-pressures the girls yielded to. Most girls conformed to parents' views about moral issues like honesty or peer solidarity and yielded to parents' opinions about conflicts over how to achieve school success, what kind of a boy to date, how to let a boy know she wants to go out with him and which extracurricular or vocational achievements to strive for. But they favoured the peer view on which classes to take in school and how to dress. Brittain felt that these differences could be accounted for by the following basic assumptions:

1. Adolescents view parents' and peers' expertise differently, so peer advice is chosen for some decisions and parental advice for others. Career choice, for example, is an area where parents' wider experience and direct contact with the world of work make their advice more valuable, while peers are seen to know more about contemporary fashion, sport, music and films.
2. Adolescents fear peer group rejection if they appear to be noticeably different from the group (e.g. they conform to peer opinions in the highly visible domain of clothing fashions).
3. Adolescents wish to avoid separation from friends. (This, in addition to presumed greater knowledge, explains conformity to their friends' choices of school classes.)
4. Perceived similarity to parents is greater in some situations and similarity to peers is greater in others. Adolescents conform to the person seen as most relevant to the specific situation.

Several of these concepts are illustrated in Box 12.4, where a real-life version of Brittain's moral conflict over the collective responsibility of the group for 'the sins of a few' is described in the first part of the entry. Later, Louise's father describes how she was caught in a cross-fire between her parents, her peers and her own opinion about whether or not she should attend the school dance. Her compromise was arriving late, thereby gaining peer approval, which she hoped might partly compensate for her unwillingness to go at all.

The fact that she had learned to dance through peer imitation without adult instruction suggests that, in this area, peer competence was respected. The incident in which the adult chaperones turned the spotlights on the seated male students is another instance of adult–peer cross-pressure. While the adults were pressuring the boys to dance, the male peer group, by remaining seated, silently pressured each individual boy to avoid appearing different.

Finally, Louise herself faced a powerful parent–peer conflict over whether or not to conform to her 13-year-old group's predominantly short hairstyle. In his explanation of this conflict, her father expressed some surprise over the fact that she had chosen a reference group of her own age in her preference for short hair, rather than that of the slightly older girls who were wearing their hair long. Her professed concern with the opinion of her age-mates makes sense in light of Brittain's hypothesis that looking physically different from members of one's group of

BOX 12.4 Parent–peer pressures and the dilemmas of a school dance

The following diary entry, written by Louise's father, describes several conflicts and cross-pressures which 13-year-old Louise and some of her peers faced at the time of a school dance.

16 December 1961. The junior high dance was held last evening, the close of school before Christmas holiday. The school authorities had threatened to cancel it if there was misbehavior among any of the student body. There was, of course, as there inevitably must have been in the face of such a threat, so the dance was duly cancelled, compelling good and bad alike to atone for the sins of a few. Better judgment evidently prevailed at the eleventh hour and we heard, when Louise got home from school yesterday, that the dance was on after all. She, however, didn't want to go because at the previous dance there were no boys, the school having thoughtfully staged it on the same evening as a football game. But she usually protests these affairs, and finally consented on condition that she'd arrive late. She said the others make a fuss over late arrivals. She did so with a vengeance, having remembered the time as 8:00 when actually it was 7:00. So she was the latest one there, but there were boys too and she was monopolized by one boy, Maurice, whom she seldom sees in school, they being in different classes.

Much of these dances is individual performance: one girl pantomiming with records for the entertainment of the group, and the girls as a group shimmying (it's now a brand new dance called the Twist) for the entertainment of the boys. Louise, with virtually no other instruction except the emulation she does at these school affairs, has caught on very well to social dancing: a process of self-instruction I long wondered about, seeing how the adult dancing schools flourish. But they, I guess, have an almost all-male student body. The boys apparently do not learn to dance as the girls do, and each school dance strains the imaginative resources of the dance managers to devise ways of getting the boys out on the floor. Last night the method was to turn a searchlight on the non-dancers, and it worked to a limited extent. Louise wore lipstick and the girls all assured her she should do so regularly; but she wisely decided to save it for dances when it would be noticed. She was one of the few eighth-grade girls who did not wear high heels, and one of only three who still have long hair. Keeping her hair long is a never-ending battle between me and conformity. Ultimately conformity will get it cut and curled unless in the meantime long hair comes back with younger teenagers, as it has with the older teenagers. Looking around in church I see only the very elderly women are uniformly short-haired; and I wonder this does not have its effect on the younger ones.

associates is dreaded. However, there is also some justification for the diarist's suggestion that conformity to a slightly older group than her immediate peers would make more sense for Louise, since this was the group she would be joining before her hair would have time to grow long again.

Cross-cultural comparisons of parent–peer relations

Another intriguing insight into parent–peer cross-pressures arose out of Urie Bronfenbrenner's (1967) comparisons of adolescents in England, Germany, the United States and the former Soviet Union. He found that in both English-speaking countries, adolescents spent more time in peer-dominated settings than German youths did, whereas the more family-dominated lifestyle of teenagers in Germany encouraged a strong adherence to the adult-approved alternative to dilemmas like those used by Brittain (1963). Unlike their German counterparts, American teenagers were almost as ready to follow the prompting of peers as of adults, while English teenagers were more peer-oriented than adult-oriented. This was especially significant since several of the dilemmas that Bronfenbrenner used depicted peer pressures towards antisocial or illegal activities. In the former Soviet Union, peer influence was weaker than in the United States.

However, the most important difference between these two countries emerged when Bronfenbrenner told his subjects that their answers, together with their names, would be posted on a bulletin board for their peers to examine. Under these conditions, American adolescents were driven to profess an increased willingness to follow their companions' antisocial lead, whereas Russian teenagers expressed an even stronger adherence to adult values than under the private conditions. Bronfenbrenner concluded that in the former Soviet Union peer group pressures tended to reinforce conformity to parental standards, whereas in the United States these two forces were more apt to be in opposition to each other.

Studies of migrant adolescents in Australia have also shown the importance of cultural background in determining adolescents' conformity to parental versus peer cross-pressures (Connell et al., 1975). One questionnaire item asked teenagers how often they found themselves 'using friends to get up the courage to do something parents would disapprove of'. Southern Italian migrant youths reported more use of this strategy than any other group. Asian- and Greek-Australians came next, followed by those from Maltese, Yugoslav and Polish migrant families. Australian-born teenagers and British and Dutch migrants used peers in opposition to parents significantly less often than any of these former groups, but the Germans used this tactic even less often than Anglo-Australians.

Thomas J. Berndt (1979) looked for age differences in conformity to antisocial peer group pressure and prosocial parental pressure with story dilemmas of the same type. His subjects were some 500 American children aged from nine to 18. He found that the peak for stating a willingness to conform to an antisocial peer suggestion occurred at age 15, while conformity to the parental suggestion decreased steadily from the age of nine.

The relationship between parent and peer conformity was not the same for all age groups. Among the youngest children, the two were in opposition to one another; that is, the children who went along with parental directives the most faithfully were the ones least willing to follow their peers in antisocial transgressions. But among 17- and 18-year-olds there was a general factor of conformity which transcended the age of the leader and the type of activity. In other words, the conformists in this age group who expressed greatest eagerness to go along with antisocial peer acts were also the most willing to conform to the prosocial suggestions of parents.

Social involvement with parents and peers

As well as exerting differing influences and pressures on the adolescent, parents and peers also offer teenagers a choice of two different styles of social companionship. There are times when the chance of a relaxed evening or weekend with familiar family members will seem preferable to the stressful bustle of a peer-group activity. Thirteen-year-old Louise would rather have endured the relative monotony of an evening at home with her parents (Box 12.4) than join her peers at a school dance, where novelty and excitement were counterbalanced by peer-group conformity pressures and the fear of social rejection. At other times, peer-group companionship seems the more attractive choice. Box 12.5 shows some of the reasons why peer activities can be more enjoyable than staying at home. Culture may also influence adolescents' choices.

Figure 12.8 shows developmental changes in the levels of emotional intimacy, instrumental helping and conflict in adolescents' interactions with their parents and friends in the United States compared with Japanese families (Takahashi et al., 2002).

Despite differences in the nature of the peer-group activities described in Boxes 12.4 and 12.5, the fact that Louise was 13 when she preferred parental company and 15 when she preferred the society of her peers was also undoubtedly relevant. Several research studies have discovered age-related increases in children's and adolescents' preferences for peer companionship. In one of the first, Bowerman and Kinch (1959) analysed the changes in family-oriented social dependency which took place between Grades 4 and 10 for 686 students in a middle-class district in Seattle, Washington. They found that 75 per cent of the fourth-graders preferred to associate with their families; by the seventh grade this percentage had fallen to 52; and by tenth grade only 15 per cent expressed a clear preference for spending time with

parents. Correspondingly, preference for the company
of peers showed an increase over the grades. The
researchers also found that, on the whole, girls disengaged from family-oriented social dependency sooner
than boys did.

Frank Musgrove (1964) conducted a similar
survey of 778 children from the English Midlands. As
in the American study, a majority of the 9-year-olds
preferred their parents when asked to choose with
whom to attend picnics, football matches and films.
The percentage of parent choices then declined
steadily with increasing age to a low of 2 per cent at
age 15. Growing older seemed to be the only factor
in this preference shift, for Musgrove found no tendency at any age for social dependence on parents to
be related to intelligence level or social-class background.

He also asked 9- and 14-year-olds to choose their
associates for three activities that differed in stressfulness:

1. a party
2. a long and difficult journey
3. 'a situation of great danger'.

Preference for adult, as opposed to peer, companionship increased with the stressfulness of the task for
both age groups. But the younger children also
wanted more adult company than their older
counterparts in all three situations.

In Australia, W. F. Connell and his associates
(1975) offered adolescents the hypothetical choice of
going on a family picnic or attending a barbecue
arranged by friends. The proportion who picked the
latter alternative increased steadily from age 11 to age
16 and then levelled off. However, when they were
asked whether they would find it harder to bear the
disapproval of their parents, of their favourite teacher
or of one of their best friends, more than two-thirds at
each age level said 'parents'. Likewise, over half the
15- to 20-year-old Australians who were still at school
reported that, if they were worried about something,
they would choose to discuss it with one of their
parents in preference to a sibling or a close friend of
either sex. So the preference for peer company seemed
to relate mainly to social enjoyment.

Susan Quine (1973) compared Aboriginal
teenagers in Australia with their Anglo peers on the
question of whose evaluation they were most concerned about – that of parents, teachers or friends.
Again, parents stood out for both races as the people
whose disapproval mattered most (Figure 12.9). Girls
appeared to be slightly more concerned about their
peers' opinions than boys, but this was equally true
among Aboriginal and Anglo groups. Nor did the
pattern of preferences appear to change with the
adolescent's socioeconomic background or level of
academic achievement.

Adolescent friendship

During early adolescence, same-sex friendship is
likely to assume greater importance than the
parent–child relationship or dating a member of the
opposite sex. The typical teenager spends up to three
hours a day in face-to-face interaction with friends,
plus extra contact by telephone (Argyle, 1986).
Adolescents are also much more sophisticated and
complex than children in their social dealings with,
understanding of, and demands on, their friends. One
early observational study of a group of American
adolescent girls resulted in the following portrait of
teenage friendship:

> Best friends may change in a moment; strange
> partnerships may come into being. If we look
> back to adolescence we may be stupified to recall
> friendships with the unlikeliest, most alien of part-
> ners, to whom we were bonded by a momentary
> yet critical mutuality of needs. Even our solid and
> enduring adolescent friendships may turn out, if
> we remember them closely enough, not to have
> been quite so unbroken and harmonious as they
> first appear in retrospect. They may in fact have
> blown hot and cold, responsive to all the rise and
> fall of feeling in self and others. (Douvan &
> Adelson, 1966, p. 179)

This tempestuous, intense and changeable mode
of relating to friends can be contrasted with adult

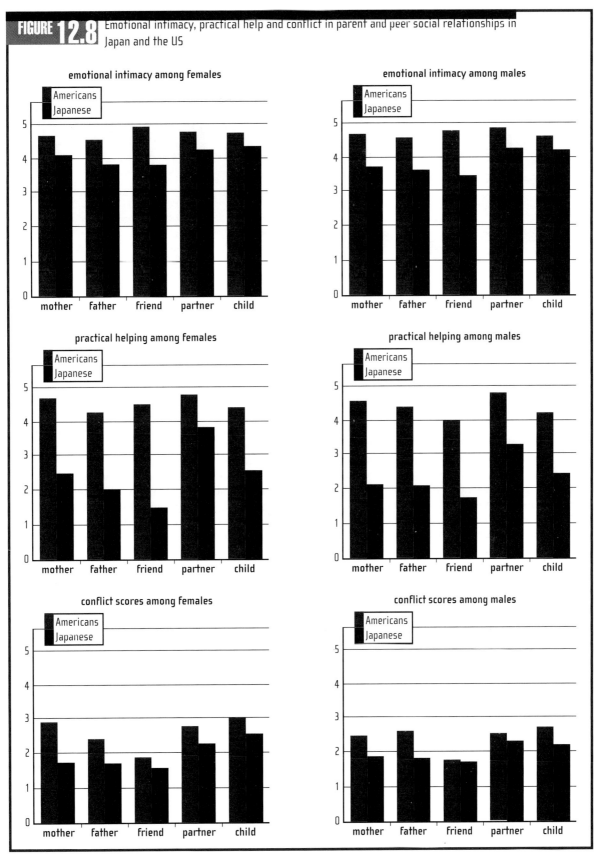

Source: Adapted from Takahashi et al. (2002).

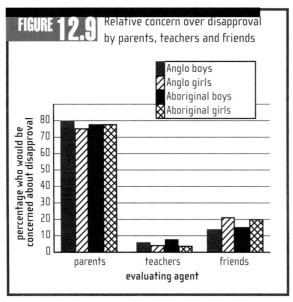

FIGURE 12.9 Relative concern over disapproval by parents, teachers and friends

Legend:
- Anglo boys
- Anglo girls
- Aboriginal boys
- Aboriginal girls

Y-axis: percentage who would be concerned about disapproval (0–80)
X-axis (evaluating agent): parents, teachers, friends

Source: Based on data in Quine (1973).

Intimate friendship with a same-sex peer may mean more during adolescence than at any other stage in life.

friendship which, according to researchers Elizabeth Douvan and Joseph Adelson, is often

> no more than a mutual flight from boredom – a pact against isolation with an amendment against intimacy. The interaction focuses on gossip or on leisure interests; in many cases the friendship centres itself on a game – bridge or golf, let us say, the understanding being that anything that does not bear on the game is gauche, embarrassing, or out of bounds. Those things which are crucial to personal integration, such as a person's history, values, or work, are studiously excluded from the interaction. (p. 178)

These authors went on to suggest that each age-related style of friendship had its own unique advantages and disadvantages. The playmate mode of childhood, with its focus on shared activity and the demand for little more than basic social decency from a friend, encourages wide-ranging interactive social involvement, but lacks the extraordinary depth of adolescent friendship. Consequently, sensitive appreciation of the friend's unique qualities and personality dispositions is of little use to children, but crucial among adolescents. Likewise, for adults who use their marital relationships to satisfy whatever needs for intimacy they may have, relatively superficial relationships with extramarital friends may provide levity and balance.

By contrast, Douvan and Adelson wrote, 'The adolescent does not choose intimate friendship, but is driven to it' (p. 179). One of the driving forces is the absence of any other feasible confidante than a like-sexed peer. Parents can no longer be taken fully into the adolescent's confidence, because of the parents' own preoccupations and also because adolescents need to undo the exclusive emotional ties binding them to their families. Heterosexual friendship, on the other hand, is too new, too superficial and too apt

to be anxiety-provoking to encourage intimacy. But another, more positive factor promoting intimacy between adolescent friends of the same age and sex is the guidance and feedback they can offer on one another's mastery of two important adolescent dilemmas: sexuality and identity. Since these problems are no longer relevant to most adults:

> The adult loses both the misery and the advantages that arise from the adolescent's peculiar openness to inner experience; thus there is little need to examine and share the internal world with others. Adulthood all too often brings with it a retreat into extraversion and, paradoxically, a loss of sensitivity to the other. (p. 178)

Person perception and the understanding of friendship

The ability of friends to understand or think about each other in psychological terms increases abruptly during early adolescence. Steve Duck (1973) found that only 5 per cent of the 12-year-olds he studied made use of psychological or personality qualities such as 'eager', 'uncertain', 'shy' or 'caring' in descriptions of their friends, but the figure rose to 25 per cent among 14- and 15-year-olds and to 63 per cent among 18-year-old university students.

Similarly, when Douvan and Adelson asked the 3000 girls in their sample to name the quality they valued most in a friend, clear age differences emerged. Preadolescents offered relatively superficial characteristics most of the time: the friend should have good manners, be amiable and cooperative, should play fairly and not be grouchy or a show-off. In other words, for children whose main purpose in friendship is the sharing of activities, the principal demand on playmates is that they not disrupt the working or playing endeavour. In adolescence, on the

Preadolescents frequently define friendship in terms of the sharing of activities together.

Adolescents are more likely than younger children to understand, and value, their friends' idiosyncratic personality characteristics.

other hand, friendship was sought in its own right and the qualities looked for in a friend reflected this new emphasis. The older girls interviewed by Douvan and Adelson wanted a friend they could confide in, who would be loyal, sensitive and a source of support in an emotional crisis.

This new meaning of friendship in early adolescence appears to come about partly as a result of the growth of the need for self-awareness, sexual understanding and social support. But another important factor in the growth of adolescent friendship is the new cognitive capacity which enables the adolescent to see beyond the superficial and obvious qualities of people into their deeper personalities. Thus, young adolescents, who are by now sensitive to personality attributes among individuals, come to choose best friends or chums with some of the same discerning selectivity that they will later apply to their choice of a marital partner. The sensitivity of older children to those qualities that make individual peers unique was brought out in a study that asked a group of 8- to 15-year-olds to describe their best friends and to say why they liked them (Livesley & Bromley, 1973). The younger children's descriptions tended to focus on superficial attributes like possessions and appearance, or on irrelevant details which revealed nothing about their friends' true characters. One child's portrait of his friend was limited to the statement that he had been to France for his holidays. Another said of a girl: 'I used to like her but I don't now because her dog bit me.' By contrast, the young adolescents produced sensitive descriptions that revealed an acute appreciation of their friends' unique personalities, including their motives, values, aspirations, needs and private idiosyncrasies.

Similar results were obtained by Barbara Peevers and Paul Secord (1973) when they asked children and adolescents to describe three of their friends. Young children tended to give global, undifferentiating descriptions which failed to draw a line between the person and his or her situation, and so told nothing about what the friend was like as an individual ('John lives in a big house'). Adolescents more often described their friends' specific personal characteris-

tics ('John is a good athlete'), and some also included personality dispositions which predicted the person's behaviour across a wide range of situations ('John is talkative').

Stephen Snodgrass (1976) found that adolescents were also more skilled than younger children at inferring personality dispositions like these when only a person's concrete actions were described. Also, his older subjects took more notice of the need for a hierarchical integration of the various descriptive qualities that make up a character sketch and of the need to resolve inconsistencies in personality descriptions. All these skills are brought out in the following adolescent's description of a friend:

> She is curious about people but naive, and this leads her to ask too many questions so that people become irritated with her and withhold information, although she is not sensitive enough to notice it. (Livesley & Bromley, 1973, p. 225)

Robert Selman (1981) concluded from findings like these that it makes sense to describe the young adolescent as a 'friendship philosopher'. He noted that teenagers, like the ancient Greeks, are often preoccupied with such problems as what qualities actually constitute an ideal friendship. Aristotle proposed a typology of three distinct kinds of friends:

1. *Congenial business partners*, who engage in pleasantries and friendly chitchat over monetary transactions
2. *Casual friends*, who treat each other kindly but know and understand one another only slightly
3. *True friends*, who enjoy a unique, mutually chosen and emotionally committed relationship.

When he tapped into children's and adolescents' philosophising about friendship by asking them the question 'What makes someone a close friend?',

Selman discovered that awareness of the three levels identified by Aristotle usually emerges only after the transition from middle childhood into early adolescence. Before that, preschoolers and school-age children seemed to think of friends in three successively emerging, but all relatively superficial, ways:

1. Momentary *companions of convenience*, or playmates who happen to live nearby and play together often
2. A *one-way partnership*, or the idea that a friend is a special playmate who is willing to engage in one's own favourite form of play (such as dolls or rocket ships)
3. '*Fair-weather cooperators*', or partners whose material likes and dislikes are known and accommodated without any genuine understanding of the underlying basis for such preferences or aversions in the individual's personality.

But, by the age of 12 or 13, Selman found, friendship philosophising came into full flower. Most prevalent between the ages of 12 and 15 was a style of thinking about friends that Selman called 'intimate and mutually shared relationships'. Numbering this new acquisition Stage 3, to distinguish it from fair-weather relationships at Stage 2, and one-way partnerships at Stage 1, Selman (1981) gave the following description of the adolescent's more advanced understanding of the meaning of friendship:

> At Stage 3 there is the awareness of both a continuity of relation and affective bonding between close friends. The importance of friendship does not rest only upon the fact that the self is bored or lonely; at Stage 3, friendships are seen as a basic means of developing mutual intimacy and mutual support; friends share personal problems. The occurrence of conflicts between friends does not mean the suspension of the relationship, because the underlying continuity between partners is seen as a means of transcending foul-weather incidents. The limitations of Stage 3 conceptions derive from the overemphasis of the two-person clique and the possessiveness that arises out of the realization that close relations are difficult to form and to maintain. (p. 251, reprinted with the permission of Cambridge University Press)

This led Selman to identify a fourth stage of thinking about friendship that did not emerge clearly until after age 14 or 15. This model of friendship, once acquired, is likely to persist throughout the lifespan. Selman (1981) described Stage 4's 'autonomous interdependency' as follows:

> The interdependence that characterizes Stage 4 is the sense that a friendship can continue to grow and be transformed through each partner's ability to synthesize feelings of independence and dependence. Independence means that each person accepts the other's needs to establish relations with others and to grow through such expe-riences. Dependence reflects the awareness that friends must rely on each other for psychological support, to draw strength from each other, and to gain a sense of self-identification through identification with the other as a significant person whose relation to the self is distinct from those with whom one has less meaningful relations. (p. 251, reprinted with the permission of Cambridge University Press)

Putting friendship into practice

By middle adolescence, the average teenager seems capable of thinking about true friendship in a manner not unlike Aristotle or other philosophers. But when it comes to behaviour, teenagers do not always practise the rational tolerance and forebearance that might seem to follow naturally from a mature awareness of the meaning of friendship. Instead, when they watched teenage girls' behaviour, Douvan and Adelson (1966) observed such an intricate interplay among the girls – who teamed up temporarily to exclude other girls and then formed alliances with the excluded parties to break up intimacies among their former bosom friends – that they could not resist drawing an analogy between female adolescent friendship and a 'da Ponte libretto'. As they put it:

> There is no end to the complexities (and the tedium) of arrangements and rearrangements within the friendship group, particularly among girls: A breaks up a close tie between B and C by retailing to B something she heard C say about B; so the displaced C will detach D from her intimacy with E and get her to join in a vendetta against A and B. (p. 184)

Two illustrations of the skilled use by adolescent girls of promises of intimacy and threats of social exclusion to control their peers, and of the insecurity that abrupt changes in friendship allegiances can foster, appear in Box 12.6. Although manipulative motives and 'vendettas' like these incline adolescent friendship towards the unstable and tempestuous, the basic needs that are served by teenage friendships tend, conversely, to encourage friendship's continuity and stability. In fact, when the stability of the 'best friend' relationship is measured, the likelihood of the same person being named as closest friend from year to year is found to increase from middle childhood to mid-adolescence (Garrison, 1965).

One important need among adolescent friends, according to Douvan and Adelson, is for effective feedback. They found that girls aged 14 to 16 who had just begun dating spent much of their time talking with each other about their experiences. They shared advice on how much heterosexual intimacy was acceptable, and how soon, and offered each other reassurance and cushioning against the inevitable disappointments which their early relationships with boys entailed.

An Australian study (Connell et al., 1975) likewise showed that 35 per cent of one group of

BOX 12.6 The horror of being 'hated'

On the eve of her 14th birthday, Louise was distressed over the possibility that she might be caught in the midst of one of the typical rearrangements of adolescent girls' friendships. Her father wrote:

4 March 1962. *She came home from Girl Scouts yesterday in tears. The meeting had been devoted to plans for camping out next weekend and a division of camping sites was made which excluded Louise and Linda from the rest of the troop. The purpose was to exclude Linda, whom Wendy, the loudest voice in the troop, happens momentarily to dislike. Louise was caught in the crossfire since the exclusion of Linda all by herself would not have been allowed. A year ago she might not have minded so much but she and Linda have been drawing farther apart in recent months. It's the same old reason: Linda wants to talk of nothing but sex, or 'boys' as Louise euphemistically puts it, and Louise doesn't. I suggested that Louise, while excusing herself from the campout, call Linda and explain her decision was not because she objected to being excluded with her but that she objected to the whole idea of creating a gang inside the troop. Louise opposed this on the grounds that Linda could simply use what Louise told her as a means to work herself into the good graces of the gang by directing its wrath against Louise. As it is, she is sure they don't dislike her, and merely used her to get at Linda.*

The generality of the phenomenon was brought out a year later when, after a move across the world to Auckland, New Zealand, Louise encountered a very similar experience. Her father described it in his diary as follows:

8 July 1963. *Angela, an English girl who has been here several years, was nearly excluded from a downtown outing of six of the girls on Friday and Louise fears she may be excluded another time. What made it worse was that Robyn, who only joined in the hue and cry against Angela at the last minute, persisted long after the others had quit. Louise wonders if Robyn, whom she thinks of as her best friend, would do the same to her.*

© Peterson, 1974, reproduced with permission

Social exclusion may be particularly trying on a camping trip where peers are ever-present.

11-year-old girls in Sydney relied heavily on their friends for 'talking over problems'. This basis for friendship rose steadily in importance with age, so that 60 per cent of the 17-year-old girls endorsed it. But 'talking' was seen as the least important of all bases for friendship by 11-year-old Australian boys and, though they grew slightly more favourable towards it with age, still only 38 per cent of them endorsed communication as a basis for friendship at age 17.

For boys, by far the most important reason for becoming friends with a male peer was the sharing of common interests and the opportunity to play sport or work on hobbies together. A steady 70 per cent of Australian boys at all ages put this forward as their main criterion for choosing friends. Common interests also underscored the friendships of Australian girls. The way in which shared interests may foster friendship was demonstrated by Theodore Newcomb (1961) in a true-to-life manipulative experiment that he conducted on a university campus. Through a newspaper advertisement, he gathered together a group of 17 male students who were total strangers. They were invited to live in a house rent-free in exchange for their participation in Newcomb's research. Using a series of questionnaires assessing attitudes about various social and political issues, a pre- and post-design was implemented. The men answered the questions before they became acquainted and then again after they had come to know each other well.

Newcomb found that similarity of attitudes was a very good predictor of friendship: men who became close friends had usually had similar social and political opinions before meeting, and, when men with dramatically different views became friends, either their views or the friendship itself was liable to be short-lived.

The saying that 'birds of a feather flock together' would thus seem to be as true of early adolescent friendship choices as it is of later friendship and heterosexual attraction. But another proverb, that 'opposites attract', also has some truth when applied to the young person's choice of a same-sex friend. While a similarity of opinions and ideas draws individuals together, complementarity of needs and personality styles also fosters friendship by enabling:

- mutual need satisfaction; and
- self-modification of undesired traits by copying their opposites as modelled by the friend.

When one child needs to talk and another prefers to listen, or one enjoys leading and another being led, both their needs can be met when they interact. On the other hand, a friendship between similar children (e.g. partners who share an equal ambition for leadership) is inevitably doomed to frustration. Both will experience conflict as they attempt to dominate each other and one will eventually be disappointed. But in a complementary friendship, the shy, retiring partner can enjoy being dominated while at the same time gaining opportunities to copy leadership tactics from an outgoing friend that would not arise in friendships between peers with similarly submissive dispositions. Another kind of complementarity is illustrated in Box 12.7.

Douvan and Adelson (1966) also proposed a complementarity explanation for their frequent observation of close friendships among pairs of adolescent girls who had reached quite different levels of involvement with boys. While a girl who is actively dating might seem to have little in common with a peer who has not yet displayed any interest in boys, and two girls who are heterosexually active might seem to have a lot of common experiences to share, Douvan and Adelson found that friendship was facilitated by the former situation and undermined by the latter. When they observed closely a typical interaction between girl A, who routinely dated, and

Similarity of interests and beliefs, along with complementary personality patterns, fosters friendship during adolescence.

girl B, who as yet showed no active heterosexual interest, they found evidence for both complementary need satisfactions and mutual learning experiences. Girl A's descriptions of her sexual exploits satisfied girl B's need to hear and learn about such things before venturing into this dangerous territory herself. Likewise, through reactions of either admiration or shocked disapproval, girl B provided valuable feedback to girl A concerning how much sexual involvement could be undertaken without endangering her reputation among her female peers.

Another study of complementarity in early adolescent friendship showed that eighth-grade boys tended to choose male friends who were opposite to themselves in social outgoingness. Those boys who enjoyed 'showing off' tended to have rather quiet and retiring best friends who preferred being the audience rather than the star performer. But among girls this relationship did not obtain. If anything, girls tended to choose friends who were as outgoing and sociable as themselves. One explanation for this sex difference might be that the eighth-grade girls, being earlier to mature sexually, placed less importance than their male classmates on an intimate same-sex friendship because they were beginning to turn their interest towards the possibility of intimacy with a boy (Berndt, 1982).

Solitude and adolescent adjustment

Despite the fact that social relationships play an important role in adolescent development, those who spend all their time in the company of others are found to score lower on some measures of adjustment and well-being than their teenage peers who spend time alone. Using an innovative observational methodology, Reed Larson (1997) had teenagers

BOX 12.7

Opposites attract, but similarity is binding

Lillian Hellman (1973) provided an eloquent description of the joy of 'just talking' and of a sensitive interplay of similarity and complementarity between adolescent friends in her recollection of her relationship with her peer, Julia. She wrote:

At night, wrapped in our blankets, the fire between us, we would talk. More accurately, I would ask questions and she would talk: she was one of the few people I have ever met who could give information without giving a lecture. How young it sounds now that, although I had heard the name of Freud, I never knew exactly what he wrote until she told me; that Karl Marx and Engels became men with theories, instead of that one sentence in my school book which mentioned the Manifesto. But we also talked like all young people, of possible beaux and husbands and babies, and heredity versus environment, and can romantic love last, mixing stuff like that in speeches made only for the pleasure of girls on the edge of growing up. One night when we had been silent for a long time because she was leaning on an elbow, close to the fire, reading a German grammar, I laughed at the sounds coming from her mouth as she repeated the sentences. She said, 'No, you don't understand. People are either teachers or students. You are a student.' 'Am I a good one?' 'When you find what you want, you will be very good.'
(p. 117)

aged 13 to 15 years old carry pagers with them throughout the day. When they were paged, they were required to report to a member of the research team on (a) their mood and (b) who they were with (if anyone). Depressive moods were more frequent in adolescents who were never alone than in those who enjoyed a moderate amount of solitude (see Figure 12.10). However, those who were alone all or most of the time were as depressed as those who were always in company. Academic achievement (as denoted by grade-point average) and independently measured psychological adjustment followed a similar pattern (see Figure 12.10), with the group who spent between 30 and 50 per cent of their time alone doing better than those who were either always or never with others.

Presumably, the stresses of developing new social relationships and new levels of social understanding during interactions with same- and opposite-sex peers eventually take their toll. Those adolescents who are able to cope with this stress by taking time out to listen to music in their bedroom, visit the library or go for a solitary walk or swim seem to cope better with the developmental demands of adolescent social life than their peers who are in the company of friends or family continuously. Of course, having no opportunity at all for social interaction is undesirable too, so that adolescents who find themselves completely isolated socially suffer depressive and maladjustment symptoms, just like those who lack the chance to be alone.

Though peer companionship is enjoyable, solitary pursuits are likewise beneficial to adolescent psychological development.

Adolescent dating

The proportion of friends who are of the opposite sex declines for both sexes from age seven to a low between ages 10 and 12, from which it rises again steadily to age 15 (Broderick, 1966). Up to the age of 16, the person chosen as the 'best friend' is usually someone of one's own sex. After age 16, the best friend is likely to be an opposite-sex boyfriend or girlfriend. In other words, while childhood is a time of easy and relatively casual relationships with an assortment of playmates of both sexes, and early adolescent friendship brings a deeper and more intense attachment to a chum, these bonds give way, in later adolescence, to a progression of heterosexual relationships, beginning with dating.

The dating game

The transition from simple friendship to a stage of going out together, or dating, marks further progress in social maturation. Dating is a distinctive social pattern, as different from the opposite-sex friendships of childhood and early adolescence as it is from later developments like living together or marriage. By definition, *dating* consists of an arrangement by a boy and girl to meet together on their own for some mutually enjoyable outing or other social activity. Unlike courtship, which has marriage as its ultimate goal, dating centres around more immediate pleasures and is viewed by most adolescents and their parents as strictly 'an end in itself'. A historical sketch of the combination of social changes over the

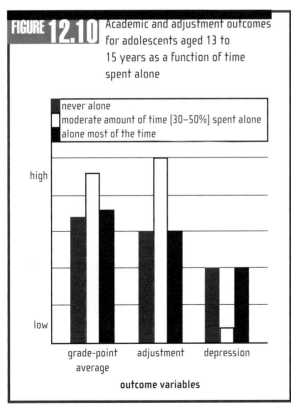

FIGURE **12.10** Academic and adjustment outcomes for adolescents aged 13 to 15 years as a function of time spent alone

never alone
moderate amount of time (30–50%) spent alone
alone most of the time

Source: Based on data in Larson (1997). Reproduced with the permission of the Society for Research in Child Development.

past few decades that helped to give rise to this distinctive style of socialising in Australia is given in Box 12.8. Australian adolescents typically begin to go out on dates between the ages of 14 and 15 (see Figure 12.11). The dating experience is now protracted. Teenagers generally continue to date for up to five years before contemplating a more serious or permanent romantic relationship such as marriage, engagement or living together. Similarly, there are generally a number of years, though decreasing today as compared with several decades ago, between the uptake of dating and the onset of the adolescent's first sexual relationship (see Figure 12.12).

Like any other game, dating has its rules. Participants do not always recognise this. But when experienced participants are probed in interviews, very clear ideas about even the most seemingly 'unruly' situations, such as fist fights among delinquent girls or riots by British football hooligans, are found to emerge from their mouths (Argyle, 1986). Dating is no exception. But, despite the fact that dating is not governed by formal laws like marriage, Michael Argyle (1986) found that British adolescent girls had a very clear set of criteria in their own minds about how to behave when asked out by a boy. All the girls he interviewed were in close accord about the informal guidelines that prescribed what to do and what not to do on a date. These rules differed in several important respects from the rules governing same-sex friendships, as Table 12.8 illustrates.

The rules of dating also changed as the girl progressed from her first dating experience to having gone out with more than one male partner. Those who had dated only one boy stressed showing an interest in the boy, being faithful and displaying unconditional positive regard. But after going out

World War I changed the pattern of dating. The shortage of males, restricted army leave, the immediacy of the situation, last-minute dates and pick-ups from dances saw the demise of the chaperone, who had to be booked in advance. Girls became the guardians of their own morals and the date took on a different meaning; it became less a part of the courtship-to-marriage process and was controlled by the young couple themselves.

A number of other factors further changed the nature of dating. During World War II, Australia saw the first real threat to her shores. The bombing of Darwin, enemy reconnaissance flights over Sydney, the shelling of Bondi, the Japanese submarine attack in Sydney Harbour, the Coral Sea Battle, the appearance of POWs in Cowra and the fighting on our doorstep in New Guinea, together with rationing, restrictions, blackouts, confusion and conscription of young men led to an atmosphere wherein parents allowed older adolescents to enjoy themselves while they could. After the war, returning servicemen dated the girls they had left behind, and younger adolescents copied their behaviour. Later the motor car provided the adolescent with the means of seeking more private rendezvous, and with the ability to travel to places where she was not known. Here she had the protection of anonymity as she ostentatiously displayed affection for her date.

With the spread of co-education, young people were provided with even greater opportunities to mix and make dates, and with the age of puberty occurring earlier, heterosexual interests appeared at younger ages. The date then became completely divorced from courtship and seemed to be more of an end in itself, where young boys and girls sought out one another's company in order to have a good time. (p. 87)

BOX 12.8 The history of dating in Australia

In this historical synopsis of the changes in adolescent dating habits in Australia, John Collins and Juliet Harper (1978) trace the origin of the word 'dating' back to Queen Victoria's era when 'date' referred to an appointment with a chaperone.

A boy had to present himself to the girl's parents and ask permission to take her to some social function, and a date was made for this outing. When the time eventually came, the speech and behaviour of the couple were monitored by the ever-present chaperone whose task was to look after the virtue of the girl. All types of surreptitious planning was needed for the boy to get the girl alone for a brief period. The chaperone was really a babysitter for adults, and some were so skilled that they were in great demand by the parents of young girls. Certain things were allowed, others were discouraged depending upon the stage of the courtship process.

In Australia, the rules of dating have changed over the years.

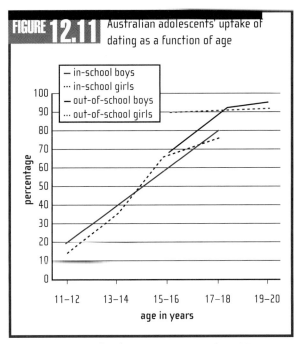

FIGURE 12.11 Australian adolescents' uptake of dating as a function of age

- in-school boys
... in-school girls
- out-of-school boys
... out-of-school girls

percentage

age in years

Source: Connell et al. (1975), reproduced with permission of the authors.

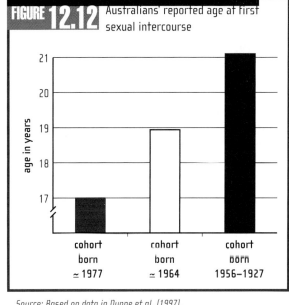

FIGURE 12.12 Australians' reported age at first sexual intercourse

age in years

cohort born ≃ 1977
cohort born ≃ 1964
cohort born 1956–1927

Source: Based on data in Dunne et al. (1997).

TABLE 12.8 British girls' rules for dating and friendship

Rules applying to friendship only	Rules applying to dating only	Rules applying to both dating and friendship
Repay debts and favours and return compliments, no matter how small.	Be willing to compromise.	Respect the other's privacy.
	Be faithful.	Share news of success.
Volunteer help in time of need.	Show interest in the other's daily activities.	Be tolerant of each other's friends.
Strive for mutual enjoyment when together.	Disclose your innermost feelings and personal problems.	Don't criticise the other in public.
		Keep a secret.
Don't be jealous or critical of the friend's other relationships.	Ask for personal advice.	Stand up for the other in his or her absence.
Don't nag.		

Source: Based on data from Argyle (1986), pp. 75–7.

with a number of boys, girls with wider dating experience rejected the faithfulness rule. Less predictably, they were also more wary than inexperienced daters of displaying interest in the partner's daily activities, or of asking the partner for personal advice. In fact, their rule was not to express any strong feelings of any kind when with a boy. Thus they were more cautious about showing affection or approval for their dating partner, and followed another rule not in the inexperienced group's repertoire: that a girl should never express anger or distress and should conceal any feelings of anxiety, shyness or unhappiness from her male partners.

This last rule, advocating emotional blandness and concealment of feelings when on dates, has been noted frequently in earlier studies of dating (Douvan & Adelson, 1966). In fact, this is one basis for the oft-expressed fear that prolonged exposure to dating as an adolescent may interfere with the young adult's subsequent adjustment to marriage. One of the first researchers to articulate this anxiety was the anthropologist Margaret Mead (1949). She complained that dating encouraged youth to place ulterior status needs ahead of feelings for others, and she described the dating male as 'longing to be in a situation, mainly public, where he will be seen by others to have a girl, and the right kind of girl' (p. 287). Mead reached this conclusion after contrasting American teenage dating patterns with the situation in Samoa in the 1920s. Even earlier, she and her close women friends at Barnard College had rejected the chance to date men when doing so would require artificial bargaining or damage to their female friendships.

A contrast between a dating and a non-dating culture also alerted Elizabeth Douvan and Joseph Adelson (1966) to the potential for negative transfer from dating into marriage. One of the girls they interviewed was a thoughtful Finnish exchange student who complained, after one year's exposure to dating in America, that it forced a superficial and unsympathetic relationship between males and females. When she was out on a date she felt she was not quite allowed to be herself. In her opinion this was because:

> A boy is supposed to bring a date, and it doesn't matter who she is as long as she says and does what's expected of her. The boy brings a date the way he might bring a pair of skis if he were going skiing. (p. 204)

Douvan and Adelson found substantial support for this Finnish girl's criticism in their discovery of a 'characterological fiction' which they dubbed the 'good date' stereotype. Its outstanding feature was moderation in everything. The 'good date' was always friendly and conversational, but never too emotional or passionate. He or she had to be bright but not serious or intellectual, agreeable but not gushing, and could on no account get into a bad mood.

In their interviews with adolescent girls, Douvan and Adelson discovered gradual increases in awareness of, and efforts to conform to, this stereotype. Preadolescent girls usually did not yet date and, when they were asked 'What do you think makes a girl popular with boys?', they focused superficially on attractive physical appearance, whereas the typical 14- to 16-year-old girl's commonest response to the same question was 'good personality' – by which they meant the kind of charm and social skill characterised in the 'good date' stereotype. Indeed, girls of this age were found to be so engrossed in building their 'good date' image that they reacted with a denial of feeling to a hypothetical situation which provoked outrage and action from both older and younger girls. When asked to imagine what they would do if their date began paying attention to their own girlfriend, 14-year-olds were more likely than any other group to advise taking no action, or pretending not to notice and hiding jealousy at all costs. In the rare cases when they suggested action at all, it was not to break off with the boy (the main choice of the under-14s) or to talk to him (favoured by older girls) but to work on him via the girlfriend. This reinforced Douvan and Adelson's view that 'early dating is a manipulative game rather than a real relationship based on mutuality and emotional interaction' (p. 204).

If dating was unfamiliar in the 1960s to Finnish teenagers such as the exchange student interviewed by Douvan and Adelson, by the early 1980s it had become an almost universal experience for adolescents throughout Europe and most other modern Westernised nations. Even in modern China, where pre-revolutionary tradition decreed that marriages should be arranged by a matchmaker without the couple's prior acquaintance, and where contemporary law prohibits marriage until late adolescence for workers, or until after graduation with a Bachelor's degree for university students, the practice of dating among contemporary Chinese teenagers has become widespread (Hooper, 1985).

Health and dating

Perhaps because of the more recent introduction of dating into Finland, researchers there have highlighted some additional problems beyond those attributable to the 'good date' stereotype as it applies in Australia, the United States and Britain (Argyle, 1986). When Hillevi Aro and Vappu Taipale (1987) examined medical records and evaluated the psychosomatic complaints in a group of 935 Finnish girls aged 14 to 16 years, they found that girls who had already begun to date suffered from more physical and stress-related ailments than their female peers who had not yet become involved with a boy. The 12 physical symptoms on the Finnish researchers' health checklist were insomnia, dizziness, nausea, vomiting, loss of appetite, heartburn, diarrhoea, breathlessness, excessive perspiration, headache, heart palpitations and hand tremors. They also included five mental health symptoms: depression, anxiety, irritability, nightmares, and weakness or lack of energy. When they summed the frequency and severity of the total range of symptoms experienced by each girl over a four-month period, Aro and Taipale discovered significantly higher rates of stress symptoms in girls who were dating, as well as in those who had experienced menarche at an earlier than normal age (see Chapter 10).

Figure 12.13 illustrates the additive contribution of both these factors to the average Finnish girl's level of mental and physical upset. Except for a small group of girls who had begun menstruating at the extremely early age of 11 years or before (who were found to suffer from equally high rates of stress symptoms irrespective of whether or not they dated), the frequency and severity of health problems reported by dating girls was dramatically higher than for their non-dating counterparts of the same age at menarche. Physiological and social maturation each seemed to make separate but similar contributions to the Finnish girls' discomfort during middle adolescence.

Although elevation of stress, the undermining of physical health and the cultivation of a superficial style of relating to members of the opposite sex are among the serious drawbacks of dating, the practice

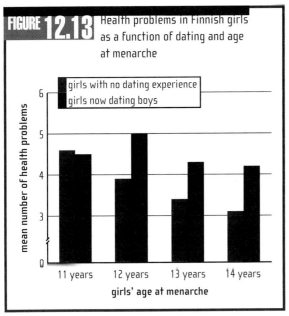

FIGURE 12.13 Health problems in Finnish girls as a function of dating and age at menarche

mean number of health problems

- girls with no dating experience
- girls now dating boys

girls' age at menarche — 11 years, 12 years, 13 years, 14 years

Source: Based on data in Aro & Taipale (1987), p. 266.

also has some compensating advantages. Elizabeth Hurlock (1973) enumerated the following:

1. the tempering of idealistic and highly romantic notions about love
2. learning how to make rapid adjustments to new situations
3. developing balance, poise and self-confidence
4. increasing one's status among one's peers
5. having a good time.

Dating also has the advantage of postponing, relatively painlessly, the more serious commitments of

The experience of dating teaches adolescents new social skills.

courtship and marriage until an age when youth are educationally and economically prepared to take them on.

Whether these advantages outweigh dating's disadvantages seems to depend in part on the age of the adolescent dater. Douvan and Adelson found that girls who began to date much earlier than their female peers differed from both average and late daters in several important respects. Predictably, the early daters had fewer intimate female friendships than other girls, and engaged in fewer organised social activities with peers of either sex. On the other hand, they were high in self-confidence and poised in their dealings with adults, and not sexually precocious, either physiologically or psychologically.

Perhaps the most disturbing finding was also the least expected in view of this group's extensive contact with males through early dating. This was their failure to understand either their own boyfriends or the nature of boy–girl relationships generally. In fact, they showed even less awareness of their boyfriends' special needs and sensitivities than girls of their own age who had not yet begun dating. It seemed that precociously early dating had not fostered the growth of mature social skills or social understanding. Whether it had actually interfered with the development of these qualities could not be determined from Douvan and Adelson's correlational study. Though dating too early could conceivably have stunted the growth of social sensitivity, it was equally plausible that girls might have gravitated to early dating because of an already more superficial personality style. Early daters were found to daydream and fantasise less than others, despite equivalent intelligence. This suggested a disposition that would have been evident well before dating began (see Chapter 7). Furthermore, it may be that a rich inner life of one's own is an important prerequisite to a sensitive understanding of another person's inner qualities.

Culture, dating and teen marriage

In Australia and New Zealand, as in North America and Europe, it is relatively rare for adolescent dating to lead immediately to courtship and marriage. In fact, as we see in Chapter 13, first marriage is typically an event that now takes place in the late 20s or early 30s. But in other countries in the Asia-Pacific region, adolescent marriage is a common event for girls, curtailing opportunities for education and the forging of a mature lifestyle as a single adult independent of the parental family. Data from the Mahbub ul Haq Human Development Centre (2000) revealed that, in India, Nepal and Pakistan, between 12 and 22 per cent of young girls were first married by the age of 12 years, with 54 per cent in India, 76 per cent in Nepal and 72 per cent in Pakistan being married by age 18. Figure 12.14 shows the link between early marriage and curtailed education for contemporary adolescent girls in Bangladesh and India (Mahbub ul Haq, 2000).

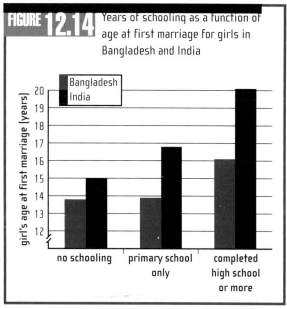

FIGURE 12.14 Years of schooling as a function of age at first marriage for girls in Bangladesh and India

Source: Based on data in Mahbub ul Haq (2000).

Sex roles in adolescence

Gender-role socialisation often becomes more intense during adolescence as puberty accentuates the physical distinctiveness of the sexes and parents respond to the advent of reproductive sexuality and the imminence of marriage by treating their sons and daughters in very different ways (Hill & Lynch, 1983). According to Jeanne Brooks-Gunn and W. S. Matthews (1979):

> Girls find themselves in another predicament during puberty. Not only are they expected to give up sports, but they find their sexual maturity is a concern rather than a joy to their parents. Girls are told to protect themselves, never walk at night alone, always to call … (p. 239)

Other authors describe a 'Chameleon Syndrome' in the socialisation of adolescent females, which prescribes not only virginity but strict adherence to traditionally feminine role behaviour, including passivity, 'sweet' sociability and coquettishness (Hill & Lynch, 1983). The prescribed accentuation of femininity may also include avoidance of competitive achievement on the sports field or in the classroom and a lowering of expectations for success in stereotypically masculine domains like chemistry, engineering or mathematics (see Chapter 9). As Aletha Huston and M. Alvarez (1990) explain:

> Social pressures for sex-appropriate behaviour are relatively benign during middle childhood, particularly for girls. With the onset of puberty, however, both psychological and social forces act to increase awareness of gender roles and efforts to adhere to them. (p. 158)

The counterpart for boys of parental intensification of the gender role may entail minimisation of traits such as empathy and sensitivity and the enhancement of cold-blooded competition, or the pursuit of power and domination in relations between the sexes. According to John Hill and Mary Ellen Lynch (1983):

> Explicated along machismo lines [this cultural ideal of mature masculinity leads parents to] respond to pubertal change in males with increased tolerance for independence and decreased tolerance for emotional display, less protectiveness, and subtle encouragement of sexual conquest. (p. 203)

In a longitudinal study of this gender-role intensification hypothesis, Ann Crouter and her colleagues (1995) compared male and female adolescents' participation in stereotypically feminine household activities like making beds and doing laundry with their involvement in masculine chores like home repairs, outdoor work and taking out garbage. The hypothesis was supported for boys and girls in traditional families where the mother and father divided household work strictly in accordance with sex-role stereotypes (see Chapters 8 and 13) and mothers performed more than 75 per cent of the overall household work. In these families, over the one-year longitudinal period spanning the transition into the teens, girls increased their involvement in feminine tasks and decreased their contribution to masculine domestic work, especially when they had younger brothers. Boys in traditional homes likewise became more involved in masculine work and less involved in feminine chores over the same period. But no clear evidence of gender intensification emerged for teenagers in egalitarian families where both parents were employed outside the home and the husband performed at least one-quarter of the regular household chores.

It would seem that parental role models continue to play an important part in adolescent sex-role development, just as they did during early and middle childhood. The process of gender-role intensification went hand-in-hand with an increasing amount of time spent with the same-sex parent, especially in families where younger siblings were of the opposite sex.

One outcome of gender-role intensification pressures may be the development of greater divergence between male and female behaviour and psychological functioning after adolescence than during childhood. This is especially likely for contemporary Australian and New Zealand children who, at the present time, are freely encouraged during childhood to engage in behaviours (from play with dolls to football) which tradition formerly reserved for only one sex (see Chapter 8). This differential socialisation of adolescent sex roles may help to explain the observed increase in sex differences during adolescence, as contrasted with the results of studies comparing the behaviour of boys and girls during early and middle childhood (see Chapter 8). The following behavioural differences between boys and girls become stronger, or are noted for the first time, during adolescence (Crouter et al., 1995; Hill & Lynch, 1983).

1. *Susceptibility to anxiety*: Girls show more self-consciousness and nervousness in social situations from early adolescence onwards.
2. *Cognitive processing*: Boys show strong superiority on spatial tasks such as reading maps, geometry, and visualising the motion of objects. Girls, conversely, show somewhat better verbal skills than boys after adolescence.
3. *Social relationships*: Mothers show increasing deference to sons but not daughters as the child moves through puberty; girls tend to develop more intimate friendships and use more sophisticated concepts when describing friendship (see page 414) than boys do during adolescence.
4. *Risk-taking*: Girls in adolescence display more cautious attitudes than boys, are less willing to take risks when making decisions and are subjected to stronger parental protectiveness.

A survey of Sydney adolescents (Richmond, 1984) likewise revealed significant differences between male and female personality patterns. At both age 12 and age 16, boys were significantly more self-assertive, while girls at both ages scored higher than boys on measures of nurturance, worry and physiological symptoms of stress and anxiety. An increase in sex stereotyping during adolescence was suggested by the observation that, while there was no sex difference in the trait of gregariousness at age 12, girls were earning significantly higher scores than boys on this stereotypically feminine personality attribute by age 16. This finding supports the view that an intensification of gender-role socialisation is triggered by parents noticing the first physical symptoms of puberty in their offspring (Hill & Lynch, 1983). That this process of intensive, role-restrictive socialisation during adolescence may prove both painful and an obstacle to integrated personality growth, at least for females, was also suggested by the finding that:

Adolescent boys are inclined to engage in riskier leisure pursuits than adolescent girls.

... for girls, to be self-assertive within the context which emphasizes cooperation and consideration for others is associated with feelings of discordance ... It is possible that the relationship is stronger in girls due to sex-role stereotype effects. (p. 1030)

Another more specific outcome of restrictive parental socialisation practices is the emergence during adolescence of double standards of dating behaviour and sexual morality. In fact, Marita McCabe (1984) noted that double standards about how to behave on dates are directly linked to the process of sex-role development:

Childhood socialization produces pressure for males to adopt a sexual orientation and females an affectionate orientation. Adolescents who adopt a masculine sex role therefore desire and experience largely sexual behaviors, while those adopting a feminine sex role desire and experience largely affectionate behaviors from a heterosexual relationship. (p. 166)

This can produce conflict between teenage boys and girls when they go out on dates together. The traditionally feminine girl is apt to desire such expressions of affection from the boy as 'companionship', 'sharing of life experiences', 'tenderness', 'reassurance' and 'mutual respect' (McCabe & Collins, 1979). She is also likely to feel worried or antagonistic towards any expressions of sexuality beyond the level of light kissing or embracing. From the age of 16, however, an Australian boy with a stereotypically masculine sex-role orientation may desire such sexual displays as 'general body contact', 'deep kissing', 'necking' and 'breast petting' from the girl on their first date together (McCabe & Collins, 1979). The incompatibility of these contrasting attitudes may create antipathy towards boyfriend or girlfriend or towards dating in general.

But another way of resolving the conflict is for each sex to adapt to the expectations of the other. By transcending stereotyped masculine and feminine roles to become androgynous, daters of both sexes can learn to appreciate the satisfactions from which they were traditionally excluded by the double standard. According to McCabe:

Males and females who adopt androgynous sex roles desire and experience both sexual and affectionate behaviours. (p. 166)

In her own research with dating couples in Sydney aged 16 to 25 years, McCabe (1984) found that sex-role orientations did influence daters' preferences for sexual and emotional intimacy. Regardless of biological gender, teenage boys and girls whose social sex roles were feminine desired more affection and less overt sexuality than masculine or androgynous adolescents. But, with increasing age, these differences gradually disappeared. By age 25, and after a steady relationship with one particular dating partner had developed, there was as strong a desire for sexual intimacy on the part of feminine males and females as among stereotypically masculine men or androgynous men and women. McCabe concluded that:

> Having experienced dating desires in a number of unions, it is possible for the individual to adopt behaviors which best suit personal needs and those of one's partner. Once acceptable behaviors have been determined, the dating partners find it necessary to create opportunities so that it is possible to experience these behaviors. This is more readily achieved in some environments than in others. Once the opportunity does arise, it is possible for dating partners to express their overall dating orientations, whether these experiences are largely sexual, affectional, or a combination of sexual and affectional behaviors. (p. 169)

The adolescent's level of moral reasoning influences acceptance of the double standard for dating and sexuality. One study used Kohlberg's ethical dilemmas (see Chapter 11) to measure the abstract moral reasoning skills of male and female college students in the United States (D'Augelli & D'Augelli, 1977). The results showed that, when men and women who were still operating at the lower levels of moral reasoning in Kohlberg's scheme were questioned specifically about their sexual code of ethics, almost all of them endorsed the double standard prescribing permissiveness for men and abstinence for women. By contrast, students whose reasoning about general moral questions was more advanced (Kohlberg's Stage 5) frequently rejected the double standard in favour of a 'non-exploitative' code of sexual ethics.

In the eyes of many of these morally mature subjects, mutual agreement, joint responsibility for contraception and a dialectical pattern of interactive decision-making were three crucial prerequisites to a dating couple's decision to engage in premarital sexual intercourse. Rather than trusting to tradition, couples who adopted this approach created their own personal norms about sexuality through probing and sensitive exploration of each other's feelings in lengthy discussion. According to their Stage 5 ethical standards, the underlying moral and pragmatic issues had to be resolved collectively before either partner could feel comfortable about engaging in sexual acts. Sexual abstinence was also viewed as perfectly acceptable when it suited the feelings of both partners.

The adolescent peer group

Concern about conforming to the stereotyped social and sexual standards endorsed by the peer group, or worry over losing status with friends of one's own sex if dating is delayed, highlights another important function of peer-group membership during adolescence. Peers regulate the individual boy or girl's development both of sexuality and of heterosexual friendship. Peers put pressure on one another to undertake a level of boy–girl friendship which corresponds to the group average (see Box 12.9). Young

BOX 12.9   **Peer pressure and dating**

When Louise moved to New Zealand at the age of 14 she entered a peer group which expected a less advanced level of boy–girl intimacy than had been the norm in the peer group she left behind in southern California. Having been one of the slower members of this Californian group, entry into a slower-paced group suited Louise very well. Her father explained some of the reasons for this in his diary.

> **15 August 1962.** *As usual Louise was unsure about wanting to go to last night's 'social' (school dance), though somewhat less unsure I thought than in California. There the question of whether any boys would ask her to dance was a far more burning one since, no matter how sincerely she might scorn the 'popular' set, she felt her prestige suffer if she got no dances at all. And it didn't improve her status if, like one or two, she got her dances by asking the boys. What Louise dreaded, before each dance, was the prospect of not being asked; and she was always sure this would be her fate. She had the same forebodings here but they were less pressing. First, only two of the girls she knows fall into the 'popular' class, and for their 'popularity' they pay a higher price than in California. Their experiences are discussed with shocked disapproval. Second, the boys of the same category, the more self-possessed ones as I believe Louise described them, are nothing like as openly competed for here.*
>
> © Peterson, 1974, reproduced with permission

But by the time Louise was 16 and had made another move, popularity among her Australian female peer group depended on dating involvement. Thus her father wrote:

> **29 August 1964** *... Louise is concerned over whether she should be dating as four or five girls in her class are already doing, on a 'steady' basis, of course. Caroline, with whom she associates most at school, is one of them; and Gillian is only too anxious to be one – and would if her parents didn't keep such a tight rein on her. Sally, who doesn't date, is a year younger than the others and Prue is overweight. Louise fears she may be considered childish like Sally or unattractive to boys unless she has a boy friend to talk about. I naturally tell her not to be in a hurry. The boys of her age who do date are either better off economically than most or out of school and working; the rest wouldn't even come to the social. Nevertheless I realize young people do grow up fast and Louise must have more social contact with boys than she does.*
>
> © Peterson, 1974, reproduced with permission

people who are too far behind or too far ahead of the rest of the group are subject to disapproval.

In fact, adolescent popularity among peers of the same sex is closely related to the sort of relationship they have with peers of the opposite sex. But the relationship between these two factors is a complex one. It depends on the adolescent's age and leadership status within the group, and also on the standards each individual peer group has about what degree of intimacy between boys and girls is appropriate at each stage in the development of heterosexual relationships.

Dexter Dunphy (1969) was able to trace this development in his studies of adolescent 'cliques' and 'crowds' in Sydney as a participant observer. This uncommon and laborious method of investigation required him to follow up the initial contacts he made with young members of formal youth clubs through all their various informal associations with each other 'on street corners, in milkbars and homes, at parties and on Sydney beaches' over a period of four to six months per group. He made an effort to mingle with the group and yet was careful not to say or do anything that would alter the group's natural course of activity. He was aided in this blending process by his youthful physique and by the adoption of a clothing style that was a compromise between teenage fashion and the clothing a man of his age would normally wear. The fruits of Dunphy's participant observation were a number of novel and important discoveries about the structure and functioning of adolescent peer groups. The fact that these results were based on direct observation rather than questionnaires also earns them a special place in the literature on adolescence.

Dunphy found that each adolescent belonged simultaneously to two structurally different kinds of groups: the clique and the crowd. *Cliques* were small, closely knit bodies of three to nine members and *crowds* were aggregates of two or more complete cliques (they averaged a membership of 20). Clique members usually lived near one another and came together often during the week to share secrets, to plan and analyse crowd functions or just to talk. Crowds usually came together only at weekends to participate in more structured social functions like dances, swim meets, beach parties and movies.

Membership of a crowd required prior membership of one of its constituent cliques, and the boundaries of cliques were rigidly enforced. To gain entry initially, the adolescent had to express an active desire to belong and had to conform to the basic outlook and interests of the rest of the group. Once accepted, continued clique membership required deference to the authority of the leader and, most critically, an equivalent rate of progress in relationships with the opposite sex to that of the other clique members.

In addition to serving, by this means, as the vehicle for entry into the age-graded teenage practice of dating, the peer groups that Dunphy observed also followed their own interesting and quite unique course of development through time. As members grew older, the peer group's size, structure and interconnections changed in consistent, systematic ways. The earliest stage consisted of isolated unisex cliques. The crowd had not yet come into existence, and even the various cliques that occupied the same Sydney neighbourhood or classroom at school had relatively little to do with one another. Ages of members of the isolated cliques of this initial stage typically ranged from 11 to 13 years. Clique membership was also inevitably segregated to a single sex. In fact, though not fully aware of the existence of opposite-sex cliques, members were apt to express generalised distaste for peers of the opposite sex when Dunphy questioned them about cliques of the other gender.

A similar pattern at this age was observed by Jane Kroger (1983) in a comparative study of New Zealand and American children. When questioned about the opposite sex, girls in New Zealand and boys in both countries made the greatest number of negative remarks at age 11, as shown in Figure 12.15. American girls, on the other hand, rarely expressed negative feelings about boys at any age, possibly as a result of their relatively early emulation of the 'good date' model discovered by Douvan and Adelson.

The second stage in the evolution of Australian teenagers' peer groups arose, according to Dunphy, when adjacent boys' and girls' cliques became aware of each other's existence and began to interact in limited, superficial ways. The membership in each clique was still strictly unisex, and the overarching crowd had not yet come into existence. But perhaps as a carry-over from the cross-gender hostility illustrated in Figure 12.15, the boys' and girls' cliques had begun to take notice of each other, largely through bantering, teasing and alternating forays into, and retreats out of, each other's territory. By the third stage, the leaders of the unisex cliques had banded together to form a superordinate heterosexual 'top' clique.

By the fourth stage, the rank-and-file membership had also redistributed themselves into cliques of mixed sex. In the fifth and final stage, the cliques and crowds began to disintegrate as couples broke out of the group to go their separate ways (see Figure 12.16).

Other research with Sydney adolescents (Connell et al., 1975) likewise saw the move from universally unisex peer groups at age 12 to universally mixed-sex peer groups by age 17 to be 'one of the most dramatic social changes found in the whole study' (p. 210).

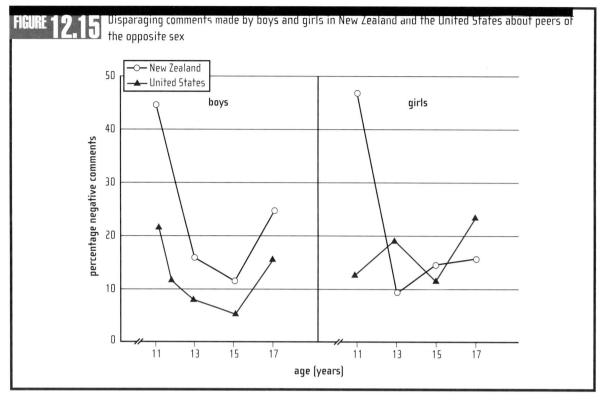

FIGURE 12.15 Disparaging comments made by boys and girls in New Zealand and the United States about peers of the opposite sex

Source: Based on data in Kroger (1983).

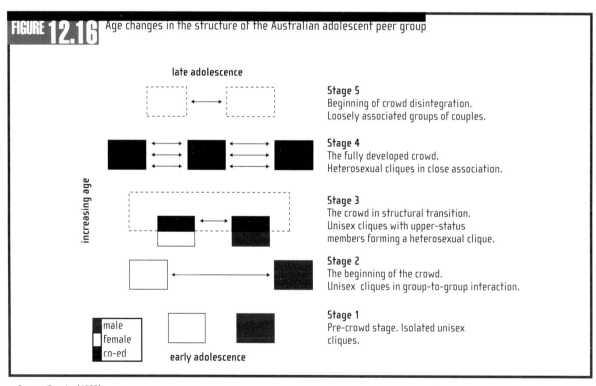

FIGURE 12.16 Age changes in the structure of the Australian adolescent peer group

late adolescence

Stage 5
Beginning of crowd disintegration.
Loosely associated groups of couples.

Stage 4
The fully developed crowd.
Heterosexual cliques in close association.

Stage 3
The crowd in structural transition.
Unisex cliques with upper-status
members forming a heterosexual clique.

Stage 2
The beginning of the crowd.
Unisex cliques in group-to-group interaction.

Stage 1
Pre-crowd stage. Isolated unisex
cliques.

male
female
co-ed

early adolescence

Source: Dunphy (1969).

Chapter summary

Few situations in life compare in difficulty to the task of parenting an adolescent son or daughter from puberty to fully fledged independence. Part of the problem stems from the lack of consistent culturally shared beliefs about how much independence is appropriate, and how soon. This leads to conflict between adolescents and their parents over bedtime hours, dating privileges, the use of the car and housework responsibilities.

Cross-pressures between the attitudes and desires of parents versus the peer group may also produce stress for individual teenagers, depending in part on their gender and age and also on their cultural background.

The emotional relationship between adolescents and their parents is disrupted, according to Anna Freud, by the need to sever the attachment bonds that made the parents the prime objects of their offspring's affection from infancy through middle childhood. When successful, this emotional emancipation process enables the young person to transfer affection to close friends of the same sex and eventually to embark on heterosexual dating relationships.

The conflicts that erupt more frequently between parents and their adolescent offspring as the teenagers pass through puberty and struggle to achieve a satisfactory balance between autonomy and responsibility serve a number of important developmental functions. Advanced logical reasoning skills, a positive self-concept and successful exploration of identity issues are all found to be linked with a style of parent–adolescent conflict resolution in which differences are openly and vigorously confronted without anxiety or violence.

Family violence, though by no means a necessary ingredient in parent–adolescent conflict, is a growing problem in Australia and New Zealand today, as are the other problem areas of delinquency, smoking, alcohol and drug abuse and adolescent suicide. Recent research on parental leadership styles indicates that warm, democratic patterns of childrearing promote a safe passage through these developmental hazards of contemporary adolescence, as do close, supportive relationships with peers.

Adolescents sometimes seek refuge from difficulties with parents by forming close friendships with peers of the same sex. But adolescent friendship itself can be a source of turmoil and unhappiness, both for the rejected child who lacks friends and for the accepted child through its sometimes tempestuous intensity. But formal-operational reasoning skills foster adolescents' social understanding and sensitivity to their friends' needs and idiosyncracies. In addition, same-sex friendship may serve as a forum for learning the mores of dating or acquiring social sensitivity from intimacy with a close friend.

Entry into a network of boy–girl relationships through co-ed peer groups and one-to-one dating serves a number of developmental functions in addition to providing enjoyment. Consequently, relationships with dating partners and the hierarchical structures of adolescent cliques, groups and gangs undergo predictable changes as their participants pass through their teens into early adulthood.

For further interest

Looking forward on the Internet

Use the Internet to visit the following websites. Examine them for further information and varied perspectives on issues raised in this chapter. Also search for other relevant websites for yourself, using keywords like 'teenagers', 'friendship', 'peer pressure', 'drugs', 'cigarettes', 'alcohol' and 'adolescent development' in your search engine.

In particular, for further ideas on adolescent physical and mental health, visit the following websites: http://www.aacap.org and http://www.aboutourkids.org and http://www.askeric.org.

For resources, ideas, activities and other items of interest in conjunction with this chapter, visit the Companion Website for this textbook at:

http://wps.pearsoned.com.au/peterson

Multimedia

For a glimpse into the lifestyles and concerns over friendship, dating and employment of Australian teenagers view the video *Greetings from Wollongong* (Street City Pictures, Sydney, 1981: 44 minutes, colour). For a glimpse into relationships within an Australian adolescent peer group, view the video *Weekend* (Film Australia, 1977: 11 minutes, colour).

Milestones of development in adolescence

Domain of development

Physical	Emotional	Cognitive	Social	Personality
By the end of the teens, the average adolescent has achieved full reproductive and sexual maturity as well as mature adult stature and build.	While pubertal growth is at its peak, at the time of menarche for girls and spermarche for boys, emotions are unstable and readily aroused, owing to hormonal changes.	Cognition develops in important ways as adolescents make the transition from concrete-operational to formal-operational thinking.	Peers become increasingly important as social-interaction partners, models for conformity, companions and confidantes as adolescents sever emotional bonds to parents in preparation for couplehood.	Throughout adolescence, teenagers grapple with the identity crisis, according to Erikson's theory. In so doing, they strive to find a personally and socially satisfactory answer to the core existential question: Who am I?
During the process of pubertal physical growth, from age 12–20, individual differences exist both within and between the sexes that can have important psychological consequences, during puberty itself and for the remainder of adult life.	Conflict with parents escalates in frequency and intensity at this time. By late adolescence emotions typically stabilise, self-esteem is boosted and angry family conflict declines.	With the attainment of formal operations, late adolescents can reason systematically about abstract and hypothetical possibilities and are aware of multiple and probabilistic causality.	In early adolescence the friendship network consists of a small clique of same-sex friends. By middle adolescence, clique leaders have joined heterosexual crowds into which the rest of the clique is gradually inducted. Mixed-sex cliques form and continue as the basis for daily peer companionship, with crowd functions (like parties) drawing cliques together at weekends.	With resolution of the identity crisis, the adolescent, who has been through a period of turmoil, exploration of alternatives and self-doubt, finds a solution in the form of plans for a future career, philosophy of life and style of relating socially with others.
Boys who reach biological puberty earlier than most of their male peers experience less stress during adolescence but run a higher risk of identity foreclosure and marriage problems in middle adulthood.	Part of the task of adolescence is to achieve emotional independence from parents, as a preparation for the emotional intimacy of couplehood in early adulthood.	For a time, the new cognitive capacities of formal operations, in conjunction with social immaturity, may produce distortions in reasoning and a temporary sense of social self-consciousness as adolescents encounter the imaginary audience and personal fable syndromes.	In order to maintain a position in these important networks of peers, the individual adolescent must conform to the group norms, particularly in regard to readiness to experiment with boy–girl friendships and dating.	Less successful outcomes to the identity crisis include the personality patterns of identity foreclosure and identity diffusion.
For girls, early menarche is associated with poorer academic achievement in the teens, but fewer clear-cut negative consequences than for boys in adult life.	Adolescents may adopt a variety of strategies to facilitate emotional emancipation from the family of origin, but the process is likely to be stressful for both generations, irrespective of which strategy is adopted.	Eventually, new logical powers are applied to social questions and moral issues, resulting in an improved awareness of one's social situation as well as important advances in ethical reasoning.	By the end of adolescence, the crowd disintegrates into dating and couplehood.	Some teens take a moratorium and resolve the identity question in early adult life.

ADULTHOOD

PART 6

Contents

Overview

The next three chapters explore developmental psychology's last frontier: the years from the end of adolescence to the beginning of old age. We now know that adulthood, like childhood, is a period devoted to growth and change in psychological functioning as significant in its own way as the developmental gains made during the years when the body is also maturing physically. An understanding of adulthood's developmental possibilities can therefore help mature men and women (along with their teachers, counsellors, caregivers and other professional helpers) to extend the boundaries of knowledge and intellectual capacity, to clarify ethical values and personal goals, to broaden and expand commitments to other people and to social institutions, and to achieve fulfilment in marriage, friendship, parenthood and careers. Perhaps the whole issue of psychological growth is even more serious during these years than earlier, not only because adulthood occupies the major portion of the lifespan but also because adults are the 'command generation' of society. Thus the ups and downs their lives go through and the examples their behaviour sets for others will have broad ramifications for the whole fabric of society.

The next three chapters trace pshychological development through adulthood in a chronological sequence: Chapter 13 looks at the period from age 20 to age 35, Chapter 14 at the next two decades and Chapter 15 at the transition to old age during the late fifties and early sixties.

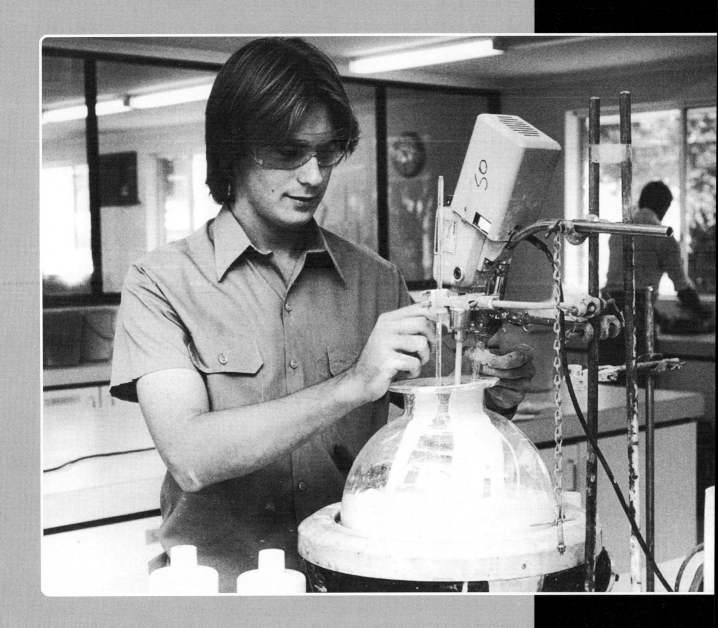

EARLY ADULTHOOD: Physical, cognitive, social and personality development

One can live magnificently in this world, if one knows how to work and how to love.

Leo Tolstoy (1828–1910)

Contents

CHAPTER OVERVIEW

Erik Erikson (1968a) reported that his mentor, Sigmund Freud, was once asked what he thought a mature adult should be able to do well. As the questioner braced himself to receive a lengthy and technical answer, Freud replied simply, 'Love and work'. Of course, when he said 'love', he was talking about parenthood and friendship as well as marriage, and about the sharing of affection, experiences and ideas with colleagues and close friends, as much as about sexual intimacy. And when he said 'work' he meant life's work, not just a place to earn a pay cheque. With his own lifelong vocation as a theorist, therapist and teacher in mind, Freud probably intended the word 'work' to describe productive activity that develops our skills, judgment and creative powers, while providing outlets for the expression of a philosophy of life and socially useful contributions to the well-being of other people and future generations.

With these caveats, Freud's description of the directions optimal lifespan development should take throughout adult life is as pertinent today as when he voiced it in the early part of last century. In this chapter we examine the changes in psychological functioning that occur when young adults set off on the developmental journey that their paths through love and work will open up during their 20s and early 30s. First, we look at the social, emotional and cognitive changes that arise in the context of the young adult's first intimate romantic and sexual relationships. Then we explore adult development in careers, marriage and the transition to parenthood. Most people would probably agree that what is most important in adulthood is loving and caring for the people we share our lives with, and putting the various talents we possess to work for causes we care about and goals we believe in.

This chapter focuses on early adulthood, or the time when men and women enter the major roles and activities that will preoccupy them in changing ways for the rest of their lives. This phase typically begins at about age 18 with the termination of adolescent physical growth, the completion of secondary schooling and a move out of the parental home. But variations in the timing of these events over a span of five or more years are not uncommon. The end of exploration and the beginning of a settled phase of adult life are even harder to pinpoint chronologically, but it is probably safe to say that the various developmental milestones of early adulthood extend from the late teens through the twenties for most contemporary Australian and New Zealand young people. These life events include falling in love, completing an education, finding a job, establishing a home, getting married and starting a family. Once each of these developmental hurdles has been crossed, the adult aged 25 to 35 has achieved sociological maturity and is ready to settle down into the various patterns of mature adult existence that are examined in detail in Chapter 14.

For most young adults, the first milestone in the passage into fully fledged adulthood involves the mysterious process of falling in love. By the age of 18, over half of young Australian adults have fallen in love at least once and consummated their emotion through sexual intercourse (see Chapter 12). For the typical contemporary young adult, the next step in the developmental sequence is the search for a place in higher education or paid employment.

In increasing numbers today, compared with their parents' and grandparents' generations, Australian and New Zealand young people are electing to remain at high school to complete the final years of secondary education. Many would prefer to enter paid employment at this point but rates of unemployment for Australian and New Zealand young people are high, and this hope is frequently frustrated. The pursuit of further education is an important stimulus to psychological development in its own right.

We study the process of career exploration and the new opportunities for cognitive, social and personality growth that arise with career entry. Then we examine the young adult's passage through the milestones of marriage and parenthood, the markers of mature adult status that anchor the 'love' pole of Freud's developmental love/work equation. The life crises and developmental opportunities created by marriage and parenthood are explored in the final sections of the chapter.

The shape of early adulthood

Unlike the teens, no fixed age in years marks the entrance into, or exit from, the *early adult phase* of the lifespan. In the absence of a culturally shared tradition of ceremonial initiation as practised in traditional Aboriginal communities (see Chapter 10), young people in their late teens or early 20s in urban, industrialised societies today often find themselves occupying for years a kind of limbo status in the life cycle where most would agree they are no longer children, yet few would be prepared to describe them as fully fledged adults. Contemporary educational,

economic and social constraints delay the attainment of full financial, residential and emotional independence from parents, especially for young people in tertiary study or who still live at home or are unemployed and seeking a job. We often agree on viewing youth as 'young adults' (rather than adolescents or teenagers) once they have made an important sociological or financial transition like renting an apartment, buying a car, entering university, finding a full-time job or getting married, though no single event is universally definitive.

Even these discrete life events are not absolutely agreed and definitive age boundaries. Consequently,

The onset of a committed couple relationship is one of the markers along the route to full adult maturity.

for convenience, it is conventional to equate *early adulthood* with the chronological period from 18 to 30 years of age.

Figure 13.1 shows one of the major transition events of early adulthood: parenthood, and the age at which this significant life event typically occurs for young women today. Some important social changes have recently transformed the timing of early adult transitions in Australia and New Zealand, as well as in Europe and North America. Marriage and parenthood are good examples. From the 1950s to the 1980s adults typically married before the age of 24 and had a first child shortly afterwards. Today, as Figure 13.1 shows, young adults usually have children closer to the end of early adulthood.

There are many ways to look at psychological development through the formative early adult years. A combination of topical and chronological approaches is used in this chapter to organise the developmental issues we chart across the early adult

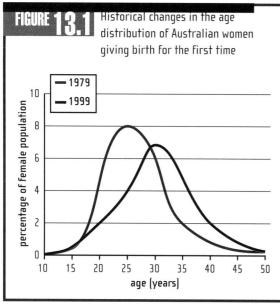

FIGURE 13.1 Historical changes in the age distribution of Australian women giving birth for the first time

Source: Based on data in ABS, Yearbook Australia (2002).

phase. The chronological approach has the advantage of emphasising the interconnected and cumulative nature of the developments and changes that arise year by year from age 18 to age 30 across the physical, cognitive, emotional, social and personality domains of psychological functioning. Figure 13.1 suggests the importance of being aware, for example, that a young adult today can count on a long period of being sexually and emotionally mature enough for couple love before having a child. The topical focus in this chapter on discrete life events, considered sequentially from falling in love to entering a career, getting married and creating a family, lends coherence to a journey that, at each developmental turning point, ushers in a host of important challenges, changes and psychological adjustments far beyond the simple progression of chronological age from one birthday to the next.

Our exploration of young people's entry into significant adult roles begins on the 'love' side of Freud's equation. The first genuine love affair is viewed by many as the dividing line between adolescence and adult maturity. After examining love as a developmental process, we explore Freud's 'work' dimension of the adult personality. Major psychological changes arise as young adults' idealistic contemplation of the wide array of career choices available in Australia and New Zealand today is tempered by the sobering fear of unemployment. Even if they do not move into jobs immediately after completing high school, the various physical and mental challenges that young adults undertake through sport, leisure pursuits or tertiary study combine to prepare them to select and achieve their major life ambitions. Work exerts a very important maturing influence on the young adult's personality.

Having found a job and established a secure economic base, many young people opt to undertake yet another important developmental transition by getting married. We examine how this important step with all its associated changes in domestic living arrangements can influence the couple's psychological functioning and emotional well-being. Deciding to have children is usually the last transition of early adulthood, chronologically, and also one of the most challenging. We examine how becoming a parent shapes adult psychological development from the point at which having a child is first considered, through pregnancy and birth, to a point of stabilisation when the first child is one or two years old.

The first adult transition: Falling in love

Falling in love is itself a developmental process. From the point of the lovers' first meeting through the climax of their affection to the affair's eventual termination, each intimate couple relationship follows a

Falling in love is itself a developmental process.

TABLE 13.1	Developmental tasks in preparation for, and initiation into, couple relationships
Developmental prerequisites for adult couple relationships	• Emotional independence from parents (see Chapter 12) • Identity crisis resolved (see Chapter 11) • Dating and/or boy–girl friendship experiences (see Chapter 12) • Understanding of contraception, reproduction and safe sex (see Chapter 10)
Developmental tasks of adult couple relationships	• Develop mutual trust and understanding • Develop roles for sharing household tasks • Develop commitment to a continuing relationship • Progressively share one another's friends, possessions, finances, leisure time, career goals and family plans • Learn skills for communicating, resolving conflict and dealing with life's problems; practise them to build deeper and deeper mutual understanding

uniquely changing course through time. Poetry describes sudden passions of love that flare up, burn brightly and die down in a compressed space of time, as well as initially mild attractions that take decades to reach their peak intensity. Romantic love and human psychological development are linked not only by their progressively changing nature but also by the fact that every love affair is shaped, in part, by the developmental status of each partner. These adults' levels of psychological maturity combine with their past experience of couplehood and romance to set the tone of their budding new relationship with one another.

We begin with a look at some of the universal changes in the emotion of romantic love that punctuate its developmental passage from acquaintance to intimacy, as illustrated in Table 13.1. We then examine how the lovers' own personality dispositions and maturity, together with their present preoccupations and past experiences, combine to play a vast array of variations on this basic theme.

What is romantic love?

In 1902 Henry Finck exclaimed that 'Love is such a tissue of paradoxes, and exists in such an endless variety of forms and shades that you may say almost anything about it that you please and it is likely to be correct'. Humorists James Thurber and E. B. White (1924) concurred with Finck's sentiments while sounding a further note of caution against the endeavour to work out a plausible theory of the love phenomenon: 'By and large, love is easier to experience *before* it has been explained' (p. 40).

Undaunted by such warnings, psychologists from Sigmund Freud (see Chapter 2) onwards have struggled with the task of accounting scientifically for the rise and fall of romantic passion. In 1974 an experiment performed by Donald Dutton and Arthur Aron on a hilly reserve in Vancouver, Canada, offered a promising lead. Two bridges played central roles in Dutton and Aron's study. The first was fear-inspiring. It was long, narrow and loosely supported, swaying

above a rocky canyon 70 metres deep. The other bridge was tame by comparison. It was short, wide and solid, and positioned only one metre above the ground. Young men who happened to be walking through the reserve were the unsuspecting participants in this scientific investigation. The researcher was an attractive young woman who positioned herself at prearranged times at the terminus of each bridge. When a potential subject crossed the bridge, she approached him to request his participation in an attitude survey she claimed to be conducting. (Actually the survey was only an excuse for engaging him in a few moments conversation and supplying him with her phone number.) The operational measure of 'romantic love' was whether any of the young men subsequently telephoned the researcher to ask her out on a date.

The results were compelling. Out of the 33 men who had been approached on the perilous bridge, nine later rang up, compared with only two of the 33 who met the researcher on the bridge that was steady. Since the woman's words, manner and appearance had been identical in both settings, the nature of the two bridges seemed to be the factor responsible for this statistically significant difference in romantic attraction.

Jane Traupmann and Elaine Hatfield (1981)

A person who believes in romantic love is apt to fall in love passionately when strong feelings are aroused by fear, anger or excitement as well as by romantic stimuli.

formulated a theory of passionate love to explain these otherwise puzzling findings. According to Traupmann and Hatfield, romantic passion arises when physiological emotional arousal is cognitively interpreted as love by the person experiencing it. The stimulus that triggers arousal in the first place need not always be romantic. Fear, anger, jealousy and other frustrations that upset physiological homeostasis (see Chapter 4) and create symptoms of arousal may be mistakenly attributed to romance by people who happen to be in the mood for love. Thus, in Dutton and Aron's experiment, a man who was unconsciously made anxious by the lurching of the bridge, but failed to infer consciously that fear was the emotion responsible for his roused feelings, might assume that the researcher's pretty face had stirred him romantically. On the steady bridge, where no emotional feelings of any kind were likely to arise, such a mental misconstruction of emotional events was less probable.

Romantic love is also an ideology (Cunningham & Antill, 1981). One of the most basic prerequisites for falling in love is a belief that the phenomenon of couple love, or romantic attraction, actually exists as a potential life experience. Some men and women are such strong believers in romantic love that they would feel cheated or abnormal unless they managed to fall 'head-over-heels' in love at least once in their lives. But to others the very notion of passionate love seems preposterous. In the extreme, a cynic about love is liable to agree with the lyrics of the song by Bob Dylan that 'Love is just a four-letter word'. A less radical stance is taken by pragmatists who believe that, although the dramatic all-compelling passion embodied in the notion of 'love at first sight' may well be a figment of history or the result of reading too many love stories, the possibility of feeling intense fondness in conjunction with sexual attraction is quite real.

Kenneth and Karen Dion (1973) devised a set of questions to identify differences like these in adults' beliefs about romantic phenomena. On the basis of the replies of some 200 male and female university students in the United States, they identified three distinctive ways of reacting to the romantic ideology. There were clear sex differences in attitudes to romantic love. The Dions found many more female than male pragmatists, while the majority of cynics and idealists were male. That many men are cynical about love fits the common-sense stereotype of the male sex, but the finding that more men than women were idealistic about love was unexpected. Past experiences of the adults in this experiment provided an explanation. The women in the sample turned out to have had a broader range of love experiences than the men. More than one-quarter of the male group had never been in love at all, compared with less than 1 per cent of the women. The women's love affairs had also lasted longer and been more intense than the men's. Thus women's greater rejection of the romantic ideology may have resulted from its proven incompatibility with their wide range of real-life encounters with the emotion of love.

Arguing that it may be hazardous to make sweeping generalisations about love on the basis of the limited experiences of 19-year-old university students, John Cunningham and John Antill (1981) extended their explorations of belief in the romantic ideology into the wider Australian community. The 293 men and women in their sample were carefully selected to represent each state and territory in Australia and to resemble the population at large in terms of educational background, socioeconomic circumstances and religious orientation.

Cunningham and Antill's findings confirmed the Dions' suggestion that adults who believed most strongly in the romantic ideology were relatively inexperienced in matters concerning the opposite sex. 'True romantics' were usually younger Australian men and women who were dating or had dated a partner but had never been married. Men and women who were or had been cohabiting or married were more likely to have pragmatic or cynical attitudes towards romantic love, and to discount the magical and stereotypic overtones of romanticism to a greater extent than inexperienced daters.

This finding is consistent with the postulate that romantic passion is a short-lived stage which gives way to a more rational or companionable style of love with age and experience as a couple. However, Cunningham and Antill also found that cohabiting couples were significantly less romantic than those who were legally married (see Figure 13.2). Married people who had lived together before taking their wedding vows resembled current cohabiters in being low in romanticism. Cunningham and Antill therefore suggested that 'their starry-eyed romanticism may earlier have come to grief, or their past life convinced them that no one partner is indispensable'

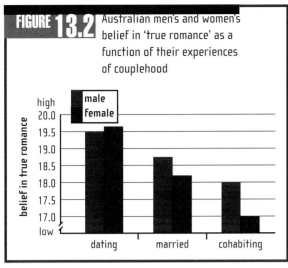

FIGURE 13.2 Australian men's and women's belief in 'true romance' as a function of their experiences of couplehood

Source: Based on data in Cunningham & Antill (1901), p. 44.

Most mature men and women believe children and early teens are too young to fall in love.

(p. 50). On the other hand, it is also conceivable that these couples' willingness to consider cohabitation as an alternative to legal marriage had developed as a result of an earlier pragmatic or cynical scepticism about the romantic ideology.

Australian couples with a wider range of sexual experiences were also found to adhere less strongly to idealistic images of romance. Cunningham and Antill reported:

> Romanticism is negatively related to the number of significant relationships and the amount of sexual experience an individual has had … The more people with whom a person has had sexual intercourse, the lower the romanticism score … Also for all groups, there was a significant negative correlation between romanticism and the view that, given the opportunity, the person would readily have intercourse with someone other than his/her partner. (p. 45)

Chronological age is a factor in adults' opportunities to taste the pains and pleasures of romantic love. The romantic ideology depicts readiness for love over the lifespan as an inverted U-shaped curve. Adolescents in their early teens are considered too young to experience full-blown romantic passion. Thus, if a 15-year-old says she has 'fallen in love', her parents and older siblings are likely to dismiss her emotions as 'puppy love', 'calf love' or mere 'infatuation'. Older teenagers and young adults are also inclined to do this when they look back to their earlier romantic experiences (Argyle, 1986). One survey of over 1000 American college students pinpointed 13 as the average age of the first *infatuation*. But the first *genuine* experience of romantic love did not occur until they were an average of 17 years old (Argyle, 1986).

Romantic love may also have an upper age boundary in popular consciousness. Kris and Richard Bulcroft (1985) interviewed a group of American dating couples who were all over the age of 50. These older men and women reported taking elaborate precautions to conceal their romantic involvements from their potentially disapproving friends, neighbours, adult children and other relatives, who perhaps agreed with a comment made by the literary critic H. L. Mencken:

> Find a man of forty who heaves and moans over a woman in the manner of a poet and you will behold either a man who ceased to develop intellectually at twenty-four or thereabout, or a fraud who has his eye on the lands, tenements and hereditaments of the lady's deceased first husband'. (Evans, 1978, p. 410)

To test whether the notion of romantic love has similarly age-specific connotations in your own immediate social environment, you may wish to complete the practical exercise in Box 13.1.

The many splendours of early romantic love

Robert Sternberg (1988) suggested that young adults' styles of love involve varied combinations of three distinct cognitive and emotional elements:

1. *Passion*: physiological sexual attraction, sex drive and the other symptoms of physiological arousal that Jane Traupmann and Elaine Hatfield identify as part of passionate love (see page 439).
2. *Commitment*: the strength of a couple's investment in their relationship and the confidence with which they plan a future together. Marriage falls at one extreme of the continuum and a casual one-night stand with a stranger at the other.
3. *Intimacy*: the degree of mutual affection, confiding and emotional closeness in the couple's relationship.

According to Sternberg, each of these three aspects of love is independent of the other two. Thus, eight different relationship styles are possible, depending on how the three factors are combined. Table 13.2 illustrates these possibilities. Apart from the state of

BOX 13.1 Media watch: The humour of love

Instructions. The cartoon here could be described as 'ageist'. Its humour depends on a stereotype of romantic involvement as inappropriate for the elderly. To assess how general this trend is, try collecting as many examples as you can of 'romantic' humour from newspapers, joke books or popular magazines. Then group the jokes according to the apparent ages of the protagonists. Compare both (a) the overall frequencies of representation of different age groups and (b) any variations in the underlying basis for humour across age. Do you conclude that love in the very old (or very young) is indeed more laughable?

'I'm afraid we will have to stop seeing each other. My children don't approve.'

Antill's work on the romantic ideology, Sternberg described 'romantic love' as an intimate passion with no commitment to a long-term future together. 'Liking', on the other hand, is a close friendship devoid of both passion and the desire to forge a committed couple relationship.

Emotional development through love experiences

While falling in love can be blissful, romantic love is also a source of intense emotional pain. One of its unpleasant side effects can be *jealousy*. Anthropologist Margaret Mead (1960) described this emotion as 'a negative and miserable state of feeling having its origin in the sense of insecurity and inferiority' (p. 94). She argued that, because jealousy is due to a fear of rejection, it can swell to crisis proportions among men and women who lack a basic confidence in their ability to inspire a partner's love. Therefore, while bound up with romantic attraction, jealousy is not intrinsically necessary. 'Jealousy is not a barometer by which the depth of love can be read,' wrote Mead (1960, p. 94). 'It merely records the degree of the lover's insecurity.'

In addition to the possibility of inner turmoil and hostile conflict between lovers due to jealousy, passionate relationships are liable to cause further heartache when the lovers break up. Unfortunately, the unstable physiology of passion makes its decline almost inevitable, according to Elaine Hatfield (formerly Walster) and G. William Walster (1978). In their experience, even the most intensely romantic of couples rarely maintains a state of emotional euphoria for more than six months, and almost never for more than a year and a half. This is partly due to passionate love's intimate connection with bodily upheavals like giddiness, a racing pulse, excess energy, pallor and loss of appetite. The human body cannot maintain such aberrant physiological states indefinitely. Even under prolonged conditions of severe stress (such as military combat) the body eventually

TABLE 13.2 Sternberg's typology of love	Emotional component		
Style of love	Passion	Commitment	Intimacy
Consummate love	+	+	+
Fatuous love	+	+	−
Infatuation	+	−	−
Companionate love	−	+	+
Empty love	−	+	−
Romantic love	+	−	+
Liking	−	−	+
Isolation (non-love)	−	−	−

'isolation', where none of the love components is present, each of these patterns can be observed when dating couples describe their love relationships (Sternberg, 1988). In line with Cunningham and

Is the thrill of passion a necessary ingredient in the experience of romantic love?

gravitates back to a stable equilibrium. Passionate love is apt to follow the same habituating course through time as the appreciation of good food and wine by jaded epicures, or splendid scenery by office workers who confront the same window day after day.

A decline in love's bodily upheavals need not always terminate the couple's involvement with one another, but this often does happen, particularly among young or inexperienced lovers who are uncertain enough about what love is to require physiological confirmation. As James Thurber and E. B. White (1924, p. 48) humorously explained:

> There is no more disturbing experience in the rich gamut of life than when a young man discovers, in the midst of an embrace, that he is taking the episode quite calmly and is taking the kiss for what it is worth. His doubts and fears start from this point ... He doesn't know whether it's love or passion. In fact, in the confusion of the moment he's not quite sure it isn't something else, like forgery. He certainly doesn't see how it can be love.

Even in the absence of physical proof of passion, the process of falling out of love is likely to cause such hurt feelings as bruised pride, frustration, self-doubt and/or loneliness. Box 13.2 illustrates this.

Sex differences are also noted in how easily young adults fall in and out of love. Men appear to cling more tenaciously than women to relationships which are on the decline. They also report longer and more intense suffering in the aftermath of a break-up (Huston & Levinger, 1978). Perhaps for this reason, women precipitate the breaking up of premarital love relationships significantly more often than men (Hill, Rubin & Peplau, 1976). Some of the reasons that men and women offer for terminating a love affair are shown in Table 13.3.

Lifespan developmental theories of love

Traupmann and Hatfield's (1981) theory of love is basically a two-stage model. They proposed that

BOX 13.2 A case in point
The morning after the ball

The following extract from a letter which Louise wrote home to her parents after attending the annual dance at her university hall of residence describes the pain of being rejected.

September 1965. *Last night it was the Ball which is about the biggest social event of the year at St Martha's. They always have it on a Friday night which made it hard for me and Gail and Trisha who have 6:30 lectures. I decided not to go to mine and Trisha didn't either. We had to get our hair done. In fact the whole David Jones hair dressing salon was made up of St Martha's girls. But Gail had to go to Economics because they take attendance so all the rest of us told our partners not to get there until about 8:00 which was just as well because we missed the handshaking with the dignitaries that Miss Combe always invites.*

Well, we just all sat around there with our partners and didn't dance much at first because it was all slow ones, but then once the floor filled up they started having the stomp, and rock-and-roll, and the twist, and all that. I only danced with my partner and he could only do the twist, so mostly we still just sat there. The band was so loud you couldn't talk and anyway I didn't know what to talk about with him. But at least he didn't go off with some other girl. I really felt sorry for poor Cathy North. Her partner dumped her and went over to Sue Wells who had this whole crowd around her—you know, she was on this one's lap with this other one playing with her fingers and all these other guys sort of clustering around her. And poor Cathy. She just sat there a little way off for the whole night because she didn't have anything else to do. And they were laughing at her and everything.

© Peterson, 1974, reproduced with permission

couples who were fortunate enough to weather the dwindling of romantic passion without deciding to

TABLE 13.3 Factors contributing to the ending of a relationship

	Women's reports (%)	Men's reports (%)		Women's reports (%)	Men's reports (%)
Couple factors			**Personal factors**		
Becoming bored with the relationship	76.7	76.7	Woman's desire to be independent	73.7	50.0
			Man's desire to be independent	46.8	61.1
Differences in interests	72.8	61.1	Woman's interest in someone else	40.3	31.2
Differences in background	44.2	46.8	Man's interest in someone else	18.2	28.6
Differences in intelligence	19.5	10.4	Living too far apart	28.2	41.0
Conflicting sexual attitudes	48.1	42.9	Pressure from woman's parents	18.2	13.0
Conflicting marriage ideas	43.4	28.9	Pressure from man's parents	10.4	9.1

Source: Adapted from Hill et al. (1976), p. 160, reproduced with permission.

separate could look forward to a new phase called *companionate love*. Companionate love can be described as a 'sturdy evergreen which thrives on contact', in contrast to the 'fragile flower' of passion. Evidence for such a contrast between fickle and lasting forms of romance came from a study in which the replies by married couples to questions about their current feelings were contrasted with those of couples who had only recently begun dating (Driscoll, Davis & Lipetz, 1972). The former group made far less mention than the latter of intense physical emotions, even including sexual arousal. Instead, the qualities of companionship, trust and mutual respect to which these experienced couples alluded sounded very similar to other adults' listings of the ingredients of simple friendship.

The notion that enduring love progresses from turbulent physiological upheaval and violent sexual desire to a stage of calm, friendly companionship is one model of the lifespan development of romantic couplehood. But there are other theories, too. Some distinguish 'mature' love from immature infatuation. Others link the growth of love to the adult development of personality. Let us examine some of these contrasting impressions of what it means to develop love over the lifespan.

Equitable love: The development from passion to the keeping of accounts

According to Elaine Hatfield (1988), the alternate ecstatic and painful emotional upheavals of romantic love are by their very nature short-lived. But, when passion fades, romance is not necessarily at an end. Over time, passion may merge into a companionate style of couple love that is marked by a preoccupation with fairness or equity. The psychological construct known as *equity* refers to a subjective sense of balance between the two lovers' contributions to the relationship and what they each gain or lose from being involved in it. Contributions may range from affection to money, clean laundry, beauty, or a warm and responsive personality. According to equity theory, the lover who contributes the lion's share of these inputs must also receive greater gains from the relationship (such as fidelity, companionship or income) in order for equity and mutual satisfaction to be maintained. Inequitable relationships evoke anger and a sense of exploitation in the partner getting less than his or her fair share, along with guilt and anxiety in the one who gains too much.

The examples from 'lonely hearts' advertisements in Box 13.3 illustrate other qualities believed by the individuals who wrote them to be desirable assets and dividends in the romantic relationships to which they aspired.

Lifespan changes in the equity balance

Using a group of 400 married women aged 50 to 92 years as subjects, Jane Traupmann and Elaine Hatfield (1983) traced the course of companionate

minded man, 40s, highly intelligent, accomplished, desirous of intimacy and commitment. Young child welcome.

TALL MALE PROFESSIONAL, SKI BUM AT HEART, seeks female professional, artist or ski bum who can read and write, to explore the coming powder.

WARM, ATTRACTIVE WOMAN, vivacious and caring, 52, professional. Loves theatre, films, art, travel and conversation. Seeks intelligent, affectionate man with sense of humour and zest for life.

BLONDE, VERY SMART AND VERY PRETTY, drama therapist. Seeks attractive, intelligent man with quick wit and integrity. Prefer divorced father 35+.

SLENDER, ATTRACTIVE MAN, 47. Enjoys art, music, history, politics, stimulating conversation, biking, travel. Seeks emotionally open, intellectually alive, slim woman.

SINGLE MAN, 30s, BLOND, seeks a special friendship with an older lady who would like to add a bit of spice to her life.

Throughout all stages of the adult life cycle, upsets in the equity balance are liable to occur.

love from dating through six or seven decades of marriage. On a scale where the wives described their own and their spouse's contributions to the love relationship in terms of an overall 'deal', the most common pattern was perfect equity. Thus, when they looked at individuals, Traupmann and Hatfield found that 52 per cent of the women had never experienced even a 'slight' disturbance of the equity balance throughout their lengthy marriages. Most of the others had had only one or two minor upheavals,

Most women report equity most of the time in their relationships.

followed by a swift return to equity. Only 10 per cent of wives reported consistent departures from equity over a period of several years. One of these was an 83-year-old woman whose marriage had been strictly equitable throughout its first six decades. Only since her 62nd wedding anniversary had she begun to feel steadily overbenefited. Traupmann and Hatfield concluded that companionate married love relationships were indeed dominated by equity throughout the lifespan.

But what happens to the unfortunate few who do encounter a disruption of marital equity? This can arise in several different ways. A wife may boost her financial contribution to the marriage by undertaking paid employment or gaining a promotion at work. A formerly overweight spouse may likewise raise the level of 'beauty' he or she contributes to the relationship by losing weight. The birth of a baby, entrance into university or a geographical separation may similarly add to or detract from partners' contributions to the companionate love equation. The equity model predicts that whenever upheavals like these arise, both lovers will immediately experience distress. This usually motivates efforts to restore an equitable balance of companionate love. But if such efforts are unavailing, each lover's enjoyment of being in love will decline and the couple may eventually decide to separate.

Elaine Hatfield (Walster) and G. William Walster (1978) tested these predictions empirically by asking a large group of American married couples whether they had ever engaged in an extramarital love affair. The rationale was that spouses who perceived the marriage as inequitable should be more willing than lovers in equitable relationships to take the risk of having an affair. If the extramarital liaison should end up threatening the marriage, an inequitably treated spouse has less to lose than an equitably treated lover whose companionate affection is, by definition, stronger. Furthermore, the changes in marriage resulting from one spouse's venturing into an overt or clandestine liaison can sometimes restore marital equity. For example, by tolerating her husband's extramarital affair, an overbenefited wife can boost the satisfactions that her unfaithful partner derives, albeit indirectly, from the marriage.

On this basis, the researchers predicted that extramarital encounters would be less common among the couples in their survey who described their marriage as perfectly balanced, or *strictly equitable*, than among those who felt themselves to be either underbenefited or overbenefited by their spouses. Their results fully supported the theory. Both underbenefited partners, who felt short-changed by marriage, and overbenefited spouses, whose marriages were already bringing them more satisfaction than they felt they deserved, were found to seek the additional gratification of extramarital liaisons more often than equitably treated lovers. The overbenefited group's inflated level of marital risk-taking was viewed by the researchers as a particularly telling testimony to the distress engendered by inequity, even in the person who profits most from the imbalance in the exchange.

Beyond companionship: Mature love

Two Sydney researchers, John Cunningham and John Antill (1981), went a step beyond Traupmann and Hatfield's two-stage model of love to propose the possibility of love developing to a higher level, where the 'score-keeping' resulting from a preoccupation with equity gradually disappears. Progress may be assisted by familiarity and the passage of time. Just as it is emotionally taxing to continue the physiological upheavals of romantic passion, it is mentally effortful to continually compute and recompute each partner's overall deal or to strive to restore equity. Cunningham and Antill explained:

> A life filled with 'Do I owe them, or do they owe me?' puts a crimp in spontaneity and free expression of one's wishes and impulses – whether prosocial or antisocial – and is costly in itself. If in love both share the same outcomes, then there is no need to keep separate tabs as to who gave and who took in any particular exchange. (p. 32, reproduced with permission from Elsevier)

However, in addition to time and familiarity, Cunningham and Antill postulated that resolution of *dialectical conflict* also contributes to the transition from equity to interdependent love. As the couple progressively comes to terms with the paradox between self and other, the focus on fair exchange is replaced by a growing sense of mutuality, 'we-feeling' or solidarity. 'The development of love pivots on this tension between concern for self and concern for the partner ... Love begins with exchange and then attempts to transcend it' (p. 34).

Sometimes the poles of the dialectic may be externalised, as when lovers quarrel. But, regardless of tactics used to resolve conflict (see Chapter 12), the development of love pivots in this model around a basic struggle for unity in the face of intrinsic contradictions between 'pre-existing values and habits, commitments to third parties, and limited resources

Over time, couples may move beyond passion and equity to interdependent love.

of time, energy, and money' (p. 34). As they fall further into love, the couple's 'increasing interdependence brings to light genuine conflicts of interest which must be resolved before further progress toward an identity of interests can be made' (p. 34).

Thus, in reality, very few couples manage to achieve the theoretically plausible ideal of perfect identity in love. But once they move beyond equity to reach Cunningham and Antill's higher level of mutual identification, or 'interdependence', clear qualitative changes in the nature of the love relationship are nonetheless evident. Instead of struggling to balance their own efforts against their private gains, or thinking only about how well their own needs are being met by their lover, mature or interdependent men and women become concerned about 'maximum joint profit to the couple'.

Cunningham and Antill explained this transition when they wrote:

> As partners fall in love, the values in the equity equation ... become transformed ... by a rule which stipulates that the outcomes of all exchanges will have the same value for both partners. 'Equality', undoubtedly a prerequisite for friendship, is not quite the proper term, as it implies that the pie is divided into halves and each partner takes his/her own half away. 'Identity' is a preferable choice; love implies that the satisfaction of the pie-eater can be savoured just as much by the pieless partner. This contrasts sharply with the marketplace metaphor, where the tit-for-tat

swap of one resource for another means that each trader loses what he had initially but acquires sole possession of the new resource. In love, both delight in one's gain and both grieve at one's loss. The loved one's pleasure and pain become one's own. (p. 32, reproduced with permission from Elsevier)

As Cunningham and Antill noted, this notion of a higher level of interdependent love that transcends Traupmann and Hatfield's equitable companionship is in keeping with Abraham Maslow's (1968) theory of a developmental progression in love during adulthood. Maslow used the concept of self-actualisation to describe this change. He viewed striving to become self-actualised in love and in life as the highest level on his needs hierarchy. To study its expression, he first identified a group of exceptionally mature and creative men and women. After analysing these adults' patterns of romance, Maslow coined the term 'being-love' (or B-love) to describe the unique style of mutual affection in their relationship. The term 'being' referred to an unqualified appreciation of the partner's entire essence as a unique human being. Maslow contrasted this with another form of couplehood distinguished by D-love (for 'deficiency' love). This is based on the lovers' mutual satisfaction of one another's basic needs. Deficiency-motivated lovers rely on their partners for companionship, emotional 'bolstering-up', sexual satisfaction, protection against loneliness and all the other major and minor blessings that participation in an intimate emotional relationship can confer on the individual. By contrast, the B-lover's attainment of self-actualisation precludes his or her dependency on any of these lower-order gratifications. Therefore, B-lovers are free to admire their partners without really *needing* them.

Maslow's self-actualising lovers were strikingly independent people. They enjoyed each other without clinging or making demands. Thus they tended to feel less competitive than other lovers and less threatened by criticism. Independence also assisted their tolerance of separation, to the point where they sometimes seemed to outsiders to be callously hard-hearted after becoming divorced or widowed. B-lovers also understood their lover's psyche unusually well, and this total appreciation made them loath to correct little flaws or 'improve' their partners in some way.

Maslow failed to observe B-love in any of the young-adult love affairs he studied. However, as well as being the norm for those relatively few older men and women who had attained self-actualisation, B-love also frequently showed itself in the marriages of non-self-actualising older couples. Maslow therefore concluded that both age and a backlog of experience in intimate living could contribute to the growth of this particular facet of emotional maturity.

Another personality theorist, Erich Fromm (1975), also viewed the development of love as a process capable of continuing throughout the lifespan. He distinguished youthful infatuations and romantic impulses from *mature love*, which he defined as follows:

> Mature love is union under the condition of preserving one's integrity, one's individuality. Love is an active power in man; a power which breaks through the walls which separate man from his fellow men, which unites him with others … In love the paradox occurs that two beings become one and yet remain two. (p. 24)

Such a view is also consistent with the developmental model of love in contemporary Australian marriages, put forward recently by Patricia Noller and her colleagues who propose that mature love supports close family ties and high levels of satisfaction with marriage. In addition, mature love creates an environment that fosters the lifespan psychological development not only of the lovers themselves but also of family members who depend on them (Noller, Feeney & Peterson, 2001).

Erikson's theory of personality growth through intimacy

Erik Erikson (1968a; see also Chapter 2) defined intimacy as the personality dimension that develops out of a successful resolution of the central developmental crisis of early adulthood. For Erikson, intimacy is:

> Mutual devotion [which] overcomes the antagonisms inherent in divided sexual and functional polarization [and] the guardian of that elusive and yet all-pervasive power … which binds into a 'way of life' the affiliations of competition and cooperation, production and procreation. (p. 137)

In other words, for Erikson, genuine intimacy implies something more than the exclusivity of 'steady' dating or sexual monogamy, and more than the togetherness of sharing a home, a bed or even one's most private thoughts and feelings. As he defined it, intimacy entails a major reorganisation of each partner's entire psychological make-up through 'a counterpointing as well as a fusing of identities'. This means that a stable, achieved identity (see Chapter 11) is one of the prerequisites for mature, intimate love.

Couples who enter a relationship before resolving their own identity crises may enjoy purely sexual intimacy but are likely to have problems in establishing the kind of emotionally intimate love relationship on which the further development of their personalities depends. As Erikson explained: 'The late adolescent wants to be an apprentice or disciple, a follower, a sexual servant, or patient' (p. 168) to his or her lover. Temporarily, this idolatrous subjugation of one's own sense of identity to that of one's lover may ease the pain of identity uncertainty and role confusion. But as a developmental strategy it is almost always doomed to fail, both as a way of love and a way of solving the identity crisis. Until a secure sense of identity is achieved by resolving the crisis, Erikson argued, 'Fusion with another becomes identity loss' (p. 108). So, the immature and identity-uncertain lover is apt to retreat from love affairs, which plunge the self-concept into an unbearable state of confusion.

Researchers Judith Hall and Shelley Taylor (1976) discovered that a mild form of idolatry was quite prevalent among the young inhabitants of Harvard University's married-student housing. They asked 26 students from this population of young couples to give detailed personality descriptions of their spouse, themselves and a friend. Ratings of the spouse were glowing and 'highly idealized' compared with the pictures painted not only of self but of friends as well. Hall and Taylor found that these idyllic visions of marriage partners were maintained by means of mental biases and the distortion of reality. Whenever something good happened, the idolatrous lover gave his or her spouse full credit for it. But bad outcomes, including unpleasant actions by the spouse, were blamed on outside circumstances and events. This discovery prompted Hall and Taylor to ask to what extent idealisation is desirable in marital relationships. They felt that, although serving a benevolent function in the short term, idealisation was a potentially unsatisfactory long-term strategy:

> Idealization may blind us to problems which if confronted honestly could be worked out to the benefit of the marriage. Idealization may also lead to unrealistically high expectations which, when violated, set the stage for a more serious confrontation than would realistic expectations. (p. 76)

Another way of coping with interpersonal relationships prior to the establishment of a secure sense of identity is by a process which Erikson labelled *interpersonal isolation*. Since intimacy threatens a weak identity and disrupts the autonomy which the adolescent's emotional emancipation from parents has conferred, many young people prefer self-contained isolation, at least for a time. They would rather suffer the pangs and deprivations of loneliness than surrender their hard-won emotional independence fully to another human being. Their relationships consequently remain superficial. However, by this means they at least avoid the risks and compromises entailed in a major personality reorganisation, or a genuine long-term commitment.

Thus, according to Erikson's theory, the development of a satisfactory and potentially lasting intimate relationship depends on both partners having previously resolved their identity crisis. In one empirical test of this idea, researchers interviewed 53 male university students to measure intimacy crisis resolution along with resolution of Erikson's preceding crisis over identity. (Orlofsky, Marcia & Lesser, 1973). The questions included such issues as the degree to which the men shared feelings and had insight into the needs of friends and dating partners, and also how enduring, intense and mutual their relationships with these people were.

Five different levels of intimacy emerged in response to these questions. At the most mature, *fully intimate* level were 14 men who had stable, deep and trusting relationships with male friends and also a steady girlfriend. These men were 'generally characterized by a good deal of self-awareness, a genuine interest in others, and the absence of significant defensiveness' (p. 213). Next came a group of 11 *pre-intimate* men who had values that disposed towards intimacy but felt ambivalent about commitment and intimate sexuality. A third category contained both *pseudo-intimate* (12 men) and *stereotyped* (9 men) patterns. The former group had gone through the motions of making a lasting commitment to one woman. However, because of a lack of responsibility, understanding and openness, the relationship was 'a mutual isolation in the guise of intimacy' (p. 213). The stereotyped men were enmeshed in superficial dating relationships. Some dated one girl steadily but understood her poorly. Others seemed merely to be 'going from one conquest to the next'. The final category consisted of seven *isolated* men who had no enduring personal relationships of any kind and tended to be 'anxious and immature and generally lacking in assertiveness and social skills' (p. 213).

These data suggest that a moderately satisfactory resolution of the identity crisis is a prerequisite to the attainment of intimacy. Men and women who have not yet completed the developmental task of working out who they are and what they want from life are likely to remain socially isolated or else to limit their emotional relationships to the stereotyped and superficial plane. But adults who have achieved a stable identity are able to embark on a mature and genuinely intimate style of couplehood.

Adult attachment and romantic love

As noted in Chapters 5 and 12, adults' approaches to love can be directly compared with young infants' patterns of attachment to their primary caregivers. Cindy Hazan and Phillip Shaver (1987) discovered that when adults were asked about (a) their attitudes to love, (b) their feelings about the person they were in love with, and (c) their lover's responses to them, three distinct patterns of adult loving emerged.

Newlyweds' idealisation of each other may interfere with identity development and with practical accommodation to the routines of married life.

Furthermore, these adult attachment styles match the three categories of attachment uncovered in Mary D. S. Ainsworth's (1973) pioneering infancy studies (see Chapter 5): (1) avoidant, (2) secure, and (3) anxious-ambivalent. Box 13.4 includes examples of three distinct styles of adult attachment.

Using a sample of young Australians as subjects, Judith Feeney, Patricia Noller and Janice Patty (1993) examined how the experience of falling in love for the first time was shaped by these three distinct styles of adult attachment. The 193 young men and women who took part in their study were assessed for attachment style using Hazan and Shaver's (1987) self-report measure. They also kept a diary in which all their interactions with friends and lovers were recorded on a daily basis. The results supported the hypothesis that attachment style helps to determine the nature and quality of early romantic relationships. As Figure 13.3 shows, the young men and women whose style of attachment was avoidant were more likely than their secure or anxious-ambivalent peers to report that they had never been in love. Perhaps these avoidant young people were still grappling with Erikson's interpersonal isolation.

The Australian young adults in the sample studied by Feeney and her colleagues who had a secure style of attachment were the ones who were most likely to have fallen in love only once by age 20, and to still be dating the person they had first fallen in love with. Those who had an anxious-ambivalent style reported multiple, though brief, affairs and only half were currently dating. Secure subjects' couple relationships were generally more affectionate, more satisfying and of longer duration than the romantic involvements of the other two attachment groups. The diary records indicated that avoidant subjects had fewer interactions of any kind with members of the opposite sex than males and females from other attachment categories. Young people with a secure style of attachment to intimate others also socialised with a larger circle of same- and opposite-sex friends than their peers with avoidant or anxious attachment styles.

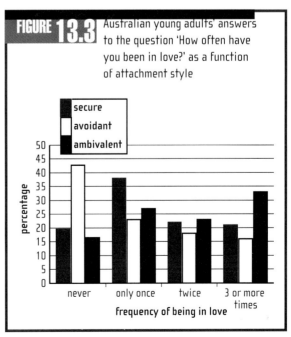

FIGURE **13.3**   Australian young adults' answers to the question 'How often have you been in love?' as a function of attachment style

Source: Based on data in Feeney et al. (1993).

When a dating relationship broke up, reactions by members of the three attachment groups were also strikingly different. Avoidant lovers expressed more relief than the others, on average describing themselves as 'quite' relieved and only 'slightly' upset. Anxious-ambivalent lovers experienced more surprise at the break-up than the other two groups, suggesting that they might have been less well-attuned to their partners' feelings and less skilled in monitoring the progress of their dating relationships.

On the other hand, anxious-ambivalents were also the group most likely to report being in love again in the immediate aftermath of breaking up with a previous lover. Feeney and Noller concluded that the 'clinging relationship style and the poor relationship quality which characterises this style may be explained in part by the persistence of issues which have not been adequately resolved in previous romantic relationships' (p. 73).

Jean Hammond and Garth Fletcher (1991) examined attachment styles in a sample of 20-year-old dating couples who were attending university in Christchurch, New Zealand. A total of 64 per cent of these students had a secure attachment style. Another 20 per cent were anxious-ambivalent and 16 per cent were avoidant. These proportions are very similar to reports on samples of young adults in the United States, according to Hazan and Shaver (1987), and in Australia, according to Feeney and Noller (1992). It would seem that adult attachment styles develop in a similar manner in all three cultures.

Hammond and Fletcher were interested in how attachment style might relate to partners' satisfaction with their dating relationships. The possibilities of longitudinal changes in attachment and its links with satisfaction over a four-month period were also considered. As predicted, romantic partners with secure attachment styles were initially found to gain greater satisfaction from their experience as a dating couple than their peers whose styles of attachment were either anxious-ambivalent or avoidant. As time went on, the quality of the dating relationship created changes in attachment style, but not vice versa. In other words, young lovers who had entered their early love affairs with anxious or avoidant attachment styles tended to progress towards greater security in their patterns of attachment over four months, provided they shared mutual trust and, were satisfied in love. On the other hand, securely attached lovers whose encounters with dating were traumatic tended to become more anxious and ambivalent as time went on.

Hammond and Fletcher concluded that, while the styles of attachment brought by individuals to their first romantic relationships may have been forged in early parent–child interaction, these styles are malleable in the face of couple love itself. This means that the adverse consequences of the unfortunate attachment experiences described in Chapter 5 can be reversed in adult life. An adult who, as an infant, was insecurely attached to both parents is not necessarily doomed to loneliness and insecurity in couple love. A satisfying and supportive relationship with a romantic partner can prove to be of great assistance in overcoming such early emotional setbacks. Conversely, a secure infant attachment style does not provide complete protection against heartbreak and attachment insecurity if the young person's early love relationships prove to be painfully harsh, mistrustful and disappointing.

These studies divided adult attachments into Ainsworth's three broad groupings, but there is another way of looking at couples' attachment patterns. Attachment styles can be subdivided into four categories on the basis of the individual's implicit model of self and his or her model of the other person in the intimate relationship (Feeney & Noller, 1996). These four categories are shown in Table 13.4. As can be seen, the resulting typology of approaches to love is similar to the three-group model of adult attachment. The main difference is that the anxious-ambivalent style subdivides into two groups: the *preoccupieds* (who have a negative view of themselves as unworthy of love, but a positive view of others as potentially loving and supportive) and the *fearfuls* (who are negative about both self and others).

Research conducted in New Zealand, Australia and the United States has shown that young adults' attachment styles are quite stable over an eight-month period (Feeney & Noller, 1996). Furthermore, the occurrence of disruptive life events such as a geographical move or a relationship break-up has not been found to diminish attachment stability in the, admittedly atypical, affluent and well-educated samples of young adults that have been studied.

When she examined the attachment styles of a group of 361 Australian couples who had been married for between one and 20 years, Judith Feeney (1994) discovered a link between secure attachment and relationship satisfaction. At every stage in the family life cycle, husbands and wives with secure attachment styles were happier with marriage than men and women who had been married for the same number of years but had anxious-ambivalent or

TABLE 13.4 The four-category model of attachment styles in relation to working models of self and other

		Model of other people in relationships	
		Positive	Negative
Model of self	Positive	Secure	Dismissing or avoidant
	Negative	Preoccupied	Fearful

avoidant styles of attachment. Communication patterns also contributed to the observed association between attachment and marital satisfaction. Australian husbands and wives who used mutually constructive methods of communication when they needed to resolve disputes, or wanted to share ideas with one another, emerged as more satisfied with marriage and more likely to have secure attachment styles than husbands and wives who routinely avoided communicating or became aggressive, sulky or anxious during disagreements. (For a more detailed discussion of the impact of conflict-resolution styles on family relationships, see Chapters 12 and 14). Feeney suggested that an anxious or avoidant attachment style may lead to maladaptive communication patterns, limiting spouses' opportunities to achieve intimacy and enjoyment in marriage:

> In marital relationships anxiety is associated with increasingly negative patterns of communication for both males and females … and, hence, may engender dissatisfaction. (pp. 345–6)

From a developmental standpoint, these Australian results suggest a move towards greater individual attachment security as marriage progresses. Compared with couples in marriages of more than 20 years duration, husbands and wives who had been married for between one and 10 years reported more anxiety about relationships and less secure patterns of attachment. Worries about the relationship breaking up and being abandoned by the partner were much more common in newer marriages than in longer-term ones. (In Chapter 14 we examine some additional developmental changes that are observed reliably in marriages spanning several decades.) One development explanation for these results could be a change in attachment patterns as a result of a positive marriage. In other words, husbands and wives who enter marriage with insecure attachments might gradually revise their internal working models (see Table 13.4) as a result of the gains in trust and mutual understanding they achieve as the marriage progresses. Based on her observation of a link between attachment and communication, however, Feeney suggested an alternative developmental possibility:

> Marriages with at least one highly anxious partner may be less likely to endure, given that anxiety is associated with … marital conflict and destructive responses to this conflict. (p. 344)

Attachments to love and work

We often think of love as a separate and unique domain of human existence that offers a completely different set of pleasures, pains and challenges from those encountered in a career. Yet, in terms of psychological development, intimacy and employment have much in common; and within the developing adult's own life, the two are inextricably entwined. Not only does an employed adult face the challenge of how to balance investments of time and energy between the two domains, but there are also important patterns of overlap and integration between love and work throughout the lifespan.

Attachment style is one such link. When Hazan and Shaver (1990) examined young adults' orientation to work alongside their emotional attachment to their romantic partner, they discovered that attachment style was a strong predictor of the way men and women approached their jobs. Individuals who were securely attached to their spouse or lover approached their career with enthusiasm and confidence. They also gained high levels of satisfaction from the job they did. But love always came first – for secure lovers, opportunities to cultivate and enjoy an intimate relationship took clear precedence over the demands and opportunities of employment. Whenever conflicts threatened to arise between needs at home and at work, securely attached intimates typically put concern about their partner ahead of the chance to fulfil an exciting vocational challenge. An opportunity for promotion, for example, might be rejected if it required a timetable or a geographical move that would jeopardise the couple bond.

Adults with an avoidant attachment style, by contrast, were inclined to immerse themselves so completely in their job that they had little time or energy left over for intimacy. While gaining high levels of satisfaction from work, their overwhelming investment in their occupation seemed somewhat defensive. Many of these men and women appeared to view their job as a legitimate excuse for not becoming involved in a close relationship. Hazan and Shaver concluded that avoidant adults who mistrust intimacy 'use work activity to avoid social interaction' (p. 278).

The remaining group of respondents had an ambivalent attachment style. You may recall that this approach to love is characterised by a preoccupation with the need for intimacy, coupled with intense anxiety over rejection and loss of love. Adults who approached close relationships in this way were found by Hazan and Shaver to possess similarly anxious and uncertain attitudes about their job. Thus, they were apt to become preoccupied with anxiety and competition at work. While they typically invested themselves wholeheartedly in their job, their motivation for doing so seemed more a fear of being laid off or demoted than genuine love of the work they were doing. In other words, young adults may express similar needs both at work and in their love relationships. At the same time, they may gain either similar, or compensatory, satisfactions from these two key domains of psychological growth (see Table 13.5).

Another important similarity between love and work is the rapid and predictable progression of changes that punctuate early adulthood. Let us now look at the steps that mark the young adult's entry into the world of work.

TABLE 13.5	Attachment styles and employment experiences	
Securely attached	**Insecure attachment**
High job satisfaction	Low job satisfaction
Friendly relations with co-workers	Poor relations with co-workers
Trust in boss/supervisor	Distrust praise
Confident of career future	Sense of job insecurity
Minimal work versus love conflict	Work conflicts with family life on a daily basis
Enjoy group work, comfortable with individual responsibility	Dislike boss and dislike group work (avoidant attachment)
Confident in job skills	Worry about own performance (ambivalent attachment)

Source: Based on data in Hazan & Shaver (1990).

Children begin to think about having a job many years before occupational entry, and skills taught in school are justified in terms of their relevance to future employment.

The first career development transition: Graduating into employment or unemployment

Though most contemporary Australians and New Zealanders do not enter permanent employment until their late teens or early twenties (see Figure 13.1), the crucial significance of having a job as a marker of adult status begins to be stressed during childhood and adolescence. Schools justify the teaching of specialised skills (from computing to legal studies or higher mathematics) on the grounds of their relevance to future employment prospects, and rules about prompt arrival, neat dress and industriousness may also be justified in school on the grounds they will be demanded in the workplace. Thus, by the time they leave high school most adolescents have already built up expectations about the careers they would like to enter and their chances of being able to secure a job (Feather, 1983).

Work is also a key factor in marking the cognitive transition from adolescence to maturity, according to Jean Piaget (see Chapters 2 and 11). 'The adolescent becomes an adult when he undertakes a real job. It is only then that he is transformed from an idealistic reformer into an achiever' (Inhelder & Piaget, 1958, p. 346). From a personality perspective, embarking on a career is seen as a route towards self-definition and a means of resolving Erik Erikson's identity crisis (see Chapter 11). A move into the workforce has the added advantages of proving to the world that the adolescent has attained full maturity as an adult, and of helping to sever any lingering ties of emotional or economic dependence on parents (see Chapter 12).

Work is also seen as a way to express the skills at learning and the specific aptitudes that decades at primary and high school have cultivated, even for young people who have ambitions other than a job that will help them grow rich. As one Melbourne adolescent told researcher Millicent Poole (1983):

> In 10 years time I'd like to be just married. I'd like to have been overseas and had a ball. I'd like to marry a popular easy-going, loving man who is interested in art and sport. I'd like to live somewhere interesting, somewhere that's exciting and different. I'll be a mother after then. I'd like to be still doing art and hopefully have achieved a name for myself somehow. I'd like to be able to sing and I'd decorate my home. I'll lead an interesting life, travelling with my husband and meeting new people all over the world. I hope my husband's a (famous) professional tennis player, and Australian. (p. 303)

In the light of all these personal hopes and proven developmental advantages, it is a source of serious concern when a young adult's first taste of the job market culminates in the pain and disappointment of unemployment. Yet in Australia and New Zealand today this is a frequent outcome. Table 13.6 shows the rates of unemployment in Australia in the years 2000 and 2001. For young people aged 15 to 19 years who have finished school and have no plans for further study, unemployment is about four times as high as in the 35- to 44-year-old group, and it remains twice as high even for 20- to 24-year-olds, many of whom would have completed university or vocational training and be eager to enter the world of work. In Table 13.6 these age differences in unemployment patterns in the Australian workforce are documented.

Table 13.7 illustrates recent historical trends in unemployment in Australia. Trends in New Zealand are comparable. The overall percentage of the New Zealand workforce aged 15 to 64 who were registered as unemployed rose dramatically from only 1 per cent in 1961 to 1.4 per cent in 1973 and then to almost 5 per cent by 1985 (Bethune & Ballard, 1986). By 1991, 9.8 per cent of the New Zealand labour force was unemployed and the level was similar in 1995 and 2000 (NZ Department of Statistics, 1995, 2000).

The very high rates of youth unemployment are worrying, not only in their own right but also because of the developmental need for young people to cross the threshold into adult status by taking on a full-time job. In line with the figures for Australia that are shown in Table 13.6, in New Zealand in 1995 the unemployment rate for young men and women aged 15 to 19 was 21.5 per cent (NZ Department of Statistics, 1995). Maoris and females are more likely to be unemployed at all ages than Pakeha males (New Zealand Department of Statistics, 1995).

Psychological consequences of unemployment

A number of Australian researchers have tackled the problem of unemployment from the standpoint of its potentially damaging influence on the psychological growth and well-being of young people. In one of the first of these studies, Alison Turtle and her associates (Turtle, Cranfield, Halse-Rogers, Reuman & Williams, 1978) found that young unemployed men and women in Sydney's low-income neighbourhoods suffered poorer levels of physical and mental health than their former high school classmates from the same neighbourhood who had been lucky enough to find paying jobs. The jobless young adults were less self-confident and more lethargic and socially isolated than their employed peers. They went out to clubs, movies and other public entertainment less often, which might have been due to economic hardship. But they also took less exercise, attended parties less often and had fewer informal chats with their friends. Since these latter activities are not directly dependent on income, the unemployed young person's failure to participate in them appears symptomatic of unemployment's adverse influence on emotional well-being. Turtle's unemployed young adults also read fewer books, magazines and newspapers than their working counterparts, despite having access to these media in the public library and more spare time than the employed to devote to constructive leisure pursuits like reading.

Such adverse correlates of the unemployment experience are found to grow more pronounced the longer joblessness continues (Feather, 1985). When Sydney young people who had just lost their jobs

TABLE 13.6 Unemployment rates for younger and older adults in Australia, 2001–2002			
	Percentage unemployed* (percentage of age cohort)		
Age cohort (years)	Males	Females	Total
15–19	21%	21%	21%
20–24	11%	9%	10%
25–34	6%	6%	6%
35–44	5%	6%	5%
45–54	4.5%	4.5%	4.5%
55 and over	5%	3.5%	4.5%

Note: * Excludes those not looking for full-time work and those in full-time study.
Source: ABS, Yearbook Australia (2002).

TABLE 13.7 Typical duration of unemployment in Australia: Annual averages						
Duration out of work (weeks)	1995–96	1996–97	1997–98	1998–99	1999–2000	2000–2001
Under 52	72.5%	73.0%	70.8%	70.3%	73.2%	76.6%
50–103	12.3%	12.8%	14.1%	13.1%	10.7%	9.7%
104 and over	15.2%	14.2%	15.2%	16.6%	16.1%	13.7%

Note: The annual average is the percentage of the total unemployed cohort who have been out of work for the specified time.
Source: ABS, Yearbook Australia (2002), p. 125.

The notion that unemployed young people can happily spend their days in a holiday-like leisure existence is a myth. Hobbies (like fishing) cost money, and the motivation to pursue them can be undermined by the stresses of joblessness.

were contrasted with a group who had been out of work for five months or more (Turtle & Ridley, 1984), the long-term unemployed were found to smoke more heavily, drink more alcohol, play less sport and visit the doctor more often than their short-term counterparts. In addition to these health hazards, the males in the long-term unemployed group slept more and had less contact with male and female friends than their peers who had only recently failed to find work.

Interviews by Norma Bethune and Keith Ballard (1986) with a group of 50 Dunedin unemployed school-leavers revealed a similarly increasing tendency to feel bored, apathetic and insecure the longer joblessness continued. Almost half their unemployed New Zealand adolescents could name no other activity besides housework or watching television when asked how they spent their time on a typical day, and one commented: 'There's lots to do, but I can't be bothered doing it' (p. 139). Fifty-four per cent likewise claimed to spend all or most of their time alone, 70 per cent blamed unemployment on their own personal deficiencies and 78 per cent felt bored, frustrated and angry.

Roy Nash (1981) likewise noted a higher incidence of petty crime and drug-taking in unemployed New Zealand young people, as well as 'restlessness, apathy, hopelessness, lowered sense of self-worth, lack of self-confidence and a loss of trust in the system' (p. 3).

Research in Sheffield, England, by Peter Warr (1983) also led to the inescapable conclusion that unemployment poses a serious psychological health hazard: 'Without doubt the psychological health of unemployed people is significantly below that of people with jobs' (p. 306). However, the extent of the psychological strain created by unemployment will vary, according to Warr, with the following factors:

1. *Commitment to work.* English men and women who accorded a relatively low personal priority to employment coped better with job loss than those who could see no meaning in life apart from working. A study of unemployed university graduates in South Australia also showed more damaging psychological consequences for those who felt strongly committed to being employed than for their unemployed classmates who had other interests in life besides employment (Feather & Bond, 1983).
2. *Age.* Warr found that middle-aged unemployed men experienced the greatest strain as a consequence of job loss, partly because they had greater financial commitments and family responsibilities than younger or older men.
3. *Activity level.* Unemployed people who managed to keep busy and found purposeful uses for their free time fared better than those whose job loss reduced them to physical, social and mental inactivity. Another English study by Marie Jahoda (1982) also showed that problems of boredom, inactivity and lack of purpose were greater for young unemployed school-leavers than older unemployed groups.

Longitudinal research on youth unemployment

A problem with the results of many cross-sectional comparisons between unemployed and employed young people is the unanswered question of whether the salient psychological problems of the unemployed arose as a result of their being out of work or, alternatively, were among the reasons for failure to find a job in the first place. To achieve a clearer insight into the probable causes and consequences of unemployment, a number of longitudinal studies of youthful unemployment have been conducted in Australia.

One of the first, by Ross Gurney (1980), tested Melbourne high school students during their final year before leaving school. Measures included levels of self-esteem, the extent to which pupils had resolved Erikson's identity crisis (see Chapter 11) and the strength of the feelings of competence, personal control and self-efficacy that we explored in detail in the context of infant development in Chapter 4. Gurney waited until the school-leavers had been on the job market for several months and then contacted them again for a second assessment session. By this time some had found jobs, some had joined the ranks of the unemployed and others had made a last-minute decision to stay on at school. Gurney administered the same set of measures in the second assessment. When he compared the young people's earlier and later scores, he found little change among the unemployed or at-school groups. But those Melbourne teenagers who had moved from high school into paid employment showed substantial gains in self-esteem, sense of control and overall personality growth. Gurney concluded that 'Unemployment has the effect of inhibiting development in

Becoming unemployed may cause psychological adjustment difficulties.

school-leavers rather than of inflicting trauma as is sometimes popularly supposed' (p. 212).

However, the results of further longitudinal studies of Australian school-leavers have combined to suggest that becoming unemployed may also cause psychological difficulties. A longitudinal study of 113 Brisbane school-leavers by Wendy Patton and Patricia Noller (1984) first measured self-esteem, locus of control and depression when the teenagers were all still at school. Five months later, some had found jobs, some had stayed at school and some had left school to become unemployed. Compared with their own earlier self-esteem scores, dramatic falls were noted in the unemployed group after just five months of futile job search. A slight contrasting boost in the self-esteem scores of the employed teenagers after finding a job supported Gurney's earlier result. Together with the drop in self-confidence, depression, gloom and apathy increased in the unemployed Brisbane youths to levels far above those registered by the same girls and boys while still in school.

Table 13.8 links the results of longitudinal comparisons of Australian school-leavers to the length of time they remained without a job.

Complex interconnections exist between the antecedents and consequences of unemployment. This was shown in the longitudinal study of

TABLE 13.8	Results of Australian longitudinal studies of unemployed adolescents	
Duration of unemployment	Source	Findings
2 months	Jones, 1980	Unemployed have lower self-esteem and more symptoms of mental illness than employed peers. Unemployed blame themselves for failure more than employed peers. Unemployed believe more strongly in the Puritan work ethic. Unemployed are less choosy about jobs they will do and have fewer requirements for an 'ideal' job.
4 months	Gurney, 1980	Unemployed blame themselves for failure more than employed peers. Unemployed girls have lower self-esteem than employed girls.
5 months	Patton & Noller, 1984	Unemployed have become more depressed and less self-confident. They feel less in charge of their fate than when they were still in school.
6 months	Tiggemann & Winefield, 1980	Unemployed are (a) more bored, (b) more lonely, (c) less satisfied with themselves, and (d) less happy than employed peers.
9 months	Jones, 1980	Unemployed have fewer requirements for jobs they would do than employed peers and than themselves 7 months earlier. No differences in self-esteem or mental health between unemployed and employed young people; significant improvements for unemployed compared to selves 7 months earlier.
1 year	Tiggemann & Winefield, 1984	Unemployed are more depressed, less well-adjusted and lower in self-esteem than employed peers.
2 years	O'Brien & Feather, 1990	Unemployed are more depressed, less satisfied and less internally controlled and self-confident than peers in challenging jobs. Those in low-quality, unskilled employment did not differ from unemployed.

Australian school-leavers by Marika Tiggemann and A. H. Winefield (1984), listed in Table 13.8. Figure 13.4 illustrates this Adelaide sample's mean scores on personality measures taken while they were still in school (T1) and after the school-leavers had either found jobs or gone on the dole (T2). No differences in boredom or feelings of 'learned helplessness' (Seligman, 1975; see also Chapter 4) were evident between the two groups at school but, after they left, the employed became less bored and helpless and the unemployed more so, just as the theory of psychological damage due to joblessness would predict. On the other hand, the observed contrasts in depression scores were consistent with the theory that an unemployed teenager's failure to find a job can be blamed partly on pre-existing personality defects. While still in school, the group destined to become unemployed scored significantly higher than their peers on standardised clinical tests of depressive feelings. Surprisingly, after several months of being unemployed, their depression declined to match the lower levels registered by their employed counterparts.

Thus, longitudinal evidence uncovers the complexity of the relationship between unemployment and personality development. While some personality problems (like learned helplessness) seem to be a direct consequence of frustrated career aspirations, others (like depression) seem to function as causes rather than consequences of being unemployed.

Gordon O'Brien and Norman Feather (1990) also tested a group of high school students in Adelaide who, two years after leaving school, had become employed, unemployed or university students. The employed Australians were subdivided into two groups. One group had found good-quality jobs which provided challenge and opportunities to utilise

skills and education. The others were employed, but in low-quality jobs that proved to be routine and unfulfilling. There were few differences between the unemployed adolescents and those working in poor-quality jobs. But young people who had gone on to university and those in high-quality employment were less depressed, less stressed, more self-confident and higher in life satisfaction than their peers. Thus, the results of this study suggest that it is not employment *per se* but rather the opportunity to work at tasks that match people's skills and challenge them to develop new ones that makes career entry such a positive influence on psychological functioning and well-being.

Taken collectively, the results of these longitudinal studies concur with cross-sectional findings in suggesting that there are likely to be adverse psychological consequences for the young Australian or New Zealand school-leaver who is unable to secure a job. Groups of adolescents who differed relatively little while still in school became markedly different after several months of being either employed or unemployed. The employment experience appears to boost development, while prolonged unemployment can be both emotionally and socially damaging.

Tiggemann and Winefield (1984) concluded that: Whatever the precise mechanism, it is clear that differences in terms of reported negative mood, self-esteem and depressive affect do exist between the young employed and unemployed, and that these differences can be attributed to their employment experience. And while it is primarily the employed who improve, such a finding should not allow us to become complacent. The results are consistent with a notion of paid work leading to growth rather than of unemployment leading to debilitation. For these young people,

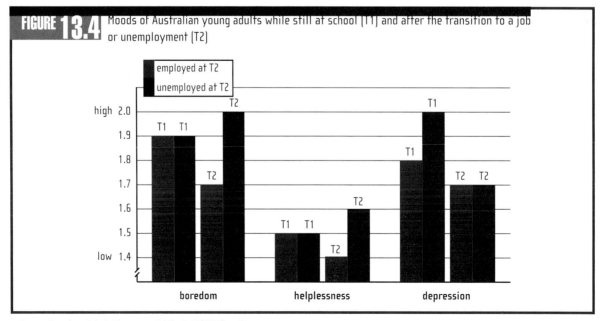

FIGURE 13.4 Moods of Australian young adults while still at school (T1) and after the transition to a job or unemployment (T2)

Source: Based on data in Tiggemann & Winefield (1984), p. 37.

getting a job, still the 'normal' and desired option in our society, provided something valuable for their identity and self-concept, something which the unemployed missed. Such a retardation of 'normal' development is hardly a pleasant finding. It appears that the unemployed individual is not given the same opportunity to grow and develop as his employed counterpart. One can as yet only speculate as to whether such consequences subside after the individual is able to obtain a job, or persist if the opportunities provided by a job are denied for a sufficiently long period of time, resulting in permanent psychological damage. (p. 41)

Thus, quite apart from developmental gains in skill or reasoning that may be acquired on the job, entry into the labour force in itself serves as a major milestone for adult psychological development. It is unfortunate that not all young adults in Australia and New Zealand today can feel assured of enjoying the benefits of a smooth transition into the world of work. Optimisers of development may strive to boost opportunities for psychological growth in at least three ways:

1. Improving employment prospects for young adults whose risk of unemployment is more than double that of older age groups in Australia and New Zealand today (see Table 13.6)
2. Combating the social prejudice and stigmatisation associated with unemployment
3. Supplying opportunities for challenging voluntary or leisure activities that will compensate for work's maturing influence (see Chapter 14).

Perhaps the sheer recognition that a problem exists is a useful first step. According to Tiggemann and Winefield:

It is important to recognize the existence of such psychological consequences as a result of the unemployment experience, in addition to the economic consequences. A large group of young people who are disqualified, unhappy, and whose self-esteem is dwindling is likely to give rise to a variety of social problems. How, or indeed if, the young may be helped to cope with the problem is not clear. Obviously more research is needed to provide a factual basis for any social policy directed to that end. Certainly the difficulties the young are facing can only be exacerbated by the perpetuation of the commonly expressed view that they 'laughingly laze on beaches ... and indulge themselves all day', a view this study helps refute. In fact, unemployment results in genuine psychological stress. We have demonstrated psychological consequences for the individual in terms of happiness and loss of self-esteem even after only a few months. We can only speculate as to the consequences, perhaps even irreparable consequences, that might result from longer periods of unemployment. (1980, p. 276)

The potential importance of work as a stimulus to adult development and adjustment can be gauged not only through the effects of its absence, as in unemployment, but also in the sheer number of hours that most adult men and many adult women spend on the job. For example, Douglas Heath (1977) estimated that a professional–managerial occupation consumes about 100 000 hours of a person's life – more time than is normally devoted to any single activity besides sleeping.

Employment also indirectly structures much of the worker's life outside working hours. Where a family lives, who their friends are, their leisure pursuits, their roles and functions in the community and their position in the economic status hierarchy all depend to a large extent on the husband's and/or the wife's occupation. Furthermore, since vocational activities change with the passage of time, adults' patterns of lifelong psychological development are also shaped by their progress into, through, and out of the world of work.

Career planning

One important stimulus to young adults' plans, and hence to their lifelong patterns of career development, is the occupational climate of the society and era in history into which they graduate from formal education. The world of work is an ever-changing one, as the cyclic unemployment fluctuations described above (see Table 13.7) aptly illustrate.

In times of full employment, when job vacancies are plentiful and workers eager to fill them are scarce, young people have a broad range of careers available as options. But when economic conditions conspire to make jobs scarce, as in Australia and New Zealand at the present time, some young people must face the frustration of being unable to embark on the psychological tasks of career development. For those who do manage to find a job, freedom of choice and the terrain available for career exploration are necessarily curtailed.

The progress of technology is another social change affecting early career development. In addition, society's attitudes to higher education, on-the-job training, and both informal expectations and formal rules about the age for leaving or entering the labour market all have a bearing on who is employed and what work they are doing. These factors help to shape employment's impact on the psychological development of the individual. Sudden societal changes such as war or a depression may radically alter the entire course of a worker's career and lifestyle. But gradual changes also occur. As W. E. Henry (1971) observed:

Work is a continuing engagement in the human community, a community presenting changing patterns of options and contingencies. The realities of the work community keep changing with changes of policy and personnel. (p. 127)

No single career pattern or family lifestyle seems normative any longer. As we see in Chapter 14, large numbers of Australian couples today are opting for the *dual-career* work–family pattern in which both spouses are employed outside the home, sharing domestic duties and childrearing, often with assistance from paid outsiders. Many men and women opt to return to study at various ages throughout adulthood and will leave one career path to embark on a very different *second career* (see Chapter 14). Couples today have fewer children and have them later than their parents' generation did, and these changes, too, have had profound effects on identity growth (see Chapter 11) and marital and family development (see Chapter 14). Technological change has led to new kinds of jobs (especially in the computing and electronics industries) and the need for advanced education has escalated correspondingly.

Men and women who are out of synchrony with the typical timing of life events in their ever-changing career and family life cycles may find their adjustment to change more difficult. Bernice Neugarten (1968) noted this in the personality problems and feelings of stress that emerged in a group of army officers who had remained 'too-long-in-grade' without being promoted to a higher rank. Dennis Hogan (1980) similarly found that:

> The scheduling of events (timing, spacing, and sequencing) by which ... males make the transition from adolescence to adulthood has lasting consequences for career attainments in the later life course. (p. 275)

Having observed that the normal sequence of life events for the sample he studied was to complete formal education, then enter a job and then marry, Hogan studied the ordering of these three events in the lives of 18 000 North American men aged 20 to 65. The results showed that men who had violated the expected sequence received a significantly lower income than their peers in the same job (from the same educational and economic background) who had progressed through the three developmental transitions in the normal order. Men who broke both

ordinal rules by marrying before graduation *and* occupational entry were found to suffer even greater earnings deficits than those who had graduated but not yet become employed before marriage. Timing seemed as important as the nature of the change for emotional adjustment. In Chapter 15 we observe similar findings with regard to the timing of late-life transitions like retirement and grandparenthood.

Consequently, effective career planning is a much more complex business for young adults today than it was for earlier generations. Fortunately, thanks to recent research in lifespan developmental psychology, career counsellors, vocational guidance personnel and workers themselves are now aware that effective career planning is a lifelong undertaking, not something to be accomplished once-and-for-all by taking an aptitude test or sitting for a job interview at the end of high school. In Chapters 14 and 15 we continue our exploration of career plans, cognitions, aspirations and motivations during the later decades of adult life.

Entering upon a career path

Entry into the workforce is an important milestone for young people, who develop psychologically in important ways as they assume the new identity of an employed adult. Three major developmental issues preoccupy young adults during the transition from school or unemployment to the world of work – (a) career goals, (b) career identity, and (c) career choice. These issues are salient irrespective of whether the move is into a job, an apprenticeship, a training scheme or a professional specialisation at a college or university. In each case, vocational preparation includes the following psychological aspects.

Career values, goals and satisfactions

To give meaning to work and derive satisfaction from the activities undertaken in the course of their careers, young adults must perceive a value in work over and above the immediate monetary incentive of taking home a pay cheque (Feather, 1979). The development of ideas about values and priorities for work typically begins while the adolescent is still in school, but the transition into a career setting greatly aids the putting of these values into perspective. Until a 'real' job is undertaken, the concrete practical meaning of values like 'a good relationship between supervisors and subordinates' or 'challenging and varied jobs to do' is not likely to be fully understood.

Like values in general, 'career values' refer to the ideals, goals and tangible and intangible end-states that a working individual holds dear. Some values apply broadly both to work and to all the non-work areas of a person's life. For example, an individual may value 'equality' both as a principle guiding fair employment, democratic decision-making and mutual respect between co-workers on the job,

Men who marry before completing their education and taking their first job may suffer lasting career setbacks through violating the normal developmental sequence.

and as a crucial determiner of the quality of marriage or political and governmental leadership. But some work values (such as skill utilisation or an aesthetic working environment) are specific to work, or even to particular kinds of jobs.

Thus the development of a valid set of vocational and career values has both general and specific aspects. At the general level, this is part of the lifelong task of evaluating and re-evaluating goals and priorities and deciding on purposes for life as a whole (Feather, 1985). But for those values that apply specifically to work, or are more readily identified, put into practice or fulfilled at work than in other arenas of living, the ordering of priorities and the development of a value hierarchy can be viewed as a crucial component of vocational preparation and career selection. As Gordon O'Brien (1985) pointed out: 'Whether or not an individual is productive and satisfied with a given job depends, to some extent, on his or her values, needs and personality' (p. 247).

Donald Super (1970) developed a test of work values which has seen extensive use in Australia (Pryor, 1980) and New Zealand (Hesketh, 1982). Figure 13.5 illustrates the relative priorities assigned to some of the most salient of these goals and values by samples of 446 Australian and 229 New Zealand young people who were in their final year at school.

Not all jobs allow such goals to be achieved. Furthermore, the link between work values and job satisfaction is not a straightforward one. In fact, when Beryl Hesketh attempted to use work values to predict the job satisfaction of a group of 82 employed New Zealand men and women, she found that the only significant predictors of extent of liking for the new job were the rather mundane material values of income, job security and pleasant physical surroundings. In other words, workers who (a) had placed a high priority on economic returns before entering the workforce, *and* (b) had been lucky enough to find a well-paying job, were happier at work than their classmates who had either not valued income so highly in the first place or else valued it highly but had ended up taking a job with a low salary. The same applied to tenured, secure jobs and physically attractive workplaces. But when it came to such work values as intellectual stimulation, altruism and creativity, no predictive links with job satisfaction were discerned, suggesting that these values may be more difficult to implement, at least during the early stages of a working life.

Gordon O'Brien (1985) similarly reviewed a large body of Australian research into the association between work values and job satisfaction and concluded that:

> The Australian studies show that work values account for a relatively small percentage of the variance in job satisfaction. Whereas job characteristics such as skill-utilisation and influence accounted for about 40 per cent of the variance in job satisfaction and work motivation, work values accounted for less than 5 per cent. The main implication of these studies is that the large majority of employees want jobs that use their skills and provide them with some control over work procedures. When they experience jobs with these characteristics they report high levels of satisfaction and work motivation. Individual differences, due to work values, do have a small effect but the magnitude of this effect is of little practical consequence. (p. 248)

Identity development at work

Erik Erikson (1959, 1968a) viewed the development of a career identity as an important component of the personality crisis over personal identity and self-definition that spans adolescence and early adulthood (see Chapters 2 and 11). The timing may be even more protracted today than when Erikson (1959) first put forward his theory of identity in the middle of last century, given that a complete resolution of the occupational identity cannot take place until young adults move into the world of work and have the chance to test their vocational interests and skills against the opportunities and requirements of their career environment. Still, when contemporary Australian and New Zealand children are asked 'What do you want to be when you grow up?', the answer is almost invariably the name of an occupation. It seems that occupational identity development is one of the most important of all the psychological needs served by entry into the world of work.

As noted earlier, Ross Gurney's studies of employed and unemployed Melbourne school-leavers showed major progress in resolution of the identity crisis by the employed group after they moved from high school into their first job. Conversely, as Betsy Wearing (1996) noted, the threat posed by unemployment to lifespan identity development is one of the most serious of the many psychological

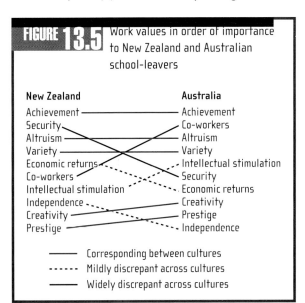

FIGURE 13.5 Work values in order of importance to New Zealand and Australian school-leavers

New Zealand / Australia

Achievement — Achievement
Security — Co-workers
Altruism — Altruism
Variety — Variety
Economic returns — Intellectual stimulation
Co-workers — Security
Intellectual stimulation — Economic returns
Independence — Creativity
Creativity — Prestige
Prestige — Independence

—— Corresponding between cultures
····· Mildly discrepant across cultures
—— Widely discrepant across cultures

Source: Based on data in Hesketh (1982).

hazards of the high rate of youth unemployment in Australia. As she explained:

> Due to the high level of unemployment there is little hope of the formation of an occupational identity for many adolescents today. Feelings of self-worth for these young people are likely to be extremely low in a society where the 'work ethic' is strongly emphasised … If they do manage to find an alternative route to identity, the definition allocated to such an identity by dominant groups in society will be that it is deviant from the norm and inferior, thus keeping them in a powerless position vis-à-vis the employed person. Even when an occupational identity has been established, the development of technology is likely to threaten its continuity throughout adult life. (p. 21)

Mary Ann Kacerguis and Gerald Adams (1980) discovered that a young adult's resolution of the occupational aspects of Erikson's identity crisis was a better predictor of future development progress through Erikson's stage system than other identity issues such as the crystallisation of personal values, moral codes and religious beliefs, or the development of a sense of identity as child, friend and future marriage partner. Among the 88 male and female university students in their sample, one group had resolved the crisis over occupational identity to the point of having explored options for themselves and settled firmly on a career that matched their own particular goals and talents. When it came to Erikson's next crisis, over intimacy, this group had made greater progress than their peers whose occupational identities were either foreclosed, diffused or in moratorium. Somewhat paradoxically, in view of the theoretical link between intimacy and the sense of self as a future spouse and lover, a student's degree of resolution of interpersonal or philosophical identity issues bore no clear relationship to his or her level of intimacy development. Evidently, the career question is central to the contemporary young adult's overall identity growth.

Career exploration

Before opting definitely for a particular career direction, most young adults in Australia, New Zealand and other industrialised societies today take time to 'test the water' by examining the advantages and disadvantages of a variety of different possible lines of work. This can be done through part-time jobs while still in school, by taking career education classes or by paying visits to vocational counsellors, workplace settings and already-employed friends. Eventually, the process of career exploration may take practical shape in the form of a first job.

Career theorist Donald Super (1957, 1990) proposed that the first step in building a career path and a career identity was one of career exploration. He proposed that the young person needs to explore the world of work to find a career matching their personal ambitions, interests and skills. Richard Pryor

A career is not only a means of earning a living but also a source of friendship and psychological impetus to resolve the identity crisis.

and Neville Taylor (1986) studied this process of career exploration in a group of 287 Australian technical college students in New South Wales. Ranging in age from 17 to 42 (the mean was 20), about half of these young adults had already discovered while in college that the ability to achieve a compromise between career ideals and available job opportunities in the real world of work was one of the most important developmental outcomes of a successful career exploration process. The other half were floundering. Without the ability to compromise, even over so basic an issue as what they would do if they failed their forthcoming examinations, this 54 per cent was in urgent need of vocational planning help. As Pryor and Taylor pointed out, even if they managed to graduate successfully and were fortunate enough to gain entry into their chosen course of apprenticeship or further study, their incapacity to compromise would place them at risk when they tried to find a job and engage in effective exploration of career alternatives in the world of work.

Pryor and Taylor (1986) found that women were better than men at achieving a sensible match between their vocational interests and the constraints and possibilities of chosen careers. In fact, only 29 per cent of male students were aiming for a future career that was in any way congruent to their stated vocational interests. The remainder seemed to have opted for careers with high visibility, income or status or difficult entry requirements without considering their own work values or whether they personally enjoyed creative, artistic, socially useful or investigative pursuits. Women's success in matching their interests to their career plans was much higher, with 67 per cent of female students having made career choices that were at least partially in keeping with their stated vocational goals and interests.

The males' difficulties appeared to have been exacerbated by failure to engage in adequate career exploration. But an additional problem was their overly rigid adherence to traditional sex-role stereotypes. In this Australian sample, the men were inclined to restrict their career horizons to male-only jobs, whereas the female students claimed to feel more at liberty to select from lists of jobs traditionally dominated by men, as well as those stereotyped as feminine or for both sexes.

The first stage of career development

Many theorists who have examined the process of career development through the lifespan have described it as a series of qualitatively distinct stages (Havighurst, 1964; Levinson, 1986; Super, 1957, 1990). We study these stage models in more detail in Chapter 14, since they have greatest relevance to psychological development during middle adulthood. Despite differences in these later stages, all developmental career theories agree that the first step in the career life cycle is a period of exploration, identity uncertainty and rapid learning. Indeed, initial entry into the paid workforce necessitates a radical lifestyle reorientation. Some of the lessons to be mastered, such as the job skills required or a professional code of ethics, will depend on the specific career the young adult happens to enter. But others are almost universal. New social roles are demanded when joining a peer group of fellow workers, and also compliance with the job's authority hierarchy and social-status structure. New relationships with parents, dating partner or spouse may also emerge, together with the new economic freedom and the reduction of free time and energy that employment brings.

As novice workers' job experience increases, the requirements and opportunities created by work in general, and by the chosen line of employment in particular, become increasingly apparent. Such issues as the hourly, daily and weekly pattern and pace of work, the pay structure, criteria for promotion and the range of tasks the worker is called on to perform vary from job to job.

Trial commitment

By 'shopping around', young adults in their first career may, when the economy is favourable, be able to move from one employer to another to find the best combination of these job characteristics. At the same time, accommodation to the job's requirements may begin to developmentally modify the individual worker's own psychological orientation, goals and ambitions. Regardless of the extent of their previous exploration of values, identity issues, careers and compromise strategies during the transition to work, the matching of workers to their new jobs at the point of career entry is likely to be as incomplete as the matching of husbands and wives on their wedding day.

Just as the development of couplehood extends over a major portion of adult life, the working out of a satisfactory relationship between workers and their chosen line of work is apt to extend over many years,

Professionals who undertake demanding careers may have little time or energy left over for recreation or intimacy.

entailing not only the changing of a job to suit the person but also the development of the person to suit the job. The first step is often the seeking of a satisfactory vocational identity by trying out a series of different jobs, or moving from one apprenticeship or course of study to another even before career entry.

Adjusting to the job

To assess the impact of the prolonged transition from formal tertiary study into the professional workforce, Mary Westbrook and Lena Nordholm (1983) followed a group of 93 female health science graduates longitudinally from entry into tertiary education until 20 months after graduation. By this time, all the women were fully employed in their chosen profession of speech pathology, physiotherapy or occupational therapy. Their average age was 23 years and 26 per cent were married. Overall, their satisfaction with their chosen career was very high. On a scale asking for agreement or disagreement with the statement 'All in all, I'm satisfied with my career choice', the average level of agreement was 6 out of a maximum of 7. However, there were also some key areas where the job had failed to live up to the women's expectations. Table 13.9 shows the various aspects of the job where these health professionals' hopes had been frustrated. Areas of gratification and indifference are also shown.

From a developmental standpoint, these disappointments were intriguing. The two most notable complaints by these Australian career entrants were feelings of (a) *personal stagnation*, or lack of opportunities to develop and extend their skills, and (b) *thwarting of achievement*, or a lack of opportunity to accomplish something meaningful and worthwhile. It would seem that even a professional career

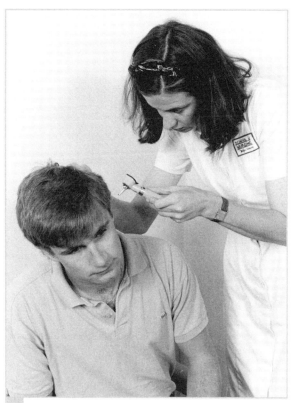
Women who enter a health science career are likely to report high levels of career satisfaction.

whose hopes and plans had been more conventional and sex-stereotyped. Higher job satisfaction was also predicted by women having adopted more radical or feminist attitudes as students, and having planned to place their careers ahead of finding a spouse or raising large numbers of children. The satisfied therapists had also placed less importance than their dissatisfied peers on the goals of making friends, enjoying life, marriage, parenthood or experiencing adventure. Presumably, these values were difficult to satisfy within the confines of a professional career.

But Westbrook and Nordholm also suggested that those health professionals who eventually gained the greatest satisfaction from their jobs had probably also modified their goals and values more than other therapists over the course of their professional training. As first-year students, almost all the women had been preoccupied with such hedonistic goals as boyfriends, adventure and enjoyment. But those who later became highly satisfied had shifted their priorities over time so that, on entry into the workforce, they accorded highest value to professional achievement and altruistic concern for their clients.

Marriage and psychological development

Most contemporary Australians and New Zealanders believe that love and marriage, in the words of the old song, 'go together like a horse and carriage'. Adults who are not in love are not supposed to marry, whereas those of the right age who fall in love with eligible partners are under strong social pressure to do so. In other cultures, such a linkage appears nonsensical. Marriage is seen as a planned family merger, arranged for eminently rational and practical reasons. Within this framework, the emotion of romantic love is treated as a dangerous aberration, or 'psychological abnormality', which without proper safeguards could

frequently fails to provide the new recruit with tasks challenging enough to encourage creative or self-actualising development, at least during the early stages of working life.

Westbrook and Nordholm (1983) also found that the women's career attitudes when they first entered tertiary study continued to predict their levels of contentment or distress with jobs some four years later. Those who, as first-year students, had held unconventional attitudes about the future were more satisfied when they entered the workforce than women

TABLE 13.9 Sources of job satisfaction, deprivation and indifference for Australian health professionals		
Gratification (i.e. 'The issue is important to me, and I am satisfied with this aspect of my job.')	**Indifference** (i.e. 'It makes no difference whether I gain this from my job or not.')	**Deprivation** (i.e. 'The issue is important to me, and my job is not bringing the satisfaction I expected.')
Job features Freedom on the job Relationship with the boss Friendly co-workers Salary Taking part in decisions	**Job features** Security or tenure Opportunity for promotion Physical surroundings	**Job features** Earning respect or recognition from others Feedback on own performance Sense of accomplishing something worthwhile Skill development Resources available to do the job properly

Source: Based on data in Westbrook & Nordholm (1983), p. 121.

Do love and marriage go together like a horse and carriage?

destroy the fabric of society (Linton, 1936). Thus well-to-do parents in prewar Japan and prerevolutionary China employed marriage brokers whose impartial judgments of personal compatibility and the mutual advantages to the bride's and groom's extended families were deemed to be sounder bases for the undertaking of a permanent commitment to couplehood than the fickle emotion of love.

Among the Australian Aborigines of Arnhem Land, tradition decreed that a female child should be betrothed at birth, ideally before the blood had ceased flowing from the placenta. Such an arrangement offered the girl economic and social security. If her parents died before she reached maturity she retained a protector concerned about her welfare. The parents' impartiality in arranging the betrothal before complicating factors like romantic love, or the son's or daughter's fickle opinions, could intervene was seen as a further advantage auguring the marriage's future success:

> If the arrangements are made before the girl, in particular, is able to voice an opinion in the matter, this union is more than whim—that is, it is a longstanding affair, thoughtfully decided on, and so has more chance of enduring. (Berndt & Berndt, 1964, p. 168)

Even when the engagement did not originate at birth, traditional Aboriginal parents preferred to have their children's marriages arranged by tribal elders rather than through romantic love (Bell, 1980). Box 13.5 illustrates the progress of one such arranged courtship and marriage.

Love and marriage

This cross-cultural difference of opinion over whether marriages based on practical and economic grounds are sounder or more durable than those based on romantic love is reconsidered in Chapter 14. But regardless of whether they decided to marry for love or at the behest of their parents or professional matchmakers, couples the world over face many of the same problems when they begin to share a household together. The decision to get married offers many attractions. Not only is there the promise of security and the opportunity to replace the emotional unrest of passionate love with the stability of companionate affection (see pages 442–6), but also important developmental opportunities that apply specifically to married or cohabiting couples.

For marriage itself is a developmental process of change that occupies most of the adult years of life and imposes a series of age-graded demands on its participants. When people fail to conform to social expectations about when to get married, when to buy a home or when to have a first and a last child, they are likely to encounter the same social pressure as is applied to such other deviations from the 'Act your age' rule as wearing inappropriately 'young' or 'old' styles of fashion, or not advancing through career milestones on schedule (see Chapter 1). Novelist Monica Dickens, out of step with these expected temporal sequences of adult life, ruefully described what it was like to get married for the first time at age 36:

> Some of my friends who had left me behind by marrying at the usual age were already divorced. Now they had lost me a second time. I was still in the wrong camp. (1978, p. 142)

Irrespective of timing, however, and contrary to myths of the overwhelming popularity of the single lifestyle that occasionally emerge in the popular press, a vast majority of Australians and New Zealanders today do end up getting married. For example, the New Zealand census of 1991 revealed that only 17 per cent of women over the age of 20 and 17 per cent of men over the age of 25 had never been married (New Zealand Department of Statistics, 1995). Similarly, in Australia at the present time only a 4 per cent minority of women and 9 per cent of men have not yet been married by age 40 (Australian Bureau of Statistics, 1995). When cohabitation is included along with marriage, it is clear that couplehood is a fact of life for most young adults. But the age for getting legally married for the first time is later now than it was in the 1970s.

The fact that most people do conform in one way or another to the demands of a sequentially organised, family-oriented life cycle has implications for the study of adult psychological development. Just as the behaviour of typical 7-year-olds can be as much a function of entry into school and learning to read as of having been alive for seven years, so psychological functioning during early adulthood needs

BOX 13.5 An Aboriginal arranged marriage

Douglas Lockwood (1962, p. 110) interviewed Waipuldanya, a full-blooded Aboriginal health worker, who described his tribal arranged marriage at Roper River in the Northern Territory. Tribal law dictated that the maternal uncle of 20-year-old Waipuldanya should choose a bride from the eligible kinship class. Neither Waipuldanya nor his intended bride, nor even the bride's or groom's parents, had any say in the matter. In fact, the couple were not even introduced or allowed to speak to each other before the wedding ceremony. Waipuldanya described the arrangement as follows:

'I have a wife for you,' my uncle said.

'Her name?' I asked.

'Dulban, Ngamayang, Wandarang,' he said, giving Hannah's personal name, her skin and her tribe ...

What could I say? The decision had been made for me. Objections would be useless. And, anyway, I did not want to object. I was secretly pleased, for Hannah was attractive by all Aboriginal standards: maiden's firm breasts, rounded abdomen, strong thighs, large eyes with long lashes, broad nostrils, full lips, and flashing teeth revealed by a spontaneous smile which broke without cause into melting feminine laughter.

'What does her gardi-gardi say?' I asked.

'He agrees,' Marbunggu said.

And I knew that nothing could now stop my immediate marriage, for Hannah had even less right than I to an opinion on whom her partner should be. I knew that whether she liked me or not she would be my wife and bear my children. If she resisted she would be taken on a walkabout holiday by her relatives. Before leaving, her uncle would invite me to a rendezvous in the bush. When I arrived he would point to the girl and say, 'Take her away. She is yours.' She would then become my wife by force under the Mungu-Mungu law of our ancestors.

Fortunately nothing like that happened. Hannah was apparently satisfied with Waipuldanya of the Bungadi skin of the Alawa tribe.

A few days later her paternal aunts made a camp for me away from my parents: a fire with wood to stoke it, water, food, and a double blanket laid out on the sand.

Then they came to me. 'Tonight you will be getting married. That is your camp,' they said.

We had no engagement, no kitchen tea, no wedding ring, no bridal gown, no bridesmaids, no groomsman, no banquet, and certainly no champagne. There was not even a brief courtship or a single word from me to Hannah.

Reproduced with the permission of Mrs Ruth Lockwood.

to be understood in relation to the task of forming an intimate commitment to a partner, and the behaviour of 50-year-olds must be studied in relation to the requirements of an 'empty nest' and preretirement couplehood (see Chapter 15). Indeed, John Flavell (1970) suggested that marriage stimulates adult cognitive development through the new challenges, conflicts and pleasures that it brings. He felt that most 'really significant and enduring changes in an adult's cognition' grow out of marriage and parenthood and 'consist of changes in the individual's implicit theories regarding self, others, and the human condition generally' (p. 250).

Nevertheless, the decision over whether to cross the threshold from being single to being legally or informally married can be a difficult one for many young adults today. Although few engaged couples or honeymooners are fully aware of the magnitude or the difficulty of the transition they are about to embark on, the shift from single to conjugal existence disrupts nearly every aspect of an individual's early mode of life. Independence and spontaneity must be sacrificed in favour of a new self-definition which includes responsibility and mutuality as a couple. At the same time, a whole host of more mundane challenges shatter the habitual outward pattern of daily existence.

When they set up residence together, couples must modify many of their old eating and sleeping habits, their former recreational patterns and the approaches to housework which they acquired either as children in their parents' home or when living independently. The potentially disruptive consequences of having to share such household accoutrements as toothpaste

Newlyweds and cohabiting couples must modify the habits of a singles lifestyle when they move into a household together.

tubes, teabags, television sets, beds and alarm clocks are well known. Marriage and cohabitation also create new duties and domestic chores which were either not present or at least not as onerous during single life. Right from the beginning, most new couples undertake a more ambitious style of entertaining than before, assume added financial burdens and take on new duties and responsibilities in relation to each other, each other's friends and both sets of relatives. A sexual relationship must also be developed or extended. So new learning, as well as changing old habits, is virtually inevitable.

Division of domestic labour

Once couples decide to marry, one of the first sources of friction they are likely to encounter in married life is how to share out the many new chores created by moving into a household together. Disputes over tidiness and expenditure, differences of opinion about who should wash dishes, do the laundry or take out the garbage, and conflicting expectations about how lavishly to entertain guests or how often floors need vacuuming, are inevitably bound up with the lengthy process of creating an acceptable domestic routine. In the end, most couples opt for one of three different styles of household role division (Duberman, 1974).

The first is the *traditional* approach. Couples who adopt this system adhere to a policy of role specialisation in which the man and the woman have totally distinct spheres of influence and responsibility. The husband (for most traditional couples are conventionally married) shoulders the major decision-making and breadwinning roles outside the home. He also controls most aspects of the couple's economic or recreational behaviour (e.g. paying bills, accepting dinner invitations or planning travel and family outings). The traditional wife becomes an equally narrow specialist in housework and childrearing and controls most other functions within the boundaries of the family circle (e.g. writing to parents and in-laws).

A second style of couplehood is *egalitarian*. This approach rejects role specialisation of any kind. In its ideal form, either partner can and does assume all the rights and all the role activities of the other partner. If the man washes dishes and scrubs floors one week while his wife cooks meals and tends the garden, they switch tasks for the next week or month. Alternatively, they may divide each job and benefit neatly down the middle so that sharing is uniform at all times. Over time, however, some specialisation normally creeps in since society makes it hard for each adult in a family to do exactly half the breadwinning and half the childrearing.

The third broad style, the *partnership*, is a compromise between the other two extremes. In a *colleague partnership* (see Table 13.10) spouses may choose to specialise in particular lines of domestic work, but the choice is made on the basis of the particular interests and aptitudes of each person

| TABLE 13.10 | Options for style of role division in marriage |

Style of role division	Description
Egalitarian	The spouses share all roles, tasks and chores in and outside the home equally.
Traditional	Husband and wife have completely separate domains of responsibility. The division mirrors traditional patterns for the two sexes, with husbands responsible for income, planning, major financial decisions and outdoor chores (car, lawn, pool, etc). Wife is fully responsible for homemaking and childrearing.
Colleague partnership	Spouses choose a domain of domestic responsibility that suits their own interests and skills irrespective of tradition (e.g. husband – chef, wife – car maintenance).
Junior–senior partnership	The wife (= junior career partner) is employed outside the home but takes the major (senior) share of the housekeeping and child-care roles inside the home; the husband is the senior career partner and part-time 'helper' of the wife in 'her' domain of child care and domestic chores.

rather than according to gender or patriarchal tradition. Thus a husband might do the cooking because he enjoys it, while the wife might opt for mechanical repairs or gardening. In the extreme, traditional roles may be completely reversed, so that the wife becomes the sole breadwinner and the father the children's primary caregiver (see Chapter 5). Junior–senior partnerships entail some specialisation in the context of equal access, in principle, for each spouse to all marriage and extra-familial roles. Thus both partners are usually employed, but one (often the woman) has senior responsibility on the home front, and the other (often the man) takes primary responsibility for breadwinning.

Each style has its advantages. The traditional style, matching the long-enduring stereotype of marriage in our culture, may meet the expectations of friends, relatives, neighbours and the larger community with a minimum of fuss. An egalitarian division of roles offers the benefit of encouraging both partners' full development of their own skills and personal effectiveness in all areas. Thus either spouse can smoothly take over from the other, if need be. Also, neither the husband nor the wife in an egalitarian marriage can complain of being exploited or denied the pleasure of the easier or more interesting jobs (though both may complain of overwork or of

The sharing of roles on an exactly equal basis, as in the egalitarian style, can create a struggle, both within the couple and between the couple and society.

getting in each other's way). Perhaps for these reasons, an ideological preference for egalitarian marriage is growing rapidly among educated young couples in Australia and New Zealand today (Feeney, Peterson & Noller, 1994). The colleague partnership style is also becoming more popular. It lessens some of the pressure for all-round competence which successful egalitarianism requires, while still allowing spouses to develop those special aptitudes and interests that do not happen to conform to traditional gender roles.

But both egalitarian and colleague styles have their disadvantages. Each clearly demands more effort than traditionalism during the early phase of marriage, if only because spouses must draw up their own plans and convince one another about how domestic roles should be allocated, rather than conforming unquestioningly to rules dictated by tradition.

Traditional, egalitarian and partnership households all depend for their long-term success not only on how skilfully the two spouses fulfil the various duties allocated to them but also on how well the style they have adopted fits in with their attitudes and ideological preferences. In a longitudinal study of 43 newlywed couples in Sydney, Alan Craddock (1980) found greater discord after several months of marriage among spouses whose preferences had initially been incongruent than among those husbands and wives who had entered marriage with an agreement either that an egalitarian role division was preferable to the traditional pattern, or vice versa. Furthermore, those households in which a traditionalist husband clashed with an egalitarian wife experienced more discord than in those where the wife's traditional beliefs were in conflict with her husband's more egalitarian attitudes. Perhaps the traditional wife's willingness to undertake most of the household drudgery made the latter situation easier. Craddock also found that individual sex-role orientations influenced

marital satisfaction in a similar manner. Husbands were more satisfied with marriage when their wives had a traditionally feminine sex-role orientation and wives were more satisfied when their husbands were feminine or androgynous. In other words, having a spouse who, regardless of biological gender, adopted the feminine social qualities of nurturance, caring, supportiveness and submissiveness was an obvious asset to marital harmony.

Another study of middle-class Australian families compared husbands' and wives' rankings of the roles they expected their partner to fulfil with the spouses' own assessments of how well they performed these same role activities (Krupinski & Stoller, 1974). The roles that these couples viewed as most important were usually divided along traditional lines. Husbands expected their wives to take charge of housework and child care, giving these two roles first and third priority, respectively, while wives expected relatively little from their husbands in these two domestic areas, and ranked them lowest of the roles on their list. Conversely, the breadwinner role, which women saw as the third most important of all their husband's activities, was viewed by men as a trivial factor in their wife's overall contribution to the home. Both men and women expected an egalitarian sharing of roles involving couple companionship, sexuality and playing with and teaching children. These three roles were placed immediately after homemaking and breadwinning in importance.

After assessing husbands' and wives' expectations about what their spouse's role priorities ideally should be, the investigators also looked at what their priorities actually were by interviewing them about one another's domestic role behaviour. Among stable, happy marriages they found that the alignment was very close: one spouse's expectations tallied almost exactly with the priorities given by the partner to the things the spouse did around the home. But, among a group of troubled couples attending a marriage guidance clinic, large discrepancies were found. It seemed that inappropriate role allocation and performance can contribute to marital breakdown.

Lawrence Kurdek (1995) studied the division of domestic labour longitudinally in a sample of 75 gay and 51 lesbian couples in the United States. The couples rated how important equality was in their cohabiting relationship on annual assessments spanning three years of living together. They also described their actual patterns of relating by using the statements listed in Box 13.6.

Kurdek found that, over time, some partners came to feel more committed to their couple relationship while others grew less committed and still others registered no change. When actual levels of equality in the relationship fell short of the partners' ideal levels, commitment to the relationship declined among both gay and lesbian lovers. But Kurdek also found that lesbian relationships were more egalitarian overall than either the gay male couple relation-

BOX 13.6 Taking things personally: Test your own relationship

Instructions: If you are presently involved in a close couple relationship, you may wish to pause for a moment and assess its egalitarianism using a scale based loosely on Kurdek's (1995).

Item	Response
1. My partner and I have equal power in the relationship.	True ☐ False ☐
2. My partner depends on me as much as I depend on him/her.	True ☐ False ☐
3. My partner and I invest equal amounts of time and energy in the relationship.	True ☐ False ☐
4. My partner and I contribute equally to the day-to-day lives we lead together, including housework, earning a living, and leisure pursuits.	True ☐ False ☐
5. When it comes to a major decision (e.g. car or home purchase, job change) we have an equal say in the final outcome.	True ☐ False ☐

Scoring: For each item that you marked 'true', give yourself one point. For 'false' choices, score zero. Add up your total. Scores of 4 or higher indicate a strongly egalitarian relationship. To see if your perceptions match those of your partner, ask him or her to take the test. If your scores differ by more than one point, you see the relationship differently from one another.

A wife who is employed outside the home does not generally escape her full quota of domestic responsibilities.

ships he studied or the typical heterosexual cohabiting relationships described earlier in this chapter. Not surprisingly, therefore, lesbian partners rated equality as more important than did gays, and decreases in actual equality over time were especially destructive to commitment and happiness in lesbian relationships.

Are roles becoming more equal?

Alan Craddock's time-lag study of unmarried Sydney university students' expectations about role division in marriage from 1973 to 1985 suggested a move towards more egalitarian beliefs over this period, especially among men. These students, however, had yet to marry and face the realities of role division on a day-to-day basis.

More recent studies do in fact suggest that, regardless of attitudes, actual marital role performance has not become noticeably more egalitarian in Australia or New Zealand in contemporary genera-

tions (Australian Bureau of Statistics, 1995, 2001). Women have moved into the workforce in far greater numbers than during the middle of last century (see Chapter 14), but on the home front they are still expected to accomplish the bulk of housecleaning, cooking and the various other domestic duties that wives traditionally undertook as full-time homemakers without the added demands of a career.

A study of New Zealand married couples by Peggy Koopman-Boyden and Max Abbott (1985) showed that the average wife in full-time or half-time paid employment was busy for about 65 hours a week, including housework. Her husband worked a total of 57 hours a week, while wives who were not employed spent 54 hours on housekeeping alone. Thus the new domestic role division resulting from the wife's employment was not only out of line with tradition but also likely to overload both spouses. Since their total combined input could not match the contribution of time and effort invested by full-time housewives, frustration and disgruntlement were almost inevitable. The domestic duties that New Zealand husbands of employed wives were prepared to undertake were also narrowly restricted by traditional sex-role stereotypes. Koopman-Boyden and Abbott found that, whereas about 40 per cent of New Zealand men participated in child care when their wives worked, only 18 per cent helped with cooking, cleaning or other forms of housework.

An Australian comparison between dual-career

and male-breadwinner households reached similar conclusions (Brewer, Cunningham & Owen, 1982). The researchers found, disturbingly, that Australian career wives had significantly less decision-making power than housewives. Furthermore:

> ... while the husband of the career wife performs somewhat more household tasks than the husband of the housewife, the bulk of the housework and responsibility still falls to the wife regardless of her employment status. (p. 84)

Australian and New Zealand migrant families from non-English-speaking backgrounds are apt to have different attitudes towards the division of domestic labour than their mainstream Anglo counterparts. Figure 13.6 shows the disapproval ratings for husbands' involvement in housework among a group of married Australian men and women as a function of their countries of origin. It would seem that many non-Anglo migrant women are far less willing than either their husbands or their Anglo-Australian counterparts to consider an egalitarian division of domestic roles (Khoo, 1985).

Pioneering marriage styles

Given the complexity of contemporary family life, the simple issue of how household chores are divided may fail to capture the most significant contrasts among marriages today. On the basis of longitudinal data from a sample of 100 rural United States newly-weds who were followed across the first two years of married life, Michael Johnson, Ted Huston, Stanley Gaines and George Levinger (1992) concluded that five aspects of the domestic role were relevant to a couple's overall marriage style. These were (a) patterns of labour force participation by each spouse, (b) sex-typing of household work, (c) amount of leisure time spouses spend together, (d) differences between spouses in amount of time spent with relatives, and (e) differences between spouses in amount of time spent with friends. Using the statistical technique of cluster analysis, they discovered four marital patterns:

1. *Parallel marriage.* This marriage style resembled the 'traditional' role patterns observed in earlier research, with the husband as primary breadwinner. These marriages operate by a rigid sex-typing of household work and spouses have few shared leisure pursuits. Twenty-seven per cent of the rural American couples adhered to this pattern.

2. *Symmetrical marriage.* This style resembled the egalitarian ideal to the extent that the breadwinning role was shared equally between spouses and household chores were not rigidly sex-typed. But couples who adopted this marriage style actually spent less time together than any other type of couple. This was the most popular style in this newlywed study, accounting for 42 per cent of the American couples during the initial years of marriage.

3. *Differentiated-companionate marriage.* Marriages of this type stood out from all the others for the intensity of spouses' investment of time in each other. But, despite their emphasis on companionship, these couples divided household chores along traditionally segregated lines and considered the husband to be the primary breadwinner, even when both spouses were employed. Twenty-one per cent of the sample adopted this pattern.

4. *Role-reversed marriage.* In this style, adopted by only 10 per cent of the couples, traditional family patterns were turned upside down. Wives in these marriages were more involved in the paid labour force than husbands, and domestic chores were also divided along non-traditional lines. Husbands were more involved with their relatives than in any other style and the couple's patterns of leisure pursuits were highly companionate.

Interestingly, no differences in marital satisfaction emerged among any of the four marriage types, either at the newlywed stage or one or two years later. Thus each of these marital patterns seemed to suit the couples that chose it, enhancing their enjoyment of married life to the same extent as the other styles. However, the pressures of child-bearing and child-rearing may make some of them unworkable. As we see in the next section of this chapter, the demands of childrearing drastically reduce the total amount of time that spouses have free to invest in relating to one another. Their emotional, practical and financial investments in the couple relationship must compete with their involvement in parenthood. The differentiated-companionate style of marriage is more vulnerable than any of the others to these pressures, and thus may not survive the transition to parenthood.

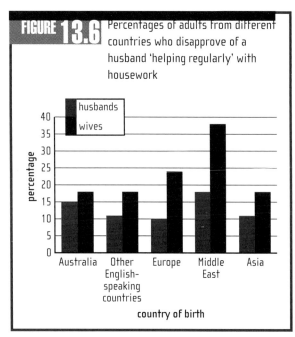

FIGURE **13.6** Percentages of adults from different countries who disapprove of a husband 'helping regularly' with housework

Source: Based on data in Khoo (1985), p. 60.

Similarly, the demands of childrearing may make it difficult to sustain the spouses' equally intense investment in their career that is at the heart of the symmetrical style.

Nevertheless, these examples of innovative marriage styles devised by contemporary newlyweds suggest that young couples today are no longer content simply to accept the traditional role divisions of past generations of married couples.

Planning for parenthood

The eventual aim of having children together is in the back of many couples' minds when they decide to get married. But the transition to parenthood is no longer a smooth and virtually unquestioned extension of early married life for every young couple today. Ready access to effective contraception, changing beliefs about the ideal size and spacing of a family, and the increased participation by young married women in higher education and demanding careers have conspired to make planning for parenthood an important developmental process in its own right (Peterson, 1982b).

Babies today begin to disrupt the steady flow of their future parents' lives long before they are born, and the married couple's decision about whether to have a family is itself likely to become a source of child-related stress and uncertainty. Though our society remains 'pro-natalistic' in its expectation that most adults will opt for parenthood eventually, the arguments in favour of child-bearing are no longer as one-sided as they used to be. The example set by the growing body of married couples in Australia, New Zealand and North America who are choosing to remain permanently childless tempts many modern young adults to pay heed to the 'cons' as well as the 'pros' of parenthood (Veevers, 1979; Callan, 1982).

Disadvantages of parenthood

When Victor Callan (1982) compared the attitudes of a group of 50 deliberately child-free Australian husbands and wives with a matched group of parents, he found that all four groups came up with essentially the same list of the disadvantages of parenthood. However, the emphasis placed on different cost factors varied somewhat as a function of gender and parental experience. Figure 13.7 shows the drawbacks perceived by these Australian couples.

While mothers seemed somewhat less aware than childless women of many of the problems associated with parenthood, experienced fathers named nearly as many disadvantages as their male peers who had opted against fatherhood. In fact, a few of the costs of fathering seemed to trouble fathers more than childless men. Thus more fathers than childless men complained about the curtailment of opportunities to travel, financial hardships and loss of spontaneity (e.g. not being

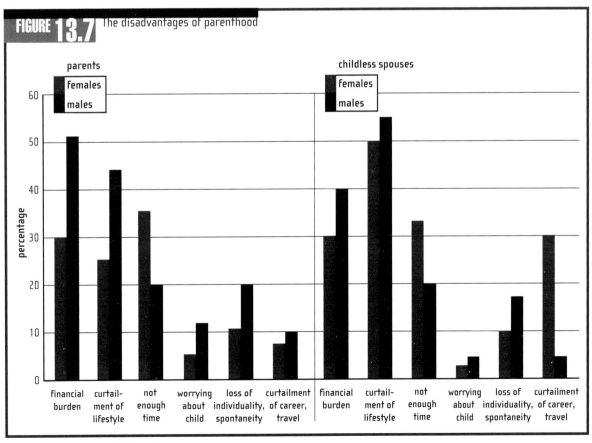

FIGURE 13.7 The disadvantages of parenthood

Source: Based on data in Callan (1982).

able to make spur-of-the-moment decisions to go out visiting or to a restaurant). Greek-Australian fathers were less likely than Anglo-Australian fathers to focus on these particular disadvantages (Callan, 1980). However, they mentioned another disadvantage of parenthood – the stress, anxiety and responsibilities connected with childrearing – almost four times as often as Anglo-Australian fathers. It would seem that, for one reason or another, a majority of Australian fathers view parenthood as a mixed blessing.

Experienced Australian mothers' perceptions of the cost of childrearing centred more than the fathers around such day-to-day hardships as fatigue and lack of free time. On the other hand, childless adults of both sexes were particularly disturbed at the thought of disrupting a lifestyle which they found satisfying, and also about whether they had stamina enough to shoulder the burden of responsibility imposed by parenthood.

After comparing a group of childless and parental couples in Canada, J. E. Veevers (1979) concluded that an additional disadvantage of parenthood for many young adults is limitation of their opportunities for psychological development. She noted that:

> For parents, especially young parents, the freedom which is gained by the attainment of full adult status is almost simultaneously curtailed by the presence of dependent children. (p. 16)

Veevers explained that childrearing may curtail adult development in any of the following four ways.

CURTAILMENT OF MARITAL INTERACTION

Couples with young children have less time for each other than childless spouses. Studies have shown that, in comparison with parents, infertile and voluntarily child-free couples not only have more opportunities to communicate but also usually manage to achieve closer and deeper levels of communication and more common points of view (Van Keep & Schmidt-Elmendorff, 1975). Childless spouses also touch each other physically more than parents do, which may have implications for communication and the resolution of disagreements as well as for sexuality (Ryder, 1973). Veevers suggested that a decrease in intensely mutual interaction after the advent of children may have a benign effect on some couples and an adverse effect on others, depending on their idiosyncratic needs for privacy versus sharing, and mutuality versus autonomy.

A RETURN TO TRADITIONAL ROLES

Childless couples are more likely than parents to practise an egalitarian division of household roles (see page 465) and to use democratic ways of reaching decisions, along with few overt disagreements. Veevers suggested that, with the advent of parenthood, 'Even couples who profess liberal ideology find their circumstances tend to buttress conventional division of labor' (p. 14).

OBSTACLES TO ANDROGYNY

This increase in traditional role allocation is apt to extend also into adult sex roles. Veevers suggested that 'the coming of children tends to accentuate biological sex differences and to reinforce traditional sex role expectations', whereas 'without the constraint of child care, men and women have a more realistic opportunity to approximate egalitarian sex roles' (p. 14). Australian women who have opted to remain childless are found to have a more balanced blend of masculine and feminine qualities in their personalities than mothers of the same age, education and economic background, who tend to be more stereotypically feminine (Callan, 1982).

CURTAILMENT OF LEISURE AND LEARNING

Veevers discovered that a substantial portion of her group of childless adults was smitten with such a mania for travel that she could only describe it as *wanderlust*. These people saw moving around as their best means of satisfying their need for new knowledge and experiences, and suggested that whatever new understanding a person might derive from childrearing would seem quite narrow and humble by comparison. Although most adults would probably agree that visits to new environments and total immersion in the sights, smells, tastes and customs of other cultures do constitute valuable educational experiences, not everyone would endorse the view that the new knowledge to be gleaned from parenthood is any less significant. Unfortunately, for individuals who would like to gain both kinds of experience, parenthood does severely curtail mobility and opportunities for vacation trips, at least while the children are small and finances are limited.

Formal education during adulthood can also be made more difficult by the presence of children. The costs of childrearing limit the family's resources, and few parents feel justified in putting their own educational interests ahead of their children's. The need to maintain a steady income also reduces working parents' freedom to take risks by making career changes that could lead to valuable new learning experiences. Although there is nothing intrinsically incompatible in being a child's guide and teacher while still an active learner oneself, the pragmatics of parenthood do tend to confine parents' learning opportunities to a narrower radius than those of childless adults.

Advantages of parenthood

Balanced against these disadvantages, parenthood also offers an impressive list of attractions. Couples who decide to have children look forward to giving and receiving love and affection, and to the pleasure of watching their children grow up. Children provide the basis for family life, cementing the couple's position in the community and their togetherness in the household, while offering the chance to sample recreational activities like holiday celebrations or simply playing and having fun. Parents may also embark on childrearing for the sake of personal growth and fulfilment, or to attain a sense of achievement. Still other expectant parents look forward to the adventure of creating a new life and to the chance of becoming more settled, mature and responsible (Callan, 1982). The relative importance of attractions like these in the minds of Australian parents and non-parents is shown in Figure 13.8.

The parents in this Australian sample seemed more conscious than non-parents of the emotional delights of parenthood. They spoke more frequently of gaining love and affection from their children, of becoming more mature and responsible through their parenting activities and of experiencing pride in their children's accomplishments. On the other hand, the saliency of certain of parenthood's other potential rewards seemed enhanced for those adults who had deliberately opted against childrearing. The childless men and women were, paradoxically, more likely than parents to mention the possibility of gaining enjoyment from watching a child develop. As we see in Chapter 15, this is also the most frequently cited satisfaction of grandparenthood for contemporary Australian grandparents (Peterson, 1999). Perhaps new parents fail to mention this pleasure because the day-to-day pressures of childrearing accord them too little time to step back and contemplate!

On the other hand, both groups of couples in Callan's study appeared highly conscious, and to an equal degree, of the pleasures to be had from the companionship of children while they were young. Yet many more childless spouses than parents mentioned the advantage of being able to enjoy an off-spring's company during old age. Looking further ahead to the very end of the life cycle, raising children can be seen not only as a worthwhile investment in the future but also as a partial consolation against disappointment and the fear of dying. The philosopher Bertrand Russell described one aspect of parental feeling as being:

> ... the hope that one's children may succeed where one has failed, that they may carry on one's work when death or senility puts an end to one's own efforts, and, in any case, that they will supply a biological escape from death, making one's own life part of the whole stream, and not a mere stagnant puddle without any overflow into the future. (1975, p. 385)

On the basis of questionnaire research, Robert Kastenbaum concluded that 'We fear death – and that is why we reproduce after our kind' (1978, p. 63). He found that virtually all the high school and university students he questioned suffered anxiety about the prospect of dying. Their concerns ranged widely. Some complained empathically of the grief their death would cause to bereaved survivors. Others were frightened of the pain of death or dreaded what might happen after they died.

Most of the remaining concerns, however, could be linked directly to the desire for heirs and successors. In particular, the students said they did not want to be forgotten after their deaths, nor to have all their plans and projects come to an end. Through further questioning, Kastenbaum discovered that having offspring was viewed as one way of offsetting some of the bad feelings inspired by thoughts about one's own death. Approximately 90 per cent of the adults he surveyed agreed that 'People with children can face

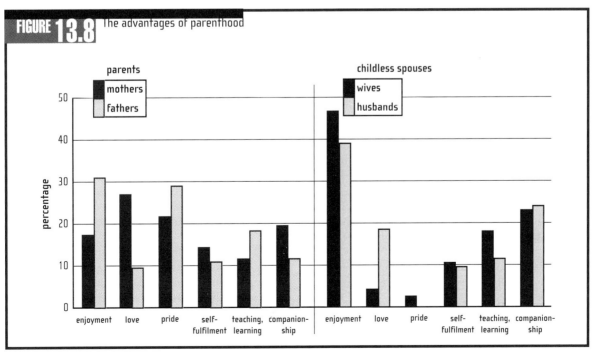

FIGURE 13.8 The advantages of parenthood

Source: Based on data from Callan (1982).

death more easily'. However, they were also prepared to consider other ways. 'Having people remember me after my death' was nearly as popular as 'Bringing children into this world' as a means of achieving partial immortality. Some males, but very few females, also endorsed 'Achievements of mine, or other accomplishments that live on after my life'. Kastenbaum's imaginative suggestion of having people's thoughts and personalities programmed into computers for access by succeeding generations met with notably little enthusiasm. Nor was there much interest in an 'impressive funeral and a well-marked resting place'.

Costs of childlessness

To complicate the decision-making process still further, the choice of remaining childless is found to entail advantages and disadvantages over and above those associated with the sheer absence of children from the couple's household. When Victor Callan (1983) interviewed a group of intentionally childless Australian wives about the ramifications of their decision, he found that social ostracism and overt hostility from friends, parents and in-laws weighed even more heavily on these women's minds than the question of children *per se*. They reported that people made negative comments, when informed that the decision not to have children was a deliberate, conscious choice, such as: 'You are very selfish,' 'You must be crazy,' 'You'll change your mind eventually, but then it will be too late,' 'You are strange, weird, unstable,' 'You are irresponsible,' 'You are overwhelmed by materialistic desires,' 'You must hate children,' 'You will be lonely when you get old.'

Making the decision

Coming to a decision for or against parenthood by weighing up gain and cost factors is not likely to be easy, particularly during the early years of marriage when couples lack decision-making experience and a sound knowledge of their own and the other's basic goals and values. Difficulty in reaching a decision is also enhanced by its all-or-nothing nature. As J. E. Veevers noted: 'Many topics of disagreement in a marriage can be worked out by varying kinds of compromises. The issue of having or not having children, however, is not one of them (1979, p. 14).

Just as one can't be 'a little bit pregnant', a couple can't really find a position halfway between the parental and the childless state. So the only real avenues open to spouses when their opinions differ are:

1. to talk out the issue and hope that one spouse will eventually be persuaded by the other's arguments
2. to wait and hope that changing circumstances will enable a mutually agreeable choice later on
3. to take unilateral action and count on the spouse eventually accepting it.

The process whereby couples reach a decision about parenthood is liable to affect their satisfaction with the outcome. Those who get pregnant unintentionally are found to make a less favourable adjustment to subsequent childrearing than couples who plan for the transition and deliberately control its timing (Furstenberg, 1976). One longitudinal study showed that the children of Czechoslovakian women who had asked for an abortion but had their request denied had more emotional and scholastic problems than a matched group of wanted offspring (Pohlman, 1969).

Developing as a parent

Though deciding whether to have children can itself be stressful, this stress is mild compared with the challenges that adjustment to life with a newborn baby imposes on first-time parents. To evaluate how stressful the transition to parenthood really is, Deborah Terry (1991) interviewed a group of 123 Canberra couples who were expecting their first child. The expectant mothers ranged in age from 20 to 43 at the time of the study, while their husbands were aged 20 to 47. During the final trimester of pregnancy (see Chapter 3), Terry asked the husbands and wives to complete a battery of questionnaires measuring their attitudes to parenthood, their styles of coping with stress, and the other existing and impending stresses in their lives besides the birth of a first baby. She returned to study the households approximately four weeks after the infant was born, and again when the baby was three months old. Hospital reports of obstetric complications and parents' ratings of infant temperament (see Chapter 5) were also obtained.

The transition to parenthood

Both sexes found the move into parenthood stressful, but the women reported significantly higher levels of stress and strain immediately after their baby was born than new fathers did. To study what could help parents to cope with the stress of having a new baby, Terry compared those families in her sample who were having the greatest difficulty with those for whom the transition to parenthood had been easiest. Highly stressed new parents stood out in a number of ways. If they had seen the birth of their child as an extremely important event in their lives while still waiting for the birth, their subsequent adjustment was more difficult than if parenthood was deemed no more significant for their identity (see Chapter 11) and their relationship in the future than other life events such as marriage or career entry. In addition, expectant couples who had anticipated that parenthood would be difficult did actually experience more stress after the event than those who had imagined it would be easy.

While these factors predated the birth itself, Terry found that the baby's own nature also made a difference. Infants who were born with the 'difficult' temperamental qualities described in Chapter 5 were a source of greater stress than those born with 'easy' natures. It is not too surprising that an infant who is irregular, slow to adapt to routines, irritable and predominantly negative in mood creates stress for new parents. However, it is possible that this particular source of stress might be alleviated somewhat if more information on the psychology of infant temperament were to be incorporated into childbirth preparation classes – another role for the lifespan developmental psychologist?

In a similar longitudinal study of new parents in the United States, Shirley Feldman and Sharon Nash (1984) confirmed that the entry into parenthood is stressful. The psychological well-being of each spouse suffered, and the quality of the marriage typically underwent upheavals during the first six months with a new baby. As in Terry's Australian sample, new mothers seemed to be hit harder by stress than new fathers. Feldman and Nash saw the women's unrealistic expectations as partly to blame for this difference. When interviewed before the birth, most of the men in their sample had anticipated difficulty and successfully predicted many aspects of their parenting behaviour, but there was virtually no consistency for women between their anticipation of motherhood during pregnancy and their later experiences as parents.

According to Feldman and Nash, many new mothers had been blinded by idealistic, stereotypic images of what motherhood would be like and had not realised how much a new baby would disrupt their lives. Their underestimation of the time and effort needed for parenting led to stress in marriage. Feldman and Nash went on to note that:

An implicit conflict seems to arise for many women between the roles of 'good wife' and 'good mother'. At motherhood, the baby begins to surpass the husband as source of greatest satisfaction. Despite general contentment with the role of wife, women reported being bothered by the decrease in time spent with their husbands, by arguments, and by sexual problems. In comparison to their feelings preceding the baby they are less happy with the quality of the marital relationship and with their own efforts at nurturing the marriage ... Expectations of continued or even enhanced communication and support during the early phases of parenthood were usually disappointed as a result of the underestimated impact of the child on most aspects of the husband-and-wife relationship. (p. 74)

Other studies show that with the birth of a first child the amount of time wives typically spend on housework doubles, while time in conversation with their husbands is cut in half (Aldous, 1978). A strain may also be imposed on the sexual relationship by fatigue, lack of a private room, frequent interruptions or the fear of a future pregnancy. New fathers are as apt to complain as new mothers about these unwelcome intrusions into a formerly stable married life.

Difficulties like these during the transition to parenthood can be blamed partly on a lack of adequate preparation. Having grown up for the most part in closely spaced nuclear families, contemporary parents rarely gain the experience of close involvement in the rearing of much younger brothers and sisters. Childbirth classes may prepare couples for the birth process (see Chapter 3) and for hospital life, but usually stop short of dealing with the practicalities of looking after an infant on a 24-hour-a-day basis at home. Nor is 'sporadic babysitting experience' a reliable guide to the realities of fully fledged parenthood. Thus many of the initial adjustment difficulties encountered by new parents may simply result from ignorance and unrealistic expectations:

A woman knows her husband as a unique real person when she enters the honeymoon stage of marriage. A good deal of preparatory adjustment on a firm reality-base is possible during the engagement period which is not possible in the equivalent pregnancy period. Fantasy is not corrected by the reality of a specific individual child until the birth of the child ... On this basis alone there is greater interpersonal adjustment and learning during the honeymoon stage of the parental role than of the marital role (Rossi, 1977, p. 231).

Ignorance about the realities of parenthood and child development can have adverse effects not only

TABLE 13.11	Factors influencing ease of adjustment to parenthood
Parent Factors	• Realistic expectations of infant's developmental status and limitations • Realistic expectations of the demands of the role of parent, time and psychological burdens of caring for young infants • Parents' attachment styles • Quality of communication, conflict-resolution styles and adaptability in parents' relationship (including role allocation)
Infant Factors	• Infant temperament (easy, difficult, slow to warm up; see Chapter 5) • Infant health (e.g. prematurity, disability) • Multiple births
Extrafamilial factors	• Social support • Extrafamilial roles

on the new mother's and father's immediate feelings and coping strategies but also on their long-term success in rearing their offspring. One study showed that new parents who had unrealistically high expectations of how easy it was going to be to care for a child, and who anticipated that developmental gains such as smiling, walking, speaking and being toilet-trained would be made by their baby at far earlier ages than actually happens, adjusted relatively poorly to parenthood (Furstenberg, 1976). These parents' skills in caring for their baby actually deteriorated as time went on. In comparison with other parents, they also tended to be more irritable and impatient and less interested in or involved with their offspring.

It seemed that the disappointment and frustration which had arisen when the realities of caring for an infant failed to live up to the naive parents' falsely high hopes had spilled over to undermine confidence in their own abilities. Thus the pleasure they derived from parenting was also diminished. Not surprisingly, these disappointed parents found less joy in being married and showed less affection for their spouses than couples whose anticipations about parenthood had been more realistic. For these reasons, it is important for expectant parents to be aware of issues such as those listed in Table 13.11 which can ease the transition to parenthood.

The later challenges of parenthood

Fortunately, for the average couple with a moderately sound knowledge of what to expect from a baby, the crisis phase of parenthood normally lasts for only a few months (Russell, 1974). The developmental gains in sleeping, crying and alertness patterns that infants typically make at about three months of age (see Chapter 4) ease the parenting burden considerably. As the parents' and baby's sleeping cycles become coordinated, as maturation of the nervous and digestive systems diminishes the infant's irritability, and as the parents themselves learn to master and streamline their various new caregiving duties, their shared lifestyle together evolves into a more comfortable routine. Thus morale improves, couples regain time for one another and their non-parenting ambitions

and they come to feel less fearful and inadequate than during the newborn period.

But the transition to parenthood is only the first of a series of developmental milestones in the parents' patterns of adult psychological growth. As children grow up they confront their parents with a changing sequence of new challenges and surprises. Thus the adults' lifestyles alter gradually to cope with the needs of their infants, toddlers, school children and adolescents, as discussed in earlier chapters of this book. These new experiences and changes all pose problems to stimulate cognitive functioning and foster the growth of additional social skills (Flavell, 1970). They may also give rise to marital stress. Table 13.12 shows some of the changes in added time commitments and responsibilities and losses of emotional support and shared leisure that arose for a sample of new parents in the United States during the first year of their new baby's life. Some of these changes arose for child-free couples, also, over the same time period. But their impact was generally less severe.

From a developmental standpoint, however, parenthood may provide the adult with an opportunity to resolve the crisis over *generativity* which Erik Erikson saw as the key personality issue of mature adulthood (see Chapters 2, 15 and 17). According to Erikson, 'mature man needs to be needed' and care for dependent offspring provides one means of expressing 'the concern for establishing and guiding the next generation', on which can be built this new feature of a mature personality. As their children grow up, parents' pride in them and their accomplishments may help the parents gain a sense of achievement, a trust in the future and a feeling that their lives have been made worthwhile. Some of these feelings are illustrated in Box 13.7.

An empirical study of generativity (Snarey, Son, Kuehne, Hauser & Vaillant, 1987) showed, in fact, that becoming a father did assist men's resolution of this important developmental crisis. The subjects were 343 men who were followed longitudinally for four decades. Of the group, 15 per cent experienced infertility. They attempted a variety of strategies for

TABLE 13.12 Changes in marriage between the newlywed stage and year 2		
Domain of change	New parents (infant 0–8 months)	Child-free couples matched for marital duration
Time spouses spend in shared leisure and recreational activity	Declines by 1.5 hours per day	Declines by half an hour per day
Wife's involvement in instrumental household roles (cleaning, cooking, laundry, etc.)	Increases by 26 new roles per day	Decreases by half a role per day
Number of emotionally positive couple events	Decreases by 20 per day	Decreases by 20 per day
Number of emotionally negative couple events	No change	Decreases by half an event per day

Source: Based on data in Huston & Vangelisti (1995).

BOX 13.7 The delights of fatherhood

Louise's father made the following entry in his diary when she, his only child, was two years old. It illustrates some of the pleasures of parenthood and the emotions an involved father can invest in the parenting role.

22 April 1950. *I wish I could describe my feelings this afternoon when Louise came outdoors after her nap. How purposeful she was as she clutched a couple of her toys and declared what she was going to do with them. It seems that being away from her for just a couple of hours makes everything fresh about her. We dug in the garden and Louise would pick little cones off some pussywillow stems left over from last year. She'd bring them over and say, 'I'll give it to Peggy (her doll) to eat and then throw it on the ground'. She did it and said it over and over again.*

© Peterson, 1974, reproduced with permission

coping with this frustrating and unexpected disruption of their planning for adult life. Some of the childless men in Snarey and his colleagues' sample developed 'self-centered substitutes' for children. Examples were intense devotion to 'body building, health foods, macho sexuality' (p. 595). Other infertile men chose such 'object substitutes' as pets, a garden or a car, which they treated like a child. Still others became involved in vicarious childrearing activities as scout leader, teacher or youth worker. When compared with the fathers in the sample, the infertile men more often failed to achieve generativity, especially when they had opted for 'self-centered' and 'object' child substitutes. But not all fathers were successful either, possibly because 'even during the mature years, not all parenting is generative parenting' (p. 594). The researchers nevertheless concluded that:

> The experience of parenting children still appears to make an additional independent contribution to the subsequent midlife achievement of generativity. Men who became fathers — both those who initially experienced infertility and those in the larger fertile sample who experienced no delay in achieving parenthood — were significantly more likely to be generative at midlife than were those who remained childless. In sum, parenting one's children appears to provide a partial foundation for subsequently guiding other adults. (p. 602)

Chapter summary

Early adulthood is a time when most people fall in love, choose a career, get married and have children. Falling in love is itself a developmental process, sometimes beginning with starry-eyed romanticism or with the physiological upheavals of passionate love. Later, couples may progress to a companionate style of affection typified by equity. Eventually, according to some theorists, couples achieve a higher, or more mature, mode of love in which concerns over equity and fairness are replaced by intimate mutuality.

Entry into the world of work is another major milestone in young adults' development. For those who are not lucky enough to find a job, the psychological costs of unemployment may include boredom, apathy, loss of self-esteem, sacrifice of vocational ideals and heightened risk of physical and mental illness.

Entry into the workforce, on the other hand, provides the opportunity to develop a set of work values and a vocational identity. But beginning workers may also face challenges and setbacks. Some 'shop around' in an effort to achieve a better fit between their private ideals and the vocational requirements of the organisation. Many are thwarted in their desire to develop their skills, achieve social recognition and gain a sense of accomplishment by dull jobs, overprotective supervisors or rigid institutional structures.

But, in the end, most workers come to accept the fact that vocational development is highly selective. Certain talents and interests are nurtured and stimulated at work, but many other abilities are allowed to grow stale through disuse.

During the early years of marriage, most couples adopt a traditional, egalitarian or colleague style of allocating domestic duties. The long-term success of the arrangement seems to depend as much on spouses' ideological preferences as on their skill at performing the roles allocated to them. Stress, marital discord, overwork and mental health problems can all result if roles are allocated inappropriately.

Decisions about when and whether to have children preoccupy most young couples. Perceived disadvantages of parenthood include inconvenience, financial hardship, the curtailment of vocational or recreational interests, and the burdens of responsibility and anxiety on the child's behalf. Motives in favour of having children include enjoyment, self-fulfilment, the exchange of love and opportunities for pride, teaching and learning.

The first few months after a child's birth are difficult for most new parents. They have only a short time in which to engineer a major reorganisation of their daily routines, their personal feelings and their marital, vocational and social role structures. The transition to parenthood is also made more difficult today by contemporary adults' lack of accurate knowledge about the realities of day-to-day parenting.

Parental morale is likely to improve steadily over the child's first year of life. However, significant challenges and changes occur throughout the life cycle of parenting and coping effectively with these can facilitate the adult's resolution of Erikson's personality development crisis over generativity.

For further interest

Looking forward on the Internet

Use the Internet to visit the following websites. Examine them for further information and varied perspectives on issues raised in this chapter. Also search for other relevant websites for yourself, using keywords like 'youth', 'adulthood', 'marriage' and 'unemployment' in your search engine.

In particular, for further ideas on adult development visit: **http://www.aging.ufl.edu/apadiv20/vidlist.htm** which has a list of educational videos on adult development, and **http://www.adultdevelopment.org** which contains information from the Society for Research in Adult Development on progressive developmental changes in adult life.

For resources, ideas, activities and other items of interest in conjunction with this chapter, visit the Companion Website for this textbook at:

http://wps.pearsoned.com.au/peterson

Activity suggestion

As a practical activity in conjunction with themes in this chapter, you may wish to invite a spokesperson or a panel from local bodies working with the unemployed in your community to come to class and talk about schemes for boosting the morale, skills and employment prospects of the young unemployed.

Multimedia

For a provocative documentary that uses vignettes and interviews to illustrate the impact of careers and unemployment on marriage, view the video *Unemployment and Marriage* (Film Australia, Sydney, 1988: 40 minutes, colour).

MIDDLE ADULTHOOD: Physical, cognitive, social and personality growth

CHAPTER 14

> Middle age – by which
> I mean anything over
> twenty and under ninety.
>
> A. A. Milne

Contents

Until recently, the years from age 35 to age 50 were seen as distinct from the rest of the lifespan as periods of unruffled psychological stability. Consequently, the bulk of adulthood held little to interest the developmental psychologist. Since maturity was believed to consist merely of the playing out of patterns of behaviour established during childhood and youth, there was no reason to expect mature men and women to change in significant ways over time. Nor did it make much sense to try to relate adult psychological functioning to chronological age if, to quote the 19th-century psychologist William James: 'In most of us, by the age of 30, the character has set like plaster and will never soften again' (Rubin, 1981, p. 18).

Today, however, such notions of static adulthood are no longer tenable. Recent research (Baltes, 2001) has shown that middle adulthood is punctuated by age-linked psychological change that is no less significant than that arising earlier and later in life. Furthermore, as we noted in Chapter 1, genuine gains in psychological capacity are just as feasible in middle adult life as they were during childhood, adolescence and youth. In middle life, as earlier, part of the impetus for change comes from outside the person, as when adults are promoted at work, a new baby is born, a child enters school, or when lifelong habits are disrupted by the death of a parent, a financial gain or loss, or a move to a new community. A married couple's feelings for one another are also liable to change with time and familiarity, while parents are forced to accommodate successively to the milestones that mark their offspring's progress from infancy to adolescence, and then to the demands of launching their children out of the family and resuming non-parental couplehood. Career issues in the modern world of work may encompass retrenchment, retraining and second careers, as well as opportunities for promotion up the ladder in the same occupation. So, even if mature adults did not voluntarily try to foster their own psychological development through such avenues as adult education, challenging leisure pursuits or commitments to leadership roles and political causes, James's 'plaster' would almost certainly be forced to crack. We examine each of these external and internal stimuli to developmental change in this chapter.

In so doing, we adopt a developmental perspective on adult life, studying situations like marriage, parenthood and career pursuits in terms of the predictable changes arising from year to year and from one decade to the next. We begin by examining the biological changes in the adult body and brain that give rise to psychological opportunities and adjustments. We look at how neurocognitive changes and adult life experiences influence changes in adult cognition, the processes of memory and problem-solving during middle life. Personality changes are explored, along with the social and relationship changes that are likely to arise over several decades of marriage and parenthood. Then we examine the stages that punctuate the career life cycle, and the developmental opportunities embodied in the approximately 60 000 hours of leisure time that many adults enjoy between age 35 and age 50 or 55 when some decide to retire from paid employment to pursue a life of leisure on a full-time basis (see Chapter 15).

Physical and motor development in middle adulthood

The body at 35 is not quite what it was at age 25, which explains why so many athletes, swimmers and tennis stars retire at around this age. Even with peak levels of training, coaching and fitness, professional sportspeople often discover that they no longer have the speed, strength or endurance to compete effectively against performers in their early 20s. This does not mean that retirement to become a couch potato is mandated, however. For athletes, as for the average adult, good health depends on energetic physical activity, and the enjoyment of sports participation and competition remains both possible and highly desirable throughout this age period.

Most of the biological changes in muscular, physiological and sensory systems that influence an adult's sporting performance are very gradual (see Table 14.1). Some (such as eyesight) are readily overcome through prosthesis (e.g. glasses or contact lenses). Others respond well to increased exercise and training. For example, a 20-year longitudinal study in Sweden showed that women who exercised regularly had lower rates of death and chronic illness than women of the same age who led sedentary and inactive lives (Lissner, Bengtsson, Björkelund & Wedel, 1996). A summary of some of the major changes of mid-adult bodily ageing appears in Table 14.1.

Neurocognitive development in middle adulthood

It was once thought that the brain aged so swiftly in early adulthood, and that brain cells died so rapidly without replacement after childhood, that the average 35-year-old was even less likely to win a mental than a physical competition against a 25-year-old. However, recent neurological, brain imaging and neuroanatomical research studies have proved this idea to be a myth. In fact, brain cells are capable of continuing to grow and regenerate throughout adult life, even during old age (Gould, Reeves, Graziano & Gross, 1999). This biological possibility gives rise to important new ideas about adult cognition, both in normal circumstances and as a result of brain injury or neurological disease.

TABLE 14.1	Changes in physical capacity and functioning for the average adult over 30	
Physiological system	Age of onset of change	Nature of change
Lungs/breathing capacity	35 years	Maximum oxygen uptake declines by about 1% per year
Systolic blood pressure	40 years	Increases owing to decreasing elasticity of blood vessels
Immune system	35 years	Thymus gland decreases in size; at 45 it is only 10% of its size at puberty; T-cell function declines correspondingly, diminishing resistance to disease
Eyesight	40 to 45 years	Lens of the eyes thicken and lose elasticity, reducing acuity for reading
Reproductive system	33 years	Reduced fertility and increased risk of congenital problems in offspring, especially chromosome abnormalities (see Chapter 3)
Muscles	45 to 50 years	Loss of tissue, reducing strength, especially for bursts of speed
Smell	40 years	Acuity diminishes
Cellular elasticity	35 years	Gradual decline, faster in areas (e.g. skin) exposed to sunlight

Neurocognitive plasticity

The phenomenon of *plasticity* in brain physiology describes the brain's capacity to repair itself following disease, injury or age-related cell damage and loss. Recent studies of the rehabilitation of victims of brain injury and cerebrovascular disease (such as stroke) show that, at all ages, many damaged neurons and neurocognitive systems can recover, at least to a certain degree. Other neurocognitive processes that fail to repair themselves outright can be replaced by alternative modules, leading to a restoration of function. However, age and timing do matter to a certain extent: neurocognitive recovery from brain damage is generally more rapid during the first three months after the injury, more complete during childhood than in adolescence or adulthood, and more so in middle age than in old age when the same degree of damage has been sustained (Gould et al., 1999).

As an example of how researchers' awareness of adult brain plasticity has led to new therapies to assist neurological recovery from stroke, Rosenzweig, Breedlove and Leiman (2002) highlighted the successes that have recently been achieved using (a) mirror rehabilitation and (b) constraint-induced-movement therapy. Using mirror rehabilitation, a stroke patient whose brain injury had restricted the use of an arm was placed before a mirror in such a way that the paralysed arm appeared to move whenever the undamaged arm moved. Visual feedback suggesting that the weak arm was moving was given on repeated occasions over several days. Eventually, brain connections were restored, and the patient was able to move the formerly paralysed arm even without the mirror.

In constraint-induced-movement therapy (Liepert et al., 2000), the arm unaffected by stroke was placed in a splint while therapists manually exercised the paralysed arm. After 80 hours of such therapy over a two-week period, approximately 75 per cent of adult patients had regained enough brain function to enable their spontaneous use of the paralysed arm. In both cases, stroke patients who a generation ago would have been diagnosed with incurable paralysis owing to permanent neural cell loss were helped to regain the use of their limbs, demonstrating that the adult brain is far more plastic than was once supposed.

Adult brain growth

In the normal adult brain, new neural connections continue to form, creating new pathways for the transmission of nerve impulses. Just as during infancy and childhood, old pathways that are unused decline and close themselves off. Myelinisation (see Chapters 4 and 6) also continues throughout adult life, improving the speed of neural conduction in response to practice and experience. Recent studies suggest that there may be two periods of unusually rapid brain growth during adulthood (Spreen, Risser & Edgell, 1995). The first occurs from the late teens through the early 20s and is centred on the frontal lobes of the cerebral cortex (see Chapter 4). This spurt may be connected with the increased logical reasoning skills that arise in early adolescence, prompting Jean Piaget (1970) to propose a new cognitive stage of formal operational thought (see Chapters 2 and 11).

The second surge in brain growth also involves the frontal lobes, but includes the limbic system and other connections among neural paths throughout the brain as well. It is seen to arise between the ages of 25 and 30 (Fischer & Rose, 1995) and may be connected with the more 'settled' and 'mature' outlook of many young men and women who, at the start of the middle adult period, are able to curb their impulsivity, consider broad goals and plan for the future in ways that were not yet possible during their late teens.

During middle adulthood, ageing of the brain also begins in the context of these continuing progressive growth changes. For example, the weight of the average human brain at autopsy declines from age 40 to age 90, as shown in Figure 14.1. However, the extent to which brain weight relates to brain function is controversial. People with large hat sizes are not necessarily smarter than adults of the same age and sex whose heads are small. A gender difference in overall brain weight is also apparent in Figure 14.1, yet it would clearly be misleading to suggest that the average woman of 40 is substantially less intelligent than the average boy at age 12.

Autopsy studies also reveal changes in the cell mass, dendrite density and synaptic connections of certain regions of the brain, beginning at age 30. Yet growth cones are also observed in the cortical cells of very old people, 'suggesting that some forms of synaptic plasticity continue throughout life' (Rosenzweig, Breedlove & Leiman, 2002, p. 206).

Personality development in middle adulthood

Many of the most important cognitive and personality changes of adult life are bound up with the important relationships and life activities to which men and women devote themselves – marriage, parenthood, a career and a rewarding set of leisure pursuits in which to be creative, productive, playful, thoughtful, friendly and socially useful. As they embark on these life pursuits, new kinds of challenges arise that draw on emotional and cognitive resources and coping skills. Conflicts arise which may provide the impetus for achieving higher levels of functioning (see Chapter 2).

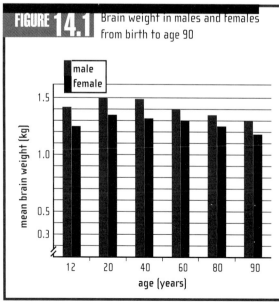

FIGURE 14.1 Brain weight in males and females from birth to age 90

Source: Based on data in Dekaban & Sadowsky (1978).

Developing the need to be needed: Generativity versus stagnation

In the personality domain, Erik Erikson (1968a) spoke of the crisis over generativity as the key to a full psychological understanding of the mature adult. The generativity crisis (see Chapter 2) involves a conflict between a sense of having made a worthwhile contribution by reaching out to others and a profound sense of boredom, self-preoccupation and doubt. According to Erikson, this crisis may continue to preoccupy the mature personality throughout midlife, as adults assess and reassess the quality of the contribution they are making to the health, growth and well-being of future generations. The social environment may support generativity by offering mature men and women opportunities to become generative by helping others at home, at work or in the neighbourhood. While contributing productively to others' psychological growth, the adult personality itself can ripen, since, as Erikson (1968a) noted, 'mature man [and woman] needs to be needed' (p. 140).

Adults may achieve a sense of personal growth through generativity when they contribute to goals that will have a beneficial impact on others and will continue to assist younger generations after their own lives draw to a close. Some may choose parenthood as a way of making a generative contribution. Other adults express the impulse for generativity through creative contributions in art, music, drama or literature, while some achieve generativity by making their mark on the workplace, perhaps by developing new tools and techniques or by mentoring younger workers who will fill their shoes after they retire. Political activism on behalf of social justice, assistance to the underprivileged, world peace or the global environment also provides a forum for the expression of generativity; according to Erikson (1982), 'a new generative ethos may call for a more universal care concerned with the lives of all children' (p. 68). Generativity is likely to increase throughout middle age, as illustrated in Figure 14.2.

For women, the challenges of making a contribution to life outside the family may be an especially important stimulus to mid-life generativity development. Table 14.2 shows the life activities that predicted high levels of generativity in one group of middle-aged graduate career women in a US longitudinal study. These women's occupations provided them with a 'career clock' against which to set new challenges and measure their levels of ongoing success (Stewart & Ostrove, 1998).

Cognitive development in middle adulthood

In addition to developing their personality strengths in the domain of generativity, adults' patterns of life activity in marriage, as parents, at work and at leisure

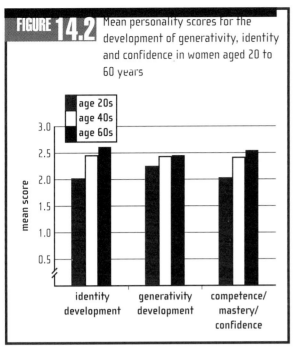

FIGURE 14.2 Mean personality scores for the development of generativity, identity and confidence in women aged 20 to 60 years

mean score

- age 20s
- age 40s
- age 60s

identity development | generativity development | competence/ mastery/ confidence

Source: Adapted from Zucker, Ostrove & Stewart (2002), Table 2, p. 239, by permission of the American Psychological Society.

TABLE 14.2 Links between generativity motivation and career women's life activity from age 18 to age 48

Dimension of life activity	Correlations with generativity motivation at age 48
Involvement in social/political movements in youth	.25*
Political involvement through adulthood	.26*
Integration of political values at mid-life	.38**
Involvement with a mentor in youth	.39**
Mastery of career challenges	.33*
Helping others at work	.48**
Career productivity	.08
Parenting	.06

Note: Statistically significant correlations are denoted * for p < .05 and ** for p < .01
Source: Based on data in Stewart & Ostrove (1998).

An occupation, such as that of teacher, which allows opportunities to help others and guide future generations, may contribute positively to the adult's resolution of the generativity crisis.

supply them with many opportunities to exercise cognitive skills. These challenges may draw on existing cognitive skills, including Piagetian formal operations (see Chapter 11). In addition, new kinds of cognitive skills may emerge through adult cognitive activity in solving the problems of everyday life in the real world. When a father is called away from an urgent deadline at work to pick up a sick child from day-care, or when a middle-aged daughter is summoned to help her elderly mother deal with a difficult landlord who will not make necessary repairs to the electrical fittings in her rented flat, 'hot' (or applied) cognitive processes are clearly required. These may not always fit neatly inside the cool, logical framework of formal operations that developed in late adolescence or early adulthood (see Chapters 2 and 11).

In everyday problem-solving situations, qualitatively new cognitive skills may develop, according to some theorists. As explained in more detail in Chapter 15, some of the theoretical models of adult cognition that include further stages beyond formal operations are summarised in Table 14.3.

Marriage development in middle adulthood

Folklore has it that once a couple who married for true love settle down into a home together with happy, healthy children they can sit back in love together to enjoy a life of 'happily-ever-after' wedded bliss. But the developmental course of a real marriage is not this easy (or this boring). In Australia, Robert Bell (1975) interviewed a group of 439 Melbourne wives aged 30 to 50 who had experienced between one and three decades of married life. He asked these women to imagine they had their lives to live over

TABLE 14.3	Postulated cognitive developmental stages beyond formal operations	
Theorist	Post-formal cognitive skill	Description
Labouvie-Vief (1990)	Contextually valid thinking	Specialised and highly pragmatic reasoning about practical real-world problems
Basseches (1988)	Dialectical thinking	Perceiving fundamental contradictions in everyday dilemmas and discovering higher-order syntheses to solve dynamic problems in a changing universe
Arlin (1990)	Problem-finding	Creative 'problem-finding': generating multiple novel-yet-workable solutions to routine problems and pulling out the core dilemma in problems that are ill-defined

again and to consider whether there was anything they might want to do differently. Severe disappointment with marriage was registered by the 20 per cent of these wives who said they would elect celibacy if they could start again. Futhermore, about the same proportion of women who felt that marriage itself was acceptable said they would prefer a different husband the next time round. Rather than being unusually unlucky, or having made a mistake in their initial choice of mate, these women were reflecting on a normal phenomenon in the life cycle of marriage that is not accurately portrayed by the 'happy-ever-after' fairy tale marriage.

The U-shaped curve of marital happiness

Using a cross-sectional design, a number of researchers have compared the average level of marital satisfaction among newlyweds with that of couples who have been married for up to six decades. Some of their findings are shown in Figures 14.3 and 14.4. The results all show a strikingly similar pattern. Very early in marriage, most couples are highly satisfied. This is not surprising. Marriage is a big decision and most rational people would not undertake it if they had no chance of feeling satisfied. However, as time goes on, the data from normal couples depicted in these graphs show that love for the spouse and happiness with being married are likely to dwindle steadily to reach a low ebb in the childrearing stage of the life cycle. But this is not simply a consequence of shedding the blinkers of romantic love (see Chapter 13). Nor does it appear to reflect a return to reality after the blissful unreality of the honeymoon. Indeed, the most interesting aspect of what has come to be known as the 'U-shaped curve' of marital satisfaction is the dramatic upward swing of the curve late in marriage. This reflects a renewed happiness with marriage among couples who have been together for between three and six decades. In fact, as Figure 14.3 suggests, couples in the 'empty-nest' stage of family life (see Chapter 15) typically report they are at least as satisfied with their marriage as honeymooners and newlyweds, and sometimes more so. But parents with

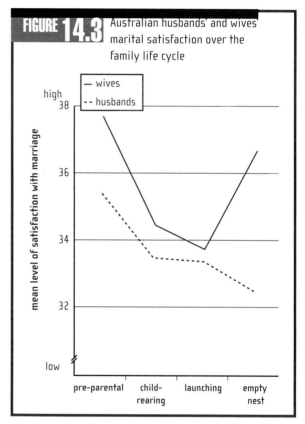

FIGURE 14.3 Australian husbands' and wives' marital satisfaction over the family life cycle

Source: Based on data in Feeney, Peterson & Noller (1994). Reproduced with the permission of Cambridge University Press.

children at home, like the childless couples who have been married for between 5 and 20 years, typically report significantly less marital satisfaction than newlyweds or older childless spouses both with the state of being married and with their relationship partners.

There are some variations in these results from study to study. Figure 14.3 is based on the responses of 373 Queensland husbands and wives to a standardised measure of marital satisfaction (Feeney, Peterson & Noller, 1994). Among wives, the results provided statistically significant confirmation that the curve is U-shaped. Wives in the empty-nest phase were

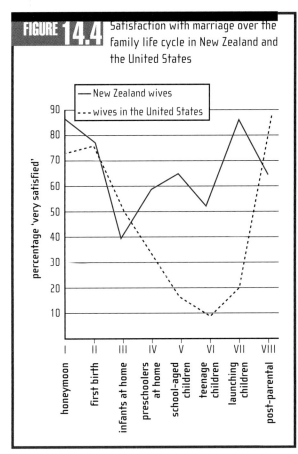

FIGURE 14.4 Satisfaction with marriage over the family life cycle in New Zealand and the United States

Source: Smart and Smart (1970), p. 411, © 1970, National Council on Family Relations, 3989 Central Avenue Northeast, Minneapolis, Minnesota 55414. Reproduced by permission.

just as happy with marriage as newlyweds. But wives who had offspring still at home were significantly less happy than either of these two groups. On the other hand, the average levels of marital satisfaction reported by Australian husbands in this study did not differ significantly across the stages of family life, and the upward swing of the U-curve during post-parental marriage was not evident among these men. Similarly, when Russell and Mollie Smart (1970) made a cross-cultural comparison of the progress of marital satisfaction across the family life cycle between wives in New Zealand and wives in the United States, there were more ups and downs in the New Zealand women's curves, possibly because the New Zealand sample was much smaller. These data are shown in Figure 14.4.

But when the results of the many dozens of studies that have mapped happiness with marriage onto a couple's progress through the life cycle are combined, a consistent picture does emerge (Glenn, 1998). In fact, the pattern is so consistent across couples, cultures and eras in history that it has been described as 'about as close to being certain as anything ever is in the social sciences' (Glenn, 1998, p. 853). Husbands and wives who have been married for five to ten years encounter a downturn in marital satisfaction, especially if they have infants or young

children at home. Over the next decade or so, marital happiness continues to decline, reaching its lowest ebb for parents with adolescent offspring, or at around 15 to 20 years into marriage among the child-free (Anderson, Russell & Schumm, 1983). This is a pattern described as *marital disenchantment*. Later, during the stages in marriage after all the grown children have left home or child-free spouses have retired from work, marital bliss increases again, often to as high a level as during the honeymoon, or even higher. This process is sometimes called 're-enchantment'. We explore some of the causes for both disenchantment and the 'second honeymoon' in the next sections of this chapter.

Marital disenchantment

Peter Pineo (1961) conducted the first longitudinal study of marital happiness by following a sample of 400 United States newlyweds over a period of up to 20 years of married life. Striking changes in these husbands' and wives' feelings about marriage occurred with the passage of time. Some of Pineo's results are shown in Table 14.4.

Pineo's longitudinal data confirm the fact that happiness with marriage deteriorates for the average couple as the years go by, while showing that such deterioration is neither an artifact of differences between generations nor simply due to an overall disgruntlement with life. (Contrary to popular stereotypes about middle age, Pineo's results revealed no change in personal happiness over two decades.) Furthermore, Pineo measured how amicably couples interacted together (see Table 14.4) as well as how satisfied they felt with marriage. The declines on both dimensions showed a souring of the entire marriage relationship during middle age. Spouses' love for one another had diminished along with their enjoyment of being married, while discord and the perceived threat of divorce had increased. Nor were such problems confined to only a few atypical couples. Though the degree of loss varied somewhat from household to household, almost every couple in Pineo's sample had suffered some deterioration since the wedding. Pineo concluded that the phenomenon that he dubbed 'disenchantment' was virtually inevitable in marriages more than a few years old. Nor was it a trivial problem. He noted:

> The term 'loss of satisfaction' is insufficient to express the fact that this is a process which appears to be generally an inescapable consequence of the passage of time in a marriage. (p. 261)

Marital re-enchantment

The initial picture of age-related changes in marriage through the child-bearing and childrearing years may seem bleak. But this is a true developmental story with a genuinely happy ending. As shown in Figures 14.3 and 14.4, the research evidence strongly indicates that couples who remain married through

TABLE 14.4	Changes in spouses' feelings after two decades of marriage		
Dimension	Sample question	Change from honeymoon for husbands	Change from honeymoon for wives
Overall satisfaction with marriage	'Taking everything into consideration, how happy are you with married life?'	Decline*	Decline*
Affection	'How much do you love your spouse?'	Decline*	Decline*
Disharmony	'How often do you disagree with your spouse?'	Increase*	Increase*
Marital instability	'Is there a chance that you may consider divorce?'	Increase*	Increase*
Personal happiness	'How content do you feel with life in general?'	No change	No change

Note: * indicates change was statistically significant.
Source: Based on data in Pineo (1968).

BOX 14.1 How can you explain it?
Marital disenchantment

Instructions. The following excerpts from interviews with couples married for 10 to 15 years illustrate aspects of the disenchantment experience. After reading through these examples (and reflecting on your own experience, if relevant) try to come up with two plausible reasons why marital satisfaction should decline for the average couple over the early years of marriage.

- *Sometimes it's like living with a stranger – without the excitement* (an American husband).
- *I used to want to be with my husband all the time. But now that we've grown older he's found his interests and his own set of friends, and I've got mine. When he's around I become irritable and bitchy. All I want is to be left alone* (an Australian wife).
- *At first I kept saying, 'Well, it'll be different after we get used to one another.' But it didn't. I kept hoping he'd change, or I would, but we didn't. Now it doesn't seem to matter much* (an American wife).

HOW DO YOU EXPLAIN IT?

_____

_____

_____

To compare your answers with those of lifespan developmental theorists, see the next sections of the text.

the low ebb of the satisfaction curve can count on improvements in marital satisfaction later in middle age. After their grown children have left home (or after the childless couple's 25th wedding anniver-

sary), the curve of marital happiness swings steadily upward again. Very high levels of satisfaction are reported by both husbands and wives during the retirement years, sometimes exceeding the dizzy heights of love that young honeymooners enjoy. Box 14.2 illustrates this.

The phenomenon of a 're-enchantment' increase in marital satisfaction during the post-parental years is observed in cross-sectional studies conducted in Australia (Feeney et al., 1994) and among British married couples (Argyle, 1986), as well as in cross-sectional studies of thousands of married couples over several decades in the United States (Rollins & Cannon, 1974). However, it does need to be borne in mind that, when applied to marriage, the cross-sectional method (see Chapter 2) has one major limitation. Since being married is a criterion for inclusion in a cross-sectional study, older couples who had grown so unhappy with marriage that they opted for divorce would not be sampled, so their experiences would not be reflected in curves like those in Figures 14.3 to 14.5. However, a number of longitudinal studies of the progress of marital satisfaction over time have been published. Unfortunately for those who prefer simplistic accounts of human behaviour, their data indicate that the phenomenon of marital disenchantment cannot be explained away as an artifact of cross-sectional methodology. Fortunately for those who hope to enjoy a happily married old age, they equally strongly support the cross-sectional observation of marital re-enchantment.

In one of these longitudinal studies, Sylvia Weishaus and Dorothy Field (1988) interviewed a group of California couples, some of whose families had taken part in the Berkeley Growth Study when the now-married adults were children. (Recall the examination in Chapter 2 of some of the provocative life-cycle surprises that emerged from this pioneering developmental study by Jean Walker MacFarlane (1975).)

A case in point
A marriage of minds

The French philosopher Simone de Beauvoir, famous for her existential theories, political activism and feminist beliefs, described the benefits of a long-term marriage in her autobiography when in her fifties:

There has been one undoubted success in my life: my relationship with Sartre. In more than thirty years, we have only once gone to sleep at night disunited. These years spent side by side have not decreased the interest we find in each other's conversation: a woman friend has observed that we always listen to each other with the closest attention ... We have a common store of memories, knowledge and images behind us; our attempts to grasp the world are undertaken with the same tools ... guided by the same touchstones. Very often one of us begins a sentence and the other finishes it; if someone asks us a question, we have been known to produce identical answers. The stimulus of a word, a sensation, a shadow, sends us both travelling along the same inner path, and we arrive simultaneously at a conclusion – a memory, an association – completely inexplicable to a third person. (1968, p. 659)

Philosopher Jean Paul Sartre, de Beauvoir's partner and colleague, also expressed a similar, slightly astonished gratitude for their lifelong intimacy in an interview he gave at the age of 71. The interviewer asked what specific advantages he felt he had gained from having maintained the same intensely loving relationship through the course of his adult life. He replied:

It is an enormous benefit, because couples each have their own ways of viewing the things, people, and events which they encounter at any given point in life. Ten years later, heaps of things have changed. What that means, simply, is that you yourself have changed. If you happen to have changed all alone, you will have a new way of looking at things which is different from the old one. But that is all. If you live with someone else, on the other hand, you can try to work out together what the changes are: what this friend, or that colleague or some other adventure or happening was like 10 years ago. You can almost bring the past back to life. Clean off and polish things that weren't clear before. And that is only possible with another person. Also, it is important that this person have a sexual relationship with you because some of the important events in life are sexual and others are directly related to sexuality. It's absolutely essential to find this unity of ideas which enables Simone de Beauvoir and me to understand each other without speaking a word. (1977, p. 66)

The couples had been married for between 50 and 69 years when Weishaus and Field interviewed them. Interview data were supplemented with each spouse's retrospective reminiscences. The researchers found that the most common pattern across the five or six decades of marriage was the U-shaped curve. The 42 per cent of couples who showed this pattern had experienced declines in satisfaction and in the quality of their marriage during the middle years. But a dramatic rise in love, mutuality and pleasure in being married had followed the last child's departure from home.

Other patterns were also observed in a smaller number of elderly Berkeley couples. Twenty-nine per cent had experienced reasonably high levels of satisfaction throughout marriage. But parts of the curve still applied. Some of these spouses reported that the intensity of their love relationship had declined as they settled into maturity, while others experienced a rise in closeness and mutuality in old age, but without any discernible trough during the childrearing years. Another 18 per cent of couples had steadily maintained a superficial but congenial marriage over time. These couples, according to Weishaus and Field, had married largely for convenience and to please their parents and 'never became intensely involved with one another' (p. 768) even after five decades of marriage. The remaining 12 per cent of couples in Weishaus and Field's sample had experienced the decline from satisfaction as newlyweds to a low ebb of disenchantment when children were born, but had yet to experience any significant increase in marital satisfaction after being together for 55 to 60 years.

All in all, these longitudinal results support the cross-sectional picture of a predictable rise and fall in marital quality over time, though some variations of the pattern in individual marriages are clearly evident. It appears that marital disenchantment and re-enchantment are stable phenomena over time, not only in familiar Western societies but in other cultures, including those where marriage is undertaken as an economic or political arrangement rather than for love.

Cross-cultural studies of the development of marriage

The Irish playwright George Bernard Shaw blamed marital disenchantment on the irrationality of modern Western culture's belief in romantic love as both a necessary and a sufficient precondition to marriage (see Chapter 13). As he explained:

If a man marries a woman after three weeks' acquaintance, and the day after meets a woman he has known for twenty years, he finds, sometimes to his own irrational surprise and his wife's equally irrational indignation, that his wife is a stranger to him, and the other woman an old friend. Also, there is no hocus pocus that can possibly be devised with rings and veils and vows and benedictions that can fix either a man's or a woman's affection for twenty minutes, much less twenty years ... A person proposing or accepting a contract not only to do something but to like doing it would be certified as mad. Yet popular superstition credits the wedding rite with the power of fixing our fancies or affections for life even under the most unnatural conditions. (1929)

It is possible to test Shaw's hypothesis that marrying for love causes disenchantment by examining the progress over time of couples' feelings about marriage in cultures where criteria other than romantic love have traditionally been used to choose a mate. Let us look at how marital happiness developed over time in three different cultures where arranged marriage was practised.

Traditional Aboriginal marriage

Anthropologists Ronald and Catherine Berndt (1964) studied the marriage patterns of Aboriginal adults who lived in remote areas of Western Australia. They discovered three different types of marriage in these traditional Aboriginal communities.

1. *The arranged betrothal.* This is the most common, and most socially accepted, marital arrangement, consisting of a contract drawn up between the prospective in-laws before the future wife reached puberty. In some cases, the betrothed girl was taken to her husband's camp to get acquainted with him, but this was not essential. When the time for marriage drew near, a simple rite such as the mutual lighting of a fire was usually performed and the two families exchanged gifts. Henceforth, the couple was publicly recognised as being married, but the union was not usually considered permanent until after the first child was born.

2. *Elopement.* The next most common way of getting married was for lovers who chose one another in the face of parental and community disapproval to elope secretly to an inaccessible spot away from the main camp. Generally, they were followed and captured and ritual punishments were meted out by the community elders. But if the wife was not already married or betrothed to a 'suitable' husband who wanted her back, the runaways might be allowed to set up house together. Once they had a child, their union was likely to be tolerated as a fact of life.

3. *Capture.* The least common wedding procedure involved warfare. The future husband, sometimes with the aid of his relatives, ambushed and seized the woman. Unless her betrothed husband, father or brothers were strong enough to overpower the aggressor, she became his recognised wife.

These marital practices, while serving to illustrate the cultural diversity that pertains to an institution with a major impact on psychological functioning

throughout adult life, also have theoretical interest in the context of possible explanations for marital disenchantment. If the loss of love over time that couples in Western-style marriages are found to suffer were due purely to the instability of the emotion of romantic love, traditional Aboriginal couples who were married by means of a community-sanctioned *betrothal* should grow less disenchanted than their eloping counterparts. But the Berndts found that differences in the happiness and durability of Aboriginal marriages could not be linked in any consistent way to the initial manner of getting married. Some couples from arranged betrothals grew disenchanted, but so did some who had eloped or used capture, whereas marriages which persisted 'into the old age of both partners with every appearance of devotion between them' had sometimes originated in sweetheart elopements and sometimes from impartial betrothal. The Berndts concluded that the interacting personalities of the two spouses were more crucial to the marriage's long-term success than the manner of getting married:

> Whether they merely tolerate each other for want of something better, or from sheer inertia, or have a more positive affection for each other, depends to some extent on their personal experience together. If a woman neglects her husband or children, or is always looking for a new erotic experience: if he is so rough and hasty-tempered that she is afraid of him, or so weak that she cannot rely on him in a crisis – that marriage may perhaps last for a long time, but largely as a matter of habit: and it is likely to come to an abrupt end if the opportunity arises. On the other hand, a marriage need not be on the verge of a rupture because husband and wife are constantly quarrelling: in fact, they may prefer it that way. (1964, pp. 174–5)

Traditional Japanese marriage

A more systematic cross-cultural test of the provocative notion that middle-aged marital disenchantment develops as a consequence of couples basing their decision to marry on love rather than convenience was conducted by Robert Blood (1967) in post-World War II Japan.

Through a fortunate accident of social change, Blood had access to two groups of otherwise identical Japanese couples who typified this polar contrast. The more traditional *miai* couples had adhered to the old system of arranged marriage. Usually, they had met one another for the first time in the office of a marriage broker who had previously set the wheels in motion by offering their parents the dossiers of a dozen or so eligible young people to choose from. Parents' choices were based on the information in the dossier, which included name, age, health, education, occupation, family background and a photograph, plus, occasionally, an investigation by a private detective or the marriage broker to eliminate the possibil-

Love-match couples are no more likely than those who marry by arrangement to weather the middle years of marriage without experiencing disenchantment.

ity of 'skeletons in the closet'. Once introduced, the traditional *miai* couple normally felt they had little freedom to reject one another, even though the possibility of this was technically allowed. Blood quoted one representative *miai* wife, as follows:

> I was the youngest among my brothers and sisters. They were all married and I was left alone as a single woman. My mother got high blood pressure from worry about my being unmarried. My family were anxious to arrange a marriage as soon as possible and showed my mother the picture of my prospective husband. I was thus in haste to marry. After the *miai* I did not love my partner but I married him. It was not for my sake but because I wanted to relieve my mother and my family of their anxiety that I decided to marry. (p. 19, reprinted with permission of The Free Press)

On the other hand, the courtships of the newer breed of Japanese 'love-match' couples were very similar to those of Blood's comparison group of Americans in Detroit. They were distinguished from *miai* arrangements by the following characteristics:

- The couple met on their own initiative rather than via others' mediation.
- Love and emotional involvement were expressed during the courtship.
- The couple relied on their own decision to marry even in the face of opposition by significant others.
- They had informal rather than traditional marriage ceremonies.

A quote from a love-match wife typifies this contrast:

> At first my parents were opposed to the marriage but we two decided to push on. As my husband strongly wished, I dared to marry him ignoring my parents' opposition. Anyhow, he was a man of good character, which I thought highly of. (p. 25, reprinted with permission of The Free Press)

Interestingly enough, Blood discovered that Japanese folk wisdom was in accord with Pineo's hypothesis that *miai* marriages should show greater resistance to disenchantment than love marriages. He was told that 'Love matches start out hot and grow cold. Arranged marriages start out cold and grow hot' (p. 60). However, when he began to examine the evidence, he found that this saying gave a rather inaccurate and overly simplistic picture of what really happened to Japanese marriages with the passage of time. He wrote:

> Hence the slogan must be revised; from the man's standpoint, arranged marriages start out cool and end up cool, but enjoy a hot spell in the middle years. The trouble with the old prediction is that it fails to recognize that time generally chills marital satisfaction. Japanese arranged marriages are no more exempt from falling temperatures than any other kind of marriage. Hence the prediction about arranged marriages had to be wrong ultimately. Only in the short run – in the early years of marriage – could it be right. Even then, it is right only for the chief beneficiary of the old system, the man. (p. 86, reprinted with permission of The Free Press)

When love rather than satisfaction was the measure of the temperature of the marriage, progressive disenchantment over time showed up almost as clearly. *Miai* wives were the only exception, and they began with so little love for their husbands that, even though their love declined after a peak attained when they had been married for about two years, it never grew quite as cool as during the engagement period. (The average changes in love in both types of marriage and both sexes of partners are shown in Figure 14.5.) In accord with Pineo's hypothesis, Blood wrote that 'love is so hot when love marriages begin that they cannot help cooling down'. But the fact that the *miai* husbands' and wives' love for each other also declined after four or so years of marriage negates the theory that marital disenchantment can be attributed solely to the irrationality of marrying while romantically in love.

Traditional Chinese marriage

Even as early as the 1950s, traditional Japanese couples who married by arrangement could not have escaped some degree of contact with the Hollywood ideal of romantic love as a necessary condition for marriage. But in recent decades in China the situation has been different. Tradition, as in Japan, decreed that couples should marry on the basis of an arrangement between the bride's and groom's families, rather than for love. The couple's parents dominated the mate-selection process, and neither spouse typically felt they had a free choice of whom to marry. Often, the bride and groom were introduced to one another for the first time by their parents or a marriage broker of their parents' generation just before the wedding. After the socialist revolution, the role of parents in the Chinese mate-selection process declined sharply. Free choice by the couple was the recommended basis

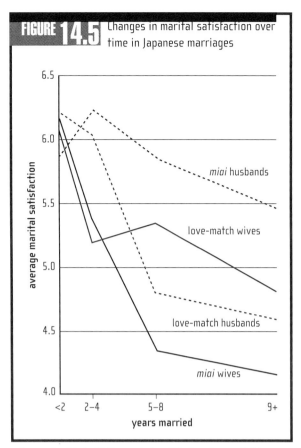

FIGURE 14.5 Changes in marital satisfaction over time in Japanese marriages

Source: Reprinted with the permission of The Free Press, a Division of Simon & Schuster Adult Publishing Group, from Love Match and Arranged Marriage: A Tokyo–Detroit Comparison, by Robert O. Blood, Jr, p. 85. Copyright 1967 by Robert O. Blood, Jr.

for selecting a mate, even though the Hollywood model of romantic love exerted relatively little influence during China's years of isolation from the West.

Xu Xiaohe and Martin Whyte (1990) studied a sample of 586 married women from the city of Chengdu in China who had been married for between one and 57 years. Those who had married before the 1949 revolution had almost all experienced an arranged marriage, of either a traditional or an intermediate variety. In fact, of the 71 Chengdu wives who married between 1933 and 1948, only 17 per cent reported having any personal choice in the decision. Similarly, only 17 per cent (possibly these same women) remembered being 'completely in love' at the time of getting married. Free choice in mate selection increased dramatically in China after the revolution. Nevertheless, arranged marriages did not disappear altogether, at least not in rural China. Four of the 210 wives (2 per cent) who were married between 1977 and 1987 experienced an arranged marriage.

The researchers discovered that a trough in marital satisfaction reflecting the development of disenchantment applied to love-based and arranged marriages alike, as shown in Figure 14.6. But there was also an overall difference in satisfaction at every age period between the wives who had married for love and those who had been wed by arrangement. Using the statistical technique of multiple regression, Xu and Whyte were able to exclude a number of background differences between the two groups of women. These included whether or not the wife was employed, the number of children she had borne, and the family's experiences during the dramatic Chinese Cultural Revolution of the 1960s. The results of these analyses confirmed that love marriages were more satisfying for wives overall than arranged marriages. In line with the disenchantment phenomenon, satisfaction was seen to decline significantly for both groups after five to 15 years of marriage.

But the rise in satisfaction in old age that is observed in other cultures did not seem to emerge for

While cultures vary in romantic ideology and marriage arrangements, the ups and downs of marital satisfaction over the life cycle are culturally universal.

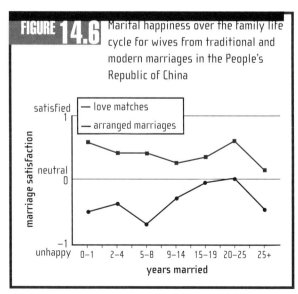

FIGURE 14.6 Marital happiness over the family life cycle for wives from traditional and modern marriages in the People's Republic of China

Source: Xu & Whyte (1990), Figure 5, © 1990 National Council on Family Relations, reproduced with permission.

these Chinese women. The authors looked to cultural variations in elderly women's lifestyles to explain the unexpected second drop in satisfaction after 25 years of marriage.

> Most older Chinese women will never see an 'empty nest', since they end their days living in a three-generation family and tending small children once again for one or more of their grown children. (p. 718)

As Figure 14.6 suggests, marital happiness seems to decline twice in the life cycle for Chinese married women: first, when the woman bears and rears children of her own, as in other cultures. But then, after a slight improvement as children grow up, marital disenchantment seems to occur again for traditional wives in China when the adult offspring bring their own young children into their elderly parents' homes and the grandmother has the duty to look after them. Thus, not arranged marriage but rather the duties of childrearing would appear responsible for the decline.

Theories of lifespan marriage development

These findings both within and across cultures are compelling. It would seem that the downward plunge in the average couple's feelings of marital happiness at the low ebb of the disenchantment curve is too robust a phenomenon to be explained away as an artifact of the use of a cross-sectional research design, as a peculiarity of the methods of mate selection in a particular culture or as the fickle vagaries of the mysterious emotion of romantic love. So what does cause disenchantment? As a predictable, age-related phenomenon of adult life, the growth of feelings of disappointment with both the institution of marriage and one's choice of mate demands an explanation. The rise in satisfaction in later marriage may seem even more puzzling. You may wish at this point to revisit your own explanations in Box 14.1.

In addition to the theories about cross-sectional evidence and love-match marriage that we have already dismissed, some other theories have been put forward to account for changes in marital happiness over time. These theories also help to define some of the important changes that arise in the marriage relationship during middle adulthood. They are:

1. Role strain and role shock in married life
2. Lifespan changes in sexual drive and sexual satisfaction
3. Parenting and childrearing
4. Communication and conflict-management skills
5. Personality development
6. Sex roles and androgyny.

Role strain and shock

Jessie Bernard (1972) proposed what she called 'the shock theory of marriage'. She noted so many discontinuities and stresses in the step from single life into marriage that she saw marriage as a genuine emotional health hazard. She argued that romanticism and each spouse's initial efforts to please the other and remain on best behaviour temporarily insulated newlyweds against the shock. But eventually couples had to confront the realities of married life – from dirty dishes and unshaven faces to loss of legal, economic and emotional freedom, as well as in-laws, house payments, housework and the rearing of children. When spouses were unable to cope with these new obligations and difficulties, their anxiety and mutual recriminations led to a decline in attraction to one another and to the institution of marriage. Efforts to negotiate a mutually acceptable way of dividing up housework may also fail, leading to hostility and disappointment (Goodnow, 1988).

Lifespan sexuality and sexual satisfaction

A sociobiological explanation for disenchantment ascribes a decline in marital satisfaction over time to sexual familiarity. It could be advantageous for survival to have a species that continually mates with new partners during the reproductive years, so that barren unions are avoided. If so, evolution may have selected humans who grow bored with the same sexual partner and crave novelty and variety. Yet Alfred Kinsey's (1953) classic study suggested that sexual pleasure (defined by orgasm) remains strong in middle-aged marriage. Indeed, sexual satisfaction is likely to improve for most wives, compared with their experiences at the honeymoon (see Table 14.5). Furthermore, the 're-enchantment' increase in marital satisfaction observed during the post-childrearing years is difficult to reconcile with the hypothesis that disenchantment is due to a dwindling of sexual excitement over time. Figure 14.7 shows the high levels of importance that men and women continued to ascribe to sexual satisfaction from age 45 to age 75.

TABLE 14.5	Percentage of marital coitus leading to female orgasm, by length of marriage				
	Year of marriage				
Coitus with orgasm (%)	1st	5th	10th	15th	20th
None	25	17	14	12	11
1–29	11	13	14	16	13
30–59	13	15	13	11	12
60–89	12	15	17	16	17
90–100	39	40	42	45	47
Number of cases	2244	1448	858	505	261

Source: Kinsey et al. (1953), p. 408. Copyright 1953 Elsevier Inc., with permission from Elsevier.

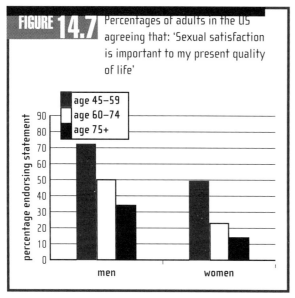

FIGURE **14.7** Percentages of adults in the US agreeing that: 'Sexual satisfaction is important to my present quality of life'

Source: Based on data in AARP (1999).

Couples who have children spend less time in intimate husband–wife interaction and more time on household chores than child-free couples.

Stresses of parenthood

The burdens and costs of parenthood, and the strains and anxieties connected with 24-hour-a-day responsibilities for infants and small children (discussed in Chapter 13), certainly contribute to making the middle years of marriage more stressful for those couples who elect to become parents within two or three years of the honeymoon than for their child-free counterparts. The presence of children also limits the time men and women have at home for recreation and communication with one another. Couples who have children spend more time on household chores than child-free couples. They share fewer recreations and have less chance to talk together, less money for luxuries and entertainment and less privacy for sexuality (Noller, Feeney & Peterson, 2001). These factors could all potentially contribute to disenchantment. Yet the picture is more complicated. Robert Blood (1967) was able to compare child-free and parental Japanese and American couples at various stages of marriage. He found that time and parenthood each made separate and statistically significant contributions to disenchantment. Using the statistical technique of multiple regression to tease apart the effects of time and children on marital satisfaction, S. Anderson, C. Russell and W. Schumm (1983) showed that, even without children, time led to disenchantment, over and above any influence due to stage in the family life cycle.

Marital communication and conflict management

Conflict is an inevitable feature of all intimate relationships, including couplehood. Early in marriage, a couple may lack the skills, motivation, cognitive resources or emotional energy needed for resolving conflict effectively. According to Joseph Forgas (1994), couples' understanding of the disagreements they inevitably encounter in everyday domestic life may be marred by mood factors. Using a sample of Australian men and women who volunteered to take part in a series of studies after being approached in public places, Forgas investigated the effects of happy and unhappy moods on subjective explanations for couple conflict.

For example, in one of his studies, 162 Sydney men and women were approached outside a number of metropolitan and suburban cinemas. The 'experimental' group consisted of adults in couple relationships who had just seen a preselected happy or sad film. (Pilot studies established that these particular films had a strong effect in elevating or depressing most viewers' moods.) The control group, elegantly matched, consisted of adults who were similarly involved in couple relationships and who were waiting in a queue outside the movie theatre intending to watch the same preselected happy or sad films. Thus, they were like adults in the experimental group except for the fact that their moods had not yet been affected by the movie. Forgas asked each adult individually to describe the causes of two serious and two trivial conflicts that had recently arisen in their couple relationship. Examples of serious conflicts included:

- level of partner's commitment to the relationship
- jealous behaviour
- depth of communication between partners.

The trivial conflicts, based on recent disagreements reported by other Sydney couples not included in the main study, included:

- which TV channel to watch
- household tidiness
- personal habits.

When Forgas analysed the explanations the Australian men and women gave for disagreeing with their partner over these issues, he found that those who had been placed in an unhappy frame of mind by viewing a sad movie blamed themselves for the conflict more than the happy adults did. This was especially true for the serious conflicts which, in themselves, were likely to exert more long-term effects on relationships. Forgas concluded that:

> The present findings suggest that sad people are more likely to feel guilty, to blame internal, stable, and global causes for their conflicts, and to rely on passive, noninterventionist conflict resolution strategies to cope with such situations ... Such a strategy is somewhat reminiscent of learned helplessness ... Increased mood bias when dealing with serious conflicts suggests that transient feelings may play a greater role in dysfunctional relationships than is commonly assumed. (1994, p. 66)

In a more recent study, Forgas (1996) induced happy, sad or neutral moods in men and women who were then asked to perform a number of cognitive tasks and social perception exercises. When in a happy mood, men and women displayed better memory scores and were more inclined to attribute other people's behaviour to their longstanding personality traits, rather than temporary external factors. Applied to marriage, this suggests that conflicts may be solved more productively when the spouses are in a good mood, and credit given more than when they are in a bad mood, even if for reasons that have nothing to do with their relationship.

The capacity to communicate intimately may increase over the duration of marriage, possibly helping to explain marital re-enchantment. The results of a study of 108 Australian married couples by John Antill and Sandra Cotton (1987) identified a process known as *self-disclosure* as a particularly important contributor to gains in marital happiness with the passage of time. Antill and Cotton defined *self-disclosure* as the voluntary communication by one spouse to the other of private, confidential or highly personal information about themselves which the recipient is unlikely to be able to discover from any other source. The specific content of the couple's self-disclosures to one another can be either positive (e.g. a sudden burst of happiness or news of an important personal achievement) or negative (e.g. expressions of anxiety or frustration).

Using a list of 20 potentially sensitive topics such as 'my worries and fears', 'my sexual dislikes', 'my personal successes' and 'anger and irritations', Antill and Cotton's married subjects rated how often they discussed sensitive issues as a couple, and also rated the overall quantity of information they revealed to their partners on a scale from 'nothing or almost nothing' to 'everything or almost everything'.

An important association was discovered between couples' rates of self-disclosure and the duration of their marriage. On average, couples who had reached the disenchantment-prone middle years of marriage disclosed less to one another than those who were still in the earlier 'enchanted' stage of couplehood. Age was also a factor. Older husbands and wives, as well as those who had been married longer, scored lower in intimate self-disclosure than younger or recently married Australian men and women. The number of children in the family also diminished intimate self-disclosure. It seemed that having three or more children to attend to meant parents had little time alone together and few opportunities or incentives for communicating at an intimate level.

A strong link was likewise found between a couple's overall level of intimate self-disclosure and the husband's and wife's reported levels of marital satisfaction. The more intimately the partners communicated, the happier they felt about being married. Even the disclosure of negative information was a positive predictor of marital happiness. While it might seem that telling a spouse one is worried or sexually frustrated could be aversive, this kind of communication was linked with optimal marriage satisfaction in Australian couples. According to Antill and Cotton:

> Marital counselling could profitably concentrate on this aspect of a relationship. This may be particularly important as couples reach their middle years and have a number of children to distract them from important aspects of their own relationship. (p. 22)

Adult personality development as a stress on marriage

Peter Pineo's (1968) explanation for his longitudinal disenchantment data was founded on his view that continuing personality growth is a necessary

The capacity to communicate intimately about personal and sensitive topics is an important ingredient in marital satisfaction.

prerequisite for individual psychological adjustment throughout mature adulthood. Therefore, if marriage interferes with this necessary psychological developmental process in some way, the resulting feelings of stagnation, maladjustment or personal unhappiness are liable to detract from satisfaction with marriage.

Even when married adults continue to develop their individual personalities in adult life, acquiring qualities like intimacy and generativity (Erikson, 1968a), there is a risk that their separate personal growth trajectories may carry them in different directions. After a decade of divergent growth, they may discover they no longer have very much in common. This can explain disenchantment since, according to Pineo (1968), when couples marry for love, the decision to wed is usually made at the point of optimal matching between the two lovers' personalities. But a similarly congenial personality match can only be maintained over 10 years of marriage in one of two ways – either no change in personality occurs in either spouse, or they both change simultaneously in compatible ways. In some cases, thwarted personal growth may be caused directly by marriage. For example, the economic burdens of home ownership, lack of free time or the other spouse's disapproval may prevent married individuals from cultivating their creative, intellectual or social talents. But even when personality growth is blocked by factors outside the marriage (such as occupational socialisation pressures, examined later in this chapter), the resulting unhappiness can nevertheless spill over to undermine marital happiness.

Conversely, gains in personal growth are likely to increase marital enjoyment, regardless of whether they are directly, or only incidentally, attributable to being married. This is one reason why men and women who gain intense psychological satisfaction (or growth towards generativity) from the experience of parenthood are likely to escape many of the vexed feelings associated with marital disenchantment (Erikson, 1968a). In line with these ideas, the husbands in Pineo's longitudinal study who reported the most substantial personal growth gains were the least disenchanted. Similarly, couples who experienced a drop in income over the first 20 years of marriage were less disenchanted than those whose economic circumstances had improved steadily over the same time period, a finding that can only be explained if the drop in income was associated with a rise in growth or satisfaction outside the sphere of working life. Presumably, declines in income allow more time to be spent with the spouse.

Unpaid leisure pursuits may also foster opportunities for personal fulfilment more effectively than one's job does (as seen later in this chapter when we look at leisure's influence on adult development). The sharing of active outdoor leisure pursuits and cultural interests between husbands and wives has been found to be more frequent among spouses in New Zealand than in North America, as Figure 14.8 shows (Parnicky, Williams & Silva, 1985). On average, New Zealand couples scored higher than their North American counterparts in the communication qualities of affectionate 'cohesion' and open expression of disagreement. These differences possibly help to explain the overall lower levels of disenchantment in New Zealand than in the United States (see Figure 14.4).

Sex roles and androgyny

Dual-career marriages, in which both husband and wife remain employed outside the home, are found to be less prone to disenchantment (Pineo, 1968).

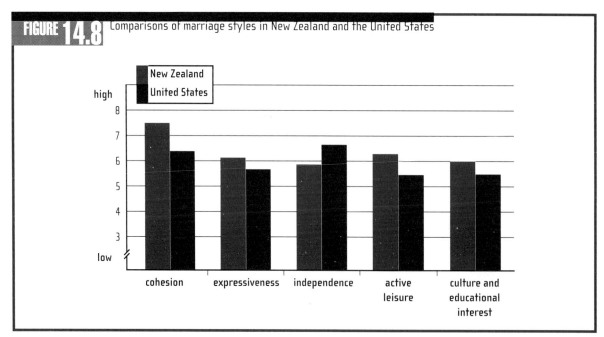

FIGURE 14.8 Comparisons of marriage styles in New Zealand and the United States

Source: Based on data in Parnicky, Williams & Silva (1985).

Marital dissatisfaction is correspondingly found to be greater when couples adopt traditional sex-role patterns and strictly segregate their home duties along rigid and conventional lines (see Chapter 13). But Antill and Cotton (1987) found that Australian husbands and wives who scored higher in femininity disclosed more intimately, and were consequently happier with marriage, than either traditionally masculine husbands or sex-role-reversed wives who opted for masculine attributes like dominance, control and self-assertion in place of feminine qualities like nurturance or sensitivity. Stereotypically masculine husbands are less likely than androgynous or feminine men to be able to carry on the process of intimate self-disclosure that contributes to shared understanding and the lifelong growth of the couple's love for one another.

From a study of Sydney couples who ranged in age from 19 to 65 years, John Antill, Kay Bussey and John Cunningham (1985) similarly concluded that spouses are happiest with marriage when their partners are either androgynous or feminine in sex-role orientation, as shown in Figure 14.9.

The empty-nest stage of couplehood

Towards the end of the middle adult years, children grow up and move away and the married couple lives alone together once again. Spouses have more time to devote to one another once they reach the empty-nest stage of family life. One might imagine they could find this trying, with boredom escalating and each getting in the other's way. Yet the empirical data shown in Figures 14.3 and 14.4 suggest the opposite. At least for those couples who escaped divorce when disenchantment was at its peak, the U-shaped curve of marital satisfaction reveals gains in happiness that are just as dramatic as the decline during the middle years. But what explains the abrupt rise in satisfaction in late adulthood?

The departure of children from home is one important factor. The emptying of the parental nest may influence marital satisfaction in both direct and indirect ways. Directly, it is apt to reduce jealousy, rivalry and the likelihood of disagreements between spouses over childrearing. Indirectly, the children's departure frees up time, energy and economic resources for investment in the couple relationship.

Having time to converse, negotiate and even argue with one another may also boost older couples' satisfaction with marriage, according to Sylvia Weishaus and Dorothy Field (1988). When they interviewed their longitudinal sample of couples in Berkeley, California, who had been married for over 50 years, they recorded frequent comments about the benefits of lively discussions and debates from those couples whose marriages had improved after the children left home. One husband commented that while the children were at home he and his wife had 'never' argued, but this was because they had not been emotionally close. When the children had grown up and left home, he and his wife found they had more time to argue, although they usually managed to resolve their disagreements amicably and rarely fought angrily or nursed a grudge. Consequently, they came to understand each other better and described their post-parental marriage as very close and satisfying.

Another elderly California couple had been so disenchanted during the middle years of marriage that they had actually separated for a while. But, according to Weishaus and Field:

> In their young-old and old-old years, however, they reported that although they still argued ('I think people should'), they 'are very much in love', they now have a good time together, and they rated the present as the happiest time of the marriage. (p. 772)

William Roberts' (1979) interviews with 50 couples who had been married for 50 to 65 years likewise showed extremely high levels of affection, mutual understanding and marital satisfaction among these long-term couples. Nearly 80 per cent of them reported 'above average' levels of happiness with their marriage and, when asked privately whether they would marry the same person again, close to 90 per cent said they would. One man whose age was over 80 said: 'I tell my wife every day that I love her. It makes her happy and it makes me feel

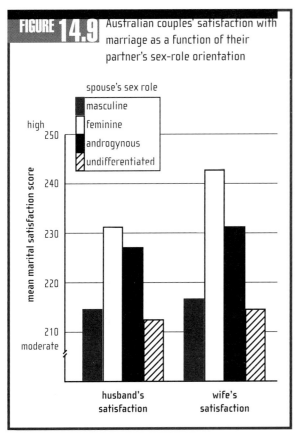

FIGURE 14.9 Australian couples' satisfaction with marriage as a function of their partner's sex-role orientation

spouse's sex role
- masculine
- feminine
- androgynous
- undifferentiated

mean marital satisfaction score

high 250

240

230

220

210 moderate

husband's satisfaction   wife's satisfaction

Source: Based on data in Antill & Cotton (1987).

Marital happiness is high in couples who have been together for four or more decades.

good to say it' (p. 269). Roberts concluded that, for most couples in this sample, the benefits of an enduring marriage far outweighed the costs.

Roberts found that 'few couples would say that there had not been adjustments over the years' and that 'time alone did not diminish the need for adapting and changing in the relationship' (p. 270). In fact, he attributed these couples' extraordinarily successful married lives to their ability to adjust to one another's needs and to handle the problems they all experienced. When asked if they had ever considered divorce, a few of them smilingly replied, 'Divorce, no; murder, yes' (p. 267). It seemed less that these couples had been exceptionally good matches for each other in the beginning than that they had gradually learned to live amicably together by confronting the stresses and upheavals of their partnership in ways that encouraged both their individual growth and their mutual development.

Robert and Jeanette Lauer and S. Kerr (1995) similarly interviewed a sample of 100 North American couples who had been married for between 45 and 64 years. In keeping with Roberts' findings, these elderly couples reported uniformly high levels of satisfaction with marriage and exceptionally frequent and effective patterns of conflict management and communication as a couple. Over 80 per cent of the spouses in this sample said that they confided in their mate all or most of the time and that they had come to agree with one another on their aims, goals and philosophy of life. The result was a renewal of marital happiness exceeding the highest levels they had experienced as newlyweds. According to the Lauers, 85 per cent of these elderly men and women reported that their spouse was more interesting to them now than when they were first married, and 94 per cent of them had come to regard their mate as their best friend. The benefits of communication and shared experience for overcoming disenchantment to achieve satisfaction in late adulthood are illustrated in Box 14.2.

Household work and marital role allocation

In Chapter 13 we explored how couples divide up the household chores during early marriage. Parenthood, as we noted, may constrain a segregated role pattern. But then, during the empty-nest stage, a return to a more egalitarian household pattern may lay a strong foundation for older couples' gains in marital satisfaction and mutual affection after three to five decades of marriage. When Timothy Brubaker (1985) interviewed a unique group of American couples who had recently celebrated their golden wedding anniversary, he found a remarkably egalitarian style of domestic role division, in contrast to the traditional, sex-stereotyped patterns typically adopted by couples in the childrearing phase of family life in the United States, as well as in Australia and New Zealand. Brubaker noted that, in contrast to younger men, most of the retired husbands in his sample undertook sole responsibility for cleaning the house and for minor repair jobs inside the house, as well as for the traditionally masculine jobs of maintaining the garden and the car. They also participated equally with their wives in other jobs such as entertaining and shopping for groceries. These domestic changes are likely to give a direct boost to marital happiness by providing more free time for each spouse, and the chance to enjoy shared leisure pursuits. They are also apt to have the added indirect benefits of fostering the other correlates of successful marriages, namely:

- personal growth (as when a retired husband discovers his talent for cooking)
- self-disclosure (as when couples converse intimately while working together on a household job)
- androgyny (as when spouses reassess their sex roles after discovering aptitudes for traditionally cross-sex stereotyped tasks)
- positive moments (as when a spouse tells a joke while doing housework together).

From a study of nearly 400 married couples in Queensland who were asked about patterns of equity, or fairness, in their marriage during different stages in the family life cycle, Judith Feeney and her colleagues concluded that *global equity*, or a sense that neither spouse was exploiting or being exploited by the other, reached a peak for wives during the empty-nest stage (Feeney, Peterson & Noller, 1994). In fact, approximately two-thirds of empty-nest wives perceived a perfectly fair balance of domestic rewards and contributions between their husband and themselves. But during the childrearing and launching stages, approximately one-third of the Australian wives felt exploited. They believed that they were putting more time, effort and skill into the marriage than their husband, yet their husband was reaping a disproportionate share of the benefits accruing from being married.

Careers, families and the roles of middle adulthood

Love may seem to fit marriage as closely as a 'horse and carriage' but few would say the same about employment. Even relationships within the family, such as parenthood or intimacy with ageing parents, may place a strain on marriage by limiting the amount and quality of time that husbands and wives can spend together on a one-to-one basis. Consequently, psychological development through careers and relationships during middle life is something of a juggling act. The challenge is to manage a wider diversity of adult roles than at any other stage in the life cycle while at the same time endeavouring to sustain and coordinate cognitive and personality growth in both spouses. With an increasing drive to achieve generativity (see page 480) as middle age progresses, men and women need to continue to develop in relationship contexts, at the same time as growing career maturity and personal psychological strength.

These pressures are not always resolved in an optimally developmental manner. In one longitudinal study of male university graduates it was discovered, sadly, that career development arose at the cost of growth through intimacy (Heath, 1977). Most of the well-educated men in this study, who had the good fortune to develop cognitive skills, moral maturity, personal stability and autonomy by coping successfully with the demands of their jobs, failed dismally when it came to development in relationships with wife and children. In fact, no man in the study believed that his job had had any beneficial influence at all on his relationship with his intimates. Several respondents were conscious of their job's degenerative (or 'immaturing') effects on domestic life. One physician explained: 'My job takes up a lot of my need for intimacy. I feel all my intimacy needs become cool: I'm cooler with my friends and perhaps with my wife' (p. 277).

Careers, marriage and parenthood

Increasing numbers of mid-adult men and women in Australia, New Zealand and other industrialised societies today strive to combine marriage, parenthood and a challenging career, so that both spouses are employed outside the home and children spend the working hours of each week in day-care or after-school care. This may have beneficial effects. Australian couples who use child care while their children are very young typically report enjoying at least some of the benefits that are listed in Table 14.6.

However, child care can also have disadvantages. One large-scale longitudinal study of a nationally representative sample of families in the United States (NICHD, 2002) revealed that, if mothers returned to paid employment when their infants were aged nine months or younger, these children had poorer levels of cognitive development as preschoolers and less

TABLE 14.6 Benefits and disadvantages of child care outside the home according to Australian parents	
Advantages	**Disadvantages**
Children in day-care learn to mix with other children and become more relaxed in social situations with peers and adults	Children in day-care are less able to amuse themselves when alone
Children in day-care receive more stimulation and educational input than those who stay at home	Children learn bad habits (e.g. aggression) from other children in day-care
Children in day-care learn to share and cooperate with peers	Children are more vulnerable to illness and accidental injury in day-care than at home
Children acquire independence and self-reliance and a sense of their own individuality through regular daily separations from parents	Children may feel lonely and upset if parents are not available
Children gain social experiences in day-care that they could not get at home	Caregivers in day-care cannot provide the same attention, care and affection to individual children as a parent can

readiness for school in areas of language, memory, reasoning, problem-solving and perceptual skill than children in statistically matched families where the mother remained at home as a full-time caregiver throughout the child's first year of life. This pattern was not observed in Sweden, however, where child care is of a generally higher standard than in the United States, and where paid maternity leave provisions are more favourable to mothers who decide to remain at home. This fact led the authors of the North American study to conclude that:

> Improving the quality of the child care used by the children of fulltime working mothers might help to mitigate the observed negative effects of mothers' early and fulltime employment on children's cognitive development. (p. 1068)

On the other hand, once children reach the age of one or two years, there can be developmental advantages for those whose mothers are employed outside the home, especially for daughters whose mothers work full-time. Figure 14.10 shows the results of one research comparison of the offspring of employed and non-working mothers in Melbourne. Sons' psychological functioning was unaffected by maternal

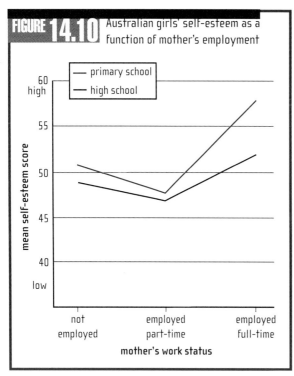

FIGURE 14.10 Australian girls' self-esteem as a function of mother's employment

mean self-esteem score

— primary school
— high school

60 high
55
50
45
40
low

not employed   employed part-time   employed full-time

mother's work status

Source: Based on data in Amato (1987), p. 190.

employment, but daughters were found to score significantly higher on measures of self-confidence and self-esteem when their mothers worked full-time than if they were either part-time employees or full-time homemakers (Amato, 1987). Presumably, the model provided by a full-time working mother of successfully bridging the gap between stereotypically masculine and feminine roles spills over to the daughter's pride in herself. Why the same should not apply to the daughters of women who worked part-time is puzzling, but perhaps the relatively low status, income and challenge of many part-time jobs for women in Australia prevented these mothers from feeling the same levels of pride and job satisfaction that are seen to accompany a full-time career.

The proportion of Australian and New Zealand dual-earner couples has increased substantially in recent years. At the beginning of the 20th century, approximately one Australian wife in five was in the paid workforce. By the late 1980s, this figure had grown to nearly half, and it remains at a high level. Almost two-thirds of two-parent households where there are dependent children now have both spouses in the labour force. One reason for the increase in dual-career families has been a change in fertility patterns and the timing of child-bearing for contemporary Australians and New Zealanders.

Women now enter marriage later than during the early 1970s. At the same time, the birth of a first child is now being delayed until the mother reaches the average age of 28 or 29. Family size is continuing to shrink. In Australia at present, a woman's total average fertility over the lifespan is estimated at only

1.9 children, in contrast to an average of 2.7 children in 1972 (ABS, 2001). These delays in the timing of child-bearing have meant that contemporary Australian and New Zealand women have gained about a decade on their mother's generation during which to work at a career before children are born. Furthermore, the tendency to bear only one or two children within an average of less than two years has meant that an Australian or New Zealand wife today can count on returning to work much sooner than her mother or grandmother did, even if she elects to drop out of the workforce completely while her children are young.

But other social changes besides these marked shifts in fertility patterns are also bound up with the increasing move towards dual-career families. A new emphasis in popular consciousness on the potential of women to contribute to society through a career has coincided with changes in the psychological motivations and values of young Australian and New Zealand women. According to Ailsa Burns and Jacqueline Goodnow (1985), women are attracted to employment because:

> Work provides mothers with income and some combination of independence, identity, interest, status, companionship, pride, purpose, security, and structure, just as it does men. (p. 90)

Women's average level of income is apt to be lower than the average married man's, as is their access to the fringe benefits of paid employment. This is partly because mothers today are still more likely than fathers to opt out of employment or to choose part-time jobs for periods while their children are young. Also, women's jobs are concentrated to a greater extent than men's in low-income clerical, sales and service positions (Burns & Goodnow, 1985). At the same time, working mothers typically assume an undue share of the burdens of housework and child care outside their working hours, contributing to feelings of stress, burnout and overload (see Chapter 13).

Role conflict and role overload: The pain of juggling love and work

As well as its potential advantages, employment for both spouses has its costs. Couples who opt to integrate work, marriage and parenthood can end up in a bind known as *role overload* in which neither spouse has enough time or energy to do any of the jobs properly. Even when enough time is available, stress can arise if the crucial features of the person's roles at work and in the home are incompatible with one another. This problem is known as *role conflict*. Examples include spouses with egalitarian marriage roles who work in leadership positions in a highly hierarchical organisation, or the wife in a traditionally stereotyped marriage who shows deference to her husband's authority when making decisions at home yet is required by her executive position to exert leadership and direction over male subordinates at work.

In an Australian study, Barry Fallon (1997) studied the problem of marriage/career role conflict. His focus was on the way husbands and wives managed interpersonal conflict at home and at work. Although an integrating, compromising style was popular in both settings, Fallon found that many Australians used different conflict styles at work and in marriage. Wives were much less likely to practise conflict avoidance with their husbands than with their co-workers. Husbands were more dominating with their co-workers than with their wives. (See Chapter 12 for additional information on these different conflict-resolution styles.)

Role overload describes the problem of having too many demanding roles to perform, at home, at work, or at both. Overwork can result in problems of stress, inefficiency and sheer exhaustion. Employed adults who become caught up in demanding occupations may find they have little time or energy left for developing deeper intimacy and increasingly satisfying interpersonal involvements. On the basis of a dialectical 'equilibrating' or 'balance' model of adult development (see Chapter 2), Douglas Heath (1977) predicted that adults on an intensive career trajectory would eventually call their vocational overspecialisation into question, perhaps after working through a *mid-life crisis* (or a critical overhauling of their life's goals, see page 502). Ultimately, by these means, they might eventually rearrange their priorities to catch up on their neglected roles as parent, husband, wife, offspring, friend, lover or grandparent. This possibility is considered in more detail later in this chapter.

Samuel Rabinowitz and Stephen Stumpf (1987) explored the problems of role conflict and overload in a sample of middle-aged American academics. Somewhat to their surprise, they discovered that role conflict was not invariably destructive or disorganising. Instead, its effects on job performance varied with the university teacher's age and seniority within the promotional system. At more junior levels, when the academic's main role involved teaching, higher levels of role conflict were associated with above-average teaching effectiveness as rated by student evaluations and peer judges. Role conflict in junior academic staff was negatively associated with administrative performance but, later on, after promotion to professor, role conflict became a positive predictor of administrative excellence. In other words, role conflict may be energising when it relates to a major focus of activity at any given stage of a career, and even though role overload and conflict consume time, effort and energy and create immediate stress, their long-term effect on development is frequently beneficial. Thus paid employment *per se* need not be incompatible with positive developmental changes in marriage and parental relationships during middle adulthood, even when both spouses' careers are highly demanding.

Love and household work

Jacqueline Goodnow and Pamela Warton (1991) interviewed a sample of Sydney mothers about their own, their husband's and their children's participation in household work. They discovered that family members, mothers especially, view love and work in the home as inextricably interconnected. When asked about their motives for performing household drudgery, these Australian women frequently remarked that by doing chores they expressed their love for their husband and children. 'I do this because I care for you' was a justification for tasks ranging from ironing a shirt to cleaning the toilet.

By the same token, a child's spontaneous participation in household work was viewed not only as a sign of maturity but, more importantly, as testimony to the child's affection for family members. Implicitly, the Sydney mothers conveyed to their children the message that: 'What you do is a sign of the way you care for me.' They read back messages of their children's love in helpfulness with household chores, especially when the child was thoughtful enough to perform the task without having to be nagged. The time parents spend in household work per day increases, especially for wives, as children grow up, despite the potential of school-aged children to make a contribution. Even in dual-earner families the wife does the lion's share of housework at all stages in the family life cycle. In their interviews with mothers, Goodnow and Warton asked the mothers to give details of a particularly 'good moment' in family life. Very often this was a time when spouse or child had spontaneously made a domestic contribution. As one mother explained:

> When they have a bath, I often warm up their slippers and place them outside the bathroom door so they can just step into them and stay nicely warm. The other day, I had a bath and when I came out, there were my slippers all nicely warmed. I felt so happy and I went and hugged them. (p. 282)

For mothers, love and household work are intimately interconnected.

Theories of career development

The experiences that adults have in the world of work exert a major influence over their psychological development. Between the ages of 20 and 60, employed adults typically spend one-third of their waking hours on their job; as well they devote a large share of time spent outside the occupational environment thinking about work, talking about it or doing work-related tasks. Thus, it is not surprising that a career affects nearly every aspect of a person's health, cognition, social relationships and personality during middle adulthood.

Though naive adolescents may idealistically imagine that, provided they choose the right job, their working lives will proceed through four or more decades of 'happily-ever-after' uneventfulness (Super, 1957, 1990), the career life cycle is in fact an ever-changing one. In addition to devising acceptable mergers between their vocation and their family life, working men and women must also find ways of coping with the sequential changes that are apt to arise in their career between early and late adulthood.

Three major career development theorists have postulated developmental changes in career orientation, activities and aspirations during middle adulthood. Let us briefly examine their theories.

Donald Super's theory

Donald Super (1957, 1990) drew his inspiration from Charlotte Buhler's theory (see Chapter 2) of lifelong, organic development of a person's central life goals, including the career. Buhler postulated that self-determination increases from early to mid-adulthood and then plateaus or declines between the ages of 40 and 50. In her view, early middle age is a time for 'stocktaking', or a critical overhauling of all one's successes and failures in life. This is frequently followed by renewed ambition, as the mature adult makes hurried efforts to remedy whatever deficiencies the stocktaking process brought to light. Some contemporary researchers, including Super, call this process the *mid-career crisis* (see page 502).

Like Buhler, Super (1990) proposed a sequence of developmental changes which he defined more fully in the context of the work situation. He believed that the worker shifts motivational emphasis at about age 45. The single-minded push for fame, achievement and personal advancement characterising early adulthood was followed by a phase in which mature workers endeavoured to consolidate earlier advances and maintain their existing level inside the organisation. Following the exploratory career phase studied in Chapter 13, Super described the phase leading up to the mid-career crisis as a period of establishment, followed by maintenance and decline phases once the crisis is resolved. These three phases are outlined below.

ESTABLISHMENT PHASE

(Age 25 to 44): Super proposed that the first half of this phase was a 'trial' period devoted to the translation of the young adult's budding self-concept into occupational terms. The 'shopping around' discussed in Chapter 13 is a normal aspect of searching for a satisfactory match between one's own interests or aptitudes and the requirements of various lines of work. During the second half of the establishment phase, experimentation is put aside and effort goes into carving out a secure place in the chosen occupation, or to advancing up that particular job's status hierarchy. There is settling into an occupational identity that suits the worker's talents and goals. Single-minded pursuit of career advancement begins and pressures outside the job – family responsibilities or community entrenchment – may also contribute to tying the worker down. Promotions and higher pay and status bring increased pay and job security.

MAINTENANCE PHASE

(Age 45 to 60): According to Super, this phase is distinguished from the earlier stage of career establishment both objectively (in terms of the worker's outwardly observable accomplishments and working style) and subjectively, through a shift in vocational attitudes and reasons for working. No longer is the impulse to get ahead paramount. By now, workers have either achieved most of the goals they set for themselves in the establishment stage, or they have abandoned their earlier unrealistically lofty ambitions. In either case, the main goal of the maintenance stage is to consolidate earlier successes and to keep from dropping below the level already achieved. Also, the self-concept is no longer being shaped by surpassing their own past feats. Past achievements yield a sense of complacency, together with the social recognition which is apt to catch up with the worker during this phase. On the other hand, workers whose self-concept depicts them as failures can only endeavour to avoid being nagged by an unfavourable self-image.

DECLINE PHASE

The onset of this phase depends partly on individual workers (and their health, stamina and capabilities) and partly on broader factors such as superannuation schemes, mandatory retirement age and the economic climate. In general, Super suggested that this phase begins earlier and lasts longer at lower levels of the occupational hierarchy. Eventually, however, all workers move from the maintenance phase of the career life cycle into what Super labelled 'decline'. Again, this broad stage includes two separate substages. The first is a period when work activities slow down, even though the worker remains on the job. The second substage usually begins with retirement, when a sudden readjustment to the relatively complete loss of the former vocational role is required.

(We examine this change in more detail in Chapter 15.) Super felt that the major psychological task of both these 'decline' substages was the 'adjustment to a new self'. Being a retired person, with its associated status changes and other cultural ramifications, forms one component of this altered self-definition; the second is the relinquishment of those aspects of the self-concept that were bound up with the individual's working activities.

Robert Havighurst's theory

Erik Erikson's theory of lifespan psychological development (see Chapter 2) has been integrated into another model of adult career development that resembles Super's in many ways (Tiedeman & O'Hara, 1963; Havighurst, 1964). Robert Havighurst (1964) endeavoured to mesh Erikson's notion of stages in adult personality growth with Super's vocational stages. He came up with three stages of career development between occupational entry and retirement, as follows.

BECOMING A PRODUCTIVE PERSON

(Age 25 to 39): This phase blends Super's notion of career 'establishment' with Erikson's identity crisis (see Chapter 11). Thus, the worker during this stage is preoccupied not only with mastering vocational skills and ascending the career ladder in the direction of higher occupational status, success and seniority, but also with an inward struggle to stabilise his or her vocational self-definition and to gain a better understanding of personal talents and incapacities.

MAINTAINING A PRODUCTIVE SOCIETY

(Age 40 to 69): During this phase in Havighurst's scheme, workers replace the personal ambitions of the previous phase with the motive to use their productive energies for the benefit of society as a whole. Thus, the developmental tasks in this stage include:

1. *Activism:* Becoming more socially aware and taking an active interest in occupational politics or social issues outside the workplace (this typically involves broadening one's scope and taking on civic responsibilities or community service roles congruent with one's vocational capabilities and position).
2. *Altruism:* Setting aside one's own personal striving for recognition, promotion or monetary rewards in favour of contributions that will serve others and be maintained apart from one's own career.
3. *Mentoring:* Becoming a guide, patron or teacher to younger workers and fostering their career growth at the expense of one's own personal ambition.

The mentor role enables the mature worker to take an active interest in the career progress of younger recruits. By replacing personal ambition with concern for the junior worker's achievement, mentoring provides an excellent forum for resolving Erikson's generativity crisis (see Chapter 2). Middle-aged men and women may therefore come to find this role more satisfying than the pursuit of personal ambition or competitive advancement. In some jobs, concern for the younger generation may be best expressed by simply stepping aside gracefully to provide room for younger newcomers.

But, regardless of how these motivations of Havighurst's second stage of career development express themselves, the older worker's resolution of the inner developmental conflict between generativity and stagnation is aided by such a refocusing of the meaning of work away from the relative egocentrism of personal success towards a more socially significant contribution to the broader concerns of the organisation, society and up-coming generations.

CONTEMPLATING A PRODUCTIVE AND RESPONSIBLE LIFE

(Age 70 and over): Havighurst amended Super's stage of career 'decline' to bring in Erikson's final conflict between 'ego integrity' and 'despair'. Thus, during the last phase in his theory, retired workers redefine the career as something already accomplished rather than as something waiting to be done. Consequently, the focus of this final stage is on the search for meaning in the career life cycle as a completed process. If they are successful, workers achieve a readiness not only to retire gracefully from their job but also to come to terms with personal mortality. This last developmental task is greatly aided, according to Havighurst, by having successfully reoriented oneself towards maintaining a productive society during the preceding career stage. If this has been done, and if society as a whole is still seen as worthy of one's contribution, the retired worker is in a fortunate position:

> He looks back over his work life with satisfaction, sees that he has made his social contribution, and is pleased with it. While he may not have achieved all of his ambitions, he accepts his life and believes in himself as a productive person. (Crites, 1969, p. 535)

Daniel Levinson's theory

Daniel Levinson (1986) devised a theory of career development that subdivides working life into the nine stages shown in Table 14.7. His theory derives jointly from an early biographical study of 40 men (Levinson et al., 1978) and a more recent, equally intensive, retrospective study of 45 women's adult lives (Levinson, 1986). On the basis of in-depth interviews, Levinson reconstructed the developmental patterns in men's and women's accounts of their life experience, 'much as the biographer does in writing a book-length life story' (p. 12). In these data, supplemented by more circumscribed information on an additional group of over 130 men and women, Levinson discerned an invariant sequence of alternating, age-linked, structure-building and transitional periods that applied equally to men's and women's lives. As he explained: 'The sequence of eras and periods holds for men and women of different cultures, classes and historical periods' (p. 8). Furthermore, despite myriad individual variations in personality, roles, life events and their timing, Levinson observed

> an underlying order in the human life course, an order shaped by the eras and by the periods in life structure development [so that] the basic nature and timing of life events are given in the life cycle at this time in human evolution. (p. 11)

According to Levinson, the life structure subsumes all facets of life activity, including career development, family development and development of values and beliefs. He discerned a fixed, cyclic alternation in the career component of the life structure between stable and transitional processes each lasting about five years. During every stable period, according to Levinson, psychological energy is devoted to 'structure-building'. In other words, the individual settles down during stable phases to the concerted pursuit of the goals, values and life activities that were selected during the previous transitional phase. But change is inevitable, and its timing is strictly

prescribed in Levinson's model. Consequently, every stable period is inevitably followed by another 'structure-changing', or 'transitional', period during which the goals and life activities that formed the basis for previous stability are called into question and gradually modified. Thus, in Levinson's model, crisis periods arise not just once in the middle of a career but once per decade of working life.

Levinson conceived of the life cycle as a series of four eras (see Table 2.2 on page 65) with career stages occupying two of these only: early and middle adulthood. The move from one to the other is punctuated by a *mid-life transition*, which consumes the entire career stage between age 40 and age 45. (We look at the mid-life transition, also called mid-life crisis, in more detail later in this chapter.) During the career stage leading up to this transition, the adult is occupied with self-advancement. Once committed to a chosen occupation, workers strive to adjust to the job's demands and to find a place in its status hierarchy. Quite often, young adults apprentice themselves in a psychological sense to an older mentor (or guide) who may be a teacher, a supervisor, an editor or even an experienced co-worker. Sponsorship by the mentor boosts the younger worker's confidence, and

TABLE 14.7 Levinson's theory

Developmental era	Career development stage	Age range (years)	Career task	Stage type
Era of Pre-adulthood (Age 0–23)	1. Early adult transition	17–23	Moving out of parents' home Finding employment Shopping around for appropriate vocation	Transitional
Era of Early Adulthood (Age 24–45)	2. Enter life structure for early adulthood	23–28	Settling on an appropriate career Creating a stable life structure with options open	Stable
	3. Age 30 transition	28–33	Reappraising and modifying the initial structure	Transitional
	4. Culminating life structure for early adulthood	33–40	Establishing a niche through ambitious goal achievement	Stable
	5. Mid-life transition	40–45	Reappraisal and reformulation of goals to allow neglected parts of the personality to express themselves	Transitional
Era of Middle Adulthood (Age 45–65)	6. Enter life structure for middle adulthood	45–50	Creating a productive self-expressive life structure	Stable
	7. Age 50 transition	50–55	Assessing, modifying and improving the middle adulthood structure	Transitional
	8. Culminating life structure for middle adulthood	55–60	Achieving the goals formulated during the fifties transition	Stable
	9. Late adult transition	60–65	Preparing for retirement	Transitional

Source: Smart & Peterson (1994b), Table 1, p. 244, reproduced with permission.

smooths the way towards the career advancement that is so important during this period.

After the midlife crisis, adults typically become less single-mindedly ambitious and strive to express qualities in their personality that were neglected during the concerted push for career advancement of the early adult era. Consequently, Levinson's model of middle adulthood resembles Erikson's in many ways. Successful development, as in the case of Erikson's generativity crisis (see page 480) entails stepping aside to make room for workers from younger generations, while at the same time cultivating nurturance, wisdom and a balanced perspective on one's own career. As Levinson explained:

> One developmental task of this transition is to begin a new step in individuation. To the extent that this occurs, we can become more compassionate, more reflective and judicious, less tyrannized by inner conflicts and external demands, and more genuinely loving of ourselves and others. Without it, our lives become increasingly trivial or stagnant. (p. 5)

Comparing career development theories

In an empirical study of career development in a sample of 498 Australian dieticians ranging in age from 22 to 60, Roslyn Smart and Candida Peterson (1994a) obtained some support for Levinson's model of the career life cycle as shown in Table 14.7. As noted above, Levinson's (1986) theory differs from Super's and Havighurst's (where the working life cycle is divided into only three qualitatively distinct stages) in its subdivision of career life into seven phases, not counting the transitional phases of initial career entry and exit into retirement. To test the differential predictions by these three theories about how the shape of the career alters over time, Smart and Peterson recruited a sample of female Australian health professionals, almost all of whom had been working steadily in their chosen career in dietetics on either a full-time or a part-time basis since career entry in their early twenties. These women were asked what satisfactions they gained from working, what their work values were, and how committed they felt to their careers and the organisations they worked in.

Statistically significant differences emerged on certain dimensions of career satisfaction between women at each successive stage of Levinson's theory of working life. Furthermore, the data partially supported Levinson's theory of a regular alternation between periods of stability and transition in psychological development across the career life cycle. The female Australian health professionals who were in the 'stable' phases of Levinson's model (see Table 14.7) reported greater satisfaction with their salary, and a perception of greater equity in the balance between their effort and their pay, than the women who were in each of the adjacent 'transitional' phases. This result is in line with Levinson's suggestion that, during the numerous transitional phases that punctuate the career life cycle, workers come to question their career goals, values and directions. They are apt to wonder if they should be earning more, or even whether their chosen career path may be carrying them in the wrong direction. But during the ensuing 'stable' phase these doubts dissipate and satisfaction is seen to rise in exactly the manner reported by Smart and Peterson's sample of Australian dieticians.

The three theories are alike in at least two important ways. First, each theory postulates an initial phase of becoming adjusted to the chosen career and then pursuing it in a single-minded fashion. (This is true of Super's 'establishment phase', of Havighurst's stage of 'becoming a productive person' and, with some ups and downs, of Levinson's entire 'era of early adulthood'.) We examine the empirical evidence supporting this first point of common agreement among the theories in the context of the process of occupational socialisation in the next section.

Second, all three of these major theories of career development agree in suggesting that the entire course of the vocational life cycle is apt to change radically at around the age of 45. In each theory, the self-centred pursuit of personal ambition, the single-minded striving for advancement and the organisational conformity characteristic of the first few stages of working life are seen to give way in mid-career to a period of self-doubt, or stocktaking, known as the *mid-career crisis*. This causes psychological upheaval. But, finally, the crisis is resolved – according to all three theorists – by changing careers, or by re-evaluating priorities and changing one's approach to the existing job, or by a despondent lowering of one's career expectations and motivational standards. This results in the development of new aspects of personality.

One longitudinal study of business recruits supported Super's theory by showing progressive changes in employed men's attitudes over time (Hall, 1976). As young men in Super's exploration stage, these men had been uncertain about specific occupational directions but had held highly idealistic work values and career ambitions. After some years at work, their values shifted to conform to those held by senior managers in their organisation and, in line with Super's establishment stage, they worked very hard for career advancement. In a different longitudinal study, disturbing decreases were found in the level of work motivation among a professional research and development team. Whereas the values these workers had brought to their jobs as new recruits had centred around the tackling of challenges and the creative expression of their personal talents and skills, their sights gradually lowered over time to the point where, as seasoned workers, their goals were confined to maintaining tenure and job security (Hall & Lawler, 1969). According to the principal investigator:

> Because of the conflict between the needs of growing individuals and the requirements of organizations for tight control and uniformity, people become less concerned about their own growth and they become less independent, less strong, and less active as they spend more time in the organization. (Hall, p. 68)

The mid-career crisis

All three career development theories agree in postulating a period of turmoil, uncertainty and upheaval known variously as 'midolescence' (Sagan & De Blassie, 1981), the 'mid-life blues' or, more aptly, the *mid-career crisis*. This phase usually begins as a cooling down of the ambitious, single-minded, purposive striving of the establishment phase into a transitional phase of strenuous critical self-analysis and finally a redirection of work-related efforts. Some recent empirical evidence also supports the view that a shift in vocational direction and vocational self-concept does normally coincide with the middle of the working lifespan.

Patrick Murphy and Harman Burck (1976) gathered together the results of seven separate studies which had examined the vocational attitudes and adjustments of men between the ages of 35 and 45. Taken as a group, these results showed a drop in self-esteem at around age 40, accompanied by a lengthy period of intense self-doubt and questioning of values, priorities and occupational and personal identities. At this point, many of the men seemed to long for a career change but feared the risks involved. Some 'questioned company policy and wondered if success is what life is all about' (p. 339). But when they reached age 45 or 50, all the men seemed to emerge from their uncertainty with a new set of values and a diminished personal investment in their job. Self-esteem also recovered, though some researchers interpreted the change as a 'resignation to reality' rather than a revival of vigour and optimism. All in all, Murphy and Burck concluded that a crisis in self-concept seems to occur at mid-life and that, as a consequence:

> One's career may no longer be an accurate expression of that changed self-concept and that a change or adjustment in career may have to be made. (p. 341)

Bernice Neugarten (1968) interviewed 100 men and women aged 45 to 55 and concluded that one of the most striking changes in this period in life was an increased self-awareness and a re-evaluation of life's priorities in relation to time. She quoted one man as saying:

> Time is now a two-edged sword. To some of my friends, it acts as a prod; to others, a brake. It adds a certain anxiety, but I must also say it adds a certain zest in seeing how much pleasure can still

be obtained, how many good years one can still arrange, how many new activities can be undertaken. (p. 97)

Douglas T. Hall (1976) also found evidence of mid-career uncertainty, of a sense of 'let-down' and of critical re-evaluation of life goals among a group of Catholic priests. This tendency to doubt and restructure the goals and values which they had hitherto accepted without question (and in some cases the decision to make the radical career change of leaving the priesthood altogether) seemed to occur despite clear outward signs of success in these priests' careers. The point in the clerical career at which promotion was normally offered frequently triggered a sense of crisis and uncertainty. In fact, after spending some 26 years as assistant pastor, even those priests who achieved sought-after promotions to the more prestigious and challenging pastor role often expressed profound dissatisfaction. Hall suggested that symptoms of bodily ageing normally combine with the shift in time perspective described by Neugarten (1968) to precipitate feelings of urgency in the middle-aged. Thus:

> Ironically, the stress may be greater if he has achieved his career goals; then he may wonder, in the words of a recent popular song, 'Is that all there is?' (p. 82)

Karen Sagan and Richard De Blassie (1981) also found mid-career crises to be very common among clergymen who had devoted intense energy throughout earlier adulthood to helping others and advancing the religious cause. They cited the example of a 46-year-old Protestant minister who commented:

> I've enjoyed my parish work very much but in the last two or three years I have increasingly questioned where I go from here ... I've changed places but never changed direction. I don't know exactly where these feelings of dissatisfaction came from, but I think the fact that I've been here ten years now precipitated some of the questioning ... I've also come to the conclusion that it has to do with my time in life. My age. I keep feeling in my head that forty-five is the big crucial time, kind of a watershed age. I have the feeling that the number of options open to me have suddenly narrowed very dramatically. (p. 38)

Box 14.3 provides an illustration of one Australian business woman's mid-career crisis.

Second careers and career recycling

One way of resolving the mid-career crisis is to drop out of the old career and embark on a new and totally different line of work. From the point of view of adult psychological development, this approach has several distinct advantages. The choice of a new career enables people to find avenues to express those aspects of their personality that were neglected

In an interview with Jan Bowen (1995, pp. 96–7), Nene King, who was described as 'the most powerful woman in Australia' during her time as editor-in-chief of Australia's two most prominent women's magazines, *Women's Day* and *Australian Women's Weekly*, described a mid-career crisis at age 30 and a sense of time running out at 50. Her experiences of both were closely in line with the theories described earlier in this chapter.

Turning thirty was my crisis. The thirties were my worst time ... I had plastic surgery when I was thirty. I had my eyes done ... I had no confidence in myself and I thought I was in love with somebody who didn't like women working and who wanted me to have a baby. I was under a lot of personal pressure and that interfered with my thinking, but I said my life is over. Really my life was just beginning ...

My forties were wonderful. My fifties are turning out to be wonderful too but I'm scared that I am running out of time because I have always been very afraid of dying, not of the pain, but I haven't come to terms yet with what is going to happen.

during the process of becoming occupationally socialised in the original job. Second, the new career is apt to require a period of new learning, which keeps cognitive development alive (see Chapter 15). Third, the person who embarks on a totally different occupation in mid-life will almost certainly meet new people, face new challenges and develop skills that would never have been possible if the original career had been pursued continuously until retirement.

L. Eugene Thomas (1980) studied the developmental benefits of changing career directions in mid-life. He interviewed a sample of 73 working men who had chosen this adventurous option. Being interested only in radical career change, Thomas limited his research to workers who had abandoned prestigious professional and managerial positions between the ages of 34 and 54 to undertake jobs very different from their earlier careers. This ruled out anyone who claimed to have made a career change but actually had merely accepted a promotion or else shifted emphasis in the original field of work (e.g. from university teaching to academic administration). Thus the career changes made by the group he interviewed were both dramatic and unconventional.

When these career-changers were asked why they had made such drastic alterations to their former vocational pattern, Thomas discovered, somewhat to his surprise, that economic motives were relatively insignificant. Only a small minority (11 per cent) mentioned the desire for better pay as having played

any part in their decision to make a career change. The economic risks of ignoring income were, however, intensified by the fact that most of their wives were not employed. Furthermore, though Super's theory argues that workers become ready to trade ambition for tenure and security at about this age, only 13 per cent of the men Thomas interviewed named insecurity in their old jobs or the promise of steady employment in their new one as a reason for changing career. The most frequently cited reason was attitudinal. Thomas found that 48 per cent had decided to make the change because they wanted 'a better fit' between their life values and their work. This is in keeping with Levinson's theory that the mid-life crisis is brought on by a need to express facets of the personality that grow stagnant through disuse when operating within the confines of a narrow initial career.

Sandra and Linda Perosa (1985) studied how well three groups of middle-aged working men and women had managed to resolve Erikson's identity crisis (see Chapter 11). One group, the *Changed*, had just completed a major career change to a totally different occupation. The second group, the *Changers*, were in the throes of making a similarly dramatic career shift. The third group were *Persisters*. Though of similar age and initial career backgrounds to the two groups of career-changers, this group had thought about changing careers but had opted instead to continue indefinitely in their first occupation. The mean identity achievement scores earned by each of these groups are shown in Figure 14.11. Higher scores reflect more mature identity patterns.

As can be seen in the figure, the Changed group scored significantly higher than the Changers, who in turn were more advanced in identity development than the Persisters. The Persisters' failure to make any salient shift in their ambitions or job values as a result of mid-career stocktaking appeared to be

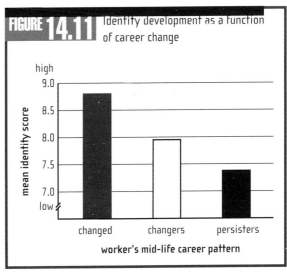

FIGURE 14.11 Identity development as a function of career change

Source: Based on data from Perosa & Perosa (1985), p. 60.

blocking their resolution of Erikson's identity crisis, compared with the progress made by the career-changers. These results lend strong support to Carol Kelleher's (1973) earlier conclusion that second careerists tend to be exceptionally psychologically healthy men and women, rather than 'failures at life' who seek escape from personal inadequacies by quitting their first occupation.

Perosa and Perosa concluded from their findings that:

> Failure to resolve an adult identity crisis may have deleterious effects on development ... In sum, the link between Super and Erikson may be that a mid-career crisis affords the individual the opportunity to complete the process of 'implementing the self-concept' or attaining 'identity achievement status' that is necessary before reaching generativity. An essential modification to both theories is the need to emphasize that establishing an identity requires time in which the individual may be recycled into exploratory (Super's theory) or moratorium (Erikson's theory) stages of development. (p. 66)

In a study of employed Australian adults, Roslyn Smart and Candida Peterson (1997) discovered that progress through Super's (1990) stages of career development was faster for adults who had voluntarily given up one career in order to embark on a second career that was very different from the first. These radical career-changers were progressing more quickly through the career stages identified by Donald Super (see page 498) than their peers who had either remained stationary or had changed areas within the same broad career path. In addition, levels of satisfaction with their job and overall career progress was higher for adults who were fully engaged in a radical, new second career than for single-career adults. Yet these latter were similar to the career-changers in other ways, including income, educational level and family commitments. These results are shown in Figure 14.12.

In line with Daniel Levinson's theory that periods of career transition are stressful, Smart and Peterson discovered that Australian men and women who were planning to change to a new career but had not yet completed the switch were less happy than a matched group who had remained in their original occupation with no thoughts of changing. Presumably, once the transitional group had completed the change their overall levels of satisfaction with their new job would rise to the level achieved by their peers who were fully embarked upon second careers.

L. Eugene Thomas (1980) catalogued hundreds of case histories of career-changers from all levels of the socioeconomic spectrum. By and large, changers reported that their new job met or exceeded all their hopes, even though many entailed a drop in salary and status. Factors that are critical to an easy transition to a second career are shown in Box 14.4.

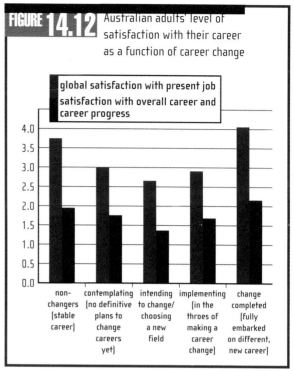

FIGURE 14.12 Australian adults' level of satisfaction with their career as a function of career change

global satisfaction with present job
satisfaction with overall career and career progress

| non-changers (stable career) | contemplating (no definitive plans to change careers yet) | intending to change/ choosing a new field | implementing (in the throes of making a career change) | change completed (fully embarked on different, new career) |

Source: Based on data in Smart & Peterson (1997).

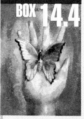

BOX 14.4 Factors associated with second-career satisfaction

- Voluntary decision to make a career change (as compared with retrenchment, ill health, etc.).
- Economic support during the transition period.
- Spouse's support for the change (both financial and moral).
- The availability of role models who have successfully accomplished a similar career change.
- Vocational counsellors who support the option of career-change as feasible and desirable.
- The timing of the transition, in relation both to family life (e.g. children's independence, wife's working) and the original career (e.g. a missed promotion, an increase in pressure on the job).
- Support and encouragement from the family of the career-changer.

Changes in career satisfaction over the lifespan

Whether in their first, second or multiple careers, adults will experience ups and downs in their enjoyment of work over their adult years. Most people view their employment as a source of income, but for many it is much more than that. Jobs may fill other needs and supply gratifications over and above the weekly or fortnightly pay cheque. In fact, when asked

In 1992 the Aboriginal musician Mandawuy Yunupingu was named Australian of the Year for his distinguished contribution to Australian culture. As the lead singer for the musical group Yothu Yindi, he was judged to have made a rich and outstanding contribution not only to music but also to Australia's cultural life in the broadest sense. International recognition of a musical style that blends the traditional rhythms of the didgeridoo with the lyrics of social protest has given an added dimension to Yunupingu's achievement. Australia has gained a distinctive place in the world music scene through his efforts. Yothu Yindi performs the traditional music of the Gumalj and Rirratjingu Aboriginal tribes of north-east Arnhem Land in the Northern Territory. By this means, the group has alerted the world to the rich cultural traditions of the Aboriginal people. Adhering closely to the Aboriginal cultural traditions of the transmission of knowledge, faith and creative expression from one generation to the next (see Chapters 1 and 10), Yothu Yindi's music also reflects the wisdom of traditional Aboriginal elders. For example, the song 'Mainstream' describes reflections on the water as a man contemplates reminiscences of pretty young girls, voices of Yolngu heroes and racial equality as black and white people live together and share their dreams.

Such an achievement by Mandawuy Yunupingu might seem significant enough to constitute the entire contribution of an exceptionally successful career life cycle. But, in his case, other equally distinguished achievements also punctuated his working life. He was the first Arnhem Land Aboriginal to graduate with a Bachelor of Education degree and became the first Aboriginal headmaster in Australia, achievements which had earned him high distinction before his decision to pursue a second career in music.

to imagine that they could quit work tomorrow and still continue to receive their normal income for the rest of their life, Australian workers' reactions were paradoxical (Burns & Goodnow, 1985). A surprising number of working men, and even more working women, opted to go on working regardless. They preferred to carry on with their jobs for no pay rather than taste the freedom of an affluent life of leisure. Presumably, they doubted their ability to find leisure-time substitutes for all the other bonuses besides money that their jobs were currently offering.

To test whether this evidently strong satisfaction with employment changes to any substantial degree over the career life cycle, Gordon O'Brien and Peter Dowling (1981) contacted a group of 1383 Australian workers by means of an ambitious door-knock campaign to every 200th household in metropolitan Adelaide. The ages of the men and women

they interviewed ranged from 15 to over 60, and all major occupational areas were represented in proportions matching the Australian working population as a whole.

When they charted workers' levels of satisfaction with their job against chronological age, O'Brien and Dowling found, as shown in Figure 14.13, that the oldest workers were the happiest, and that disgruntlement appeared steadily worse at younger ages and with shorter time on the job. To see whether other factors might be responsible for this apparent developmental trend, the researchers performed a partial correlational analysis. By statistical means they were able to separate out from age such age-linked variables as income, the levels of variety and skill involved in the job and the worker's own level of seniority, tenure and influence within the organisation. With all these extraneous variables removed, older workers were still found to gain greater enjoyment from their job than younger workers. As time on the job increased, the man's image of an ideal job grew steadily closer to his description of what his actual job entailed. Women's notions of their ideal job also grew closer to their real job with time, but even this fact did not fully account for the simple growth of vocational happiness as the women aged.

O'Brien and Dowling suggested that older workers' greater contentment with their job could possibly be due to a general improvement in morale as a function of growing older, or a process of becoming more 'mellow' with age. In fact, veteran workers do appear to gain more enjoyment than new recruits from the very same job. They also seem to have a more positive attitude towards their colleagues, their supervisors, the organisation and work in general. They make fewer complaints than younger workers about pay, pressure and supervision, their physical working conditions, the level of skill demanded by their job or the opportunities they are offered for

FIGURE 14.13 Australian workers' enjoyment of their job as a function of age

Source: Based on data from O'Brien & Dowling (1981), Table 4.

promotion and further education (O'Brien & Dowling, 1981).

Of course, other factors besides a mellowing with age may plausibly account for such differences. Veteran workers have, by definition, remained in the system longer. Perhaps this is mainly by choice, with the more disgruntled new recruits opting out before becoming veterans. Also, since salaries, seniority and various benefits like a prime parking space or a well-lit office are apt to accumulate with time on the job, older workers are likely to have more objective reasons for feeling contented with the nature of their work and their job conditions and earnings. So perhaps the apparent link between age and job satisfaction is really an artefact of time spent working.

Still another reason for older workers' greater job satisfaction may be their having learned to make compromises. Perhaps time and experience combine to make people more realistic. Rather than expecting work to match up to the ideals they may have subscribed to in their youth (see Chapters 11 and 13), mature workers may scale down these ideals to fit the more modest sources of pleasure that their job routinely offers. Alternatively, younger workers may be subjected more often than their experienced peers to the frustrations of not finding their talents utilised, as described to Westbrook and Nordholm (see Chapter 13) by Australian health professionals during their first two years on the job. If so, young adults' disappointment with their job would have a realistic basis.

Leisure pursuits and adult development

According to Bertrand Russell (1935): 'To be able to fill leisure intelligently is the last product of civilization' (p. 12). His contemporary and fellow peer, Lord Avebury, similarly remarked that:

> The advantage of leisure is mainly that we may have the power of choosing our own work, not certainly that it confers any privilege of idleness. (Evans, 1978, p. 383)

Thus, to these members of the English 'leisured class', activities undertaken for interest, recreation or altruistic reasons had at least as much potential as paid work for fulfilling an adult's psychological needs and for providing development-inducing stimulation, conflict and challenge. But, as noted above, few Australian working men and women today appear to share such an enthusiasm for leisure. Instead, a great many would rather work for no pay than not work at all (Burns & Goodnow, 1985). Thus, mature adults in Australia and New Zealand today seem to view leisure pursuits as a relatively poor substitute for employment, even when economic considerations are put aside. Studies of young unemployed Australians (Turtle et al., 1978) reveal a similar pattern of feelings.

In addition to creating a serious challenge at the time of retirement, a negative outlook on leisure is also clearly maladaptive for those unemployed young adults and housebound housewives who have no access to paid employment. Furthermore, this devaluation of leisure is likely to become even more of an issue in future years when the continuation of current social trends towards more pervasive unemployment, wider utilisation of part-time work and early retirement are liable to provide all adults with more spare time than they know what to do with.

What is leisure?

Like play in childhood, adult leisure activity defies succinct definition. Leisure resembles play (see Chapters 6 and 7) in being undertaken voluntarily and for no ulterior motive. Some would argue that, for this reason, leisure is less serious than work. But many adults take their leisure pursuits very seriously and, from a cultural, intellectual or economic standpoint, the products of one adult's leisure activity can have at least as much value as the contributions made by another adult at work. Sometimes, a leisure interest becomes an economically viable vocation, as illustrated in Box 14.4. People also make friends, develop knowledge, and express nurturance and creativity as much through their leisure pursuits as through paid work. According to Michael Argyle (1972), the avenues of vocational and avocational self-expression in adulthood are essentially the same. They include the six categories shown in Box 14.6.

Sporting activities are favoured leisure pursuits throughout adulthood.

BOX 14.6

Taking things personally: Career versus leisure satisfactions

Instructions: In order to assess the kinds of satisfactions your job and leisure interests bring you, and to compare the two (if you have both), write down on a piece of paper the 10 things you like best about the paid job you do, and your 10 favourite things to do in your leisure time. Once your lists are complete, try to categorise each item on each list into the groupings shown below. How do job and leisure satisfactions compare? The spill-over theory (see the text) predicts that your top sources of satisfaction will be the same in both areas. The compensation theory (see the text) predicts that your leisure satisfactions will fall into different categories.

Satisfactions adults gain from productive activity at leisure or on the job	
Constructive/creative activity	**Intellectual and cultural pursuits**
Constructive activity may include farming, gardening, being an artist, sewing, home renovations or carpentry. Vocational and avocational constructive activities both provide such satisfactions as: • a feeling of being useful • pride in one's skills and accomplishments • expressing creativity • exercising imagination • pleasure of contemplating or using the finished product.	Cultural pursuits can include reading, doing crosswords, going to or giving lectures and enjoying or producing music, dance or drama. In leisure, amateur actors, teachers, musicians, writers and artists have the freedom that professionals lack to produce and attend what they want when they want. However, they often miss out on the social recognition, financial compensation and stimulation which the competitive situation of the workplace can provide. Both vocational and avocational cultural activities provide such satisfactions as: • solving challenging problems • learning new things • developing special talents and skills • enjoying the finest achievements of human civilised, cultural life • performing before an audience and earning recognition • exercising the imagination.
Family activity	**Social activity**
Family activities include cooking and dining, visiting, casual conversation, hosting celebrations, going on outings and the care of children. Vocational and avocational family activities provide such satisfactions as: • sense of being useful • pleasure in involvement with people of different ages • intimacy and friendship.	Socialising includes all the varied voluntary entertainments that are motivated primarily by a desire to share time and experiences with friends – such as dinner parties, playing cards and dancing. These social activities are unlike most paid work in their content. However, the gratifications they provide, such as pleasant interpersonal contact, intimacy and a feeling of belonging to a group, are also named as important reasons for working by workers in jobs that allow for social contact (Hall, 1976).
Ideological commitment	**Sport/physical exercise**
In work and at leisure, some adults prefer to spend their time expressing their political, religious or ideological beliefs through activities they believe will make a difference. Examples include organising political campaigns or political protests, environmental design and enhancement, church activities, philosophical debates and so on.	Organised physical sports resemble manual labour in that they release tensions, demand planning, test physical skill and provide muscular exercise. Quite often, both sport and manual labour involve social contact and team cooperation. Professional and avocational physical and sporting activities provide such satisfactions as: • development of muscular strength, speed and motor skills • health-promoting physical fitness and aerobic exercise • strategic planning skills • team cooperation and stimulating competition • social prestige through athletic success • self-esteem and self-confidence through trim athletic physique and skilled coordination.

Developmental potential of leisure pursuits

As the examples in Box 14.6 illustrate, leisure activities can potentially foster important cognitive, social and practical skills during adulthood, as well as providing a respite from boredom or from the stresses of other kinds of adult life activity. The adult's need to meet and surmount challenges, be productive and creative, enjoy intimacy or aesthetic stimulation, develop social skills, stretch all their physical and mental talents and capacities beyond their previous limits and find meaning in their life can all be fulfilled if they choose their pastimes judiciously and engage wholeheartedly in the pursuit of leisure. In one sense, the fact that leisure activities are freely chosen ends-in-themselves may actually enhance their developmental effectiveness, in comparison with work, since adults can choose new challenges to grapple with at leisure and develop talents that their employment may not require of them.

On the other hand, leisure may fail to serve as an adequate substitute for work when it comes to earning social status, gaining power and influence or satisfying the adult's needs for pride, commitment and solidarity, owing to the lesser social prestige that is accorded to leisure pursuits than career activity in contemporary society. Being a paid worker may likewise serve to validate the usefulness of one's activity while demonstrating to the world one's virtue in conforming to the 'work ethic'. All these factors, as well as financial need, are apt to enhance the value of work over leisure for most contemporary men and women. But the problem for society is that technological change is steadily reducing the amount of paid employment available to the adult population. Futurists estimate that in future decades the working week may be as short as 16 hours. Alternatively, people may be forced to retire by the age of 38 if young adults are to have the option of entering a career at all (Kaplan, 1960). Under such circumstances, adults may well be required to find avenues other than work for satisfying the needs described above. If they discover leisure pursuits that offer challenges and opportunities for intellectual, creative or social self-expression, avocational life may open developmental avenues towards self-actualisation and the development of cognitive, social and personality strengths.

Theories of leisure's place in lifespan development

Rather than being mutually exclusive alternatives, work and leisure can be considered as two interconnected routes towards optimal well-being and psychological development in adulthood. As Douglas Kleiber (1999) explained:

> Relaxation can have the momentary value of enabling one to adjust effectively to circumstances throughout life but its existential value is especially important during midlife. Pausing and relaxing [helps the adult to] make judgments and effective decisions about how best to use the life that is left to live. (p. 124)

The selection of leisure pursuits that will assist men and women to develop their full potential is a serious business. The leisure activity should be rewarding, challenging and relevant to a person's self-chosen developmental directions. For employed adults, the nature of their job may also help to determine their leisure interests, and vice versa. Two opposing theories have been put forward to explain the way in which work decides the choice of leisure activities: *compensation* and *spill-over*. The compensation theory (also known as *complementarity*) suggests that workers select recreational activities that offer the satisfactions to which their jobs deny them access. The spill-over theory (also known as *similarity* or *generalisation*) proposes, instead, that people are attracted to leisure pursuits that satisfy the same needs and make use of the same talents and skills as their paid occupations (Kabanoff & O'Brien, 1980). Despite their mutual opposition, there is research evidence to support both theories.

In one classic comparison of the two theories, the leisure interests of 100 air-traffic controllers were studied, together with those of a comparable group of public servants and college students (Hall, 1976). Since the job of controlling airport flight patterns involves a much higher level of risk-taking (defined as placing oneself and others in jeopardy) than a desk job, the compensation theory predicts that air-traffic controllers should show less interest than the other two occupational groups in such risky leisure activities as racing-car driving and mountaineering. On the other hand, spill-over predicts that the air-traffic controllers should be the ones to take up hobbies such as hang-gliding. In support of the latter hypothesis, the

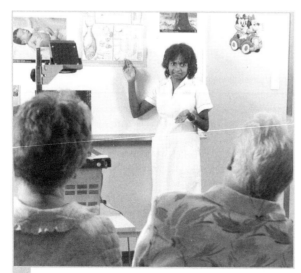

According to the generalisation hypothesis, people who work with people intensively in their careers will prefer social leisure pursuits, whereas the compensation view predicts they will favour solitary recreation.

authors found that the controllers were more disposed than the students and public servants towards a whole range of outdoor activities which involved thrills, adventure, danger and speed. The controllers also expressed the greatest interest in other risky or thrill-oriented leisure activities, such as:

- experience-seeking (which included drug-taking, exhibitionism in dress and behaviour, and wanderlust)
- 'swinging' (i.e. a hedonistic, or 'playboy', leisure style which included heavy drinking, sexual mate-swapping and gambling)
- varying their leisure activities from time to time to cope with restlessness or the need for change.

In other words, in line with the spill-over model, it seems that risk-loving adventurers choose jobs and leisure activities that allow for the expression of a generalised sensation-seeking personality style.

On the other hand, when Arthur Adams and Thomas Stone (1977) measured the strength of the need for achievement among 104 Iowa business people, they found support for the compensation theory of leisure. Workers who had a strong need to achieve and few opportunities to tackle challenges at work were the ones most likely to engage in competitive, success-oriented hobbies like team sports, bridge or do-it-yourself engineering. When asked to justify their choice of leisure interests they gave achievement-oriented reasons ('It's enjoyable to build something complicated and see it function'). In contrast, workers whose level of ambition was matched or exceeded by the demands of their job picked leisure activities like television, the beach or parties, which allowed them to relax and socialise.

Complementarity between leisure and work is also seen in the frequency with which painting is chosen as a hobby by physicians, since art and medicine are at opposite ends of such dichotomies as social involvement, precision versus free creativity, and stressfulness. In this case, the need to find relief from the job and to exercise complementary skills seems to predominate, as it does for the car salesman whose hobby is fishing alone on a remote lake (Bischof, 1976, p. 250).

A third theory, known as the *segmentation* hypothesis, argues that people keep their work and leisure lives so distinct from one another that there are no consistent relationships of either similarity or contrast between the two (Kabanoff, 1980). The results of research studies that have failed to support the complementarity or the generalisation theory have sometimes been interpreted as support for the segmentation position (London, Crandall & Seals, 1977). However, Boris Kabanoff suggests that such

results may instead reflect the fact that there are large individual differences among workers, with some people showing similarity between work and leisure interests, while others display compensation. These differences are obscured when one overall average is computed for the entire population.

Kabanoff's own studies of a representative sample of Adelaide residents provided some support for this idea. Male workers with low income and education were found to employ a pattern of passive generalisation between work and leisure. In other words, their relatively low levels of skill use and social interaction at work spilled over into the choice of simple and passive forms of recreation (such as drinking or watching television). But older women with similarly low incomes tended to employ a compensation pattern in which active, family-centred recreation made up for the lack of challenge and social involvement on the job. Still another group of highly educated, well-paid workers appeared to have generalised the search for self-actualisation from their complex challenging jobs into the choice of equally complex and skill-oriented styles of leisure (e.g. playing chess or writing and producing amateur theatricals).

Argyle's (1972) suggestion that leisure can serve several different ends is consistent with these results which, when taken together, indicate that compensation and generalisation are *both* true for some of the people some of the time. The search for recuperation via leisure implies complementarity between vocational and recreational pursuits, whereas, when leisure is used as a stimulus to personal growth, the seeking of challenges should generalise from work to leisure and back again. Still another reason why the actual relationship between adults' vocational and avocational preferences may be more complex than either the complementarity or the similarity hypothesis implies is the fact that, in practice, leisure activities are not always freely chosen ends-in-themselves. Donald Super (1957) explained that vocations and avocations are linked, not only by the sometimes similar and sometimes complementary needs and personality characteristics to which they each give expression, but also by the following additional social realities:

- The exigencies of work determine the amount of money, time and energy available for leisure pursuits.
- People frequently choose their leisure-time social contacts from among their workmates.
- Leisure activities are often used to serve such vocational ends as seeking a promotion or cultivating social influence with co-workers (e.g. when the boss is invited home to dinner).

Chapter summary

Middle adulthood, the period stretching from approximately age 30 to age 55, is now recognised as an important and dynamic phase in lifespan psychological development. Along with physical, physiological and neurocognitive changes, mature men's and women's personalities, intellectual and social skills, careers and intimate relationships are all subject to a regular series of highly predictable changes with the passage of time.

Peak levels of strength and speed in athletic and sporting pursuits decline gradually in middle adulthood, and many physiological and sensory systems become somewhat less efficient. Yet regular and vigorous physical exercise remains possible and highly desirable throughout the adult years and those adults who exercise regularly enjoy better health and wellbeing than an adult who is purely sedentary.

The same is true of mental exercise. Recent neurocognitive studies show that the brain remains plastic in adult life, enabling new connections to form and some recovery from all but the most severe brain injuries or disease.

Marriage undergoes a predictable sequence of changes over the adult years. From the honeymoon to the empty-nest stage of family life, the average couple's satisfaction with marriage is found to describe a U-shaped curve. Peaks of happiness occur after the honeymoon and during post-parental or retirement phases, with a low ebb known as disenchantment arising for most couples during the middle years.

This pattern applies cross-culturally in societies such as prewar Japan and pre-revolutionary China where arranged marriage was practised, as well as in Australia, New Zealand, Britain and the United States today. While the presence of children in the household may intensify it, disenchantment has been found to apply to child-free and parental couples alike.

Marrying purely for love does not eliminate disenchantment, nor does marriage based on a brokered arrangement or economic practicality as is practised in other cutures. Nor is the phenomenon an artifact of cross-sectional developmental methodology. Plausible explanations for changes in marital satisfaction over time emerged as we examined middleadult marriage in terms of sexual satisfaction, communication, conflict resolution, career and parenting pressures and partners' sex roles.

Couples who manage to survive the first 15–20 years of marriage without deciding to separate often experience a renewal of satisfaction and marital intimacy once their children leave home. This phenomenon, sometimes called a 'second honeymoon', emerges on questionnaire surveys as well as in interviews with couples who have been happily married for several decades. Older couples often show an exceptional ability to negotiate conflict and extremely close emotional ties.

Dual-career couples are likely to encounter more stress and role conflict or overload than spouses in traditional marriages. But neither they nor their children are seen to suffer emotionally as a result of this. Instead, the challenges of merging two committed careers may stimulate husbands' and wives' psychological growth.

Household work provides another medium through which family members can express love and consideration for one another.

During the middle years of a working life, a shift is apt to occur from single-minded striving for achievement to a 'crisis' phase of stocktaking, and then to the selection of a new set of career goals. Three different theories of career development all postulate a transition near the age of 45.

Some workers emerge from this 'mid-life crisis' with renewed confidence and self-assurance, allowing them to slow down a little and enjoy the status achieved through earlier efforts, tangible accomplishments and promotions. Others suffer disappointment and may make hurried attempts to set their careers back in line with the ambitions they inadvertently lost sight of during earlier adulthood.

A growing number of mature men and women avail themselves of the opportunity provided by a mid-career crisis to embark on a totally new occupation during middle age. Leisure interests afford rich opportunities for psychological development, in conjunction with work or when undertaken in place of a paid occupation.

Changes from one decade of adulthood to the next exert a reverberating impact on individual adult cognition, social roles and personality. The myth of adulthood as a static period in life when behaviour is fixed in a plaster-like rigidity is no longer tenable in light of recent research. When we followed people through the sequential stages of family life and a career, clear support emerged for the chronological predictability of development.

Psychological development as qualitative change (see Chapter 1) shows up just as clearly among adults as during the traditional growth periods of infancy, childhood and adolescence. The major difference is that, in adulthood, longer spans of time separate each of the qualitatively distinct chronological stages, or age periods.

For further interest

Looking forward on the Internet

Use the Internet to visit the following websites. Examine them for further information and varied perspectives on issues raised in this chapter. Also search for other relevant websites for yourself, using keywords like 'adulthood', 'maturity', 'marriage', 'career development', 'recreation', 'leisure activity' and 'family life' in your search engine.

In particular, visit **http://www.healthinsite.gov.au** and select the button titled *Life Stages/Events*. This provides useful information on the transition events and turning points in adult development, along with suggested coping strategies. Information on the family life cycle is also provided here, including parenting, marriage, sexuality and mental health issues.

For resources, ideas, activities and other items of interest in conjunction with this chapter, visit the Companion Website for this textbook at:

http://wps.pearsoned.com.au/peterson

Activity suggestion

As a practical activity in conjunction with themes in this chapter, try interviewing a group of employed men and women from your range of personal acquaintances about their attitudes to their jobs. Ask about the prime sources of satisfaction at work and the major drawbacks, disappointments and job-related difficulties they may be experiencing now, or have experienced in the past. Compare the themes raised to the research evidence about age-related changes in job satisfaction and career concerns that was described in this chapter.

Multimedia

For an interesting glimpse of adult development through the eyes of an Indigenous Australian woman, view the film/video *My Survival as an Aboriginal* (Film Australia, Sydney, 1979: 50 minutes, colour) in which Essie Coffey, musician and activist, tells of her experiences and progress towards generativity.

CHAPTER 15

THE FIFTIES: Physical, cognitive, social and personality development

> The man who views the world at 50 the same as he did at 20 has wasted 30 years of his life.
>
> Muhammad Ali (1942–)

Contents

CHAPTER OVERVIEW

Physical markers of biological ageing like menopause, wrinkles or the first grey hairs draw the mature adult's attention to the imminence of old age, as do 50th-birthday celebrations, recording the fact of having lived for half a century. Yet most contemporary adults at 50 do not feel 'old' in any conventional sense of the word. Their physical, cognitive and creative powers are apt to be at their height, career success often peaks, the social world is rich with more time for friends than in the busy childrearing and career establishment years and with a family full of teenage and adult offspring the mature adult has stimulating contact with a family circle that may include aged parents and grandchildren as well. The personality mellows and ripens and new interests and leisure pursuits may blossom at the threshold of retirement, offering a new set of challenges to stimulate psychological growth. But developmentally optimistic psychological growth is not inevitable in late middle age, any more than it was earlier. In this chapter we study the factors that lead some adults to develop enthusiastically and productively throughout their 50s, while others suffer disappointment, stagnation or a paralysing fear of the onset of the final phases of the lifespan.

In contrast to earlier centuries when average human longevity was briefer than today (see Chapter 18) and the debilitating frailties of old age struck most of those lucky enough still to be alive at 50, the decade of the 50s is rich with the promise of developmental opportunities for many adults in Australia, New Zealand and other parts of the contemporary world, who can count on many more years of vigorous good health even after this 'golden' decade draws to a close. Of course, as with any other phase in lifespan development, chronological age in years is only a rough guide to psychological maturity. Many of the physical, physiological, social, cognitive and personality changes that we explore in this chapter, while becoming more noticeable at 50, have been shaping up for decades before that.

What is so special about turning 50? Are there really discernible features of this period in adult life that make it different from both middle adulthood at one end and old age at the other? In this chapter we examine some of the distinctive changes in biological, social and psychological functioning that arise for most adults at some point between age 50 and age 60 or 65. These include the onset of menopause for women and changes in the metabolic rate and gradual alterations to patterns of sexual responsiveness in men. The greying or balding of hair and the wrinkling of skin, though equally gradual, have left some indelible marks on the outward appearance of most people before they turn 50.

At the same time, according to personality theorists like Erik Erikson and Charlotte Buhler (see Chapter 2), as well as Donald Super and Daniel Levinson (see Chapter 14), mature adults become psychologically more focused on concerns for the younger generation. They also tend to develop a preoccupation with life's abiding meaning or the abstract future that gradually comes to replace the unquestioning pursuit of family goals and personal ambition that drive psychological functioning during the first three decades of adult life.

These biological and personality changes typically coincide with a set of rather dramatic upheavals to the average middle-aged man's or woman's social roles and family relationships. At home, adult children are being launched into marriage, careers and parenthood. Meanwhile, the adult of 50 may have ambitions to redirect career energies or to undertake a challenging occupation for the first time, now that the financial and emotional burdens of parenthood have eased. For some, the needs of a frail elderly parent replace the needs of dependent children for the middle-aged adult's nurturant care. Changes like these in the outward shape of the social life space alter the middle-aged adult's goals and plans. At the same time, a realignment of the inner balance of goals to nurture and to achieve is likely to combine in middle age with the search for answers about how and when to effect the transition from employment into retirement to bring about a radically altered orientation to one's career.

This chapter begins with a look at how the process of adult cognitive development can give rise to new mental abilities, new creative strengths and a new orientation to questions of philosophy, morality and religious faith in later adulthood. We then examine the biological changes of middle age, including menopause and changes in sex drive and sexual expression.

The major milestones of social development that punctuate middle age are examined in roughly chronological sequence. We begin with the process of launching offspring into independent adult lives, and the effects on marital and parent–child relationships of the transition to the empty-nest phase of family life. Then we examine grandparenthood, with its effects on adult psychological development as well as on the growth and development of the grandchildren.

The chapter concludes with a detailed analysis of how the process of retiring from work shapes adults' cognitive, social and personality development and, possibly, their physical health.

The prime of life

In Japan, Shigeo Hori (1994) asked a group of more than 500 adults who were either middle-aged (30 to 50 years) or elderly (over age 60) how old a person is when they are in the prime of life. He found that their responses varied depending on whether the target of their judgment was a man or a woman, as shown in Table 15.1. But, on average, Japanese adults deemed the prime of life to occur in the 40s. A similar study

TABLE 15.1	The 'prime of life' according to Japanese adults	
	Middle-aged respondents	Elderly respondents
Prime of life for a man	42 years (range: 35 to 50 years)	48 years (range: 40 to 56 years)
Prime of life for a woman	38 years (range: 30 to 46 years)	45 years (range: 37 to 53 years)

in New Zealand conducted by Mark Byrd and Trudy Breuss (1992) asked a group of 150 adults ranging in age from 18 to 75 years to pinpoint the time in adulthood when people should have the greatest sense of accomplishment and the strongest self-respect. New Zealanders of all ages typically named the late 50s as the average age for the former and the early 60s for the latter.

Many adults in their 50s would agree that they have reached their prime. In her pioneering studies of middle age in midwest North America during the middle of last century, Bernice Neugarten (1968) found that many adults in their 50s described themselves as the 'command generation' of society. Top positions in the occupational hierarchy are often held by adults in their 50s, and the individual worker typically reaches his or her career peak by then. Levels of income and social prestige both at work and in the community are as high as they will ever be, and cognitive powers, while capable of further growth, are in advance of those of early adulthood, as we see later in this chapter. Even physically, although adults of 50 may no longer possess the strength, speed or endurance of sporting adults aged 20 or 30, they are generally not constrained by any severely detrimental effects of physical ageing, and can still enjoy vigorous exercise while winning the occasional contest at tennis, golf or marathon running through outsmarting opponents with the benefit of experience (see Chapter 16).

Thus middle-aged adults today are likely to continue to pursue the same vigorous, physically demanding vocational or leisure interests they enjoyed when younger. Furthermore, the experiences that build up over two or three decades of adult life are likely to give middle-aged adults the edge over younger people in any task requiring planning, broad vision or leadership (Chalmers & Lawrence, 1993). It often makes good sense that senior managerial roles in politics, finance, business, education, religious institutions and most other social organisations in Australia and New Zealand today are likely to be occupied by middle-aged men and women.

In Neugarten's study, the sense of achievement enjoyed by 50-year-olds was often tempered by a bitter-sweet savouring of 'time running out', coupled with a clear consciousness of ageing. They felt they had to achieve whatever else they were going to achieve before retirement or the anticipated losses of biological ageing set in. This self-conscious fear of losing everything one has achieved and invested in

life, by growing old or dying, is one of the factors that makes middle age such a unique phase in the life-span. Time is now a two-edged sword. Family relationships may take on a new meaning as career doors close with retirement. The pleasures of life, large and small, acquire a fresh poignancy with the sense that the remaining time in which to savour them is short.

Some of the mixed feelings accompanying one adult's passage through the 50s are illustrated in Box 15.1.

BOX 15.1 **A case in point**
'The end'

The last entry in Louise's father's diary record of her growing up provides an eloquent statement of many feelings that the 'empty nest' can inspire in a parent. She had been living away from home for some eight months when she returned for a brief visit to her parents' home in Sydney. On the final day of this visit, her father closed his diary of her childhood with the following entry.

28 August 1965. We were at the station in plenty of time – time enough to have a light breakfast and with less tension than at the close of the last holiday. We are saddened by the need to part – an augury of the time, all too close I am afraid, when Louise will be going her own way for good. Goodbyes like this seem to foreshadow goodbyes to life itself – as each is indeed a goodbye to some of life. Perhaps, as the sentimentalists have it, the regret is in seeing a child grow up, envying those who will enjoy her adult companionship when we no longer can.

We wrote a letter in Hyde Park this morning so she will have it on Monday; and we shopped for meat and groceries before the stores closed and before taking the ferry. Coming back along the cove we saw children in Manly pool and thought of Louise perhaps finding it warm enough today so she could have the swim we had promised her. Then in the flat her tumbled bed reminded me again that she won't be around to be cozened, cautioned, and chided. I'll miss discussing her problems, helping with her lessons, helping to plan her future. Peggy will miss being jumped on by two instead of just one.

In a way this brings my journal of Louise to a close. The journal as such had long ago drifted away from its original frame of reference more and more into family adventures and finally a travel notebook. Lately of course she had been writing most of her part of it herself in her regular letters. But, thinking of her again as a person whose growing up I resolved to record, I realize she is indeed too grown up, too adult to have her privacy thus invaded.

When she was younger, when she was still as it seemed more 'our child' than a person in her own right, I could do it. And even now I could if I loved her less. But there's the big stumbling block. I can't, never could, be dispassionate about her, but while she was mine, a thing of my own like a book or a painting, I could write about her with some detachment. Now I can't even venture a physical description: my eyes water and my throat tightens when I think about it.

And perhaps this is the real source of my sadness. She is changing but there is nothing about her I can bear to see changed. I want her always to look just as she does now. Not always to stay 17 however, for I want her to grow in experience, to have as rich and full a life as she can. It's just her looks I wouldn't have changed: her hair which causes her so much worry because it isn't curly, her temporary skin blemishes, her way of scraping her right toe when she walks, her splendid strong figure and delightfully candid face, her excellent hands, her bright lively smile.

© Peterson, 1974, reproduced with permission

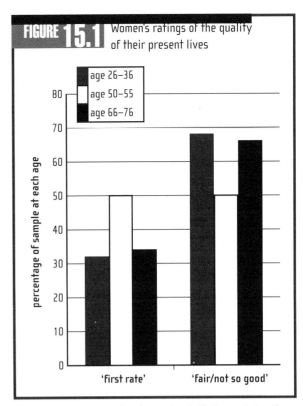

FIGURE 15.1 Women's ratings of the quality of their present lives

Source: Mitchell & Helson (1990). Reproduced with the permission of Cambridge University Press.

Life satisfaction at 50

The benefits of being over 50 are likely to outweigh the drawbacks, according to the results of an ambitious study of North American women ranging in age from 30 to 80 years. The researchers, Valory Mitchell and Ravenna Helson (1990), used a combination of cross-sectional and longitudinal approaches to identify enduring feelings about each decade of adult life in successive cohorts of women (see Chapter 2 for a discussion of these methodologies). By combining evidence in this way, they were able to examine general reactions to lifespan development separate from the unique effects of reaching 50 at one particular point in history. Their conclusions were striking. The cross-sectional and longitudinal data agreed in showing that the decade beginning on the 50th birthday is likely to bring peak levels of satisfaction with life to most contemporary women.

Compared with young women in their 30s, as well as with elderly women aged 66 to 76, significantly more women of 50 in Mitchell and Helson's sample chose the highest possible rating, 'first rate', to describe their lives at present (see Figure 15.1). As well as being happier, the 50-year-olds earned significantly higher scores both for feeling healthy and for being in good overall physical health on objective indicators than did women in their 30s and were, perhaps not surprisingly, healthier also than women in their 60s – although a number of even the oldest

women in Mitchell and Helson's sample had not yet begun to complain of the biological losses associated with physical ageing (see Chapter 16). Finally, the women in their 50s were more content with their finances than women in their 30s, 60s or 70s.

In a similar study, Ravenna Helson and Paul Wink (1992) examined subjective feelings about life in a longitudinal sample of North American women at age 52. A majority noted improvements in their lives compared with when they were in their 30s and 40s. Some of the areas of improvement are shown in Table 15.2, together with the percentages of 52-year-

Women are likely to achieve a peak of life satisfaction during the decade between age 50 and age 60.

TABLE 15.2	Changes in women's attitudes to their lives during their 50s	
Item	'More true now' than at 40	'Less true now' than at 40*
A sense of being my own person	90%	3%
A new level of productivity	70%	11%
Discovering new parts of myself	72%	11%
Feeling the importance of time's passing	76%	10%
Feeling secure and committed	71%	12%
Feeling my life is moving well	74%	15%
Feeling established	78%	11%
Feeling optimistic about the future	58%	20%
Appreciating my complexity	69%	10%

* Percentages do not sum to 100 as some women were undecided.
Source: Based on data in Helson & Wink (1992).

old women who rated the item 'more true now' than a decade earlier.

Turning points and transition events of late middle age

In addition to the chronological marker of turning 50, a number of life events are likely to arise at this age that draw the adult's attention to the sense of 'time's passing' (see Table 15.2). As we noted earlier, *turning points*, or *transition events*, are changes in one's life situation that demand new patterns of coping. Some of these (like menopause) are *normative*, or regularly associated with age, while others (like divorce) are idiosyncratic and can occur at any age. As Robert Atchley (1975) explained:

> A turning point is a change in situation that alters the individual's usual strategy for coping with day-to-day life. Turning points often carry along with them immediate demands for action. Turning points represent change beyond the threshold that can be dealt with routinely. They are points at which the individual ceases to be one thing and becomes something else; and many turning points are mandated by age norms. The disintegration and subsequent reintegration associated with turning points can occur as a result of a long

process of erosion or as a sudden shift. (1975, p. 275)

For contemporary Australian or New Zealand adults, the salient normative turning points of the fifth decade in life typically include (a) menopause or the male climacterium, (b) the empty nest (launching of adult offspring from the family), (c) the birth of grandchildren, and (d) preparation to retire from paid employment. These changes close off certain avenues of life activity while simultaneously opening up others. Thus retirement disrupts most aspects of daily life inside and outside the home as well as ushering in a possible turning point in self-definition as a '*retired* teacher', '*former* bank manager' or an '*ex*-politician'. The emptying of the family nest similarly demands a reorganisation of the domestic timetable and the discovery of new couple-centred goals and priorities to replace childrearing. But the easing of the burden of parenthood also enables older couples to achieve new intimacy and closer sharing, while they shift their concepts of themselves back to a couple rather than a family.

Stimulated by the new coping demands bound up in a turning point, new inner psychological developments are likely to come about at key transition stages, and new bursts of creative energy or a heightened philosophical awareness of faith, morality and the interconnectedness of human existence are seen to arise for many adults in their 50s. The overall improvement in the quality of the older couple's marital relationship that is likely to occur after the empty-nest transition is noted in Chapter 14. In addition, the birth of grandchildren provides opportu-

Boredom may ease the adult's transition out of one life phase into the next.

nities for the development of relationships with infants and children that may either mirror or complement the adult's earlier parenting style. Finally, retirement from paid employment may open up the opportunity to undertake a new set of self-expressive or goal-directed pursuits. Potentially, these can assist psychological growth, but, as during each earlier stage in life, the opportunities provided by the transition events of middle age do not in themselves guarantee psychological development.

The 'turning point' concept, with its implication of sudden, radical change, suggests that adults may encounter stress or psychological difficulties while endeavouring to cope, and the fact that changes of late middle age (like menopause) are largely irreversible may increase feelings of stress and loss. Furthermore, whereas the turning points of early adulthood mostly involve the expansion of a person's sphere of competence and range of endeavour, in middle age the balance shifts towards the relinquishment of hitherto significant avenues of activity and developmental opportunity. But the process of giving things up need not imply that psychological growth must cease. Instead, the challenge created by such physiological events as female menopause and male climacteric is to find a new style of sexuality which is valued in its own right instead of as a means of getting pregnant. The youngest child's departure from home, or retirement from paid employment, can likewise afford lively opportunities for free choice and personality growth gains, as well as possibly causing passing or enduring hardship and unhappiness.

In the end, how well a person adjusts to a new status in middle age, how much room for continuing growth the new style of life includes, and even whether the turning point is a source of crisis or simply ignored will depend heavily on many idiosyncratic situational and personality factors. For an individual who has never viewed work as anything more than a means of obtaining a pay cheque, retirement is less of an issue than for those whose entire

psychic life was invested in their job. Menopause is likewise a much more difficult hurdle for a woman who 'ties her worth to her reproductive ability' (Huyck, 1974) than for one who views it as merely a 'natural' form of contraception.

Boredom may also play a role in easing the transition through all the major turning points of late middle age. According to Atchley (1975): 'Having spent as long as several decades in a given position, people often welcome and even seek the new experiences that turning points bring' (p. 276). Furthermore, the factor of being 'on time', 'early' or 'late' in relation to peers may make a transition easier or harder for the individual to adjust to (Neugarten, 1968, 1979). While being 'precocious' can confer the pride of achievement (e.g. the youthful grandmother who enjoys alerting people to the incongruity between her own status and the norm), at the same time it lessens the opportunity for social support from one's peers, or for emulating the coping strategies of friends who have already successfully adjusted to a particular transition.

The social clock

Publicly evident marker events like the first grey hairs, the launching of grown children into independence, the termination of paid employment and the birth of grandchildren can have an impact not only on the adult's self-definition as 'middle-aged' or 'old' but on most aspects of the person's everyday social existence. In Helson and Wink's (1992) study (see Table 15.2), over 60 per cent of women found that 'being treated by others as an older person', a change they greeted less enthusiastically than the others listed in Table 15.2, was more frequent in their 50s than at age 40.

Social forces also shape adult development in another way. Cultures share expectations about the lifespan (Goodnow, 1996), including beliefs about the age at which it is appropriate to pass through a milestone event like getting married, entering the workforce, having a first child, graduating from university or retiring from work. People who deviate from these normative expectations by passing through one of the turning points at too young or too old an age are subject to social censure. So are those who take on age-typed leisure pursuits at atypical ages. Thus, even though 50-year-olds might possess all the necessary strength, stamina, cardiac fitness and enthusiasm to enjoy sports like abseiling, hanggliding or surfing, they can incur disapproval for taking up these strenuous leisure activities for the first time during middle age.

When Bernice Neugarten (1979) questioned a group of middle-aged adults in Kansas City during the mid-20th century about the appropriate timing for the major transition events of the adult life cycle, she found that the vast majority prescribed very narrow age limits for every significant life event. In fact, an allowable age range of five years or less

The empty-nest transition is a turning point in parents' lives.

surrounded each of the events shown in Figure 15.2, according to these adults' tightly calibrated social clocks. The penalties for deviating from the social clock were also severe. Thus, people of that era were apt to feel strong social pressure to marry or have a first child once they reached their early 20s, even though their own personal preferences and life circumstances might motivate them to delay these transitions. By the same token, a middle-aged couple who decided to have another child were criticised not only because of possible health risks but also because of the presumed social embarrassment to their adolescent or married children (Neugarten, Moore & Lowe, 1965, p. 712).

Such prescriptive components of age norms can still influence the quality of adults' coping with the developmental milestones of mature life today. Indeed, whether or not a particular life transition evokes enough stress or psychiatric imbalance to qualify as a 'crisis' may be a function of the discrepancy between its timing and normative social expectations. Neugarten (1979) argued that: 'For the majority of middle-aged women the departure of children is not a crisis. It is, instead, when children do not leave home on time that a crisis is created for both parent and child' (p. 889).

However, in Australia in recent years, the age boundaries set by the social clock have become much more generous than they were several generations ago. Figure 15.2 shows a group of contemporary Australian adults' beliefs about the upper and lower age boundaries for various milestone events of adult life (Peterson, 1996). As this figure shows, a person

It no longer seems out of place to see an older face in a group of recent university graduates.

today is considered 'on time' for a first marriage for a total of 49 years (between being 'too young' at 18 and 'too old' at age 67). Similarly, the contemporary social clock prescribes a generous band of 28 years between the age at which an Australian adult is too young to retire with social approval (40 years) and the age (70) when to remain at work without taking up the option of retirement would incur the social disapproval of being 'off time'.

Intellectual and cognitive development in late middle age

As noted in Chapter 14, there are many important differences between solving a logical problem as an adolescent in school and grappling as a mature adult with a real-life problem such as whether to invest company finances in a new venture or have a first child (Baltes, 1993). In the same way that a formal-operational adolescent might consider all possible combinations of chemical substances on a Piagetian reasoning task (see Chapter 11), a mature adult might weigh up all possible costs and benefits when deciding whether to move to another city to pursue a new career challenge or to return to university to study for a second career. But, unlike the adolescent, the adult must evaluate potential solutions at an emotional as well as a cognitive level, and must live with the consequences of a real-life decision.

There are other differences as well. In school, problems tend to be imposed on the thinker from the outside. A teacher might quiz the audience while lecturing, or set an assignment or a question on a test. In these situations, 'academic' problems may be just that – abstract, arbitrary tests of reasoning with little

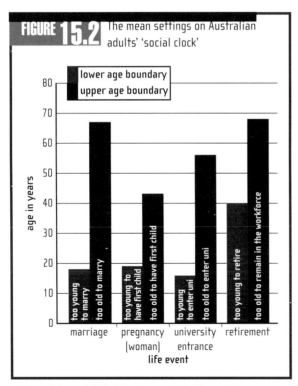

FIGURE 15.2 The mean settings on Australian adults' 'social clock'

Source: Peterson (1996), Table 1, reproduced with permission.

direct relevance to the student's own interests and plans. But, in adult life, the problems that arise in the context of one's chosen life pursuits – marriage, career, raising a family, deciding how to care for an elderly relative and so on – have a very personal meaning. More importantly, the wrong solution to one of the cognitive problems of adult life is likely to carry far heavier penalties than when an adolescent gives the wrong answer to a homework problem in school. Thus, cognitive development in adult life is shaped by different kinds of challenges from those that guided the child's progress through Piaget's concrete-operational stage (see Chapter 7) or the late adolescent's progress into the stage of formal-operations (see Chapter 11). The intellectual skills that adults use to solve the genuine dilemmas of everyday life may develop to a correspondingly higher degree of complexity and sophistication.

Schaie's stage theory

K. Warner Schaie (1997) proposed that the new intellectual demands of mature adult life usher in new stages of cognitive growth beyond that achieved with Piagetian formal operations at the end of adolescence. Schaie (2000) summarised the results of his ambitious 35-year cohort-sequential longitudinal study of cognitive functioning in a sample of over 5000 Seattle men and women. He found there were gains in all cognitive abilities from early adulthood to early middle age. Between the ages of 50 and 60 most of the adults in his study had reached their peak mental performance in the domains of language ability, reasoning, memory, geometry and creatively fluent thinking. By age 67, some decline in numeric ability was apparent with some tasks for some individuals, but Schaie concluded that verbal abilities and logical reasoning powers showed modest gains throughout this period.

The improvements in cognitive performance that Schaie observed from the end of adolescence to the onset of old age led to his formulation of the stage theory of adult cognitive development that is illustrated in Figure 15.3. From this perspective, adolescent cognitive growth can be seen as a stage of preparation for the new developmental opportunities afforded by mature adult responsibilities. Schaie argued that cognitive progress through Piaget's childhood and adolescent stages readied the mind for the genuine cognitive growth that arises for the first time in response to the everyday challenges of adult life.

In Schaie's model, not everyone passes through all the stages, since growing older does not in itself guarantee that cognitive challenges are confronted, with corresponding qualitative gains in cognitive growth. But for those adults who enjoy good mental and physical health, whose lifestyle exposes them to novelty and challenge, and who choose to think deeply about their lives and to exercise and improve their intellects by studying, reading and engaging in

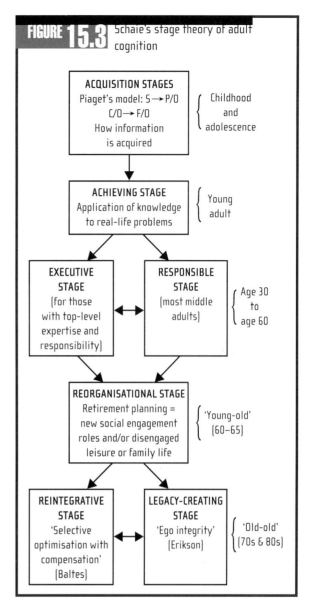

FIGURE 15.3 Schaie's stage theory of adult cognition

Source: Schaie (1997).

lively discussions, progress to higher levels of cognition than formal operations is a definite possibility.

In the first adult stage, labelled 'achieving' (see Figure 15.3), young adults are preoccupied with tangible goals like getting a job, being promoted, establishing a home or gaining social recognition. The driving force behind cognitive development in this stage is the thirst for personal success gained against long odds or in competition with others. This ambitious, goal-directed orientation leads, according to Schaie, to 'more efficient and effective cognitive function with respect to tasks which have role-related achievement potential' than was possible for formal-operational thinkers during adolescence. While it is a qualitative improvement on formal operations, early adult cognition has its own intrinsic limitations. For adults in their 30s and 40s who are firmly embarked upon ventures like parenthood or leadership within an organisation, the concrete goals of the achieving stage are apt to seem too immediate, narrow or self-oriented to prove optimally cognitively challenging.

Thus, according to Schaie, the central developmental tasks of the *responsible stage* of cognitive development revolve around nurturing others' cognitive growth as well as one's own (this mature focus on fostering, protecting and guiding the younger generation is in line with Erikson's ideas about adult personality development through the crisis over generativity that we examined in Chapter 14).

In Schaie's model, when they act as mentors to their younger colleagues at work, adults develop new intellectual skills for planning their solutions to life problems (Chalmers & Lawrence, 1993). As a consequence, adults in the responsible stage gain expertise in their areas of special interest and also in the process of problem-solving at its broadest level. Schaie's fourth period, known as the *executive stage*, is reserved for a very few exceptional adults who are usually well into middle age by the time they reach it. This stage involves a far-reaching cognitive concern about solving the problems faced by those social institutions for which the adult has assumed a significant degree of personal responsibility. By their late 40s or early 50s, some adults have become senior managers in the organisations they work for. Others have gained positions of leadership as volunteers in church or community organisations to which they belong, or attained executive roles in politics, sport, art or music. Over and above the specific demands of the adult's chosen field of endeavour, the challenge of being responsible for many others besides oneself and one's immediate family unit prompts cognitive growth into Schaie's executive stage. The result is a more astute and well-balanced sense of judgment than was possible in the responsible stage, and an exceptional ability to resolve conflicts and coordinate the incompatible needs of each individual in the organisational unit into a cooperative synthesis.

As they progress into their 60s, adults are apt to shift their cognitive focus in a *reorganisational stage* that emphasises preparation for retirement and the thoughtful life planning needed to create a social, creative, financial and personal future that is independent of the lifelong career.

Still later, on a more contemplative plane, elderly men and women may put their minds to the task of leaving a legacy for others (*legacy-creating stage*) or to striving to make sense of their own lives and fit all their significant achievements during adulthood into a larger picture (*reintegrative stage*). This often, though not inevitably, leads to a preoccupation with spiritual concerns, as we see when we examine faith development later in this chapter. The reintegrative stage of cognitive development in Schaie's scheme may trigger a process of life review. We examine this process in more depth in Chapter 16.

Dialectical thinking

Another theory of adult cognitive development depicts intellectual progress after Piaget's stage of formal operations as a transition from formal logic to *dialectical reasoning* (Basseches, 1988). According to this view, formal operations, though more sophisticated and versatile than concrete operations, suffer from an inherent logical limitation. As we saw in Chapter 11, formal-operational thought is organised around the logic of induction and deduction. The formal-operational thinker reaches rational solutions to problems by systematically following a set of 'premises', or propositions, to their inescapable, logical conclusion. In Piaget's theory, the operations themselves form a closed system of interconnected concepts. Thus the mental models acquired in the formal-operational stage enable logical solutions to problems that have a single correct answer. But this system breaks down when probabilistic or changing situations are considered. Because it is a closed system, formal-operational logic has difficulty solving problems that involve multiple systems and their relationships to one another. Open, changing systems that are characterised by a continual process of radical transformation of the status quo are also problematic for this style of thinking (Basseches, 1988).

The dialectical approach to logical reasoning has a different basis. In this scheme, inner conflict drives the continual coordinating, or synthesising, of polarised contradictions into more encompassing, higher-order solutions. In philosophical terms, cognitive problems can be broken down into two contradictory elements, a *thesis* (or core idea), which implies a contrary idea known as an *antithesis*. Before development takes place, the thesis and antithesis are in opposition, each fraught with seemingly irreconcilable contradictions. But cognitive development creates a higher-order integration that melds thesis and antithesis into a more advanced or more complete unity, known as a *synthesis*. Here thesis and antithesis are no longer contradictory. Instead they coexist as complementary facets of the more complex, embracing concept. However, this peaceful synthesis is never the final answer. For, as we saw in Chapter 2, dialectical models of development view instability as normal and inevitable, with periods of stability as unusual temporary pauses in a continuing progression of change. Thus, each new synthesis sows the seeds of further contradiction, and cognitive development is ever punctuated with doubt, disagreement and uncertainty.

To give an example of dialectical adult cognition, Michael Basseches presented the dilemma of a small nation under threat of war. The citizens all realise they must form a militia to protect their national territory, their dependants and the nation's core values against the threat posed by an invading enemy. But no individual wants to risk his or her own life in military service. How do they decide who should be drafted to join their national army?

Basseches suggested that, using formal-operational logic, a thinker who had reached Lawrence Kohlberg's highest 'principled' level of moral development (see Chapter 11) would solve a dilemma like this by coming up with a rule that all members of the social group would be able to accept. For example, the citizens might agree that a random lottery to select soldiers would be fairest.

By contrast, a dialectical thinker might argue that the conception of a national interest that demands military service is intrinsically contradictory to the goals of a democratic community, where no member feels sufficient antipathy to the enemy to want to volunteer to fight. Thus, a dialectical thinker might integrate the core humanitarian interests of the citizenry with the core interests of the other people who were previously seen as 'the enemy'. In this way, a dialectical synthesis of opposing propositions redefines the concept of national interest in a manner that does not require war.

Basseches studied the development of dialectical thinking among a group of highly committed faculty members and gifted undergraduates at a small liberal arts college in the United States. He found that faculty members tended to think more dialectically than fourth-year university students. But these advanced students showed more dialectical thinking than first-years who had only recently completed high school. Similarly, another study in a large American university revealed that graduate students who were completing Masters or PhD degrees used dialectical logic to solve everyday problems and moral dilemmas more often than advanced undergraduates who had been taught by the same instructors in the same departments at the same university.

Basseches therefore concluded that the development of dialectical reasoning is stimulated by higher education during early adulthood. However, at least for individuals like university instructors, who follow intellectually demanding career paths, dialectical cognitive development apparently does not cease with the completion of higher education. Instead, as a lifelong process of change, the dialectical model of cognitive development proposes that every apparent attainment of a new stage of thought or a new level of certainty about life issues simply sets the stage for further contradictions. As Basseches explained:

> In this way of thinking, the constant epistemic task of life is building better and better understandings. New experiences and unexpected changes which occur can all be employed in addressing this task … I believe that events in life, which show us that the views and beliefs we were most sure about with respect to ourselves and our world no longer make workable sense because we've changed or our environment has changed, serve as opportunities for the development of dialectical thinking. (p. 337)

As they move into late middle age, men and women are likely to spend time thinking about what the future holds in store.

The development of faith, religion and spirituality

As they progress through adult life, many men and women, irrespective of their religious background and education, begin to consider what the future may hold in store, both for themselves as unique identities and for the world they will leave behind when they die. This may lead to new sociopolitical activism on behalf of the global environment, world peace or other cherished causes. Many mature adults are also disposed to think about philosophical dilemmas over what ethical, social or religious values to believe in, what lasting contribution their overall pattern of life will make to future generations, and how to confront their own mortality in cognitive, emotional and practical ways (see Chapter 18). Many of these core questions come under a rubric that a psychologist would describe as the development of faith.

The growth of faith during adult life has much in common with the dialectical views of adult cognitive development considered earlier, according to James Fowler (1981). He conceived of faith development as a sequence of six stages (Table 15.3). Throughout each stage, Fowler viewed faith as a kind of knowing. He argued that the content of faith knowledge embraces all human impulses to understand the furtherest limits of existence and the essence of spirituality. Thus faith includes religious belief, but also goes beyond it. Fowler suggested that the growth of a sense of faith reflected a person's efforts to give meaning to human existence. Faith epitomises a person's ultimate concerns. For some people, these

Stage number	Stage name	Age period	Focus of concern	Cognitive prerequisites
1	Intuitive projective faith	3–7 years	Power, control, the mystery of birth, and what happens after death	Preoperational thought
2	Mythic literal faith	8 years to adult	Religious symbolism and parables; the personal qualities of God	Concrete-operational thought
3	Synthetic conventional faith	Adolescence to adult	Tacit acceptance of culturally ordained or religious spiritual codes; finding a meaning for self and one's everyday tasks; seeking a justification for moral behaviour	Formal-operational thought
4	Individual reflective faith	Late adolescence or adult	Self-awareness of personal choices and decisions about what to believe in; a personally chosen, active commitment to one's own values replaces Stage 3's passive conformity to cultural or religious codes	Formal-operational thought
5	Conjunctive faith	Middle age to old age	Synthesising mystical symbols with rational and personally chosen moral values; recognition of the integrity and truth in positions other than one's own; commitments freed from the confines of culture, tribe, nation or religious community	Formal operations plus dialectical schemata
6	Universalising faith	Middle age to old age	Self-sacrificing devotion to compassion, justice and humanity's welfare; using one's life in the service of these beliefs; efforts to transform and transcend religious or moral doctrine on behalf of a universal community of self-actualised human beings	Formal or post-formal (e.g. dialectical) operations

TABLE 15.3 Fowler's stages of faith development

are religious; for others with an equally mature and well-developed sense of faith, the content that inspires hope may have nothing to do with any organised religion or even a god figure. Adults may place their faith in a group of people, in their nation, in a political system, in the natural environment or in a philosophic moral code.

Fowler's six stages of faith development (outlined in Table 15.3) were identified on the basis of interviews with children and adults of all ages. He found that people's thinking about faith and religion was a lifespan process of psychological growth. Though a few exceptionally thoughtful individuals managed to reach Stage 4 while still in late adolescence, the final three stages in his scheme typically do not emerge before adulthood. Often the transition to marriage and the workforce triggers the self-reflection needed

to achieve Stage 4. The making of firm lifelong commitments to a spouse, career and the rearing of children may stimulate a corresponding desire to articulate a personal belief system during the 20s and 30s. While not a necessary precondition, university education is another frequent stimulus to the transition from Stage 3 to Stage 4.

Fowler noted that Stage 4 often develops in reaction to dialectical conflicts over issues bound up with the teaching of formal religion, as well as the debates over morality, lifestyle and personal responsibility that may arise in the context of university life, including:

- individuality vs belonging to a community
- subjectivity vs objectivity
- self-fulfilment vs service to others
- the relative vs the absolute (p. 6).

Stage 4 dialectically synthesises these contradicting ideas at an advanced level of complexity. But some adults never make the developmental step from Stage 3 to Stage 4 (some can remain fixated at Stage 2 throughout their adult lives, especially if, as outlined in Chapter 11, they are among those adolescents and adults who fail to make the transition from Piaget's concrete to formal operations).

According to Fowler (1981), development of Stage 5 faith almost never happens until middle or old age:

> This stage's commitment to justice is freed from the confines of tribe, class, religious community or nation. And with the seriousness that can arise when life is more than half over, this stage is ready to spend and be spent for the cause of conserving and cultivating the possibility of others' generating identity and meaning. (p. 198)

Stage 6 is even rarer. In fact, the saintly individuals who achieve Stage 6 are often viewed as deviants by society because their style of faith is so atypical and their self-sacrificing devotion to it so extreme. Examples of the attainment of Stage 6 in late adulthood can be seen in the lives of such exceptionally committed individuals as Gandhi, Martin Luther King, Albert Schweitzer and Mother Theresa. As Fowler (1981) explained, these individuals' 'strategies of nonviolent suffering and ultimate respect for being constitute affronts to our usual notions of relevance. It is little wonder that persons best described by Stage 6 so frequently become martyrs to the visions they incarnate' (p. 200).

Personality development in late middle age: Generativity

As noted in Chapter 2, Erik Erikson's (1968a) theory of lifespan personality depicts the key development-inducing conflict of middle age as the challenge to achieve *generativity*, or a sense of being needed by, and useful to, future generations. Some adults achieve generativity through parenthood, as was illustrated in Box 15.1. Others do so through artistic, literary or musical contributions or in the professional fields of education, science, medicine or politics.

Evidence of mature generativity emerged from a longitudinal study in the United States. Louis Terman (1959) began the study by examining a group of gifted girls in 1921 when they were still in school. Sixty-six years later, in 1987, G. E. and C. O. Vaillant (1990) went back to the same female group, who had been selected for study initially out of some 250 000 others (Schwartz, 1986) because of their exceptional intellectual ability. All the women were now in their seventies, with an average age of 77. The Vaillants' goal was to discover what had led some of the women to put their intellectual talents to creative use in generative pursuits in the community in adult life

and, conversely, what factors had inhibited others from ever realising the potential for genius they had displayed during childhood.

As adults, the cognitively gifted women fell into two clearly distinct groups. One group of women stood out for their creative accomplishments. Either throughout their adult lives or, for some, on completion of childrearing, these women had made contributions to culture or society that were significant enough to earn them public recognition. Some had distinguished themselves in art, literature, theatre, music or publishing. Others had achieved elected offices or public honours in service to their community. The other group had achieved no such distinction. Nor were they creative in any way that extended beyond their own immediate household. A number had hobbies, but these tended to be activities like knitting, cooking, pet breeding and gardening that were never subjected to public scrutiny.

To discover the basis for the difference between the gifted women who had turned their exceptional cognitive abilities to creative achievements and those who had not, the Vaillants went back through the longitudinal data in search of the contrasts in their early lives. There were no differences in IQ scores between the accomplished and undistinguished women either in childhood or when their intelligence was tested again during adulthood. Nor did the two groups differ in terms of their parents' income, level of education, father's or mother's occupation or attitudes to women's achievement. But there were differences in the women's adult personalities. The creative achievers were more optimistic, enthusiastic and full of *joie-de-vivre* (joy of living) compared with the less creative group. They were also more likely to have achieved Erikson's generativity (see Figure 15.4).

In addition, the creative women possessed a more lively sense of humour than their less creative peers, reminiscent of the contrast uncovered in the studies of highly creative and high-IQ preadolescents described in Chapter 9. Finally, the Vaillants noted that the self-actualising women who had realised their creative potential had a more realistic and emotionally healthy attitude to their own biological and social ageing than the underachieving elderly women.

Age and generativity
Some of the exceptionally creative women in the Vaillants' subgroup of high achievers had made their first recognised creative contribution late in their adult lives. For example, one woman had her first book published at the age of 65. Another, at the age of 75, became the editor of a small newspaper. Two others, who had enjoyed music all their lives but had only played in private while their children were growing up, gave their first public recitals when in their early 60s. These examples highlighted the positive developmental opportunities that ageing can bring about.

In another study of middle-aged generativity,

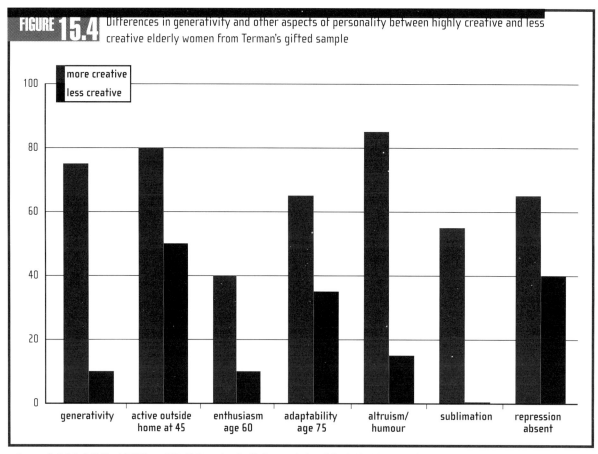

FIGURE **15.4** Differences in generativity and other aspects of personality between highly creative and less creative elderly women from Terman's gifted sample

Source: G. E. & C. O. Vaillant (1990), pp. 612–14. Reproduced with the permission of Cambridge University Press.

Carol Ryff (1984) examined the impact of stressful life events such as job loss, the death of a parent and the emptying of the family nest. She found that adults encountered varying numbers of these events at different times during middle age. Individual differences existed, also, in their methods of coping with those events they perceived as stressful (see Chapter 17 for a further discussion of age differences in adult coping strategies).

When she tested how well these adults had resolved Erikson's personality crisis over generativity, Ryff observed an association with the timing and number of stressful life events. Adults with the highest generativity scores (indicating they were well advanced in resolving the crisis) were not the ones who had escaped stress and upheaval entirely. To the contrary, there was a statistically significant positive association between generativity and numbers of stressful life events for women, indicating that the more upheavals (like the empty nest, bereavement, etc.) a woman experienced, the higher was her generativity score. In line with Erikson's dialectical model of development, stress seemed to have triggered the woman's development of productive contributions to benefit future generations. For men the correlation, though positive, was not statistically significant. These results are shown in Figure 15.5.

An interesting sex difference also emerged, as

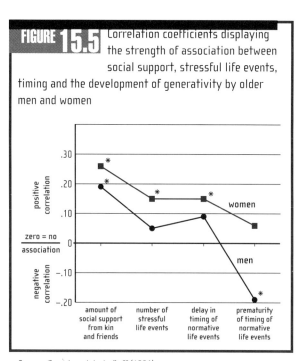

FIGURE **15.5** Correlation coefficients displaying the strength of association between social support, stressful life events, timing and the development of generativity by older men and women

Source: Based on data in Ryff (1984).
Note: * denotes statistically significant association.

shown in Figure 15.5. Whereas more life events and more social support predicted higher generativity in women, for men it was the timing that mattered. If life events arose unusually early, they were linked with low generativity, somewhat in line with the identity foreclosure problems that arose for early physically maturing males, as noted in Chapter 11.

Age, generativity and creativity

Examples like these contradict the popular belief that older people are too rigid, conventional and set in their ways to do anything outstandingly original or creative. But is it true that for most people the creative flame burns brightest in early adulthood and then fades steadily? Or is ageing completely irrelevant to creativity and talented achievement? One of the first researchers to try to find a scientific answer to these questions was Harvey Lehman (1953). After early exposure to the common-sense belief that intellectual and aesthetic powers invariably grew worn with use, Lehman devoted his scholarly career to testing the scientific truth of this conjecture. His first effort to gather data involved scanning numerous historical and contemporary anthologies, public documents and books of records to find the ages at which famous contributors to a wide range of academic disciplines and non-scholastic fields of creative endeavour had made their contributions. Box 15.2 shows some examples.

Lehman was aware that, due to mortality, fewer potential contributors would have been alive at older ages. He therefore grouped the data not only by the age of the creator but also according to the number of potential contributors to each creative field who had lived to be at least that old. Some of his findings are shown in Figure 15.6 and Table 15.4. Lehman also drew a distinction between the quality of a creative contribution and the total number of works an individual produced at a particular age. He argued that if talent declines after early adulthood, top quality products might disappear, yet older adults could still go on producing lesser works. He looked at the greatest contributions ever made to a range of ten different avenues of endeavour (including writing, scholarship, science and performing arts), according to contemporary experts in the discipline. Then he examined their creators' age at the time when these works were produced. Great achievements did tend to be produced by workers in their 30s. Even those rare geniuses of earlier eras in history who had lived past the age of 80 made relatively few contributions once they reached the age of 60. Figure 15.6 illustrates the quantity of work produced in a range of disciplines by workers of various ages.

If illness and bodily decline sap workers' mental alertness and creative energies during later adulthood the elderly might perhaps be the hardest hit. However, if this were the major factor accounting for Lehman's results, people who remained healthy and vigorous into extreme old age would be expected to

BOX 15.2 How can you explain it?
Age and achievement

Here are some examples that support Lehman's hypothesis of people's peak achievements arising in early adulthood.

- Jane Austen wrote the novel *Sense and Sensibility* at age 19.
- Walt Disney made his first cartoon film at age 22.
- Isaac Newton developed the law of gravity at age 23.
- Guglielmo Marconi invented the radio at age 27.
- Fidel Castro led his revolutionary government to power at age 32.
- Edmund Hilary climbed Mount Everest at age 33.
- Maria Montessori opened her first school at age 37.
- Jonas Salk developed a vaccine against polio at age 39.

Activity suggestion 1. Search the archives of a field of creative endeavour that interests you and note down the ages at which the accomplishments you admire most were produced by their creators. Does early adulthood stand out ahead of middle age or old age on your list?

Activity suggestion 2. Can you think of two different explanations for why these adults achieved their best work before the age of 40? (Write them out and then compare your answers with the text.)

It is important to take longevity into account when examining creative output in different decades of adult life.

FIGURE 15.6 Age and achievement in a variety of professions

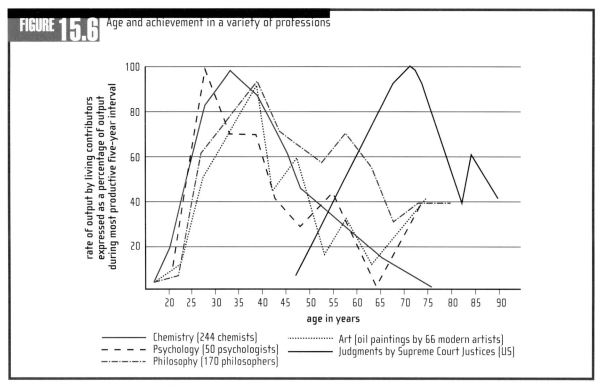

Chemistry (244 chemists)
Psychology (50 psychologists)
Philosophy (170 philosophers)
Art (oil paintings by 66 modern artists)
Judgments by Supreme Court Justices (US)

Source: Lehman (1953), Figure 15.4, © 1953, American Philosophical Society, reprinted by permission of Princeton University Press.

TABLE 15.4 Academic and scientific achievement as a function of longevity

Age (in years) at death	Percentage of notable contributions per decade of life							
	Under 20	20–29	30–39	40–49	50–59	60–69	70–79	80–89
Before 50	5	32	50	14	–	–	–	–
50–59	0	23	39	28	9	–	–	–
60–64	1	17	32	27	20	4	–	–
65–69	0	8	38	28	16	10	–	–
70–74	2	15	36	28	13	6	0	–
75–79	0	10	28	27	20	10	4	–
80–84	0	12	32	28	15	9	3	1
85 and over	0	8	29	26	22	9	3	2

Source: Based on data in Lehman (1953).

continue to produce longer than those who died prematurely. Paradoxically, Lehman found that 'those who live to age 85 and beyond and those who die at 40 both do their best work in the thirties' (p. 309).

Even after making allowances for early mortality, Lehman concluded that the overall quantity of creative achievements declined in late middle age. Thus, he defined the period between age 29 and age 39 as the 'golden decade' of creative achievement, summing up his findings by quoting the following lines from George Miller Beard (1874; cited in Lehman, 1953, p. 241):

The golden decade is between 30 and 40
The silver decade is between 40 and 50
The bronze decade is between 20 and 30

The iron decade is between 50 and 60
The tin decade is between 60 and 70
The wooden decade is between 70 and 80.

Jock Abra (1989) suggested a social reason for the apparent decline in creativity in middle age: people in their 40s and 50s are typically married with children and are often caregivers for older family members. Thus, they are generally more heavily encumbered by responsibilities for other people's welfare and creative development than young men and women. Or young people may simply be more self-preoccupied than middle-aged adults. As Abra explained:

Since creativity does demand time and energy, and since Muses are jealous mistresses whose speech cannot be timetabled, devotees must put their work before all else, including social obligations, personal relationships and the needs of others. Insufficient selfishness has compromised more than one talent. (p. 113)

Increased strivings for generativity in late middle age, coupled with the age-graded promotional system, may help to explain Lehman's results. For example, in academia, older academics who achieve promotion may become so encumbered with administrative duties that they have little time or energy to devote to creative research or writing. Opportunities to share ideas and credit with younger scholars may also increase along with the supervision of advanced students. When Davis Haber (1979) studied the creativity of mature university professors, he found that both the amount and nature of their creative accomplishment changed with age. Their total output declined in middle age and, rather than producing tightly reasoned, rigorous and precise pieces of work, the older scholars were more inclined to range widely and to attempt to put their lifetime's accumulation of wisdom to the task of integrating and synthesising large fields of knowledge. Because such work is risky, and does not easily fit within traditional paradigms and scientific frameworks, it may not earn prestige or promotion. Nor is it as apt as the more traditional scholarship characteristic of young academics to result in a mention in the anthologies consulted by Lehman. But this should not necessarily be taken as a slur upon its usefulness.

Haber (1979, p. 310) quoted Hans Selye:

There must remain a few of us who train men and perfect tools to scan the horizons rather than to look ever closer at the infinitely small.

These observations fit in well with Erikson's theory of generativity and with Havighurst's and Super's extensions of these ideas to career development (see Chapter 14). In employment, if talented older workers reorient their interests away from personal achievement towards promoting the development of their younger colleagues, data similar to Lehman's (see Table 15.4) would emerge. Levinson's theory of the development of a mentor role in mid-life (see Chapter 14) also predicts a transfer of personal achievement striving to the seeking of vicarious satisfaction by nurturing the achievements of younger protégés.

Another possibility considered by Lehman is that some gifted individuals may have only a single message to communicate. Thus, if they achieve early, their mature works may simply become redundant copies of this initial contribution. But if their opportunities to be creative are delayed until mid-life, genius might still emerge at this later age, in line with the Vaillants' findings of exceptional creativity by gifted elderly women. As the Vaillants' data would seem to suggest, the 'golden decade' for women's creativity may arise in the 50s rather than the 20s or 30s. The same could well be true of adults who switch careers at mid-life to enter totally different

fields of creative endeavour. Indeed, even if age does limit creativity for some, examples like those in Box 15.3 suggest that the barrier is by no means insurmountable.

Biological changes in late middle age

Sometime between the ages of 45 and 55, most women gradually cease menstruation. This brings to a close the reproductive phase of the lifespan. At the same time, menopause ushers in a number of other important changes to female physiological functioning.

Menopause

The lengthy process of the tapering off of menstruation typically begins in the early forties with irregular periods, a gradual lowering of *estrogen* (female hormone) levels in the bloodstream and decreased fertility as fewer ova are produced (see Chapter 3). The decline in estrogen production leads to a decrease in the size of the uterus to about half the weight it had at age 30. The walls of the vagina grow thinner and secretions diminish. Once estrogen levels in the bloodstream drop to about one-sixth, menstruation ceases and the habitual cyclic ups and downs of the menses are replaced by a steadier hormonal balance.

During the tapering-off period, many women are troubled by 'hot flushes' or a feeling of sudden sweating or blushing, due to a vascular change. Some also suffer from additional physical problems, including numbness, dizziness, constipation, insomnia, breast pains, headache, poor circulation, chills and weight gain. After the complete cessation of menstruation, most of these side effects disappear spontaneously. But the continued lower level of estrogen is responsible for drier skin, and approximately one in every four postmenopausal women is affected by a condition known as *osteoporosis*, or a weakening of the bones' resistance to fractures, to which lowered estrogen levels may be a contributing factor.

Folklore suggests that all these temporary, or enduring, physical symptoms are insignificant by comparison with the overwhelming psychological impact of the menopause. If you would like to test the accuracy of your own impressions of the psychological consequences of menopause, try doing the quiz in Box 15.4 before reading the next section.

Psychological consequences of menopause

The quiz in Box 15.4 taps into some of the most commonly held stereotypes about the adverse psychological impact of menopause. When they gave a longer version of this quiz to a group of American women ranging in age from 21 to 65 years, Bernice Neugarten, Vivian Wood, Ruth Kraines and Barbara Loomis (1963) found that approximately half the inexperienced women in their 20s and 30s did believe that depression, selfishness and marital difficulties were virtually inevitable by-products of menopause. But the experienced women aged 56 to 65, who had already passed through this transition in their life, were sceptical about most of the supposed negative psychological consequences of menopause. They were inclined to consider it a relatively minor upset, even physically.

Going still further, a substantial proportion of this older group believed that menopause actually boosted a woman's happiness, self-confidence and self-esteem, while at the same time improving sex and marriage and her involvement in community pursuits. Nearly half the postmenopausal women described menopause as 'the best thing that ever happens to a woman'. Very few of the younger women believed that this could be true. Consequently, very few premenopausal women looked

BOX 15.4 Activity suggestion
Do you understand menopause?

Instructions. This quiz tests the accuracy of your knowledge of the psychological consequences of menopause, or 'the change of life'. Mark each item *True* or *False* and then check your answers against the scoring key, which is upside down at the bottom of this box.

Note: Answers are scored 'true' or 'false' on the basis of majority agreement by a group of experienced, postmenopausal women (Neugarten et al., 1963).

True or False?

1. Women generally feel better after the menopause than they have for years.
2. A woman has a broader outlook on life after menopause.
3. A woman gets more confidence in herself after the change of life.
4. Women are generally calmer and happier after the change of life than before.
5. Life is more interesting for a woman after the menopause.
6. After the change of life, a woman feels freer to do things for herself.
7. After the change of life, a woman has a better relationship with her husband.
8. Many women think menopause is the best thing that ever happened to them.
9. After the change of life, a woman becomes more interested in community affairs.
10. Women often get self-centred at the time of the menopause.
11. After the change of life, women often don't consider themselves 'real women' any more.
12. In truth, just about every woman is depressed about the change of life.
13. Women worry about losing their minds during the menopause.
14. A woman is concerned about how her husband will feel towards her after the menopause.

Activity suggestion. Once you have taken the quiz yourself, you may wish to try giving it to your friends and acquaintances to check whether the accuracy of people's impressions varies consistently with age or gender.

Answers: (1) true (2) true (3) true (4) true (5) false (6) false (7) true (8) false (9) true (10) false (11) false (12) false (13) false (14) false.

forward to any beneficial outcomes of the change of life. It seemed that, in the absence of direct experience of the change, younger women relied on popular myths about it and consequently saw menopause as an impending psychological catastrophe.

But despite the pervasive cultural expectation that menopause will constitute a severe psychological trauma, most women do not experience this and are pleasantly surprised when they encounter menopause. Ruth Kraines (1963) suggested that the psychological difficulties encountered by the minority of women who do find the change of life stressful are not specific to menopause itself. In her sample, the same women who suffered from postmenopausal depression had also undergone emotional problems when they began menstruating, and during pregnancy and childbirth. Furthermore, these women's medical histories were complicated by a host of other serious health problems which the untroubled group had been spared. At any stage in life, poor physical health can interfere with effective psychological functioning. But we must be wary of equating illness and abnormality with the effects of normal ageing.

Bernadette Lyon (1985) compared older and younger Australian women's beliefs about menopause and found that postmenopausal women, aged 52 to 57, were somewhat less likely than immediately premenopausal women, aged 40 to 45, to believe that negative psychological consequences were an inevitable component of the change-of-life transition. But the tendency to ascribe negative moods, depression and mood swings to the biological event of menopause was not strong in either Australian age group. Lyon also noted that the anecdotal accounts given by postmenopausal Australian women of their own experiences with menopause depicted the change as overwhelmingly positive. Very few of the women in her sample reported experiencing any emotional upsets themselves during the climacterium, though some knew of a friend or relative who had had 'a terrible time' (p. 202).

BOX 5.5
Lessons from culture
Menopause in Mexico

The following accounts by rural Mayan women in the Yucatan peninsula of Mexico (Beyene, 1992) suggest a generally positive experience.

Interviewer: How did you feel after the menopause?
Mayan women:
- A sense of release
- Happy again
- Like a young girl
- Young again
- Carefree and alive

Interviewer: What symptoms, apart from your periods stopping, did you have during the menopause?
Mayan women: None

Is there a male menopause?
There is no single event in the ageing of the male reproductive system to correspond to the female's cessation of monthly periods. But gradual changes do occur for the man, leading to some speculation of possible psychological repercussions (Huyck, 1974). The production of *testosterone* (the male hormonal counterpart to estrogen) decreases slowly from age 40 to age 60. The result is a lowering of the sperm count, though usually not to the point of complete infertility. Endocrinologists have suggested that the drop in testosterone could influence men's moods, but the gradual nature of the change renders the assumption of inevitable psychological difficulties even more problematic than in the case of female menopause. A Canadian medical investigation showed that, when a group of 30 men presenting with symptoms that seemed to be of hormonal origin were treated with testosterone-replacement therapy, their purely physical ailments such as headache, sweating, hot flushes and numbness disappeared completely, but the replenishment of a youthful hormone balance had no visible effect on more complex psychologically mediated difficulties like depression, anxiety or sexual impotence (Lear, 1974).

A further complication is the fact that, for men, serious psychological upsets such as job loss or divorce can boost the production of the stress hormone *adrenal cortisone* to the point where it interferes with the body's normal manufacture of testosterone. Thus the afflicted man may encounter all the physiological symptoms of hormone deficiency and, if he is middle-aged, may erroneously blame the ageing process for troubles actually caused by experiences at home or at work. Martha Weinman Lear's description of the male 'menopause' brings out the plethora of interacting factors which may be implicated if and when a man does encounter emotional upheaval during late middle age:

> The hormone-production levels are dropping, the head is balding, the sexual vigor is diminishing, the stress is unending, the children are leaving, the parents are dying, the job horizons are narrowing, the friends are having their first heart attacks; the past floats by in a fog of hopes not realized, opportunities not grasped, women not bedded, potentials not fulfilled, and the future is a confrontation with one's own mortality. (1974, p. 43)

So, as in the case of female menopause, middle-aged adults should probably resist putting too much faith in the biological inevitability of a traumatic male 'change of life'. This way they will avoid the pitfall of creating real problems out of imaginary or anticipated forebodings.

Sexuality after age 50
The lowering of testosterone levels after the age of 40 can have an effect on male sexual performance. On average, it takes longer for a middle-aged man to

Love, intimacy and sexual pleasure are as feasible after the menopause as before.

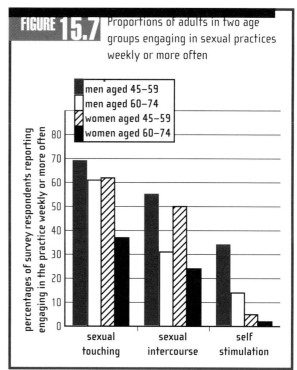

FIGURE 15.7 Proportions of adults in two age groups engaging in sexual practices weekly or more often

Legend:
- men aged 45–59
- men aged 60–74
- women aged 45–59
- women aged 60–74

Source: Based on data in AARP (1999).

become sexually aroused. Direct tactile stimulation of the penis is also more important for maintaining the older man's erection, and the climax itself is apt to be less dramatic, with fewer genital spasms, less seminal fluid ejected and a milder feeling of release during orgasm. These changes, along with the fact that the body's rate of production of ejaculate slows down, may help to explain why most men come to desire intercourse less frequently as they grow older. But when the older couple's style of lovemaking is modified to take account of these changes, no loss of overall enjoyment of sexuality need result. Indeed, the new taste which mature husbands are apt to acquire for a broad range of sensual experience, lengthy foreplay and supplementary forms of sexual expression, in addition to intercourse, may even improve the couple's sexual relationship by opening up new options to them, and by increasing empathy and compatibility between the needs of husband and wife. As shown in Figure 15.7, sexual activity is reported by a majority of men and women as occurring on a weekly basis (or more often) up to the age of 60. Even after that age, sexual pleasure is more a question of the availability of a partner than it is of any biological or psychological consequence of the ageing process. From a study of men and women aged 60 to 80 in the United States (AARP, 1999), it was found that over half of the men and women with a partner engaged in intercourse on a weekly basis, but less than 10 per cent of widows and widowers without a partner did so.

For women, social factors appear to take the place of biological changes in accounting for any alteration of sexual performance or enjoyment which may occur during middle age or later adulthood. Owing to their longer life expectancy (see Chapter 18) and tendency to marry husbands older than themselves, women are more likely than men to be without a sexual partner during old age. For those that remain married, sexual pleasure is just as likely after as before the menopause. Despite the relative suddenness and far-reaching hormonal and reproductive consequences of the menopause, it has surprisingly little influence on the purely physical side of female sexuality. Apart from the decrease in vaginal moisture, there is nothing in the woman's body to correspond to the male's testosterone-based loss of sex drive. Postmenopausal women are as capable as younger women of becoming sexually aroused and achieving orgasm. If anything, biological ageing may improve the older woman's sexual motivation and involvement by enabling her to dispense with the distractions and limitations of contraceptive paraphernalia, while the experience that grows over decades of marriage, and the increased self-confidence that often arises in middle age, may facilitate her communication of her sexual wishes to her partner.

Some women nonetheless do experience a cooling of sexual passion after menopause. Social factors such as unfavourable attitudes, inappropriate social conditioning and unfortunate past experiences can combine to block the expression of mature female sexuality. Many women accept the myth that beauty depends on youthfulness. When their bodies begin to show signs of age, they may feel disgusted with themselves and hesitate to expose their nakedness to their husband for fear of 'turning him off' or incurring ridicule. Public opinion may also undermine the older woman's enthusiasm for intercourse by intimating that post-reproductive sexuality is 'dirty' or abnormal. Alternatively, women whose experiences with sexuality in earlier years have proved routine or unenjoyable may welcome the menopause as a socially sanctioned excuse for opting out of an irksome duty.

Kris and Richard Bulcroft (1985) explored the sexual practices of a group of currently unmarried 60-year-old American men and women who, after varying periods of celibacy following divorce or death of their former spouses, had begun to date members of the opposite sex. They found that cohabitation was quite common in this age group. The average elderly dating couple spent two to four nights a week together in one or other partner's home. But even among the elderly daters who did not cohabit, sexual intimacy was the norm. In fact, as the Bulcrofts explained:

> Sexuality appears to be a vital part of the dating relationship in later life. Sexual intercourse is expected from the dating partner; this is true for women as well as men. The normative standard of sexuality tends to imply that if sexual intercourse does not occur by the fourth or fifth date, then other dating partners will be sought. The majority of those interviewed report that sexual intercourse is better in later life; there is evidence that new learning can and does take place in the sexual activities and behaviours in later life. Kissing, hugging, and petting behaviours are deemed appropriate in the dating relationship, and do not appear to differ radically from the expression of intimacy at earlier stages in the life cycle. The nuances of the sexual relationship appear to remain constant over time and contribute to overall satisfaction with the sexual aspect of the dyadic relationship. (pp. 121–2)

These data combine with the results of numerous studies of married couples (see Chapter 14) to suggest that neither the female menopause nor the corresponding physiological and hormonal changes in men during late middle age is likely to prevent mature sexual enjoyment, provided attitudes are conducive and a willing and supportive partner is available.

Family relationships after age 50

Birthday cards aimed at adults turning 50 sometimes strike an optimistic note of congratulation for entering an era where 'life begins'. Others strive to console the middle-aged adult for the social, physical and cognitive losses that are presumed to be just around the corner for a person of 50. But, either way, the 50th birthday is a socially momentous occasion. Like the 13th, 18th and 21st birthdays earlier in life, the passage into the second half-century of a person's life is marked by a change in social status. The alterations to the shape of social life that cluster around the age of 50 for most men and women provide new opportunities for psychological development. In the next sections we examine the changes in personality, cognition and social behaviour that tend to occur during the empty-nest and grandparenting stages of the family life cycle.

The empty nest

The youngest child's departure from the parental household marks a transition known as the *empty nest*. Some of the effects of child-free status on the older couple's marital relationship are examined in Chapter 14. The empty nest also paves the way for a new mode of relating to grown offspring. Instead of being intimately involved in their children's daily lives, the vast majority of Australian empty-nest parents can count on a visit from at least one adult son or daughter either once a month or more often (Peterson, 1999).

However, though frequent contact during the children's daily, weekly or monthly visits may help to make the transition easier, the last child's moving away from home can be painful, especially for a traditional housewife or house-husband who undertook parenthood as their life's principal career. Even employed mothers and fathers with other major commitments besides parenthood are apt to feel nostalgic, as illustrated in Box 15.1.

Adult children and their parents

The quality of the relationship that parents and adult children manage to evolve for themselves after the offspring leave home is likely to be far more important than sheer frequency of contact as a basis for both generations' happiness and psychological well-being. But the development of mature, tolerant and mutually supportive relationships between two people is never easy. Ageing parents and their young adult offspring appear to find it particularly difficult

The empty nest paves the way for a new mode of relating together as a couple.

to achieve this goal. After studying a large number of North American families with offspring in their 30s, one researcher concluded:

> A state of uneasy truce is characteristic of the relationship with parents of more than half of these young people, while a sixth of them are angry and condemning. Only a third of the group genuinely enjoy and value their parents. (Cox, 1970, p. 221)

On the basis of a three-year longitudinal research study of adult offspring and their parents in Boston, Kathleen White, Joseph Speisman and Daryl Costos (1983) likewise concluded that, even by the age of 26, most men still viewed their mother egocentrically in terms of the mother's capacity and willingness to minister to the son's emotional, material or practical needs. But by the same age the typical Boston daughter had moved beyond this egocentric stage to consider her mother as an individual in her own right. The following comment by one of the young women in the sample typifies this change in attitude:

> I am understanding her more now than I ever did before. I have started to understand that I had to stop blaming her for everything in my life. I felt she had been a lousy parent. Now, I'm more understanding that my mother is a person and that she has her own problems and her own life … which I wasn't understanding of before. I accepted her as a mother – but she actually is a human being, and as an individual she had personality, and she had good days and bad days. I only saw her as a mother until recently. (p. 73)

Cultural factors may make elderly parents' transition to interdependent, mutually enjoyable relationships with their adult children either easier or more difficult. Daphne Keats (1987) noted that the multicultural fabric of Australian society encompasses many conflicting ideals about how family members should relate together in adulthood. She reported the results of an unpublished study by Alice Munnings on migrant Australian families of Chinese, Greek and British descent. Clear differences in expectations about old age arose among these cultural groups. The Chinese, in particular, appeared to adhere to a three-stage model of family relations in adulthood instead of the two stages usually anticipated by mainstream Australians and British migrants. After their grown children had achieved independence, married and given birth to children of their own, elderly Chinese parents (and to a lesser extent their Greek counterparts) anticipated the continuation of filial respect, ultimately culminating in the aged parents' dependency on their mature children for care and support in old age. As Keats explained:

> We have a theme which goes across some quite diverse cultural groups both in Australia and the countries from which these respondents come. I believe the notion of interdependence … is one which must be seriously considered in any theory of life-span development. If autonomy is reached, for many of these Asian respondents it is not an

ultimate level of development at all, but an intermediate stage which must lead on, if the person is to develop satisfactorily, to a further stage of responsibility and interdependence. (p. 151)

Though their manner of relating to one another is apt to change with the offspring's final departure from home, the relationship between middle-aged parents and their adult children typically persists throughout the ageing parents' lives. In fact, a new phenomenon called social-age peership (Peterson, 1993b) has grown up in Western societies in recent decades. This describes a tendency for all the adult generations of a family to pursue similar lifestyles. This pattern contrasts sharply with traditional families several decades ago, in which each adult generation had its own distinct role to play. But now we find parents attending university, going sailing, attending fitness classes or driving to work alongside their adult children. Newlyweds and retirees can belong to any generation and today, much more than in the past, the trend for divorce to lead to remarriage has meant that numbers of older parents (especially fathers) re-experience the bearing and rearing of infants at the same time as their grown children's first venture into parenthood.

One consequence of such a shift in family lifestyle patterns has been a narrowing of the gap in attitudes between the generations. On issues like religion, politics, sexual behaviour and gender equity, young adults' views may now be mirrored by those of their middle-aged parents more closely than ever before (Miller & Glass, 1989).

Grandparenthood

Despite the trauma they may experience over their grown children's departure from the family home and the consequent struggle to establish a new style of intimacy between adult generations, many older Australian and New Zealand men and women look forward eagerly to the empty-nest transition for one main reason – it signals the likely approach of grandparenthood. The birth of a son's or daughter's child is a very desirable event in the lives of most elderly parents. It symbolises biological continuity of the family line, as well as providing a second chance to taste the pleasures of involvement in the exciting early years of a child's development. When the grandchild is born, further satisfactions present themselves, as shown in Figure 15.8.

The most frequent source of gratification for both grandfathers and grandmothers was the chance to be involved in the grandchild's growing up, with affectionate contact between grandparent and grandchild running a close second. Some grandparents felt the role made them feel young again, though others mentioned how tired they became after a day with a grandchild and relished the luxury, not accorded to parents, of being able to give the child back.

Grandparenting can also have its down side, clearly illustrated by the responses of one sample of

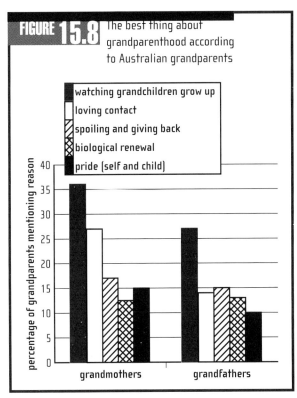

FIGURE 15.8 The best thing about grandparenthood according to Australian grandparents

watching grandchildren grow up
loving contact
spoiling and giving back
biological renewal
pride (self and child)

percentage of grandparents mentioning reason

grandmothers   grandfathers

Source: Adapted from Peterson (1999), p. 83, Table 2, by permission of Baywood Publishing Co., Inc.

Australian grandparents in Queensland to the question 'What is the worst thing about being a grandparent?' (Peterson, 1999). While a minority of grandmothers and grandfathers rejected the question by claiming that nothing was bad about it, most could name some disadvantages, as shown in Figure 15.9.

Styles of grandparenting

So many factors influence the way grandparents interact with their children and grandchildren that it is difficult to draw broad conclusions about what is 'normal' or 'typical' grandparenting. Cohort membership and age at becoming a grandparent for the first time are highly influential. A classic study conducted several decades ago by Bernice Neugarten and Karol Weinstein (1964) identified a group of *formal* grandparents over the age of 65 who provided special outings and special favours at birthdays and Christmas coupled with a careful avoidance of intrusion into their married children's affairs, an unwillingness to offer 'grandmotherly advice' and a reluctance to undertake any significant day-to-day care of their grandchildren. Younger grandparents often either avoided the role altogether (*distant figures*) or were *fun-seekers* who, as the name implies, viewed grandparenting as a second chance to enjoy the pleasures of playful companionship with a young child. They were more closely and emotionally involved with their grandchildren than any other group in the study. Their style of interaction tended

BOX 15.6 **Lessons from culture**
Grandparenting in Fiji

Many grandparents value the opportunity to become involved in the lives of their grandchildren and to offer advice (Peterson, 1999). Yet in cultures or eras in history where social change is rapid, the grandparent's efforts to give advice are apt to be greeted with derision rather than respect. This description of a family patriarch in Fiji shows a mixture of two distinct cultural patterns (Stewart, 1982, p. 253).

Pulling and tugging and burying my face in my mother's skirt, I cried in fear at the sight of the huge man as he squeezed his way out of the taxi. His grey hair was neatly kept and trimmed almost to his scalp. He wore a black linen *sulu* bound to his waist by a *magimagi* string. He was about six feet four inches tall, weighed about sixteen stone and had a shoulder span of about three feet.

The man was Sakaraia Sivo, my great-grandfather, who had just arrived all the way from Lakeba ...

The fear that I had of him lessened as the days went by, and a sense of attachment began to build up. In the evenings my brothers and sisters and I would sit around his chair or bed and listen to his interesting stories. At times he would sing Tongan psalms and we would make fun of him trying to make up the words. This would usually end up in brief friendly arguments, where we would give in when he started pinching our behinds.

These arguments were nothing in comparison to how he would criticise us, especially my sister, about our behaviour, manners, the clothes we wore and how we went about using our allowances. I can still remember the evening when, returning from our shopping, my brother and I proudly displayed our purchases to the rest of the family. My brother had bought himself a cricket bat, while I had bought a tennis racquet. After bitterly criticising us on our reckless misuse of the money, he said that a twelve-by-one board would do just as well for a racquet and a coconut stem shaped like an oar for a cricket bat. We all laughed at his idea, but his expression remained stony.

to be informal, with minimal assertion of authority, and they frequently remarked on how much enjoyment both generations gained from their involvement together.

Other less common styles included grandparents who were *parent surrogates* rearing their grandchildren full-time in cases of parental absence due to death, travel or divorce, and *reservoirs-of-wisdom*, or authoritative patriarchal figures (see Box 15.6) who saw the special duty of the grandparent to be the maintenance of familial and historical tradition. Their main activities with their grandchildren

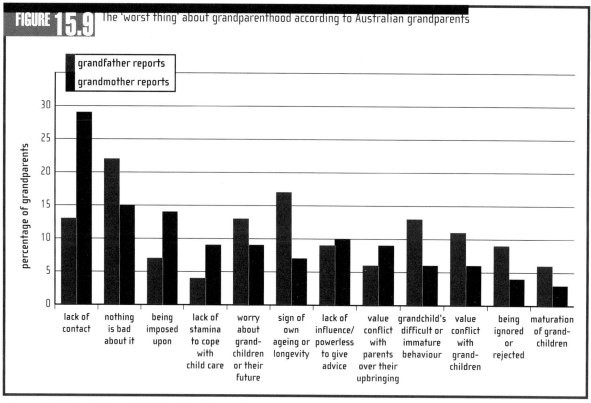

Source: Adapted from Peterson (1999), p. 85, Table 3, by permission of Baywood Publishing Co.

involved reminiscence and the imparting of their own special wisdom, skills, memories and resources to the youngest generation.

Grandparents and generativity

When grandparents become involved in their grandchildren's lives and exert a positive influence on their development, the grandparent may gain opportunities to develop the personality attribute of generativity (see pages 523–6). Karen Roberto and Johanna Stroes (1995) examined North American grandparents' influence on the values of their grandchildren as a function of grandparenting style. A number of dimensions of value orientation were assessed in late adolescents and young adults, including:

1. religious beliefs
2. political ideology
3. sexual mores
4. work ethic
5. moral values
6. personal identity.

Grandmothers played a significantly larger part than grandfathers in the value development of their grandsons and granddaughters, possibly because grandchildren spent more time with their grandmothers in childhood, adolescence and early adulthood.

Using interviews and naturalistic-observational procedures (see Chapter 2), Barbara Tinsley and Ross Parke (1987) studied a sample of first-time grandparents in the United States shortly after their first

grandchild was born. They found that high levels of contact between grandparents of both sexes and their infant grandchildren were the norm.

Furthermore, more frequent contact with grandparents was linked with accelerated psychological development in the infant. Using the Bayley Scales (a measure of infant 'IQ', or cognitive and sensorimotor maturity: see Chapter 4), Tinsley and Parke found that certain kinds of contact between grandparents and grandchildren were especially strong predictors of the infant's high scores. Grandfathers who were rated as highly playful when observed naturalistically tended to have developmentally precocious grandchildren. Among grandmothers, frequent verbalisation and demonstrative teaching was the best predictor of the infant's cognitive maturity.

These findings give a new meaning to cross-generational social contact. It would seem that the emotionally involved grandparent has a more important role to play than that of occasional babysitter or parent-substitute. Indeed, frequent intergenerational contact appears to provide not only enjoyment to the grandparents and a welcome respite for the parents but also a new source of input to stimulate the baby's cognitive and social development.

A second hypothesis tested by Tinsley and Parke was derived from a theory outlined in Chapter 5. This is the view that primary and secondary caregiving roles are complementary. According to this theory, the caregiver who is 'secondary' (i.e. the father in a traditional nuclear family, or the spouse with the longest hours of employment outside the home in a non-traditional household) has more freedom to engage in a playful, egalitarian style of interaction with infants and toddlers. If this applies also to grandparenting, both grandmothers and grandfathers (who are both secondary caregivers) should show more playful behaviour during face-to-face interaction than mothers or primary-caregiver fathers. On the other hand, if the adult's gender is the operative factor, grandfathers should be playful whereas grandmothers should engage in nurturant and serious patterns of interaction (such as teaching) to the same extent as the mother of the infant (see Chapter 5).

The results lent partial support to each of these hypotheses. Grandfathers were found to do less caregiving (checking on the infant or changing nappies) and less serious teaching than grandmothers. But grandparents of both sexes were highly affectionate and playful with their grandchildren, suggesting that the playful role is an important feature of grandparenting. Fathers played more vigorous physical games with their infants than either grandfathers or grandmothers, possibly because of their greater strength and endurance at their younger age.

In another study of three-generation North American families, the teaching strategies used by grandmothers were found to differ systematically from those used by mothers, supporting the stereotype of the indulgent grandmother who makes the parents' lives more difficult by 'spoiling' her grandchildren (Blackwelder & Passman, 1986). This study used a laboratory-experimental procedure (see Chapter 2). The measure of parental behaviour consisted of a teaching task with mothers and grandmothers alternating as the teachers. They had a choice of whether to reward, punish or ignore each correct or incorrect response the youngster made. They could also control the intensity of whatever rewards and punishments they chose to administer. Unbeknown to the 'teacher', the child's performance was rigged by the experimenter so that errors increased steadily over the teaching session.

The results showed that, as the accuracy of the child's responses dropped from 80 per cent to less than 20 per cent, the typical mother steadily increased the intensity of her punishments for error, while still continuing to reward the child's occasional successes. The typical grandmother, on the other hand, stopped punishing errors and concentrated only on rewarding accurate responses once the child's success rate fell below half correct. Grandmothers were also less punitive and more forgiving than mothers throughout the experiment, as well as more generous in the actual amount of reward they delivered to their grandchildren.

However, important individual differences among grandmothers were also found. Those grandmothers who regularly assumed primary caregiving responsibility for their grandchildren as babysitters when the parents worked tended to behave more like mothers. Thus it seemed that the relatively indulgent style adopted by the typical grandmother was more a byproduct of her freedom from parental responsibility than of any intrinsic difference between parenting and grandparenting relationships *per se*. Overall, it would appear that grandparenthood means many different things to mature adults.

The significance of the role in contemporary Australian and New Zealand society has been shaped by a number of recent social changes, including the geographical mobility of young adults and their tendency to have small, closely spaced families (see Chapters 13 and 14), as well as the increased prevalence of divorce and remarriage in both the grandparental and the parental generations, leading to blended families of step-grandparents and step-grandchildren. Although the lack of any single recipe for how to be a 'good' grandparent may be disconcerting, recognition of the diversity of their options should help modern-day grandparents to work out their own personally satisfying ways of becoming involved in the lives of their young descendents.

The social changes that have extended life expectancy (see Chapter 18) have also begun to alter the position of grandparenthood in the life cycle. As Nina Nahemow (1984) explained:

Grandparenthood has become a middle-aged phenomenon ... That is, grandparents are no longer the oldest generation. Indeed, since grand-

Grandfathers, as well as grandmothers, enjoy teaching new skills to the grandchildren while engaging with them in play and leisure activities.

parenthood is occurring earlier in the family life cycle and lasting longer, the meaning of the role itself is in flux. There are more surviving grandparents per child today, and grandchildren interact with their grandparents into adulthood, which necessitates redefinition of the role. Grandparents are juggling their own time and energy between their grandchildren on the one hand and their own aged parents on the other. (pp. 274–5)

The transition to retirement

The final turning point in the mature adult's transition into old age is likely to be retirement from paid employment. After finishing his last day at work and leaving an office career behind him, the writer Charles Lamb felt like a prisoner being released from the dungeons of the Bastille prison. But fellow author Ernest Hemingway called retirement 'the most repugnant word in the language'. The rest of this chapter examines recent data on the psychological underpinnings of the retirement transition.

When to retire?

In the United States, as in some other countries today, the mandate for a fixed retirement age has been abolished and the question of whether such a policy should be extended to Australia and New Zealand is the subject of popular debate. There are arguments in favour of a universally agreed retirement age at 65. Workers who have performed the same job for four or five decades may well have grown bored and be ready for change. The cumulative experience of having set their alarm for the same hour every weekday, taken the same route to work and had coffee at the same time with the same collection of co-workers can similarly motivate a desire for change. Many workers feel they have earned the right to enjoy a period of leisure after spending a lifetime in paid employment. When retirement is mandatory, their enjoyment is not blighted by any feelings of guilt that a reprieve from work might otherwise inspire in a strong believer in the Protestant work ethic. A legal mandate to retire by a certain age likewise obviates the need for a medical or executive decision about each individual's fitness to continue at work. Finally, the knowledge that retirement must occur by a certain age helps people plan more effectively for retired living, while also helping the organisation to plan and phase in new recruits to take over from veteran employees.

On the other hand, the policy of demanding that a worker depart from the workforce purely on the grounds of chronological age is open to challenge as an inequitable and discriminatory practice. In fact, when people are required to retire as soon as they reach a certain age, without any regard for their individual capacities or characteristics as a person, the charge of *ageism* (see Chapter 1) can be seen to apply. The issue is clearly complex.

Workers who have performed the same physically demanding job for several decades may be eager to retire, if for no other reason than to have a rest and a break from the routine.

In an ambitious cross-national survey, Bernadette Hayes and Audrey Van den Heuvel (1994) compared beliefs about mandatory retirement in Australia, Germany, Britain and the United States. Sharp differences in attitude emerged between countries. British men and women were the most accepting of a national standard prescribing a mandatory retirement age, while the American citizens were the most strongly opposed to the notion that a person should have to retire at a certain age, believing the issue to be a personal decision in which the law had no right to intervene.

Australians fell mid-way between these two extremes. Approximately one in three Australians agreed with a majority of Britons that workers should be compelled to leave their jobs at age 65, but only 18 per cent of Americans felt this way. There were also strong national differences in levels of support for government intervention in labour force practices, and these differences mirrored each culture's level of opposition to mandatory retirement. Within Australia, higher levels of education and self-ratings as middle class rather than working class were found to be significant predictors of opposition to the government's setting a mandatory age for retirement.

Another consequence of the questioning of whether retirement at age 65 is a social or psychological necessity has been increasing popular support for the possibility of early retirement. This trend has grown in recent years in Australia, New Zealand and other industrialised nations boasting high standards of living, effective superannuation policies and incentive schemes in many organisations to reward early retirement. Figure 15.10 shows the working versus retired status of Australian men and women. A substantial number had opted to move out of the paid workforce (ABS, 2002). The magical age of 65 no longer seems absolute, with many men and women opting, instead, for early retirement.

Preparing for retirement

Long before they reach the age of 65 or 70, and well before the day when they are given a gold watch or a final handshake on departure from the workplace, most employed adults begin to consider retirement seriously. Opportunities for early retirement make such forward planning advisable. But even workers who hope to remain employed for as long as possible are apt to spend time imagining, either with dread or eager anticipation, what their lifestyles will be like once they have retired and no longer have a job to go to.

One of the first evaluation studies of formal retirement programs showed beneficial effects (Thompson, 1958) and recent research confirms this conclusion (Hayslip, 1993). Workers who attend classes or seminars, plan ahead, read books and seek advice from others before retiring are found to adjust better to retirement than unprepared retirees. In particular, planners display more realistic expectations about retired life, better financial management, more

effective and satisfying uses of their leisure time and greater overall satisfaction with retirement than older men and women from the same organisations who opt out of any form of retirement planning.

Findings like these have motivated the introduction of a wide range of 'retirement-education' programs into businesses, government departments and private industries in Australia, New Zealand and the United States (Hayslip, 1993). The advice given ranges from financial management and investment seminars, to information on over-50s housing and health arrangements, to training in new recreational skills and further education so as to give adults new challenges to fill their new expanses of free time. The repercussions that retirement can have on marriage may also be discussed in planning seminars. These include the benefits of being able to spend more time with one's spouse and to share housework, shopping, grandchild babysitting and networks of friends. But there is also a risk of friction through getting in each other's way or curtailing the desire for privacy and independence. Finally, retirement planning normally includes a consideration of the worker's future social status and opportunities for achieving respect and influence within the community. The tenor of the advice given may range from Alex Comfort's blunt message that 'Retirement is another name for dismissal and unemployment. It must be prepared for exactly as you would prepare for dismissal and unemployment' (1977, p. 29) to Murray Hoyt's (1974) rosy picture of retirement as 'the best years yet'.

Individuals who have received this kind of retirement counselling in the form of classes or lectures sponsored by their companies have generally benefited from the experience. But exposure to news media and casual personal contacts with retired friends may be equally effective, if not more so. Of course, it is also hard to tell whether the personalities and positive attitudes of individuals who elect to prepare for retirement would have made the transition easier for them anyway, irrespective of any specific benefits of the type of planning they chose to undertake (Hayslip, 1993).

In addition to concrete plans and formal counselling, a worker's preparation for retirement takes account of a lifetime of work experience and encompasses skills developed for coping with stress and changes during previous phases in the life cycle. All life's earlier transitions, from marriage and career entry through to the empty nest, involve a similarly radical reorganisation of lifestyle and one's inner patterns of thinking and feeling. Thus retiring workers are in a position to profit from past experience. Good use can continue to be made of adjustment strategies that facilitated a smooth passage through these earlier changes in life (see Chapters 13 and 14). Lessons learned from previous mistakes can likewise be brought to bear. Even the knowledge of having 'survived' earlier, more drastic life changes can

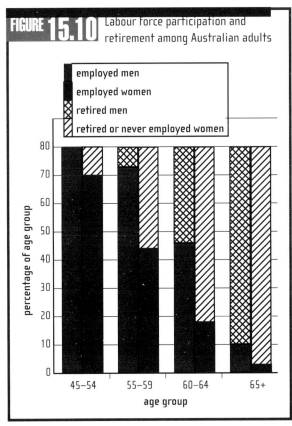

FIGURE 15.10 Labour force participation and retirement among Australian adults

- employed men
- employed women
- retired men
- retired or never employed women

percentage of age group

age group: 45–54, 55–59, 60–64, 65+

Source: Based on data from ABS (2002).

provide consolation and confidence to help cope with retirement. Furthermore, the unique set of goals, values and leisure interests which people evolve for themselves over their lifetime will help to specify the style of retirement that will suit them best. As Robert Atchley (1976) noted: 'Much of what leads up to an individual's retirement is haphazard and the result of his own unique biography' (p. 32).

It is important to plan realistically for retirement and to beware of the myths about the state that abound without any sound basis in fact. Box 15.7 illustrates some of these myths.

The process of retiring

Robert Atchley (1976) divided the retirement process into the series of steps shown in Figure 15.11. The honeymoon phase is a euphoric period when retirees indulge in a busy round of activities, which may include golf, sewing, card-playing, hunting and fishing, parties, theatre or even world travel – in short, they strive to make up for all the things they didn't have time for while working. This phase may

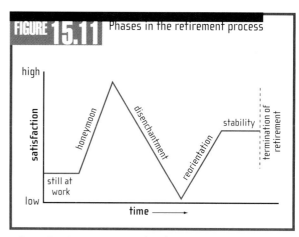

FIGURE 15.11 Phases in the retirement process

Source: Based on data in Atchley (1976).

be quite brief or it may last for many years. Some retirees never have a chance to experience it due to health, financial or family constraints. A disenchantment phase was seen by Atchley as a probable, though not inevitable, sequel to the retirement honeymoon. It resembles the marital disenchantment of middle age (see Chapter 14). To the extent that the preretirement fantasies lived out during the honeymoon period were empty, unrealistic or out of character for the individual, an emotional 'letdown' is apt to accompany the return to the routines of everyday life. Depression and uncertainty may be intensified if retirees lack options, income or social contact, or if the skills they need for planning their own future and making their own decisions are underdeveloped.

The successful weathering of disenchantment leads to a reorientation phase in which people explore the options offered by retired life in a systematic fashion. Rather than being motivated primarily by hedonism, as in the honeymoon phase, retirees now seek a lifestyle they will be able to feel comfortable with on a long-term basis. It must offer interest and challenge and allow for the utilisation of their talents and skills to serve goals that have meaning for them. If reorientation is accomplished, it is followed by a stability phase in which the chosen retirement role is performed smoothly and confidently. Satisfaction consequently returns to a high level. For some individuals, this period of stable retired living is followed by a protracted termination phase, when retirement is traded either for a return to full-time employment or for a disabled role as a patient in a hospital or nursing home.

To test the empirical validity of the stages proposed by Atchley, David Ekerdt, Raymond Bosse and Sue Levkoff (1985) contacted a cross-sectional sample of 293 retired men in the United States who typified the American retired population in income, marital status, type of housing and range of jobs they had occupied when working. The men had been out of work for between one month and three years at the time of the interviews. In an effort to capture the rapid patterns of change postulated by Atchley,

Retirement mythology

BOX 15.7

Myth 1: Retirement is a health hazard.

Fact: The notion that retirement causes the ex-worker to fall ill or drop dead is based on a false inference from cross-sectional data. For an explanation see the text.

Myth 2: Retirement is financially impossible.

Fact: Though their incomes may drop by up to about 50 per cent after retirement, most retirees in Australia (Donovan, 1978) and the United States (Palmore et al., 1984) report still having enough to live on. Where economic difficulties do arise, they are likely to be a continuation of problems encountered before retirement.

Myth 3: Women adjust better to retirement than men.

Fact: Contrary to popular belief, married women are often the ones hardest hit by the shock of retirement. While problems vary with previous occupation, marital status and career orientation while working, there is presently no evidence to support the view that the average working woman is either any happier to give up work or any freer of retirement problems than the average man. For a more detailed discussion, see the text.

the researchers divided the men into the following five subcategories:

1. retired less than 6 months
2. retired between 6 and 12 months
3. retired 13 to 18 months
4. retired 19 months to 2 years
5. retired 2 to 3 years.

They then compared the groups across a wide array of standardised measures of psychological well-being, life satisfaction, mood quality and activity patterns.

The results lent some support to the stages illustrated in Figure 15.9. Ekerdt and his colleagues found that men who had been retired for less than six months generally felt more positive about retirement, and enjoyed greater overall optimism and life satisfaction than their counterparts who had been out of work for longer periods. This was consistent with Atchley's postulated 'honeymoon'. Furthermore, those who had been retired for between 13 and 18 months stood out from all other groups for their generally bleak moods, lower levels of participation in physical or recreational activities and poor psychological adjustment. This supported Atchley's suggestion that a period of disenchantment with retirement normally arises during the second year out of work. Fortunately for the long-term success of the retired lifestyle, the scores earned on measures of mood, life satisfaction and activity by the group that had been out of work for two to three years were all significantly higher than those earned by the 13- to 18-month group. The researchers concluded that letdown, or disenchantment, was only a temporary problem for the average retired man.

While supportive of Atchley's theory, this study's conclusions suffer the limitations of cross-sectional data. It is possible, for example, that rather than recovering from a period of post-retirement depression and adjusting to the lifestyle, workers who had found themselves disenchanted during the second year after retiring had opted to rejoin the workforce at that point. If so, they would not have been included in the cross-sectional sample of individuals two or more years past retirement. Thus the evident recovery from letdown in the Ekerdt, Bosse and Levkoff study could have been an artifact of sample selection rather than a genuine age change.

A number of longitudinal studies of adjustment to retired life have also been conducted in the United States (Streib & Schneider, 1972; Ward, 1984). In one of these, Gordon Streib and Clement Schneider (1972) maintained contact with a group of 1486 men and 483 women, representing a wide variety of occupations, social classes and geographical locales throughout the United States, from the time when they were still employed until several years after retirement. In partial confirmation of Atchley's theory, the proportion of this group who agreed that 'retirement is good for a person' increased substantially at each successive assessment period after the event. Thus, though no evidence of a drop from honeymoon-like euphoria to disenchantment appeared, the steady rise in life satisfaction which these researchers observed is consistent with the theory that retired people reorient themselves gradually over time to achieve progressive stabilisation.

Many workers are unnecessarily frightened of retirement because of its supposedly adverse influence on health and longevity (see Box 15.7). Folklore certainly supports the idea that job deprivation can induce sudden death. According to Robert Atchley, almost everyone knows of someone who dropped dead within days, weeks or months of his or her retirement from work. Early cross-sectional data reinforced the myth by showing the average retired worker's health to be poorer than that of employed workers of the same age and social class. However, the limitations of cross-sectional data were not considered in reaching this conclusion (see Chapter 2). In fact, one of the major reasons why workers of any age elect to retire from their jobs is precisely because their health is poor. In some cases, a terminal condition has already been diagnosed. Therefore, any cross-sectional sample of retired people will include a greater proportion who are in ill health, or near death, than a corresponding sample of workers who are still in the labour force at the same age. Longitudinal evidence is needed to tease apart whether poor health causes workers to retire, or vice versa. Collectively, present longitudinal results in which the same individuals are studied before and after they retire reveal no clear evidence of a deterioration in health as a function of retirement *per se*. The health of a majority of unskilled workers in one longitudinal study actually improved significantly during the first six months after they retired (Streib & Schneider, 1972).

Erdman Palmore, Gerda Fillenbaum and Linda George (1984) examined six longitudinal data sets to explore the consequences of retirement for health, income and social activity. They concluded that little or no change in health could be attributed to retirement. Income did decline, but not normally to the point of inhibiting social activity or life satisfaction. Retirement by itself also had few effects on social activity. But in the few cases where declines in health or social contact coincided with departure from the workforce, retirees were apt to show poorer life satisfaction and mental health than other ex-workers of the same age. Thus, even though the myth (see Box 15.7) that retirement *per se* damages health and survival is not supported by longitudinal data, the data do suggest that the social quality and stimulation potential of the ex-worker's post-retirement milieu is essential to health, well-being and life satisfaction.

Adjusting to retired life

Retirement, as a life event, demands at least as much cognitive, emotional and social readjustment as ealier life transitions, such as entry into marriage, a career and parenthood. But the retired worker has certain assets in this process that the young adult typically has not yet developed. These include the skills acquired while coping with major transitions earlier in life, and the sense of identity as a person and a worker that adults gain over many years on the job. Nevertheless, the transition can still be stressful. In modern Western cultures where youth, productivity and managerial leadership are highly valued, a move out of the paid workforce can bring a sense of diminished social and personal worth. These negative consequences may affect men and women differently, and may depend as much on the retired worker's personality and psychological maturity as on the outward shape of his or her life before and after retirement.

An Australian comparison of the attitudes of a group of middle-aged employed men and women from a range of professional, white-collar and blue-collar jobs (Burns & Goodnow, 1985) revealed that 'career-oriented' women (who worked because of interest in their job rather than merely in order to boost the family income) were more anxious at the thought of retirement than similarly career-oriented Australian working men in the same occupations. The women were also more likely than their male peers to mention other rewards from work besides income ('satisfaction', 'independence', 'a sense of accomplishing something'). When compared with non-working women of similar economic backgrounds, the Australian career wives scored higher in overall life satisfaction. Presumably these women would find it hard to leave jobs that were bringing them so much gratification. However, when John McCallum (1984) surveyed a group of over 1000 elderly men and women in Sydney, he found that almost identical proportions of males (67 per cent) and females (68 per cent) reported having adjusted completely satisfactorily to the transition, as Figure 15.12 shows.

Kaaren Hanson and Seymour Wapner (1994) studied a group of 94 recently retired men and

With retirement, women (and to a lesser extent men) can gain a new sense of personal identity, for example as a gardener.

women in the United States and found that their personal identity (sense of self) had changed as a result of retirement. In fact, more than half the women felt they gained a new sense of self as a result of retirement, while only one in four men did. But, while women who experienced retirement as a time to wind down and seek a disengaged style of living (see Chapter 17) were more likely than men with the same attitude to feel disgruntled with retirement, more women than men correspondingly reported a positive attitude to old age. The researchers concluded:

> In general women appear to be more positively influenced by retirement than men ... The overwhelming numbers of women who experience the transition to retirement as a 'continuation' may be ... because women tend to give relatively greater importance to informal roles such as 'friend' [than men. Thus], when they retire and lose the formal role of 'worker', continuity in their life remains.

As the women in this sample had also undertaken a greater amount of formal and informal preretirement planning than their male peers, their favourable adjustment outcomes may have been partly due to the beneficial effects of planning noted earlier in this chapter.

Sharon Winocur, Linda Rosenman and Jeni Warburton (1994) studied the retirement decisions of employed Australian women in Brisbane, Queensland, and found that women in professional occupations tended to retire later than women in manual, skilled and semi-skilled careers or in sales. They

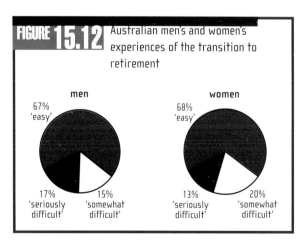

FIGURE **15.12** Australian men's and women's experiences of the transition to retirement

men

67% 'easy'

17% 'seriously difficult'

15% 'somewhat difficult'

women

68% 'easy'

13% 'seriously difficult'

20% 'somewhat difficult'

Source: Based on data from McCallum (1984), p. 15.

found that professional women had more choice about when they could retire and were in jobs that took less of a physical toll so that retirement was not a physical necessity. In addition, many of the women in non-professional careers, especially when they came from non-English-speaking backgrounds, earned so little at work that they were financially better off on the retirement pension.

Leisure activities in retirement

As they seek meaningful new activities to replace those lost with the job, older adults are forced to evaluate their goals, values and interests. Initially, such intensive stocktaking may prove painful to people who are faced for the first time with the realisation that many of the ambitions with which they began their careers have remained unfulfilled. But, even in this case, retirement may offer an exciting and promising chance to make amends for such short-comings. Older workers who elect to stay on and do the same job for another decade are not likely to have the same freedom or incentive for this evaluation and redirection. According to Atchley (1976), the retired worker's first task is to assess what their new goals are and then to find leisure activities which may permit their fulfilment. The process of matching goals with recreational pursuits may be assisted by the parallels between vocational and avocational satisfactions that were drawn in Chapter 14. In fact, Atchley found that when retired workers listed their goals and values, most could be grouped into two main categories: *personal* and *material*. The former

group included the desire for personal qualities such as honesty, kindness, creativity and self-control, as well as aims that involve personal relationships – such as being a good father, husband, neighbour or grandparent. Material goals involved the desire for money, prestige and promotion, or for a comfortable home or a motor boat.

Materialistic goals are the hardest to satisfy outside work, because they demand a certain level of income and also because they are the most transitory. 'After material goals are achieved,' wrote Atchley, 'they seem to turn to ashes in the mouth of the achiever' (p. 20). Thus, when a worker's preretirement self-examination reveals a predominance of material goals, they might be well advised to remain employed or else seek a lucrative retirement hobby. Personal goals, on the other hand, depend less on participation in the workforce, since they may be achieved in any situation. Individuals who place personal goals high in their value hierarchies not only have less internal reorganisation to do in order to take on the retirement role gracefully, but may even find it easier to maintain personal development and goal attainment by means of leisure activity during the retirement years than they did while working. Leisure can be shared with intimate family members and friends, enabling the satisfaction of goals involving these relationships. The freedom of choice provided by leisure likewise enables the efficient selection of activities which optimally fulfil personal aims and values.

Chapter summary

The 50s is an exciting decade in lifespan psychological development. Biological and personality changes inside the person are likely to coincide with equally radical changes to the outward shape of men's and women's lives after turning 50. According to stage theories of adult cognition, the changing tasks and responsibilities of adult life give rise to qualitatively new modes of reasoning. Dialectical thinking and the ability to plan may develop correspondingly.

Fowler's stage theory of spiritual thinking depicts the adult development of faith as a sequence of six distinct stages. For Fowler, faith is the knowledge connecting the individual with the boundaries, peaks and depths of human experience.

But, as in Kohlberg's theory of adult moral development (see Chapter 11), progress through all the stages of faith or adult cognition is not necessarily automatic or universal, even in late adulthood. Experience and personality appear to exert stronger pressure for adult developmental change than simple maturation from one birthday to the next.

Creativity, or the expression of talent and originality through notable achievement, may develop significantly during middle and old age. Among men who persist in the same career from early adulthood to retirement, the peak of creative productivity typically arises on the border between early and middle adulthood (see Chapters 13 and 14).

The decade of the 50s heralds the onset of menopause in most women. Menopause terminates monthly periods and the natural capacity for biological reproduction, but rarely interferes with psychological well-being. For men the hormonal changes of middle age are gradual, but may lead eventually to a decrease in the frequency of intercourse or to a slower climb to the peak of sexual arousal.

The empty-nest phase, defined by the final departure of all adult offspring from their parents' home, is another turning point in family development which proves traumatic for some mature adults. During the period of launching, when the youngest child is about to move away, middle-aged women who lack interests and commitments other than parenthood are especially vulnerable to anxiety, stress and an impending sense of loss. But, by creating opportunities for a new style of marital intimacy and, eventually, grandparenthood, the changes that follow the empty-nest transition can also have positive ramifications.

Grandparents today have adopted diverse styles, ranging from the traditional family patriarch to a playful fun-seeking approach, and from being a parent substitute to distant non-involvement. Regardless of the mode of grandparenting adopted, most find the role enjoyable. Grandchildren gain developmental benefits from frequent intimate contact with grandparents during childhood, adolescence and early adulthood.

The final transition from middle age to old age is likely to come with the worker's retirement from paid employment. Successful adjustment to retired living is aided by favourable attitudes, advance planning, cultural background and the retiree's desire to pursue personal, as opposed to material, goals.

Career-oriented professional working women may miss their work more than retired men, but in contemporary society retirement is not directly to blame for adverse changes to health, finances or longevity for either sex.

Adults in their 50s who keep mentally alert through challenging creative and cognitive activities at work and leisure can count on intellectual development beyond the boundaries reached in adolescence or younger adulthood.

Intimacy with grandchildren is another possible developmental benefit of late adult life which, coupled with socially oriented or personal goals, can help to ensure optimal psychological development during retirement. Through effective social planning, society of the future has the scope to optimise educational provisions for, and social utilisation of, these psychological assets of middle age.

For further interest

Looking forward on the Internet

Use the Internet to visit the following websites. Examine them for further information and varied perspectives on issues raised in this chapter. Also search for other relevant websites for yourself, using keywords like 'maturity', 'late adulthood', 'empty nest', 'grandparenthood' and 'menopause' in your search engine.

In particular, for further ideas on retirement planning and adjustment to retired life, visit: **http://www.aarp.org** and **http://www.retirenet.com**. For a report on a longitudinal study of health in retirement, visit: **http://www.hrsonline.isr.umich.edu**.

For further ideas on menopause and women's health in late adulthood, visit: **http://www.menopause.org** and **http://www.nim.nih.gov/medlineplus/menopause.html** and **http://www.healthinsite.gov.au**.

For resources, ideas, activities and other items of interest in conjunction with this chapter, visit the Companion Website for this textbook at:
http://wps.pearsoned.com.au/peterson

Activity suggestion

Many banks and businesses provide free pamphlets and brochures that are aimed at retirement planning. You may also find ads for retirement communities and products in newspapers and glossy magazines. Compile a selection of these and examine the issues and advice they give. Compare the potential problems and concerns that these media suggest may arise during retirement within the research evidence described in this chapter.

Multimedia

For an interesting glimpse of some Australian adults' reactions to retirement, view the video *Hitting a Brick Wall* (Film Australia, 1983: 16 minutes, colour).

Milestones of development in adulthood

Domain of development

Physical	Sensory-perceptual	Cognitive	Personality	Social
Physical and athletic capacities instilling strength, speech and latency of reaction rise to a peak during the 20s and then slowly and gradually decline.	From the age of 40, adults typically require glasses for reading.	The consolidation of formal-operational thinking, begun in adolescence, typically continues through the early 20s. At the same time, moral reasoning ability may advance, in thoughtful young adults, to Kohlberg's higher stages.	During early adulthood, personality development centres around the tasks involved in the growth of an intimate couple relationship.	Adults develop socially in the context of intimate family relationships, including marriage and parenthood, as well as in the context of their life's work or vocational career.
From the 30s to the 50s, there are gradual losses in the elasticity of the skin and the colour and thickness of hair and by the end of the 50s, many men show signs of baldness and many women have partially, or completely, grey hair.	Hearing also diminishes with age, especially in men after the age of 55, and especially in adults who have been exposed to noise earlier in life at work, musical concerts or in noisy residential neighbourhoods.	The capacity to solve problems involving real-life events, uncertainty, compromises and responsibility for others increases in adult life as mature men and women gain practice in everyday cognition.	According to Erikson's theory, a crisis arises in the personality during the 20s over the dialectic between independence and relationship commitment, or intimacy versus isolation.	Theories of career development highlight regular progressions of change in career goals, attitudes, performance and satisfaction over working life from age 20 to age 65.
The hormonal changes of the menopause (women) and climacteric (men) can create mood swings and other mild symptoms during the early 50s, though culture plays a major role in whether or not negative symptoms are experienced.	The sense of smell declines very gradually with age. Again, changes are typically more pronounced in men than in women.	Stages in advance of formal operations may develop, according to some theorists, increasing the adult's skill in contextually valid thinking, dialectical thinking, creativity, problem-finding and heuristic cognitive expertise.	The adult who resolves the crisis successfully acquires a capacity for mature love that extends the personality and sets the stage for the middle-age crisis in Erikson's model.	Studies of the life course of marriage similarly reveal a predictable sequence of changes.
Women are no longer fertile after the change, while men's fertility declines but usually does not completely disappear. Risks of birth defects rise rapidly for parents of both sexes from the late 30s on.	**Neurobiological**	Philosophical, spiritual or religious issues become grist for the cognitive mill and the challenges at work or in leisure pursuits hone cognitive powers still further.	This crisis is between generativity (the production of achievements, creations and social influences that make a difference to future generations) and stagnation (a sense of having wasted one's life).	Many of these (intensity of love, satisfaction, commitment to marriage, and so on) describe a U-shaped curve, with intense positive feelings arising most often very early in marriage and again in late adulthood after grown children leave home and spouses retire from paid employment.
The internal physiological systems of the body and brain also change gradually, beginning in the late 30s. The blood vessels become less elastic, breathing capacity declines and blood pressure increases.	The brain's capacity to recover from accidental injury or illness also diminishes, though some plasticity to facilitate recovery does remain throughout adulthood.		The generativity crisis may include, but is not confined to, parenthood and may be bound up with career development issues arising at the time of a midlife crisis around age 45.	
	The brain continues to grow in adult life, with gains in myelinisation and synaptic connections.		Other theories of personality development in adult life highlight changes in sex roles, personal control, self-esteem and self-directedness.	

OLD AGE AND THE END OF THE LIFESPAN

PART 7

Contents

Overview

Charlotte Buhler (see Chapter 2) suggested that the story of the human lifespan was more interesting when approached from its end than its beginning. Though this book has followed psychological development in the conventional chronological direction, the narrative is certainly not finished yet. In the next two chapters we study the fascinating and somewhat mysterious period known as old age. Some see this phase in life as the peak of the climb, or a pinnacle of wisdom and personal integrity in which all earlier psychological developments culminate. The poet Cicero epitomised this view in his remark: 'Old age ... is of more value than all the pleasures of youth' (*De Senectute*, p. 245). But many modern adults fear old age, seeing it as anything but a pleasant stage in life. Fears may centre around presumed physical or cognitive declines or a belief that social losses and reduced self-worth are inevitable during old age.

The next two chapters weigh evidence on both sides of this dichotomy as we explore recent research into the various physiological, intellectual, social and personality changes that are apt to take place in people whose lifespan extends beyond the age of 65. Chapter 18 closes the book with an exploration of death, the final phase through which every developing human life must eventually pass.

OLD AGE: Physical, neurobiological, sensorimotor and cognitive development

CHAPTER 16

Old age is full of enjoyment, provided you know how to use it right.
Lucius Armaeus Seneca (4 BC–65 AD)
Youth longs, manhood strives, but age remembers.
Oliver Wendell Holmes (1809–94)

Contents

CHAPTER OVERVIEW

'Come grow old along with me!' wrote the poet Robert Browning. 'The best is yet to be, the last of life for which the first was made.' Unfortunately, it is unusual for contemporary adults to agree with Browning that old age is really the best segment of the life cycle. When researchers ask people to pinpoint the 'prime of life', the years after age 60 are rarely mentioned, even by people who are over this age themselves (Hori, 1994), and when Mark Byrd and Trudy Breuss (1992) asked New Zealanders aged 18 to 75 to name 'the worst time of life for a man or woman', the mid-60s was most often nominated. Many people have an image of the years from 60 or 65 onward as a time when health, the senses, the mind, body and energy deteriorate, when widowhood and loneliness set in and when society rejects and discriminates against the individual, so that the transition to old age is not a happy one for most adults. But are these adverse images and stereotypes accurate?

In this chapter we evaluate recent research evidence on how people grow old both biologically and psychologically. We look at the physical changes in health, fitness and physiological capacity that arise after age 60. We critically compare theories to explain the physiological ageing process and the individual differences that exist in rates of biological ageing. Cultural variations in attitudes to old age are explored, along with a close look at the ways in which the ill-founded myths and stereotypes about old age that prevail in many contemporary societies can limit older people's social and psychological opportunities and create setbacks and challenges that have nothing directly to do with biological ageing.

Clearly, the biological changes of old age do influence the process of psychological ageing. So do cultural attitudes to the elderly. But neither of these processes is synonymous with the ways men and women adjust psychologically to the transition into old age. As in all the earlier stages of life, older people's bodily and neuropsychological capacities, their state of health, and their age-related physical and sensory weaknesses and disabilities may influence their cognitive, emotional and social functioning, but only in conjunction with their style of living, their personality and the coping skills and expertise they have built up over decades of adult living.

Even when the old person's biological systems slow down, when sensory acuity and physiological reserves weaken and when chronic ailments develop, their level of life satisfaction is likely to remain high and their overall quality of life is not automatically undermined. Paul Baltes' (2002) S-O-C (selective optimisation with compensation: see Chapter 1) model of psychological ageing is examined again in this chapter. We learn how older adults can use psychology to outwit younger competitors in a variety of sports and mental games.

In an overview of late adult psychological functioning, we explore the predictable emotional, intellectual and personality developments that arise during the decades of the 60s, 70s, 80s and 90s as old people adjust to changes in their physiological and social situation. Some of these changes are genuinely developmental in the progressive psychological sense that aligns clearly with Browning's promised 'best' that life can be. In particular, we explore the adult's opportunities during the final decades of life to cultivate wisdom, self-understanding, elderhood, wise mentoring and advisorship and a sense of integrity in a life well lived.

BOX 16.1

A case in point
How does it feel to be 70 years old?

Louise's mother's contribution to the diary which her husband kept of their daughter's growing up was quite significant, but mainly behind the scenes. Here (having been pressed by her daughter to give an 'honest' and 'unrehearsed' answer to the question above) she speaks for herself.

Since I have reached the age of comparison (that is, I am able to compare my age with the rest of life's normal duration), it is one of the best ages to be. I am reminded of a remark of one of my old (young) sweethearts who said, 'The perfect state for man is to be engaged.' 'Why?' I asked. He replied, 'Because he has all the privileges of marriage without the responsibilities.' Of course, isn't that just like a man?

But for me being an old lady is the same sort of perfect state, because I have all the privileges of family life without the responsibilities. Not that there is anything wrong with responsibilities because I am always willing to assume them, but there is a certain freedom. You know you don't have to do such and such unless you want to.

After having had the responsibilities of a marriage and family for nearly forty years and enjoying every minute of it (or so it seems now), it is a great relief not to have them anymore. Because what my old boyfriend said about marriage goes doubly for a woman. Her responsibilities not only equal the man's if she has a job as I did, but they exceed his, because society expects her to keep a neat house, cook three meals a day, wash clothes, wash dishes, make beds, take care of the children and scrub the floors as well. It is true, most men I have known are willing to help, but as for responsibility, they feel it ends when they get home from work, while a woman's usually continues.

Perhaps my considering old age to be the perfect state of existence is because I have everything so good ... a wonderful daughter, married to a wonderful man, with a wonderful granddaughter, my health, my freedom, enough money, and millions of interesting things to do. I have enjoyed all the other periods of my existence, but they have been very different from this one. The main thing that distinguishes this one for me is the sense of freedom. It is nice to have the ability to look back on all the past ages with pleasure because the trials and tribulations don't last. For example, I can read my old love letters and remember what it was like to love and be loved by a man, but none of the pangs of that love remains. Likewise I can remember all the joys of being a mother, but all the problems escape me now. My having to quit school at the age of sixteen and settle down to a humdrum job seemed a major catastrophe at the time. I loved going to high school. However, when I look back on this period now, I can only remember how lucky I was that this happened to me. Because my getting a job just when I did enabled me to have an income all during the depression when millions of people were on the breadlines and without adequate clothing and shelter, which was very tough in northern climates.

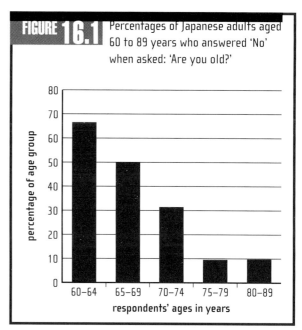

Source: Based on data in Hori (1994).

What age is old age?

Perhaps understandably in light of the fact that old age is not always greeted optimistically, there is some disagreement in people's minds, including the elderly themselves, about what the chronological age boundary between middle and old age actually is, and what criteria besides the years one has been alive should be used to define a person as 'old'.

In Japan, Shigeo Hori (1994) asked a group of 400 adults over the age of 60: 'Do you think you are an old man/woman?' Only one-third of the group aged 60 to 64 years answered 'Yes' to this question, and even at age 70 to 74 about one-third continued to say 'No!' and to refer to themselves as middle-aged. Figure 16.1 shows these findings. Furthermore, the vast majority of Japanese adults in their 60s reported feeling uncomfortable when someone referred to them as old, and even in the late 70s and 80s sizeable proportions (35 per cent and 26 per cent) continued to do so. For these Japanese men and women, old age was defined not so much by their age in years as by a change in life situation that undermined their capacity to function as they had during younger adulthood. Figure 16.2 shows the events the very elderly Japanese typically named when asked what had finally made them feel old.

As well as in popular culture, there is disagreement in the scientific literature about what chronological age period the phrase 'old age' demarcates. As Paul Baltes (2002) explained:

Whereas it is obvious that an individual must have lived 100 years in order to be called a centenarian,

there is little consensus about the characteristics of old age or the chronological age associated with its average onset ... Depending on country, culture, birth cohort and idiosyncratic factors, the period of old age could extend over 20 to 40 years of an individual's life (e.g. age 60 to 100+) (p. 10 843).

Baltes suggested the following ways of defining old age independently of one's age in years:

1. *Sociological*: retired from paid employment
2. *Biological*: onset of age-linked frailty and physical disability
3. *Longevity/Demographic*: last 10 years of life before natural death
4. *Cognitive*: onset of cognitive decline or first symptoms of Alzheimer's disease or senile dementia
5. *Institutional*: after the transition into sheltered living in a retirement village or nursing home.

The young-old versus the old-old

An alternative way of conceptualising old age is to subdivide into separate phases the four or more decades of later life that an adult with optimal longevity can enjoy, as illustrated in Table 16.1. These categorisations are useful for defining differences in expected psychological characteristics of different groups of elderly men and women. Yet the term 'old age' has a perjorative social significance which new labels can only partially overcome.

Ageism and fear of ageing

Prejudice against the elderly is widespread in contemporary society and can be elicited by very subtle cues.

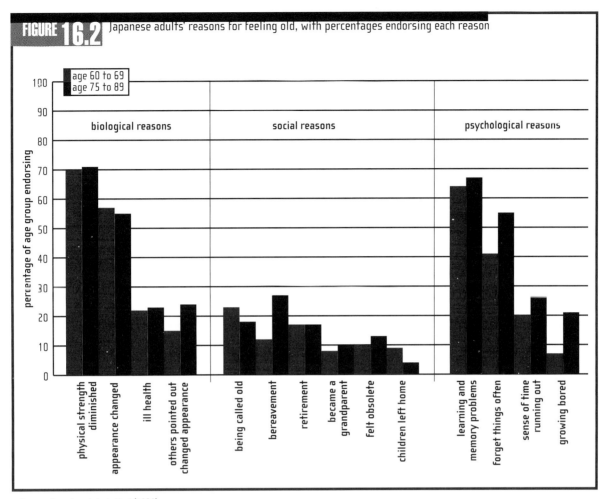

FIGURE 16.2 Japanese adults' reasons for feeling old, with percentages endorsing each reason

age 60 to 69
age 75 to 89

biological reasons | social reasons | psychological reasons

Source: Based on data in Hori (1994).

TABLE 16.1 Substages of old age according to various theorists

	Hippocrates	Neugarten (1974)	Baltes (2002)
Age 60 to 69	Green old age	Young-old	Third Age
Age 70 to 79	True old age	Mid-old	Third Age until 50% of birth cohort has died, then Fourth Age
Age 80 to 89	Ultimate old age	Old-old	Fourth Age
Age 90 to 100	Caducity	Old-old	Fourth Age

In a study to test the influence of speech manner on listeners' attitudes to speakers and their discourse, Howard Giles and Nikolas Coupland (1991) presented groups of British, New Zealand and United States adults with transcripts of a man talking about his car. The man's manner of speaking (i.e. rate of speech, tone of voice, accent and so on) and what he said were identical in two experimental conditions. The only difference was that in one situation he was described as a young adult in his early 30s, while in the other he was said to be an elderly man in his early 60s. Despite their identical utterances, the older speaker was perceived as more 'egocentric', 'stupid', 'confused' and 'vague' than the younger speaker. In addition, the 62-year-old man was described as 'losing his grip', 'living in the past' and 'weak'.

In a further study where the interview included mention of a car crash with no personal injury involved, even greater ageist stereotyping against the elderly emerged. Not only were older speakers described in more negative terms than younger speakers, but what they said was dismissed as irrelevant and not worth paying attention to. Thus, on a recognition test two days later, the listeners who had heard the older speaker recalled significantly less about the car accident than those who had listened to

There is a large difference in physical health, life activity and capacity between young-old and old-old adults.

a younger man saying exactly the same thing in exactly the same way.

Giles and Coupland observed that many of the same forms of subtle prejudice and patronising dismissal were levelled against older adults in New Zealand as in the UK. But there was an interesting difference between the two cultures. In New Zealand, ageism appears to come into play at a surprisingly early age. In contrast to British adults, who mostly displayed ageist attitudes against targets who were over the age of 60, in New Zealand 'a decrement perception of growing older is well grounded for middle-age targets, and increases drastically with a target of around 31 years of age' (Giles & Coupland, 1991, p. 101).

In most English-speaking countries, including New Zealand and the UK, items from popular culture like birthday card slogans, songs and jokes (see Box 17.5) equate growing older with frailty, ugliness and unhappiness. Giles and Coupland suggested that the essentially well-meaning efforts of our peers to advise us to be careful of our health and to cut down on strenuous physical activities once we reach 30 or

Contrary to widespread stereotypes, adulthood after age 60 has many pleasures and developmental opportunities in store.

40 can also have adverse repercussions. With his colleagues Nikolas and Justine Coupland, Howard Giles (1991) argued that:

> The admixture of fear, reticence and regret with which, facetiously or not, many middle-aged adults appear to represent their own ageing undoubtedly forms part of the interactional means by which negative images of ageing and the elderly are reproduced. (pp. 129–30)

In Australia, Valerie Braithwaite (1990) drew a distinction between negative impressions of old people and negative beliefs about ageing as a process. Using a sample of first-year university students as subjects, she measured stereotypes about old age using a questionnaire with items like 'I feel uncomfortable when I have to talk with an old person: true or false?' and beliefs about ageing with responses to statements like 'In my old age I will be as enthusiastic about life as I am now: true or false?' She found that the respondents' age, gender and frequency of contact with the elderly all predicted their ideas about both the ageing process and old people as individuals. Students who had frequent contact with their grandparents and elderly friends had more positive attitudes than students who rarely or never mixed socially with older adults. Mature-aged students also had more positive attitudes overall than students who had just completed high school, and women's attitudes were generally more favourable than men's.

If ageist attitudes are the basis for discriminatory treatment of older Australian citizens, Braithwaite reasoned that students' responses to these attitude measures should predict their behaviour in an experimental discrimination task. The design of the task was simple. Students read a description which they were told was the transcript of a female applicant's job interview for a tutorship in psychology. For some groups the applicant was said to be age 27 while for others her age was 59. The woman's qualifications and responses to the interview questions were otherwise identical.

Ageism and bigotry against older people were distressingly evident in this Australian sample. Many more students wanted the 27-year-old woman rather than the 59-year-old to be their tutor. The younger applicant was also rated as more likely to be successful at interview than the older woman. However, the students who had the most negative attitudes to ageing on the questionnaire and old people in general were not necessarily the ones most likely to reject the older tutor when discriminatory behaviour was measured in this more personalised way. Australian university students' open-ended descriptions of old people reflect similarly bleak expectations of what this phase in the life cycle is likely to hold in store. They are apt to see the elderly as 'weak', 'sick', 'dull', 'rigid', 'unhappy', 'unproductive', 'dogmatic', 'narrow-minded', 'selfish' and 'ugly' (Braithwaite, 1990). Ageist stereotypes about the elderly emerge at quite a young age. Figure 16.3 illustrates Australian children's generally pessimistic impressions of old age. From the age of seven, three out of four Melbourne young people used derogatory terms like 'sick', 'lonely', 'senile', 'decayed', 'dying', 'irritable' and 'broken bones' to portray the elderly (Goldman & Goldman, 1982).

Old people are also devalued when indirect measures of attitude are used. Donald Schwab and Herbert Heneman (1978) found that personnel specialists rated work they thought had been done by a secretary of 24 as superior to identical work by a secretary aged 61. Employers in another study were more impressed by the dossiers of 30-year-old job applicants than when the same dossier was said to belong to a 60-year-old (Rosen & Jerdee, 1976). When Rochelle Reno (1979) asked adults to explain a student's failing a university course, she likewise found that failure by an elderly person was attributed to irremediable lack of ability, while consensus held that a young student had simply not tried hard enough. Such attributional biases led Joel Cooper and George Goethals (1981) to conclude that:

> The elderly cannot be and are not immune from the influence of such evaluations. Although people will differ in the degree to which they will be affected by stereotypes, old age is a time at which people may be more than usually vulnerable ... Thus, the self-concept of the elderly is not only a function of attributions made about the cause of their behavior but also a function of the reflection the elderly see of themselves when looking in the mirror held by society's stereotypes. (p. 441)

Mary Luszcz and K. M. Fitzgerald (1986) explored stereotypes about old age in three cohorts of South Australians: adolescents, middle-aged and the elderly. They found that some negative stereotypes were shared by all three age groups, including the elderly themselves. For example, old people were viewed by the entire Adelaide sample as weaker and more dependent and disorganised than the young or the middle-aged. Also, while slightly less ignorant than younger men and women, the elderly were likewise found to share serious misconceptions about their own cohort, such as underestimating their physical and mental health and overestimating their tendency to be lonely. However, on a personal level, each aged individual rated him- or herself as superior to old people in general. In fact, they seemed to identify themselves personally with the image of a middle-aged Australian, rather than feeling in any way akin to the devalued stereotype of the 'typical' elderly citizen.

Evidently, many older people have come to grips with the discrepancy between the adverse myths and stereotypes about old age which prevail in society and their own happier experiences with this life phase. They seem to conclude that they themselves are lucky exceptions to the general rule. But if most people are the exceptions, the rule itself appears dubious. Some recent research evidence challenging popular stereotypes and images of old age is considered in this chapter. First, a glance at one individual's personal account of her own old age, in Box 16.1, may provide a more optimistic antidote to pessimistic stereotypes about ageing, for this woman saw the years after 65 as the prime of life.

In other cultures, stereotypes about the elderly are not always bleak. Recall (see Chapter 1) the example of the Himalayan Lepcha who valued longevity so highly that they congratulated one another on looking old, displayed politeness by estimating acquaintances ages as older than they really were, and showed strong respect for seniority in most of their life activities and cultural pursuits. Optimistic impressions abound along with pessimism in images of old age in poetry and prose, as Box 16.2 illustrates.

Is optimism justified?

Some losses in old age are unavoidable. Unless the old person has lived throughout adulthood in as quiet an environment as the African bush (see Chapter 2), hearing acuity declines. Visual acuity likewise diminishes, as do muscular strength and endurance and the body's resilience in the face of temporary illness. That is the bad news. But the better news is that, for old people who maintain health and fitness, even these inevitable biological losses are by no means as sudden or dramatic as younger adults tend to imagine. But wait for the really good news – as compared with their own parents and grandparents, old people in

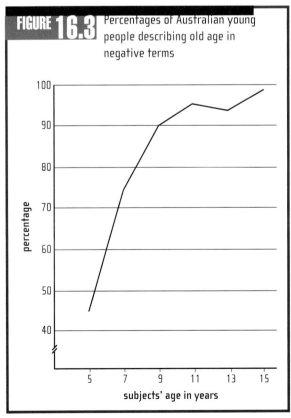

FIGURE 16.3 Percentages of Australian young people describing old age in negative terms

Source: Based on data in Goldman & Goldman (1982), p. 93.

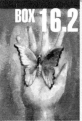

BOX 16.2 Literary images of old age

Optimism

I shall grow old, but
never lose life's zest,
Because the road's
last turn will be the
best.
Henry Van Dyke

With years a richer life begins,
The spirit mellows:
Ripe age gives tone to violins,
Wine, and good fellows.
John Townsend Trowbridge

The year grows rich as
it groweth old,

And life's latest sands are
its sands of gold!
Julia C. R. Dorr

To be seventy years young
is sometimes far more cheerful
and hopeful than to be forty
years old.
Oliver Wendell Holmes

I believe that one has to be seventy
before one is full of courage. The young
are always half-hearted.
D. H. Lawrence

The heads of strong old age are
beautiful beyond all grace of youth.
Robinson Jeffers

Old age has its pleasures which,
though different, are not less than
the pleasures of youth.
W. Somerset Maugham

Pessimism

Age I do abhor thee,
Youth I do adore thee.
Shakespeare

A stone's a stone
And a tree's a tree.
But what's the use of ageing me?
It's no improvement that I can see.
Steven Vincent Benet

How strange it seems with so much
  gone
Of life and love, to still live on!
J. G. Whittier

Weep not, my wanton, smile
upon my knee; when thou art
old there's grief enough on thee.
Robert Greene

Australia and New Zealand today are healthier, wealthier, better educated, more likely to be living independently and possessed of more leisure time. Thus, they can count many positive developmental gains as well as some inevitable biological, cognitive and social losses. As Ross Thompson (1991) explained:

> Maturity is also distinguished by expertise, perspective, wisdom, generativity, experience, self-management, and consistency in behavioural and personality attributes. These are the positive features of social portrayals of ageing that older adults are motivated to acquire rather than avoid. (p. 253)

Recent Australian evidence supports these conclusions. For example, in a study comparing emotional attitudes and life satisfaction of younger Australian adults (mean age 20 years) with that of Australian men and women (mean age 75.6 years), Elise Maher and Robert Cummins (2001) discovered significantly higher levels of optimism and capacity to cope with change (secondary control) in the older group. Some of their results are illustrated in Figure 16.4.

In later sections of this chapter we examine research evidence on the growth of wisdom, expertise and mature personality strengths in old age. But first let us look at impressions of old age across cultures. The pessimism about old age expressed by many contemporary urban Australian, New Zealand,

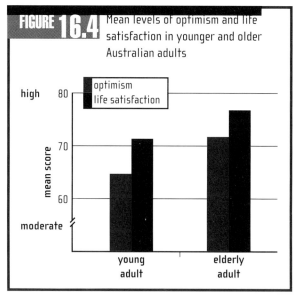

FIGURE 16.4 Mean levels of optimism and life satisfaction in younger and older Australian adults

Source: Based on data in Maher & Cummins (2001).

American and European adults is not shared by men and women in all other parts of the world.

Cross-cultural perspectives on ageing

In a classic cross-cultural investigation, Donald Cowgill and Lowell Holmes (1972) studied old peo-

In cultures where the old person's contribution to younger generations in the family is valued, old age gains respect.

ple in 14 cultures, looking both for worldwide universals and for cultural variations in how the elderly felt and were treated. The lists of differences they found across cultures turned out to be much longer and more impressive than the similarities. Cowgill and Holmes concluded that a society's degree of (1) industrialisation, (2) advanced technology, (3) urbanisation and (4) modernisation all tended to undermine the status and opportunities accorded to old people. In other words, the adverse stereotypes and unfair treatment (see Chapter 1) which are apt to blight enjoyment of the final years of the life cycle for city dwellers in America, Britain, Australia and New Zealand are not as likely to be observed among 'primitive' tribespeople who reside in the remote deserts or jungles of Africa, Indonesia or the Australian outback.

Other cross-cultural studies of ageing have specified further stresses often incurred by the contemporary elderly in modern industrial societies. The 'suburban sprawl' of recent generations in Australia, Britain, North America and Italy, for example, has led to a concentration of older people in inner-city neighbourhoods, which often have higher crime rates than rural or suburban communities. A study of 808 elderly women who lived alone in Bologna, Milan and Rome showed that one-third had perpetual grounds for anxiety: they feared muggers whenever they went out of their homes and burglars when they remained inside (Florea, 1980). Neville Brooke (1985) found that a large percentage of urban Australians experienced age discrimination at work. The view that older workers gave 'less value for money' was also found to be widespread in the Australian labour market. A recent survey of employment practices in Australia (Horin, 2002) revealed

that only one job in 10 is currently being filled by applicants who are over the age of 45. Furthermore, out of a sample of 1000 large Australian companies in the financial and business sector, nearly half had no employees who were over the age of 50. In line with the cultural contrasts shown in Figure 16.4, Australian employers cited obsolete skills as a major reason for refusing to hire middle-aged workers. They are 'out of touch', 'lacking in current skills' or 'lacking in relevant technical expertise', the Australian bosses claimed (Horin, 2002).

An inflationary economy is likewise especially disadvantageous to the elderly who have moved out of the workforce on a fixed pension, or to those relying on diminished savings and dwindling bank interest. According to many social observers (Kimmel, 1974; Comfort, 1977), the maintenance of an adequate income is the greatest social problem of ageing in modern industrialised societies. Poverty has repercussions for the maintenance of a comfortable style of housing, nutrition, transportation, health care and access to varied leisure activities, and may increase vulnerability to consumer fraud.

In other words, the opportunities available to the aged seem to be undermined in cultures:

- where health technology and birth control have created a disproportionately large elderly population
- where economic technology, child-oriented education and adult literacy have diminished the value of accumulated traditional wisdom, making the unique skills of older generations obsolete
- where contact between older and younger members of the extended family has been blocked by geographic mobility, suburbanisation and age prejudice.

Box 16.3 illustrates some of these cultural contrasts.

Robert Atchley (1977) developed the chart shown in Figure 16.5 in order to place the major societal differences in relating to the elderly into a theoretical framework. While much of the recent research described in earlier chapters has had the effect of modifying the old notion that nothing changes between age 21 and age 50 except chronological age (see Chapter 14), the impact of lifespan developmental psychology on popular beliefs about old age has been rather the opposite. It has tended to show that old age is less strange and less different from the rest of adulthood than most young people imagine. As Robert Kastenbaum (1979) noted:

> Ageing does not take hold of us like some powerful force that bends our personality this way or that. More often we continue to work upon our own experiences and cope with our own life challenges according to the patterns set in earlier years. (p. 49)

One reason why the changes brought about by old age are less striking when viewed objectively instead of in stereotypic myths or the anxious fore-

Lessons from culture
Age and etiquette

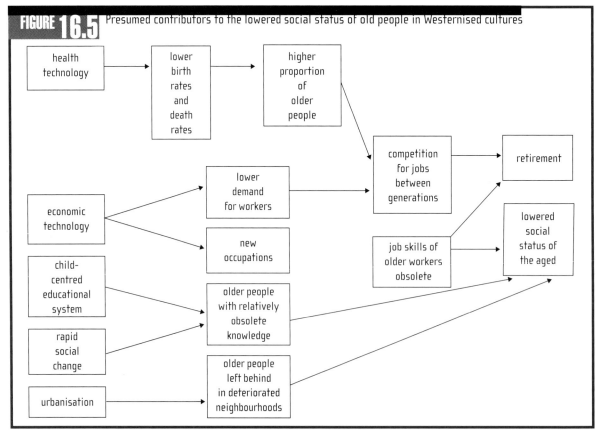

Nyeedura, an aged Aboriginal woman from a traditional tribal camp, enters a shop where a group of young women, both Aboriginal and white, are waiting to be served. Nyeedura pushes up to the counter. When the shop assistant turns to look at her she begins ordering her groceries. The shop assistant refuses to take her order. 'It's not your turn yet,' she tells Nyeedura curtly. 'All of these other women were here ahead of you. You'll have to wait at the end of the queue.' She turns back to the shopper on whom she was waiting before the interruption, muttering 'silly old woman' under her breath.

This incident reflects a clash between two cultures' contrasting approaches to ageing. Nyeedura, a respected elder in her tribe, was operating on the premise that her seniority entitled her to be served ahead of the younger women. It would have been a breach of tribal etiquette to give precedence to them, in view of their junior status. The anthropologist Robert Tonkinson (1978) described the following additional benefits accruing to elderly Aboriginal women:

For married women, too, prestige and authority in matters connected with their own as well as certain male rituals increase with age. Provided they remain alert and responsive, the older people derive considerable stature from their accumulated wisdom. Becoming older, or being an elder, means less active participation in subsistence and ritual concerns, but greater responsibility for the caretaking and directing of the religious life.

In keeping with this changing role, elderly people can expect material assistance, in the form of foodstuffs, from younger relatives who respond willingly to the strongly expressed imperative that old people must be fed and looked after in return for having reared their children. The norms of classificatory kinship assure older, less active hunters and gatherers that there will always be relatives to support them. Also, a number of choice foodstuffs are normally reserved for old people; for example, the porcupine-like echidna whose flesh is considered a delicacy. In the religious life, too, hunting commitments by younger men assure their elders of meat (pp. 82–3, reprinted by permission of Holt, Rinehart & Winston, CBS College Publishing).

While old age is accorded respect in a traditional culture, the Western approach is quite the opposite. The shop assistant's interpretation of Nyeedura's behaviour as due to rudeness, with a possible admixture of senility, reveals the contrasting Western point of view.

FIGURE 16.5 Presumed contributors to the lowered social status of old people in Westernised cultures

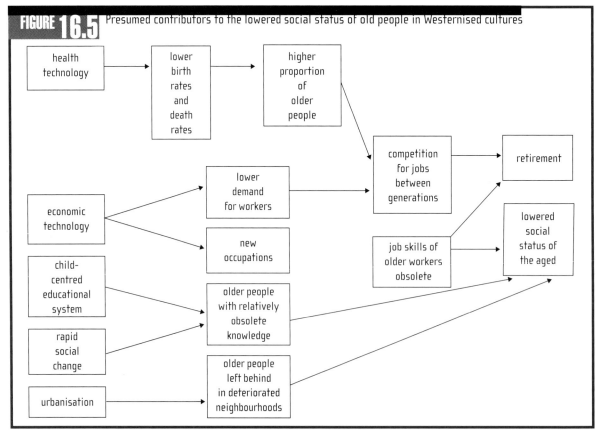

Source: Based on data in Atchley (1977), p. 25.

While physical declines in strength and speed are common across cultures, the older person's roles, responsibilities and social prestige are largely culturally determined.

bodings of young adults is that losses tend to be both gradual and cumulative. Most of the physical declines of ageing (such as increasing slowness or diminished hearing) build up imperceptibly, though steadily, over the bulk of the adult years. Also, they are quite often due to idiosyncratic past experiences (such as a lifetime of exposure to loud rock music or traffic noise) rather than being the 'pure' consequences of ageing itself. Finally, individual differences among people are greatest in old age, after a lifetime of diverse, idiosyncratic formative influences. As Bernice Neugarten (1968) noted, the members of one's high school graduating class tend to be less alike at 40 (or 70) than at age 18.

But favourable cultural traditions and values are not sufficient in themselves to guarantee each individual a smooth passage through old age. Even in a culture that accords high respect to old age, such as traditional Australian Aboriginal communities, status as an elder is earned, not automatic, and social account is clearly taken of individual differences and incapacities. Only those old people who are fortunate enough to possess health, intellectual competence and leadership skills qualify to be venerated. Aboriginal Australians in former times distinguished two categories of old people. There were the respected elderly religious leaders who held senior status over all other members of the community, and the 'closed-up-dead' old people who were too physically frail or mentally infirm to assume active social or religious roles (Storer, 1985). The latter group might elect to remain in their own familiar country when the rest of the tribe migrated and could sometimes be left to die there when conditions of extreme hardship made their care a threat to the survival of the rest of the group.

As Janice Reid (1985) pointed out, two extreme contrasts coexisted in Aboriginal attitudes to the elderly – one stressing care, respect and veneration, the other neglect and disdain for infirmity.

Along similar lines, Jenny Noesjirwan, Una Gault and June Crawford (1983) conducted a cross-cultural comparison of beliefs about age-related memory loss among adults in Sydney versus the tribal Minangkabau people of western Sumatra. On the grounds that the status of the elderly is higher in Sumatra than Australia, and tribal Minangkabau old people frequently hold the respected positions of clan leader, religious teacher or *dukun* (traditional healer), the researchers predicted less expectation of senile mental deterioration among Indonesians than Australians. But their results showed just the opposite, as Figure 16.6 illustrates. This could mean that ageism is even more rampant in tribal Sumatra than in urban Australia.

On the other hand, the fact that both cultures expected old people to forget more trivial than important information suggests an alternative interpretation. It is possible that the observed cross-cultural difference reflected an accurate impression of the lesser need for memorisation of items such as the location of the nearest post office, or the age of nieces and nephews, on the part of tribal elders in Sumatra who enjoy a less stressful and more socially supportive lifestyle than their aged counterparts in Sydney.

In traditional cultures where the information and skills an old person needs in order to contribute effectively to society change very little from one generation to the next, it is perhaps understandable that old people are held in higher esteem than modern cultures where a person's command of the latest computer technology replaces stored personal memories as a source of expertise. But in contemporary Japan, the pace of technological advance has not swept older adults aside, and the special wisdom of old age continues to earn the highest social respect. In domestic life, older family members occupy the rooms with the best views, the finest silks and the most expensive bedding. They are ushered through doors in front of younger kin and get first use of the family bath. In working life, a similar order of seniority applies. Erdman Palmore (1990) explains:

> The legislature, corporations, universities, religious organizations and most other such institutions are largely controlled by the elderly. This is a result of the seniority system in which prestige and power tend to increase with age ... Most Japanese believe that this is as it should be since they assume that maturity and wisdom tend to increase with age and that power should be given to those who are most mature and wise – the elders. (p. 260)

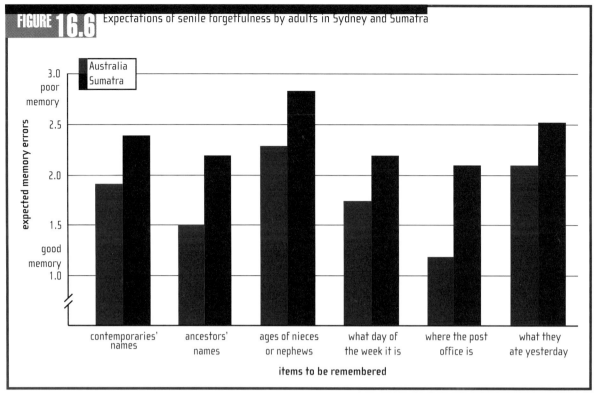

FIGURE 16.6 Expectations of senile forgetfulness by adults in Sydney and Sumatra

Source: Based on data in Noesjirwan, Gault & Crawford (1983), p. 465.

The interaction of biology and culture in human ageing

Whereas wide cultural variations distinguish what it feels like socially to be an old person in different societies, the biological markers of old age are largely universal. These may include grey hair, wrinkled skin and baldness, as well as a distinctive set of internal physiological changes that gradually conspire to undermine physical functioning, as shown in Figure 16.7.

Variations on the ageing theme: Lifestyle and culture

In practice, it is often difficult to separate the 'normal' ageing of the body from abnormal events like illnesses and accidents, which may occur suddenly during old age or accumulate so slowly over time that they do not show up clearly until late in the life cycle. For example, hearing losses build up gradually in most adults, but can arise prematurely in young people who, like rock musicians, are exposed to heavy doses of loud noise. Similarly, in the average adult over 50, the walls of the arteries gradually weaken and plaques of hard, clogging build-up accumulate in them, restricting blood flow (a process known as *arteriosclerosis* or *atherosclerosis*). Sometimes pieces of plaque break off, blocking the artery and causing a heart attack or stroke. But not all adults suffer hardening of the arteries, and for some the process begins well before 50. Diet and exercise are con-

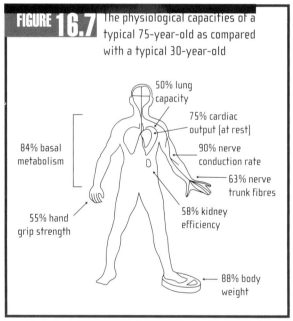

FIGURE 16.7 The physiological capacities of a typical 75-year-old as compared with a typical 30-year-old

Source: Based on data in Shock (1962).

tributing factors. So are culture, lifestyle and health practices.

The building up of arterial blockages through arteriosclerosis was once thought to be a normal, universally inevitable consequence of ageing. But studies of Bantu, Yoruba and Kurumba tribe members in Africa have shown that diet and lifestyle exert moderating influences on this deterioration process. Tribal Africans who leave the bush to dwell in urban areas develop age-related arteriosclerotic patterns comparable to their Afro-American counterparts in the United States. But adults in Africa of the same chronological age who have led a traditional Bantu, Yoruba or Kurumba lifestyle show a much lower incidence of arterial damage. Furthermore, when James Birren (1964) measured the brain functioning of a group of very healthy American men in their 70s, he found no differences from younger men in brain wave patterns, blood flow or oxygen consumption. Given that an unavoidable deterioration of blood vessels with age would have undermined these processes in the 70-year-olds, Birren concluded that when such changes do occur in old age they are the result of specific disease processes like arteriosclerosis or Alzheimer's disease, rather than due to normal ageing.

The hearing deficits frequently associated with ageing in noisy industrialised societies are likewise less pronounced among aged individuals whose environments have been gentler on their ears. Robert Kastenbaum (1979) noted that 'One year of exposure to the din of heavy machinery might have the effect of a decade of gradual ageing' (p. 20).

Health attitudes, preventative health practices and physiological ageing

Since all normal human environments include at least a few hazards and insults that wear down the body's machinery over time, it is realistic for everyone to expect to suffer some form of diminished physical capacity eventually. But it is a mistake to assume that age 65 (or 50 or 70) is a catastrophic point at which a hitherto intact organism suddenly falls apart. Nor are all age-related declines in physical functioning untreatable or irreversible. In fact, one of the greatest health problems associated with old age is fatalistic acceptance of potentially remediable health complaints.

When Sue Levkoff, Paul Cleary and Terri Wetle (1987) asked a group of 460 middle-aged and elderly adults to rate their present state of physical health on a four-point scale from 'good' to 'poor', they found the group aged 65 to 89 gave themselves significantly lower health ratings than the 45- to 64-year-olds did. This might at first appear to testify either to the old person's greater vulnerability to physical disabilities, or to elderly adults' more accurate awareness of the true state of their health in contrast to their middle-aged peers who may have been anxiously avoiding recognition of the bodily declines of the ageing process. But a further analysis by Levkoff, Cleary and Wetle revealed that neither of these explanations was true.

Instead, when the researchers examined objective medical measures of the state of health of their subjects, they found that the middle-aged group's subjective health ratings much more accurately reflected their true medical condition than the older group's. In fact, the elderly sample as a whole tended to possess a very distorted view of how their bodies were functioning. Instead of being clearly conscious of the limitations on their fitness and health that resulted from ageing, this group's subjective impressions were distorted in a much more pessimistic direction than any actual health problems would warrant. Furthermore, when the researchers controlled for (a) number and severity of all medically diagnosed acute illnesses and chronic conditions such as arthritis or high blood pressure, (b) number of days spent sick in bed or in hospital over the recent past, and (c) mental health status, they still found a significant difference between the middle-aged and older groups' self-perceptions. When all these objective reasons for feeling ill were statistically removed, the old people still took an unrealistically bleak view of their state of health. It seemed that their ability to feel healthy had been undermined by belief in ageist stereotypes about physiological decline. Like the philosopher Seneca, they had gone into old age expecting it to be 'an incurable disease'. According to Levkoff, Cleary and Wetle:

> The increased monitoring of normal sensations, more frequent experience of physical illness, and normative expectations may all combine to increase the elderly person's tendency to perceive and label dysphoric experiences as somatic … We believe that for some elderly individuals, with no previous history of exaggerated symptom reporting, unfounded pessimistic assessments of health may result from the stresses imposed by ageing. This is not to say that all elderly people will be overly pessimistic in their health assessments and be at risk of hypochrondriacal illness behavior … We believe, however, that certain individuals may use the sick role more in old age in response to social stresses imposed by life transitions, isolation, and chronic illness. Although age *per se* may not be the factor precipitating overly negative health assessments, the situational changes that accompany ageing might place elderly individuals at risk for hypochondriacal illness behavior. (p. 119)

The implications of these findings for health professionals who work with the aged are clear. While ensuring accurate diagnosis and treatment of all objectively presenting medical problems, it is perhaps even more important to help old people to gain a realistic appraisal of their level of fitness and health potential. At the same time, preventive efforts to improve the intellectual, social and emotional qualities of old people's lives may discourage them from prematurely accepting the 'sick role'. Optimisation strategies towards these ends are considered later in this chapter and also in discussions of social influences on happiness and mental health in Chapter 17.

Paradoxically, the fatalistic acceptance of old age as an incurable disease is a two-edged sword. While limiting old people's utilisation and enjoyment of whatever level of health and fitness they possess, it is also liable to prevent them seeking diagnosis or

Health professionals who work with older men and women can minimise the fears and unnecessary worries that stereotyped beliefs about ageing may induce.

treatment for genuine health problems that require active medical intervention. According to physician J. A. Muir Gray (1983):

> Many old people believe that everything that happens in old age is caused by the ageing process. The consequences of this belief are serious, because persons who hold such beliefs see no reason to seek help for breathlessness or dizziness or incontinence, or for any other symptom of disease. Even when such persons do consult a doctor they will not necessarily follow the doctor's advice unless they are helped to understand that their problem is the result of a treatable disease and not the result of the intractable ageing process. In prevention also, the belief that all symptoms are the result of the ageing process can have undesirable consequences. Persons holding such beliefs are unlikely to change their lifestyle or adopt any preventive measure suggested by the health educator. (p. 7, reproduced by permission of Dr Muir Gray)

Maladaptive beliefs about health problems in old age could result in part from old people's ignorance about contemporary research evidence showing how the most common age-related health complaints can be prevented or cured. In fact, research shows that old people are apt to be less aware than younger adults of the availability or usefulness of prosthetic devices (such as spectacles, hearing aids and walking supports), or of recent medical advances in the treatment of cataract blindness, operable cancers and so on. They also tend to seek help less often even when they are aware of its availability. One study of preventive dental health practices in Australia showed that older Australians were less likely than younger men and women to visit the dentist for tooth cleaning or a check-up when not in dental distress (Cameron, 1980).

According to Gray, ignorance and inertia are not the only reasons why old people avoid medical or dental help. Some resistance is due, he argued, to a more basic philosophy of resignation or hopelessness:

> Some old people are very pessimistic and respond to suggestions that problems can be prevented or solved by saying that 'It is a waste of time', or 'You should help someone who is younger, I'm too old'. In some people, this reflects the belief that all problems are due to ageing. Other older people, however, hold this view even though they know that the problem is theoretically preventive or treatable. Such persons have experienced so many disappointments and defeats in life that they have become hopeless and helpless, and are reluctant to try any new activity. Persons holding such views are often unwilling to try any preventive measure or obtain a service that is known to be in short supply. (p. 9, reproduced by permission of Dr Muir Gray)

Such complacent or fatalistic resignation to poor health and disability may interfere not only with the older person's ability to enjoy the last years of life to the full, but also with the optimal timing of the diagnosis and treatment of those conditions which are more susceptible to cure during their early stages.

The view that acute disease is inevitable during old age is another widely held but erroneous myth. Alex Comfort (1977) reported that a longitudinal medical study in North Carolina showed that more than half the group aged 65 and over who returned for regular check-ups had suffered no detectable deterioration in health over periods from three to 13 years. Some, in fact, registered measurable health *improvements* over this time span. Living in an institution can also influence health independently of age itself (see Chapter 17).

The physiological ageing process

The physical functioning of the body is less efficient for the average person by the age of 75 than it was at age 30, as illustrated in Figure 16.7. Some of these typical changes affect outward appearance, influencing social perceptions of the individual, as explained earlier, while at the same time alerting the older adult to the fact that ageing is progressing, with consequent repercussions for the psychological self-concept. Other changes involve internal organs and physiological systems, with implications for exercise capacity and overall health. Still others involve the sense organs and perception. Let us examine some of the key physiological changes arising in most adults after age 60.

Ageing of the hair and skin

The greying of the hair and progressive baldness in men are among the best known physical changes of ageing. The timing of both these events is largely genetically determined. This means that individual differences tend to be large. Some women go grey and some men turn bald at 30, while others live to a ripe old age without encountering either change (Comfort, 1977). Illness (such as thyroid deficiency, which may lead to baldness) or environmental insult can accelerate these age-related changes in pigmentation and thickness of hair.

The wrinkling and drooping of the skin on face and body is another tell-tale sign of age. The skin cells gradually lose their elasticity, while some muscles and fatty tissues disappear under the surface of the skin, producing crevices and sagging. Skin cells dry out more with age as oil production diminishes, and dark patches known as 'age spots' are likely to appear, beginning in the late 40s and becoming clearly evident in most adults by age 70.

The skin's ageing process begins in early adulthood. However, because it is cumulative (i.e. wrinkles are not readily erasable) and because it accelerates markedly in the later adult years, wrinkles normally do not become conspicuous until late middle age. At this point, some affluent adults who find the psychological acceptance of age difficult to handle may elect to undergo cosmetic surgery to 'lift' their face by removing patches of skin to stretch the remaining facial skin into a more youthful appearance. Another cosmetic age-denying therapy that has recently become popular in the United States (Park, 2002) involves botox injections. Botox (short for botulinum toxin) is a deadly poison which, when injected into the facial muscles in very dilute doses, causes a temporary paralysis that can appear to smooth out facial wrinkles while the toxin remains active.

Lifestyle is relevant to the ageing of the skin since exposure to sunlight accelerates the skin's age-related changes. Adults in sunny climates who spend their summer months outdoors without adequate sunscreen or hats and clothing to protect them from the sun's harmful rays not only display a more weathered appearance but also run a high risk of skin cancer later in life.

Ageing of the blood vessels

The walls of the veins and arteries throughout the body and brain have a crucial role to play in older men's and women's health, fitness, cognitive capacity and longevity. As was noted earlier, the process known as arteriosclerosis is a leading cause of death and disability in older adults in Australia, New Zealand and other Western countries. This building up of fatty deposits in the lining of the blood vessels is illustrated in Figure 16.8.

When the blood supply to muscles, brain, lungs, heart and other organs is restricted through atherosclerotic narrowing of the blood vessels, the supply of oxygen is reduced. The consequence is a decrement in the organ's rate and efficiency of functioning. In addition, the deposits of the fatty substance, *plaque*, on the walls of the arteries can break away, producing blood clots that may lead to a stroke.

Arteriosclerosis becomes more common with age.

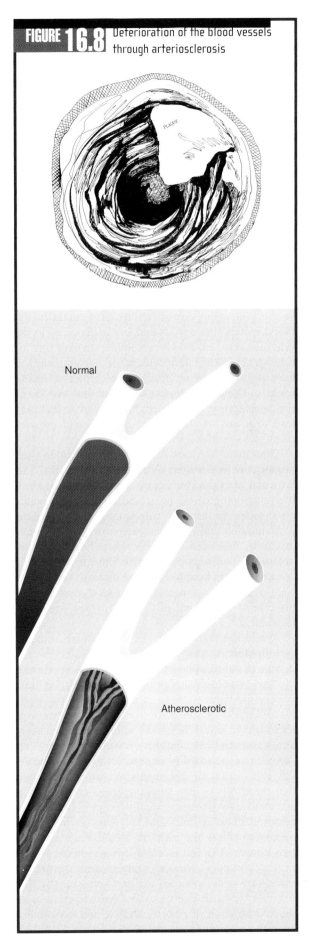

FIGURE 16.8 Deterioration of the blood vessels through arteriosclerosis

Normal

Atherosclerotic

Incidence rates rise for men after age 45 and for women after menopause at age 50 or so. However, it is important to remember that arterosclerosis is a disease, not a normal component of the ageing process. The risk can be reduced by health precautions such as stopping smoking, reducing consumption of saturated fats and taking regular exercise, as discussed in a later section of this chapter.

Ageing of muscles and internal organs

Like the skin cells, the muscles tend to become progressively less elastic over time. Muscle cells increase in size and strength until about age 39 but are then gradually lost without replacement so that strength slowly declines. *Collagen* is a connective tissue found throughout the body (including in the skin, muscles and the joints between bones). The finding that collagen changes character with advancing age may help to explain age-related increases in pain and stiffness of the joints, the slower healing of wounds to the blood vessels and muscles and loss of elasticity in the skin (Timaras, 1972). The accumulation over time of a substance known as *lipofuscin* (or 'age pigment') in various body cells is another aspect of the ageing process. The cause remains as mysterious as that of the deterioration of collagen, but it likewise seems to lead to a loss of elasticity in the skin and muscles (Hendricks & Hendricks, 1977).

The most obvious consequence of diminished muscle tone is tiredness and decreased physical and muscular strength (see Figure 16.7). However, since the functioning of the heart and lungs also depends on muscle, the internal consequences of lipofuscin accumulation and collagen changes may be far more insidious. American children's hearts begin to show deposits of lipofuscin at age 10. Since it builds at a constant rate in both healthy and diseased heart muscle, this substance typically comes to take up some 4 per cent of the volume of the heart by the age of 70 (Strehler, 1962).

While age-related changes in muscular collagen and lipofuscin may help to explain some of the decline in functioning of the heart and lungs during old age, arteriosclerosis of the blood vessels, as illustrated in Figure 16.8, can also play a part. Psychological variables are likewise highly relevant. Exposure to stress heightens vulnerability to heart attack, especially in conjunction with a hard-driving, competitive personality pattern known as Type A. Lifestyle factors are also highly relevant and the fact that the effects of diet, smoking, stress and pollution accumulate over time eventually means that the older person's fitness declines and they become more vulnerable to killers like heart and lung disease or stroke (see Chapter 18). Individual differences in the health of the coronary arteries, muscles and connective tissues are wide, as noted earlier. Consequently, vulnerability to cardiac or vascular disease tends to be as much a function of culture, lifestyle and personality as of the ageing process *per se*.

Hormonal changes

As noted in Chapter 15, the female menopause and corresponding changes in the male's production of testosterone and other masculine sex hormones typically occur in the mid to late 50s. As well as reducing the likelihood of conceiving a child, the progressive loss of estrogen from the female bloodstream, culminating in menopause, can have other effects on the facial and bodily appearance, including drying of the skin, thinning of hair on the scalp and, for some women, an increase in unwanted hair on other parts of the body. For these reasons, as well as to overcome the sometimes unpleasant symptoms of hot flushes and malaise during the climax of the menopause (see Chapter 15) some women elect to undergo hormone replacement therapy (HRT) in which estrogen supplements are administered orally or transdermally to mimic premenopausal levels. Some women elect to continue HRT into old age, even after the transitional symptoms of the menopause itself have dissipated.

While helping to slow some of the superficial changes in the physical appearance of ageing, long-term HRT can be risky, according to the results of a recent large-scale clinically controlled drug trial in the United States (Park, 2002). In fact, the trial was halted owing to a perception of risk, and women in the HRT group were quickly taken off their estrogen supplement. After five years of controlled administration either of HRT or a placebo, it had already become clear that the hormone therapy was associated with an elevated probability of premature death. In contrast to the placebo group, matched on other variables, the women taking HRT were found to have a significantly elevated risk of breast cancer, heart disease and stroke (see Figure 16.9).

The lesson for understanding the normal ageing process would appear to be that the physiological changes of ageing are so intimately interconnected that the artificial slowing of the ageing of one part of the system will not necessarily halt the ageing process as a whole. Indeed, piecemeal intervention in an effort to delay ageing may sometimes undermine health and normal functioning, thereby shortening life.

Ageing of the bones and teeth

Bone cells differ from muscle cells in their capacity to regenerate and the rate of replacement of bone declines with increasing age. During early adulthood, it is estimated that 10 per cent of the skeleton is rebuilt each year (Exton-Smith, 1985), but in old age calcium from the bones is absorbed by the body at a faster rate than bone is replaced, resulting in increased vulnerability to fractures. This normal aspect of the skeleton's ageing can be exacerbated by a problem known as osteoporosis (see Chapter 15), a disease-like condition related to cigarette smoking and inactivity, particularly in postmenopausal women.

The teeth wear down so slowly that an adult who

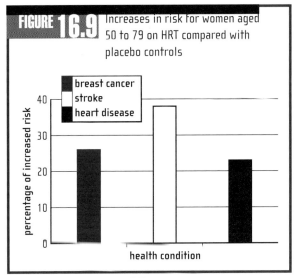

FIGURE 16.9 Increases in risk for women aged 50 to 79 on HRT compared with placebo controls

Source: Based on data in Park (2002).

TABLE 16.2 Changes in the visual system in old age

Part of eye	Change
Cornea	Becomes flatter and less transparent
Lens	Proteins in the lens change and elasticity is reduced, and cataracts may develop
Pupil	Dilation of the pupil becomes less efficient, owing to changes in the autonomic nervous system
Retina	Becomes thinner and contains fewer rods
Cataracts	Cloudy areas of the lens, known as cataracts, are common in the elderly (up to 50 per cent of those over 65 have one)

escaped other dental problems would retain youthful chewing capacity for up to 200 years (Perlmutter & Hall, 1992). But few adults completely escape tooth decay or inflammation of the gums, causing periodontal disease. Nevertheless, with good oral hygiene and regular dental check-ups, a contemporary old person need not anticipate the transition to false teeth that was once almost inescapable in extreme old age.

Sense organs and perception

Vision and hearing become less sensitive with age. Again, most of this deterioration is cumulative, beginning early in life. Table 16.2 lists some changes that arise in the visual system in old age. The average old person's need for reading glasses is due to the hardening of the lens of the eye (known as *presbyopia*) which reduces the ability to focus on near objects. This process proceeds at a constant rate from age five to about age 60, thereafter showing no further change (McFarland, 1968). More serious losses of vision in old age are often caused by cataracts, which cloud the lens and eventually cause blindness. The reason for this progressive clouding is unknown, though a build-up of cholesterol has been implicated (Weale, 1963), along with a lifetime's exposure to bright light. Cataracts are relatively rare before the age of 80 but afflict about one in every three octogenarians. They can often be removed by surgery.

The ability to hear high-pitched sounds declines relatively early, with adults as young as 25 performing less well in this respect than adolescents. A person's rate of hearing loss is determined partly by the environment. The hearing of elderly Africans from quiet bushland areas is nearly as efficient as that of young adults who live in cities, while men who work in noisy factories suffer the fastest rate of hearing decline (McFarland, 1968). Exposure to loud music or living on a noisy street can also accelerate the ageing of the auditory system.

Cross-sectional studies of olfactory acuity through the sense of smell reveal poorer performance in old age than in adults under 70, as shown in Figure 16.10 (Doty et al., 1984). However, there are at least two possible explanations for this observed effect. The sense of smell may genuinely decline in acuity with age. Alternatively, or in addition, older adults may be less familiar with certain smells than younger men and women owing to different life experiences as a cohort. The lack of familiarity with odours in the test set, rather than lack of acuity, almost certainly explains the poor performance of the children aged 5 to 9 years in Figure 16.10. As with vision and hearing, decreased smell sensitivity has implications for quality of life (from enjoyment of fine perfume or the

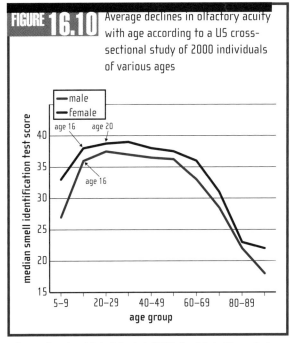

FIGURE 16.10 Average declines in olfactory acuity with age according to a US cross-sectional study of 2000 individuals of various ages

Source: Based on data in Doty et al. (1984). Reprinted with permission. Copyright American Association for the Advancement of Science.

rich bouquet of a well-aged wine to the social ills befalling adults whose insensitivity to body odour leads to their inadvertently offending younger noses). Health and safety may also be affected if an elderly adult fails to smell smoke from a dangerous fire or serious chemical pollution.

The other senses of taste, touch and balance also often decline with age, though the implications of these changes are generally less serious than for vision and hearing. Nevertheless, taste loss may motivate old people to oversalt or overspice their foods, with adverse consequences for blood pressure or digestion. A loss of balance sense, due to the degeneration of small crystals in the inner ear known as *otoliths*, may help to explain the older adult's susceptibility to falls, while decreased temperature sensitivity may result in injury from scalds and burns.

All these changes to the sensory system have broad ramifications, some of which were brought out in Leon Pastalan's (1974) imaginative old-age-simulation studies. To heighten younger students' sensitivity to the difficulties old people may experience as a result of the accumulation of sensory losses, he created a kit containing goggles, finger patches and earplugs. When these were put on, the wearer's sensory inputs declined to about the average level of sensory awareness of octogenarians. Pastalan found that students who wore the kit even for just a few hours suffered stress, encountered many physical hazards (particularly in traffic and on stairs) and often felt inadequate or even paranoid (laughter, which was robbed by the earplugs of its conversational context, was wrongly interpreted by the subjects as being at their expense). Illuminating as these results are, their applicability to the understanding of old age is limited by the following considerations:

1. If sensory deficits develop gradually, which is the case for normal old people (though not for Pastalan's subjects), they should cause less stress and the learning of compensatory strategies should be easier.
2. Properly fitted prosthetic devices (such as spectacles and hearing aids) can neutralise the effects of age-related sensory deterioration among the elderly.
3. Marked differences between older people and, for the same person, between one sensory process and another mean that the group deficits on which Pastalan's kit were based were probably much greater than any one octogenarian would ever encounter.

Neurocognitive ageing

As was noted in earlier chapters (see Chapters 9, 14 and 15), the brain's volume declines in old age and dendrite density decreases. It is not presently known to what extent, if any, these changes influence cognitive functioning. However, changes in the synaptic and neural transmission processes do occur with age, and these are influential. In particular, the structure of nerve cells changes in old age, dendrites shrink and this contributes gradually to a slowing of neuro-motor and neurosensory processes with age. The age pigment, lipofuscin, also builds up in the brain during old age and its rate of accumulation seems to be increased by factors that stem the flow of oxygen into the central nervous system, suggesting a relationship with reduced neural conduction speed. The ventricles (spaces in the brain containing fluids) enlarge and the grooves on the surface of the cortex widen. As noted earlier, brain functioning in old age can be threatened by cerebral arteriosclerosis, or the build-up of fatty tissues and calcium inside the arteries supplying the brain with blood. This process reduces the brain's oxygen intake, while increasing the likelihood of a stroke (or cerebrovascular accident), due to the rupture of one of the blood vessels in the brain. A stroke can be fatal, or it may lead to temporary or permanent mental incapacity. Diet and lifestyle are implicated along with age in raising the individual's risk of developing cerebral arteriosclerosis. Many very old people suffer minor strokes that may go largely unnoticed when they happen but can diminish cognitive functioning as minor episodes of brain damage accumulate over time (Coffey & Cummings, 2000).

The aged brain weighs less, on average, than the brain of a young adult, partly owing to deeper cortical grooves. These changes are probably due to oxygen loss and dehydration, the normal loss of brain cells (which begins in early infancy and accelerates after age 60), environmental insults, damage due to mild strokes (see above) or even, possibly, a slow-acting virus which selectively attacks nerve tissue (Comfort, 1977).

Consequently, the brain at age 75 is noticeably smaller than the brain in early adulthood. It weighs about 5 to 10 per cent less and has lost about 10 per cent of its overall volume within the cranial cavity (Coffey & Cummings, 2000). Although this may seem significant to the lay person, researchers are now aware, as noted in earlier chapters, that brain size does not directly predict brain functioning except in cases of severe injury, malformation or disease.

Furthermore, as noted in Chapters 7, 9 and 14, the brain remains highly plastic in adulthood so that, when existing cells die or decline in function, other brain cells are able to replace them and connections among surrounding neurons proliferate in such a way as to compensate to a large degree (Coffey & Cummings, 2000). As a result, the average person's intelligence is not likely to be seriously impaired before age 70 or 75, as we see later in this chapter. By the age of 80, perhaps 20 per cent of normal, healthy adults are found to have some symptoms of senile brain disease (such as seriously slowed cognitive function, severe memory loss, impaired speech or word recognition, or inability to perform routine habits), possibly due to one or more of these degenerative changes in brain structure. Even so, it is important to bear in mind that this is often the result of an age-related disease. Brain impairment is not a normal and inevitable consequence of the ageing process, clearly shown by the 80 per cent or so of healthy very old men and women without discernible cognitive loss. In fact, according to the gerontologist Alex Comfort:

> Becoming 'senile' is statistically an unlikely misfortune. The word 'senile' itself is less a diagnosis than a term of abuse – you're senile if you make a fuss. That indicates only that your brain is still functioning and they haven't washed it for you. (1977, p. 47)

The brain's patterns of electrical activity (EEG) typically change during old age and the conduction speed of the impulses along neuronal fibres throughout the body also slows down, owing to a reduced rate of production of certain biochemical substances involved in neurotransmission, including serotonin, glucamate, dopamine and acetylcholine (Rosenzweig, Breedlove & Leiman, 2002).

The slowing of nerve conduction speed has a direct bearing on psychophysiological and behavioural tests of *reaction time* (or the average time lag between the presentation of a signal, such as a red traffic light, and a person's response to it, such as stepping on the brake). Reaction time also slows down gradually over age. It has been suggested that lengthened reaction and movement speeds are the direct result of physiological declines in nerve conduction rate, but other explanations are also possible.

In a classic study, Jack Botwinick (1967) found that older test recruits were more cautious than younger participants and seemed to choose to go slowly in order to increase the accuracy and precision of their responses. Alan Welford (1976) likewise found that mood, health, personality, motivation and expectancy of success may all contribute to how well a person performs on tests of reaction time. If old people expect to be slow, or if they are feeling ill, angry, bored or depressed, their measured performance rate will suffer. Extensive practice diminishes age differences in reaction time (Baltes, Staudinger & Lindenberger, 1999), suggesting that such non-physiological considerations do account for at least some part of the older person's apparent slowness on speed of reaction tasks and timed psychological tests like IQ tests. Box 16.4 illustrates another method of speeding older people's performance.

Whatever its cause, the normal slowing of the older adult's speed of reaction has an important bearing on the measurement of adult intelligence – as we see later in this chapter, most standard intelligence tests require rapid response to at least some of the test items to earn a high score.

Theories of biological ageing

The exact cause, or causes, of the biological ageing process remains something of a mystery. But several

BOX 16.4 Erasing the effects of neurocognitive ageing by playing video games

The fact that older people's reaction speed slows down is well documented. When tested in the laboratory, and when doing everyday jobs such as dialling a telephone number or cutting cabbage, the elderly move more slowly than the young. But Jane Clark, Ann Lanphear and Carol Riddick (1987) discovered a way to reverse this age-related speed deficit. They asked a group of 70-year-olds to play video games for a total of at least 14 hours over a period of seven weeks. The group's average scores on the two games, *PacMan* and *Donkey Kong*, more than trebled over the seven-week period.

But this was not the only change. Their reaction speed was measured in the laboratory before and after they played the video games. Their speeds after play were significantly faster than on the pretest. Furthermore, the game-players improved more than a matched control group of the same age from the same senior citizens' centre who did not play with video machines. Perhaps our local video arcades could contribute to the optimisation of physiological ageing by acquiring a new image to attract an older clientele.

Playing video games improves reaction speed in the elderly.

intriguing hypotheses have been put forward, including the notion that the body's ageing may be due to the same chemical process as the spoiling of milk or the perishing of rubber, or that it may resemble a contagious disease, or be caused by a breakdown of the immune system, by environmental pollution or by a genetic blueprint engraved in the cells at conception. These theories are analysed briefly in this section.

Disease theories

The view that old age is a disease goes back to the scientist Roger Bacon, who, many centuries ago, looked to alchemy for its cure (de Beauvoir, 1977, p. 23). Today, disease factors continue to be implicated in the processes leading up to ageing and death, but in a more complex manner than Bacon foresaw. For one thing, the infectious diseases and illnesses (from colds to hepatitis or rheumatic fever) that people suffer through the life cycle may progressively weaken both the bodily organs themselves and the immune system's capacity to ward off future infections. Second, some diseases (such as chronic hypertension and some forms of cancer) are both slow and cumulative, so that their influence is most likely to be witnessed later in life. A third, more extreme, disease theory is that ageing itself is an illness (maybe a virus) to which everyone is eventually exposed and to which no organism can develop a complete and lasting immunity (Rosenfeld, 1976).

A fourth theory turns the tables by suggesting that ageing occurs when the immune system runs amok, so that the body's own cells are fought against as though they were foreign disease agents. This 'autoimmune civil war' could be brought about either by age-related mutations in the body cells (causing them to seem foreign) or by mutation and deterioration in the cells of the immune system itself, reducing its capacity to distinguish host cells from invaders. The autoimmune theory was supported in an experiment that linked the bloodstreams of aged and youthful hamsters. After a short time, the young hamsters began to show non-specific symptoms of senility (Walford, 1965, p. 85).

A fifth theory has equated ageing with genetic disease. This grew out of the discovery of a form of premature ageing (known as Werner's syndrome, or progeria) which accelerates an apparently normal ageing process (including lipofuscin build-up) to such a degree that afflicted individuals can die grey, wrinkled and senescent while still in their 20s. *Progeria* is a genetic disease caused by a single pair of faulty recessive genes (see Chapter 3). The theory is that, if deviant genes can trigger the ageing process abnormally early in progeria patients, the non-deviant counterparts of these genes may eventually perform a similar function in the normal body. Still in the realm of science fiction, at present, is the consequent hope that human ageing may be halted by genetic substitution.

Homeostasis and the compression of morbidity

A concept of *homeostasis*, similar in some ways to Piaget's psychological *equilibration* construct (see

Chapters 2 and 7), forms the basis for James Fries' (1990) theory of ageing. He argues that healthy physiological functioning can be viewed as the continual striving for balance (homeostasis) in the body's internal physiological environment. Thus regulatory systems, including the pituitary gland, the hypothalamus and the pancreas, monitor and readjust levels of hormones, sugar, insulin and other chemicals in the brain, internal organs and bloodstream. In youth, these mechanisms tend to be sensitive, flexible and effective and so the compensating balance of functioning in organs such as the heart, lungs, liver and kidneys is maintained within strict limits.

The reserve capacity of these organs at age 20 is estimated to be four to ten times that needed to sustain life but, over time, this reserve declines. Serious illnesses undermine the body's reserve capacity at a rapid rate, according to Fries (1980), so that the sicker one is during younger life the earlier one will die of 'natural' (i.e. not illness-related) causes in old age. Eventually, even a slight imbalance can block the restoration of homeostasis and so the individual dies.

On the basis of this model, Fries (1990) explained the apparent improvement in longevity over the past century (see Chapter 18) as due primarily to the elimination of traumatic illness and injury, or their reduction in severity. He called this the *compression-of-morbidity* hypothesis. According to this view, advances in medical science that have led to improved innoculation against infectious disease, and better treatments to curb the diseases that do strike, leave bodily organ systems in better shape for most adults now than in past centuries. This improves human longevity but does not retard natural ageing. Consequently, old people live longer (see Chapter 18) and suffer less from periods of infectious and chronic illness owing to improved population health care. But these measures do not genuinely retard the ageing process that is caused by impaired homeostasis, according to Fries. Eventually the homeostatic mechanism will disintegrate and 'natural death' will occur, even in the absence of any discernible injury, morbid illness or sudden disease.

Cellular theories of ageing

It was once thought that cells that were taken out of the body and cultured in glass dishes under ideal laboratory conditions were, for all practical purposes, immortal (Comfort, 1977). More recently, however, it has been shown that, with the possible exception of some malignant cells, all cells grown in any environment reach a fixed number of reduplications and then cease dividing and die. Furthermore, cells removed from a fetus or immature animal divide more times under glass than cells from an aged organism. It seems that all the cells in the body have a preset 'clock', or a fixed maximum lifespan, known as the *Hayflick limit* after the researcher, Leonard Hayflick, who discovered that human cells cannot replicate themselves indefinitely. In life outside the laboratory, the answer to the question of whether the Hayflick limit coincides with normal human life expectancy, or extends so far beyond it as to be practically irrelevant to the timing of ageing, is not yet clear.

Alex Comfort (1977) humorously compared another cellular theory, known as the *free-radical* explanation of ageing, to the action of a group of convention delegates who, as soon as they break free from their wives, frantically begin to attach themselves to all the single bodies in sight. At the cellular level, a comparable process (in which portions of molecules break free and recombine with hitherto independent molecules) is already known to be involved in the souring of milk, the spoilage of meat and the perishing of rubber.

Intriguingly, Comfort (1970) reported on a somewhat counter-intuitive technique that proved effective in extending the lives of laboratory mice. They were fed some of the same antioxidant (or 'preservative') chemicals used in the food industry to retard spoilage and lived longer than the controls. Comfort remained dubious of the relevance to human ageing, however, as the effect may have only 'removed one important cause of presenile death' rather than actually prolonging the mouse's lifespan. In addition, the mice who were fed the unpalatable chemicals ate less. Thus, even if ordinary ageing really was delayed, it might have been as the indirect result of dietary restriction.

A third cellular theory ascribes ageing to cross-linkage of molecules in the body's cells. Cross-links are irreversible bonds caused by a chemical reaction that lead molecules to become rigid, impairing their normal functioning. With increasing age, cross-links

emerge in connective tissues and the DNA of cells, diminishing elasticity and producing leathery rigidity. (The tanning of leather involves a similar process of cross-linking cells.) It is thought that cross-linkage may explain the visible changes to the skin that ageing brings, as well as stiff joints and age-related damage to arteries. The process is accelerated by ultraviolet radiation, a serious concern in the contemporary climate of depletion of the earth's ozone layer owing to human environmental mismanagement.

Environmental insult theories of ageing

Through many avenues, in addition to exposure to ultraviolet radiation, human ageing is accelerated by environmental and lifestyle factors. The analogy between human ageing and the perishing of food or rubber or the tanning of leather implicates the destructive influence on the human body of exposure to sunlight and gamma radiation, which are known to speed the action of free radicals on organic substances. The accumulation of daily doses of sunshine and cosmic radiation could cause cell damage to the human body through either mutation of genetic material or disruption of the immune system. Human mutation rates are known to increase with radiation exposure (see Chapter 3).

In addition, there is evidence to suggest that abnormally high doses of radiation from X-rays or radioactive fallout accelerate ageing. In one study, animals who were dosed with sublethal levels of radiation over a long period died prematurely of 'natural' physical symptoms which mimicked normal ageing. Another intensive medical study of 14 survivors of the Hiroshima bombing likewise found symptoms of the premature ageing of the connective tissues throughout these radiation victims' bodies (Anderson, 1965).

A radiation theory of bodily senescence brings these observations together in the suggestion that the gradual exposure over the course of a lifetime to radiation bombardment culminates in cellular and organ damage. In a normal environment we recognise the process as ageing; when accelerated in an abnormally radioactive environment, similar cell changes lead to radiation disease. Individual differences in susceptibility to radiation insult may modify the rate of decline and eventual longevity.

Voluntary abuse of our body can also contribute to ageing. Abuse includes such environmental insults as emotional stress, poor diet, excess alcohol consumption, use of recreational drugs, tobacco, smog, sports injury and sunburn. Too much hard work can also build up over time to undermine physical wellbeing and therefore the length of a person's life. But it remains to be seen whether the normal ageing process can be viewed as a simple accumulation of the cellular *wear-and-tear* caused by these insults, or whether ageing that results from environmental damage should be considered, like traumatically debilitating diseases and accidents, as a factor that operates independently of 'natural' ageing to shorten life.

Exposure to the sun 'weathers' the skin, according to the environmental insult theory of ageing.

However, even if all of ageing could be ascribed to wear and tear, the fact that the damage occurs to all cells within the body as well as to their internal strands of DNA (see Chapter 3) makes it highly unlikely that the human machine can be rejuvenated in the same way as a car by simple engine replacement. Consequently, the surgical replacement of 'worn-out' body parts such as hearts and kidneys through organ transplant holds little hope of prolonging human life indefinitely.

Optimising health and fitness in old age

Slowed reaction times, muscular weakness, breathing problems and sensory losses can all make getting around, doing things and meeting people quite difficult for an older adult. But the decision about whether to curtail activity during old age in response to one or more of these bodily deficits depends to a surprising degree on mental attitude. Alex Comfort (1977) recalled that his own father experienced a mere two months of restrictive 'old age' during his 94-year lifetime, and these two months of disability were the consequence of accident rather than of chronological ageing. (They followed a lengthy trip on the subway, with a broken rib, on a stiflingly hot day.) Although it could be argued that his father was exceptionally lucky, Comfort attributed his vigour to the fact that he chose 'to face old age like a Cyrano de Bergerac rather than like a doormouse' (p. 181). People's mental attitudes may also shape their idiosyncratic reactions to the changes in physical appearance which ageing brings about, and hence their satisfaction with life. Some of these important differences among individuals during old age are illustrated in Box 16.5.

Chronic illness or debilitating injury to the body can occur at any age. When such calamities strike, they invariably demand psychological and social adjustment. This may include coming to terms with limitations on one's activity or increased dependence on other people. Such adjustments may be more difficult to make during old age as a result of the old person's longer backlog of practice in living independently and more firmly entrenched habits of self-reliance. It is also likely that youthful victims of ill health or accident will gain more sympathy and social support than infirm elderly people as a result of the stereotypes that equate old age with disability. Individual differences in attitude again play a major role in impeding or facilitating coping with disability during old age. Box 16.5 illustrates one individual's relatively easy adaptation to physical losses which might have proved catastrophic earlier in life.

Though Bacon's alchemy could not invent a potion to combat the ageing process (see page 563), a sensible style of living can go a long way towards improving the health and vigour of contemporary

BOX 16.5 Three adults in France show different psychological reactions to biological ageing

Philosopher Simone de Beauvoir gave the following description of her personal reaction to her appearance at age 55.

I often stop, flabbergasted, at the sight of this incredible thing that serves as my face ... I had the impression once of caring very little about what sort of figure I cut. In much the same way, people who enjoy good health and always have enough to eat never give their stomachs a thought. While I was able to look at my face without displeasure, it could look after itself. The wheel eventually stops. I loathe my appearance now: the eyebrows slipping down toward the eyes, the bags underneath, the excessive fullness of the cheeks, and that air of sadness around the mouth that wrinkles always bring. Perhaps the people I pass in the street see merely a woman in her fifties who simply looks her age, no more, no less. But when I look, I see my face as it was, attacked by the pox of time for which there is no cure. (1968, pp. 672–3)

In other words, Simone de Beauvoir felt as though the changes of age resembled a disease which had attacked her face, robbing it of all beauty and turning it into an alien reflection of the self she sensed behind it. Her compatriot, however, the actress Simone Signoret (1978), revealed a different attitude to similar changes in her face. Enjoying the challenge of acting older roles, she noted that 'for me, wrinkles have been allies' (p. 39). Despite (or perhaps because of) belonging to a profession where facial appearance is a prime asset, Signoret valued the lines on her face and the grey hair which enabled her to develop beyond beautiful but shallow theatrical roles to reach a new level of serious acting excellence. She concluded 'the ageing process has helped me pass through a number of toll gates' (p. 39).

The lines on a wrinkled face can be either an asset or a liability, depending on attitude.

In an interview given just before his 70th birthday, another contemporary, the French existential philosopher Jean Paul Sartre, was asked how he was feeling. He replied:

It is difficult to say that I am feeling well, but I can't say that I am feeling bad either. . . . My legs begin to hurt us soon as I walk more than one kilometer, so I don't usually walk any farther than that. I've also had considerable problems with my blood pressure . . . Worst of all, I had hemorrhages behind my left eye – the only eye that I can see out of, since I lost almost all vision in my right eye when I was three years old. Now I can still see forms vaguely, I can see light and colors, but I do not see objects or faces distinctly, and as a consequence, I can neither read nor write . . . Without the ability to read or write, I no longer have even the slightest possibility of being actively engaged as a writer: my occupation as a writer is completely destroyed . . .

Apart from that I am in fine shape, I sleep extremely well. This work with my comrades is going well and I am participating fully. My mind is probably as sharp as it was ten years ago – no more, but no less – and my sensibility has remained the same. Most of the time my memory is good, except for names which I recall only with great effort and which sometimes escape me. I can use objects when I know where they are in advance. In the street I can get along by myself without too much difficulty.

His interviewer then asked how he could remain cheerful in the face of the disabilities which had taken away his vocation as a writer. Sartre replied, highly optimistically:

In a sense, it robs me of all reason for existing: I was, and I am no longer, you might say. I should feel very defeated, but for some unknown reason I feel quite good. I am never sad, nor do I have any moment of melancholy in thinking of what I have lost. (1977, pp. 3–4, used by permission of Pantheon Books, a division of Random House, Inc.)

A balanced diet is an important prerequisite for optimal physical health and psychological functioning during old age

pleasure of eating nutritious food, or when widowhood leads to loneliness and lack of motivation to cook and eat without company. Living in an institution may also lead to poor nutrition if menus and methods of food preparation are very different from those a person has grown accustomed to at home, or simply because residents cannot order the foods that would supplement an unbalanced diet.

Even relatively affluent old people, residing in their own homes in Australian and New Zealand cities and rural areas, may be at risk of poor nutrition, according to a number of surveys (Stuckey, Darnton-Hill, Ash, Brand & Hain, 1981). Community efforts in Australia to improve the nutritional status of widowed or impoverished old people include two important services. The 'meals-on-wheels' program delivers a balanced lunch or dinner to the housebound elderly person's home. In addition, the local seniors' clubs or activity centres in many cities and country towns provide lunches cooked on the premises to aged men and women who attend the centre on a daily basis. But even these interventions are far from adequate in combating the problem of malnutrition among the elderly.

One study of a group of 80 Sydney men and women who received midday meals daily, either from meals-on-wheels or at their activity centre canteen, revealed that a full 81 per cent were at dietary risk as a result of inadequate intake of one or more essential nutrients (Stuckey et al., 1981). Approximately half the aged men and women in this sample were receiving less than the recommended daily allowance of protein and energy. Despite access to vitamin pills, a substantial proportion were also undernourished with calcium, iron and vitamins B and C. The researchers concluded:

These results confirm that the elderly are nutritionally at risk. Males receiving meals-on-wheels appear to be most vulnerable. (p. 118)

Other methods of optimising the elderly person's nutritional intake may therefore involve anything from providing more money to spend on groceries to

older adults. Three ingredients of a health-promoting pattern of life are diet, exercise and the sensible avoidance of risks.

Diet

Nutritional intake is essential for health and growth during childhood and adolescence, but many adults believe they can stop worrying about a balanced diet once their full stature has been achieved. This is untrue. Much ill health during adulthood and old age is caused directly by vitamin deficiency, iron depletion, obesity or the protein malnutrition that may arise from inappropriate dieting or excessive consumption of 'empty calories' in junk food. During old age, poor diet habits developed earlier in life are likely to grow worse – through economic hardship, or when diminished taste sensitivity takes away the free transport to the supermarket, or the social facilitation of dining that the companionship of visiting a married son or daughter's house or chatting over a meal with the local meals-on-wheels volunteer can offer. In one nursing home in Kansas, the nutritional intake of elderly residents was boosted by a simple modification of the menu to eliminate 'either/or' choices. Before this intervention, beverages like milk and Milo had been offered strictly as alternatives to tea and coffee, while fresh fruit was allowed only in substitution for a cooked pudding. When given free access to all these nutritious items, the old people who enjoyed *both* tea and Milo corrected their previous dietary deficiencies by themselves (Risley, 1982).

Exercise

Though the body's strength and mobility may diminish in old age, regular physical exertion remains essential to fitness and good health throughout life. Moderately strenuous exercise like cycling, brisk walking or swimming stimulates the flow of oxygen to the brain and aids kilojoule consumption and the removal of wastes, diminishing the risk of such health problems as obesity and heart disease. One fitness program in which older people were encouraged to jog, dance and do push-ups resulted in significant improvements to many of the aspects of age-related physical loss shown in Figure 16.7, including better cardiac output, breathing capacity and basal metabolism.

A healthy lifestyle: Avoiding avoidable risks

The fact that life expectancy increases with intelligence and education (see Chapter 18) suggests that taking sensible precautions to avoid accidents and unnecessary disease is another way of lengthening life and retarding the physiological ageing process. Such precautions may include breathing smoke-free or smog-free air, avoiding noisy concerts and adopting defensive driving, sexual, eating and drinking habits.

Many older adults are also exposed to special risks from prescription drugs. This is partly because they consume more medication than any other age group (Aiken, 1982) and also because the multiple physical disabilities of old age may require the use of a variety of drugs that interact badly. Furthermore, the elderly often forget what tablets they have taken, or have trouble reading labels, or measure out incorrect quantities of medicine, or misunderstand the doctor's warnings or instructions. Optimisation of this avoidable cause of death and disability may require education as well as restraint when prescribing drugs to treat such chronic, age-related health problems as arthritis, depression and high blood pressure. The avoidance of unnecessary emotional stress may also help to promote the older person's health, though challenging activity is needed in moderation to keep the mind active and to maintain an optimal hormone balance in the bloodstream (Selye, 1979). We return to this issue in Chapter 17 when looking at how social activity influences the ageing process.

Regular daily exercise through participation in sport can assist older adults to maintain optimal health.

Ageing and sport

Olympic athletes age early. Swimmers reach their peak performance at an average age of 18 years (17 for females and 19 for males). Sprint runners, pole-vaulters and long-jumpers show peak records at the average age of 22 (Perlmutter & Hall, 1992). This does not mean that an older athlete is incapable of taking part in these sports, or even of winning the occasional gold medal. But the fact that top performance in each Olympic event depends on an optimal blend of reaction time, strength, coordination and rapid movement means that the first signs of bodily ageing in the late teens and early twenties are a serious disadvantage to professional athletes.

On the other hand, when it comes to playing sport for recreation, the expertise that comes with long years of practice and the sophisticated cognitive strategies that an experienced older sportsperson can bring to a game may outweigh the physical advantages of youth. An Australian study by Ray Over and Patrick Thomas (1995) compared the skills of young (33-year-old) and elderly (62-year-old) amateur golfers. The overall expertise of the young and old groups was matched by choosing golfers from each group who played at the same handicap level (shots taken per round of golf). In line with the age-related changes in physical strength and endurance that were noted earlier in this chapter, Over and Thomas found that older golfers drove the ball a shorter distance on each shot and played fewer risky or unusually difficult shots than their younger peers. But what they lost in energy, vision or global strength, the older golfers gained back through planning, confidence and a positive mental attitude. The older players adopted a more conservative approach to shot-making, prepared mentally for each shot to a greater extent than young players and experienced fewer negative emotions regardless of winning or losing. Some of these differences are illustrated in Figure 16.11.

The processes of cognitive ageing: Memory

Health and biological capacity affect the mind's ability to take in, store, retrieve and process information. But, as we have already noted, an older person's cognitive capacity is also heavily influenced by personality and social factors. Reciprocally, old people can sometimes 'use psychology' to outsmart the purely physical impediments of ageing like slowed reaction time or sensory weakness, as we see when we look at Paul Baltes' (1989) S-O-C model of cognitive ageing later in this chapter.

Lifespan changes in memory performance

Older people sometimes complain that they forget things. But it is difficult to know how much older adults' impressions of forgetfulness reflect genuine loss of memory due to ageing and how much they are a product of social stereotyping. When a younger adult forgets something, the lapse is typically attributed to causes other than age: 'She's feeling overworked', 'He's an absent-minded professor distracted by ideas', 'He's too busy with the kids to notice'. But if an older person displays the same lapse of memory, the ageing of the brain is likely to be blamed.

When it comes to people and events from the past, the old person's memory may be even more vivid than a younger adult's.

Not all elderly men and women report increased forgetfulness during old age. Indeed, the results of one large-scale survey of nearly 15 000 men and women over age 55 in the United States (Cutler & Grams, 1988) revealed that memory loss was an atypical complaint. Only 15 per cent of the sample claimed that they were frequently troubled by forgetfulness, while 20 per cent of those over the age of 85 said they *never* had trouble remembering anything.

Yet when adults are tested in scientific laboratories under controlled conditions, memory performance is typically found to decline with age. Older adults typically recall fewer items when required to commit lists of words to memory and are slower in recalling even the items they do manage to remember. Although the declines with age are often more marked when researchers use cross-sectional designs that confound cohort differences with age (see Chapter 2), memory problems also emerge when using longitudinal methodologies among adults who are over the age of 70 (Coffey & Cummings, 2000; Schaie, 1983).

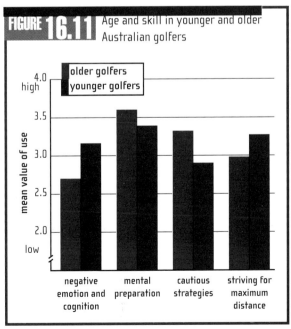

FIGURE 16.11 Age and skill in younger and older Australian golfers

- older golfers
- younger golfers

Source: Based on data in Over & Thomas (1995), p. 6.

Though immediate memory may grow less efficient with age, it is the older student who has the edge when life experience is called upon.

The biographical extract in Box 16.6 illustrates one of the most common memory complaints of older people who do experience forgetfulness: lapses in the recall of people's names.

Strategic compensation: Optimising memory performance in old age

The fact that memory skill typically declines in older adults does not necessarily mean that the neural structure of the brain that supports memory has inexorably deteriorated. In fact, quite the contrary is true, as our earlier discussion of neurocognitive plasticity indicates. Part of the reason why young adult university students typically outperform elderly experimental participants on psychological tests of memory seems to be differences in rates of use of deliberate memorisation strategies. University students learn and practise strategic memorisation techniques like rehearsal and word association (see Chapter 7) to assist their preparation for exams. However, many contemporary elderly adults in countries like Australia and New Zealand did not attend university in their youth. Even if they did, it may have happened so long ago that the need to cram for exams is itself a distant memory rather than the automatic response to an experiment structured around learning words for a test that it may be for a younger student.

Paul Baltes (1993) studied older adults' spontaneous use of memory strategies and found they rarely reported using them; when they did, the types of strategies used were relatively inefficient. Baltes designed a series of experiments to test his theories (a) that deliberate compensation is an effective means of overcoming cognitive losses due to ageing and (b) that the limits of the human mind's plasticity to overcome age-linked declines is far greater than has previously been supposed. In the studies he conducted with Reinhold Kliegl and other colleagues in Germany, Baltes (1993) taught older men and women to use the strategy called the Method of Loci, or Memory Walk. Using this technique, the participant in a memory experiment thinks of each word on the training list as an object located at a fixed position along a familiar walk, such as the route from home to the nearest set of shops. For example, if the list began 'scissors, motorcycle, abacus', the person might visualise scissors on the front door knob, a motorcycle on the front steps, an abacus in the letterbox, and so on.

Baltes and his colleagues found that healthy elderly Berliners responded well to this training and their memory spans improved systematically. After training, many older men and women more than doubled the number of words they could remember. Furthermore, after as little as five hours of training, the average 70-year-old was able to remember as much as an untrained 60-year-old, and a trained 60-year-old could recall as many words as an untrained adult of 50. Nevertheless, there were age-related limits to the brain's plasticity (see Chapter 1). Trained young adults improved even more than an elderly person who had had the benefit of the same amount of training.

Conversely, when university students are prevented from using strategies, their memory performance declines more substantially than an older adult's. For example, in one study (Zacks, 1982) 20-year-old students and 70-year-old community resident adults were asked to recall lists of words drawn from categories that lent themselves readily to two other strategies – *organisation* (in which items are hierarchically categorised; see Chapter 7) or *clustering* (where similar items are mentally grouped together; see Chapter 7). Use of these strategies was prevented in one condition of the experiment by having subjects repeat each word in the list out loud, over and over again until the next one appeared. Under this condition, the elderly and the young adults performed on a par with one another. But when they were free to use these strategies again, the students did better, in line with Baltes' (1993) findings.

When Marion Perlmutter (1986) asked groups of young and elderly men and women to keep diaries in which they recorded their use of strategies to boost memory in everyday life, both age groups made lists, used mnemonics, carried a diary or adopted other deliberate techniques to assist recall of doctors'

BOX 16.6 Absent-minded professors

The psychologist Jean Piaget noted in his autobiography that his memory for recent information had weakened when he was in his seventies. He wrote:

A while ago, it so happened that I congratulated two of my collaborators on a paper they had given me, and which I believed they had written; but they had a good laugh because I was the one who had written it. (1976a, p. 35)

Another elderly psychologist, B. F. Skinner (1983), used the behavioural strategies he had pioneered in his theories of learning (see Chapter 2) as an antidote to his memory lapses when he reached the age of 79. Like many younger people, 79-year-old Skinner had trouble remembering his umbrella, especially if the sun was shining when he left to go outdoors on a day when showers had been predicted. To cope with this memory problem behaviourally, Skinner developed the habit of hanging his umbrella over the knob of the front door or through the handle of his briefcase as soon as he heard a weather forecast of rain. By this means, he minimised the load on his memory by linking it to the habit of going out of the same door and carrying a briefcase that he had built up over a lifetime.

appointments, shopping needs, friends to phone and letters to mail, but the elderly did so more often. Furthermore, Perlmutter found that the adults aged 60 to 80 did better than young adults on these every-day memory tasks, probably owing to the fact that the need for memory strategies in everyday situations was more obvious to them. Older people may, conversely, make less use of strategies in laboratory tests of memory because they are less motivated than younger adults to try hard in the unfamiliar, daunting environment of a scientific laboratory.

Motivation, lifestyle and memory

Motivational changes may also contribute in other ways to observed decreases with age in the efficiency of immediate memory (Welford, 1976). One example is the increase in cautiousness often seen in the elderly. In practice, it is difficult to separate caution from forgetfulness – if people are loath to risk the embarrassment of remembering wrongly (as when an acquaintance is called by an incorrect surname), they may refrain from voicing anything that they recall with less than perfect certainty, whereas less cautious people with equally imperfect memories might seem to remember more simply because of their greater willingness to submit what they think they know to public scrutiny. On speeded memory tasks where items for memorisation are presented at very rapid rates, participants over age 60 are found to make more and more *errors of omission* (not remembering an item which had in fact been presented) as their study time decreases. But *errors of commission* (naming something which had not actually been presented) remain infrequent at all study intervals. Fast pacing therefore seems particularly to boost the tendency to be cautious.

Older people may also put less effort into memorisation in everyday life because they have come to expect fewer rewards for such effort than younger adults who are caught up in the memory-demanding 'exigencies of work and bringing up children' (Welford, 1976, p. 197). Slowness of reaction speed could also make them more cautious by decreasing self-confidence and the motivation to memorise. In cross-sectional laboratory studies, differences between the generations might likewise help to explain motivational differences in the decision as to whether to stretch memory capacity to its furthest limit. Cohort differences in familiarity with nonsense syllables, or beliefs about the usefulness of scientific research might unfairly bias the results of memory comparisons in favour of younger adults. It may be, as Welford (1976) suggests, that as age augments the mental exertion required for memorisation and/or correspondingly diminishes the older person's expectation of a favourable result (either because mistakes cost more than they used to or because being able to remember correctly does not mean as much), less and less effort is put into the task of trying to remember.

Welford also drew attention to the prevalence of individual differences in memory skill among the aged, making the important point that these could reflect either capability or motivation or both. He noted that 'anyone who has observed older people knows that some individuals use limited powers to the utmost, while others leave much greater powers idle' (p. 189).

In studies of memory, it is often difficult to separate the influence of changes in lifestyle and living environment during old age from the influence of the ageing process itself. One study that did effectively separate these two variables (Rabbitt, 1993) began by matching two groups of elderly volunteers on the basis of age and general intelligence. One group consisted of older men and women who had recently moved into age-segregated nursing homes. The other group were still living in their own homes in mixed-age neighbourhoods. When their memories for recent and long-distant autobiographical events were compared, the nursing-home elderly were found to be better at remembering events from their early years than things which had happened to them quite recently. But the opposite was true of the elderly still living in the community. Thus, the supposedly old-age-specific effect of 'living in the past' and consequent loss of memory from the present appeared to be confirmed in men and women whose current environment and lifestyle afforded them relatively few opportunities for personal initiative and decision-making (see Chapter 17: discussion of personal control in the nursing home environment).

In addition, Rabbitt suggested that people in residential care spend more time rehearsing the past than do community elderly. Nursing home staff and fellow residents are apt to encourage reminiscence and life review, whereas old people living in a mixed-age neighbourhood may be too busy dealing with the present to have time to reminisce about their childhood, adolescence or early adult life.

Metamemory, self-efficacy and personal control

Feelings of confidence can be a product of social expectations about elderly forgetfulness as much as of one's own awareness of memory capabilities. On the basis of her extensive studies of memory performance in Australian adults, Mary Luszcz (1993) wondered whether older people know as much about the way memory operates as the young adult university students with whom they are often compared in laboratory studies of memory. Recall (see Chapter 7) that the term *metamemory* refers to an individual's knowledge and beliefs about memory as distinct from actual memorisation itself.

It is quite conceivable that older men and women would have less well-developed metamemories than young adults, since fewer members of the cohort now in their 60s and 70s had the opportunity to complete higher education and, of those who did, the experience of using memory in the context of passing exams is much further in the past than for the average 20-year-old. To test this possibility, Luszcz presented a questionnaire on metamemory to a sample of 40 Australians, 20 of whom were under age 30 and the remainder over the age of 65. Their knowledge of memory strategies, memory capacity and span limitations, and the influence of task characteristics on memory performance were explored. In addition, these adults were asked to complete two actual memorisation exercises. They were asked to read and remember a passage from a Grimm Brothers fairy tale and a passage from a non-fiction text on Antarctica.

The results indicated that younger and older Australians did equally well in remembering the narrative passage from the fairy tale, and both groups recalled this information better than the expository passage of scientific text. Possibly because of their significantly higher formal educational attainments, the young adults did better than the older group at remembering the scientific textual information. Both groups had quite impressive metamemories when it came to straightforward factual knowledge about how memory operates. But the elderly Australians had a diminished sense of self-efficacy about their own memory capacities. In contrast to young adults, the older men and women attributed their memory lapses mainly to internal factors like lack of ability. The younger group, on the other hand, were inclined to blame any memory problems they experienced on bad luck, on the difficulty of the task, or on the fact that the passage was too long for anyone to be able to memorise it without error. Recall the findings reported in Chapter 9 that children's attribution of their poor academic performance to external factors, like the ones the young adults were using, was linked with academic success and strong motivation to achieve. On the other hand, children who make the same sort of internal attributions for failure that the elderly Australian group in Luszcz's study were using are found to perform badly in school. Luszcz concluded that:

> Older adults are more sensitive to memory limitations and maintain strong beliefs in their personal

responsibility for memory performance. If, with advancing age, memory self-efficacy is eroded, its possible role in moderating memory performance warrants further examination. For instance, low memory self-efficacy may interfere with adopting effective strategies even though one is aware of their utility. (p. 19)

Autobiographical memory

Memory of the distant past seems to suffer less (if, indeed, it suffers at all) from the ravages of time. In one study of memory for real events out of recent decades of modern history, the best recall was shown by people who had been in their 20s at the time the events had happened, *regardless of their age when memory was tested* (Botwinick & Storandt, 1974). Klaus Riegel (1972) likewise found that older people remembered as many people from their early childhood as from among their recent range of acquaintances, whereas young and middle-aged adults' memories for people were disproportionately biased in favour of those first met within the previous five years.

Gillian Cohen and Dorothy Faulkner (1987) asked 154 British adults to think over their past lives and report six of the most vivid memories that came into their minds. They were divided into three age groups: 20-year-olds, 50-year-olds and the over-60s. All three groups remembered a greater proportion of events from childhood and youth than from any other age period in their lives. Births, marriages and deaths of immediate kin were the events recalled most frequently, followed by holidays, trivia and illnesses. World War II was a common memory for old people who had served in it, and for middle-aged and elderly men and women who recalled blitz bombings and evacuations.

The adults were also asked to rate their memories in terms of emotional and pictorial vividness. Contrary to what might have been predicted on the basis of decline theories of ageing, the elderly people's memories were more vivid overall than younger adults'. Frequent rehearsal appeared to be one factor responsible for the aged group's superiority, but many of their memories of childhood and early adulthood also had special meaning for the elderly during old age. Thus, use of memory via *life review* in a productive way to achieve an effective resolution to the personality crisis over integrity (see Chapter 17) may also have enhanced the vividness of autobiographical memories for the older group. These data combine with findings cited earlier and with other evidence of superior autobiographical memory in the elderly (Baltes, 1993) to suggest that, although memory functions differently in old age than in youth, it is by no means deficient. In fact, some of the memories of older people are extremely well preserved.

Morris Moskovitch and Gordon Winocur (2002) compared the autobiographical memories of older and younger adults. Two examples appear in the exercise in Box 16.7. In these examples, the older

Younger and older adults are likely to do equally well at remembering a narrative passage, as in this illustration, but young students are better at memorising passages of scientific text.

BOX 16.7 Activity suggestion
Who remembers what?

Instructions. *The two passages below, adapted from the materials used in a study of semantic and episodic memory described in the text (Moskovitch & Winocur, 2002), typify responses by an elderly person and a young adult to the task of reporting a salient recollection from the previous year. Can you guess which is which? Also (a) try to guess the age (in years) of the adults who reported these memories and (b) try to identify an instance of an episodic and a semantic memory feature in at least one of the transcripts. For answers, see the text.*

RESPONDENT A

I'm very close to my youngest sister's family, but she died four years ago. I'm very close to all her great kids. I've always had Friday night dinners with that branch of the family since my husband and I are no longer together. So after my sister died my brother-in-law kept up the family dinners and that's always a big do. I'm fond of the family and it's something I look forward to very, very much. In the winter, when he goes away on business, I go over all the same. So we keep this thing going on every Friday night. I am closer to them, actually, than I am to my own branch of the family. This is an ongoing thing that is very precious to me.

RESPONDENT B

An Italian restaurant. It was on the second floor of this restaurant and it was busy. I was at this little table. It was tiny. The man I was with was a big man. He was 6 foot 4 inches and he looked really huge. Too big for the table. He was a bit impatient with the service and I remember talking to him about Italian food. He ordered pizza and I think his had eggplant on it and I don't like eggplant. I don't remember what mine had on it though. I remember I didn't eat the whole thing. I asked the waiter to wrap it up so I could take it home. I remember the waiters were wearing white aprons, white shirts with a tie. We were going to order wine but we didn't.

adults' memories are rich in *semantic* memory features, including narrative accounts, meaningful connections, emotional associations and general patterns. The young adults, by contrast, excel at *episodic* memory for discrete lists of highly specific dates, times, numbers and other particular facts and figures.

Moskovitch and Winocur found that there were systematic declines with age, from early adulthood through the 70s, in episodic memories involving highly specific factual details and one-off events, such as Respondent B's memory of the eggplant on the pizza in Box 16.7. However, more emotionally significant and generic memories, known as semantic memories, showed no decline with age. An example of a semantic memory is Respondent A's memory of

the 'big do' and pleasant experiences associated with Friday night dinners with her widowed brother-in-law's family. As you may have guessed from the differential distribution of memories of each type in the two adults' transcripts, Respondent B was in her 20s and Respondent A was in her 70s.

Memory and personality: Life review and reminiscence

The use of memory or reminiscence to evoke an image of a deceased friend or relative is one aspect of a more general phenomenon known as *life review*. This term describes the old person's tendency to talk and think about the past, as a means of putting their psychological house in order as a preparation for death (see Chapter 18). Often, very old people will reminisce to the point of seeming to lack interest in, or contact with, the present. In addition to feeling bored by a garrulous elderly relative, or by a patient's continual reiteration of the same often incoherent anecdotes dredged up from the distant past, old people's caregivers often worry that such intense preoccupation with the past may be psychologically damaging. But Robert Butler (1968), who was one of the first psychologists to study the process scientifically, concluded that the act of engaging in life review could serve a potentially therapeutic function, especially during old age. As he explained, life review is:

> A naturally occurring universal mental process characterized by the progressive return to consciousness of past experiences, and particularly, the resurgence of unresolved conflicts; simultaneously, and normally, these revived experiences and conflicts are surveyed and reintegrated. It is assumed that this process is prompted by the realization of approaching dissolution and death, and by the inability to maintain one's sense of personal invulnerability. (p. 266)

Butler concluded that, when old people are allowed to reminisce freely, the outcome of the life review is generally beneficial:

> In the majority of the elderly, life review enables substantial reorganization of the personality [and] the evolution of such qualities as wisdom and serenity, long-noted in some aged persons. (p. 271)

Such serenity might even help to mitigate the fear of death (see Chapter 18). However, life review can also become detrimental to elderly people's emotional well-being when they find they are unable to come to terms with the past events and failures that memory dredges up. The consequences may be anxiety, depression, panic, guilt, obsession, schizophrenic withdrawal or even suicide.

In a further study of the life review process, Victor Molinari and Robert Reichlin (1985) endeavoured to distinguish more precisely between its evidently beneficial and its pathological aspects. They began by defining life review as 'that form of reminiscence in which the past is actively evaluated and conflict is necessary for resolution to occur' (p. 83). In other words, life review differs from other forms of thinking or talking about the past, such as:

- *Oral history,* or recounting anecdotes from the past to inform others of one's own experience and maintain the thread of continuity between past and future generations
- *Defensive fantasising,* or telling a distorted account of a past event in order to allay one's own anxieties or overcome guilt feelings
- *Escapist reminiscing,* or the individual's use of private recollection or storytelling as a means of substituting memories of a more pleasant past for the painful present.

These forms of reminiscence lack the essential feature of conflict resolution that is central to life review as Molinari and Reichlin defined it. Their model of the life review is a dialectic one (see pages 40–42). They argued that, as with any other dialectical conflict, the outcome of the life review process can conceivably take any one of three different forms – development, deterioration or a return to the preconflict state. For example, the conflict brought out in the life review might involve the person's memory of an action that clashes with their overall self-concept (e.g. an instance of exceptional courage, a violation of ethical standards or an uncharacteristic, but serious, neglect of a friend in need).

If the person is able to integrate the dissonant remembered action into a better understanding of self, the outcome may be the development of a new level of wisdom or 'integrity' (Erikson, 1968a). But conflict does not always create progressive developmental change. Sometimes the outcome is disintegrative, and the individual becomes more anxious, depressed or self-recriminating through being unable to synthesise opposing elements brought out by the review process. When this happens, the obsessive or defensive forms of reminiscence described above may be used to escape the conflict.

Molinari and Reichlin's review of empirical studies of reminiscence showed that both destructive and constructive developmental resolutions were indeed possible. But the latter seemed to be much more frequent than the former, at least among healthy community-dwelling adults. One study, comparing widows who reminisced frequently with those who indulged in reminiscence rarely or never, found that the reminiscers scored lower in depression than the others. Additional studies showed more adaptive reactions to stress and greater consistency between past and present self-concepts, the more frequently elderly men engaged in life review. Also, despite the suggestion that friends and acquaintances may grow bored with the reminiscence process, Molinari and Reichlin found that affluent older men and women who reminisced frequently had a wider and more intimate circle of friends than their income-matched peers who rarely or never engaged in life review. However, studies of the institutionalised elderly have linked reminiscing about the past with unhappiness, stress, hopelessness and psychological impairment. The difference may be that an institutionalised old person has fewer social or personal resources than an integrated community member to aid the healthy, developmental resolution of *dialectical conflicts* (see Chapters 2 and 15). Molinari and Reichlin concluded:

> Unsuccessful life review [may be] more commonly found in institutional settings. From this point of view, institutionalized individuals would be seen as lacking the opportunity to resolve the conflict that arises in the course of reminiscence given that their environment tends to reflect a failure of autonomy. In addition, there are few possibilities for becoming involved in the activities that enhanced self-esteem prior to institutionalization. (p. 86)

Life review and psychological well-being

After reviewing a total of 97 studies of the effects of the life review process on psychological functioning and emotional well-being, published between 1960 and 1990, Barbara Haight (1991) concluded that the evidence is overwhelmingly in favour of the benefits of life review, even for institutionalised and housebound elderly. In fact, less than 5 per cent of the large number of studies she analysed showed any statistically significant adverse effects of life review or reminiscence. But many showed clearly significant benefits for elderly institutional and community residents.

As a typical example of the studies revealing these positive outcomes, Haight described a longitudinal investigation of life reviews by a group of institutionalised Canadians, undertaken in the context of anthropological research (Holzberg, 1984). The 25 Jewish men and women who took part in this study were residents in an integrated geriatric care facility. Their ages ranged from 70 to 95 years. Over a period of 11 months, they met once a week with an anthropologist who questioned them about their life experiences, especially their early lives in Europe and their first encounters with Canadian culture as Jewish immigrants. Their responses were tape-recorded and they were also encouraged to write further memoirs privately. As well as providing valuable data for anthropology and oral history, the life review process had a clearly positive impact on the mental health and emotional well-being of the elderly institutional residents. In fact, the speaking and writing of their memoirs helped these older adults to achieve personal growth and the sense of personal integrity that is highlighted in Erik Erikson's theory of old age (see Chapter 2). In addition, they reported increased life satisfaction and self-confidence as a consequence of the opportunity to help in the preservation of important historical data.

From the perspective of her own clinical interests as a nurse and nurse educator, Haight concluded that clinicians working with the institutionalised and community-dwelling elderly should continue to use reminiscing as a therapeutic tool, while researchers should devote further attention to identifying those aspects of reminiscence that contribute most strongly to its effectiveness.

The processes of cognitive ageing: Intelligence

Neither Jean Paul Sartre (Box 16.5) nor Jean Piaget (Box 16.6) appeared to feel too bothered by the difficulties with immediate memory brought on by old age. Possibly this was because what really mattered to them both was their thinking capacity. Clearly, the intellect had undergone no age-related decline in either case. One of Piaget's anecdotes about his intellectual capacity as an octogenarian is reported in Box 16.8.

BOX 16.8 **A case in point**
Taking a PhD exam at 80

In his autobiography Jean Piaget gave this account of a proposal for celebrating his 80th birthday. It clearly testifies to his confidence that his intellectual powers remained unimpaired.

Let us end with an anecdote which will show better than any other that our house is still filled with teachers and authors whose first rule is: 'Don't take yourself too seriously.' In order to celebrate my coming 80th birthday in a pleasant rather than a sad and solemn manner, my colleagues suggested that I should sit for an oral exam in defense of my doctoral thesis before an examining panel made up of themselves and some invited students, who would offer a critique of my last book on 'Equilibration' and would see how well I could defend my position. In fact I never actually passed any exams in psychology, and the oral defense of my doctorate in 1918 had to do with alpine molluscs. The idea of being able to put this scandalous situation to rights, especially before a jury of former pupils, was therefore both appealing and amusing. The Chancellor and Vice Chancellors were also amused by this initiative which they recognized as coming from a faculty which delights in the unexpected. A few members of the university unfortunately decided that the exercise 'was not being taken seriously', however, with the result that my orals will not be official and must be treated as a private game among ourselves. This means that I shall still die without the right diplomas, and shall have to carry with me to the grave the secret of the gaps in my knowledge. (1976a, p. 43)

As discussed in Chapter 2, the results of cross-sectional studies of mental ability that were conducted during the middle of last century to standardise widely used intelligence tests (IQ tests), like David Wechsler's (1989), suggested such a steep decline in IQ during middle and late adulthood that a bonus score, known as the *deterioration quotient*, was automatically added on to the scores of older men and women who took the test. Yet in more recent longitudinal studies, cognitive abilities have been shown to improve from early to later adulthood (see Figure 16.12).

The mythical equation of old age with 'senility' (see page 562) and the consequent worry that any person's mental capacity will deteriorate, provided they live long enough, is a very real one for many people – so much so that it probably accounts for more dread and mistrust of old age than all its purely physical ailments put together. But recent research has indicated that suffering senile dementia or cognitive incapacity from Alzheimer's disease or degenerative neurological conditions has a low probability of arising in most adults' lives. The notion that senility is inevitable is another ill-founded myth about ageing. In part, this view reflects the same confusion between 'normal' ageing and abnormal disease and injury that was seen to cloud understanding of the physical ageing process, as we noted earlier. In part, confusion is understandable. Some of the methods researchers used in the past to evaluate intellectual capacity in old age led to controversial findings. Thus conclusions about whether intelligence declines, remains stable or, indeed, increases with the transition from middle to old age need to be carefully evaluated in light of the methodologies used to study age-related changes (see Chapter 2).

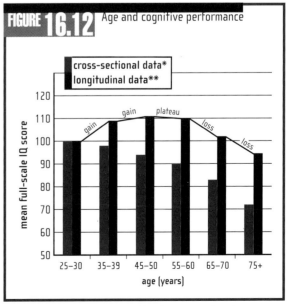

FIGURE 16.12 Age and cognitive performance

Source: Based on data in Kaufman (1990)* and Schaie (2000)**.

Age and IQ scores:
A critical look at the scientific evidence

The issue of whether we can expect to lose cognitive capacity in old age is of crucial significance to every adult. As we have seen, prejudices and stereotypes about the inevitability of aged senility abound. But what does the research evidence say? Unfortunately, the research evidence itself is mixed, partly because of the difficulty of designing a 'pure' test of the effect of chronological age on intellectual functioning. At least four distinct methodological issues are likely to complicate any conclusions to be drawn from studies examining changes in a person's IQ score (intelligence quotient) from early adulthood to old age:

1. increased risks of illness in old age which may become confounded with healthy ageing in a random sample of participants
2. the fact of *terminal drop* – namely a decline in IQ scores in the years immediately preceding natural death
3. cohort confounds with age in cross-sectional studies
4. contamination from practice effects and selective attrition in longitudinal evidence.

Let us briefly examine each of these issues.

DISEASE VERSUS HEALTHY AGEING AS CAUSES OF COGNITIVE DECLINE

None of us thinks best when ill or seriously injured. Whenever possible, young adults will postpone cognitively demanding tasks, like sitting an exam or giving an oral presentation, until they have recovered

Their more recent and more extensive exposure to formal education may be more important than age in boosting young adults' IQ scores relative to those of older men and women.

from flu, fever or pain. But for older adults in experimental studies of intelligence, postponement may not be possible. Many older men and women suffer chronic illnesses, like arthritis, which cause pain. Others have been the victim of one of the many injuries and diseases (such as alcohol abuse, arteriosclerosis or viral encephalitis) which can damage the brain in ways that reduce thinking capacity. Some of these (e.g. car accidents or meningitis) are relatively sudden and can occur at any age. But other cumulative degenerative processes (e.g. arteriosclerosis and Alzheimer's disease) become more evident with the passage of time.

Statistically, the risk of incurring a senile brain disease, even in old age, is extremely remote. Douglas Kimmel (1974) estimated that only about 2 per cent of the aged population are admitted to hospital for any form of cerebral arteriosclerosis, senility or mental dysfunction. Though the proportion of people suffering from these diseases in the community could be somewhat higher, it is nonetheless unrealistic to view senile brain disorder as an automatic consequence of ageing.

TERMINAL DROP IN IQ

There are two ways to measure a person's age. One, the familiar approach, is to count the years since they were born. Another, rarely used, is to count backwards in years from their death (e.g. an individual who died at 60 was five years pre-death at age 55). The latter approach is illuminating when applied to IQ scores. It seems that the belief that old age causes cognitive decline is due in part to a confusion between old age and nearness to death, when age since birth is the index of ageing. In fact, the ill health immediately preceding death frequently does diminish mental alertness (Riegel, 1971). Thus, when R. W. Kleemeier (1962) measured the intellectual functioning of a group of 13 elderly patients (who had all been of comparable intelligence four years previously), he found that the four men who scored lowest were the first to die. Imminent death, and not age itself, seemed to have produced their mental deterioration.

Other longitudinal studies have likewise shown that a *terminal drop* in intelligence occurs consistently, though not invariably, several months before a person dies. But since death can occur at any age, the terminal drop is not properly identifiable with ageing. Statistically, however, older populations will include a larger proportion of individuals who are nearing death, so it is common to confuse the two when contrasting the intelligence scores of various adult age groups using the cross-sectional method (see Chapters 1 and 2).

LIMITATIONS OF CROSS-SECTIONAL AND LONGITUDINAL EVIDENCE ON AGE AND INTELLIGENCE

Early studies, which used exclusively cross-sectional research designs, agreed almost unanimously that intelligence declined steadily after early adulthood. In fact, as noted above, the large-scale standardisation studies that went into the development of the WAIS intelligence test led David Wechsler (1955, 1989) to conclude that peak IQ was attained at age 25; thereafter a continuous drop resulted in an average loss of 25 per cent of a person's total intelligence as it was at age 25 by the time they reached the age of 60. In addition to the problem of terminal decline, the cross-sectional method that Wechsler employed incorporates the serious flaw of confounding age differences with generational differences. Thus, what appears to be the effect of growing older might in fact be the effect of differences in educational background or other life experience between recent and earlier cohorts. More recent studies show a similar pattern, as illustrated in Figure 16.13.

Historical changes in general knowledge and vocabulary can also lead to revision of the tests favouring one generation over another. (Being asked the meaning of a word like 'cybernetics', for example, could unfairly disadvantage a person who left school before the concept was invented, while the reverse might be true of relatively archaic words like 'soughing', 'davenport' or 'wimple'.)

The cross-sectional method's inability to tease out the contribution of cohort or generational difference to apparent age trends is a serious problem. Cohort factors do contribute substantially to intellectual functioning in adulthood. For example, one *time-lag* (see Chapter 2) study of 53-year-olds over the period from 1890 to 1930 showed variations in IQ irrespective of age (Baltes, 1987). Those born in 1890 were substantially better on tests of word fluency than their age peers born between 1900 and 1930. But the group born before the turn of the century did sub-

Can you name these objects? If so, you would probably score higher on Wechsler or Binet's original intelligence tests than on their revised editions being used today.

stantially worse than more recent generations on measures of word meaning and reasoning by induction. Paul Baltes concluded that:

Depending on the prevailing cultural conditions, the level and course of intellectual ageing can vary markedly. Any single cohort-specific observation does not tell the final story on the nature of intellectual ageing. (p. 620)

To overcome the problem of cohort differences, researchers as early as the 1950s began to study intelligence by the alternative longitudinal procedure (see Chapter 2). Intriguingly, their results contradicted Wechsler's. Louis Terman and Melita Oden (1959) found steady *increases* in intelligence among a group of gifted adults and their spouses from age 30 'at least through 50 years of age', and Nancy Bayley and Oden (1955) found similar intellectual growth among a more average group of Californian adults across the same age range.

Subsequent longitudinal studies following individuals into their 60s and 70s have offered further proof of the fallibility of the cross-sectional approach, as well as registering considerable agreement among themselves. R. D. Savage summarised the results of his own and eight other major longitudinal studies as showing that the retesting of subjects below the age of 74 generally results in an increase in IQ over age, whereas the two studies that tracked their subjects past age 75 showed drops after this point (see Table 16.3).

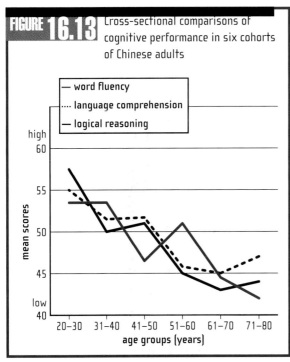

Source: Schaie et al. (2001), p. 199, Figure 1.

TABLE 16.3	Longitudinal studies of normal aged samples: Mean differences between initial and second assessment			
Nationality of sample	Number of subjects	Age at second assessment (in years)	Difference in full-scale IQ score between initial and second assessment	Time between initial and second assessment
United States	85	64.80	4.14	41.1 months
United States	80	74.60	0.527	38.67 months
United States	184	64.97**	–3.01*	8.65 years
United States	64	61.20**	3.05	104 days
German	51	60–64	2.7	60 months
German	48	65–69	0.5	60 months
German	44	70–74	1.9	60 months
German	34	75+	–3.4*	60 months
British	111	77.00	–2.6*	3 years

Indicates that performance at second assessment is lower than at initial assessment.
**Age at initial assessment.*

SELECTIVE ATTRITION IN LONGITUDINAL STUDIES

Terminal declines were consistently observed in the longitudinal studies that Savage, Britton, Bolton and Hall (1973) reviewed. For example, in their own research in the UK, Savage and his colleagues found that, over a seven-year span, the old people who survived to complete each subsequent test had averaged significantly higher scores on the previous tests than their peers who died in the interim. Savage concluded that:

> In a longitudinal study, an originally representative sample of elderly subjects can become biased in favour of higher intelligence since those with initially lower intelligence scores tend to die, or at least drop out earlier. (1973, p. 125)

On the other hand, the terminal drop also invalidates the attribution of group differences in cross-sectional intelligence studies to the pure influence of age, since each cross-sectional group may incorporate an unknown proportion of individuals who are currently in the midst of the terminal drop.

R. D. Savage (1973) also examined developmental changes in several separate components of intelligence, using the longitudinal method. The Wechsler test breaks the overall IQ score down into a 'verbal' and a 'performance' component. Verbal intelligence encompasses abilities like vocabulary size and sentence comprehension, whereas performance tasks include copying patterns made up of coloured blocks and creating a story from a sequence of wordless cartoons. Savage found that verbal intelligence began to decline after the first test (given when the subjects' average age was 71) and dropped significantly across the seven-year interval through which the old people

were followed (see Figure 16.14). Performance intelligence, on the other hand, increased markedly with age up to 76 and then levelled off. The overall rise in IQ was thus largely confined to the performance domain.

One IQ or many?
The different kinds of intelligence

To understand fully how intellectual capacity changes in old age, we need to be aware of the distinctions that researchers often draw among the various components of an intelligence test score. The contrast between verbal IQ items (like word knowledge) and performance IQ items (like puzzle completion) that R. D. Savage and his associates drew was discussed earlier. As shown in Figure 16.14, this contrast made an important difference to the patterns of longitudinal change in IQ from age 70 to 80 that Savage and his team observed. In their UK community sample, performance IQ scores rose from age 71 to age 76, while verbal scores declined from age 71 to age 74. Some of the gains in the performance domain may reflect the benefits of practice with specific test items. For example, an adult might play with the task of reciting number sequences backwards between visits to the lab for a formal IQ test. Indeed, practice effects, like selective attrition, plague the results of most longitudinal studies. Once exposed to a test item, a participant is apt to retain some memory for it. But it is also conceivable that the evidence of differential gains in performance IQ in old age is genuine. Perhaps no new opportunities for vocabulary

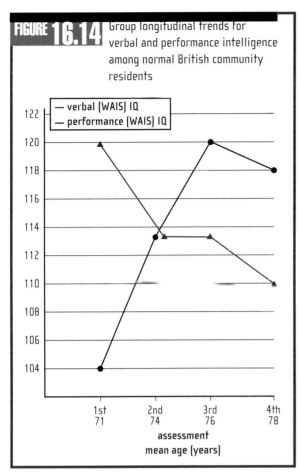

FIGURE 16.14 Group longitudinal trends for verbal and performance intelligence among normal British community residents

— verbal (WAIS) IQ
— performance (WAIS) IQ

assessment
mean age (years)

Source: Reproduced from Savage et al. (1973). Intellectual functioning in the aged, with permission of the authors and Methuen & Co.

and language growth arose for the older men and women in Savage's sample. However, these adults could have undertaken leisure activities in their 70s, such as jigsaw puzzles or computer games, that may genuinely have boosted their performance capacities (see Box 16.4).

Another important distinction for the study of adult intelligence is that between 'crystallised' and 'fluid' mental abilities. *Crystallised intelligence* reflects the long-term memory storage, the lasting mechanics of knowledge and distilled information, and is heavily shaped by the effects of schooling, experience and past knowledge. *Fluid intelligence* involves short-term memory and abilities that may be bound up in rapid thinking and the learning of new material or may reflect perceptual processes involving spatial and pattern detection and other non-verbal cognitive skills.

As might have been expected on the basis of the studies of reaction time and memory that were discussed earlier in this chapter, crystallised intelligence is often found to withstand the detrimental consequences of ageing more readily than fluid intelligence, which may rely on speeded components. For example, in their longitudinal studies, Savage and his colleagues (1973) discovered that adults' crystallised

mental abilities remained constant for a longer stretch through the early and mid 70s than fluid intelligence, or learning ability, which displayed some decline from age 71 onward. This was true in both the verbal and the performance areas. It also applied equally well to normal old people who lived in the community and to a hospitalised sample who were suffering from psychotic breakdown and organic brain damage.

An important application of this result is that the aged should be given the greatest possible opportunity to make use of the knowledge and information they have acquired over the course of a lifetime. When they are expected to learn everything afresh as a result of such changes in lifestyle as the shift from their own home to a retirement community, or from one hospital or nursing home to another, they are forced to rely on their weakened learning ability, rather than on the crystallised intelligence which remains relatively immune from the effects of ageing.

The cohort-sequential research design combines both cross-sectional and longitudinal information to make independent estimates of generational change and average age-related change. K. Warner Schaie (2000) described the results of cohort-sequential studies as showing declines in most adults on at least some IQ subscales in very advanced old age.

Yet Schaie also found that the declines in IQ did not begin until after age 60 for the average adult on any of the subtests apart from one measure of 'word fluency', which was heavily dependent on rapid responding. (Recall the age-related changes in motor reaction speed that were discussed earlier in this chapter.) Furthermore, an overall improvement from one generation to the next (which these researchers described as 'cultural obsolescence') tended to overshadow any declines due purely to age. Variance attributable to age was generally much less than that attributable to cohort differences. Furthermore, K.W. Schaie and Iris Parham (1977) found that individual differences were also so great, relative to age differences, that none of the older adults fell below the average range of performance of the younger adults except on the speeded word task. This observation led to the conclusion that:

> There is ... little justification to limit or restrict privileges or opportunities for the elderly on the basis of presumed generalized decline. (p. 653)

Jack Block's (1971) longitudinal studies at Berkeley also illustrate the importance of individual personality differences in determining whether intellectual assets and liabilities are developed or lost over the course of the lifespan. In general, Block concluded that:

> For the lower ranges of ability ... intelligence appears to be a shaping force on character and the consequences of life; for the upper ranges, character and life are more likely to determine the [eventual] shape of one's intelligence. (p. 275)

Successful cognitive ageing

Paul Baltes (1987) used the phrase 'selective optimization with compensation' to describe his observations of the balance of gains and losses in cognitive functioning during old age. An example would be a skilled elderly chess player overcoming the handicap of slower mental processing speed by using his expert knowledge of his opponent's probable strategies, built up over a lifetime of playing with diverse adversaries. At the level of motor performance, experienced older secretaries are found to compensate for slower typing speed with more efficient reading forward through the copy they are typing from.

According to Baltes, cognitive functions normally become more smooth, specialised and efficient with age and practice. Therefore, if losses arise due to accident, disease or biological ageing, the individual has a reserve capacity to fall back on. As a result, existing 'knowledge systems ... can continue to evolve and function at peak levels' (p. 617) even during old age. But once these reserves are depleted, people cope by narrowing the range of tasks they put their minds to, or by developing compensatory mechanisms to substitute for the skills they have lost. While more evident during old age, the same processes of specialisation and compensation also arise earlier in life, as when the school child substitutes verbal memorisation for the vivid pictorial imagery of the preschooler (see Chapter 7) or ceases to draw expressively after achieving literacy. As Baltes explained:

> Development at all points of the life course is a joint expression of features of growth (gain) and decline (loss). It is assumed that any developmental progression displays at the same time new adaptive capacity as well as the loss of previously existing capacity. No developmental change during the life course is pure gain. (p. 616)

Baltes' (1993) model of cognitive functioning in old age is illustrated in Figure 16.15.

Most old people suffer one or more of the biological losses we looked at earlier in this chapter at some point during old age. But, when selective-optimisation-by-compensation is practised, people draw on experience to find ways of continuing to perform important cognitive tasks that minimise dependency on their declining biological capacity. For example, elderly long-distance runners who wish to continue running in old age after muscular strength and endurance have begun to decline might, as a first step, cut out other energy-draining activities from their everyday routines. This is Baltes' process of *selection*. Then they might begin to pay closer attention to their diet. By monitoring daily rises and falls in energy levels they can plan new strategies to maximise energy and endurance (such as eating more iron-rich foods or running only early in the morning). This is the process of *compensation*. Finally, the runner might learn new strategies for preventing injury such as new warm-up techniques or running in better shoes. This is *optimisation*. As a real-life example, Baltes (1993) cited the cognitive planning for running that his psychologist colleague Herschel Leibowitz had engaged in during his 50s. Discovering that no one pair of specialised running shoes was optimal, Leibowitz bought himself 10 different pairs. By rotating these so as to wear a different pair every day on his run, he was able to avoid the damage to his feet and leg muscles that exclusive use of any one type of shoe might produce in conjunction with physical ageing.

Another example of compensating cognitively for the physical losses of ageing emerged earlier in this

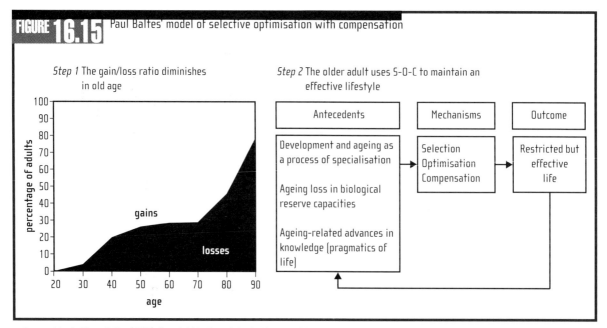

FIGURE 16.15 Paul Baltes' model of selective optimisation with compensation

Step 1 The gain/loss ratio diminishes in old age

Step 2 The older adult uses S-O-C to maintain an effective lifestyle

Antecedents | Mechanisms | Outcome

Development and ageing as a process of specialisation

Ageing loss in biological reserve capacities

Ageing-related advances in knowledge (pragmatics of life)

Selection Optimisation Compensation

Restricted but effective life

Source: Adapted from Baltes (1993). Copyright by Gerontological Society of America. Reproduced with permission of Gerontological Society of America in the format textbook via Copyright Clearance Center.

chapter in the study of elderly Australian golfers. In line with Baltes' model, the older golfers in this study found ways of compensating for the physical losses of ageing through planning and cognitive skill. They learned to substitute a series of shorter shots (compensation) for the long swings they no longer had the strength to deliver or the visual acuity to direct with accuracy. Similarly, golfers use optimisation when they exercise off the golf course to build up muscles they will need in the game, and selection when they rely on memory or maps in place of ageing eyesight to work out distances on the green.

Wisdom

Intelligence was defined by David Wechsler as the 'global capacity of the individual to act purposefully, to think rationally, and to deal effectively with his environment' (Matarazzo, 1972, p. 79).

The term *wisdom*, while similar to intelligence in many respects, has a slightly different connotation. Reflecting an integrated and distilled understanding associated with the accumulation of life experience, the adjective 'wise' is more often used in popular speech to describe elderly people than children or young adults. Paul Baltes (1993) defined wisdom as 'expertise in the fundamental pragmatics of life' (p. 615). He cited research in which groups of adults of different ages were given dilemmas to solve that involved everyday choices that hypothetical story characters in familiar predicaments had to make. For example, one dilemma involved a woman in her 50s who had an opportunity to take up a challenging new career, but wondered whether she should instead devote her time to caring for her recently widowed son's preschool-aged children. Another involved an unmarried pregnant teenager's decision about whether to keep her baby or put it up for adoption. In the advice they offered to characters in dilemmas like these, Baltes discerned the elements of wisdom. Wise solutions took account of the context the person in the story was operating in and made allowances for differences due to age, gender, religious background and each person's unique backlog of relevant life experience.

In addition, wisdom, according to Baltes, entails:

1. rich factual knowledge
2. rich procedural knowledge (e.g. of how to prioritise and weigh risks against probabilistic gains)
3. the capacity to avoid dogmatism or being judgmental
4. a philosophic tolerance for uncertainty and the possibility of change.

Wise solutions containing all these elements were rare at any age but they were somewhat more common in older than younger adults. Baltes concluded that, with age, people learn to plan better and use a 'knowledge system that is more elaborated than that of younger adults' (p. 615).

However, the simple fact of growing older does not guarantee access to wisdom. According to Vivian Clayton (1975), wisdom is attained when an elderly man or woman achieves successful resolution of Erikson's central personality conflict between integrity and despair. As she explained:

Wisdom emerges in the last stage of development if the individual has committed himself to integrity rather than despair. It signals the time when the individual can see and accept that his own life is coming to a conclusion and when he can see and accept the cycle of his generation concluding itself in the next … According to Erikson, wisdom includes qualities ranging from ripened wits to accumulated knowledge and matured judgment. It is the essence of knowledge freed from temporal relativity, permitting the individual to have a detached concern for life itself in the face of death. (p. 121)

Vivian Clayton and James Birren (1980) studied American adults' perception of wisdom and found the concept was indeed associated with old age. The researchers asked three age groups of volunteers (mean ages 21, 49 and 70) to rate the similarity of 105 words describing personal and intellectual characteristics (e.g. 'practical', 'intuitive', 'gentle', 'wise', 'empathetic', 'young', 'aged'). They found a striking tendency for subjects of all ages to link wisdom with old age. However, elderly subjects did so somewhat less consistently than younger men and women, suggesting that they realised that, although some old men and women do become wise, the gaining of wisdom is not inevitable.

In fact, Clayton suggested that wisdom and integrity may be achieved more readily by old people in traditional cultures where old age is accorded high respect, and where the knowledge an old person has accumulated is still relevant to the young, than in modern industrialised societies where the elderly are viewed as old-fashioned and obsolescent. Janice Reid (1985) explained how the status of traditional Aboriginal women in the western desert regions of Australia, as wise and respected authorities, was accumulated with their progress through the successive informal milestones and formal ceremonial passages that punctuated their life cycle:

… women assume more authority, become more assertive and tender their advice more frequently as they become older. They have a profounder knowledge of and interest in mythology and possess a fund of experience drawn from journeys, attendance at inter-tribal meetings and quarrels witnessed. Taboos and social restrictions have been relaxed; the women have surmounted the dangers believed to be inherent in the approach of puberty, introcision [a pubertal rite], childbirth and lactation. They, like men, have little to fear from the supernatural and much to hope for. They preside over the rites associated with women's activities, birth and puberty … Together with the old men, they are the repositories of myth, are responsible for the handing on of tribal law and custom, and are one of the forces which make possible the stability and continuity of tribal life. (p. 72, reproduced with the permission of Cambridge University Press)

Box 16.9 offers an illustration from Reid of an Aboriginal man who achieved the status of wise elder in traditional Aboriginal society, partly as a result of his own intellectual and leadership qualities but also as a consequence of the traditional Aboriginal legal–political system, which made old men 'the final repositories of all the sacred knowledge which can be obtained' and gave them the right to control younger men's progress through the age-graded initiation rites leading up to elder status in old age.

The cultivation of wisdom during old age in the Asian cultures of China, Korea and Japan can be

BOX 16.9 Lessons from culture
A wise elder

As an example of the possibility of attaining the pinnacle status of elder statesman in old age, Janice Reid (1985) recorded a brief biography of a tribal Aboriginal leader named Badawuy, who was born in 1904 at Yirrkala and died there in 1975. He was already a mature husband and father when the Yirrkala mission was established and continues to be remembered, years after his death, as a 'redoubtable fighter and sage leader'. According to Reid:

In his 75 years Badawuy married, successively, a total of twelve wives and had 46 children. His last marriages were serial rather than polygamous and in his last years he sat for most of each day on the verandah of his house, cared for by his twelfth wife, surrounded by his youngest children and visited often by older children or ex-wives who lived nearby, particularly by his daughters and grandchildren. He and his wife relied on his old-age pension and occasional gifts of hunted or store food from sons and daughters. Whenever a family member arrived at Yirrkala from elsewhere he or she always went and greeted him, sitting for a time to talk ... Family members showed not only deference and respect towards Badawuy. They loved him. If, as some said, he could be cantankerous in his youth, in his old age he seemed a calm, humorous and immensely knowledgeable man and a wise and interested father.

When he was sick he was the focus of attention of scores of his descendants. In 1975 he was sent to Darwin Hospital for an operation after some time in Nhulunbuy Hospital. On the day of his removal to Darwin, 50 adults and a multitude of children crowded into vehicles to accompany him to the airport. The women wailed and his son-in-law, a clan leader, cried openly. As the flight was called, family members went

up to him, took his hand and said goodbye, clearly fearing they would not again see him alive. Many of the women were prostrate with emotion.

During Badawuy's two-week stay in Darwin any news of his condition was immediately passed around the camp. He returned home, weak but recovering from his surgery, and was taken to his verandah where he sat receiving the joyous welcome of a growing group of relatives. A lasting impression, in a society in which public displays of affection between men and women are very rare, is of his twelfth wife who sat next to him, beaming with joy and relief, and suddenly threw her arms around his ample torso in a spontaneous gesture of affection (pp. 79–80, reproduced with the permission of Cambridge University Press).

While acknowledging how well this particular life history conforms to the modernisation hypothesis that special advantages are gained through being elderly in close-knit, traditional societies, Reid nevertheless points out that not everyone in Badawuy's age group at Yirrkala enjoyed the same advantages and prestige as he did. She concludes that:

Different old people in different situations have different opportunities to negotiate status and to influence the balance between the costs to their families and societies of maintaining them and the contributions they can make. (p. 92)

traced back to Confucius, whose account of his own personal stage-like progression towards higher understanding is described in Chapter 1. Many contemporary Chinese and Japanese adults echo Confucius's preference for an old age devoted to reading, formal study or philosophical discussion. But, as is the case in the West, neither the accumulation of years nor devotion of one's old age to scholarly pursuits was considered by Confucius, or his followers, to guarantee the acquisition of a level of wisdom that would earn the respect of younger generations. As Tu Wei-ming (1978) explained:

Old age in itself commands little admiration. Respect for the old is actually based on the assumption that, in the long and unavoidable journey of self-improvement, an old man ought to have forged way ahead in furnishing his life with inspiring contents. Ideally, therefore, being advanced in age is a sign of wisdom and resourcefulness as well as of experience and perseverance. But this hardly implies that in practice seniority of age automatically becomes an undisputable value. Simply 'being old and not dying' does not get one very far. (p. 118)

Confucius is likewise said to have described an old man who had done 'nothing in middle age that was worth being handed down' as 'merely living on, getting older and older' and as 'a useless pest' (Tu, 1978, p. 118).

Chapter summary

Attitudes to ageing are shaped by individual expectations and these in their turn reflect the culture's attitudes and treatment of old age. Few contemporary urban Anglo-Australians look forward so eagerly to growing old that they would rather be described as 'elderly' than 'middle-aged', yet in other cultures, such as the Himalayan Lepcha, it is a compliment to be called 'old'.

In traditional Australian Aboriginal communities, high social status is accorded to the older men and women who pass through ceremonial inductions into elder roles and are seen to have greater wisdom, social prestige, religious seniority, and accumulated skills and experience than younger adults. Yet in many modern industrial societies, ageist bigotry excludes old people from high-status social roles and ageist attitudes and stereotypes portray them as senile, lethargic, ill, rigid, lonely, sexless and unfit.

A reluctance to grow old, bred from stereotypes like these, may be accentuated by social changes which isolate old people in high-crime neighbourhoods or impersonal institutions. But people over age 65 report pleasant surprise when they discover that there are attractions and compensations in being elderly, even in modern society.

The biological ageing process brings about changes to the skin, hair, nerves, eyes, ears, muscles, bones, connective tissue and internal organs, resulting in a characteristic aged appearance. While the brain retains plasticity throughout life, the neurocognitive changes of ageing diminish aspects of the older adult's neuromotor and neurocognitive functioning, especially reaction speed. Slowness may combine with sensory losses and muscular weakness to diminish physical and sporting performance while increasing the elderly adult's vulnerability to falls, injuries like broken bones and a decline in the sense of personal control.

Fortunately, many of these age-related losses can be remedied or prevented by sensible living or medical intervention, and Paul Baltes' S-O-C theory reveals how older men and women can often 'use psychology' to overcome the physical impediments of age.

Several theories have been put forward to explain these changes in the anatomy during old age. Among the most promising are the notions that ageing may be due to the building-up over time of cell-copying errors or faults in the body's immunological defence system, or to the cumulative consequences of wear and tear and insults from such environmental pollutants as radiation and viruses, or to a preprogrammed genetic clock built into the cells at conception.

Cognitive capacities are also subject to change in old age, though at a slower rate and less universally than was once supposed. Some loss of episodic memory and short-term memorisation and retrieval capacities commonly occurs during old age, though this may be largely circumvented with practice and training in the use of memory strategies. Life review processes and autobiographical memory remain highly functional in old age and can be instrumental in optimising personality development and life satisfaction.

Although IQ scores show an age-linked decline in many cross-sectional studies that confound cohort membership with age, the opposite is often found during the 50s, 60s and early 70s using longitudinal methodologies. Though longitudinal studies, too, suggest possible declines in cognitive abilities from the late 70s or early 80s, differences in intelligence test scores between cohorts and among individuals within a cohort are marked and may often outweigh any differences due to ageing.

To the extent that intelligence does decline in very old age, changes are more striking for verbal than performance abilities, and for fluid than crystallised intelligence. With astute compensation for sensory deficits and slowed reaction times, older adults who actively use their brains can expect to retain their mental powers until close to the time of death (terminal drop) unless non-normative injury or disease processes intervene to upset the predictable trajectory of cognitive ageing.

Today there is little or no scientific support for the view that senility, or any serious loss of intellectual capacity, is a normal accompaniment to the ageing process. When intellectual declines do occur, they are more often the result of specific diseases (such as Alzheimer's disease, arteriosclerosis, mild strokes or prolonged alcohol abuse) or of a socially isolated and cognitively unstimulating way of life.

The new cognitive attribute known as 'wisdom', seen in many cultures as the special purview of old age, may develop in those old people who manage successfully to integrate cognitive ability with distilled understanding from experience.

For further interest

Looking forward on the Internet

Use the Internet to visit the following websites. Examine them for further information and varied perspectives on issues raised in this chapter. Also search for other relevant websites for yourself, using keywords like 'aging', 'ageing', 'seniors', 'life stages', 'old age', 'elderly', 'family' and 'health' in your search engine.

In particular, for further ideas on health and fitness in old age, visit: **http://www.yalenewhavenhealth. org** and **http://www.healthinsite.gov.au** and **http:// www.aarp.org**. Also visit: **http://www.healthandage. net** for latest news on age-related health problems (including Alzheimer's disease) and preventative health suggestions to optimise cognitive and physical functioning in old age. For information on the older Australian population, visit: **http://www.aihw.gov.au/ publications/welfare/oag03/index.html** and for practical tips on how to promote wellbeing and self-efficacy in old age, visit: **http://www.aoa.gov/ eldfam/healthy_lifestyles/healthy_lifestyles.asp**.

For resources, ideas, activities and other items of interest in conjunction with this chapter, visit the Companion Website for this textbook at:

> **http://wps.pearsoned.com.au/peterson**

Activity suggestion

As a practical activity in conjunction with themes in this chapter, collect news clippings on old people from the local newspaper. Also visit **http://www. aarp.org** and explore news items about the elderly there. After you have collected 20 or more items, group them into categories: (a) positive, (b) neutral, or (c) negative, depending on the image of old age that is portrayed. Do negative impressions outweigh positive ones? What topics (e.g. health, achievements, etc.) bring old people to the attention of the news media most often?

Multimedia

To gain a visual picture of the physiological ageing process and theoretical explanations for it, consider viewing the following films:

- *Ageing and Mortality* (LTS/UK, 1994: 28 minutes), which explores theories of the biological ageing process and scientific discoveries about how ageing can be slowed in animal species
- *How the Body Ages* (CSA/Video Education Australasia, 1992: 36 minutes, colour), which gives an up-to-date account of the physiological ageing process and implications for health and psychological functioning
- *Ageing Successfully* (Davidson Films, San Luis Obispo, CA, 1998: 31 minutes, colour), which provides details on Paul Baltes' S-O-C model and other contemporary theories and research on cognitive ageing.

OLD AGE: Social, emotional and personality development

CHAPTER 17

Age, like love, cannot be hid.
Thomas Dekker (1572–1632)

Age does not protect you from love. But love, to a degree, protects you from age'
Jeanne Moreau (1928–)

Contents

CHAPTER OVERVIEW

In the field of lifespan development, a controversy has raged for more than five decades over what optimally healthy social, personality and emotional adjustment during old age actually consists of. Should the older adult behave like a younger adult for as long as possible, retaining social roles and adding new relationships and commitments to the repertoire as losses occur due to retirement from paid employment, departure of adult children from the family nest, bereavement and so on? (This model is known as *activity theory*.) Alternatively, is the best adjusted old person one who retires in old age to a placid, contemplative, 'rocking-chair' mode of existence, thinking about life as it has been, no longer striving to keep active at all costs so as to fight against the bodily frailties and losses of social roles that come about naturally in old age? (This model is known as *disengagement theory*.)

Theoretical debates between these two models, along with two recent, compromise positions (*personality continuity theory* and *socioemotional selectivity theory*), form the cornerstone for an understanding of ageing as a social process. In this chapter, we study recent research into the developmental changes in social functioning late in life that has been guided by this debate. We look at the definitions of optimal ageing that emerge from each of the theories and at how these can assist in the optimisation of contentment, social relationship quality, mental health and life satisfaction after age 60.

We compare and contrast the postulates of disengagement theory with those of activity theory, personality continuity theory and socioemotional selectivity theory and examine the research that has supported and contradicted each of them. We examine the implications of each theory for individual life planning, and then for social policies and provisions for older adults' residential and lifestyle opportunities, and for access to social interaction with partners, friends, siblings, children and grandchildren.

The chapter then explores recent research evidence on personality development, coping styles and psychological adjustment in old age. We study how older men and women deal with stress and change, noting some unexpected 'life-cycle surprises' in the superior coping skills that may sometimes emerge in wise old people with a lifetime of challenging experience to draw on. We also study developmental changes during old age in the adult's sense of personal control, self-esteem, skilled competence and personal responsibility. The stresses of frail health, reduced income on a pension and bereavement may challenge these important prerequisites for emotional well-being. Yet opportunities to express them still continue in old age, and doing so may benefit not only physical and mental health but even biological longevity.

The key personality issue of old age in Erikson's theory, namely a dialectical conflict over the need to achieve a sense of integrity in a life well lived versus the pain and despair of coming to feel one's life has been wasted, is closely examined. At the end of the chapter we look at other determinants of life satisfaction and healthy emotional adjustment in old age, including an active sex life and opportunities to interact with a social confidante who might be a spouse, a close friend, a sibling or an adult child.

Successful social ageing

What is the recipe for enjoying a happy old age? On reaching the remarkable age of 120 years and 8 months, the French widow Jeanne Calmet celebrated with laughter, wine and chocolates. Reminiscing about her hardworking, active life, which had included the sale of paints and canvas to the artist Vincent Van Gogh in her youth during 1888, Calmet suggested that her recipe for ideal ageing was simple. She claimed that her lively sense of humour had contributed to her extreme longevity, and the port wine that she routinely drank had probably done her no harm either (*Time* magazine, 1995).

Lifespan developmental psychologists, too, have searched for the recipe for successful ageing, conducting research and formulating theories about how best to cope with the physical losses (like weakened muscle strength, poor eyesight and failing hearing) that we examined in the context of biological ageing in Chapter 16. One approach to describing what it means to age 'successfully' builds on evaluative beliefs and life goals which most members of a culture share. Carol Ryff (1989) used such an approach to obtain the picture of a healthy old-aged personality that appears in Figure 17.1.

On the grounds that older people's experiences of the transition from middle age to old age would supply them with personal insights about successful ageing, Ryff interviewed a sample of 171 adults in the United States ranging from age 50 to age 80. Some of her results are shown in Figure 17.1. As these data indicate, the most important criterion of success in old age for these adults was being socially responsible and interested in others. Such a personality pattern includes the qualities of compassion, caring and responsiveness to friends and family. Outgoing and productive social relationships with intimates is also a crucial component.

Next most important was a quality developmental psychologists also highlight, namely the capacity to accept change. Many of these older respondents had weathered biological declines as part of the ageing process, and some had suffered widowhood and other serious social losses. These experiences had taught them that flexibility and adaptability are essential for a healthy personality in old age. Given that change in psychological functioning is inevitable

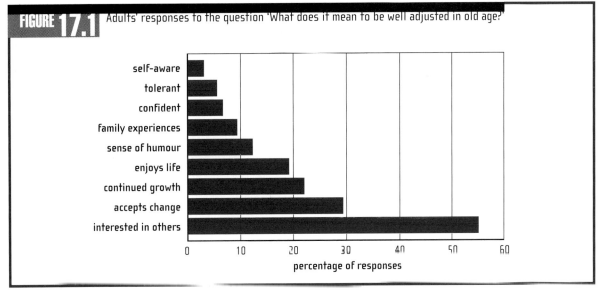

FIGURE 17.1 Adults' responses to the question 'What does it mean to be well adjusted in old age?'

Source: Ryff (1989), © 1989, American Psychological Association, reprinted by permission.

throughout life, the capacity to adjust to new challenges and cope productively with the stress and uncertainty that changes can create is a hallmark of maturity for people over 60, as we see later in this chapter.

In line with the theories of lifespan psychological development highlighted throughout this book, these lay conceptions of successful ageing emphasised continued psychological growth and development as a marker of good adjustment.

Social roles and relationships in old age

According to the adults whose responses are shown in Figure 17.1, one of the most important criteria for successful adjustment in old age is the acceptance of change. This idea is equally central to many psychological researchers' and theorists' definitions of healthy psychological adjustment to lifespan development and ageing. But too much acceptance of negative outcomes or pessimistic stereotypes about old age may lead to apathy, resignation or learned helplessness (see Chapter 4). Thus the question becomes to what extent old people should accept change gracefully and to what extent they should actively confront the challenges posed by reduced strength, slowed speed, diminished memory or a narrowed circle of friends in old age. Theorists who study the mature personality are perplexed by similar questions. They too ask whether successful ageing consists of passive acceptance of age-related change or active rejection of biological or psychological decline in an increasingly effortful struggle to maintain the same lifestyle in old age as during mid-life.

Is the rocking chair the way to go?

Issues like these are at the root of a controversy that has raged for several decades in the field of social gerontology, the discipline devoted to the study of the

old person's functioning in society. One pole of the controversy was articulated by the psychoanalyst Carl Gustav Jung (1969) who was a contemporary of Sigmund Freud's (see Chapter 2). Jung argued that an optimally healthy adjustment to old age requires social withdrawal and quiet contemplation:

> Ageing people should know that their lives are not mounting and expanding, but that an inexorable inner process enforces the contraction of life. For a young person it is almost a sin, or at least a danger, to be too preoccupied with himself; but for the ageing person it is a duty and a necessity to devote serious attention to himself. After having lavished its light on the world, the sun withdraws its rays in order to illuminate itself. Instead of doing likewise, many old people prefer to be hypochondriacs, niggards, pedants, applauders of the past or else eternal adolescents – all lamentable substitutes for the illumination of the self, but inevitable consequences of the delusion that the second half of life must be governed by the principles of the first. (p. 399)

Jung argued that, because their personality needs were different from those of younger adults, old people's patterns of social life had to be less active and more self-centred than during middle age. To neglect their new needs while endeavouring to perpetuate a style of existence no longer appropriate to their mature years was as dangerous to the elderly man or woman's psychological health and developmental opportunity as an infant's unwillingness to be weaned from the bottle, or an adolescent's refusal to venture out of the family into an independent role in society. Jung felt that old people had to cut their links with other people in order to gain sufficient time and energy for inner contemplation, and for putting their psychic affairs in order in readiness for death.

Disengagement theory

Disengagement theory holds that healthy old age consists of a deliberate divorcing of oneself from other people, from social roles and from the active concerns with others and their lives that preoccupies much of mature adulthood. As a theory of social ageing, it was originally put forward by Elaine Cumming and William Henry (1961) to account for the results of a five-year longitudinal study, conducted in Kansas City with a sample of 275 healthy 50- to 90-year-olds during the 1950s.

Disengagement theory is provocative and controversial. It has inspired a large amount of research, social policy-making and critical commentary (Cath, 1975; Gordon, 1975). Let us first examine its three main postulates. Then we analyse some of the criticisms and alternative theoretical positions that have been put forward in opposition to it as part of the healthy debate that has raged in the literature of adult developmental psychology for almost half a century.

Postulate 1: Disengagement is normative

'The fully engaged person acts in a large number and wide variety of roles in a system of divided labor, and feels an obligation to meet the expectations of his role partners', wrote Cumming (1964, p. 3). In other words, the first postulate of Cumming's disengagement theory is that old people do, in fact, disengage themselves from social roles. Consequently, the following social changes arise in old age as part of this typical, or normative, disengagement process.

- Emotional ties with others are severed.
- Vocational and social roles are eliminated from the repertoire.
- Depth of involvement and participation in remaining roles is radically reduced.

Postulate 2: Disengagement is mutually desired by old people and by society

The second postulate states that disengagement is internal to the old person as part of a normal and natural process of social ageing. Cumming (1964) described the urge to shed social roles and cut social ties to friends, kin and acquaintances as:

> an intrinsic process or a mutual withdrawal ... between the aging person and others in the social system to which he belongs – a withdrawal initiated by the individual himself, or by others in the system. (p. 3)

Irrespective of whether old people actually do pull out of some or all of their middle-aged social roles, the real question is whether they genuinely need and want to do so. If the choice to disengage is forced on them by society without their consent, as ageist practices (see Chapter 16) might sometimes encourage, this is not true disengagement in the theoretical sense implied by Cumming. She and other disengagement theorists view disengagement as a process that origi-

The theory of disengagement may be culture-bound. For this aged Aboriginal spear fisherman, there is no respite from the exercise of skills developed over a lifetime.

nates with a developmental need that emerges organically inside ageing individuals, provided they live long enough. Society may contribute to the process by reducing the number and attractiveness of the social roles that are available to older people. For example, mandatory retirement from work (see Chapter 15) cuts off one option, while grown children's departure from home closes off another.

However, the fact that it is deemed theoretically to be both 'mutual' and 'intrinsic' means that disengagement as a genuine psychological process is still the older person's own decision. The disengaged adult has voluntarily opted to make a break with society, rather than having been forced unwillingly out of social roles that they would have preferred to continue occupying.

That a desire to reduce social activity should arise in old age makes some intuitive sense. For one thing, recognition that death may be just around the corner grows ever more compelling the older a person becomes. By gradually relinquishing intimate ties voluntarily, aged adults may assist themselves as well as their survivors to accept the final separation with grace and dignity. Old people may need to use the time and energy gained by relinquishing social ties for the *psychic contemplation* suggested by Jung, for resolving the *integrity crisis* postulated by Erikson (see Chapter 2 and page 612) or for carrying out the *life review* process described by Butler (see Chapter 16).

Also, certain social roles may be surrendered

Retired adults who maintained a social role (such as that of golfer) for extraneous reasons while working are likely to disengage from it when free to do so. But older men and women who genuinely enjoy golf will continue to play it actively in old age.

of the disengagement process itself. Cumming (1964) argued that, as the older adult comes to have less and less to do with other people and takes less and less interest in social activity, possible topics of conversation are lost through disuse. With little to say, social interaction becomes even more limited and awkward. At the same time:

> the seduction of freedom, preoccupation with the accumulated symbols of the past, and a license for a new kind of self-centeredness cannot be resisted, so that idiosyncratic personal behavior becomes possible. (pp. 9–10)

So the third postulate of the theory is that a basic human wish to behave egocentrically, which is held in check during the middle years of life by societal demands and role expectations, emerges during old age when these expectations are relaxed. An essential ingredient of the disengaged personality is self-centredness, or an emotional distance which reduces the need to take other people's feelings and thoughts into account. Cumming and Henry wrote:

> We have thought of the inner process as being an ego change . . . The fully disengaged person can be thought of as having transferred much of his cathexis to his own inner life; his memories, his fantasies, his image of himself as someone who was something, and did accomplish things. (cited in Savage, 1973, p. 674)

All three components of disengagement are illustrated in the individual life history described in Box 17.1.

Thinking critically about disengagement theory

Despite its applicability both to individual life stories (see Box 17.1) and to the population of elderly Kansas City men and women who took part in Cumming's (1964) research, disengagement theory has not gone without serious criticism. The three postulates of the theory, namely: that older people *do* disengage from society, that they *want* and *need* to do so and that they *change* cognitively as a result, have been researched carefully over many decades. However the jury is still out and support for the theory is limited, at best. We examine some of the research evidence about each of the three postulates in a later section of this chapter, after considering an alternative theory. But it is important to note that disengagement theory is also open to criticism on logical grounds as a model that may be more in keeping with the way a person of any age might react to loss, social stigmatisation and curtailment of future opportunities than as a model of social ageing. Indeed, the way a person adjusts psychologically to terminal illness (see Chapter 18) resembles Cumming and Henry's disengagement process in a number of ways.

As with disengagement, the dying individual frequently chooses to curtail social contact, to pull back from social roles and to erect emotional barriers around the people, places and interests that formed the focus of healthy life activity. But in this case it is

gladly because they were undertaken in the first place for reasons of expediency rather than out of any real interest or desire. For example, some business executives may belong to golf clubs, not because they enjoy the sport but because club membership is necessary for entertaining clients and maintaining status. In old age, such a person is now free to choose a more compatible, perhaps solitary, style of leisure. Or he may keep up golf, but for the sake of the game rather than for business advancement. This, too, constitutes disengagement at the social level. Cumming said:

> In some ways, an aging person is like an adolescent; he is allowed more freedom and expressiveness than a middle-aged adult. Later, when he is very old, he is permitted the dependency and individuation of the small child. (1964, p. 10)

People of all ages might opt to disengage from strenuous and demanding social roles and allow themselves to be passively nurtured and cared for by others, were it socially acceptable for them to do so.

Postulate 3: Disengagement produces changes in thought patterns

The third postulate of disengagement theory is that, once the mutual social withdrawal process has been initiated, the older individual's inner dynamics, cognitions, emotions and social interaction patterns undergo important changes. The switch to a more egocentric and dependent mode of relating is seen as a desire that motivates disengagement in the first place, and also as an almost automatic consequence

A case of disengagement

During her youth and the years of her marriage to a famous Parisian theatre director, the actress Camille was such a vibrant, active, sparkling personality that her friend Simone de Beauvoir (1975) wrote:

When I was young, Camille's beauty, her independence, the furious strength of her ambition and her immense eagerness for work filled me with an envious wonder (p. 73).

In early middle age, Camille acted, taught theatre and produced plays. Though she was his pupil and many years his junior, Camille's director-husband, Dullin, was similarly in awe of her remarkable powers. He worshipped her, believing her to be a genius and not trusting his own judgment until he had sought her advice. But after Dullin's death, Camille left the theatre and became a virtual recluse. She tried writing, but lacking talent and perseverance turned eventually to alcohol and talking aloud to her dolls. She lost interest in seeing friends and broke off her relationship with her married daughter. After her death, which followed a period of complete isolation and abject lack of awareness of herself or her surroundings, de Beauvoir discovered Camille's diary. 'I had not expected the papers to be as childish as all that,' she wrote.

It still surprises me. The emptiness we detected in her when we heard her [attempts to write scripts] had invaded the whole of Camille; and drink and loneliness had completed the destruction – she had sunk into formlessness (pp. 83–4).

De Beauvoir attributed Camille's mental and physical decline in part to the social disengagement which followed the simultaneous loss of her husband and her role in the theatre:

Camille had never been gifted for give and take: she would ask a few quick questions; we would give brief answers; and then she would launch into a monologue. In the days when she still saw a great many people, and read, and acquired information, her soliloquies were full of meat. But you cannot live shut in on yourself without paying for it. The mind grows rusty; interests diminish. (p. 78)

Camille's sudden withdrawal from her major activities and network of friends had been accompanied, as Cumming and Henry's theory predicted, by a loss of interest in the outside world and by spiralling cognitive egocentrism. But in her case, widowhood and alcoholism rather than old age seemed to have precipitated the crisis. Camille was less than 50 when the process began, and in her early 60s at the time of her death.

awareness of imminent death, not old age, that triggers the need for change. Studies of unemployed Australians and New Zealanders (see Chapter 13) have also highlighted changes similar to the process described by Cumming and Henry, in which social activity and contact with friends decline, and attitudes become increasingly disinterested and apathetic. But, in the case of the unemployed, social disengagement is both involuntary and unrelated to ageing. The social apathy displayed by patients suffering from clinical depression can also occur at any age (Cath, 1975). Furthermore, since Cumming and Henry's subjects were all over 50, these authors had no means of assessing whether disengagement was more complete or more pervasive in old age than during these other kinds of retreats from major social roles at earlier points in the life cycle.

Ideologically, Cumming and Henry's theory has been criticised for lending itself so readily to segregatory, prejudicial and discriminatory treatment of the aged (Gordon, 1975). Granted that the theory's stress on the mutuality of disengagement should preclude its serving as a political or dogmatic bludgeon for forcing old people out of roles they are not yet ready to relinquish voluntarily, it has nevertheless been used to justify just such unfair social treatment (Comfort, 1977, p. 65). Also, as Judith Gordon pointed out, even when the theory is not explicitly put forward as a political alibi, it may blind us to real social issues or to alternative interpretations of old people's conduct. She wrote:

> We see old women alone and cut off from intimate sexual relationships. This theory tells us we see them acting by choice. We see old people busily playing bingo at a Senior Center. This theory tells us that the old can now choose to play because they are freed from the obligations of work ... But before we can conclude that this is the way people want to age, we must find methods for looking at the meaning of aging for people doing it in the world of everyday life. (p. 224)

Another serious methodological criticism of the research basis on which disengagement theory rests was Cumming's (1964) generalisation of the theory far beyond the small, homogeneous group of healthy, white, middle-class, mid-western Americans she studied. Despite her claim that disengagement theory is 'culture-free', it has never been studied closely in non-Western cultures and probably would not closely fit the experiences of elders in many of these cultures, who are seen to become progressively more socially active and more fully 'engaged' as religious leaders, therapists and teachers as they accumulate seniority and experience (see Box 17.2).

The possibility of cultural differences in old people's attitudes towards disengagement was suggested by the results of a cross-cultural study that compared elderly people in Japan and the United States. The investigators, Yutaka Okura, Robert

BOX 17.2 The continued pursuit of a committed life

- Elizabeth Blackwell, the first woman to qualify as a medical doctor in the United States, continued to practise gynaecology and to occupy a professorial chair until disabled by an accident at age 86.
- Albert Schweitzer developed his famous mission hospital in West Africa at age 43 and was still in charge of it and treating patients at the age of 89.
- Maggie Kuhn was 64 when she organised the Gray Panther network to fight ageism in the United States. A firm believer in social experimentation, she moved into a communal household at age 69.
- Michelangelo, the Italian Renaissance artist, was 71 when he began work on the Sistine Chapel. He continued painting for 18 years while at the same time directing a team of artists and architects and writing some of his finest poetry.
- Mao Zedong shepherded his nation through its socialist revolution while in his 50s and through its cultural revolution while in his 70s. He continued his innovative leadership of China and contributions to world diplomacy until the time of his death in his 80s.

When disengagement from society is caused by poverty, ill health or social ostracism, the anticipated boost in morale will not occur.

Ziller and Hiroshi Osawa (1986), employed an innovative method. Participants were handed a camera and asked to take six photographs to describe themselves as they believed they were, along with their feelings and how they felt about life. The elderly Americans usually included other people in their photos, suggesting a preference for social activity and an engaged, active, people-filled style of ageing. For example, one typical photograph taken by an old man in the United States portrayed himself in a boater hat posed with the other older 'minstrels' in his recreational singing group. Older women in the United States likewise often posed with members of their leisure groups (such as a book club or an aerobic exercise class), or with members of their families or in front of collections of photos of their children and grandchildren.

The elderly Japanese, on the other hand, were more likely to photograph themselves in solitary or contemplative activities such as meditating in the garden, reading a book or admiring a piece of sculpture. More Japanese than Americans took still-life and landscape photographs with no people in them at all. This suggested a more socially disengaged outlook on the part of elderly Japanese. The researchers linked these differences to the two countries' contrasting philosophical orientations and religious traditions, suggesting that 'Peace is sought through self-harmony in the orient but through social harmony in the occident' (p. 247).

Activity theory

There are other ways of adjusting socially to the changes brought on by old age that contrast sharply with the ideal epitomised in disengagement theory. One model is its mirror image. Activity theory depicts continued social activity, commitment and role involvement as essential in order to age successfully (Havighurst, Neugarten & Tobin, 1963). Activity theorists argue that high morale and robust mental health are best maintained during old age through active participation in as many social roles and interpersonal relationships as during early and middle adulthood. In the event that a role is lost with retirement or bereavement, activity theory recommends that the old person seek new roles as substitutes. If this is not possible, the best way of maintaining healthy adjustment is by becoming more intensely involved in whatever roles remain in the repertoire. Thus activity theory challenges the notion that disengagement is normal, desirable or voluntarily chosen by a disengaged old person.

According to proponents of the activity model, some elderly people may indeed disengage from society and, once disengaged, they may well become selfish and mentally lazy. But neither of these changes is either a requisite developmental task or a component of healthy ageing. Instead, society is blamed for excluding the elderly from interesting, though highly demanding, social roles and for relieving them of the various duties, obligations and cognitive challenges

Activity theory maintains that older men and women need to find new roles to replace those lost with age. Thus a worker might retire to a life of growing and selling fruit and vegetables.

person's participation in a wide repertoire of social roles. For each of the 11 social relationships shown in Table 17.1, respondents rated themselves on a scale from 'inactive' to 'highly involved'. A summary score was then constructed to reflect total overall levels of role activity.

When they examined the relationship between age and the range and intensity of a person's investment in these roles, Cumming and Henry discovered a steady decline in role activity for men from the age of 50, and a sharp decline for women after age 65. More than half the men and women in the Kansas City study were involved in at least six roles before age 65, with a sharp drop after that age. Thus, by age 75, only 8 per cent of the group remained active in six roles or more. Some three-quarters of the Kansas City women under the age of 55 had a relatively large life space (as measured by the number of people they had contact with each day), but this fell to one-third

that, when tackled, might help to prevent cognitive decline into egocentrism.

Despite its opposing focus, activity theory is similar to disengagement theory in one respect: both theories make the assumption that a single pattern of social ageing is ideal, and that every old person's life satisfaction can be maximised by adhering to this one ideal model.

Research answers to key questions

In the end, the acceptance or rejection of any psychological theory is decided not so much by intuitive appeal or practical considerations as by research evidence. Studies which have a bearing on the postulates of disengagement theory and on the alternative formulation of activity theory will therefore be considered next. Three key questions have provoked considerable critical and empirical attention. From the perspective outlined in Chapter 2, the first is a *descriptive* question. It asks a question of fact: Do old people typically relinquish social roles as they age, or do they not? The second two questions are *explanatory*. They test disengagement theory's controversial postulates that disengagement is (a) a beneficial change for psychological adjustment and (b) a step towards further changes in cognition and personality. Let us look at the current research evidence surrounding these three questions.

Do old people disengage?
Cumming and Henry's (1961) initial measure of disengagement assessed the range and intensity of the

TABLE 17.1	Social role activity scale with examples of high investment in each role
Role	**High involvement**
Spouse	live together, intensely interested in one another, share all recreation and travels
Parent	frequent contact, advice-giving, shared recreation, mutual help
Grandparent	frequent contact, babysitting, talk together daily
Kin-network member	frequent contact, advice-giving, mutual help
Worker/employee	long hours at work, mentoring, occupational identity, promotion-seeking
Caregiver to aged/disabled relative	frequent contact, advice-giving, mutual help, practical daily assistance
Citizen/ politician/ public affairs/ local government	attend meetings, office-bearer, shoulder responsibilities, manage teams of volunteers, make decisions, frequent social contact
Friend	frequent contact, entertainment, mutual advice, confidante
Neighbour	practical help, socialising, shared projects
Club member/ office-bearer	attend meetings, assume positions of importance, organise activities and special functions
Church activities	attend church regularly, take on roles in the church organisation, fundraising, charity volunteer work

during the next five years and down to only 12 per cent at age 70. All the men were above average on this measure at age 60, but only one-quarter remained so a decade later.

These results suggested that, regardless of any possible motivation to remain active, elderly Kansas City adults in the middle of last century did indeed disengage socially, beginning even before retirement from work and continuing at an escalating rate thereafter. However, later studies in other countries yielded a somewhat different picture. When R. D. Savage and his associates (Savage, Faber, Britton, Bolton & Cooper, 1977) gave the role activity measure outlined above to a group of elderly British men and women who lived in their own dwellings in Newcastle-on-Tyne, they found no statistically significant change in range or intensity of role involvement during the period from 70 to over 85 years of age. Furthermore, the mean score of the British group as a whole was over 22. While a score this high could also be earned through intense investment in a smaller number of roles, when spread across the range of 11 roles listed above it indicates at least a mild investment in each of them. Thus it would seem inappropriate to describe these aged Britons as fully 'disengaged' from role activity, even at the advanced age of 80.

Other research using different measures of role activity has similarly failed to substantiate disengagement theory. The average elderly person in Australia and New Zealand is typically involved in social roles involving kinship, recreation, church and community service for many years after retirement (Feather, 1989). Daily or weekly contact with adult children also tends to be maintained well into old age (Brooke, 1985; Peterson, 1999). Seventy-four per cent of the men over the age of 75 in an urban Australian sample had contact with at least one of their children at least once a week, as did 69 per cent of women in the same age range. Furthermore, half the Australian women and 43 per cent of Australian men over age 75 had social contact with a friend weekly or more often

(Brooke, 1985). In the United States, a recent survey of grandparents revealed that more than two-thirds saw a grandchild at least once every two weeks and over 90 per cent had personal contact at least every few months, while 80 per cent were in contact by phone on a fortnightly basis (AARP, 2002).

Living alone becomes more frequent as Australians grow older, as Figure 17.2 indicates. But even so, older men and women who live completely alone are in the minority, even at very advanced ages (Brooke, 1985; Cameron, 1992; Peterson, 1999).

Sometimes old people *feel* lonely even when they live with close family members and have additional daily or weekly contact with other relatives and friends. But as these subjective feelings relate directly to the second postulate by disengagement theorists, that the dropping of roles is voluntary and deliberate, the issue of loneliness is considered in the next section. In summing up the evidence regarding the

FIGURE 17.2 Living arrangements of elderly men and women in Sydney

Source: Based on data in Rowland (1982).

Most older men and women have contact with younger family members on a regular basis, even if they do not live with them.

first postulate, it would seem that some modification is needed. For the contemporary Australian, New Zealand or American adult who retains good health and an adequate income, complete disengagement from social roles with family and friends is uncommon, even at the advanced ages of 75 to 80 years or older.

Should old people disengage?

The second postulate of disengagement theory is that older adults' healthy development and emotional adjustment are aided by relinquishing social roles, so that social withdrawal is typically instigated by old people at their own desire. A consequent prediction is that morale and life satisfaction should be higher among healthy older people who have disengaged successfully than among those who are still socially engaged. Unfortunately, it is difficult to test this prediction through observational research, due to the complexity of the social forces that intrude into an older person's everyday life. Some old people are forced into inactivity by ill health. But illness limits happiness and optimism at any age. Other elderly men and women lose mobility and social contact as a result of such potentially depressing life events as economic losses, bereavement, sensory impairments, and so on. These, again, are quite independent of any need or wish to disengage. But they may lead to an involuntary form of disengagement that is difficult to separate, in a research design, from the deliberate shedding of social roles. The problem is that depression resulting from these unfortunate life events is likely to outweigh whatever boost to morale the process of disengagement itself might engender.

On the other hand, as Stanley Cath (1975) pointed out, a rise in morale could likewise coincide with disengagement for reasons other than those articulated by disengagement theory. The elderly may respond favourably to reductions in social contact not because they need to be alone, but rather through self-sacrifice:

> Old people may believe the last gift to those who remain on the face of this earth will be to lay down or sacrifice needs and preferences in the service of others. Accordingly they may minimize illness or ignore the rage felt at their own decline in order not 'to rock the boat'. (p. 202)

All these factors complicate the interpretation of the limited amount of data that researchers have so far gathered about the relationship between morale and social engagement status. Furthermore, the evidence itself is contradictory. While Cumming and Henry (1961) found morale to be higher among the fully disengaged than the partially disengaged portion of their Kansas City sample of old people, a subsequent study of the same population reached the opposite conclusion – that the lower an old person's activity level, the less satisfied he or she was likely to be with life, and that the loss of roles with age was bitterly regretted (Havighurst, Neugarten & Tobin,

1963). In North Carolina, a group of older volunteers whose activity had increased over three years likewise reported increases in happiness and satisfaction over the same time period, while those who had lost role involvement suffered a concomitant drop in morale (Maddox, 1963).

Activity theory seems a better explanation than disengagement theory for these research results. But the finding that widowhood, health problems, reduced income and occupational retirement were also more frequent in the group with diminished activity could mean that the drop in activity and the loss of morale were each caused independently by factors like ill health, poverty or outside trauma, rather than being in any way related to 'normal' ageing.

Norman Feather (1989) studied a sample of Adelaide men and women in their 50s and 60s who were forced to change their patterns of social role activity by becoming unemployed. He found that there were significant changes in a number of social role activities for the group as a whole as a result of unemployment. These changes are summarised in Table 17.2.

To see whether the patterns of role change that had been forced on them by unemployment were more in line with the disengagement or the activity theory of social ageing, Feather assessed the self-esteem, life satisfaction and psychological distress of his sample of unemployed older Australians. In

TABLE 17.2 Changes in social role activities of Adelaide men and women as a result of late-life unemployment	
Comparison with working life	
Activities increased	**Activities decreased**
• *Domestic roles* (cooking, cleaning, shopping)	• *Recreational roles* (going to the pub, cinema, theatre, concerts)
• *Private activities* (reading, television, library, window shopping)	• *Work-related social roles* (entertaining colleagues from work)
• *Home improvements* (gardening, repairs, jobs for neighbours, decorating)	• *Costly recreational pursuits* (expensive restaurants, travel)
• *Social activities* (visit neighbours, help charities, volunteer work)	

Source: Based on data in Feather (1989).

keeping with the activity model, he discovered that those older men and women who had increased their unpaid social role activities and contacts with neighbours and friends were better adjusted psychologically and happier with their lives than those who had decreased social role activity. Conversely, those who had allowed passive, aimless activities, like sitting around the house or watching television, to fill in the time they had formerly spent at work were coping poorly with unemployment and were less well-adjusted psychologically than the socially active unemployed group.

Feather concluded that, when unemployment leads to a sense of resignation, social isolation and loss of control, the prognosis is poor, even for older men and women who have a spouse and close friends to rely on (81 per cent of his sample were married and living with a spouse). But when middle-aged and elderly adults respond to the loss of a job (whether through retrenchment or retirement) by finding new leisure roles (see Chapter 14) that allow opportunities for (a) skill utilisation, (b) social influence, (c) varied activity, (d) purposive goal direction, and (e) structured use of time, their satisfaction with life can be maintained or even enhanced when compared with their middle-aged, employed levels of social role involvement.

Are active adults happier?

Of course, the cross-sectional method is not ideal for uncovering the consequences of job loss or role loss in old age (see Chapter 2). This method cannot readily distinguish between root causes and subsequent consequences. In the case of disengagement, poor morale or depression could conceivably cause role loss, or they could both be caused independently by some third factor (e.g. ill health). The longitudinal method (see Chapter 2) provides clearer insight into cause–effect relationships. An early longitudinal study by Erdman Palmore and his colleagues (Palmore, Fillenbaum & George, 1984) indicated that the best predictor of surviving to the age of 75 in good health and high spirits was neither disengagement nor activity *per se*, but rather the initial level of happiness measured when the subjects were 66 years old. People tended to maintain a similar mood throughout the decade, regardless of whether their social commitments dwindled or increased. On the other hand, physical exercise did distinguish the subjects who were happiest and healthiest from the remainder, supporting suggestions about the value of fitness and vigorous activity made in Chapter 16.

K. S. Markides and H. W. Martin (1979) used the statistical method of path analysis to tease apart the complex pattern of interconnections between poor health, low social activity and poor morale among the elderly. Their results indicated that social engagement had both direct and indirect effects on life satisfaction, particularly for men. Socially active older men tended to be happier overall than their disengaged counterparts. This could have been due partly to the disengaged group's poorer health. But by using statistical controls this research was able to demonstrate that, over and above the limitations on social role activity that resulted from illness and disability, inactivity was also directly linked with lower morale.

A longitudinal follow-up of a group of exceptionally gifted Americans who had been studied since childhood by Louis Terman (see Chapter 15) likewise revealed that those who were happiest at the age of 75 had maintained high levels of social role activity with family and friends after retiring from paid employment. They rated continuing personal growth to be a major source of satisfaction in life and were continuing to use their talents to benefit society. But these adults also enjoyed exceptionally good health in their 70s (Holahan & Holahan, 1987).

When they measured life satisfaction in a sample of more than 200 men and women over the age of 60 who lived in houses and flats in urban and suburban Melbourne and Adelaide, Neville Brooke (1985) discovered a similarly complex set of links between morale, social role activity and other interconnected factors such as income, marital status and health. Some of these links are illustrated in Table 17.3.

In summary, while it seems clear from these results that socially active older adults are often more content with life overall than their socially isolated, fully disengaged peers, it is difficult to draw any clear theoretical conclusions about the effect of voluntary disengagement from these results for people who were forced to disengage by ill health or other adverse circumstances. Lonely, unhappy old people who have been compelled to drop social commitments as a result of poor health, low income or an inability to get along with their spouse, friends or neighbours in no way represent the model postulated by disengagement theorists as the ideal way of

TABLE 17.3 Correlates of happiness in elderly Australians

Life satisfaction status	
Very happy with life	**Poor morale**
• Excellent health	• Poor health
• Presently married or never married	• Divorced, separated or widowed
• No financial problems	• Serious financial problems
• Daily contact with friends	• Two or less contacts with friends in the last five years
• Frequently visits, phones and helps neighbours	• No contact with neighbours
• Voluntary worker or social club member	• No voluntary work or clubs

Source: Based on data in Brooke (1985).

Adults who are active physically, mentally and socially are happiest in old age, according to activity theory.

Substituting devotion to a pet for the parenting role is one way of reorganising the social and emotional life space during old age.

ageing. But without explicit questioning about their motives, and without longitudinal tracking of disengagement-related decisions and their outcomes, it is difficult to pull out voluntary disengagers from the lonely, disappointed group who were driven to social inactivity against their will.

Age also complicates the search for a clear link between happiness and either active or disengaged role involvement. Robert Hansson (1986) found that a wide social network was a positive predictor of morale in the 'young-old' – those aged in their late 60s and early 70s and enjoying good health. But neither social activity nor disengagement predicted happiness for 'old-old' widows, who ranged in age from 75 to 95 years. This suggested that chronological age differences within the broad 'old age' category need to be taken more carefully into account by the disengagement model, and also that extreme old age may bring about a new mode of social interaction not adequately encompassed by the disengagement–activity contrast. According to Hansson:

> The very old often experience a less prescribed and less evaluative social environment with fewer opportunities or role functions. (p. 1050)

Personality continuity theory

Instead of prescribing either disengagement or social activity as universal models of healthy ageing, an alternative possibility is a compromise between the two. There may be individual differences in strategies for confronting old age, just as there are individual differences in effective solutions to the developmental challenges arising earlier in life. According to this view, social withdrawal suits some old people best, a fast-paced social life suits others, and an intermediate course is the ideal social style for still other members of any given group of elderly citizens. This model of individual personality variation forms the basis of Robert Atchley's (1972) *continuity theory* of social involvement during old age.

Atchley argued that one of the most important spin-offs of a lifespan developmental approach is recognition of the links between earlier and later phases in the life cycle. Thus, according to Atchley, older people's accumulation of experience throughout their life comes to shape a unique set of habits, values and goals. As long as society allows it, and health permits, most people continue to work at these goals for as long as possible. The hardships of bodily decline or disease, and the crises caused by widowhood or retirement from work may eventually force people to change their habitual social and psychological patterns. But Atchley argued that disengagement and activity were only two from among 'literally hundreds' of possible adaptations to ageing that a person might make, and that people's prior predispositions have as much to do with the level of social involvement they opt for as do the special exigencies of old age. He therefore felt that both disengagement and activity might enable healthy psychological adjustment by some old people some of the time, especially when closely aligned with the elderly person's personality dispositions and earlier style of life.

Bernice Neugarten (1968) was led to the study of individual differences between old people empirically by her observation that neither disengagement theory nor its opposite, activity theory, seemed to characterise adequately the relationship between social involvement and life satisfaction for all old people all of the time. Some of the oldest Kansas City residents she interviewed had high activity levels and high levels of life satisfaction. But others who were equally active socially were profoundly dissatisfied with their lives. A similar range of moods was found among the socially disengaged portion of Neugarten's sample. As Stanley Cath explained:

> When we present any image of man to other people, we must take into account unique variations. Not only are the whorls of each fingertip of

Old people are individuals. While disengagement may suit some, and activity others, the individual's lifelong personality must also be taken into account.

each individual different from others, but life styles have remarkable individual variations stamped into them. (1975, p. 213)

Neugarten rank-ordered the personality patterns that emerged from her detailed six-year longitudinal study of 59 Kansas City septuagenarians along a continuum of increasing mental health or 'successfulness'. This outcome measure was based jointly on the subject's own report and on independent assessments by a team of psychologists.

Integrated adults

At the top rung of this ladder were the personalities Neugarten labelled *integrated*. The 17 elderly men and women in the category 'integrated adults' were best adjusted. They stood out from the other participants in the following ways:

- They took unusually great pleasure in the everyday business of living.
- They accepted their lives for what they had been and saw them as meaningful.
- They felt they had been reasonably successful in achieving their major life goals.
- They had a favourable self-image and high self-esteem.
- They were rated as happy, enthusiastic and optimistic in mood by trained psychologists.

In addition, the psychologists who interviewed them noted that these adults had 'a complex inner life and, at the same time, intact cognitive abilities and competent egos'. In short, people with integrated personalities seemed to be coping exceptionally well with all the varied challenges of the last decades of life.

To test the predictions of disengagement against those of activity theory, Neugarten examined the level of social role activity of the old people in this

integrated category. She found that they ran the gamut from almost complete disengagement to almost frenetic activity. On the basis of this range of difference, she discerned the following three subtypes of integrated personality.

Neugarten speculated that, during an earlier era

Reorganisers

These nine individuals defied disengagement by maintaining, or even increasing, their extent and depth of role involvement relative to what it had been during middle adulthood. They seemed to equate happiness with youthfulness, and youthfulness with activity, and they eagerly embraced all three. Inevitable losses due to the death of friends, widowhood or retirement from work had all been replaced as a result of their vigorous seeking of new friendships and intimacies and their devotion to church, club and community affairs.

Reorganisers eagerly embrace continued social activity, and may develop new friendships along with devotion to new volunteer or family pursuits.

Focused personalities

The five old people who made up this subgroup had about the same level of overall role activity as the reorganisers, but the nature of their role involvement was different and a change, also, from what it had been during earlier stages of their own lifespan. Focused adults had become more deeply and selectively involved in one or two chosen roles to which they

Focused adults become selectively and single-mindedly devoted to one or two chosen social roles, such as home handyman.

currently devoted most of their energy, and from which they gained no less satisfaction than the more 'thinly spread' reorganisers. A typical focuser was a retired man who had left his roles as club member and community leader behind, along with retirement from his job. His time was now exclusively, but happily, devoted to his wife and grandchildren.

Disengaged personalities

As the name implies, this personality style was the one that supported Cumming and Henry's original equation of high morale with a contemplative style of ageing. The three adults in this category had all voluntarily chosen to relinquish the role commitments of their earlier years. Furthermore, they had done so not in response to loss or external pressures, but because they wanted to 'sit back in their rocking chairs and relax'. They were interested in the world, and their personalities were not shallow, but they seemed content now to watch life from the sidelines with no real temptation to re-enter the fray and spent much time passively in front of the TV.

The integrated disengaged adults in Neugarten's sample were happy to retreat to an armchair and contemplate life, rather than remaining actively involved.

in history, the disengagers' arena for contemplation would have been limited to the view from their own front verandah. However, the advent of television (which William Henry had described as the 'great disengager') offered these old people as wide a vista on the world as they chose to select. As Henry explained:

> American TV programming permits that the individual older person can, with complete physical and psychic immobility, contemplate and passively re-examine many values inherent in his earlier life and in the social system at large. The virtues, or at least the common attributes, of achievement motivation, of over-determined social engagement, of complex mutually dependent relations, are all fully displayed. Their merits and their relation to self can easily be re-examined with no commitment whatsoever. (1965, p. 28)

Armoured and defended personalities

Down a rung on the ladder of mental well-being from the integrated personalities was a global style which Neugarten described as *armoured and defended personalities*. Again, this overall personality pattern encompassed several subtypes that were unified by their somewhat precarious and anxiety-ridden acceptance of old age. More than half the armoured old people rated themselves on a level of life satisfaction equal to that of the integrated group. But, because their happiness was achieved by dint of immense effort and abnormally tight control over all their feelings, instincts and impulses, the psychologists viewed their stance as a vulnerable one. The odds of their suffering an abrupt downturn in mood seemed greater than among the integrated, whose adjustment to life rested on a realistic awareness of both the assets and the liabilities which ageing held in store. Again, the armoured personality pattern was more consistent with continuity theory than either disengagement or activity, since it included both a disengaged and an active subgroup. Neugarten described these subcategories as follows.

HOLDING-ON

The 11 old people in this group had ambitious, achievement-oriented personalities but, because they defined success in middle-aged terms, they tended to perceive old age as a threat to their well-being. They responded to the threat by defiantly maintaining the same active roles and life patterns that they had established for themselves during middle age. Although this worked well enough to keep their morale high, weak spots in their 'armour' were illustrated in comments that betrayed their anxiety, such as one man's vow that 'I'll work until I drop'.

CONSTRICTED PERSONALITIES

A disengaged version of the armoured personality style was adopted by five old people who, in a sense, had rushed to accept the defeat they perceived old age to be. Like the integrated-disengaged, they had voluntarily chosen to decrease their role involvement and to constrict their social interactions after middle age. Their reasons for making the choice were different, however. They appeared to believe that, if they had tried to remain active, the inevitable disabilities of ageing would result in pain, humiliation and a loss of self-respect. Since they feared these consequences more than the unpleasantness of being inactive, they had elected to remove themselves from the social scene. Thus they had restructured their world 'to keep off imminent collapse'. This style was somewhat less successful than those outlined earlier, though most of the constricted individuals managed to enjoy at least moderate levels of life satisfaction.

Passive-dependent personalities

A still less effective style overall was the *passive-dependent personality* category. It incorporated two subtypes: succourance-seekers and the apathetic elderly.

SUCCOURANCE-SEEKERS

This group of six old people had maintained reasonably high life satisfaction but, since they relied heavily on other people, their future was precarious. Succourance-seekers also led a rather passive style of existence, not extending their capacities to the full by meeting new challenges.

APATHETIC ELDERLY

Another form of the 'rocking-chair' lifestyle was much less satisfying and fulfilling than the integrated-disengaged style and was practised by seven people. These *apathetic* personalities were all alike in having opted for a minimally active, almost vegetative, life pattern during old age. One man could not even be bothered to answer questions: he let his wife tell the interviewer what he thought and felt; a woman in the same group appeared to have no interests left except her own basic physical comfort.

Disorganised personalities

The least well-adjusted of all the aged personalities in Neugarten's sample were something of a mixed bag. Labelled *disorganised*, all 11 members of this category showed signs of serious mental and emotional disturbance. In view of this, they perhaps did not belong within the framework of any general theory of normal ageing. Indeed, the only consistency among them seemed to have been very low life satisfaction.

It is not clear to what extent these old-age personality patterns mirrored idiosyncracies which would have been found in the same people at earlier stages in their lives had longitudinal studies been conducted. But Neugarten's results tend to support personality-continuity theory's compromise between the polar opposites in the theoretical controversy between activity and disengagement. All in all, an individual's own nature – as optimist or pessimist, as gregarious extrovert or retiring introvert, as active achiever or passive follower – would seem to offer better predictions of the style of social ageing that that person will opt for than any universal model of successful ageing that is designed to define success for everyone.

A further study

A further study, using a similar method, was conducted in Newcastle-upon-Tyne, England, by R. D. Savage and his associates (1977). Its results also highlighted the important contribution of personality differences to successful ageing. The 82 healthy, elderly urban community dwellers included in Savage's study grouped themselves into four broad personality types, as follows.

THE SILENT MAJORITY

This group of intense, wary and self-sufficient old people made up 54 per cent of the British sample. While shrewd, analytic and deliberate in their actions, they tended to be rather intolerant of change and suspicious of outsiders, resenting any interference with their private lives.

THE MATURE

This group of resourceful, self-sufficient, tough-minded elderly men and women stood out for their intelligent decision-making skills, their even tempers and their personal strength and courage. Approximately 16 per cent of the total sample fell into this category.

THE INTROVERTED

This 20 per cent subgroup of the sample had reserved, introspective natures coupled with shyness and conscientious self-restraint. While apprehensive about meeting other people, particularly in large groups, they also displayed above-average social sensitivity and concern.

THE PERTURBED

This group of difficult-to-get-along-with elderly comprised 11 per cent of the Newcastle sample, and stood out for their irrational anxiety, their irritable and uncontrolled emotional behaviour and their consequent personal and interpersonal problems. However, despite some signs of personality disturbance, their problems were not severe enough to place them in the category of 'mentally ill'.

When they examined the links between life satisfaction and social role activity for these four personality groups, Savage and his colleagues reached conclusions very similar to Neugarten's. Disengagement seemed to suit some personality patterns best while social activity was ideal for others. Thus, although

The 'silent majority' comprised British old people who were shrewd but intensely private and intolerant of change.

the *silent majority* and *introverted* groups scored almost identically high in life satisfaction, the former group was high in social role activity while the latter typified a disengaged model of ageing. As Savage and his associates explained:

> The results of this study confirm and substantiate the point of view ... that both theories – activity and disengagement – may be applicable to the explanation and understanding of aged personality functioning depending on individual and social differences. Neugarten's ... assertion that personality is a 'pivotal dimension in predicting relationships between levels of social role activity and life satisfaction' has been reaffirmed and has gained further credence on the basis of the present study. (p. 161)

Socioemotional selectivity theory

More recently, Laura Carstensen (1992, 1995) proposed the theory of *socioemotional selectivity* as an explanation for healthy social ageing. According to this view, healthy old people who are coping well do not simply disengage or remain active in the all-or-nothing manner proposed by earlier theorists. Instead, they become more astutely selective in their social relationships, disengaging from some of them and remaining highly active and involved in others. As a consequence, the older person's social network changes systematically in old age. It becomes both narrower and deeper. After the 'less essential' social ties are shed, the older adult invests emotions and energies heavily in the selected few social relationships that have been voluntarily and deliberately retained.

According to this model, marriage is likely to become more emotionally intimate, deeper and more intensely satisfying in late middle age, in line with the U-shaped curve for marital satisfaction that we analysed in Chapter 14. In research with elderly married couples, Carstensen and her colleagues (Carstensen, Gottman & Levenson, 1995) discovered that relationships that had lasted for four or five decades were characterised by higher levels of positivity, enjoyment of being together, intimate affection and mutual trust than the marriages of young or middle-aged adults. In addition, the older couples spent more time in one another's exclusive company than younger couples whose time together as husband and wife was often shared with offspring, other family or friends.

In sharp contrast to the sociobiological theory of sexual and emotional boredom in adult marriage (see Chapter 14), elderly couples who spent the most time alone together as couples were found to be the ones who reported the highest levels of satisfaction with their marriage, their spouse and life in general (Carstensen, 1995). The older married couples also differed from younger spouses in reporting fewer angry conflicts, more success in resolving any conflicts that did erupt between them, and pleasure in sharing ideas with one another in open, affectionate and energetic discussion. In line with Carstensen's theory, they seemed to have selectively chosen to invest dwindling cognitive and emotional energy into their couple relationship, learning to understand one another better and to find constructively dialectical solutions to their points of controversy. By contrast, younger adults, whose marriages were only one component of a multitude of satisfying social roles, seemed to put less energy into learning to understand and appreciate the spouse, and hence felt less satisfied and involved in the marital relationship.

Carstensen developed her theory partly out of careful analysis and interpretation of empirical research findings like these, and partly on inspiration from Paul Baltes' S-O-C (selective optimisation with compensation) model of successful ageing that we examined in Chapter 16. According to Baltes, healthy older men and women can 'use psychology' to outwit the physical and social losses that are bound to arise if they live long enough. By astutely *selecting* capacities that have remained more immune to the detrimental effects of ageing, by strategically *optimising* their functioning through planning, practice or other deliberate interventions and by *compensating* for losses with options that remain available, an older adult can overcome many of the problems that old age might otherwise have brought about.

Applied to social roles and relationships, the result is Carstensen's socioemotional selectivity theory. As an alternative to activity and disengagement theories, it represents a compromise position, with withdrawal from certain social roles and heightened investment in others. To cope with the physical energy losses, reduced mobility, weaker sight and hearing and frail health that may make social interaction more difficult, and to offset the social disappointments and losses that may arise during old age, the elderly strategically narrow their social networks and then invest more heavily in the relationships that they have elected to retain. Consequently, these desired bonds become richer and more satisfying in old age, while the need to disengage from superficial roles is fulfilled without the threat of total loneliness and social isolation. As Carstensen (1992) explained:

> In the socioemotional selectivity model, social patterns observed in old age reflect gradual changes that unfold over the life course. The theory ... posits that although the basic functions of interaction remain consistent across the life cycle, place in the life cycle influences the salience and effectiveness of specific functions ... [O]ver the course of many years, emotional closeness to family and close friends – having shared innumerable joys and sorrows – may increase. Simultaneously, however, interaction with unfamiliar social partners becomes less likely to yield gains sufficient to warrant the necessary energy expenditure. Rather, contact with strangers or

acquaintances comes to cost more than it's worth. Thus, over the life course, the potential risks and benefits of social interaction change. There is a reduced likelihood that interaction with casual social partners will be rewarding; yet, interaction with a select group of significant others becomes increasingly valuable. (pp. 331–2 © American Psychological Association, reprinted by permission)

The research evidence

As noted earlier, Cumming, Havighurst and Neugarten each drew support for their theories of (a) disengagement, (b) activity and (c) personality continuity, respectively, from interviews with the same longitudinal sample of Kansas City men and women who were tracked over several decades. Carstensen also consulted longitudinal data in her efforts to assess the validity of socioemotional selectivity theory. Recall the Berkeley longitudinal studies that we considered in Chapters 1 and 10. Carstensen (1992) returned to study 50 members of this California sample of men and women when they were in their 50s. When she examined the quality of the relationship that each of these individuals had enjoyed with their best friend as teenagers and throughout adulthood, she found that the nature of the friendship bond had changed systematically over the period from age 17 to age 52. Less time was spent with best friends in middle and late adulthood than during adolescence and youth. At the same time, however, the relationships grew closer over time and produced stronger feelings of intimacy, emotional empathy and mutual trust. Figure 17.3 shows some of these changes.

Similar patterns of change applied to the adults' relationships with their siblings and parents, as shown in Figure 17.4. By age 50, the quality of the mature adults' relationships with their elderly parents and adult siblings had improved markedly. Low

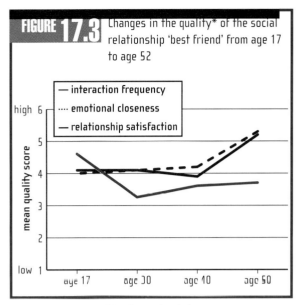

FIGURE 17.3 Changes in the quality* of the social relationship 'best friend' from age 17 to age 52

* Quality = close, satisfying, frequent contact
Source: Based on data in Carstensen (1992), Table 1. © American Psychological Association, adapted with permission.

points in the life cycle for both these types of family relationship arose around age 30. Carstensen argued that, as older adults reduce their social involvement with casual friends and acquaintances, they become more selective in their decision to spend positive, quality time with family members. As energy dwindles, the benefits of social involvement can be optimised by renewing old bonds and investing more deeply in ties with close kin (e.g. spouse, children, siblings and aged parents). As Carstensen explained:

> Results provide strong support for socioemotional selectivity theory, which maintains that reductions in social contracts across the life span reflect increasing selectivity in one's choice of social partners. Although rates of interaction with acquaintances decline steadily from early adulthood on, interactions in significant relationships

FIGURE 17.4 Increases with age in satisfaction and closeness of ties with siblings and aged parents, from age 17 to age 52

Source: Carstensen (1992). © American Psychological Association, reprinted by permission.

increase. Thus, interactions with a core group of social partners, from whom people derive affective gains, become more frequent, satisfying, and emotionally close over the adult life course. However, interactions with more casual social contacts, which provide fewer affective rewards, become less satisfying and frequent. (pp. 336–7 © American Psychological Association, reprinted by permission)

Table 17.4 shows how the S-O-C model, incorporating Paul Baltes' (2002) concepts of selection, optimisation and compensation, can be applied to intimate relationships in old age according to Carstensen's theory.

Cross-cultural evidence of socioemotional selectivity

In a Japanese study, Keiko Takahashi, Junko Tamura and Makiko Tokoro (1997) assessed life satisfaction, self-esteem, subjective health and the nature and quality of social relationships in a group of 148 men and women, all over the age of 65. These authors observed high levels of life satisfaction, self-esteem and well-being in most of the elderly, who still lived in the same community where they had spent the bulk of their adult life. While their social networks were smaller than in earlier adult life, the vast majority of the community-dwelling elderly had maintained at least one close relationship with a friend or family member. Their choice of relationship partners resembled the patterns observed by Carstensen (1992) in the United States – most of these older Japanese were closest to an intimate family member, either their spouse (33 per cent of women; 67 per cent of men) or an adult son, daughter or daughter-in-law (22 per cent of women; 11 per cent of men). But among the institutionalised elderly, many of whom had moved into institutions because their family members could no longer care for them, 'friends' were the most commonly cited intimates; and a full one-third of these institutionalised elderly Japanese men and women, compared with only 14 per cent of the sample as a whole, were what the investigators described as 'lone wolves' – people who had no close and mutually satisfying intimate relationships.

In support of Carstensen's theory and in contradiction to disengagement theory, the elderly Japanese men and women who had at least one selected close relationship reported very high levels of life satisfaction and were well adjusted on each of the other psychological measures included in the study, whereas the 'lone wolves', who had not managed to selectively retain any close social contacts, were coping poorly. They scored significantly lower in life satisfaction and other aspects of emotional adjustment than their institutionalised peers of comparable age and health status who had selectively maintained a relationship with a relative or close friend. Figure 17.5 illustrates these results. As shown in this figure, some Japanese adults had selected their spouse as the major focus of social connectedness, while others had chosen their adult children or close friends. All of these adults were approximately equally satisfied with their lives, and significantly more so than the 'lone wolf' elderly who had disengaged completely from social roles and relationships.

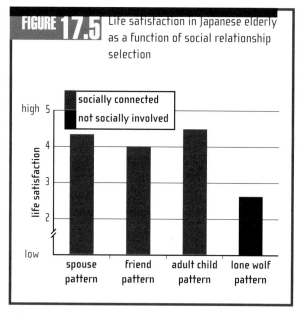

FIGURE 17.5 Life satisfaction in Japanese elderly as a function of social relationship selection

Source: Based on data in Takahashi et al. (1997).

TABLE 17.4 Selection, optimisation and compensation in aged adults' close relationships		
Selection	Optimisation	Compensation
Choose social ties that matter and bring rewarding emotional experiences (e.g. deeming marriage the most important bond of old age).	Make the most of chosen social relationships by working hard to sustain frequent contact and emotionally positive interactions, while resolving conflict thoughtfully and amicably (e.g. travelling together or engaging in household projects with the spouse).	Overcome problems in chosen relationships (e.g. disagreements in marriage or separation by geographical distance from adult offspring) by familiar methods (mutual discussion) or novel techniques (e.g. long-distance phone calls and the Internet).

Personality, culture and where to live

The results discussed above clearly indicate that the question of whether, and when, an older adult should move from the home community into a sheltered institution or retirement community is a complex one involving social and personality considerations as well as issues of income, health and physical or cognitive capacity. Older people's selection of social network members and their unique personality pattern, developed over a lifetime, must be taken into account before prescribing either residential or community living. To caregivers, social planners and other would-be optimisers of lifespan psychological development, the research on disengagement, activity, personality continuity and socioemotional selectivity theories that we have just reviewed underscores the need to offer a range of social options for old people to select from.

Some residential communities for the elderly attempt to take account of this diversity of needs by offering a continuum of graded options from fully independent to highly assisted and supported living. At one extreme, the well-equipped and well-staffed resort-style 'over-55s' community can offer its healthy and affluent elderly residents new options for theatrical, artistic, musical, handyman and sporting recreational pursuits that they would not have had access to in an ordinary, mixed-aged suburban environment. New social contacts with other residents of like mind can offer options for satisfying friendships, and role activities and commitments may increase, at least for a time. But as health declines, other choices in the residential home may encourage retirement from the fray into a life of passive leisure pursuits and self-reflective contemplation. The research evidence reviewed above highlights the need at this point for voluntary choice so that frail older residents can exercise their need for selectivity

Age influences the level of activity an older resident desires and also the decision to move into residential care during old age in the first place. Figure 17.6 shows the age distribution of residents in aged care facilities

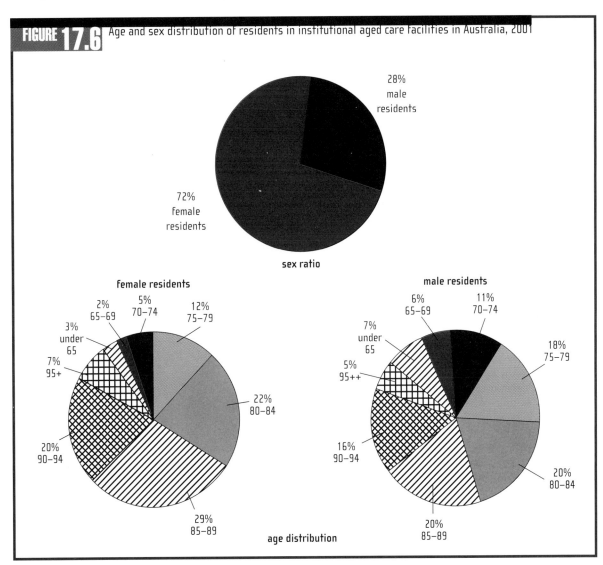

FIGURE 17.6 Age and sex distribution of residents in institutional aged care facilities in Australia, 2001

Source: Based on data in Australian Institute of Health and Welfare (2002).

Many old people prefer to spend their final years in mixed-age company.

in Australia in 2001. As can be seen in this figure, relatively few adults under age 75 select this style of residence, with increases thereafter.

Perhaps too few nursing homes take sufficient account of gender, age and other individual differences among old people. As the research on personality continuity and socioemotional theories shows, there are wide individual differences among old people in their level of desire for social involvement and companionship versus privacy, and in the kinds of social contacts that are likely to bring them optimal satisfaction. Frail health, failing senses and mobility problems may discourage elderly nursing-home residents from undertaking social initiatives, social selection and socially meaningful role activity.

Culture, gender, ethnicity and adjustment to nursing home life

Cultural background, native language and experience contribute, together with personality, to create variations in the needs and desires of elderly men and women who live in institutional environments. Box 17.3 illustrates cultural variation with an example of a nursing home in contemporary China.

In 'melting pot' societies like Australia, New Zealand, Canada and the United States today, older individuals from ethnic minority groups may have more difficulty than members of the cultural mainstream in finding a congenial style of residential accommodation and having their needs effectively catered for when they take up residence in institutions that are staffed and run by Anglo-Australians or New Zealanders. Mary Westbrook and V. Legge (1990) studied the patterns of tension associated with caring for elderly members of three ethnic minority groups in a sample of 163 nursing homes in Sydney. As expected, tensions experienced by nursing staff were greater when caring for patients from non-English-speaking backgrounds than for Anglo-Australian residents.

But the old person's ethnic background also influenced the patterns of tension experienced, as Figure 17.7 shows. Meals were especially problematic for the Chinese and Greek-Australian elderly, less so for Italian-Australians. The sexual and social behaviours of the Greek-Australian elderly stood out from those of the other two ethnic groups as sources

BOX 17.3 — Lessons from culture
Residential care in China

During prerevolutionary times in China, the lot of an old person without living relatives was severe. This changed after the socialist revolution. For example, the Lingshui Commune in Dalian, China, set up a retirement home in the former landlord's manor house. Its rules of operation are designed to foster dignity in the aged and respect for them (Su, 1982).

- *Freedom to move in and out.* A resident is free to leave the home at any time. Some residents opt to visit for a trial period initially before making a final decision about whether to move in.
- *Freedom to entertain.* Visiting hours are completely open. Friends and relatives are welcome to visit at any time. The home provides close relatives with free board whenever they visit.
- *Freedom to travel.* Residents are free to go in and out during the day, and to take longer trips away from the home to visit friends and relatives. The home pays their travelling expenses.
- *Freedom to work.* In order to keep fit and active, retirees can volunteer to do light jobs such as raising poultry or flowers. Exercise and calligraphy are also popular hobbies.
- *Freedom to drink liquor.* Despite concern about the ex-workers' health, the directors of the home decided to permit free access to alcohol out of respect for the dignity and autonomy of the residents.

Some older nursing home residents value social activities while others may gain most satisfaction from solitary pursuits.

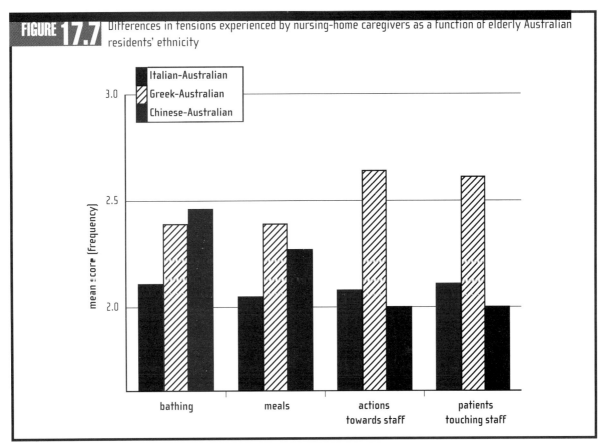

FIGURE 17.7 Differences in tensions experienced by nursing-home caregivers as a function of elderly Australian residents' ethnicity

- Italian-Australian
- Greek-Australian
- Chinese-Australian

mean score (frequency)

bathing meals actions towards staff patients touching staff

Source: Based on data in Westbrook & Legge (1990).

of special tension, while bathing was especially stressful when Anglo-Australian nurses cared for Chinese-Australian elderly patients.

Residential disengagement

A nursing home is one residential option for an elderly adult, though it is often forced on the person

The Internet can reduce social isolation for older men and women who find it difficult to leave home.

by ill health or chronic disability rather than chosen voluntarily. But, even in the absence of physical incapacity, many older people and their families are preoccupied with the question of where to live. Common options in Australia and New Zealand range from beachside resorts to granny flats; from urban ghettos to bucolic, age-segregated 'cities-of-seniors'; from nursing homes or retirement villages to caravan parks; and from single-tenant apartments to communal households. As well as having a likely impact on such mental health issues as anxiety and life satisfaction, an older person's residential decision-making is bound up with possibilities for involvement with, or disengagement from:

- younger, older and co-generational family members
- friends and neighbours of other generations
- social contact with long-term friends
- new friends and social acquaintances
- community participation in clubs, church groups, volunteer organisations, political networks, etc.
- previous household duties, routines and recreational pursuits.

The older person and the Internet

One way to overcome the enforced isolation that may come about in old age through restricted mobility, living alone in a high-rise apartment or on a secluded farm or after moving into a nursing home or other care facility is via the Internet. In an Australian study, Carol Irizarry, Deborah West and Andrew Downing (2001) examined older adults' use of the Internet facilities that were available to them at home or within convenient reach of their place of residence. They found that fewer elderly men and women (only 9 per cent of those over 55 in one survey) had computer access to email or the Web from home than younger adults (about 24 per cent of young men and women, on average, had home access). But when the option of taking an Internet class and learning to use email and other facilities in their community libraries, schools and recreation centres was made available to them free of charge, many older Australians in rural communities jumped at the chance.

The investigators examined older men's and women's reasons for undertaking to learn the new technology and found, as shown in Figure 17.8, that social contact with family, friends, children and grandchildren via email ranked high on the list. In fact, the most frequently used applications of new technology by older Australians who had completed an Internet class were social ones. Over two-thirds (69 per cent) had used email to contact friends and family, about half (54 per cent) played games on the Net, some of which (like bridge and chess) were social, and only one person in the sample had employed it for the more mundane, non-social purpose of Internet banking!

Neighbourhood crime and the elderly

Fear of crime, exploitation or victimisation is both a frequent instigator and a frequent consequence of a change of residence during old age. Aged widows and widowers may elect to move out of their home into an institution because they no longer feel safe living alone, or lest a sudden accident, illness or intrusion prevents them from being able to summon help, the police or an ambulance. The perceived risk of being attacked or robbed also prompts many aged people to move out of inner-city neighbourhoods, despite the economic advantage of a paid-off mortgage. A move into a nursing home, a granny flat, a caravan park, a son's or daughter's household or a retirement village may alleviate these worries while creating new ones to do with dependency or loss of status, the hardship

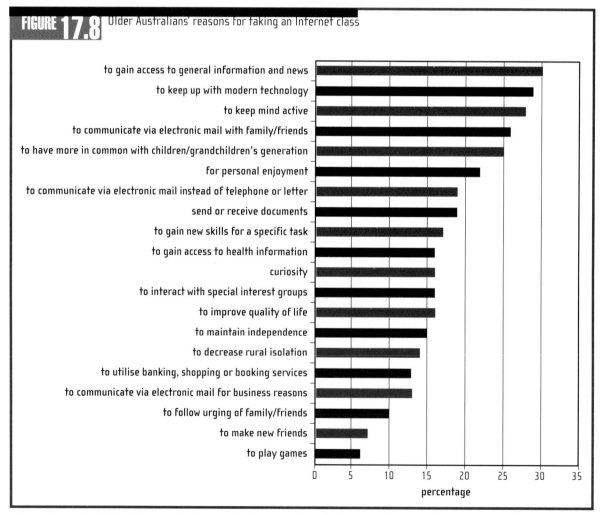

FIGURE 17.8 Older Australians' reasons for taking an Internet class

Source: Irizarry et al., Australasian Journal on Ageing, 20, September 2001. Reproduced with permission of the Council on the Ageing (Australia).

of losing contact with former friends and relatives, or the loss of a pet or a garden.

A large-scale survey of older people in Denmark (Ensomme Gamles Vaern, 1980) revealed, for example, that the inability to take care of a multi-storey suburban family home was the most common reason for moving into sheltered housing, followed by the desire to be able to summon help in emergencies. But after the move was made, the further away the new residence was from the old person's former abode the fewer were his or her social contacts with family and friends.

People over age 70 were especially apt to be neglected. Also, residents of high-rise buildings and those with physical impairments reported relatively little opportunity to chat with their new neighbours, and the problems of social isolation made them doubt whether the decision to move had been the right one. Some of the benefits of mixed-age residential integration and of maintaining continuity of home and neighbourhood through the adult life cycle were brought out in Peter Townsend's (1962) classic large-scale survey of old people in Britain; his results remain current today for many old people whose disengagement from their community of a lifetime is instigated by the threat of crime or disability rather than voluntary choice. Townsend found that most of the elderly who had moved into old-age institutions deplored the transfer and suffered lower morale and less life satisfaction than their peers of comparable age and economic circumstances who had remained in their lifelong dwelling places in the community.

On the other hand, Wayne Seelbach and Charles Hansen (1980) found that, in comparison with their non-institutionalised peers, a group of 151 80-year-old American residents of sheltered health-care housing projects for the aged had higher morale and better attitudes about their health. The fact that both groups in Seelbach and Hansen's study had more health problems and less income than average for their age may have helped to explain these results.

Yonina Talmon (1968) suggested that many older people desire protection from the feelings of competition or inferiority that arise when they make invidious comparisons between themselves and younger members of the community. This could explain the higher morale and more positive impressions about 'old people in general' found among affluent residents of resorts for the aged than among their equally prosperous counterparts living in mixed-age neighbourhoods.

Christine Dunkel-Schetter and Camille Wortman (1981) likewise suggested that age-segregated housing increases opportunities for contact with aged peers, thus helping old people to give vent to their feelings and gain support from others in a similar situation. As they explained:

> We suspect that because elderly persons share common experiences, they are much more capable of meeting one another's support needs

than are family or younger friends. A first step in providing peer support is to increase the likelihood that elderly people will meet and get to know others of their own age. To this end, it might be worthwhile to consider various living arrangements that offer proximity to other older people (e.g. communal households, retirement communities, public housing for senior citizens) ... Contrary to some opinions that the elderly should not be segregated in this way, there may be some important psychological advantages to age-segregated housing and recreational facilities because they provide primary access to age peers ... It is therefore important to ... develop interventions that aim to facilitate the formation of friendships and communication among older people. (pp. 372–3)

But not all old people feel isolated or threatened when they contrast themselves with the young, and many relish exchanging views with a younger generation of neighbours. Clearly, the choice of where and with whom to live is as idiosyncratic and multi-dimensional as the issues to do with social disengagement (considered earlier in this chapter) or sexuality. A major benefit of recent research has been to explode the myth that any one single style of residence will ideally suit *all* old people. Not everyone wishes to spend the last years of their life in an institution but, equally, not all old people prefer not to. The same can be said of most of the other residential opportunities offered to the elderly in a complex, economically affluent society.

Personality and adjustment in old age

Carstensen's theory of socioemotional selectivity (see page 600) highlights the importance of voluntary choice as old people use mechanisms of selection and optimisation to compensate for social changes and losses. There is clearly a need to make sure that free choice and a wide range of social and residential options are as available to the aged as to the young. This applies also to personality and emotional adjustment. For optimal well-being and the option to develop their personality fully, free choice and voluntary decision-making are both essential. Not only do old people need to have input into major choices such as whether to live alone or with relatives or in an institution, they also need to make their own decisions about simple day-to-day matters like what and when to eat, how long to sleep, who and what to see or do, and how to spend their time. Unfortunately, many widowed, poor or disabled old people find their range of choice limited even at the simplest everyday level. For those old people who live in their own house or flat in the community, lack of access to transport or a telephone may limit their choice of social companions and leisure activities. Lack of housekeeping or shopping help may likewise limit their choice of what to eat, as well as undermining nutrition (see Chapter 16).

Conversely, residence in an institution restricts the individual's choice to whatever range of options this closed environment happens to provide. One study of the unmet needs of a small group of elderly Queensland nursing home residents suggested that institutional living is liable to seriously hamper the Australian old person's range of free choice (Brown, Davey & Halladay, 1986). Some of the deprivations experienced by this group are shown in Table 17.5.

Motivation, personality and the sense of personal control

When old people's choices are limited to the point where they feel they no longer have an impact on events, decisions or people that matter, they risk developing a problem known as *learned helplessness* (see Chapter 4). In fact, learned helplessness can pose a serious threat to the older person's physical and mental well-being.

Martin Seligman (1975) cited a doctoral study by N. A. Ferrari, who interviewed a group of 55 elderly women who had applied for admission to a nursing home in the United States. One major issue explored in the interview was how much freedom of choice the woman felt she had had when making the decision to go into the home. For 17 of the women the decision to move was not an act of free will. Either her relatives had forced her into making the application or she herself felt she had no other realistic option available. Of these 17 women, eight (47 per cent) died after less than four weeks of residence in the home and 16 (94 per cent) were dead within 10 weeks, compared with only one of the 38 who had applied

The decision to move out of the home of a lifetime into a retirement village or nursing home is a difficult one for many older men and women.

voluntarily. While poor health might conceivably have been one of the reasons why relatives had urged the move, no seriously life-threatening conditions had been diagnosed in any of the women by the medical staff who examined them on entry. Furthermore, the physician attending at the time of death had not anticipated a fatality in any of the involuntary entrants and described the event as 'unexpected' on the death certificate. Thus, in Seligman's view, the sense of profound helplessness engendered in these women by a forced move into a nursing home had contributed to their premature demise.

An even more striking demonstration of the link between personal control and longevity arose in the study by Ellen Langer and Judith Rodin (1976), outlined briefly in Box 17.4. In this experiment, feelings of personal control were manipulated by giving one group of healthy nursing home residents sole charge over a pot-plant in their room, while a matched group of residents of similar age, health and socio-economic status received their plant without the control manipulation.

| TABLE 17.5 | Unmet needs of elderly people living in residential care in Queensland |

Unmet need	Percentage who mentioned the need*
More intimate social contact	32
More aged persons' settlements and age accommodation	23
Financial resources	18
Recreational services	14
Better transport	14
GPs who will make house calls	9
Telephones	9
Assistance with shopping	9
Information services	9
More complete housekeeper service	5
More facilities for people in wheelchairs	5

* Percentages total more than 100 because some adults named more than one need.
Source: Based on data in Brown, Davey & Halladay (1986).

BOX 17.4 A life-or-death experiment in a nursing home

The following 'natural' experiment was conducted by Ellen Langer and Judith Rodin (1976) in a clean, modern, well-staffed nursing home in the state of Connecticut, USA. Government inspectors had previously rated this particular nursing home as one of the finest in the entire United States. The outcome of the experiment (or dependent variable: see Chapter 2) was also dramatic. It consisted of life itself, operationalised as a comparison of the survival rates of the two experimental groups of elderly residents, all of whom had been equally fit and free of all diagnosable life-threatening conditions at the start of the study. A reliable difference did emerge. If you would like to test your own scientific intuition, try predicting which group of old men and women suffered the highest death rate, before you read the answer in the text.

The survival rate of residents who were made responsible for the plant was 85 per cent after 18 months, compared with only 70 per cent in the group whose sense of responsibility had not been boosted. Langer and Rodin (1976) also found that the responsible group made significant gains in happiness, general activity and alertness over the course of their time with the plant in contrast to slight negative changes among their counterparts whose plant was tended by the nurses. The researchers concluded that the seemingly minor intervention of being put in charge of the survival of a pot-plant had had the optimising effect of diminishing the responsible group's feelings of learned helplessness, and had consequently helped to boost their health, longevity and life satisfaction.

When asked to comment on the results of the experiment a decade later, Judith Rodin (1984) explained that ageing itself is apt to create such profound feelings of learned helplessness that access to even apparently trivial choices and control options becomes significant. According to Rodin:

During the later years, the environment is so drastically altered that people must feel restricted, and that might influence their sense of control … The changes [of responsibility for a pot-plant] seem trivial to people with a broad range of choices. But against the background of no choice at all, having any choice is dramatic. We believe that by providing choices we changed people's sense of being able to alter their environment. That's a profound psychological state. The residents had a greater sense of efficacy, so they responded to others differently, and that enabled their families and nurses to respond to them more positively. That dynamic process reverberated in all areas of their lives. (p. 44)

The optimising strategy developed by Langer and Rodin (1976) also led to new ideas about how to design and implement nursing care for the disabled elderly. In place of comprehensive, totally supportive custodial care, some hospitals and nursing homes are now experimenting with the curtailment of non-essential services, combined with advice and encouragement to help old people assume responsibility for as many of their own decisions, health routines and services as possible. For example, an aged patient who could walk slowly with the aid of a cane or walker might be encouraged to do so rather than being placed immediately in a wheelchair and pushed. To the extent that such interventions provide a sense of personal competence and efficacy, Langer and Rodin's findings indicate they could potentially trigger a spiral of improved activity and further gains in physical mastery and competence.

Another approach is to train mastery-oriented coping skills directly (Rodin, 1984). For example, an elderly nursing home resident who complained that her daughter rarely visited her might be coached to think of ways to take control of the problem, such as telephoning the daughter and inviting her to come. Rodin found that old people who were coached in this way did gain better morale and feelings of control, as well as mastery over a range of specific goal-related strategies.

The elderly adult's need for freedom and personal choice is also reflected in the organisational structure of institutions for the elderly established in China to cater for childless widows and widowers and aged singles (see Box 17.3). It is interesting to speculate on contrasts between residents' experiences there and the problems of Chinese-Australian residents of Sydney nursing homes that were discussed earlier in this chapter.

Broader cultural attitudes to old age can also enhance or detract from an older adult's sense of competence and self-efficacy. In one study of memory using standardised tasks to evaluate the encoding, retention and retrieval of information as a function of age (see Chapter 16), comparisons were made between samples of family-dwelling elderly in the People's Republic of China and in the United States (Daniel, 1994). The Chinese performed markedly better than the elderly Americans on every dimension of memory performance and the researchers concluded that: 'The results can be explained entirely by the fact that the Chinese have the most positive, active and 'internal' image of ageing across the … cultures studied' (Daniel, 1994, p. 64).

Stress and coping

The types of stresses that adults encounter are apt to change with age. This is partly because people's life circumstances change in predictable ways as they grow older. During early and middle adulthood, the most stressful events in life typically revolve around marriage, parenthood, finances and the pursuit of a career. Finances continue to create stress for older men and women. But with the emptying of the family nest and retirement from work, other sources of stress abate somewhat and older men and women may find time to relax and enjoy a lower stress lifestyle than younger adults. They are also likely to perceive the stressful events they do encounter in less negative terms (Chiraboga, 1993). But there is one major exception to this rule. The death of a spouse, and the consequent challenges imposed by having to adjust to single life as a widow or widower, constitutes perhaps the most severe of all the stresses an adult will ever encounter in life. We examine older adults' patterns of adjustment to the stress of bereavement in more detail in Chapter 18.

Nonetheless, an optimistic aspect of lifespan development through old age is the fact that the elderly suffer fewer daily stresses and hassles than younger adults. In a study of 1000 men and women aged 25 to 74 years, David Almeida (2002) found that only 8 per cent of young adults averaged one stress-free day per week, whereas 19 per cent of adults aged 60 and over did so.

The types of situations and events that cause stress for an older person differ from the stresses that plague young and middle-aged adults. For the elderly, politics, the environment, crime, personal health and the vicariously experienced difficulties of loved ones and friends are among the most commonly reported sources of stress (Folkman, Lazarus, Pimley & Novacek, 1987), and older adults tend to rate these concerns as more stressful than do younger people. It may be that personality development plays a role here. In a later section of this chapter, we examine Erik Erikson's theory of a personality crisis in old age over the conflict between *integrity* and *despair* (see Chapter 2). Perhaps the efforts of older adults to give meaning to their finite life cycle by resolving the integrity crisis make war, political upheavals, problems in the environment or the uncertain future of the world seem more personally threatening than during earlier stages in life. The vicarious experience of stress when other people face hardships, a phenomenon more common among elderly than young adults, could also stem from a similar cause.

The older person's relative lack of power and influence in modern, industrialised society (see Chapter 16) can also make political issues and concerns with the immediate environment seem more stressful. Vulnerability to financial losses through inflation or reduction of the pension, to loss of living quarters and to inner-city crime through environmental decline increases with the transition from middle to old age. Thus political, environmental and social issues may loom larger as sources of stress to older people because of their enhanced personal relevance.

Coping with stress

Earlier in this chapter, as well as in Chapter 16, we looked at Paul Baltes' (1993) S-O-C theory and at how older adults may use processes of *selection*, *compensation* and *optimisation* as cognitive strategies in coping with biological and social losses due to ageing. But strategies for coping with stress are also influenced by personality. During old age, as at earlier stages in life, it is not so much the nature or magnitude of the stressful event itself as (a) the way a person appraises it and (b) the coping mechanisms used to deal with it that determine the effect of stress on physical or mental health. Figure 17.9 illustrates this process. The sequence of strategies in the left-hand column, beginning with perception of the event as a controllable challenge rather than a threat, enables both elderly and younger adults to deal with most stresses successfully.

Developmental gains in coping skills during old age

Apart from the institutionalised elderly, who may need special help in learning to cope with pain, frailty and an impersonal environment low in opportunities to exert personal control, older men and women seem to do better than younger adults at coping with stress (Chiraboga, 1993). Recent research on normal populations of dwellers in mixed-age urban, rural and suburban communities has consistently shown that the elderly typically possess at least as wide and effective a range of problem-solving strategies as their younger peers.

When Jane Irion and Fredda Blanchard-Fields (1987) contrasted the strategies used by North American 15-year-olds, 20-year-olds and 60-year-olds to cope with everyday threats, problems and challenges in their lives, they found 'support for a growth perspective' (p. 504). The researchers discovered that adolescents and young adults made more use than middle-aged and older men and women of such immature and maladaptive coping methods as escapism, fantasy, hostility and self-blame. Not only are these techniques unlikely to lead to meaningful and lasting solutions to problems, they are also associated with increases in emotional distress, depression and powerlessness.

On the other hand, their wider range of life experience had evidently taught the adults over 40 to use

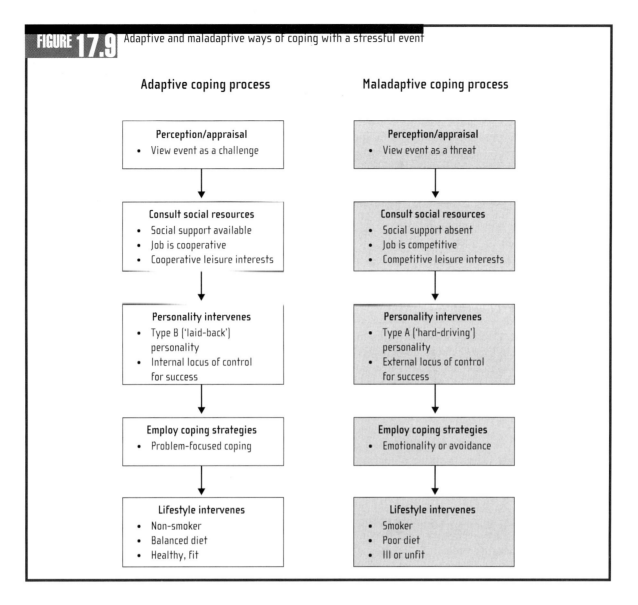

Adaptive coping process

Perception/appraisal
- View event as a challenge

↓

Consult social resources
- Social support available
- Job is cooperative
- Cooperative leisure interests

↓

Personality intervenes
- Type B ('laid-back') personality
- Internal locus of control for success

↓

Employ coping strategies
- Problem-focused coping

↓

Lifestyle intervenes
- Non-smoker
- Balanced diet
- Healthy, fit

Maladaptive coping process

Perception/appraisal
- View event as a threat

↓

Consult social resources
- Social support absent
- Job is competitive
- Competitive leisure interests

↓

Personality intervenes
- Type A ('hard-driving') personality
- External locus of control for success

↓

Employ coping strategies
- Emotionality or avoidance

↓

Lifestyle intervenes
- Smoker
- Poor diet
- Ill or unfit

a gamut of highly effective problem-solving techniques. When coping with problems that ranged from serious accidents and potentially life-threatening illnesses all the way to an argument with the spouse or the breakdown of a domestic appliance, the middle-aged and elderly groups more often came up with effective solutions. These might include seeking help or social support from others, exploring any optimistic overtones or possibilities bound up in the problem and considering the situation altruistically. The frustration of a broken-down lawnmower, for example, might be converted by a positively reappraising older adult into a plan for an enjoyable social visit to borrow a friend's mower, or a welcome excuse to indulge in a new gardening venture to replace an unwanted patch of lawn. An adolescent who used hostile or escapist coping might, on the other hand, simply kick the mower or pull the curtains in an effort to forget that the lawn still needed mowing.

Irion and Blanchard-Fields concluded that their data supported an incremental theory of coping.

Over a lifetime of experience with frustrations of various kinds, adults gain a rich store of data about effective and ineffective tactics. This teaches them to use potentially effective coping methods more often, leading to a higher rate of successful problem-solving. When problems are solved effectively, the adult overcomes feelings of helplessness and acquires the sense of mastery needed to motivate the tackling of more difficult challenges. This explains why the older problem-solvers were also less likely than adolescents and young adults to distort reality by over- or underestimating their own problem-solving capabilities.

Carole and Charles Holahan (1987) conducted a longitudinal assessment of coping skills in 52 elderly Texans living in mixed-age communities. As was expected, those with better skills had stronger feelings of personal control, less depression and more drive to tackle challenges than those whose personal resources for dealing with problems were rigid, immature or impaired. Furthermore, those individuals who had the best coping skills at the beginning of the study were found to have the strongest social support networks one year later. A spiralling sequence of advantages was again postulated to explain this optimal situation – the person with effective problem-solving skills believes he or she is worthy of friendship and is capable of obtaining social support. Active implementation of social coping skills proves that this is the case. The support network thereby mobilised continues to encourage optimism and subsequent successful coping.

The causes of stress also change with age. Young adults are more likely to report stress over relationship problems, middle-aged men and women encounter stress through overwork and role overload (see Chapter 14), whereas the elderly are more often stressed by health problems than are younger adults (Almeida, 2002).

The integrity crisis

According to Erik Erikson's lifespan theory of the growth of personality (see Chapter 2), the final developmental stage arises in old age and revolves around people's need to attach meaning, coherence and significance to their own lives in the context of faith in human life in general. From a dialectical standpoint (see Chapters 2 and 15), a secure sense of integrity emerges as a synthesis of the clash between a desire to believe that all one's choices earlier in life were the right ones and, at the opposite pole of the dialectic, a sense of despair over mistakes made, opportunities lost or unrealised personality potentials, intellectual capacities or creative talents. A number of forces in contemporary society conspire to create despair, thus strengthening the negative pole of the integrity dialectic. As Erik Erikson and his colleagues (Erikson, Erikson & Kivnick, 1986) explained:

> Life brings many quite realistic reasons for experiencing despair; aspects of the present that cause unremitting pain; aspects of a future that are uncertain and frightening. And, of course, there remains inescapable death, that one aspect of the future which is both wholly certain and wholly unknowable. Thus, some despair must be acknowledged and integrated as a component of old age. (p. 29)

On the other hand, according to Erikson's theory, elderly adults are helped to achieve integrity by their successful experiences in resolving the earlier crises of personality development that punctuate the lifespan. In addition, the process of life review that we explored in detail in Chapter 16 may prove beneficial.

The attainment of integrity may be somewhat easier in non-Western cultures. In a society where old people are generally deemed to be wise, where tradition accords the elderly strong social respect (see Box 16.9), and where the progress of modernisation does not threaten to disrupt the old person's contributions to society or make them obsolete, it is easier

for old people to accord personal value to their life's contributions. But even in modern cultures, the attainment of integrity, and of the related cognitive attribute, wisdom, are possible, as we saw in Chapter 16. When synthesis is achieved, integrity interconnects lifespan personality growth with the process of adult cognitive development. As Marion Perlmutter and Elizabeth Hall (1992, p. 270) pointed out: 'Wisdom is as dependent on personality as it is on cognition and that is why great wisdom is so rare. Extreme wisdom entails exceptional growth in both personality and cognition.'

The development of a sense of integrity also assists in the individual's acceptance of death. We will explore this process in more detail in Chapter 18.

Sexuality in old age

Sexuality is an important component of personal adjustment and intimate social relationships throughout adult life. But the expression of mature sexuality takes on new meanings and new importance for many adults during old age. Traditionally, Western societies adhered strongly to the implicit creed that disengagement, leading to sexual abstinence, was the only normal model of healthy ageing. Thus, during the 1950s and 1960s, Nathan Kogan and his colleagues found that old and young adults alike consistently believed that one major difference between the elderly and 'people in general' was that the former considered sex to be of negligible importance (Kogan & Shelton, 1962; Golde & Kogan, 1959). A majority of all age groups likewise expressed the belief that the need for companionship was greater during old age than in many of the earlier stages in life, but appeared not to find this contradictory to the assumption of aged asexuality.

However, by the 1970s and 1980s the situation had begun to change and today sexual pleasure is generally deemed to be as important to healthy older men and women as to younger adults. Indeed, one recent survey in the United States (Purnine & Carey, 1998) indicated not only that sex was important to older adults but that they (old women especially) were more adventurous in their experimentation with varied sexual postures and practices than were middle-aged adults. The frequency of engaging in sexual intercourse does decline in the population as a whole in old age, according to recent US data (AARP, 1999). However, this is more a reflection of increasing percentages of ill and widowed adults in older cohorts than a falling away from sex among those older men and women who are still healthy and married. Indeed, during the 80s, the proportion who had experienced full sexual intercourse within the month of the US longitudinal survey had not fallen to zero (AARP, 1999). Figure 17.10 shows changes in the populations of sexually active men and women over the decades from the 50s through the 70s.

However, even though sex is likely to remain

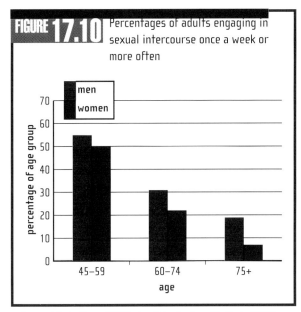

FIGURE 17.10 Percentages of adults engaging in sexual intercourse once a week or more often

Source: Adapted from AARP/Modern Maturity Sexuality Study (1999).

BOX 17.5 Is sex in old age a joke?

Some illustrations of society's views of sexual disengagement.

NEGATIVE

'At your age dentures are superfluous. No one cares how a 70-year-old woman looks.'

POSITIVE

'An 80-year-old lady wanted a physical check-up because she noticed she was losing her sexual desires. When asked by her doctor when she first noticed this, she replied, 'Last night and then again this morning.' (Palmore, 1986, p. 102)

AMBIVALENT

'Oh, and could you keep track of the score silently? The mention of 'love' is upsetting at my age.'

important to the individual in old age, society may disapprove. Erdman Palmore (1986) studied the community's attitude to sexual activity among old people by the indirect means of analysing jokes made at old people's expense. He collected a set of 264 jokes about ageing from newspapers, magazines, greeting cards and joke books. Of the total, 31 (or 12 per cent) made explicit reference to sexuality and a further 93 (or 35 per cent) alluded to it indirectly with references to physical appearance, attractiveness to the opposite sex or the marital relationship. Of the explicitly sexual jokes, Palmore found that 41 per cent depicted aged sexual relationships in a purely negative light and an additional 10 per cent were ambivalent. But a surprising 48 per cent were positive, suggesting that the popular image of sexuality as ugly or inappropriate for the old may not be as pervasive as was once supposed.

Examples of the types of jokes Palmore classified into each of his three categories are shown in Box 17.5.

When asked about their own sexuality, the elderly are not so likely to agree that disengagement is either desirable or a practical necessity. Bernard Starr and Marcell Bakur (1980) found that an overwhelming majority of 60- to 91-year-old New Yorkers (or, at least, of those aged volunteers who felt relaxed enough about sexuality to fill out a questionnaire) were still sexually active and still enjoyed sex. Many of them felt more comfortable and satisfied with their sexual behaviour than during their younger years. Furthermore, they appeared to be coping realistically with the special sexual problems caused by old age; many women said they would consider oral sex, masturbation and lesbianism as solutions to male impotence and the scarcity of male partners. Starr and Bakur concluded that the recent 'revolution' from Victorian prudery towards more permissive and more positive beliefs about sexuality (see Chapter 10) had

affected this elderly generation, despite the fact that many of them were born before 1900.

As in the case of social disengagement generally, a variety of different patterns and preferences for sexual involvement are found among old people. Simone de Beauvoir (1977) described the widely diverse attitudes of several of her personal acquaintances whose backgrounds and objective experiences with aged sexuality were quite similar. She knew two old women whose reactions to the sexual disengagement which old age had brought about for them both

Recent evidence indicates that romance is possible in old age as in youth, and sexual desire is a frequent accompaniment at all ages.

were completely different. The first had welcomed it so heartily that she had gone to her doctor to obtain a written certificate stating that her age disqualified her from continuing her 'conjugal duties'. The other was so frustrated by the sexual continence necessitated by her husband's ill health that she 'felt like beating her head against a wall'.

Among men, de Beauvoir found major differences not only in attitude but also in the degree to which sexual disengagement was actually practised. Examples of men in their 70s and 80s who marry women in their 20s and 30s are well known, and include such famous figures as Pablo Picasso, Charlie Chaplin, Pablo Casals and Henry Miller. The late-life sexual vigour of these men carried over into their creative work. André Gide, who continued to record 'passionate nights of love' in his journal when he was over 75, saw his sexuality as a major stimulus to his literary creativity:

> If it were abstract my thought would go out ... it is my carnal self that feeds the flame, and now I pray that I may retain carnal desire until I die. (Gide, cited in de Beauvoir, 1977, p. 391)

Other old men with no health impairments prefer to disengage from sexuality. As the playwright George Bernard Shaw explained:

> I am ageing very quickly. I have lost all interest in women, and the interest they have in me is greater than ever and it bores me. (de Beauvoir, 1977, p. 390)

The results of another longitudinal study of the sexual behaviour of middle-aged and elderly married men and women in the United States have suggested that most old people do not decide to disengage from sexuality simply because they are old (Weiler, 1981). Until illness or death of a spouse forces a change, the most common pattern is to maintain the same frequency of sexual intercourse as during middle age. Furthermore, when sexual disengagement does occur, the decline is likely to be sudden rather than gradual. That is, when they decide to stop, most people discontinue sexual relations altogether, rather than remaining active but engaging in lovemaking less and less often. For a woman, the main cause for cessation is illness, sexual dysfunction or the death of her husband. Men cease having sex for a wider variety of reasons, including boredom, mental and physical fatigue, illness or fear of illness, a troubled marriage, overindulgence in food or drink, or the fear of sexual or erectile failure.

However, all these reasons combined accounted for less than 18 per cent of Stephen Weiler's longitudinal sample aged 46 to 71 years. Over a six-year period, 58 per cent of these couples continued the same pattern of regular sexual activity they had enjoyed throughout their younger married years.

Chapter summary

Lay models of successful ageing emphasise social responsibility and adaptability in the face of the biological and cognitive changes of ageing, as well as the social losses due to retirement and bereavement. Changing one's social roles to suit the demands of ageing is an issue for all the major theories of social gerontology.

The theory of disengagement proposes that old people need to relinquish the various social roles which gave meaning to their lives during early and middle adulthood. Activity theory argues that socially engaged lifestyles are healthiest in old age, and continuity theory suggests that individuals age socially according to personality dispositions acquired earlier in life.

Recent research indicates that social involvement diminishes for many old people, particularly after the age of 70. But there is currently only modest support for the view that disengagement is initiated by the older person, or that it results in egocentric patterns of thought. The accumulating data suggest that old people are too diverse in their temperaments, goals and abilities for any one model of social involvement to serve as a universal recipe for successful ageing.

One factor that assumes as much importance for the mental health of elderly men and women as it did during earlier phases in the lifespan is the opportunity to gain control of important decisions and life events. Institutionalised old people who develop feelings of learned helplessness may become depressed or even die prematurely. But when elderly nursing home residents are allowed to assume responsibility and make choices freely, their health, longevity and life satisfaction are all enhanced.

Older adults may experience less stress than younger adults and their sources of stress are different. Politics, the environment, health and vicarious concerns with other people's problems are frequent causes of stress in old age. Mature men and women often show better coping skills and problem-solving strategies than younger adults, based on years of experience.

The final stage of personality development in Erikson's theory revolves around acceptance of one's life decisions and equanimity at the prospect of its close. The personality attribute known as *integrity*, which develops out of a successful resolution of this dialectical conflict, is closely related to the cognitive asset of *wisdom*.

Older people's sexual needs, desires and behaviours vary widely, but contemporary research evidence dispels the myth that sexuality is irrelevant in old age. For adults who are healthy and interested in life, old age has many desirable social opportunites and developmental challenges in store

For further interest

Looking forward on the Internet

Use the Internet to visit the following websites. Examine them for further information and varied perspectives on issues raised in this chapter. Also search for other relevant websites for yourself, using keywords like 'old age', 'elders', 'grandparenting', 'social gerontology', 'aging/ageing' and 'retirement living' in your search engine.

In particular, for further ideas on elderly adults' financial, recreational and residential options and decisions, visit: **http://www.aarp.org/life**.

For information on transition events and coping strategies in old age, visit: **http://www.healthinsite. gov.au** and select *Life Stages/Events* button.

For resources, ideas, activities and other items of interest in conjunction with this chapter, visit the Companion Website for this textbook at:

http://wps.pearsoned.com.au/peterson

Activity suggestion

Are grandparents getting younger? (1) As a practical activity in conjunction with themes in this chapter, ask as many grandparents as you know in your range of personal acquaintances (including your own grandparents, if they are still alive) to tell you (a) how old they were when they first became grandparents and (b) how old they are now. Once you have sampled a large group, graph age of onset of grandparenthood against birth year (or decade) of the grandparent. If there is a systematic trend towards younger onset, you will see it in the slope of the line. Compare your findings with the results of a recent survey in the United States (AARP, 2002) that found that age 48 was the average age of the grandparent at the birth of the first grandchild (visit: **http://www. aarp.org/press/2002/nr071502.html** for more information on the survey). (2) As a second practical activity, collect jokes and cartoons depicting love, romance and sexuality in the elderly. Group the items you have gathered according to Palmore's (1986) criteria (see Box 17.5). Do positive or negative messages predominate? For more information on jokes and a broader sampling of age-related humour, visit: **http://www.ahajokes.com/old_age_jokes.html**. (3) Alternatively, you may wish to visit an environment used by old people. If you are well acquainted with a resident in a nursing home or retirement community, pay him or her a visit; alternatively, seek permission from the facility's director. Rate the opportunities for social contact the environment provides and consider how happy or unhappy you yourself would be to live there (a) now and (b) when you are over 60.

Multimedia

To get a clear picture of successful sexual and social ageing, you may wish to view these films:

- *Love, Intimacy and Sexuality* (CSA/Video Education Australasia, 1992: 60 minutes) in which older men and women discuss their intimate relationships and enjoyment of sexuality and sensuality.

- *The Psychology of the Elderly* (Malcolm J. Brown, 1990: 58 minutes) which discusses cultural differences in successful social ageing.

THE END OF THE LIFESPAN:
Death, dying and bereavement

CHAPTER 18

Do not go gentle into that good night. Rage, rage against the dying of the light.

Dylan Thomas (1914–53)

The key to the question of death unlocks the door of life.

Elisabeth Kübler-Ross (1975)

Contents

Death is a normal, natural and inevitable part of lifespan human development. Without death, there would be no birth and no new life. Without psychological consciousness of death, individuals would not develop psychologically in the ways that we have witnessed through earlier chapters of this book, undertaking new challenges, honing their finest cognitive, emotional and social capacities, and expressing their unique personalities through their connectedness with other developing lives. Sigmund Freud (cited in Evans, 1978, p. 148) commented that: 'The goal of all life is death.' By being aware throughout our lives that death is eventual, final and inevitable, we are motivated to use all our available years of life to the fullest extent, relishing each new opportunity for psychological growth. Thus, over time, we all develop our own life stories to their eventual endings, the point where they connect with the life histories of the human race. As the poet Algernon Swinburne (1837–1909) put it in 'The Garden of Prosperine':

From too much love of living,
From hope and fear set free,
We thank with brief thanksgiving
Whatever gods may be
That no life lives forever;
That dead men rise up never;
That even the weariest river
Winds somewhere safe to sea.

In this chapter we examine death as an aspect of lifespan psychological development. Death can occur at any age, and its timing will influence the ways in which it is experienced and accepted psychologically by the dying person and the bereaved survivors. In industrialised societies like Australia and New Zealand today, death is more likely to occur at the end of old age than at any earlier time, and happens at a later chronological age now than even a decade or two ago. We examine some of the reasons for, and consequences of, historical and cross-cultural variations in death's timing and look at individual predictors of longevity.

Death is a developmental psychological issue partly because of the fact that people throughout their lives think about death and prepare both consciously and unconsciously for their own dying and for the deaths of the intimate others with whom their lives are interconnected. In the chapter we examine how children, adolescents and adults understand death. We explore how thoughts about dying and attitudes to death change as people grow up and grow older. We chart the developmental changes that culminate in the child's understanding that death is a biological process, closely connected with life and birth. Eventually children become aware that death is final, a completion of living rather than a temporary state like sleep.

The fear of dying in adults of different ages is explored and we look at psychological adjustment processes and coping mechanisms, including the cognitive completion of life review (see Chapter 16), personality processes involved in the resolution of Erikson's integrity crisis (see Chapters 2 and 17) and styles of adapting psychologically to the physical losses associated with biological ageing (see Chapters 16 and 17), processes that may help older men and women to accept their own dying and adjust peacefully to the deaths of significant others. This is central to the theme highlighted throughout this book of the connectedness of psychological processes earlier in life to development through all subsequent phases. According to Paul Baltes, Hayne Reese and Lewis Lipsitt (1980):

The propositions of a life-span developmental psychology are that ... these themes of the dying process are properly identified and investigated as developmental phenomena. (p. 70)

The process of dying is a very significant component of the life history and, like other major issues in life, partly a product of earlier psychological developments. The demands for adjustment and change during the dying process cover a wider terrain than at any of life's other turning points, for imminent death impinges on all the person's coping mechanisms and social and psychological supports. But though the crisis of death is unique, in many ways the strategy a person adopts for dealing with it also shows lifespan continuity. Personality dispositions and the unique set of skills and values developed earlier in life make each death different from any other because that death is consistent with the individual's lifespan developmental trajectory. Death also fits into the human life cycle by providing closure to the complex pattern of lifelong psychological changes described in earlier chapters of this book, regardless of whether it arises at 2, 12, 20 or 80 years of age.

We begin this chapter by examining the timing of death through the lifespan, together with the related questions of the statistically probable causes of death for people of different ages, and the roles of lifestyle factors, heredity and historical and cultural environments in shaping the odds of dying at different times. The social consequences of the changes in population longevity are considered, and we analyse how individuals develop fears, attitudes and understandings about life and death from childhood through adolescence and from adulthood into old age.

Bereavement is also examined in this chapter from a psychological perspective. The deaths of others constitute crisis events that exert a major impact on the lifespan development of bereaved survivors. Sigmund Freud saw the death of a parent in early childhood as an almost certain setback to healthy personality growth. Although recent studies do not fully support this simplistic pronouncement, contemporary researchers nonetheless agree that few

Adjusting to bereavement challenges all of a person's psychological coping mechanisms.

events in life have as much influence on a person's emotions or patterns of social organisation as the death of an intimate loved one. While it is usually easy to imagine the distressing and psychologically disorganising effects of bereavement, we may be much less aware of how often progressive psychological development is boosted in the wake of such a loss (Schultz, 1978).

For parents, teachers, counsellors, members of the clergy, health and helping professions, and all other would-be optimisers of lifespan human development, death has special significance. The tasks of coping psychologically with dying and being bereaved stand out as two of the most difficult adjustments a person is ever called upon to make. In addition to assisting and supporting the individual's passage through the immediate crises and challenges posed by these events, professionals have a role to play in assisting those in their care to prepare for them and then make long-term adjustments to them through the remainder of the lifespan. Some of the characteristics of our society that may help by providing choices and yet, at the same time, may intensify the need for long-term preparation are considered in later sections of this chapter.

Death is significant to psychological researchers who study what the concept of a 'healthy' or 'dignified' death implies, to both the dying individual and the bereaved survivors. We explore research that has endeavoured to clarify how variations in death's timing, causes and surroundings shape both the immediate and the long-term impact of dying and bereavement. We examine bereavement as a crucial component of healthy lifespan development, first in the context of a bereaved survivor's psychological coping processes in the immediate aftermath of a loved one's dying, and then through the rest of the bereaved survivor's lifespan as new roles (e.g. that of widow or widower) take the place of the roles and relationships that were lost through death and that eventually come to offer new opportunities for psychological growth.

The timing of death through the lifespan

Death can occur at any age from the moment of conception but, as Figure 18.1 shows, it is more likely at certain ages or critical points in life. Infancy is one such high-risk period. Infections, accidents, congenital defects and complications of the birth process (see Chapter 3), along with the mystery killer SIDS (see Chapter 4), account for varying proportions of infant deaths, depending on hygiene, economic factors and social conditions in the infant's environment. Today, as noted in Chapter 4, SIDS is the leading cause of infant death in Australia, as in many other industrialised nations. After infancy, the odds of survival rise rapidly to a high point during middle childhood and early adolescence (see Figure 18.1). Deaths rise sharply in the late teens and early twenties. As noted in Chapter 12, problems like drug abuse, youth suicide and violent deaths by automobile-, weapons-, drug- and alcohol-related misadventures are partially to blame for this increase. From then on, death rates in the population rise steadily with increasing age. But there is a sex difference in favour of survival for females. On average, an infant boy born today in an industrialised nation of the world can count on more than seven decades of life and a baby girl can count on eight (see Tables 18.1 and 18.2).

Longevity in the world today

Recent historical changes have altered the shape and duration of the typical human lifespan through a dramatic boost in the average length of life. As Figure 18.2 shows, an infant born in Australia or New Zealand today can count on a lifespan that is

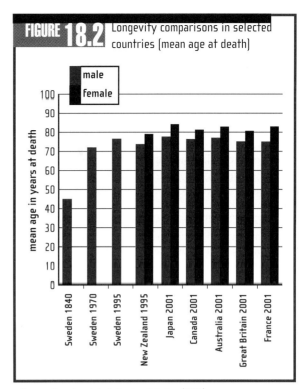

FIGURE 18.2 Longevity comparisons in selected countries (mean age at death)

Source: Based on data in Smelser & Baltes (2001).

almost twice as long as average human longevity in 1840 (as recorded in Sweden, a nation with population health statistics that are exemplary for their accuracy over several centuries). Changes in the average duration of the human lifespan have had particularly pronounced impacts on the two tails of the longevity chart shown in Figure 18.1. As noted in Chapter 3, the likelihood of death during the first risk period (early infancy) declined markedly over the 20th century in industrialised nations, largely owing

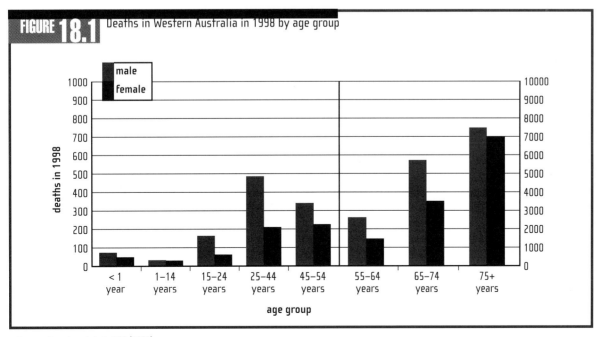

FIGURE 18.1 Deaths in Western Australia in 1998 by age group

Source: Based on data in ABS (1999).

to improved nutrition, antibiotics and other medical advances that contributed to increasingly efficient control over the infectious diseases that used to claim a disproportionate share of neonatal lives. Some of the major killers of adults in the early part of the 20th century, such as tuberculosis, pneumonia and certain gynaecological fatalities, have also been conquered, resulting in the improvement in life expectancy at older ages. As we see in Chapter 16, the medical conquest of biological ageing has likewise boosted the lifespan in the years past 60, resulting in a new age distribution of the Australian population, as shown in Figure 18.3.

Table 18.1 illustrates some of these recent historical changes in longevity in Australia and New Zealand, as well as in a selection of other countries.

Centenarians

In very recent years another dramatic change in the shape of the typical human lifespan has occurred at the upper extreme (McCormack, 2000). There has been a disproportionate increase in numbers of Australian, New Zealand, European and North American adults living to very advanced old ages. Box 18.1 illustrates a few examples.

Figure 18.3 shows the prevalence of centenarians, or adults who have lived to be over 100 years old, in Australia, New Zealand and the United States (McCormack, 2000). At present, in Australia, population projections suggest that the proportion of centenarians will double by the year 2006

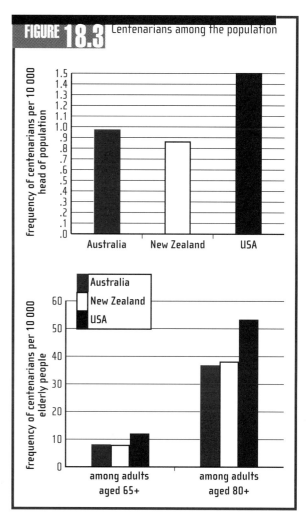

FIGURE 18.3 Centenarians among the population

Source: Based on data in McCormack (2000) and US Department of Health and Human Services (1996).

(McCormack, 2000). In Japan, a nation of greater longevity even than Australia (see Table 18.1), the estimate is that a girl born in 2001 will have a roughly 50 per cent chance of living to be 100 (Smelser & Baltes, 2001). Already, approximately one in four Japanese women lives to the age of 93. Female life expectancy rose dramatically in Japan throughout the 20th century, at a rate of about 3 months per year, or 2.5 years per decade.

No single cause is seen to be responsible for these average gains in expected length of life. According to John McCormack, an Australian researcher on centenarians: 'The data show heterogeneity in the centenarians' social circumstances such that they do not necessarily fit a frail stereotype' (p. 75).

Survival is a good predictor of further longevity, especially at advanced ages. Table 18.2 shows a person's expected length of life as computed from birth. The gender difference again appears. What is not clear from this table, however, is how the odds of long life continue to improve for individuals who have survived beyond the longevity projections that could be forecast statistically for them at birth. In fact, individuals who have already outlived the average lifespan

TABLE 18.1 Mean longevity in selected nations in 1966–1970 and 1995–2000

| | 1966–1970 | | 1995–2000 | |
	Men	Women	Men	Women
Japan	68.5	74	76.5	83
Sweden	72	76.5	76.5	82
Switzerland	69.5	75	75	82
France	68	75.5	74.5	83
Greece	69.5	73	75	81
Canada	69	75	75	81
Australia	67	74	76	81
Iceland	71	76	76	80
UK	68	74.5	74	80
Germany	68	73.5	73.5	80
New Zealand	68	74.5	74	79
USA	67	74	72.5	79
Ireland	69	73.5	73	78

Source: Based on data in Smelser & Baltes (2001), p. 8824.

BOX 18.1 A case in point
Extreme longevity

When the remarkable French woman Jeanne Calmet (whose recipe for successful ageing was described in Chapter 16) died at the age of 122 years and 5 months (McCormack, 2000) she became a statistic as the oldest person to live through the longest verifiably recorded human lifespan. Other remarkable survivors included the following.

- Sarah Knauss, from Pennsylvania, US, died on 30 December 1999, narrowly missing the feat of living a lifespan across three historical centuries. Knauss was born in 1880 and was 119 years old at the time of her death.

Born in 1880, Sarah Knauss narrowly missed living across three centuries of history.

- Hadj Mohhammed El Mokri of Morocco became the oldest airline passenger and oldest actively serving diplomat when he flew to Paris in 1955 to lead a Moroccan delegation from the Sultan to discuss the independence of Tangier at the age of 114. Much earlier in his life, he had led a political delegation to the same city to petition the court of Napoleon III! El Mokri died at the age of 116 soon after independence came to Morocco (Morris, 1983).

TABLE 18.2 Selected projections of average mean years of life expectancy at birth for infants born in 1996 to 1998

Country	Males	Females
Australia (excluding Aboriginal and Torres Strait Islander Australians)	76.2	81.8
Canada	76.2	81.9
China	68.1	72.3
India	62.5	63.3
Indonesia	63.7	67.5
Japan	76.9	83.0
Korea	69	76.2
New Zealand	74.3	79.5
Papua New Guinea	56.6	59.1
Singapore	75.1	79.5
United States	73.5	80.2
Aboriginal Australians in WA	53.7	58.9
Aboriginal Australians nationwide	56.9	61.7

Source: Based on data in ABS, Yearbook Australia (2000) and Smelser & Baltes (2001).

Zealand Department of Statistics, 2000). Similarly, although an infant Anglo-Australian boy born at the end of the 20th century could count on living to age 76, an Australian man who is 76 years old now is likely to live to be over 80.

The most worrying aspect of the data presented in Table 18.2 concerns the longevity projections for Indigenous Australians. As shown in the table, the average longevity projection for an Aboriginal boy born in 1998 is almost a quarter of a century shorter than for his Anglo-Australian peer. Some of the possible reasons for this unfortunate situation are explored in Box 18.2 (on page 624).

The psychological impact of longevity gains

The changes in average life expectancy that have arisen in recent decades have implications for psychological development through the lifespan. They are also relevant to our understanding of how people cope with their own deaths and with bereavement when loved ones die. The decreased risk of infant mortality guarantees that more and more of the children born in recent times will have the opportunity to live through all the phases in life described in earlier chapters of this book. Also, in concert with the recent decrease in the birth rate in most modern Western nations, these gains in longevity have contributed to build up the ratio of older to younger members of the population, and, consequently, to alter the frequency

shown in Tables 18.1 and 18.2 can, for the most part, count on living still longer. For example, a woman who is aged 90 in New Zealand today can expect to live a total of 93.5 years, whereas a New Zealand baby girl born today has an expected life of only 79 years, according to the data in Table 18.2 (New

of various kinds of problems typically encountered by members of the helping professions (e.g. widowhood counselling versus marriage counselling; retirement planning versus vocational planning).

In relation to death itself, increases in longevity will mean, among other things, that the loss of a child is a less common event today than it was for families in the past and therefore more traumatic for those who do encounter it. Also, the fact that most adults today are bereaved of their own parents at about the same time as the empty-nest crisis may help to explain the turmoil associated with both events (see Chapter 15). Furthermore, psychological preparation for dying is made more difficult for the contemporary child and adult by lack of direct contact with people who have died or are dying.

Age, gender, culture and the causes of death

The changing patterns for death's timing can also be linked with historical changes in the leading causes of death, and the emergence of cancer and cardiovascular disease (such as heart attack and stroke) as the leading killers at the present time. Both these ailments are age-related, with more than 10 times as many deaths caused by each of them among 55- to 64-year-olds than among people under 40 (see Figure 18.1).

Since the risk of lung cancer rises with the accumulation of insults over many years (including a lifetime of smoking cigarettes or breathing polluted air), and since many diseases of the heart and arteries are made worse by lifestyle factors (like diet and stress) which build up over time, the observed clustering of deaths in the later years of life is understandable.

The sex difference in longevity illustrated in Figures 18.1 and 18.2 and in Tables 18.1 and 18.2 may be caused in part by differences between men's and women's styles of life. The male typically travels to and from work each day, exposing himself to the risk of a fatal motor vehicle accident. Stresses, physical danger or environmental pollution on the job may likewise increase the man's odds of succumbing to cancer, heart attack or stroke. Suicide rates are higher among men than women, and it has been suggested that a male proclivity for violence (see Chapter 8) is another lifelong sex difference that may diminish masculine longevity (through accidents, homicide and military fatalities as well as suicide).

But in most infrahuman species without these special lifestyle characteristics the female likewise tends to outlive the male, suggesting that chromosomal or hormonal sex differences (see Chapter 3) may also exert an independent influence over the programming of life's duration.

Intriguingly, a statistically reliable basis for guessing a husband's longevity is to know the age of his wife. Men married to women much younger than themselves have the best odds of a long life. Those who fit the standard pattern of having wives who are within four years of their own age come next. But men whose wives are much older than they are run a significantly higher risk of an early death. The differences can be quite dramatic. Dorothy Foster, Laurel Klinger-Vartabedian and Lauren Wispe (1984) found that a man of 60 whose wife was under 45 ran only half the mortality risk of a 60-year-old with similar health and income who was married to a woman of exactly his own age. On the other hand, his odds of death were 30 per cent higher if his wife was between 65 and 70 years old than if she was 60.

The researchers suggested two contrasting reasons for this surprising relationship. First, it is possible that a man endowed with such favourable correlates of longevity as good health, a slim physique, low blood pressure and an adequate income finds himself advantaged in the marriage stakes and may elect to marry (or remarry) a much younger wife. Conversely, marriage to a relatively young woman could actively boost longevity by providing lifestyle advantages that men with older wives miss out on – such as going jogging together or having younger children or a wide circle of active, young friends. Unfortunately, the researchers' data did not afford a choice between these possibilities. Nor did they examine the effect on wives' longevity of having younger versus older husbands.

Aboriginal longevity

Like gender, culture and ethnicity also exert important influences on the predicted span of life. In Australia, it is a tragic fact that Aboriginal longevity is significantly shorter than for an Australian of European ancestry (see Table 18.2 and Figure 18.4). According to Rosemary Neill (2002):

> Australia has the dubious distinction of being the only First World country with a dispossessed indigenous minority whose men, on average, will not live long enough to claim a retirement pension. (p. 22)

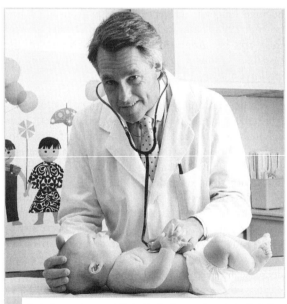

Medical advances have contributed to the improved survival of infants and children, as well as adding years at the upper end of the lifespan.

In fact, on average, the life expectancy of an Aboriginal Australian is about 20 years shorter than that of an Anglo-Australian of the same age and sex (see Box 18.2). The Australian Bureau of Statistics (2002) estimated that the average life expectancy for an Aboriginal boy born at the start of the 21st century is only 56 years, and only 64 years for an Aboriginal baby girl, whereas comparative figures for non-Indigenous Australians are 77 and 83 years respectively (see Table 18.2). This greatly reduced longevity for Indigenous Australians contrasts sharply with the situation in other countries, even including neighbouring New Zealand, where Maori life expectancy is only an average of five or six years shorter than for Anglo (or Pakeha) New Zealanders.

Nature versus nurture:
Heredity, environment and longevity

Figure 18.4 shows the racial difference in longevity that is highlighted in Box 18.2. One possible explanation for the difference is genetic. Other evidence for a hereditary contribution to longevity comes from comparisons among individuals of the same racial background. Long and short lives tend to run in families, as shown by the significant correlation between a person's own lifespan and the ages at death of their parents and grandparents (see Box 18.3). Identical twin pairs live to more similar ages than fraternal twin pairs, further reinforcing the implication of a longevity factor within each individual's genetic make-up (see Chapter 3). *Species genes* (see Chapter 3) are also relevant, since different animals each have their own average and maximum spans of life (Kendig & Hutton, 1981). There may be genetic dif-

ferences in susceptibility to illnesses like diabetes that claim a disproportionate number of Aboriginal lives (see Table 18.3). Thus the racial contrast in longevity discussed in Box 18.2 may have a partially genetic basis. But nurture is also relevant.

Idiosyncratic habits, attitudes and lifestyle patterns may also help to predict how long a person is likely to live, as mentioned in Box 18.3. The causes of some of the correlations between habits and length of life illustrated in Box 18.3 remain unknown, but many are consistent with the theories of physiological ageing discussed in Chapter 16. In particular, diet,

Environmental factors (like cigarette smoking) combine with hereditary dispositions to influence longevity.

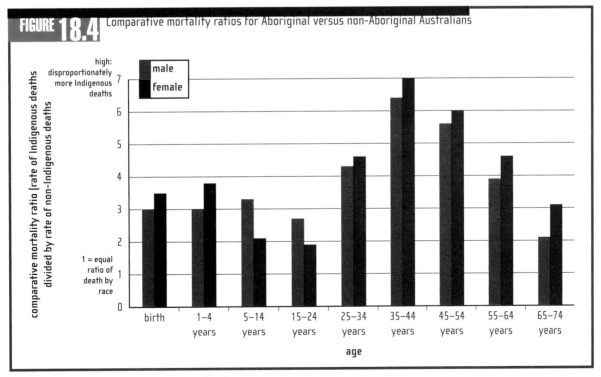

FIGURE 18.4 Comparative mortality ratios for Aboriginal versus non-Aboriginal Australians

Source: Based on data in ABS, Yearbook Australia (2002).

BOX 18.2

How can you explain it?
Contrasts between life expectancies of Aboriginal and non-Aboriginal Australians

Instructions. These figures illustrate the dramatic difference that exists between the average life expectancy of an Aboriginal man or woman and that of Australians of non-Aboriginal descent. Can you think of two different explanations for these disturbing findings? (For answers, see the text.)

Age profile of the Australian population by age, gender and Indigenous/non-Indigenous status in 2000

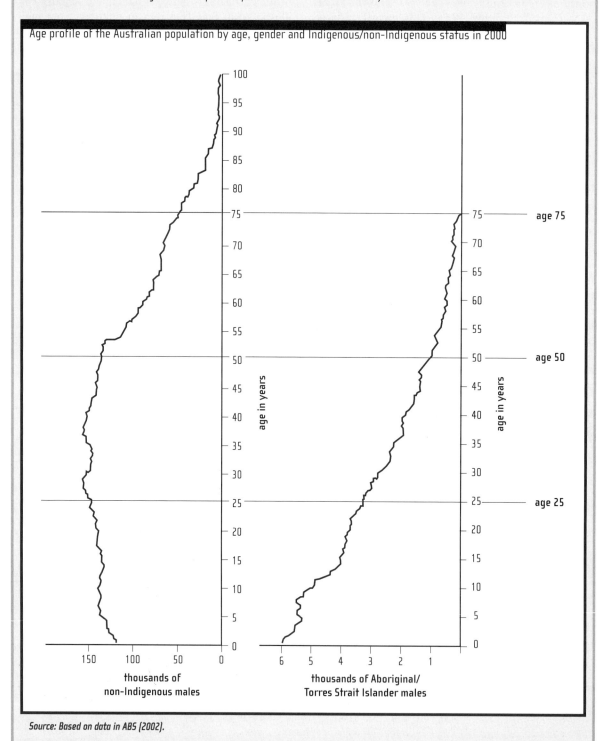

Source: Based on data in ABS (2002).

BOX **18.3**

Activity suggestion
How long will you live?

The following rules of thumb, which have been abstracted from demographic statistics, can help to serve as science's answer to the fortune teller, palm-reader or tea-leaf reader in prophesying longevity. Though no one knows for sure, you may find it interesting to compute your own odds for a long life. Beginning with the Biblical three score and ten (70 years), compute a more exact forecast by means of the following additions and subtractions:

1. *Family tree*
   - If two or more of your grandparents lived past 80, add two years.
   - If a parent, brother or sister has had cancer, a heart condition, stroke or diabetes, or died before 50, subtract four years.
2. *Health habits*
   - If you smoke cigarettes at all, subtract three years; then subtract three more years for each pack you smoke per day.
   - If you formerly smoked but have quit, you need only subtract two years if you have not touched a cigarette for 5 years or more.
   - For every five kilos you are overweight, subtract one year.
   - If you sleep more than nine hours a night, subtract three years.
3. *Personal factors*
   - If you are male, subtract two years; if you are female, add four.
   - If your work keeps you seated at a desk, subtract two years; if it supplies physical exercise, add two.
   - If you earn an income well above the national average, subtract two years.
   - If you're a university or college graduate, add two years.
   - If you are married or living with someone, add four years; if you live alone, subtract a year for each decade alone since age 25.
   - If you are happy and enjoy your life, add two years.

BOX **18.4**

Tapping the fountain of youth: Optimising longevity

The question of whether the progress of medical technology will eventually make it possible for most people to live to be 100 is subject to much scientific debate (Cutler, 1981). But recent longevity research has highlighted a number of health precautions which, even if they do not actually stretch the maximum limit of life, can reduce the odds of a person's dying prematurely far short of the limit they could have reached with care. Some of these strategies are listed below.

- *Balanced diet*. Nutritional status, achieved by consuming a balanced diet, affects fitness and health throughout the lifespan. But recent research indicates that adequate nutrition plays a special role in fostering the effective functioning of the immune system in old age. Thus a balanced diet may be especially crucial in prolonging life once the biological limits of longevity draw near.
- *Dietary restriction*. Exceptionally long lived groups such as the Hunzas of the Himalayas and the Georgian Abkhasians of the former Soviet Union consume fewer calories per day than the average Australian or New Zealander, suggesting that dietary restriction to (say) around 1900 calories (7953 kilojoules) might help to prolong life in our society.
- *Exercise*. Steady exercise which gets the heart pumping and keeps it working steadily for 20 minutes a day has also been advocated to improve fitness and reduce the risk of one of the major killers: heart disease. Studies of monkeys and hogs made to do daily exercise revealed better oxygenation of the blood and less clogging of arterial pathways, providing hints about the reduction of one important human ageing symptom: hardening of the arteries.
- *Avoiding sunlight*. Shielding the skin from extreme doses of sunlight partially protects against such visible signs of ageing as wrinkles, dryness and brown-pigmented 'age spots', proved by the difference in appearance between skin on an old person's buttocks and skin on the face and hands. Too much exposure to the sun has also been linked to potentially fatal skin cancers. You should wear a hat, protective clothing or sunscreen lotion if you spend time in the sun.
- *Cigarettes*. On average, a regular smoker's lung capacity is equal to that of a non-smoker who is 10 to 20 years older. Quitting the habit reduces the risk of heart disease and lung cancer.
- *Vitamins*. Vitamin E is sometimes promoted to slow the rate of ageing. However, though serious vitamin deficiencies can be problematic at any age, there is no firm evidence that extra intake of Vitamin E or any other vitamin supplements beyond the levels in a normal balanced diet will actually influence longevity.
- *Avoiding risks*. At all ages, safety precautions such as wearing seat belts and avoiding drink driving, hard drugs and unsafe sex can reduce the risk of a premature fatality.
- *Light drinking*. If you enjoy a glass of wine or beer,

exercise and freedom from avoidable risks like smoking, alcohol abuse or car accidents seem to be as important for ensuring longevity as they are for maintaining optimum levels of health and vigour during old age.

Box 18.4 (on page 625) suggests some specific strategies for preventing premature death and stretching the lifespan to its full potential.

Racial differences in longevity, as shown in Box 18.2, might reflect these lifestyle factors to a certain extent. But factors beyond the individual's power to control are also strongly implicated in the Aboriginal longevity problem. Good health care beginning in childhood and freedom from diseases that can cut life short are strongly implicated in the gains in human longevity that have occurred in most parts of the world in recent years. Unfortunately, Aboriginal Australians are clearly disadvantaged, relative to the rest of the population, when it comes to health care and protection from preventable chronic and infectious disease. For example, Dr Joan Cunningham (2002) found that barriers existed at the levels of (a) diagnosis, (b) access to medical tests and health services, (c) hospital admissions, and (d) access to surgical and medical procedures for Indigenous Australians compared with other members of the population. Thus the longevity differential may be just another manifestation of political injustice and profound social disadvantage. Table 18.3 shows some of the variations in causes of death that may have links with health and access to health care across the lifespan.

Development of knowledge, beliefs and feelings about death

Children's beliefs

Most modern children apparently know a lot more about death than most adults give them credit for. Robert Kastenbaum (1974) described an incident when a 16-month-old boy watched with alarm as an adult's foot descended unknowingly on a wriggling caterpillar. On inspecting the remains, the child exclaimed matter-of-factly: 'No more'. Kastenbaum concluded that 'glimmers' like these show that a basic awareness of death's finality and its distinctiveness from life is present at a very early age.

More systematic research has likewise led to the conclusion that children have a notion of death that partially matches the adult's from at least 18 months of age (Speece & Brent, 1984). But there are impor-

TABLE 18.3	Causes of death and comparative incidence rates in Australia in 2000
Cause	**Comparative incidence rate** (actual incidence for Indigenous Australians relative to expected rates based on remainder of the Australian population)
Fatal accidents and injuries (motor vehicles, homicide, suicide, etc.)	3.5 times more common than expected
Respiratory diseases	3 to 5 times more common than expected
Cancer (lung, cervical, liver, brain tumour, etc.)	Though incidence rates of cancer illnesses are similar in Indigenous and non-Indigenous Australians, deaths are much higher among Indigenous Australians owing to poorer health care and more advanced stage at diagnosis.
Diabetes	Deaths were 9 times more common than expected for Indigenous males in WA in 1997 and 16 times more common for females.
Renal disease	7 to 8 times more common than expected
Infectious diseases	Notifications and fatalities more common than expected

Source: Based on data in Jupp (2001).

tant differences between preschoolers' and adults' ideas. Between the ages of three and five years, the child's concept of death is influenced by preoperational *egocentrism* and magical or wishful thinking (Koocher, 1973). Thus, a child may believe that the dead are inactive but are still capable of hearing things or sensing what is happening around them. Or they may assimilate 'death' to the more familiar experience of sleep and assume that a dead person will eventually wake up again.

With her colleagues Raquel Jaakkola and Susan Carey, Virginia Slaughter (1999) studied Australian children's understanding of death. They gave the children interviews that included questions similar to those shown in Box 18.5 (on page 628).

Slaughter and her colleagues found that some children as young as four to six years could correctly answer a number of these questions, but only if they had a concept of 'life' as a core biological concept about human beings. Specifically, the young 'life-theorisers' in their Australian sample could accurately distinguish between living and non-living things (e.g. by agreeing that a mouse is alive but a bicycle is not) and avoid the pitfalls of Piagetian animistic reasoning (see Chapter 7). Eighteen of the 38 children aged four to six years in Slaughter and her colleagues' sample (47 per cent) were life-theorisers who reasoned biologically rather than animistically. Their ages were no different from the other half of the group who were still displaying animistic thinking about life concepts. Significantly more life-theorisers than animistic thinkers answered the death interview correctly, as shown in Figure 18.5.

Despite their budding awareness of some of the distinctive features of death, children's understanding remains limited through the preschool years. In fact, results of this Australian study combine with those of other studies conducted overseas to suggest that, until they reach the age of seven, eight or even older, many children do not fully appreciate three properties of death, all of which are essential to a mature definition of the concept (Slaughter et al., 1999; Speece & Brent, 1984). These properties are irreversibility, non-functionality and universality.

IRREVERSIBILITY

Irreversibility refers to the awareness that once death occurs the dead person, animal or plant cannot be brought to life again. Some ambiguities over unusual cases such as resurrection, 'near-death' experiences with subsequent resuscitation and the revival of apparently dead trees are apt to perplex adults as well as children. But the young child's belief in reversibility is more extensive than this. When asked 'Can dead things come back to life?', 6-year-olds are likely to assert that this is almost always possible. They are likely to mention familiar interventions such as giving a dead human an injection, or water to a dead plant, as effective methods of reversing death. This suggests that they view death as a temporary condition rather than a final, irreversible state.

NON-FUNCTIONALITY

Another criterion of death for an adult is the cessation of all life functions. In the case of humans, this includes physiological processes like breathing, brain activity and heartbeat as well as psychological or behavioural capacities for moving, speaking and

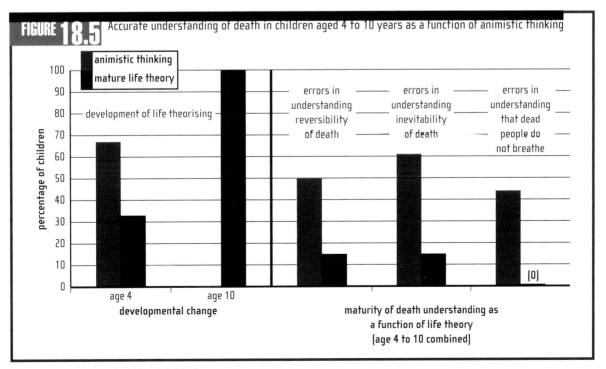

FIGURE 18.5 Accurate understanding of death in children aged 4 to 10 years as a function of animistic thinking

Source: Based on data in Slaughter et al. (1999).

Many children from as young as age 4 are aware that a tree is alive and a bicycle is not.

sensation. Younger children often consider it possible to maintain many of these life functions after death has occurred. Thus a large proportion of children under the age of seven believe that dead people can perform the cognitive activities of thinking, dreaming, hearing and feeling. At very young ages, they may also think that the dead eat, breathe and have a heartbeat (Kane, 1979).

UNIVERSALITY

A third feature common to all adults' understanding of death is its inevitability. While species differences and the factors listed in Boxes 18.3 and 18.4 may influence when death will occur, the mature thinker realises that every human, plant and animal will die eventually. But younger children are likely to believe that certain special categories of people do not die. For example, they may believe it possible to escape death by being clever, lucky or famous. They may realise that all animals are mortal before believing it true of all people, or accept the inevitability of strangers' eventual death before agreeing that they themselves, or their parents, will die sometime.

Developmental changes in children's death understanding

After reviewing more than 40 separate studies of children's thinking about death, Mark Speece and Sandor Brent (1984) concluded that healthy children gain an awareness of the irreversibility, non-functionality and universality of death between the ages of five and seven. (Less is known of the death consciousness of terminally ill children, but it is believed they may develop a unique understanding of death at a younger age than normal children by beginning to

think about death and having direct experience of the deaths of others in hospital.) By the age of eight, the vast majority of healthy children in all 40 of the research samples Speece and Brent surveyed clearly understood death as a process that is irreversible, non-functional and universal.

Gerald Koocher (1973) endeavoured to relate children's understanding of death both to age and to their levels of cognitive maturity on Piaget's tests of operational thinking (see Chapters 2 and 7). The participants in his research were 75 children aged six to 15 years. When asked about the causes of death, they almost all gave realistic suggestions, naming events which frequently do prove to be fatal (e.g. getting shot by a gun, car accidents). Only a few of the children, all of whom scored as 'preoperational' on Piaget's tests, seemed to have a 'magical' or improbable conception of death's causality (e.g. 'eating a dirty bug'). Similarly, the only ones who believed that death was reversible were preoperational children, who said that a corpse could be brought back to life if it was looked after properly.

Koocher also asked the children when they were going to die. He considered very young (e.g. age 13) or very old (e.g. age 100) expectations to be unrealistic. These unrealistic replies were given most often by the children in the sample who were at the lowest levels of Piagetian cognitive development. Age seemed to have no independent influence over and above cognitive maturity on any aspect of death awareness in this sample. Finally, when the children were asked 'What will happen when you die?', most confined their replies to descriptions of objective external events (funeral, burial) but a few (7 per cent) volunteered the belief that death was like sleeping. Some even made explicit mention of an afterlife (21 per cent).

Barbara Kane (1979) found that children's descriptions of death fell into three discrete groupings, which corresponded roughly to increasing age and bore similarities to general Piagetian cognitive stages. She also found that, while children's actual experiences with the deaths of close family members accelerated their understanding of the concept up to the age of six, direct encounters bore no relation to the maturity of their understanding after this age.

Young children's relative immunity from anxiety about death may result from their unique patterns of belief about it. Wayne Gartley and Marion Bernasconi (1967) found that very few children aged five to 12 years were frightened, possibly because they saw death as reversible, or as something far in the future for themselves. The researchers concluded that, despite the pervasive denial of death among adults in modern societies, and our corresponding cultural belief that children should be kept away from dying people, today's younger generations have made good use of the ample opportunities provided by television to learn about the causes and consequences of dying. Several of Gartley and Bernasconi's young subjects remarked spontaneously that they had gleaned much of their knowledge of death from medical dramas or from watching police gun battles, the television news or cowboys' last moments in television westerns.

Death understanding and death anxiety in adolescence and adulthood

While young children's confusion over the finality and universality of death can largely be attributed to simple ignorance or inexperience, most adults today are aware that these concepts are themselves some-

what relative and subject to advances in science and medical knowledge in the future. Yet the development of concepts of death and dying continues to evolve throughout adolescence and into adulthood, as Box 18.6 illustrates.

Whereas the average child of eight or nine has moved out of preoperational belief in death as an idiosyncratic temporary state, with some functional capacities, into a notion that death is absolutely irreversible, universal and devoid of all physiological function, a well-educated contemporary adult might disagree. In their conception of death, many adults entertain the possibility of some limited life functions (as when a respirator sustains breathing after the brain has 'died') and generally display more sophistication than an average eight-year-old. According to Sandor Brent and Mark Speece (1993), children in Piaget's concrete-operational stage possess 'pre-modern' concepts of death whereas most adults in Western culture have concepts that are distinctively 'modern'. According to the modern view, there is a vague and constantly changing boundary zone between unambiguous life and unambiguous death. This zone includes those instances noted earlier where patients are maintained on mechanical life support systems, as well as some instances of resuscitation, in which a person who has been pronounced clinically dead is restored to independent life through medical techniques. Thus, paradoxically, an adult may respond in a manner reminiscent of a preschooler to questions about the reversibility of death that a child of eight or nine years would consider unambiguously wrong. For example, Brent and Speece (1993, p. 207) asked adult university students the following questions:

1. 'Can a dead person become alive again?'
2. 'If I gave some medicine to a dead person, could he become alive again?'
3. 'If I said some magic words to a dead person, could he become alive again?'

When used as a test to distinguish magical from logical thinking about death by young children, the correct answer to questions is an unequivocal 'no'. But adults with a fluid, or modern, conception of death could argue persuasively for 'yes' answers, at least under special circumstances. This is exactly what Brent and Speece found. They decided to exclude all those adults who said 'yes' on religious grounds (e.g. 'Spiritually he can, physically he cannot once dead', p. 206) as these men and women might have been interpreting the questions as a test of faith rather than logical understanding. But even after the religious answers were eliminated, Brent and Speece discovered that beliefs in the reversibility of death were more pronounced among adults than among school-age children, as illustrated in Figure 18.6. Thanks to the miracles of modern medical science, most adults are aware that the state of death is not always absolutely irreversible, at least for a time.

Children may learn about death through watching television.

A case in point
Thoughts about death from toddlerhood to adolescence

When Louise was three her mother had a near brush with death. Her father described this event and Louise's reactions to it in his diary.

5 July 1951. ... Much has happened since my last entry. Peggy was seriously ill with a ruptured ectopic pregnancy that might have cost her her life if by chance I had not come home extra early that afternoon. She was suffering so much from shock that she had not been able to telephone. But they rushed her to the hospital and operated on her. While Peggy was away Louise stayed alone with me. We went out for dinner and managed on light breakfasts and lunches at home. After her nap Louise stayed with a neighbor while I visited Peggy in the hospital. Louise said once, 'Dot, I don't need Mom as long as I have you to take care of me.' Just the same she was pretty happy to see Mom come home. And I certainly was.

© Peterson, 1974, reproduced with permission.

Louise's spontaneous remark suggests she was aware that her mother's illness might lead to a permanent separation from her. Louise's 'utterly matter-of-fact' style of verbalisation about this possibility has also been found to characterise young children's replies to interview questions about death (Gartley & Bernasconi, 1967, p. 83). Some eight years later, Louise's father was again struck by her similarly matter-of-fact approach to the possible sequels to death. He made the following diary entry:

2 September 1959. This evening after a late supper, having attended a movie matinee in Santa Barbara, Louise expressed a fear of something happening to her (as happened to a child in the picture) like catching polio. I told her she need not fear. She had received her Salk injections. 'But something else,' she said, 'maybe not polio.' 'Oh you're just a worrier,' I replied. 'I know I am,' said Louise ruefully. 'Well,' I said, 'there's no sense worrying. You're dead a long time.' 'But don't you go to Heaven when you die?' 'I suppose so, but I don't know. Nobody knows. Nobody has ever died and come back to tell us.' 'Except Jesus.' 'Yes, but even Jesus didn't say anything about being dead. He told Thomas to feel his wounds and that was about all.' 'Well, just as long as you don't lie there being bored it's all right.' 'Oh, I'm sure of that at least. Either you go to sleep and are conscious of nothing or else you live very much as you are living now.' 'That's good,' Louise said and was satisfied. All these centuries men have debated these two alternatives as if their lives depended on it being one way or the other. Some have felt that annihilation was unspeakable, even unthinkable. Others have argued just as warmly that life of any kind beyond death is fantastic. But to an eleven-year-old child it makes no

real difference. Life would be all right but then so would extinction. And how right she is.

© Peterson, 1974, reproduced with permission.

Later still, when Louise was 17 and home on holiday from the university, her father wrote:

22 May 1965. Louise and I have been alternately reading Stanislaus Joyce's diary and discussing James Joyce, this decadent era, death, psychology, and Freud ... Louise, like so many young people today, knows for a certainty that death is the end of all consciousness. I argue how consoling such a conviction must be since to be altogether convinced of this is to remove all terror of death. Death then becomes merely the pleasure of going to sleep.

© Peterson, 1974, reproduced with permission.

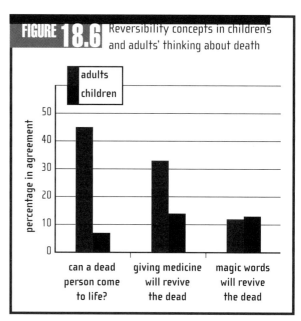

FIGURE 18.6 Reversibility concepts in children's and adults' thinking about death

Source: Based on data in Brent & Speece (1993).

Thus cognitive development in adolescence and adulthood (see Chapters 11 and 15) combines with the adult's access to new information about scientific discoveries to stimulate new *relativistic* and *dialectical* modes of thought. As Brent and Speece explained:

> These results appear to imply that the conventional naturalistic form of a concept – such as the concept of death – which the child achieves at about age 10, subsequently comes to serve as merely the stable nucleus, or core, of a connotational sphere that the child continues to enrich and elaborate throughout the remainder of life by the addition of all kinds of exceptions, conditions, questions, doubts, and so forth. (pp. 222–3)

Unlike young children, almost all adolescents are aware that death is inevitable and irreversible, and brings to a close all physiological and psychological life processes. However, the tendency to ponder about death does not end with the development of these realisations, as the example in Box 18.6 illustrates. Instead, concerns about the possibility of a transformed consciousness, or other outcomes or modes of existence after death, are liable to intensify during late adolescence with the acquisition of formal-operational reasoning skills. In fact, preoccupations with sophisticated philosophical or religious ideas about death and its consequences are apt to continue throughout the adult lifespan, as are concerns or anxieties about the process of dying itself. Research into the suicidal thoughts and behaviour of the small, though growing, fraction of adolescents who attempt to take their own lives is described in Chapter 12. But normal, non-suicidal adolescents also spend a good deal of their time thinking about their own death and the death of people they know or read about. Most of the systematic research into the death-related cognitions of adolescents and adults has focused on emotional feelings and reactions.

One of the first to embark on this line of study was Donald Templer (1970), who created the 15-item scale shown in Box 18.7 to assess individuals' preoccupation with death and the intensity of their fear of dying. Agreement with such statements as 'I often think how short life is', 'The sight of a dead body horrifies me', 'The subject of life after death troubles me greatly' and 'I am very much afraid to die' were taken to indicate high levels of *death anxiety*. Using this measure, Templer (1970, 1971) reached several unexpected conclusions about the type of person who is most afraid to die. He found, for example, that religious believers who attended church regularly each week were neither more nor less afraid to die than self-avowed atheists. Enthusiasts for the death-defying sport of parachute-jumping have likewise been found to earn similar scores on death anxiety measures to their peers who prefer more cautious recreational pursuits like gardening or lawn bowls (Alexander & Lester, 1972). Perhaps most worrying of all is the recent finding that students who complete courses on death and dying at university experience greater death anxiety at the end of the course than at the beginning (Knight & Elfenbein, 1993).

Gender also influences death anxiety, with women reporting more fear of death than men, especially on questionnaire measures like the one in Box 18.7. Sex differences are not so consistent in studies using such indirect measures as galvanic skin responses to slides of death scenes, or speed of reacting to death-related versus neutral words (Pollack, 1980), so they may in part reflect women's greater willingness to communicate their fears openly on survey instruments. But in interviews women also speak more about the negative consequences of their own death for others and the devastating consequences of others' deaths for themselves.

Death anxiety also tends to run in families. On the basis of comparisons within a group of 2500 North American adolescents and their parents, Donald Templer and his colleagues (Templer, Ruff & Franks, 1971) discovered a number of significant relationships between the intensity of parents' fears about death and death anxiety in their offspring. The strongest correlations arose within the same sex. In other words, fathers who were extremely anxious about death were likely to have sons who were also well above average in death anxiety, and anxious mothers tended to have anxious daughters. Impressive similarities between mothers and fathers in the same family were also observed. Thus, the stronger link between attitudes of mothers and daughters than fathers and daughters, and vice versa, seemed to have an environmental rather than a genetic basis (see Chapter 3).

The authors concluded that 'environmental events in general' and 'intimate interpersonal relationships in particular' have profound effects on the formation and development of an individual's attitudes towards death. Perhaps adolescents feel more confident in disclosing their feelings about a socially taboo topic like death to their same-sex parent. Parents may feel the same way when needing to talk about death to a son or daughter. Thus attitudes to death can be shaped by the individual processes that occur within the family – for example, discussing death with family members (see Box 18.6), the sharing of one's deepest emotional reactions with a spouse, parents or grown children, and each family's unique set of personal experiences with dying and bereavement. These forces appear to exert more of an effect than chronological age on the formation of death attitudes after early childhood.

According to Robert Kastenbaum (2000), death anxiety is not a unidimensional construct, but rather a collection of four distinct elements: (a) concern about physical degeneration, (b) concern about time left to live, (c) concern about pain, stress and fear accompanying the experience of death, and (d) spiritual and emotional feelings bound up with thoughts of death and what may come after. The overarching concern is with losses of developmental acquisitions that are most highly valued, including a sense of personal identity (see Chapter 11) and the pleasures of close relationships (see Chapters 5, 12 and 13).

Death anxiety in old age

It is popularly believed that elderly men and women fear death less than young or middle-aged adults, and possibly for good reason. An older person's successful completion of a process of life review (see Chapter 16) and attainment of Erikson's personality attribute of integrity (see Chapters 2 and 17) could well make the acceptance of dying easier. So could the satisfaction of having lived a long life. On the other hand, impairments of the elderly person's health or physical well-being (see Chapter 16) or social connectedness (see Chapter 17) could make life seem less worth living in old age than during young or middle adulthood.

But the notion that widows and widowers, or the retired or impoverished elderly, are less fearful of dying than other men and women has not received consistent empirical support. Instead, most studies of widows' attitudes to death have suggested that these women are no more or less frightened of dying than married women of the same age and social background (Kalish & Reynolds, 1974). However, owing to social desirability biases, a widow may be more inclined to deny her fear than a married woman when direct questions are asked (Swenson, 1961). Indeed, when widowhood brings loneliness and loss of social

While the loss of an intimate loved one may make the thought of one's own death easier to bear, there is no consistent evidence that the elderly fear death any less than younger adults.

support, the fear of death may intensify rather than diminish. Adults, both young and old, who feel socially isolated report brooding and feeling terrified of death. These lonely men and women score higher on Templer's death anxiety measure than their peers who are actively involved in a wide and supportive network of social roles and relationships.

One study of elderly people who were in good versus poor health did show that the ill were more complacent than the healthy at the thought of death (Swenson, 1961). But, since younger subjects were not included in this study, its results do not bear directly on the hypothesis of a decline in death anxiety during old age. The issue of achieving an emotional acceptance of death over the course of a lengthy terminal illness is considered later in this chapter.

Eena Job (1984) interviewed a group of 352 Queensland men and women who were all over the age of 80 at the time of the interview. An initial impression of a reduction in death anxiety with age came from the fact that 83 per cent of them denied ever worrying about death. But when Job probed their feelings in more detail she discovered a diversity of views, matching those of the Australian population at large (Warren & Chopra, 1979). She was able to group the attitudes of her elderly Brisbane sample into the five categories shown in Figure 18.7. The most common reaction was to accept death as natural and inevitable eventually. Some who were in poor health or lonely welcomed the thought of dying soon. Others wished to postpone it for as long as possible or simply preferred not to think about it.

Another possible reason for inconsistencies in conclusions about the nature or direction of any possible link between age and fear of death may be variations over the adult lifespan in the way the basic attitudes shape a fear of dying. During old age, the statistical averages illustrated in Figure 18.1 and Table 18.1 may boost death anxiety by suggesting

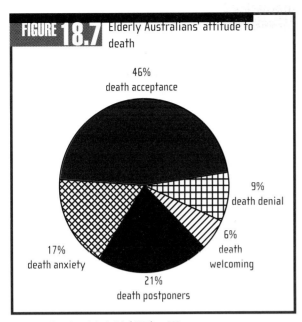

FIGURE 18.7 Elderly Australians' attitude to death

46%
death acceptance

9%
death denial

6%
death
welcoming

17%
death anxiety

21%
death postponers

Source: Based on data in Job (1984), p. 203.

that the event is going to happen soon. But the old person's wider range of recent and personal experiences of the deaths of friends and relatives may conversely help to minimise anxiety, relative to the fears of young adults who have not yet encountered the death of a parent, spouse or close friend.

Stress researcher Hans Selye (1979) explained how his own death anxiety was diminished by contact with a dying colleague, the bacteriologist Hans Zinsser, during the latter's final stages of terminal cancer. According to Selye:

> Zinsser felt that even his desperate condition could be used to an advantage, because only a man who knows he will soon die can speak with real detachment, without wishing to influence anyone or obtain any benefits for himself. Those of us who knew him were full of admiration for his wise adaptability to an apparently hopeless situation. His motivation helped him to keep the inevitable out of his mind and, at the same time, this great scientist earned the gratitude of innumerable people, up to the very moment of his death. I know that his writings helped me immensely during my own periods of pain and trouble. (p. 246)

As well as possibly boosting death anxiety for a time, realisation of the nearness of the end of the lifespan could conceivably aid the older person to allay fear eventually, and thus come to peaceful terms with death. This would be less likely in the case of young people, who do not see their own death looming on the horizon. But it is also quite possible that young or middle-aged adults in Australia and New Zealand today derive relatively little consolation from statistical longevity projections like those illustrated in Table 18.2. Instead of assuming that their own deaths will safely be postponed until they reach the far-off

ages of 70 or 80, young people today may fear death just as intensely as septuagenarians because of an identical belief that they will die sometime during the next decade of their lives. One of the big surprises of scientific research into people's concepts about dying, according to Robert Kastenbaum and Paul Costa (1977), is that young adults are found to be as apt as older people to have very short subjective future life expectancies: 'An appreciable number of adolescents and young adults expect to die within a few years' (p. 232). Perhaps the global nuclear threat, the news media's wide coverage of premature deaths by violence or fatal afflictions like AIDS are partly responsible for this effect.

Several recent studies of beliefs about the future among contemporary Australian and New Zealand adolescents and young adults have confirmed that their faith in surviving into old age is generally quite weak (Kissane, 1988). Fear of nuclear holocaust is one major reason for mistrusting the future (see Chapter 9). In one 1988 Australian opinion poll survey, two out of three teenagers were found to believe that a nuclear war or catastrophe was inevitable during their lifetime and to agree that 'the future is so uncertain that it's best to live from day to day' (Kissane, 1988, p. 8). Fear of dying through a nuclear accident, terrorist attack, war or other environmental or political disaster continues to be widespread among Australian and New Zealand teenagers today and a new fear has been added to their list of anxieties: fear of contracting AIDS (see Chapter 10). In this climate of opinion, the absence of age differences in fear of death could therefore be due to an equalisation of subjective personal life expectancy across all age groups, as a result of concern over contemporary risk factors in the global future of the world.

To test the possible link between death anxiety and concern about nuclear disaster more directly, Dianne Storey (1987) constructed a 48-item death anxiety measure, broken down into three subscales measuring concern about one's own death, the deaths of loved ones and the annihilation of the human race. This measure is illustrated in Table 18.4. Factor analysis confirmed the distinctiveness of these three separate dimensions of death-related worry. In other words, people who scored as most fearful when asked about their own death were not necessarily the ones most anxious about the death of loved ones or the dying out of the human race. Many of those who worried most about the extinction of the human species were less fearful than other adults about themselves or their intimates dying.

When she gave this test to a group of 200 male and female Western Australians aged 16 to 83, Storey did discover a relationship betwen death anxiety and fear of nuclear disaster. The adults in her sample who were most worried about the risk of nuclear war also experienced more anxiety than other men and women about the extinction of the human race.

TABLE 18.4	Three dimensions of Australian adults' death anxiety		
	Death of self	Death of loved ones	Death of the human species
Sample items	'I am disturbed by the physical degeneration involved in a slow death.' 'I would avoid death at all costs.' 'I am very disturbed by discussions about dying.'	'If someone close to me died, I would miss him/her very much.' 'Death is only disturbing if it happens to someone you care about.' 'If someone close to me was dying, I could not discuss it.'	'It disturbs me that everyone on earth could die at the same time.' 'I do not expect the human species to survive beyond my lifetime.' 'I often worry about the entire human species dying out.'
Highest scores relate to	Male gender Lack of religious belief Younger age	Female gender	Female gender Concerns over nuclear threat Political participation Viewing films about global disasters and nuclear pollution

Source: Based on data in Storey (1987), pp. 70–8.

Greater fear of species death was also observed among Australian men and women who (a) had viewed films like *Threads* and *The Day After*, depicting nuclear holocaust, and (b) had a more accurate and detailed knowledge about nuclear weapons and nuclear-related accidents.

Storey also found that Australian men tended to worry more than women about their own death and dying. But the gender difference was reversed for worry about the dying of loved ones or the human species. Women felt more anxious about both these outcomes than men.

Influence of close encounters with death

Anecdotal reports from adults who have come close to dying and then been resuscitated suggest that the survival of a 'close call' may diminish death anxiety. One reason may be that such an experience explodes the popular fear that death is painful. Edwin Schneidman (1971) found that for 15 per cent of a large sample of average American adults, fear of pain was the most distasteful aspect of their contemplation of death. But the people who had survived close calls had found their moments before resuscitation to involve pleasant floating sensations and to be easy and relaxing. Another reason for the lessened fear of death after a near-death experience may be a sense of reprieve and gratitude for being granted further 'borrowed' time to live.

The process of dying

Previous sections of this chapter explore how attitudes about death and the timing and causes of death fit within the framework of an age-ordered human lifespan. But death can also be seen as a developmental process in its own right.

The consideration of death as a discernible stage in the life cycle with its own special needs, concerns and developmental tasks has gained impetus in recent

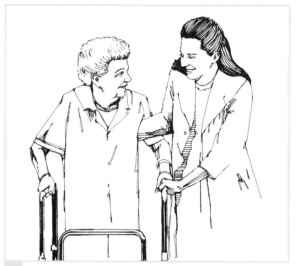

Personal courage, success in coping with previous life crises and an understanding attitude on the part of medical helpers can all encourage the patient's progress towards death acceptance.

years. Partly this has been the result of the increasing frequency of illnesses like cancer, which stretch the terminal phase of life across a lengthy span of time. But the theorising of Elizabeth Kübler-Ross (1975) has also had a major impact.

Kübler-Ross deplored contemporary Western culture's denial of death, which she saw epitomised in 'the drive-in funeral homes … where you drive up in your sports car, look through a glass window, sign a guest book, and take off' (1975, p. 370), and in modern cemeteries where graves are concealed immediately with artificial grass and flowers, 'in the pretence that nothing has happened'. In her view, a complete conscious awareness of death is necessary to the full psychological health of the dying and the bereaved alike.

Stages in adjustment to death

Her interviews with dying hospital patients led Kübler-Ross to conclude that awareness and acceptance of death develops through a series of five stages which she described as follows.

DENIAL

This is a stage of shock and disbelief that most people go through when they are first told that their illness or injury is terminal. It can endure from a few seconds to several months, depending on the duration of the illness. It may also lead to 'shopping around' for a doctor who will give a more hopeful prognosis. But Kübler-Ross found that less than 1 per cent of the dying patients she interviewed continued to believe they were going to get better right up to the moment of their death. So denial is not a stable state in which to adjust to dying. Also, the bereaved relatives (who tend to go through the same stages, though not necessarily in synchrony with the dying person) cannot easily maintain denial once the death has become a fact. The impulse towards denial is potent; however, Robert Kastenbaum (1998) explained that social taboos against discussing difficult topics like sexuality (see Chapter 10) and death can persist so strongly that, unless a dying patient makes clear his or her desire to do so, relatives and medical staff may try to sustain the pretence of death denial.

ANGER

After denial, according to Kübler-Ross, comes a period of generalised anger in which the dying person (or the bereaved relative) complains, criticises and rages against everyone they encounter. She suggested that this was a particularly difficult time for loved ones and medical personnel, as these groups were the most frequent targets of the angry patient's abuse. However, she argued that the expression of rage should not be quelled, lest its repression impede progress to the next stage. The root source of the anger is an inescapable sense of being singled out unfairly. The dying person asks 'Why me?' and the grieving person, 'Why my loved one?' If death had to strike, why couldn't it have been against someone older, or someone without relatives to miss them, or someone with less potential to contribute to life, and less wish to live?

BARGAINING

Once a tentative compromise with anger has been achieved, pleading or bargaining for more time sets in. The individual recognises that to beg for a cure is unrealistic, but is willing to promise almost anything for a temporary extension of life. Sometimes the pleas are addressed to a religious authority, sometimes to a doctor, or sometimes merely internalised. The promises are not usually kept if a miracle does happen and the threat of imminent death is lifted. One of the inevitable outcomes of bargaining, however, is a greater economy of time and a decision to make the fullest use of whatever time remains (see Box 18.8). The bargaining stage is also a time for completing 'unfinished business' and for making arrangements for others to carry on the most important of one's life concerns.

DEPRESSION

Kübler-Ross proposed that once all of the dying patient's practical affairs have been sorted out, bargaining is given up. But there is still one issue to be dealt with: profound sadness. With nothing else to think of except dying, the patient or bereaved person ordinarily enters a period of profound depression. According to Kübler-Ross, this depression takes two forms. The first is a *reactive depression*, or mourning for the losses already suffered. The dying person may complain of no longer being able to travel or to go outside to the park or the beach.

Simone de Beauvoir's (1969) description of riding in a taxi away from her mother's death-bed, and sensing the futility of all the life in the hub of Paris in which her mother would no longer take part, is a poignant illustration of how this kind of depression can affect a survivor. She wrote:

> How desolate I was, that Wednesday evening, in the cab that was taking me away! I knew this journey through the fashionable quarters by heart: Lancome, Houbigant, Hermes, Lanvin. Often a red light stopped me; in front of Cardin's I saw ridiculously elegant hats, waistcoats, scarves, slippers, shoes. Farther on there were beautiful downy dressing-gowns, softly coloured: I thought, 'I will buy her one to take the place of the red peignoir.' Scents, furs, lingerie, jewels: the sumptuous arrogance of a world in which death had no place: but it was there, lurking behind this facade, in the grey secrecy of nursing homes, hospitals, sick-rooms. And for me that was now the only truth. (p. 69)

Since almost everyone has at least some experience with limitations and losses of this kind, most people can understand and sympathise with reactive depression in a dying patient. But the next stage, *proactive depression* (or 'preparatory grief'), is much harder to conceptualise because it encompasses mourning for the future loss of everyone and everything the dying patient has loved. Kübler-Ross described this as 'a thousand times more sad' than the nearest equivalent which most healthy people have experienced – namely, the death of one beloved individual.

ACCEPTANCE

Gradually, out of this immense grief, Kübler-Ross saw that a stage of final acceptance began to take form in most of her patients. During this last stage, most people endeavour to separate (or 'decathect') from others. First, they may ask to see their more distant friends for the last time, and then may gradually say farewell to all but (usually) one close confidant with whom they are content to sit without speaking. The silent physical presence of another

A memorial to the life of someone who has died may assist bereaved survivors to accept that person's death and, eventually, to reinvest themselves in living.

person does not disguise the solitary isolation of the dying individual, however, and the fact that one really does die alone is usually not faced until the acceptance stage. During her mother's funeral, Simone de Beauvoir (1969) reflected that:

> We were taking part in the dress rehearsal for our own burial. The misfortune is that although everyone must come to this, each experiences the adventure in solitude. We never left Maman during those last days which she confused with convalescence and yet we were profoundly separated from her. (p. 87)

When acceptance is finally achieved, it is characterised by a kind of serenity which distinguishes it from resignation. Resignation is more like giving up or an exhausted and unhappy defeat, whereas, while acceptance is not a joyful state, it is without bitterness.

A critique of Kübler-Ross's theory

Kübler-Ross's theory has been criticised by those who argue that evidence derived solely from a theorist's own intuition-based counselling procedures requires independent and objective validation. Also, the question of whether the stages apply to everyone and occur in the same order must remain open until the theory has been subjected to the rigorous tests for sequentiality and universality which have been developed for stage theories in other domains of psychological development (Kohlberg, 1969).

A more subtle criticism concerns what some feel is an implicit prescription in Kübler-Ross's theory that the stage system outlines the ideal, 'right' way to die. Individuals who fail to traverse all five stages are sometimes made to feel guilty, as though they have not fully mastered the major developmental task of the terminal phase of psychological functioning. Kübler-Ross (1975) herself adamantly denied the view that acceptance is an intrinsically better state in which to meet death than (say) rage or denial.

In other words, the stage theory of dying is seen by its author to describe a possible developmental progression which may be appropriate to some individuals but not at all appropriate to others. Robert Kastenbaum (1975, 1998) analysed some of the variables that may influence the possibility of a dying person's progression through the various attitudinal and adjustment changes described in Kübler-Ross's theory. The following factors were included. They may also help to explain individual differences in adjustment to dying.

CAUSE OF DEATH

Some terminal illnesses are never diagnosed as such and give no warning to the victim, while others offer virtually undeniable evidence to everyone that death is imminent. Likewise, some accidental deaths are sudden and involve loss of consciousness, while others are more gradual. In the former cases, the dying person may be able to go through the stages only in an abstract or vicarious way, while, in the latter, inescapable knowledge in itself may force some kind of psychological accommodation.

SEX DIFFERENCES

Kastenbaum's own research suggested that men suffered more than women from the pain, dependency and loss of occupational role that accompany a terminal illness, whereas women were more worried than men by the impact their illness and death would have on the feelings of others. This being the case, the rate and style of coping with each hurdle in the Kübler-Ross stage system may differ between the sexes. A man, for example, might be unable to move past anger and outrage if his illness turned out to be an extremely painful one, while a woman might be pushed towards acceptance by the sense that achieving the final stage would comfort her survivors.

CULTURAL, ETHNIC AND SOCIOECONOMIC FACTORS

Cultural, racial and socioeconomic differences may determine the surroundings in which death is encountered, and thus the experiences that the dying individual must integrate psychologically. In this context,

Ethnic variations in beliefs, kinship structures and funeral rites can all have a bearing on how death is experienced.

Late in the winter of 1995, Franciszek Gajowniczek died peacefully at the age of 94, more than half a century after his initial brush with death. As a Polish army sergeant during World War II, he was captured by the Nazis and imprisoned in the concentration camp at Auschwitz in 1939. When a fellow inmate escaped, Gajowniczek was condemned to die slowly of starvation in the 'hunger bunker' at Auschwitz along with nine other inmates also implicated in the escape. He pleaded for mercy, unable to accept the thought of abandoning the wife and children he had left behind in Poland. In answer to his pleas, the Franciscan monk, Reverend Maksymilian Kolbe volunteered to die in Gajowniczek's place. Celibate himself, Kolbe argued that Gajowniczek should be allowed to survive for the sake of his wife and children. The concentration camp authorities accepted the exchange and Kolbe was sent to the 'hunger bunker' to die of slow starvation. He survived in the dungeon for 10 days, spending his time leading the other condemned prisoners in prayer. In the end, the Nazis killed Kolbe and three others by injection.

Upon his release from the concentration camp at the end of the war, Gajowniczek devoted much of the remainder of his life to speaking of Kolbe's heroism and helping to dedicate churches to this courageous cleric's name. As his widow explained, Gajowniczek's own acceptance of dying in old age was made easier by the memory of Kolbe's bravery and willingness to use his own final hours to assist his dying fellow prisoners. (*Time*, 27 March 1995, p. 21)

Simone de Beauvoir (1969) described her mother's death as 'a very easy death: an upper-class death' because it had occurred in a private hospital room surrounded by her close family members. She contrasted this with death in the public wards at the same hospital, where:

> when the last hour is coming near, they put a screen round the dying man's bed: he has seen this screen round other beds that were empty the next day: he knows. (p. 83)

Ethnic and cultural differences in beliefs about the meaning of life and death, and traditional funeral rituals and styles of expressing emotion may also have an important bearing on how death is experienced (see Boxes 18.8 and 18.9).

HISTORICAL EVENTS

During times of peace and prosperity, a society may become complacent and death may seem an issue only for the very old or very ill. But in times of war, social upheaval, catastrophe or natural disaster, even the young and able-bodied may be called upon to come to terms with the possibility of dying. In such situations, acts of heroism and humane generosity may emerge, as illustrated in Box 18.8.

PERSONALITY AND COGNITIVE STYLE

Kastenbaum argued that because 'we approach our death to some extent as the type of person we have always been—reflective or impulsive, warm or aloof, whatever', it follows that: 'A view of the dying process that excludes personality ... must also exclude much of reality' (1975, p. 43). So whether a person will be most comfortable by dying in a state of denial or rage or acceptance depends on the mode in which that person has lived and the strategies developed earlier in life for coping with crisis situations. Individual differences in death attitudes and anxiety may also play a part (see Box 18.7), as will the duration of the terminal phase itself. Though

death is called 'the great equaliser', each individual's way of dying must remain as unique as his or her mode of living throughout the life that preceded it.

DEVELOPMENTAL LEVEL AND CURRENT GOALS

We noted that children's levels of cognitive maturity influence their beliefs about death, and these beliefs may in their turn influence the experience of dying. However, the timing of death in relation to an individual's ongoing life activities may also be crucial, according to Kastenbaum. He described an 82-year-old woman who had been complacently ready to die when she first entered the hospital. But life in the ward offered her so many opportunities for friendship, social activity and the utilisation of her organisational skills that she rejected death as a regrettable and unwelcome interruption when it eventually did occur. The moment of her greatest psychological acceptance of death failed to coincide with the physical event. On the other hand, psychologist Abraham Maslow reported being able to accept his own death more readily because it followed the completion of an important piece of work:

I think actors and dramatists have that sense of the right moment for a good ending, with a phenomenological sense of good completion and that there was nothing more you could add. (1970, p. 16)

Some adults set deliberate goals for their lives which, when accomplished, make the acceptance of death easier. In such cases, the process of bargaining with death for more time (see page 635) may be seen to begin many years before the terminal phase of the life cycle.

SOCIAL AND PHYSICAL SURROUNDINGS

Some people die alone. Others are in the company of fellow victims at death, or with relatives and friends, or watched over by unknown spectators or by trained medical personnel. The differences in social supports and social demands implied by these varied situations may also modify the experiences and attitudes of terminal patients. Dying in a hospital is different from dying at home or at work. The degree of pain and the availability of pain-reducing medication may be further differentiating factors.

In summary, Kastenbaum argued that 'the dying person is also a living person' and that the issue of how he or she will adjust psychologically to the process of dying is as much a function of his or her prior psychological development through the lifespan and of 'general laws of personality and behaviour' as of the unique requirements imposed by death *per se*. He concluded, in view of these considerations, that it was premature to 'declare that people die according to certain stages' (p. 48).

Choice and personal control

Kübler-Ross's writings have also helped to alert the modern-day public to the dying patient's right of free choice. She noted that 'when a patient is severely ill, he is often treated like a person with no right to an opinion' (1975, p. 7). Particularly today, when so many medical and technological devices are available for prolonging life and for treating lingering illnesses amid the comforts and companionship of home, it is necessary that dying individuals be offered options concerning where and how to die.

During the past few years, self-help groups, legal and political lobbies and information-giving agencies have formed themselves around the issues of 'death with dignity', the 'right to die' and the 'living will' or medical advance directive. These groups argue that, since dying is a psychological as well as a physical process, and since the individual is the one who is in the best position to know what his or her own psychological needs are, the dying patient's wishes must be consulted.

Rights of the dying and living wills

The issue of whether and to what extent individuals should have the right to self-determination and free choice during the dying process has many facets. Some of the most important include:

- The right to choose to know (or not to know) the exact nature of the terminal condition which has been diagnosed
- The right to refuse medical treatment or 'heroic artificial means' which might prolong life in a manner unacceptable to the dying individual
- The related right to choose to die at home or in the company of chosen friends, children and relatives rather than in a hospital intensive-care unit, where visitors and routines are regulated by hospital personnel
- The right to opt for euthanasia (or mercy-killing).

The advance directive, or *living will*, is typically constructed as a legal document that includes information on the kinds of medical treatments the individual wishes to receive, and those that he or she wishes to do without. Signed and dated before two witnesses, it becomes a legally binding document in many jurisdictions. Another approach is a legal document known as *enduring* (or 'durable') *power of attorney*. This specifies a particular person as the legally authorised decision-maker who has the power to determine the kinds of resuscitation measures, medical interventions and other procedures that should be attempted if the dying patient is too ill or incapacitated to decide these things independently. Often a spouse or adult child will serve as the power of attorney, though some adults prefer to appoint a doctor or lawyer whom they have briefed thoroughly about their wishes before becoming ill.

Robert Kastenbaum (1979) discovered in his clinical work with the dying that it is quite common for beliefs among relatives about the patient's wishes concerning life-sustaining measures to be at sharp variance with one another. The living will makes these wishes clear and lightens the burden of responsibility.

But the danger is that overreliance on a legally prepared written document or prescribed decision surrogate (the power of attorney) could diminish efforts to communicate with the dying person at the time. The anthropologist Margaret Mead, who pioneered the construction of a living will during the mid-20th century, was careful to note that her notarised document was to apply *only* if she was unconscious or otherwise unable to express her wishes intelligibly. Western culture's general tendency to deny death and to isolate the dying from healthy members of the community already facilitates such communication breakdowns during the terminal phase (see page 635). Special efforts may therefore be needed to ensure that dying patients are offered as much choice and mutual human interchange as they desire, including the right to modify a living will in the light of current circumstances.

The hospice

According to Harry Shanis (1985), the dying person's chance to make effective use of the final period in life depends on three things. First, they must be free from pain and be as alert and intellectually competent as the progress of the terminal condition will permit. Second, the opportunity for privacy should be available when needed, along with the freedom to seek social contact with family members, medical staff or fellow terminal patients. Third, both the patient and the family should have as much help as necessary to maintain physical health care, alleviate stress and ease the dying person's and the survivors' progression through the phases leading up to their final separation. These three focal needs of terminal patients form the basis for the *hospice* movement which has grown up as an alternative to traditional hospital care in many parts of the world today. According to Lawrence Maloney (1985):

> 'Taking control' is an idea heard often in reference to the process of dying and the events after someone dies ... One step in regaining that control is the growing hospice movement, which attempts to put dying patients in a more humane, relaxed environment. Whether the care takes place in a special hospital wing or in a patient's home, the concept is the same: A team of health practitioners, clergy and volunteers deals with the patient's physical, psychological and spiritual needs – and counsels the family as well. Pain-reducing drugs keep the dying person as comfortable as possible, but expensive life-sustaining machinery is avoided. (p. 172)

In order to facilitate dying with dignity, members of the hospice health team may visit a dying patient at home so that death can occur in familiar surroundings.

The first hospice for cancer patients was created by Dr Cicely Saunders and her colleagues at St Christopher's in London in 1967 (Kastenbaum, 1985). Since then, the concept has spread to many countries throughout the world, including Australia and New Zealand. The benefits of the hospice system include maintaining the dignity of the dying person and providing assistance for the survivors in coping with terminal care and eventual bereavement. Most hospices offer counselling services and grief therapy as well as opportunities for patients to move freely from their own homes into the hospice and back again. When the patient's presence at home becomes too much of a burden for the family, a short stay at the hospice allows the support network at home to regroup. A visiting team, staffed by volunteers as well as paid hospice nurses, may also be provided in the patient's own home when needed. Thus the patient, family and medical staff have firmer ideas about what is happening and a better chance to support and assist one another in a collaborative atmosphere. Shanis described a typical follow-up by one hospice team to help the bereaved survivors adjust to the loss of a family member:

> Memories of the patient were shared among the hospice team, family, and friends. The trained and experienced hospice team helped the loved ones understand what they had experienced during the terminal illness and after the death. The team empathized with the loved ones, having known the patient themselves. In a number of cases the family and friends of the patient established friendships with the members of the hospice team. After the patient died family and friends were encouraged to continue these contacts with members of the hospice team. Consequently, the patient's death did not cause an abrupt halt to these meaningful relationships. (p. 379)

Research contrasting the attitudes and feelings of dying patients in a hospice versus the traditional hospital setting has generally supported the belief that a hospice environment is superior (Shanis, 1985). In one typical study, Susan Silver (1981) measured the emotional well-being of a group of elderly hospice patients each week. She found that the longer the treatment continued, the greater the improvement in patients' feelings of relaxation, acceptance of death and overall morale. Compared with traditional hospital inpatients, hospice clients are also found to suffer less anger, depression, anxiety and hostility towards a spouse (Shanis, 1985).

Cultural variations in dying and the acceptance of death

Culture also shapes the choices made by a dying person about how to spend the final period of life and also the observances that their survivors will practise following the death. Among the traditional

Australian Aborigines, the period of terminal illness preceding an old person's anticipated death was often an important social event for the whole community, as the example in Box 16.9 illustrates. Some traditional Aboriginal health care practices that contrast sharply with the situation of an ailing Anglo-Australian patient in hospital were described by Annette Hamilton on the basis of two years of living in a remote Aboriginal community in the early 1970s. Hamilton (1974) wrote:

> When an Aborigine is ill, he advertises this by the way in which he sits or lies in a public place – outside his shelter, in full public view. When it becomes known that he is ill, the local practitioners come to attend him. All the group gather around to offer sympathy and aid. Others fetch firewood or boil tea for the sick person, while the therapist spends endless time in massaging, rubbing, and manipulating the body. All ministrations are carried out in public, there is much speculation about the source of the illness and the likelihood of cure, and all members of the community show their care and concern, in some cases by public wailing in sympathy for the suffering of the afflicted. If a person has fallen out of harmony with the community, a period of illness, with all the concern and attention that goes with it, serves to override the tensions and re-unite the group. Physical therapy is at the same time psychological therapy and emotional therapy, and it is a group concern, not an individual one. There are no time restrictions placed on the therapy. The practitioner takes as long as he likes, and when he is tired another is likely to take over. No one expects the night to be free of disturbance. If a child cries unreasonably at night the local practitioner feels just as obliged to come and attend to it as he does in the daytime. (p. 21)

The death of a member of a traditional Aboriginal group was likewise viewed as a loss shared by the entire community, rather than a private and personal affliction applying only to members of the deceased's immediate family. According to Des Storer (1985), traditional Aboriginal funeral practices were central to the religious, social and political life of the community as a whole. The inquest formed an essential part of the tribal reaction to one of its member's death. Traditionally, the Aborigines rarely ascribed a death to 'natural causes' except in the case of a very young infant or a very old or decrepit person. Thus the rituals connected with the inquest were designed to establish the cause of death, to discover the perpetrator and to restore the community's shaken faith in life's meaning and their collective chances of survival that untimely death inevitably brings about. Once a culprit was discovered, either by police work or by reading mystical signs or dreaming, the elders decided on a form of vengeance, recompense or retribution to fit the circumstances. Avenged in this way, the soul of the dead person was thought to achieve tranquillity.

During the protracted inquest and lengthy judicial consultation over retributive measures, the remains of the dead person were often placed in a temporary grave site. Ritual moaning and wailing and other public exhibitions of mourning went on during this time to placate the troubled spirit of the deceased. The spirit was thought to be released from the dead person's body at the moment of death, remaining in a limbo state near the body until the cause of death was discovered and all the legal proceedings connected with it were concluded. Other funeral rituals varied somewhat from group to group but might include ceremonial fumigation or burning of the deceased's possessions, mummification of the corpse, temporary burial of the body in a hollow tree or its exposure on a decorated platform, followed by eventual cremation or permanent interment of the decomposed corpse.

Once all these funeral rites were completed, there were still some long-term observances connected with a death. A taboo against ever again speaking the dead person's name was observed in most traditional Aboriginal groups, and severe penalties could be levelled against a forgetful offender who broke the rule. Sometimes, members of the tribe whose own names sounded similar to the deceased's would go so far as to take a new name for themselves to prevent inadvertent infringement of the taboo. However, though reference to them by name was prohibited, deceased people themselves were not forgotten. Tributes would be paid to a respected Aboriginal dead person's memory for many years. The example in Box 16.9 illustrates how respect was accorded in traditional Aboriginal communities.

However, while cultural traditions shape the funeral procedures and socially accepted ways of expressing grief, the emotions felt by dying people and their bereaved survivors are likely to be similar throughout the world. Box 18.9 is an example from the South Pacific island of Vanuatu. Here, as in urban Auckland or Sydney, or in the Chicago cancer wards studied by Kübler-Ross, the acceptance of death was made easier by the social support of relatives and completion of 'unfinished business'.

In achieving an acceptance of death, terminally ill individuals may take comfort, or suffer stress, in looking forward to the observances that will be practised by their survivors to mark the death. Here again, culture plays an important role. Funeral practices vary widely from one ethnic group to another within Australia and New Zealand, as well as from nation to nation, over eras in history.

In some cultures, the rapid progress of social change has had a dramatic impact on attitudes to burial, funeral rites and bereavement. For example, in traditional Japan of two generations ago, the accepted practice was to bury a wife in her husband's burial plot, and single women in their father's. But recent trends towards divorce and remarriage have created complications for this tradition. Often the

BOX 18.9 Lessons from culture
Wishes fulfilled

A student from the island of Vanuatu (Stewart, 1982) described the life plan of an old woman who had narrowly escaped death during her childhood.

One day my grandmother told me that if she had been killed a long time ago in that tribal war, I wouldn't have been here today. Then she went on to say that what she had expected of her children had been fulfilled. 'What I am hoping now is to see one of you become a priest like your father, and the next thing is to see one or two of my great-grandchildren before I die.' (p. 255)

Some 15 years later both these wishes had been granted. The old lady's eldest grandson married, had two children and was ordained a priest. Ailing and nearly blind, she had one final request. Her grandchild wrote:

We knew now that she was ready to die, but there was something else she wanted to do before she died. One day she sent for my brother. When he went into the house she asked to celebrate Holy Communion beside her bed. My brother's children were kneeling beside her bed during the service. She could not see them very well because of her poor eyesight, but she called them to come closer to her so that she could touch them.

After the Holy Communion Service, she told my brother to tell everybody that all she wished had come to pass. A few days later she died peacefully. (p. 256)

Though ways of managing it may differ from family to family and culture to culture, the experience of grief over the death of an intimate loved one is universal.

eldest son of a first wife, who inherits the family grave, will not allow his stepmother to be buried there. The rise of the women's movement in recent decades in Japan has also motivated many women to want their own funeral and burial rites, rather than being considered an appendage of their husband. Thus, in recent years societies have formed in Japan to raise money to build 'women-only' tombs, allowing remarried and never-married women the option of an independence in their final decision in life (Sodei, 1993).

Bereavement

Death terminates a person's own life cycle, but remains a factor that must be integrated into the ongoing life cycles of the other people who are affected by it. Grieving for the dead person, fulfilling the claims of the will or dealing with unfinished business, and achieving a better understanding both of the dead individual's unique life and of the survivors' own mortality are all important components of this process. We have noted Kübler-Ross's suggestion that bereaved people progress through the same sequence

of stages as their dying loved ones. She stressed the importance of individual differences in ways of achieving acceptance, and declared it impossible to state categorically that any one stage or approach is better, or a psychologically more mature or healthy reaction to bereavement, than any other. The nature of the relationship that the dead and bereaved individuals had with one another during their lives together will influence what style of symbolic relationship the survivor feels most comfortable with after death, as will other personal, religious and environmental dimensions of the survivor's life.

Preparation is another factor in an individual's coping with bereavement. Some married couples 'rehearse' for each other's death and funeral by attempting to equip the other with whatever survival skills (like cooking or managing finances) they may have taken charge of as a result of the marriage's style of role allocation (see Chapter 13). But the emotional loss caused by a spouse's death cannot usually be sorted out so easily. John Riley (1970) found that the overwhelming majority of a representative sample of 1500 American adults believed that death was more of a tragedy for the survivors than for the victim, and the proportion who thought this increased steadily with age.

A similar survey of 171 elderly retirees in Florida revealed that concern over the effect of one's death on loved ones ranked with fear of pain during the process of dying as the two major reasons why the thought of death was distressing (see Figure 18.8).

The management of grief

For some, the ideal way of handling grief after bereavement is to erase all memory of the dead person so that a full and independent life can be resumed. Others prefer to collect photographs, letters and clothing or even to keep the dead person's room arranged exactly as it was during their lifetime. By

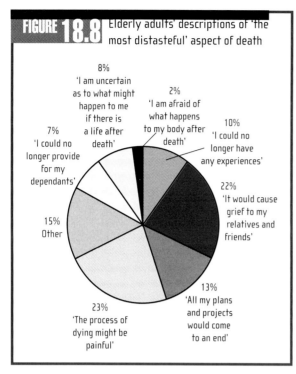

FIGURE 18.8 Elderly adults' descriptions of 'the most distasteful' aspect of death

- 8% 'I am uncertain as to what might happen to me if there is a life after death'
- 2% 'I am afraid of what happens to my body after death'
- 10% 'I could no longer have any experiences'
- 7% 'I could no longer provide for my dependants'
- 22% 'It would cause grief to my relatives and friends'
- 15% Other
- 13% 'All my plans and projects would come to an end'
- 23% 'The process of dying might be painful'

Source: Based on data in Wass et al. (1979), p. 342.

creating memorials like these, the aim is to permanently integrate the dead person's influence into the survivors' lives. Still others see the only valid outcome of bereavement to be the perpetuation of anger. This may involve a refusal either to accept death's unjustifiable outrage or to forgive the dead person for abandoning the living. But whichever resolution or non-resolution is reached, the crisis of death imposes a major demand for emotional reorganisation on the bereaved person. From the moment of the first shock of being told that a loved one is dead until the time at which the survivors become aware that some more or less stable resolution of the struggle to integrate that death into their pattern of life has been reached, the inner changes are probably greater than those required by any of the other developmental tasks of adulthood, such as marriage, changing jobs, parenthood, moving to a new city or retirement. Also, since bereavement is as universal as death itself, this developmental task is one which no adult escapes from. In some cases it turns out to be 'a meaningful growth-inducing aspect of life' (Kübler-Ross, 1975, p. 145).

An interview study with a group of widows and widowers in Cambridge, Massachusetts, reinforced the view that major and beneficial developmental changes often follow in the wake of overcoming the grief of bereavement (Glick, Weiss & Parkes, 1974). Most of these mourners suffered severely during the weeks immediately following their partners' death. But, after several months, 61 per cent were able to agree that 'I'm beginning to feel more like myself again', and by the end of a year many were astounded at the progress they had made. Almost all

the widows had developed new skills they had never considered themselves capable of while their husbands were alive, including car repairs, carpentry, bookkeeping and driving a car. Boosts to their inner strength and overt self-confidence testified even more eloquently to the developmental opportunity which mastery over bereavement can provide. The simple knowledge of having pulled through showed many of these widows that they were stronger and more capable people than they would ever have believed before the bereavement experience. An individual's account of her bereavement in Box 18.10 vividly captures some of its universal and unique aspects.

Widows and widowers

Over the long term, members of most older married couples will encounter the painful event of the spouse's death. This is perhaps the most stressful experience the average man or woman is ever called on to face (Rahe, 1979). The immediate emotional calamity of bereavement gives way eventually to the difficult task of rebuilding a single life after many years of marriage. For these reasons, widows and widowers are found to encounter more physical and psychological ill health during the first months and years after their spouse's death than do married people of the same age (Stroebe & Stroebe, 1983). Their own risk of death is also elevated during this time. Suicide accounts for part of the inflation of mortality rates among the recently bereaved. But physiological or biochemical stress reactions may possibly also undermine the grieving survivor's bodily

BOX 18.10 **A case in point**
Staying involved after death

Playwright Lillian Hellman wrote about her reactions to the loss of her lifelong friend, adviser and partner, the writer Dashiell Hammett, as follows:

I know as little about the nature of romantic love as I knew when I was eighteen, but I do know about the deep pleasure of continuing interest, the excitement of wanting to know what somebody else thinks, will do, will not do, the tricks played and unplayed, the short cord that the years make into rope and, in my case, is there, hanging loose, long after death. I am not sure what Hammett would feel about the rest of these notes about him, but I am sure that he would be pleased that I am angry with him today ... But I do not wish to end this book on an elegiac note. It is true that I miss Hammett, and that is as it should be. He was the most interesting man I've ever met. I laugh at what he did say, amuse myself with what he might say, and even this many years later speak to him, often angry that he still interferes with me, still dictates the rules. (1973, pp. 223–4)

immune system, according to Judith Rodin (1984), leading to a greater risk of death from infectious or chronic illnesses. Finally, there are many more practical and mundane reasons why a married person's lifestyle is liable to be healthier than a widow's or widower's.

The married adult has an intimate companion at home to chat to and confide in (Fiske, 1979), as well as a partner to provide nursing care when ill and to help out with the daily jobs of cooking, cleaning, shopping and paying bills. Familiarity is another advantage for elderly married couples. Support from extended kin and friendship networks are also more readily available to elderly married couples than to their widowed contemporaries (Kastenbaum, 1985). With the exception of adult children, who visit and support widowed and married parents equally, networks of extended kin and couple friendships are more often closed off to widowed than married members.

Statistically, the married woman's odds of becoming and remaining a widow are much higher than the married man's odds of either becoming a widower in the first place or remaining in the unmarried state. The average sex difference in life expectancy (see Figure 18.1 and Table 18.1) helps to explain this phenomenon, since more women than men can count on living to advanced ages. Most Australian and New Zealand wives are married to men who are older than they are. Widows are also much less likely to remarry after becoming widowed than men are. Thus, survival of the death of a spouse as a long-term life adjustment is an overwhelmingly female experience.

The immediate stresses of bereavement are traumatic for widows and widowers alike. But among women who are still vigorous and healthy when widowhood occurs, a long-term adjustment to the widowed lifestyle may eventually open up rich opportunities for personal growth and self-development.

Development as a widow

Robert Woodfield and Linda Viney (1984–85) studied Australian widows from the initial crisis point when news of the husband's death was broken to them through to their eventually stable adjustment to a widowed style of life. The theory underpinning their research was that death disrupts the widow's system of *personal constructs* (Kelly, 1955) – her entire gamut of previously integrated feelings and beliefs about herself as a married woman. As a result, she is apt to find herself confused, unable to anticipate events and unsure of how to interpret the events impinging on her from the outside world.

During the initial phase of bereavement, the widow's emotional states are apt to fluctuate across a combination of any of the following reactions.

SHOCK AND NUMBNESS

Surprise and disbelief are very common during the initial stages of bereavement. Even after the funeral, a widow is apt to have periods of imagining her husband's continued presence or anticipating his return as though he has merely gone away on a trip. Grief may be held in abeyance by such disbelief, creating a sense of numbness. According to Woodfield and Viney, this shock reaction is due to the widow's implicit realisation that her entire existing personal construct system has been overturned by her husband's dying.

STRESS AND THREAT

As efforts to cope with the loss begin, the widow 'becomes aware of imminent comprehensive change of her core structure' (p. 5) and may feel either challenged or overwhelmed by stress, depending in part on how heavily she relied on her husband for her own sense of personal identity or as a way of giving her life a meaning during the course of their marriage.

ANGER

A series of superficial and more serious frustrations are apt to follow in the wake of bereavement. The widow may find that her friends treat her differently or even exclude her from couple-based friendship networks. This invalidates her construction of herself as a friend as well as a wife. Smaller problems with finances, home maintenance and eating and sleeping habits can also provoke anger through sheer frustration.

ANXIETY

'Waves of discomfort' lasting between 20 minutes and an hour were also found by Woodfield and Viney to be a normal part of the grief reaction to widowhood. The anxious widow is thrown into a state of panic by the realisation that her former beliefs about herself and her life have failed her. The more extensive the implications of her husband's death for her sense of self, the stronger will be her feeling of anxious dislocation and worry over the future.

GUILT

According to Woodfield and Viney, feelings of guilt and self-blame are a component of both normal and pathological grief reactions. The widow who finds herself the most vulnerable to guilt is one who reacts to bereavement and widowed life in ways she would not have expected of herself. For example, she may feel less unhappiness than she believes a devoted wife should feel after losing her husband. Alternatively, she may find herself performing the masculine jobs that her husband formerly took charge of with a degree of skill that challenges her belief in her own essential femininity.

SADNESS AND DESPAIR

Beginning to come to realistic terms with the permanence of the loss leads to a process of grieving. The widow mourns not only her deceased husband but also the loss of those 'aspects of herself which were formerly amplified by her husband' (p. 6).

Identity as a widow

While these emotional states can be extremely painful, the pain may serve the useful function of motivating the widow to find a new identity. The ultimate resolution of the crisis of widowhood can be developmentally progressive, according to Woodfield and Viney (1985). The widow who completes the painful task of discarding her former married identity is faced with the challenge of defining a new sense of self. To be effective, her new 'self', or the revised set of personal constructs she creates for herself, will entail a developmental reorganisation and reconstruction process. Woodfield and Viney explain that components of the new identity are tried out and revised according to (a) how well they suit the widow's basic personality and (b) how effectively they enable her to predict reality and extend her range of life experience. A new and effective set of personal constructs represents a final resolution of the grief reaction and equips the widow to resume a normal and fulfilling widowed style of life. In some cases, the options afforded by the revised self-concept are richer and more developmentally stimulating than a perpetuation of the wifely role would have been.

But the resolution of this unique identity crisis during widowhood will also be influenced by the quality of the widow's previous identity development, extending far back into the life cycle (see Chapter 11). Women who escaped the adolescent identity crisis by adopting diffused or foreclosed identities are likely to have a harder time reconstructing an identity after widowhood than their counterparts who did at one time engage in a serious, dialectical process of identity exploration, however long ago. According to Woodfield and Viney:

> The widow who has defined her identity and the meaning of her life inflexibly in terms of her marriage and husband may become a prisoner of her own construct system. The widow whose prior beliefs about herself and her marriage have encompassed a broader perspective has a better chance of discovering those choices which lead her to freedom. (p. 11)

The notion of venturing into 'freedom' to resolve a new wave of the identity crisis also forms the basis for Helena Lopata's (1975) developmental theory of widowhood. Lopata studied the adjustments made by a group of widows of all ages who lived in metropolitan Chicago. She found that they all suffered from shock, depression and the practical disruption of their lives immediately after bereavement. But some told her that the most difficult time of all had arisen several months after the funeral when the social support of relatives and friends was withdrawn and they were expected to recover emotionally and find new ways of occupying themselves. Like their Australian counterparts, these American widows experienced the same feelings of having 'no place to go', either physically or in relation to their own sense of personal identity, as outlined by Woodfield and Viney (1985).

Lopata argued that the absence of a clearly defined *widowhood role* intensifies this identity crisis for the modern widow in Western society. Unlike her counterpart in most parts of the non-Western world, she has many potentially rewarding options available to her. She is not compelled to remain unmarried or to return to her parents' or in-laws' household, let alone immolate herself on her husband's funeral pyre or go into seclusion with a shaved head as was the custom in India last century (Lopata, 1975). Nor is remarriage automatic, as among the traditional Aborigines of Australia (Tonkinson, 1978). But this very lack of structure and the corresponding freedom to make an individualised choice may prove painfully disorienting at first.

Eventually, most of the widows studied by Lopata did manage to work out satisfactory new styles of living. Furthermore, despite the breadth of their options and the diversity of their ages and backgrounds, Lopata discovered only seven main patterns of widowed life.

The first two of these were the least common, but stood out as models of successful identity reconstruction by reason of the women's eager receptiveness to new experience and vigorous seeking and meeting of challenges. Lopata called these two styles 'liberated widows' and 'merry widows' respectively. The former included women who lived their lives as individuals and displayed a secure, well-rounded sense of personal identity. They made full use of the varied resources that a big city like Chicago has to offer, and their styles of activity were 'multidimensional'; that is, they were intensely involved in several different spheres of life endeavour. The 'merry widows' had less of this all-round quality and tended to devote most of their energies to social activity. But they led

A widow may substitute involvement in hobbies and volunteer pursuits (such as caring for injured wildlife) for the activities she lost with the death of her spouse.

lively, vigorous lives that revolved around dating, seeing friends and being a recognised member of the city's social life.

The other four styles of adjustment to widowhood were more frequent but slightly less adaptive than the first two. 'Individualistic working widows' had jobs that absorbed most of the energy, effort and feeling that had formerly been devoted to their husband and household. Most of the women in this category had worked before being widowed. A few were 'career widows' – extremely self-confident in their work and enjoying high job satisfaction. But the majority had taken up employment after many years as full-time housewives. Their choice of job had been rather haphazard and they were largely untrained, so the work they did tended to be routine and unchallenging. Nevertheless, they liked being able to get out of their empty house and had adjusted reasonably well to widowhood. Despite this, Lopata remarked on the narrowness of their focus of interest relative to that of the liberated women and queried how well these widows would adjust to changes later in the lifespan, such as retirement from work (see Chapters 15 and 17).

The category of 'widow's widows' was made up of women who had adopted widowhood itself as the new centre of their lives. They lived independently in their own home but spent most of their waking hours with other widows in a busy round of social meetings and projects. Their participation in both formal and informal widows' groups consumed all the time they had formerly shared with their husband, and many became much more socially active than during their married years. New intimacies with one or two fellow widows replaced former friendships with married couples, and these women tended to have relatively little to do with their children or any of the other people they had known before widowhood. Again, life satisfaction was high for the widow's widow, but Lopata argued that the narrowness and homogeneity of her social circle reduced her opportunities for challenge and stimulation.

The sixth category was made up of 'traditional widows' who had found substitutes for their former married role in devotion to their extended family. Much of their time was taken up with visiting and assisting their married children and grandchildren, but they also renewed contacts with relatives of their own generation. Many of the latter relationships had been forced to lie dormant during the marriage, either through lack of time or because of the husband's dislike of members of the wife's family. Traditional widows seemed to enjoy life and reported levels of satisfaction and activity that were as high as the other groups'. But, unlike liberated and merry widows, their options were limited and less likely to stimulate growth, as a result of being confined within the family circle.

'Grieving widows' were the only women in Lopata's sample who appeared not to have made even a partially satisfactory adjustment to the loss of their husband. They found themselves unable to enter into new social relationships and even lost ground in relationships with lifetime friends or their own children because of their withdrawal and lack of interest in life. Thus their unhappiness spiralled through a vicious circle of progressive social isolation. Many had been widowed for more than a decade. Throughout this time they had remained bitter, depressed and unappeased in their longing for the company of their dead husband.

Lopata's study revealed variety as well as certain commonalities in widows' adaptations to the alteration in their lifestyle caused by bereavement. Such factors as the woman's own personality (whether she tended to be shy or outgoing, for example), her past experiences (such as whether she was employed outside the home while her husband was alive) and her present opportunities (perhaps living near married children or in a city or on a farm) all affected the style of widowhood she chose to adopt. In terms of her psychological well-being and her opportunities for personal fulfilment, however, the most decisive factor would appear to be to what extent the widow is able to reinvest her interest, energy and involvement in her new style of living. All but the grieving group in Lopata's study had managed to find at least one new focus to build their life purpose around and thus had 'that something still which prompts the eternal sigh, for which we bear to live or dare to die' (Alexander Pope, cited in Evans, 1978).

Widowhood and culture

Culture also influences widows' sources of social support. Helena Lopata (1975) found that, in contrast to Chicago widows, women from highly patriarchal cultures who became widowed tended to turn to their sons rather than their daughters for emotional support. Thus, when she asked widows in India, Korea and Turkey who they were most likely to turn to in a crisis and tell their problems to, they most often named their sons, while Chicago widows typically named their daughters. Lopata suggested that, in a traditional, patriarchal society, the widow is often unable to inherit her husband's property and hence depends economically on her son. Often she lives with her son, whereas her daughters move away after marriage. Also, in traditional societies the widow is embedded in a narrow social network of family members. By contrast, as Lopata (1975, p. 127) notes, the modern Australian, New Zealand or American widow has the advantages of 'mass education, a new view of women as competent to function outside the home and resources for social engagement'.

Gender, bereavement and divorce

Because of the male's statistically shorter life, the tendency for husbands to marry wives younger than themselves and for widowers to remarry within two years of bereavement (Stroebe & Stroebe, 1983), the typical older man will never be required to make the same long-term personal reconstruction and practical reorganisation of life's goals as was studied among widowed women by Woodfield and Viney (1985) and Lopata (1975). However, divorce has become more frequent in recent years and, in many respects, the challenge of rebuilding a new mode of living as an unmarried adult presents the same difficulties to the divorced as to the widowed. A period of grieving for the lost partner and the broken marriage is nearly as common among the divorced as the recently bereaved. And the divorced person is faced with many of the same practical difficulties as the widow – problems such as finding a social network of friends for whom partnership as a couple is not an entry requirement, managing on a reduced income, not knowing how to do the household jobs the spouse used to handle, or needing to look after children.

The divorced person's coping tends to be made especially difficult by emotional strain during marital breakdown, separation and court proceedings. Like widowed people, the divorced tend to complain of loneliness, economic hardship, household role overload (see Chapters 13 and 14) and the discomfort that comes with the disruption of longstanding habits and routines. Nevertheless, like their widowed counterparts, divorced adults are offered a wide range of new options by contemporary society. Many achieve satisfaction and *self-actualisation* through the same kinds of independent activities that formed the focus of Lopata's liberated widows' lives. Others escape the challenges of a divorced pattern of life by remarrying. They then face the task of setting up a new household (see Chapter 13) armed with the benefits of age and experience but disadvantaged by old habits which may prove inappropriate to the new relationship. And so the everchanging process of lifelong development continues.

Long-term adjustment

Beverley Raphael (1992) studied bereavement in Australian adults from the perspective of how to provide counselling, support and therapeutic care for those who find themselves unable to cope with their grief without assistance. She discovered a number of risk factors that predicted a person's need for counselling or therapy before grief processes could follow the 'natural' path of healing:

1. *The nature of the relationship disrupted by bereavement.* When a widow, widower or other bereaved adult has been highly emotionally dependent on the deceased, loss may give rise to feelings of helplessness, hopelessness or anger over abandonment, as well as simple grief.
2. *Circumstances of death.* Sudden and violent death (murder or suicide) produces more shock, distress and lasting problems than death that is anticipated. In recent years, a new problem has arisen to add stress to the bereavement process: *social stigma*. Because of the connotations of homosexuality or sexual promiscuity associated with HIV infection (see Chapter 10) in many people's minds, bereaved survivors' reactions to the loss of an AIDS victim may be made more traumatic by social stigmatisation. On the other hand, within the gay community itself, social support networks can ease the suffering of individuals.
3. *Social support and rituals surrounding the death.* According to Raphael (1992), the recognition and social responses displayed by other people at the funeral and informally afterwards may ease the pain of bereavement. When others' social reactions are in synchrony with the bereaved survivor's expectations and are symbolic of respect, acceptance and fond farewell, adaptation to bereavement is facilitated.
4. *Multiple stresses.* If the grieving survivor encounters multiple losses all at once, or in close sequence, bereavement can become an overwhelming catastrophe.

Raphael argued that health professionals' awareness of the factors associated with difficulty in coping with bereavement should enable them to provide sensitive care and expert help in dealing with grief and in eventually achieving acceptance of the loss.

Chapter summary

Death completes the life cycle. We examined longevity statistics and projections and discovered that, whereas death can occur at any age, it is more likely during early infancy and old age than at other phases in life. Death also occurs earlier for the average man than the average woman, both of whom live longer in Australia and New Zealand today than in earlier eras in history. Lifestyle factors such as diet, smoking, exercise and ancestors' longevity help to predict a person's length of life.

Beliefs about death begin to develop during childhood and correspond closely to a child's cognitive level. But death anxiety persists through the lifespan for many adults, and is linked to family experiences and political concerns.

The process of adjusting to dying was described by Elisabeth Kübler-Ross as consisting of five stages: denial, anger, bargaining, depression and a final placid acceptance. A person's progress through the stages may depend on age, sex, culture, temperament, the nature of the final illness and the social surroundings. Because of individual differences like these, the dying person's right to information, social support and freedom of choice must be respected.

Adjustment to bereavement is apt to be an equally protracted process, possibly encompassing similar stages. But besides coping with grief at an emotional level, widows and widowers, like their divorced counterparts, are faced with many practical problems of developing a new identity and constructing a new and enduring lifestyle as a single person. So development continues, in the wake of one individual's death, throughout the lives of all the other people with whom the dying person's life was formerly interconnected.

For further interest

Looking forward on the Internet

Use the Internet to visit the following websites. Examine them for further information and varied perspectives on issues raised in this chapter. Also search for other relevant websites for yourself, using keywords like 'longevity', 'death and dying', 'Indigenous health' and 'death anxiety'.

In particular, for further ideas on topics related to death, dying and bereavement, visit: **http://www.nim.nih.gov/medlineplus/deathanddying.html** and for more information on living wills and advance directives, visit: **http://www.mindspring.com/~scottr/will.htm** and **http://www.aarp.org**.

For resources, ideas, activities and other items of interest in conjunction with this chapter, visit the Companion Website for this textbook at:
http://wps.pearsoned.com.au/peterson

Activity suggestion

As a practical activity in conjunction with themes in this chapter, compile information on the range of options that are available in your community for funeral services, burial or cremation, and the costs and availability of each. Visit a funeral home or crematorium to obtain more information, paying special attention to the kinds of materials that might assist a terminally ill person to choose from among the alternatives that are available.

Multimedia

For an intriguing portrait of Dr Elisabeth Kübler-Ross and a sensitive account of deaths of children and their parents' coping with bereavement, view the award-winning video *We're Almost Home Now* (Rites of Passage Videos, PO Box 226, Vanderpool, Texas, USA, 1993: 30 minutes, colour).

The whole lifespan

Through this book we have followed the progress of a human life from conception through childhood, adolescence, adulthood and old age to death, the final developmental transition. At each stage in the lifespan, we noted the qualities all healthy human beings share, regardless of their age. These include a vigorous physical body, idiosyncratic temperamental traits, bonds of affection for other people, a sophisticated information-processing system and the drive to continue growing psychologically throughout life. Other characteristics are peculiar to certain phases in the life cycle and so serve as distinctive milestones marking each age period off from the next. Infancy and early childhood, the traditional growing years, include dramatic gains in motor skills during the first months of life, a remarkable transition between age one and age three from making noise to using language with adult-like precision and versatility, and the onset, during the preschool years, of rich theories about the world and the human mind, and an inventive imagination. With the advent of formal schooling come revolutionary changes in problem-solving capacity, as well as literacy and numeracy. During adolescence, the universal markers of psychological growth begin to reflect more clearly the uniqueness of culture and individual choice. Shaped in part by encounters with specific cultural experiences, ranging from pubertal initiation ceremonies to the onset of sexual experience in a climate of fear of sexually transmitted disease, distinctively adolescent modes of relating to peers, parents and the abstract problems of life are seen to emerge between the ages of 12 and 20.

A few decades ago most of the important age markers of adult life were yet to be identified. Many psychologists, health professionals and educators mistakenly assumed that opportunities for genuine psychological growth declined after puberty. But our analysis of recent research into the period between the ages of 20 and 60 reveals the error of this assumption. In fact, the latest studies now show convincingly that the adult years of life are rich with developmental opportunities. As they progress, decade by decade, through adult life, most adults show quite predictably age-specific ways of coping with the various career milestones intervening between job entry and retirement, or the similarly universal ups and downs of love, domestic couplehood and parenthood. As a consequence, it is no longer feasible to divide the lifespan into two halves, one characterised by freshness, growth and excitement and the other by ageing, decay and loss. Instead, the two dialectic processes of development and decline are part of the entire pattern of lifelong psychological growth, beginning from the moment of conception and not ending until the last breath is drawn. As Eena Job (1984) explained:

We lose our tail and our gills to become more human. Similarly we shed old skills such as crawling to develop new ones such as walking. According to one theory, we discard brain cells, without constantly replacing them, as the price of the consolidation of memory ... Youth is a period when development is more evident than decay; middle age is a period when more or less of a balance is achieved; and though decay becomes more obvious in old age, there is a plethora of evidence that possibilities for continuing development are still present ... There is no evidence that the rate of change in physiological characteristics can be related to any specific chronological age, and some physiological systems are maintained with minimal alteration almost to the point of death. [pp. 5–7]

While development remains possible throughout life and the identifying features of each age period are unmistakeable, idiosyncratic differences are also apparent in any collection of people of the same age. Even newborn identical twins do not always mimic one another's behaviours, as their exhausted parents, struggling to cope with nightly variations in their patterns of eating and sleeping, will readily confirm. With the accumulation of the choices and diversifying experiences that punctuate the life cycle, individuality becomes magnified. As Desmond Morris (1983) noted:

Although there are typical ways of behaving at every age, there are always exceptions to the rule – individuals who break the pattern, being either unusually early or unusually late in their progress from childhood to old age. There are the amazingly mature children who become virtuosos at tender ages and there are childlike adults who refuse to age, either physically or mentally, at the usual rate. The significance of these two messages is clear enough: age rules exist, but they are there to be broken. Exceptional individuals will always ignore them and will write symphonies at 9 and elope at 90. [p. 203]

In this book we explored broad variations like these in human development in the context of universal trends. We also explored the unique patterning resulting from gender, ethnicity, family structure and personality style. One particular variation, however, received special emphasis. This was the factor of developing as an Australian or New Zealander as compared with growing up and growing older in some other corner of the globe. We saw that, although the broad outlines of development are the same the world over, development in Australia and New Zealand has its own unique characteristics. Distinctive features of the physical and social environments help to shape these quirks, as well as the special consequences of blending Aboriginal, Maori and migrant European, Asian and Polynesian traditions into the mainstream Anglo-Australian or Pakeha way of life. By observing these variations, developmental researchers working in Australia and New Zealand have contributed important new insights to our psychological understanding of the universal processes of human growth.

However, while many important advances in knowledge have recently arisen out of the Australian, New Zealand and overseas research that is summarised in these pages, lifespan developmentalists rarely congratulate themselves on discovering *final* answers. Thus the end of this book is really a beginning. Exciting new research horizons continue to beckon, we all have many uncharted developmental opportunities before us, and the formal or informal study of our own and other people's lifespan development, along with the progress of future scientific research, is bound to turn up new surprises, further puzzles and fresh insights. Let us wish each other well in this lifelong undertaking as observers of human lives from beginning to end.

GLOSSARY

Terms in *italics* are included as separate entries in the glossary.

abortion Termination of a *pregnancy* before the *fetus* or *embryo* is capable of independent survival. Spontaneous abortion is also known as miscarriage.

abuse Acts of physical, verbal and/or emotional violence aimed at hurting another person.

academic achievement Attainments in scholastic tasks including reading, writing, social studies, science and mathematics.

accommodation Piaget's term for the alteration of a thought process, or *schema*, to incorporate new information.

achievement motivation The drive to accomplish things and to achieve success.

achievement tests Standardised measures of *academic achievement*.

acquired immune deficiency syndrome See *AIDS*.

activity level A dimension of *temperament* based on vigour and frequency of body movements.

activity theory A view of psychological adjustment in old age that stresses the need to maintain commitment, social involvement and physical and mental activity. See also *disengagement theory*.

actualisation, self See *self-actualisation*.

adaptation A general term for developmental changes which increase the individual's adjustment to the environment. In Piaget's theory, adaptation consists of an interplay between the processes of *assimilation* and *accommodation*.

addiction A state of physical or psychological dependency.

admixture studies A method of estimating *heritability* by comparing pure with *hybrid populations*.

adolescence The years between *childhood* and *adulthood*; often identified with the teens, or with the period from *puberty* to full skeletal and reproductive maturity.

adoption design A method of estimating *heritability* by comparing individuals related to one another by biology versus adoption.

adrenal cortisone A hormone produced by the adrenal cortex.

adultery See *infidelity*.

adulthood The period of mature life that follows *adolescence*.

adultomorphism The mistake of viewing child behaviour in light of concepts or rules actually relevant only to adults.

advance directive A document specifying the person's wishes with regard to medical intervention in the event of cognitive incapacity. See also *living will*.

affective role-taking The ability to understand or infer another person's emotional state.

age change A relatively permanent alteration of behaviour which reliably accompanies the passage from one *chronological age* to the next (also called *ontogenetic change*).

age difference Observed contrasts between two or more *cohorts*, or age groups.

age grading Cultural or societal rituals, regulations or social practices that draw distinctions among age groups.

age norm Behaviour that is typical or average at a particular *chronological age* as determined by systematic observation and quantitative measurement. In adult psychology, the term is also used to describe expectations within a society about behaviours which are prescribed at one age but considered deviant at an older or younger age.

ageing Normal changes arising in most people with increasing age. The term is frequently restricted to degenerative changes in contrast to the progressive gains known as *growth* or *development*.

ageism Bigotry, stereotyping or discriminatory treatment unfairly disadvantaging one age group.

aggression A deliberate act of physical or verbal violence with the intent to do harm. See also *abuse*.

AID Artificial insemination of the *ovum* by donor's *sperm*.

AIDS (acquired immune deficiency syndrome) A potentially fatal condition caused by infection with the HIV virus, often resulting from unprotected sexual intercourse with an infected partner. The virus is also spread by blood exchange (e.g. transfusion) and unhygienic intravenous drug use.

alienation A sense of powerlessness and lack of interest. At work, alienation can be brought about by automated tasks which leave no room for variety or initiative.

allele Members of pairs of *genes* that correspond to one another in their coding for a given trait.

alliteration Words that share the same initial phoneme, or sound pattern (e.g. ball, beach, boat).

altruism Self-sacrifice on behalf of another.

Alzheimer's disease A common form of *dementia*, involving gradual mental deterioration and memory loss with increasing age.

alz-ism The erroneous overestimation of proportions of elderly adults afflicted with *Alzheimer's disease* and other forms of dementia.

Ameslan See *ASL*.

amniocentesis A test for *chromosome abnormalities* in the unborn *fetus*. The test requires the insertion of a needle through the mother's stomach to remove a small amount of *amniotic fluid*.

amniotic fluid A cushioning liquid which fills the *amniotic sac* and protects the *fetus* from shock and temperature change.

amniotic sac A thick membrane forming a closed bag around the *fetus* in the womb, encasing it in a protective liquid. See also *amniotic fluid*.

anaclitic attachment Freud's term for the infant's primitive and total dependency on the caregiver's nurturance.

anal stage In Freudian theory, the period during which a child's pleasures and concerns centre around elimination.

androgyny A *personality* disposition which allows for the expression of both masculine and feminine *sex-role* qualities.

anencephaly A *congenital malformation* marked by the absence of most of the brain and spinal cord.

animism The child's belief that inanimate things (e.g. trees, dolls, the moon) are alive and behave like people.

anorexia nervosa A pattern of self-imposed starvation that can prove fatal.

anoxia Oxygen deprivation which, if prolonged, may lead to brain damage or death.

antithesis The argument opposing the *thesis* in *dialectical reasoning*.

anxious attachment See *attachment classification*.

apathetic personality Neugarten's term for an elderly personality pattern marked by a vegetative lack of interest in life.

apportioned grandmother A woman whose frequent contact with her grandchildren provides a major focus for her life.

arteriosclerosis A disease of the arteries restricting blood flow to the brain and other bodily organs. It is seen more frequently in the elderly, but is not an inevitable consequence of *ageing*.

arthritis Degenerative inflammation of joints in the body that can make movement stiff and painful.

articulation of rules An index of *conscience* in which the individual explains why something is right or wrong.

artificialism The child's belief that natural phenomena are fabricated by people.

asceticism Anna Freud's term for the adolescent's extreme rejection of all pleasurable experiences and impulses.

ASL (American Sign Language) The sign language used by deaf people in the USA.

assimilation Piaget's term for the incorporation of new information into an existing mental category or *schema*.

asynchrony Discrepancies in growth rates either among the various parts of one person's body (*intra-individual asynchrony*) or between people of the same chronological age (*inter-individual asynchrony*).

athletic skills Skills involving physical exertion, sport and motor performance.

attachment An affectional bond between people (e.g. an infant's emotional link to his or her primary caregiver).

attachment classification A typology of infant attachment behaviour based on behaviour in the *strange situation* where Type A denotes an avoidant, insecure attachment, Type B denotes a secure attachment and Type C denotes an anxious, ambivalent attachment.

attachment styles An adolescent's or adult's approach to intimate relationships in relation to infant *attachment classifications*.

attention   Directing awareness at specific stimuli.

Auslan   Australian Sign Language, the native language used by many deaf people in Australia. Similar to the American equivalent, *ASL* or *Ameslan*, it represents words through gesture, movement and positioning of the hands.

authoritarian parenting   See *autocratic discipline.*

authoritative discipline   A style of child-rearing in which parents discuss important issues with their offspring and allow for a certain amount of democratic decision making, within limits the parents set.

autism   A developmental disorder characterised by abnormal social interaction, impaired imagination and language problems.

autocratic discipline   An authoritarian child-rearing style in which parents demand unquestioning obedience from their offspring.

autoimmune theory   The theory that *ageing* is caused by the body's natural immunological defence system turning upon the body's own healthy cells and structures.

autonomy   Independence, self-control and self-direction. See also *emancipation.*

avocation   A hobby or voluntary leisure pursuit.

avoidant attachment   See *attachment classification.*

axon   The cable containing neural fibres that stretches away from the cell body and conducts impulses to other neurons.

babbling   Strings of vowel–consonant sequences uttered by babies without the apparent intent to represent, or speak meaningfully.

baby talk   See *motherese.*

barking-at-print   A style of oral 'reading' in which little or no comprehension is evident. See also *parroting.*

basal metabolism   The body's rate of energy conversion while resting.

behaviour   An aspect of human conduct that lends itself to objective measurement or *description.*

behaviour genetics   The study of biological inheritance and its influence on behaviour.

behaviour modification   The practical application of learning principles to treat behaviour problems.

bereavement   The loss of an intimate friend or relative through death.

blastocyst   See *blastula.*

blastula   A hollow sphere of cells which develops out of the early cell divisions of the fertilised *ovum.*

bonding   See *attachment.*

Broca's area   A region in the left *cerebral hemisphere* that is involved in speech production.

bulimia   An eating disorder characterised by gorging and purging.

buratya   A cradle used by Aboriginal Australians to carry infants.

bystander apathy   The failure of witnesses to an assault, emergency or accident to come forward to give assistance.

cardiac output   Heart rate.

cardiovascular disease   An ailment compromising the heart and/or blood vessels.

career development   Regular psychological changes punctuating progress through a career.

career exploration   The first stage of *career development* in Super's theory.

caregiver   A parent or surrogate who tends infants or young children.

caregiver sensitivity   The *caregiver's* ability to accurately discover and effectively satisfy a baby's varied needs.

castration fear   Freud's term for boys' unconscious dread of attacks by the father against the penis during the *phallic stage.*

cataract   A progressive clouding of the lens of the eye, leading eventually to blindness.

cathexis   Freud's term for an emotional *attachment,* or the concentration of one's psychic energy on a particular person or thing.

causality   An awareness of the laws of cause and effect.

centration   Being fixated on some salient feature of the overall situation to the exclusion of other features.

cephalocaudal   The direction of physical growth from head to trunk to limbs.

cerebral cortex   The convoluted surface of the brain. The cortex governs higher mental processes.

cerebral hemispheres   The two sides of the brain, left and right.

cerebrovascular accident   Cerebral haemorrhage, embolism or thrombosis of the blood vessels in the brain.

cervix   The neck of the womb; the narrow outer opening of the *uterus.*

childhood   The stage in the lifespan between the end of *infancy* and the onset of *adolescence.*

chorionic villus sampling   A procedure in which a sample from the placenta is taken to diagnose fetal genetic problems.

chromosome abnormality   A developmental disorder caused by an error in the chromosomes, often an abnormal number. See also *Down syndrome.*

chromosomes   Microscopic threadlike particles composed of DNA and serving as vehicles for the *genes.* Chromosomes come in pairs in every cell of the normal person's body except the *gametes,* where the chromosome complement is halved.

chronological age   The time that has elapsed since a person's birth, as measured in years, months and days.

chum   A close friend of the same sex in Sullivan's theory.

chumship   Sullivan's term for a close friendship among pre-adolescents of the same sex.

circumcision   The operation of cutting away the foreskin of a male child's penis.

classical conditioning   The repeated pairing of an unconditioned stimulus with a previously neutral stimulus to produce an eventual response to the latter alone.

classification   A Piagetian problem which requires the grouping of objects into categories (e.g. arranging blocks by colour, shape and size).

climacterium   A period in middle adulthood marked by changes in the hormones and reproductive organs, including female *menopause.*

climax   A peak of sexual excitement.

clique   A small, cohesive group of three to nine adolescent friends.

clustering   A strategy for organising information in memory.

cognition   A general term for thought or intellectual functioning. Cognition involves mental processes such as perception, reasoning, language, judgment and imagination.

cognitive-developmental theories   Explanations for development which attribute changes in behaviour to the growth of mental capacity.

cognitive egocentrism   Pigget's term for the inability to conceptualise alternative viewpoints.

cognitive monitoring   The introspective act of keeping track of one's own thought processes during problem-solving.

cognitive role-taking   The ability to understand or infer another person's mental viewpoint.

cognitive stategies   Planful methods of solving problems.

cognitive tempo   A dimension of cognitive style that ranges from *impulsivity* to *reflectivity.*

cohabitation   Living together as husband and wife without a legal marriage contract.

cohort   A group of people who were born in the same year or at roughly the same era in history (e.g. everyone born in the year 1920).

cohort contrast   See *cohort difference.*

cohort difference   A dimension of behaviour which distinguishes the members of one *cohort* from their counterparts in other cohorts. Cohort differences may be confused with *age differences* when using the *cross-sectional method.*

coitarche   The individual's first experience of complete sexual intercourse.

coitus   Sexual intercourse.

colic   Protracted bouts of crying in early infancy that commonly occur in the early evening or when the infant is over-excited but not necessarily hungry, wet or in pain.

collagen   A protein substance found in connective tissue, bone and cartilage. Its composition changes continually with age.

colleague role allocation   Dividing household duties to suit each spouse's interests and skills. See also *egalitarian role allocation* and *traditional role allocation.*

collective monologue   Children's use of the superficial form of conversation exchange to convey private thoughts without modification to suit the needs or interests of a listener.

commonality   Similarity; the sharing of interests and personality characteristics, especially in the context of married couples' relationships.

companionate love   A calm, friendly mode of affection which may gradually replace *passionate love,* according to the Walsters.

compensation hypothesis The theory that workers select leisure pursuits which make up for deficiencies in their paid occupation.

complementarity The matching of two people whose dispositions are opposite to one another.

comprehension The reader's understanding of the meaning of printed text.

conception The moment of fertilisation when the *sperm* and *ovum* unite to begin the new individual's life cycle.

concrete-operational stage Piaget's term for the third stage of cognitive development (7–11 years); it normally begins during *middle childhood* and involves an organised logic which can deal effectively with concrete experience but not with the abstract or hypothetical. See also *formal-operational stage*.

condom A prophylactic or *contraceptive* device consisting of a latex sheath that is worn over the penis.

confession Acknowledging wrongdoing.

conflict Discord, argument or discrepancy of points of view.

conflict avoidance The anxious failure to discuss or to acknowledge issues that may prove contentious or controversial.

conflict-habituated marriage A marriage characterised by habituation to overt or covert hostility between spouses.

conflict-resolution style Habitual patterns of dealing with inter-personal disagreement.

conformity The tendency to behave like others or to change one's attitudes or expressed beliefs to make them coincide with those of other people.

congenital defect A physiological problem acquired in the uterus (e.g. rubella deafness).

congenital malformation A birth defect involving the structure of a bodily organ, most often caused by problems during the *embryonic period*.

conjunctive faith Fowler's term for the fifth stage in *faith development*.

conservation A Piagetian term for an awareness that certain physical properties such as mass, quantity and weight remain invariant after transformations of their shape, grouping or location.

constitutional defect A problem caused by *prenatal* or *postnatal* illness or injury.

constricted personality Neugarten's term for a personality pattern characterised by a defensive rejection of social involvement during *old age*.

contingency A reliable 'if . . . then' association in the physical or social environment (e.g. an infant learns that 'If I cry when I wake up from my nap, then someone will come into the room and pick me up').

continuity Consistency in behaviour over age.

continuity theory The view that earlier experience creates styles of living which aged people will strive to maintain for as long as possible. See also *activity theory* and *disengagement theory*.

contraception Birth control; deliberate prevention of pregnancy.

contrast effect The tendency to emphasise minor differences between pairs of *identical twins*.

control group A group included in an experimental design to provide a neutral comparison against which to judge the manipulation applied to the *experimental group*.

controversial peer status The *sociometric classification* for children who score high in both 'like' and 'dislike' nominations.

conventional level Kohlten's second level of moral reasoning.

co-operative play Play in which children collaborate on shared tasks or work together to reach a common goal.

corpus callosum A bundle of nerve fibres that connects the two *cerebral hemispheres* and allows information to flow between them.

correlation A statistically determined association between two separate variables. The existence of a strong correlation does not prove that change in one variable causes the other to change. They may both be influenced by some third factor.

cortical See *cerebral cortex*.

cot death See *SIDS*.

courtship Keeping company with a member of the opposite sex for the purpose of persuading him/her to marry.

creativity Fluent, flexible, original or unusual thinking or production. Creativity is associated with divergent thinking, or the ability to generate a wide range of alternatives or problem solutions.

critical period A specific point in time when the developing individual is unusually vulnerable to a particular type of influence (e.g. the organ structures of the body are critically vulnerable to traumas that occur during the first three months after conception).

cross linkage A theory of ageing based on damage to cells.

cross-pressure Attempts at influence that converge on the individual from two conflicting directions at once.

cross-sectional study A research design which compares different age groups measured at one point in time.

crowd A collection of two or more adolescent *cliques* brought together by common interests.

crystallised intelligence Mental abilities entailing previously learned habits or information. See also *fluid intelligence*.

cuddliness The personality disposition to seek close physical contact with another person.

cumulative changes Changes that build successively on the groundwork created by previous change.

cyclic change Change that follows a regularly recurring pattern (e.g. the seasons of the year).

cynicism An attitude towards romantic love characterised by profound scepticism.

dating Going out together; a relationship with a member of the opposite sex that is undertaken more for mutual enjoyment than as a long-term commitment.

day-care Substitute care for infants and preschool children during parents' working hours.

death The cessation of all physical signs of life, including brain activity, heartbeat, breathing and reflexes.

death anxiety A person's fearful thoughts concerning death of self or others.

decoding The reader's ability to convert printed letters or words into spoken sounds.

deductive reasoning A process of logical inference which involves drawing a specific conclusion from a given broad premise (e.g. 'All men are mortal; therefore Mr Jones will die sometime'). See also *inductive reasoning* and *transductive reasoning*.

defensive identification Freud's term for the resolution of the *phallic stage* conflict by endeavouring to become identical to the same-sex parent.

deformation professionelle Occupational distortion; the shaping of workers' personalities by the job they do.

deliberate memory The process of actively encoding and committing designated information to mental storage.

delinquency Serious misbehaviour or criminal activity on the part of children or adolescents.

dementia The loss of cognitive capacity through brain damage or disease. See also *Alzheimer's disease*.

democratic discipline A style of parenting in which children's preferences are sought and attended to and decisions are made by consensus.

dendrites Nerve endings that receive information from other *neurons* in the form of electrical impulses.

denial Freud's term for an unconscious defence mechanism involving the failure to perceive or to attend to anxiety-provoking impulses.

dependency Reliance on someone else for assistance, nurturance or emotional support.

dependent variable The measurable outcome of an *experiment*.

description Information that provides a detailed account, or picture, of some existing pattern of behaviour. See also *explanation*.

descriptive grammar A theory of language embracing all the rules underlying everyday speech. See also *prescriptive grammar*.

development Changes in behaviour as a function of increasing age, especially those which are cumulative, irreversible and enhancing of the organism's capacity for *self-regulation*.

developmental receptive dysphasia A disorder limiting the child's ability to comprehend spoken language.

devitalised marriage A mode of mature couplehood in which fondness remains but love and togetherness are less complete and intense than formerly.

dialectical conflict Clash between polar opposites, such as thesis and antithesis.

dialectical model A view of development as a continual process of change resulting from the constant occurrence, resolution and then higher-order recurrence of conflicts and contradictions.

dialectical reasoning A mode of thinking in which contradictions are resolved into higher order *synthesis*.

dialectical synthesis   Resolution of dialectical conflict.

differential sociability   An indicator that an infant has developed a specific attachment.

differential vulnerability   The heightened risk of negative outcomes from change to individuals for whom the changing characteristic held unusually high values.

differentiated companionate marriage   Intense, intimate, though traditional marriage.

differentiation   The separation of a global whole into discrete parts (e.g. in embryonic development the organs of the body are differentiated out of an originally uniform mass of cells).

difficult temperament   A dispositional pattern involving a negative mood and irregularity.

diffusion   See *identity diffusion.*

discontinuity   Development characterised by uneven rates of change or by a lack of uniform sequentiality.

discrimination   The ability to distinguish between non-identical stimuli.

disenchantment   A progressive loss of love and satisfaction with marriage.

disengaged personality   Neugarten's term for an exceptionally healthy personality pattern characterised by a contented distancing of the self from social roles and involvements.

disengagement   A state of detachment from society, social roles and close personal contact.

disengagement theory   The view that successful adjustment to *old age* entails mutual withdrawal between the old person and society.

displacement   Anna Freud's term for the adolescent's rejection of parents and compensatory attachment to someone outside the family.

distant-figure grandparent   A grandparent in name only who has minimal contact or involvement with grandchildren. See also *remote grandparent.*

distributive justice   Rules governing the fair distribution of resources or rewards.

divergent thinking   See *creativity.*

divorce   The formal, legal dissolution of a marriage.

dizygotic twins   See *fraternal twins.*

DNA (deoxyribonucleic acid)   The chemical compound that carries genetic information in the cells. See also *chromosomes.*

dominant gene   In the single-gene pair mode of genetic inheritance, the dominant gene in any given pair determines the *phenotype*, or the observed characteristics, of the individual. See also *genotype; recessive gene.*

double standard   Discrepancy in expectations for the two sexes (e.g. the greater degree of premarital sexual restraint expected from females).

Down syndrome   A congenital abnormality caused by the presence of an extra member of the 21st *chromosome* pair (hence its other label 'Trisomy 21') and marked by *mental retardation.*

drug abuse   The excessive or inappropriate ingestion of chemical substances.

dual career   Marriage in which both spouses are involved in paid employment.

dyad   A pair of people; a couple.

early adulthood   The years between the end of *adolescence* and the beginning *of middle age.*

early childhood   The preschool and early school-age years, spanning ages three to six or seven.

early maturer   An individual who reaches *puberty* well ahead of the *age norm* for his or her sex.

ecology   The relationship between living individuals and their external environment.

ectoderm   The layer of cells in the *embryo* that will develop into skin, hair, sense organs and nervous system.

EEG   See *electroencephalogram.*

egalitarian role allocation   The equal sharing of all household duties and functions by spouses. See also *colleague role allocation* and *traditional role allocation.*

ego   An aspect of *personality* which, according to *psychoanalytic theory*, is reality-oriented and mediates conflicts between the *id* and the *superego.*

egocentrism   In Piaget's theory, egocentrism is a limitation on *cognition* which prevents individuals from clearly conceptualising viewpoints other than their own. Cognitive development consists of the gradual overcoming of egocentrism. More generally, the term can also refer to a motivational unwillingness to consider others. See also *imaginary audience.*

eidetic memory   A special ability to summon a vivid mental picture (or image) of a visual display which has vanished from view.

ejaculation   The release of semen from the penis.

Electra conflict   A psychoanalytic term for the girl's unconscious *phallic stage* conflict concerning her sexual attraction towards her father. See also *Oedipal conflict.*

electroencephalogram (EEG)   A technique for measuring the electrical activity of the brain. The recorded EEG patterns are sometimes called brain waves.

emancipation   The adolescent's process of becoming emotionally independent of parents.

embryo   The unborn child during the *embryonic period*, roughly the first three months of prenatal development.

embryonic period   The period in prenatal development that begins when the fertilised *ovum* implants itself in the wall of the *uterus* and ends when *differentiation* of organs is complete and bone cells appear. See also *fetal period.*

emotional arousal   A state of elevated feeling.

empathy   The sympathetic, vicarious feeling of another person's needs, thoughts or emotional states.

empirical   Based on direct observation or *experiment.*

empty-calorie foods   Foods that cause weight gain without contributing substantially to the body's nutritional requirements (e.g. a lollipop).

empty nest   The stage in the marriage relationship after the youngest child has grown up and left home.

endoderm   The layer of cells in the *embryo* from which the internal organs (heart, lungs, intestines and the like) will develop.

engagement   The status of being committed, involved or socially active.

engrossment   A father's intense fascination with his newborn offspring.

entertainment   Leisure activities whose main purpose is to provide pleasure and diversion.

environment   The total pattern of external conditions and events affecting the life and development of an organism.

environmental engineering   The tendency for individuals to actively select environments to match their hereditary dispositions.

environmental insult theories   *Explanations* of ageing in terms of *cumulative change* due to wear-and-tear, or the destructive effects of stressors in the *environment.*

epigenesis   A process of *qualitative change* leading to the emergence of new capacities which are planfully and functionally integrated.

equilibration   The act of achieving *equilibrium.*

equilibrium   A state of harmony or stability. In Piaget's theory, relative (or temporary) equilibrium occurs whenever *assimilation* and *accommodation* are in balance with one another.

equity   A state of balance or fairness. In marriage, equity describes a situation where each spouse's overall 'deal' (as denoted by the ratio of investments into, and outcomes from, the relationship) balances that of the partner.

error of commission   Mistakenly recalling an item that was not actually presented for memorisation. See also *error of omission.*

error of omission   Failing to recall an item that was presented for memorisation. See also *error of commission.*

estrogen   *Hormone* that occurs predominantly in the female body. Estrogens help to regulate a girl's reproductive development during puberty, and are involved in menstruation and fertility later on. Estrogen replacement is sometimes prescribed to control *menopausal* symptoms.

ethnicity   A person's cultural background as determined by ancestry, national origin and/or self-identification with a subculture or social grouping in society.

euthanasia   Mercy-killing; the act of actively or passively hastening the death of a suffering or severely incapacitated person or animal.

expansion   A language-teaching device whereby the adult repeats the sense of a child's spoken sentence while extending or correcting its grammatical structure.

expatiation   A language-teaching device whereby an adult responds to a child's utterance by putting forward further related ideas.

experience   See *environment.*

experiment   A research method in which the intrusion of irrelevant factors is controlled while manipulating one condition (*independent variable*) and gauging the effect of this manipulation on a behavioural outcome (*dependent variable*).

experimental group   The group subjects receiving the experimental manipulation. See *control group*.

explanation   Information which provides a reason for particular behaviour or its pattern of change over age; a theoretical account of development which enables understanding and prediction. See also *description*.

extinction   A term used in learning theories to describe the reduction of a conditioned response through non-reinforcement (*operant conditioning*) or discontinuation of stimulus pairing (*classical conditioning*).

extraversion   A sociable, outgoing *personality* disposition. See *introversion*.

faith development   The maturation of a system of belief for giving meaning to human existence.

fallopian tubes   The tubes connecting the *ovaries* to the *uterus* in the female reproductive system.

false belief tasks   Cognitive problems that require a child to take account of the thought processes of someone with a false idea and are used to test for *theory of mind*.

family life cycle   Successive stages from bearing through rearing to launching of offspring.

fear of success   Negative emotional reactions to a real or anticipated accomplishment.

fetal alcohol syndrome   A problem in *prenatal* development involving congenital malformation of eyes, nose and brain; often appears in babies born to mothers who seriously abuse alcohol during pregnancy.

fetal period   The final period in *prenatal* development which begins when bone cells appear (at about three months after *conception*) and continues until birth.

fetus   An unborn child during the *fetal period* of *prenatal* life.

floundering   Career uncertainty; inability to become committed to a chosen occupation.

fluency   The number and breadth of creative solutions to a problem.

fluid ability   A generalised learning ability. See also *crystallised intelligence*.

focused personality   Neugarten's term for an exceptionally healthy personality pattern which entails the narrowing and intensifying of an old person's commitment to one or more social relationships.

foreclosure   The failure to confront and resolve a developmental crisis. In Eriksons's theory, *identity* foreclosure describes a young person who prematurely settles on a role without exploring all the options available.

formal grandparent   A grandparent adhering to a traditional role which entails providing special favours for a grandchild while eschewing major responsibility for the child's care or discipline.

formal-operational stage   The final stage in Piaget's theory of *cognitive development*. The new logical organisation acquired enables the thinker to deal with hypothetical concepts and to use *inductive* and *deductive reasoning* to solve abstract problems.

fragile X syndrome   A structural defect of the X *chromosome*; may lead to learning problems or *mental retardation*, especially in boys.

fraternal twins   Twins formed through the simultaneous unions of two separate *sperm* cells and two separate *ova*; also called dizygotic twins. Unlike their monozygotic counterparts, they do not share identical *genotypes*.

free-radical theory   The view that physiological ageing is caused by the breakage and reconnection of molecules in a manner analogous to the perishing of rubber or the spoilage of milk.

frustration   The blocking or thwarting of attainment of a goal.

full-term infant   A baby born after a normal gestation period of 38 to 40 weeks and who weighs at least 2.5 kilograms. See also *prematurity*.

fun-seeking grandparent   A grandparent who adopts a playfully informal style of grandparenting, emphasising mutual pleasure and enjoyment.

gamete   A cell from which a new organism can develop; a *sperm* or *ovum*.

gender   A person's biological sex as determined by *chromosomes*, *hormones* and *gonads*.

gender aschematic   A child who makes relatively little use of *gender schemas* in cognitive processing.

gender consistency   Awareness that superficial transformations (such as a boy putting on a dress) do not alter biological gender.

gender constancy   The knowledge that one's biological gender cannot be altered by growing older or by superficial alterations to hair and clothing.

gender identity   A person's sense of himself or herself as a biologically male or female individual.

gender preference   The child's attraction to the attributes of his or her own sex and corresponding rejection of toys, clothes, etc. associated with the opposite sex.

gender-role intensification   The increased emphasis on traditional *sex roles* often arising during adolescence.

gender schema   Bem's term for a conceptual distinction between biological or social masculinity and femininity to create a scheme for processing information.

gender schema theory   The view that children acquire sex roles by fitting their observations, memories and predictions about the social world into schemes based on gender.

gender schematic   A child for whom the gender distinction is highly salient.

gender stability   The child's awareness that a person's biological gender remains the same over the lifespan.

gene–environment interactions   Situations in which *heredity* and *environment* come together in a non-linear manner to influence development.

generalisation   The transfer of learned responses to similar situations.

generalisation hypothesis   The theory that workers choose leisure activities entailing similar demands and satisfactions to those of their paid job.

generation   A synonym for *cohort* (or all the people born at a particular point in history); also refers to the ancestors and descendants in a particular biological family unit (e.g. parents, children and grandchildren each represent different generations of the family).

generation gap   Discrepancies between the attitudes, beliefs or social behaviour of earlier and later *cohorts*.

generativity   A stage (also known as 'generativity-*vs*-stagnation') and process in Erikson's theory of human development, characterised by the need to create a lasting contribution to society.

generosity   Willingness to donate one's own resources to needy recipients.

genes   The units of *heredity*, carried by the *chromosomes*. They contain the coded chemical information which determines how characteristics are inherited.

genital stage   The final stage in Freud's theory of psychosexual development. Pleasure centres around mature eroticism, and defence mechanisms evolve which permit higher cultural achievement.

genotype   The genetic composition of an individual (as distinguished from *phenotype*) or outward appearance of inherited characteristics.

germ cell   A *gamete*; *sperm* or *ovum*.

gerontology   The medical, sociological and psychological study of *old age*.

gestation period   The period from *conception* to birth.

gestural symbol   A form of *symbolic representation* involving stereotyped manual or bodily communication (e.g. waving goodbye).

glial cells   Cells within the brain that support and assist *neurons*.

gonads   The sex organs. See *ovaries* or *testes*.

gonorrhoea   A *venereal disease* marked by inflammation of the genitourinary tract, causing pain and/or a discharge of mucus and pus.

good-child orientation   The third stage in Kohlberg's system of moral judgment, marked by a desire to earn the commendation of significant others.

gooing   The infant's first non-crying vocalisations, consisting of gutteral sounds and usually beginning six to eight weeks after birth.

grammar   The rules which underlie the combination of words in meaningful language. *Prescription grammar* identifies a set of rules that can be explicitly taught while *descriptive grammar* contains all the implicit rules that enable language to be spoken and understood.

graphic symbol   A form of *symbolic representation* involving the creation of a permanent record, as by writing or drawing.

grasp reflex The inborn reflex that causes *neonates* to grip their fists tightly around something touching their palms.

grouping Piaget's term for a mental structure composed of aspects of the algebraic group and the lattice, which results in the *concrete-operational* mode of thought.

growth Gains in size, strength, capacity or complexity with increasing age.

growth asynchrony An imbalance in the timing of growth events either between people (*inter-individual asynchrony*) or within the same person between one part of the body and another (*intra-individual asynchrony*).

growth spurt The rapid increase in height that occurs during *puberty*.

guilt Feelings of discomfort after transgressing.

habituation The reduction in strength or frequency of response to a stimulus as a result of its uninterrupted repetitive occurrence.

Hayflick limit The upper limit on a cell's capacity to divide.

health professionals Members of the allied health professions (e.g. doctors, nurses, OTs, speech therapists, physiotherapists and health educators). After obtaining formal qualifications, usually accompanied by registration as practitioners, health professionals are involved in the diagnosis, treatment and prevention of illness or injury.

helpfulness Willingness to provide practical assistance to a person in need.

helplessness A situation in which the individual lacks control over important contingencies in the environment. See also *learned helplessness*.

hereditary birth defect A disorder caused by the *genotype* that was inherited through the family line.

heredity The biological transmission of characteristics from parent to offspring.

heritability An estimate of the degree to which *heredity* governs the development of a physical or behavioural characteristic. Twin comparisons provide one means of estimating the heritability of a trait within a particular population.

heterozygosity Mixed genetic composition; a gene pairing containing unlike members. See also *homozygosity*.

heuristic A cognitive principle, or 'rule-of-thumb' that guides mental organisation and problem-solving.

HIV Human immunodeficiency virus.

holding-on personality Neugarten's term for an elderly personality pattern marked by anxious perpetuation of the same level of social activity as during *middle age*.

holophrastic speech The use of a single word to express the meaning of an entire sentence.

homeostasis A continuing search for balance in living organisms.

homozygosity Genetic homogeneity; a gene pair in which both members are identical.

hormone replacement therapy The artificial restoration of *estrogen* or *testosterone* to their preclimacteric levels.

hormones Chemical substances produced by glands and carried through the bloodstream to exert specific effects on some other bodily process. For example, adrenal hormones influence the body's reaction to stress, pituitary hormones influence the timing of bodily growth, and *estrogen* and *testosterone* are involved in the development and functioning of the *gonads*.

hospice An alternative to the traditional hospital environment for terminal care.

humanistic psychology The theoretical approach which emphasises positive self-determination and the ideals of human existence.

Huntington's chorea An inherited degenerative disease of the nervous system resulting in dancelike movements and intellectual deterioration.

hybrid population A group with genetically mixed ancestry.

hyperactivity A behaviour pattern involving high activity, poor attention span and high distractability.

hypertension Chronic high blood pressure.

hypothalamus The part of the brain which regulates the production of hormones, as well as many other important aspects of physiological functioning.

hypothesis An 'educated guess', or a working theory, to be subjected to experimental test.

iconic symbol A type of mental imagery or *symbolic representation* that is based on a sensory record (e.g. picturing the item being symbolised in the mind's eye, or calling up a memory of the scent of an item).

id Freud's term for the primitive part of the *personality* made up of pleasure-seeking instincts and impulses.

identical twins See *monozygotic twins*.

identification The process of endeavouring to become identical to some key person. In Freud's theory, identification with a parent is the mechanism which accounts for the acquisition of *sex roles* and *morality*.

identity In Erikson's theory, an all-encompassing answer to the question 'Who am I?'. With the attainment of a secure sense of identity the adolescent or adult moves beyond role-playing and *identification* to achieve a stable sense of his or her own personality.

identity achievement The attainment of a sense of personal *identity* following a period of crisis and self-examination.

identity crisis The developmental process of achieving an *identity*. See also *foreclosure, identity diffusion, moratorium* and *negative identity*.

identity diffusion Inability to resolve the *identity crisis*. The symptoms are general indecisiveness and anomie.

identity foreclosure See *foreclosure*.

identity moratorium A delayed or protracted grappling with the *identity crisis*.

idiographic record An idiosyncratic portrait describing the behaviour and development of a single individual.

idolatry An immature style of love characterised by blind 'worship' of one's partner coupled with abasement of oneself.

imaginary audience The adolescent's impression that he or she is the prime focus of nearly everyone's interest and attention.

imaginary companion The child's playful interaction with an invisible partner invented through *pretence*.

imitation Copying the behaviour of other people. See also *modelling*.

immanent justice Piaget's term for a young child's belief in justice or retribution deriving from misdeeds rather than logical connections between events.

immunological system The body's mechanisms for resisting and combating disease.

implantation The embedding of the *blastula* into the wall of the *uterus*.

imprinting Very rapid learning which occurs during critical periods early in the life of certain animals.

impulsivity A conceptual tempo characterised by a rapid response rate and a relatively high error rate (for certain kinds of problems). See also *reflectivity*.

incentive A motivating condition or object; something which *reinforces*.

incidental memory The recall of details which were not deliberately memorised. See also *deliberate memory*.

independent variable A factor the researcher manipulates in an *experiment*.

individual reflective faith Fowler's fourth stage in *faith development*.

individualised grandparent Grandparents who seek pleasure in their grandchildren's company without undue worry over discipline, teaching or setting a good example.

induction Parents explaining to their children the reasons behind disciplinary prohibitions. For example, in other-oriented induction, the parent points out to the child the hardships his or her act could impose on other people.

inductive discipline See *induction*.

inductive reasoning The logical formulation of general principles to encompass sets of more specific propositions; in parenting — the use of *induction*.

infancy The period from birth until the acquisition of meaningful language; roughly the first two years of postnatal life.

infant mortality Death occurring during the first year of life.

infantile sexuality Freud's notion that sexual aims and urges are present in the *personality* from earliest childhood, though in a qualitatively different form from mature sexual motivation.

infatuation Early romantic attraction, sometimes dubbed 'puppy love'.

infertility The biological incapacity to conceive offspring. See also *voluntary childlessness; IVF*.

infidelity A married person's undertaking of a sexual relationship with someone other than his or her spouse.

inflection A change in word form to indicate certain grammatical relationships such as gender, past tense, plural, etc.

information processing Cognitive activity involved in the encoding, storage, retrieval and manipulating of ideas and concepts.

initiation ceremony (or *rite de passage*)   A religious ritual by which certain cultures mark an abrupt transition from childhood to adulthood.

innate birth defect   A problem that is due to *genes* or chromosomes but not strictly hereditary (e.g. abnormalities of chromosome number).

inner speech   In Vygotsky's theory, the covert use of language to aid reasoning.

insecure attachment   A child's anxious, resistant or ambivalent pattern of emotional connectedness with a *caregiver*.

institutions   Organisational living environments which specialise in caring for homogeneous groups of needy people (e.g. orphanages, hospitals and nursing homes for the elderly).

instrumental hedonism   Kohlberg's second stage of moral reasoning.

instrumental-relativist orientation   The second stage in Kohlberg's system of moral judgment, marked by belief in hedonistic reciprocity.

integration   A developmental process by which separate parts are brought together into unified, complex systems of organisation. See also *differentiation*.

integrity (or *ego integrity*)   In Erikson's theory, the final attainment of psychological development. It includes a sense of order, completeness, self-worth and an awareness of the meaning of one's own completed life cycle in relation to the wider scheme of things.

integrity crisis   The epigenetic stage in Erikson's theory that arises in old age and is devoted to a conflict between *integrity* and despair.

intelligence   A measure of mental ability, usually based on *IQ tests*.

intentionality   Buhler's term for the lifelong process of selecting, elaborating and assessing one's basic goals in life.

interaction   The non-additive contribution of two or more factors (such as *heredity* and *environment*) to a developmental outcome.

intercourse   *Coitus* or sexual intimacy involving penetration.

interdependence   A higher order of love in which concerns over equity are replaced by the drive for maximum joint profit for the couple.

inter-individual asynchrony   Differences in rate of physical growth between individuals of the same age.

internal working model   A component of *attachment* development involving unconscious expectations about availability of emotional support and affection in relationships.

internalisation of conscience   The process by which the child's respect for social rules and ethical values becomes self-directed, so that resistance to temptation no longer depends on surveillance or punishment by external authorities.

intimacy   In Erikson's theory, the mutual love and respect between partners who both possess a mature *identity*; closeness and mutual *self-disclosure*.

intra-individual asynchrony   Variations in growth rates of different parts of one individual's body.

introversion   A personality pattern characterised by preference for solitude and contemplation. See *extraversion*.

intuitive projective faith   A *preoperational* concept of religion.

invulnerable   Garmezy's term for an individual who displays exceptional *resilience* and effective coping in the face of problems that could upset the course of normal development in others.

IQ score   A measure of mental ability based on a standardised test.

IQ tests   Various tests which enable the calculation of an 'intelligence quotient' or IQ. Among the most commonly used are the tests developed by Wechsler, known as WAIS, WISC and WPPSI; they include a verbal component (word meaning) and a performance component (such as picture arrangement).

irritability   The quality of being easily aroused or excessively sensitive to mild stimulation.

isolation   In Erikson's theory, an unfavourable outcome to the crisis over intimacy. The isolated individual is unwilling to risk committing his or her *identity* to a mutual loving relationship with someone else.

isolette   An incubator which sustains the premature infant's life by aiding breathing and food intake and protecting him or her from infection.

IVF (in vitro fertilisation)   A treatment for *infertility* in which *ova* are removed surgically, fertilised with sperm outside the woman's body and then re-implanted.

jealousy   Resentment of a real or imagined rival for a lover's affections; a barometer of the jealous lover's insecurity according to Mead.

Klinefelter syndrome   A chromosome problem involving too many copies of the *X chromosome*.

labelling   A memory strategy involving verbal cues.

labour   The period in the birth process during which the *fetus* is moved through the birth canal by contractions of the *uterus*.

laissez-faire discipline   A child-rearing method in which parents place virtually no limits on their offspring's behaviour.

Lamaze method   An approach to childbirth preparation involving breathing and relaxation exercises.

language-acquisition device (LAD)   A theoretical *hypothesis*-testing mechanism, postulated by *nativist theories* of language development.

lanugo   Downy hair with which some *neonates* are covered at birth.

late maturer   An individual who reaches *puberty* at a much older age than the norm for his or her sex.

latency stage   The stage in Freud's theory between the *phallic* and *genital* stages, during which psychosexual development lies dormant.

lateralisation   The developmental process whereby specific sensory, motor and cognitive functions (e.g. language and handedness) become localised in the brain so that one *cerebral hemisphere* is more involved than the other.

launching phase   The stage in family life when adult children begin to move out of their parent's home.

learned helplessness   A psychologically debilitating feeling of powerlessness or apathy; may be acquired by curtailment of one's options or by the frustration of being unable to solve problems or master *contingencies*.

learning   Changes in behaviour resulting from experience.

Leboyer birth   The use of techniques such as warm baths and dim lights to minimise the *neonate*'s shock in making the transition from the womb to the outside world.

leisure   Time devoted to rest or recreation; often refers to that part of the adult life cycle which is not spent in paid employment. Colloquially, according to Comfort (1977, p. 130), it may be 'time in which you are expected to do trivial things for which you have to pay money'.

lexicon   One's mental dictionary, or store of word meanings.

libido   Freud's term for sexual drive and also, broadly, for the vital energy which motivates all human behaviour.

life cycle   See *lifespan*.

life events   Stressful happenings with implications for health.

life expectancy   The length of time, based on statistical average, a particular individual or group of similar individuals can be expected to live.

life review   A process, described by Butler, whereby the older person reminisces about his or her earlier life and endeavours to reorganise the self in preparation for dying.

life satisfaction   Overall feelings of pleasure or displeasure with one's current pattern of life.

lifespan   For an individual, the time between *conception* and *death*; in general, the course of human life from the *prenatal* period through to *old age*.

linguistic universals   Features of language which characterise all speech communities (e.g. the combination of subject and predicate to form sentences).

lipofuscin   Any one of a group of fatty substances which build up in nerve cells and other parts of the body over age and give rise to a yellow pigmentation. At present, they seem more important as a symptom of *ageing* than as a cause for declines in cell functioning.

living will   A document prepared by a person while in sound health to explain his or her preferences for terminal care in the event of being rendered incapable of making these known at the time.

locomotion   Moving from one place to another (e.g. crawling and creeping are forms of locomotion which precede another form, walking).

longevity   The chronological duration of life.

longitudinal study   A developmental research design in which individuals are retested at regular intervals as they age. See also *cross-sectional study*.

look–say A strategy for teaching reading, based on recognition of whole words.

love withdrawal A mode of discipline in which a parent's expression of affection for the child is made contingent upon the child's good behaviour. See also *induction* and *power assertion*.

ludic symbol Piaget's term for pretending, or the use of one item to represent another in the context of a playful game (e.g. a clothes peg for a person).

maintenance activities Basic survival skills and routines, including feeding, sleeping and elimination.

make-believe Dramatic play which involves pretending, or the use of *ludic symbols*.

mandatory retirement A legal upper age limit on employability.

Maori A New Zealander of indigenous Polynesian descent.

mastery orientation Converse of helplessness; effective drive to achieve in the face of challenge.

materialistic goals Atchley's term for values and ambitions centred around income and social status.

maternal deprivation The baby's lack of the opportunity to become involved on a close one-to-one basis with the biological mother or a mother-substitute.

mateship An adult masculine sex-role ideology characterised by the sharing of leisure interests with male companions in preference to family.

maturation Growth process which is relatively independent of environmental factors.

mature love Affection between adults which is founded on *autonomy*, a secure sense of *identity* and mutual respect.

maturity The state of being fully developed.

mechanistic model An analogy that equates psychological development with the assembly of a complex machine from a set of simple component parts.

mediation A process assumed to intervene between external stimuli and responses; in Kendler and Kendler's theory, a symbolic representational response and its covert feedback cue (e.g. the concept, or verbal label, 'food' mediates between perception of an edible item and taking a bite of it).

meiosis A special process of cell division in the *gametes* which produces *sperm* and egg cells, each containing only 23 unpaired *chromosomes*.

memorisation Committing information to storage in memory. See also *mnemonic*.

memory span The amount of material that can be held in memory at a given time.

menarche The onset of *menstruation* (or monthly periods) in adolescent girls.

mendelian inheritance The biological transmission of parental characteristics to offspring by means of a single pair of genes.

menopause A process that occurs in women at mid-life and includes the cessation of monthly periods, changes in hormone balance and the loss of fertility.

menstruation The periodic discharge of blood and uterine lining among women of reproductive age.

mental retardation Intellectual ability which is significantly below average.

mentor A guide or teacher; often a senior member of the employing organisation who takes responsibility for career development of junior workers.

mesoderm The layer of cells in the *embryo* from which the muscles, bone structure and circulatory system will develop.

metacognitive awareness An ability to reflect on the goals, organisation and implementation of one's own cognitive processing (e.g. a skilled reader's awareness that the super-ordinate goal of reading is to extract meaning from print).

metamemory What a person knows about the phenomenon of memory and about how to remember effectively.

metapelet A substitute mother in charge of care for infants and children in Israeli kibbutzim.

miai An arranged betrothal in traditional Japan.

mid-career crisis A period of self-critical stocktaking and reorientation of vocational aims and ambitions.

mid-career transition See *mid-career crisis*.

middle age The phase of adult life which follows *early adulthood* and precedes *old age*. The *chronological age* limits are relatively arbitrary and subjective. Many adults see middle age as covering the late 40s through to the early 60s.

middle childhood The period (roughly) from ages eight to 12.

mid-life crisis A personal upheaval that occurs towards the beginning of *middle age* for some adults. It may involve a reorganisation of one's life goals and values.

mid-life transition See *mid-life crisis*.

mini-theory An explanatory account of a circumscribed aspect of *behaviour* or *development*.

miscarriage See *abortion*.

mnemonic A strategy or device to facilitate memory.

model A set of analogies or general assumptions which guide theory construction.

modelling Learning by observation or imitation of someone else.

moko A facial tattoo used in traditional Maori society to mark the achievement of a distinguished adult role.

Mongolism See *Down syndrome*.

monitoring Parental supervision of children's activities and whereabouts.

monozygotic twins Twins formed when a single fertilised *ovum* divides into two and develops into two separate individuals. Unlike dizygotic (or *fraternal*) twins, monozygotic (or identical) twins have the same *genotype*.

mood quality The emotional tone of an individual's habitual manner of reacting to people and experiences (e.g. cheerfulness or peevishness).

morality Standards of right and wrong; ethical values which relate to justice, fairness and human welfare.

morality of care Gilligan's term for moral reasoning based on nurturant concern for others, and compassion rather than blind justice.

moratorium In Erikson's theory, a prolongation of the *identity crisis* past *adolescence*. During the moratorium, a person's overt behaviour may suggest *identity diffusion*, but the crisis is in fact being worked on during this period, and the eventual outcome of the moratorium is a resolved sense of identity.

Moro reflex The response of the newborn infant to sudden loud sounds or loss of support. It involves throwing the arms out, drawing them back and crying.

motherese A special style of simplified speech which many mothers use when speaking to their infants and toddlers.

motivational expectancy The child's beliefs about which tasks require effort and which can be safely ignored. Such beliefs are acquired through *socialisation* and may vary from culture to culture.

motor co-ordination The control and interrelation of bodily movements.

motor skills Capabilities which involve muscular movement, control and coordination (e.g. reaching, grasping, throwing, skipping).

motor symbol A form of *symbolic representation* involving bodily movement.

multiple regression A statistical technique for teasing apart the separate contributions of individual variables in the context of multiple causality.

mutation A spontaneous alteration in the chemical structure of a gene producing unpredictable variations in inherited characteristics.

myelin The white fatty sheath around nerve fibres.

myelinisation The developmental process whereby neural fibres become coated with a fatty substance (*myelin*) that speeds neural transmission.

mythic literal faith Fowler's second stage in *faith development* corresponding to Piaget's *concrete operational stage*.

narcissism Anna Freud's term for the adolescent's unconscious conversion of affection for parents into self-centredness.

nativist theories Theoretical positions that stress the predominance of hereditary over experiential factors as causes for developmental change.

naturalistic observation A research technique which involves observing people in their natural habitat with minimal intrusion by the investigator.

negation In language, rules of *grammar* for converting an affirmative statement into an opposing denial or refusal. In Piaget's theory, a form of *reversibility*.

negative identity In Erikson's theory, the adolescent's adoption of an undesirable, inappropriate or antisocial self-definition when his or her favourable resolution of the *identity crisis* is thwarted.

negativism A pattern of intentional non-compliance seen frequently during *toddlerhood*.

neglected peer status (or *social isolation*) The *sociometric classification* for children who are not nominated as either 'liked' or 'disliked', but are simply ignored.

neonate A newborn *infant*.

neuron Nerve cells in the brain and body that transmit information as electrical impulses.

non-normative influences Factors affecting development that are unpredicted and not regularly associated with age.

normative description An account of the average or typical behaviour of a group of people of a particular age.

normative social clock See *social clock*.

NREM sleep The stages in the sleep cycle which are not characterised by *REMs* (rapid eye movements) and not normally thought to include dreaming.

nuclear family A family unit comprising a mother, a father and their dependant children.

numeracy Understanding of number and mathematical processes.

nurturance The quality of offering comfort, care and sustenance to needy or dependant individuals.

obesity Weight in excess of the ideal or average, often defined as 20% or more over the average weight for a given height, age and sex.

object permanence The notion that an object which is out of sight and hearing continues to exist.

observational learning See *modelling*.

occupational socialisation The shaping of a worker's attitudes and behaviour by the demands of his or her job.

octogenarian A person aged between 80 and 90 years.

Oedipal conflict A psychoanalytic term for the boy's unconscious *phallic stage* conflict concerning his sexual attraction towards his mother. See also *Electra conflict*.

old age The age period which succeeds *middle age*; often thought to begin after age 65, although there is no universally accepted chronological age limit. Recently, the term 'young-old' has been used to describe individuals over age 60 or 65 who remain fit, healthy and active.

old-old Elderly adults who have begun to show signs of physical frailty and age-related decline (see *young-old*).

ontogenetic change See *age change*.

operant conditioning Learning which takes place as a result of direct *reinforcement* of the desired behaviour.

operating procedures Inbuilt strategies for testing the rules of *grammar* as postulated by *nativist theories* of language acquisition.

optimisation The practical application of knowledge about development to enhance the welfare, well-being and opportunities of all growing human beings.

oral stage The first stage in Freud's system of psychosexual development. Pleasures and concerns are thought to be centred around oral gratifications, such as eating.

organic model An analogy which equates the development of human behaviour with the life cycle of a plant.

organisation A memorisation technique that consists of grouping items together into memorable categories.

orgasm The climax of sexual excitement during *coitus*.

originality The uniqueness of answers given on a *creativity test*.

osteoporosis A degenerative change to the bones making them vulnerable to fracture.

otoliths Small calcite crystals in the inner ear which assist the vestibular senses of posture and balance.

ova Plural of *ovum*.

ovaries The female *gonads*, which contain the *ova*.

overextension In language acquisition, the young child's tendency to confer a broader meaning upon a word than is normal in mature speech (e.g. calling all men 'Daddy').

overgeneralisation See *overextension*.

overregularisation A too-inclusive application of a grammatical rule, which fails to take account of exceptions or irregularities in the language (e.g. 'my foots' instead of 'my feet').

ovum The *gamete*, or reproductive cell of the human female. *Ova* are present in the *ovaries* from the time of a girl's birth and are ordinarily shed singly at roughly monthly intervals between *menarche* and *menopause*.

Pakeha A New Zealander of Anglo descent.

parallel marriage Traditional sex-role stereotype marriage patterns.

parental imperative The directing role exerted by parenthood over men's and women's *sex roles* and life activity.

parroting The act of repeating a spoken utterance, or *decoding* a written phrase, without comprehending its meaning.

participant observation A research technique in which the researcher joins the group he or she is studying.

passion See *passionate love*.

passionate love The first stage in a love affair, usually marked by intense emotional arousal and rarely lasting for more than a few months.

passive-congenial marriage A style of mature couplehood in which amicable relations are maintained without great intensity of feeling or extensive mutual involvement.

paternal deprivation The baby's lack of the opportunity to become involved on a close one-to-one basis with the biological father or a father-substitute.

peer pressure Attempts to influence an individual, made by a group of age-mates.

peers Unrelated individuals of about the same *chronological age*.

performance IQ A subscale of Wechsler's intelligence test assessing non-linguistic abilities (e.g. the completion of a geometric puzzle).

person permanence The infant's awareness that key people (e.g. the mother) continue to exist even when they are out of sight and earshot.

personal agency See *self-efficacy*.

personal construct A person's theory about self and the world.

personal control The responsiveness of the *environment* to influence by the individual.

personal fable The adolescent's egocentric fantasy of personal greatness and a charmed existence.

personal goals Atchley's term for values and ambitions centred around humanistic concerns, such as honesty and *generosity*.

personality The sum total of an individual's characteristic dispositional patterns and distinctive modes of behaviour.

personality convergence Spouses' characters growing more alike the longer the marriage lasts.

perspective taking The ability to cognitively shift vantage points and see situations from a variety of opposing points of view.

phallic stage The third stage in Freud's developmental theory. Pleasures and concerns shift to the genital region and the *Oedipal conflict* arises.

phenotype The observed characteristics of an individual. In contrast to the *genotype*, the phenotype is influenced by *environment* as well as *heredity*.

phenylketonuria (PKU) A disease caused by a pair of *recessive genes*, resulting in the body's inability to metabolise certain food substances. Mental retardation may result unless PKU is detected early and treated through dietary intervention.

pheromones Odourous chemical compounds secreted by humans and animals that affect the behaviour of other members of their species.

phoneme The simplest sound units in spoken language.

phonics A strategy for teaching reading which involves breaking words down into their component consonant and vowel sounds.

phonological awareness The awareness of sound patterns of spoken and written languages.

physical skills Abilities involving bodily movement, strength and coordination.

pictograph A symbolic style of drawing by a young child of about three to six years. Pictographs convey meaning without seeming to strive for photographic realism.

pivot grammar A rule for the construction of two-word sentences; it involves pairing a word of the pivot class with a word from the non-pivot (or open) portion of the child's vocabulary.

placenta The organ that forms between the unborn child and the wall of the *uterus* during the *embryonic* stage of *prenatal* development, through which fetal nourishment is provided and waste products are eliminated.

plasticity In neurobiological development, the capacity of brain cells to respond flexibly to experience and to recover function after brain injury or cell death.

polygenic inheritance Characteristics which are influenced by several separate pairs of *genes*.

popular peer status The *sociometric classification* for children who earn many 'like' nominations and are rarely (or never) chosen as 'disliked'.

popularity   The extent to which an individual is favoured by others as a social companion.

postnatal   Refers to the period after the *infant* is born.

power assertion   Methods of discipline in which parents manage children by a show of force (e.g. spanking or confinement to a bedroom as punishment for misdeeds).

pragmatism   An approach to romantic love characterised by openness to opportunity.

pregnancy   The period between *conception* and giving birth to a baby; the state of carrying a *fetus* in the womb.

prematurity   Babies born more than three weeks before term and weighing less than 2500 grams.

premoral level   Kohlberg's first level of moral reasoning.

prenatal   Pertaining to the period between *conception* and the birth of the baby, some nine months later.

preoperational stage   The stage in Piaget's theory which follows the *sensorimotor* period and precedes the acquisition of *concrete operations*.

prerequisite skill   An initial step in a developmental sequence which is essential to further progress through the sequence.

presbyopia   An age-related degenerative disease of the eye marked by hardening of the lens and consequent difficulties with detailed vision.

prescriptive grammar   A set of rules correcting popular linguistic usage or ordaining how people ought to speak (e.g. 'Don't say ain't').

pretence   *symbolic representation* expressed through play or fantasy.

primary caregiver   The person who assumes major responsibility for the day-to-day tending of an infant's basic needs. See also *secondary caregiver*.

primary memory   Immediate memory for information recently received by the sense organs and still the focus of conscious attention.

prime of life   The period of the *lifespan* when one's abilities and pleasures are optimal.

principled level   Principled morality. See *principled orientation*.

principled orientation   The highest level in Kohlberg's system of moral judgment; marked by adherence to benefits and justice for the whole of society and self-chosen ethical rules.

proactive depression   Kübler-Ross's term for the grief which arises when a dying patient prepares to face the loss of everything and everyone he or she has loved.

problem contingency   The causal factor or action on which a solution to a problem depends (e.g. pressure on a response lever to yield a food pellet in a Skinner box apparatus).

problem solving   The cognitive act of perceiving a problem, attending to relevant information and consulting memory or a reasoning process for a solution.

production   The output of spoken sounds, words or manual signs.

progeria   An inherited recessive-gene disorder resulting in accelerated physiological ageing.

prosocial behaviour   Behaviour which has a favourable social impact (e.g. altruism, cooperation).

prosthetics   Artificial substitutes for damaged or deteriorating parts of the body (e.g. spectacles, dentures).

proximodistal growth   The tendency for growth and maturation to proceed from the centre of the body outward to the extremities.

pseudo-conversation   A dialogue between parent and child which conforms to the structural requirements of mature conversation without the customary exchange of meaning.

psychoanalysis   The method of treatment of mental illness based on Freudian theory.

psychoanalytic theory   The theory of *personality* development formulated by Freud and elaborated by followers, including Erikson and Jung.

psycholinguistics   The psychological study of language development and *grammar*.

psychopathology   Mental illness; serious emotional disturbance.

puberty   The biological growth changes of *adolescence*, culminating in reproductive maturity.

pubescence   The process of growing through *puberty*.

pubic hair   Hair emerging in the genital region after *puberty*.

punishment   An unpleasant event which decreases the likelihood of the behaviour it is consistently associated with.

punishment-obedience orientation   The first stage in Kohlberg's system of moral judgment, marked by the blind desire to escape negative sanctions.

qualitative change   The emergence of new characteristics which are radically different from those previously existing (e.g. the transformation from a caterpillar to a butterfly). See also *quantitative change*.

quantitative change   A change in the number or degree of some pre-existing characteristic (e.g. an increase in height). See also *qualitative change*.

racism   Bigotry, antagonism or prejudicial treatment of one racial group by another.

raising the ante   A language-teaching technique whereby the adult gradually escalates his/her demands for complete or grammatically complex utterances from the child.

rape   Forcing sexual intercourse on a person against their will.

reaction formation   A Freudian defence mechanism involving the substitution of directly opposite wishes for one's true wishes.

reaction time   The interval between the presentation of a stimulus and initiation of a response to it.

reactive depression   Kübler-Ross's term for the dying patient's grief over losses or hardships already suffered (such as the immobility or pain caused by the person's illness).

reading comprehension   The translation of written text into meaningful ideas.

reading prerequisites   Skills that are essential before learning to read.

realism   Piaget's term for the child's over-reliance on superficial, objective or visible features of an abstract or intangible concept.

recall   A method of testing memory which demands the reproduction of the memorised material. See also *recognition*.

reception   A term for the language-user's intake and processing of linguistic material.

recessive gene   The subordinate member of a single gene pair, which will only be expressed in a *phenotype* when combined with a recessive gene. See also *dominant gene*.

reciprocity   A give-and-take relationship where influence is mutual, as when parent and child each modify their own actions in response to the partner's reactions.

recognition   A method of testing memory which relies on the ability to identify memorised material when it is presented again. See also *recall*.

recuperative leisure   *Avocations* whose main purpose is to enhance fitness and provide respite from the demands of one's paid occupation.

reflectivity   A conceptual tempo characterised by slow thoughtfulness and the protracted evolution of various problem solutions. It may be associated with high levels of accuracy on tasks of moderate uncertainty when no time limit is imposed.

reflex responsivity   How readily and reliably an infant's inborn response patterns (e.g. the *rooting reflex* and the *grasp reflex*) can be elicited.

regression   Loss of a developed capacity as a result of illness, injury or other abnormality.

regression towards the mean   A tendency for scores to cluster more closely around the group average as sampling continues.

regulator genes   Units of *heredity* which govern the timing of genetic inheritance. See also *structural genes*.

reinforcement   A term used in learning theories to describe an event which changes the probability of behaviour it is associated with. Positive reinforcement (or reward) increases the likelihood of the associated response.

rejected peer status   The *sociometric classification* for children who earn many 'dislike' nominations and few (or no) 'like' votes.

reliability   The extent to which repeated measurements of the same phenomenon concur with one another.

REM sleep   A stage in the sleep cycle which is characterised by rapid movements of the eyelids and is thought to involve dreaming.

remote grandparent   Term for grandparents in name only who have little to do with their children's offspring. See also *distant-figure grandparent*.

reorganised personality   Neugarten's term for an exceptionally healthy personality pattern in which roles relinquished due to age are replaced by equally intense commitments to new social relationships.

representation   See *symbolic representation*.

resilience See *invulnerable*.

resistance to temptation An index of *internalised conscience* shown when an individual refrains from transgressing.

reticular formation A brain structure that is involved in the attention cycle from sleep through wakefulness to alert attentiveness (also known as 'reticular activating system' or RAS).

retirement The end of the employed portion of a person's life. 'Retirement' can describe the process of moving out of the work force, the phase in life during which a person who once worked no longer does so, or a legal policy. See also *mandatory retirement*.

retroactive interference The distortion of memory for earlier information by more recently memorised material.

reversal of affect Anna Freud's term for the adolescent's conversion of positive feelings for parents to their negative opposites.

reversibility A Piagetian term for the inversion or *negation* of an action or mental operation to return it to its original state.

Rh incompatibility The production of antibodies by the mother's Rh-negative blood, causing damage to the fetus's Rh-positive blood supply.

rhyme sensitivity A child's awareness of rhyming sound patterns.

rite de passage See *initiation ceremony*.

role conflict A state in which a person's various prescribed or self-appointed duties clash with one another (e.g. when being a docile, compliant wife is incompatible with also being the husband's assertive business partner).

role overload Occurs when people undertake more activities or duties than they have time to perform effectively.

role strain Difficulty in fulfilling the requirements of a role.

romantic love A passionate and often irrational attraction towards a member of the opposite sex.

rooting reflex An inborn behaviour pattern which causes *neonates* to turn the mouth towards a stroke on the cheek.

rubella German measles; can produce abnormalities in the unborn child if contracted by the mother during the first months of *pregnancy*.

sampling The choice of an appropriate group of people on whom to conduct a psychological investigation.

schema Piaget's term for a cognitive unit that coordinates related actions and perceptions.

schema discrepancy A mismatch between an observed *stimulus* and the mental template built up through exposure to similar stimuli in the past.

second career A switch to a completely different type of work at some point after having become established in an initial occupation.

secondary caregiver A person who assumes occasional responsibility for the care of an infant, either as an adjunct to, or as a temporary substitute for, the *primary caregiver*.

secondary circular reaction Piaget's term for infants' repetition of actions which they perceive as producing interesting and predictable outcomes.

secondary memory Long-term storage of information.

secondary sex characteristics Physical attributes which distinguish mature male from female bodies but are not involved directly in reproduction (e.g. facial hair; breasts).

secular change Historical changes which have an impact on behaviour and may therefore bias measurements made before and after the change (e.g. adolescents' attitudes to military service may vary from wartime to peacetime or with changing levels of employment).

secular trend A trend which shows up across a span of history. The term is most often used to describe the gradual hastening of the average time of onset of *puberty* across the past century.

secure attachment See *attachment classification*.

segmentation The use of pauses in spoken language (or spaces in written language) to divide sound sequences into discrete word units.

segmentation hypothesis The theory that work and leisure are totally separate spheres of activity with no uniform interrelationship.

selective attrition The loss of subjects from a research design in a manner likely to influence interpretation of the outcome.

self-actualisation The highest level of need in Maslow's theoretical hierarchy. It involves the expression of *creativity* and the realisation of the highest human talents and potentials.

self-concept The total pattern of ideas one has about oneself.

self-disclosure Communication of intensely personal information.

self-efficacy The individual's expectation of competency in a learning or problem-solving situation.

self-esteem A person's evaluative estimation of his or her self-worth.

self-regulation The ability to cope independently with changes in the *environment*. See also *autonomy*.

self-report A method of investigation in which the subjects supply their own accounts of phenomena of interest in face-to-face interviews or on written questionnaires.

senile brain diseases A group of degenerative disorders of the brain and nervous system which can become apparent after age 60 or 65. See e.g. *Alzheimer's disease; arteriosclerosis*.

sensation The reception of a *stimulus*.

sensitive period See *critical period*.

sensorimotor stage The first major period in Piaget's system. It spans the first two years of life and is characterised by the perfection of an infant's preverbal understanding of, and control over, his or her *environment*.

sequential designs See *sequential methodology*.

sequential methodology Complex research designs in which *cross-sectional, longitudinal* and *time-lag* information is pooled.

seriation A Piagetian task demanding the ordering of objects, qualities or events along a quantitative continuum (e.g. lining up a series of sticks from longest to shortest).

sex differences Observable contrasts between the average or typical performance of males and females.

sex education Teaching designed to acquaint children with basic information concerning sexual activity, *contraception* and reproduction.

sex-linked genes Genes which are carried on the X or Y *chromosomes*.

sex role A pattern of attitudes and behaviour distinguishing males from females within a particular culture.

sex-role development The acquisition of a *sex role*.

sex-role identity The individual's definition of himself or herself in relation to cultural expectations for masculinity and femininity.

sex-role polarisation Rigid separation of masculine from feminine role attributes.

sex-role stereotypes Generalised expectations about the appropriate behaviour of males and females, many of which are based on inaccurate knowledge or prejudice.

sex-role transcendence A stage in sex-role development in which the limitations of traditional conceptions of masculinity and femininity are discarded and the individual is free to create his or her own unique blend of masculine and feminine attributes.

sex stereotypes See *sex-role stereotypes*.

sex typing See *sex-role development*.

sexism Bigotry based on gender or prejudicial beliefs and practices that unfairly disadvantage either males or females.

sexual preference An individual's preference for romantic, sexual or relationship partners of their own or the opposite sex.

sexual revolution A marked change over time in sexual attitudes or behaviour.

shopping around A stage in Super's theory of career development, marked by job change and exploration of a variety of vocational possibilities.

sibling rivalry Conflict or competition among brothers and/or sisters in the same family.

sibling tutoring effect Cognitive gain through teaching a younger sibling.

SIDS (sudden infant death syndrome) A fatal breathing failure that strikes most often when infants aged one month to one year are asleep (also called *cot death* or 'crib death').

simulation A contrived experimental situation set up to duplicate certain crucial aspects of the natural *environment*, often used deliberately as a research tool.

singleton An only child; a child who grows up in a family without brothers or sisters.

slow-to-warm-up temperament A dispositional pattern involving withdrawal in response to new phenomena and very gradual acceptance of change.

small-for-dates birth An infant born on schedule but weighing less than 2500 grams.

social age peership The sharing of a common lifestyle by several adult generations in the same family.

social clock Society's expectations about the ages at which various life events like marriage or university entrance should occur.

social cognition Reasoning about social behaviour, others' thoughts, or the values and institutions of society.

social construction Youniss's term for the adolescent's dialectical negotiation of the emancipation process with parents through dialogue.

social-contract orientation The fifth stage in Kohlberg's system of moral judgment, marked by belief in the democratic process and the welfare of the majority.

social conventions Arbitrary rules which prescribe appropriate behaviour for a particular cultural group without appealing to *morality* or justice.

social gerontology The study of social factors and social adjustment in *old age*.

social isolate A child who is rarely or never included by peers on a *sociometric* scale of liking.

social isolation See *neglected peer status*.

socialisation The process of acquiring the values, roles and behaviour which all members of a given society are expected to possess.

social learning theory An explanation of development in terms of the learning principles of *modelling, imitation* and *internalisation*.

social reject A child who is frequently named by peers as someone they dislike.

socioeconomic status (SES) An individual's position on a continuum determined by income, education and occupational prestige.

sociometric measurement A method for measuring preference relationships within a social group.

solitary play Playing alone, physically apart from other children.

soothability The infant's readiness to be comforted when in distress.

spatial memory The ability to recall the position of objects in an array.

speech comprehension The hearer's ability to understand the words or sentences uttered by a speaker. See also *speech production*.

speech production The utterance of spoken language. See also *speech comprehension*.

sperm The male *gamete*, released into the *vagina* during *ejaculation*.

spermarche The boy's first *ejaculation* of *sperm*.

spina bifida A *congenital malformation* in which the spinal canal fails to close completely.

stage A phase or period in development during which particular behaviours differ qualitatively from those of other periods.

stagnation Erikson's term for an unfavourable outcome to the crisis over *generativity*, in which feelings of failure, apathy and disillusionment are dominant.

standards Evaluative reactions about appropriate behaviour for self and others.

STDs Sexually transmitted diseases; also known as VD, or *venereal disease*.

stereotypes Simple, rigid and often unrealistic concepts about the behaviour of individuals or particular groups of people, especially those stigmatised by prejudice (e.g. the stereotype that all Italians have violent tempers).

stimulus A property of the environment to which the organism is capable of reacting.

stimulus deprivation A situation devoid of varied, interesting or attention-getting sensory input, such as a bland nursery with no interesting people, objects or events.

strange situation A method developed by Ainsworth to measure the quality of an infant's *attachment* to a *caregiver*.

stranger anxiety Infants' fearful reaction to unfamiliar people; it normally peaks during the last quarter of the first year of life.

structural genes Units of *heredity* that govern the nature of inherited characteristics. See also *regulator genes*.

succourance-seeking personality Neugarten's term for an elderly personality pattern involving extreme dependency on other people.

superego Freud's term for the part of the unconscious *personality* which corresponds to the *conscience* and motivates conformity to the dictates of society.

superordinate concept A concept which encompasses several identifiable subclasses (e.g. 'flower' is a superordinate for 'roses', 'daisies' and 'violets').

superstition An irrational belief which defies the laws of physical causality.

surfactin A biochemical coating of the lungs that appears during the final weeks of prenatal development and assists breathing if birth is premature.

swaddling The practice of wrapping infants up tightly in bands of cloth which restrict the movements of the limbs.

symbolic grandmother Matriarchal figure whose involvement with her grandchildren is predicated on the teaching of proper behaviour.

symbolic play Play involving fantasy, imagination, representation or pretending.

symbolic representation The mental act of using something to stand for, or signify, something else (e.g. the child's use of the word 'bow-wow' to represent a dog's barking, or the mathematician's use of *x* to symbolise an unknown quantity).

symmetrical marriage See *egalitarian role allocation*.

synapse The juncture between nerve endings.

synaptic pruning The brain's selective discarding of unnecessary neural pathways.

syncretic See *syncretic reasoning*.

syncretic reasoning Reasoning which fails to take account of important logical distinctions.

syntax See *grammar*.

synthesis A developmental gain that results when a dialectical conflict is resolved by bringing the two poles of the initial contradiction into a higher-order integration.

syphilis An infectious *venereal disease* which, when untreated, may pass through three stages: (1) a hard sore at the point of inoculation; (2) lesions spreading over the skin and mucous membranes; and (3) disablement of bones, muscles and nerve tissue.

telegraphic grammar A set of rules for constructing sentences from major content words while omitting articles, inflections, prepositions, etc.

temperament Personal characteristics and behaviour dispositions which differentiate members of the same age group (e.g. cheerfulness, timidity, irritability).

teratogen Something which can damage the developing baby in the womb, giving rise to a birth defect.

terminal drop A decline in intellectual functioning during the final months of life.

terminal illness An illness which is anticipated to lead to *death* after a finite period of time.

testes The male sex glands which secrete *sperm*.

testosterone A male sex hormone involved in the maturation of the masculine reproductive system and male *secondary sex characteristics*.

thalidomide A sedative medication prescribed to pregnant women a generation or more ago as an antidote to morning sickness; subsequently implicated in severe birth defects.

theoretical model A simplified analogy which guides theory construction.

theory of mind The recognition that people's behaviour is guided by thoughts, feelings and beliefs that may not correspond directly to objective reality.

thesis In *dialectical reasoning* a proposition contradicted by the *antithesis*.

time-lag method The measurement of individuals of the same *chronological age* at different points in history (e.g. all five-year-olds entering kindergarten in 1960, 1970 and 1980).

time-of-test effect An influence on the behaviour or scores of a particular age group due to the historical era when the measurement was taken. Such influences may be mistaken for genuine *age change* when using the *longitudinal method*.

toddlerhood The years from age two to three or four.

total marriage A style of couplehood characterised by complete mutual involvement in one another's life activities and intense expressions of affection.

traditional role allocation A type of marriage in which the wife specialises in housekeeping and child care while the husband is the major breadwinner. See also *colleague role allocation* and *egalitarian role allocation*.

transductive reasoning Reasoning from one particular instance to another, rather than from the general to the particular (see *deductive reasoning*) or from the particular to the general (see *inductive reasoning*).

transfer   The influence of learning one task on the learning of other tasks.

transient exuberance   The rapid proliferation of neural interconnections early in development.

transitive inference   The logical co-ordination of discrete items in an ordered relationship, for example — if A > B and B > C, then A > C.

Turner syndrome   A *chromosome* problem involving an XO chromosome complement.

turning point   A change in the *environment* creating a challenge or demanding a new adjustment on the part of the individual.

ultrasound   The use of sound waves to provide a photographic image of the *fetus* inside the womb.

uncompromising   Anna Freud's term for a mode of adolescent personality development involving extreme rejection of normal social and physical comforts.

unemployment   The state of being unable to find paid employment.

universalising faith   Fowler's term for the highest stage in *faith development*.

uterus   The womb; the part of the mature female anatomy in which the *embryo* and *fetus* develop.

vagina   The canal in the female reproductive system which extends from the external opening of the genitalia back to the *cervix*.

validity   The extent to which a test measures what it purports to assess.

venereal disease   Any of several diseases transmitted by sexual contact (e.g. *gonorrhoea* and *syphilis*).

verbal IQ   A subscale of Wechsler's intelligence test that assesses various language-related abilities (e.g. word definition).

virgin   An individual with no previous experience of penetrative sexual intercourse.

visually directed reaching   The ability to use vision to co-ordinate the hand's aim for, and seizing of, a target object.

vital marriage   A style of marriage characterised by intense mutuality and enthusiasm for one another.

vocational life cycle   The sequence of events marking an individual's passage from career entry through to *retirement*.

vocational satisfaction   The pleasure workers derive from their job.

voluntary childlessness   A married couple's deliberate decision never to bear or rear offspring. See also *infertility*.

wanderlust   An intense desire to travel.

weaning   The process of withdrawing an infant from breast or bottle feeding by substituting food or another source of milk.

wear-and-tear theory   An explanation for the *ageing* process on the basis of the cumulative insults on the body of use and environmental stress.

Wechsler Adult Intelligence Scale (WAIS)   A commonly used *intelligence test* that provides summary scores for *verbal IQ* and *performance IQ*.

Werner's syndrome   See *progeria*.

Wernicke's area   A region in the left *cerebral hemisphere* that is involved in comprehension and interpretation of language.

widowhood   The period of time during which a woman remains unmarried following the death of her husband.

wisdom   A cognitive capacity, often emerging in old age, that combines rich knowledge with a keen pragmatic ability to give useful advice.

work values   Beliefs, attitudes and ideals related to one's occupation.

X chromosome   A sex-determining *chromosome*. When paired with itself (XX), the offspring is a female.

X-linked disease   Hereditary disorder carried by a *recessive gene* located on the X *chromosome* (e.g. haemophilia).

Y chromosome   A sex-determining *chromosome*. When paired with an X *chromosome* (XY), the offspring is a male.

young-old   Adults over 60 who are still physically and mentally fit and who may gravitate to middle-aged interests while resisting being considered 'old'.

zone of proximal development   Vygotsky's term for the region of potential growth lying between the child's capacity to perform a task with assistance and the capacity to perform the same task independently.

zygote   The single-celled organism resulting from the fertilisation of an *ovum* by a *sperm*.

REFERENCES

AARP. (1999). *AARP/Modern Maturity Sexuality Study*. Washington DC: AARP Public Policy Institute.

AARP. (2002). *Grandparenting Study*. Washington DC: AARP Public Policy Institute.

Abel, E. (1980). Fetal alcohol syndrome. *Psychological Bulletin, 87*, 29–50.

Abel, E. (1998). *Fetal alcohol syndrome*. New York: Plenum.

Abra, J. (1989). Changes in creativity with age: Explanations and further predictions. *International Journal of Aging and Human Development, 28*, 105–126.

Abrahams, B., Feldman, S. S., & Nash, S. C. (1978). Sex-role self-concept and sex-role attitudes: Enduring personality characteristics or adaptations to changing life situations? *Developmental Psychology, 14*, 393–400.

Achenbach, T. M. (1978). *Research in developmental psychology: Concepts, strategies, methods*. New York: Free Press.

Acredolo, L. P., & Goodwyn, S. W. (1990a). Sign language among hearing infants: The spontaneous development of symbolic gestures. In V. Volterra & C. J. Erting (Eds.), *From gesture to language in hearing and deaf children*. New York: Springer-Verlag.

Acredolo, L. P., & Goodwyn, S. W. (1990b). Sign language in babies: The significance of symbolic gesturing for understanding language development. In R. Vasta (Ed.), *Annals of Child Development* (Vol. 7). Greenwich, CT: JAI Press.

Adams, A. J., & Stone, T. H. (1977). Satisfaction of need for achievement in work and leisure time activities. *Journal of Vocational Behavior, 11*, 174–181.

Adams, G. R., & Jones, R. M. (1981). Imaginary audience behavior: A validation study. *Journal of Early Adolescence, 1*, 1–10.

Adelson, J. (1979). Adolescence and the generalization gap. *Psychology Today, 12*(9), 33–37.

Ahammer, I. (1973). Social learning theory as a framework for the study of adult personality. In P. B. Baltes & K. W. Schaie (Eds.), *Life-span developmental psychology: Personality and socialization*. New York: Academic Press.

Ahammer, I., & Baltes, P. (1972). Objective versus perceived age differences in personality: How do adolescents, adults and older people view themselves and each other? *Journal of Gerontology, 27*(1), 46–51.

Aiken, L. R. (1982). *Later life*. New York: Holt, Rinehart & Winston.

Ainsworth, M. D. S. (1973). The development of infant–mother attachment. In B. M. Caldwell & H. N. Ricciuti (Eds.), *Review of child development research* (Vol. 3): *Child development and social policy*. Chicago: University of Chicago Press.

Ainsworth, M. D. S. (1979). Infant–mother attachment. *American Psychologist, 34*(10), 932–937.

Ainsworth, M. D. S. (1983). Patterns of infant–mother attachment as related to maternal care. In D. Magnusson & V. Allen (Eds.), *Human development: An interactional perspective*. New York: Academic Press.

Akhtar, N., Carpenter, M., & Tomasello, M. (1996). The role of discourse novelty in early work learning. *Child Development, 67*, 635–645.

Aldous, J. (1978). *Family careers: Developmental change in families*. New York: Wiley.

Alexander, M., & Lester, D. (1972). Fear of death in parachute jumpers. *Perceptual and Motor Skills, 34*, 338.

Allen, E. (1992). Adolescent imaginary audience. Unpublished. Honours thesis, University of Queensland.

Almeida, D. (2002). Stress and age. *American Psychological Association Annual Meeting*. Chicago, August.

Altman, I., Vinsel, A., & Brown, B. (1981). Dialectic conceptions in social psychology: An application to social penetration and privacy regulation. *Advances in Experimental Social Psychology, 14*, 108–160.

Amato, P. (1987). *Children in Australian families*. Sydney: Prentice Hall.

Amato, P. R., & Keith, B. (1991). Parental divorce and the well-being of children: A meta-analysis. *Psychological Bulletin, 110*, 26–46.

Amato, P. R., & Ochiltree, G. (1986). Children becoming independent: An investigation of children's performance of practical life skills. *Australian Journal of Psychology, 38*, 59–68.

Ames, L. B. (1974). *Readings in human development*. Guildford, CT: Dushkin.

Ames, R. (1957). Physical maturing among boys as related to adult social behavior. *California Journal of Educational Research, 8*, 69–75.

Amundsen, D. W., & Diers, C. J. (1973). The age of menarche in Medieval Europe. *Human Biology, 45*, 363–370.

Anastasi, A. (1958). Heredity, environment, and the question 'How?' *Psychological Review, 65*, 197–208.

Anders, T. F., & Roffwarg, H. P. (1973). The effects of selective interruption and deprivation of sleep in the human newborn. *Developmental Psychobiology, 6*, 77–89.

Anderson, D. S., & Western, J. S. (1972). Professional socialisation. In F. J. Hunt (Ed.), *Socialisation in Australia*. Sydney: Angus & Robertson.

Anderson, R. E. (1965). Aging in Hiroshima atomic bomb survivors. *Archives of Pathology, 79*, 1–6.

Anderson, S. A., Russell, C. S., & Schumm, W. R. (1983). Perceived marital quality and family life-cycle categories: A further analysis. *Journal of Marriage and the Family, 46*, 127–139.

Anstey, K., Stankov, L., & Lords, S. (1993). Primary aging, secondary aging, and intelligence. *Psychology and Aging, 8*, 562–570.

Antill, J. K., Bussey, K., & Cunningham, J. D. (1985). Sex roles: A psychological perspective. In N. T. Feather (Ed.), *Australian psychology: Review of research*. Sydney: Allen & Unwin.

Antill, J. K., & Cotton, S. (1987). Self disclosure between husbands and wives: Its relationship to sex roles and marital happiness. *Australian Journal of Psychology, 39*, 11–24.

Apgar, V. (1953). A proposal for a new method of evaluation of the newborn infant. *Current Research in Anesthesia and Analgesia, 32*, 260–267.

Argyle, M. (1972). *The social psychology of work*. Ringwood, VIC: Penguin.

Argyle, M. (1986). Social behavior problems in adolescence. In R. K. Silbereisen (Ed.), *Development as action in context*. Berlin: Springer-Verlag.

Aries, P. (1962). *Centuries of childhood*. London: Jonathan Cape.

Arlin, P. K. (1990). Wisdom: The art of problem finding. In R. J. Sternberg (Ed.), *Wisdom. Its nature, origins, and development* (pp. 230–243). New York: Cambridge University Press.

Aro, H., & Taipale, V. (1987). The impact of timing of puberty on psychosomatic symptoms among fourteen- to sixteen-year-old Finnish girls. *Child Development, 58*, 261–268.

Aronfreed, J., & Paskal, V. (1965). Altruism, empathy, and the conditioning of positive affect. Unpublished manuscript, University of Pennsylvania.

Aronoff, C. (1974). Old age in prime time. *Journal of Communication*, Autumn, 86–89.

Asher, S., & Hymel, S. (1981). Children's social competence in peer relations: Sociometric and behavioral assessment. In J. D. Wine & M. D. Syme (Eds.), *Social competence*. New York: Guilford.

Asher, S. R., Renshaw, P. D., & Hymel, S. (1982). Peer relations and the development of social skills. In S. G. Moore (Ed.), *The young child: Reviews of research* (Vol. 3). Washington DC: National Association for the Education of Young Children.

Ashman, A., & Elkins, J. (1990). *Children helping children*. New York: Academic Press.

Aslin, R. N., Pisoni, D. B., & Jusczyk, P. W. (1983). Auditory development and speech perception in infancy. In M. M. Haith & J. J. Campos (Eds.), *Handbook of child psychology* (Vol. 2). *Infancy and developmental psychobiology*. New York: Wiley.

Astington, J. (2001). The future of theory of mind research. *Child Development, 72*, 685–687.

Astington, J., & Jenkins, J. M. (1999). A longitudinal study of the relation between language and theory-of-mind development. *Developmental Psychology, 35*(5), 1311–1320.

Atchley, R. C. (1972). *The social forces in later life: An introduction to social gerontology*. Belmont, CA: Wadsworth.

Atchley, R. C. (1975). The life course: Age grading and age-linked demands for decision-making. In N. Datan & L. H. Ginsberg (Eds.), *Life-span developmental psychology: Normative life crises*. New York: Academic Press.

Atchley, R. C. (1976). *The sociology of retirement*. Cambridge, MA: Schenkman.

Atchley, R. C. (1977). *The social forces in later life*. Belmont, CA: Wadsworth.

Au, T., Romo, L., & DeWitt, J. (1999). Considering children's folk biology in health education. In M. Siegal & C. Peterson (Eds.), *Children's understanding of biology and health*. New York: Cambridge University Press.

The Australian. Ageing nation (2002, April 8).

The Australian. Humans to get life for a century (2002, May 11).

The Australian. Chef's oodles of noodles (2002, May 11).

Australian Bureau of Statistics. (1993). *Statistics profile of young people*. Canberra: ABS.

Australian Bureau of Statistics. (1995). *The labour force*. Canberra: ABS.

Australian Bureau of Statistics. (1999). *Deaths: Australia*. Canberra: ABS.

Australian Bureau of Statistics. (2001). *Yearbook Australia 2001*. Canberra: ABS.

Australian Bureau of Statistics. (2002). *Yearbook Australia 2002*. Canberra: ABS.

Australian Institute of Health and Welfare (AIHW). (2002). *Residential aged care in Australia 2000–2001: A statistical overview*. AIHW cat. no. AGE 22. Canberra: AIHW (Aged Care Statistics Series no. 11).

Australian Psychological Society, Ltd. (1995). Guidelines relating to the reporting of childhood memories. *Bulletin of the Australian Psychological Society*, February.

Ausubel, D. P. (1958). *Theory and problems of child development*. New York: Grune & Stratton.

Avery, D., & Winokur, G. (1978). Suicide, attempted suicide, and relapse rates in depression. *Archives of General Psychiatry*, 27, 675–687.

Baer, D. M. (1973). The control of developmental process: Why wait? In J. R. Nesselroade & H. W. Reese (Eds.), *Life-span developmental psychology: Methodological issues*. New York: Academic Press.

Bailey, J. A. (1994). Phonological sensitivity in novice readers and nonreaders. *Journal of Experimental Child Psychology*, 58, 134–159.

Bakan, D. (1974). Adolescence in America: From idea to social fact. In A. E. Winder (Ed.), *Adolescence: Contemporary studies*. New York: Van Nostrand.

Baltes, P. B. (1979). On the potential and limits of child development: Life-span developmental perspectives. *Society for Research in Child Development Newsletter*, Summer.

Baltes, P. B. (1987). Theoretical propositions of life-span developmental psychology: On the dynamics between growth and decline. *Developmental Psychology*, 23, 611–626.

Baltes, P. B. (1989). The dynamics between growth and decline. *Contemporary Psychology*, 34, 983–984.

Baltes, P. B. (1993). The ageing mind: Potential and limits. *The Gerontologist*, 33, 580–594.

Baltes, P. B. (1997). On the incomplete architecture of human ontogenesis: Selection, optimization and compensation as foundations of developmental theory. *American Psychologist*, 52, 366–381.

Baltes, P. B. (2001). Lifespan developmental psychology. In N. Smelser & P. B. Baltes (Eds.), *International encyclopedia of the social and behavioural sciences*. Oxford: Elsevier Science.

Baltes, P. B., Lindenberger, U., & Staudinger, U. M. (1998). Life-span theory in developmental psychology. In R. M. Lerner (Ed.), *Handbook of child psychology* (5th ed.). New York: Academic Press.

Baltes, P. B., Reese, H. W., & Lipsitt, L. (1980). Life-span developmental psychology. *Annual review of psychology*, 31, 65–110.

Baltes, P. B., Reese, H. W., & Nesselroade, J. R. (1977). *Life-span developmental psychology: Introduction to research methods*. Monterey, CA: Brooks/Cole.

Baltes, P. B., & Schaie, K. W. (1973). On life-span developmental research paradigms: Retrospects and prospects. In P. B. Baltes & K. W. Schaie (Eds.), *Life-span developmental psychology: Personality and socialization*. New York: Academic Press.

Baltes, P. B., & Staudinger, U. M. (1996). *Interactive minds: Life-span perspectives on the social foundation of cognition*. New York: Cambridge University Press.

Baltes, P. B., Staudinger, U. M., & Lindenberger, U. (1999). Life-span psychology: Theory and application to intellectual functioning. *Annual Review of Psychology*, 50, 471–507.

Bandura, A. (1969). Social learning theory and identification processes. In D. A. Goslin (Ed.), *Handbook of socialization theory and research*. Chicago: Rand McNally.

Bandura, A. (1973). *Aggression: A social learning analysis*. Englewood Cliffs, NJ: Prentice Hall.

Bandura, A. (1986). *Social foundations of thought and action: A social cognitive theory*. Englewood Cliffs, NJ: Prentice-Hall.

Bandura, A. (1989). Social cognitive theory. In R. Vasta (Ed.), *Annals of Child Development*, 6, Greenwich, CT: JAI Press.

Bandura, A. (1997). *Self-efficacy: The exercise of control*. New York: Freeman.

Bandura, A., & Walters, R. H. (1963). *Social learning and personality development*. New York: Holt, Rinehart & Winston.

Bank, B. J., Biddle, B., Anderson, D. S., Hauge, R., Keats, D. M., Keats, J. A. et al. (1985). Comparative research on the social determinants of adolescent drinking. *Social Psychology Quarterly*, 48, 164–177.

Barak, B., Stern, B., & Gould, S. (1998). Ideal age concepts: An exploration. In M. Houston (Ed.), *Advances in consumer research* (Vol. 15, pp. 146–152). Ann Arbor, MI: Association for Consumer Research.

Barling, N., & Moore, S. (1990). Adolescents' attitudes towards AIDS precautions and intentions to use condoms. *Psychological Reports*, 59, 364.

Barnhart-Thomson, G., & Stacey, B. G. (1987). Nuclear war issues: Reaction of New Zealand adolescents. *New Zealand Family Physician*, 14, 60–63.

Baron-Cohen, S. (1995). *Mindblindness*. Cambridge, MA: MIT Press.

Baron-Cohen, S., Leslie, A. M., & Frith, U. (1985). Does the autistic child have a Theory of Mind? *Cognition*, 21, 37–46.

Barr, H., Stressguth, A., Darby, B., & Sampson, P. (1990). Prenatal exposure to alcohol, caffeine, tobacco and aspirin. *Developmental Psychology*, 26, 339–348.

Barresi, C. M. (1990). Ethnogerontology. In K. Ferrero (Ed.), *Gerontology: Perspectives and issues*. New York: Springer.

Barry, R. J. (1978). Development of sex-role stereotyping in rural Aboriginal children. *Psychological Reports*, 43, 412–414.

Bart, P. B. (1971). Depression in middle-aged women. In V. Gornick & B. K. Moran (Eds.), *Woman in sexist society: Studies in power and powerlessness*. New York: Basic Books.

Basseches, M. (1988). *Dialectical thinking and adult development*. Norwood, NJ: Ablex.

Bates, D. M. (1966). *The passing of the Aborigines: A lifetime spent among the natives of Australia*. London: John Murray Publishers Ltd.

Bates, E. (1999). On the nature of language. In R. Levi-Montalcini, D. Baltimore, R. Dulbecco, F. Jacob, E. Bizzi, P. Calissano & V. Volterra (Eds.), *The brain of homo sapiens*. Rome: Giovanni Trecanni.

Baumrind, D. (1971). Current patterns of parental authority. *Developmental Psychology Monographs*, 1, 1–103.

Baumrind, D. (1978). Parental disciplinary patterns and social competence in children. *Youth and Society*, 9(3), 239–267.

Baumrind, D. (1991). The influence of parenting style on adolescent competence and substance use. *Journal of Early Adolescence*, 11, 56–95.

Bavin, E. (1993). Socialisation in a Walpiri community. In M. Walski & C. Yallop (Eds.), *Language and culture in Aboriginal Australia*. Canberra: Aboriginal Studies Press.

Bayley, N. (1965). Research in child development: A longitudinal perspective. *Merrill-Palmer Quarterly*, 11, 183–208.

Bayley, N. (1993). *Bayley scales of infant development* (2nd ed.). New York: Psychology Corporation.

Bayley, N., & Oden, M. H. (1955). The maintenance of intellectual ability in gifted adults. *Journal of Gerontology*, 10, 91–107.

Beaglehole, R., Eyles, E., & Harding, W. (1978). Cigarette smoking habits, attitudes, and associated factors in adolescents. *New Zealand Medical Journal*, 87, 239–242.

Becker, H. S., & Strauss, A. L. (1968). Careers, personality, and adult socialization. In B. L. Neugarten (Ed.), *Middle age and aging. A reader in social psychology*. Chicago: University of Chicago Press.

Beckwith, J. B. (1973). The sudden infant death syndrome. *Current Problems in Pediatrics, 3,* 1–36.

Bell, D. (1980). *Desert politics.* New York: Praeger.

Bell, R. Q. (1968). A reinterpretation of the direction of effects in studies of socialization. *Psychological Review, 75,* 81–95.

Bell, R. Q. (1971). Stimulus control of parent or caretaker behavior by offspring. *Developmental Psychology, 4,* 63–72.

Bell, R. R. (1975). Significant roles among a sample of Australian women. *Australian and New Zealand Journal of Sociology, 11,* 2–12.

Bell, S. (1970). The development of the concept of object as related to infant–mother attachment. *Child Development, 41,* 291–311.

Belsky, J. (1988). The 'effects' of infant care reconsidered. *Early Childhood Research Quarterly, 3,* 235–272.

Belsky, J., & Steinberg, L. D. (1978). The effects of day care: A critical review. *Child Development, 49,* 929–949.

Bem, S. L. (1975). Androgyny versus the tight little lives of fluffy women and chesty men. *Psychology Today, 9*(4), 59–62.

Bem, S. L. (1983). Gender schema theory and its implications for child development: Raising gender aschematic children in a gender-schematic society. *Signs: Journal of Women in Culture and Society, 8,* 598–616.

Bem, S. L. (1987). Gender schema theory and the romantic tradition. In P. Shaver & C. Hendrick (Eds.), *Sex and gender.* London: Sage.

Bem, S. (1989). Genital knowledge and gender constancy in preschool children. *Child Development, 60,* 649–662.

Bennett, A., Hewson, D., Booker, E., & Holliday, R. (1985). Antenatal preparation and labor support in relation to birth outcomes. *Birth, 12,* 9–16.

Bergemen-Klackenberg, C. S., Plomin, R., McClearn, G., Pederson, N. L., & Friberg, L. T. (1988). Genotype-environment interaction in personality development: Identical twins reared apart. *Psychology and Aging, 3,* 399–406.

Berk, L. E. (2003). *Child development* (6th ed.). Boston, MA: Allyn & Bacon.

Bernard, J. (1972). *The future of marriage.* New York: World.

Bernard, J. (1975). Notes on changing life styles: 1970–74. *Journal of Marriage and the Family, 37,* 582–593.

Berndt, R. M., & Berndt, C. H. (1964). *The world of the first Australians.* Sydney: Ure Smith.

Berndt, T. J. (1979). Developmental changes in conformity to peers and parents. *Developmental Psychology, 15*(6), 608–616.

Berndt, T. J. (1982). The features and effects of friendship in early adolescence. *Child Development, 53,* 1447–1460.

Berzonsky, M. (1983). Adolescent research: A life span developmental perspective. *Human Development, 26,* 213–221.

Best, D. L., Williams, J. E., Cloud, J. M., Davies, S. W., Robertson, L. S., Edwards, J. R. et al. (1977). Development of sex-trait stereotypes among young children in the United States, England, and Ireland. *Child Development, 48,* 1375–1384.

Bethune, N., & Ballard, K. D. (1986). Interviews with 50 young job seekers on their experience of unemployment. *New Zealand Journal of Educational Studies, 21,* 133–144.

Bettleheim, B. (1969). *The children of the dream.* New York: Macmillan.

Beyene, Y. (1989). *From menarche to menopause: Reproductive lives of peasant women living in two cultures.* Albany: State University of New York Press.

Beyene, Y. (1992). Menopause: A biocultural event. In A. J. Dann & L. L. Lewis (Eds.), *Menstrual health in women's lives.* Urbana, IL: University of Illinois Press.

Bigler, R. S., & Liben, L. S. (1990). The role of attitudes and interventions in gender-schematic processing. *Child Development, 61,* 1440–1452.

Bingham, C. R., & Crockett, L. J. (1996). Longitudinal adjustment patterns of boys and girls experiencing early, middle and later sexual intercourse. *Developmental Psychology, 32,* 647–658.

Birdwhistell, M. (1971). Adolescents and the pill culture. In M. Powell & A. H. Frerichs (Eds.), *Readings in adolescent psychology.* Minneapolis, MN: Burgess.

Birns, B., Blank, M., & Bridger, W. H. (1966). The effectiveness of various soothing techniques on human neonates. *Psychosomatic Medicine. 28,* 316–322.

Birren, J. E. (1964). *The psychology of aging.* Englewood Cliffs, NJ: Prentice Hall.

Birren, J. E., & Birren, B. A. (1990). Concepts, models and examples. In J. E. Birren & K. W. Schaie (Eds.), *Handbook of ageing.* New York: Academic Press.

Birren, J. E., Butler, R. N., Greenhouse, S. W., Sokoloff, L., & Yarrow, M. R. (Eds.). (1963). *Human aging: A biological and behavioral study.* Pub. No. (HSM). 71–9051. Washington, DC: US Government Printing Office.

Bischof, L. J. (1976). *Adult psychology.* New York: Harper & Row.

Blackwelder, D. E., & Passman, R. (1986). Grandmothers' and mothers' disciplining in three-generation families: The role of social responsibility in rewarding and punishing grandchildren. *Journal of Personality and Social Psychology, 50,* 80–86.

Blakemore, J. E. O. (1981). Age and sex differences in interaction with a human infant. *Child Development, 52,* 386–388.

Blieszner, R. (1981). Social relationships and life satisfaction in late adulthood. Paper presented at XII International Congress of Gerontology, Hamburg, July.

Block, J. in collaboration with N. Haan. (1971). *Lives through time.* Berkeley, CA: Bancroft Books.

Block, J. H. (1973). Conceptions of sex role. *American Psychologist, 28,* 512–526.

Block, V. L. (1937). Conflicts of adolescents with their mothers. *Journal of Abnormal and Social Psychology, 32,* 192–206.

Blood, R. (1967). *Love-match and arranged marriage.* New York: Free Press.

Bloom, L. (1970). *Language development.* Cambridge, MA: MIT Press.

Bloom, L., Hood, L., & Lightbown, P. (1974). Imitation in language development: If, when, and why? *Cognitive Development, 6,* 380–420.

Bocknek, G. (1976). A developmental approach to counseling adults. *Counseling Psychologist, 6,* 37–40.

Bodmer, W. F., & Cavalli-Sforza, L. L. (1970). Intelligence and race. *Scientific American, 223*(4), 19–30.

Bok, S. (1978). *Lying: Moral choices in public and private life.* Sussex, UK: Harvester Press.

Boldizar, J. P. (1991). Assessing sex typing and androgyny in children: The children's sex role inventory. *Developmental Psychology, 27,* 505–515.

Bond, M. (1986). *The psychology of the Chinese people.* Hong Kong: Oxford University Press.

Bond, N., & McConkey, K. (2001). *Psychological science: An introduction.* Sydney: McGraw-Hill.

Boocock, R. M., & Trethewie, K. J. (1981). Body image and weight relationships in teenage girls. *Proceedings of the Nutrition Society of Australia, 6,* 166–167.

Bornstein, M. H. (1976). Infants are trichromats. *Journal of Experimental Child Psychology, 21,* 425–445.

Borrie, W. D., Smith, L. R., & Di lulio, O. B. (1978). *National Population Inquiry.* Canberra: Commonwealth of Australia.

Boswell, D. A. (1979). Metaphoric processing in the mature years. *Human Development, 22,* 373–384.

Botvin, G. J., & Murray, F. B. (1975). The efficacy of peer modeling and social conflict in the acquisition of conservation. *Child Development, 46,* 796–799.

Botwinick, J. (1967). *Cognitive processes in maturity and old age.* New York: Springer.

Botwinick, J. (1970). Geropsychology. *Annual Review of Psychology, 21,* 239–272.

Botwinick, J., & Storandt, M. (1974). *Memory, related functions, and age.* Springfield, IL: Charles C. Thomas.

Bouchard, T., Jr., Lykken, D. T., McGue, M., Segal, N. L., & Tellegen, A. (1990). Sources of human psychological differences: The Minnesota study of twins reared apart. *Science, 250,* 223–228.

Bouchard, T., & McGue, M. (1981). Familial studies of intelligence: A review. *Science, 212,* 1055–1059.

Bourliere, P. (1977). Cited in S. de Beauvoir, *Old age.* Ringwood, VIC: Penguin.

Bourne, E. (1978). The state of research on ego identity: A review and appraisal. *Journal of Youth and Adolescence, 7,* 223–351, 371–392.

Bowen, J. (1995). *The fabulous fifties.* Sydney: Angus and Robertson.

Bower, T. G. R. (1966). The visual world of infants. *Scientific American, 215.*

Bower, T. G. R. (1974). *Development in infancy.* San Francisco: W. H. Freeman.

Bower, T. G. R. (1977). A *primer of infant development.* San Francisco: W. H. Freeman.

Bowerman, C. E., & Kinch, J.W. (1959). Changes in family and peer orientation of children between the fourth and tenth grades. *Social Forces, 37*, 206–211.

Bowerman, M. (1973). *Early syntactic development: A cross-linguistic study with special reference to Finnish.* Cambridge, UK: Cambridge University Press.

Bowey, J. A. (1994). Phonological sensitivity in novice readers and non-readers. *Journal of Experimental Child Psychology, 58*, 134–159.

Bowey, J. A., Cain, M. T., & Ryan, S. (1992). A reading-level design study of psychological skills underlying fourth-grade children's word reading difficulties. *Child Development, 63*, 999–1011.

Bowlby, J. (1973). *Attachment and loss* (Vol. 2). London: Hogarth Press.

Bowlby, J. (1982). *Attachment and loss* (Vol. 1): *Attachment* (2nd ed.) New York: Basic Books.

Boyd, D. R. (1986). The ought of is: Kohlberg at the interface between moral philosophy and developmental psychology. In S. Modgil & C. Modgil (Eds.), *Lawrence Kohlberg: Consensus and controversy,* London: The Falmer Press.

Brackbill, Y. (1979). Obstetrical medication and infant behavior. In J. D. Osofsky (Ed.), *Handbook of Infant Development,* 76–125. New York: Wiley.

Bradley, L., & Bryant, P. E. (1983). Categorizing sounds and learning to read: A causal connection. *Nature, 301*, 419–421.

Brain, D. J., & Maclay, I. (1968). A controlled study of mothers and children in hospital. *British Medical Journal, 1*, 278–280.

Braine, M. D. S. (1963). The ontogeny of English phrase structure: The first phase. *Language, 39*, 1–13.

Braine, M. D. S. (1976). Children's first word combinations. *Monographs of the Society for Research in Child Development, 41*(1).

Braithwaite, V. (1990). *Bound to care.* Sydney: Allen & Unwin.

Braungart, J. M., Fulker, D. W., & Plomin, R. (1992). Genetic mediation of the home environment during infancy: A sibling adoption study of the HOME. *Developmental Psychology, 28*, 1048–1055.

Braungart, J. M., Plomin, R., DeFries, J. C., & Fulker, D. W. (1992). Genetic influences on tester-rated infant temperament as assessed by Bayley's Infant Behaviour Record: Non-adoptive and adoptive siblings and twins. *Developmental Psychology, 28*, 40–47.

Brazelton, T. B. (1984). *Neonatal behavioural assessment scale.* Philadelphia, PA: Lippincott.

Brent, S. B., & Speece, M. W. (1993). 'Adult' conceptualization of irreversibility: Implications for the development of the concept of death. *Death Studies, 17*, 203–224.

Bretherton, I., & Waters, E. (1985). Growing points of attachment theory and research. *Monographs of the Society for Research in Child Development, 50*(209), 1–211.

Brewer, A., Cunningham, J. D., & Owen, J. (1982). Self esteem, sex roles and domestic labour in single-career and dual-career couples. *Australian Journal of Sex, Marriage and Family, 3*, 77–86.

Brittain, C. V. (1963). Adolescent choices and parent–peer cross-pressures. *American Sociological Review, 28*, 385–391.

Broderick, C. B. (1966). Sexual behavior among preadolescents. *Journal of Social Issues, 22*, 6–21.

Brody, A. M. (1998). Emily Kame Kngwarreye: Portraits from the inside. In M. Neale (Ed.), *Emily Kame Kngwarreye.* Brisbane: Queensland Art Gallery.

Brody, G. H. (1998). Sibling relationship quality: Its causes and consequences. *Annual Review of Psychology, 49*, 1–24.

Broerse, J., Peltola, C., & Crassini, B. (1983). Infants' reactions to perceptual paradox during mother–infant interaction. *Developmental Psychology, 19*, 310–316.

Bronfenbrenner, U. (1961). The changing American child: A speculative analysis. *Journal of Social Issues, 17*, 6–18.

Bronfenbrenner, U. (1966). Response to pressure from peers versus adults among Soviet and American school children. In *Social Factors in the Development of Personality,* 2–18. XVIII International Congress of Psychology, Symposium 35, Moscow.

Bronfenbrenner, U. (1967). Response to pressure from peers versus adults among Soviet and American school children. *International Journal of Psychology, 2*, 199–207.

Brook, J. (1986). Perceptions of employment and other life activities. *Australian Psychologist, 21*, 101–102.

Brook, J. S., Whiteman, M., Gordon, A. S., Nomura, C., & Brook, D. W. (1986). Onset of adolescent drinking: A longitudinal study of intrapersonal and interpersonal antecedents. *Advances in Alcohol and Substance Abuse, 5*, 91–101.

Brooke, N. (1985). *Older people at home.* Canberra: Australian Government Publishing Service.

Brooks-Gunn, J., Han, W.-J., & Waldfogel, J. (2002). Maternal employment and child cognitive outcomes in the first three years of life: The NICHD study of early child care. *Child Development, 73*(4), 1052–1072.

Brooks-Gunn, J., & Matthews, W. S. (1979). *He and she: How children develop their sex-role identity.* Englewood Cliffs, NJ: Prentice Hall.

Brooks-Gunn, J., Petersen, A. C., & Eichorn, D. (1985). The study of maturational timing effects in adolescence. *Journal of Youth and Adolescence, 14*, 149–161.

Brown, C., Davey, J., & Halladay, A. (1986). Elderly consumers and social care policy. *Australian Journal of Social Issues, 21*, 299–311.

Brown, R. (1965). *Social psychology.* New York: Free Press.

Brown, R. (1973). *A first language: The early stages.* Cambridge, MA: Harvard University Press

Brown, R., & Bellugi, U. (1964). Three processes in the child's acquisition of syntax. *Harvard Educational Review, 34*, 133–151.

Brown, R., Cazden, C., & Bellugi-Klima, U. (1969). The child's grammar from I to III. In J. P. Hill (Ed.), *Minnesota symposium on child psychology* (Vol. 2). Minneapolis, MN: University of Minnesota Press.

Brubaker, T. H. (1985). Responsibility for household tasks: A look at golden anniversary couples. In W. A. Peterson & J. Quadagno (Eds.), *Social bonds in later life.* London: Sage.

Bruch, H. (1973). *Eating disorders: Obesity, anorexia nervosa, and the person within.* New York: Basic Books.

Bruner, J. (1983a). Formats and contexts. Paper presented at the Australian and New Zealand Association for the Advancement of Science. Perth.

Bruner, J. S. (1983b). The acquisition of pragmatic commitments. In R. M. Golinkoff (Ed.), *The transition from prelinguistic to linguistic communication* (pp. 27–42). Hillsdale, NJ: Erlbaum.

Brunswick, A. F., & Messeri, P. (1984). Causal factors in onset of adolescents' cigarette smoking: A prospective study of urban black youth. *The Addictive Behaviors, 2*, 35–52.

Bryan, J. H., & Schwartz, T. (1971). Effects of film material upon children's behavior. *Psychological Bulletin, 75*, 50–59.

Bryan, J. H., & Walbeck, N. H. (1970). The impact of words and deeds concerning altruism upon children. *Child Development, 41*, 747–757.

Bryant, P. E., & Goswami, U. (1987). The causes of children's reading. Invited lecture to IXth Biennial International Society for the Study of Behavioural Development Meetings, Tokyo.

Bryson, L. (1983). Thirty years of research on the division of labour in Australian families. *Australian Journal of Sex, Marriage and Family, 4*, 125–132.

Buchanan, C. M., Eccles, J. S., & Becker, J. B. (1992). Are adolescents the victims of raging hormones? Evidence for activational effects of hormones on moods and behaviour at adolescence. *Psychological Bulletin, 111*, 62–107.

Buhler, C. (1968). Introduction. In C. Buhler & F. Massarick (Eds.), *The course of human life: A study of goals in humanistic perspective.* New York: Springer.

Bulcroft, K., & Bulcroft, R. (1985). Dating and courtship in later life: An exploratory study. In W. A. Peterson & J. Quadagno (Eds.), *Social bonds in later life.* London: Sage.

Burnet, MacF. (1973). *Genes, dreams, and realities.* Harmondsworth, UK: Penguin.

Burns, A., & Goodnow, J. (1985). *Children and families in Australia.* Sydney: Allen & Unwin.

Burns, A., Homel, R., & Goodnow, J. J. (1984). Conditions of life and parental values. *Australian Journal of Psychology, 36*, 219–237.

Burton, L. M., & Bengston, V. L. (1985). Black grandmothers: Issues of timing and continuity of roles. In V. L. Bengston & J. F. Robertson (Eds.), *Grandparenthood* (pp. 61–78). Beverley Hills: Sage.

Bushnell, J. A., Wells, J. E., Hornblow, A. R., & Oakley-Browne, M. (1990). Prevalence of three bulimia syndromes in the general population. *Psychological Medicine, 20*(3), 671–680.

Buss, D. M., & 48 others. (1990). International preferences in selecting mates. *Journal of Cross-Cultural Psychology, 21*, 5–47.

Bussey, K. (1983). A social-cognitive appraisal of sex-role development. *Australian Journal of Psychology, 35*, 135–143.

Bussey, K. (1992). Lying and truthfulness: Children's definitions, standards, and evaluative reactions. *Child Development, 63*, 129–137.

Bussey, K., & Bandura, A. (1984). Influence of gender constancy and social power on sex-linked modeling. *Journal of Personality and Social Psychology, 47*, 1292–1302.

Bussey, K., & Bandura, A. (1992). Self-regulatory mechanisms governing gender development. *Child Development, 63*, 1236–1250.

Bussey, K., & Maughan, B. (1982). Gender differences in moral reasoning. *Journal of Personality and Social Psychology, 42*, 701–706.

Butler, N. (1974). Late postnatal consequences of fetal malnutrition. In M. Winick (Ed.), *Nutrition and fetal development*. New York: Wiley.

Butler, R. N. (1968). The life review: An interpretation of reminiscing in the aged. In B. L. Neugarten (Ed.), *Middle age and aging: A reader in social psychology*. Chicago: University of Chicago Press.

Butler, R. N. (1969). Ageism: Another form of bigotry. *Gerontologist, 9*(4), 243–246.

Butler, R. N. (1974). Successful aging and the role of the life review. *Journal of the American Geriatric Society, 22*, 529–535.

Butler, R. N. (1975). *Why survive? Being old in America*. New York: Harper & Row.

Butler, R. N., & Lewis, M. I. (1977). *Love and sex after sixty*. New York: Harper & Row.

Butterfield, E., & Siperstein, G. (1972). Influence of contingent auditory stimulation on non-nutritional suckle. In J. F. Bosma (Ed.), *Third Symposium on Oral Sensation and Perception: The mouth of the infant*. Springfield, IL: Charles C. Thomas.

Byrd, M., & Breuss, T. (1992). Perceptions of sociological and psychological age norms by young, middle-aged and elderly New Zealanders. *International Journal of Aging and Human Development, 34*, 145–163.

Byrne, D. G., Byrne, A. E., & Reinhart, M. I. (1993). Psychosocial correlates of adolescent cigarette smoking: Personality or environment. *Australian Journal of Psychology, 45*(2), 87–95.

Caffin, N. A., Binns, C. W., & Miller, M. R. (1981). Dietary patterns of Perth primary school children. *Proceedings of the Nutrition Society of Australia, 6*, 119–120.

Cain, L. D., Jr. (1964). Life course and social structure. In R. E. L. Faris (Ed.), *Handbook of modern sociology*. Chicago: Rand McNally.

Callan, V. J. (1980). The value and cost of children: Australian, Greek and Italian couples in Sydney, Australia. *Journal of Cross-Cultural Psychology, 11*, 482–497.

Callan, V. J. (1982). How do Australians value children? A review and research update using the perceptions of parents and voluntarily childless adults. *Australian and New Zealand Journal of Sociology, 18*, 384–399.

Callan, V. J. (1983). Factors affecting early and late deciders of voluntary childlessness. *Journal of Social Psychology, 119*, 261–268.

Cameron, R. J. (1980). *Social indicators No. 3*. Canberra: Australian Bureau of Statistics.

Cameron, R. J. (1992). *Social indicators Australia 1992*. Canberra: Australian Bureau of Statistics.

Canestrari, R. E. (1968). Age changes in acquisition. In G. A. Talland (Ed.), *Human aging and behavior*. New York: Academic Press.

Cantor, P. (1977). Suicide and attempted suicide among students: Problem prediction and prevention. In P. Cantor (Ed.), *Understanding a child's world*. New York: McGraw-Hill.

Carlsson-Paige, N., & Levin, D. E. (1985). Helping young children understand peace, war, and the nuclear threat. *Australian Journal of Early Childhood, 10*, 24–27.

Carr, D. H. (1970). Chromosome studies in selected spontaneous abortions. *Canadian Medical Association Journal, 103*, 343–348.

Carstensen, L. L. (1992). Social and emotional patterns in adulthood: Support for socioemotional selectivity theory. *Psychology and Ageing, 7*, 331–338.

Carstensen, L. L. (1995). Evidence for a life-span theory of socioemotional selectivity. *Current Directions in Psychological Science, 4*, 151–156.

Carstensen, L. L., Gottman, J. M., & Levenson, R. W. (1995). Emotional behaviour in long-term marriage. *Psychology and Ageing, 10*, 149–159.

Carstensen, L. L., Isaacowitz, D. M., & Charles, S. T. (1999). Taking time seriously: A theory of socioemotional selectivity. *American Psychologist, 54*, 165–181.

Cartwright, L. (1978). Career satisfaction and role harmony in a sample of young women physicians. *Journal of Vocational Behavior, 12*, 184–196.

Case, R. (1992). *The mind's staircase: Exploring the conceptual underpinnings of children's thought and knowledge*. Hillsdale, NJ: Erlbaum.

Cashmore, J. (1982). Parent–child agreement on attributional beliefs: Differences associated with ethnic background and gender of child. In T. G. Cross & L. M. Riach (Eds.), *Issues and research in child development*. Melbourne: Institute of Early Childhood Development.

Caspi, A., Lynam, D., Moffitt, T. E., & Silva, P. A. (1993). Unravelling girls' delinquency: Biological, dispositional, and contextual contributions to adolescent misbehaviour. *Developmental Psychology, 29*, 19–30.

Caspi, A., & Moffitt, T. E. (1991). Individual differences are accentuated during periods of social change: The sample case of girls at puberty. *Journal of Personality and Social Psychology, 61*(1), 157–168.

Caspi, A., & Silva, P. (1995). Temperamental qualities at age three predict personality traits in young adulthood: Longitudinal evidence from a birth cohort. *Child Development, 66*, 486–498.

Cath, S. H. (1975). The orchestration of disengagement. *International Journal of Aging and Human Development, 6*(3), 199–211.

Cazden, C. (1965). Environmental assistance to the child's acquisition of grammar. Unpublished doctoral dissertation, Graduate School of Education, Harvard University.

Centre for Education and Information on Drugs and Alcohol of the NSW Department of Health. (1986). *An Australian guide to drug issues*. Canberra: Australian Government Publishing Service.

Chalmers, D., & Lawrence, J. A. (1993). Investigating the effects of planning aids on adults' and adolescents' organisation of a complex task. *International Journal of Behavioral Development, 16*(2), 191–214.

Chapman, J. W. (1984). The self concept of Maori school pupils revisited: A critique of Ranby's study and some new data. *New Zealand Journal of Educational Studies, 19*, 45–54.

Chapman, J. W., & Nicholls, J. G. (1976). Occupational identity status, occupational preference and field dependence in Maori and Pakeha boys. *Journal of Cross-Cultural Psychology, 7*, 61–72.

Chapman, S., & Hodgson, J. (1988). Showers in raincoats: Attitudinal barriers to condom use in high-risk heterosexuals. *Community Health Studies, 12*, 97–105.

Chavkin, W. (1995). Substance abuse in pregnancy. In B. Sachs, R. Beard, E. Papiernik & C. Russell (Eds.), *Reproductive health care for women and babies*. Oxford: Oxford University Press.

Chen, X., Rubin, K., & Li, Z. (1995). Social functioning and adjustment in Chinese children: A longitudinal study. *Developmental Psychology, 28*, 484–490.

Chi, M. T. H. (1978). Knowledge structures and memory development. In R. S. Siegler (Ed.), *Children's thinking: What develops?* Hillsdale, NJ: Erlbaum.

Chiraboga, D. A. (1993). Stress. In R. Kastenbaum (Ed.), *Encyclopedia of adult development*. Phoenix, AZ: Oryx Press.

Chivian, E. & Goodman, J. (1984). What Soviet children are saying about nuclear war. *International Physicians for the Prevention of War Newsletter, 2*(1), 10–12.

Chomitz, V., Cheung, I., & Lieberman, E. (2000). The role of lifestyle in preventing low birthrate. In K. I. Freiberg (Ed.), *Human development*. Guilford, CT: McGraw-Hill.

Chomsky, N. (1967). The formal nature of language. In E. H. Lenneberg (Ed.), *Biological foundations of language*. New York: Wiley.

Christie, M. I. (1983). The ritual reader: Guiding principles for teaching reading to Aboriginal children. In D. Lapp (Ed.), *Teaching reading to every child*. New York: Macmillan.

Cicchetti, D., & Sroufe, L. A. (1976). The relationship between affective and cognitive development in Down's syndrome infants. *Child Development, 47*, 920–929.

Clark, E. V. (1978). Strategies for communicating. *Child Development, 49*(4), 953–959.

Clark, E. V. (1983). Meanings and concepts. In J. H. Flavell & E. M. Markman (Eds.), *Handbook of child psychology* (Vol. 3), *Cognitive development*. New York: Wiley.

Clark, H. H., & Clark, E. V. (1977). *Psychology and language: An introduction to psycholinguistics*. San Diego, CA: Harcourt Brace Jovanovich.

Clark, J. E., Lanphear, A. K., & Riddick, C. C. (1987). The effects of videogame playing on the response selection processing of elderly adults. *Journal of Gerontology, 42*(1), 82–85.

Clay, M. M. (1980). Engaging with the school system: A study of interactions in new entrant classrooms. *New Zealand Journal of Educational Studies, 20*, 20–38.

Clay, M. M. (1983). *Observing young readers*. Exeter, NH: Heinemann.

Clayton, V. P. (1975). Erikson's theory of human development as it applies to the aged: Wisdom as contradictive cognition. *Human Development, 18*, 119–128.

Clayton, V. P., & Birren, J. E. (1980). The development of wisdom across the lifespan: A reexamination of an ancient topic. In P. B. Baltes & O. G. Brim (Eds.), *Life-span development and behavior*. New York: Academic Press.

Clifford, A. (1968). *Send her down, Hughie! An Australian experience*. Adelaide: Rigby Ltd.

Clopton, N., & Sorrell, G. (1993). Gender differences in moral reasoning: Stable or situational? *Psychology of Women Quarterly, 17*, 85–101.

Clopton, W. (1973). Personality and career change. *Industrial Gerontology*, Spring, 9–17.

Coffey, C., & Cummings, J. (2000). *The American Psychiatric Press textbook of geriatric neuropsychiatry*. Washington DC: AP Press.

Cohen, G., & Faulkner, D. (1987). Life span changes in autobiographical memory. Technical Report No. 24, September. Human Cognition Research Laboratory, Milton Keynes, UK.

Cohen, L. B., DeLoache, J. S., & Strauss, M. S. (1979). Infant visual perception. In J. D. Osofsky (Ed.), *Handbook of infant development*. New York: Wiley.

Colby, A., & Kohlberg, L. (1987). *The measurement of moral judgment*. London: Cambridge University Press.

Colby, A., Kohlberg, L., Gibbs, J., & Lieberman, M. (1983). A longitudinal study of moral judgment. *Monographs of the Society for Research in Child Development, 49*, Serial No. 200.

Cole, M., & Cole, S. (2001). *The development of children* (4th ed.). New York: Worth.

Cole, M., Gay, J., Glick, J. A., & Sharp, D. W. (1971). *The cultural context of learning and thinking*. New York: Basic Books.

Coles, P., Sigman, M., & Chessel, K. (1977). Scanning strategies of children and adults. In G. Butterworth (Ed.), *The child's representation of the world*. New York: Plenum Press.

Collins, J. K. (Ed.). (1975). *Studies of the Australian adolescent*. Stanmore, NSW: Cassell.

Collins, J. K., & Harper, J. F. (1978). *The adolescent girl: An Australian analysis*. Stanmore, NSW: Cassell.

Collins, J. K., & Harper, J. F. (1985). Sexual behaviour and peer pressure in adolescent girls. *Australian Journal of Sex, Marriage and Family, 6*, 137–142.

Collis, F. (1991). Parents' and teachers' beliefs about adolescent sexuality and HIV/AIDS. Unpublished thesis. Melbourne University.

Comfort, A. (1970). Biological theories of aging. *Human Development, 13*, 127–139.

Comfort, A. (1977). *A good age*. North Sydney: Macmillan.

Comings, D., Muhleman, D., Johnson, J., & MacMurray, J. (2002). Parent–daughter transmission of the androgen receptor (AR) gene as an explanation of the effect of father absence on age of menarche. *Child Development, 73*, 1036–1042.

Condon, W. S., & Sandor, L. (1974). Synchrony demonstrated between movements of the neonate and adult speech. *Child Development, 45*, 456–462.

Condry, J., & Condry, S. (1976). Sex differences: A study of the eye of the beholder. *Child Development, 47*, 812–819.

Confucius. *Analects*. London: George Allen & Unwin, 1938.

Conger, J. J., & Petersen, A. C. (1984). *Adolescence and youth*. New York: Harper & Row.

Connell, W. F., Stroobant, R. E., Sinclair, K. E., Connell, R. W., & Rogers, K. W. (1975). *Twelve to 20: Studies of city youth*. Sydney: Hicks Smith.

Conner, K., Powers, E., & Bultena, G. (1979). Social interaction and life satisfaction: An empirical assessment of late-life patterns. *Journal of Gerontology, 34*, 116–121.

Coope, P. A., Gabb, D. C., MacDonald, G., Pears, R. K., Wells, J. E., & Woolfield, F. J. (1984). Age at menarche: A 1981–82 Christchurch sample. *New Zealand Family Physician*, Summer, 18–19.

Cooper, C. R., & Grotevant, H. D. (1987). Gender issues in the interface of family experience and adolescents' friendship and dating identity. *Journal of Youth and Adolescence, 16*(3), 247–263.

Cooper, C. R., Grotevant, H. D., & Condon, S. M. (1983). Individuality and connectedness in the family as a context for adolescent identity formation and role-taking skill. In H. D. Grotevant & C. R. Cooper (Eds.), *Adolescent development in the family*. San Francisco: Jossey-Bass.

Cooper, J., & Goethals, G. R. (1981). The self-concept and old age. In E. J. G. March (Ed.), *Aging: Social change*. New York: Academic Press.

Coopersmith, S. (1967). *The antecedents of self esteem*. San Francisco: W. H. Freeman.

Corah, N. L., Anthony, E. J., Painter, P., Stern, J. A., & Thurston, D. L. (1965). Effects of perinatal anoxia after seven years. *Psychological Monographs, 79*(3), whole No. 596.

Coren, S. (1989). Left-handedness and accident-related injury risk. *American Journal of Public Health, 79*, 1040–1041.

Coren, S., Porac, C., & Duncan, P. (1981). Lateral preference behaviours in preschool children and young adults. *Child Development, 52*, 443–450.

Covey, H. C. (1992). The definitions of the beginning of old age in history. *International Journal of Aging and Human Development, 34*, 325–337.

Cowgill, D. O., & Holmes, L. D. (Eds.). (1972). *Aging and modernization*. New York: Appleton-Century-Crofts.

Cowley, G. (2001). Generation XXL. In K. L. Frieberg (Ed.), *Human development 01/02* (29th ed., pp. 120–121). Guilford, CT: McGraw-Hill/Duskin.

Cowley, R. (1968). Rousseau: The toll collector's riddles. *Horizon, 10*, 30–43.

Cox, R. O. (1970). *Youth into maturity: A study of men and women in the first ten years after college*. New York: Mental Health Materials Center.

Craddock, A. (1980). The effect of incongruent marital role expectations upon couples' degree of goal-value consensus in the first year of marriage. *Australian Journal of Psychology, 32*, 117–125.

Craddock, A. E. (1983). Correlations between marital role expectations and relationship satisfaction among engaged couples. *Australian Journal of Sex, Marriage and Family, 4*, 33–46.

Craddock, A. E. (1991). Relationships between attitudinal similarity, couple structure, and couple satisfaction within married and de facto couples. *Australian Journal of Psychology, 43*, 11–16.

Crassini, B., & Broerse, J. (1980). Auditory-visual integration in neonates: A signal detection analysis. *Journal of Experimental Child Psychology, 29*, 144–155.

Crites, J. O. (1969). *Vocational psychology*. New York: McGraw-Hill.

Croake, J. W. (1969). Fears of children. *Human Development, 12*, 239–247.

Crook, T., & Elliot, J. (1980). Parental death during childhood and adult depression: A critical review of the literature. *Psychological Bulletin, 87*, 252–259.

Cross, T. G. (1978). Motherese: Its association with syntactic development in young children. In N. Waterson & C. Snow (Eds.), *The development of communication: Social and pragmatic factors in language acquisition*. London: Wiley.

Cross, T. G. (1981). Parental speech as primary linguistic data: Some complexities in the study of the effect of the input on language acquisition. In P. Dale & D. Ingram (Eds.), *Child language*. Baltimore: University Park Press.

Cross, T. G., Nienhugs, T. G., & Kirkman, M. (1983). Parent–child interaction with receptively disabled children: Some determinants of maternal speech style. In K. E. Nelson (Ed.), *Children's language* (Vol. 5). New York: Gardner Press.

Crouter, A. C., Manke, B. A., & McHale, S. M. (1995). The family context of gender intensification in early adolescence. *Child Development, 66*, 317–329.

Cuber, J. F., & Haroff, P. B. (1965). *Sex and the significant Americans.* Baltimore: Penguin.

Cumming, E. (1964). New thoughts on disengagement. In R. Kastenbaum (Ed.), *New thoughts on old age.* New York: Springer.

Cumming, E., & Henry, W. (1961). *Growing old: The process of disengagement.* New York: Basic Books.

Cunningham, A. S., Jelliffe, D. B., & Jeliffe, E. F. P. (1991). Breastfeeding and health in the 1980s: A global epidemiological review. *Journal of Pediatrics, 118*, 659–666.

Cunningham, C. J. (1987). The geography of children's play: Australian case studies. Paper presented to 56th Congress of the Australian and New Zealand Association for the Advancement of Science, Palmerston North, New Zealand.

Cunningham, J. (1990). Becoming men and women. In P. C. L. Heaven & V. J. Callan (Eds.), *Adolescence: An Australian Perspective.* Sydney: Harcourt Brace Jovanovich.

Cunningham, J. (2000). Diagnostic and therapeutic procedures among Australian hospital patients identified as Indigenous. *Medical Journal of Australia, 176*, 58–62.

Cunningham, J. D., & Antill, J. K. (1981). Love in developing relationships. In S. Duck & R. Gilmour (Eds.), *Personal relationships 2: Developing personal relationships.* New York: Academic Press.

Cunningham, J. D., & Antill, J. K. (1994). Cohabitation and marriage: Retrospective and predictive comparisons. *Journal of Social and Personal Relationships, 11*, 77–93.

Cutler, R. G. (1981). Life-span extension. In J. G. March (Ed.), *Aging: Biology and behavior.* New York: Academic Press.

Cutler, S. J., & Grams, A. E. (1988). Correlates of self-reported everyday memory problems. *Journal of Gerontology, 43*, 582–590.

Damon, W. (1975). Early conceptions of positive justice as related to the development of logical operations. *Child Development, 46*, 301–312.

Damon, W. (1988). *The moral child.* New York: Free Press.

Damon, W., & Hart, D. (1982). The development of self-understanding from infancy through adolescence. *Child Development, 53*, 831–857.

Damon, W., & Hart, D. (1988). *Self understanding in childhood and adolescence.* New York: Cambridge University Press.

Daniel, J. (1994). Learning to love growing old. *Psychology Today*, October.

Daniels, D., & Plomin, R. (1985). Origins of individual differences in infant shyness. *Developmental Psychology, 21*, 118–121.

Daniels, P., & Lachman, M. (1975). The prime of life. In F. Rebelsky (Ed.), *Life: The continuous process.* New York: Alfred A. Knopf.

Darling, C. A., & Hicks, M. W. (1982). Parental influence on adolescent sexuality: Implication for parents as educators. *Journal of Youth and Adolescence, 11*, 231–245.

Dasen, P. R. (1973). Piagetian research in Central Australia. In G. E. Kearney, P. R. de Lacey & G. R. Davidson (Eds.), *The psychology of Aboriginal Australians.* Sydney: Wiley.

Datan, N., Rodeheaver, D., & Hughes, F. (1987). Adult development and ageing. *Annual Review of Psychology, 38*, 153–180.

D'Augelli, J. F. & D'Augelli, A. R. (1977). Moral reasoning and premarital sexual behavior: Toward reasoning about relationships. *Journal of Social Issues, 33*, 46–66.

Davis, A. (1992). Suicidal behaviour among adolescents: Its nature and prevention. In R. Kosky, H. S. Eshkevari & G. Kneebone (Eds.), *Breaking out: challenges in adolescent mental health in Australia* (pp. 89–103). Canberra: Australian Government Publishing Service.

Davis, D. M. (1990). Portrayals of women in prime-time network television: Some demographic characteristics. *Sex Roles, 23*(5–6), 325–332.

Day, K. C., & Day, H. D. (1984). Kindergarten knowledge of print conventions and later school achievement: A five-year follow-up. *Psychology in the Schools, 21*, 393–396.

de Beauvoir, S. (1963). *Memoirs of a dutiful daughter.* Ringwood, VIC: Penguin.

de Beauvoir, S. (1965). *The prime of life.* Ringwood, VIC: Penguin.

de Beauvoir, S. (1968). *Force of circumstance.* London: André Deutsch.

de Beauvoir, S. (1969). *A very easy death.* Ringwood, VIC: Penguin.

de Beauvoir, S. (1975). *All said and done.* New York: Warner Books.

de Beauvoir, S. (1977). *Old age.* Ringwood, VIC: Penguin.

Debus, R. L. (1975). Modification of an impulsive tempo through modelling and training procedures. Unpublished manuscript, University of Sydney.

DeCasper, A.J., & Spence, M. J. (1986). Prenatal maternal speech influences newborns' perception of speech sounds. *Infant Behaviour and Development, 9*, 133–150.

DeFries, J. C., Plomin, R., & LaBuda, M. (1987). Genetic stability of cognitive development from childhood to adulthood. *Developmental Psychology, 23*, 4–12.

Dekaban, A. S., & Sadowsky, D. (1978) Changes in brain weights during the span of human life. *Annals of Neurology, 4*, 345–356.

De Lemos, L. W. (1969). The development of conservation in Aboriginal children. *International Journal of Psychology, 4*, 255–269.

De Lisi, R., & Staudt, J. (1980). Individual differences in college students' performance on formal operations tasks. *Journal of Applied Developmental Psychology, 1*, 163–174.

de Mause, L. (Ed.). (1976). *The History of Childhood.* London: Souvenir Press.

Dement, W. C. (1975). Studies on the function of rapid eye movement (paradoxical) sleep in human subjects. In M. Jouvet (Ed.), *7 Aspects Anatomo-fonctionnels de la Physiologie du Sommeil*, 571–611. Paris: Centre National de la Recherche Scientifique.

Demos, J., & Demos, V. (1972). Adolescence in historical perspective. In D. Rogers (Ed.), *Issues in adolescent psychology.* New York: Meredith.

Dentler, R. A., & Pineo, P. (1960). Sexual adjustment, marital adjustment and personal growth of husbands: A panel analysis. *Marriage and Family Living, 22*, 45–48.

Derbyshire, R. L. (1968). Cited in J. Harris (1980), *Report No. 22, Educational Research and Development Council (Australia)*, 15.

Deutsch, M. (1975). Equity, equality and need: What determines which value will be used as the basis for distributive justice? *Journal of Social Issues, 31*, 137–149.

Deutscher, I. (1964). The quality of post-parental life. *Journal of Marriage and the Family, 26*(1), 263–268.

Deutscher, I. (1968). The quality of post-parental life. In B. L. Neugarten (Ed.), *Middle age and aging: A reader in social psychology.* Chicago: University of Chicago Press.

De Varon, T. (1972). Growing up. In J. Kagan & R. Coles (Eds.), *Twelve to sixteen: Early adolescence.* New York: W. W. Norton.

de Villiers, J., & de Villiers, P. (1999). Linguistic determinism and the understanding of false beliefs. In P. Mitchell & K. Riggs (Eds.), *Children's reasoning and the mind.* New York: Psychology Press.

De Vries, H. (1975). The physiology of exercise and aging. In D. Woodruff & J. Birren (Eds.), *Aging: Scientific perspectives and social issues.* New York: Van Nostrand.

DeVries, M. W. (2001). Culture, community and catastrophe: Issues in understanding communities under difficult conditions. In S. E. Hobfoll & M. W. DeVries (Eds.), *Extreme stress and communities: Impact and intervention.* New York: Kluwer Academic Publishers.

De Vries, R. (1969). Constancy of generic identity in the years three to six. *Monographs of the Society for Research in Child Development, 34*(3), Serial No. 127.

Dickens, M. (1978). *An open book.* Harmondsworth. UK: Penguin.

Dien, D. S. F. (1982). A Chinese perspective on Kohlberg's theory of moral development. *Developmental Review, 2*, 331–341.

Dietz, W., & Gortmaker, S. (1985). Do we fatten our children at the television set? *Pediatrics, 175*, 807–812.

Dimant, R. J., & Bearison, D. J. (1991). Development of formal reasoning during successive peer interactions. *Developmental Psychology, 27*(2), 277–284.

Dion, K. L., & Dion, K. K. (1973). Correlates of romantic love. *Journal of Consulting and Clinical Psychology, 41*.

Dizard, J. (1968). *Social change and the family*. Chicago: Community and Family Study Center, University of Chicago.

Dobkin, P., Tremblay, R., Masse, L., & Vitaro, F. (1995). Individual and peer characteristics in predicting boys' early onset of substance abuse. *Child Development, 66*, 1198–1214.

Dodge, K. A. (1983). Behavioral antecedents of peer social status. *Child Development, 54*, 1386–1399.

Dodge, K. (1994). Studying mechanisms in the cycle of violence. In C. Thompson & P. Cowas (Eds.), *Violence*. Oxford: Butterworths-Heinemann.

Doherty, N., & Feeney, J. (2003). An attachment perspective on adult sibling relationships. Paper presented at 32nd Annual Meeting of the Society of Australasian Social Psychologists. Bondi Beach, Sydney.

Dollard, J., Doob, L. W., Miller, N. E., Mowrer, O. H., Sears, R. R., Ford, C. S. et al. (1939). *Frustration and aggression*. New Haven, CT: Yale University Press.

Donaldson, M. (1978). *Children's minds*. Glasgow: Fontana/ Open Books.

Donelson, E., & Gullahorn, J. E. (1977). *Women: A psychological perspective*. New York: Wiley.

Donovan, R. J. and associates. (1978). *Survey of leisure activities, interests, opinions and concerns of pre-retired and retired*. Perth: Community Recreation Council of Western Australia.

Donovan, W., & Leavitt, L. (1985). Simulating conditions of learned helplessness: The effects of interventions and attributions. *Child Development, 56*, 594–603.

Doob, L. W. (1966). Eidetic imagery: A cross-cultural will-o'- the-wisp? *Journal of Psychology, 63*, 13–34.

Doty, R. L., Shaman, P., Applebaum, S. L., Bigerson, R., Sokorski, L., & Rosenberg, L. (1984). Smell identification and disability. *Science, 226*, 1441–1443.

Douvan, E., & Adelson, J. (1966). *The adolescent experience*. New York: Wiley.

Douvan, E., & Pleck, J. (1978). Separation as support. In R. Rapoport & R. N. Rapoport (Eds.), *Working Couples*. Brisbane: University of Queensland Press.

Drillien, C. M. (1970). The small-for-dates infant: Etiology and prognosis. *Pediatric Clinics of North America, 17*, 9–23.

Drinkwater, B. A. (1976). Visual memory skills of medium contact Aboriginal children. *Australian Journal of Psychology, 28*(1), 37–43.

Driscoll, R., Davis, K. E., & Lipetz, M. A. (1972). Parental interference and romantic love. *Journal of Personality and Social Psychology, 24*, 1–10.

Duberman, L. (1974). *Marriage and its alternatives*. New York: Praeger.

Duck, S. (1973). *Personal relationships and personal constructs: A study of friendship formation*. New York: Wiley.

Duncan, B. L., Kraus, M. A., & Parks, M. B. (1986). Children's fears and nuclear war: A systems strategy for change. *Youth and Society, 18*, 28–43.

Dunkel-Schetter, C., & Wortman, C. B. (1981). Dilemmas of social support. In J. G. March (Ed.), *Aging: Social change*. New York: Academic Press.

Dunn, J. (1983). Sibling relationships in early childhood. *Child Development, 54*, 787–811.

Dunn, J. (1993). *Young children's close relationships: Beyond attachment*. Newbury Park, CA: Sage.

Dunn, J. (1994). Changing minds and changing relationships. In C. Lewis & P. Mitchel (Eds.), *Children's early understanding of mind: Origins and development* (pp. 297–310). Hove, UK: Erlbaum.

Dunn, J. (1996). Brothers and sisters in middle childhood and early adolescence: Continuity and change in individual differences. In G. H. Brody (Ed.), *Sibling relationships: Their causes and consequences*. Norwood, NJ: Ablex.

Dunn, J. (1999). Mindreading and social relationships. In M. Bennett (Ed.), *Developmental psychology: Achievements and prospects*. Philadelphia, PA: Psychology Press.

Dunn, J., & Kendrick, C. (1982). *Siblings: Love, envy, and understanding*. Cambridge, MA: Harvard University Press.

Dunne, M. P., Martin, N. G., Statham, D. J., Slutske, W. S., Dinwiddie, S. H., Bucholz, K. K. et al. (1997). Genetic and environmental contributions to variance in age at first sexual intercourse. *Psychological Science, 8*(3), 221–224.

Dunphy, D. C. (1969). *Cliques, crowds and gangs*. Melbourne: Cheshire.

Durkin, K. (1985). Television and sex role acquisition. *British Journal of Social Psychology, 24*, 101–113.

Durkin, K., & Akhtar, P. (1983). Sex roles and children's television: A report to the Independent Broadcasting Authority. Canterbury, UK: Social Psychology Research Unit.

Dutton, D. G., & Aron, A. P. (1974). Some evidence for heightened sexual arousal under conditions of high anxiety. *Journal of Personality and Social Psychology, 30*, 510–517.

Dweck, C. S. (1978). Achievement. In M. E. Lamb (Ed.), *Social and personality development*. New York: Holt, Rinehart & Winston.

Dweck, C. S. (1999). *Self theories: Their role in motivation, personality and development*. Philadelphia, PA: Psychology Press.

Dweck, C. S., Davidson, W., Nelson, S., & Enna, B. (1978). Sex differences in learned helplessness II: The contingencies of evaluative feedback in the classroom. *Developmental Psychology, 14*, 268–276.

Dwyer, J., & Mayer, J. (1968–69). Psychological effects of variations in physical appearance during adolescence. *Adolescence, 3*, 353–368.

Eccles (Parsons), J. (1983). Expectancies, values, and academic behaviors. In J. Spence (Ed.), *Achievement and achievement motives*. San Francisco: W. H. Freeman.

Eccles, J. S., Wigfield, A., & Schiefele, U. (1998). Motivation to succeed. In W. Damon (Series Ed.) & N. Eisenberg (Vol. Ed.), *Handbook of child psychology* (Vol. 3): *Social, emotional and personality development*. New York: Wiley.

Edgar, D. E. (1974). *Adolescent competence and sexual disadvantage*. Working Papers in Sociology. Melbourne: La Trobe University.

Edgar, D., & Glezer, H. (1992). A man's place? *Family Matters*. Melbourne: Australian Institute of Family Studies.

Edgar, P., & McPhee, H. (1974). *Media She*. Melbourne: Heinemann.

Egeland, B., & Farber, E. A. (1984). Infant–mother attachment: Factors related to its development and changes over time. *Child Development, 55*, 753–771.

Eimas, P. D., Siqueland, E. R., Jusczyk, P., & Vigorito, J. (1971). Speech perception in infants. *Science, 171*, 303–306.

Eisenberg, N., Guthrie, I. K., Fabes, R. A., Shepard, S., Losoya, S., Murphy, B. C. et al. (2000). Predictions of elementary school children's externalising problem behaviours from attentional and behavioural regulation and negative emotionality. *Child Development, 71*, 1367–1382.

Eisenmajer, R., & Prior, M. (1991). Cognitive linguistic correlates of 'theory of mind' ability in autistic children. *British Journal of Developmental Psychology, 9*, 351–364.

Eisenstadt, S. N. (Ed.). (1960). *From generation to generation*. New York: Free Press.

Ekerdt, D. J., Bosse, R., & Levkoff, S. (1985). An empirical test for phases of retirement: Findings from the normative aging study. *Journal of Gerontology, 40*(1), 95–101.

Elder, G., Liker, J., & Jaworski, B. (1984). Hardship in lives: Depression influences from the 1930s to old age in postwar America. In K. McCluskey & H.W. Reese (Eds.), *Life-span developmental psychology*. New York: Academic Press.

Eldredge, N., & Gould, S. (1972). Punctuated equilibria. In T. M. Schopf (Ed.), *Models in psychobiology*. SanFrancisco: Freeman Cooper.

Elkind, D. (1967). Egocentrism in adolescence. *Child Development, 38*, 1025–1034.

Elkind, D. (1978). *The child's reality: Three developmental themes*. Hillsdale, NJ: Erlbaum.

Elkind, D., & Bowen, R. (1979). Imaginary audience behavior in children and adolescents. *Developmental Psychology, 15*, 38–44.

Ellerman, D. A. (1980). Self-regard of primary school children: Some Australian data. *British Journal of Educational Psychology, 50*, 114–122.

Ellerman, D. A. (1993). Parental support and control in relation to children's self-esteem. *Australian Journal of Marriage & Family, 14*(2), 76–80.

Emde, R. N., & Metcalf, D. R. (1970). An electroencephalographic study of behavioral rapid eye movement states in the human newborn. *Journal of Nervous and Mental Disease, 150*, 376–386.

Emde, R. N., Plomin, R., Robinson, J., Corley, R., DeFries, J.,

Fulker, D. W. et al. (1992). Temperament, emotion and cognition at fourteen months: The MacArthur longitudinal twin study. *Child Development, 63*, 1437–1455.

Emde, R. N., Zeynep, B., Clyman, R. B., & Oppenheim, D. (1991). The moral self of infancy: Affective core and procedural knowledge. *Developmental Review, 11*, 251–270.

Enright, R. D., Shukla, D. G., & Lapsley, D. K. (1980). Adolescent egocentrism–sociocentrism and self-consciousness. *Journal of Youth and Adolescence, 9*, 101–116.

Ensomme Gamles Vaern. (1980). The housing desires of the elderly. *Ageing International, 7*(2), 19–20.

Epstein, L., & Wing, R. R. (1987). Behavioral treatment of childhood obesity. *Psychological Bulletin, 101*, 331–342.

Erikson, E. H. (1950, 1963). *Childhood and society.* New York: W. W. Norton.

Erikson, E. H. (1959). *Identity and the life cycle: Selected papers.* New York: International Universities Press.

Erikson, E. H. (1968a). *Identity: Youth and crisis.* New York: W. W. Norton.

Erikson, E. H. (1968b). The life cycle. In D. L. Sills (Ed.), *International encyclopedia of the social sciences.* New York: Macmillan.

Erikson, E. H. (1982). *The life cycle completed: A review.* New York: Norton.

Erikson, E. H. (1983). A conversation with Elizabeth Hall. *Psychology Today,* June, 22–30.

Erikson, E. H., Erikson, J. M., & Kivnick, H. Q. (1986). *Vital involvement in old age.* New York: Norton.

Ervin, S. M. (1964). Imitation and structural change in children's language. In E. H. Lenneberg (Ed.), *New directions in the study of language.* Cambridge, MA: MIT Press.

Escalona, S., & Corman, H. H. (1967). The validation of Piaget's hypotheses concerning the development of sensori-motor intelligence: Methodological issues. Paper presented at the biennial meeting of the Society for Research in Child Development, March.

Espenschade, A. (1960). Motor development. In W. R. Johnson (Ed.), *Science and medicine of exercise and sport.* New York: Harper & Row.

Evans, B. (1978). *Dictionary of quotations.* New York: Avenel.

Exton-Smith, A. N. (1985). Mineral metabolism. In C. Finch & E. Schneider (Eds.), *Handbook of the biology of aging.* New York: Van Nostrand.

Eysenck, H. J. (1970). *Crime and personality.* London: Paladin Books.

Fagot, B. I. (1985). Beyond the reinforcement principle: Another step toward understanding sex-role development. *Developmental Psychology, 21*, 1097–1104.

Fagot, B. I., & Leinbach, M. D. (1989). The young child's gender schema: Environmental input, internal organisation. *Child Development, 60*, 663–672.

Fagot, B., & Leinbach, M. (1995). Gender knowledge in egalitarian and traditional families. *Sex Roles, 32*, 513–526.

Fairburn-Dunlop, P. (1986). Samoan parents and pre-school education: New Zealand. *Australian Journal of Early Childhood, 11*(1), 21–26.

Falbo, T., & Poston, D. (1993). The academic, personality and physical outcomes of only children in Chile. *Child Development, 64*, 18–35.

Fallon, B. J. (1997) Conflict management at home and at work. *Australian Journal of Psychology, 49*, 97.

Fantz, R. L., & Fagan, J. R. (1975). Visual attention to size and number of details by term and pre-term infants during the first six months. *Child Development, 46*, 3–18.

Faran, D., & Ramey, C. (1977). Infant day care and attachment behaviors toward mothers and teachers. *Child Development, 48*, 1112–1116.

Farber, S. (1981). Telltale behavior of twins. *Psychology Today.* January, 58–62, 79–80.

Farberow, N. L. (1989). Suicide: Youth. In R. & B. Kastenbaum (Eds.), *Encyclopedia of death.* Phoenix, AZ: Oryx Press.

Farnham-Diggory, S. (1972). *Cognitive processes in education: A psychological preparation for teaching and curriculum development.* New York: Harper & Row.

Farnill, D. (1987). Gender differences in the granting of behavioural autonomy to adolescents. *Australian Educational and Developmental Psychologist, 4*, 5–10.

Faust, M. (1983). Pubertal growth and the media. In J. Brooks-Gunn & A. C. Petersen (Eds.), *Girls at puberty.* New York: Plenum.

Faust, M. S. (1977). Somatic development of adolescent girls. *Monographs of the Society for Research in Child Development, 42*, Serial No. 169.

Feather, N. T. (1979). Human values and the work situation: Two studies. *Australian Psychologist, 14*, 131–141.

Feather, N. T. (1980). Values in adolescence. In J. Adelson (Ed.), *Handbook of adolescent psychology.* New York: Wiley.

Feather, N. T. (1983). Causal attributions and beliefs about work and unemployment among adolescents in state and independent secondary schools. *Australian Journal of Psychology, 35*, 211–232.

Feather, N. T. (1985). The psychological impact of unemployment: Empirical findings and theoretical approaches. In N. T. Feather (Ed.), *Australian psychology: Review of research.* Sydney: Allen & Unwin.

Feather, N. T. (1989). Behaviour changes after job loss. *Australian Journal of Psychology, 41*, 175–185.

Feather, N. T., & Bond, M. J. (1983). Time structure and purposeful activity among employed and unemployed university graduates. *Journal of Occupational Psychology, 56*, 241–254.

Feather, N. T., & Simon, J. G. (1975). Reactions to male and female success and failure in sex-linked occupations: Impressions of personality, causal attributions, and perceived likelihood of different consequences. *Journal of Personality and Social Psychology, 31*, 20–31.

Feeney, J. A. (1994). Attachment style, communication patterns and satisfaction across the life cycle of marriage. *Personal Relationships, 1*, 333–348.

Feeney, J. A., & Noller, P. (1990). Attachment style as a predictor of adult romantic relationships. *Journal of Personality and Social Psychology, 58*, 281–291.

Feeney, J. A., & Noller, P. (1991). Attachment style and verbal descriptions of romantic partners. *Journal of Social and Personal Relationships, 8*, 187–215.

Feeney, J. A., & Noller, P. (1992). Attachment style and romantic love: Relationships dissolution. *Australian Journal of Psychology, 44*, 69–74.

Feeney, J. A., & Noller, P. (1996). *Adult attachment.* Thousand Oaks, CA: Sage.

Feeney, J. A., Noller, P., & Patty, J. (1993). Adolescents' interactions with the opposite sex: Influence of attachment style and gender. *Journal of Adolescence, 16*, 169–186.

Feeney, J., Peterson, C., & Noller, P. (1994). Equity and marital satisfaction over the family life cycle: A study of Australian couples. *Personal Relationships, 1*, 83–99.

Fein, G. (1981). Pretend play in childhood: An integrative view. *Child Development, 52*, 1095–1118.

Fein, G. G. (1986). The affective psychology of play. In A. W. Gottfried & C. C. Brown (Eds.), *Play interactions: The contribution of play material and parental involvement to children's development.* Lexington, MA: Lexington Books.

Fein, G., Johnson, D., Kosson, N., Stork, L., & Wasserman, L. (1975). Sex stereotypes and preferences in the toy choices of 20-month-old boys and girls. *Developmental Psychology, 11*, 527–528.

Feldman, S. S., & Nash, S. C. (1984). The transition from expectancy to parenthood: Impact of the firstborn on men and women. *Sex Roles, 11*, 61–69.

Fergusson, D. M., Beautrais, A. L., Horwood, L. J., & Shannon, F. T. (1981). Working mothers and day care. *New Zealand Journal of Educational Studies, 16*, 168–176.

Fergusson, D. M., Lloyd, M., & Horwood, L. J. (1991). Family ethnicity, social background and scholastic achievement: An eleven year longitudinal study. *New Zealand Journal of Educational Studies, 26*(1), 49–63.

Ferrari, J. (2002). Antioxidants. *The Australian* (2002, June 29).

Feshbach, N. D. (1973). Cross-cultural studies of teaching styles in four-year-olds and their mothers. In A. Pick (Ed.), *Minnesota Symposium on Child Development* (Vol. III, 87–116). Minneapolis: University of Minnesota Press.

Feshbach, S. (1970). Aggression. In P. H. Mussen (Ed.), *Carmichael's Manual of Child Psychology.* New York: Wiley.

Field, J. (1982). Infants' localization of very brief sounds. In T. Cross & L. Riach (Eds.), *Issues and research in child development.* Melbourne: Institute of Early Childhood Development.

Field, T. (1978). Interaction behaviors in primary versus

secondary caregiver fathers. *Developmental Psychology, 14,* 183–184.

Finck, H. (1902). Romantic love and personal beauty. In E. Walster & G. W. Walster (1978), *A new look at love.* Reading, MA: Addison-Wesley.

Fischer, C. T. (1992). A humanistic approach to lifespan development. In V. B. Van Hasselt & M. Hersen (Eds.), *Handbook of social development: A lifespan perspective.* New York: Plenum.

Fischer, G. (2001). Lifelong learning. In N. Smelser & P. B. Baltes (Eds.), *International encyclopaedia of the social and behavioural sciences* (Vol. 13, pp. 8836–8840). Oxford: Elsevier Science.

Fischer, K. W., & Rose, S. P. (1995). Concurrent cycles in the dynamic development of the brain and behavior. *SRCD Newsletter, Fall,* 3–4, 15–16.

Fiske, M. (1979). *Middle age: The prime of life?* Melbourne: Thomas Nelson.

Fitzgerald, F. Scott. (1963). *The letters of F. Scott Fitzgerald.* New York: Charles Scribner's Sons.

Flavell, J. H. (1963). *The developmental psychology of Jean Piaget.* New York: Van Nostrand.

Flavell, J. H. (1970). Cognitive changes in adulthood. In L. R. Goulet & P. B. Baltes (Eds.), *Life-span developmental psychology: Research and theory.* New York: Academic Press.

Flavell, J. H. (1971). First discussant's comments: What is memory development the development of? *Human Development, 14,* 272–278.

Flavell, J. H. (1975). *The development of role-taking and communication skills in children.* Huntington, NY: Krieger.

Flavell, J. H. (1985). *Cognitive development.* Englewood Cliffs NJ: Prentice Hall.

Flavell, J. H. (2000). Development of children's knowledge about the mental world. *International Journal of Behavioral Development, 24,* 15–23.

Flavell, J. H., Flavell, E. R., Green, F. L., & Moses, L. J. (1990). Young children's understanding of fact beliefs versus value beliefs. *Child Development, 61,* 915–928.

Flavell, J., Green, F., & Flavell, E. (1995). The development of children's knowledge about attentional focus. *Developmental Psychology, 31,* 706–712.

Flavell, J. H., Miller, P. H., & Miller, S. (2002). *Cognitive development.* Upper Saddle River, NJ: Prentice-Hall.

Flavell, J. H., Mumme, D. L., Green, F. L., & Flavell, E. R. (1992). Young children's understanding of moral and other beliefs. *Child Development, 63,* 960–977.

Fletcher, G. J. O. (1984). Psychology and common sense. *American Psychologist,* March, 206–212.

Florea, A. (1980). Needs and aspirations of elderly women living alone. *Ageing International, 6,* 10–11.

Folkman, S. R., Lazarus, S., Pimley, S., & Novacek, J. (1987). Age differences in stress and coping procedures. *Psychology and Aging, 2,* 171–184.

Folvern, R., & Bonvillian, J. D. (1991). The transition from non-referential to referential language in children acquiring American sign language. *Developmental Psychology, 27,* 806–816.

Forgas, J. P. (1994). Sad and guilty? Affective influences in the explanation of conflict in close relationships. *Journal of Personality and Social Psychology, 66,* 56–68.

Forgas, J. (1996). Emotion and social behaviour. *Australian Journal of Psychology, 48,* 60.

Forger, N. G., & Breedlove, S. M. (1987). Seasonal variation in mammalian striated muscle mass and motorneuron morphology. *Journal of Neurobiology, 18,* 155–165.

Foster, D., Klinger-Vartabedian, L., & Wispe, L. (1984). Male longevity and age differences between spouses. *Journal of Gerontology, 39,* 117–120.

Fowler, J. W. (1981). *Stages of faith: The psychology of human development and the quest for meaning.* New York: Harper & Row.

Fowler, J. W. (1986). Faith and the structuring of meaning. In C. Dykstra & S. Parks (Eds.), *Faith development and Fowler.* Birmingham, AL: Religious Education Press.

Fox, G. L., & Inazu, J. K. (1980). Mother-daughter communication about sex. *Family Relations, 29,* 347–352.

Fox, N. (1977). Attachment of kibbutz infants to mother and metapelet. *Child Development, 48,* 1228–1239.

Fox, R. (1979). Margaret Mead. In D. L. Sills (Ed.), *International encyclopedia of the social sciences.* New York: Macmillan.

Francher, J. S. (1973). 'It's the Pepsi generation . . .' Accelerated aging and the television commercial. *International Journal of Aging and Human Development, 4*(3), 245–255.

Frank, A. (1954). *The diary of Anne Frank.* London: Pan.

Frankenberg, W. K., & Dodds, J. B. (1967). The Denver developmental screening test. *Journal of Pediatrics, 71,* 181–191.

Freedman, D. G. (1958). Constitutional and environmental interactions in rearing of four breeds of dogs. *Science, 127,* 585–586.

Freedman, D. G. (1974). *Human infancy.* New York: Wiley.

Freidman, H. S., Hawley, P. H., & Tucker, J. S. (1994). Personality, health and longevity. *Current Direction in Psychological Science, 3,* 37–41.

Freud, A. (1958). Adolescence. *Psychoanalytic Study of the Child, 13,* 255–278.

Freud, S. (1957). Five lectures on psychoanalysis. In J. Strachey (Ed.), *The standard edition of the complete psychological works of Sigmund Freud.* London: Hogarth.

Freud, S. (1973). *An outline of psychoanalysis.* London: Hogarth (first published 1938).

Frey, K. S., & Ruble, D. N. (1987) What children say about classroom performance. *Child Development, 58,* 1066–1078.

Friedenberg, E. Z. (1969). *The vanishing adolescent.* Boston: Beacon Press.

Friedman, I. A., & Mann, L. (1993). Coping patterns in adolescent decision making: An Israeli–Australian comparison. *Journal of Adolescence, 16,* 187–199.

Fries, J. F. (1980). Aging, natural death and the compression of morbidity. *New England Journal of Medicine, 303,* 130–135.

Fries, J. (1990). Medical perspectives on successful ageing. In P. Baltes & M. Baltes (Eds.), *Successful ageing.* Cambridge: Cambridge University Press.

Frieze, I. H. (1981). Children's attribution for success and failure. In S. Brehm, S. Kassin & F. Gibbons (Eds.), *Developmental social psychology.* London: Oxford University Press.

Frieze, I. H., Parsons, J. E., Johnson, P. B., Ruble, D. N., & Zellman, C. L. (1978). *Women and sex roles.* New York: W. W. Norton.

Frith, U. (1989). *Autism: Explaining the enigma.* Oxford: Blackwell.

Frodi, A. M., & Lamb, M. E. (1978). Sex differences in responsiveness to infants: A developmental study of psychophysiological and behavioral responses. *Child Development, 49,* 1182–1188.

Frodi, A. M., & Lamb, M. E. (1980). Child abusers' reactions to infant smiles and cries. *Child Development, 51,* 238–241.

Frodi, A. M., Lamb, M. E., Leavitt, L. A., Donovan, W. L., Neff, C., & Sherry, D. (1978). Fathers' and mothers' responses to the faces and cries of normal and premature infants. *Developmental Psychology, 4,* 490–498.

Fromm, E. (1975). *The art of loving.* London: Allen & Unwin.

Fry, P. S., & Grover, S. C. (1982). The relationship between father absence and children's social problem solving competencies. *Journal of Applied Developmental Psychology, 3.*

Furman, W., Simon, V., Shaffer, L., & Bouchey, H. (2002). Adolescents' working models for relationships. *Child Development, 73,* 171–183.

Furstenberg, F. F., Jr. (1976). *Unplanned parenthood: The social consequences of teenage childbearing.* New York: Free Press.

Furth, H. G., Ross, B. M., & Youniss, J. (1974). Operative understanding in reproductions of drawings. *Child Development, 45,* 63–70.

Futterweit, L. R., & Ruff, H. A. (1993). Principles of development: Implications for early intervention. *Journal of Applied Developmental Psychology, 14,* 153–173.

Gaddis, A., & Brooks-Gunn, J. (1985). The male experience of pubertal change. *Journal of Youth and Adolescence, 14,* 61–69.

Gale, F. (1978). Introduction. In F. Gale (Ed.), *Women's role in Aboriginal society* (pp. 1–33). Canberra: Australian Institute of Aboriginal Studies.

Gallois, C., & Callan, V. (1990). Sexuality in adolescence. In P. Heaven & V. Callan (Eds.), *Adolescence: An Australian perspective.* Sydney: Harcourt Brace Jovanovich.

Gallup, G. G., Jr. (1979). Self-recognition in chimpanzees and man: A developmental comparative perspective. In M. Lewis & L. A. Rosenblum (Eds.), *Genesis of behaviour* (Vol. 2): *The child and its family.* New York: Plenum.

Gardner, R. A., & Gardner, B. T. (1969). Teaching sign language to a chimpanzee. *Science, 165,* 664–672.

Garfield, J. L., Peterson C. C., & Perry, T. (2001). Social cognition, language acquisition and the development of theory of mind. *Mind & Language, 16*(5), 494–541.

Garmezy, N. (1987). The role of competence in the study of risk and protective factors in childhood and adolescence. Paper presented at IXth Biennial International Society for the Study of Behavioural Development Meetings, Tokyo.

Garrett, C. S., Ein, P. L., & Tremaine, L. (1977). The development of gender stereotyping of adult occupations in elementary school children. *Child Development, 48,* 507–512.

Garrison, K. C. (1965). *Psychology of adolescence.* Englewood Cliffs, NJ: Prentice Hall.

Garrison, K. C. (1968). Physiological changes in adolescence. In J. F. Adams (Ed.), *Understanding adolescence. Current developments in adolescent psychology.* Boston: Allyn & Bacon.

Gartley, W., & Bernasconi, M. (1967). The concept of death in children. *Journal of Genetic Psychology, 110,* 71–85.

Garvey, C. (1977). *Play.* Cambridge, MA: Harvard University Press.

Gately, B. C., & Whalley, W. F. (1990). Elder abuse: The response and role of the police. *Australian Journal on Aging, 9,* 18–21.

Gatz, M., & Pearson, C. G. (1988). Ageism revisited and the provision of psychological services. *American Psychologist, 43,* 184–188.

Geber, M., & Dean, R. F. (1964). Le developpement psychomoteur et somatique des jeunes enfants Africains en Ouganda. *Courrier, 14,* 426–433.

Gelman, R. (1979). Preschool thought. *American Psychologist, 34*(10), 900–905.

Gelman, R., & Gallistel, C. R. (1978). *The child's understanding of number.* Cambridge, MA: Harvard University Press.

Gesell, A. (1940). *The first five years of life.* New York: Harper.

Getzels, J. W., & Jackson, P. W. (1962). *Creativity and intelligence.* New York: Wiley.

Gewirtz, J. L., & Boyd, E. F. (1976). Mother–infant interaction and its study. In H. W. Reese (Ed.), *Advances in child development and behavior* (Vol. II), pp. 141–163. New York: Academic Press.

Gibson, E. J. (1969). *Principles of perceptual learning and development.* New York: Appleton-Century-Crofts.

Gibson, E. (1989). Exploratory behaviour in the development of perceiving, actions and the acquiring of knowledge. *Annual Review of Psychology, 39.*

Gibson, E. J., & Walk, R. D. (1961). The 'visual cliff'. *Scientific American, 202*(4), 64–72.

Giles, H., & Coupland, N. (1991). *Language: Contexts and consequences.* Milton Keynes, England: Open University Press.

Giles, H., Coupland, N., & Coupland, J. (1991). *Language, society and the elderly.* Oxford: Blackwell.

Gilligan, C. (1977). In a different voice: Women's conceptions of self and morality. *Harvard Educational Review, 47,* 481–517.

Gilligan, C. (1982). *In a different voice.* Cambridge, MA: Harvard University Press.

Gilligan, C., Lyons, N. P., & Hanmer, T. J. (1960). *Making connections.* Cambridge, MA: Harvard University Press.

Gilligan, C., Murphy, J. M., & Tappan, M. B. (1990). Moral development beyond adolescence. In C. N. Alexander & E. J. Langer (Eds.), *Higher stages of human development.* New York: Oxford University Press.

Gillis, J. R. (2001). Life course in history. In N. Smelser & P. B. Baltes (Eds.), *International encyclopaedia of the social and behavioural sciences.* New York: Elsevier Science.

Ginsburg, H. J., & Miller, S. M. (1982). Sex differences in children's risk-taking behavior. *Child Development, 53,* 426–428.

Glenn, N. (1981). Age, birth cohorts, and drinking. An illustration of the hazards of inferring effects from cohort data. *Journal of Gerontology, 36,* 362–369.

Glenn, N. D. (1998). The course of marital success and failure in five American 10-year marriage cohorts. *Journal of Marriage and the Family, 60,* 569–576.

Glick, I., Weiss, R. S., & Parkes, C. M. (1974). *The first year of bereavement.* New York: Wiley.

Glynn, T. J. (1981). From family to peer: Transitions of influence among drug-using youth. In D. J. Lettieri & J. P. Ludford

(Eds.), *Drug abuse and the American adolescent.* Rockville, MD: National Institute on Drug Abuse Research.

Goetting, A. (1986). The developmental tasks of siblingship over the life cycle. *Journal of Marriage and the Family, 48,* 703–714.

Gold, D. P., Andres, D., Etezadi, J., Arbuckle, T., Schwartzman, A., & Chaikelson, J. (1995). Structural equation model of intellectual change and continuity and predictors of intelligence in older men. *Psychology and Ageing, 10,* 294–303.

Golde, P., & Kogan, N. A. (1959). A sentence completion procedure for assessing attitudes toward old people. *Journal of Gerontology, 14,* 355–363.

Goldenberg, R. L. (1995). Small for gestational age infants. In B. Sachs, R. Beard, F. Papiernik, & C. Russell (Eds.), *Reproductive health care for women and babies.* Oxford: Oxford University Press.

Goldenring, J. M., & Doctor, R. M. (1985). *Children's fear of war.* Washington, DC: House Select Committee on Children, Youth, and Families.

Goldin-Meadow, S. (2000). Beyond words: The importance of gestures to researchers and learners. *Child Development, 71,* 231–239.

Goldman, J. (1990). The importance of an adequate sexual vocabulary for children. *Australian Journal of Marriage and the Family, 11,* 136–148.

Goldman, R. J., & Goldman, J. D. G. (1981). Children's perceptions of clothes and nakedness: A cross-national study. *Genetic Psychology Monographs, 104,* 163–86.

Goldman, R. J., & Goldman, J. D. G. (1982). *Children's sexual thinking.* Melbourne: Routledge & Kegan Paul.

Golomb, C., & Cornelius, C. B. (1977). Symbolic play and its cognitive significance. *Developmental Psychology, 13*(3), 246–252.

Goode, M., Alexander, L., & Arthur, G. (1982). Transition to parenthood. In T. G. Cross & L. M. Riach (Eds.), *Issues and research in child development.* Melbourne: Institute of Early Childhood Development.

Goodenough, F. L. (1931/1975). *Anger in young children.* Minneapolis: University of Minnesota Press.

Goodnow, J. J. (1977). *Children's drawing.* Cambridge, MA: Harvard University Press.

Goodnow, J. J. (1985). Change and variation in ideas about childhood and parenting. In I. Sigel (Ed.), *Parental belief systems: The psychological consequences for children.* Hillsdale, NJ: Erlbaum.

Goodnow, J. J. (1988). Children's household work: Its nature and functions. *Psychological Bulletin, 103,* 5–26.

Goodnow, J. J. (1996). Collaborative rules: How are people supposed to work with one another? In P. B. Baltes & U. M. Staudinger (Eds.), *Interactive minds: Life-span perspectives on the social foundation of cognition.* New York: Cambridge University Press.

Goodnow, J. J. (2001). Towards a cultural developmental psychology. Paper presented at Australasian Human Development Association Biennial Conference, Brisbane, Queensland.

Goodnow, J. J., & Bowes, J. M. (1994). *Men, women and household work.* Melbourne: Oxford University Press.

Goodnow, J. J., Cashmore, J., Cotton, S., & Knight, R. (1984). Mother's developmental timetables in two cultural groups. *International Journal of Psychology, 19,* 193–205.

Goodnow, J. J., & Collins, W. A. (1990). *Development according to parents.* Hove, UK: Lawrence Erlbaum.

Goodnow, J. J., & Warton, P. M. (1991). The social bases of social cognition: Interactions about work and their implications. In K. M. McConkey & N. W. Bond (Eds.), *Readings in Australian psychology.* Sydney: Harcourt Brace Jovanovich.

Goossens, F. A., & van Ijzendoorn, M. (1990). Quality of infants' attachments to professional caregivers. *Child Development, 61,* 832–837.

Goossens, L. (1984). Imaginary audience behavior as a function of age, sex and formal operational thinking. *International Journal of Behavioral Development, 7,* 77–83.

Gordon, J. B. (1975). A disengaged look at disengagement theory. *International Journal of Aging and Human Development, 6*(3), 215–227.

Gortmaker, S. L., Must, A., Perrin, J. M., Sobol, A. M., & Dietz, W. H. (1993). Social and economic consequences of overweight in adolescence and young adulthood. *New England Journal of Medicine, 329,* 1008–1012.

Gosden, C., Nicolaides, K., & Whitting, V. (1994). *Is my baby all right?* Oxford: Oxford University Press.

Goswami, U., & Bryant, P. (1990). *Phonological skills and learning to read.* Hove, UK: Erlbaum.

Gottesman, I. I. (1963). Heritability of personality: A demonstration. *Psychological Monographs, 77*(9), Serial No. 572.

Gottman, J. M. (1994). *What predicts divorce? The relationship between marital processes and marital outcomes.* Hillsdale, NJ: Erlbaum.

Gould, E., Reeves, A., Graziano, M., & Gross, C. (1999). Neurogenesis in the neocortex of adult primates. *Science, 286,* 548–552.

Goulet, L. R., & Baltes, P. B. (1970). *Life-span developmental psychology: Theory and research.* New York: Academic Press.

Gove, F. L., & Keating, D. P. (1979). Empathic role-taking precursors. *Developmental Psychology, 14.*

Graber, J. A., Brooks-Gunn, J., Paikoff, R. L., & Warren, M. P. (1994). Prediction of eating problems: An 8-year study of adolescent girls. *Developmental Psychology, 30,* 823–834.

Graber, J. A., Brooks-Gunn, J., & Warren, M. P. (1995). The antecedents of menarcheal age. *Child Development, 66,* 346–359.

Gracey, M., Sullivan, H., Burke, V., & Gracey, D. (1989). Factors which affect health, growth and nutrition in young children in remote Aboriginal communities. *Australian Paediatric Journal, 25,* 322–323.

Grainger, S., Dispenzieri, A., & Elsenberg, J. (1983). Age, experience and performance on speed and skill jobs in an applied setting. *Journal of Applied Psychology, 68,* 469–475.

Gratch, G., & Landers, W. F. (1971). The stage IV error in Piaget's theory of infants' object concepts. *Child Development, 42,* 359–372.

Gray, J. A. M. (1983). Health beliefs and attitudes as they affect preventive practices and self-care. *Ageing International, 10*(3), 7–10.

Gray, W. M., & Hudson, L. M. (1984). Formal operations and the imaginary audience. *Developmental Psychology, 20,* 619–627.

Greenberg, M., & Morris, N. (1974). Engrossment: The newborn's impact upon the father. *American Journal of Orthopsychiatry, 44,* 520–531.

Grey, A. (1993). *Mothers and daughters.* Wellington, NZ: Bridget Williams Books.

Grieg, R., & Raphael B. (1989). AIDS prevention and adolescence. *Community Health Studies, 13,* 211–219.

Grieve, R., & Garton, A. F. (1981). On the young child's comparison of sets. *Journal of Experimental Child Psychology, 32,* 443–458.

Griffith, P. (1988). Midwives' attitudes: Promoting normal birth. *Australian Journal of Advanced Nursing, 5,* 33–39.

Grotevant, H. D., & Cooper, C. R. (1985). Patterns of interaction in family relationships and the development of identity exploration in adolescence. *Child Development, 56,* 415–428.

Grusec, J. E., & Goodnow, J. J. (1994). Impact of parental discipline methods on the child's internalization of values: A reconceptualization of current points of view. *Developmental Psychology, 30*(1), 4–19.

Gunn, P. (1993). Characteristics of Down syndrome. In Y. Burns & P. Gunn (Eds.), *Down syndrome: Moving through life.* London: Chapman & Hall.

Gunnar-Vongnechten, M. R. (1978). Changing a frightening toy into a pleasant toy by allowing the infant to control its actions. *Developmental Psychology, 14,* 157–162.

Gurin, G., Veroff, J., & Feld, S. (1960). *Americans view their mental health.* New York: Basic Books.

Gurney, R. M. (1980). The effects of unemployment on the psychosocial development of school leavers. *Journal of Occupational Psychology, 53,* 205–213.

Gutmann, D. L. (1975). Parenthood, key to comparative study of the life cycle. In N. Datan & L. H. Ginsberg (Eds.), *Life-span developmental psychology: Normative life crises.* New York: Academic Press.

Guttmacher, A. F. (1973). *Pregnancy, birth, and family planning: A guide for expectant parents in the 1970s.* New York: Viking Press.

Haan, N., Millsap, R., & Hartka, E. (1986). As time goes by: Change and stability in personality over fifty years. *Psychology and Ageing, 1,* 220–232.

Haan, N., Smith, M. B., & Block, J. (1968). Moral reasoning

of young adults: Political social behavior, family background and personality correlates. *Journal of Personality and Social Psychology, 10,* 185–201.

Haber, D. A. (1979). The broadening of perspective over the career course: An exploratory study of self-reported creative research acts. *International Journal of Aging and Human Development, 9*(4), 305–311.

Haber, R. N. (1969). Eidetic images. *Scientific American, 220,* April, 36–44.

Hagen, J. W. (1971). Some thoughts about how children learn to remember. *Human Development, 14,* 262–271.

Haight, B. (1991). Reminiscing: The state of the art as a basis for practice. *Journal of Aging and Human Development, 33,* 1–32.

Halford, G. (1982). *The development of thought,* Hillsdale, NJ: Erlbaum.

Halford, G. (1985). Cognitive development. In N. T. Feather (Ed.), *Australian psychology: Review of research.* Sydney: Allen & Unwin.

Halford, G. S. (1993). *Children's understanding: The development of mental models.* London: Lawrence Erlbaum.

Halford, G., & Boyle, F. (1985). Do young children understand conservation of number? *Child Development, 56,* 165–176.

Halford, G. S., Maybery, M. T., & Bain, J. D. (1986). Capacity limitations on children's reasoning. *Child Development, 57,* 616–627.

Halford, G., Maybery, M., & Bennet, D. (1985). The role of strategies in the development of memory span assessed by running probes. *International Journal of Behavioral Development, 8,* 301–312.

Halford, G. S., Maybery, M. T., O'Hare, A. W., & Grant, P. (1994). The development of memory and processing capacity. *Child Development, 65,* 1338–1356.

Hall, D. T. (1975). Pressures from work, self and home in the life stages of married women. *Journal of Vocational Behaviour, 6,* 121–132.

Hall, D. T. (1976). *Careers in organizations.* Pacific Palisades CA: Goodyear.

Hall, D. T., & Lawler, E. E. (1969). Unused potential in research and development organizations. *Research Management, 12,* 339–354.

Hall, E., Lamb, M., & Perlmutter, M. (1982). *Child psychology today.* New York: Random House.

Hall, G. S. (1907). *Aspects of child life and education.* New York: Appleton.

Hall, J. A., & Taylor, S. E. (1976). When love is blind: Maintaining idealized images of one's spouse. *Human Relations, 29*(8), 751–761.

Halliday, J., McNaughton, S., & Glynn, T. (1985). Influencing children's choice of play activities at kindergarten through teacher participation. *New Zealand Journal of Education, 20,* 48–58.

Halpern, D., & Coren, S. (1993). Left-handedness and life span: A reply to Harris. *Psychological Bulletin, 114*(2), 235–241.

Halpern, L. F., Maclean, W. E., Jr., & Baumeister, A. A. (1995). Infant sleep–wake characteristics: Relation to neurobiological status and the prediction of developmental outcome. *Developmental Review, 15,* 255–291.

Hamilton, A. (1974). The traditionally oriented community. In B. S. Hetzel (Ed.), *Health services for Aborigines.* Brisbane: University of Queensland Press.

Hamilton, A. (1981). *Nature and nurture.* Canberra: Australian Institute of Aboriginal Studies.

Hammond, J., & Fletcher, G. (1991). Attachment styles and relationship satisfaction in the development of close relationships. *New Zealand Journal of Psychology, 20,* 56–62.

Hansen, J., & Bowey, J. A. (1994). Phonological analysis skills, verbal working memory and reading ability in second-grade children. *Child Development, 65,* 938–950.

Hanson, K., & Wapner, S. (1994). Personality in retirement. *Educational Gerontology, 20,* 452–461.

Hansson, R. O. (1986). Relational competence, relationships, and adjustment in old age. *Journal of Personality and Social Psychology, 50,* 1050–1058.

Happé, F. (1995). The role of age and verbal ability in the ToM performance of subjects with autism. *Child Development, 66,* 843–855.

Hardy, J. B. (1973). Clinical and developmental aspects of congenital rubella. *Archives of Otolaryngology, 98,* 230–236.

Harkness, S., & Super, C.M. (1985). Child–environment interactions in the socialization of affect. In M. Lewis & C. Saarni (Eds.), *The socialization of emotions*. New York: Plenum Press.

Harlow, H. F., & Harlow, M. K. (1966). Learning to love. *American Scientist, 54*, 244–272.

Harper, J., & Collins, J. K. (1975). The effects of early or late maturation on the prestige of the adolescent girl. In J. K. Collins (Ed.), *Studies of the Australian adolescent*. Stanmore, NSW: Cassell.

Harris, D. B. (1957). *The concept of development*. Minneapolis: University of Minnesota Press.

Harris, J. (1980). *Report No. 27, Educational Research and Development Council* (Australia), 15.

Harris, M., & Hatano, G. (1999). *Learning to read and write*. Cambridge, UK: Cambridge University Press.

Harris, P. L. (1989). *Children and emotion: The development of psychological understanding*. Oxford: Blackwell.

Harrison, P. (1978). Living with old age. In V. Carver & P. Liddiard (Eds.), *An aging population*. Sevenoaks, Kent, UK: Hodder & Stoughton.

Harter, S. (1980). A model of intrinsic mastery motivation in children: Individual differences and developmental change. In W. A. Collins (Ed.), *Minnesota symposium on child psychology*. Hillsdale, NJ: Erlbaum.

Harter, S. (1987). The determination and mediational role of global self-worth in children. In N. Eisenberg (Ed.), *Contemporary topics in developmental psychology* (pp. 219–242). New York: Wiley.

Harter, S. (1990). Processes underlying adolescent self-concept formation. In R. Montemayor, G. R. Adams & T. P. Gullota (Eds.), *From childhood to adolescence: A transitional period?* (pp. 205–239). Newbury Park, CA: Sage.

Harter, S., & Pike, R. (1984). The pictorial scale of perceived competence and social acceptance for children. *Child Development, 55*, 1969–1982.

Hartshorne, H., & May, M. A. (1928). *Studies in deceit*. New York: Macmillan.

Hartup, W. W. (1964). Friendship status and the effectiveness of peers as reinforcing agents. *Journal of Experimental Child Psychology, 1*, 154–162.

Hartup, W. W. (1970). Peer interaction and social organization. In P. H. Mussen (Ed.), *Carmichael's manual of child psychology* (Vol. 2), 361–456. New York: Wiley.

Hartup, W. W. (1987). The developmental significance of close relationships. Paper presented at China Satellite International Society for Behavioural Development Conference. Beijing.

Hartup, W. W. (1992). Peer relations in early and middle childhood. In V. B. Van Hasselt & M. Hersen (Eds.), *Handbook of social development: A lifespan perspective* (pp. 257–281). New York: Plenum Press.

Hartup, W. W., Glazer, J. A., & Charlesworth, R. (1967). Peer reinforcement and sociometric status. *Child Development, 38*, 1017–1024.

Hassall, I. B. (1987). The cot death enigma. *Medical Journal of Australia, 147*, 214–216.

Hatfield, E. (1988). Passionate and companionate love. In R. J. Sternberg & M. L. Barnes (Eds.), *The psychology of love*. New Haven: Yale University Press.

Havighurst, R. J. (1964). Youth in exploration and man emergent. In H. Barrow (Ed.), *Man in a world at work*. Boston: Houghton Mifflin.

Havighurst, R. J. (1973). History of developmental psychology: Socialization and personality development through the lifespan. In N. Datan & J. R. Nesselroade (Eds.), *Lifespan developmental psychology*. New York: Academic Press.

Havighurst, R. J. (1974). Obituary: Charlotte Buhler. *Human Development, 17*, 1.

Havighurst, R. J., Neugarten, B. L., & Tobin, S. S. (1963). Disengagement and patterns of aging. Unpublished paper presented at the meeting of the International Association of Gerontology, Copenhagen, August.

Haviland, J. M., & Walker-Andrews, A. S. (1992). Emotion socialization: A view from development and ethology. In V. B. Van Hasselt & M. Hersen (Eds.), *Handbook of social development: A lifespan perspective* (pp. 29–49). New York: Plenum Press.

Haviland, W. A. (1975). *Cultural anthropology*. New York: Holt, Rinehart & Winston.

Hay, D. A. (1985). *Essentials of Behaviour Genetics*. Oxford: Blackwell.

Hay, D. A. (1986). Children at risk. *Australian Journal of Early Childhood, 11*, 6–10.

Hay, D. A., & O'Brien, P. J. (1983). The La Trobe twin study: A genetic approach to the structure and development of cognition in twin children. *Child Development, 54*, 317–330.

Hay, L., Blampeid, N. M., Church, R. J., & Priest, H. (1981). Family relationships over three generations: A comparative study of distressed and nondistressed parent–teenage triads. *New Zealand Journal of Educational Studies, 16*, 81–87.

Hayes, B., & Van den Heuvel, A. (1994). Attitudes toward mandatory retirement: An international comparison. *International Journal of Aging and Human Development, 39*, 209–231.

Hayflick, L. (1987). Origins of longevity. In H. R. Warner, R. N. Butler, R. L. Sprott & E. L. Schneider (Eds.), *Ageing: Vol 31. Modern biological theories of ageing* (pp. 21–34). New York: Raven Press.

Hayflick, L. (1994). *How and why we age*. New York: Ballantine Books.

Hayslip, B. (1993). Retirement preparation. In R. Kastenbaum (Ed.), *Encyclopedia of adult development*. Phoenix: Oryx.

Hazan, C., & Shaver, P. (1987). Romantic love conceptualized as an attachment process. *Journal of Personality and Social Psychology, 52*, 511–524.

Hazan, C., & Shaver, P. (1990). Love and work: An attachment theoretical perspective. *Journal of Personality and Social Psychology, 59*, 270–280.

Hazan, C., & Shaver, P. R. (1994). Attachment as an organizational framework for research on close relationships. *Psychological Inquiry, 5*, 1–22.

Hazan, C., & Zeifman, D. (1994). Sex and the psychological tether. In K. Bartholomew & D. Perlman (Eds.), *Advances in personal relationships* (Vol. 5): *Attachment processes in adulthood* (pp. 151–178). London: Jessica Kingsley.

Heath, D. H. (1977). Some possible effects of occupation on the maturing of professional men. *Journal of Vocational Behavior, 11*, 263–281.

Hefner, R., Rebecca, M., & Oleshansky, B. (1975). Development of sex-role transcendence. *Human Development, 18*, 143–158.

Heibeck, T., & Markman, E. (1987). Word learning in children: An examination of fast mapping. *Child Development, 58*, 1021–1034.

Hellman, L. (1973). *Pentimento*. Boston: Little Brown.

Helson, P., & Wink, P. (1992). Personality change in women from the early 40s to the early 50s. *Psychology and Ageing, 7*(1), 46–55.

Hemmer, J., & Kleiber, D. (1981). Tomboys and sissies: Androgynous children? *Sex Roles, 7*, 1205–1212.

Hendricks, J., & Hendricks, C. D. (1977). *Aging in Mass Society*. Cambridge, MA: Winthrop.

Henneborn, W. J., & Cogan, R. (1975). The effect of husband participation on reported pain and probability of medication during labor and birth. *Journal of Psychosomatic Research, 19*, 215–222.

Henry, W. E. (1965). Engagement and disengagement: Toward a theory of adult development. In R. Kastenbaum (Ed.), *Contributions to the psychobiology of aging*. New York: Springer.

Henry, W. E. (1971). The role of work in structuring the life cycle. *Human Development, 14*, 125–131.

Hesketh, B. (1982). Work values of a group of potential school leavers in two New Zealand high schools. *New Zealand Journal of Educational Studies, 17*, 68–73.

Hetherington, E. M. (1965). A developmental study of the effects of sex of the dominant parent on sex-role preference, identification, and imitation in children. *Journal of Personality and Social Psychology, 2*(2), 188–194.

Hetherington, E. M. (1972). Effects of father absence on personality development in adolescent daughters. *Developmental Psychology, 7*, 313–326.

Hetherington, S. E. (1990). A controlled study of the effects of prepared childbirth classes on obstetric complications. *Birth, 17*, 86–90.

Hicks, D. J. (1965). Imitation and retention of film-mediated aggressive peer and adult needs. *Journal of Personality and Social Psychology, 2*, 97–100.

Higbee, K. L. (1979). Factors affecting obedience in preschool children. *Journal of Genetic Psychology, 134*, 241–253.

Hill, C. T., Rubin, Z., & Peplau, L. A. (1976). Breakups before marriage: The end of 103 affairs. *Journal of Social Issues,* 32(1), 147–153.

Hill, J. P., & Lynch, M. E. (1983). The intensification of gender-related role expectations during early adolescence. In J. Brooks-Gunn & A. C. Petersen (Eds.), *Girls at puberty.* New York: Plenum Press.

Hill, P. (1993). Recent advances in selected aspects of adolescent development. *Journal of Child Psychology and Psychiatry,* 34(1), 69–99.

Hill, P., Smith, I., & Terare, C. (1993). Tradition and culture: Aboriginal and Torres Strait Islander HIV/AIDS posters. *Health Promotion Journal of Australia,* 3(3), 42–43.

Hill, R., Foote, N., Aldous, J., Carlson, J., & McDonald, R. (1970). *Family development in three generations.* Cambridge, MA: Schenkman.

Hinde, R. A. (1979). *Towards understanding relationships.* New York: Academic Press.

Hinde, R. A. (1992). Human social development: An ethological/relationship perspective. In H. McGurk (Ed.), *Childhood social development: Contemporary perspectives* (pp. 191–207). Hillsdale, NJ: Hemisphere

Hindley, C. B., Filliozat, A. M., Klackenberg, G., Nicolet-Meister, P., & Sand, A. A. (1966). Differences in age of walking in five European longitudinal samples. *Human Biology,* 38, 364–379.

Hoffman, L. W., & Nye, F. I. (1974). *Working mothers.* San Francisco: Jossey-Bass.

Hoffman, M. L. (1970). Moral development. In P. H. Mussen (Ed.), *Carmichael's manual of child psychology* (Vol. 2). New York: Wiley.

Hoffman, M. L. (1979). Development of moral thought, feeling, and behavior. *American Psychologist,* 34(10), 958–966.

Hoffman, M. L. (1993). Empathy, social cognition, and moral education. In A. Garrod (Ed.), *Approaches to moral development: New research and emerging themes.* New York: Teachers College Press.

Hogan, D. P. (1980). The transition to adulthood as a career contingency. *American Sociological Review,* 45, 261–276.

Holahan, C. K., & Holahan, C. J. (1987). Self-efficacy, social support, and depression in aging: A longitudinal analysis. *Journal of Gerontology,* 42(1), 65–68.

Holden, D. (1985). Genes, personality, and alcoholism. *Psychology Today,* January, 38–44.

Holman, C. D. J. and 41 others. (1986). *Our state of health: An overview of health and illness in Western Australia in the 1980s.* Perth: Steering Committee for the Review of Health Promotion and Health Education in Western Australia, Health Department of Western Australia.

Holmes, V. M., & Wales, R. J. (1985). Psycholinguistics and language acquisition. In N. T. Feather (Ed.), *Australian psychology: Review of research.* Sydney: Allen & Unwin.

Holstein, C. B. (1976). Irreversible stepwise sequences in the development of moral judgments. *Child Development,* 47, 51–61.

Holzberg, C. S. (1984). Anthropology, life history, and the aged: The Toronto Baycrest Centre. *International Journal of Aging and Human Development,* 18(4), 255–275.

Hook, E. B. (1978). Extra sex chromosomes and human behavior: The nature of the evidence regarding XYY, XXY, XXYY and XXX genotypes. In H. Vallet & I. Porter (Eds.), *Genetic aspects of sexual differentiation.* New York: Academic Press.

Hooper, B. (1985). *Youth in China.* Ringwood, VIC: Penguin.

Hopkins, J. R. (1977). Sexual behavior in adolescence. *Journal of Social Issues,* 33(2), 67–85.

Hori, S. (1994). Beginning of old age in Japan and age norms in adulthood. *Educational Gerontology,* 20, 439–451.

Horin, A. (2002). Employers biased against over-45s. *The Australian* (2002, April 8).

Horne, D. (1975). *The education of young Donald.* Ringwood, VIC: Penguin.

Horner, M. (1972). Toward an understanding of achievement-related conflicts in women. *Journal of Social Issues,* 28, 157–176.

Horsborough, R., Cross, T. G., & Ball, I. (1982). Conversational interactions between mothers and their autistic, dysphasic, and normal children. In T. G. Cross & L. M. Riach (Eds.), *Issues and research in child development.* Melbourne: Institute of Early Childhood Development.

Houseknecht, S. (1978). Childlessness and marital satisfaction. *Journal of Marriage and the Family,* 41, 259–265.

Howes, C. (1985). Sharing fantasy: Social pretend play in toddlers. *Child Development,* 56, 1253–1258.

Hoyt, M. (1974). *Creative retirement: Planning the best years yet.* Charlotte, VT: Garden Way.

Hsu, L. K. G. (1990). *Eating disorders.* New York: Guildford.

Hughes, C. (1998). Finding your marbles: Does preschoolers' strategic behavior predict later understanding of mind? *Developmental Psychology,* 34, 1326–1339.

Hughes, T. (1889). *Tom Brown's school days.* London: Macmillan.

Hunter, E. M. (1991). An examination of recent suicides in remote Australia: Further information from the Kimberly. *Australian and New Zealand Journal of Psychiatry,* 25, 197–202.

Hurlock, E. (1973). *Adolescent development.* New York: McGraw-Hill.

Huser, W. R., & Grant, C. W. (1978). A study of husbands and wives from dual-career and traditional-career families. *Psychology of Women Quarterly,* 3(1).

Huston, A., & Alvarez, M. (1990). The socialization context of gender role development in early adolescence. In R. Montemayor, Cr. Adams & T. Gullota (Eds.), *From childhood to adolescence.* Newbury Park, CA: Sage.

Huston, T. L., & Levinger, G. (1970). Interpersonal attraction. *Annual Review of Psychology,* 29, 118–157.

Huston, T. L., & Vangelisti, A. L. (1995). How parenthood affects marriage. In M. A. Fitzpatrick & A. L. Vangelisti (Eds.), *Explaining family interactions* (pp. 147–176). Thousand Oaks, CA: Sage.

Hutt, C. (1972). Neuroendocrinological, behavioral, and intellectual aspects of sexual differentiation in human development. In C. Ounsted & D. C. Taylor (Eds.), *Gender differences – their ontogeny and significance.* London: Churchill.

Huyck, M. H. (Ed.). (1974). *Grow older: Things you need to know about aging.* Englewood Cliffs, NJ: Prentice Hall.

Huyck, M. H., Eschen, C., & Tabachnik, R. (1973). Women's attitudes toward radical hysterectomy. Paper presented at the 26th Annual Scientific Meetings of the Gerontological Society, Miami.

Hyde, J. S. (1984). How large are gender differences in aggression? A developmental meta-analysis. *Developmental Psychology,* 20, 722–736.

Inagaki, K., & Hatano, G. (1999). Children's understanding of mind–body relationships. In M. Siegal & C. Peterson (Eds.), *Children's understanding of biology and health.* Cambridge: Cambridge University Press.

Ingram, D. (1971). Transitivity in child language. *Language,* 47, 888–910.

Inhelder, B., & Piaget, J. (1958). *The growth of logical thinking from childhood to adolescence.* New York: Basic Books.

Irion, J. C., & Blanchard-Fields, F. (1987). A cross-sectional comparison of adaptive coping in adulthood. *Journal of Gerontology,* 42(5), 502–504.

Irizarry, C., West, D., & Downing, A. (2001). Use of the internet by older rural South Australians. *Australasian Journal on Ageing,* 20(3), 153–155.

Izard, C. E., Fantauzzo, C. A., Castle, J. M., Haynes, O. M., Rayais, M. F., & Putnam, P. H. (1995). The ontogeny and significance of infants' facial expressions in the first 9 months of life. *Developmental Psychology,* 31, 997–1013.

Jackson, S. (1965). The growth of logical thinking in normal and subnormal children. *British Journal of Educational Psychology,* 35, 255–258.

Jahoda, M. (1982). *Employment and unemployment: A social–psychological analysis.* Cambridge, UK: Cambridge University Press.

James, W. (1890). *Principles of Psychology.* New York: Holt.

Janowsky, J. S., & Carper, R. (1996). Is there a neural basis for cognitive transitions in school-aged children? In A. J. Sameroff & M. M. Haith (Eds.), *The five to seven year shift: The age of reason and responsibility.* Chicago, IL: University of Chicago Press.

Jasny, B. R., & Kennedy, D. (2001). The human genome. *Science,* 291, 1153.

Jenkins, J. M., & Astington, J. W. (1996). Cognitive factors and family structure associated with theory of mind development in young children. *Developmental Psychology,* 32, 70–78.

Jersild, A., & Holmes, F. B. (1935). *Children's fears.* New York: Columbia University Press.

Jersild, A., & Tasch, R. J. (1949). *Children's interests.* New

York: Bureau of Publications, Teachers College, Columbia University.

Jessor, R. (1992). Risk behaviour in adolescence. *Developmental Review, 12,* 374–390.

Jessor, R., & Jessor, S. L. (1980). Adolescent development and the onset of drinking. In R. Muuss (Ed.), *Adolescent behavior and society.* New York: Random House.

Job, E. (1984). *Eighty plus: Outgrowing the myths of old age.* Brisbane: University of Queensland Press.

Johnson, M. P., Huston, T., Gaines, S. O., & Levinger, G. (1992). Patterns of married life among young couples. *Journal of Social and Personal Relationships, 9,* 343–364.

Johnson, R. C., & Medinnus, G. R. (1968). *Child psychology: Behavior and development,* 2nd ed. New York: Wiley.

Jones, D. (1979). The effects of teacher style on year one Aboriginal children's reading achievement. *The Aboriginal Child at School, 7*(3), 48–57.

Jones, D. L., Hemphill, W., & Meyers, E. S. A. (1973). *Height, weight and other physical characteristics of NSW children.* Sydney: NSW Department of Health.

Jones, H. E. (1954). The environment and mental development. In L. Carmichael (Ed.), *Manual of child psychology.* New York: Wiley.

Jones, M. C. (1957). The later careers of boys who were early- or late-maturing. *Child Development, 28,* 113–128.

Jones, M. C. (1965). Psychological correlates of somatic development. *Child Development, 36,* 899–911.

Jones, M. C., & Bayley, N. (1950). Physical maturing among boys as related to behavior. *Journal of Educational Psychology, 41,* 129–148.

Jones, M. C., & Mussen, P. H. (1958). Self-conceptions, motivations, and interpersonal attitudes of early- and late-maturing girls. *Child Development, 29,* 491–501.

Jones, N. (1980). Work values and adjustment in unemployed school leavers. Unpublished Master's thesis, Murdoch University.

Jordan, V. (1978). Searching for adulthood in America. In E. H. Erikson (Ed.), *Adulthood.* New York: Norton.

Jorm, A. F., Christensen, H., Henderson, A. S., Korten, A. E., & Australian National University's NHMRC Social Psychiatry Research Unit. (1994). Complaints of cognitive decline in the elderly: A comparison of reports by subjects and informants in a community survey. *Psychological Medicine, 24*(2), 365–374.

Jung, C. (1969). *The collected works.* Translated by R. F. C. Hull. London: Routledge & Kegan Paul.

Jupp, J. (2001). *The Australian people.* Melbourne: Cambridge University Press.

Kabanoff, B. (1980). Work and nonwork: A review of models, methods, and findings. *Psychological Bulletin, 88*(1), 60–77.

Kabanoff, B., & O'Brien, G. E. (1980). Work and leisure: A task attributes analysis. *Journal of Applied Psychology, 65,* 596–609.

Kacerguis, M. A., & Adams, G. R. (1980). Erikson stage resolution: The relationship between identity and intimacy. *Journal of Youth and Adolescence, 9,* 117–126.

Kagan, J. (1964). Acquisition and significance of sex-typing and sex-role identity. In M. Hoffman & L. W. Hoffman (Eds.), *Review of Child Development Research.* New York: Russell Sage.

Kagan, J. (1970). Attention and psychological change in the young child. *Science, 170,* 826–832.

Kagan, J. (1976). Emergent themes in human development. *American Scientist, 64,* 186–196.

Kagan, J., & Coles, R. (1972). *Twelve to sixteen: Early adolescence.* New York: W. W. Norton.

Kagan, J., & Kogan, N. (1970). Individual variation in cognitive processes. In P. H. Mussen (Ed.), *Carmichael's manual of child psychology.* New York: Wiley.

Kail, R. (1979). *The development of memory in children.* San Francisco: W. H. Freeman.

Kalish, R., & Reynolds, D. (1974). Widows view death. *Omega, 5,* 187.

Kallman, F. J. (1953). *Heredity in health and mental disorder.* New York: W. W. Norton.

Kane, B. (1979). Children's concepts of death. *Journal of Genetic Psychology, 134,* 141–153.

Kaplan, M. (1960). *Leisure in America.* New York: Wiley.

Kastenbaum, R. (1964). *New thoughts on old age.* New York: Springer.

Kastenbaum, R. (1974). Childhood: The kingdom where creatures die. *Journal of Clinical Child Psychology, 3,* 11–14.

Kastenbaum, R. (1975). Is death a life crisis? In N. Datan & L. H. Ginsberg (Eds.), *Life-span developmental psychology: Normative life crises.* New York: Academic Press.

Kastenbaum, R. (1978). Fertility and the fear of death. *Journal of Social Issues, 30,* 63–78.

Kastenbaum, R. (1979). *Growing old: Years of fulfilment.* Melbourne: Thomas Nelson.

Kastenbaum, R. (1985). Death, dying, and bereavement in old age. In H. Cox (Ed.), *Aging.* Guildford, CT: Dushkin.

Kastenbaum, R. (1993). *Encyclopedia of adult development.* Phoenix, AZ: Oryx Press.

Kastenbaum, R. (1998). *Death, society and the human experience.* Boston, MA: Allyn and Bacon.

Kastenbaum, R. (2000). *The psychology of death.* New York: Springer.

Kastenbaum, R., & Costa, D. T., Jr. (1977). Psychological perspectives on death. *Annual Review of Psychology, 28,* 225–249.

Katchadourian, H. A., & Lunde, D. T. (1975). *Biological aspects of human sexuality.* New York: Holt, Rinehart & Winston.

Katz, P., & Ksansnak, K. (1994). Developmental aspects of gender role flexibility and traditionality in middle childhood and adolescence. *Developmental Psychology, 30,* 272–282.

Kaufman, A. S. (1990). *Assessing adolescent and adult intelligence.* Boston: Allyn & Bacon.

Kazuhiko, A., & Suzuki, T. (1986). Prevalence of some symptoms in adolescence and maturity: social phobias, anxiety symptoms, episodic illusions and idea of reference. *Psychopathology, 19,* 200–205.

Kearins, J. (1981). Visual spatial memory of Australian Aboriginal children of desert regions. *Cognitive Psychology, 13,* 434–460.

Kearins, J. (1986). Visual spatial memory in Aboriginal and white Australian children. *Australian Journal of Psychology, 38*(3), 203–214.

Keats, D. M. (1982). Cultural bases of concepts of intelligence: A Chinese versus Australian comparison. Paper presented at Second Asian Workshop on Child Development, Bangkok.

Keats, D. M. (1987). New windows on the world. *Australian Psychologist, 22,* 143–157.

Keats, D. M., Keats, J. A., & Liu, F. (1982). The language and thinking relationship in bilingual Chinese children. *Australian Journal of Chinese Affairs, 7,* 125–135.

Keats, J. A., & Keats, D. M. (1978). The role of language in the development of thinking: Theoretical approaches. In J. Keats, K. Collis & G. Halford (Eds.), *Cognitive development: Research based on a neo-Piagetian approach.* Brisbane: Wiley.

Kelen, J., & Griffiths, J. A. (1983). Housing for the aged: New roles for social work. *International Journal of Aging and Human Development, 19,* 125–133.

Kelleher, C. (1973). Second careers: A growing trend. *Industrial Gerontology,* Spring, 1–8.

Keller, H. (1902). *The story of my life.* Garden City, NY: Doubleday.

Kellogg, R. (1969). *Analyzing children's art.* Palo Alto, CA: National Press.

Kelly, E. L. (1955). Consistency of the adult personality. *American Psychologist, 10*(9), 659–681.

Kelly, G. A. (1955). *The psychology of personal constructs.* New York: W. W. Norton.

Kendig, R., & Hutton, R. (1981). *Lifespans.* London: Methuen.

Kendler, H. H., & Kendler, T. S. (1972). Discrimination and development. In W. K. Estes (Ed.), *Handbook of learning and cognitive processes.* New York: Halsted.

Kenrick, D. T. (1987). Gender, genes, and the social environment. In P. Shaver & C. Hendrick (Eds.), *Sex and gender.* London: Sage.

Kerr, M., Lambert, W. W., & Bem, D. J. (1996). Life course sequelae of childhood shyness in Sweden: Comparison with the United States. *Developmental Psychology, 32,* 1100–1105.

Khoo, S. E. (1985). Family formation and ethnicity. Working Paper No. 9, June. Melbourne: Institute of Family Studies.

Kiell, N. (1967). *The universal experience of adolescence.* Boston: Beacon Press.

Kim, K. H., Relkin, N. R., Lee, K. M., & Hirsch, J. (1997). Distinct cortical areas associated with native and second languages. *Nature, 388,* 171–174.

Kimmel, D. (1974). *Adulthood and aging*. New York: Wiley.

King, M. (1972). *Moko*. Wellington: Alister Taylor.

King, N. J., Ollier, K., Iacuone, R., Schuster, S., Bays, K., Gullone, E. et al. (1989). Fears of children and adolescents: A cross-sectional Australian study using the reversed-fear survey schedule for children. *Journal of Child Psychology and Psychiatry, 30*(5), 775–784.

Kinney, H. C., Filiano, J. J., Sleeper, L. A., Mandell, F., Valdes-Dapena, M., & White, W. F. (1995). Decreased muscarinic receptor binding in the arcuate nucleus in sudden infant death syndrome. *Science, 269*, 1446–1450.

Kinsey, A. C., Pomeroy, W. B., Martin, C. E., Gebhard, P. H. and associates. (1953). *Sexual behavior in the human female*. Philadelphia: Saunders.

Kirkman, M., & Cross, T. G. (1982). A conversational analysis of the speech of mothers to their deaf or hearing children. In T. G. Cross & L. M. Riach (Eds.), *Issues and research in child development*. Melbourne: Institute of Early Childhood Development.

Kirkpatrick, L. A., & Hazan, C. (1994). Attachment styles and close relationships: A four-year prospective study. *Personal Relationships, 1*, 123–142.

Kisilevsky, B., & Muir, D. (1991). Human fetal and subsequent newborn responses to sound and vibration. *Infant Behaviour and Development, 14*, 1–26.

Kissane, K. (1988). Grave new world, *Time*, January 6–13.

Kleemeier, R. W. (1962). Intellectual changes in the senium. *Proceedings of the Social Statistics Section of the American Statistical Association*. Washington, DC: American Statistical Association.

Kleiber, D. (1999). *Leisure experience and human development*. New York: Basic Books.

Klima, E., & Bellugi, U. (1966). Syntactic regularities in the speech of children. In J. Lyons & R. Wales (Eds.), *Psycholinguistic Papers*. Chicago: Aldine Press.

Knight, K. H., & Elfenbein, M. H. (1993). Relationship of death education to the anxiety, fear and meaning associated with death. *Death Studies, 17*, 411–425.

Kogan, N., & Shelton, F. C. (1962). Images of 'old people' and 'people in general' in an older sample. *Journal of Genetic Psychology, 100*, 3–21.

Kohlberg, L. (1963). The development of children's orientations toward moral order: I. Sequence in the development of moral thought. *Vita Humana, 6*, 11–33.

Kohlberg, L. (1966). A cognitive-developmental analysis of children's sex-role concepts and attitudes. In E. E. Maccoby (Ed.), *The development of sex differences*. Stanford, CA: Stanford University Press.

Kohlberg, L. (1969). Stage and sequence: The cognitive–developmental approach to socialization. In D. A. Goslin (Ed.), *Handbook of socialization theory and research*. Chicago: Rand McNally.

Kohlberg, L. (1984). *The psychology of moral development*. New York: Harper & Row.

Kohlberg, L., & Gilligan, C. (1971). The adolescent as a philosopher: The discovery of the self in a post-conventional world. *Daedalus, 100*, 1051–1086.

Kohlberg, L., & Kramer, R. (1964). Continuities and discontinuities in childhood and adult moral development. *Human Development, 12*, 93–120.

Kohlberg, L., Levine, C., & Hewer, A. (1983). *Moral stages: The formulation of Kohlberg's theory and a response to critics*. Harvard University: Laboratory of Human Development.

Kojima, H., & Aoi, N. (1987). How do people represent their life course in retrospect and prospect? Paper presented at IXth Biennial International Society for the Study of Behavioural Development Meetings, Tokyo.

Komarovsky, M. (1946). Cultural contradictions and sex roles. *American Journal of Sociology, 52*(3), 184–189.

Kommenich, P., McSweeney, M., Noack, J., & Elder, N. (1980). *The menstrual cycle*. New York: Springer-Verlag.

Koocher, G. P. (1973). Childhood, death, and cognitive development. *Developmental Psychology, 9*, 369–375.

Koopman-Boyden, P. G., & Abbott, M. (1985). Expectations for household task allocation and actual task allocation: A New Zealand study. *Journal of Marriage and the Family, 48*, 211–219.

Korn, S. J. (1984). Continuities and discontinuities in difficult temperament: Infancy to young adulthood. *Merrill-Palmer Quarterly, 30*, 189–199.

Kosky, R. (1987). Is suicidal behaviour increasing among Australian youth? *Medical Journal of Australia, 147*, 164–166.

Kovacs, G. T., Dunn, K., & Selwood, T. (1986). Teenage girls and sex: The Victorian Action Centre survey. *Australian Journal of Sex, Marriage and Family, 7*, 217–224.

Kraines, R. (1963). The menopause and evaluation of the self: A study of women in the climacteric years. Unpublished doctoral dissertation, University of Chicago, Committee on Human Development.

Krashen, S. D. (1988). *Second language acquisition and second language learning*. Englewood Cliffs, NJ: Prentice-Hall.

Kraus, J. (1977). Causes of delinquency as perceived by juveniles. *International Journal of Offender Therapy and Comparative Criminology, 21*, 79–86.

Krebs, D. L. (1970). Altruism – an examination of the concept and a review of the literature. *Psychological Bulletin, 73*(4), 258–322.

Krebs, D. L., & Rosenwald, A. (1977). Moral reasoning and moral behavior in conventional adults. *Merrill-Palmer Quarterly, 23*, 77–87.

Kreutzer, M. A., Leonard, C., & Flavell, J. H. (1975). An interview study of children's knowledge about memory. *Monographs of the Society for Research in Child Development, 40*, 1–57.

Kroger, J. (1983). Relationships during adolescence: A developmental study of New Zealand youths. *New Zealand Journal of Educational Studies, 18*, 115–126.

Kroger, J. (1989). *Identity in adolescence*. London: Routledge.

Kroger, J. (1995). The differentiation of 'firm' and 'developmental' foreclosure identity statuses: A longitudinal study. *Journal of Adolescent Research, 10*, 317–337.

Kroger, J. (1996). Identity, regression and development. *Journal of Adolescence, 19*, 203–222.

Kroger, J., & Haslett, S. J. (1991). A comparison of ego identity status transition pathways and change rates across five identity domains. *The International Journal of Aging and Human Development, 32*, 303–321.

Krupinski, J., & Stoller, A. (1974). *The family in Australia*. Sydney: Pergamon Press.

Kübler-Ross, E. (1969). *On death and dying*. London: Tavistock.

Kübler-Ross, E. (1975). *Death: The final stage of growth*. Englewood Cliffs, NJ: Prentice Hall.

Kuczynski, L. (1983). Reasoning, prohibitions and motivations for compliance. *Developmental Psychology, 19*, 126–134.

Kuhn, D. (1988). Cognitive development. In M. H. Bornstein & M. E. Lamb (Eds.), *Developmental psychology: An advanced textbook*. Hillsdale NJ: Lawrence Erlbaum.

Kuhn, D., Nash, S. C., & Brucken, L. (1978). Sex role concepts of two- and three-year-olds. *Child Development, 49*, 445–451.

Kurdek, L. A. (1995). Developmental changes in relationship quality in gay and lesbian cohabiting couples. *Developmental Psychology, 31*, 86–94.

Kutner, B., Fanshel, D., Togo, A. M., & Langner, T. S. (1956). *Five hundred over sixty: A community survey of aging*. New York: Sage.

Kyrios, M., Prior, M., Oberklaid, F., & Demetriou, A. (1989). Cross-cultural studies of temperament in Greek infants. *International Journal of Psychology, 24*, 585–603.

Labouvie-Vief, G. (1990). Modes of knowledge and the organization of development. In M. L. Commons, C. Armon, L. Kohlberg, F. A. Richards, T. A. Grotzer & J. D. Sinnott (Eds.), *Models and methods in the study of adolescent and adult development* (Vol. 2). New York: Academic Press.

Lachman, M. E., & Burack, O. R. (1993). Planning and control processes across the lifespan: An overview. *International Journal of Behavioral Development, 16*(2), 131–143.

Ladd, G. W., & Oden, S. L. (1979). The relationship between children's ideas about helplessness and peer acceptance. *Child Development, 50*, 402–408.

LaFarge, P. (1972). An uptight adolescence. In J. Kagan & R. Coles (Eds.), *Twelve to sixteen: Early adolescence*. New York: W. W. Norton.

Lamb, M. (1975). Fathers: Forgotten contributors to child development. *Human Development, 18*, 245–266.

Lamb, M. E. (1976). *The role of the father in child development*. New York: Wiley.

Lamb, M. E. (1997). *The role of the father in child development*. New York: Wiley.

Landers, A. (1977). If you had to do it all over again, would you marry the same person? *Family Circle*, 90(8), 2, 52, 54.

Landers, A. (1979). 1976 readership survey. Reported in S. Ambron & D. Brodzinsky. *Lifespan human development*. New York: Holt, Rinehart & Winston.

Landis, P. H. (1954). The ordering and forbidding technique and teenage adjustment. *School and Society, 80,* 105–106.

Langer, E. J., & Rodin, J. (1976). The effects of choice and enhanced personal responsibility for the aged: A field experiment in an institutional setting. *Journal of Personality and Social Psychology,* 34(2), 191–198.

Langlois, J. H., & Downs, A. C. (1979). Peer relations as a function of physical attractiveness: The eye of the beholder or behavioral reality. *Child Development, 50,* 409–418.

Langlois, J. H., & Roggman, L. A. (1990). Attractive faces are only average. *Psychological Science, 1,* 115–121.

Langlois, J. H., Roggman, L., & Rieser-Danner, L. (1990). Infants' differential responses to attractive and unattractive faces. *Development Psychology, 26,* 153–159.

Lapsley, D. K., & Murphy, M. N. (1985). Another look at the theoretical assumptions of adolescent egocentrism. *Developmental Review, 5,* 201–217.

Larson, R. (1995). Secrets in the bedroom: Adolescents' private use of media. *Journal of Youth and Adolescence, 24,* 535–541.

Larson, R. W. (1997). The emergence of solitude as a constructive domain of adolescence. *Child Development, 68,* 80–93.

Larzelere, R. (1986). Moderate spanking. *Journal of Family Violence, 1,* 27–37.

Latack, J. (1984). Career transitions: Connections between love and work. *Organizational Behavior and Human Performance, 34,* 296–322.

Lauer, R., Lauer, J., & Kerr, S. (1995). The long-term marriage: Perceptions of stability and satisfaction. In J. Hendricks (Ed.), *The ties of later life.* New York: Baywood.

Lawrence, B. M. (1984). Conversation and cooperation: Child linguistic maturity, parental speech and helping behavior of young children. *Child Development, 55,* 1926–1935.

Lawrence, J. A. (1991). The importance of planning in education. In J. B. Biggs (Ed.), *Cognitive processes in education.* Melbourne: ACER.

Lawrence, J. A., & Valsiner, J. (1993). Conceptual roots of internalisation. *Human Development, 36,* 150–167.

Lawton, M. P. (1990). Residential environment and self-directedness among older people. *American Psychologist, 45,* 638–640.

Lear, M. W. (1974). In M. H. Huyck (Ed.), *Growing older: Things you need to know about aging.* Englewood Cliffs, NJ: Prentice Hall.

Lechner, C. R., & Rosenthal, D. A. (1984). Adolescent self-consciousness and the imaginary audience. *Genetic Psychology Monographs, 110,* 289–305.

Lecours, A. R. (1982). Correlates of developmental behaviour in brain maturation. In T. Bever (Ed.), *Regressions in mental development.* Hillsdale, NJ: Lawrence Erlbaum.

Lehman, H. C. (1953). *Age and achievement.* Princeton, NJ: Princeton University Press.

Le Masters, E. E. (1957). Parenthood as crisis. *Marriage and Family Living,* 19(4), 352–355.

Lempert, H. (1984). Topic as a starting point for syntax. *Monographs of the Society for Research in Child Development, 49,* Serial No. 208.

Lenneberg, E. H. (1964). *New directions in the study of language.* Cambridge, MA: MIT Press.

Lenneberg, E. H. (1969). On explaining language. *Science, 164,* 635–643.

Lenz, W. (1966). Malformations caused by drugs in pregnancy. *American Journal of Diseases in Children, 112,* 99–106.

Leonard, R. J. (1993). Requests, refusals and reasons in children's negotiations. *Social Development, 2,* 131–144.

Lerner, R. M. (1996). Relative plasticity, integration, temporality, and diversity in human development: A developmental contextual perspective about theory, process and method. *Developmental Pychology, 32,* 781–786.

Lerner, R. M., Fisher, C. B., & Weinberg, R. A. (2000). Applying developmental science in the 21st century: International scholarship for our times. *International Journal of Behavioral Development, 24,* 24–29.

Lerner, R., Palemo, M., Spiro, A., & Nesselroade, J. R. (1982). Assessing the dimensions of temperamental individuality across the life span: The dimensions of temperament survey (DOTS). *Child Development, 53,* 149–159.

Leslie, G. R. (1979). *The family in social context.* New York: Oxford University Press.

Lester, D. (1984–85). The fear of death, sex and androgyny. *Omega, 15,* 271–274.

Levinson, D. J. (1978). *The seasons of a man's life.* New York: Knopf.

Levinson, D. J. (1986). A conception of adult development. *American Psychologist, 41,* 3–13.

Levinson, D. J. (1996). *Seasons of a woman's life.* New York: Knopf.

Levkoff, S. E., Cleary, P. D., & Wetle, T. (1987). Differences in the appraisal of health between aged and middle-aged adults. *Journal of Gerontology,* 42(1), 114–120.

Lewis, M. (1993). Self-conscious emotions: Embarrassment, pride, shame and guilt. In M. Lewis & J. M. Haviland (Eds.), *Handbook of emotions.* New York: Guilford Press.

Lewis, M., & Brooks-Gunn, J. (1979). *Social cognition and the acquisition of self.* New York: Plenum Press.

Lewis, M., Sullivan, M., Stanger, C., & Weiss, M. (1989). Self development and self conscious emotions. *Child Development, 60,* 146–156.

Liben, L. S., & Signorella, M. L. (1993). Gender-schematic processing in children: The role of initial interpretations of stimuli. *Developmental Pychology, 29,* 141–149.

Licht, B. G., & Dweck, C. (1984). Determinants of academic achievement: The interaction of children's achievement orientations with skill area. *Developmental Psychology, 20,* 628–636.

Liebert, R. M., & Baron, R. A. (1972). Some immediate effects of televised violence on children's behavior. *Developmental Psychology, 6,* 469–475.

Lieblum, S., Bachmann, G., Kemmann, K., Colburn, D., & Swartzman, L. (1983). Vaginal atrophy in postmenopausal women. *Journal of the American Medical Association, 249,* 2195–2198.

Liepert, J., Bauder, H., Wolfgang, H., Miltner, W. et al. (2000). Treatment-induced cortical reorganization after stroke in humans. *Stroke, 31,* 1210–1216.

Light, P. (1988). Context conservation and conversation. In K. Richardson & S. Sheldon (Eds.), *Cognitive development to adolescence.* Hove: Erlbaum.

Lin, C., Verp, M., & Sabbagha, R. (1993). *The high risk fetus.* New York: Springer-Verlag.

Linden, E. (1977). *Apes, men, and language.* Harmondsworth, UK: Penguin.

Linn, M. C., & Petersen, A. C. (1985). Emergence and characterization of sex differences in spatial ability: A meta-analysis. *Child Development, 56,* 1479–1498.

Linton, R. (1936). *The study of man.* New York: Appleton Century-Crofts.

Lipman-Blumen, J. (1972). How ideology shapes women's lives. *Scientific American,* 226(1), 34–42.

Lipsitt, L. (1979). Critical conditions in infancy. *American Psychologist, 34,* 973–980.

Lissner, J. A., Bengtsson, C., Björkelund, C., & Wedel, H. (1996). Physical activity levels and changes in relation to longevity: A prospective study of Swedish women. *American Journal of Epidemiology, 143,* 54–62.

Livesley, W. J., & Bromley, D. B. (1973). *Person perception in childhood and adolescence.* New York: Wiley.

Livson, F. B. (1981). Personality continuity and change. In D. H. Eichorn, J. A. Clausen, N. Haan, M. Honzik & P. Mussen (Eds.), *Present and past in middle age.* New York: Academic Press.

Livson, N., & Peskin, H. (1980). Perspectives on adolescence from longitudinal research. In J. Adelson (Ed.), *Handbook of adolescent psychology.* New York: Wiley.

Lobel, M. (1994). Conceptualisations, measurement and effects of prenatal maternal stress on birth outcomes. *Journal of Behavioural Medicine, 17,* 225–272.

Lockwood, D. (1962). *I, the Aboriginal.* Adelaide: Rigby.

Loehlin, J. C. (1985). Fitting heredity–environment models jointly to twin and adoption data from the California Psychological Inventory. *Behaviour Genetics, 15,* 199–221.

London, M., Crandall, R., & Seals, G. W. (1977). The contribution of job and leisure satisfaction to the quality of life. *Journal of Applied Psychology, 62,* 328–334.

Lopata, H. Z. (1975). Widowhood: Societal factors in lifespan disruptions and alternatives. In N. Datan & L. H. Ginsberg

(Eds.), *Life-span developmental psychology: Normative life crises.* New York: Academic Press.

Luce, G. G., & Segal, J. (1966). *Sleep.* New York: Coward-McCann.

Luckey, E., & Nass, G. A. (1969). A comparison of sexual attitudes and behaviour in an international sample. *Journal of Marriage and the Family, 31,* 364–379.

Luria, A. R. (1961). *The role of speech in the regulation of normal and abnormal behaviour.* New York: Liveright Publishing.

Luria, A. R. (1973). *The working brain.* New York: Basic Books.

Luria, A. R. (1981). *Language and cognition.* New York: Wiley.

Luszcz, M. A. (1993). When knowing is not enough: The role of memory beliefs in prose recall of older and younger adults. *Australian Psychologist, 28,* 16–20.

Luszcz, M. (1996). Beliefs about control in later life. *Hong Kong Journal of Gerontology, 10,* 502–506.

Luszcz, M. A., & Fitzgerald, K. M. (1986). Understanding cohort differences in cross-generational, self, and peer perceptions. *Journal of Gerontology, 41,* 234–240.

Lyon, B. M. (1985). Causal attribution of mood in the climacterium. *International Journal of Aging and Human Development, 20*(3), 191–204.

Lyons-Ruth, K., Connell, D., Zoll, D., & Stah, J. (1987). Infants at social risk. *Developmental Psychology, 23,* 223–232.

Lytton, H. (1980). Parent–child interaction. New York: Plenum.

Maas, H. S. (1968). Preadolescent peer relations and adult intimacy. *Psychiatry, 31,* 161–172.

Maccoby, E. E. (1966). *The Development of Sex Differences.* Stanford, CA: Stanford University Press.

Maccoby, E. E., & Jacklin, C. N. (1974). *The psychology of sex differences.* Stanford, CA: Stanford University Press.

Maccoby, E. E., Snow, M. E., & Jacklin, C. N. (1984). Children's dispositions and mother–child interaction at 12 and 18 months: A short-term longitudinal study. *Developmental Psychology, 20,* 459–472.

MacFarlane, A. (1975). Olfactory sensation in the development of social preferences in the human neonate. *Parent–infant interaction (CIBA Foundation Symposium 33).* New York: Elsevier.

MacFarlane, A. (1977). *Psychology of Childbirth.* Cambridge, MA: Fontana.

MacFarlane, J. W. (1975). Perspectives on personality consistency and change. In F. Rebelsky (Ed.), *Life: The continuous process.* New York: Alfred A. Knopf.

Mack, J. E., & Snow, R. (1986). Psychological effects on children and adolescents. In R. K. White (Ed.), *Psychology and the prevention of nuclear war.* New York: New York University Press.

Mackie, D. (1980). A cross-cultural study of intra-individual and inter-individual conflicts of centration. *European Journal of Social Psychology, 10,* 313–318.

Maddock, K. (1974). *The Australian Aborigines: A portrait of their society.* Harmondsworth, UK: Penguin.

Maddox, G. L. (1963). Activity and morale: A longitudinal study of selected elderly subjects. *Social Forces, 42*(2), 195–204.

Maddux, J. E., Roberts, M. C., Sledden, E. A., & Wright, L. (1986). Developmental issues in child health psychology. *American Psychologist, 41,* 25–34.

Mahbub ul Haq Human Development Centre. (2000). *Human development in South Asia.* Oxford: Oxford University Press.

Maher, E., & Cummins, R. A. (2001). Subjective quality of life, perceived control and dispositional optimism among older people. *Australasian Journal on Ageing, 20*(3), 139–144.

Malin, M. (1990). The visibility and invisibility of Aboriginal students in an urban classroom. *Australian Journal of Education, 34,* 312–329.

Maloney, L. (1985). A new understanding about death. In H. Cox (Ed.), *Aging.* Guildford, CT: Dushkin.

Mangelsdorf, S., Shapiro, J., & Marzoff, D. (1995). Developmental and temperamental differences in emotion regulation in infancy. *Child Development, 66,* 1817–1828.

Mann, L., Radford, M. H., & Kanagawa, C. (1985). Cross-cultural differences in children's use of decision rules: A comparison between Japan and Australia. *Journal of Personality and Social Psychology, 49,* 1557–1564.

Marceau, J. (1976). Marriage, role division, and social cohesion: The case of some French upper-class families. In

D. L. Barker & S. Allen (Eds.), *Dependence and exploitation in work and marriage.* London: Longman.

Marcia, J. E. (1976). Identity six years after: A follow-up study. *Journal of Youth and Adolescence, 5,* 145–160.

Marcia, J. E. (1980). Identity in adolescence. In J. Adelson (Ed.), *Handbook of adolescent psychology.* New York: Wiley.

Marcus, D. E., & Overton, W. F. (1978). The development of cognitive gender constancy and sex role preferences. *Child Development, 49,* 434–444.

Marder, K., Harvey, J., & Russo, P. F. (1975). The age of menarche in Sydney schoolgirls in 1973 with comment on the secular trend. In J. K. Collins (Ed.), *Studies of the Australian adolescent.* Stanmore, NSW: Cassell.

Markides, K. S., & Martin, H. W. (1979). A causal model of life satisfaction among the elderly. *Journal of Gerontology, 34,* 86–93.

Markman, E. M., & Siebert, J. (1979). Classes and collections: Internal organisation and numerical abilities. *Cognitive Psychology, 11,* 395–411.

Marquis, K. S., & Detweiler, R. A. (1985). Does adopted mean different? An attributional analysis. *Journal of Personality and Social Psychology, 48,* 1054–1066.

Marschark, M. (1993). *Psychological development of deaf children.* New York: Oxford University Press.

Marsh, H. W., Barnes, J., Cairns, L., & Tidman, M. (1984). Self-description questionnaire: Age and sex effects in the structure and level of self-concept for preadolescent children. *Journal of Educational Psychology, 76,* 940–958.

Marshall, W. A., & Tanner, J. M. (1969). Variations in the pattern of pubertal changes in girls. *Archives of Disease in Childhood, 44,* 291.

Martin, T. W., Berry, K. J., & Jacobsen, R. B. (1975). The impact of dual-career marriages: An empirical test of a Parsonian hypothesis. *Journal of Marriage and the Family, 37,* 734–742.

Masataka, N. (1996). Perception of motherese in a signed language by 6-month-old infants. *Development Psychology, 34,* 241–246.

Maslow, A. H. (1954). *Motivation and personality.* New York: Harper & Row.

Maslow, A. H. (1968). *Toward a psychology of being* (2nd ed.). Princeton, NJ: Van Nostrand.

Maslow, A. H. (1970). Interview. *Psychology Today, 4,* 16.

Maslow, A. H. (1971). *The farther reaches of human nature.* Middlesex, UK: Viking Press.

Masten, A. S. (1986). Humour and competence in school-aged children. *Child Development, 57,* 461–473.

Masters, W. H., & Johnson, V. E. (1966). *Human sexual response.* Boston: Little Brown.

Matarazzo, J. D. (1972). *Wechsler's measurement and appraisal of adult intelligence.* Baltimore: Williams & Wilkins.

Mathias, J. (1992). Cycles of violence and abuse. In R. Kosky, H. S. Eshkevari & G. Kneebone (Eds.), *Breaking out: Challenges in adolescent mental health in Australia,* Canberra: Australian Government Publishing Service, Chapter 8, pp. 105–119.

Matthews, P. (1996). *Guinness book of records.* London: Guinness Publishing.

Maude, D., Wertheim, E. H., Paxton, S., Gibbons, K., & Szmukler, G. (1993). Body dissatisfaction, weight loss behaviours and bulimic tendencies in Australian adolescents with an estimate of female data representativeness. *Australian Psychologist, 28*(2), 128–132.

Maziade, M., Boudreault, M., Cote, R., & Thivierge, I. (1986). Influence of gentle birth delivery procedures and other perinatal circumstances on infant temperament: Developmental and social implications. *Journal of Pediatrics, 108,* 134–143.

Mazzella, C., Durkin, K., Cerini, E., & Buralli, P. L. (1992). Sex role stereotyping in Australian television advertisements. *Sex Roles, 26,* 243–259.

McAlpine, L. M., & Moore, C. L. (1995). The development of social understanding in children with visual impairments. *Journal of Visual Impairment and Blindness, 89,* 349–358.

McBride-Chang, C., & Kail, R.V. (2002). Cross-cultural similarities in the predictors of reading acquisition. *Child Development, 73,* 1392–1407.

McCabe, M. P. (1982). The influence of sex and sex role on the dating attitudes and behavior of Australian youth. *Journal of Adolescent Health Care, 3,* 29–36.

McCabe, M. P. (1984). Toward a theory of adolescent dating. *Adolescence, 14*, 159–170.

McCabe, M. P., & Collins, J. K. (1979). Sex role and dating orientation. *Journal of Youth and Adolescence, 8*(4), 407–425.

McCallum, J. (1984). The educational challenge of the Australian retirement boom. *Australian Journal of Adult Education, 24*, 11–20.

McCallum, J. (1986). A right to retire but not to work. *Australian Journal of Social Issues, 21*, 93–104.

McCandless, B. R. (1970). *Adolescents: Behavior and development*. Hinsdale, IL: Dryden Press.

McCandless, B. R., & Marshall, H. R. (1957). A picture socio-metric technique for preschool children and its relation to teacher judgments of friendship. *Child Development, 28*, 139–147.

McCann, T. E., & Sheehan, P. W. (1985). Violence content in Australian television. *Australian Psychologist, 20*, 33–42.

McClearn, G. E. (1970). Genetic influences on behavior and development. In P. H. Mussen (Ed.), *Carmichael's manual of child psychology*. New York: Wiley.

McClelland, D. C. (1955). *Studies in motivation*. New York: Appleton-Century-Crofts.

McComas, J., & Field, J. (1984). Does early crawling experience affect infants' emerging spatial orientation abilities. *New Zealand Journal of Psychology, 13*, 63–68.

McConaghy, M. (1979). Gender permanence and the genital basis of gender: Stages in the development of constancy of gender identity. *Child Development, 50*, 1223–1226.

McConkey, K. (1995a). Guidelines relating to the reporting of recovered memories. *Bulletin of the Australian Psychological Society*, February, 20–21.

McConkey, K. (1995b). Hypnosis, memory and the ethics of uncertainty. *Australian Psychologist, 30*, 1–10.

McCormack, J. (2000). Hitting a hundred: Centenarians in Australia. *Australasian Journal of Ageing, 19*, 75–81.

McCoy, C. M. (1952). Chemical aspects of ageing and the effect of diet upon ageing. In A. I. Lansing (Ed.), *Sowdry's problems of ageing* (pp. 139–202). Baltimore: Williams & Wilkins.

McFarland, R. A. (1953). *Human factors in air transportation*. New York: McGraw-Hill.

McFarland, R. A. (1968). The sensory and perceptual processes in aging. In K. W. Schaie (Ed.), *Theory and methods of research on aging*. Morgantown: West Virginia University Press.

McGarrigle, A., & Donaldson, M. (1974). Conservation accidents. *Cognition, 3*, 341–350.

McGhee, P. E. (1979). *Humor: Its origin and development*. San Francisco: W. H. Freeman.

McGrade, B. J. (1968). Newborn activity and emotional response at eight months. *Child Development, 39*, 1247–1252.

McGraw, M. (1939). Later development of children specially trained during infancy. *Child Development, 10*, 1–19.

McGuffin, P., Riley, B., & Plomin, R. (2001). Behavior genetics and the human genome. *Science, 291*, 1232–1249.

McGuire, K. D., & Weisz, J. R. (1982). Social cognition and behavior correlates of preadolescent chumship. *Child Development, 53*, 1478–1484.

McGurk, H. (1995). *Australian families*. Seminar presented at University of Queensland, August 25.

McIntire, W. G., Nass, G. D., & Battistone, D. L. (1974). Female misperception of male parenting attitudes and expectancies. *Youth and Society, 6*, 104–110.

McIntosh, J. L. (1989). Suicide: Native American. In R. & B. Kastenbaum (Eds.), *Encyclopedia of death*. Phoenix: Oryx Press.

McIntyre, L. A. (1976). An investigation of the effect of culture and urbanization on three cognitive styles and their relationship to school performance, In G. E. Kearney & D. W. McElwain (Eds.), *Aboriginal cognition: Retrospect and prospect*. Newark, NJ: Humanities Press.

McKenzie, A. F. (1985). The locus of control construct. Unpublished thesis, Murdoch University.

McKenzie, B., Day, R., & Ihsen, E. (1984). Localization of events in space. *British Journal of Developmental Psychology, 2*, 1–9.

McKenzie, B. E., Tootell, H. E., & Day, R. H. (1980). Development of visual size constancy during the first year of human infancy. *Developmental Psychology, 16*, 163–174.

McNeill, D. (1966). The creation of language by children. In J. Lyons & R. Wales (Eds.), *Psycholinguistic Papers*. Edinburgh: University of Edinburgh Press.

McNeill, D. (1970). The development of language. In P. H. Mussen (Ed.), *Carmichael's manual of child psychology* (Vol. 1), 1061–1161. New York: Wiley.

Mead, M. (1949). *Male and female*. New York: William Morrow.

Mead, M. (1960). Jealousy: Primitive and civilised. In A. M. Krich (Ed.), *The anatomy of love*. New York: Dell.

Mead, M. (1961). *Coming of age in Samoa*. New York: William Morrow. (Originally published in 1928.)

Mead, M. (1972). *Blackberry winter: My earlier years*. New York: William Morrow.

Mead, M. (1974). Adolescence. In H. V. Kraemer (Ed.), *Youth and culture: A human-development approach*. Monterey, CA: Brooks-Cole.

Meilman, P. W. (1979). Cross-sectional age changes in ego identity status during adolescence. *Developmental Psychology, 15*(2), 230–231.

Menyuk, P. (1971). *The Acquisition and development of language*. Englewood Cliffs, NJ: Prentice Hall.

Menyuk, P., & Bernholtz, N. (1969). Prosodic features and children's language production. *Massachusetts Institute of Technology Research Laboratory of Electronics Quarterly Progress Reports, 93*, 216–219.

Messer, S. B. (1976). Reflection-impulsivity: A review. *Psychological Bulletin, 83*, 1026–1052.

Middleton, M. R., & Francis, S. H. (1976). *Yuendumu and its children*. Canberra: Australian Government Publishing Service.

Mill, J. S. (1960). *The Autobiography of John Stuart Mill*. New York: Columbia University Press.

Miller, D. C., & Form, W. H. (1964). *Industrial society*. New York: Harper & Row.

Miller, M. R., & Binns, C. W. (1979). Cultural differences in children's T.V. viewing habits and implications for nutritional status. *Proceedings of the Nutrition Society of Australia, 4*, 120–121.

Miller, N. E., & Dollard, J. (1941). *Social learning and imitation*. New Haven, CT: Yale University Press.

Miller, P. H., & Weiss, M. G. (1982). Children's and adult's knowledge about what variables affect selective attention. *Child Development, 53*, 543–549.

Miller, R., & Glass, J. (1989). Parent–child attitude similarity across generations. *Journal of Marriage and the Family, 51*, 991–997.

Miller, V., Ontera, R. T., & Deinard, A. S. (1984). Denver developmental screening test: Cultural variations in Southeast Asian children. *Journal of Pediatrics, 104*(3), 481–482.

Minkowski, A. (1967). *Regional development of the brain in early life*. Oxford: Blackwell.

Minnigerode, F. A., & Lee, J. A. (1978). Young adults' perceptions of social sex roles across the life span. *Sex Roles, 4*(4), 563.

Minuchin, S., Rosman, B. L., & Baker, L. (1978). *Psychosomatic families: Anorexia nervosa in context*. Cambridge, MA: Harvard University Press.

Mitchell, J. J. (1975). *Human life: The early adolescent years*. Toronto: Holt, Rinehart & Winston.

Mitchell, P. (1997). *Introduction to Theory of Mind: Children, autism and apes*. London: Arnold Publishers.

Mitchell, V., & Helson, R. (1990). Women's prime of life: Is it the 50s? *Psychology of Women Quarterly, 14*, 451–470.

Miyake, K., Chen, S., & Campos, J. (1985). Infant temperament, mother's mode of interaction and attachment in Japan. *Monographs of the Society for Research in Child Development, 50*, 276–297.

Molinari, V., & Reichlin, R. E. (1985). Life review reminiscence in the elderly: A review of the literature. *International Journal of Aging and Human Development, 20*, 81–92.

Money, J., Cawte, J. E., Bianchi, G. N., & Nurcombe, B. (1970). Sex training and traditions in Arnhem Land. *British Journal of Medicine, 43*, 383–399.

Money, J., & Ehrhardt, A. (1972). *Man and woman, boy and girl*. Baltimore: Johns Hopkins University Press.

Montemayor, R. (1983). Parents and adolescents in conflict: All families some of the time and some families most of the time. *Journal of Early Adolescence, 3*(1–2), 83–103.

Montepare, J. M., & Lachman, M. E. (1989). 'You're only as old as you feel': Self-perceptions of age, fears of ageing and life satisfaction from adolescence to old age. *Psychology and Ageing, 4*(1), 73–78.

Moon, C., Cooper, R., & Fifer, W. (1993). Two-day-olds prefer their native language. *Infant Behaviour and Development, 16*, 495–500.

Moore, B., Underwood, B., & Rosenhan, D. L. (1973). Affect and altruism. *Developmental Psychology, 8*, 99–104.

Moore, C., & Frye, D. (1986). The effect of experimenter's intention on the child's understanding of conservation. *Cognition, 22*, 283–298.

Moore, K. L. (1993). *Before we are born: Essentials of embryology and birth defects*. Philadelphia: Saunders.

Moore, S., & Rosenthal, D. (1993). *Sexuality in adolescence*. London: Routledge.

Moore, S. M., & Rosenthal, D. (1991a). Adolescent invulnerability and perceptions of AIDS risk. *Journal of Adolescent Research, 6*, 164–180.

Moore, S. M., & Rosenthal, D. (1991b). Adolescents' perceptions and friends' and parents' attitudes to sex and sexual risk-taking. *Journal of Community and Applied Psychology, 1*, 189–200.

Moore, W. E. (1969). Occupational socialization. In D. Goslin (Ed.), *Handbook of socialization theory and practice*. Chicago: Rand McNally.

Morawski, J. G. (1987). The troubled quest for masculinity, femininity, and androgyny. In P. Shaver & C. Hendrick (Eds.), *Sex and gender*. London: Sage.

Morelli, G., Rogoff, B., Oppenheim, D., & Goldsmith, D. (1992). Cultural variations in infants' sleeping arrangements. *Developmental Psychology, 28*, 604–613.

Morris, D. (1983). *The book of ages*. London: Jonathan Cape.

Moshman, D. (1998). Cognitive development beyond childhood. In W. Damon (Series Ed.), D. Kuhn & R. Siegler (Vol. Eds.), *Handbook of child psychology* (Vol. 2): *Cognitive, language and perceptual development*. New York: Wiley.

Moskovitch, M., & Winocur, G. (2002). The frontal cortex and working memory. In D. T. Struss & R. T. Knight (Eds.), *The frontal lobes*. Oxford: Oxford University Press.

Moss, H. A. (1967). Sex, age and state as determinants of mother–infant interaction. *Merrill-Palmer Quarterly, 13*, 19–36.

Mumford, M. D. (1984). Age and outstanding occupational achievement: Lehman revisited. *Journal of Vocational Behavior, 25*, 225–244.

Munley, P. H. (1977). Erikson's theory of psychosocial development and career development. *Journal of Vocational Behavior, 10*, 261–269.

Munro, D., & Mann, L. (Eds.). (1989). *Heterogeneity in cross-cultural psychology*. Amsterdam: Swets & Zeitlinger.

Murphy, D. P. (1947). *Congenital malformations: A study of parental characteristics with special reference to the reproductive process* (2nd ed.). Philadelphia: Lippincott.

Murphy, P. P., & Burck, H. D. (1976). Career development of men at mid-life. *Journal of Vocational Behavior, 9*, 337–343.

Murray, A. (1979). Infant crying as an elicitor of parental behavior. *Psychological Bulletin, 86*, 191–215.

Murray, A. D., Dolby, R. M., Nation, R. L., & Thomas, D. P. (1981). The effect of epidural anesthesia on newborns and their mothers. *Child Development, 52*, 71–82.

Musgrove, F. (1964). *Youth and the social order*. Bloomington: Indiana University Press.

Mussen, P. H., & Jones, M. C. (1957). Self-conceptions, motivations, and inter-personal attitudes of late and early maturing boys. *Child Development, 28*, 243–256.

Mussen, P. H., & Rutherford, E. (1963). Parent–child relations and parental personality in relation to young children's sex-role preferences. *Child Development, 34*, 489–607.

Myers-Walls, J. A., & Fry-Miller, K. M. (1985). Nuclear war: Helping children overcome fears. *Australian Journal of Early Childhood, 10*, 43–46.

Nagel, E. (1957). Determinism and development. In D. B. Harris (Ed.), *The concept of development*. Minneapolis: University of Minnesota Press.

Nahemow, N. R. (1984). Grandparenthood in transition. In K. A. McCluskey & H. W. Reese (Eds.), *Life-span developmental psychology*. New York: Academic Press.

Nash, R. (1981). Schools can't make jobs: Structural unemployment and the schools. *New Zealand Journal of Educational Studies, 16*, 1–20.

Natapoff, J. N. (1982). A developmental analysis of children's ideas of health. *Health Education Quarterly, 9*, 130–141.

National Institute of Child Health & Development (NICHD). (1997). The effects of infant childcare on mother–infant attachment security. *Child Development, 68*, 860–879.

Neill, R. (2002). Black lives white lies, *The Australian*, June 29, p. 22.

Neimark, E. D. (1975). Intellectual development during adolescence. In F. D. Horowitz, E. M. Hetherington, S. Scarr-Salapatek & G. Siegel (Eds.), *Review of child development research* (Vol. 4). Chicago: University of Chicago Press.

Nelson, C., & Dolgin, K. (1985). The generalized discrimination of facial expressions by seven-month-old infants. *Child Development, 56*, 58–61.

Nelson, K. (1973). Structure and strategy in learning to talk. *Monographs of the Society for Research in Child Development, 38*, Serial No. 2.

Nelson, K. (1979). Explorations in the development of a functional semantic system. In W. A. Collins (Ed.), *Minnesota Symposium on Child Psychology*. Hillsdale, NJ: Erlbaum.

Nelson, K., Carskaddon, G., & Bonvillian, J. (1973). Syntax acquisition: Impact of experimental variation in adult verbal interaction with the child. Paper presented at the Society for Research in Child Development meeting.

Nelson, K., Denninger, M. M., Bonvillian, J. D., Kaplan, B., & Baker, N. (1984). Maternal input adjustments and non-adjustments as related to children's linguistic advances and to language acquisition theories. In A. Pellegrini & T. Yawkey (Eds.), *The development of oral and written language in social contexts*. Norwood, NJ: Ablex.

Nelson, K., Rescorla, L., Gruendel, J., & Benedict, H. (1978). Early lexicons: What do they mean? *Child Development, 49*, 960–968.

Nemeroff, C. J., & Cavanaugh, C. J. (1999). The ethics of emancipation: Moral connotations of body, self and diet. In M. Siegel & C. C. Peterson (Eds.), *Children's understanding of biology and health*. Cambridge, UK: Cambridge University Press.

Nesdale, A. R., & Pope, S. (1982). Young children's performance attributions and expectancies. In T. G. Cross & L. M. Riach (Eds.), *Issues and research in child development*. Melbourne: Institute of Early Childhood Development.

Nesdale, L. H., & Nesdale, A. R. (1987). Young children's detection of communication failures. *Australian Journal of Early Childhood, 12*, 15–19.

Nesselroade, J. R., & Baltes, P. B. (1974). Adolescent personality development and historical change 1970–1972. *Monographs of the Society for Research in Child Development, 39*(1), whole no. 154.

Nesselroade, J. R., Schaie, K. W., & Baltes, P. B. (1972). Ontogenetic and generational components of structural and qualitative change in adult behavior. *Journal of Gerontology, 27*, 222–228.

Neuendorff, D. (1986). Teenage awareness of family planning matters. *Australian Journal of Social Issues, 21*, 57–66.

Neugarten, B. L. (Ed.). (1968). *Middle age and aging: A reader in social psychology*. Chicago: University of Chicago Press.

Neugarten, B. L. (1969). Continuities and discontinuities of psychological issues into adult life. *Human Development, 12*, 121–130.

Neugarten, B. L. (1979). Time, age and the life cycle. *American Journal of Psychiatry, 136*, 887–894.

Neugarten, B. L. (1987). Understanding psychological man. *Psychology Today*, May, 54–56.

Neugarten, B. L., Moore, J. W., & Lowe, J. C. (1965). Age norms, age constraints and adult socialization. *American Journal of Sociology, 70*, 710–717.

Neugarten, B. L., & Weinstein, K. K. (1964). The changing American grandparent. *Journal of Marriage and the Family, 26*(2), 199–204.

Neugarten, B. L., Wood, V., Kraines, R. J., & Loomis, B. (1963). Women's attitudes toward the menopause. *Vita Humana, 6*(3), 140–151.

Neuhauser, C., Amsterdam, B., Hines, P., & Steward, M. (1978). Children's conceptions of healing: Cognitive development and locus of control factors. *American Journal of Orthopsychiatry, 48*, 334–341.

Neville, H., Bavelier, D., Corina, D., Rauschecker, J. et al. (1998). Cerebral organization of language in deaf and hearing subjects. *Proceedings of the National Academy of Sciences, USA, 95*, 922–929.

Neville, H. J., Coffey, S. A., Lawson, D. S., Fischer, A.,

Emmorey, K., & Bellugi, U. (1997). Neural systems mediating American sign language: Effects of sensory experience and age of acquisition. *Brain and Language, 57,* 285–308.

Newcomb, T. M. (1961). *The acquaintance process.* New York: Holt, Rinehart & Winston.

New Zealand Department of Statistics. (1993, 1995, 2000). *New Zealand Official Yearbook.* Wellington: Government Printer.

Ney, P. G. (1988). Transgenerational child abuse. *Child Psychiatry and Human Development, 18,* 151–168.

Ng, S. H. (1983). Children's ideas about bank and shop profit: Developmental stages and the influences of cognitive contrasts and conflict. *Journal of Economic Psychology, 4,* 209–221.

Nienhuys, T., Cross, T. G., & Horsborough, K. M. (1984). Child variables influencing maternal speech style. *Journal of Communication Disorders, 17,* 189–207.

Nilsson, E., Gillberg, C., Gillberg, I., & Rastam, M. (1999). Ten-year follow-up of adolescent-onset anorexia nervosa: personality disorders. *Journal of the American Academy of Child and Adolescent Psychiatry, 38,* 1389–1395.

Noesjirwan, J., Gault, U., & Crawford, J. (1983). Beliefs about memory in the aged. *Journal of Cross-Cultural Psychology, 14,* 455–468.

Noller, P. (1996). What is this thing called love? Defining the love that supports marriage and family. *Personal Relationships, 3,* 97–115.

Noller, P., & Bagi, S. (1985). Parent–adolescent communication. *Journal of Adolescence, 8,* 125–144.

Noller, P., & Callan, V. J. (1990). Adolescents' perceptions of the nature of their communication with parents. *Journal of Youth and Adolescence, 19,* 349–362.

Noller, P., Feeney, J. A., & Peterson, C. (2001). *Personal relationships across the lifespan.* Philadelphia, PA: Taylor & Francis.

Noller, P., Feeney, J., Peterson, C., & Sheehan, G. (1995). Learning conflict patterns in the family. In T. Socha & G. Stamp (Eds.), *Parents, children and communication.* Hove, UK: Erlbaum.

Noller, P., Feeney, J. A., Sheehan, G., & Peterson, C. (2000). Marital conflict patterns: Links with family conflict and family member's perceptions of one another. *Personal Relationships, 7,* 79–94.

Nowakowski, R. S. (1987). Basic concepts of CNS development. *Child Development, 58,* 568–595.

Nusberg, C. (1979). Do people want to retire? *Ageing International, VI*(2), 13–15.

Nusberg, C. (1980). Access to grandchildren a growing problem. *Ageing International, VII* (2), 14–16.

Nye, F. I., & Hoffman, L. W. (1963). *The employed mother in America.* Chicago: Rand McNally.

O'Brien, G. (1985). The effect of employment on behaviour: Recent developments in Australian organisational psychology. In N. T. Feather (Ed.), *Australian psychology: Review of research.* Sydney: Allen & Unwin.

O'Brien, G., & Dowling, P. (1981). Age and job satisfaction. *Australian Psychologist, 16,* 49–61.

O'Brien, G., & Feather, N. T. (1990). The relative effects of unemployment and quality of employment on the affect, work values and personal control of adolescents. *Journal of Occupational Psychology, 63,* 151–165.

O'Connell, A. (1976). The relationship between lifestyle and identity synthesis and resynthesis in traditional, neo-traditional, and non-traditional women. *Journal of Personality, 44,* 675–688.

O'Connell, E. M. (1987). An investigation into children's concepts of death of familiar animate and inanimate objects and vegetable matter. Unpublished thesis, Murdoch University.

O'Connor, B. P., & Nikolic, J. (1990). Identity development and formal operations as sources of adolescent egocentrism. *Journal of Youth and Adolescence, 19*(2).

Okura, Y., Ziller, R. C., & Osawa, H. (1986). The psychological niche of older Japanese and Americans through auto-photography: Aging and the search for peace. *International Journal of Aging and Human Development, 22,* 247–255.

Oliver, P. (1990). Nuclear freedom and students' sense of the efficacy about prevention of nuclear war. *American Journal of Orthopsychiatry, 60*(4), 611–619.

O'Loughlin, M. A., & Sinclair, K. E. (1982). Social change and the transition from adolescence to adulthood: A study of three generations of Australians. *Australian Journal of Education, 26,* 155–169.

Orlofsky, J. L., Marcia, J. E., & Lesser, I. M. (1973). Ego identity status and the intimacy versus isolation crisis of young adulthood. *Journal of Personality and Social Psychology, 27,* 211–219.

Osofsky, J. D., & Connors, K. (1979). Mother–infant interaction: An integrative view of a complex system. In J. D. Osofsky (Ed.), *Handbook of infant development.* New York: Wiley.

Over, R. (1989). Age and scholarly impact. *Psychology and Aging, 4,* 222–225.

Over, R., & Thomas, P. (1995). Age and skill. *Australian Journal of Psychology, 47,* 112.

Overton, W. F., & Reese, H. W. (1972). Models of development: Methodological implications. In J. R. Nesselroade & H. W. Reese (Eds.), *Life-span developmental psychology: Methodological issues.* New York: Academic Press.

Oviatt, S. L. (1980). The emerging ability to comprehend language: An experimental approach. *Child Development, 51,* 97–106.

Owles, E. (1975). A comparative study of nutrient intakes of migrant and Australian children in Western Australia. *Medical Journal of Australia, 26* July, 130–133.

Paabo, A. (2001). The human genome. *Science, 291,* 1155.

Pachana, N. M., Gallagher-Thompson, D., & Thompson, L. W. (1994). Assessment of depression. In M. P. Lawton & J. A. Teresi (Eds.), *Annual Review of Gerontology and Geriatrics* (Vol. 14, pp. 234–256). New York: Springer Publishing Company.

Pakizegi, B. (1985). Gender classification by infants. *Journal of Genetic Psychology, 46,* 135–136.

Palmore, E. (1986). Attitudes toward aging shown by humor: A review. In E. Palmore (Ed.), *Humor and aging.* New York: Academic Press.

Palmore, E. B. (1990). *Ageism: Negative and positive.* New York: Springer.

Palmore, E., Fillenbaum, G., & George, L. K. (1984). Consequences of retirement. *Journal of Gerontology, 39,* 109–116.

Papousek, H. (1967). Conditioning during early postnatal development. In Y. Brackbill & S. G. Thompson (Eds.), *Behavior in infancy and early childhood.* New York: Free Press.

Papousek, H. (1974). The course of conditioning in newborns. In L. J. Stone, H. T. Smith & L. B. Murphy (Eds.), *The competent infant.* London: Tavistock.

Paris, S. (1986). Teaching children to guide their reading and learning. In T. Raphael (Ed.), *The context of school-based literacy.* New York: Random House.

Paris, S., & Oka, E. (1986). Children's reading strategies, meta-cognition, and motivation. *Developmental Review, 6,* 25–56.

Park, A. (2002). What did the study show? *Time,* July 22, pp. 49–50.

Parke, R. D. (1977). The father of the child. *The Sciences, 14*(4), 12–15.

Parke, R. D. (1979). Perspectives on father–infant interaction. In J. D. Osofsky (Ed.), *Handbook of infant development.* New York: Wiley.

Parke, R. D. (1981). *Fathering.* Glasgow: Fontana.

Parke, R. D., & Kellum, S. G. (1994). *Exploring family relationships with other social contexts.* Hillsdale, NJ: Erlbaum.

Parke, R. D., & Stearns, P. (1993). Fathers and childrearing. In G. Elder et al. (Eds.), *Children in time and place.* New York: Cambridge.

Parks, C. M. (1972). *Bereavement.* New York: International Universities Press.

Parnicky, J. J., Williams, S., & Silva, P. A. (1985). Family environment scale: A Dunedin (New Zealand) pilot study. *Australian Psychologist, 20,* 195–204.

Parsons, D. St. J. (1978). Continuous dual career families: A case study. *Psychology of Women Quarterly, 3*(1), 30.

Parsons, T. (1955). Family structure and the socialization of the child. In T. Parsons & R. F. Bales (Eds.), *Family socialization and interaction process.* Glencoe, IL: Free Press.

Passman, R. (1977). Providing attachment objects to facilitate learning and reduce distress: Effects of mothers and security blankets. *Developmental Psychology, 13*(1), 25–28.

Pastalan, L. A. (1974). The simulation of age-related sensory losses. A new approach to the study of environmental barriers. *The New Outlook for the Blind,* October, 356–362.

Patterson, G., & Stouthamer-Loeber, M. (1984). The correlations of family management practice and delinquency. *Child Development, 55,* 1299–1307.

Patton, W., & Noller, P. (1984). Unemployment and youth: A longitudinal study. *Australian Journal of Psychology, 36,* 399–413.

Pavlov, I. P. (1927). *Conditioned Reflexes.* Translated by G. V. Anrep. London: Oxford University Press.

Paxton, S. J., Wertheim, E. H., Gibbons, K., Szmukler, G. I., Hillier, L., & Petrovich, J. L. (1991). Body image satisfaction, dieting beliefs, and weight loss behaviours in adolescent girls and boys. *Journal of Youth and Adolescence, 20,* 361–379.

Pears, J., & Noller, P. (1995). Youth homelessness: Abuse, gender and the process of adjustment to life on the streets. *Australian Journal of Social Issues, 30,* 405–424.

Peevers, B. H., & Secord, P. F. (1973). Developmental changes in attribution of descriptive concepts to persons. *Journal of Personality and Social Psychology, 27*(1), 120–128.

Pellegrini, A. (1984). The effects of classroom ecology on preschoolers' functional uses of language. In A. Pellegrini & T. Yawkey (Eds.), *The development of oral and written language in social contexts.* Norwood, NJ: Ablex.

Penner, S. G. (1987). Parental responses to grammatical and ungrammatical child utterances. *Child Development, 58,* 376–384.

Perlmutter, M. (1986). A life-span view of memory. In P. B. Baltes, D. L. Featherman & R. M. Lerner (Eds.), *Lifespan development and behavior.* Hillsdale, NJ: Lawrence Erlbaum.

Perlmutter, M., & Hall, E. (1992). *Adult development and aging* (2nd ed.). New York: Wiley.

Perner, J., Ruffman, T., & Leekam, S. (1994). Theory of mind is contagious: You catch it from your sibs. *Child Development, 65,* 1228–1238.

Perosa, S. L., & Perosa, L. M. (1985). The mid-career crisis in relation to Super's career and Erikson's adult development theory. *International Journal of Aging and Human Development, 20,* 53–67.

Perret-Clermont, A. N. (1980). *Social interaction and cognitive development in children.* London: Academic Press.

Perry, D. G., & Bussey, K. (1984). *Social development.* Englewood Cliffs, NJ: Prentice Hall.

Perry, J., & Perry, E. (1977). *Pairing and parenthood: An introduction to marriage and the family.* San Francisco: Canfield Press.

Pesce, R. C., & Harding, C. G. (1986). Imaginary audience behavior and its relationship to operational thought and social experience. *Journal of Early Adolescence, 6,* 83–94.

Peskin, H. (1972). Pre- and postpubertal personality and adult psychologic functioning. *Seminars in Psychiatry, 4,* 343–353.

Peskin, H. (1973). Influence of the developmental schedule of puberty on learning and ego functioning. *Journal of Youth and Adolescence, 2,* 273–290.

Petersen, A. C., Compas, B. E., Brooks-Gunn, J., Stemmler, M., Ey, S., & Grant, K. E. (1993). Depression in adolescence. *American Psychologist, 48,* 155–168.

Petersen, K. L., & Roscoe, B. (1991). Imaginary audience behaviour. *Adolescence, 26,* 195–200.

Peterson, C. C. (1974). *A child grows up.* New York: Alfred.

Peterson, C. C. (1975). Distributive justice within and outside the family. *Journal of Psychology, 90,* 123–127.

Peterson, C. C. (1981). Are young people biased against older teachers? *Journal of Genetic Psychology, 136,* 309–310.

Peterson, C. C. (1982a). The imaginary audience and age, cognition and dating. *Journal of Genetic Psychology, 140,* 317–318.

Peterson, C. C. (1982b). *Should we have a baby?* Adelaide: Rigby.

Peterson, C. C. (1987). Middle age in urban Australia versus an Israeli kibbutz. *Journal of Social Psychology, 127,* 405–407.

Peterson, C. C. (1990). Disagreement, conflict and negotiation in families with adolescents. In P. Heaven & V. Callan (Eds.), *Adolescence: An Australian perspective.* Sydney: Harcourt Brace Jovanovich.

Peterson, C. C. (1993a). The accuracy of older and younger Australians' understanding of mental health and aging. *International Journal of Aging and Human Development, 36,* 129–138.

Peterson, C. C. (1993b). Adult children and their parents. In R. Kastenbaum (Ed.), *Encyclopedia of adult development.* Phoenix, AZ: Oryx Press, pp. 1–6.

Peterson, C. C. (1995). Husbands' and wives' perceptions of global equity in marriage over the family life cycle. In

J. Hendricks (Ed.), *The ties of later life.* New York: Baywood.

Peterson, C. C. (1996). The ticking of the social clock: Adults' beliefs about the timing of transition events. *International Journal of Aging and Human Development, 142,* 189–203.

Peterson, C. C. (1999). Grandfathers' and grandmothers' satisfaction with the grandparenting role: Seeking new answers to old questions. *International Journal of Ageing and Human Development, 49,* 61–78.

Peterson, C. C. (2000). Kindred spirits: Influences of siblings' perspectives on theory of mind. *Cognitive Psychology, 15,* 435–455.

Peterson, C. C. (2001). The early years of development. In N. Bond & K. McConkey (Eds.), *Psychological science: An introduction.* Sydney: McGraw-Hill.

Peterson, C. C. (2002). Commentary: A propitious time to study lifespan close relationships, both old and new. *International Society for the Study of Behavioural Development, Newsletter, Number 1,* Serial No. 41, 19–20.

Peterson, C. C. (2003). Looking forward to old age: Images of the adult lifespan in Australians aged 20 to 89 years. Symposium paper: Australasian Human Development Association Conference, Auckland, July.

Peterson, C., Beck, K., & Rowell, G. (1992). *Psychology: An introduction for nurses and allied health professionals.* Sydney: Prentice Hall.

Peterson, C. C., & McDonald, L. (1980). Children's occupational sex-typing. *Journal of Genetic Psychology, 136,* 145–146.

Peterson, C. C., & Peterson, J. L. (1975). Issues concerning collaborating careers. *Journal of Vocational Behavior, 7,* 173–180.

Peterson, C. C., & Peterson, J. L. (1986). Children and cigarettes: The effect of a model who quits. *Journal of Applied Developmental Psychology, 7,* 293–306.

Peterson, C. C., Peterson, J. L., & Carroll, J. (1983). Children's attitudes toward imagination. Paper presented at 53rd Australian and New Zealand Association for the Advancement of Science Conference, Perth, May.

Peterson, C. C., Peterson, J. L., & McDonald, N. (1975). Factors affecting reward allocation by preschool children. *Child Development, 46,* 942–947.

Peterson, C. C., Peterson, J. L., & Seeto, D. (1983). Developmental changes in ideas about lying. *Child Development, 54,* 1529–1535.

Peterson, C. C., Peterson, J. L., & Skevington, S. (1986). Heated argument and adolescent development. *Journal of Social and Personal Relationships, 3,* 229–240.

Peterson, C., Peterson, J., & Webb, J. (2000). Factors influencing the development of a Theory of Mind in blind children. *British Journal of Developmental Psychology, 18,* 431–447.

Peterson, C. C., & Siegal, M. (1995). Deafness, conversation and the theory of mind. *Journal of Child Psychology and Psychiatry, 36,* 459–474.

Peterson, C., & Siegal, M. (1998). Changing focus on the representational mind. *British Journal of Developmental Psychology, 16,* 301–320.

Peterson, C. C., & Siegal, M. (1999a). Cognitive development and the competence to consent to medical and psychotherapeutic treatment. In M. Siegel & C. C. Peterson (Eds.), *Children's understanding of biology and health.* Cambridge, UK: Cambridge University Press.

Peterson, C., & Siegal, M. (1999b). Representing inner worlds: Theory of mind in autistic, deaf and normal hearing children. *Psychological Science, 10,* 126–129.

Peterson, C., & Siegal, M. (2000). Insights into theory of mind from deafness and autism. *Mind & Language, 15,* 123–145.

Peterson, C., & Siegal, M. (2002). Mindreading and moral awareness in popular and rejected preschoolers. *British Journal of Developmental Psychology, 20,* 205–234.

Peterson, C., & Slaughter, V. (in press). Opening windows into the mind. *Cognitive Development.*

Peterson, D. R. (1983). Conflict. In H. H. Kelley, E. Berscheid, A. Christensen, J. H. Harvey, T. L. Huston, G. Levinger et al. (Eds.), *Close relationships.* New York: W. H. Freeman.

Peterson, S. A. (1985). Death anxiety and politics. *Omega. 16*(2), 169–173.

Pfeiffer, E., & Davis, G. C. (1971). The use of leisure time in middle life. *Gerontologist, 11*(3, Part 1), 187–195.

Pflaum, S. W., Walberg, H., Karegianes, M., & Rasher, R. (1980). Reading instruction: A quantitative analysis. *Educational Research, 9,* 12–18.

Phillips, B. S. (1957). A role theory approach to adjustment in old age. *American Sociological Review, 22*, 212–217.

Phillips, D. (1984). The illusion of incompetence among academically competent children. *Child Development, 55*, 2000–2016.

Phillips, J. R. (1973). Syntax and vocabulary of mothers' speech to young children: Age and sex comparisons. *Child Development, 44*, 182–185.

Phillips, M., Nicholson, J., & Peterson, C. (2002). The relationship between the parenting styles of biological parents and stepparents. *Journal of Divorce and Remarriage, 36*(3/4), 57–76.

Phillips, M., Nicholson, J., Peterson, C., & Battistutta, D. (2002). Relationship between the parenting styles of biological parents and step-parents and the adjustment of young adult stepchildren. *Journal of Divorce and Remarriage, 36*, 57–76.

Phillips, S. (1982). Adult attitudes to children and childrearing practices in Sydney. In T. G. Cross & L. M. Riach (Eds.), *Issues and research in child development*. Melbourne: Institute of Early Childhood Development.

Phinney, J. S. (1990). Ethnic identity in adolescents and adults: A review of research. *Psychological Bulletin, 108*(3), 499–514.

Phinney, J. S. (1993). A three-stage model of ethnic identity development in adolescence. In M. E. Bernal & G. P. Knight (Eds.), *Ethnic identity: Formation and transmission among Hispanics and other minorities*. Albany, NY: SUNY Press.

Phinney, J. S. (1995). Ethnic identity and self-esteem: A review and integration. In A. M. Padilla (Ed.), *Hispanic psychology: Critical issues in theory and research*. Thousand Oaks, CA: Sage.

Phinney, J. S. (1996). When we talk about American ethnic groups, what do we mean? *American Psychologist, 51*(9), 918–927.

Phinney, J. S., & Alipuria, L. L. (1990). Ethnic identity in college students from four ethnic groups. *Journal of Adolescence, 13*, 131–183.

Phinney, J. S., & Rosenthal, D. A. (1993). Ethnic identity in adolescence: Process, context and outcome. In G. R. Adams, R. Montemayor & T. P. Gullotta (Eds.), *Adolescent identity formation*. London: Sage Publications.

Piaget, J. (1929/1973). *The child's conception of the world*. Frogmore, UK: Paladin.

Piaget, J. (1932/1965). *The moral judgment of the child*. New York: Free Press.

Piaget, J. (1952a). *The language and thought of the child*. London: Routledge & Kegan Paul.

Piaget, J. (1952b). *The origins of intelligence in children*. New York: International Universities Press.

Piaget, J. (1955). *The language and thought of the child*. New York: Meridian Books.

Piaget, J. (1959). *Judgment and reasoning in the child*. Paterson, NJ: Littlefield, Adams.

Piaget, J. (1962). *Play, dreams, and imitation in childhood*. New York: W. W. Norton.

Piaget, J. (1970). Piaget's theory. In P. H. Mussen (Ed.), *Carmichael's manual of child psychology*. New York: Wiley.

Piaget, J. (1972). Intellectual evolution from adolescence to adulthood. *Human Development, 15*, 1–12.

Piaget, J. (1973). *The child's conception of the world*. St Albans, UK: Frogmore.

Piaget, J. (1976a). *Autobiographie*. Unpublished manuscript, University of Geneva.

Piaget, J. (1976b). *The grasp of consciousness*. Cambridge, MA: Harvard University Press.

Piaget, J., & Inhelder, B. (1968). *The psychology of the child*. New York: Basic Books.

Piaget, J., & Inhelder, B. (1973). *Memory and intelligence*. New York: Basic Books.

Piaget, J., Inhelder, B., & Szeminska, A. (1960). *The child's conception of geometry*. New York: Basic Books.

Pike, A., & Plomin, R. (1997). A behavioural genetic perspective on close relationships. *International Journal of Behavioural Development, 21*, 647–667.

Piliavin, J., & Piliavin, I. (1972). Effects of blood on reactions to a victim. *Journal of Personality and Social Psychology, 23*, 353–361.

Pineo, P. (1961). Disenchantment in the later years of marriage. *Marriage and Family Living, 23*, 3–11.

Pineo, P. (1968). Disenchantment in the later years of marriage.

In B. L. Neugarten (Ed.), *Middle age and aging: A reader in social psychology*. Chicago: University of Chicago Press.

Pines, M. (1981). Only isn't lonely (or spoiled or selfish). *Psychology Today*, March, 11–19.

Pingree, S., & Hawkins, R. (1981). US programs on Australian television: The cultivation effect. *Journal of Communication, 31*, 97–105.

Pipe, M. E., & Goodman, G. S. (1991). Elements of secrecy: Implications for children's testimony. *Behavioral Sciences and the Law, 9*, 33–41.

Plomin, R. (1986). *Development, genetics, and psychology*. Hillsdale, NJ: Erlbaum.

Plomin, R. (1994). *Genetics and experience*. Newbury Park, CA: Sage.

Plomin, R. (2000). Behavioral genetics in the 21st century. *International Journal of Behavioral Development, 24*, 30–34.

Plomin, R., & DeFries, J. C. (1983). The Colorado adoption project. *Child Development, 54*, 276–289.

Plomin, R., DeFries, J. C., & McClearn, G. E. (1980). *Behavioral genetics: A primer*. San Francisco: W. H. Freeman.

Plomin, R., DeFries, J., McClearn, G. E., & Rutter, M. (1997). *Behavioural genetics*. New York: Freeman.

Plomin, R., Loehlin, J., & DeFries, J. (1985). Genetic and environmental influences in maternal and sibling interaction in middle childhood: A sibling adoption study. *Developmental Psychology, 28*, 484–490.

Plomin, R., & Rutter, M. (1998). Child development, molecular genetics and what to do with genes once they are found. *Child Development, 69*, 1223–1242.

Plumb, J. H. (1971). The great change in children. *Horizon, 13*(1), 4–13.

Podd, M. H. (1972). Ego identity status and morality: The relationship between the two constructs. *Developmental Psychology, 6*, 497–507.

Podmore, V., & St George, R. (1986). New Zealand Maori and European mothers and their 3-year-old children: Interactive behaviors in pre-school settings. *Journal of Applied Developmental Psychology, 7*, 373–382.

Pohlman, E. (1969). *The Psychology of Birth Planning*. Cambridge, MA: Schenkman.

Pollack, J. M. (1980). Correlates of death anxiety: A review of empirical studies. *Omega, 10*, 97–121.

Pollitt, E., Golub, M., Gorman, K., Grantham-McGregor, S., Levitsky, D., Schurch, B., Strupp, B. et al. (1996). A reconceptualization of the effects of undernutrition on children's biological, psychosocial and behavioral development. *SRCD Social Policy Report, 10*. Ann Arbor, MI: Society for Research in Child Development.

Poole, M. (1983). *Youth: Expectations and transitions*. Melbourne: Routledge & Kegan Paul.

Poole, M., De Lacey, P., & Randhawa, B. (1985). *Australia in transition*. Sydney: Harcourt Brace Jovanovich.

Poole, M. E., & Low, B. C. (1982). Who stays? Who leaves? An examination of sex differences in staying and leaving. *Journal of Youth and Adolescence, 11*, 49–63.

Poole, M., Sundberg, N. D., & Tyler, L. E. (1982). Adolescents' perceptions of family decision-making and autonomy in India, Australia and the United States. *Journal of Comparative Family Studies, 13*(3), 349–357.

Porac, C., Coren, S., & Duncan, P. (1980). Life-span age trends in laterality. *Journal of Gerontology, 35*, 715–721.

Porter, R. H., Makin, J. W., Davis, L., & Christensen, K. (1992). Breastfed infants' responses to olfactory cues from their own mother and unfamiliar lactating females. *Infant Behavior & Development, 15*, 85–93.

Power, D., & Carty, B. (1990). Cross-cultural communication and the deaf community in Australia. In C. Hendrick & R. Holton (Eds.), *Cross-cultural communication and professional education*. Adelaide: Flinders University Centre for Multicultural Studies.

Preston, G. A. N. (1986). Dementia in elderly adults: Prevalence and institutionalization. *Journal of Gerontology, 41*(2), 261–267.

Price-Williams, D. R., Gordon, W., & Ramirez, M. (1969). Skill and conservation: A study of pottery-making children. *Developmental Psychology, 1*, 296–334.

Prior, M. R., Dahlstrom, B., & Squires, T. L. (1990). Autistic children's knowledge of thinking and feeling states in other people. *Journal of Child Psychology and Psychiatry, 31*, 587–602.

Prior, M., Garina, E., Sanson, A., & Oberklaid, F. (1987). Ethnic influences on 'difficult' temperament and behavioural problems in infants. *Australian Journal of Psychology, 39,* 163–172.

Pritchard, C. (1992). Youth suicide and gender in Australia and New Zealand compared with countries of the Western world (1973–1987). *Australian and New Zealand Journal of Psychiatry, 26,* 609–617.

Pruchno, R., & Smyer, M. (1983). Mental health and aging: A short quiz. *International Journal of Aging and Human Development, 17,* 123–138.

Pryor, R. G. L. (1980). Some types of stability in the study of students' work values. *Journal of Vocational Behavior, 16,* 146–158.

Pryor, R. G. L., & Taylor, N. (1986). What would I do if I couldn't do what I wanted to do? Investigating career compromise strategies. *Australian Psychologist, 21,* 363–376.

Pumariega, A. J. (1986). Acculturation and eating attitudes in adolescent girls. *Journal of the American Academy of Child Psychiatry, 25,* 276–279.

Purnine, D., & Carey, M. (1998). Age and gender differences in sexual behavior preferences: A follow-up report. *Journal of Sex & Marital Therapy, 24,* 93–102.

Putallaz, M. (1983). Predicting children's sociometric status from their behavior. *Child Development, 54,* 1417–1426.

Quine, S. (1973). Relative concern over evaluation by others in two ethnic cultures. *Australian and New Zealand Journal of Sociology, 9*(3), 65–66.

Rabbitt, P. (1993). Does it all go together when it goes? *Quarterly Journal of Experimental Psychology: Human Experimental Psychology, 46A,* 385–434.

Rabinowitz, S., & Stumpf, S. A. (1987). Facets of role conflict, role-specific performance, and organizational level within the academic career. *Journal of Vocational Behavior, 30,* 72–83.

Radke-Yarrow, M., Cummings, E. M., Kuczynski, L., & Chapman, M. (1985). Patterns of attachment in two- and three-year-olds in normal families and families with parental depression. *Child Development, 56,* 884–893.

Radloff, L. (1975). Sex differences in depression: The effects of occupation and marital status. *Sex Roles, 1*(3), 249–265.

Ragon, B. M., Kittelson, M. J., & St Pierre, R. W. (1995). The effect of a single effective HIV/AIDS educational program on college students' knowledge and atittudes. *AIDS Education and Prevention, 7*(3), 221–231.

Rahe, R. H. (1979). Life change events and mental illness: An overview. *Journal of Human Stress, 5,* 2–10.

Randhawa, B. S., de Lacey, P. R., & Saklofske, D. H. (1986). Personality and behavioral measures: Gender, age, and race contrasts in an Australian setting. *International Journal of Psychology, 21,* 389–402.

Rands, M., Levinger, G., & Mellinger, G. D. (1981). Patterns of conflict resolution and marital satisfaction. *Journal of Family Issues, 2*(3), 297–321.

Raphael, B. (1992). *Anatomy of bereavement.* London: Routledge.

Reaves, J., & Roberts, A. (1983). The effect of type of information on attraction to peers. *Child Development, 54,* 1024–1031.

Rebelsky, F., & Hanks, C. (1971). Fathers' vocal interaction with infants in the first three months of life. *Child Development, 42,* 63–68.

Reedy, M. N., Birren, J. E., & Schaie, K. W. (1981). Age and sex differences in satisfying love relationships across the adult life span. *Human Development, 24,* 52–66.

Rees, J. M., & Trahms, C. M. (1989). Nutritional influences on physical growth and behavior in adolescents. In G. R. Adams, R. Montemayor & T. P. Gullotta (Eds.), *Biology of adolescent behavior and development.* Newbury Park, CA: Sage Publications.

Reese, H. W. (1976). The development of memory: Lifespan perspectives. In H. W. Reese (Ed.), *Advances in child development and behavior.* New York: Academic Press.

Reese, H. W., & Overton, W. F. (1970). Models of development and theories of development. In L. R. Goulet & P. B. Baltes (Eds.), *Life-span developmental psychology: Theory and research* (pp. 116–145). New York: Academic Press.

Reid, J. (1985) 'Going up' or ' going down': The status of old people in Aboriginal society. *Ageing and Society, 5,* 69–95.

Reiser-Danner, L. (1994). Infant day care, attachment and the 'file drawer' problem. *Child Development, 65,* 1429–1443.

Rende, R., Slomkowski, C., Stocker, C., Fulker, D., & Plomin, R. (1992). Genetic and environmental influences on maternal and sibling interaction in middle childhood: A sibling adoption study. *Developmental Psychology, 31,* 531–539.

Reno, R. (1979). Attribution for success and failure as a function of perceived age. *Journal of Gerontology, 34,* 709–715.

Renshaw, P., & Brown, P. (1993). Loneliness and sociometric status. *Child Development, 46.*

Retschitzki, J. (1989). Evidence of formal thinking in Baoule airele players. In D. M. Keats, D. Munro & L. Mann (Eds.), *Heterogeneity in cross-cultural psychology.* Amsterdam: Swets & Zeitlinger.

Reznick, J. S., & Goldfield, B. A. (1992). Rapid change in lexical development in comprehension and production. *Developmental Psychology, 28,* 406–413.

Rheingold, H. L., & Cook, K. V. (1975). The contents of boys' and girls' rooms as an index of parents' behavior. *Child Development, 46,* 459–463.

Rheingold, H. L., Gewirtz, J. L., & Ross, H. W. (1959). Social conditioning of vocalization in the infant. *Journal of Comparative and Physiological Psychology, 52,* 68–73.

Richards, M. P. M., Bernal, J. F. & Brackbill, Y. (1976). Early behavior differences: Gender or circumcision? *Developmental Psychobiology, 9,* 89–95.

Richardson, A. (1961). The assimilation of British immigrants in a Western Australian community: A psychological study. *Research Group for European Migration Problems, 9,* 1–75.

Richmond, P. C. (1984). An aspect of sex-role identification with a sample of twelve year olds and sixteen year olds. *Sex Roles, 11,* 1021–1032.

Rickwood, D., & Bussey, K. (1984). Sex differences in gender schema and scriptal knowledge. Unpublished manuscript, Macquarie University.

Ridenour, M. (1982). Infant walkers: Developmental tool or inherent danger? *Perceptual and Motor Skills, 55,* 1201–1202.

Riegel, K. F. (1971). The predictors of death and longevity in longitudinal research. In E. Palmore & F. C. Jeffers (Eds.), *Handbook of aging.* New York: Academic Press.

Riegel, K. F. (1972). Time and change and the individual. In H. W. Reese (Ed.), *Advances in child development research.* New York: Academic Press.

Riegel, K. F. (1975). *The development of dialectical operations.* Basel: Karger.

Riegel, K. F. (1976). The dialectics of human development. *American Psychologist, 31,* 689–700.

Riley, J. W., Jr. (1970). What people think about death. In O. Brim, H. E. Freeman, S. Levine & N. A. Scotch (Eds.), *The dying patient.* New York: Sage.

Riley, M., & Foner, A. (1968). *Aging and society.* New York: Sage.

Risley, T. (1982). Personal communication. Lecture given at Selby Clinic, Perth, April.

Ritchie, J., & Ritchie, J. (1978). *Growing up in New Zealand.* Hornsby, NSW: Allen & Unwin.

Roberto, K., & Stroes, J. (1995). Grandchildren and grandparents. In J. Hendricks (Ed.), *The ties of later life.* New York: Baywood.

Roberts, W. L. (1979–80). Significant elements in the relationship of long-married couples. *International Journal of Aging and Human Development, 10*(3), 265–271.

Robertson, J. F. (1977). Grandmotherhood: A study of role conceptions. *Journal of Marriage and the Family, 39,* 165–174.

Robinson, J., Kagan, J., Reznick, J. S., & Corley, R. (1992). The heritability of inhibited and uninhibited behaviour: A twin study. *Developmental Psychology, 28,* 1030–1037.

Rodin, J. (1984). A sense of control. *Psychology Today,* December, 38–45.

Roffwarg, H., Muzio, J., & Dement, W. (1966). Ontogenetic development of the human sleep–dream cycle. *Science, 152,* 604–619.

Roggman, L., Langlois, J., Hubbs-Tait, L., & Reiger-Danner, L. (1994). Infant day care, attachment and the file drawer problem. *Child Development, 65,* 1429–1443.

Rogoff, B. (1981). Schooling and the development of cognitive skills. In H. C. Trandis & A. Heron (Eds.), *Handbook of cross-cultural psychology,* Vol. 4. Boston: Allyn & Bacon.

Rogoff, B. (1990). *Apprenticeship in thinking.* New York: Oxford University Press.

Rollins, B. C., & Cannon, K. L. (1974). Marital satisfaction over the family life cycle: A reevaluation. *Journal of Marriage and the Family, 36*(2), 271–283.

Rollins, B. C., & Feldman, H. (1970). Marital satisfaction over the family life cycle. *Journal of Marriage and the Family, 32*(1), 20–28.

Rose, S. P. R. (1973). *The conscious brain.* New York: Alfred A. Knopf.

Rosekranz, M. (1967). Imitation in children as a function of perceived similarity to a social model and vicarious reinforcement. *Journal of Personality and Social Psychology, 7,* 307–315.

Rosen, B., & Jerdee, T. H. (1976). The nature of job-related age stereotypes. *Journal of Applied Psychology, 61,* 180–183.

Rosenfeld, A. (1976). *Prolongevity.* New York: Alfred A. Knopf.

Rosenkrantz, A. L. (1978). A note on adolescent suicide: Incidence, dynamics and some suggestions for treatment. *Adolescence, 13,* 209–214.

Rosenthal, D. A. (1982). Influence of ethnicity on parent–adolescent conflict. In T. G. Cross & L. M. Riach (Eds.), *Issues and research in child development.* Melbourne: Institute of Early Childhood Development.

Rosenthal, D. A., & Chapman, D. C. (1982). The lady spaceman: Children's perceptions of sex-stereotyped occupations. *Sex Roles, 8,* 959–965.

Rosenthal, D. A., & Feldman, S. S. (1992). The relationship between parenting behaviour and ethnic identity in Chinese-American and Chinese-Australian adolescents. *International Journal of Psychology, 27*(1), 19–31.

Rosenthal, D. A., Gurney, R. M., & Moore, S. M. (1981). From trust to intimacy: A new inventory for examining Erikson's stages of psychosocial development. *Journal of Youth and Adolescence, 10,* 525–537.

Rosenthal, D. A., Moore, S. M., & Taylor, M. J. (1983). Ethnicity and adjustment: A study of the self-image of Anglo-, Greek-, and Italian-Australian working class adolescents. *Journal of Youth and Adolescence, 12,* 117–135.

Rosenthal, D., Moore, S., & Brumen, I. (1990). Ethnic group differences in adolescents' responses to AIDS. *Australian Journal of Social Issues, 25*(3), 220–239.

Rosenthal, D. A., & Paltiel, M. (1982). Children's knowledge and use of gender stereotypes. *Psychological Reports, 51,* 849–850.

Rosenzweig, M., Breedlove, M., & Leiman, A. (2002). *Biological psychology* (3rd ed.). Sunderland, MA: Sinauer Associates.

Ross, G. (1985). Use of the Bayley Scales to characterize abilities of premature infant. *Child Development, 56,* 835–842.

Rossi, A. S. (1977). Transition to parenthood. In L. R. Allman & D. T. Jaffe (Eds.), *Readings in adult psychology: Contemporary perspectives.* New York: Harper & Row.

Rotenberg, K. J. (1985). Causes, intensity, motives and consequences of children's anger from self-reports. *Journal of Genetic Psychology, 146,* 101–106.

Roth, J. (1971). *Adolescence.* New York: Atherton.

Rovee, C. K., Cohen, R. Y., & Shlapack, W. (1975). Life span stability of olfactory sensitivity. *Developmental Psychology, 11,* 311–318.

Rowland, D. I. (1982). The vulnerability of the aged in Sydney. *Australian and New Zealand Journal of Sociology, 18,* 229–247.

Roybal, E. R. (1988). Mental health and aging. *American Psychologist, 43,* 189–194.

Rozin, P. (1990a). Social norms and moral aspects of food and eating. In I. Rocks (Ed.), *The legacy of Solomon Asch: Essays in cognition and social psychology* (pp. 97–110). Hillsdale, NJ: Erlbaum.

Rozin, P. (1990b). Towards a psychology of food and eating: From motivation to model to meaning, morality and metaphor. *Current Directions in Psychology, 5,* 1–7.

Rozin, P. (1991). Family resemblance in food and other domains. *Appetite, 16,* 93–102.

Rozin, P., & Fallon, A. E. (1981). The acquisition of likes and dislikes for foods. In J. Solms & R. L. Hall (Eds.), *Criteria of food acceptance: How man chooses what he eats. A symposium* (pp. 35–48). Zurich: Forester.

Rozin, P., & Fallon, A. E. (1987). A perspective on disgust. *Psychological Review, 94,* 23–41.

Rozin, P., Fallon, A. E., & Augustoni-Ziskind, A. (1986). The child's conception of food: The development of contamina-

tion sensitivity to disgusting substances. *Developmental Psychology, 21,* 1075–1079.

Rozin, P., Fallon, A., & Mandell, R. (1984). Family resemblance in attitudes to foods. *Developmental Psychology, 20,* 309–314.

Rozin, P., Millman, L., & Nemeroff, C. (1986). Operation of the laws of sympathetic magic. *Journal of Personality and Social Psychology, 50,* 703–712.

Rozin, P., Nemeroff, C., Horowitz, M., Gordon, B., & Voet, W. (1995). The borders of the self: Contamination sensitivity and potency of the body apertures and other body parts. *Journal of Research in Personality, 29,* 318–340.

Rozin, P., Nemeroff, C., & Markwith, M. (1993). Magical contagion, beliefs and fear of AIDS. *Journal of Applied Social Psychology, 23,* 1081–1092.

Rozin, P., Nemeroff, C., Wane, M., & Sherrod, A. (1989). Operation of the laws of sympathetic magic in the interpersonal domain in American culture. *Bulletin of Psychonomic Society, 27*(4), 367–370.

Rubenstein, J. L., Howes, C., & Boyle, P. A. (1981). Two-year follow-up of infants in community based day care. *Journal of Child Psychology and Psychiatry, 22,* 209–218.

Rubin, K. H., Burgess, K., & Hastings, P. (2002). Stability and sociobehavioral consequences of toddlers' inhibited temperament and parenting behavior. *Child Development, 73,* 483–495.

Rubin, K. H., Hastings, P., Chen, X., Stewart, S., & McNichol, K. (1998). Interpersonal and maternal correlates of aggression, conflict and externalising problems in toddlers. *Child Development, 69,* 1614–1629.

Rubin, K. H., Maioni, T. L., & Hornung, M. (1976). Free play behaviours in middle- and lower-class preschoolers: Parten and Piaget revisited. *Child Development, 47,* 414–419.

Rubin, J. Z., Provenzano, F. J., & Luria, Z. (1974). The eye of the beholder: Parents' views on the sex of newborns. *American Journal of Orthopsychiatry, 43,* 720–731.

Rubin, Z. (1981). Does personality really change after 20? *Personality Today,* May, 18–27.

Ruffman, T., Perner, J., Naito, M., Parkin, L., & Clements, W. A. (1998). Older (but not younger) siblings facilitate false belief understanding. *Developmental Psychology, 34,* 161–174.

Runyan, W. (1978). The life course as a theoretical orientation. *Journal of Personality. 46,* 569–593.

Ruoppila, R., & Takkinen, S. (2001). Life functioning in old age. *International Journal of Ageing and Human Development, 53,* 231–232.

Russell, B. (1935). *In praise of idleness and other essays.* London: Allen & Unwin.

Russell, B. (1975). *The autobiography of Bertrand Russell.* London: Allen & Unwin. (Originally published in 1926.)

Russell, C. S. (1974). Transition to parenthood: Problems and gratifications. *Journal of Marriage and the Family, 36,* 294–301.

Russell, G. (1978). The father role and its relation to masculinity, femininity, and androgyny. *Child Development, 49,* 1174–1181.

Russell, G. (1982). Shared-caregiving families: Australian study. In M. Lamb (Ed.), *Nontraditional families: Parenting and child development.* Hillsdale, NJ: Erlbaum.

Russell, G., & Russell, A. (1987). Mother–child and father–child relationships in middle childhood. *Child Development, 58,* 1573–1585.

Rutter, M. (1974). Protective factors in children's responses to stress and disadvantage. In M. W. Kent & J. E. Rolf (Eds.), *Primary prevention of psychopathology* (Vol. III). Cambridge, UK: Cambridge University Press.

Rutter, M., & Garmezy, N. (1983). Developmental psychopathology. In E. M. Hetherington (Ed.), *Handbook of child psychology* (Vol. 4): *Socialization, personality, and social development.* New York: Wiley.

Rutter, M., & Quinton, D. (1984). Long-term follow-up of women institutionalized in childhood: Factors promoting good functioning in adult life. *British Journal of Development Psychology, 2,* 191–204.

Ryder, R. G. (1973). Longitudinal data relating marriage satisfaction and having a child. *Journal of Marriage and the Family, 35,* 605–606.

Ryff, C. (1984). Personality development from the inside. In P. B. Baltes & O. G. Brim (Eds.), *Life-span development and behavior.* New York: Academic Press.

Ryff, C. D. (1989). Happiness is everything, or is it?

Explorations on the meaning of psychological wellbeing. *Journal of Personality & Social Psychology, 57,* 1069–1081.

Ryff, C. D. (1989). In the eye of the beholder: Views of psychological well-being among middle-aged and older adults. *Psychology and Ageing, 4,* 195–210.

Ryff, C., & Heincke, S. (1983). The subjective organization of personality in adulthood and aging. *Journal of Personality and Social Psychology, 44,* 807–816.

Saarni, C. (1999). *The development of emotional competence.* New York: Guilford.

Sagan, K., & De Blassie, R. (1981). The male midlife crisis and career change. *Journal of Employment Counseling, 18,* 34–42.

Sales, E. (1978). Women's adult development. In I. H. Frieze, J. E. Parsons, P. B. Johnson, D. K. Ruble & G. L. Zellman (Eds.), *Women and sex roles.* New York: W. W. Norton.

Salk, L. (1973). The role of the heartbeat in the relations between mother and infant. *Scientific American, 288,* 24–29.

Sanson, A., & Di Muccio, C. (1993). The influence of aggressive and neutral cartoons and toys on the behaviour of preschool children. *Australian Psychologist, 28,* 93–99.

Sanson, A., Prior, M., & Oberklaid, F. (1985). Normative data on temperament in Australian infants. *Australian Journal of Psychology, 37,* 185–191.

Santrock, J. W. (1997). *Life-span development.* Maddison, WI: Brown & Benchmark Publishers.

Sartre, J. P. (1967). *Words.* Ringwood, VIC: Penguin.

Sartre, J. P. (1977). *Life situations.* Translated by P. Auster and L. Davis. New York: Pantheon Books.

Savage, R. D. (1973). Old age. In H. Eysenck (Ed.), *Handbook of abnormal psychology.* London: Methuen.

Savage, R. D., Britton, P. G., Bolton, N., & Hall, E. H. (1973). *Intellectual functioning in the aged.* London: Methuen.

Savage, R. D., Faber, L. B., Britton, P. G., Bolton, N., & Cooper, A. (1977). *Personality and adjustment in the aged.* London: Academic Press.

Savin-Williams, R., & Small, S. (1986). The timing of puberty and its relationship to adolescent and parent perceptions of family interactions. *Developmental Psychology, 22,* 322–347.

Scarr, S. (1992). Developmental theories for the 1990s: Development and individual differences. *Child Development, 63,* 1–19.

Scarr, S., & McCartney, K. (1983). How people make their own environments: A theory of genotype–environment effects. *Child Development, 54,* 424–435.

Scarr-Salapatek, S. (1975). Genetics and the development of intelligence. In F. D. Horowitz, E. M. Hetherington, S. Scarr-Salapatek & G. Siegel (Eds.), *Review of child development research* (Vol. 4). Chicago: University of Chicago Press.

Schaefer, E. S., & Edgerton, M. (1985). Parent and child correlates of parental modernity. In I. E. Sigal (Ed.), *Parental belief systems.* Hillsdale, NJ: Erlbaum.

Schaffer, H. R. (1996). *Social Development.* Oxford: Blackwell.

Schaffer, H. R., & Emerson, P. (1964a). The development of social attachments in infancy. *Monographs of the Society for Research in Child Development, 29,* whole No. 94.

Schaffer, H. R., & Emerson, P. (1964b). Patterns of response to physical contact in early human development. *Journal of Child Psychology and Psychiatry, 5,* 1–13.

Schaie, K. W. (1965). A general model for the study of developmental problems. *Psychological Bulletin, 64,* 92–107.

Schaie, K. W. (1973). Methodological problems in descriptive developmental research on adulthood and aging. In J. R. Nesselroade & H. W. Reese (Eds.), *Life-span developmental psychology: Methodological issues.* New York: Academic Press.

Schaie, K. W. (1983). *Longitudinal studies of adult psychological development.* New York: Guilford Press.

Schaie, K. W. (1996). *Intellectual development in adulthood.* New York: Guilford.

Schaie, K. W. (1997). Cognitive components of late life contributions. Paper presented at the 16th World Congress of the International Association of Gerontology, Adelaide: August.

Schaie, K. W. (2000). The impact of longitudinal studies on understanding development from young adulthood to old age. *International Journal of Behaviour Development, 24,* 257–266.

Schaie, K. W., & Gribbin, K. (1975). Adult development and aging. *Annual Review of Psychology, 26,* 65–83.

Schaie, K. W., Nguyen, H., & Willis, S. (2001). Environmental factors as a conceptual framework for examining cognitive performance in Chinese adults. *International Journal of Behavior Development, 25,* 193–202.

Schaie, K. W., & Parham, I. A. (1977). Stability of adult personality traits: Fact or fable? *Journal of Personality and Social Psychology, 34,* 146–157.

Schneidman, E. S. (1971). You and death. *Psychology Today, 5*(1), 43–46.

Schultz, R. (1978). *The psychology of death, dying and bereavement.* Reading, MA: Addison-Wesley.

Schwab, D. P., & Heneman, H. G. (1978). Age stereotyping in performance appraisal. *Journal of Applied Psychology, 63,* 573–578.

Schwartz, L., & Markham, W. (1984). Sex stereotyping in children's toy advertisements. *Sex Roles, 11,* 677–690.

Schwartz, S. (1986). *Classic studies in psychology.* Mountain View, CA: Mayfield.

Schwebel, M. (1982). Effects of nuclear war threat on children and teenagers: Implications for professionals. *American Journal of Orthopsychiatry, 52,* 608–618.

Scott, W. A., Scott, R., Boehnke, K., Shall-Way, C., Kwola, L., & Masamichi, S. (1991). Children's personality as a function of family relations within and between cultures. *Journal of Cross-cultural Psychology, 22*(2), 182–208.

Seagrim, G. N., & Lendon, R. J. (1980). *Furnishing the mind.* New York: Academic Press.

Sears, R. R., Maccoby, E. E., & Levin, H. (1957). *Patterns of child rearing.* Evanston, IL: Row Peterson.

Seelbach, W. C., & Hansen, C. J. (1980). Morale among the institutionalized and non-institutionalized elderly. *Ageing International, 7*(2), 20–21.

Seitz, S., & Stewart, C. (1975). Imitations and expansions: Some developmental aspects of mother–child communications. *Development Psychology, 11,* 763–768.

Seligman, M. E. P. (1975). *Helplessness: On depression, development, and death.* San Francisco: W. H. Freeman.

Selman, R. (1980). *The growth of interpersonal understanding.* New York: Academic Press.

Selman, R. (1981). The child as a friendship philosopher. In S. R. Asher & J. M. Gottman (Eds.), *The development of children's friendships.* Cambridge, UK: Cambridge University Press.

Selye, H. (1979). *The stress of my life.* New York: McGraw-Hill.

Serbin, L. A., O'Leary, K. D., Kent, R. N., & Tonick, I. J. (1973). A comparison of teacher response to the pre-academic and problem behavior of boys and girls. *Child Development, 44,* 796–804.

Shanis, H. S. (1985). Hospice: Interdependence of the dying with their community. In W. A. Peterson & J. Quadagno (Eds.), *Social bonds in later life.* London: Sage.

Shantz, C. (1983). Social-cognitive development. In J. H. Flavell & E. M. Markham (Eds.), *Carmichael's manual of child psychology.* New York: Wiley.

Sharps, M. J., Sharps, J. L. P., & Hanson, J. (1998). Attitudes of young adults towards older adults: Evidence from the United States and Thailand. *Educational Gerontology, 24,* 655–660.

Shatz, M., & Gelman, R. (1973). The development of communication skills. *Monographs of the Society for Research in Child Development, 38,* whole No. 152.

Shaw, G. B. (1929). *Back to Methuselah.* New York: Brentano's.

Shea, J. D. C. (1983). Sex typing in Australian children as a function of social class, sex and age. *Australian Psychologist, 18,* 243–250.

Sheehan, P. W. (1983). Age trends and the correlates of children's television viewing. *Australian Journal of Psychology, 35,* 417–431.

Sherman, J. A. (1973). *On the psychology of women: A survey of empirical studies.* Springfield, IL: Charles C. Thomas.

Sherman, L. W. (1975). An ecological study of glee in small groups of preschool children. *Child Development, 46,* 53–61.

Shipley, E. F., Smith, C. S., & Gleitman, L. R. (1969). A study of the acquisition of language: Free responses to commands. *Language, 45,* 322–342.

Shipman, C. (1971). The psychodynamics of sex education. In R. E. Muuss (Ed.), *Adolescent behavior and society: A book of readings.* New York: Random House.

Shipman, W. G. (1964). Age at menarche and adult personality. *Archives of General Psychiatry, 10,* 155–159.

Shirley, M. M. (1933). *The first two years: A study of twenty-five babies.* Minneapolis: University of Minnesota Press.

Shock, N. W. (1962). The physiology of aging. *Scientific American, 206*(1), 100–111.

Sidorowicz, L. S., & Lunney, G. S. (1980). Baby X revisited. *Sex Roles, 6*(1), 67–73.

Siegal, M. (1984). Social cognition and the development of rule-guided behaviour. *Australian Journal of Psychology, 36,* 387–398.

Siegal, M. (1985). *Children, parenthood and social welfare in the context of developmental psychology.* Oxford: Oxford University Press.

Siegal, M. (1991). *Knowing children.* Hove, UK: Erlbaum.

Siegal, M. (1997). *Knowing children: Experiments in conversation and cognition.* Hove, UK: Psychology Press Ltd.

Siegal, M., & Peterson, C. C. (1994). Children's theory of mind and the conversational territory of cognitive development. In C. Lewis & P. Mitchell (Eds.), *Children's early understanding of mind: Origins and development.* Hove, UK: Erlbaum.

Siegal, M., & Peterson, C. C. (1996). Breaking the mold: A fresh look at questions about children's understanding of lies and mistakes. *Developmental Psychology, 32,* 322–334.

Siegal, M., & Peterson, C. C. (1998). Children's understanding of lies and innocent and negligent mistakes. *Developmental Psychology, 34,* 332–343.

Siegal, M., & Peterson, C. C. (1999). *Children's understanding of biology and health.* Cambridge, UK: Cambridge University Press.

Siegal, M., & Share, D. L. (1990). Contamination sensitivity in young children. *Developmental Psychology, 26,* 455–458.

Siegal, M., & Storey, R. M. (1985). Daycare and children's conceptions of moral and social rules. *Child Development, 56,* 1001–1008.

Siegel, L. (1974). Development of number concepts: Ordering and correspondence relationships and the role of length cues. *Developmental Psychology, 10,* 907–912.

Sigel, I., & Hooper, F. (Eds.). (1968). *Logical thinking in children: Research based on Piaget's theory.* New York: Holt, Rinehart & Winston.

Sigel, I., & McGillicuddy-DeLisi, A. (1984). Parents as teachers of their children. In A. Pelligrini & T. Yawkey (Eds.), *The development of oral and written language in social contexts.* Norwood, NJ: Ablex.

Signoret, S. (1978). *Nostalgia isn't what it used to be.* London: Granada.

Silcock, A. (1984). Crises in parents of prematures: An Australian study. *British Journal of Developmental Psychology, 2,* 257–268.

Silver, S. (1981). Evaluation of a hospice program: Effects on terminally ill patients and their families. *Evaluation and the Health Professions, 4,* 3.

Silverberg, S., Tennenbaum, D. L., & Jacob, T. (1992). Adolescence and family interaction. In V. B. Van Hasselt & M. Hersen (Eds.), *Handbook of social development: A lifespan perspective* (pp. 347–370). New York: Plenum Press.

Simmons, R. G., & Blyth, D. A. (1987). *Moving into adolescence: The impact of pubertal change on school and context.* New York: Aldine De Gruyter.

Simmons, R. G., Blyth, D. A., & McKinney, K. L. (1983). The social and psychological effects of puberty on white females. In J. Brooks-Gunn & A. C. Petersen (Eds.), *Girls at puberty.* New York: Plenum Press.

Simmons, R. G., Blyth, D. A., Van Cleave, E. F., & Bush, D. M. (1979). Entry into early adolescence: The impact of school structure, puberty, and early dating on self-esteem. *American Sociological Review, 44,* 948–967.

Simpson, E. L. (1974). Moral development research: A case study of scientific cultural bias. *Human Development, 17,* 81–106.

Simpson, I. H., Harper, G., & McKinney, J. C. (Eds.). (1966). *Social aspects of aging.* Durham, NY: Duke University Press.

Singer, J. L. (1973). *The child's world of make-believe: Experimental studies of imaginative play.* New York: Academic Press.

Singer, J. L., & Singer, D. G. (1981). *Television, imagination, and aggression: A study of preschoolers.* Hillsdale, NJ: Erlbaum.

Sinnott, J. D. (1975). Everyday thinking and Piagetian operativity in adults. *Human Development, 18,* 430–443.

Sirignano, S. W., & Lachman, M. E. (1985). Personality change during the transition to parenthood: The role of perceived infant temperament. *Developmental Psychology, 21,* 558–567.

Skinner, B. F. (1953). *Science and human behaviour.* New York: Macmillan.

Skinner, B. F. (1983). Intellectual self-management in old age. *American Psychologist, 38,* 239–244.

Slaby, R. G., & Frey, K. S. (1975). Development of gender constancy and selective attention to same-sex models. *Child Development, 46,* 849–856.

Slaughter, V., Jaakkola, R., & Carey, S. (1999). Constructing a coherent theory: Children's biological understanding of life and death. In M. Siegel & C. C. Peterson (Eds.), *Children's understanding of biology and health.* Cambridge, UK: Cambridge University Press.

Slee, P. (1993). *Child, adolescent and family development.* Sydney: Harcourt Brace Jovanovich.

Smart, R., & Peterson, C. (1994a). Stability versus transition in women's career development: A test of Levinson's theory. *Journal of Vocational Behaviour, 45,* 241–260.

Smart, R., & Peterson, C. (1994b). Super's stages and the four-factor structure of the Adult Career Concerns Inventory in an Australian sample. *Measurement and Evaluation in Counselling and Development, 26,* 33–47.

Smart, R., & Peterson, C. C. (1997). Super's career stages and the decision to change careers. *Journal of Vocational Behavior, 51,* 358–374.

Smart, R., & Smart, M. (1970). Recalled, present and predicted marital satisfaction. *Journal of Marriage and the Family, 32,* 20–27.

Smart, R. C., & Smart, M. S. (1980). Complexity of pre-adolescents' social play and games. *New Zealand Journal of Educational Studies, 25,* 81–92.

Smelser, N. J., & Baltes, P. B. (2001). *International encyclopaedia of the social and behavioural sciences.* New York: Elsevier Science.

Smetana, J. G. (1981). Preschool children's conceptions of moral and social rules. *Child Development, 52,* 1333–1336.

Smith, A. (1970). *The body.* Ringwood, VIC: Penguin.

Smith, G., & Carlsson, I. (1985). Creativity in middle and late school years. *International Journal of Behavioral Development, 8,* 329–343.

Smith, M. B. (1970). Morality and student protest. In M. Wertheimer (Ed.), *Confrontation: Psychology and the problems of today.* Glenview, IL: Scott, Foresman.

Smith, R. M., Spargo, R. M., & Cheek, D. B. (1982). Zinc status and growth of Aboriginal children in the north-west of Australia. *Proceedings of the Nutrition Society of Australia, 7,* 37–44.

Snarey, J., Son, L., Kuehne, V. S., Hauser, S., & Vaillant, G. (1987). The role of parenting in men's psychosocial development: A longitudinal study of early adulthood infertility and midlife generativity. *Developmental Psychology, 23,* 593–603.

Snodgrass, S. R. (1976). The development of trait inference. *Journal of Genetic Psychology, 120,* 163–172.

Snow, C. E. (1972). Mothers' speech to children learning language. *Child Development, 43,* 549–565.

Snow, C. E. (1977). The development of conversation between mothers and babies. *Journal of Child Language, 4,* 1–22.

Snow, C. E., & Hoefnagel-Hohle, M. (1978). The critical period for language acquisition: Evidence from second language learning. *Child Development, 49,* 1114–1128.

Snow, M. E., Jacklin, C. N., & Maccoby, E. E. (1980). Cry episodes and sleep–wakefulness transitions in the first 26 months of life. *Infant Behavior and Development, 3,* 387–394.

Sodei, T. (1993). Old age policy as a women's issue. In R. N. Butler & K. Kiikuni (Eds.), *Who is responsible for my old age?* (pp. 73–95). New York: Springer Publishing Co.

Solem, P. E. (1978). Paid work after retirement age and mortality. *Ageing International, 5*(2), 20.

Sommerland, E. A., & Bellingham, W. P. (1972). Cooperation–competition: A comparison of Australian European and Aboriginal school children. *Journal of Cross-Cultural Psychology, 3*(2), 149–157.

Sontag, L. W. (1966). Implications of fetal behavior and environment for adult personalities. *Annals of the New York Academy of Sciences, 134,* 782–786.

Speece, M. W., & Brent, S. B. (1984). Children's understanding of death: A review of three components of a death concept. *Child Development, 55*(5), 1671–1686.

Spence, D. L. (1975). The meaning of engagement. *International Journal of Aging and Human Development, 6*(3), 193–197.

Spence, S. H., & McCathie, H. (1993). The stability of fears in children: A two-year prospective study: A research note. *Journal of Child Psychology and Psychiatry, 34*(4), 579–585.

Spreen, O., Risser, A., & Edgell, D. (1995). *Developmental neuropsychology*. New York: Oxford University Press.

Sroufe, L. A. (1979). Emotional development. In J. D. Osofsky (Ed.), *Handbook of infant development*. New York: Wiley.

Sroufe, L. A. (1983). Infant–caregiver attachment and patterns of adaptation in preschool: The roots of maladaptation and competence. In M. Perlmutter (Ed.), *Minnesota symposium on child development*. Hillsdale, NJ: Erlbaum.

Sroufe, L. A. (1985). Attachment classification from the perspective of infant–caregiver relationships and infant temperament. *Child Development, 56*, 1–14.

Sroufe, L. A., Egeland, B., & Kreutzer, T. (1990). The fate of early experience following developmental change. *Child Development, 61*, 1363–1373.

Sroufe, L. A., & Waters, E. (1977). Attachment as an organizational construct. *Child Development, 48*, 1184–1199.

Staats, A. (1970). Linguistic–mentalistic theory versus an exploratory S–R learning theory of language development. In Dr D. Slobin (Ed.), *The ontogenesis of grammar*. New York: Academic Press.

Stacey, B. G. (1987). Economic socialization. In S. Long (Ed.), *Annual review of political science*. Norwood, NJ: Ablex.

Staffieri, J. R. (1967). A study of social stereotype of body image in children. *Journal of Personality and Social Psychology, 7*, 101–104.

Stanhope, J. M., & Prior, I. A. M. (1975). Smoking behavior and respiratory health in a teenage sample: The Rotorua Lakes study. *New Zealand Medical Journal, 82*, 71–76.

Stanley, F. (1994). *Research for a healthy society*. Canberra: Office of the Chief Scientist.

Stanley, F. (2003). *Before the bough breaks: Doing more for our children in the 21st century*. Academy of the Social Sciences in Australia: Canberra.

Starr, B., & Bakur, M. (1980). United States: Sexual behavior. *Ageing International, 7*(2), 13.

Statistics New Zealand (1995). *New Zealand Official Yearbook* (98th ed.) Wellington.

Stattin, H., & Klackenberg-Larsson, I. (1991). The short- and long-term implications for parent–child relations of parents' prenatal preferences for their child's gender. *Developmental Psychology, 27*, 141–147.

Stattin, H., & Magnusson, D. (1990). *Paths through life (Vol. 2): Pubertal maturation in female development*. Hillsdale, NJ: Erlbaum.

Staub, E. (1970). A child in distress: The influence of age and number of witnesses on children's attempts to help. *Journal of Personality and Social Psychology, 14*, 130–140.

Stein, A. H., & Bailey, M. M. (1973). The socialization of achievement orientation in females. *Psychological Bulletin, 80*(5), 345–366.

Steinberg, L. (1988). Reciprocal relation between parent–child distance and pubertal maturation. *Developmental Psychology, 24*, 122–128.

Steinberg, L. (1989). Pubertal maturation and parent–adolescent distance. In G. R. Adams, R. Montemayor & T. P. Gullota (Eds.), *Biology of adolescent behaviour and development*. London: Sage Publications.

Steinberg, L. (1990). Autonomy, conflict and harmony in the parent–child relationship. In S. Feldman & G. Elliott (Eds.), *At the threshold: The developing adolescent*. Cambridge, MA: Harvard University Press.

Steinberg, L. (1996). *Adolescence* (4th ed.). New York: McGraw-Hill.

Steinberg, L., Lamborn, S., Darling, N., Mounts, N., & Dornbusch, S. (1994). Over time changes in adolescent competence. *Child Development, 65*, 754–770.

Stephan, C. W., & Langlois, J. H. (1984). Baby beautiful: Adult attributions of infant competence as a function of infant attractiveness. *Child Development, 55*, 576–585.

Stern, W. (1905). *Person und Sache*. Leipzig: J. A. Barth.

Sternberg, R. J. (1988). Triangulating love. In R. J. Sternberg & M. L. Barnes (Eds.), *The psychology of love*. New Haven: Yale University Press.

Stetson, D. (1973). Second careers. *Industrial Gerontology,* Spring, 9–12.

Stewart, A., & Ostrove, J. (1998). Women's personality in middle age. *American Psychologist, 53*, 1185–1194.

Stewart, R. A. (1982). *Pacific profiles*. Fiji: Extension Services of the University of the South Pacific.

St George, A. (1983). Teacher expectations and perceptions of Polynesian and Pakeha pupils and the relationship to classroom behaviour and school achievement. *British Journal of Educational Psychology, 53*, 48–59.

Stocker, C. (1995). Difference in mothers' and fathers' relationships with siblings. *Development and Psychopathology, 7*, 499–513.

Stone, C. P., & Barker, R. G. (1939). The attitudes and interests of premenarcheal and postmenarcheal girls. *Journal of Genetic Psychology, 54*, 27–72.

Storer, D. (1985). *Ethnic families in Australia*. Sydney: Prentice Hall.

Storey, D. (1987). *Death anxiety*. Unpublished honours thesis: Murdoch University.

Straus, M. A., & Gelles, R. J. (1986). Societal change and change in family violence from 1975 to 1985 as revealed by two national surveys. *Journal of Marriage and the Family, 48*, 190–194.

Straus, M. A., & Sweet, S. (1991). Verbal/symbolic aggression in couples: Incidence rates and relationships to personal characteristics. *Journal of Marriage and the Family, 54*, 346–357.

Strehler, P. L. (1962). *Time, cells and aging*. New York: Academic Press.

Streib, G. F., & Schneider, C. J. (1972). *Retirement in American society: Impact and process*. Ithaca, NY: Cornell University Press.

Stroebe, M., & Stroebe, W. (1983). Who suffers most? Sex differences in health risks of the widowed. *Psychological Bulletin, 93*, 279–301.

Stuckey, S. J., Darnton-Hill, I., Ash, S., Brand, J. C., & Hain, D. L. (1981). Dietary patterns of the elderly in Sydney. *Proceedings of the Nutrition Society of Australia, 6*, 117.

Su, Wen-ming (Ed.). (1982). *From youth to retirement*. Beijing: Beijing Review.

Sullivan, H. S. (1953). *The interpersonal theory of psychiatry*. New York: W. W. Norton.

Super, C. M., & Harkness, S. (1997). The cultural structuring of child development. In J. W. Berry, Y. Poortinga & J. Pandey (Eds.), *Handbook of cross-cultural psychology*. Boston: Allyn & Bacon.

Super, D. E. (1957). *The psychology of careers*. New York: Harper.

Super, D. E. (1970). *Manual of the Work Values Inventory*. Boston: Houghton Mifflin.

Super, D. E. (1990). A life-span, life-space approach to career development. In D. Brown et al. (Eds.), *Career choice and development* (2nd ed.). San Francisco: Jossey-Bass.

Swenson, W. M. (1961). Attitudes toward death in an aged population. *Journal of Gerontology, 16*, 49–52.

Taft, R. (1985). The psychological study of adjustment and adaptation of immigrants in Australia. In N. T. Feather (Ed.), *Australian psychology: Review of research*. Sydney: Allen & Unwin.

Tager-Flusberg, H. (1992). Autistic children's talk about psychological states: Deficits in the early acquisition of a theory of mind. *Child Development, 63*, 161–172.

Takahashi, K., Ohara, N., Antonucci, T., & Akiyama, H. (2002). Commonalities and differences in close relationships among the Americans and Japanese. *International Journal of Behavior Development, 26*(5), 453–465.

Takahashi, K., Tamura, J., & Tokoro, M. (1997). Patterns of social relationships and psychological well-being among the elderly. *International Journal of Behavioural Development, 27*(3), 417–430.

Takahashi, M. (2000). Toward a culturally inclusive understanding of wisdom. *International Journal of Aging and Human Development, 46*, 109–124.

Takkinen, S., & Ruoppila, I. (2001). Meaning in life as an important component of functioning in old age. *International Journal of Behaviour Development, 53*, 211–231.

Talmon, Y. (1968). Aging in Israel: A planned society. In

B. L. Neugarten (Ed.), *Middle age and aging: A reader in social psychology*. Chicago: University of Chicago Press.

Tanner, J. M. (1962). *Growth at adolescence*. Oxford: Blackwell.

Tanner, J. M. (1968). Earlier maturation in man. *Scientific American, 218*, 21–27.

Tanner, J. M. (1970). Physical growth. In P. H. Mussen (Ed.), *Carmichael's manual of child psychology* (Vol. 1). New York: Wiley.

Tanner, J. M. (1972). Sequence, tempo, and individual variation in growth and development of boys and girls aged twelve to sixteen. In J. Kagan & R. Coles (Eds.), *Twelve to sixteen: Early adolescence*. New York: W. W. Norton.

Tanner, J. M. (1974). Variability of growth and maturity in newborn infants. In M. Lewis & L. A. Rosenblum (Eds.), *The effect of the infant on its caregiver*. New York: Wiley.

Tanner, J. M. (1990). *Foetus into man: Physical growth from conception to maturity* (2nd ed.). Cambridge, MA: Harvard University Press.

Taylor, M., & Carlson, S. (1997). The relation between individual difference in fantasy and theory of mind. *Child Development, 68*, 436–455.

Taylor, S. E., & Langer, E. J. (1977). Pregnancy: A social stigma? *Sex Roles, 3*, 27–35.

Templer, D. (1970). The construction and validation of a death anxiety scale. *Journal of Genetic Psychology, 82*, 165–177.

Templer, D. (1971). Death anxiety as related to depression and health of retired persons. *Journal of Gerontology, 26*.

Templer, D., Ruff, C., & Franks, C. (1971). Death anxiety: Age, sex, and parental resemblance in diverse populations. *Developmental Psychology, 4*, 108.

Tenezakis, M. D. (1975). Linguistic subsystems and concrete operations. *Child Development, 46*.

Terman, L. (1921–1959). *Genetic studies of genius*. London: Oxford University Press.

Terman, L. M., & Oden, M. H. (1959). *The gifted group at mid-life*. Stanford, CA: Stanford University Press.

Terry, D. J. (1991). Predictors of subjective stress in a sample of new parents. *Australian Journal of Psychology, 43*, 29–36.

Thatcher, R. W. (1991). Maturation of the human frontal lobes: Physiological evidence for staging. *Developmental Neuro-psychology, 7*(3), 397–419.

Thatcher, R. W. (1994). Cyclic cortical reorganisation: Origins of human cognitive development. In G. Dawson & K. W. Fischer (Eds.), *Human Behaviour and the Developing Brain* (pp. 232–266). New York: Guilford.

Thomas, A., & Chess, S. (1977). *Temperament and development*. New York: Brunner/Mazel.

Thomas, A., Chess, S., & Birch, H. (1963). *Behavioral individuality in early childhood*. New York: University Press.

Thomas, A., Chess, S., & Birch, H. (1970). The origins of personality. *Scientific American, 223*, 102–109.

Thomas, D. R. (1986). Culture and ethnicity: Maintaining the distinction. *American Journal of Psychology, 38*, 371–380.

Thomas, D. R. (1988). Development of a test of Maori knowledge. *New Zealand Journal of Psychology, 17*, 59–67.

Thomas, J. L. (1986). Age and sex differences in perceptions of grandparenting. *Journal of Gerontology, 41*, 417–423.

Thomas, L. E. (1980). Midlife career changes. *Journal of Vocational Behavior, 16*, 173–182.

Thomas, M. B., & Neal, P. A. (1978). Collaborating careers: The differential effects of race. *Journal of Vocational Behavior, 11*, 33–42.

Thompson, L., & Walker, A. J. (1989). Gender in families. *Journal of Marriage and the Family, 5*, 845–871.

Thompson, R. A. (1991). Maturing the study of aging: Discussants' comments. *Nebraska symposium on motivation, 39*, 250–259.

Thompson, R. A. (2000). The legacy of early attachments. *Child Development, 71*, 145–152.

Thompson, R. F. (2000). *The brain: A neuroscience primer*. New York: W. H. Freeman.

Thompson, S. K. (1975). Gender labels and early sex role development. *Child Development, 46*, 339–347.

Thompson, W. E. (1958). Pre-retirement anticipation and adjustment in retirement. *Journal of Social Issues, 14*, 35–45.

Thurber, J., & White, E. B. (1924). *Is sex necessary?* New York: Harper.

Tidman, M., & Renshaw, P. D. (1987). Case studies of peer isolation and rejection amongst preadolescent girls. Paper presented at IXth Biennial International Society for the Study of Behavioural Development Meetings, Tokyo.

Tiedeman, D. V., & O'Hara, R. P. (1963). *Career development: Choice and adjustment*. New York: College Entrance Examination Board.

Tietjen, A. (1986). Prosocial reasoning among children and adults in a Papua New Guinea society. *Developmental Psychology, 22*(6), 861–868.

Tiggemann, M., & Winefield, A. H. (1980). Some psychological effects of unemployment in school leavers. *Australian Journal of Social Issues, 15*, 269–276.

Tiggemann, M., & Winefield, A. H. (1984). The effects of unemployment on the mood, self-esteem, locus of control, and depressive affect of school-leavers. *Journal of Occupational Psychology, 57*, 33–42.

Timaras, P. S. (1972). *Developmental Physiology and Aging*. New York: Macmillan.

Time. Milestones. (1995, March 27).

Time. Milestones. (1995, April 2).

Tinsley, B., & Parke, R. D. (1987). Grandparents as interactive and social support agents for families with young infants. *International Journal of Aging and Human Development, 25*, 259–276.

Tobin-Richards, M., Boxer, A., & Petersen, A. C. (1983). The psychological significance of pubertal change. In J. Brooks-Gunn & A. C. Petersen (Eds.), *Girls at puberty*. New York: Plenum Press.

Tolstoy, L. (1917). *My confessions, My religion*. New York: Charles Scribner's Sons.

Tonkinson, R. (1978). *The Mardudjara Aborigines: Living the dream in Australia's desert*. New York: Holt, Rinehart & Winston.

Townsend, P. (1962). *The last refuge: A survey of residential institutions and homes for the aged in England and Wales*. London: Routledge & Kegan Paul.

Traupmann, J., & Hatfield, E. (1981). Love and its effect on mental and physical health. In J. G. March (Ed.), *Aging: Stability and change in the family*. New York: Academic Press.

Traupmann, J., & Hatfield, E. (1983). How important is marital fairness over the lifespan? *International Journal of Aging and Human Development, 17*, 89–101.

Trehub, S. E. (1976). The discrimination of foreign speech contrasts by infants and adults. *Child Development, 47*, 466–472.

Trehub, S. E., & Rabinovitch, M. S. (1972). Auditory-linguistic sensitivity in early infancy. *Developmental Psychology, 6*, 74–77.

Trewin, D. (2002). *Year Book of Australia*. Canberra: Australian Bureau of Statistics.

Trlin, A. D., Krishnamoorthy, S., & Khoo, S. E. (1983). Premarital sex: Differentials and predictors of never-married males and females. *Australian Journal of Sex, Marriage and the Family, 4*, 201–214.

Troll, L., & Schlossberg, N. (1971). How 'age-biased' are college counselors? *Industrial Gerontology*, Summer, 14–20.

Troth, A., & Peterson, C. C. (2000). Factors predicting safe-sex talk and condom use in early sexual relationships. *Health Communication, 12*, 195–218.

Tu, Wei-ming (1978). The Confucian perception of adulthood. In E. H. Erikson (Ed.), *Adulthood*. New York: W. W. Norton.

Tunmer, W. E., & Bowey, J. (1984). Metalinguistic awareness and reading acquisition. In W. E. Tunmer, C. Pratt & M. L. Herriman (Eds.), *Metalinguistic awareness in children*. New York: Springer-Verlag.

Tunmer, W. E., & Nesdale, A. R. (1985). Phonemic segmentation skill and beginning reading. *Journal of Educational Psychology, 77*, 417–427.

Tunmer, W. E., Nesdale, A. R., & Pratt, C. (1983). The development of young children's awareness of logical inconsistencies. *Journal of Experimental Child Psychology, 36*, 97–108.

Turiel, E. (1977). Distinct conceptual and developmental domains: Social convention and morality. *Nebraska Symposium on Motivation, 25*, 77–97.

Turiel, E. (1983). *The development of social knowledge: Morality and convention*. Cambridge, UK: Cambridge University Press.

Turiel, E., & Wainryb, C. (2000). Social life in culture: Judgments, conflicts and subversion. *Child Development, 71*, 250–256.

Turtle, A., Cranfield, D., Halse-Rogers, D., Reuman, B., & Williams, J. (1978). Life – not in it: A psychological comparison of employed and unemployed Sydney youth. *Vocational Guidance Bulletin, 4*, March.

Turtle, A., & Ridley, A. (1984). Is unemployment a health hazard? Health-related behaviours in a sample of unemployed Sydney youth in 1980. *Australian Journal of Social Issues, 19*, 27–42.

Tvrethewey, J. (1989). *Aussie battlers: Families and children in poverty*, Melbourne: Collins Dove.

Tzuriel, D., & Klein, M. M. (1977). Ego identity: Effects of ethnocentrism, ethnic identification and cognitive complexity in Israeli, Oriental and Western ethnic groups. *Psychological Reports, 40*, 1099–1110.

Udry, J. R. (1971). *The social context of marriage*. Philadelphia: Lippincott.

Ungerer, J., Dolby, R., Barnett, B., Kelk, N., & Lewin, V. (1990). The early development of empathy: Self regulation and individual differences in the first year. *Motivation and Emotion, 14*, 93–106.

United Nations. (1991). *World population trends and policies: 1991 monitoring report*. New York: United Nations.

Uotinen, V. (1998). Age identification: A comparison between Finnish and North American cultures. *International Journal of Aging and Human Development, 51*, 217–230.

Urberg, K., & Robbins, R. (1981). Adolescents' perceptions of the costs and benefits associated with cigarette smoking: Sex differences and peer influence. *Journal of Youth and Adolescence, 5*, 353–361.

US Department of Health and Human Services. (1996). *Vital statistics of the United States*. Washington, DC: US Government Printing Office.

Vaillant, G. E. (1990). Avoiding negative life outcomes. In P. B. Baltes & M. M. Baltes (Eds.), *Successful ageing* (pp. 332–355). New York: Cambridge University Press.

Vaillant, G. E., & Vaillant, C. O. (1990). Determinants and consequences of creativity in a cohort of gifted women. *Psychology of Women Quarterly, 14*, 607–616.

Valkonen, T. (2001). Life expectancy and adult mortality in industrialised countries. In N. Smelser & P. B. Baltes (Eds.), *International encyclopaedia of the social and behavioural sciences*. New York: Elsevier Science.

Vandell, D. L., Minnett, A. M., & Santrock, J. W. (1987). Age differences in sibling relationships during middle childhood. *Journal of Applied Developmental Psychology, 8*, 247–258.

Van Doren, C. (1941). *The Oxford dictionary of quotations*. Oxford: Oxford University Press.

Van Gennep, A. (1960). *The rites of passage*. London: Routledge & Kegan Paul.

van Ijzendoorn, M. H., & De Wolff, M. S. (1997). In search of the absent father: Meta-analysis of infant–father attachment. *Child Development, 68*, 604–609.

Van Keep, P. A., & Schmidt-Elmendorff, H. (1975). Involuntary childlessness. *Journal of Biosocial Science, 7*, 37–48.

Van Lieschout, C., & Van Aken, M. A. G. (1987). Peer acceptance and rejection and the structure of children's self-concept. Paper presented at IXth Biennial International Society for the Study of Behavioural Development Meetings, Tokyo.

Vaughan, B., & Langlois, I. (1983). Physical attractiveness as a correlate of peer status and social competence in preschool children. *Developmental Psychology, 19*, 561–567.

Vaughan, G. M. (1986). Social change and racial identity: Issues in the use of picture and doll measures. *Australian Journal of Psychology, 38*, 359–370.

Veevers, J. E. (1979). Voluntary childlessness: A review of issues and evidence. *Marriage and Family Review, 2*, 2–19.

Vuchinich, S. (1987). Starting and stopping spontaneous family conflict. *Journal of Marriage and the Family, 49*, 591–601.

Vygotsky, L. S. (1962). *Thought and language*. Cambridge, MA: Harvard University Press.

Vygotsky, L. S. (1978). *Mind in society: The development of higher psychological processes*. Cambridge, MA: Harvard University Press.

Wales, R., Colman, M., & Pattison, P. (1983). 'How a thing is called': A study of mothers' and children's naming. *Journal of Experimental Child Psychology, 36*, 1–17.

Walford, R. L. (1965). Immunology and aging. In R. Kastenbaum (Ed.), *Contributions to the psychobiology of aging*. New York: Springer.

Walker, L. J., & Taylor, J. H. (1991). Family reasoning and the development of moral reasoning. *Child Development, 62*, 264–283.

Walker-Andrews, A. S., & Lennon, E. M. (1985). Auditory–visual perception of changing distance by human infants. *Child Development, 56*, 544–548.

Wallach, M. (1970). Creativity. In P. H. Mussen (Ed.), *Carmichael's manual of child psychology*. New York: Wiley.

Wallach, M., & Kogan, N. (1965). *Modes of thinking in young children: A study of the creativity–intelligence distinction*. New York: Holt, Rinehart & Winston.

Walsh, M., & Yallop, C. (1993). *Language and culture in Aboriginal Australia*. Canberra: Aboriginal Studies Press.

Walster, E., & Walster, G. W. (1978). *A new look at love*. Reading, MA: Addison-Wesley.

Ward, R. (1984). *The Aging Experience*. New York: Harper & Row.

Warr, P. B. (1983). Work, jobs, and unemployment. *Bulletin of the British Psychological Society, 36*, 305–311.

Warren, M. P. (1980). The effects of exercise on pubertal progression and reproductive function in girls. *Journal of Clinical Endocrinology and Metabolism, 51*, 1150–1157.

Warren, M. P. (1983). Physical and biological aspects of puberty. In J. Brooks-Gunn & A. C. Petersen (Eds.), *Girls at puberty*. New York: Plenum Press.

Warren, W. G., & Chopra, P. N. (1979). An Australian survey of attitudes to death. *Australian Journal of Social Issues, 14*, 134–142.

Wass, H., Christian, M., Myers, J., & Murphey, M. (1978–79). Similarities and dissimilarities in attitudes toward death in a population of older persons. *Omega, 9*(4), 337–353.

Waterman, A. S. (1982). Identity development from adolescence to adulthood: An extension of theory and review of research. *Developmental Psychology, 18*(3), 341–348.

Waterman, C. K., & Nevid, J. S. (1977). Sex differences in the resolution of the identity crisis. *Journal of Youth and Adolescence, 6*, 337–341.

Waterman, R. A. (1956). Aboriginals of Yirkalla. In V. Fern (Ed.), *Encyclopedia of morals*. New York: Greenwood Press.

Waterman, R. A. (1971). Aboriginal ethics. In J. Hastings (Ed.), *Encyclopedia of religion and ethics*. Edinburgh: T. T. Clark.

Watkins, D., Alabaster M., & Freemantle, S. (1988). Assessing the self-esteem of New Zealand adolescents. *New Zealand Journal of Psychology, 17*, 32–35.

Watson, A. (1983). *Reading as a conceptual reasoning task: Towards a cognitive developmental theory of learning to read*. Canberra: Education Research and Development Committee.

Watson, A. J., & Sinclair, K. E. (1987). Conceptual reasoning in reading: A complex seriation of meaning. *Australian Journal of Education, 31*(2), 161–172.

Watson, J. B. (1928). *The psychological care of infant and child*. New York: W. W. Norton.

Watson, J. S. (1971). Cognitive-perceptual development in infancy: Setting for the seventies. *Merrill-Palmer Quarterly, 17*, 139–152.

Watson, M., & Fischer, K. (1980). Development of social roles in elicited and spontaneous behavior during the preschool years. *Developmental Psychology, 16*, 483–494.

Weale, R. A. (1963). *The aging eye*. London: H. K. Lewis.

Wearing, B. (1996). *Gender: The pain and pleasure of difference*. Melbourne: Longman.

Wechsler, D. (1955). *Manual for the adult intelligence scale*. New York: Psychological Corporation.

Wechsler, D. (1989). *Manual for the Wechsler Scale of Intelligence*. New York: Psychological Corporation.

Weiler, S. J. (1981). Aging and sexuality and the myth of decline. In R. W. Fogel, E. Hatfield, S. B. Kiesler & E. Shanas (Eds.), *Aging: Stability and change in the family*. New York: Academic Press.

Weinberg, R., & Scarr, S. (1987). A ten-year follow-up study of transracially adopted children and biological offspring of the adoptive families: Achievement and adjustment at adolescence. Paper presented at IXth Biennial International Society for the Study of Behavioural Development Meetings, Tokyo.

Weishaus, S., & Field, D. (1988). A half-century of marriages: Continuity or change. *Journal of Marriage and the Family, 50*, 763–774.

Weitzman, L., Eifler, D., Hokada, E., & Ross, C. (1972). Sex-role socialization in picture books for preschool children. *American Journal of Sociology, 77*, 1125–1150.

Welford, A. T. (1976). Motivation, capacity, learning and age. *International Journal of Aging and Human Development, 7*(3), 189–199.

Wellman, H. M. (1977). Preschoolers' understanding of memory-relevant variables. *Child Development, 48,* 1720–1723.

Wellman, H. M. (1993). Early understanding of mind. In S. Baron-Cohen, H. Tager-Flusberg & D. Cohen (Eds.), *Understanding other minds*. Oxford: Oxford University Press.

Wellman, H. M., Cross, D., & Watson, J. (2001). Meta-analysis of theory of mind development: The truth about false belief. *Child Development, 72,* 655–684.

Wellman, H. M., & Inagaki, K. (1997). *The emergence of thought*. San Francisco: Jossey Bass.

Wenar, C. (1982). On negativism. *Human Development, 25,* 1–23.

Wente, A. S., & Crockenberg, S. B. (1976). Transition to fatherhood: Lamaze preparation adjustment difficulty and the husband–wife relationship. *Family Coordinator, 25,* 351–357.

Werner, E., & Smith, R. (1992). *Overcoming the odds: High risk children from birth to adulthood*. Ithaca, NY: Cornell University Press.

Wertheimer, M. (Ed.). (1970). *Confrontation: Psychology and the problems of today*. Glenview, IL: Scott Foresman.

Westbrook, M. T., & Legge, V. (1990). Staff perceptions of caring for Italian, Greek and Chinese nursing home residents. *Australian Journal on Aging, 9,* 22–28.

Westbrook, M. T., & Nordholm, L. A. (1983). Career development among female health professionals: Correlates and predictors of job satisfaction. *Australian Psychologist, 18*(1).

Wheeler, D. K. (1975). The adolescent at school in Western Australia. In J. K. Collins (Ed.), *Studies of the Australian adolescent*. Stanmore, NSW: Cassell.

White, B. L. (1971). *Human infants: Experience and psychological development*. Englewood Cliffs, NJ: Prentice Hall.

White, B. L. (1975). *The first three years of life*. Englewood Cliffs, NJ: Prentice Hall.

White, B. L., & Watts, J. C. (1973). *Experience and environment: Major influences on the development of the young child*. Englewood Cliffs, NJ: Prentice Hall.

White, I. (1985). *Daisy Bates*. Canberra: National Library of Australia.

White, K. M., Speisman, J. C., & Costos, D. (1983). Young adults and their parents: Individuation to mutuality. In H. D. Grotevant & C. R. Cooper (Eds.), *Adolescent development in the family*. San Francisco: Jossey-Bass.

White, R. W. (1952). *Lives in progress*. New York: Dryden Press.

White, S. (1965). Evidence for a hierarchical arrangement of learning processes. In L. P. Lipsitt & C. C. Spiker (Eds.), *Advances in child development and behavior* (Vol. 2). New York: Academic Press.

Whiting, B. B., & Whiting, J. W. M. (1975). *Children of six cultures: A psychocultural analysis*. Cambridge, MA: Harvard University Press.

Widdowson, E. M. (1951). Mental contentment and physical growth. *Lancet, 260,* 1316–1318.

Wilcox, M. M. (1986). Contributions of Kohlberg's theory to theological epistemology. In S. Modgil & C. Modgil (Eds.), *Lawrence Kohlberg: Consensus and controversy*. London: The Falmer Press.

Wilson, G., & Nias, D. (1976). *Love's mysteries*. Glasgow: Fontana/Collins.

Wilson, H. (1980). Parental supervision: A neglected aspect of delinquency. *British Journal of Criminology, 20,* 203–235.

Wilson, J. C., & Pipe, M. E. (1992). *Children's secrets*. Paper presented at the Seventh Australian Developmental Conference, Brisbane, July.

Wilson, R. S. (1974). Twins: Mental development in the preschool years. *Developmental Psychology, 10,* 580–588.

Wilson, R. S. (1980). Risk and resilience in early mental development. *Developmental Psychology, 21,* 795–805.

Winch, R. F. (1958). *Mate selection: A study of complementary needs*. New York: Harper.

Windschuttle, K. (1979). *Unemployment: A social and political analysis of the economic crisis in Australia*. Ringwood, VIC: Penguin.

Winefield, A., Tiggemann, M., & Goldney, R. (1988). Psychological concomitants of satisfactory employment and unemployment in young people. *Social Psychiatry and Psychiatric Epidemiology, 23,* 149–157.

Winer, G. A. (1982). A review and analysis of children's fearful behavior in dental settings. *Child Development, 53,* 1111–1133.

Winner, E. (1988). *The point of words*. Cambridge, MA: Harvard University Press.

Winocur, S., Rosenman, L., & Warburton, J. (1994). *The retirement decisions of women from a non-English-speaking background*. Bureau of Immigration Research, Canberra: AGPS.

Wode, H. (1977). Four early stages in the development of negation. *Journal of Child Language, 4,* 87–102.

Wolff, P. (1969). Crying and vocalization in early infancy. In B. Foss (Ed.), *Determinants of infant behavior* (Vol. IV). New York: Wiley.

Wolff, P. (1974). Observations on newborn infants. In L. J. Stone, H. T. Smith & L. B. Murphy (Eds.), *The competent infant*. London: Tavistock.

Woodfield, R. L., & Viney, L. L. (1984–85). A personal construct approach to the conjugally bereaved woman. *Omega, 15*(1), 1–11.

World Health Organization. (2000). *World health statistics annual 1999*. Geneva: Author. (http://www.who.int).

Xu, X., & Whyte, M. K. (1990). Love matches and arranged marriages: A Chinese replication. *Journal of Marriage and the Family, 52,* 709–722.

Yando, R. M., & Kagan, J. (1968). The effect of teacher tempo on the child. *Child Development, 39,* 27–34.

Yankelovich, D. (1974). The meaning of work. In J. M. Roscow (Ed.), *The worker and the job: Coping with change*. Englewood Cliffs, NJ: Prentice Hall.

Youniss, J. (1983). Social construction of adolescence by adolescents and parents. In H. D. Grotevant & C. R. Cooper (Eds.), *Adolescent development in the family*. San Francisco: Jossey-Bass.

Youniss, J., & Smoller, J. (1985). *Adolescent relations with mothers, fathers and friends*. Chicago: University of Chicago Press.

Yudkin, M. (1984). When kids think the unthinkable. *Psychology Today,* April, 18–25.

Zacks, R. T. (1982). Encoding strategies used by young and elderly adults in a keeping track task. *Journal of Gerontology, 37,* 203–211.

Zajonc, R., & Hall, E. (1986). Mining new gold from old research. *Psychology Today,* February, 46–51.

Zakin, D. F., Blyth, D. A., & Simmons, R. G. (1984). Physical attractiveness as a mediator of the impact of early pubertal changes for girls. *Journal of Youth and Adolescence, 13,* 439–450.

Zaporozhets, A. V., & Elkonin, D. B. (1971). *The psychology of the preschool child*. Translated by J. Shybut and S. Simon. Cambridge, MA: MIT Press.

Zucker, A., Ostrove, J., & Stewart, A. (2002). Generativity and personality. *Psychology & Aging, 17,* 337–348.

AUTHOR INDEX

Taylor, Marjorie 238
Taylor, N. 10
Taylor, Neville 460
Taylor, Shelley 448
Templer, Donald 631
Terare, Colin 349
Terman, Louis 26, 523, 577, 595
Terry, Deborah 472
Thatcher, R.W. 291
Thivierge, I. 143
Thomas, Alexander 139, 141, 146–7
Thomas, David 384
Thomas, Dylan 616
Thomas, L. Eugene 503, 504
Thomas, Patrick 568–9
Thompson, R.F. 117–18, 291
Thompson, Ross 552
Thompson, Spencer 266
Thompson, W.E. 537
Thurber, James 439, 443
Tidman, Marjorie 260
Tiedeman, D.V. 499
Tietjen, Anne Marie 373–5
Tiggemann, Marika 455–6, 457
Timaras, P.S. 560
Tinsley, Barbara 534
Tobin, S.S. 591, 594
Tobin-Richards, Maryse 333–4
Tokoro, Makiko 602
Tolstoy, Leo 436
Tomasello, Michael 180–1
Tonkinson, Robert 327, 554, 644
Tootell, H.E. 125
Townsend, Peter 607
Trahms, Christine 286, 337–8
Traupmann, Jane 439–40, 441, 443–4, 445, 447
Trehub, S.E. 174
Tremaine, L. 274
Tremblay, R. 409
Troth, Ashlea 346–7, 396
Tu Wei-ming 582
Tunmer, William 211, 304–5, 306
Turiel, E. 280
Turtle, Alison 453, 454, 506
Twain, Mark 386
Tyler, Leona 401–2

United Nations 350
Uotinen, V. 7, 8
Urberg, K. 404
US Department of Health 286

Vaillant, C.O. 63, 523, 524, 527
Vaillant, George 26, 63, 474–5, 523, 524, 527

Valdes-Dapena, M. 116
Valsiner, J. 9
Van Aken, M.A.G. 258
Van Buren, Abigail 333
Van den Heuvel, Audrey 536
van Doren, C. 5
van Ijzendoorn, M.H. 160
Van Keep, P.A. 470
Van Lieschout, C. 258
Vandell, Deborah 253
Veevers, J.E. 469, 470, 472
Verp, M. 100
Vigorito, J. 174
Viney, Linda 643, 644, 646
Vinsel, A. 42
Vitaro, F. 409
Vuchinich, S. 399
Vygotsky, Lev S. 42, 59–60, 170, 172, 175–6, 225, 238

Wainryb, C. 280
Wales, R. 180
Walford, R.L. 564
Walk, R.D. 125
Walker MacFarlane, Jean 25–6, 43, 484
Walker-Andrews, A.S. 127, 293
Walsh, M. 193
Walster, G. William 442, 445
Wapner, Seymour 540
Warburton, Jeni 540
Ward, R. 539
Warr, Peter 454
Warren, Michelle 331–2, 336
Warren, W.G. 632
Warton, Pamela 263, 343, 389, 497
Wass, H. 642
Waterman, A.S. 380
Waters, Everett 152, 155–6, 158–9
Watson, Alan 299, 307–8
Watson, John B. 60
Watson, J.S. 134
Watson, Julianne 232
Watson, Malcolm 235
Watts, J.C. 43
Weale, R.A. 561
Wearing, Betsy 459–60
Webb, J. 233
Wechsler, David 575, 577, 581
Wedel, H. 478
Weiler, Stephen 614
Weinberg, Richard 79
Weinstein, Karol 533
Weishaus, Sylvia 484–5, 493
Weiss, M. 149
Weiss, M.G. 300

Weiss, R.S. 642
Welford, Alan 563, 571
Wellman, Henry 172, 229, 230, 232
Wells, J.E. 337
Wenar, Charles 196–7
Wente, A.S. 97
Werner, Emmy 100–2
Wertheim, E.H. 337
West, Deborah 606
Westbrook, Mary 461, 462, 506, 604, 605
Wetle, Terri 557
White, B.L. 43
White, E.B. 439, 443
White, I. 14–15
White, Kathleen 532
White, Sheldon 298
White, W.F. 116
Whiteman, M. 407
Whiting, B.B. 254
Whiting, J.W.M. 254
Whitting, V. 92
Whyte, Martin 488–9
Wilcox, M.M. 371
Wilde, Oscar 160
Williams, J. 453
Williams, S. 492
Winefield, A.H. 455–6, 457
Wing, Rena 286
Wink, Paul 515–16, 517
Winner, E. 294
Winocur, Gordon 572–3
Winocur, Sharon 540
Winokur, G. 410
Wispe, Lauren 622
Wode, Henning 186
Wolff, Peter 108–9
Wood, Vivian 528
Woodfield, Robert 643, 644, 646
World Health Organization 290
Wortman, Camille 607
Wright, L. 205

Xiaohe, Xu 488–9

Yallop, C. 193
Youniss, James 227, 389, 391–2

Zacks, R.T. 570
Zajonc, R. 254
Zakin, D.F. 335
Zaporozhets, A.V. 228
Zeifman, D. 394–5
Ziller, Robert 590–1
Zucker, A. 481

SUBJECT INDEX

families *(cont.)*
  violent 403–4
family planning 70, 253, 469, 496, 535
family resemblance studies 73
fantasy play *see* make-believe play
father-adolescent relationships 343
father-child relationships
  father as primary caregiver 161–2
  fostering creativity 303
  in infancy 102, 159–63
  nature of involvement 162–3
fathering 159–63, 343
favouritism 253, 254
fear
  of crime 553, 606
  of death 471–2, 629, 633
  in middle childhood 294–6
  of retirement 539
  see also death anxiety
fertility 528, 529
  Australia's changing pattern 496
fetal alcohol effects 394
fetal alcohol syndrome 394
fetus
  gender 97
  response to auditory stimulation 95, 142
fetus phase of prenatal development 89–90
fifties, the *see* late middle age
Fiji, grandparenting 533
filial piety 12–13
fine motor development, early childhood 205, 207
Finland
  adults' ideal age 7–8
  girls' health problems 424–5
  stress before and after menarche 341
fluid conservation 214–15
foetus *see* fetus
folic acid 94
food aversions 84–5
formal-operational stage of cognitive development 59, 353–63, 481
  all-combinations reasoning 356–7
  heated family debates 395
  hypothesis formation 357–8
  limitations of formal operations 365–7, 520
  logical propositions 359
  measurement of 356–60
  proportionality and reversibility 358–9
  summary of characteristics 359
fragile X syndrome 73
Freud, Anna 344
  on adolescence 387, 388, 390–1
Freud, Sigmund
  adolescent sexuality 390
  on death 617
  gender-role development theory 271–2
  life of 54–5
  'love and work' 437
  psychosexual theory of development 54–5
friendships
  best friend relationship over time 601
  complementarity 419–20
  friendship philosophising 418
  mutual 261
  rules for 423
  same-sex, in adolescence 391, 399, 414–20
Fries, James, theory of ageing 564
frustration 199, 210

G

gametes 69, 72, 87
Gaucher's disease 72
gay men *see* homosexuality

gender
  and adolescent autonomy 389
  in adolescent-parent communication 398–9
  and moral reasoning 375–6
gender consistency 266, 267, 269
gender constancy 265–7
gender differences
  brain weight 480
  death anxiety 631, 634
  generativity 524
  suicide 622
  survival 619, 620–1, 622, 643
  terminal illness 636
gender identity 261, 266
gender preference, prenatal 97
gender roles *see* sex roles
gender schemas 274–6
gender stability 266
gender-role intensification 271, 426
generalisability 33
generalisation 61
  theory of leisure pursuits 508–9
generation gap 325–6
generativity 474–5, 480–1, 492
  grandparenthood 534–6
  late middle age 523–7
genes 69, 86
  delayed action 87
  and individual differences 69–70
genetic counselling 71–2
genetic disorders *see* chromosomal abnormalities
genital stage of development (Freud) 55
genitalia, determinant of gender 267–8
genome, human 69
genotypes 69
  overlap of 78–9
genotyping 72
gestures 169–70, 183
gift-giving 234
giftedness 35, 362
  creativity and personality 523, 524
  personal growth in old age 595
glial cells 116, 118
goal-direction 63
gonads 89
goodness-of-fit hypothesis 146–7
grammar
  descriptive (syntax) 181–2, 185
  growth of 180, 181
  pivot grammar 184
  prescriptive 182
  transformational 186
grandparent-grandchild relationship 516–17, 532, 534
grandparenthood 471, 532–6
  childrearing, participation in 532, 534–5
  and generativity 534–6
  grandmothers' teaching strategies 535
  position in life cycle 535–6
  relationships with grandchildren 516–17, 532, 534
  styles of grandparenting 533–4
grasping reflex 108
Great Depression, effect on education 37–8, 48
Greece, childrearing strategies and growth of personality 145
Greek-Australians, nursing home life 604, 605
grief 641–2, 646
growth 5, 10
  see also body growth; personality growth
Guatemala, fathering 161
guilt 56
  in widows 643
gun use, in suicides 409–10

H

habituation task 95, 126
Hadj Mohhammed El Mokri 621
haemophilia 72
hair loss 558–9, 560
handedness 48–9, 50–1, 208
Harvard, married students' rating of spouse 448
Havighurst, Robert, career development theory 499, 527
Hayflick limit 564–5
'Head Start' program 43
health
  and dating 424–5
  optimising in old age 557, 566–8
  understanding of 290, 363–5
health professionals
  and bereavement 646
  interaction with infants 181
  prejudices 29
  use of age norms 35
hearing
  acuity 40
  fetal 90, 95
  infants 126
  newborns 125
  old age 551, 555, 556, 557
hearing loss
  babbling in deaf neonates 173
  lateralisation 209
  prenatal 93
  and schooling 313
  sign language 172, 194, 209
  and theory of mind 233–4
  use of gestures 171
heart 560
heart attack 560, 622
heart defects, in embryo 93
heartbeat, mother's 110
height 71, 206
  adolescence 3
  infancy 118
  middle childhood 285–6
helpfulness 281
heredity 68–9, 70, 79
  changing influence 86
  and growth of intelligence 79
  and shyness 79, 82
  and time of death 87
heredity-environment interaction 81–3
heritability coefficient 75
heterozygosity 70
heuristics 275
Hippocrates, substages of old age 16–17, 549
Hiroshima, premature ageing of survivors 565
HIV/AIDS 347–9, 633
  and drug use 408
  ethnic differences in awareness of 348–9
  stigma of death from 646
  young adults' understanding of 364–5, 367
holophrastic speech 182–4, 187
homosexuality
  division of couples' domestic labour 466–7
  support networks 646
  see also HIV/AIDS
homozygosity 70
hormone replacement therapy (HRT) 560, 561
hospice system 639
household work *see* domestic chores
human development, historical perspective 15–18
human genome mapping 69
Huntington's chorea 71–2, 73, 87
Hunza people, longevity 625

hypertension 564
hypotheses 38

I

id 54
idealisation 448
identity achievement 378, 540
  ethnic identity and 380
  and intimacy 447–8
  occupational 459–60
identity crisis 56, 376–80, 447, 448
  and career change 503–4
  cultural variations 380–2
  identity statuses 377–80
identity diffusion 379
  ethnic identity and 380
identity foreclosure 377, 378–9, 398
  ethnic identity and 380
identity moratorium 378
  ethnic identity and 380
idolatry 448
illness, understanding of 290, 363–5
imaginary audience syndrome 365–7, 368
imaginary companions 238
imitation 62
immune system 564
incest anxiety 390
India, parenting style 401–2
individuation 501
induction 211, 250
  other-oriented 250
infancy 107
  24-hour clock at age 2 months 112
  attention 129–30
  beauty, growth of 120
  boredom 129, 130
  brain growth 115–18
  cognition 128–9
  crying 107, 108–10
  cultural beliefs and sleep 114–15
  curiosity 129–30, 134
  dreaming 113–14
  emotional development 148–9
  face perception 120, 126
  feeding 107
  gaining trust 133, 134, 196
  hearing 126
  infant mortality 619, 620, 621
  learned helplessness 134
  learning 128–9
  life expectancy 621
  milestones 165
  motor skill development 121–4
  norms for locomotor skill 36
  perceptual development 126–8
  personal control 133–4
  physical growth 118–19
  reflex behaviours 107–8
  self-efficacy 135–6
  sensorimotor stage (Piaget) 58, 130–2
  sensory development 124–6
  sleeping 107, 111–13, 147
  sociability 149–50
  soothing crying baby 110–11, 149–50
  temperament 139–42, 473
  timing of first steps 37
  transition from creeping to walking 23
  vision 125–6
  see also attachment
infatuation 441
infertility, in men 474–5
inheritance see Mendelian inheritance; polygenic inheritance
initiation ceremonies, at puberty 326–8, 383
institutionalised elderly, and reminiscence 574
integrity 574, 581

integrity crisis (Erikson) 57, 574, 581, 588, 612
intelligence
  adoption studies 78–9
  in aged people 562, 575–8
  crystallised 579
  fluid 579
  and heredity 79
  twin studies 75
intelligence tests (IQ tests) 33, 578–9
  adult test scores 50
  age differences in adults' scores 34
  ageist nature of 38
  deterioration quotient 575
  and old people 576–8
  terminal drop 576
  WAIS 577, 578, 579
intentionality 63
Internet 48
  use by elderly 605–6
interpersonal isolation 448
intimacy 56, 441, 492
  and employment 451–2, 495
  late middle age 516
  and personality growth (Erikson) 447–8
IQ tests see intelligence tests
irreversibility, of death 627, 629–31
Italian-Australians
  adolescent emancipation 393
  nursing home life 604, 605
Italy, fears of elderly women 553

J

Japan
  adults' ideal age 7–8
  age boundaries of adult life 12
  burial practices 640–1
  deaf infants and sign language 194
  defining old age 548, 549
  disengagement in the elderly 590–1
  female life expectancy 620
  life satisfaction in the elderly 602
  marriage
    'love-match' couples 487, 488
    traditional (miai couples) 486–7, 488
  peer debate discouraged 220
  prime of life 513–14
  respect for age/wisdom 555, 582
jobs see employment
Jung, Carl, theory of old age 587
juvenile delinquency 402–3

K

Kansas City study of social ageing 588, 592–3, 594, 596
kicking, in womb 92, 95, 113
Kimberley study, Aboriginal infants' growth rates 119–20
King, Nene, mid-career crisis 503
Klinefelter syndrome 73
Knauss, Sarah 621
Kohlberg, Lawrence
  cognitive-developmental theory 273–4
  moral reasoning theory 368–71
Kübler-Ross, Elizabeth, stages of dying theory 634–6
  critique 636–8

L

laboratory experiments 46
labour pains see contractions
labour stages 98–9
language
  pragmatics 175
  second-language learning 209, 223
Language Acquisition Device (LAD) 188

language development 169
  babbling 173–4
  complex sentences 187
  conversation and 190–3
  first words 180
  holophrastic speech 182–4, 187
  imitation and 189–90
  and lateralisation 208–9
  learning theories 188–90
  motherese 191–2, 198
  nativist theory of 187–8, 191
  negation 186–7
  negotiating skills 199–200
  and outgrowing negativism 198–9
  overextension 177–9
  overregularisation 185–6
  and personality 194
  pivot grammar 184
  prelanguage skills 173–5
  pseudo-conversations 175, 190, 191
  questions 107
  reinforcement 189
  and social play 235, 236
  and social skills 198–9
  speech sounds 172–5
  speech-perception abilities 174
  symbolic representation 169–72
  sympathetic listening 194
  synchrony in mother-child dialogue 194, 195
  syntax 181–7
  telegraphic speech 184–5, 192
  two-word sentences 184
  underextension 177, 179
  vocabulary development 176–81
  word meaning 175–6, 177–9
  see also grammar
late middle age 513
  50th birthday 531
  cognitive powers 514
  consciousness of ageing 514
  faith development 520, 521–3
  generativity 523–7
  intellectual and cognitive development 518–23
    Schaie's stage theory 519–20
  loss of parents 622
  menopause 527–9, 530
  prime of life 513–14
  quality of life 515–16
  sexuality 529–31
  social clock 517–18
  social-age peership 532
  see also empty-nest phase; grandparenthood; retirement
lateralisation 207, 208–9, 291
learned helplessness 456, 491
  in infancy 134
  loss of personal control 608–9
  versus mastery orientation 310–11
  about weight 337, 338
  about word meaning 181
learning 60–1
  infancy 128–9
  observational 62
  terminology 61
  theories of 60–3
learning environment 60
Lebanese-Australians
  expectations of obedience in children 220, 252–3
  self-assertion in children 200
left-handedness 48–9, 50–1
legacy-creating stage of cognitive development 520
leisure pursuits 506–8
  compensation theory 508–9
  and personal fulfilment 492, 508, 509
  in retirement 541
  segmentation theory 509

weight (cont.)
  middle childhood   285–6, 287, 288
Werner's syndrome   564
widows and widowers   612–6
  remarriage   645–6
  widowhood   9, 632
    emotional states   643
    identity as a widow   644–5
    Lopata's seven patterns of   644–5
    widowhood role   644
winner takes all   282
wisdom   25, 574, 581, 612
womb, ecology of   94
women, societal situation over time   49

word meanings   175–6, 177
  early   178
work see employment
work ethic   257, 508, 536
wrinkles   559, 566, 625

X

X chromosome   71
X-rays   86, 87, 94

Y

Y chromosome   71
young adults, fear of death   633
youth, homeless   404

youth unemployment   459–60, 506
  longitudinal research   454–7

Z

zone of proximal development (ZPD)
  60, 225
zygote   68, 72
zygote phase of prenatal development
  88, 92